To Mot
from.
Alec

INDUSTRIALISED EMBAYMENTS AND THEIR ENVIRONMENTAL PROBLEMS

A Case Study of Swansea Bay

RELATED PERGAMON TITLES OF INTEREST

Books

ANDERSON & OWEN:
The Structure of the British Isles, 2nd Edition

BOWEN:
Quaternary Geology

JENKINS:
Mediterranean Pollution

LOWE et al:
Studies in the Lateglacial of North-West Europe

OWEN:
The Geological Evolution of the British Isles

PARSONS & TAKAHASHI:
Biological Oceanographic Processes, 2nd Edition

PICKARD:
Descriptive Physical Oceanography, 3rd Edition

POND & PICKARD:
Introductory Dynamic Oceanography

RAYMONT:
Plankton and Productivity in the Oceans, 2nd Edition

TCHERNIA:
Descriptive Regional Oceanography

YALIN:
Mechanics of Sediment Transport, 2nd Edition

*Journals**

Geoforum (The International Multi-disciplinary Journal for the Rapid Publication of Research Results and Critical Review Articles in the Physical, Human and Regional Geosciences)

Journal of Structural Geology

Long Range Planning

Marine Pollution Bulletin

Progress in Oceanography

Progress in Water Technology

*Free specimen copy of any Pergamon journal available on request

INDUSTRIALISED EMBAYMENTS AND THEIR ENVIRONMENTAL PROBLEMS

A Case Study of Swansea Bay

*Proceedings of an Interdisciplinary Symposium
held at University College, Swansea
26th - 28th September, 1979*

Edited by

**M. B. COLLINS, F. T. BANNER, P. A. TYLER,
S. J. WAKEFIELD AND A. E. JAMES**

Department of Oceanography, University College, Swansea, UK

PERGAMON PRESS
OXFORD · NEW YORK · TORONTO · SYDNEY · PARIS · FRANKFURT

U.K.	Pergamon Press Ltd., Headington Hill Hall, Oxford OX3 0BW, England
U.S.A.	Pergamon Press Inc., Maxwell House, Fairview Park, Elmsford, New York 10523, U.S.A.
CANADA	Pergamon of Canada, Suite 104, 150 Consumers Road, Willowdale, Ontario M2J 1P9, Canada
AUSTRALIA	Pergamon Press (Aust.) Pty. Ltd., P.O. Box 544, Potts Point, N.S.W. 2011, Australia
FRANCE	Pergamon Press SARL, 24 rue des Ecoles, 75240 Paris, Cedex 05, France
FEDERAL REPUBLIC OF GERMANY	Pergamon Press GmbH, 6242 Kronberg-Taunus, Hammerweg 6, Federal Republic of Germany

Copyright © 1980 Pergamon Press Ltd.

All Rights Reserved. No part of this publication may be reproduced, stored in a retrieval system or transmitted in any form or by any means: electronic, electrostatic, magnetic tape, mechanical, photocopying, recording or otherwise, without permission in writing from the publishers.

First edition 1980

British Library Cataloguing in Publication Data

Industrialised embayments and their environmental problems.
1. Marine ecology - Wales - Swansea region
- Congresses
2. Marine ecology - Case studies - Congresses
3. Bays - Wales - Swansea region - Congresses
4. Bays - Case studies - Congresses
I. Collins, M B
574.5'2636   QH144   80-40507
ISBN 0-08-023992-7

In order to make this volume available as economically and as rapidly as possible the authors' typescripts have been reproduced in their original forms. This method has its typographical limitations but it is hoped that they in no way distract the reader.

Printed in Great Britain by A. Wheaton & Co. Ltd., Exeter.

TO PERCY TUCKER

In memory of the boatswain of R.V. *Ocean Crest*,

University College of Swansea,

March 1971 to May 1980

with gratitude and affection.

PAPERS COVER THE FOLLOWING SUBJECT AREAS

Geological Evolution and Geomorphological Setting
(Chapters 2 to 5)

Archaeological and Historical Influences
(Chapters 6 and 7)

The Dynamic Fluid Environment (Tides, Waves and Currents)
(Chapters 8 to 12)

Sediment Distribution and Transport
(Chapters 13 to 19)

The Chemical Environment and Inputs
(Chapters 20 to 23, 27 and 28)

Dispersion and Numerical Modelling
(Chapters 24 to 26)

Productivity, Phytoplankton and Zooplankton
(Chapters 29 to 31)

Benthic Ecology
(Chapters 32 to 34)

Economic Developments
(Chapters 35 to 37)

The Influence of Industrial Development on the Western Foreshore
(Appendix)

CONTENTS

PREFACE
    M.B. Collins and S.J. Wakefield   xi

1. INTRODUCTION
    H. Cronshaw   1

2. THE GEOLOGICAL HISTORY OF SWANSEA BAY IN POST-CARBONIFEROUS TIMES
    T.R. Owen and E.M. Bridges   5

DISCUSSION I   21

3. SWANSEA BAY: BEDROCK GEOLOGY AND ITS INFLUENCE OVER GEOMORPHOLOGICAL DEVELOPMENT
    C.R. Price and M. Brooks   23

4. THE QUATERNARY DEPOSITS OF SWANSEA BAY
    S.J. Culver and P.A. Bull   39

5. THE USE OF THE SYMAP/SYMVU COMPUTER PACKAGE TO EXAMINE BATHYMETRY, SEDIMENTOLOGY AND OFFSHORE GEOLOGY
    J.K. Rigler and M.B. Collins   51

6. PALAEOLITHIC TO IRON AGE ARCHAEOLOGY AND PALAEOENVIRONMENT IN THE SWANSEA AREA
    S.J. Culver   59

7. CHANGES IN HISTORICAL TIME
    A.P. Carr and M.W.L. Blackley   71

8. TIDAL AND NON-TIDAL VARIATIONS IN SEA LEVEL
    A.J. Wilding and M.B. Collins   85

9. STORM SURGES IN SWANSEA BAY
    A.J. Wilding   101

10. LONG WAVES AND HARBOUR SEICHES AT PORT TALBOT
    W.H. Jackson   115

Contents

11. TIDAL CURRENTS AND RESIDUAL CIRCULATION IN THE SWANSEA BAY AREA OF THE BRISTOL CHANNEL
    A.D. Heathershaw and F.D.C. Hammond ... 123

12. WAVES, CURRENTS AND LITTORAL DRIFT
    R.H. Wilkinson ... 157

DISCUSSION II ... 173

13. SEDIMENTARY BED FORMS AND LINEAR BANKS
    R.C. Britton and S.R. Britton ... 177

14. THE SUPPLY OF SAND TO SWANSEA BAY
    M.B. Collins, C.B. Pattiaratchi, F.T. Banner and G.K. Ferentinos ... 193

15. TRANSPORT AND DEPOSITION OF NON-COHESIVE SEDIMENTS IN SWANSEA BAY
    A.D. Heathershaw and F.D.C. Hammond ... 215

16. MINERALOGY OF NONCOHESIVE SEDIMENTARY DEPOSITS
    J.V. Barrie ... 249

17. SWANSEA BAY: BEACHES AND SUPRALITTORAL DEPOSITS
    M.W.L. Blackley and A.P. Carr ... 259

18. RHEOLOGY OF COHESIVE SUSPENSIONS
    R. Bryant, A.E. James and D.J.A. Williams ... 279

19. SUSPENDED SEDIMENT DISTRIBUTIONS IN NORTHERN SWANSEA BAY
    C.M. Davies ... 289

DISCUSSION III ... 303

20. INPUTS TO SWANSEA BAY
    C.J. Chubb, R.P. Dale and J.H. Stoner ... 307

DISCUSSION IV ... 327

21. TRACE METAL STUDIES IN THE RIVER TAWE AND SWANSEA BAY
    C.M.G. Vivian ... 329

22. OCCURRENCE AND SURVIVAL OF VIRUSES IN SEAWATER
    J.M. Tyler ... 343

23. THE DISCHARGE OF MEDICAL RADIONUCLIDES FROM A NEARSHORE OUTFALL, MUMBLES, WESTERN SWANSEA BAY
    J.L. Birks ... 353

DISCUSSION V ... 365

24. DIFFUSION AND DISPERSION CHARACTERISTICS IN SWANSEA BAY: SOME PRELIMINARY RESULTS
    I. Borthwick ... 367

25. ENVIRONMENTAL HYDRODYNAMIC MODELLING PROBLEM IDENTIFICATION AND A STRATEGY TO MODEL ASSESSMENT
    G.D. Tong ... 383

26. NUMERICAL MODELLING OF DISPERSION IN TIDAL AREAS
    C. Taylor ... 393

Contents

27. WATER QUALITY STUDIES IN SWANSEA BAY
    N.C. Humphrey, C. Pattinson and J.H. Stoner 409

28. CHEMISTRY OF SWANSEA BAY

    PART I: GENERAL DESCRIPTION
    A.W. Morris and R.F.C. Mantoura 439

    PART II: SPATIAL HETEROGENEITY AND PROCESSES
    R.F.C. Mantoura and A.W. Morris 453

DISCUSSION VI 465

29. PHYTOPLANKTON PRODUCTION IN SWANSEA BAY
    I.R. Joint 469

30. THE PHYTOPLANKTON OF INSHORE SWANSEA BAY
    P.J. Paulraj and J. Hayward 481

31. THE ZOOPLANKTON OF SWANSEA BAY
    M.J. Isaac 487

32. NEARSHORE SUBLITTORAL ECOSYSTEMS ALONG THE GOWER COAST
    K. Hiscock, D. Cartlidge and S. Hiscock 507

33. ANNUAL MACROFAUNA PRODUCTION IN AN *ABRA* COMMUNITY
    R.M. Warwick and C.L. George 517

34. THE BENTHIC ECOLOGY OF LINEAR SANDBANKS: A MODIFIED *SPISULA* SUB-COMMUNITY
    P.A. Tyler and S.E. Shackley 539

DISCUSSION VII 553

35. FISH AND FISHERIES IN GREATER SWANSEA BAY
    S.E. Shackley, P.E. King and J. Rhydderch 555

36. DOCK AND HARBOUR PLANNING, MAINTENANCE AND DEVELOPMENT IN RELATION TO THE SWANSEA BAY PORTS
    B.L. Flower 565

37. PORT TALBOT - ACCRETION AND DREDGING IN THE HARBOUR AND ENTRANCE CHANNEL
    W.H. Jackson and D.R. Norman 573

DISCUSSION VIII 583

APPENDIX: THE POTENTIAL INFLUENCE OF INDUSTRIALISATION OF SEDIMENT DISTRIBUTIONS IN WESTERN SWANSEA BAY
    A.D. Moran 587

CONTRIBUTING AUTHORS 613

ADDITIONAL PARTICIPANTS 615

PREFACE

This volume contains the Proceedings of an interdisciplinary Symposium on Swansea Bay, held at University College, Swansea on 26th-28th September, 1979. This industrialised embayment has been studied intensively over a period of many years by investigators from a number of Institutions. Prominent among these Institutions have been University College of Swansea, Institute of Oceanographic Sciences, Taunton (I.O.S.), Institute for Marine Environmental Research (I.M.E.R.), Welsh National Water Development Authority (W.N.W.D.A., now Welsh Water Authority), and the British Transport Docks Board (B.T.D.B.). Invited contributions relating to these studies form the main part of the Symposium Proceedings and the accompanying Discussion.

Swansea Bay is located on the northern coastline of the Bristol Channel, a large inlet situated within the western coastline of the British Isles (Fig. I). The Bristol Channel separates the coastline of South Wales, to the north, from that of England, to the south.

In terms of its physical oceanographic setting, the Bay experiences one of the largest tidal ranges in the world (8.5m on mean Spring tides and 4.1m on mean Neaps); this is created by accentuation of the tidal wave from the North Atlantic Ocean, passing through the Celtic Sea, into the converging coastlines and sea bed of the Bristol Channel. Further, the orientation of the Bristol Channel permits long wavelength swell from the western Atlantic to break upon the eastern coastline of the embayment. The combined influence of tides (tidal currents) and waves (wave-induced currents) creates a high energy environment, susceptible to extremes of energy input.

The specific area under discussion is that contained between the coastlines of the south Gower Peninsula and west West Glamorgan and a line of longitude passing through Worm's Head and a line of latitude through Nash Point (Fig. II). This area of approximately 270km^2 is slightly larger than that referred to as Greater Swansea Bay, in a review of research interest there, by Shackley (1978). The Swansea Bay area is no greater than 40m in depth (below chart datum) and is bounded to the north by a series of semicircular embayments separated by Carboniferous Limestone headlands; the latter are more resistant to erosion than the formations from which the embayments have been cut. Offshore, the bathymetric contours run generally parallel to the coastline but, in detail, are perturbed by the presence of topographic highs such as the White Oyster Ledge and the east-west aligned Helwick, Scarweather and Nash Sands (Fig. II). Freshwater input to the area is from the Rivers Tawe and Neath, from the north, and the Avon, Kenfig and Ogmore, from the east.

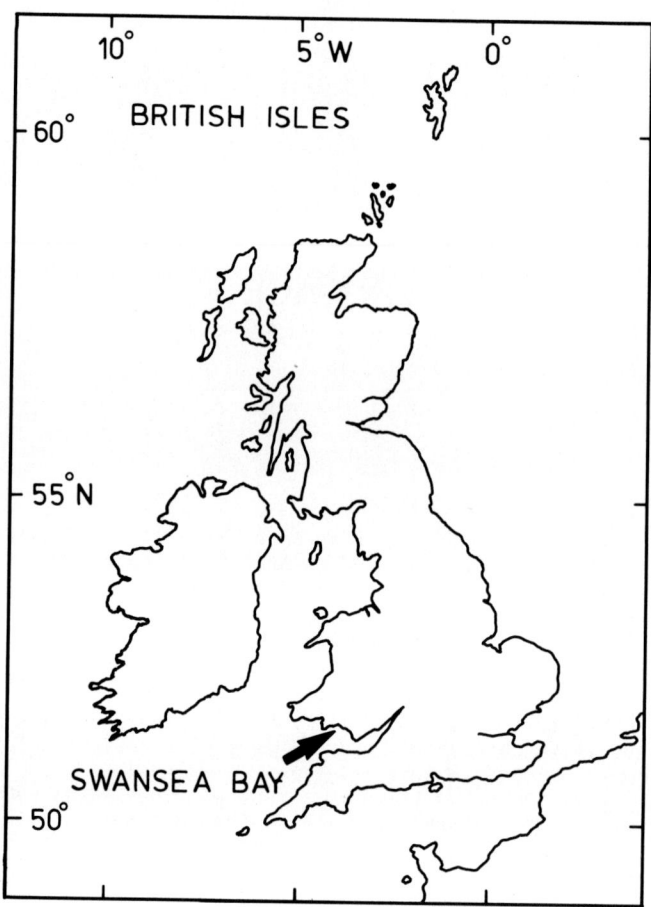

Figure I.   Location of Swansea Bay.

The Gower Peninsula, to the west of the city of Swansea was one of the first regions to be designated an "area of outstanding natural beauty" and is very popular in terms of tourism and local recreation. By way of contrast (see Plate 1), the narrow coastal strip along the eastern side of the embayment supports areas of major industrialisation such as the B.P. Chemicals complex, and the British Steel Corporation works at Port Talbot. The City of Swansea (City status was granted to the Town in 1969, by Royal Charter), with a population of some 200,000 is the main urban development in the area. Waste products from both this and the extensive areas of industrial development find their way, either directly or indirectly, into the Swansea Bay area. A Report of the Working Party on Possible Pollution in Swansea Bay was published in 1974 (Welsh Office, 1974).

"Swansea and its Region" was the subject of a Meeting of the British Association for the Advancement of Science in 1971, subsequently published. This collection of essays (Balchin, 1971) briefly dealt with some aspects of the marine environment, but was concerned predominantly with the land area. However, the associations between Town (City) and Sea are well established, principally through the extensive port facilities.

Mr. W.D. King, Docks Manager (Swansea), in a recent radio interview (January, 1980) outlined the present status of the Port of Swansea, as follows:

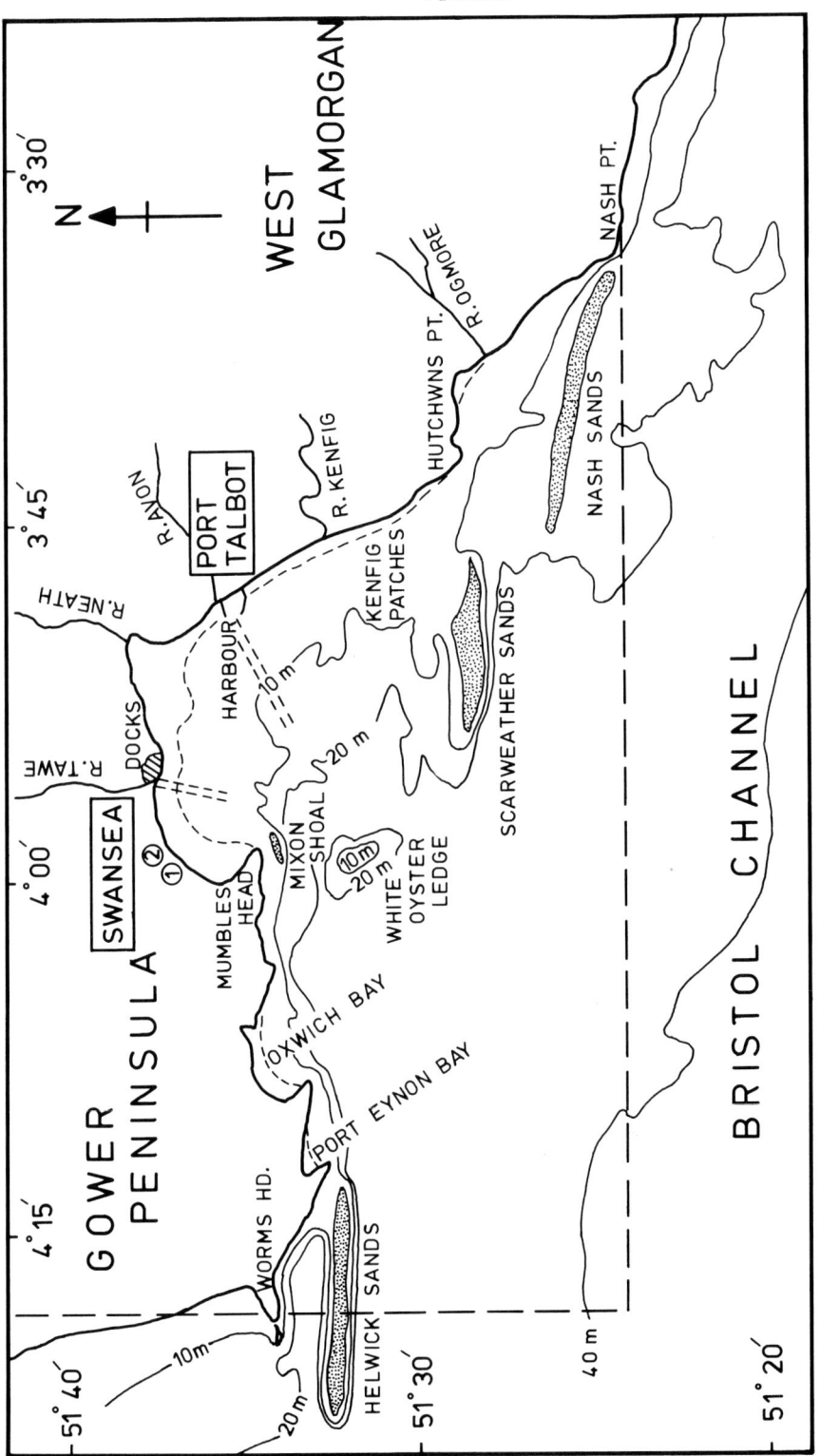

Figure II. Map of Swansea Bay area, showing geographical locations referred to in the text. (1) and (2) refer to the positions from which the photographs forming Plat I were taken.

PLATE I: (a) Mumbles Head, from the north (Position (1) in Figure II), and (b) View over the eastern side of the City of Swansea, looking towards Port Talbot (from Position (2) in Figure II); Swansea Docks are shown in the centre of the photograph and the industrial development along the eastern coastline in the distance.

Preface

"....we are still the busiest South Wales port. We handle around 6,000,000 tonnes of goods a year and we handle more ships than all the other South Wales Ports put together. Our business, these days, consists principally of refined petroleum from B.P's refinery at Llandarcy and also petrochemicals from B.P's installation at Baglan Bay. The next major flow of traffic would be anthracite coal from the Welsh Coalfields. Some suckers go out into the Severn Estuary and suck up sand for building purposes and, with the construction of the M4 making big demands on sand, we are dealing with about 400,000 tonnes/year of sand imported from the Severn Estuary. We still have the iron and steel industry here and the products of the steel industry flow out through Swansea Docks, with the heavy material being loaded in the bottom of the ship and attracting other middle and top stowage to the Port for shipment to many parts of the world. We have liner sailings to India, to Pakistan, and to Bangladesh, South America, Egypt and to many other places. So these would be the principal flows of traffic that we deal with these days".

In addition to Swansea Docks, there is a major deep-water tidal harbour located at Port Talbot; the two small ports of Briton Ferry and Neath, located between Swansea and Port Talbot, complete the port facilities of the region. Extensive dredging in the approach channels to Swansea Docks and Port Talbot Harbour (Fig. II) is required to maintain the navigation channels.

The preceding summary has provided some indication of the extent of industrialisation in the area and its dependence upon the marine environment; the purpose of this Symposium was to examine, in detail, the interaction of one upon the other and to collate the most recent research investigations.

The 39 papers (37 Chapters and an Appendix) presented here fall naturally into the following sub-divisions: (a) geological evolution and geomorphological setting (Chapters 2 to 5); (b) archaeological and historical influences (Chapters 6 and 7); (c) the dynamic fluid environment (tides, waves and currents)(Chapters 8 to 12); (d) sediment distribution and transport (Chapters 13 to 19); (e) the chemical environment and inputs (Chapters 20 to 23, 27 and 28); (f) dispersion and numerical modelling (Chapters 24 to 26); (g) productivity, phytoplankton and zooplankton (Chapters 29 to 31); (h) benthic ecology (Chapters 32 to 34); (i) economic developments (Chapters 35 to 37); and (j) the influence of industrial development on the western foreshore (Appendix).

In addition to the above, an edited version of the oral discussion at the Symposium (subsequently agreed by participants (see affiliations at the end of the Volume)) is presented, in sections, following the relevant Chapters. Editing of both the text and (taped) discussion was carried out by members of the academic staff of the Department of Oceanography, University College of Swansea; consequently, the final responsibility for any misrepresentation must rest with them.

University College of Swansea is to be thanked for its facilities used for this Symposium, including the assistance provided by Mr. D. Gabriel and Mr. J.D.S. Morgan of the Reprographic Unit. Mrs. A. Carr and Mr. K. Naylor are warmly thanked for their general assistance and draughtsmanship, respectively, during the production of this Volume. Secretarial assistance was provided by Ms. J. Greengo, who also typed the complete Volume and without whose much appreciated help its production would have been impossible.

Approximately one third of all the contributions to this Volume have relied upon field data collected using the University College of Swansea's R.V. *Ocean Crest*; the continuing assistance of Captain B. Davies and the ship's complement (Mr. N. Ledger, Mr. P. Tucker, Mr. R. Harris and Mr. L. James) are gratefully acknowledged.

Finally, the organisers/editors would like to thank the Estuarine and Brackish-Water Sciences Association (E.B.S.A.) and the Institute for Marine Studies (University College, Swansea) for their financial support for the Symposium (as a loan, and donation, respectively) and the Welsh Office for their donation towards the publishing costs.

REFERENCES

Balchin, W.G.V. (1971). *Swansea and its Region*. University College of Swansea, 391pp.

Shackley, S. (1978). *Past, present and future work in the Greater Swansea Bay area; including littoral zone to H.W.S. and sublittoral zone within the region Worm's Head to Nash Point, extending to a line drawn through the Scarweather Light*. Institute for Marine Studies, University College of Swansea, 44pp.

Welsh Office, (1974). *Report of the Working Party on Possible Pollution in Swansea Bay*. Welsh Office, Cardiff, Volume 1, 33pp. Volume 2, 110pp.

M.B. Collins,

S.J. Wakefield,

Swansea,

February, 1980.

1. INTRODUCTION

H. Cronshaw

Welsh Office, Greyfriars Road, Cardiff, U.K.

KEYWORDS

Research; Working Parties; Swansea Bay; Bristol Channel.

Although research has been going on in the Bristol Channel and Severn Estuary certainly since the early 1940's and indeed as long ago as the early 1800's, it was not until the late 1960's that, quite independently, various bodies, including Bristol University and N.E.R.C. were also considering a co-ordinated research programme for the Estuary and the Channel. The general feeling at the time was that the Estuary and Channel was "dirtier than it was before" but there was little information available on the state of the marine environment in the Estuary and Channel. Work had already been done in Swansea Bay, but as far as I can recollect the amount of work actually done was quite limited in scope. University College, Swansea, did not begin systematic studies until 1970. N.E.R.C. held an Estuaries Forum in the summer of 1971 and set up a working party on Estuaries Research (I.M.E.R. had then been recently formed) and this working party subsequently reported in 1975. It so happens that the Working Party on Possible Pollution in Swansea Bay was set up by Welsh Office and had its first meeting in April 1972. The Severn Estuary Joint Consultative Committee of the then River Authorities bordering the estuary was still continuing its deliberations although they had no statutory powers to take any effective action. At a later stage, water reorganisation took place in 1974 and after some loss of momentum, the Severn Estuary Technical Working Party (comprising members of the 3 Water Authorities bordering the Severn Estuary) then took up the work of the old Joint Consultative Committee, but did not pick up the threads of the former Committee until March 1975. In short, it would seem that the move towards some co-ordination of research in the Severn Estuary really did not bear fruit until the early seventies and even now, after almost a decade there is still much to do. Only a few baselines have been established both in the Estuary and Channel and Swansea Bay itself, much work remains to be done, and much is needed in the future to monitor the marine environment throughout the whole of the area of the Estuary and Channel including localised spots such as Swansea Bay.

As to Swansea Bay itself, it is fairly well recognised that this is a unique embayment in several respects. It is bordered by a fairly heavily industrialised area, it receives the flow from rivers which are bringing down the remains of toxic materials which have been derived from the metals processing activities of the past and is probably also unique in the complexity and extent of water movement in the

Bay. All these peculiarities, together with the very high tidal range and exposure to the Atlantic, lead to a complex environment in the Bay which is not easily or readily understood.

In short, there appears to have been an upsurge in research activity in the Estuary and Channel in the last decade and this includes the localised research in Swansea Bay and that while sufficient information is not yet available, certain studies have produced indications of baseline conditions which will be valuable for future monitoring.

As to the Symposium itself, we shall be told initially about the geological history of the Bay, together with the rapid changes that have occurred over the last 250,000 years. Variations in sea-water levels will be discussed including storm surges and their effect on residual currents. The above will reflect the influences and effects that the environment is having on man. Other papers will tell us what effect man is having on the marine environment including the effect of industrial and sewage effluents. We look forward to being told what efforts are being made to control pollution in the Bay and work that is being carried out to identify the ultimate fate of pollutants. The important subject of sediment transport and deposition will be discussed and the influence of the dynamic environment on the sub-tidal and inter-tidal zones. The incidence of trace metals resulting from previous industrial activities will be mentioned as will the possible environmental consequences resulting from the discharge of radio-active wastes from a local hospital. We also look forward to a paper on the occurrence and survival of viruses in sea-water - a comparatively new and important subject for research. The variability of chemical components will be discussed as will the study of plankton. Surveys of the littoral and sub-littoral ecosystems of the greater Swansea Bay area will be reported and the effect of natural and man-made occurrences on these systems discussed.

Accretion and dredging in the approaches to Port Talbot Harbour, together with the problems of changing trade patterns in the development of South Wales ports, will add some docks engineering aspects to the subjects of the Symposium. Finally, the history of fishing in the Greater Swansea Bay area will be traced over the last 100 years and the causes for its decline will be discussed.

The main questions which we might consider are:-
(a) Whether, as a result of man's activities, there is any evidence of adverse effects on the human population - either on the population generally or perhaps on highly exposed individuals?
(b) Could the Bay contribute more positively to man by being developed as a richer asset?
(c) Have our research activities so far taken us in the right direction and could Swansea Bay become a natural laboratory for the rest of the world?
(d) Are our research and monitoring activities designed so as to be of real, practical value to people locally and internationally?

There are many remaining questions which might be kept in mind during the Symposium; for example:-
(i) Do we have a clear idea of what we want the Bay to be? As far as the community can afford it, we want the Bay to be clean and attractive, even though several rivers drain into it from our industrialised hinterland; but it would be absurd to try to make it better than the local geography or the nature of the Bristol Channel will allow. This leads us to the further questions:-
(ii) What is the importance of this embayment to man and does its natural marine environment have any effect on him?
(iii) What effect is man having on the marine environment and, if there is an effect, what action is needed to remedy the situation?
(iv) Is our monitoring of the environment in the Bay sufficient?

When we have answers to these questions, we will find that they lead us to new questions, thus:-
How much effort must we put into future monitoring?
In what directions should our research go - and how far should they go especially in the present climate of financial restraint?

Much of our discussion must, I realise, by circular, as a question leads, not to an answer, but to another question. But we must persist until we have acquired enough knowledge and understanding of this network of problems for us to break the circle and produce answers that will benefit both Man and Nature - and at a price both can afford

2. THE GEOLOGICAL HISTORY OF SWANSEA BAY IN POST-CARBONIFEROUS TIMES

T. R. Owen[*] and E. M. Bridges[**]

[*]Department of Geology, University College of Swansea
[**]Department of Geography, University College of Swansea, Swansea SA2 8PP, U.K.

KEYWORDS

Swansea Bay; Marine Geology; Geomorphology

GEOLOGICAL RECONSTRUCTION

It is first necessary to consider the main elements of the solid geology and the geological structure of the Bay its margins - Gower to the west, the Swansea-Neath area to the north and the Port Talbot-Porthcawl coastal strip to the east. An attempt to reconstruct the probable geology and structure of the area under study is given in Fig. 2.1. One says "attempt" because over much of the Bay the solid geology is concealed beneath a superficial cover, and direct observations of outcrops are difficult.

The "solid" succession ranges from Devonian to Lower Jurassic. The Permian and much of the Triassic is unrepresented, probably because these were times of active erosion. As a result, the Palaeozoic-Mesozoic boundary is one of considerable unconformity, the Triassic resting on the Carboniferous Limestone in the Porthcawl district and on the Namurian shales at Port Eynon (Gower), whereas in places south of Gower and across the front of the Bay it is the Lias which forms the base of the unconformable cover (see Evans and Thompson, 1979, Figs. 1 and 4).

The Devonian in its surface outcrop is restricted to the anticlinal cores of Gower. These grits and conglomerates are tough and resistant and form the highest ridges of the peninsula - Cefn Bryn, Rhossili Down and Llanmadoc Hill, all reaching to about 190 metres above sea level. The Carboniferous Limestone forms large tracts of southern Gower and its resistant character is demonstrated by the striking headlands of Oxwich Point, Pwll du Head and Mumbles Head. Carboniferous Limestone is probably also the bedrock of extensive areas just offshore from the south coast of Gower (Fig. 2.1) and probably also across the front of the Bay for some distance ESE of Mumbles Head. Towards the Porthcawl coast, the Limestone probably disappears in places beneath some Mesozoic cover.

The Namurian ("Millstone Grit") is essentially a shaley sequence with only very occasional grit bands and from an erosive point of view is therefore a softer unit. The synclines of Oystermouth, Oxwich and Port Eynon in Gower all preserve Namurian shales, forming hollows flanked by resistant limestone. The bays at Oxwich and

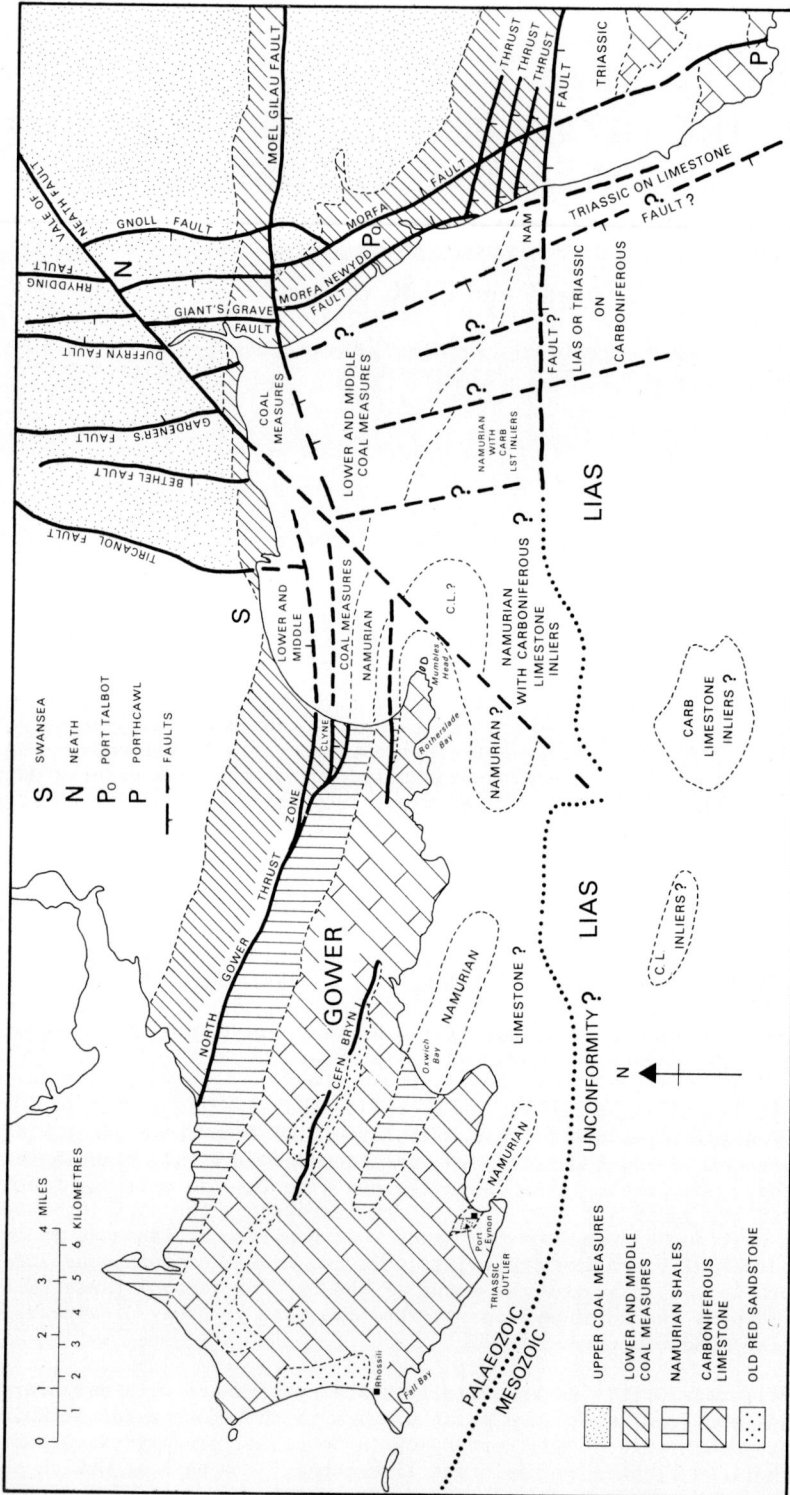

Figure 2.1. Geological sketch map of the hinterland of Swansea Bay with postulated offshore geological structures. Mesozoic southern fringe after Evans and Thompson (1979).

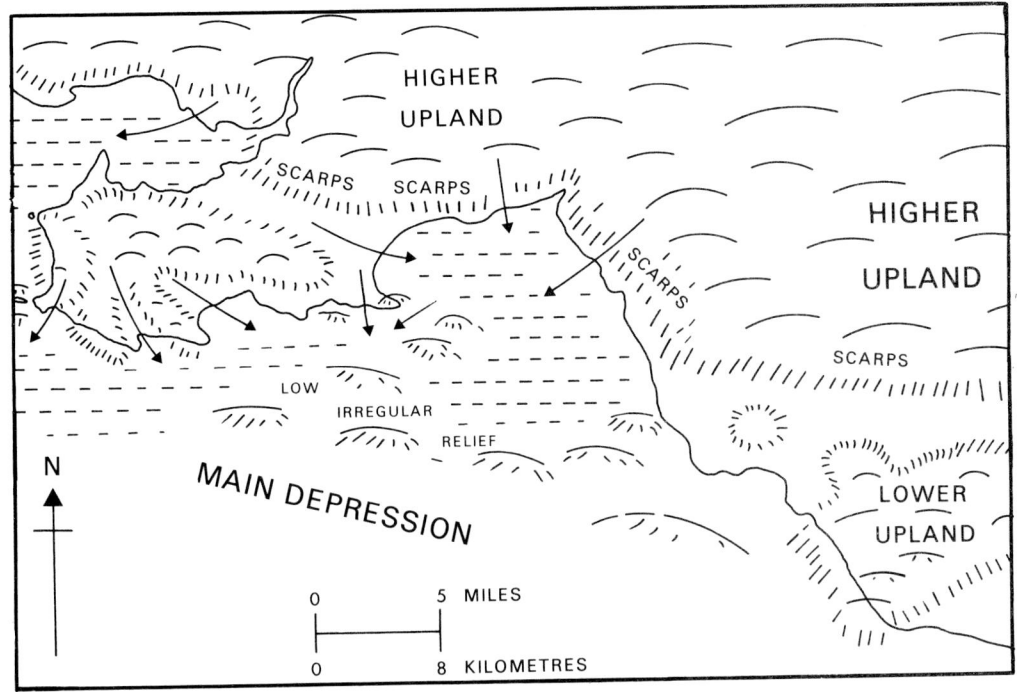

Figure 2.2. Triassic palaeogeography

Port Eynon have been excavated by the sea into these softer rocks. It is difficult to assess the offshore extent of these synclinal Namurian tracts. Those of Oxwich and Port Eynon could terminate east-southeastwards, as suggested in Fig. 2.1. Such a termination is in keeping with the general impersistent, "*en echelon*" nature of the Gower folds.

The main Namurian outcrop of Gower runs across northern Gower from Whitford Point to West Cross and this important tract embracing almost 600 metres of Namurian shales with just occasional thin grits must run across the Swansea Bay to link up with the Namurian south of the Coalfield in the Bridgend-Pyle district. How this Namurian belt runs across the Bay is a matter for conjecture. Figure 2.1 suggests that the outcrop must be frequently offset by cross faults, probably with a NNW-SSE trend. There are a considerable number of such fractures in the Swansea-Neath district (Fig. 2.1 only shows the more important of these) and it would be indeed surprising if at least some of these did not continue into the Bay. Fig. 2.1 suggests that some of these Bay fractures would downthrow eastwards in order to bring the Namurian belt down to the more southerly position of the Pyle area. Further extensive synclinal outliers of Namurian could also occur in the western portion of the front of the Bay (see Fig. 2.1), as indicated by the Whitethorn boreholes, each of which showed a solid floor of shale and sandstone.

The Coal Measures of the region, like the succession for the whole South Wales Coalfield, falls into two distinct halves, a lower (softer) sequence and an upper (resistant) unit. The Lower and Middle Coal Measures consist mainly of shales and mudstones with only occasional arenaceous interruptions. The Upper Coal Measures, on the other hand, comprise thick arenites of "Pennant" type. This contrast in resistance to erosion between the lower and upper halves of the Coal Measure succession has played an important role in the form and the evolution of Swansea Bay. Today, the contrast is plainly visible as the steep front presented to the sea by the twin hills of Swansea City (Townhill and Kilvey Hill) and again by the steep rises overlooking Port Talbot and Margam.

The Lower and Middle Coal Measures outcrop as a broad belt across northernmost Gower from Crofty in the west to Blackpill and Singleton in the east. The belt reappears across the Bay in the Baglan-Cwmavon area, and if the general structure on this South Crop of the Coalfield was straightforward, this Baglan Coal Measure outcrop would have been succeeded southwards immediately by parallel belts of Namurian shales and then Carboniferous Limestone - on the same latitude positions as in East Gower. Instead these Namurian-Limestone belts to the east of Swansea Bay are shifted well southwards and the cause lies in the great southerly downthrow of one of the most important fractures in South Wales - the Moel Gilau Fault (Fig. 2.1). This E-W fracture has a southerly downthrow which reaches to over 1000 metres near Baglan and as a result a large area of resistant Upper Coal Measures outcrop to the east of Port Talbot and Margam.

One important effect of the Moel Gilau Fault is to introduce a second, more southerly, "South Crop" of Lower and Middle Coal Measures, this time from Margam Moors to Tondu, at a latitudinal position well south of much of Gower.

Two other fractures, however, prevent this important mass of resistant Pennant Measures (south of the Moel Gilau Fault) from continuing westwards into Swansea Bay. These are the Morfa faults which trend NNW-SSE through the Briton Ferry-Aberavon areas. Both fractures *upthrow* to the west. It is difficult to assess the maximum throws because of the extensive blanketing of these coastal flats by sand. However the throw of the Morfa Newydd Fault was claimed by the 1905 Geological Survey Sheet (Glam. 33NW) to be 300 yards at a point 500 yards NW of Morfa village whilst a throw of 108 yards was placed on a fracture which could be part of the Morfa Fault (shown as a continuous extensive line on the new Swansea Sheet 247, published in 1973).

The combined effect of these two Morfa faults is to cut off any westward extent of the Upper Coal Measures into the Bay and (in combination with the southerly downthrow of the Moel Gilau fracture) to probably result in a substantial tract of Lower and Middle Coal Measures in the eastern half of Swansea Bay (Fig. 2.1). One additional aid to this extension of sub-Pennant Coal Measures in the Bay (as also on the mainland south of Morfa) is the presence of a number of E-W thrusts (including the Newlands Thrust) all of which downthrow to the south and thereby stretch even further south the base of the Coal Measures (see Fig. 2.1).

The Gower representative of the Moel Gilau Fault is not easy to detect. Strahan (1907, p.45) pointed out that at its point of intersection with the coast, the fracture points slightly south of west and that "it was suggested by Mr. Tidderman that the Mumbles Fault...might be the Moel Gilau Fault". "The Mumbles Fault" is the Oystermouth Fault which cuts off the northern limb of the Oystermouth Syncline. Strahan preferred however to link the Moel Gilau Fault with contorted measures near Clyne Castle. The newer geological survey sheet shows an east-west fracture with a southerly downthrow between Blackpill and West Cross (SS617 900) and this seems to be the more logical continuation of the Moel Gilau Fault than the Oystermouth fracture.

Two other major fractures have probably also played a major role in the evolution of Swansea Bay. One is the east-west fracture which faults Triassic against Coal Measures between Pyle and Kenfig Hill. This fault has therefore moved in post-Triassic times, downthrowing to the south. It could continue at least some way into Swansea Bay. The Palaeozoic-Mesozoic (surface) contact across the front of Swansea Bay may therefore be, in part, a faulted one (Fig. 2.1) before becoming one of unconformity further west.

The other important fracture is the southwestward continuation of the Vale of Neath Disturbance. This continuation is believed by Al-Saadi and Brooks (1973) to traverse the deep channel which lies just to the east of Mumbles Head. It is difficult to assess the structural effects of this continuation under the western half of the Bay. The Vale of Neath Fault is known to have suffered both lateral and vertical movements (Owen 1954, p.350). Near Jersey Marine, the fault has a westerly downthrow, but it must be remembered that the fracture has a notorious habit of reversing its direction of downthrow along the Vale of Neath and northeastwards (Owen 1954, p.349). The nature of the deep channel off Mumbles Head could indicate the presence of rigid rocks on both sides of the fracture line of weakness. The likelihood is that some Carboniferous Limestone outcrops east of the Vale of Neath Fault, S.E. of Gower. What is not known is the detailed fold structure. That there are several synclinal areas is suggested by the detection of shale or sandstone at the lowest depths reached in the Whitethorn boreholes (I.G.S.) in this western portion of the front of the Bay (see Evans and Thompson, 1979, Fig. 10). It may even be that the Namurian sequence develops more grit horizons eastwards across the Bay to ultimately compare with the succession N. of Bridgend.

What is also not known, of course, is whether this Mumbles continuation of the Vale of Neath Fault disrupts the Carboniferous/Lias boundary - in other words has the fracture suffered post-Liassic movement? Later movements (probably mainly vertical) have been suggested by Owen along this fracture in its Glynneath-Crickhowell tract. Late movements along the Swansea Bay portion may well have disrupted and thereby weakened any Mesozoic blanket.

PERMO-TRIASSIC EROSION

Permo-Triassic erosion in Britain may well have been as extensive and as intense as in any other part of geological time. It was a time of hot, arid climate with the active erosion of completed or still growing Hercynian structures. Erosion may in places have kept pace with the growth of structures. O.T. Jones, in particular has drawn attention to the degree of erosion and removal of material (1956, p.347). He believes the amount of strata removed from the crests of anticlines in the Vale of Glamorgan to have been of the order of nearly 5000 metres (and this removal prior to the deposition of any Trias). In South Pembrokeshire, up to 5500 metres may have removed.

Similar intense removal must have occurred in Gower. The most revealing piece of evidence, as far as this early history of Swansea Bay is concerned, occurs at Port Eynon (Fig. 2.1). Here Triassic conglomerates rest on Namurian shales and occur very close to the Namurian-Limestone boundary. The conglomerate was seen to rest almost horizontally on nearly vertical Namurian shales in a pit described in the West Gower and Pembrey Survey Memoir (1907, p.18). The shales were stained red and purple. The boulders and pebbles in the conglomerate were mostly of limestone, pointing to the erosion of the Carboniferous Limestone by these later (?) Triassic times. This occurrence has two important significances. Firstly, it shows that by Keuper times (the conglomerate being probably of the same Keuper age as similar lithologies in the Vale of Glamorgan), the whole of the Coal Measure sequence (which could be as much as 3500 metres, if not more) and almost all the Namurian (another 600 metres) had been removed from this Port Eynon locality. Secondly, the conglomerate outcrop rests at a present-day height range of only 30 to 45 metres above sea level, in a kind of topographical hollow with the Limestone plateau rising to 109 metres to the northwest near Littlehills. The Port Eynon Triassic locality must have been the site of a gulley or depression, carved into the softer Namurian shales with the more resistant limestone rising higher on either side. The Old Red Sandstone hills of Cefn Bryn and Rhossili Down must inevitably have stood well above the level of this Triassic depression.

Across the modern Bay, Triassic conglomerates rest unconformably across different divisions of the Carboniferous Limestone in the Porthcawl and Ogmore districts, again pointing to the vast removal of Upper Carboniferous strata by Keuper times. George (1933) has drawn attention to the pre-Triassic topography of the Porthcawl area. "It is manifest that the scarp of the Oolite was marked out in all essentials in pre-Triassic times; the planation of Ogmore Down is also of ancient date, for recent erosion has had no effect in defining the line of the Rhiw Fault by differential weathering" (George, 1933, p.265). Low erosive levels were therefore present in Gower and in the west of the Vale of Glamorgan by Triassic times. One is strongly tempted to suggest that the present topographical outline of Gower had a broadly comparable Triassic ancestor. The flat bevelled surfaces were not there then but a surface ranging in a height amplitude of some 150-200 metres was roughly in existence. Pliocene to Pleistocene sea-level changes were to do the final trimming.

There have probably been several movements along the Moel Gilau Fault, the ages of which are not easy to determine. The fracture is believed to have suffered both vertical and lateral movements (Woodland and Evans, 1964), the latter probably being later. The presence of Triassic conglomerates on a much eroded Limestone surface at Porthcawl and Ogmore does however, have some further significance with respect to the movements along the Moel Gilau fracture. This low level surface lies to the south of the higher Pennant plateaux occurring east of Port Talbot. The implication is that these Pennant Scarps also dominated the Triassic scene and this geological situation could only have arisen if the Moel Gilau Fault had already dropped down a Pennant block prior to Triassic erosion. In other words, the large southerly downthrows along the Moel Gilau Fault occurred during the Hercynian earth-movements (perhaps as late adjustments).

If low levels of erosion were already in existence in parts of Gower and the Vale of Glamorgan by Triassic times, what of the topography elsewhere in the Swansea district? Active pre-Triassic erosion along the Vale of Neath Fault could have opened up a depression across the west of the modern Bay. Moreover, in the eastern portion of the Bay, the combined westerly *upthrows* along the Morfa faults would have brought up the softer Lower and Middle Coal Measures (to the west) against the tough Pennant sandstones (to the east) resulting in a westward facing scarp along the Port Talbot fringe. The present day Port Talbot-Margam scarps may then have had their Triassic ancestors (Fig. 2.3a) (red-stained Pennant Sandstone can, in fact, be seen in a quarry at 100 metres O.D. above Dan-y-Graig, near Baglan).

It is suggested that,by late Triassic times, erosion had excavated down to Lower and Middle Coal Measure levels in the Swansea Bay area with the tough Pennant sandstones forming scarps to the north and to the east (as in fact they do today). To the south lay isolated ridges of tougher limestone (or even Namurian grit) broken along lines of weakness, such as cross faults or along the Vale of Neath depression. Fig. 2.2 is an attempt to reconstruct the topography of a Swansea Bay that was virtually there in Triassic times. To the east lay the higher Pennant Block (south of the Moel Gilau Fault but east of the Morfa fractures), bordered southwards by a lower-lying, *but undulating,* "Vale of Glamorgan". Gower, to the west, also undulated in height, from low gulleys to the higher ridges of Old Red Sandstone (perhaps still even capped by some residual limestone).

It is doubtful whether more than a thin veneer of Triassic gravels, screes or dusts was ever deposited across the ancestral Gower or Swansea Bay areas. Slightly higher limestone ridges and hills would not even have had these veneers, and the first blanketing deposits of the Mesozoic would then have been the Lias. This seems to have been the case across much of the western front of the Bay.

Post-Carboniferous Geology

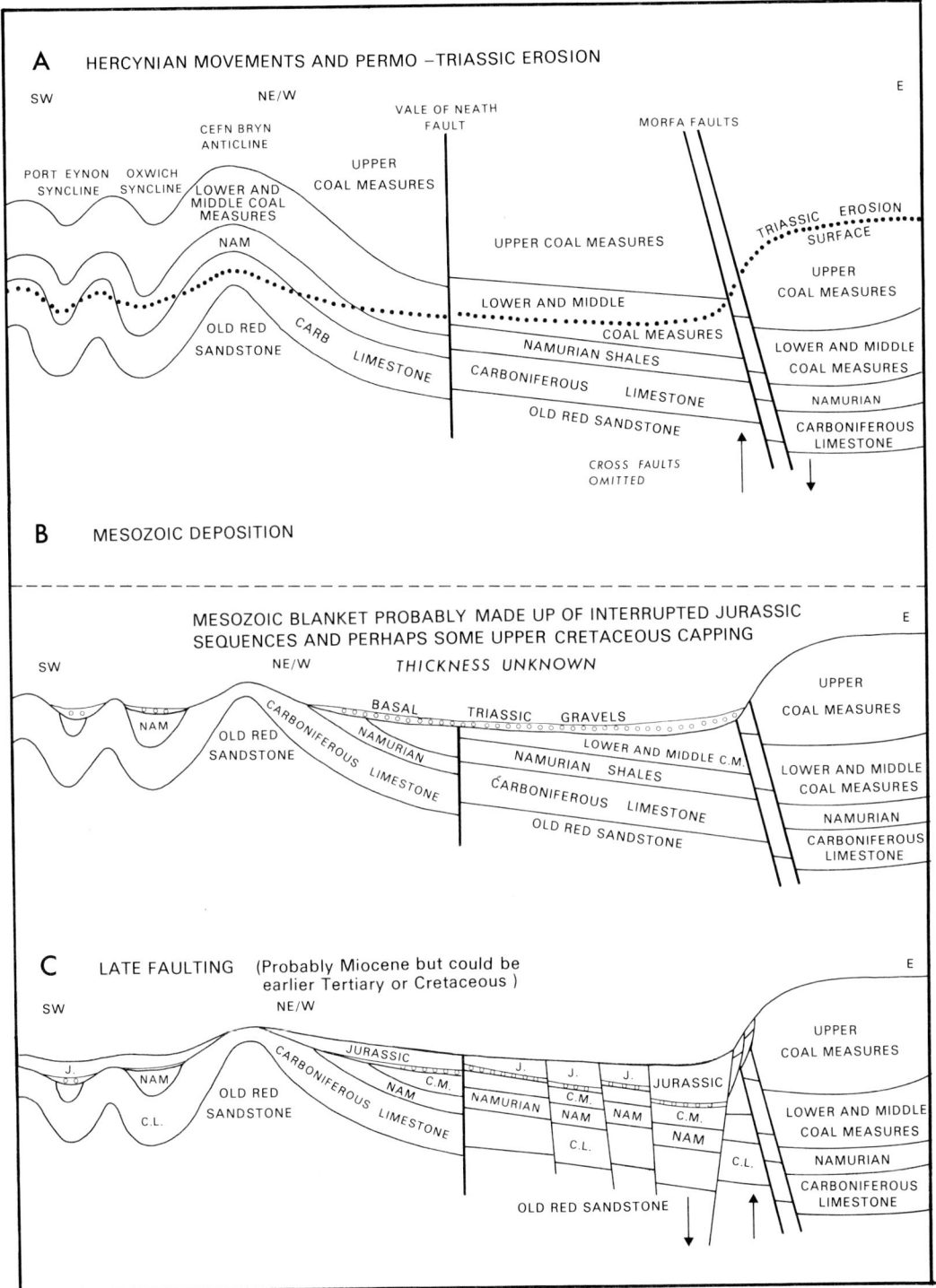

Figure 2.3. Suggested structural evolution of the Swansea Bay area.

JURASSIC-MIOCENE HISTORY

During Lower Jurassic times, however, the Liassic seas flooded northwards into South Wales and the Mesozoic blanket spread more and more inland. The South Wales Coalfield must ultimately have become drowned beneath Jurassic (probably even Early Jurassic) waters and our Triassic Swansea "embayment" was to be covered up (and thereby preserved) for some considerable time to come.

The nature of the Mesozoic blanket over the South Wales Coalfield is of course unknown. The probability is that the blanket, though present, was never thick over the main body of Wales. As areas such as the Bristol Channel and the Celtic Seas were subsiding continually (and thereby amassing thick Jurassic successions), at the same time Wales was a positive region prone to periodic rising with repeated removals of any Mesozoic deposits that were laid down. The Jurassic succession over the South Wales Coalfield was probably a condensed one with numerous interruptions in the sequence (Fig. 2.3b). Lower Cretaceous deposits were almost certainly absent as this was the time of appreciable earth movement in the British area, in fact the time of the main downfolding of the Bristol Channel syncline (Owen, 1976, p.129; Evans and Thompson, 1979, p.13), and by inference possibly the time of appreciable upwarping of the neighbouring Welsh and Exmoor masses. Rising Chalk seas however returned to once again drown the Welsh area and to probably deposit some carbonate sheets over the attenuated (and by now even more eroded) Jurassic cover.

End Cretaceous uplifts and marine recession would then have once again exposed the South Wales area and the final removal of a Mesozoic blanket began. Palaeogene seas probably now lay to the west (Celtic Seas) and south (English Channel) though Eocene tongues may have penetrated into the western end of the Bristol Channel. Palaeogene crustal unrest is however evidenced by the injection of the Lundy igneous complex and the sharp subsidence of the elongated Oligocene troughs along a Devon-E. Lundy-Flimston line.

This crustal unrest continued during the Tertiary, possibly culminating in the Miocene climax when renewed faulting occurred in the Bristol Channel and neighbouring land areas. Some of the fault movement took place along already existing (even Hercynian) fractures. It could be that reversed directions of downthrow (now to the west) occurred along the Morfa faults, now downthrowing the eastern portion of Swansea Bay. New faults may also have formed. The E-W fracture near Pyle may date from Miocene times, as also may a probable fracture just offshore from the Vale of Glamorgan's western coast (Fig. 2.3c).

THE POST-MIOCENE HISTORY

The geomorphologist seeks to explain the development of the landscape following the uniformitarian reasoning familiar to geologists. In the first place, the shape of the land is considered, particularly the erosional facets of the land; secondly the pattern and form of the drainage network is analysed, and thirdly any sedimentary deposits associated with facets of the landscape must be evaluated. Until the mid-20th century geomorphologists paid great attention to the development of a denudation chronology based almost entirely upon morphology. Present day approaches require support from stratigraphical evidence and where available, absolute dates. A consideration of the geomorphology of the Swansea Bay Area can be sub-divided into four sections; erosion surfaces above 213m (700ft), marine abrasion platforms below 213m, the river valleys, the chronology of events which preceeded the present landscape.

Upland Erosion Surfaces: The development of Welsh scenery has been the object of research and subject of discussion for over 100 years. E.H. Brown (1960) reviews these facts and theories beginning with Ramsey's (1846) concept of 'a single inclined surface formed by marine erosion' from which the relief of Wales has been carved.   Successive researchers on this topic have identified an increasing number of geomorphologically significant surfaces, for, despite the popular image of a mountainous country, Wales is a land of plateaux deeply incised by streams.

In an attempt to make sense of the multiplicity of surfaces which may be observed in Wales, Brown (1960) identifies four groups of surface remnant in Upland areas. These are: Summit plain 2100-3500 ft (640-1070m) O.D.
High plateaux 1700-1900 ft (520-580m) O.D.
Middle peneplain 1200-1600 ft (366-488m) O.D.
Low peneplain 700-1100 ft (214-336m) O.D.

Remnants of these surfaces are found on interfluves and only rarely do sufficient of them remain in the form of accordant summits of hills to enable a reasonable attempt to decipher the history of landscape development. The problem of their origin is suggested by Brown's nomenclature in that he refers to the older, higher surfaces as 'plain' and 'plateau', both terms being non-commital regarding the origin of the feature. The younger, lower surfaces are referred to as 'peneplains' with a greater air of confidence as this term suggests a particular developmental process. A peneplain results from the long-continued operation of sub-aerial denudation which ultimately reduces the landscape to low relief. Sub-aerial denudation includes weathering and removal of the regolith from the land surface through the combined forces of gravity and water operating downslope. The end result, which is interrupted only by changes in climate and baselevel, is the production of a gently undulating landscape.

These upland surfaces, which form an important part of the Welsh landscape, result from a series of alterations of base level caused by uplift. The usual result has been that each 'pulse' of uplift renewed the power of erosion so that a lower surface was created at the expense of the more elevated surfaces. An observed fact which counts against their development by marine agency is that the lower surfaces penetrate far into the older surfaces especially along old-established drainage lines.   This would have necessitated a coastline of extremely complex nature, which seems unlikely.

Around Swansea Bay the Low Peneplain cuts across the Pennant Sandstones, bevelling the escarpments north and east of the embayment to give several pronounced plateaux such as Mynydd Sylen (284m), Mynydd Garn fach (297m), Mynydd Drumau (272m), Cefn Morfydd (307m) and Mynydd Margam (344m). In this area the low peneplain has a relief which ranges from about 260m (850ft) up to rounded summits between 305 and 328m (1000-1075ft)(Fig. 2.4).

Surfaces which are attributed to the Middle Peneplain can be seen in Mynydd March Hywel (418m) and Hirfynydd (380m) between the Tawe and Neath rivers and this surface is more extremely developed in the upper Afan (Avan) Valley inland from Port Talbot between 360 and 430m (1200-1400ft).   Only Craig-y-Llyn (600m) and Mynydd Llangeiner (568m) are placed in the High Plateau Stage 520-565m (1700-1850ft) by Brown and the highest peaks of Bannan Sir Gaer (750m) and the Brecon Beacons Pen-y-Fau (886m) form monadnocks rising above.

The presence of these erosion surfaces is an observable fact and, as they occur throughout most of Upland Wales, it would appear that the country remained continuously land during the period when they were cut. However, as George (1961) is at pains to point out, mere altitudinal accordance is insufficient evidence for a common origin, especially when a considerable range of heights is involved and there are strong breaks of slope within Brown's groupings which suggest these surfaces are complex in origin and not so easily placed into four simple groups (George, 1961).

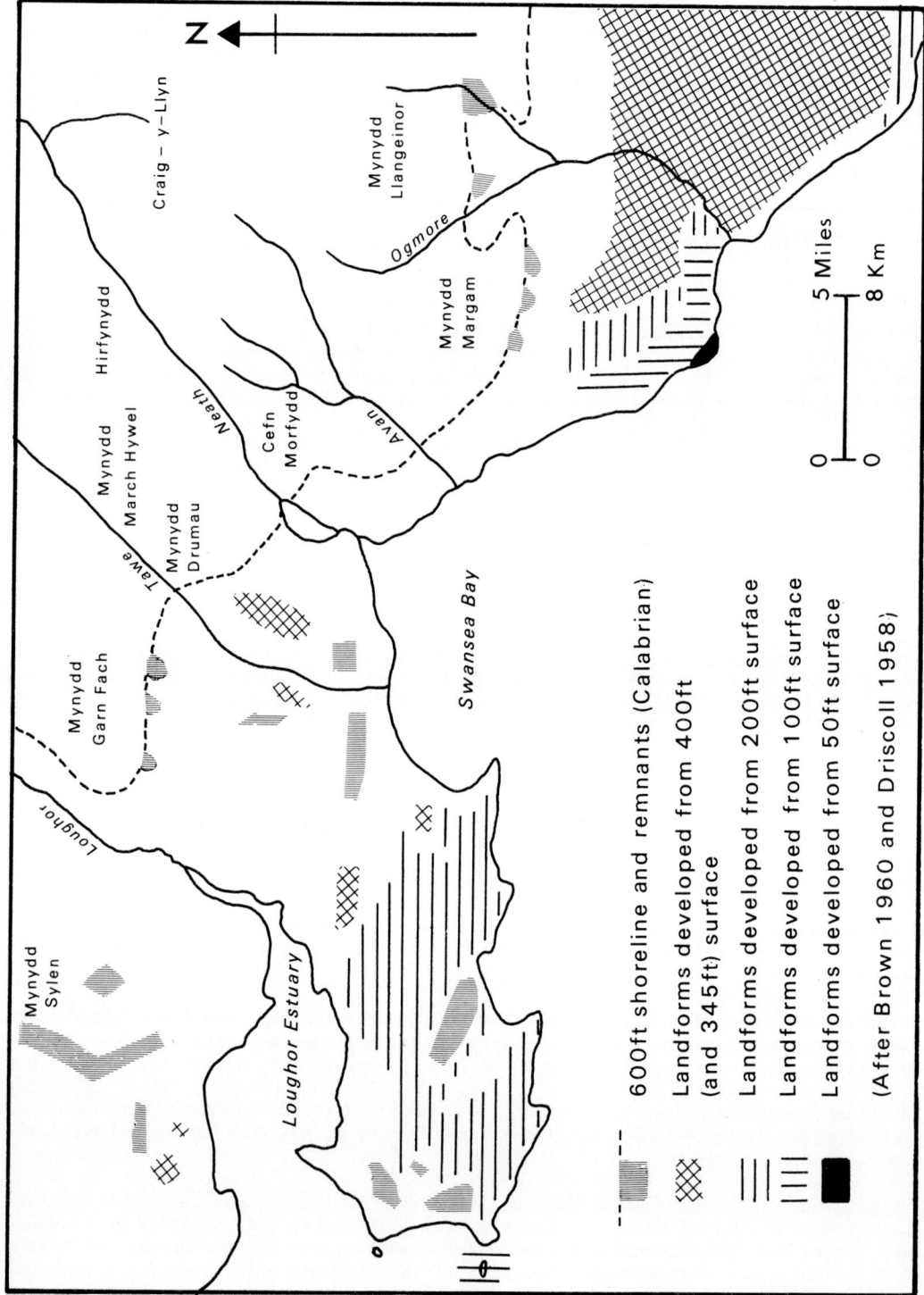

Figure 2.4. Erosional surfaces of the Swansea Bay hinterland.

Marine Abrasion Platforms: The picture is clearer in respect of land forms below 213m (700ft) and there is agreement upon the origin of the coastal platforms which surround Wales. These features are step-like in appearance, sloping gently seaward, and are backed by an abrupt rise to higher land. Their geographical distribution is such that they can be seen all around the coast from Gwent to Clwyd. Where they occur, these coastal platforms cut across many different rock formations irrespective of structure and lithology. The evidence suggests that successive changes of sea level caused the withdrawal of the sea from the coast revealing the plains of marine erosion and subjecting them to sub-aerial denudation. Although subjected to weathering and erosion these features are not so fragmented as the erosion surfaces of the uplands and are more easily traced.

In South Wales, Goskar and Trueman (1934), Driscoll (1958) and Brown (1952) have identified marine platforms at several different elevations. The highest of these is known as the 600ft platform (183m). It is well developed in South Wales and around Swansea Bay remnants of it include Rhossili Down (193m), Llanmadoc Hill (186m) Cefn Bryn (186m) Townhill (173m), Kilvey Hill (193m). On the eastern side of the Bay the fault scarp bounding the west face of Mynydd Margam rises directly from the alluvial deposits and no remnants have been identified upon it.

Below the accordant summit levels of the 600ft surface, a further coincidence of levels occurs at 122m (400ft). In Gower only a small area is preserved on Clyne Common and limited areas have been identified in the Vale of Glamorgan, where there is the development of a more extensive 115m (345ft) shoreline (Driscoll, 1958). The most extensive of these plains of marine abrasion is referred to as the 200ft surface (61m). This is widely developed in Gower but less so in the Vale of Glamorgan, where Driscoll has mapped a 210ft (64m) shoreline. In spite of an overall uniformity upon this surface, there is still considerable variation in relief. Along the south coast of Gower, for example, the surface relief of Oxwich Point lies between 76m and 85m whilst Pennard Head also on the 200ft platform rises to 97m (320ft) without perceptible break.

In his paper on the Vale of Glamorgan, Driscoll draws attention to shoreline remnants at 100ft and 50ft above present sea level but no investigators have described similar features in Gower. A most dramatic example of a planed surface occurs across the folded Carboniferous Limestone of the Worm's Head where at 33m (100ft) a horizontal surface independent of the underlying structure occurs. Although morphology suggests lower benches at Rhossili and Slade, near Oxwich, similar in height to the 50ft surface of the Vale of Glamorgan, both are constructional features produced by solifluction and not by marine erosion. However, it must be recorded that many of the small dry valleys (slades) which lead down to the south coast of Gower are not graded to present day sea level but to one 8-15m above. Several of the famous 'bone caves' of Gower also appear to have been developed at this height as well (see also Chapter 6).

In his account of the evolution of the Bristol Channel, North (1955) draws attention to the present coast and off-shore-platform suggesting that should there be another uplift the present cliff and shore-platform would add another step to the series. Temporary lowering of sea-level during the Pleistocene achieved this result, but the post-glacial rise of sea-level has brought land and sea back to approximately the same position. The presence of cemented beach material may be observed at Fox Hole in process of being eroded away. This confirms that the present cliffs are fossil (relict) and that little post-glacial change has taken place (Groom, 1971). As this beach material and other more obviously "raised" beaches are thought to be of Ipswichian interglacial date (Bowen, 1974) these features are outside the scope of the present review

The River Valleys: The plan-form and profile of the rivers in Wales give the geomorphologist an alternative approach to the study of land forms. It also brings

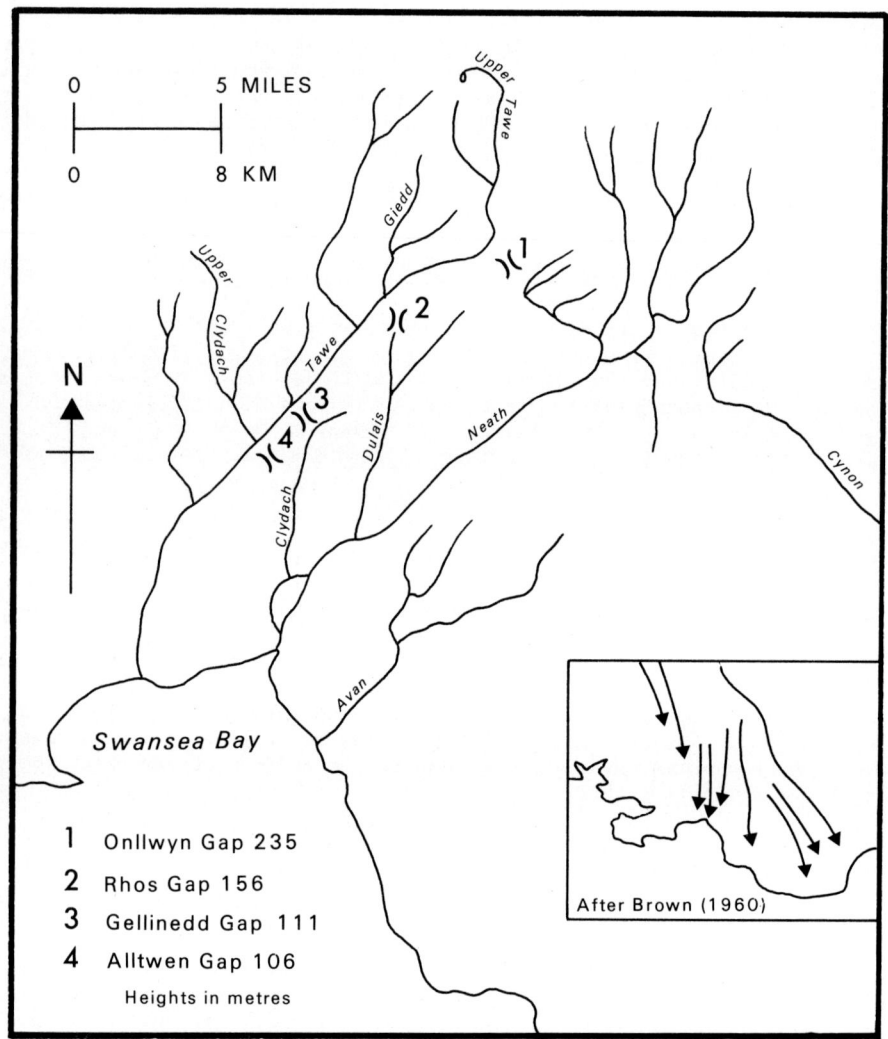

Figure 2.5. Probable changes in the drainage pattern of the Neath and Tawe river systems.

together the previous information on upland erosion surface and the plains of marine abrasion.

Evidence for the earliest drainage pattern of Wales has been interpreted in two ways. Brown (1960) follows Strahan (1902) and O.T. Jones (1952) in suggesting a radial form originating from a point south of Snowdonia. In contrast Linton (1951) makes a strong case for eastward-flowing consequents forming the headwaters of the proto-Trent and proto-Thames respectively. Which of these two theories is taken is not important in our present discussion other than to say the original drainage of South Wales probably had a northwest-southeast trend (Fig. 2.5).

Previous authors see this earlier drainage pattern superimposed upon the Palaeozoic rocks of Wales by a cover rock, now removed (Linton, 1951; Brown, 1960), or by the more straight forward extension of consequent streams across an emergent landmass

(George, 1974) without an intervening cover-rock. In both cases consequent streams are initiated on an uplifted surface and proceed to grade their valleys. As erosion of their valleys proceeds the less competent strata or fault-zones are exploited and diversion by river-capture occurs. Gradually the original consequent pattern is disrupted leaving "wind gaps" at high elevation on the interfluves.

There has been considerable discussion regarding the history of the major streams entering Swansea Bay (Strahan, 1902; R.D. Jones, 1931, 1939; O.T. Jones, 1952). In both cases, vigorous subsequent streams, exploiting the shattered rocks of the Swansea Valley and Neath disturbances, are thought to have cut back rapidly disrupting the pattern of south or south-easterly flowing streams. An examination of the interfluves to the southeast of the Tawe led O.T. Jones (1952) to suggest that the Upper Tawe may once have flowed through the gap at Onllwyn at 235m to join the line of the present Dulais. Similarly, the Afon Giedd at Ystradgynlais could have continued across a col at 145m and, near Pontardawe, the Cwm Du and Upper Clydach could have continued across cols at Gellinedd (111m) and Alltwen (106m). Although these cols are impressive features, aligned very nicely with the supposed original consequents, capture took place after a remarkable degree of incision. This does not point to river capture in the normal sense, even with the aid of a rapidly eroding Tawe along the Swansea Valley Disturbance, and diffluent ice action may be a more satisfactory explanation (Linton, 1951, 1963).

If it is accepted that the 600ft, 400ft and 200ft marine abrasion platforms were successively exposed by a sequence of uplifts, then the lower reaches of the Neath and Tawe rivers were the last to be integrated into the river systems as the consequents were extended. Unfortunately, any evidence for this has been lost by subsequent glaciation in the lower valleys, although knick-points and graded sections of valleys inland point to headward erosion, working upstream as a result of changing base-levels (O.T. Jones, 1952).

The Pre-glacial Landscape History: A study of the rivers and upland surfaces of Wales indicates a long and complex history extending back through geological time. Earlier in this Chapter, the importance of the former Triassic landscape has been stressed, and both Strahan (1902) and O.T. Jones (1952) thought the Triassic surface and its rivers to be an important stage in Welsh landscape development, extending the sub-Triassic surface across the Welsh massif. In the past, Jurassic and Tertiary deposits were not usually considered to have influenced the area of Wales, except peripherally, but most investigators thought that the Cretaceous rocks extended across the country. Consequent streams, developed on the Chalk surface, were believed to form the initial drainage pattern. Discoveries since the late 1960's, indicating faulting of considerable magnitude in the Mochras basin and in the down-faulted area near Lundy, make it clear that the sub-Cenomanian surface was already disrupted in the early Tertiary, and the 600m of sediment at Mochras does not include any signs of derived Cretaceous material. In the light of these findings, it is now difficult to support the hypotheses of a Chalk cover from which the drainage was superimposed. If it existed at all, it was probably removed by the end of the Eocene.

The age of the High Plateau erosion surface across Wales still causes controversy and Linton (1964) advanced the possibility that the older surfaces, observed in Brittany, Cornwall and Devon, Wales and Scotland, could be "of a single age but unequally elevated". He subscribed to an early Tertiary age for the High Plateau which was then disrupted by the Alpine earth movements. This does not necessarily conflict with Brown's idea that the Welsh High Plateau is undeformed: Wales simply acted as a unit throughout Tertiary and Pleistocene times. Alternatively, the High Plateau is post-Alpine, probably early Pliocene in age. No deposits have been described in Wales which would help to date these uplifted surfaces, but, in east Devon and west Dorset, Waters (1960) has described gravels between 280m and 412m above sea level lying upon a pre-Miocene surface.

George (1974) states that the Welsh landscape appears to be deceptively old but in fact - as a result of marine planing and subaerial denudation - it is much younger, late Neogene or even Pleistocene. His concept of repeated 'pulsed' emergence has the advantage of fitting both inland and coastal evidence, although the mechanism is not readily explained. It is perhaps significant that crustal movements associated with the opening of the northwest Atlantic began at the end of the Cretaceous, and that the British Isles suddenly found itself on the trailing edge of the European plate. This may have initiated the pulses of uplift. Flemming and Roberts (1973) have explained how eustatic changes in sea level can result from either glacial accumulation or loss but also changes in the mid-Atlantic ridge can result in up to 10 percent changes in ocean depth. This explanation could help to throw light upon some of the changes of sea level during the Tertiary. Each upward pulse was probably followed by a slight settlement which enabled an extension inland of the marine planing. In this way, the already emergent relief from beneath the Triassic deposits was trimmed, leaving remnants preserved in faults or in pre-existing valleys, as at Port Eynon. Associated with these sea level changes, river erosion would work inland, grading the rivers as R.O. Jones (1939) and George (1942) have shown for the 200ft feature.

Although a 'stratigraphical' position can be argued for these erosional features in the landscape of Wales, it is clearly difficult to place an absolute date upon them. The present authors are in agreement with George (1974b) when he describes the coastal platforms as pre-glacial. In view of the tectonic instability, it is difficult to subscribe to the correlation of the 600ft surface in Wales with the Calabrian (earliest Pleistocene) shoreline. However, King (1977) points to the importance of the Calabrian in the development of landforms in southeast England. Even if it could be correlated with the 600ft surface in Wales, it does not preclude the possibility that the lower surfaces had an earlier, rather than a later date, as has commonly been assumed from their lower position. This has the great benefit of allowing a late Pliocene time for the development of all the coastal platforms, rather than telescoping them all into the early Pleistocene. With their cover of drifts, we can at least be sure that the platforms are pre-glacial, but even this lacks precision.

The major relief features of Swansea Bay at the beginning of the Pleistocene were probably not too dissimilar to those we can observe today. Although ice has twice affected the area, its impact has been limited to deepening the river valleys and some gouging in Swansea Bay. Glacial or glacio-fluvial action has breached the Pennant scarps in a number of places but these are relatively minor changes to a basic landscape which has proved to be surprisingly persistent.

ACKNOWLEDGEMENTS

The authors wish to thank Mrs. Glenys Bridges for her careful preparation of the text-figures.

REFERENCES

Bowen, D.Q. (1974). The Quaternary in Wales. *In*: Owen, T.R. (Ed.). *Upper Palaeozoic and Post-Palaeozoic Rocks of Wales*, 373-426.
Brown, E.H. (1952). The 600-foot Platform in Wales. *Proc. 8th Gen. Ass. - 17th Congress Internat. Geogr. Union, Washington*, 304-312.
Brown, E.H. (1960). *The Relief and Drainage of Wales*, Cardiff.
Driscoll, E.M. (1958). The denudation chronology of the Vale of Glamorgan. *Trans. Inst. Brit. Geogr.*, 25, 45-57.
Evans, D.J., and Thompson, M.S. (1979). The Geology of the central Bristol Channel and the Lundy area, South Western Approaches, British Isles. *Proc. Geol. Ass.*, 90,

1-14.

Flemming, N.C., and Roberts, D.G. (1973). Tectono-eustatic changes in sea level and seafloor spreading. *Nature, Lond., 243* (5401), 19-22.

George, T.N. (1933). The Carboniferous Limestone Series in the West of the Vale of Glamorgan. *Q. Jl. geol. Soc. Lond., 89*, 221-72.

George, T.N. (1942). The development of the Towy and Upper Usk drainage pattern. *Q. Jl. geol. Soc. Lond., 98*, 89-137.

George, T.N. (1961). The Welsh Landscape. *Science Progress, 49*, 242-264.

George, T.N. (1974a). The Cenozoic Evolution of Wales. *In:* Owen, T.R. (Ed.). *Upper Palaeozoic and Post-Palaeozoic Rocks of Wales*, 341-371.

George, T.N. (1974b). Prologue to a Geomorphology of Britain. *In:* Brown, E.H., and Waters, R.S. (Eds.). *Progress in Geomorphology*. Inst. Brit. Geog. Special Pal. No. 7, 113-125.

Goskar, K.L., and Trueman, A.E. (1934). The Coastal Plateaux of South Wales. *Geol. Mag., 71*, 468-477.

Groom, G.E. (1971). Geomorphology. *In:* Balchin, W.G.V. (Ed.). *Swansea and its Region*. B.A.A.S., Swansea.

Jones, O.T. (1952). The drainage system of Wales and the adjacent regions. *Q. Jl. geol. Soc. Lond., 107*, 201-225.

Jones, O.T. (1956). The Geological Evolution of Wales and the adjacent regions. *Q. Jl. geol. Soc. Lond., 111*, 323-51.

Jones, R.O. (1931). The development of the Tawe Drainage. *Proc. Geol. Assoc., 44*, 305-321.

Jones, R.O. (1939). The evolution of the Neath-Tawe drainage. *Proc. Geol. Assoc., 50*, 530-566.

King, C.A.M. (1977). The early Quaternary landscape with consideration of neo-tectonic matters. *In:* Shotton, F.W. (Ed.). *British Quaternary Studies*, Oxford.

Linton, D.L. (1951). Midland Drainage - some considerations bearing on its origin. *The Advancement of Science, 7*, (28), 449-456.

Linton, D.L. (1963). The Forms of Glacial Erosion. *Trans. Inst. Brit. Geogr., 33*, 1-28.

Linton, D.L. (1964). Tertiary Landscape Evolution. *In:* Watson, J.W., and Sissons, J.B. (Eds.). *The British Isles: A systematic geography*, 110-130.

North, F.J. (1955). *The Evolution of the Bristol Channel*. National Museum of Wales, Cardiff.

Owen, T.R. (1954). The Structure of the Neath Disturbance between Bryniau Gleision and Glynneath, South Wales. *Q. Jl. geol. Soc. London, 109*, 333-65.

Owen, T.R. (1976). *The Geological Evolution of the British Isles*. Pergamon Press, Oxford, 161pp.

Ramsay, A.C. (1846). The Denudation of South Wales and the adjacent English Counties. *Mem. Geol. Surv., 1*.

Strahan, A. (1902). On the origin of the river system of South Wales and its connection with that of the Severn and Thames. *Q. Jl. geol. Soc. Lond., 58*, 207-25.

Strahan, A. (1907). The geology of the South Wales Coalfield. Part VIII. The Country around Swansea. *Mem. geol. Surv. UK.*, 170pp.

Strahan, A. (1907). The geology of the South Wales Coalfield. Part IX. West Gower and the Country around Pembrey. *Mem. geol. Surv. UK.*, 50pp.

Waters, R.S. (1960). The bearing of superficial deposits on the age and origin of the upland plain of east Devon, west Dorset and south Somerset. *Trans. Inst. Br. Geogr., 28*, 89-95.

Woodland, A.W., and Evans, W.B. (1964). Geology of the South Wales Coalfield. Part IV. The Country around Pontypridd and Maesteg. 3rd Ed. *Mem. Geol. Surv. UK.*, 391pp.

DISCUSSION I

Owen: Could I ask Mr. Price about the I.G.S. boreholes? I.G.S. noted penetration of shale or sandstone in the solid rock; have you any ideas what the precise age of these horizons might be?

Price: The boreholes haven't provided any evidence which enables the ages of the materials to be determined; they are just fine glauconitic sandstones. I have seen the cores and, despite the lack of evidence, I agree with I.G.S's opinion that they believe them to be Millstone Grit or Lower Coal Measures. All three of them are very, very similar. They detect a fault in one of the cores which is right on the fault zone I have plotted on the map, which is quite pleasing, but apart from that, there is no evidence at all.

Tait: Could I ask Prof. Owen how his account ties in with the opening up of the North Atlantic? Was the Bristol Channel left as a sort of tear as the plates tore themselves apart? Was the opening up of this part of the North Atlantic something which occurred after or at the beginning of the faulting?

Owen: Not an easy question to answer. The first real sign of British events of the opening of the North Atlantic is the Cenomanian or Chalk transgression, but all the studies of the North Sea and Celtic Sea and sea basin have some geophysical evidence of much earlier infillings to rifts or graben structures. I think we've got to think of, at least, attempts to stretch and open as happening very much earlier. In fact, it has been suggested that there was even a Midland valley of Scotland stretching right back to Carboniferous and Permian times. Early openings of the Atlantic probably spread up the Spanish areas or thereabouts relatively early (Triassic) and then even further north. But what we really don't know about is the motion that goes on beneath the lithocrust preceding actual ripping movements. And this might be a considerable factor here. There were all sorts of underlying things happening underneath Britain long before the tear in the Atlantic had spread.

Ager: It all depends what you mean by "ocean". Personally, I think that there were lots of Swansea Bays and Bristol Channels all along the east side of the North Atlantic, going back to Triassic times. I think there are strong indications of the late Triassic Sea coming in from the west and a very, shallow "Irish Sea" across the central ocean floor.

Price: Has Prof. Owen any further comments on the NW and SE trending faults bisecting the centre of Swansea Bay?

Owen: As far as what I call the cross-faults are concerned, the South Wales Coalfield is riddled with fractures which run from NNW to SSE on the mainland north of Swansea Bay and south of Jersey Marine. There are innumerable faults in the region of the new bridge at Jersey Marine. We must expect them in the Bay as well. It would be silly to expect a completely unfaulted area from Mumbles across to Sker Point and what we've done in our map is to plot a number of tentative lines running that way. You have detected at least one major fault and the interesting thing about that is that it affects not just Palaeozoic but effects Mesozoic too, which is, again, evidence of post-Hercynian movements, which can be anything up to Miocene in age. To "excavate" Swansea Bay erosion would have used all the main faults, like the Swansea Valley Fault, the Dyffryn Fault, the Neath Valley Fault and the Rhyddings Fault; some of these have got throws of over 1,000ft. If you suppose that one of them (the major one which is post-Mesozoic) ties up with the post-Mesozoic faults on the Somerset side (on the west side of the Quantocks and the Minehead Faults) then they must go across the Bay. In terms of any economic development in the next century, when we may work coals undersea, these fractures will have to be borne in mind. It can never be an easy area to work economically, because there are bound to be many cross faults and also, as you indicated on your map, many folds as well (minor contortions). In the Margam (Newlands) area, for example, there are at least four thrusts running from east to west.

3. SWANSEA BAY: BEDROCK GEOLOGY AND ITS INFLUENCE OVER GEOMORPHOLOGICAL DEVELOPMENT

C. R. Price* and M. Brooks**

*Comap Project Management Services Ltd., Trafford House, Chester Road, Strafford, Manchester M32 0RS, U.K.
**Department of Geology, University College, Cardiff CF1 1XL, U.K.

ABSTRACT

High resolution continuous seismic profiling has shown that Millstone Grit and Lower Coal Measures floor the inner part of Swansea Bay. The breaching of the Carboniferous Limestone outcrop to the south by erosional processes to form the present day bay has probably been controlled by zones of structural weakness. Major faults cross the Bay, including a NNW-SSE fault, parallel to the Vale of Glamorgan coast, downthrowing Liassic limestones and shales to the west against Upper Palaeozoic rocks to the east. An unconformity between Liassic and Carboniferous rocks runs west to east across the mouth of the Bay, terminating at the fault line. To the east of the fault, thin Triassic deposits overlie the Upper Palaeozoic rocks, whereas to the west, strata up to probable Kimmeridgian age occupy the eastward extension of the Helwick syncline. Erosion by ice and meltwaters during the Pleistocene period exploited the structures and different lithologies present, vastly modifying the topography of the embayment and its approaches. Subsequent outwash and marine deposits have buried the resulting landscape, and reworking at the present sea level has given rise to the morphology of the modern Swansea Bay.

KEYWORDS

Seismic profiling (high resolution); Marine geology; Glacial processes; Overdeepened basins; Quaternary sedimentation; Swansea Bay; Bristol Channel.

INTRODUCTION

Although the geology of the Swansea area, South Wales, has been studied extensively during the last hundred years, very little is known about the geology of the immediately adjacent sea bed because it is masked by thick superficial deposits. The only relevant data are those of Al-Saadi and Brooks (1973), concerning the buried valleys of the area, of Culver (1976), describing the origins and distribution of the superficial deposits as revealed by gravity coring, and the logs of five boreholes drilled in 1972 by the Institute of Geological Sciences from the M.V. *Whitethorn*.

This chapter presents the results of a geophysical survey which was designed, firstly, to produce a geological map of the sea floor of Swansea Bay and its approaches comparable in detail to maps of adjacent land areas, secondly, to map the topography of the buried bedrock surface and, thirdly, to identify and map the thickness and distribution of the associated superficial deposits.

The combined results presented here elucidate the degree of geological control over the development of the present day morphology of the embayment and its approaches.

METHODS OF STUDY

An area of approximately 650km^2, between the coastline and 51°25'N., and between 3°44'W and 4°24'W (See Fig. 3.1), was surveyed from the University College of Swansea Research Vessel *Ocean Crest*, as well as N.E.R.C. vessels, M.V. *Edward Forbes* and R.R.S. *John Murray* at various times during the period from November, 1973 to October, 1976. A grid of traverses was established (Fig. 3.1) using an echosounder, a side-scan sonar and a continuous seismic profiler.

Navigation and position fixing was by Decca Main Chain, supplemented by sextant fixing and Decca Hi-Fix readings for calibration purposes. By the application of normal fixed error corrections and corrections to account for residual errors revealed by sextant readings and/or Hi-Fix positions in various parts of the the area, the maximum expected error in position fixes was reduced to $\pm$ 50m from the $\pm$ 150m normally expected from Decca Main Chain in this area.

A Kelvin Hughes MS26A echosounder was run during all traverses, with calibration checks being carried out at Swansea lock sill before and after each survey period. Tidal curves were computed for the area for the duration of the survey, using the Admiralty predicted values for the Standard Port of Swansea, and the bathymetric data measured off the records were reduced to Ordnance Datum (Newlyn) before plotting. These data were then used to reduce all sub-bottom levels to O.D. (Newlyn), as well as to produce a contoured bathymetric chart which displays the present morphology of the area (Fig. 3.2).

Various side-scan sonar systems were used, including the E.G.& G. Mark 16, the Waverly 'E' Type and a Kelvin Hughes MS 48 Transit Sonar. Their use was confined to the mapping of sediment boundaries and sedimentary structures between traverses because virtually no rock is exposed in the survey area.

The continuous seismic profiling survey was carried out using high resolution boomer equipment. This comprised an E.G. & G. 'Uniboom' transducer and surface towed catamaran (owned by the British Transport Docks Board), an eight-element hydrophone array and a 300 Joule energy source. Recordings were made on a Gifft recorder, via external filters and a signal processing unit. This system has several important features. The output of the transducer is a very short, broad-band acoustic pulse giving a resolution of 0.5m or better and a depth penetration to 70m through favourable substrates. The towing configuration of the transducer and hydrophone can be arranged so as to dramatically supress multiple reflections, thus preventing complete masking of the deeper sub-bottom reflectors in shallow water. Band-pass filtering, usually in the frequency range from 900 to 1200Hz, resulted in a high signal to noise ratio, and amplification in a time-variable gain mode was used to enhance later arrivals. By transmitting three pulses per second and recording the reflected signals at a scale of 125 milliseconds per 19" sweep, high visual resolution was achieved, and full use could be made of the extremely wide range of seismic reflection characteristics displayed by the various substrates.

Examination of the seismic profiles suggests a subdivision of the bedrock of the survey area into a series of distinct units, based on reflection characteristics and associated structural and stratigraphical features. These seismic units have been given geological descriptions and stratigraphical equivalents by consideration of

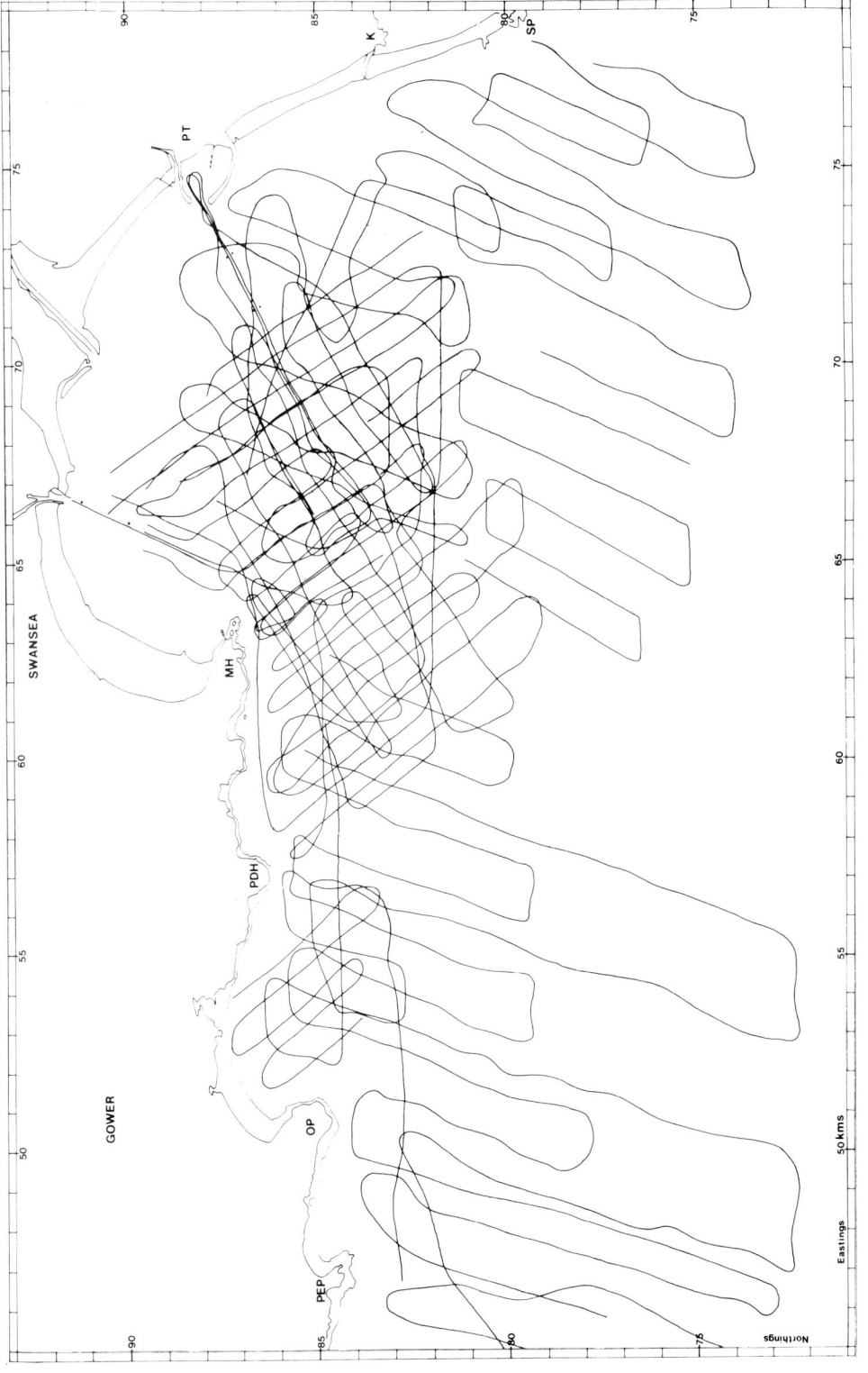

Figure 3.1. Survey area and vessel track chart (Symbols as in Figure 3.2).

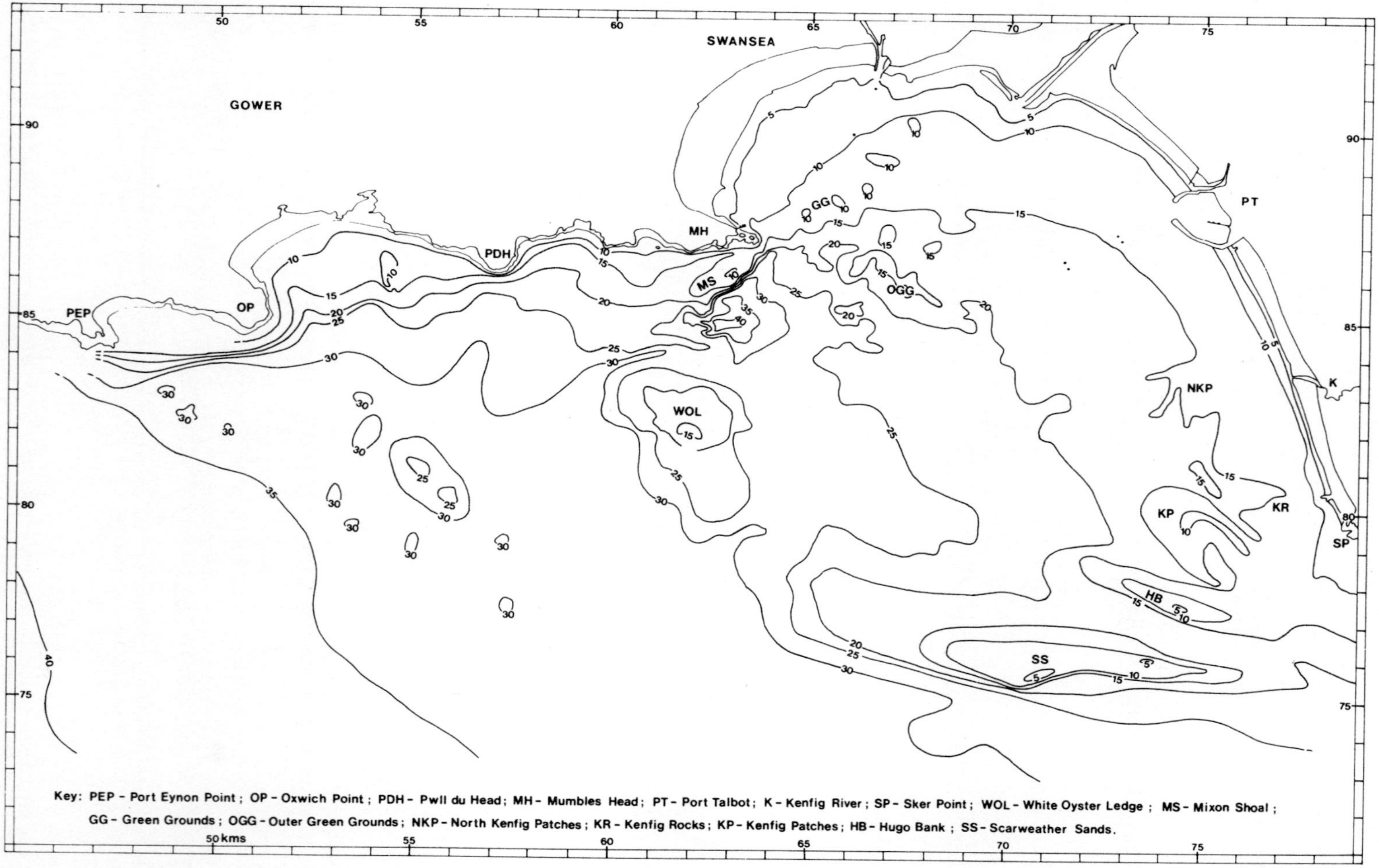

Figure 3.2. Bathymetry and present-day morphology: isobaths in metres below Ordnance Datum (Newlyn).

Key: PEP - Port Eynon Point; OP - Oxwich Point; PDH - Pwll du Head; MH - Mumbles Head; PT - Port Talbot; K - Kenfig River; SP - Sker Point; WOL - White Oyster Ledge; MS - Mixon Shoal; GG - Green Grounds; OGG - Outer Green Grounds; NKP - North Kenfig Patches; KP - Kenfig Patches; KR - Kenfig Rocks; HB - Hugo Bank; SS - Scarweather Sands.

the onshore geology and rock types, by extrapolation of onshore boundaries and structures, and by incorporating the very limited relevant borehole information available from the present survey area. The resulting units and their boundaries are presented on the geological map (Fig. 3.3). Also on the map are faults, revealed as vertical dislocations on the seismic records, and fold axes with associated dip values. Apparent dip values along the traverse directions were measured using seismic velocity estimates of 2.4km/s for the Mesozoic strata and 3.0km/s for the Upper Carboniferous rocks, from which bedding structures could be traced. True dips were then calculated at traverse intersection points using formulae given by Brooks (1970). Tests showed that the source-receiver separation was small enough to be ignored without introducing significant errors into the computed dip values, and therefore equations taking this separation into account (Curry, Hersey, Martin and Whittard, 1965) did not need to be used.

In order to map systematically the depth to bedrock surface, an average seismic velocity of 1.7km/s was assumed for the overlying deposits. This is a reasonable estimate based on velocity measurements in similar materials elsewhere (unpublished commercial report) and refraction results from the Lower Swansea Valley summarised by Al-Saadi and Brooks (1973). This velocity was used to calculate the thickness of the superficial deposits as measured off the seismic profiles using the simple formula given by Brooks (1970), which ignores the separation of source and receiver and the effect of steeply dipping reflectors. The validity of this method was tested by comparison with depths calculated by the more rigorous approach of Harrison (1970) and nowhere were significant differences produced. The sediment thickness values were plotted along the traverses and contoured to produce an isopachyte map, on which the distribution of the major contributory sediment types were also displayed (Fig. 3.5). The sediment thickness values were then combined with the bathymetric data to give depths to the bedrock surface in metres below Ordnance Datum (Newlyn), which were then contoured to produce the topographic chart (Fig. 3.4). It is these two maps which show the true morphology of the floor of the embayment and, together with Figure 3.3, indicate the degree of geological control over its development.

BEDROCK GEOLOGY (FIG. 3.3).

The Carboniferous Limestone outcrops of eastern Gower can be traced offshore seismically as submarine extensions of the anticlinal structures of Port Eynon Point, Oxwich Point, Pwll Du Point and Mumbles Head. The massive limestones can be followed away from the coast for a kilometre or more, characteristically appearing on the seismic records as areas of intense internal scattering with no coherent reflectors below a very strong, irregular reflector marking the top surface of the limestones, before the south-easterly plunge of each fold takes them beneath a cover of younger rocks. Similarly, the Carboniferous Limestone of the Vale of Glamorgan can be traced offshore, to the north of Sker Point, as the Sker Point to Bridgend anticlinal axis plunges WNW under the Bay taking the Limestone beneath the younger rocks. These are *en-echelon,* strike-replacing periclinal folds which are typical of the structural style of the rim of the South Wales Coalfield.

The synclinal areas between these structures contain Millstone Grit and Lower Coal Measures in stratigraphical sequence, and it is these rocks which underlie the sea floor of Swansea Bay and the bays of the south Gower coast as far west as Port Eynon. Three I.G.S. boreholes have been drilled within this area (Numbers 72/46, 72/58 and 72/59) and all terminated in fine grained, micaceous sandstone and mudstone. No stratigraphically useful microfossils are present, but the lithologies are clearly indicative of Millstone Grit or Lower Coal Measures. These rock series are very similar in lithology and structure and cannot be differentiated on the seismic records, so they have been mapped as one unit. This seismic unit is characterised

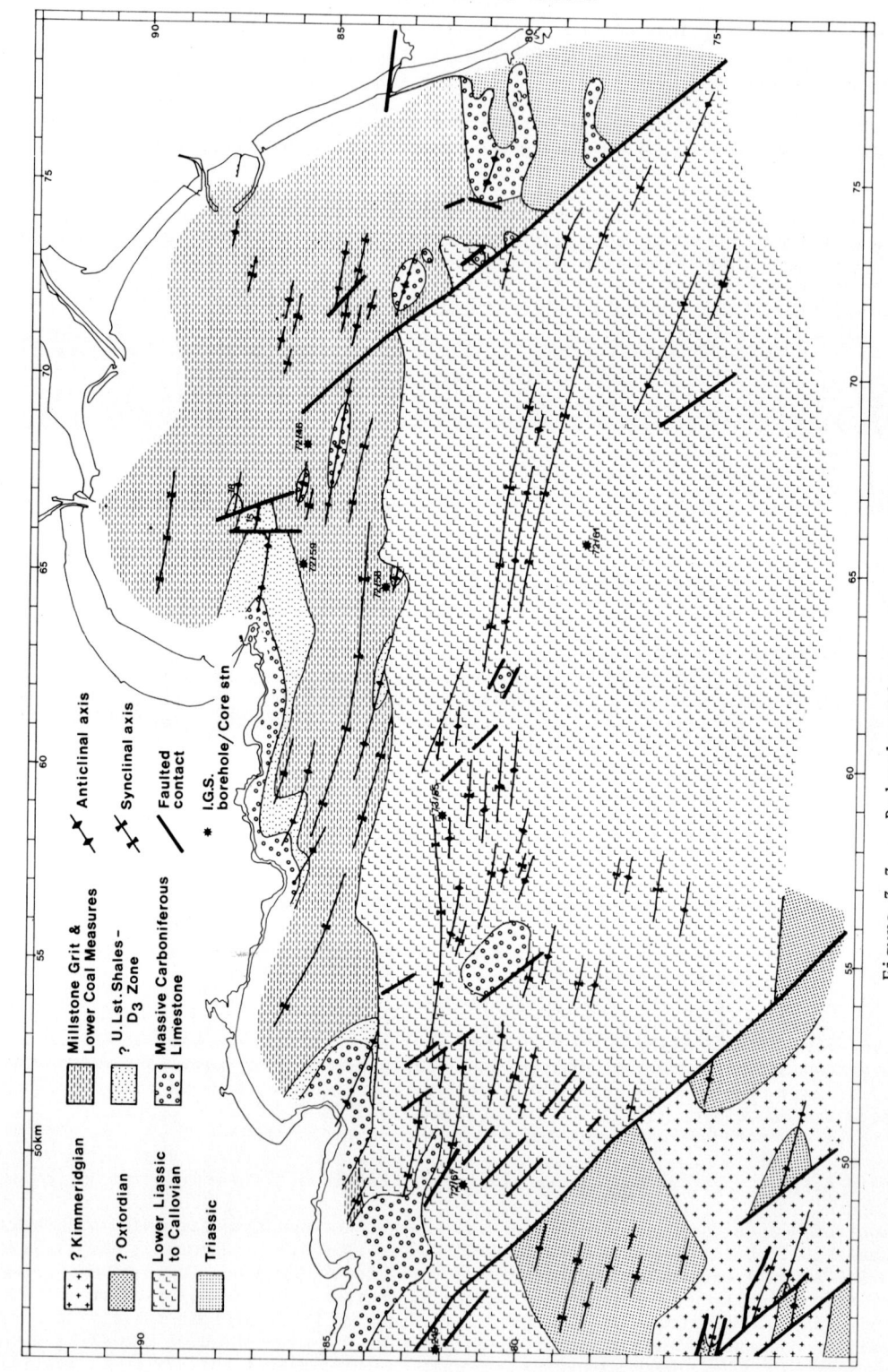

Figure 3.3. Bedrock geology and sample locations.

by a weak, irregular upper surface with much scattering, and a fairly dense reflection character with steeply dipping, closely spaced, impersistent bedding plane reflectors. Several fold axes can be traced, striking 100°, and true dips of up to 30° are encountered. The anticlinal structures in the Millstone Grit/Lower Coal Measures unit in the centre of Swansea Bay show cores of massive rocks, suggesting that the Carboniferous Limestone is nowhere very far from surface.

Between the massive Carboniferous Limestone and the Millstone Grit/Lower Coal Measures divisions a third, seismically distinct unit is present around the Gower coast. It shows very persistent, strong bedding plane reflectors, which are parallel and closely spaced, and it is relatively transparent acoustically, with no major internal scattering effects. This reflection character is consistent with a thinly bedded limestone and shale sequence and therefore the unit has been interpreted as approximating to the Upper Limestone Shales, D_3 zone, of the Carboniferous Limestone, the known thickness of which is compatible with that of the seismically mapped unit.

A striking angular unconformity, between the Upper Palaeozoic rocks described above and the Mesozoic strata of the Bristol Channel, runs from west to east across the mouth of Swansea Bay, passing some 3.5km south of Mumbles Head. At the western limit of the survey area the Mesozoic rocks overlap directly onto Carboniferous Limestone at Port Eynon Point, but elsewhere they overlie the Millstone Grit/Lower Coal Measures unit. Seismically, the Mesozoic rocks south of the unconformity show very strong and persistent bedding plane reflectors which are similar to those of the Carboniferous Upper Limestone Shales unit, but stronger and generally wider apart. I.G.S. boreholes in this area, (Numbers 72/61, 72/67 and 73/55) have identified the rockhead as limestones and shales of Liassic age, Lower Pliensbachian being specified in the case of 72/67. Gravity core 249 of D.J. Evans (Evans and Thompson, 1979) sampled Sinemurian mudstone 4km south-west of Port Eynon Point. This situation is entirely analogous to the Vale of Glamorgan where a similar unconformity can be seen. Fold axes, trending 100°, are numerous but true dips rarely exceed 5°, except where faulting has caused localised drag effects. Immediately south of the unconformity in the centre of the area, several small inliers of Carboniferous Limestone can be seen in the records. Although the seismic evidence is not conclusive, these do not appear to be fault-defined blocks and are believed to demonstrate the irregularity of the Palaeozoic surface and the extremely thin nature of the Mesozoic cover in this area.

The Mesozoic unconformity is terminated at its eastern end by a major fault, running NNW-SSE parallel to the Vale of Glamorgan coast, and bisecting the opening to Swansea Bay. This fault has downthrown Liassic rocks to the west, whereas to the east erosion has removed all but a thin, patchy remnant of the Mesozoic cover, exposing the Palaeozoics below. The remaining few metres of bedded strata, lying directly on top of the Carboniferous Limestone outcrop in the vicinity of Sker Point, have been interpreted as Triassic sediments, mainly because of their location and attitude. The throw on the fault cannot be determined accurately but it is unlikely to exceed 50m. The NNW trend is closely parallel to that of several faults in the South Wales coalfield to the north of Swansea Bay but no direct correlation with any onshore fault can be made. It is of interest to note that if the fault is projected to the SSE across the Bristol Channel, it aligns with the Timberscombe fault zone (Webby, 1965) of Somerset.

Three more major faults, all trending NNW-SSE and downthrowing to the west, are present towards the western edge of the survey area. They cut across a relatively major synclinal structure of the Mesozoic strata, which is probably the eastern end of the Helwick syncline, and by a combination of downfolding and downfaulting two new, seismically distinct, younger units are preserved in the core of the syncline. Whilst no cores younger than Lower Pliensbachian have been obtained from the Helwick syncline (I.G.S. borehole 72/67), these units have a seismic character strikingly similar to that exhibited on profiling records obtained across Oxfordian and Kimmeridgian outcrops in the nearby Bristol Channel syncline. However, the thicknesses of these units in the Helwick syncline are much reduced in comparison with those documented from the Bristol Channel syncline by Evans and Thompson (1979).

BEDROCK TOPOGRAPHY (FIG. 3.4).

The general level of the bedrock surface rises normally with a fairly uniform gradient from its deepest point in the south west of the survey area towards the coastline to the north and to the north east. The only appreciably bathymetric steps occur across the entrance to Swansea Bay, along a line between White Oyster Ledge and Scarweather Sands, and within the bays of the south Gower coast, where rockhead rises to meet the coastline. Projecting noticeably above this level are the areas of Carboniferous Limestone, where they have been exposed by the general level of erosion. Of much more significance are the deep channels eroded into the bedrock below this general level.

The main channel trends diagonally across Swansea Bay from north east to south west, passing south of Mumbles Head. It contains two main basins, with severl overdeepened portions, and has been mapped previously by Al-Saadi and Brooks (1973). To the east of this channel is a system of rock basins with three overdeepened portions trending from north west to south east towards the Kenfig River. South of these large features a series of narrow, linear sub-parllel channels runs from west to east across the mouth of the Bay. These also have several overdeepened portions along their courses. To the east these channels turn south eastwards, parallel to the coast, before terminating. To the west only the northernmost channel continues, running along the line of the Mesozoic - Palaeozoic unconformity before turning north westwards into Oxwich Bay, where it dies out.

A general division can be made between the bedrock surface inside the step at the mouth of Swansea Bay, which is channelled and irregular, and that outside the step, which is extremely regular and flat.

SEDIMENT TYPES AND DISTRIBUTION (FIG. 3.5).

Seven distinctive sediment types can be differentiated by means of their seismic characteristics within this survey area. Each sediment type has been sampled and described by S.J. Culver (1976) and all detailed references to sediment composition are based on personal communication with Dr. Culver: they are also described in Chapter 4, following.

(i) _Hummocky boulder clay_: typically a stiff clay with inclusions of unsorted material up to boulder size. This is probably a basal, lodgement till and is found in patches over the whole of the inner embayment of Swansea Bay and as far south as White Oyster Ledge and Kenfig Rocks. It reaches a thickness of 15m in places and characteristically has an irregular, hummocky surface profile.

(ii) _Quaternary lag gravels_: very poorly sorted sub-angular pebbles, cobbles and boulders in sand or mud matrix, found as a thin, flat sheet over most of the bedrock surface of the approaches to Swansea Bay, but also found over other glacial deposits. Probably a remnant after winnowing of mixed glacial tills.

(iii) _Late Devensian lacustrine silts and clays_: occurring in all major overdeepened portions of the bedrock channels and easily identifiable on seismic records. These are extremely well laminated fine silts and clays.

(iv) _Outwash deposits_: fairly well sorted intercalations of silt, sand and gravel

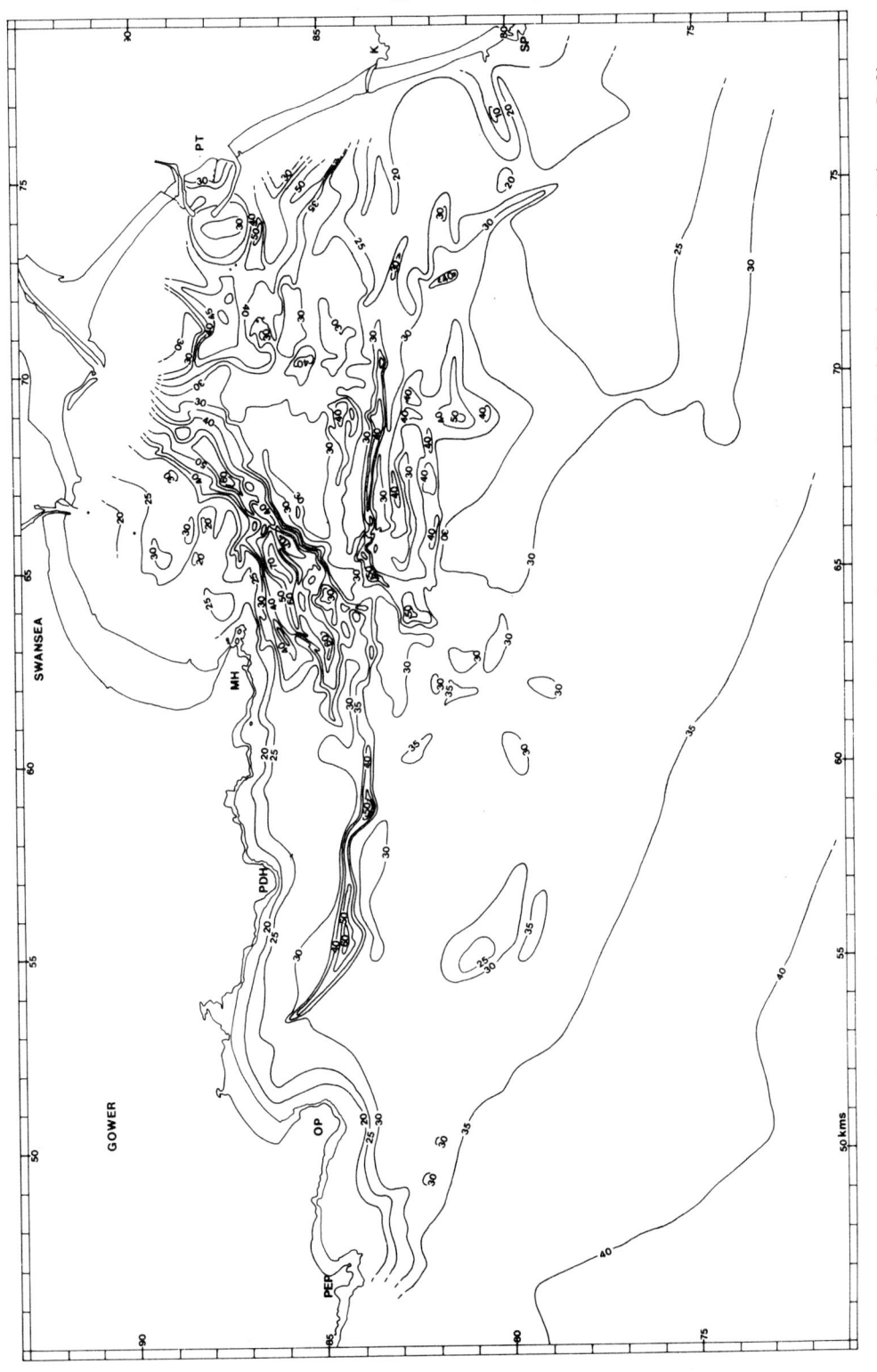

Figure 3.4. Bedrock topography: contours in metres below Ordnance Datum (Newlyn) (Symbols as in Figure 3.2).

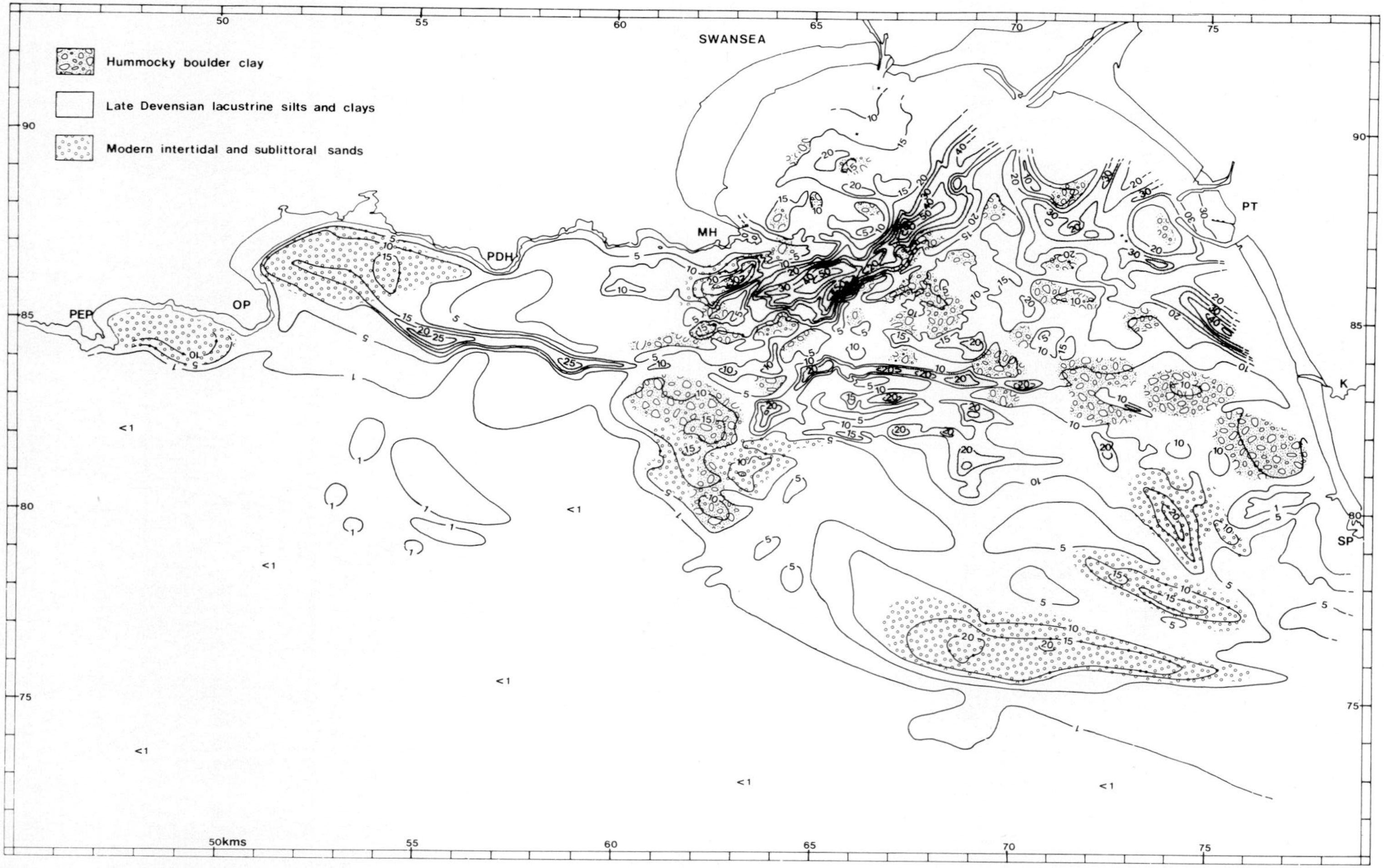

Figure 3.5. Sediment thickness and distribution of major contributory types: isopachs in metres (Symbols as in Figure 3.2).

with sub-horizontal layering, occurring over the whole of the inner Bay area as an infilling of the topography left when the ice retreated for the last time.

(v) *Flandrian materials:* mainly silts, clays and peats, with occasional sands, laid down in predominantly intertidal conditions as the marine transgression proceeded, following the retreat of the ice. These sediments are sometimes difficult to separate from the outwash deposits, although they are generally less well layered and usually have a very strong reflector at their base.

(vi) *Mixed modern sediments:* a variable layer of mud, silt and sand in varying proportions which includes all mobile materials under present conditions, of which one of the major sources is dumped dredged material.

(vii) *Modern intertidal and sublittoral sands:* relatively well sorted sands concentrated in thick wedges in all the bays of the south Gower coast, on the offshore banks of the Helwick Sands (Britton, 1978), Mixon Shoal, White Oyster Ledge, Kenfig Patches, Hugo Bank and Scarweather Sands (Turner, 1976), and on the sand flats and berm around Swansea Bay.

DEVELOPMENT OF THE PRESENT GEOMORPHOLOGY (FIG. 3.2)

As the Palaeozoic surface was exhumed during the Cenozoic, differential erosion preferentially removed the softer, argillaceous Mesozoic and Millstone Grit/Lower Coal Measures series, leaving the massive Carboniferous Limestone and Pennant sandstones upstanding. The Carboniferous Limestone rim of the South Wales Coalfield was breached along zones of faulting to open up Swansea Bay, and along the Gower coast embayments were formed, delineated by the outcrop pattern of the more resistant rocks. In this manner the gross features of the present coastline were established by differential erosion during the early Cenozoic, although T.R. Owen has suggested a much earlier date for the shaping of the basic morphology of the area (see Chapter 2). Certainly, by between late Miocene and late Pliocene times, marine erosion at fluctuating levels had modified the gross landscape to produce many of the details seen today. Little evidence exists for the nature of the early and middle Pleistocene development of South Wales and few morphological changes occurred which can be seen today. Bowen (1970) has suggested that the details of the shore platforms and cliffs of the Gower peninsula may be of Hoxnian Interglacial age, or older.

The Wolstonian stage saw the area completely covered by the ice of two ice sheets: the Irish Sea ice, advancing from the west, and the Welsh ice pressing southwards from the mountainous interior of Wales. During the Ipswichian Interglacial stage, sea level rose from more than 120m below present sea level to approximately 10m above the present level. The second glaciation of the area took place during the Devensian, when only Welsh ice from the north reached Swansea Bay at a period of ice maximum some 20,000 to 17,000 years B.P. (Bowen, 1970).

The Wolstonian Irish Sea ice reached this area as a fairly powerful ice sheet advancing from Pembrokeshire, across Gower south of Cefn Bryn, across the mouth of Swansea Bay and into the Vale of Glamorgan (Griffiths, 1937). It may also have extended eastwards up the Bristol Channel as far as the Bristol area (Hawkins and Kellaway, 1971). Its effects are seen in the form of the relatively flat, bevelled surface left across the soft argillaceous rocks of the area by the unconfined ice sheet. (See also Chapter 2). The only noticeable topographic highs occur where the harder Carboniferous Limestone outcrops are present (Fig. 3.3). The only glacial deposit in this area is a thin, flat sheet of till, which is a lag deposit of gravels and pebbles in a silty matrix, representing a basal till from which the sands and clays have been selectively winnowed by marine reworking.

Towards the northern edge of this area, parallel to the suggested line of contact between the Irish Sea ice and the Welsh ice, are the linear buried channels described in the section on bedrock topography, above. It is suggested that these were cut along weaknesses in the bedrock by volumes of meltwater flowing in sub-glacial tunnels, under considerable hydrostatic pressure, and that they were sub-marginal channels to the Irish Sea ice. The long profiles of the channels show the classic 'in-and-out' pattern produced by this type of erosion. The northernmost channel can be traced from the weak Namurian shales of the Oxwich syncline, southeastwards to the Mesozoic/Palaeozoic unconformity where it turns eastwards to follow the line of weakness provided. The channels to the south are cut into weaker bands within the Mesozoic succession. At the eastern side of Swansea Bay the channels swing to the southeast and run towards the Vale of Glamorgan coast, where evidence of occupation by Irish Sea ice can be found (Crampton, 1966). The channels all show layered fill materials, which are likely to be outwash deposits, and the larger, deeper basins contain laminated, acoustically transparent sediments which have proved to be lacustrine clays (I.G.S. borehole 72/58). These are presumably well sorted glacial outwash materials deposited as deltaic sediments into lakes formed in overdeepened rock basins (see also Chapter 4).

The thick deposit of unstructured, hummocky boulder clay which forms White Oyster Ledge is probably a basal, lodgement till of the Irish Sea ice, plastered onto the slight rock step which occurs at the mouth of the Bay. It may, however, be composed of this till mixed with end moraine from the Welsh ice. Extensive sampling would be required to investigate this possibility. Further deposits of hummocky boulder clay occur along the proposed line of contact between the Welsh and Irish Sea ice, just to the north of the submarginal channel traces. These could also be lodgement till from the Irish Sea ice sheet, but it is likely that they are mixed with end moraine from the Welsh ice.

During the Wolstonian glaciation the Welsh ice advanced southwards from the mountains onto the lowlands of Gower, Swansea Bay and the Vale of Glamorgan where it met the Irish Sea ice sheet (Bowen, 1970). The proposed line of contact across Swansea Bay has been detailed above, occurring to the north of the sub-marginal channel zone and being marked by lodgement till deposits. The evidence for glacial action by the Welsh ice during the Wolstonian cannot be separated from the effects of the later Devensian advance in the survey area. It is assumed that ice movements, erosion processes and depositional characteristics would have been very similar during both glaciations, the main difference being that the Devensian ice was unconfined to the south, whereas the Wolstonian Welsh ice was confined by Irish Sea ice to the south. Thus it is probable that erosional features produced by the first ice advance were increased and accentuated by the second, and that the second advance would have removed and redistributed the deposits of the first. A description of features produced by Welsh ice therefore implies production by a combination of both glacial periods.

The main feature of the area affected by Welsh ice is the NE-SW trending buried channel which cuts down 50m into the bedrock surface. This has been described by Al-Saadi and Brooks (1973), and attributed to erosion by active ice along the proposed extension of the Neath Disturbance zone of weakness, with overdeepening on less resistant materials caused by the mechanism of Nye (1959). This theory was developed to explain the overdeepened basins found on land, beneath both the Tawe and the Neath valleys. While this explanation is adequate for the land area, it is suggested here that, when the Welsh ice entered the lowland area of Swansea Bay, it was so near its maximum southern limit as to be entering a semi-stagnant depositional stage, and very little active ice erosion would have been achieved.

The position and trend of the offshore buried valley are such that the structural and lithological controls over its development, postulated by Al-Saadi and Brooks, are undisputed, although the Neath Disturbance fault zone cannot be traced offshore on the seismic records due to the shallow water, the extreme depth to rockhead beneath the buried valley and the nature of the strata. The main agency of erosion, however, is more likely to have been meltwater, following a series of preparatory stages. The pre-glacial drainage lines were probably dictated by the zones of major faulting and the river valleys produced would have been the sites of deep permafrost penetration into the fractured rocks during the periglacial phases in this area. Active ice pushing down these valleys during the glacial periods would undoubtedly have removed this extremely shattered layer, with overdeepening being caused on less resistant, more highly fractured rocks. Where the ice flowed out onto the lowlands a certain amount of ice gouging may have taken place, but the vast volumes of meltwater flowing in sub-glacial tunnels under considerable hydrostatic pressure would have been more effective agents of erosion, as they coursed towards a pressure release point on the ice front. Overdeepening would have taken place where the less resistant, more highly fissured and shattered rock units occurred, and the channel would cease to be eroded at the pressure release point. This can be seen south of Mumbles Head, close to the line of ice contact during the Wolstonian and the proposed ice limit of Bowen (1970), during the Devensian (Fig. 3.6). A similar mechanism is proposed for the cutting of the second major overdeepened buried valley, trending NW to SE on the eastern margin of the Bay. No apparent structural control can be demonstrated over the alignment of this channel, but it is known that the Welsh ice spilled out onto the lowlands of the Vale of Glamorgan and that a piedmont lobe occupied the Margam-Pyle area (Bowen, 1970). The eastern channel was probably eroded by meltwaters trapped between this ice and the coastal slope seeking the shortest route to a low pressure escape point on the ice front (Fig. 3.6). Feeder channels can be seen entering the main buried channel, indicating several sources of meltwater, and overdeepening has produced three separate basins. This pattern is hard to explain in terms of active ice erosion alone. No overdeepened extension to the Swansea valley can be traced along its offshore projection, which is contrary to what would be expected if the theory of active ice erosion along structural weaknesses is to be upheld. However, a deep buried channel is known to occur under Swansea Docks (Godwin, 1940), and this may have been eroded by meltwaters escaping from the confining Swansea Valley when the ice spread out onto the lowland area, turning to flow towards the nearest low pressure escape route, in this case the deeper and larger meltwater channel of the Neath Valley to the southeast.

The bedrock surface between the two main overdeepened channels is undulating and irregular as a result of weak erosion by the piedmont lobe of Welsh ice. Patches of hummocky boulder clay material are present over the rock surface with thicker patches associated with the topographic highs. These are stiff lodgement tills deposited from the base of the ice lobe and, where they are exposed, they form the bathymetric expressions of the Outer Green Grounds and the North Kenfig Patches. The absence of similar deposits south of a line from White Oyster Ledge to North Kenfig Patches indicates the maximum extent of the Welsh ice. White Oyster Ledge lodgement tills probably consist of mixed Irish Sea and Welsh materials, and the ice limit indicated by these deposits (Fig. 3.6) is not very different from that extrapolated across Swansea Bay by Bowen (1970).

During deglaciation, the bedrock and basal till surface was covered by ablation tills and glacial outwash materials, accumulating in all the hollows and slowly burying the irregular surface, except for the thicker boulder clay areas mentioned above. Isolated blocks of 'stagnant' ice, separated from the ice sheet by ice-thinning, would have remained in the deeper rock basins for some time. When these eventually melted, lakes formed and the resulting laminated fine clays and silts were deposited (Culver, 1977). These are easily traceable on seismic records, completely filling the rock basins up to the level of normal, layered, coarser outwash deposits. In places, the lakes were dammed by moraine, and lacustrine sediments can be seen overlapping boulder clay mounds. The absence of basal lodgement tills beneath these sediments is further evidence for the erosion of the rock basins by melt-

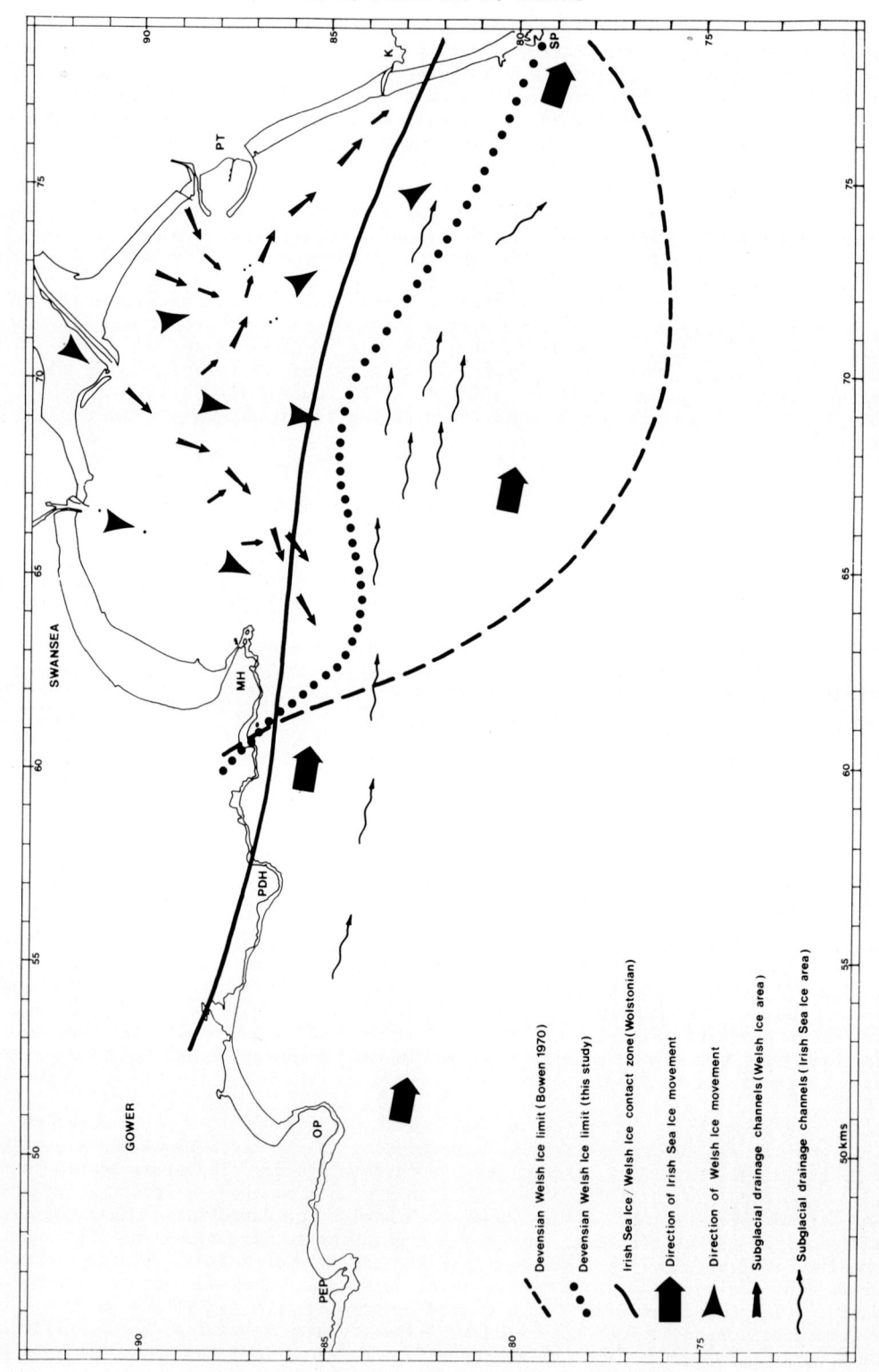

Figure 3.6. Glacial limits and associated ice and meltwater directions (Symbols as in Figure 3.2).

water, rather than ice.

The top of the glacial outwash material is marked by a strong, sub-horizontal erosion surface on the seismic records. This is the result of the Flandrian marine transgression which reached the outer part of the area by 10,000 years B.P. (Culver, 1976; Culver and Banner, 1979). Erosion and reworking of the tills and outwash materials resulted in the lag deposit covering most of the outer part of the survey area and occurring at the top of the outwash materials. Subsequent deposition of Flandrian intertidal sand, silt, clay and peat materials completed the burying of the glacial landscape beneath up to 25m of layered sediments, with the exception of the boulder clay 'islands' already mentioned. These Flandrian sediments floor the embayment today and have been only slightly eroded since 2,000 years B.P., when present day beach and sand flat environments were established.

Modern sediments in the area are of two types. The bays of Port Eynon, Oxwich, Three Cliffs and Caswell are occupied by wedges of relatively clean, well layered sand-size material, overlying glacial tills. This sediment was probably derived by winnowing of the glacial tills and outwash materials during the Flandrian transgression, as noted by Culver and Banner (1979). It has been concentrated in these bays by wave and tide action, where it is largely protected from subsequent removal. Similar sandy material was carried forward by the advancing seas into Swansea Bay where it was deposited as barrier sand dunes around the margins (Chapters 6 and 7). The prominent sand banks of Helwick Sands, Mixon Shoal, Kenfig Patches, Hugo Bank and Scarweather Sands probably originated as offshore bars, or have subsequently been built by hydrodynamically controlled deposition of the sands winnowed from the glacial material (Chapter 13). They are all well layered structures sitting on surfaces of glacial deposits or Flandrian-type materials. Some transportation of sand from these banks is occurring (Chapters 12 and 14), sand waves indicating movement to the west across the surface of the glacial deposits.

Within the inner embayment a thin layer of modern sediment consisting of variable muddy sand and sandy mud exists over the surface of the relict Flandrian deposits. Very little natural erosion of the Flandrian materials has occurred since present sea level was established some 2,000 years B.P. and this sediment is largely the result of dredging operations within the Bay removing and dumping relatively large quantities of sediment (Chapter 14).

ACKNOWLEDGEMENTS

This work was funded by means of a research contract, at University College of Swansea, awarded by the British Transport Docks Board (South Wales), for which the authors are grateful. We wish to thank Dr. B.N. Fletcher and the Institute of Geological Sciences for making available the results of their offshore drilling programme in the study area. Dr. S.J. Culver's sampling programme carried out in conjunction with this survey provided valuable control and his interest and cooperation throughout is gratefully acknowledged. The captins and crews of the N.E.R.C. vessels used and Captain B. Davies and the crew of the R.V. *Ocean Crest* are especially thanked for their assistance with all aspects of the fieldwork.

REFERENCES

Al-Saadi, R., and Brooks, M. (1973). A geophysical study of Pleistocene Buried Valleys in the Lower Swansea Valley, Vale of Neath and Swansea Bay. *Proc. Geol. Assoc.*, 84, 135-153.

Bowen, D.Q. (1970). South-East and Central South Wales. In: Lewis, C.A. (Ed.)., *The Glaciations of Wales and adjoining regions*. Longmans, London, 197-227.

Britton, R.C. (1978). *Structure of some marine sedimentary bodies and their dynamic environments*. Ph.D. Thesis, University of Wales, (Unpub.), 255pp.

Brooks, M. (1970). Some Trigonometric formulae for the Interpretation of continuous seismic profiles. *Int. Hydrogr. Rev., 47,* 65-72.

Crompton, C.B. (1966). Certain affects of glacial events in the Vale of Glamorgan, South Wales. *Jl. Glaciol., 6,* 261-266.

Culver, S.J. (1976). *A study of the post-glacial Foraminiferida of Swansea Bay, South Wales*. Ph.D. Thesis, University of Wales, (Unpub.), 442pp.

Culver, S.J. (1977). The development of the Swansea Bay area during the past 20,000 years. *Gower Jl., 27,* 58-62.

Culver, S.J., and Banner, F.T. (1979). The significance of derived pre-Quaternary foraminifera in Holocene sediments of the north-central Bristol Channel. *Mar. Geol., 29,* 187-207.

Curry, D., Hersey, J.B., Martin, E., and Whittard, W.G. (1965). The geology of the Western Approaches of the English Channel. II, Geological interpretation aided by boomer and sparker records. *Phil. Trans. R. Soc. B., 248,* 315-351.

Evans, D.J., and Thompson, M.S. (1979). The geology of the central Bristol Channel and the Lundy area, South Western Approaches, British Isles. *Proc. Geol. Assoc., 90(1),* 1-14.

Godwin, H. (1940). A Boreal transgression of the sea in Swansea Bay. Data for the study of post-glacial history. VI. *New. Phytol., 34,* 308-321.

Griffiths, J.C. (1937). *The glacial deposits between the River Tawe and the River Towy*. Ph.D. Thesis, University of Wales, (Unpub.),

Harrison, C.H. (1970). Reconstruction of subglacial relief from radio echosounding records. *Geophys., 35,* 1099-1115.

Hawkins, A.B., and Kellaway, G.A. (1971). Field meeting at Bristol and Bath with special reference to new evidence of glaciation. *Proc. Geol. Assoc., 82,* 267-292.

Nye, J.F. (1959). The deformation of a glacier below an ice-fall. *Jl. Glaciol., 3,* 386-408.

Turner, S.R. (1976). *Some aspects of sedimentary bodies in parts of the Bristol Channel*. Ph.D. Thesis, University of Wales, (Unpub.), 235pp.

Webby, B.D. (1965). The stratigraphy and structure of the Devonian rocks in the Brandon Hills, West Somerset. *Proc. Geol. Assoc., 76,* 39-60.

4. THE QUATERNARY DEPOSITS OF SWANSEA BAY

S. J. Culver* and P. A. Bull**

*Department of Paleobiology, Smithsonian Institution, Washington, D.C., U.S.A.
**Christ Church, Oxford OX1 1DP, U.K.

ABSTRACT

The floor of Swansea Bay has been sampled by gravity coring and the material recovered has been analysed sedimentologically and micropalaeontologically. As well as gross sedimentological characters, foraminiferal assemblages and scanning electron microscopy of quartz grain surface features have proved useful in attempting to delimit different sedimentary deposits.

Six sedimentary facies are recognised to occur at the seabed in Swansea Bay. These are (a) poorly sorted, consolidated boulder clay, (b) grey-brown, well-laminated lacustrine silty clays, (c) consolidated greyish sands, sandy silts and clays with associated peats, (d) intertidal sand-flats, sand bars (recent beach sands), (e) pebbles, cobbles and boulders sometimes mixed with unconsolidated mud, sand and silt, (f) silty mud. Their environments of deposition and their formation are discussed in relation to Quaternary events in the South Wales and Bristol Channel area.

KEYWORDS

Sedimentology, Quaternary, Swansea Bay.

INTRODUCTION

The floor of Swansea Bay has been sampled in order to determine the distribution of sediment textural groups and to enhance the understanding of hydrodynamic regimes within the bay (Collins, Ferentinos and Banner, 1979). Cores of seabed deposits from (unspecified) sites in Swansea Bay have already been subjected to Pb-210 chronological study (Clifton & Hamilton, 1979), and average sedimentation rates of 0.14 to 0.19cm/yr (0.12-0.15g/cm^2/yr) have been calculated for them. However, micropalaeontological studies in Swansea Bay (Culver, 1976a; Culver & Banner, 1978) have indicated that not all sediment at or near the seabed is of modern origin and that many owe their characters to earlier sedimentary processes, and are either 'relict' or 'palimpsest' (Banner with Culver, 1979).

Using micropalaeontological and scanning electron microscope (SEM) data as tools of interpretation, this paper outlines the events which have ultimately controlled the nature of the Quaternary sedimentary 'basement' in Swansea Bay and also describes

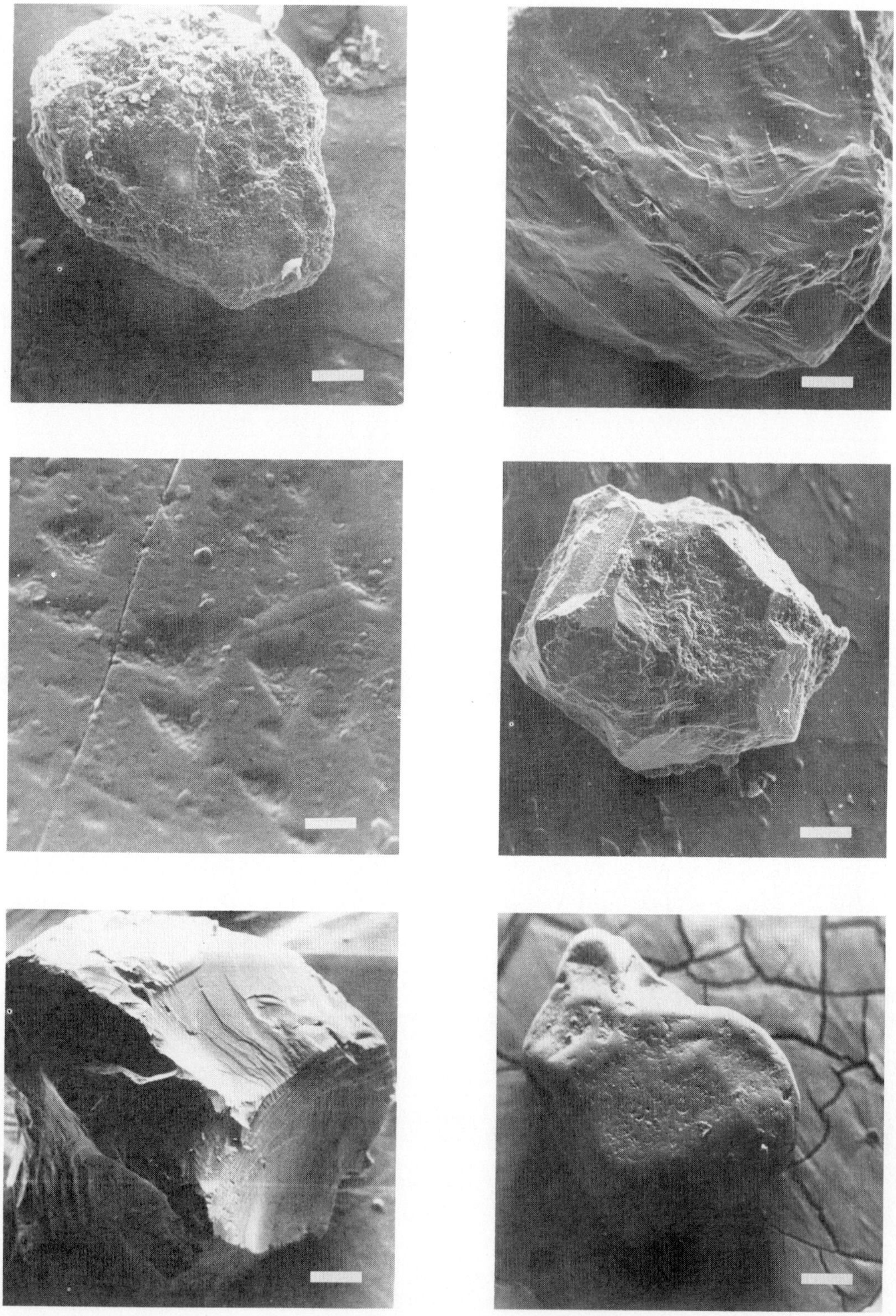

PLATE 4.1.   (OPPOSITE).

Some examples of surface textures found on the surfaces of quartz sand grains.

> Top Left: Well rounded, 'amorphous' silica precipitation.
> Top Right: Large and small scale conchoidal fractures and breakage blocks, medium relief, sub-angular outline, semi-parallel arcuate steps.
> Centre Left: Chemically produced oriented etch-pits, surface fractures.
> Centre Right: Euhedral crystal growth, chemical solution, medium/high relief.
> Bottom Left: Sharp angular outline, conchoidal fractures and breakage blocks, high relief, fresh surface appearance, sub-parallel steps.
> Bottom Right: Sub-rounded outline, low relief, disoriented mechanical impact pits.

Bar Scales = All are 40 microns except Centre Left (8 microns).

each of the major sedimentary deposits (facies) found within the bay.

MATERIAL AND METHODS

The seafloor of Swansea Bay was sampled by gravity coring, over a period of two years, at 179 stations (Fig. 4.1). Fifty-three cores with a maximum length of 1m were recovered. Non-recovery evidence, for example a pebble stuck in the corer nose-cone or mud on the outside of the core barrel, also proved to be of importance in interpretation of the sediment distribution of the sampled area. Samples taken from various depths in the cores were analysed for their sedimentological and microfaunal characteristics.

RESULTS

Six major sedimentary facies are present in Swansea Bay:

Facies 1: Poorly sorted, consolidated deposits containing clay, silt, sand, gravel, pebbles, cobbles and boulders. The larger sedimentary particles are of Coal Measures, shales and sandstones, Millstone Grit sandstones and grits, Carboniferous Limestone and Old Red Sandstone. Some better sorted sands and gravels, encountered in boreholes in the littoral zone around Swansea Bay (Culver, 1976b) are associated with these pebbly deposits. Quartz grains taken from these sands and also from the sandy clays with pebbles have been examined by SEM analysis. The surface textures of the sand grains (set out in Table 4.1, appended to this Chapter and illustrated in Plate 4.I) suggest that modification has occurred consistent with relatively high energy mechanical action. This is shown by the preponderance of large and small scale conchoidal fractures and breakage blocks, the random scratches and grooves, meandering ridges and step fractures. Limited edge rounding has occurred to both the general grain boundaries and to the smaller-scale surface features. Chemical modification, adjudged to be post-depositional, has altered the surface textures surprisingly little since deposition. However, etching consistent with a subaqueous environment of modification can be identified (oriented v-shaped etch pits, solution pits and fretting). When compared to results obtained from the other lithofacies examined, the mechanical modification features, lack of disoriented v-pits and the relatively low percentage of chemical etching and precipitation features are all highly significant.

No microfauna was recovered from Facies 1, which is exposed in places in the littoral zone of Swansea Bay. This deposit has an undulating surface and underlies facies 3 and 4. Offshore gravity cores (Culver, 1976a) and continuous seismic profiling (Price, pers. comm.) indicate similar relationships with the sublittoral zone of Swansea Bay.

Facies 2: Consolidated, grey-brown, well-laminated silty clays. These deposits, containing only 1-22% sand, have no recovered microfauna although a few fragments of freshwater gastropods were present in some samples. SEM analysis of the surface textures of the quartz grains from this facies suggests that the grains may have undergone glacio-fluvial modification (Table 4.1). The grain surfaces exhibit a relatively fresh appearance (little post-modification chemical alteration) with many conchoidal fractures and breakage blocks. Together with the size range of these fractures and the association of scratches, steps and grooves, the assemblage of mechanically derived surface features suggests modification in high energy mechanical environments. It is unlikely that such a complete suite of features could be found upon first cycle quartz grains and most likely are the result of some form of glacial action (Whalley & Krinsley, 1974). Under high magnification a small-sized suite of breakage blocks and chemical etching could be identified;

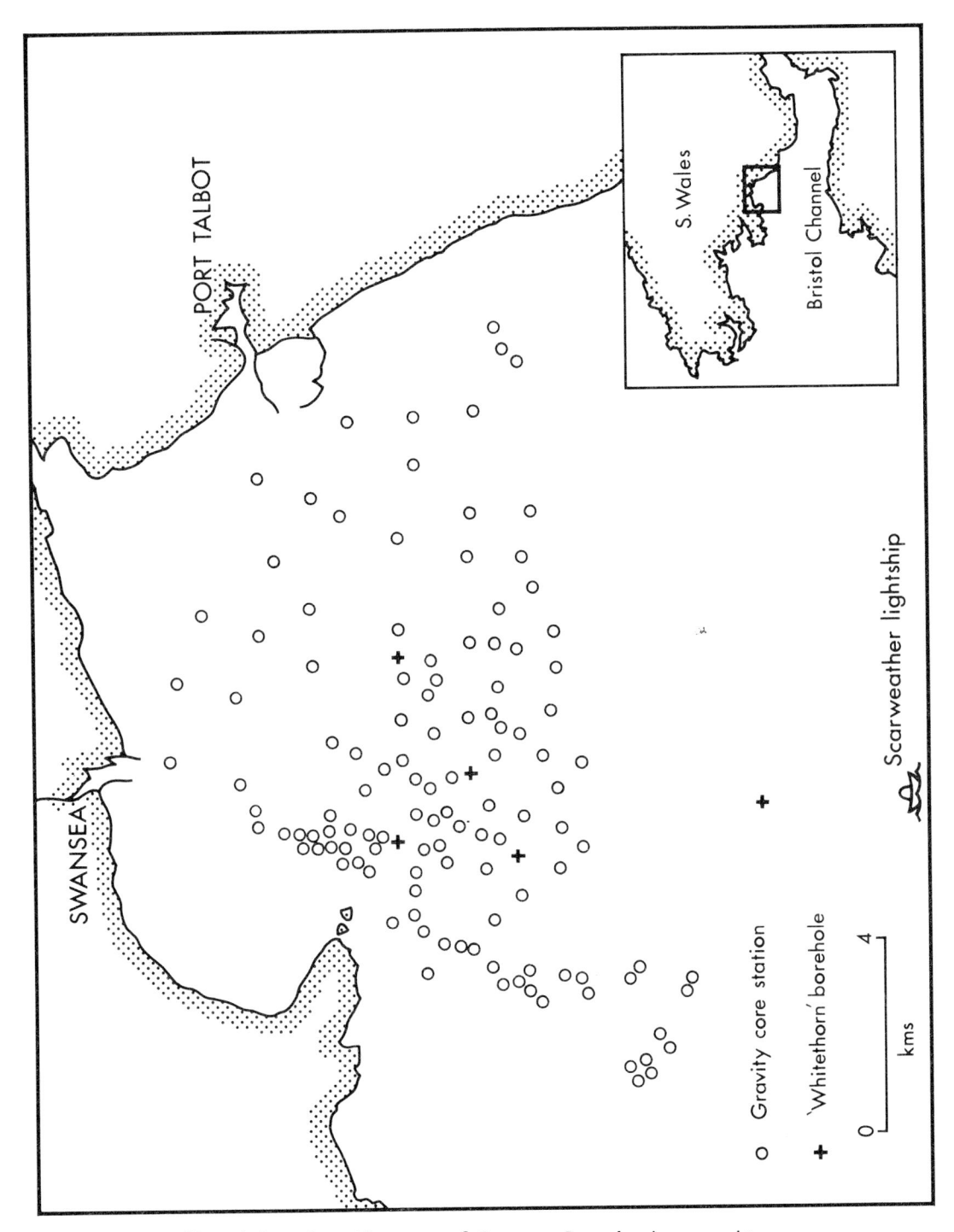

Fig. 4.1. Location map of Swansea Bay showing gravity core and "Whitethorn" borehole stations.

associated in this instance with limited post-depositional *in situ* modification. Limited edge rounding (large and small scale) both by chemical and mechanical (sub-aqueous rolling) means, together with the almost complete lack of disoriented v-shaped impact pits, is particularly noticeable. Facies 2 was only encountered directly at the seabed in one gravity core (Figs. 4.1 and 4.2), but additional information concerning its characteristics was supplied by data from boreholes drilled in Swansea Bay by the Institute of Geological Sciences.

Facies 3: Consolidated, greyish, clayey sands, sandy silts and clays (with associated peats). The benthic foraminiferal fauna recovered from these deposits is dominated by euryhaline forms such as *Haynesina germanica* (Ehrenberg), *Elphidium williamsoni* Haynes and *Ammonia tepida* (Cushman). Both juvenile and adult specimens of these forms are present and, thus, they represent the indigenous foraminiferal fauna (see Culver & Banner, 1978; where *Protelphidium anglicum* Murray = *Haynesina germanica*, see Banner & Culver, 1979). Some stenohaline forms are also present; their size sorting and often poor preservation indicates that they are transported specimens washed into Swansea Bay from the central and outer Bristol Channel (Culver & Banner, 1978; compare Murray & Hawkins, 1976). All foraminiferid tests are white and opaque due to slight etching of the test surface following burial in a slightly acidic environment (see Murray, 1967 and Murray & Wright, 1970).

SEM analysis of the surface features of quartz sand grains obtained from these deposits show (Table 4.1) that the grains have been derived from a similar high energy mechanical-modification environment as those in facies 2, but appear to have undergone some degree of subsequent shallow-marine reworking. The high percentages of conchoidal fractures, breakage blocks and associated features suggest the mechanical alteration, whilst the very high percentage of grains exhibiting relatively dense patterns of disoriented v-shaped impact pits is most diagnostic of high energy subaqueous action. Associated with these impact pits and, indeed, superimposed upon them is chemical etching both of oriented v-shaped pits and of diagenetic fretting. Both of these patterns are commonly found upon the surfaces of sand grains taken from high-energy subaqueous environments.

Facies 4: Unconsolidated sand and mud. This material (its distribution shown on Fig. 4.2) is available for present-day transportation in both the littoral and sub-littoral zones. It forms intertidal sand-flats, sand bars and the sand deposits of the berm. The mud-and-silt is often concentrated in the lee of intertidal sand bars. Offshore, the sand forms large sand banks (Mixon Shoal, for example) and other smaller sand bodies.

SEM surface texture analysis reveals the same underlying mechanically-derived breakages and fractures, perhaps indicative of glacial modification, that can be seen on sand grains from facies 1, 2 and 3. However, in these deposits modification by subsequent subaqueous action is easily seen. Edge rounding, both to grains and smaller scale features, superimposed v-shaped disoriented etch pits, chemically produced etch pits and diagenetic fretting are all indicative of shallow-marine, high energy subaqueous modification (Table 4.1).

The foraminiferal fauna consists of (probably local) stenohaline forms which originally live on, or attached to, hard substrates such as rocks and seaweeds (*Cibicides lobatulus* (Walker & Jacob), *Rosalina globularis* d'Orbigny, *Planorbulina mediterranensis* d'Orbigny, *Quinqueloculina seminulum* (Linnaeus)). After death, the tests of the animals were transported as sedimentary particles away from their habitat and were incorporated in the unconsolidated sand bodies in Swansea Bay. Also present are modern benthic forms which live sub-littorally on sand or muddy substrates and which are transported into Swansea Bay from as far away as the central and outer Bristol Channel as pseudoplankton (Murray, 1965; Murray & Hawkins, 1976; Culver & Banner, 1978). Due to their transportation as sedimentary particles, foraminiferal

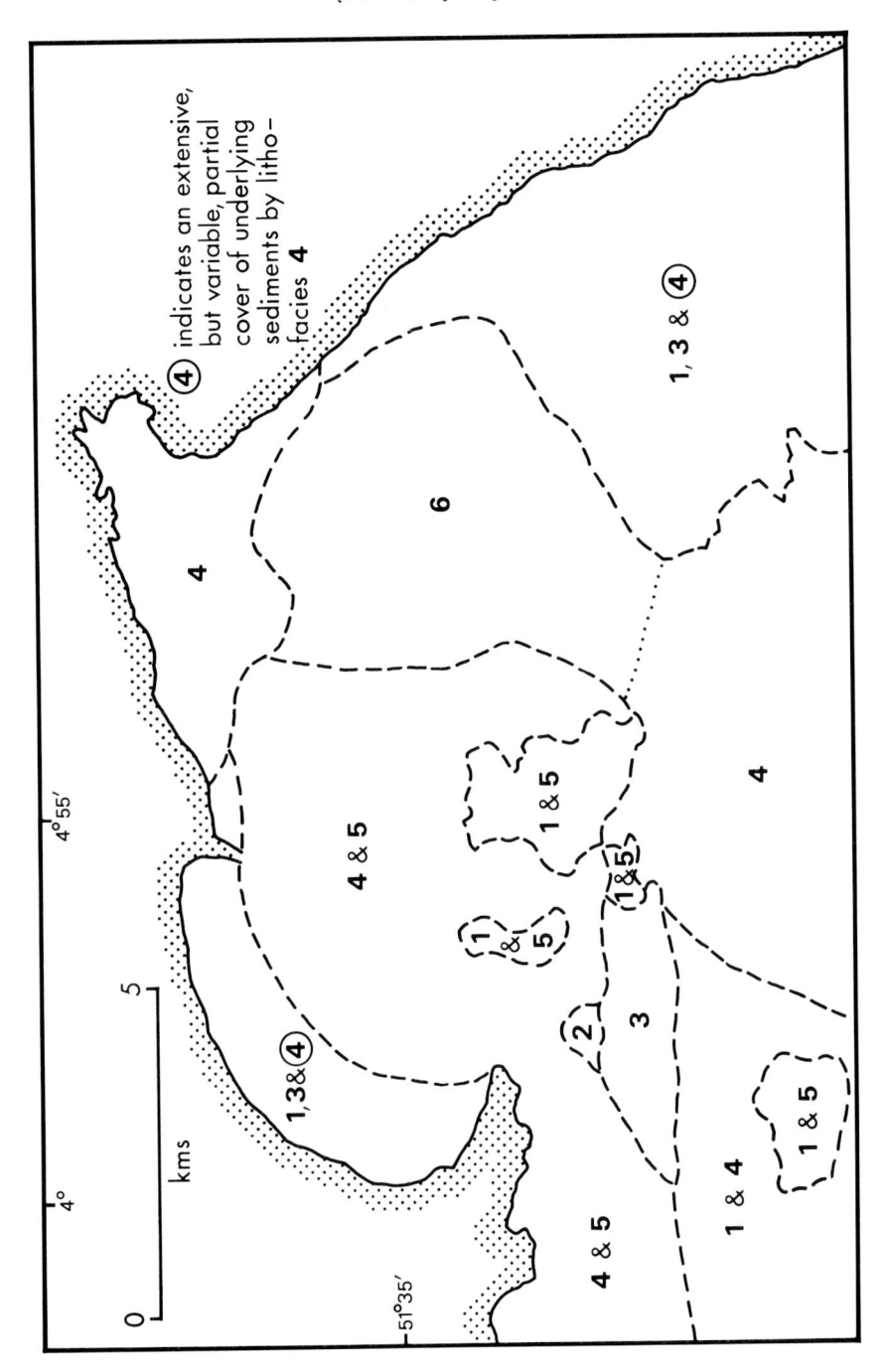

Fig. 4.2. Distribution at the seabed of the six facies referred to in the text.

tests present in the unconsolidated sands show size-sorting to varying degrees and thus differ from foraminiferal assemblages of facies 3. They also differ in their preservation showing breakages due to transportation and also little evidence of etching typical of the foraminiferid tests of facies 3. A few euryhaline benthic foraminifera are also present.

Facies 5: Pebbles, cobbles and boulders, sometimes mixed with unconsolidated mud, sand and silt. Pebbles and cobbles were often recovered in the gravity core nose-cone thus precluding the recovery of sediment cores. Subangular pebbles, cobbles and boulders of allochthonous (not colluvial) rocks (Millstone Grit, Coal Measures, Old Red Sandstone) have been recovered also by grab and dredge sampling. Most pebbles were encountered in areas of unconsolidated sand and mud but some were also picked up over areas where facies 1 is exposed on the seabed.

Facies 6: Sandy mud. A large area of Swansea Bay is covered by a layer of relatively fluid sandy mud up to a metre or more thickness. These deposits are mobile at times of maximum current speed, under present-day hydrodynamic conditions.

QUATERNARY DEPOSITION IN SWANSEA BAY

Facies 1 is the oldest Quaternary deposit encountered in Swansea Bay. These pebbly deposits are the boulder clays deposited very close to the maximum southern extent of the last (Devensian) glaciation at about 20000 to 17000 bp (Charlesworth, 1929; Bowen, 1970; Culver, this volume, Table 6.1 and Fig. 6.1). The pebbles are typical of 'Welsh Drift' and were picked up as glacier ice moved southwards over the South Wales Coalfield. The better sorted sands and gravels are possibly of fluvioglacial origin. The facies is 'relict' in the sense of Emery (1952, 1968).

Facies 2 has the characteristics of a lacustrine deposit. These laminated silts and clays occur in rock basins (Culver, 1976b) which were recognised by geophysical means (Al-Saadi & Brooks, 1973). Lacustrine sedimentation is considered to have occurred between approximately 16000 and 10000 bp (Culver & Bull, 1979) during which time Swansea Bay was a dry land area of hummocky topography, the lakes being fed by meltwater draining from the glaciers to the north. Again, this is a relict facies, which owes none of its characteristics to present-day hydrodynamics.

Around 9500 bp the rising sea invaded the Swansea Bay area and rapid deposition of mainly clay and silt, winnowed from subaqueously eroded boulder clays in the Bristol Channel, initiated intertidal mud flat deposition over most of the bay. The grey clays, silts and sands of facies 3 are the result of this low energy, littoral deposition which continued until approximately 2500 bp (Culver & Banner, 1978). This deposit is relict, in that it is stable under modern hydrodynamic conditions, but it betrays even earlier origins, and is "relict palimpsest" (Banner with Culver, 1979).

It is probable that the low energy environment, in which facies 3 accumulated, was protected by sand-dune complexes. This sand was derived by erosion of the boulder clays in Swansea Bay and the Bristol Channel. It has been potentially mobile since derivation and is represented by the modern palimpsest sand of facies 4 of this paper. The sand dune complex mentioned above has now migrated inland to form a supra-littoral coastal fringe rather than a littoral barrier feature. Some of the sand and probably the mobile mud has been eroded from facies 3 as indicated by the presence of size-sorted, euryhaline benthic foraminifera.

As the sea transgressed into Swansea Bay in the early Holocene (see Culver, Chapter 6, Table 6.1) the erosion and sorting of boulder clays (which produced the clays and silts of facies 3 and the sands of facies 4) left behind the pebbles, cobbles and boulders as a lag deposit. These have been described above as facies 5. Where these pebbles are in areas of unconsolidated sand and mud, they represent relict lag

Quaternary Deposits 47

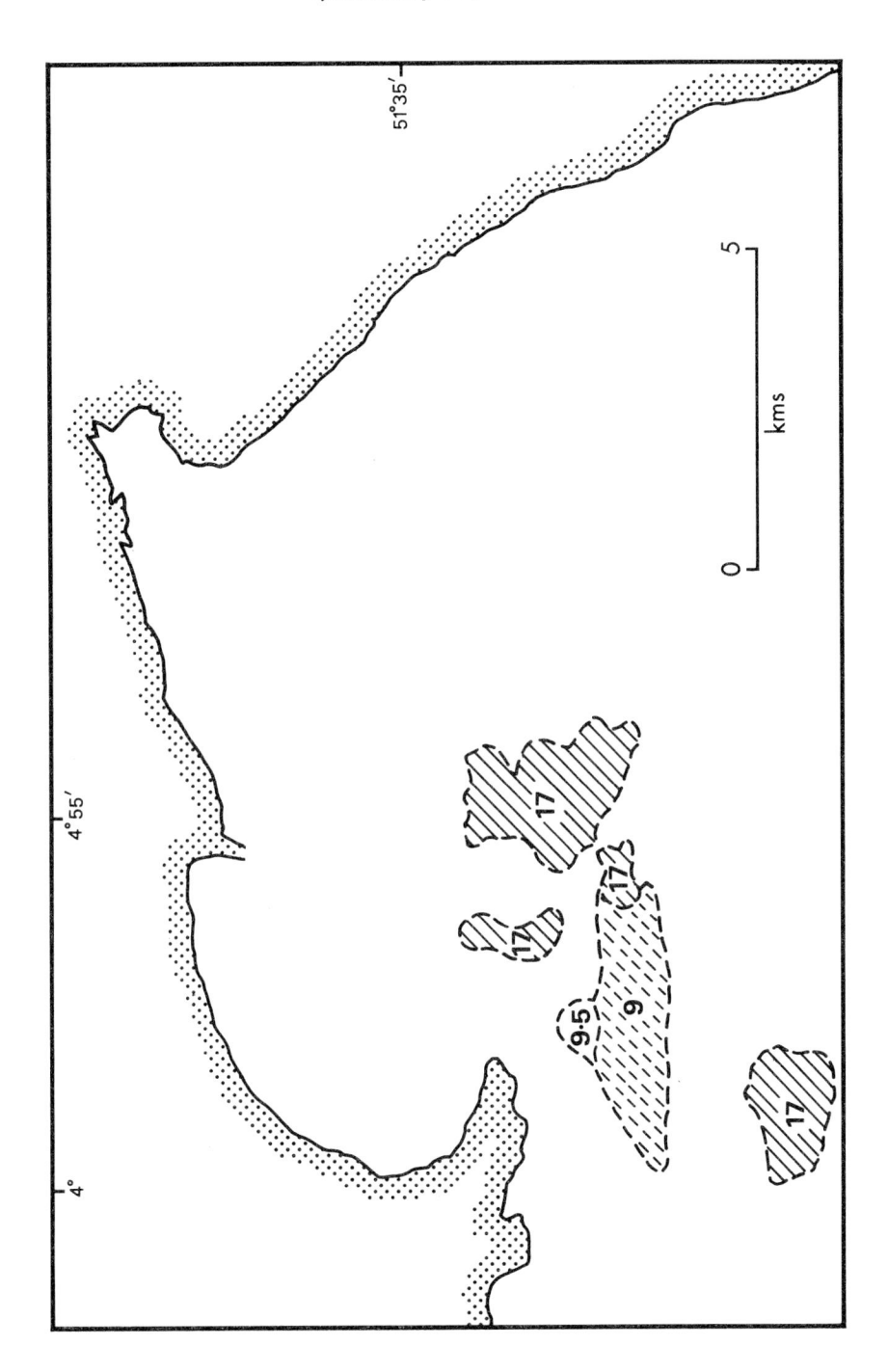

Fig. 4.3. Major areas, and approximate length of time (year x 10^3), of nil net-deposition in Swansea Bay.

gravels to which sand and mud have been supplied and added later by current action (to become relict palimpsest deposits).

The mobile sandy mud of facies 6 is the material constantly being dredged from the channels approaching the mouths of the Tawe and Neath rivers and Port Talbot harbour. This material is dumped mainly on the eastern side of the bay and is often redeposited in the dredged channels. This deposit originated when dredging first began in this area very recently. Most of the sediment particles were obtained by the dredging of facies 1 and 3 and still show evidence of their earlier deposition environment, and are "modern palimpsest" in the genetic terminology (Banner with Culver, 1979).

To summarise, Quaternary deposition in Swansea Bay has taken place in glacial, fluvio-glacial, lacustrine, aeolian, low-energy littoral and high-energy littoral natural environments. Much is immobile and 'relict' or 'relict palimpsest', playing no part in contemporary sedimentation except as a source of sedimentary material. Thin veneers of mobile sediments have been derived from these sources. Final admixtures of material have been introduced as a result of human activity.

NON-DEPOSITION AREAS

Much of the offshore, sublittoral zone of Swansea Bay is now covered by mobile sand of facies 4 and 6, but much is also bare of modern sediment. Figure 4.3 indicates the number of years of nil net-deposition for these areas in Swansea Bay. The maximum extent of the Devensian ice age occurred around 20000 to 17000 bp (Bowen, 1970). At this time, ice flowing southwards from central Wales reached the Bristol Channel only in Swansea Bay and Carmarthen Bay to the west (Charlesworth, 1929; Bowen, 1970). Thus, the boulder clays (facies 1) now exposed on the seabed of Swansea Bay must have been deposited at least 17000 years ago and possibly slightly earlier. Therefore, areas of boulder clay exposure must have been areas of net nil-deposition for at least 17000 years (Fig. 4.3). Pollen analysis of freshwater peats recovered in gravity cores in Swansea Bay at -29m O.D. (Culver & Bull, 1979) show that the peat accumulated on a hummocky boulder clay surface around 10000 to 9500 bp. Areas where this peat occurs on the seabed must, therefore, have been areas of net nil-deposition for around 9500 years (Fig. 4.3). The peats are sometimes overlain by Holocene intertidal deposits (facies 3). These areas where the clays and silts are exposed on the seabed around -29m O.D. have been areas of nil net-deposition for approximately 9000 years. Lacustrine sedimentation in over-deepened basins in Swansea Bay came to a close when the transgressing Flandrian sea entered the bay around 9500 bp. Thus, seabed exposures of lacustrine deposits (facies 2) must have been areas of nil net-deposition for at least 9500 years.

ACKNOWLEDGEMENTS

Thanks are due to the Institute of Geological Sciences (Leeds) for supplying samples from "Whitethorn" boreholes 72/58 and 72/59. Dr. Q.O.N. Kay kindly provided the pollen analysis of the Swansea Bay peats. PAB thanks Christ Church, Oxford, for financial support and the School of Geography for aid during the production of this paper.

REFERENCES

Al-Saadi, R. and Brooks, M. (1973). A geophysical study of Pleistocene buried valleys in the Lower Swansea Valley, Vale of Neath and Swansea Bay. *Proc. Geol. Ass.*, 84, 135-153.

Banner, F.T., and Culver, S.J. (1979). Quaternary *Haynesina* n.gen. and Palaeogene *Protelphidium* Haynes. *J. Foram. Res.*, 8, 177-207.

Banner, F.T., with Culver, S.J. (1979). Sediments of the North-western European Shelf. In F.T. Banner, M.B. Collins and K.S. Massie (Eds.). *The North-West European Shelf Seas: the seabed and the sea in motion*, Vol. 1, Elsevier Oceanographic Series, 24A, Elsevier Scientific Publishing Co., Amsterdam, Chap. 8, pp.271-300.

Bowen, D.Q. (1970). In C.A. Lewis (Ed.), *The glaciations of Wales and adjoining regions*. Longmans, London. 197-228.

Charlesworth, J.K. (1929). The South Wales end moraine. *Q. Jl. geol. Soc. Lond.*, 85, 335-358.

Clifton, R.J., and Hamilton, E.I. (1979). Lead-210 chronology in relation to levels of elements in dated sediment core profiles. *Estuarine and Coastal Marine Science*, 8, 259-270.

Collins, M.B., Ferentinos, G., & Banner, F.T. (1979). The hydrodynamics and sedimentology of a high (tidal and wave) energy embayment (Swansea Bay, northern Bristol Channel). *Estuarine and Coastal Marine Science*, 8, 49-74.

Culver, S.J. (1976a). *A study of the post-glacial Foraminiferida of Swansea Bay, South Wales*. Ph.D. Thesis, Univ. Wales (unpub.).

Culver, S.J. (1976b). The development of the Swansea Bay area during the past 20,000 years. *Gower*, 27, 58-62.

Culver, S.J. (1980). Palaeolithic to Iron Age archaeology and palaeoenvironment in the Swansea area. *Problems of an Industrialised Embayment - Swansea Bay*. (this volume).

Culver, S.J., and Banner, F.T. (1978). Foraminiferal assemblages as Flandrian palaeoenvironmental indicators. *Palaeogeogr., Palaeoclimatol., Palaeoecol.*, 23, 53-72.

Culver, S.J., and Bull, P.A. (1979). Late Pleistocene rock-basin lakes in South Wales. *Geol. Jl.*

Emery, K.O. (1952). Continental shelf sediments of southern California. *Geol. Soc. Amer. Bull.*, 63, 1105-1108.

Emery, K.O. (1968). Relict sediments on continental shelves of the world. *Amer. Assoc. Pet. Geol. Bull.*, 52, 445-464.

Hamilton, E.I., and Clifton, R.J. (1979). Isotopic abundances of lead in estuarine sediments, Swansea Bay, Bristol Channel. *Estuarine and Coastal Marine Science*, 8, 271-278.

Margolis, S.V. and Kennett, J.P. (1971). Cenozoic paleoglacial history of Antarctica recorded in subAntarctica deep-sea cores. *Amer. J. Sci.*, 270, 1-36.

Murray, J.W. (1965). Significance of benthonic foraminiferids in plankton samples. *Jl. Paleontology*, 39, 156-157.

Murray, J.W. (1967). Transparent and opaque Foraminiferid tests. *Jl. Paleontology*, 41, 791.

Murray, J.W. and Hawkins, A.B. (1976). Sediment transport in the Severn Estuary during the past 8,000-9,000 years. *Jl. geol. Soc. Lond.*, 132, 385-398.

Murray, J.W. and Wright, C.A. (1970). Surface textures of calcareous foraminiferids. *Palaeontology*, 13, 184-187.

Whalley, W.B. and Krinsley, D.H. (1974). A scanning electron microscope study of surface textures of quartz grains from glacial environments. *Sedimentology*, 21, 87-105.

TABLE 4.1.   Sand Grain Surface Features*

Surface Feature	Facies 1	Facies 2	Facies 3	Facies 4
Small scale breakage blocks	68	82	86	72
Small scale conchoidal fractures	58	88	60	64
Large scale breakage blocks	86	82	82	78
Large scale conchoidal fractures	92	86	72	78
Straight grooves and scratches	48	38	28	4
Curved grooves (random or trails)	8	16	4	6
Randomly oriented striations	24	8	12	6
Step-like fractures	58	42	40	42
Arc-shaped steps	38	48	50	34
Meandering ridges	76	52	32	24
V-shaped disoriented pits	0	8	64	82
Crack propagated fractures	16	20	14	4
Sharp angular outline	24	32	20	8
Sub-angular outline	64	54	46	48
Sub-rounded outline	12	12	32	26
Well rounded outline	0	2	2	18
Low relief	10	18	14	20
Medium relief	28	22	48	68
High relief	62	60	38	12
Oriented v-shaped pits	20	32	24	42
Irregular, finely pitted surface	16	28	38	24
Diagenetic etching (anastomosing)	28	22	42	40
Smooth featureless surface	8	14	8	0
Cryptocrystalline overgrowths	42	60	96	90
Euhedral overgrowths	0	0	0	0

*Figures represent the percentage number of grains in each sample exhibiting the surface feature.   Table and method based on Margolis and Kennett (1971).

5. THE USE OF THE SYMAP/SYMVU COMPUTER PACKAGE TO EXAMINE BATHYMETRY, SEDIMENTOLOGY, AND OFFSHORE GEOLOGY

J. K. Rigler and M. B. Collins

Department of Oceanography, University College, Swansea, S. Wales, U.K.

ABSTRACT

Three-dimensional perspective views produced by the SYMAP/SYMVU package have been used to represent the bathymetry of the Bristol Channel and Swansea Bay. These projections are used to examine the bedrock geology of the Channel, superficial sediment cover in Swansea Bay and a small bathymetric feature, the Mixon Shoal.

KEYWORDS

Bristol Channel; Swansea Bay; Bathymetry; Marine geology; Computer graphics; SYMAP; SYMVU.

INTRODUCTION

The central section of the Bristol Channel and its northern coastal area in particular have been studied extensively in terms of bathymetry, sedimentology and offshore geology (e.g., Evans and Thompson, 1979; Collins and Banner, 1980). The general method of representation of this data is two-dimensional. An attempt is made here to depict the bathymetry in a three-dimensional perspective view, produced by use of the SYMAP/SYMVU computer package. Available sedimentological and geological data are superimposed upon the plots to provide an alternative method of interpretation. In a further attempt to explain the surficial sediment distribution in Swansea Bay, generalised tidal current patterns are shown.

The SYMAP (Synographic Mapping System)/SYMVU (Synographic Mapping View) has been developed by H.T. Fisher at the Laboratory for Computer Graphics at Harvard University. Briefly, it is a computer program written to produce a regular matrix of data points (in this case, depth) and plot the two-dimensional matrix as a three-dimensional diagram, the value at each point representing the vertical axis. The SYMVU package generates perspective views of surfaces on the offline graph plotter and the user has full control of orientation, symbolism and scaling. As an example of the versatility of the package, SYMAP/SYMVU has been used (F.L.E. Robles, pers. comm.) to present dynamic topography in an area of upwelling.

AREA OF STUDY AND SOURCES OF INFORMATION

The Bristol Channel is a southwesterly facing funnel-shaped inlet, approximately 70 km wide at its mouth, narrowing progressively inwards towards the Severn Estuary. The hydrodynamics of the Channel is complicated by the interaction of high tidal currents and dominant swell wave approach from the southwest. The area is one of high tidal ranges; the Spring range at Swansea is 10.5m, whilst upchannel this increases to 14.5m at Avonmouth. The associated tidal currents are correspondingly high, reaching 250cm/s at the surface up-channel (von Sager, 1968). The current patterns are rectilinear in the main part of the channel (Admiralty Chart 1179) but are modified, by headlands and coastal discontinuities, along the northern coastline (Collins et al., 1979).

Hypothetical accounts of the bedrock and basement of the Bristol Channel have been presented by North (1955) and Owen (1970). Donovan et al. (1961) produced an early map showing the present surface distribution of bedrock and sediments in the Channel. This study confirmed that an extensive sequence of Jurassic beds is preserved in a synclinal structure in the southern part of the Channel. Lloyd et al. (1973), Evans (1973, MS) and Evans and Thompson (1979) have provided further detailed work concerning the stratigraphy, whilst information concerning the large scale structure and concealed geology has been presented by Brooks (1970), Brooks and Thompson (1973), Brooks and James (1975), Al-Saadi (1976) and Evans and Thompson (1979). Specific areas of the Bristol Channel have been studied geologically in detail; these include papers by Banner et al. (1971), covering the approaches to Barry Harbour, and Al-Saadi and Brooks (1973), who used geophysical techniques in Swansea Bay (see also Chapter 3).

Extensive investigations into the sediment distributions in the Bristol Channel and Swansea Bay have provided a fairly detailed picture of the grade and bedforms of the deposits. Present day accumulation is taking place upon a substrate of Pleistocene and Early Flandrian deposits on the northern side of the central Bristol Channel (Chapter 4; compare Belderson et al., 1971). Sand waves, large sand banks and a thin veneer of sand cover these earlier glacial and interglacial deposits. Quaternary deposits terminate south of the latitude of Nash Point in the form of a low scarp (Evans, 1973, MS), south of which Mesozoic and older bedrock is exposed almost to the Devon coast (Evans and Thompson, 1979). Bedforms in the Channel have been identified by Kenyon (1970) and Warwick and Davies (1977); sediment transport and distribution have been considered by Belderson and Stride (1966), Belderson et al. (1971), Donovan and Stride (1961), Stride (1963) and Collins and Banner (1980).

Detailed work has been carried out within Swansea Bay and along the Gower coastline. Johnson (1975, MS) and Hildred (1976, MS) have given accounts of the sedimentology and hydrology in eastern Swansea Bay and the Mixon Shoal, respectively. Turner (1976, MS) has investigated the Scarweather and Nash Sands (see also Chapter 13). Culver and Banner (1978) and Collins et al. (1979) have described in detail the seabed deposits and the sediment transport processes in Swansea Bay (see also Chapter 9 and Chapters 13-19).

TYPICAL RESULTS AND THEIR INTERPRETATION

An upchannel perspective view of the Bristol Channel is shown as Fig. 5.1. The bathymetry is based on information abstracted from the Admiralty Fair Sheets used to compile Admiralty Chart 1179. Some 850 data points were used, being more concentrated around the most important bathymetric features; interpolation of the data points to form a regular matrix is carried out by the SYMAP package. The bedrock geology, superimposed on the SYMVU output (Fig. 5.1), is adapted from Evans (1973), Lloyd et al. (1973), Al-Saadi and Brooks (1973) and Banner et al. (1971).

SYMAP/SYMVU Representations 53

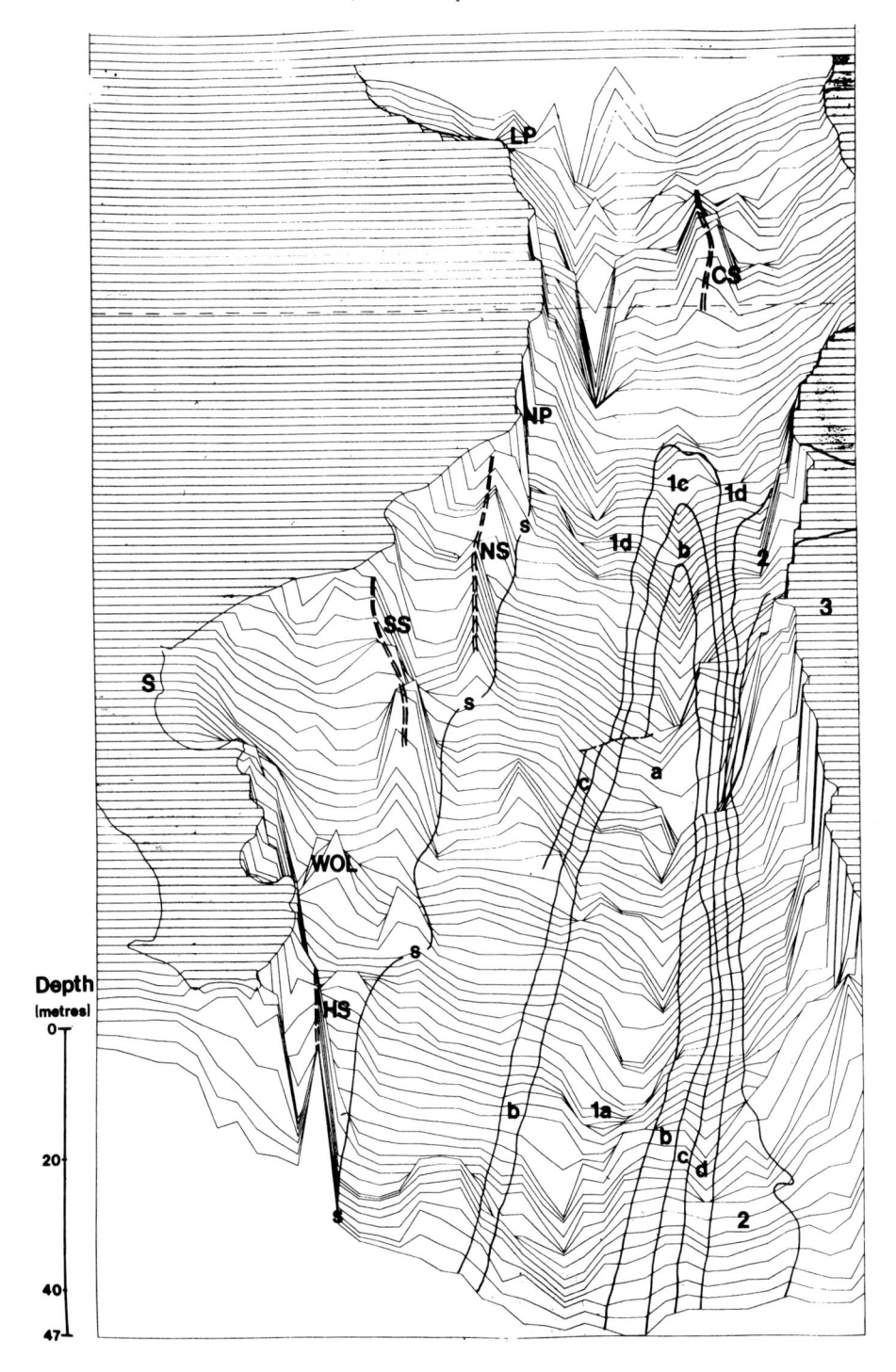

Figure 5.1. (For Caption, please see overleaf).

Fig. 5.1 demonstrates how the bathymetry is influenced by the major geological structural controls. The deepest portion of the Channel is coincident with the axis of the Bristol Channel syncline. Combinations of extensive scour and easily erodible substrate have allowed a deepening of the Channel along this axis, as shown by the exposure of Late Jurassic clays and shales. The southern limit of the extensive surficial sediment cover (Fig. 5.1) is latitudinally aligned with the northern coastline between Nash Point and Lavernock Point. This limit appears to reflect the demarcation between the tidally-scoured areas of the central and southern Channel (Stride, 1963; Donovan and Stride, 1961), which have, at most, only a thin (<2m thick) cover of muddy gravel (Evans, 1973, MS), and the wave-influenced shallow water areas to the north (Chapter 14).

Fig. 5.2. Shows the bathymetry and the superimposed surface sediment distribution in Swansea Bay. The SYMVU projection has been compiled from 1000 data points abstracted from Admiralty Fair Sheets of the 1949 (H.M.S. *Seagull*) and 1974 (H.M.S. *Woodlark*) hydrographic surveys. The sediment "provinces" have been adapted from Fig. 10 of Collins et al. (1979); these "provinces" were recognised by sediment textures, not by genetic facies as in Chapter 4. Surface flood tidal currents are taken from the same publication.

The dominant bathymetric features shown in the projection are the White Oyster Ledge, the Mixon Shoal and a deep submarine hollow at the southern limit of the Mixon Shoal (see Fig. 5.3). Geophysical evidence suggests that the White Oyster Ledge is a Carboniferous Limestone feature covered with glacial till (Chapter 3 and Collins et al., 1979). The submarine hollow to the north of the ledge reaches depths of approx. 35m below Chart Datum (Admiralty Chart 1161). This basin is floored by lacustrine Devensian sediments (Culver, 1976) with a thin cover of modern silts (Chapter 4). The SYMVU projection (Fig. 5.3) reinforces the suggestion that this feature owes its origin to glacial scour along the trend of the Neath Disturbance fault line (Al-Saadi and Brooks, 1973; see also Chapters 2 and 3).

The largest area of modern sediment (textural "province 1", Fig. 5.2) in Swansea Bay is that of sandy mud and muddy sand. The configuration of the "province" can be conveniently divided into a northeasterly area of muddy sand and a south-westerly area of sandy mud (Collins et al., 1979). The northeasterly portion may be associated with tidal current divergence (Fig. 5.2) in an area of extensive fine-grained sediment supply.

Fig. 5.3. represents an enlargement of the Mixon Shoal, a small sand body lying to

Figure 5.1. SYMVU projection of bathymetry of the Bristol Channel (viewed from the West). The exposed bedrock is superimposed on the Figure (faults have been omitted for the sake of clarity).
<u>Location and Feature Notations</u>:
CS - Culver Sands, HS - Helwick Sands, LP - Lavernock Point, NP - Nash Point, NS - Nash Sands, S - Swansea, SS - Scarweather Sands, WOL - White Oyster Ledge, S-S maximum extent of thick surficial sediment cover.
<u>Geological Notations</u>:
1a - Kimmeridgian, 1b - Oxford clays and sands, 1c - Upper Lias, 1d - Lower Lias, 2 - Permo-Trias, 3 - Pre-Permo-Trias.

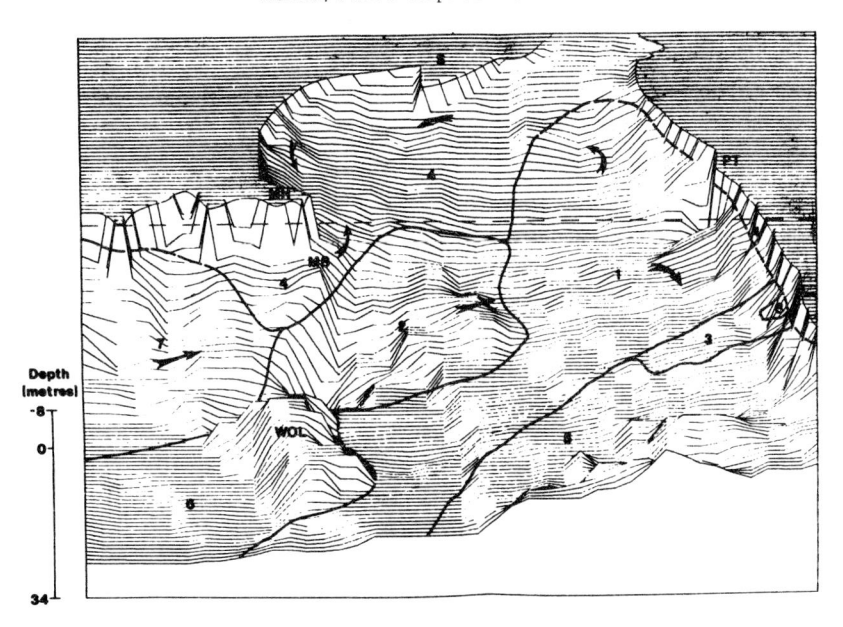

Figure 5.2. SYMVU projection of the bathymetry of Swansea Bay (viewed from the South). Boundaries between the sedimentary Provinces and the directions of maximum flood tidal currents are superimposed on the Figure.
Location Notations:
MH - Mumbles Head, MS - Mixon Shoal, PT - Port Talbot (deep water port), S - Swansea, WOL - White Oyster Ledge.
Province Notations (after Collins et al., 1978):
1 - sandy mud and muddy sand, 2 - gravelly muddy sand, muddy sandy gravel, 3 - gravelly muddy sand, sandy gravel, 4 - (gravelly) sand and sand, 5 - (gravelly) sand and sand, 6 - (gravelly) sand, 7 - sandy gravel and gravel, 8 - mud.

the south of Mumbles Head, Swansea Bay. The bathymetric data is based on a recent detailed hydrographic survey (Hildred, 1976). It is presented as an example of the value of the package in viewing data from small-scale bathymetric features.

CONCLUSIONS

Three examples from the Bristol Channel and Swansea Bay have been presented to demonstrate the use of SYMAP/SYMVU in sedimentological investigations. The technique is ideal for the representation of generalized data. Limitations are imposed by the positioning of absolute values and boundary definitions on the three-dimensional projections.

ACKNOWLEDGEMENTS

The authors gratefully acknowledge the assistance provided by Mr. F.L.E. Robles (Oceanography Department) and Mr. S. Morgan (Computer Centre) of University College, Swansea.

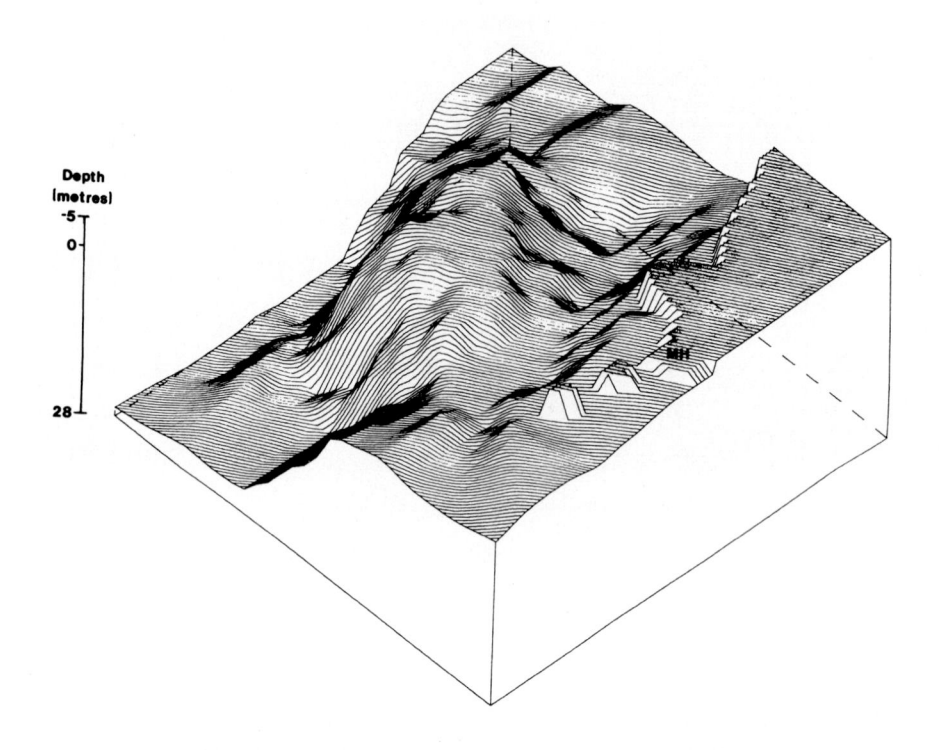

Figure 5.3. SYMVU projection of the bathymetry of the Mixon Shoal (viewed from the northeast). (MH - Mumbles Head).

REFERENCES

Al-Saadi, R.H. (1976). *Seismic studies of geological structure in the inner Bristol Channel area.* Unpub. Ph.D. thesis, Univ. of Wales.

Al-Saadi, R.H., and Brooks, M. (1973). A geophysical study of Pleistocene buried valleys in the Lower Swansea Valley, Vale of Neath and Swansea Bay. *Proc. Geol. Ass., 84,* 135-153.

Banner, F.T., Brooks, M., and Williams, E. (1971). Geology of the approaches to Barry. *Proc. Geol. Ass., 82,* 231-248.

Belderson, R.H., and Stride, A.H. (1966). Tidal current fashioning of a basal bed. *Mar. Geol., 4,* 237-257.

Belderson, R.H., Kenyon, N.H., and Stride, A.H. (1971). Holocene sediments on the continental shelf west of the British Isles. *Inst. Geol. Sci., Report No. 70,* 157-170.

Brooks, M. (1970). Discussion of 'Geology of the Bristol Channel' by Donovan, D.T., Lloyd, A.J., and Stride, A.H. *Proc. Geol. Soc. London, 1664,* 295.

Brooks, M., and James, D.G. (1975). The geological results of seismic refraction surveys in the Bristol Channel, 1970-1973. *Jour. Geol. Soc., 131,* 163-182.

Brooks, M., and Thompson, M.S. (1973). The geological interpretation of a gravity survey in the Bristol Channel. *Jour. Geol. Soc. London, 129,* 245-274.

Collins, M.B., Ferentinos, G., and Banner, F.T. (1979). The hydrodynamics and sedimentology of a high (tidal and wave) energy embayment (Swansea Bay, northern Bristol Channel). *Estuar and Coast. Mar. Sci., 8,* 49-74.

Collins, M.B., and Banner, F.T. (1980). Sediment transport by waves and tides: problems exemplified by a study of Swansea Bay, Bristol Channel. Chapter 11. *In:*

Banner, F.T., Collins, M.B., and Massie, K.S. (Eds.). *The North-west European Shelf Seas: the seabed and the sea in motion. 2*, Elsevier Oceanographic Series, 24B, 369-389.

Culver, S.J. (1976). *A study of the post-glacial foraminiferida of Swansea Bay, South Wales.* Unpub. Ph.D. thesis, Univ. of Wales.

Culver, S.J., and Banner, F.T. (1978). Foraminiferal assemblages as Flandrian palaeoenvironmental indicators. *Palaeogeogr., Palaeoclimatol., Palaeoecol., 23*, 53-72.

Donovan, D.T., and Stride, A.H. (1961). Erosion of a rock floor by tidal sand streams. *Geol. Mag., 98*, 393-398.

Donovan, D.T., Savage, R.J., Stride, A.H., and Stubbs, A.R. (1961). Geology of the floor of the Bristol Channel. *Nature, London, 189*, 51-52.

Evans, D.J. (1973). *Stratigraphy of the central part of the Bristol Channel.* Unpub. Ph.D. thesis, Univ of Wales.

Evans, D.J., and Thompson, M.S. (1979). The geology of the central Bristol Channel and the Lundy area, South Western Approaches, British Isles. *Proc. Geol. Ass., 90*, 1-14.

Hildred, K. (1976). *The Mixon Shoal: an investigation into the bathymetry, hydrodynamics and sedimentology.* Unpub. B.Sc. diss., Univ. Coll. Swansea.

Johnson, N.A. (1975). *The sedimentology and hydrology of eastern Swansea Bay.* Unpub. B.Sc. diss., Univ. Coll. Swansea.

Kenyon, N.H. (1970). Sand ribbons of European tidal areas. *Mar. Geol., 9*, 25-39.

Lloyd, A.J., Savage, R.J., Stride, A.H. and Donovan, D.T. (1973). The geology of the Bristol Channel floor. *Phil. Trans. Royal Soc. (A), 274*, 595-626.

North, F.J. (1955). *The evolution of the Bristol Channel.* National Museum of Wales, Cardiff.

Owen, T.R. (1971). The structural evolution of the Bristol Channel. *Proc. Geol. Soc. London, 1664*, 289-294.

Stride, A.H. (1963). Current swept sea floors near the southern half of Great Britain. *Quart. Jour. Geol. Soc. London, 119*, 175-199.

Tritton, D.J. (1977). *Physical Fluid Dynamics.* Van Nostrand Reinhold Company, 362p.

Turner, S. (1976). *Some aspects of sedimentary bodies in parts of the Bristol Channel.* Unpub. Ph.D. thesis, Univ. of Wales.

Von Sager, G. (1968). *Atlas der gezeitenstrome für die Nordsee, den Kanal und die Irische See.* Rostock Institut für Meereskunde, 45p.

Warwick, R.M. and Davies, J.R. (1977). The distribution of sublittoral macrofauna communities in the Bristol Channel in relation to the substrate. *Estuar. and Coast. Mar. Sci., 4*, 267-288.

6. PALAEOLITHIC TO IRON AGE ARCHAEOLOGY AND PALAEOENVIRONMENT IN THE SWANSEA AREA

S. J. Culver

Dept. of Paleobiology, National Museum of Natural History, Smithsonian Institution, Washington, D.C. 20560, U.S.A.

ABSTRACT

The Palaeolithic to Iron Age archaeological finds in the Swansea area are reviewed and the palaeoenvironmental and palaeogeographical changes that have occurred over the past approximately 250,000 years are briefly described.

The South Wales area experienced limited human occupation in the Late Lower Palaeolithic approximately 225,000b.p. and again towards the end of the Lower Palaeolithic between 100,000 and 70,000b.p. During the period between 200,000 and 100,000b.p., Wales was completely covered by the ice of the Wolstonian glaciation. South Wales was again probably free of human habitation in the early Devensian around 70,000 to 45,000b.p. but the following climatic amelioration until 30,000b.p. enabled Middle Palaeolithic man to migrate again into South Wales.

Although it has been suggested that the South Wales area was uninhabited during the Devensian glacial maximum from 25,000 to 17,00b.p., the 'Red Lady' of Paviland has been radiometrically dated at 18,460 ± 340b.p. indicating that perhaps a sparse population of Upper Palaeolithic man existed in the Swansea area.

During the post-glacial maximum late Devensian and early Holocene, the Swansea Bay area was a low-lying basin surrounded by a ring of hills. Fresh-water lakes occupied at least two glacially-deepened rock-basins and ribbon lakes existed in the Tawe and Neath valleys. Later changes in the palaeogeography and palaeoenvironment of the Swansea area are directly related to the Holocene rise in sealevel which reached its present level around 3,000b.p. during the Bronze Age.

South Wales was continuously inhabited during the Holocene, through the Mesolithic, Neolithic, Bronze and Iron Ages as evidenced by long barrows, round barrows, hill forts and various implement and pottery finds.

In summary, the Palaeolithic to Iron Age inhabitants of the South Wales coastal area experienced a rapidly changing physical environment controlled by the Wolstonian and Devensian ice ages with their subsequent climatic ameliorations and associated sea-level changes.

KEYWORDS

South Wales; Pleistocene; Holocene; archaeology; palaeoenvironment; palaeogeography;

sea-level.

The South Wales area has undergone numerous extreme climatic variations over the past million years and man has endured these fluctuations for at least the last 250,000 years. This essay summarises the archaeological evidence that man lived in the Swansea area and describes the variations in palaeogeography and palaeo-environment that our ancestors experienced.

The surface find of an Acheulian hand-axe near Cardiff is the only evidence we have that man inhabited the South Wales area in the Lower Palaeolithic (McBurney, 1965). This apparently extremely limited occupation of the South Wales area was terminated by the onset of full glacial conditions during the Wolstonian Ice Age (Table 6.1) Wales was then completely covered by an ice sheet and the Bristol Channel area was occupied by ice flowing south-eastwards from the Irish Sea.

TABLE 6.1. Geological, Archaeological and Cultural Divisions of the Quaternary.

PERIOD	EPOCH	YEARS B.P. APPROX.	GEOLOGICAL STAGE	ARCHAEOLOGICAL AGE	CULTURES	YEARS B.P. APPROX.
QUATERNARY	Holocene	—10000—	Flandrian	Historical		—1600—
				Roman		—2000—
				Iron Age		—2400—
				Bronze Age	Beaker	—3800—
				Neolithic	Megalithic	—5000—
				Mesolithic		—10000—
	Pleistocene Late	—26000—	Late Devensian	Late Upper Palaeolithic	Cresswellian	—15000—
				Man absent from the British Isles?		—22000—
		—50000—	Middle Devensian	Early Upper Palaeolithic	Aurignacean	—35000—
		—70000—	Early Devensian	Middle Palaeolithic	Mousterian	—70000—
		—100000—	Ipswichian	Late Lower Palaeolithic	Levalloisian	
		—200000—	Wolstonian		Acheulian	
	Early and Middle	—?—	Hoxnian		Clactonian	—?—
			Anglian to Waltonian	Early Lower Palaeolithic		—2000000—

Around 100,000b.p., the ice retreated northwards and the temperate conditions of the Ipswichian Interglacial ensued. Evidence of human occupation in the South Wales area during this period is again limited to one artifact. One of the excavations in Paviland Cave, South Gower, produced a Levalloisian-type flaked cutting tool which, as indicated by its worn state, was probably derived from the Ipswichian *Patella* Beach (McBurney, 1965), the basal Quaternary deposit at Paviland (George, 1933).

A cooling of climate at the beginning of the Devensian stage from around 70,000 to to 45,000b.p. probably drove the early inhabitants of Wales southwards, but the subsequent climatic amelioration during the Upton Warren Interstadial Complex until around 30,000b.p. resulted in Wales being inhabited again. No evidence of this occupation has been forthcoming from the immediate vicinity of Swansea but Mousterian implements, normally associated with Neanderthal Man (*Homo sapiens neanderthalis*), have been recovered from Coygan Cave, Dyfed and from Plas-y-Cefn, Clwyd.

Around 30,000b.p., modern-type man (*Homo sapiens sapiens*) and his culture arrived in Europe from the Near East (McBurney, 1965) and continued to migrate westwards to the British Isles. Thus, during Upper Palaeolithic times, although climatic cooling was again occurring, *Homo sapiens sapiens* was living in the South Wales area. Longhole (SS 451851) on Gower has yielded remains of mammoth, wolf, giant deer and Aurignacian-Solutrean stone artifacts (Campbell, 1977).

In 1923, W. Buckland discovered the skeleton of a young man in deposits of cemented scree in Paviland Cave, South Gower (SS 437859). The bones of the skeleton had been coated with red ochre and the find became known as the 'Red Lady' of Paviland. The artifacts associated with the skeleton were collected by Professor Sollas and proved to be typical Aurignacian scrapers, wide blades, plano-convex spear heads and bone awls. Radiocarbon dating of the 'Red Lady' gave an age of 18,460 ± 340

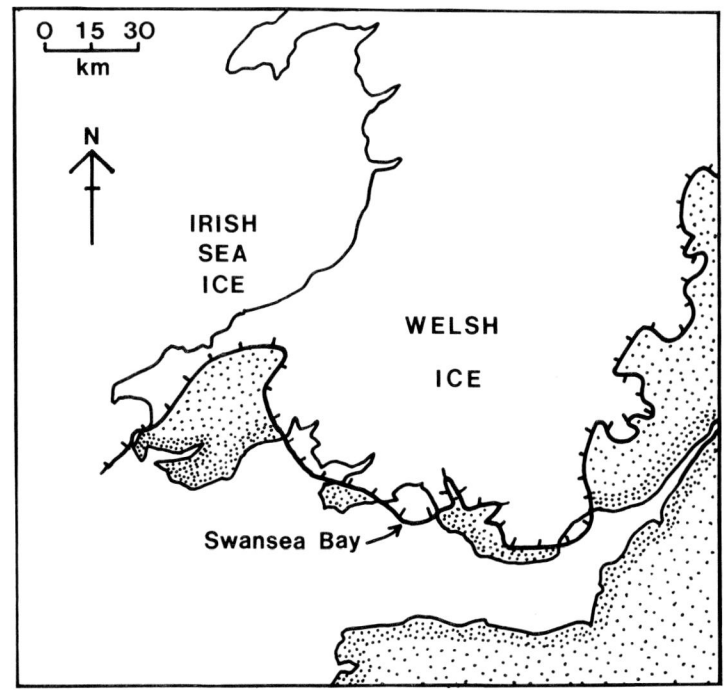

Fig. 6.1. Maximum extent of the Devensian glaciation in Wales. (Modified from Bowen, 1974).

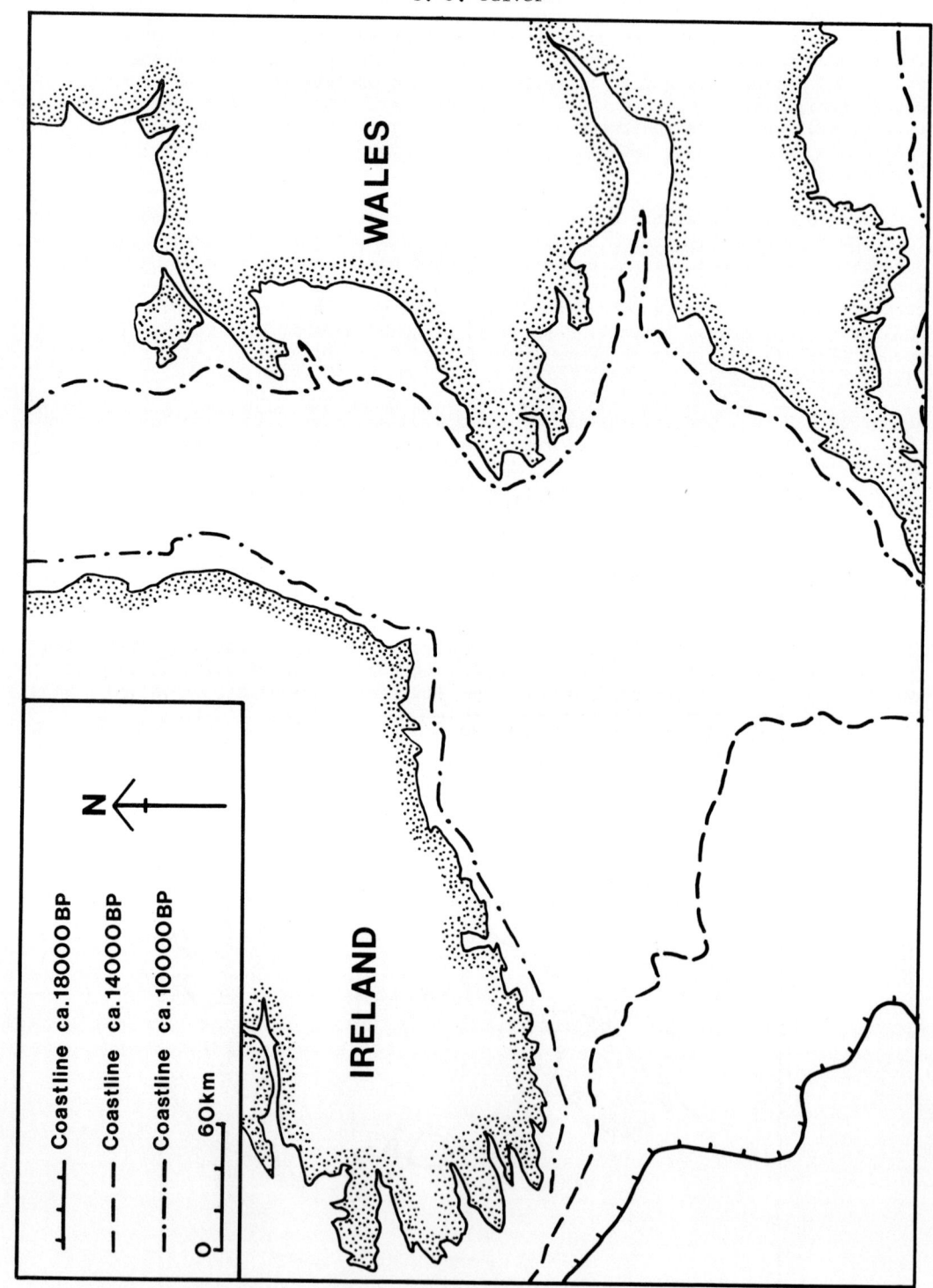

Fig. 6.2. The coastline around southwest Britain at 18,000, 14,000 and 10,000 b.p. (Modified from Culver and Banner, 1979).

(Oakley, 1968).

Bowen (1970a) has shown that the maximum extent of the Devensian glaciation occurred around 20,000 to 17,000b.p. (Fig. 6.1). At this time sea-level was up to 130m lower than at the present day (Donn and others, 1962; Fairbridge, 1977) and the Bristol Channel area was dry land (Hawkins, 1971a; Culver and Banner, 1979) crossed by rivers fed by glacial meltwater. Using the date of 18,460b.p., Bowen (1970b) reconstructed the palaeoenvironment of the 'Red Lady' and suggested that Upper Palaeolithic man lived in an unfriendly, extremely cold environment just south of the Devensian ice cap with Paviland Cave overlooking the broad lowland plain of the dry Bristol Channel area. This would contradict the idea that man was absent from the British Isles during the main Devensian ice advance (Evans, 1975) and it may well be that the radiometric date of 18,460b.p. is erroneously young (Campbell, 1977).

In the late Devensian (late Upper Palaeolithic) from around 17,000 to 10,000b.p., sea-level rose as the ice sheets retreated northwards or melted *in situ* (Fig. 6.2). The Bristol Channel area was a low-lying marshy plain similar to that which existed in the North Sea area from Britain to southern Sweden (Evans, 1975). It is probable that small lakes and bogs existed in hollows in hummocky Wolstonian and Devensian glacial drift that covered most of the Bristol Channel area.

In addition to these small temporary lakes, it has been shown (Culver, 1976a; Culver and Bull, 1979) that in the Swansea area, at least four large lakes existed for several thousand years. These lakes occupied deep rock-basins, down to -150m OD (Al-Saadi and Brooks, 1973), which were probably gouged out by Devensian ice along structural lines of weakness, the Tawe and Neath disturbances. The lakes show the characteristic ribbon-shape similar to the lakes of the Lake District in northwest England and contain laminated, fine sediment of a varved nature.

Just south of the Scarweather area, towards the centre of the Bristol Channel due south of Swansea Bay, freshwater organic mud has been recovered by gravity coring at a depth of -35m OD (Evans, 1973; Evans and Thompson, 1979). Pollen analysis of this 'peat' showed it to be of Pollen Zone IV age (about 10,000b.p.). It was overlain by marine clays and silts which indicate that the eastwards migrating shoreline of the rising sea had reached the Scarweather area at the end of the Palaeolithic around 10,000b.p.

Just south of Mumbles Head, between two rock-basin lakes (Fig.6.3) freshwater, upland bog peats have been recovered over a wide area by gravity coring at a depth of -29m OD (Culver, 1976b). The top of these peats has been dated (Q.O.N. Kay, pers. comm.) as Pollen Zone IV to V and they are overlain by marine clays and silts indicating that the Holocene transgression had reached the outer parts of Swansea Bay around 9,500b.p. when sea-level was 29m lower than at the present day.

Large pieces of solidifed resin, indicating the presence of conifer woodlands (perhaps *Pinus*), have been dredged from Carmarthen Bay, and these are probably of about this age.

Thus the palaeogeography of the Swansea area, from about 16,000b.p. to 10,000b.p., can be envisaged. A ring of hills (Mumbles Head, Town Hill, Margam Mountain) surrounded the lowland area of Swansea Bay which exhibited a hummocky topography of glacial drift. Ribbon lakes existed in the Tawe and Neath valleys, and the Tawe and Neath rivers, where they reached the lowland area, probably split up into braided streams which meandered across the drift and flowed into the rock-basin lakes south of Mumbles Head. The braided nature of the rivers is suggested by the lack of well-developed extensions of the Neath and Tawe valleys beneath the present Swansea Bay (Price and Culver, 1977). Around these lakes, some over 100m deep,

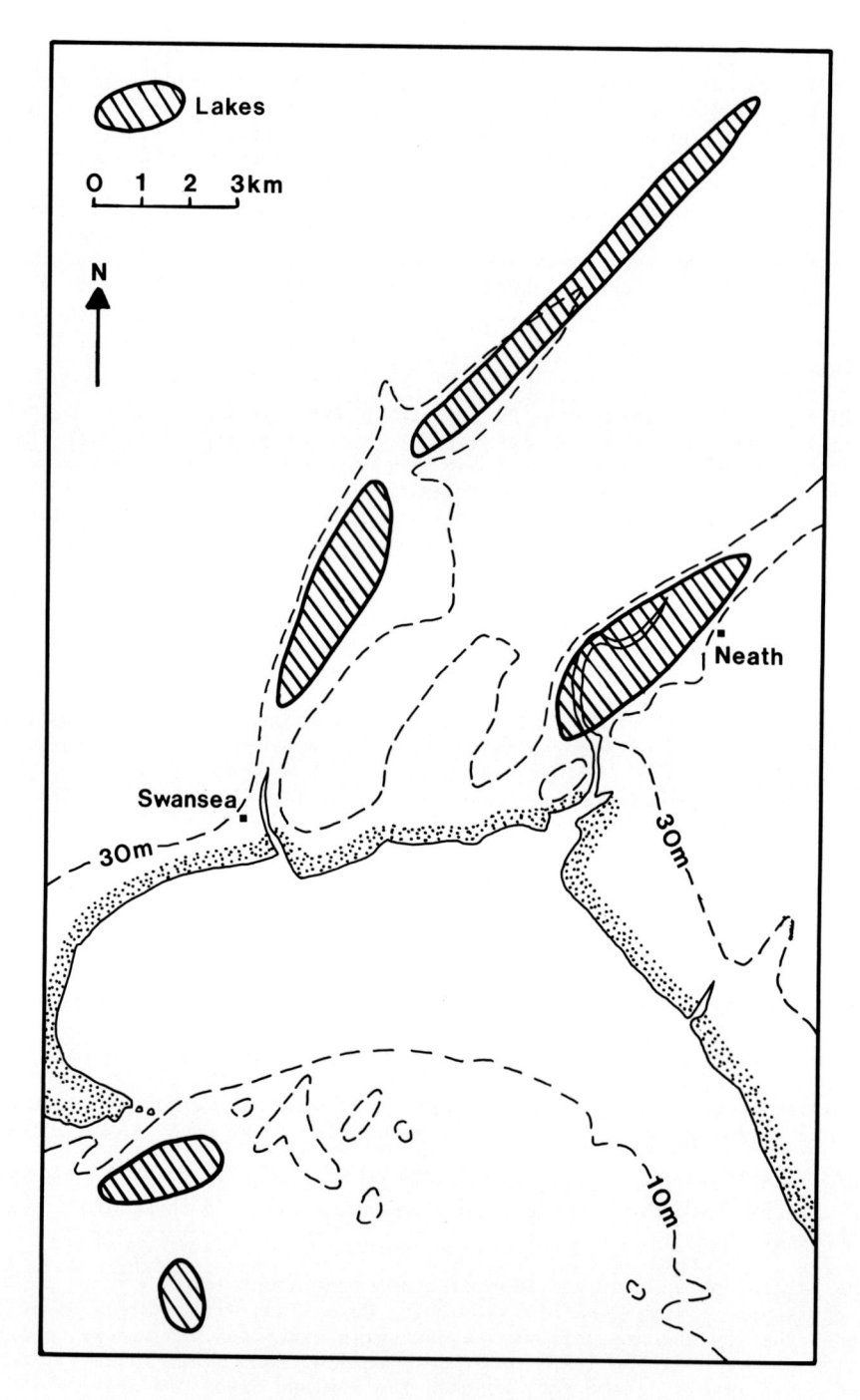

Fig. 6.3. Late Pleistocene lakes in the Swansea area.
(Modified from Culver and Bull, 1979).

Period	Culture	Years BP	Flora	Site/Fauna	Geological Period	Sea Level / Environment
NEOLITHIC		4000	SubBoreal	BLACKPILL Peats and muds *Cervus elephas*	EARLY FLANDRIAN	Dunes from Crymlyn Bog and Margam Moors. "Submerged Forest" peats of Swansea Bay western foreshore
MESOLITHIC (Maglemoisian)		5000				
		6000	Atlantic			sea penetrates inland beyond present shore
		7000		CATHOLE, PARKMILL Upper Scree *Capreolus capreolus, Ovis, Bos*; Artifacts.		
		8000	Corylus Pinus Betula / Boreal			
		9000	Boreal			Sea reaches Port Talbot: lakes and valleys flooded in SW Swansea Bay
Later UPPER PALÆOLITHIC (Creswellian-Cheddarian)		10,000	Pinus Betula / Pre-Boreal	SCARWEATHER muds and peats PORT TALBOT muds and peats	LATE DEVENSIAN	marshes and peats from Scarweather to Port Talbot
		11,000	Betula Park Tundra	PORT TALBOT muds and peats CATHOLE, PARKMILL Lower Scree: *Vulpes vulpes, Alopex lagopus, Ursus arctos, Coelodonta antiquitatis, Equus przewalskii, Cervus elephas, Megaloceros giganteus, Rangifer tarandus*; Artifacts.		
		12,000	Juniperus Park Tundra			Channel flooded to south of Swansea Bay, at 60m bsl isobath.
		13,000	Betula Park Tundra			
		14,000	Salix Tundra			
	not known?	15,000				sealevel rises to flood Bristol Channel Valley eastward to Lundy.
		16,000				
		17,000				
Earlier UPPER PALÆOLITHIC (Aurignacian- Proto-Solutrean)		18,000 14c— 19,000		PAVILAND CAVE? *Homo sapiens sapiens*, *Nerita littoralis* artifacts, Ivory artifacts.	MIDDLE DEVENSIAN	Maximum ice advance: Welsh Ice reaches Bay. Celtic Sea shelf exposed to 7°W. Firnfields in Bristol Channel Valley.
		20,000		LONGHOLE, GOWER *Lutra lutra, Canis lupus, Vulpes vulpes, Mammuthus primigenius, Bison priscus, Equus, Coelodonta antiquitatis, Rangifer tarandus, Megaloceros giganteus, Crocuta crocuta*; Artifacts.		
		21,000				
		22,000				m below modern s.l. 120 100 80 60 40 20 0

were areas where extensive upland bogs existed and large quantities of peat accumulated. Around 10,000b.p. the coastline was 3 to 5km to the southwest of the present Mumbles Head.

This, then, is the environment in which late Upper Palaeolithic man lived following the retreat of the glaciers. The lower screes of Cathole Cave at Parc le Breos in Gower (SS 537900) has provided the remains of cave bear, Przewalski's horse, red and giant deer, and numerous implements of Creswellian type including small delicate blades and a finely polished bone sewing needle (McBurney, 1965). Similar Creswellian tools have also been recovered in abundance from Paviland Cave showing that this site was occupied on at least three occasions during the Palaeolithic period.

Evidence of Mesolithic habitation in the Swansea area is limited to a chipping site at Burry Holmes in west Gower (Cousens, 1971). Mesolithic man probably hunted in the surrounding upland areas but also in the marshy coastal margins where red deer (*Cervus elephas*) were probably abundant. Red deer antlers of Mesolithic age were recovered from excavations at Port Talbot dock at a depth of -8m OD (Stevens, 1928).

Also at Port Talbot (SS 728920), freshwater peats which accumulated on a drift surface have been recorded in a borehole (Godwin and Willis, 1964). Pollen analysis and radiocarbon dating showed that this peat accumulated from 11,900b.p. (Pollen Zone II) to 8,900b.p. (early Pollen Zone VI). This peat bed, its upper

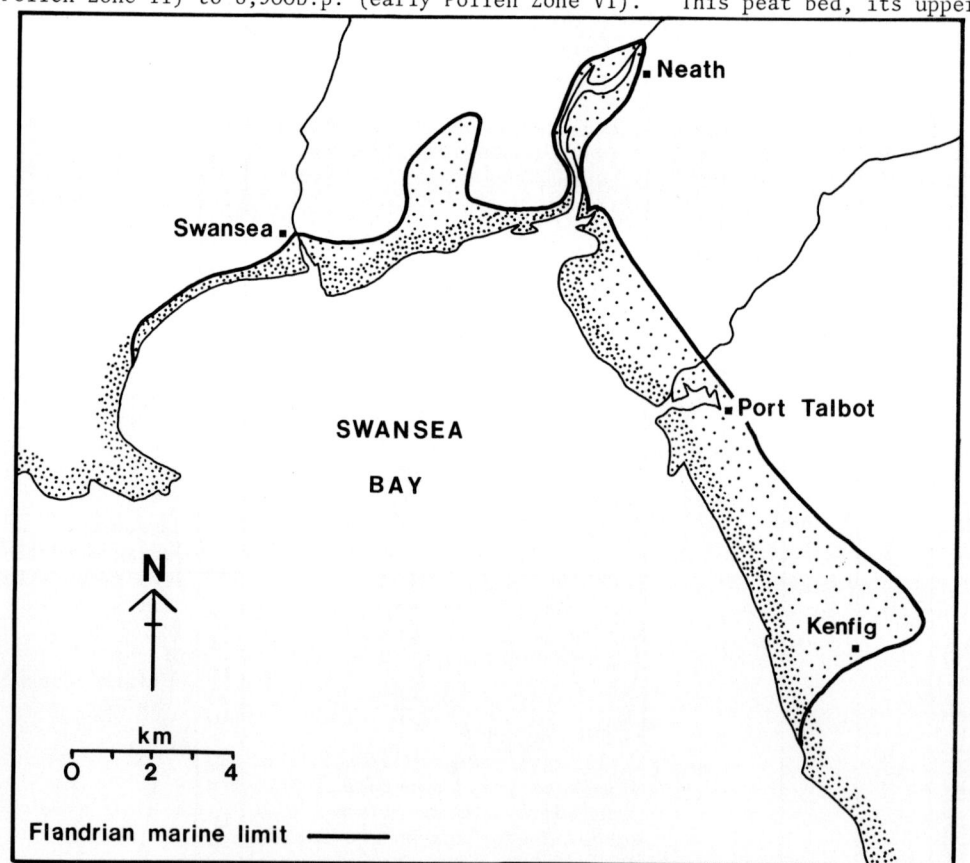

Fig. 6.4. Flandrian marine limit in the Swansea area. (Modified from Culver, 1976).

surface at -18m OD, is overlain by marine silts and clays. Thus, the Holocene
sea-level had reached a height of -18m OD by 8,900b.p. In agreement, peats
recorded from Swansea docks (Godwin, 1940) at -16m OD were dated at Pollen Zones
IV to middle VI.

In summary, the eastwards transgression of the sea had reached -35m OD and covered
the Scarweather area by the end of the Palaeolithic around 10,000b.p. (Fig. 6.2).
By early Mesolithic times (9,500b.p.), the sea had risen to -29m OD and had invaded
the Swansea Bay lowland area. The sea reached the approximate position of the
present coastline, at a level of -16m OD, by 8,900b.p.

The eustatic rise of sea-level (the Boreal transgression described by Godwin, 1940)
continued throughout the Mesolithic at a rate of 20mm per year (Hawkins, 1971b)
until about 5,500b.p. when it had reached a level of about -3m OD (Godwin and
Willis, 1961). Although sea-level was slightly lower than at the present day, the
sea penetrated further inland (Fig.6.4)beyond the present coastline as the thick
Holocene deposits had not yet accumulated and the sand dunes, which at the present
day fringe Swansea Bay on its northern and eastern coasts, had not yet formed.
After 5,500b.p. the sea-level rise continued but at a slower rate until the present
rate of rise, 0.12m per century, was reached (Hawkins, 1971b).

The silts and clays overlying the freshwater peats and the glacial drift surface in
Swansea Bay have been shown, by their foraminiferal assemblages, to be mainly intertidal deposits (Culver and Banner, 1978). These deposits formed broad tracts of
mud and sand flats crossed by meandering creeks, with areas of salt marsh where
peats accumulated. The environment was similar to that of the present day marshy
areas of the Wash or of the Burry Inlet north of the Gower peninsula. These
littoral deposits accumulated throughout the Mesolithic, Neolithic and Bronze Age
until 2,500b.p. This date is of a nearly contemporaneous peat (at approximately
-3m OD) at Llanwern near Newport, radiocarbon dated at 2,660b.p. (Godwin and Willis,
1964). Its level approximates to that of the peat at Blackpill, Swansea Bay,
which, on the basis of pollen analysis was ascribed to the Iron Age (early Pollen
Zone VIII) by Von Post (Bodwin, 1940).

Thus, during the Mesolithic, Neolithic, Bronze and Iron Age times, although the
climate was relatively constant, the palaeogeography and palaeoenvironments of the
Swansea area were changing rapidly due to the rising sea-level.

The number of inhabitants in this area rose rapidly during the Neolithic. Mega-
lithic communal tombs (long barrows) were built at Parc le Breos and Penmaen
Burrows (Grimes, 1965) while a log cairn was constructed at Nicholaston and smaller
round barrows are represented by Sweyne's Houses near Rhossili and Arthur's Stone
at Reynoldston. Evidence of life as well as death is provided by bone needles and
a polished axe fragment recovered from peat at Barry (Grimes, 1965)(these implements
have been attributed to the Bronze Age; North, 1955), by arrowheads from Merthyr
Mawr (Cousens, 1971), and by a rectangular timber house whose foundations have been
exhumed at Mount Pleasant near Nottage (Grimes, 1965; Burl, 1976).

Neolithic man probably continued to hunt herds of red deer (*Cervus elephas*) but it
is certain that he also kept domestic cattle, pigs, goats and possibly sheep; their
remains have been found at various sites along the South Wales coast often embedded
in peats on the foreshore (eg. George, 1928; North, 1955). Grimes (1965) also
pointed out that, by analogy with other areas, the Neolithic Welsh were also
cultivators, the crops grown being emmer, wheat, einkorn and barley (Cousens, 1971).
Bronze Age inhabitants continued this way of life in the Swansea area; settlements
have been found at Whitford Burrows in west Gower and at West Cross where a
circular hut has been uncovered (Cousens, 1971).

Substantial changes in the geography of the Swansea area occurred in Bronze Age and

and Iron Age times. The peat exposed on the foreshore of Swansea Bay from Blackpill around to Morfa Mawr probably accumulated behind barrier sand dunes which had begun to form just before and during the early Bronze Age, around 4,000-3,500b.p. (Higgins, 1933a). This date is suggested by the presence of Bronze Age artifacts on a 'beach' deposit exposed near Porthcawl after the removal of wind-blown sand. This areas was inhabited in the Early Bronze Age, during the Beaker period in particular, around 3,800 to 3,500b.p. (Higgins, 1933a). It was considered (Higgins, 1933b) that at about 3,500b.p., and for the subsequent 1,000 years, periods of storms caused the formation of barrier sand dunes in Swansea Bay which subsequently migrated inland and became fixed around 2,000b.p. The low-lying areas of Crymlyn Bog and Margam Moors became land permanently free of marine influence due to the presence of this sand dune barrier.

Iron Age man stamped his imprint on the Swansea area in the form of ten hill forts in the Gower Peninsula and seven more on the eastern side of Swansea Bay behind Port Talbot (Hogg, 1965). Other evidence of his habitation in the Swansea area comes from some fragments of haematitic iron ore found partially buried in peat and clay on the beach at Port Eynon (George, 1928). George (1928) suggested that the wood in the now submerged forests forming the peat beds around South Wales was utilized for the smelting of iron ore. Indeed, some fragments of charcoal have been found within peat beds in Pembrokeshire.

This essay has concentrated on the development of the Swansea Bay area over the past few thousand years. Similar environmental changes, however, took place along the entire South Wales coast. Large developments of sand dunes are found along the coastline from Pembrokeshire to Glamorgan (Higgins, 1933b). Similarly, Holocene littoral clays, silts, sands and peats are found along the length of this coastline (North, 1955): changes of environment have been traced by variations in Holocene foraminiferal assemblages and sediments recovered from boreholes located in the Burry Inlet, north Gower (Culver and Carling, 1977).

Thus, from the Palaeolithic to the Iron Age, the inhabitants of the South Wales coastal area experienced a rapidly changing physical environment vastly different from that of the present day. The geomorphological effects of the Wolstonian and Devensian ice ages, with their subsequent climatic ameliorations and sea-level rises, were the major factors in controlling palaeoenvironment and palaeogeography in the Swansea area.

ACKNOWLEDGEMENTS

Thanks are due to F.T. Banner, M.A. Buzas and A. Lanham for critical reading of a draft of this essay.

REFERENCES

Al-Saadi, R., and Brooks, M. (1973). A geophysical study of Pleistocene buried valleys in the Lower Swansea Valley, Vale of Neath and Swansea Bay. *Proc. Geol. Assoc., 84*, 135-153.
Bowen, D.Q. (1970a). South-east and central South Wales. In C.A. Lewis (Ed.), *The Glaciations of Wales and Adjoining Regions*. Longman, London, 197-228.
Bowen, D.Q. (1970b). The palaeoenvironment of the 'Red Lady' of Paviland. *Antiquity, 44*, 134-136.
Bowen, D.Q. (1974). The Quaternary of Wales. In T.R. Owen (Ed.), *The Upper Palaeozoic and Post-Palaeozoic rocks of Wales*. Univ. Wales Press, 373-426.
Burl, A. (1976). *The Stone Circles of the British Isles*. Yale Univ. Press, New Haven and London.
Campbell, J.B. (1977). *The Upper Palaeolithic of Britain*. Clarendon Press, Oxford.

264pp., 53 tables, 175 figs., 48 maps.

Cousens, S.H. (1971). Settlement before the Norman conquest. In. W.G.V. Balchin (Ed.), *Swansea and its Region*. British Assoc. Adv. Sci., 133-145.

Culver, S.J. (1976a). The development of the Swansea Bay area during the past 20,000 years. *Gower, 27,* 58-62.

Culver, S.J. (1976b). *A study of the post-glacial Foraminiferida of Swansea Bay South Wales*. Ph.D. Thesis, Univ. Wales (unpub.).

Culver, S.J.and Banner, F.T. (1978). Foraminiferal assemblages as Flandrian palaeoenvironmental indicators. *Palaeogeogr., Palaeoclimatol., Palaeoecol., 23,* 53-72.

Culver, S.J.and Banner, F.T. (1979). The significance of derived pre-Quaternary Foraminifera in Holocene sediments of the north-central Bristol Channel. *Mar. Geol., 29,* 187-207.

Culver, S.J., and Bull, P.A. (1979). Late Pleistocene rock-basin lakes in South Wales. *Geol. Jl.,* (In press).

Culver, S.J., and Carling, P.A. (1977). Sedimentology and Foraminifera of two cores, Burry Inlet, South Wales, In A. Nelson-Smith and E.M. Bridges (Eds.). *Problems of a Small Estuary*. Quadrant Press, xxxiii-xxxvii.

Donn, W.L., Farrand, W.R., and Ewing, M. (1962). Pleistocene ice volumes and sea-level lowering. *Jl. Geol., 70,* 206-215.

Evans, D.J. (1973). *The stratigraphy of the central part of the Bristol Channel*. Ph.D. Thesis, Univ. Wales (unpub.).

Evans, D.J., and Thompson, M.S. (1979). The geology of the central Bristol Channel and the Lundy area, Southwestern Approaches, British Isles. *Proc. Geol. Assoc., 90,* 1-20.

Evans, J.G. (1975). *The Environment of Early Man in the British Isles*. Paul Elek, London.

Fairbridge, R.W. (1977). Global climatic change during the 13,500b.p. Gothenburg geomagnetic excursion. *Nature, 165,* 430-431.

George, T.N. (1928). The submerged forest in Gower. *Proc. Swansea Sci. Field Nat. Soc., 1,* 100-108.

George, T.N. (1933). The coast of Gower. *Proc. Swansea Sci. Field Nat. Soc., 1,* 192-206.

Godwin, H. (1940). A Boreal transgression of the sea in Swansea Bay. *New Phytol., 39,* 308-321.

Godwin, H., and Willis, E.H. (1961). Cambridge University natural radiocarbon measurements, III. *Radiocarbon, 3,* 60-76.

Godwin, H. and Willis, E.H. (1964). Cambridge University natural radiocarbon measurements, VI. *Radiocarbon, 6,* 116-137.

Grimes, W.F. (1965). Neolithic Wales. In. I. LL. Foster and G. Daniel (Eds.), *Prehistoric and Early Wales*. Routledge and Kegan Paul, London, 35-70.

Hawkins, A.B. (1971a). Sea-level changes around south-west England. *Proc. 23rd Symp. Colston Res. Soc.,* 67-88.

Hawkins, A.B. (1971b). The Late Weichselian and Flandrian transgression of south-west Britain. *Quaternaria, 14,* 115-130.

Higgins, L.S. (1933a). Coastal changes in South Wales. The excavation of an old beach. *Geol. Mag., 70,* 541-549.

Higgins, L.S. (1933b). An investigation into the problems of the sand dune areas on the South Wales coast. *Arch. Camb., 88,* 26-67.

Hogg, A.H.A. (1965). Early Iron Age Wales. In I. LL. Foster and G. Daniel (Eds.), *Prehistoric and Early Wales*. Routledge and Kegan Paul, London, 109-150.

McBurney, C.B.M. (1965). The Old Stone Age in Wales. In. I. LL. Foster and G. Daniel (Eds.), *Prehistoric and Early Wales*. Routledge and Kegan Paul, London, 17-34.

North, F.J. (1955). *The Evolution of the Bristol Channel*. Nat. Mus. Wales, Cardiff.

Oakley, K.P. (1968). The date of the 'Red Lady' of Paviland. *Antiquity, 42,* 306-307.

Price, C.R., and Culver, S.J. (1977). The Quaternary history of Swansea Bay, South Wales. *3rd. Meeting, Geol. Soc. British Isles.* Swansea.

Stevens, P.G. (1928). A note on the geology of Swansea Bay. *Proc. Swansea Sci. Field Nat. Soc.,* 1, 31-32.

APPENDIX

THE LATE PALÆOLITHIC - NEOLITHIC TERRESTRIAL FAUNA:

Alopex lagopus, Arctic fox
Bison priscus, Steppe bison
Bos sp., Aurochs
Canis lupus, Wolf
Capreolus capreolus, Roe deer
Cervus elephas, Red deer
Coelodonta antiquitatis, Woolly rhinoceros
Crocuta crocuta, Cave hyena
Equus przewalskii, Przewalski's horse
Lutra lutra, Otter
Mammuthus primigenius, Mammoth
Megaloceros giganteus, Giant deer
Ovis sp., Ox
Rangifer tarandus, Reindeer
Ursus arctos, Brown bear
Vulpes vulpes, Red fox

7. CHANGES IN HISTORICAL TIME

A. P. Carr and M. W. L. Blackley

Institute of Oceanographic Sciences (I.O.S.), Crossway, Taunton, Someset TA1 2DW, U.K.

ABSTRACT

An examination has been made of the topographic changes within Swansea Bay, based on literary records, supplemented from about 1840 AD by maps and charts.

Onshore, along the E. side of Swansea Bay, there is an emphasis on the sea flooding reclaimed marshlands, and the instability of sand-dune systems. Maps show accretion and erosion in the Crymlyn-Witford area and erosion near Port Talbot docks: both areas have been particularly affected by engineering structures. The rate of change appears to have increased over time.

Offshore, comparison of the 1859 and 1974 hydrographic surveys suggests that Hugo Bank has been displaced towards the south while Scarweather Sands has extended westward and been realigned. The volume of material in the banks as a whole has remained roughly constant.

KEYWORDS

Beaches, Sand-dunes, Offshore Banks, Historical Coastal Changes, Erosion, Sedimentation, Bristol Channel, South Wales.

INTRODUCTION

This Chapter describes some of the evidence, both literary and cartographic, for the evolution of the coastline and offshore banks on the eastern side of Swansea Bay. The written record dates from the 12th century onwards but reliable maps and charts are not available until about the mid-nineteenth century. The physical characteristics of the coastline are described more extensively later by Blackley and Carr (Chapter 17).

LITERARY EVIDENCE

Sources falling into this field are of two types although both are almost exclusively land-orientated. They are the historical sources, either in the form of original documents and papers or derived from them, and the various topographies written to describe the local or regional scene at different periods of time. One of the difficulties incurred in using the latter is the extent to which the compilers

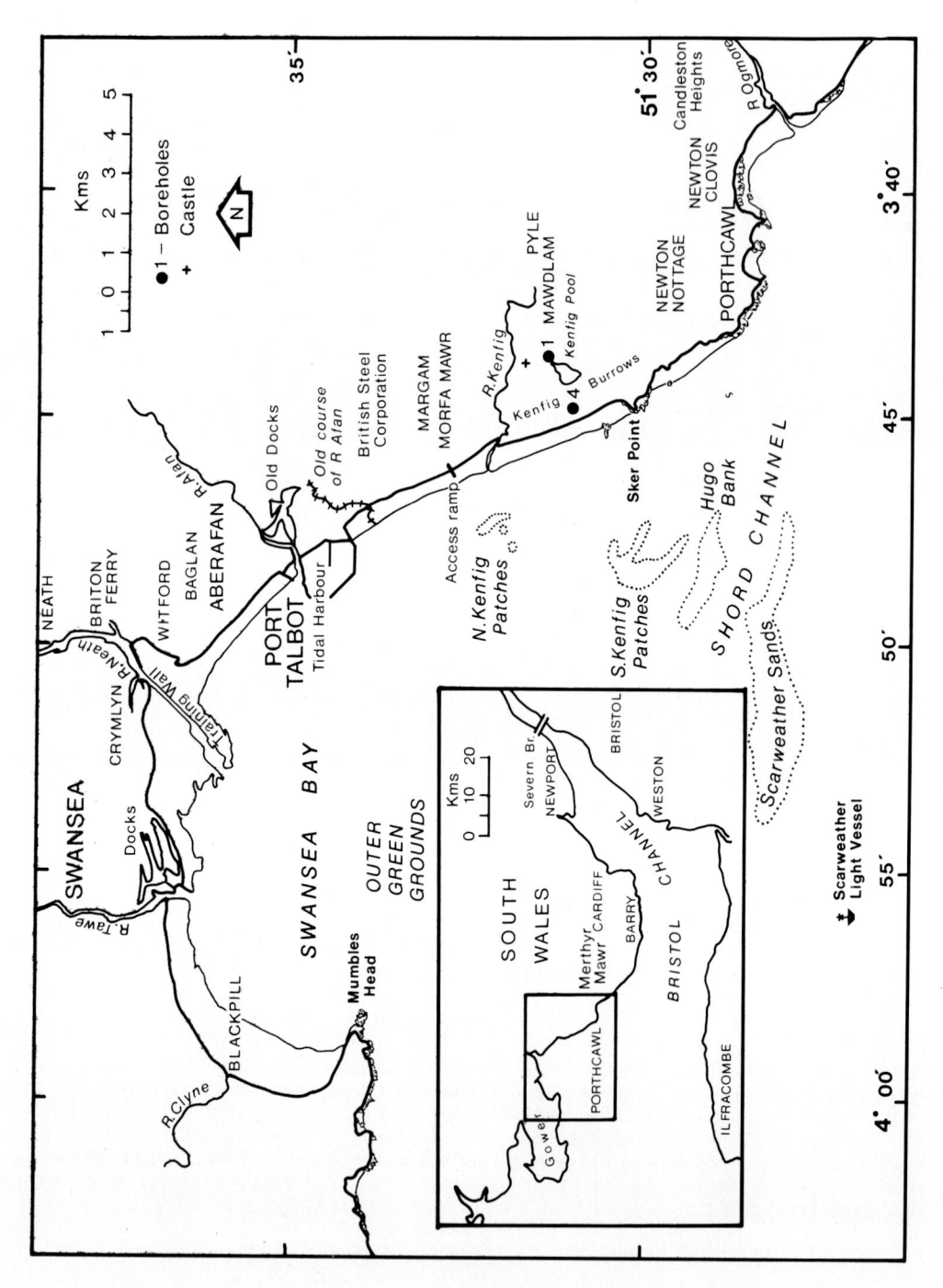

Figure 7.1. Site map, Swansea Bay.

have resorted to earlier rather than contemporary sources of information without acknowledgement. A further problem often lies in accurately identifying the area to which reference is made either because it is not specific enough or because the place-names are no longer extant. This applies especially in the context of land charters and leases.

Nevertheless three themes stand out above all others. They are the mobility of sand in the coastal zone, the maintenance of the dune system (either in the context of rabbit warrening or artificial planting and stabilisation), and the struggle to build and maintain sea walls to protect the low-lying marsh areas from flooding. Each of these will be dealt with in turn in a chronological, rather than a geographical, sequence. Place names are shown in Figure 7.1.

Sand Mobility

In prehistoric and Roman times, sand instability does not appear to have been a problem (Grimes, in Higgins, 1933). Peat was recovered at a subsurface depth of 4m (+6.2m O.D.) from a borehole put down NE of Kenfig Pool. The sample gave a radio-carbon date of 793 ± 40 years b.p. indicating that as late as the 12th century this part of Kenfig Burrows was free of sand. Although Kenfig castle and the nearby church also date from the 12th century, a time when Kenfig's port could deal with 24 vessels at once, there are contemporaneous records referring to sand accumulation at Kenfig dunes, as well as at other locations outside the immediate area of concern, such as Merthyr Mawr and on the Gower peninsula (O'Brien, 1927). Richards (1927) describes storms in 1188 AD, and again in 1222 AD, which resulted in both sand-blowing and in flooding. By about 1300 AD, the sand problem was becoming more acute - sufficient to warrant the word "drowning" (Grey, 1909) - while in 1326/1336 AD, the Abbot of Margam complained of sand drift (O'Brien, 1927). The hermitage of Theodoric (now under Margam steelworks) was probably already buried by then. Evans (1960) notes encroachment of sand in 1316 AD also. Rhys (1911) put the first serious invasion of the Glamorgan coastline by sand at 1384 AD. The old town of Kenfig, some 1.7 km from the coastline, was subject to progressive inundation while the navigational value of the River Kenfig also deteriorated. One reference suggests a specific date for Kenfig's demise as 1470 AD (Evans, 1960, quoting Leland, 1538). There is strong circumstantial evidence for this period as being one of particular instability, because round about 1400 AD the old coast road was abandoned and a new inland route was chosen for communication between Cardiff and Swansea. Although Kenfig castle was still occupied in 1403, Pyle church superseded that of Kenfig in 1485 (Richards, 1927).

In common with the Oxwich area of the Gower peninsula (Higgins, 1933), the coastline between the River Neath and Sker Point appears to have been affected relatively early as compared to that elsewhere. Thus, by 1538/9, Leland described Kenfig village and castle as "almost shokid and devourid with the sandes that the Severn Se ther castith up". By 1526 AD, too, Kenfig parish was recorded as being half drift sand (Grey, 1909), yet Candleston Heights, to landward of Merthyr Mawr (Randall, 1928) were still clear of sand as late as 1600 AD. The parliamentary Act of 1554 AD was in many respects too late to be of benefit to Kenfig but it demonstrates the degree of concern. Part of the preamble reads:
"to refourme the greate hurte nuysaunce and losses that comethe and chaunceth to the Quenes Highnes and her Subjectes, by reason of Sande rising out of the Sea and dryven to Lande by Stormes and Windes, whereby muche good Grounde lyeing on the Seacoastes in sundrye places of this Realme and especially in the Countye of Glamorgan, bee covered with suche Sande rising out of the Sea that ther comethe no Profitte of the same, to the greate loss of the Quenes Highnes and her loving Subjectes, and more ys lyke to ensue yf spedye Remedie be not therein provided......"

In 1572 a clause added to the Kenfig ordinances described the loss to the borough from blowing sand (Higgins, 1933), while there was a further reference in 1607, this time to the Margam area. Between the surveys of 1582 and 1633 fields near the River Afan had become overwhelmed with sand. Both the Survey of Kenfig dating from 1660/61 and Lhwyd's description of Kenfig in 1696-1700 show that there was still, possibly, a considerable amount of mobile sand. Lhwyd also refers to Newton Nottage being afflicted in the same way, while Baglan had "great drifts of sand wch may well be called mountaines". Wyndham, in his lurid description written in 1774, refers to Kenfig Castle as being "surrounded by naked sands, blown up in irregular heaps and subject to alteration by every storm"; the 1832 report undertaken for the Home Department (prior to the legislation which deprived Kenfig of its borough status) recorded the continuing inroad of sand. However, Strahan (1907), in evidence to the Royal Commission on Coast Erosion, considered that there was then no new supply of sand to the dunes at Baglan, Crymlyn and Kenfig Burrows, but simply a redistribution of existing material.

The picture, then, is of long-term instability of sand throughout the recorded history of over 700 years, probably reaching a maximum in the 15th century. Archaeological sections at Kenfig suggest gradual accumulation with considerable periods between violent storms (Richards, 1927).

The Maintenance of the Dunes.

The coastal sand dune systems had an economic value for rabbit warrening; the destruction of the vegetation by rabbits may, in part, account for the instability of the dunes themselves. However, attempts to maintain the stability of the dunes by marram (*Ammophila arenaria*) planting were practised from a very early date and careful management appears to have been practised. Thus, there is a reference to rabbit warrening around 1316 (Evans, 1960) while in 1330 there is an ordinance prohibiting 'sedge' (i.e., marram grass) cutting (Rhys, 1911; Evans, 1960): "Noe manner of person or persons whatsoever shall reap any sedges neither draw nor pull any rootes nor cut any furzes in any place whatsoever, nor do any other thing that may be to the ruin, destruction and overthrow of the said burrough".

A similar injunction applied to Newton Clovis around 1400 (Rhys, 1911). Although in 1344 Hugh le Despenser granted the right of free warrening in Afan and Kenfig, the Kenfig burgesses exerted strong pressure in trying to ensure dune stability.

Lhwyd (1696-1700) refers to reclamation in Newton Nottage and the stabilisation of sand dunes with sedges. He relates that while near both the rivers Neath and "Avan" the "best of the parish is now swallowed up by the sea and over run by sand", between these two areas the mobility had been almost stopped by the use of a certain matting, in Welsh called "Myrydd". Thus, the technique of dune "thatching" appears to have had a long history.

Estate records dating from 1732 refer to expenditure on sedge planting at Margam Burrows, while those from 1744, 1745 and 1747 all relate to warrening at Kenfig and Afan. That for 1745 links one with the other. Warrening and dune reclamation were clearly to the fore at the end of the 18th century, coinciding with the active encouragement by the then government's Board of Agriculture. For example, Marshall (1796) wrote, in respect of another area,"....there appears to me to be much land.......which would pay better in a state of Rabbit warren than in any other state of occupancy....". The 1832 Home Department survey (mentioned above) refers to planting, as follows:
"The inroad of sand still continues, and if it were not for the precautions taken in planting 'bent', a grass or sand rush, which has been found to be the best means of checking it, large quantities of valuable land would soon be covered" (Llewellyn, 1898).

Both Lewis (1849) and Rhys (1911) describe tenancy agreements which include a clause on marram planting whereby the tenant covenanted to give a day (or more depending on the size of his holding) to help with planting and enhance stability. In spite of these efforts, it was still possible for Stuart (1924) to detect microscopic fragments of tin from Swansea tin works at the base of 15m-high dunes west of Aberafan and Margam; these dunes could not have been more than a century old.

Sea Walls and Flooding

In the same way that there is an inter-relation between warrening and dune planting, there is a close link between reclamation of the marshlands and their flooding by the sea. This struggle refers to Baglan , Afan and Margam in particular. As noted above, flooding in 1188 AD caused considerable loss of cattle and of some men also (Richards, 1927). Early in the following century, there are definite records of sea walls being built at Margam. Further storms ensued in 1222 AD, while by 1316 AD some rents had fallen appreciably (Richards, 1927) owing to inundation by the sea as well as burial by sand. The rent of a piece of land known as the Rabbits Pasture was reduced "because the greater party is drowned by the sea" (Rhys, 1911). In 1336, Margam Abbey was complaining of losses caused by, amongst other things, the fact "that no small part of the land adjacent to the shore is subject to inundation by the sea" (Clark, in Higgins, 1933).

It is very much chance as to what events are recorded and what documents survive. As a result, it is not clear whether the next two to three centuries were less critical or not, but the same quiescent period also appears to occur at an east-coast site, Sizewell-Dunwich, Suffolk. At any rate, in the well-known storm of 1607 in which over 500 people died along the Welsh coast, there is a reference to flooding and the subsequent financial assistance by Swansea to Afan (O'Brien, 1927). The 1626 Survey of Sea Walls refers to land being covered with sand as well as being flooded (Higgins, 1933). In 1657 the use of stones to repair a sea wall at Afan is recorded in Estate records, while Lhywd (1969-1700) refers to Baglan and Aberafan marshes now being below high water spring tides and to the flooding which occurred a decade before. He writes:
".....for at this day, were it not for banks rais'd, all our and Aberavan's marsh would be at high springs overflowed by the sea, as some ten years agoe....it did .....and, indeed it has not to this day recovered its fertility..."(Lhwyd, ed. Morris, 1911).

Further flooding - possibly fluvial - occurred at Aberafan in 1768, when the town "was covered with mud and slime" (O'Brien, 1927). Another reference to the relative height of the marshes and spring tides, this time at Port Talbot harbour, occurs in a letter dated 1840, as".....an ancient sea wall......which could not keep out the present high water by several feet". The same letter describes various artifacts, together with the remains of old fences and building foundations, found during harbour construction at between 5 and 25 feet below that which was then ground level. These remains included Bronze Age and Roman relics as well as more recent material. Along with the earlier references, it appears to provide historical support for the physical evidence for relative changes in sea level, but the relative timescales, the effects of aeolian processes, and the results of compaction and wastage must also be borne in mind. Geuze (1954) suggested that the soils of the Ijsselmeer, with 30-35 per cent silt content, compress to about half their thickness during the first hundred years after reclamation.

The documentary evidence focusses attention towards the long-term struggle of man versus natural forces on the coastline, the problems of sand stabilisation, reclamation and the susceptibility of marshland areas to marine incursion through flooding. Rhys (1911) was conscious of the tendency towards erosion when he wrote: "The sea had been there before; just as certainly the sea is gaining upon this coast again".

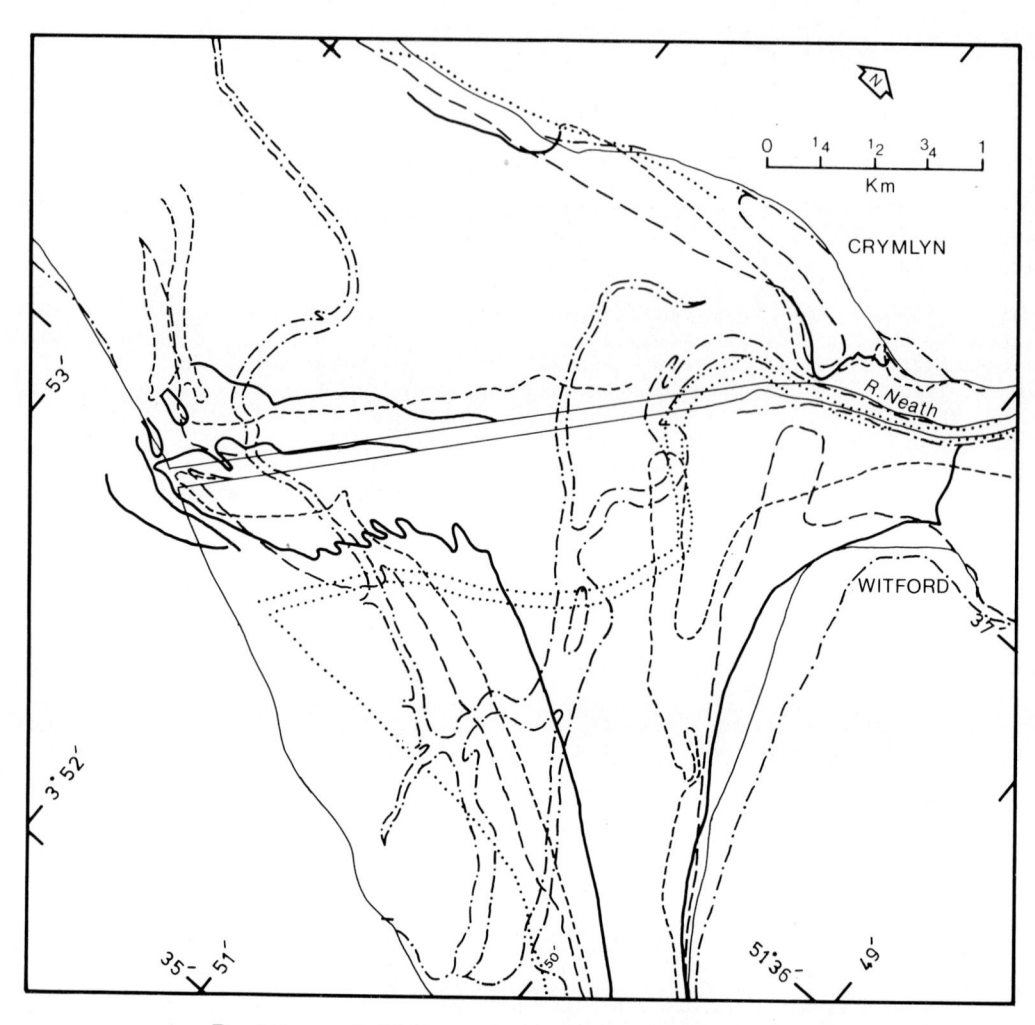

Position of High and Low Water Marks 1840's – 1960's

.... 1842-7 TITHE MAPS
—·—·— 1859   (LWOST as 1876
———— 1876   except where shown)
— — — 1897
------- 1914
▬▬▬ 1962-5

Figure 7.2. Changes in the Neath Estuary area.
The training wall was constructed about 1870.

EVIDENCE FROM LAND CARTOGRAPHY

In common with most other areas, the early (i.e., pre-19th century) maps of the Swansea region are either small scale or inaccurate and are not infrequently both. The fact that much of the eastern side of the Bay was in single ownership reduced the need for any accurate plans for litigational purposes; indeed, there is not even a Tithe Map for the parish of Margam. Thus, useful cartographic evidence is concentrated within the 19th and 20th centuries and effectively falls into two categories, the series of Tithe Maps dating from around 1840 and the medium and large scale Ordnance Survey maps. Figure 7.2 gives an indication of the change in high and low water marks between around 1840 and 1949-65, mostly 1962-65. It must be borne in mind in this context that there is always an element of uncertainty in this form of comparison (especially as far as low water is concerned). The Ordnance Survey changed their water mark criteria in 1868, so surveys before and after that date are on a somewhat different basis; other reservations included the facts that the date of publication is not necessarily closely related to the date of the survey and that revisions are only selective; that maximum development may occur between surveys, while the Tithe Maps are neither explicit nor consistent. In spite of all these reservations, there is a reasonably coherent picture and this is summarised in Table 7.1, appended to this Chapter. The location of the section lines used in the comparison is shown in Fig. 7.3.

Erosion and Accretion

The land surveys show 2 major areas of change over the period 1842-1965. These are the Crymlyn-Witford area bisected by the River Neath, and the coastline both immediately north and south of Port Talbot harbour. Elsewhere net changes are relatively minor.

River Neath area: While most of the coastline along the eastern shore of Swansea Bay has been revised by the Ordnance Survey over the period 1949-65, this is not true of the Crymlyn section (Section 1) shown on Table 7.1. However, the series of surveys from those of the 1840's Tithe Maps to that of the OS in 1914 indicates consistent accretion on a modest scale. The picture for low water is confused, partly as a result of the varying degree of generalisation between surveys, but primarily because of the construction of the training wall for the River Neath during the 1870's (Fig. 7.2). This had the effects of reducing the maze of tidal creeks, evident previously, and of causing marked scour of the coastline south of the embankment within the intertidal zone. Sections 2 and 3 for Witford reflect this phenomenon and suggest recession of the low water mark by about 1.2km overall. The trend for the high water mark for the corresponding sections is again complicated, but this time by the effect of the bar/spit which is recorded at its apparent maximum during the 1914 survey.

Afan/Port Talbot harbour area: Sections 4 and 5 are located north of the harbour, 6 to the south of it. All these show a progressive steepening of the beach over time. In the case of sections 4 and 5, high water mark has shown very little change between 1859 and 1955-63; both lines are now artificially stabilised by sea defences to landward. Section 6 shows net accretion (124m between 1859 and 1955-63) at high water mark. This is almost certainly attributable to the silting up and final reclamation of the old entrance of the River Afan, together with tipping of slag and other material by the British Steel Corporation at the edge of the dune system. There is some suggestion of local erosion previous to this, as Stuart (1924) noted.

The picture for low water mark on Section 4 is somewhat inconsistent until 1876 but shows progressive erosion thereafterwards. Sections 5 and 6 show constant erosion from 1876 onwards. This is about 342m and 214m respectively. Allowing

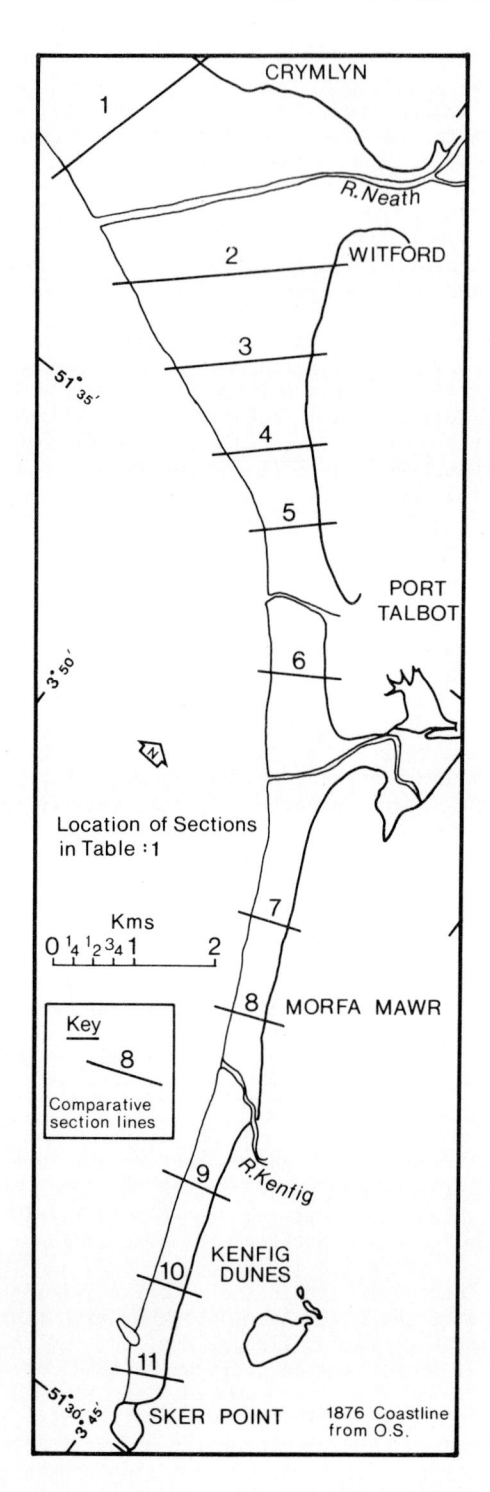

Figure 7.3. Location of section-lines referred to in the text.

for the accretion at the top of the beach on Section 6 (124m), the steepening of
the beach gradient is almost identical in each case; high and low water lines are
342 and 338m closer together for Sections 5 and 6 over the period 1876 to 1963.
The initial southern breakwater of the "old" Port Talbot harbour was built in 1865
and extended twice during the 1890's and again about 1912 (Cleaver, 1913). Low
water mark receded landward by 370m in this area between 1843 and 1963, i.e., mar-
ginally more than on the sections immediately to north and south.

Morfa Mawr: Section 7 is essentially transitional. Negligible recession is shown
for high water mark; a rather moderate degree of erosion is reflected in the landward displacement of low water mark by some 77m between 1859 and 1963.

River Kenfig to Sker Point: Sections 8 to 11 cover the area from immediately north
of the River Kenfig to Sker. The changes indicated by the surveys from 1859 onwards up until the early 1960's are small, variable and inconsistent.

The two areas of maximum change, that around the River Neath and that adjacent to
the old entrance to Port Talbot docks, are both associated with 19th and early 20th
century engineering works. Such a correlation between coastal instability and
man-made physical structures has been widely reported elsewhere, for example by
Bruun (1954) for the Danish coast, Edelman (1967) for the Netherlands, Prasada Rao
and Mahadevan (1958) and Weigel (1964) for specific sites in India and California,
USA, respectively. Komar (1976) gives a good review of the subject. The precise
effect is influenced by the design and scale of the structure in relation to such
features as the wave energy and magnitude of longshore sediment transport.

Beach Gradient

The steepening of the beach slope over the period 1876 - 1965 is a striking feature
of the overall pattern of change. Although there are topographic and hydrographic
complications at various locations between Crymlyn and Sker there is a remarkably
consistent picture taking the area as a whole. Thus, for Sections 2 to 7, the
reduction in distance between high and low water marks are 1417, 1160, 687, 331, 338,
and 77m respectively. Corresponding beach gradients would be from 1:300 to 1:140,
1:200 to 1:65; 1:130 to 1:50, and 1:85 to 1:45 for both Sections 5 and 6, and 1:60
to 1:50 for Section 7.

Sections 1 to 3 may be regarded as complicated by the creeks in and around the River
Neath; those further south, however, are on a potentially exposed beach environment.
For the particle mean size grade now present (230μm:2.12ϕ where ϕ = $-\log_2$ diameter
in millimetres), Bascom (1951) considered the minimum likely beach gradient under
such conditions to be about 1:75. The 1876 values are of about this order. Over
the last century, the recession of the coastline, as distinct from the beach, has
not been great but this may be because recession only comes about when a profile
reaches maximum steepness (Bruun, 1954).

EVIDENCE FROM HYDROGRAPHIC CHARTS

Data Sources

Of the various charts available for the whole or parts of the Swansea Bay area, only
those for 1859 (Cdr. Alldridge) and 1974 (Cdr. Pugh) effectively cover the whole
area of interest although the combination of those by Cdrs. Tizard (1881) and Arch-
deacon (1884), and the 1938 revision of the Scarweather area (Cdr. Hardy) provide
useful corroborative evidence of the trends indicated over the whole period (Carr
and Blackley, 1977).

For comparative purposes all the charts were adjusted photographically onto a common scale (1:25,000) and datum. While the slight reduction to 1:25,000 of the 1859

and 1884 surveys from 1:22,600 and slight increase to 1:25,000 of the 1881 and 1938 surveys presented little problem, the need to obtain a common datum proved rather more difficult. The basis on which this was done is explained in Carr and Blackley (1977). All values were metricated to conform with the 1974 survey.

All 5 charts were contoured at 2m intervals in relation to the chart datum employed in the 1974 survey. This is 5.20m below Ordnance Datum (Newlyn). This chart datum corresponds closely to the water level for lowest astronomical tides while OD is approximately mean sea level. Figure 7.4 shows the changes in terms of erosion and accretion between 1859 and 1974; similar comparisons were also made between the other, partial, surveys and that of 1974.

Bathymetric Changes.

The main changes shown by the hydrographic surveys are:

Scarweather Sands: Some growth towards the west has occurred during the timespan of a century and a quarter. This is not well shown by the Admiralty Charts, because the 1859 survey did not extend as far west - it did not need to - as later ones. More conspicuous is the elimination of the swatchway (at 51°28'30"N, 3°49'30"W) over the intervening period. As a consequence, the Scarweather Bank has become progressively less sinuous over time.

Hugo Bank and Kenfig Patches: Unlike the relative stability of Scarweather, both the position of Hugo Bank and the relationship between it and the South Kenfig Patches have shown appreciable change between 1859 and 1974. Hugo Bank appears to be variable in length on its western extremity but the South Kenfig Patches indicate little change in relative position. Their eastern end (i.e., that nearest the coastline towards Sker Point) appears particularly constant. The most marked change is the elimination of a link between Kenfig Patches and Hugo Bank. This was prominent in 1859, tenuous in 1938 and non-existent in 1974. As a result, the two banks are now clearly separated.

Between 1859 and 1974 a maximum net change of 13m of erosion and 12m of accretion occurred. Figure 7.4 demonstrates the scale at which long-term change has operated and indicates changes of 10m at a number of places on and around the banks. Apart from the realignment there is a tendency for the mass of the banks to be located further southward over time, although, as Robinson (1966) has noted of another area, the crests are more constant in position. This displacement can be confirmed by examining the references to leading marks in the early editions of the relevant Admiralty Coastal Pilot (e.g., 1891).

Further north in the Bay there are only relatively minor bathymetric changes. This probably reflects the greater resistance of the glacial sediments and the existence of local rock outcrops together with more subdued bed topography and lower velocity tidal currents. The 1859, 1884 and 1974 surveys cover the area, together with a further one by Cdr. Lowry dated 1949.

Volume of Material

Calculations have been made to assess the difference in the volume of material covering the eastern half of the Bay and extending as far south as Lat. 51°25'30"N (i.e. the deep water immediately south of Scarweather Sands) between 1859 and 1974. This suggests a loss of $12.3 \times 10^6 m^3$ over the period. Unfortunately, the whole of this amount, and more, could be eliminated by a change in the relative datum between the surveys of only 0.1m and there are also other considerations that have a bearing on the calculations. No firm conclusion can be drawn.

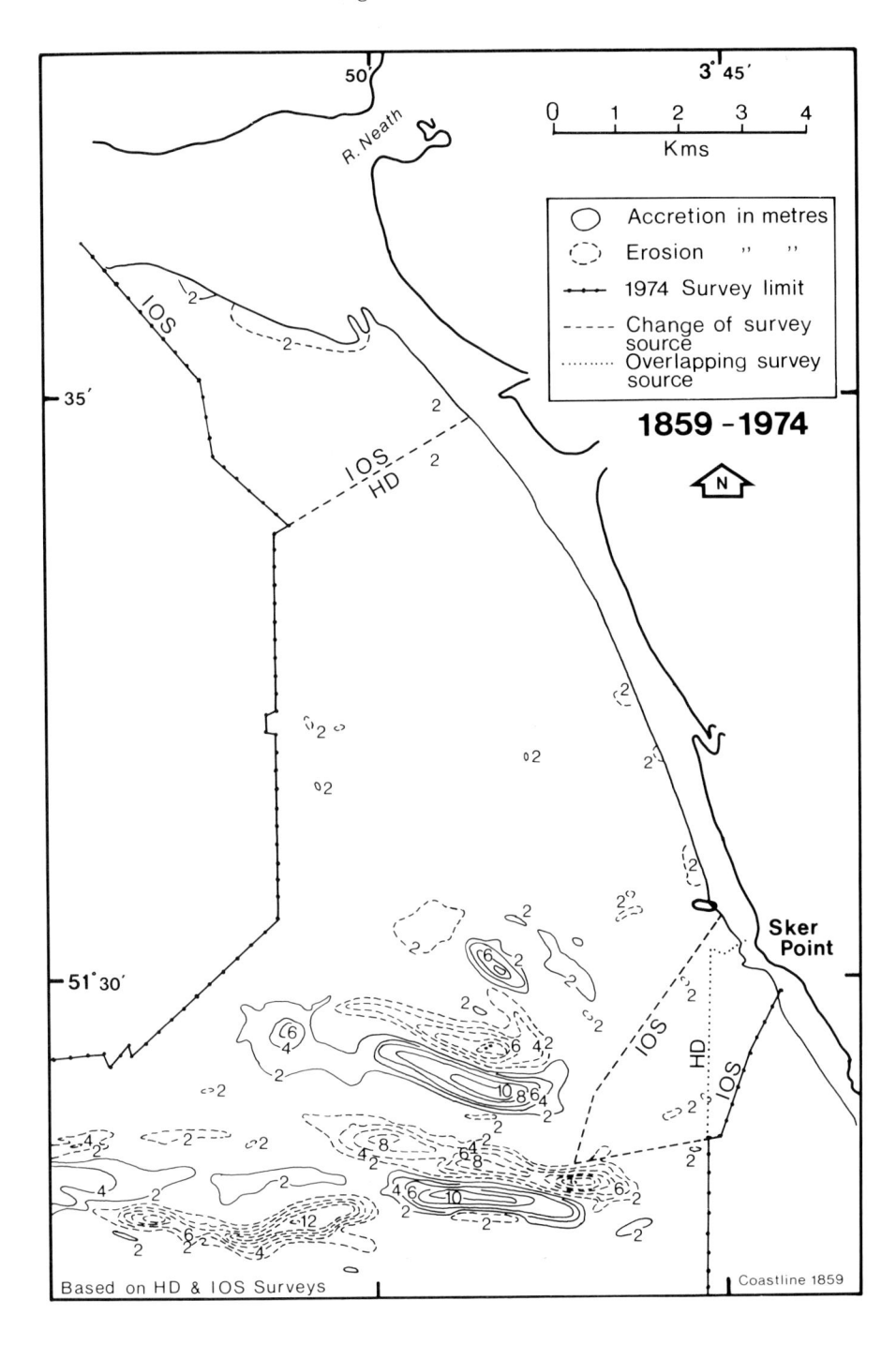

Figure 7.4. Comparison between 1859 and 1974 hydrographic charts, to show erosion and accretion in the eastern part of Swansea Bay.

TABLE 7.1. Foreshore sections.   (+Accretion, -Erosion, in m).
(1876=0, because of complete survey then.   Survey dates generalised).

		1842-7°	1859	1876	1897	1914	1962-5	Notes
1. Crymlyn	HW	- 11	0	0	94	208	-	Progressive growth seawards. Net accretion 1844-1914.
	LW	-	- 29	0	-386	-289*	-	Complex. Net erosion?
2. Witford	HW	-	-237	0	293	588	129	Effect of bar. Net accretion 1859-1914= 824m.
	LW	-216	0*	0	858	1036	-1288	Complex. Net erosion 1876-1962=1288m.
3.	HW	-	- 96	0	48	184	68	Net accretion 1859-1914=280m. Erosion 1914-62=116m.
	LW	-715	0*	0	-831	-947	-1092	Net erosion 1876-1962/5=1092m. Complex
4.	HW	-	0	0	11	37	- 15	Now artificially fixed. Negligible.
	LW	- 40	-447	0	-597	-658	- 702	Variable before 1876, erosion thereafter.
5. Port Talbot (N)	HW	-	0	0	7	-	- 11	Negligible
	LW	8	0	0	-208	-285	- 342	Net erosion 1843-1962/5= 351m
6. Port Talbot (S)	HW		- 55	0	87	64	124	Net accretion 1859-1962/5=178m
	LW		0	0	-131	-146	- 214	Net erosion 1859-1962/5=214m
7. Morfa Mawr	HW		- 17	0	56	0	0	Negligible
	LW		0	0	- 70	- 70	- 77	Net erosion 1859-1962/5=77m
8. River Kenfig (N)	HW		0	0	- 24	36	2	
	LW		- 15	0	- 90	18	- 36	
9. River Kenfig (S)	HW	-	- 16	0	39	-	6	
	LW	-	0	0	6	-	14	Variable, small and
10. Kenfig Dunes	HW	-	0	0	55	-	46	inconsistent.
	LW	-	46	0	- 3	-	14	
11. Sker	HW	-	0	0	63	-	44	
	LW	-	- 34	0	- 55	-	- 27	

(Annotations within table: "Training wall built" between 1859 and 1876 columns for rows 1-3; "No tithe map" in 1842-7° column for rows 6-8; "Beach Progressively Steepens" for rows 5-6.)

*Complex outline; °=Tithe maps; positions shown on Fig. 7.3.

Conclusions

The documentary evidence extends over a timespan of about eight hundred years. Throughout the whole of that period there appears to have been a continuing struggle with the natural forces of the environment. Although the marshes have become less subject to flooding, and the remaining dune systems more stable, over time the coastline appears to have continued its landward retreat (compare Chapter 6). Man's activities, from the nineteenth century, may well have expedited this. The map and chart record of the past 125 years merely refines the nature of the changes and demonstrates their existence offshore also.

ACKNOWLEDGEMENTS

The work described in this paper formed part of a project financed by the Department of the Environment. The authors are grateful for facilities provided by the Hydrographic Department (MOD). The radiocarbon dating was carried out by the Scottish Reactor Centre under their reference SRR-968. Figure 7.4 is based, in part, on Fig. 6.1 in 'Timescales in Geomorphology' edited by R.A. Cullingford, D.A. Davidson and I. Lewin. Copyright 1980. Reprinted by permission of John Wiley & Sons, Ltd.

REFERENCES

Admiralty (1891). West Coast of England Pilot, 4th edition, 146-153.
Anon (1813). *A description of Swansea and its environs.* D. Jenkins, Swansea, 63pp.
Birch, W. de G. (1893). A descriptive catalogue of the Margam and Penrice manuscripts. 6 vols.
Bascom, W.N. (1951). The relationship between sand size and beach-face slope. *Am. Geophys. Union Trans.*, 32, 866-874.
Bruun, P. (1954). Coast erosion and the development of beach profiles. US Beach Erosion Board. *Tech. Mem.*, 44. 79pp. and appendix.
Cleaver, W. (1913). Alterations and improvements of the Port Talbot Docks and Railways during the last decade. *Minut. Proc. Inst. Civ. Engrs.*, 191, 103-118.
Edelman, T. (1967). Systematic measurements along the Dutch Coast. *Proc. 10th Conf. Coast. Eng.*, Tokyo, 1966, 489-501.
Evans, A.L. (1960). *The story of Kenfig*, 80pp.
Geuze, E.C.W.A. (1954). In: Bennema, J. et al. Soil compaction in relation to Quaternary movements of sea-level and subsidence of the land, especially in the Netherlands. *Geologie Mijnb. (NS)* 16, 173-178.
Gray, T. (1909). *The buried city of Kenfig.* T. Fisher Unwin, London, 348pp.
Higgins, L.S. (1933). An investigation into the problem of the sand dune areas on the South Wales coast. *Arch. Camb.*, 88, 26-67.
Komar, P.D. (1976). *Beach processes and sedimentation.* Prentice-Hall, Englewood Cliffs, N.J., 429pp.
Leland, (1538). Leland's itinerary in Wales, ed. L.T. Smith, 1906.
Lewis, S. (1849). Topographical dictionary of Wales, 2 vols. London.
Lhwyd, E. (1696-1700). Parochialia. A summary of parochial queries, part 3. In: R.H. Morris (Ed.), *Arch. Camb.*, Supplement, 1911.
Llewellyn, R.W. (1898). Borough of Kenfig, *Arch. Camb.* (5th Series), 15, 132-153.
Marshall, W. (1796). *The rural economy of the West of England.* Vol. 1.
Morris, Z.B. (1802). *The Swansea guide from the exemplifications of ancient and modern Authors.* Swansea, 198pp.
O'Brien, J. (1927). *Old Afan and Margam,* Aberavon, 196pp.
Prasada Rao, R. and Mahadevan, C. (1958). Evolution of Viskhapatnam beach. *Andrha Univ. Mem. in Oceanog.* (Series 62), 2, 33-47.
Randall, H.J. (1928). Beauties and histories in mid-Glamorgan. *Arch. Camb.* (7th Ser.) 8, 316-329.
Rhys, E. (1911). *The South Wales coast from Chepstow to Aberystwyth.* T. Fisher Unwin, London, 390pp.
Richards, A.J. (1927). Kenfig Castle. *Arch. Camb.*, (7th Series), 7, 161-182.

Robinson, A.H.W. (1966). Residual currents in relation to shoreline evolution of the East Anglian coast. *Mar. Geol. 4,* 57-84.

Strahan, A. (1907). In *Royal Commission on Coast Erosion and the Reclamation of Tidal Lands in the United Kingdom, 1907, 1,* (Part 2). Minutes of evidence accompanying 1st Report. 504pp and 516pp Appendix.

Stuart, A. (1924). The Petrology of the dune sands of South Wales. *Proc. Geol. Assoc., 35,* 316-331.

Weigel, R.L. (1964). *Oceanographical engineering,* Prentice-Hall, Englewood Cliffs, N.J., 532pp.

Wyndham, H.P. (1774). *A gentleman's tour through Wales.*

8. TIDAL AND NON-TIDAL VARIATIONS IN SEA LEVEL

A. J. Wilding and M. B. Collins

Department of Oceanography, University College, Swansea, U.K.

ABSTRACT

The analyses of tide gauge data from stations around Swansea Bay have shown that the water level variations consist of both tidal and non-tidal components.

The tidal component is dominated by the M_2 constituent (3.2m at Swansea), whose phase angle varies by only a few degrees around the embayment, indicating an overall standing tidal wave.

The non-tidal components predominantly consist of free oscillations (30 to 50 mins. in period and approx. 0.15m in amplitude), semi-diurnal residuals, long-period (less than 0.25 cycles/day) residuals and storm surges. The free oscillations and semi-diurnal and long period residuals are discussed in this paper. Free oscillations relate to changes in wind speed and direction, whilst the semi-diurnal and long period residuals relate to larger-scale free oscillations of the Bristol Channel/Celtic Sea system and local meteorological conditions, respectively.

KEYWORDS

Tides; Tidal analyses; Residuals; Free oscillations; Swansea Bay; Bristol Channel

GENERAL INTRODUCTION

The present investigation of water level variations is based primarily on two years data obtained from the permanent tide-gauge at Kings Dock Lock, Swansea (see also Wilding, 1979). In addition, short periods of data were obtained from the permanent tide gauge at Port Talbot and temporary gauges installed at Mumbles and Rhossili.

TIDAL VARIATIONS

The tides in the Bristol Channel are amongst the largest in the world and Swansea Bay being situated on its northern coastline approximately midway between its mouth, near Milford Haven, and its head, near Avonmouth, consequently has a large tidal range (mean spring range 8.6m and mean neap range 4.1m). The latest (1977 Edition) Admiralty co-tidal and co-range chart of the Bristol Channel (Cdr. N.C. Glen, *pers. comm.*) is reproduced as Fig. 8.1. Solid lines in the figure represent the mean

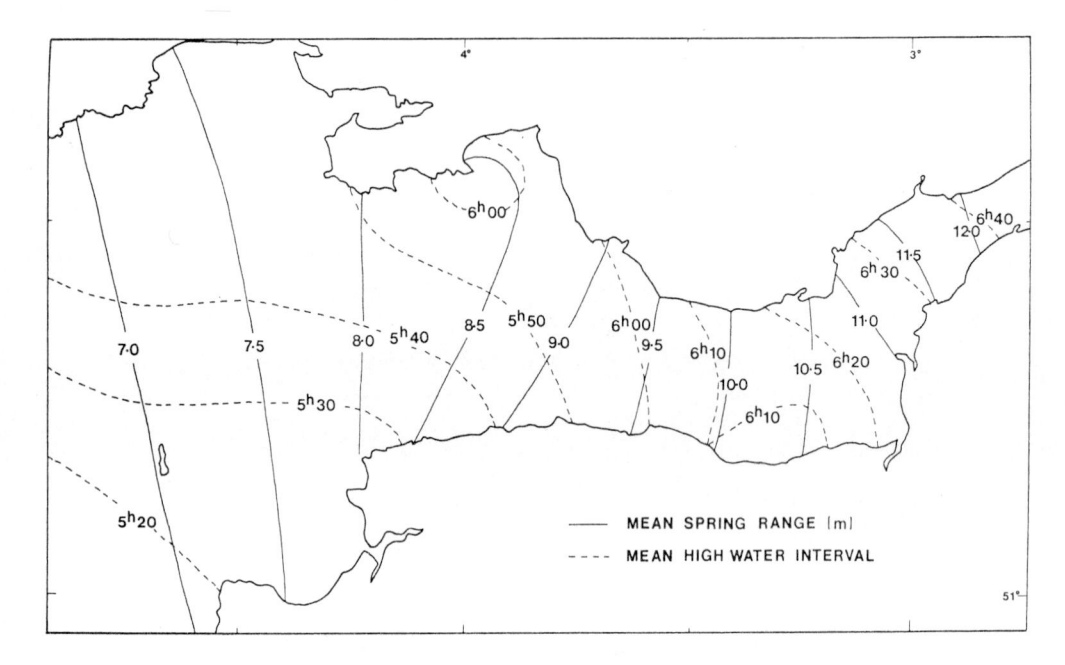

Figure 8.1. Admiralty co-tidal and co-range chart of the Bristol Channel (1977 Edition).

spring tidal range and the dashed lines show the mean high water interval (M.H.W.I.). The mean spring range increases almost linearly, from the mouth (5m) to the head (12m) of the Channel. Along the southern coastline the M.H.W.I. increases in value from the mouth to the head; this represents a steady progression of the tidal wave up the Channel. This progression can also be seen in the results for the northern coastline, to the east of Porthcawl. To the west of Porthcawl, the M.H.W.I. contours run almost parallel to the coastline, indicating that high water occurs almost simultaneously along this stretch of the coastline (these results compare with the analyses of Heaps (1968)). Swansea Bay is therefore situated within the area which is affected by a standing wave.

The results of the harmonic analyses of tidal data from Swansea, Mumbles, Port Talbot, Porthcawl and Rhossili are presented in Table 8.1. (for locations see Fig. 8.2). The principal lunar semi-diurnal constituent (M_2) has the largest amplitude (3.2m at Swansea) and the second most important constituent is the principal solar semi-diurnal constituent (S_2) (1.1m at Swansea). The M_2 phase values from these stations are all close to the Swansea value of 174° indicating the presence of a standing wave within the embayment (see also Collins and Banner (1980), Table 11.1). The value of the M_2 phase at Rhossili is slightly less than the values for stations in the Bay, indicating a progression of the tide along the south Gower coastline.

Between 20th March 1977 and 24th April, 1977, extensive tidal observations were made by the Admiralty along both the northern and southern coastlines of the Bristol Channel, as part of the so-called Admiralty "Tidal Month". The results obtained are shown in the latest version of the Bristol Channel co-tidal and co-range chart (Fig. 8.1). As part of this study, data were collected from 3 stations within Swansea Bay (Mumbles, Swansea and Port Talbot).

Figure 8.3. shows the high water time differences between the stations within Swansea

TABLE 8.1. Amplitude and phase of major diurnal and semi-diurnal constituents at stations around Swansea Bay and along the South Gower Coastline.

	M_2 Amplitude (m)	M_2 Phase (°)	S_2 Amplitude (m)	S_2 Phase (°)	K_1 Amplitude (m)	K_1 Phase (°)	O_1 Amplitude (m)	O_1 Phase (°)
SWANSEA (mean value 1976 & 1977)	3.16	174	1.13	221	0.07	126	0.07	355
PORT TALBOT (March/April 1977)	3.18	173	1.15	221	0.09	154	0.07	353
MUMBLES (March/April 1977)	3.17	176	1.09	218	0.06	125	0.06	020
PORTHCAWL (Admiralty, 1949)	3.17	173	1.25	228	0.09	123	0.03	343
RHOSSILI (September 1977)	2.79	171	0.99	214	0.12	158	0.09	002

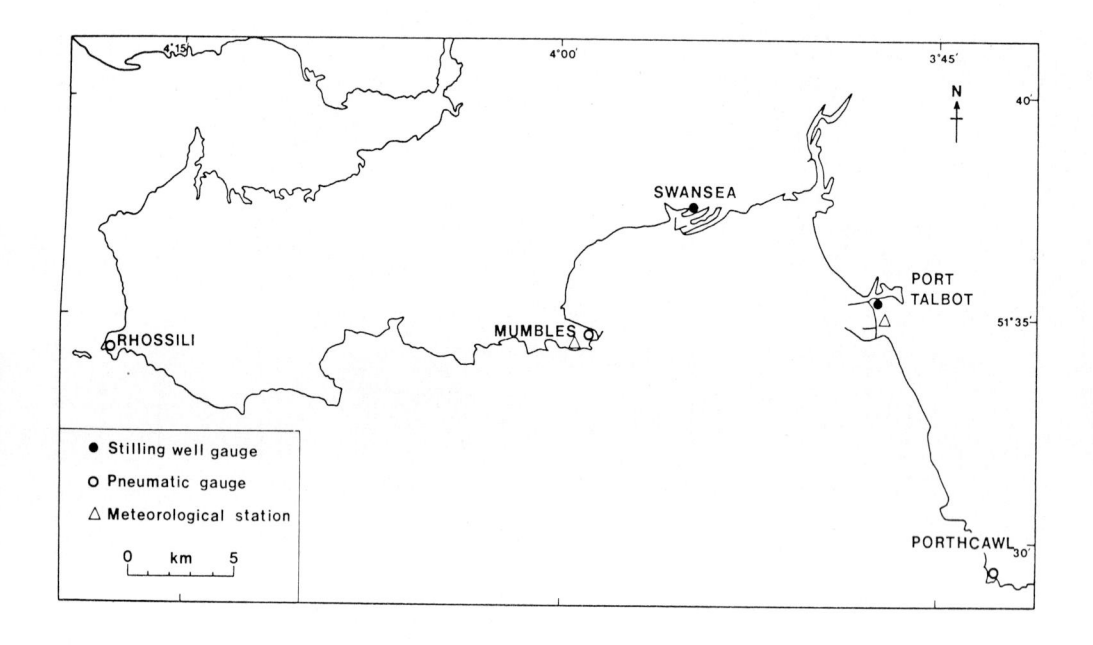

Figure 8.2. Location of tide gauges and meteorological stations.

Bay and Avonmouth (Lt. Dr. W.M. Powell, *pers. comm.*). The differences for Swansea and Port Talbot are very similar, with a maximum difference between them of 5 minutes. The Mumbles data shows a similar pattern with differences of between 5 and 15 minutes; high water occurring later at Mumbles than at Swansea and Port Talbot.

For the low water time differences (Fig. 8.4) a similar pattern exists. The maximum time difference between Swansea and Port Talbot is 8 minutes. Mumbles, however, shows a marked time difference, with low water occurring up to 30 minutes later at Mumbles than at both Swansea and Port Talbot.

From these results, it is possible to conclude that the time differences between Swansea and Port Talbot are very small. As these data were not collected simultaneously (due to gauge malfunctioning at Swansea during the period of the tidal month), the meteorological conditions would not have been the same and so it is not possible to confirm whether these small variations are of tidal or meteorological origin.

Other short periods of data collected from in and around Swansea Bay have been compared and in general validate the conclusions outlined above. Comparisons were made between the recorded times of high and low water at Swansea and those at Mumbles, Port Talbot and Rhossili. In all cases, the observed times at the various ports were subtracted from the recorded times at Swansea. The time differences for both high and low water are shown in Fig. 8.5.

Between Swansea and Port Talbot the majority of time differences are small; 53% of the observations occurring concurrently and 80% are within ± 5 minutes. Thus (from the data available) the times of high water and low water are not significantly different at these 2 ports.

Between Swansea and Mumbles the differences are extremely variable in magnitude

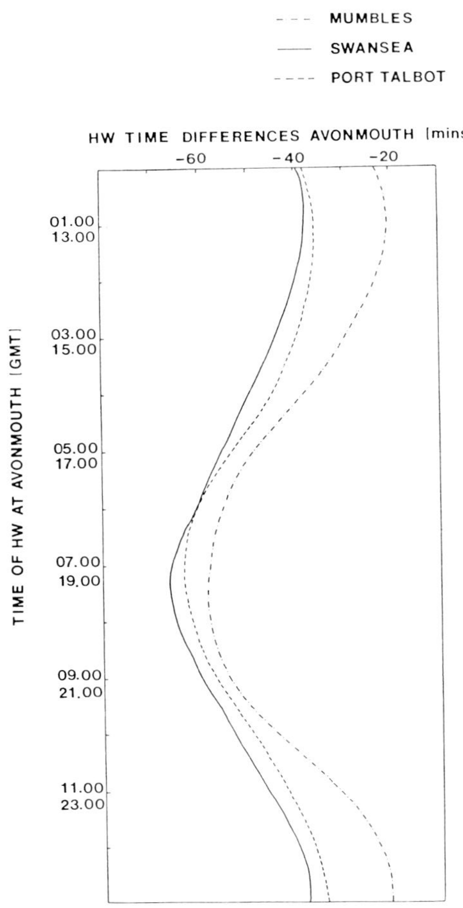

Tidal and Non-Tidal Variations

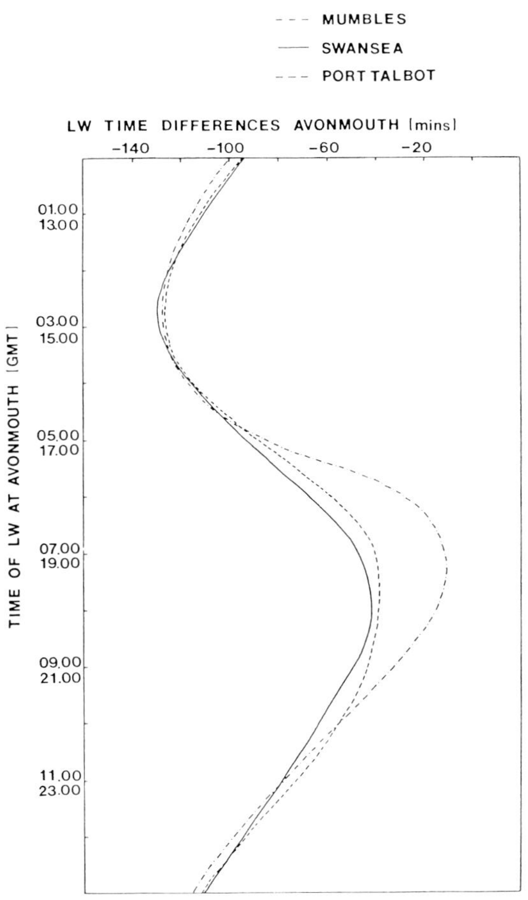

Figure 8.4. Low water time differences between Avonmouth and Swansea, Port Talbot and Mumbles.

Figure 8.3. High water time differences between Avonmouth and Swansea, Port Talbot and Mumbles.

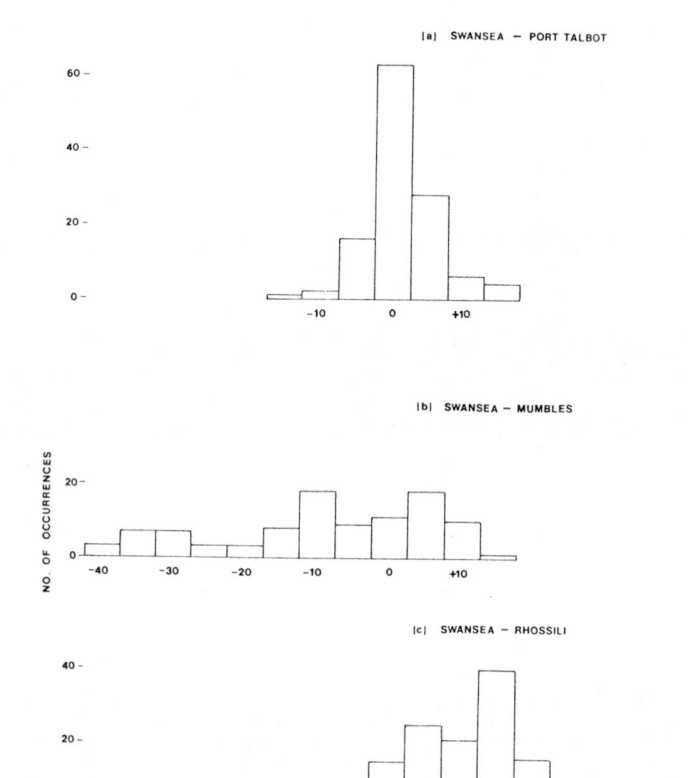

Figure 8.5. Distribution of high and low water time residuals for: (a) Swansea - Port Talbot; (b) Swansea - Mumbles; and (c) Swansea - Rhossili.

ranging from -40 min to +20 min. The majority of the time differences (71%) are negative indicating that the HW and LW occur earlier at Swansea than at Mumbles. However, as 67% of the values fall between ± 10 minutes and the time differences measured are probably accurate to only ± 5 minutes, it appears that there is generally very little differences between high water and low water times at Swansea and Mumbles. When significant time differences do occur, the low waters and high waters are generally later at Mumbles than at Swansea.

The time differences between Swansea and Rhossili are also very variable in magnitude, ranging from -35 to +40 minutes. The majority of the time differences (77%) are positive indicating that the high waters and low waters occur earlier at Rhossili than at Swansea. Similarly, the majority of the values fall between +5 and +15 minutes, indicating that the tide is usually at least 10 minutes earlier at Rhossili than Swansea.

These additional comparisons generally confirm the almost simultaneous tides within Swansea Bay and the slight progression of the tide along the south Gower coastline.

The larger time differences between Swansea and Mumbles are probably related to the local recirculating eddy system causing (Collins et al., 1979; Ferentinos and Collins, 1979), in relation to "Bernoulli's effect", the development of a hydraulic head and water level differences.

NON-TIDAL VARIATIONS.

General Introduction

The water movements within Swansea Bay are dominated by tidal oscillations, but significant non-tidal variations do occur. The most important non-tidal variations are free oscillations, semi-diurnal residuals, long-period residuals and storm surges. The last mentioned variation will be discussed in the succeeding Chapter (Wilding, Chapter 9).

Free Oscillations

The shortest period (30-50 minutes) and smallest amplitude (0.08-0.22m) non-tidal variations of sea level in Swansea Bay are the free oscillations of the water mass within the embayment. These free oscillations were observed in the records from both Swansea and Port Talbot and were found to be of approximately equal amplitude and in phase.

Spectral analyses of the water level records from Swansea both with and without the pronounced free oscillations have been compared. For this analysis, 2 (3-day) records of sea level from Swansea were sampled, at 5-minute intervals, and the data were used as input to a spectral analysis routine. The results (Fig. 8.6) demonstrate that a considerable amount of energy is concentrated between periods of 30 and 50 minutes for the record with free oscillations indicating that the free oscillations of Swansea Bay have periods of between 30 and 50 minutes. The spectral analysis also demonstrates that the free oscillations consist of a range of frequencies and thus the results obtained by direct measurement from the records, which are generally of the order of 30 mins, are simplistic representations of the overall characteristics.

Assuming Swansea Bay to be represented by a semi-circular bay with a semi-parabolic bed, theoretical studies (Wilson et al., 1965) have shown that the most likely mode of oscillation for both the high and low water situations is the Fundamental mode (Table 8.2). Such an oscillation would be associated with a nodal line at the mouth of Swansea Bay (See Fig. 8.7)(i.e., passing south-eastwards through Mumbles Head); this is practically feasible in terms of the data collected as the records from Swansea and Port Talbot show oscillations which are in phase. In order to confirm the existence of such a nodal line at the mouth of the Bay, concurrent sea level records from Mumbles would be required. Unfortunately, at the present time, such records are not available. The broad-band nature of the frequency components of the free oscillations in the embayment appears to indicate a complex situation; therefore, the simple theoretical model might not be totally representative.

Free oscillations must be initiated by external forces. Atmospheric disturbances can act as such external forces and can produce variations by two distinct mechanisms. Firstly, the action of the atmospheric pressure on the water mass can cause disturbances; secondly, the horizontal wind stress on the sea surface can influence levels (Silvester, 1974).

The synoptic meteorological conditions for the periods during which free oscillations were observed in Swansea Bay showed that the majority of free oscillations

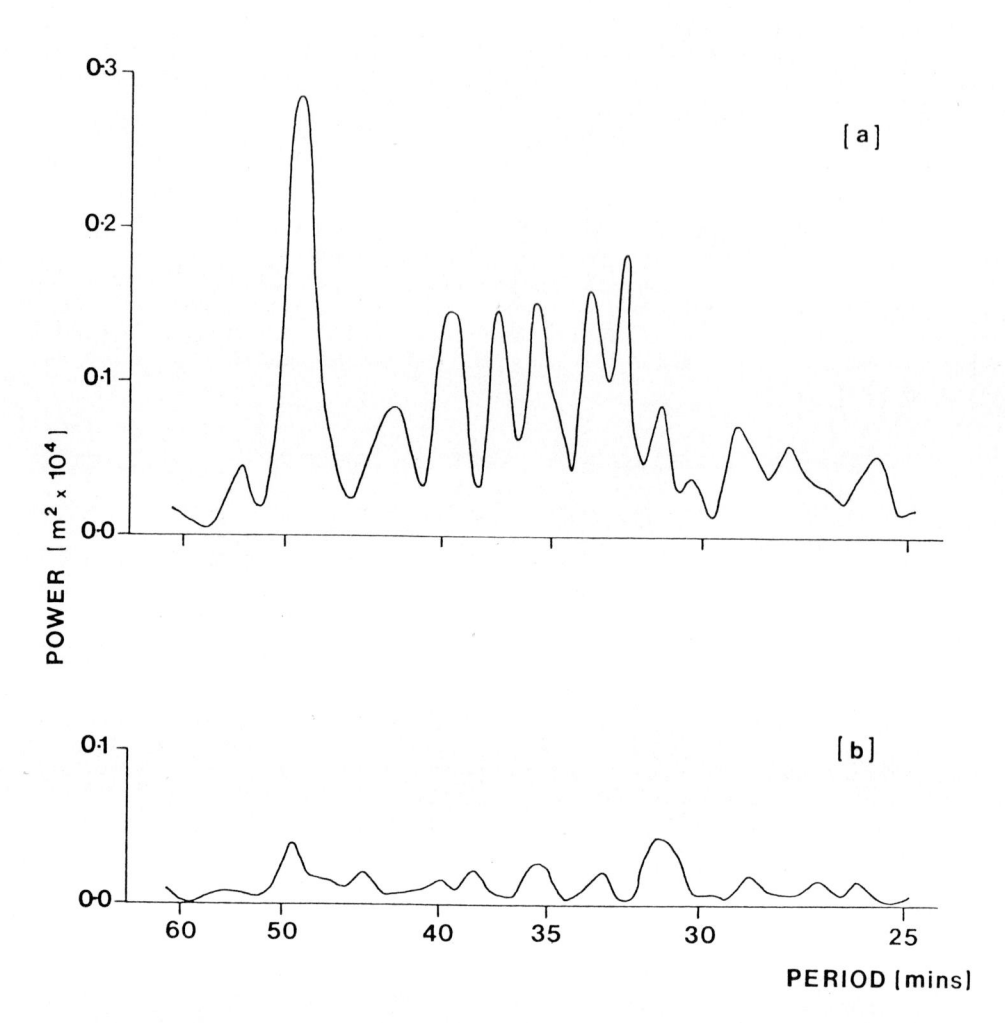

Figure 8.6. Power spectra of sea level at Swansea relating to typical section of records: (a) with free oscillations (28th - 30th Nov., 1976) and (b) without free oscillations (3rd - 5th Nov., 1976).

were associated with the passage of a trough of low pressure over the British Isles. Continuous records of barometric pressure, wind speed and wind direction from Port Talbot were used for a detailed analysis of the local meteorological conditions associated with the free oscillations. Generally, the changes in barometric pressure at the time of oscillations were insignificant. In contrast, the occurrence of free oscillations with changes in wind conditions was very noticeable. Nearly all the oscillations could be associated with peak wind speeds and a change in wind directions, with both of these characteristics occurring no more than one hour prior to the onset of the oscillations. The wind data associated with the oscillations all showed a clockwise rotation of the wind direction, which is indicative of the passage of a front over the area. A typical example of such an occurrence is shown in Figs 8.8 and 8.9. Figure 8.8. shows the presence of sea level oscillations at both Swansea and Port Talbot at 08.00 hrs G.M.T. which was just after low water. Figure 8.9. shows the corresponding wind speed and direction. In this particular

TABLE 8.2. Theoretical Periods of Free Oscillation of the Water Mass in Swansea Bay.

	PERIOD (MINS.)			
MODE	1	2	3	4
MEAN HIGH WATER SPRINGS*	43	30	25	22
MEAN LOW WATER SPRINGS+	41	29	24	21

*High water situation

+Low water situation

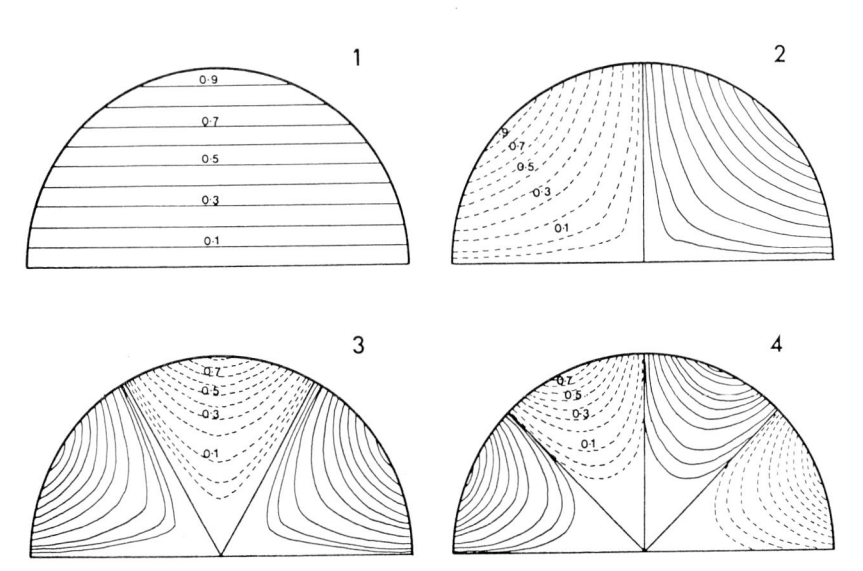

Figure 8.7. The first four theoretical modes of oscillation of a semi-circular embayment, with a semi-parabolic bed (values on diagrams relate to normalised amplitude).

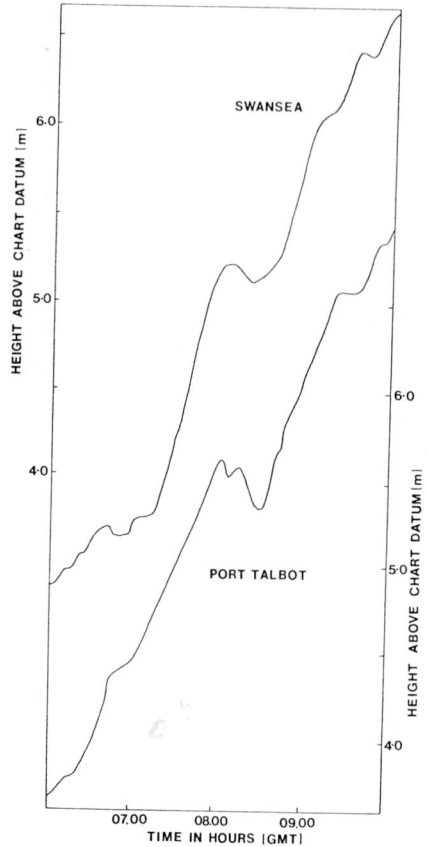

example, peak wind speed and a clockwise rotation of the wind direction occurred just before 08.00 hrs, confirming the association between the free oscillations and sudden changes in wind speed and direction.

HOURLY HEIGHT RESIDUALS

In the present investigation hourly residuals for Swansea were calculated using hourly height predictions from I.O.S. (Bidston). Due to gaps in the data, it was not possible to analyse the 2 years data as a single continuous record; consequently, in order to obtain the longest series possible, the data were divided into 6 three-monthly records.

Spectral analysis of these six records enabled the calculation of an average distribution of energy between certain frequency bands (Fig. 8.10). The two most important energy bands are the long-period (92 hr) and the semi-diurnal bands. The percentage of the total energy in the long-period band ranged from 29% to 63% (with an average of 42.5%). The percentage of the total energy in the semi-diurnal band ranged from 22% to 48% (with an average of 40.2%). Thus, the combined energy in these 2 bands generally accounts for at least 80% of the total energy in the record.

Figure 8.8. Comparison of free oscillations on the tide gauge records from Swansea and Port Talbot (29th Nov., 1976).

Long-Period Residuals

The position of the major energy peak in the low frequencies was not constant throughout the six records but varied from 0.08 to 0.02 cpd (i.e., periods of 12.5 to 50 days, respectively). The low frequency variations in the residuals are probably the result of low frequency meteorological variations.

The hourly height residuals from Swansea were compared with hourly meteorological data. The meteorological data were obtained from the Mumbles Coastguard Station and consisted of hourly values of barometric prrssure, wind speed and wind direction. The wind data were resolved into east-west and north-south components, with winds from the north and east assumed positive.

In order to calculate the correlation between two series within specific frequency bands, coherence squared analyses (see Rodriguez-Iturbe and Nordin, 1969) were carried out on the 6 three-month records. The highest values of coherence squared were found to occur between the residuals and the barometric pressure. A typical example is shown in Fig. 8.11 and shows that the coherency is particularly high in the low frequencies (the dotted line on the Figure represents the 95% confidence

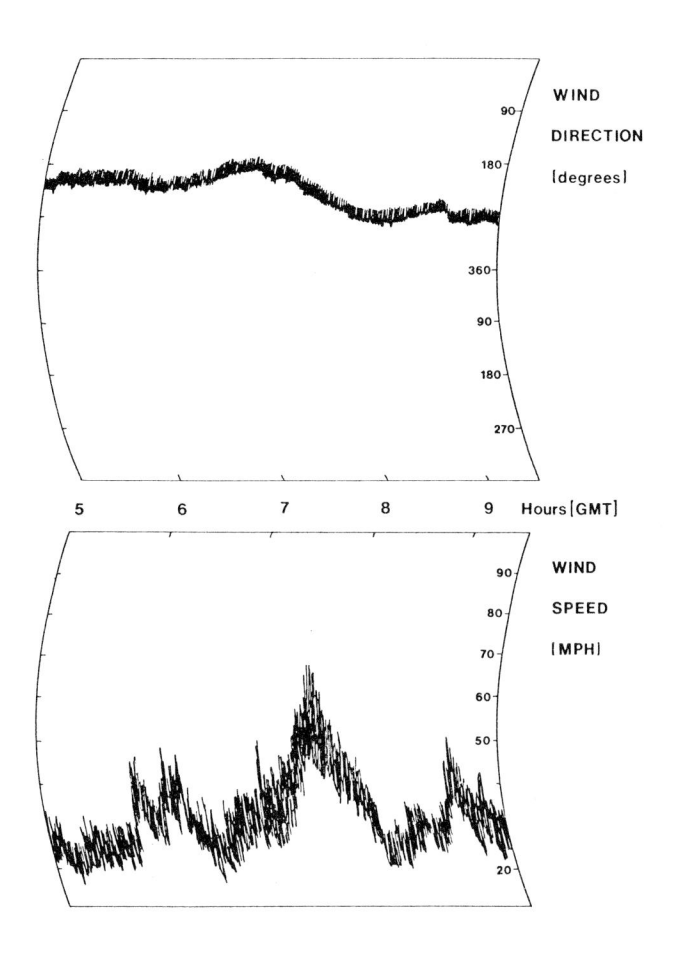

Figure 8.9. Wind data for 29th Nov., 1976 from Port Talbot

limits (see Munk et al., 1959)); this was especially true during the winter months. The low frequency coherency is probably due to the large-scale pressure systems which cross the British Isles and which are more frequent in the winter months. Generally the phase values are around ± 180° at <u>low frequencies</u>, indicating an inverse relationship between the barometric pressure and the residuals (i.e., an increase in the barometric pressure decreases the sea level).

In general, the coherence between the residuals and the wind speed is low. Significant peaks occur on most of the records in the low frequencies and the phase values indicate a direct relationship between the residuals and wind speed. These low frequency peaks are again more predominant in the winter months.

Generally the residuals and the east-west wind components are not highly correlated. In contrast, the residuals and the north-south wind components show high values of coherence at low frequencies. In all cases the values are approximately ± 180° indicating an inverse relationship (i.e., an increase in the southerly (on-shore)

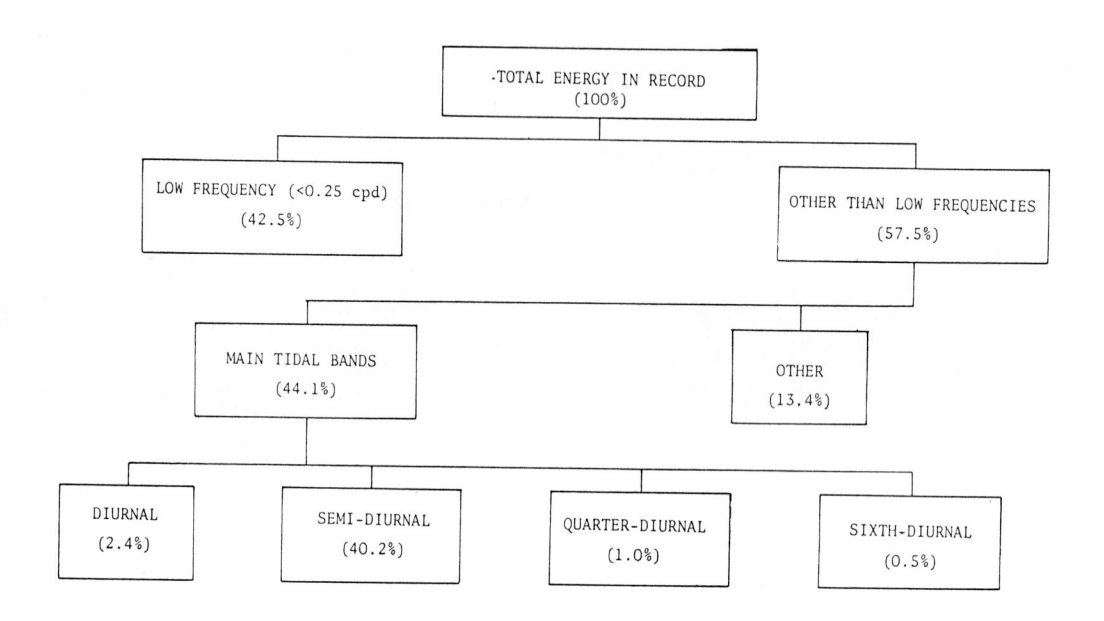

```
                    ┌─────────────────────────┐
                    │ TOTAL ENERGY IN RECORD  │
                    │        (100%)           │
                    └───────────┬─────────────┘
                ┌───────────────┴───────────────┐
  ┌─────────────────────────┐      ┌──────────────────────────────┐
  │ LOW FREQUENCY (<0.25 cpd)│      │ OTHER THAN LOW FREQUENCIES   │
  │        (42.5%)           │      │          (57.5%)             │
  └─────────────────────────┘      └──────────────┬───────────────┘
                                    ┌─────────────┴─────────────┐
                          ┌──────────────────┐        ┌──────────────┐
                          │ MAIN TIDAL BANDS │        │    OTHER     │
                          │     (44.1%)      │        │   (13.4%)    │
                          └────────┬─────────┘        └──────────────┘
         ┌──────────────┬──────────┴──────────┬──────────────────┐
  ┌────────────┐ ┌────────────┐ ┌──────────────────┐ ┌────────────────┐
  │  DIURNAL   │ │SEMI-DIURNAL│ │ QUARTER-DIURNAL  │ │ SIXTH-DIURNAL  │
  │   (2.4%)   │ │  (40.2%)   │ │     (1.0%)       │ │    (0.5%)      │
  └────────────┘ └────────────┘ └──────────────────┘ └────────────────┘
```

Figure 8.10. Energy distribution of the hourly height residuals

wind increases the positive residual height).

Thus the low frequency residuals appear to be most highly correlated with the barometric pressure and the north-south wind components.

Semi-Diurnal Residuals

In all 6 records studied the semi-diurnal residual energy had a peak at 1.97 cpd (i.e., 12.2 hours) which is not equivalent to a tidal constituent. Oscillations of semi-diurnal frequency have often been noticed in tidal residuals elsewhere. Several possible causes for this characteristic were suggested by George & Thomas (1976); these were inaccuracies in the tidal predictions, variable errors in the tide gauge, tide-surge interaction and unspecified tidal modulation. The occurrence of very similar semi-diurnal oscillations at other ports around the British Isles, including Avonmouth, Milford Haven and Newlyn, would tend to suggest that the first 2 possible causes put forward by George and Thomas (*op.cit.*) are unlikely to be the reason for the semi-diurnal residuals as it seems very improbable that all these gauges could be affected by the same combination of errors. In addition the gauge at Swansea is regularly monitored by the Ordnance Survey and so should not suffer from variable errors, and the predictions should be reliable as Swansea is a Standard Port. It appears therefore that the semi-diurnal oscillations observed in the residuals at Swansea are primarily caused either by tide-surge interaction or by unspecified tidal modulation. In such a shallow water area as Swansea Bay, tide-surge interaction might be anticipated and could account for some, if not all, of the semi-diurnal residual energy. In addition, it has been shown recently (Fong & Heaps, 1978) that the natural period of oscillation of the Bristol Channel/Celtic Sea system (defined as the area extending from the head of the

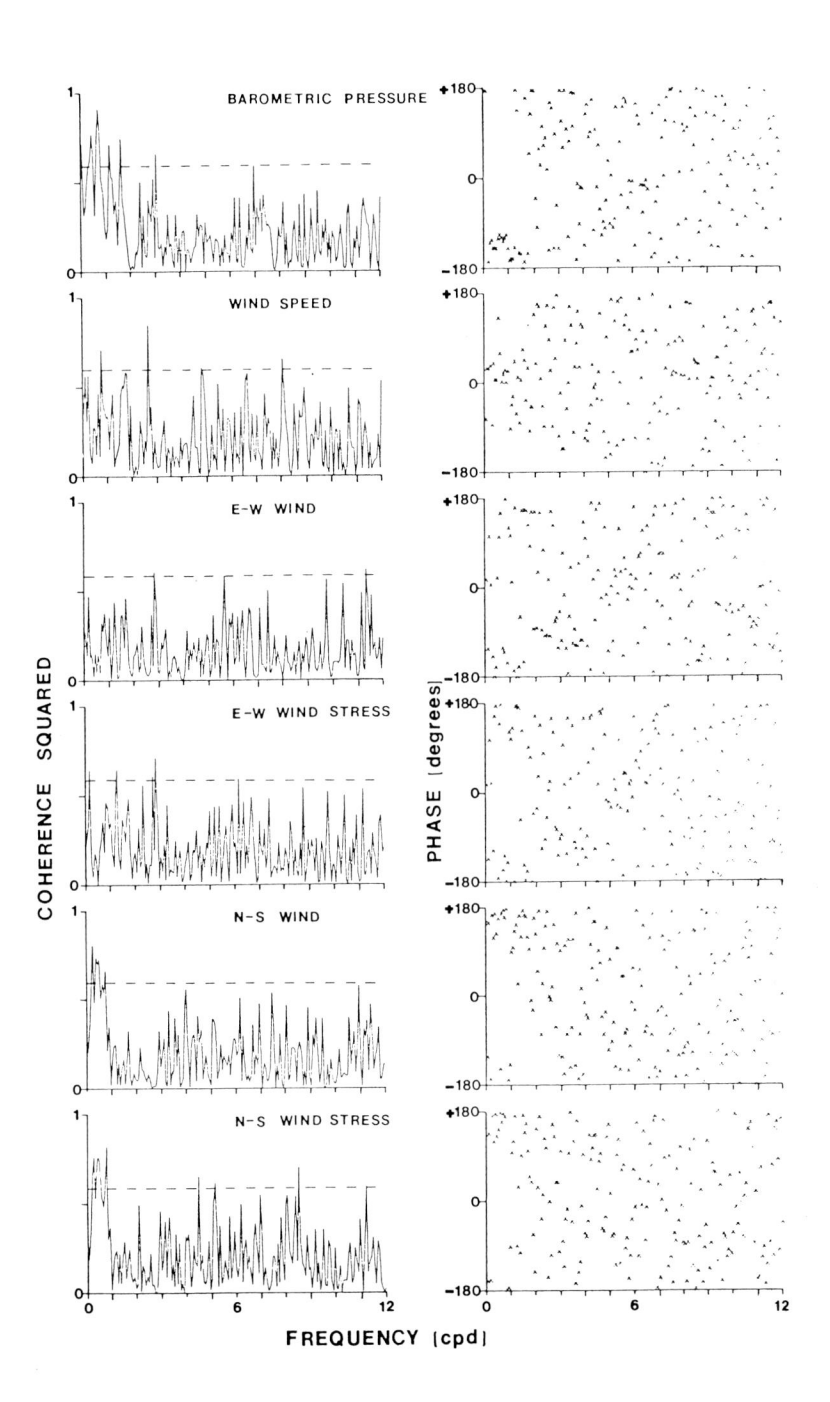

Figure 8.11. Typical coherency plots for hourly height residuals for Swansea and meteorological variables at Mumbles (Winter, 1976).

Bristol Channel to the continental shelf edge) lies between 12.2 and 12.6 hours. These free oscillations could therefore be the cause of the semi-diurnal residuals at Swansea and other ports in the Bristol Channel.

As with all free oscillations, an external force would be required to initiate them. A study of the Daily Weather Reports issued by the Meteorological Office has shown that, just prior to the onset of the more pronounced periods of semi-diurnal fluctuations, fronts passed over the continental shelf edge to the west of Great Britain. It is possible that these fronts could initiate free oscillations in the Bristol Channel/Celtic Sea area and hence cause semi-diurnal residuals at ports along the Channel. In order to confirm this hypothesis, a detailed study of meteorological data collected from a station located in the vicinity of the shelf edge would be required.

CONCLUDING REMARKS

In conclusion, therefore, an investigation of the water level fluctuations within Swansea Bay has shown that both tidal and non-tidal variations in water level occur. These variations and their generating mechanisms are summarised in Table 8.3 (storm surges are discussed in Chapter 9).

The analysis of the dominant tidal oscillations has shown that, within Swansea Bay, the tides are almost simultaneous at Swansea and Port Talbot and often occur slightly later at Mumbles. Thus the presence of a standing wave within the embayment, as suggested by the phase values of the M_2 constituent (obtained from the harmonic analyses), has been confirmed by field observations. The time variations between Rhossili and Swansea indicate the progression of the tide eastwards along the south Gower coastline. This progression is also shown in the M_2 phase difference between the two ports.

Non-tidal variations of sea level have also been found to occur, the most important being the free oscillations, the long-period residuals, the semi-diurnal residuals and the storm surges (the last mentioned being considered in a separate presentation).

The free oscillations of the water mass in Swansea Bay have the shortest periods (30 - 50 minutes) and smallest amplitudes (0.08 - 0.22m) of all the non-tidal oscillations described. The oscillations at Swansea and Port Talbot are in phase and of almost equal amplitude indicating that the theoretical model put forward (assuming a semi-circular bay with a semi-parabolic bed) may be representative. The free oscillations appear to be generated by sudden changes in wind speed and direction, related to the pasage of meteorological fronts over the area.

Spectral analysis of the hourly height residuals for Swansea have shown that the majority of the residual energy is contained within the long period (96 hr) and the semi-diurnal (approximately 2 cpd) band.

The long-period non-tidal variations appear to be closely related to meteorological conditions, in particular the barometric pressure and the north-south wind component. The sea level is increased by decreases in the barometric pressure and increases in the southerly wind component.

The semi-diurnal residuals all have a frequency of 1.97 cpd and it has been proposed that these residuals, which are also seen on the records from Milford Haven and Avonmouth, represent the free oscillations of the Bristol Channel/Celtic Sea system.

TABLE 8.3. Summary of Vertical Water Movements in Swansea Bay.

Feature	Vertical Displacement*(m)	Period (hours)	Generating Mechanism	Comments
Tides M_2	3.16	12.42	Astronomical	Principal lunar semi-diurnal constituent. Phase values at stations within Bay indicate standing wave.
S_2	1.13	12.00		Principal solar semi-diurnal constituent.
M_4	0.06	6.21		Shallow-water constituent.
M_6	0.04	4.14		Shallow-water constituent.
Storm Surges	0.79-1.58	1.5-9.5	Large-scale synoptic meteorological conditions	Secondary depressions approaching British Isles from W or SW. Amplitude related to synoptic meteorological conditions (as described by the depression).
Significant Surges	0.60-1.58	1.0-6.0	Local meteorological conditions	Negative surges increased by high barometric pressure and N winds. Positive surges increased by low barometric pressure and W winds.
Semi-Diurnal Residuals	Variable	12.2	Free oscillations of the Bristol Channel - Celtic Sea System.	
Long-Period Residuals	Variable	>40.0	meteorological conditions	Positive amplitudes increased by decreased barometric pressure and increased on-shore wind
Free Oscillations	0.04-0.22	0.5-0.8	Local meteorological conditions	Sudden changes in wind speed and direction related to passage of meteorological fronts.

REFERENCES

Collins, M.B., and Ferentinos, G. (1979). Tidally-induced secondary circulations and their associated sedimentation processes. *J. Oceanogrph. Soc. Japan, 35,* 65-74.

Collins, M.B., Ferentinos, G. and Banner, F.T. (1979). The hydrodynamics and sedimentology of a high (tidal and wave) energy embayment (Swansea Bay, Bristol Channel). *Estuar. and Coast. Mar. Sci., 8,* 49-74.

Collins, M.B., and Banner, F.T. (1980). Sediment Transport by Waves and Tides: Problems exemplified by a study of Swansea Bay, Bristol Channel. *In:* Banner, F.T., Collins, M.B., and Massie, K.S., (Eds.). *The North-West European Shelf Seas: the seabed and the sea in motion. 2.,* Elsevier Oceanographic Series 24B, (Chapter 11).

Fong, S.W., and Heaps, N.S. (1978). Note on quarter-wave tidal resonance in the Bristol Channel. I.O.S. Report No. 63, 11pp. (Unpub. manuscript).

George, K.J., and Thomas, D.K. (1976). Two notable storm surges of the south coast of England. *Hydrogr. J., 2*(4), 13-16.

Heaps, N.S. (1968). Estimated effects of a barrage on tides in the Bristol Channel. *Proc. Instn. civ. Engrs., 40,* 495-500.

Munk, W.H., Snodgrass, F.E., and Tucker, M.J. (1959). Spectra of low-frequency ocean waves. *Bull. Scripps Instn. Oceanogr., 7,* 283-361.

Rodriguez-Iturbe, I., and Nordin, C.F. (1969). Some applications of cross spectral analyses in hydrology: rainfall and runoff. *Wat. Resour. Res., 5,* 608-621.

Silvester, R. (1974). *Coastal Engineering, II.,* Elsevier Scientific, Amsterdam, 338pp.

Wilding, A.J. (1979). *Numerical Studies of Tides, Free Oscillations and Surges in Swansea Bay.* Unpub. Ph.D. Thesis, University of Wales, 184pp.

Wilson, B.W., Hendrickson, J.A., and Kilmer, R.E. (1965). *Feasibility study for a surge-action model of Monterey Harbour, California.* U.S. Army Corps. of Engineers, 166pp.

9. STORM SURGES IN SWANSEA BAY

A. J. Wilding

Department of Oceanography, University College, Swansea, U.K.

ABSTRACT

A number of storm surges occurred in Swansea Bay between January 1976 and January 1978. The surges ranged in amplitude from 0.79m to 1.58m and in their duration of influence from 1.5 to 9.5hr.

The synoptic meteorological conditions associated with the storm surges were found to be in general agreement with the conditions described by Lennon (1963), for surges at Avonmouth. The overall meteorological situation was also found to be more important in controlling surge height than the local meteorological conditions.

In the analysis, the surges at Swansea were compared with those occurring at Avonmouth. The behaviour of the surges was very similar to that of the tide in the Bristol Channel, in terms of their progression and amplification up the channel.

The combined influence of surge and tide can cause the exceedance of extreme water levels (e.g., H.A.T.) over the region; this occurred in November 1977, causing extensive flooding along the Neath Estuary.

KEYWORDS

Storm surges; Meteorological conditions; Extreme levels; Swansea Bay; Bristol Channel.

GENERAL INTRODUCTION

In Swansea Bay investigations have shown that the largest non-tidal sea level variations are the result of storm surges. The term 'storm surge' refers to a temporary rise or fall of the sea level produced by both changes in atmospheric pressure and the action of the wind over the sea surface. These phenomena are commonly associated with the passage of a meteorological disturbance. The storm surges observed along the coast of the British Isles are generally associated with the passage of deep barometric depressions across part of the surrounding sea region. The storm surge at any location, derived from observations of sea level, may therefore be regarded as being generated partially by barometric pressure and partially by the tangential wind stress over the sea surface. Storm surges are most frequently defined by means of the residuals left after the predicted tide has been subtracted from the observed level. The duration of a surge usually varies between a few hours and two to three days; those on the west coast of the British Isles generally have a duration of between nine and fifteen hours (Heaps, 1967).

West Coast Storm Surges.

Storm surges along the west coast of the British Isles have not been studied as extensively as those in the North Sea. Present knowledge of west coast surges derives mainly from the investigations of Lennon (1963a, 1965) and Heaps (1967). The more recent investigations by Milne (1971, 1975) and Graff (1977, 1978) have also considered west coast surges, although the latter investigator is concerned primarily with the extreme levels caused by these surges. Lennon (1963a) has identified the weather conditions associated with the generation of major storm surges at Avonmouth and Liverpool. He found that these surges are generally caused by secondary depressions which approach the British Isles from the west or south-west. The approach zone of potentially dangerous depressions likely to cause major surges at Avonmouth is shown in Fig. 9.1.

Figure 9.1. Approach zone of potentially dangerous depressions for Avonmouth (from Lennon, 1963a).

The hatched area indicates the position of the centres of the depressions at the time of maximum surge. Lennon (1963a) also defined four conditions which, if satisfied by the meteorological situation, could cause a major storm surge along the west coast. The conditions are:
(i) A deepening and well-developed secondary depression approaches the country, in the zones indicated, so that its right-rear quadrant has latitude to act upon the water surface *en route* to the port (of observation).

(ii) The speed of approach of this depression is of the order of 74 kmh^{-1} (40 knots).
(iii) The depression can be represented by an independent and roughly concentric system of isobars up to a radius of 280 to 370 km (150 - 200 nautical miles, respectively).
(iv) The depression is likely to reach a depth of approximately 50 mb (relative to a mean level of 1012 mb) over the country, and will be associated with a pressure gradient of approximately 30 mb in 450 km (250 nautical miles) in its right-rear quadrant.

Of these four conditions, the first two are considered by Lennon (*op.cit.*) to be more important in surge generation than the latter two. In particular, at Avonmouth (where the response of the water level is so closely connected with the ability of the Bristol Channel as a whole to respond to external influence) the rate of onset of the influence (i.e., condition (ii)), is more critical than at other west coast ports.

STORM SURGES IN SWANSEA BAY

General description

In this investigation, the storm surges were defined in terms of hourly height residuals which were calculated using hourly predictions of tidal height obtained from I.O.S. (Bidston). During the period of investigation (January 1976 to January 1978), six storm surges were observed in the tidal records from Swansea. These were in January 1976, January 1977, November 1977, two in December 1977 and January 1978; they ranged in amplitude from 0.79m to 1.58m above the predicted level. It is interesting to note here the relationships of the storm surges with the tidal situation. None of the surge maxima coincided with the time of high or low water, 4 occurring on the falling tide and 2 on the rising tide. The general appearance of the raw residuals (i.e., observed minus predicted) is of high frequency oscillations superimposed upon a more slowly varying background. The six storm surges are shown in Fig. 9.2. Oscillations of tidal frequencies, particularly semi-diurnal, are apparent on all the curves. These semi-diurnal fluctuations are particularly dominant in the January 1978 surge. The five surges in 1976 and 1977 are all very similar in appearance, having a major peak with associated minor peaks before and after the major peak. The surge of January 1978 does not show the predominant major peak but shows several large semi-diurnal oscillations. The large surges of December 1977 show very pronounced peaks, especially that of 10th December 1977 which was a very short period phenomena. In general, the rapidity with which the surges develop (and diminish) can be described quantitatively by the half-level time; i.e., the time required for the surge to develop from one-half its maximum to the maximum water level achieved (Redfield and Miller, 1957). Table 9.1 shows the half-level times for both the rise and fall of the storm surge, based on the analysis of the raw residuals.

TABLE 9.1. Half-Level Times of the Surges

Date	Surge Height (m)	Rising (hr)	Falling (hr)
02/01/76	0.79	4.0	1.5
25/01/77	0.92	9.0	0.5
11/11/77	0.91	2.0	2.0
10/12/77	1.58	0.5	1.0
24/12/77	1.54	2.5	1.5
10/01/77	0.88	2.5	2.0

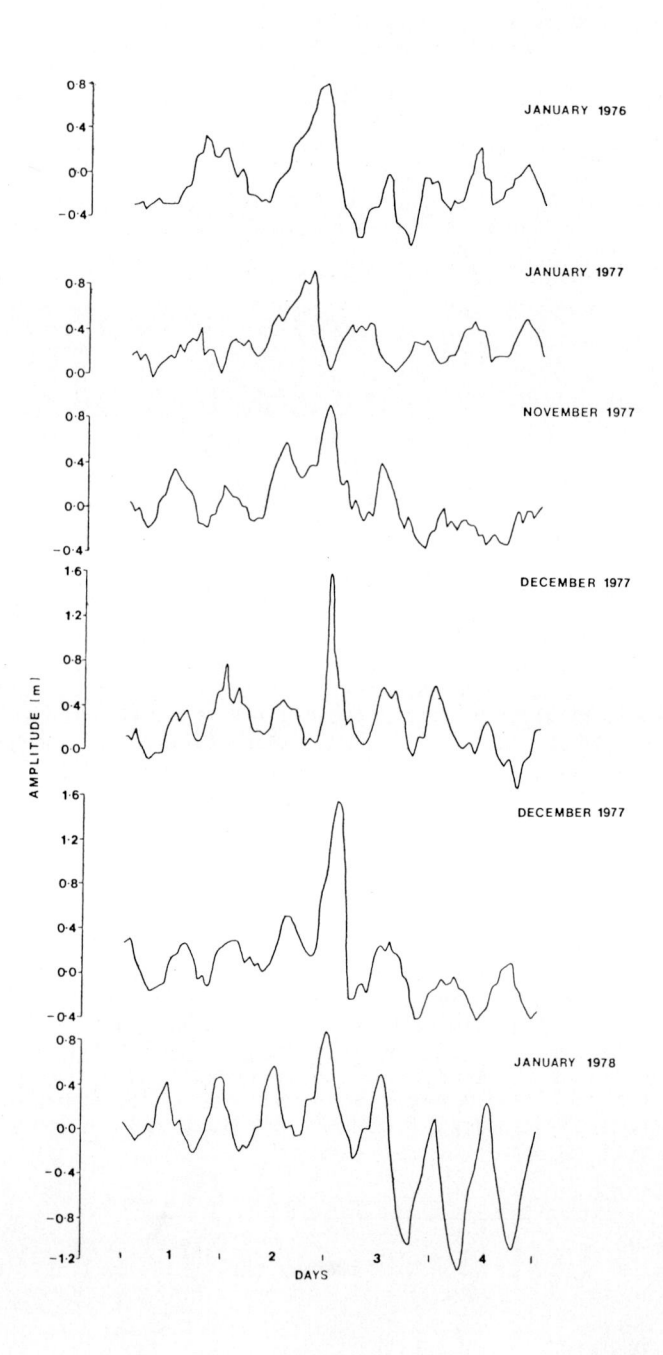

Figure 9.2. Storm surges at Swansea (January 1976 - January 1978).

On five occasions the surge took longer to rise from its half-level than to fall to it, indicating that the decay of the surge is a more rapid process. An indication of the duration of the surge may be given by the length of time during which the level is above its half-level values; for Swansea, this ranged from 1.5 to 9.5 hr. Thus the Swansea surges are normally of shorter duration than those generally described for the west coast which have durations of 9-15 hr. The high-frequency nature of the surge of 10th December 1977 is shown, being above its half-level for only 1.5 hr.

The Effect of Barometric Pressure

Earlier work (Chapter 8) has shown that when the high frequency components were removed from both the sea level and barometric pressure variations, the hourly height residuals were more highly correlated with hourly values of barometric pressure than in the presence of the high frequency components. To ascertain whether this was also the case for storm surges the raw residuals were low-pass filtered, using a Butterworth digital filter having a half-power point of 1.6 cpd (40 hr).

In order to quantify the effect of static pressure on each surge, the predictable variance attributable to the static barometric pressure (i.e., a change of 1 mb in the barometric pressure causes a change of 1cm in the sea level) has been calculated, using the method described by George and Thomas (1978). The equation used is:

$$\text{predictable variance} = \frac{\sum_{i=1}^{n} R_i^2 - \sum_{i=1}^{n} r_i^2}{\sum_{i=1}^{n} R_i^2} \times 100\%$$

where R_i is the residual height at the ith hour
r_i is the height of the residue (residual minus barometric pressure effect) at the ith hour
n is the total number of hourly heights available

The summation was carried out over two-day periods covering the storm surge, with hourly values being used. The results for the six surges at Swansea are given in Table 9.2.

TABLE 9.2. Percentage Predictable Variance

Date	Surge Height	Maximum Static Pressure Effect	Percentage Predictable Variance Raw Residuals	Filtered Residuals
01/01/76	0.79	0.16	27	34
25/01/77	0.92	0.38	76	84
11/11/77	0.91	0.14	26	39
12/12/77	1.58	0.29	50	71
24/12/77	1.54	0.14	21	32
10/01/78	0.88	0.26	-5	1

For all the surges the percentage predictable variance is greater for the filtered residuals than for the raw residuals. This is due to the removal from the residuals, by the low-pass filter, of the high frequency components; these would not be expected to correlate with the barometric pressure effects. There is no constant relationship between the values for the filtered and the raw residuals, neither does the percentage appear to be related to the surge amplitude. There is, however, a relationship between the percentage and the maximum static pressure effect (i.e., the maximum difference between the actual barometric pressure and mean barometric pressure, taken as 1012 mb), with the percentage increasing as the maximum static pressure increases. The values for the surge of January 1978 are inconsistent with the other surges. This may be due to the presence of the large negative surge which followed the positive surge (Fig. 9.2); it was not due to the large semi-diurnal residuals as these had been removed by the low-pass filter. Generally, it appears that for those surges which have a large static pressure effect (i.e., 25th January 1977 and 24th December 1977),the percentage predictable variance is high, indicating that the barometric pressure accounts for a high proportion of the variation. The other surges show that the barometric pressure plays a minor role accounting for only about 30% of the water level variation.

General Description of the Meteorological Conditions Associated with Storm Surges.

Large-scale meteorological conditions: The synoptic meteorological conditions (obtained from the Daily Weather Reports issued by the Meteorological Office) associated with the surges at Swansea were in good agreement with those given by Lennon (1963a) for the west coast. Figure 9.3 shows the depression tracks associated with the six surges and they all fall within the specified approach zone.

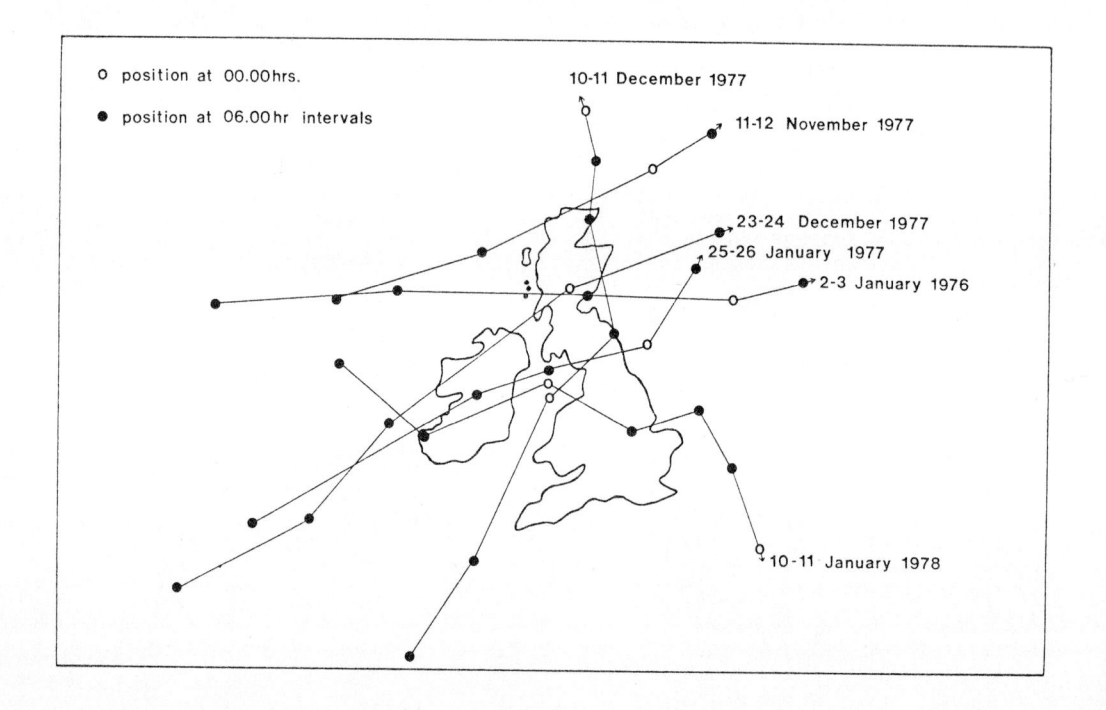

Figure 9.3. Depression Tracks for the Six Storm Surges.

Three of the surges attained their maximum heights while their depression centres were within the hatched area (Fig. 9.1), while two had centres to the north of the area (30 km and 175 km) and one had a centre on the southern edge of the area. This indicates that the position of the hatched area may not be truly representative for the surges at Swansea.

Table 9.3 gives the values for the Swansea surges for four of the meteorological parameters defined by Lennon (1963a). These parameters are the speed of approach of the depression, the radius of the depression, the depth of the depression, and the pressure gradient; they will subsequently be referred to as the "Lennon parameters".

TABLE 9.3. Synoptic Meteorological Conditions.

Surge	Speed of Approach (kmh^{-1})	Radius (km)	Depth (relative to 1012 mb)(mb)	Pressure Gradient (mb/450 km)
West Coast*	74	278-370	50	30
02/01/76	108	324	40	12
25/01/77	78	463	40	12
11/11/77	108	93	36	12
10/12/77	86	185	36	16
24/12/77	108	185	28	12
10/01/78	86	370	32	10

*Lennon (1963a).

The west coast values have been included in Table 9.3 for comparative purposes. In general, there is good agreement between the values for Swansea and those for the west coast. The speeds of approach were higher than those given by Lennon and the depths and pressure gradients were much lower. These differences indicate that the meteorological conditions associated with the Swansea surges are less effective at surge generation than those described by Lennon; this is,in fact,the case as Lennon's investigations were based on considerably larger surges than those studied at Swansea. Differences between the values for Swansea and the west coast might also be expected as Lennon was dealing with surges at different ports.

In order to study the importance of the Lennon parameters , a multiple regression analysis was carried out. The maximum surge height was taken as the dependent variable and the Lennon parameters were taken as the independent variables (these parameters are obviously inter-related as they are all associated with the same depression and so cannot be considered totally independent). The Lennon parameters were used in this method to estimate the importance of these parameters in determining surge height. Using the six storm surges studied, a multiple correlation coefficient of 0.99 was obtained. The regression equation using these four parameters therefore accounts for 98% of the variation in surge amplitude. The analysis has shown therefore that the surge amplitude is largely determined by the nature of the associated depression which has been defined here by the four Lennon parameters . These four parameters are insufficient to define the true nature of a depression and some of the parameters used are somewhat arbitrarily defined, for example, not all depressions may be conveniently divided into quadrants. However, it does appear that the use of these four Lennon parameters provides a very good estimate for determining surge amplitude at Swansea.

Local meteorological conditions: Hourly values of barometric pressure, wind speed and wind direction were obtained from the Mumbles Coastguard Station and were considered to represent the local meteorological conditions. Values for the east-west and north-south wind components were calculated assuming winds blowing from the north and east to be positive.

The local meteorological conditions were generally consistent between surges and the details of the maxima and minima of the meteorological variables associated with the surges are presented in Table 9.4.

The maximum surge heights tended to coincide with the occurrence of minimum barometric pressure and maximum wind speed. On two occasions the surge maxima lagged

TABLE 9.4. Local Meteorological Conditions Associated with the Storm Surges.

Date	Maximum Surge Height (m)	Time	Minimum Barometric Pressure (mb)	Time	Maximum Wind Speed (ms^{-1})	Time	Maximum E-W Wind (ms^{-1})	Time	Maximum N-S Wind (ms^{-1})	Time
02/01/76	0.79	21.00	997.8	19.00	33.6	19.00	-33.1	19.00	-10.6	17.00
25/01/77	0.92	18.00	975.3	18.00	23.3	18.00	-20.2	18.00	-17.0	14.00
11/11/77	0.91	22.00	999.0	19.00	28.4	19.00	-27.5	21.00	-16.0	18.00
10/12/77	1.58	23.00	983.9	23.00	31.0	23.00	-23.8	23.00	-19.9	23.00
24/12/77	1.54	01.00	999.4	01.00	31.0	01.00	-29.5	03.00	-19.9	01.00
10/01/78	0.88	23.00	986.3	04.00	38.0	23.00	-37.4	18.00	-13.0	23.00

behind the wind and pressure by 2 to 3 hr and in January 1978 the minimum barometric pressure occurred after the surge maxima. A lag in the response of the sea level to the changing meteorological conditions may well be expected but why the minimum pressure occurred after the maximum surge in January 1978 is unclear.

It is apparent that the surge magnitude is related to more than one meteorological variable. A multiple regression analysis was therefore carried out using the following independent variables: minimum barometric pressure (relative to 1012 mb); maximum wind speed; maximum east-west wind component; and maximum north-south wind component. Using the six storm surges studied, a multiple correlation coefficient of 0.95 was obtained, indicating that the regression accounted for 90% of the variation. The multiple correlation coefficient for the local meteorological conditions is lower than that for the synoptic meteorological conditions indicating that the more distant meteorological conditions affect the surge amplitude to a greater extent than the local meteorological conditions.

COMPARISON OF STORM SURGES AT SWANSEA AND AVONMOUTH

For all six storm surges at Swansea, described previously, the corresponding records were obtained for Avonmouth, in order to study the variations between the surges at these two ports. Figure 9.4 shows the hourly height residuals for both stations for one of the surges; this is typical of all the results and the similarity between them is clearly visible indicating that these surges are not localised phenomena and that their appearance is not greatly changed on travelling up the Bristol Channel

Table 9.5. gives values of Av/Sw, which is the ratio of surge magnitude at Avonmouth to that at Swansea, and TAv-TSw which is the time lag (in hours) of the surge maximum at Avonmouth upon that at Swansea. Values for the heights and times of the surge maxima at the two ports are also included in the Table. As the residuals were only calculated at hourly intervals (a restriction imposed by the predictions), residuals of greater magnitude than those derived may have occurred between the calculated values; hence, the derived ratios and also the time lags may represent only approximate values.

On most occasions the maximum surge height occurs at Swansea before it occurs at Avonmouth; this might be expected as the depressions causing these surges approach from the west. The effects of shallow water on the tide means that it takes approximately one hour for the tide to progress from Swansea to Avonmouth at high water

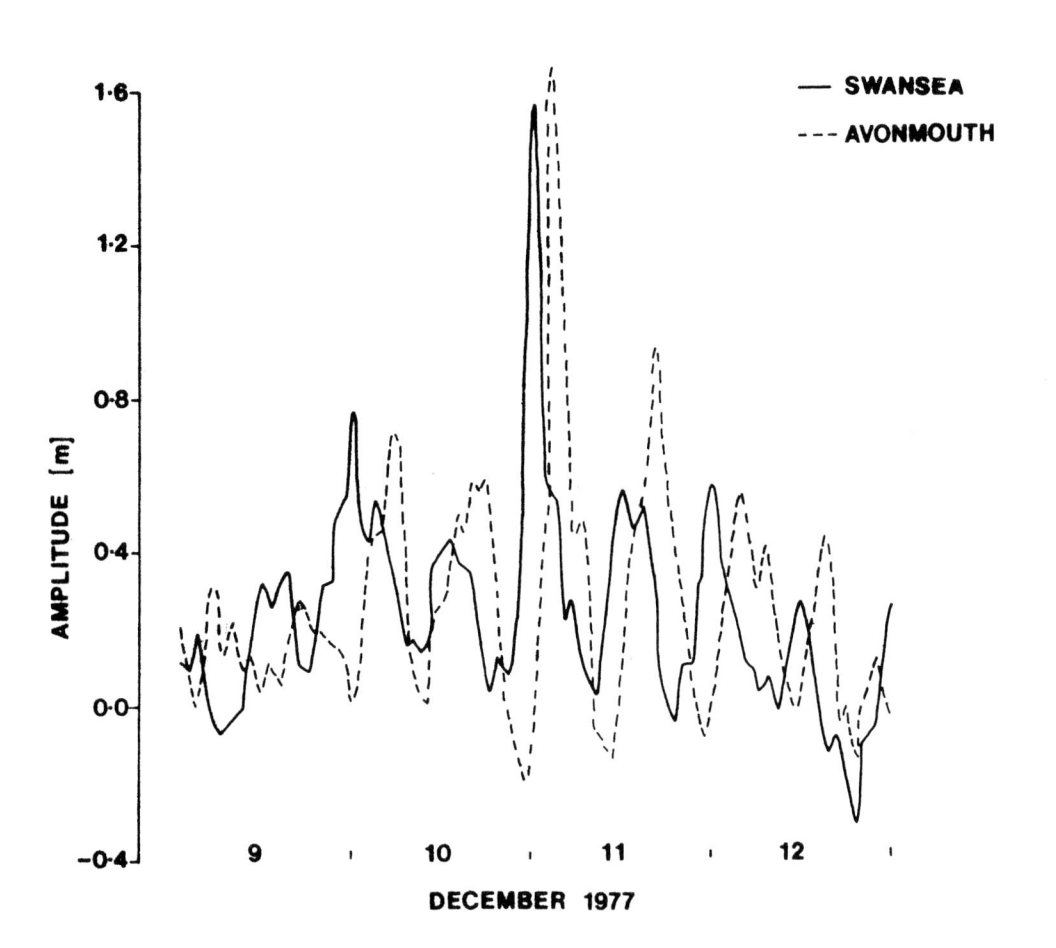

Figure 9.4. Comparison of surges at Swansea and Avonmouth.

and two hours at low water. Some of the variation in the time lags may therefore be caused by these different rates of progression at different states of the tide. It was found that the surge which took longest to progress from Swansea to Avonmouth occurred closer to low water than any of the others; for example, the surge on 10th

TABLE 9.5. Comparison of Surges at Swansea and Avonmouth.

Date	AVONMOUTH Height(m)	Time(GMT)	SWANSEA Height(m)	Time(GMT)	Av/Sw	TAv-TSw (hours)
02/01/76	1.30*	19.30*	0.79	21.00		
25/01/77	1.60	19.00	0.92	18.00	1.7	+1
11/11/77	1.10	21.00	0.91	22.00	1.2	-1
10/12/77	1.66	02.00**	1.58	23.00	1.1	+3
24/12/77	2.40	03.00	1.54	01.00	1.6	+2
10/01/78	0.75	04.00	0.88	23.00	0.9	+5

*At Avonmouth on 02/01/76 the gauge stopped working during the occurrence of the surge and the reading given is the last one obtained.
** This value occurred on 11/12/77.

December 1977 occurred 1 hour 20 minutes before low water and took 3 hr to progress to Avonmouth, whereas the surge on 25th January 1977 occurred 2 hr 15 min after low water and took only one hour to progress to Avonmouth. On 11th November, however, the surge maxima occurred at Avonmouth first. The local meteorological conditions associated with this surge show that the surge peak at Swansea occurred three hours after both the minimum barometric pressure and the maximum wind speed. At Avonmouth however, the surge peak and the maximum wind speed occurred simultaneously. This characteristic indicates that the meteorological conditions controlling the surge did initially occur at Swansea and then progress to Avonmouth; however, why there should be such a time lag between the meteorological conditions and the surge maximum is not clearly understood. Perhaps, as the surge at Avonmouth was of such a long duration, the time of the peak should have been taken for its central value (i.e., 2 hr later) rather than its maximum. If this value is adopted the surge at Avonmouth would lag behind the meteorological conditions and would occur one hour after the surge at Swansea; the lag of one hour being in agreement with its occurrence near to high water.

The amplitude ratios (Table 9.5) also show a wide variation and range from 0.9 to 1.7. Only the surge of January 1978 has a ratio which is less than unity; but the surge of 10th December 1977 has a ratio very close to unity indicating that the surge was of comparable magnitude at the two ports. Both these surges had different appearances from the others (Fig. 9.2), the January 1978 surge showing very marked semi-diurnal oscillations and the December 1977 surge being a very sudden phenomenon. All the amplitude ratios, except January 1978, show an amplification of the surge between Swansea and Avonmouth. This increase in magnitude of the surge up the channel has also been noted by Heaps (1967) in describing the amplification of surge between Milford Haven and Avonmouth. The average values for the four amplitude ratios (excluding January 1978) is 1.4; it is interesting to note that this is equivalent to the spring tidal range amplification between Swansea and Avonmouth. Lennon (1963a) found that the surge magnitudes at Avonmouth and Milford Haven were of the order of 2:1. This value is also equivalent to the corresponding spring tidal range amplification between the latter ports and, possibly, indicates the great similarity between tides and surges in the Bristol Channel. The reason for the lack of amplificiation of the January 1978 surge is unclear but may be associated with the marked semi-diurnal oscillations. The negative surge which occurred after the positive does however show an amplification, having a magnitude of -1.80m at Avonmouth and -1.25m at Swansea.

Only a limited number of surges have been compared; consequently, it is not possible to formulate any definitive criteria for the variation of surges between Swansea and Avonmouth. In general, however, it appears that the surge occurs initially at Swansea and as it progresses up the Channel to Avonmouth at approximately the same speed as the tide, so it is amplified; this occurs in the same ratio as the tidal range.

EXTREME LEVELS

The occurrence of storm surges does not necessarily mean that flooding will occur. For flooding to occur it is generally necessary for a storm surge to occur at or near the time of tidal high water and also during spring tides. Therefore levels in excess of extreme levels (e.g., H.A.T.) depend upon both tide and surge.

Lennon (1963b) investigated the frequency of occurrence of abnormally high tidal levels at certain west coast ports. For Swansea the analysis was based on 20.5 years of tide pole data and using six different statistical techniques Lennon calculated the probability of occurrence of extreme levels. The results for Swansea for the probable maximum level to be attained once in 100 years and once in 200 years are presented in Table 9.6.

TABLE 9.6.   100 and 200 Year Maximum Levels for Swansea.

Statistical Technique	Once in 100 year level(m)	Once in 200 year level(m)
Linear logarithmic function	10.92	10.98
Gumbel's Solution	10.86	10.95
Normal frequency distribution	10.61	10.64
Barricelli's Solution	10.64	10.67
Jenkinson's Solution	10.61	10.64
Normal frequency distribution including skewness and kurtosis	10.67	10.70

Note: All heights relative to Chart Datum (i.e., -5.0m O.D.)

These values can be seen to range from 10.61 to 10.92m (above C.D.) for the 100 year maximum and from 10.64 to 10.98m (above C.D.) for the 200 year maximum. The maximum level reached during the period of the present investigation (January 1976 to December 1977) was 10.58m (i.e., 0.08m above H.A.T.). The probability of occurrence of this level was calculated using the 6 techniques suggested by Lennon and the results are presented in Table 9.7.

TABLE 9.7.   Statistical Analysis of the Extreme Level of 11th November 1977.

Statistical Technique	Frequency of Occurrence
Linear logarithmic function	Once in 7 years
Gumbel's Solution	Once in 13 years
Normal frequency distribution	Once in 50 years
Barricelli's Solution	50 year maximum
Jenkinson's Solution	50 year maximum
Normal frequency distribution including skewness and kurtosis	40 year maximum

Depending on the method used, the probabilities vary from once in 7 years to once in 50 years. Lennon (1963b) indicated that probably the most reliable method for Swansea is the Normal Frequency distribution and this technique gave a value of once in 50 years. However, when considering such results it must be remembered that they are based on the analysis of data which excludes not only the 1976 and 1977 surges but all the recent observations since the analyses were published.

It appears therefore, that this level of +10.58m, which caused extensive flooding of the Neath Estuary, is a fairly infrequent occurrence.

CONCLUDING REMARKS

Six storm surges were observed at Swansea during the period of investigation; they ranged in amplitude from 0.79 to 1.58m and in duration from 1.5 to 9.5 hours. The five surges in 1976 and 1977 were all similar in appearance, with a major peak and associated peaks (on either side). The surge of January 1978 had a very different appearance showing very marked semi-diurnal oscillations and comprising of both a positive and a negative surge. The semi-diurnal oscillations in the residuals are not reflected in either the barometric pressure or the wind speed records but do appear in the residual elevations at Avonmouth and so probably represent the free oscillations of the Bristol Channel-Celtic Sea System (see also Chapter 8).

The effect of static barometric pressure on the storm surges was found to vary considerably between surges. For two surges, it was extremely important accounting for some 70% of the total predictable variance; for the other surges, it was of much less importance accounting for approximately 30%. Again, the January 1978 surge showed marked differences, probably due to the presence of the negative surge just after the positive surge.

The synoptic meteorological conditions associated with the storm surges at Swansea were found to be very similar to those described by Lennon (1963a) for surges on the west coast. It was found that the four Lennon parameters accounted for some 98% of the variation in surge amplitude; in comparison the local meteorological variables selected were found to account for only 90% of the total variation. These analyses tend to infer that the large-scale (synoptic) meteorological conditions are more important in determining surge amplitude; such forces act upon the surge in its region of generation.

A comparison of surges at Swansea and Avonmouth has shown that surges in the Bristol Channel behave very much like the tidal wave and they appear to be governed more by the hydrodynamics of the Channel than by the meteorological conditions. Hence it would appear that the surge height is determined within its region of generation (where it is affected by the synoptic meteorological conditions) rather than in the Channel (where it is affected by the local meteorological conditions).

The nature of the surge propagation up the Channel has demonstrated the importance of dynamic effects on surge generation and propagation; consequently, statistical analyses are of only limited value in surge forecasting in this region and that it may be that a numerical model similar to those developed for the North Sea and Thames Estuary (Banks, 1974) is required.

The investigation of extreme levels has shown that flooding of low-lying areas occurs when surges occur near to the time of high water on a spring tide. During the period of investigation the highest level reached was 10.58m above Chart Datum, which although only 0.08m above the H.A.T. caused extensive flooding along the Neath Estuary. However predictions indicate that this is a fairly infrequent level and likely to occur only once in 50 years.

REFERENCES

Banks, J.E. (1974). A numerical model of a river - shallow sea system used to investigate tide, surge and their interaction in the Thames - Southern North Sea region. *Phil. Trans. R. Soc. Ser. A.*, 275, 567-609.

George, K.J., and Thomas, D.K. (1978). The 'Morning Cloud' storm surge in the English Channel. *Weather, Lond., 33,* 227-235.

Graff, J. (1977). The one in a hundred year tide. *Dock Harb. Auth., 57,* 201 and 204.

Graff, J. (1978). Abnormal sea levels in the north west. *Dock Harb. Auth., 58,* 366-368 and 371.

Heaps, N.S. (1967). Storm surges. *Oceanogr. and Mar. Biol., 5,* 11-47.

Lennon, G.W. (1963a). The identification of weather conditions associated with the generation of major storm surges along the west coast of the British Isles. *Q. Jl. R. met. Soc., 89,* 381-394.

Lennon, G.W. (1963b). A frequency investigation of abnormally high tidal levels at certain west coast ports. *Proc. Instn. civ. Engrs., 25,* 451-483.

Lennon, G.W. (1965). Storm surges on the west coast of the British Isles in January, November and December 1965. I.C.O.T. Internal Report No. 29, 9pp (Unpub. manuscript).

Milne, P.H. (1971). Storm surge research on Scottish west coast. *Dock Harb. Auth., 52,* 150-152.

Milne, P.H. (1975). Tide level predictions are essential for platform float-outs. *Offshore Serv., 8,* 61-66.

Redfield, A.C., and Miller, A.E. (1957). Water levels accompanying Atlantic coast hurricanes. *Met. Monogr., 2(10),* 1-23.

10. LONG WAVES AND HARBOUR SEICHES AT PORT TALBOT

W. H. Jackson

British Transport Docks Board, Research Station, Hayes Rd, Southall, Middlesex, U.K.

ABSTRACT

Long period surges occur, on occasions, at Port Talbot Harbour; at such times a large ore-carrier moored at the jetty ranges from the jetty with periods of oscillation (usually) between 160 and 240s. This can lead to ropes parting with subsequent danger to the ship. The seiches can be clearly seen on the tide recorder charts and these are not solely a function of the natural period of resonance of the harbour, because they are found to occur elsewhere in the estuary at the same time. A limited amount of detailed data is available which has not yet been fully analysed.

The purpose of this paper is to look at the phenomenon from a practical engineering and navigational standpoint, and hope that it will encourage further, more detailed and thorough, studies by other researchers.

KEYWORDS

Surging; Seiching; Ranging; Port Talbot Harbour; Swansea Bay; Bristol Channel

PORT TALBOT HARBOUR

The present harbour at Port Talbot was built in the late 1960's and was officially opened by the Queen on the 12th May 1970. The berths are protected by two breakwaters, the main one is approximately 1.6km long and the shorter lee breakwater is approximately 1.1km long. The harbour was built to accommodate fully loaded ore-carriers of 100,000 tonnes and larger vessels, part-laden, which supply iron ore for the nearby steel works. The design of the harbour is such that it could be dredged deeper at a later date to allow larger fully-laden ships to be accommodated if required. The present entrance channel depth is 8.6m below Admiralty Chart Datum (L.A.T.). For details of the planning and design of the harbour readers are referred to McGarey and Fraenkel (1970).

A glance at a map shows that there is no land to protect Port Talbot from the large waves generated in the Atlantic Ocean and there is a maximum fetch from the southwest of over 6000km (4,000 miles). Ordinary storm waves, with periods up to 20s and wave heights of up to 6m, are not uncommon and it has been predicted that even larger

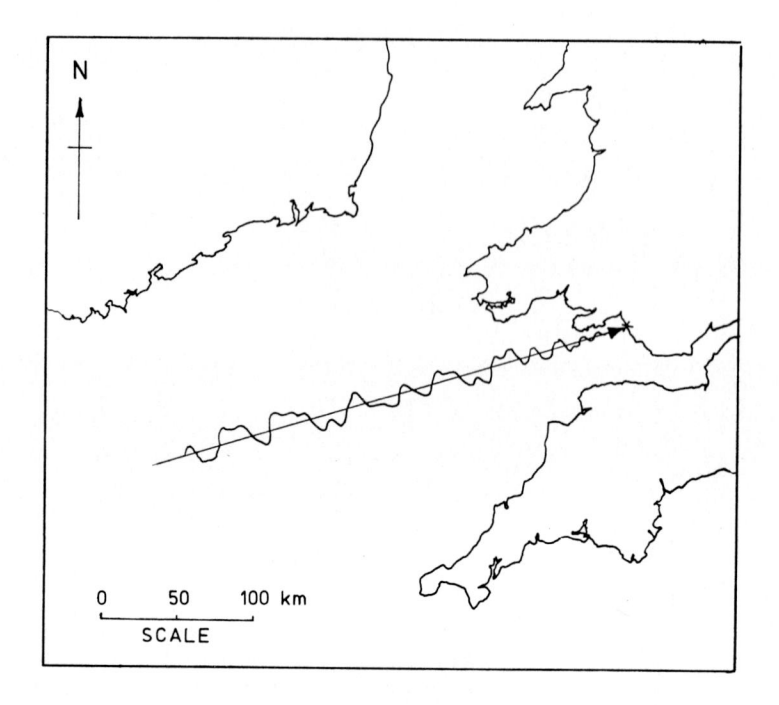

Figure 10.1.   Port Talbot Harbour - location.

waves could occur in the approaches to Port Talbot under exceptionally heavy storm conditions (see also Chapter 14; compare with Chapter 12).

A detailed study was made at the B.T.D.B. Research Station, on a 1:180 scale model, to find the effectiveness of the breakwaters in storm waves of up to 18s period (BTDB, 1968) but no hydraulic model tests were made with the final design to predict the effect of long period waves on ships moored at the jetty. The problem was, however, very much in mind at the design stage and when the concept of the new harbour was first envisaged, the Hydraulics Research Station (Wallingford) made a detailed analysis of the available tide gauge records supplied to them by the British Transport Docks Board (HRS, 1963).   This report concluded that long period waves existed in the estuary near to Port Talbot and produced a relationship between vertical and horizontal movement for long period waves.   With a natural period of 3min it was estimated that the horizontal particle movement is approximately 25 times the vertical movement.   Thus, with long period waves, the effect on moored ships is very much greater than would be expected from consideration of vertical amplitude alone.

An analysis of tidal data from the Severan Estuary has been carried out recently (Wilding, 1979; see also Chapters 8 and 9) and showed that long period surges of widely varying periods could occur.   The period of a "seiche" within Swansea Bay has been found to be 30-50min (Chapter 8) but waves of this period are no danger to moored ships; in contrast, it is waves of periods between 30s and 2min which are the most troublesome.

Long period waves can be generated, in general, by earthquakes and moving pressure fronts; however, the most likely cause of such waves of up to 2 or 3min is wave grouping, which is an irregular sea phenomena.   Individual waves travelling at different velocities, dependent upon their wave length, get into and out of phase with a frequency which can cause the ranging of ships.

FIRST SERIOUS OCCURRENCE OF SHIP RANGING

The harbour become operational in 1970, but it was not until 7th September 1974 that the first serious case of ship ranging was reported. This does not mean that there were no long period surges between 1970 and this date but that any surges that occurred were either not of sufficient magnitude to cause serious concern for the safety of large ships berthed at the jetty, or occurred when there was no large ship in

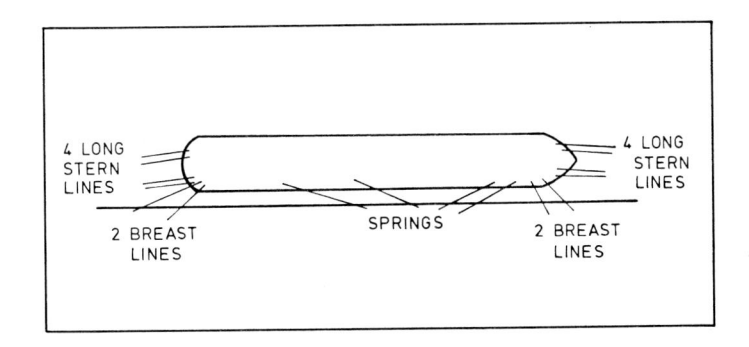

Figure 10.2. Port Talbot - Diagram of method of mooring

the harbour. Some ship movement had, in fact, been reported on 17th December 1972 and on 8th January 1974. On the 7th September 1974, however, the ranging was indeed both disturbing and dangerous.

The large ships at Port Talbot are normally moored using four long headlines, four long sternlines, two breastlines from the forecastle, two breastlines from the poop, two springs from the forward maindeck and two springs from the maindeck aft making a total of sixteen ropes (See Fig. 10.2). On the day in question, there was a heavy storm with gale strength winds and a rapidly rising barometer. The weather forecast was that the gale winds would continue for some hours. The harbour master and ships captain checked the mooring ropes and these were considered to be adequate.

By 12 noon on that day, the ship was ranging up to 2m off the jetty and one of the breastlines had parted. Further lines were put ashore, but despite this, severe ranging continued and there was grave concern that the ship might break loose from its moorings. At times the ship was as much as 6m from the berth. During the ten hours when the ranging occurred, 6 x 25cm (10 inch) circumference nylon ropes and 3 x 10cm (4 inch) wire ropes had parted. Some idea of the forces involved can be appreciated if one considers that a 25cm nylon rope has a breaking load of 108 tonnes.

Such extreme surge conditions are fortunately not a common occurrence, but happen sufficiently frequently to justify some research into the problem. There have been a few occasions since 1974 when special precautions have had to be taken.

TIDE GAUGE RECORDS

If the cause of the ship movements during 7th September 1974 was in any doubt, a glance at the tide gauge record dispelled these (Fig. 10.3).

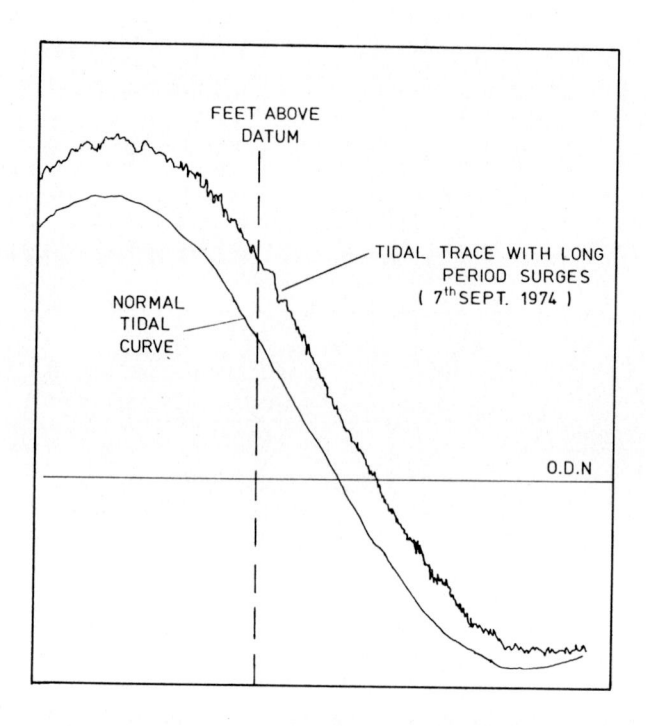

Figure 10.3. Port Talbot - tide curves.

Although a tide gauge leaves much to be desired as a "seiche-type" wave recorder, it nevertheless shows unmistakably the presence of waves of several minutes period on that particular day.

One question which came to mind at the time was whether the surges were created within the harbour or whether they were generated outside of it. To ascertain this, it was necessary to see whether similar surges were occurring elsewhere at the same time. An examination of the tide recorder chart for Swansea showed similar long period surges; similarly, at Milford Haven the disturbance was sufficiently pronounced to necessitate the use of tugs to hold some of the large vessels at their quays. It was clear, therefore, that surges were not generated within the harbour but came from some distance away.

OTHER OCCURRENCES OF RANGING

Ranging has occurred on several occasions since the serious conditions on 7th September 1974. A summary of what happened on these occasions is given in Table 10.1. As can be seen from the Table, ranging problems have been recorded on ten occasions since 1972. This frequency of occurrence is sufficient to justify a more detailed study, bearing in mind the damage that could occur if a large ship got out of control.

USE OF IDASAT TO MEASURE SHIPS RANGING

To assist in the safe berthing of ships at Port Talbot an IDASAT (Integrated System for Safer Berthing) has been installed (Cooper and Tomlinson, 1979). Basically,

TABLE 10.1. Occurrences of Ranging Since 1972.

Date	Ship	Remarks
17th December, 1972	Chelsea	Vessel ranging - tension winches not holding.
07th September, 1974	Aegean Wave	Severe ranging - many ropes and wires parted.
27th December, 1974	Gene Trefethen	Tug used to keep ship alongside jetty.
12th January, 1975	Motilal Nehru	Extra mooring had to be put out.
27th September, 1975	Vimeira	Ranging - extra moorings required.
12th March, 1976	Gene Trefethen	Severe swell effects - extra moorings and tugs on standby.
02nd February, 1978	Mount Eden	Some ranging problems.
08th December, 1978	Vassilios Bacolitsas	Moderate ranging - two wires parted.
12th December, 1978	Norvegia Team	Moderate ranging.
11th February, 1979	Oslo	Ships ranged 3-5 metres off fenders.

it is an echo sounder with the transducers fixed to the outer face of the jetty and pointing in a horizontal direction. When a ship approaches the berth the pulse is reflected from the ships hull and as with a conventional echo sounder the time between the transmitted and reflected signal measured. From this the distance of the ship from the jetty is found and from consecutive distances the velocity of approach is obtained. The velocities of both the bow and the stern of the ship are found in this way and displayed in the form of large coloured lights on the jetty. The data is also recorded on tape for subsequent detailed analysis.

During the time when the ship 'Gene Trefelthen' was ranging (see Table 10.1), this equipment was switched on so that a complete record of its movements was obtained. A typical pattern of movement of the vessel is given in Fig. 10.4.

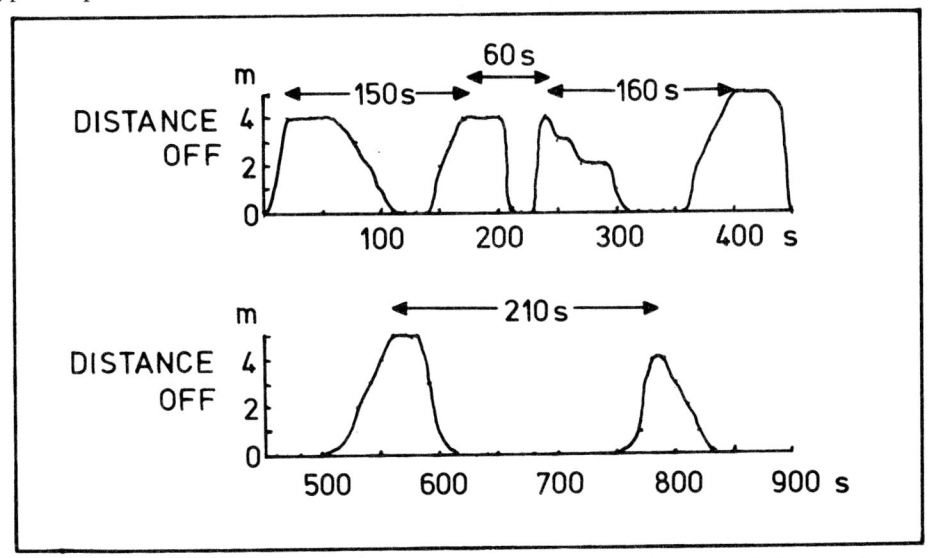

Figure 10.4. Port Talbot - ranging of ship from IDASAT record

Although mooring and other conditions change during the time of the records, a ranging of approximately 180s period occurs frequently and, on occasions a superimposed period of one half of this is observed. Further, such data will be collected in the future which will enable a more detailed analysis to be made.

POSSIBLE DAMAGE TO FENDERS

Another cause of concern was whether a ranging ship might strike the fenders with speeds causing impact forces in excess of the design loading. An impact velocity of 8cm/s occurs frequently, but this is well within the design criterion for the fendering for a ship of 100,000 tonnes. This factor would have to be seriously considered if larger ships are to be berthed at the jetty in the future. The results showed that the impact velocity during surging is about the same as the maximum impact velocity during berthing and, hence, not likely to cause damage to the fendering.

METHODS OF DEALING WITH THE PROBLEM

There does not seem to be any simple answer to the problem. A large reflecting wall outside the harbour which would reflect the waves back has been suggested, but the cost of building such a wall is high. If of adequate size and correctly placed, it could be effective for a specific wavelength where the reflected wave is out of phase with the wave at the harbour entrance; hence it would cause a reduction in the magnitude of the surge in the harbour. This would only work satisfactorily for one wavelength and could worsen the position for other wavelengths.

It has also been suggested that surges could be reduced by the use of a series of 'basins', tuned to special frequencies and located at the entrance to the harbour. Such a system has been used in several harbours to reduce storm waves but it is doubtful whether such a system would be economic or feasible with waves of long wave length and several minutes period, in more than a very limited number of harbour developments.

Until some elegant solution is found, it is necessary to accept the forces caused by ships trying to move and provide adequate mooring. In the case of Port Talbot, one storm bollard was provided when the harbour was built and a second such bollard is now being considered.

MOORING OF SHIPS

In practice, ships are usually moored to the jetty using a mixture of ropes of various materials (steel, sisal, manilla, nylon, polypropylene, etc.), all of which have widely different elasticities. The range of stiffness in a rope system is very great and the mixing of ropes of widely varying stiffness in mooring of ships is a major cause of ropes parting.

When the force on a ship changes, the least stiff ropes stretch easily and experience little increase in load whilst the stiffest ropes sustain almost all the extra load. Under conditions of increasing load, one would therefore expect the stiffest ropes to part first, which in fact happens. In the ideal situation, all the ropes should stretch equally for a given increase in force. This is a function of the length as well as the stiffness of the rope.

The ideal situation is to have a load measuring device connected, so that the actual load in each rope is displayed and the tension continually equalized. Systems are available for measuring and displaying such loads.

PREVIOUS WORK

Long period surges in harbours are no new phenomena and a detailed analysis and study of these phenomena at Table Bay Harbour, South Africa, was carried out by Wilson (1951, 1967). Wave heights, diagrams of instantaneous water levels, modes of oscillation, ship movement and a number of other factors were studied in detail by this investigator. There are many similarities between the situation at Table Bay, Capetown, and those at Port Talbot Harbour but there are a number of differences. Similar problems have arisen more recently at the Port of Acajutla, El Salvador (HRS, 1976). Although the same detailed analysis has not been carried out for Port Talbot Harbour, because there is not presently adequate data to do so, it is thought to be of interest to report the present state of the study which may encourage others to give thought to this phenomena.

FUTURE RESEARCH

More use will be made in the future of the berthing aid for recording ship's movements during times of surging.

The Hydraulics Research Station (Wallingford) are interested in this phenomena and are testing out long period wave recorders; information from these, when used with the records of ship's movement provided by the British Transport Docks Board, should enable a better understanding of this phenomenon to be obtained. Difficulties are being experienced in obtaining a satisfactory long period wave recorder to work in a high tidal range area.

Another aspect which is being studied is whether, by an analysis of wave and tide gauges records and other data, a prior warning of coming seiches can be forecast sufficiently in advance to enable extra precautions to be taken.

CONCLUSIONS

Long period "seiches" occur in the Severn Estuary (Bristol Channel) which cause severe ranging of ships at the berth in Port Talbot Harbour. Up to now, no satisfactory way of reducing the magnitude of such "seiches" has been found and it is considered that the way to deal with the problem is to provide adequate mooring facilities.

This chapter is not intended to be a detailed mathematical study of the phenomena such as that of Wilson (1951, 1967) in the case of Table Bay Harbour (Capetown) and others, but draws attention to the effects that have been observed at Port Talbot. It is hoped, that the paper will encourage researchers to look further into the theory and origin of surges of 4 or 5min duration, in Swansea Bay, and to consider practical solutions to problems associated with them.

ACKNOWLEDGEMENTS

The study into the ranging of ships at Port Talbot is a joint exercise between the staff of the Dock Master, Swansea and Port Talbot and the British Transport Docks Board Research Station. The author wishes to thank the Dock Manager for permission to publish the information. Details of the ranging of the ships and the remedial action taken was supplied by the Dock and Harbour Master.

REFERENCES

British Transport Docks Board. (1968). *Port Talbot Harbour Model Investigation.* Research Report No. R.209, 26pp.

Cooper, D.H., and Tomlinson, P. (1979). Berthing data. *Dock and Harbour Authority, LX (704)*, 75-76.

Hydraulics Research Station, (1963). *Port Talbot Harbour Investigation: Part II - Long Waves*, Report No. 203, 25pp.

Hydraulics Research Station, (1976). *Port of Acajutla, El Salvador*, Report Ex 739, Vol. I: Text and Tables, 43pp.

McGarey, D.G., and Fraenkel, P.M. (1970). Port Talbot Harbour: Planning and Design. *Proc. Instn. civ. Eng., 45*, 561-592.

Wilding, A.J. (1979). *Numerical studies of Tides, Free Oscillations and Surges in Swansea Bay.* Ph.D. Thesis, University of Wales, 184pp (Unpub.).

Wilson, B.W. (1951). Ship response to range action in harbour basins. *Trans. Am. Soc. civ. Eng., 116*, 1129-1157.

Wilson, B.W. (1967). The threshold of surge damage for moored ships. *Proc. Instn. civ. Eng., 38*, 107-134.

11. TIDAL CURRENTS AND RESIDUAL CIRCULATION IN THE SWANSEA BAY AREA OF THE BRISTOL CHANNEL

A. D. Heathershaw and F. D. C. Hammond

Institute of Oceanographic Sciences, Crossway, Taunton, Somerset, U.K.

ABSTRACT

Observed currents have been used to determine the tidal and tidally induced residual circulation in Swansea Bay. The M_2 and S_2 tidal dynamics of the area are consistent with a standing wave tidal oscillation in the Bristol Channel and it is shown that non-linear effects in the equations of motion lead to the generation of strong M_4 tidal currents in regions where the flow is accelerating or decelerating. The M_4/M_2 tidal current amplitude ratio increases moving into shallow water reaching a maximum of about 0.15, which is an order of magnitude larger than the same ratio in the elevations. Over the Neap-Spring cycle there is nearly an order of magnitude variation in tidal mixing and energy dissipation in the area as a whole.

Salinity and temperature data have shown that in the north of the Bay density currents resulting from the freshwater discharges from the rivers may be of order 1-2 cm/s and are thus comparable with the tidal residuals. These currents result in a flow which is predominantly towards the coast near the sea-bed and along the coast towards the west at the surface.

The tidal elevations and residual circulation have been found to be sensitive to meteorological forcing. In particular, during the November 1977 storm surge, strong southwest and northwest winds leading to a wind induced set-up and set-down were found to modify the residual circulation appreciably.

KEYWORDS

Tidal dynamics; Tidal currents; Residual currents; Density currents; Meteorological forcing; Surges; Swansea Bay; Bristol Channel.

INTRODUCTION

The tidal dynamics of any area will ultimately determine the movement of sediment on or near the sea bed and the fate of pollutants or any other passive contaminants in the water column.

A full understanding of these processes can only be gained from a detailed study of the relevant physical processes. Numerical models of tidal and residual currents still fall far short of being able to reproduce faithfully those processes which occur in nature and there thus remains a good deal which can be done by observation. This is particularly true of tidal processes in coastal waters where the horizontal non-uniformity of the flows and the effects of bottom friction generate higher harmonics through the non-linear terms in the equations of motion.

Swansea Bay therefore provides an excellent opportunity to study these non-linear effects and in particular to examine their implications for sediment movement and pollution control.

The object of this paper, therefore, is to describe the tidal and residual current circulation patterns in Swansea Bay; however, a complete description of the current system in the area should include a consideration of wind driven currents, surge currents and density currents. The effects of meteorological forcing and salinity and temperature distributions on the water circulation are therefore considered.

TIDAL DYNAMICS

The tidal dynamics of Swansea Bay are essentially those of the Bristol Channel with flow patterns and magnitudes being influenced by bathymetry and coastline geometry. It is beyond the scope of this chapter to review in full the physical oceanography of the Bristol Channel and reference should therefore be made to the review articles by Cooper (1967), Pugh et al. (1971/72) and N.E.R.C. (1972). More detailed accounts of recent work are given in Heaps (1968), Abdullah et al. (1973), Hamilton (1973), Bennett (1975) and Robinson (1978). Further details may also be found in Heathershaw and Hammond (1979a).

Tidal oscillations in the Channel are usually considered (e.g., Defant, 1961; Proudman, 1953) to be co-oscillations of the tides in the Celtic and Irish Seas. Thus, in the Channel, the tidal oscillations may be considered as standing wave solutions to the equations of motion leading to the times of High Water in the area being synchronous. However, co-tidal and co-range data (see Fig. 8.1) show that in general this is not the case, except for an area on the north side of the Channel in the vicinity of Swansea and Carmarthen Bays. In fact on the south shore of the Channel, between Hartland Point and Portishead there is a progression in the times of HW with HW at Portishead lagging that at Hartland Point by about 90 minutes (Fig. 11.1). Therefore, tidal oscillations in the Bristol Channel may be viewed as a mixture of standing and progressive wave components (see also Chapter 8). Since the phase relationship between surface elevations and currents in each of these cases is different it is important that we have a correct understanding of the tidal physics.

The earliest theoretical treatment of the tides in the Bristol Channel was carried out by G.I. Taylor in 1920. Noting that the breadth (b) and depth (h) of the channel varied linearly with distance (x) along its axis (see Fig. 11.1), Taylor obtained a solution of the linearized equations of continuity and motion:

$$\frac{\partial (bh\hat{U})}{\partial x} = -b\frac{\partial \zeta}{\partial t} \qquad (1)$$

$$\frac{\partial \hat{U}}{\partial t} = -g\frac{\partial \zeta}{\partial x} \qquad (2)$$

where $\hat{U}$ is the cross sectionally averaged flow at the particular harmonic which is being modelled, and

$$b = \frac{b_o x}{x_o}$$

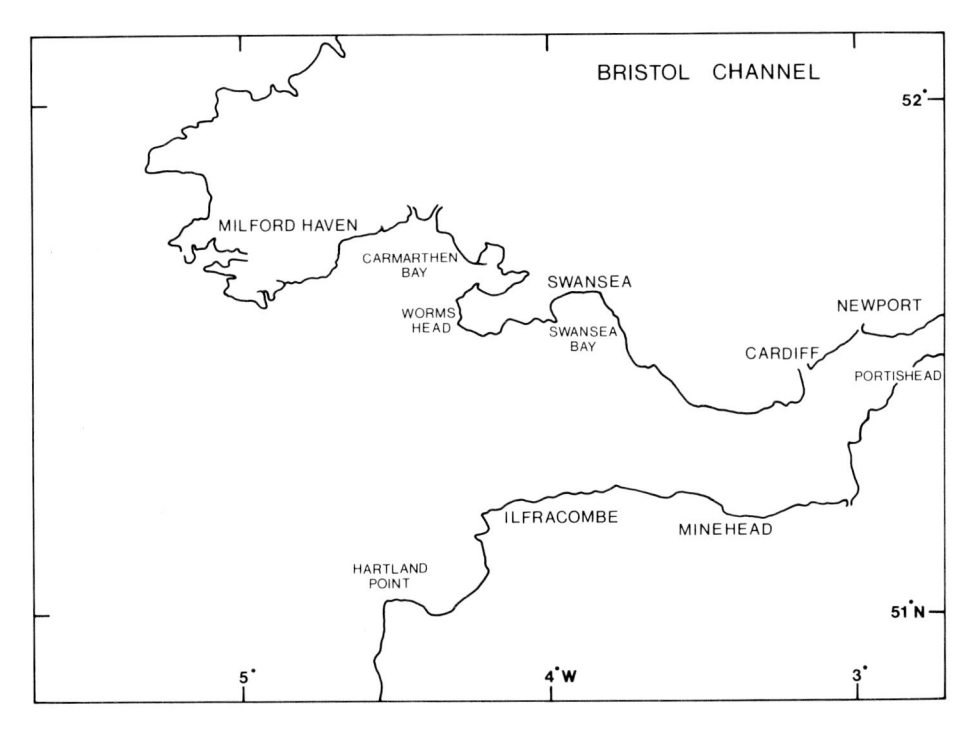

Figure 11.1. The Bristol Channel and locations referred to in the text.

$$h = \frac{h_o}{x_o} x \qquad (3)$$

Here ζ is the height of the sea surface above its undisturbed level, g is the acceleration due to gravity and b_o and h_o are the breadth and depth at a distance x_o from the head of the Channel. Thus, friction was neglected as were the non-linear terms in the equations of motion and continuity (see Equations (1) and (2)). Additionally, Coriolis forces were not considered in (2). By a rearrangement of terms, Taylor obtained a solution for (2) of the form:

$$\zeta = KJ_1\{2(kx)^{\frac{1}{2}}\}/(kx)^{\frac{1}{2}} \qquad (4)$$

where K is a constant, J_1 represents a Bessel function of the first order and the wavenumber k is given by:

$$k = \sigma^2 x_o / h_o g \qquad (5)$$

σ being the tidal frequency.

It is important to note that the solution (2) obtained by Taylor represents a standing wave with no net flow of energy into or out of the estuary and with the phase everywhere the same. However, while Taylor's work gave good agreement between predicted and observed amplitudes along the Channel it left unexplained the observed progression in the times of HW (see Fig. 8.1).

As we have already seen, the immediate effect of neglecting friction is to make the times of HW everywhere the same. Grace (1936) using observed amplitude and phase relationships, estimated the effects of friction in terms of a friction coefficient. However Heaps (1968), in an analytical study of the tides in the Channel appears to have been the first to include friction in the equations of motion and to compare both amplitude and phase with tidal observations along the coasts. By numerically integrating the equations of continuity and motion, Heaps obtained good agreement between the predicted and observed harmonic constants for the M_2 tidal elevations. Therefore, friction should be considered as important in modifying the phase of the tide in the Channel. In many respects Heaps' (1968) results confirm an earlier finding of Hunt (1964), from a study of tidal oscillations in the Thames Estuary, that the effect of friction on the tidal oscillations in a wedge shaped estuary is to introduce a progression in the times of HW along the estuary while maintaining the phase difference between currents and elevations as that of a standing wave. Hunt used the linearised equations of continuity and motion, (1) and (2) with the addition of a frictional term. Thus (2) becomes:

$$\frac{\partial \hat{U}}{\partial t} = -g\frac{\partial \zeta}{\partial x} - C\hat{U} \qquad (6)$$

where C is a linear friction coefficient given by:

$$C = \frac{8}{3\pi} \cdot \frac{C_D}{h}|\hat{U}_0|, \quad \hat{U} = \hat{U}_0(x)e^{i\sigma t} \qquad (7)$$

and C_D is a quadratic friction coefficient of order 0.002 - 0.003. In this case the usual quadratic friction term $C_D\hat{U}|\hat{U}|/h$ has been linearized. Hunt (1964) examined the solutions of (1) and (6) for various estuary configurations and obtained solutions for the elevation (ζ) and the current ($\hat{U}$) which are important in as much that they indicate a motion which resembles a standing wave with amplitude and phase varying slowly along the estuary and show clearly that there is a $\pi/2$ phase difference between the elevations and currents.

In contrast to this approach, Bennett (1975) has more recently used a non-standing wave solution to examine tides in the Bristol Channel. Whereas the classical standing wave solutions are energy conserving with no energy dissipation, a non-standing wave solution permits an energy flux to be transmitted into the estuary. Thus by taking a solution to the linearized and frictionless equations of motion (1) and (3) of the form:

$$\begin{aligned}\zeta = & \{A_1 J_1[2(kx)^{\frac{1}{2}}]/(kx)^{\frac{1}{2}} + A_2 Y_1[2(kx)^{\frac{1}{2}}]/(kx)^{\frac{1}{2}}\}\cos\sigma t \\ + & \{A_3 J_1[2(kx)^{\frac{1}{2}}]/(kx)^{\frac{1}{2}} + A_4 Y_1[2(kx)^{\frac{1}{2}}]/(kx)^{\frac{1}{2}}\}\sin\sigma t \end{aligned} \qquad (8)$$

where J_1 and Y_1 are Bessel functions of the first and second kinds of order 1 and by matching the solution for ζ at two places, Bennett was able to obtain the coefficients A_1, A_2, A_3 and A_4. Good agreement was obtained with the observed amplitudes and phases of the elevations between the calibration sections at Minehead and Wormshead. However, above Minehead and towards Newport the agreement was not so good. It is interesting to note however that Bennett's solution (8) represents a partly progressive and partly standing wave.

More recently, Robinson (1978) has reverted to the use of a linearized and frictionless analytical model to study the effects of a barrage on the tides in the Bristol Channel and found that while the predicted elevation of the tides gives reasonable agreement with observation there is a considerable disparity between observed and predicted currents. This model can of course only reproduce a standing wave oscillation and is thus unable to reproduce the observed progression in times of HW along the Channel.

In many respects, Robinson's work serves to highlight one of the major shortcomings of both analytical and numerical models; that is their poor predictive ability when the amplitudes of tidal streams and residual currents are considered. Here we are still heavily dependent upon observation.

Therefore, although the observed tides in the Channel (Fig. 8.1) exhibit both standing and progressive wave characteristics, theoretical considerations, particularly those of Hunt (1964), lead us to believe that in this area the tides are correctly described by standing wave oscillations with the inclusion of friction leading to the observed progression in the times of HW but at the same time maintaining the correct phase relationship between the elevation and currents.

TIDAL CURRENTS

Between October 1975 and November 1977, the Institute of Oceanographic Sciences carried out extensive current measurements at those positions indicated in Fig. 11.2. Near-bottom and mid-depth current measurements were made using Plessey MO21 and Aanderaa RCM4 recording current meters on conventional 'U' shaped moorings. Full details of the current meters, moorings and preliminary analysis of the data are described elsewhere (Heathershaw, 1977; Heathershaw and Hammond, 1979a). Current speed and direction values have been recorded at 10 min intervals and record lengths have been typically 30-40 days.

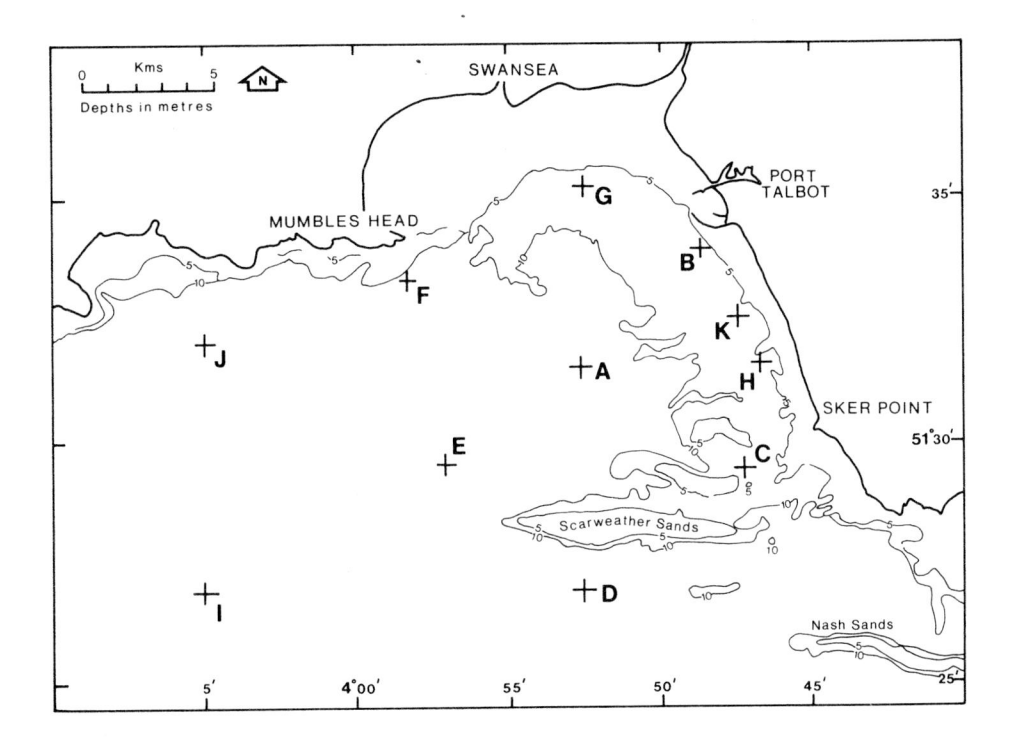

Figure 11.2. Location of current meter moorings in Swansea Bay.

Current meter data have been used to construct tidal ellipses for the constituents of interest, using a rotary analysis method (Gonella, 1972; Godin, 1972). The following description of the method is based upon that given by Maddock and Pingree (1978).

Current meter records, of an optimum 29 days' duration and corrected for timing errors, were first resolved into east-west (U) and north-south (V) components and then harmonically analysed using a standard least squares regression technique for 8 related and 27 given constituents, using the equilibrium tide for the related constituents (this assumes that currents behave in the same way as elevations - see Robinson, 1979, for discussion of this problem).

Any vector time series may be expressed in terms of two orthogonal components each of which can in turn be expressed as a Fourier series. Therefore, by resolving the measured currents into E and N flowing components U and V we may express the velocity components at a particular frequency, σ, as:

$$U_\sigma = a_u \cos\sigma t + b_u \sin\sigma t \qquad (8)$$

$$V_\sigma = a_v \cos\sigma t + b_v \sin\sigma t \qquad (9)$$

In complex notation the vector describing the ellipse for a constituent having frequency σ is given by:

$$\underline{U}_\sigma = U_\sigma + iV_\sigma \qquad (10)$$

It can be shown that by substituting (8) and (9) and (10) and expanding $\cos\sigma t$ as $(e^{i\sigma t} + e^{-i\sigma t})/2$ and $\sin\sigma t$ as $(e^{i\sigma t} - e^{-i\sigma t})/2i$ the complex quantity $\underline{U}_\sigma$ is given by:

$$\underline{U}_\sigma = \frac{1}{2}\left[(a_u+b_v)+i(a_v-b_u)\right]e^{i\sigma t} + \frac{1}{2}\left[(a_u-b_v)+i(a_v+b_u)\right]e^{-i\sigma t} \qquad (11)$$

which may be written as:

$$\underline{U}_\sigma = \underline{U}_+ e^{i\sigma t} + \underline{U}_- e^{-i\sigma t} \qquad (12)$$

Thus the vector describing the tidal ellipse for a constituent having a frequency σ is described by two contra-rotating vectors $\underline{U}_+$ and $\underline{U}_-$ having constant amplitudes and rotating anticlockwise and clockwise respectively with frequencies σ and $-\sigma$. The maximum value of the current for this particular constituent occurs when $\underline{U}_+$ and $\underline{U}_-$ lie in the same direction. The semi-major and semi-minor axes of the ellipse are given respectively by:

$$\begin{aligned} a &= |\underline{U}_+| + |\underline{U}_-| \\ b &= |\underline{U}_+| - |\underline{U}_-| \end{aligned} \qquad (13)$$

The phases of the anticlockwise and clockwise components are given respectively by:

$$\begin{aligned} \theta_+ &= \tan^{-1}\left(\frac{a_v - b_u}{a_u + b_v}\right) \\ \theta_- &= \tan^{-1}\left(\frac{a_v + b_u}{a_u - b_v}\right) \end{aligned} \qquad (14)$$

which gives the phase of constituent with frequency σ as:

$$g_\sigma = \frac{\theta_+ - \theta_-}{2} \qquad (15)$$

and the orientation of the major axis of the ellipse as:

$$\phi_\sigma = \frac{\theta_+ + \theta_-}{2} \qquad (16)$$

from the harmonic analysis of the U and V time series we obtain sets of amplitudes

H_u and H_v and phases g_u and g_v for the required tidal constituents. The results of this analysis for the principal tidal constituents at Station A are summarised in Table 11.1 and from this information it is possible to calculate the Fourier coefficients a_u, b_u, a_v and b_v and so construct the tidal ellipses.

TABLE 11.1. Amplitudes and Phases of Principal Tidal Constituents in the Currents at Station A (See Figure 11.2).

Height	Component		H(cm/s)			g(°)	
		μ	σ	$\sigma/N^{\frac{1}{2}}$	μ	σ	$\sigma/N^{\frac{1}{2}}$
M_2	U	47.97	2.40	1.07	89.47	2.07	.92
	V	2.61	1.97	.88	291.00	116.96	52.31
10m S_2	U	18.29	1.37	.61	143.09	4.00	1.79
(N=5)	V	2.02	2.53	1.13	251.65	188.34	84.23
M_4	U	3.45	.33	.15	322.29	14.60	6.53
	V	1.43	.90	.40	264.89	175.07	78.30
M_2	U	37.91	1.73	.55	85.56	5.14	1.63
	V	4.10	2.85	.90	186.48	39.65	12.54
2m S_2	U	11.21	3.00	.95	145.50	44.08	13.94
(N=10)	V	1.57	1.43	.45	262.43	58.33	18.45
M_4	U	3.46	.81	.26	328.31	9.41	2.98
	V	.83	.76	.24	246.69	159.90	50.57

Amplitudes and Phases of Same Constituents in the Tidal Elevations at Swansea

		H(m)	g(°)
M_2	ζ	3.1443	173.10
S_2	ζ	1.1308	220.80
M_4	ζ	.0549	29.40

H = amplitude; g = phase; μ = mean; σ = standard deviation; $\sigma/N^{\frac{1}{2}}$ = standard error; N = number of monthly analyses; ζ = tidal elevations in m; U = east-west component of tidal current in cm/s; V = north-south component of tidal current in cm/s. All phases are in degrees relative to the equilibrium tide at Greenwich. Values of H and g for other tidal constituents are given by Heathershaw and Hammond (1979a).

Records from Stations A-J have been routinely analysed in this manner and typical tidal ellipse characteristics from Station A are shown in Figure 11.3. This shows the semi- and quarter-diurnal constituents M_2, S_2, N_2 and K_2 and M_4 and MS_4 respectively, in a record of the current at 2m above the sea-bed at Station A. This diagram gives a good indication of the degree of rectilinearity of the currents with M_2 ellipticities, that is the ratio b/a expressed as a percentage, being of the order of 10%. It is interesting to note that ellipticity of the near bottom currents has been found to be larger than that at mid-depth and that the sense of rot-

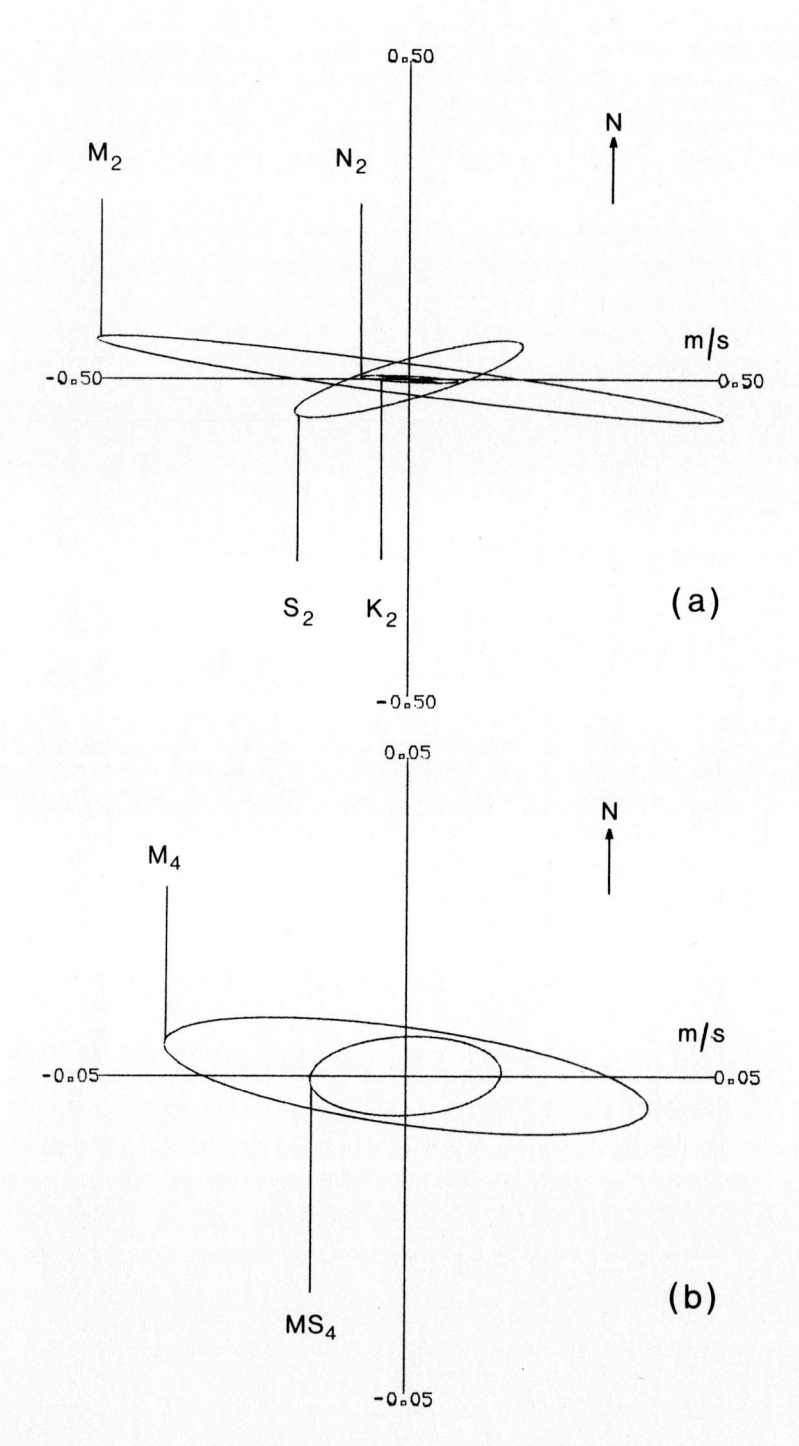

Figure 11.3. Typical tidal current ellipses showing the principal semi-diurnal (a) and quarter-diurnal (b) constituents in the mid-depth tidal currents at Station A in Swansea Bay.

ation of the currents is different. In fact, over the area as a whole we have found that the mid-depth ellipses rotate clockwise whereas the near bottom ellipses rotate anticlockwise. This feature has been observed consistently at Station A in the long term current measurements and over the area as a whole. Tidal ellipticities, orientations and phases for the M_2 tidal constituent are summarised in Fig. 11.4.

From the tidal ellipse data it has been possible to map out the distributions of the M_2 and S_2 bottom currents in the area and these are shown in Fig. 11.5. Broadly speaking, the dynamics of the M_2 and S_2 currents are similar with the ratio S_2/M_2 not varying by more than about 10% from a mean value for the area of 0.39 which compares with a figure of 0.36 for the same ratio in the elevations. The M_2 and S_2 contours, however, do illustrate the horizontal non-uniformity of the flow. From the ellipse orientation data shown in Fig. 11.4 we can see that currents flowing into and out of the Bay undergo considerable acceleration and deceleration on the west and east sides of the Bay respectively. These spatial accelerations lead to important non-linear effects in the currents which, in turn, have special implications for sediment transport.

The depth integrated equations of motion and continuity, including the effects of friction and Coriolis forces may be written (see Heaps, 1978) as:

$$\left. \begin{array}{l} \dfrac{\partial \hat{U}}{\partial t} + \hat{U}\dfrac{\partial \hat{U}}{\partial z} + \hat{V}\dfrac{\partial \hat{U}}{\partial y} - f\hat{V} = -g\dfrac{\partial \zeta}{\partial x} - \dfrac{C_D \hat{U}(\hat{U}^2 + \hat{V}^2)^{\frac{1}{2}}}{h + \zeta} + \nu_H\left(\dfrac{\partial^2 \hat{U}}{\partial x^2} + \dfrac{\partial^2 \hat{U}}{\partial y^2}\right) \\[1em] \dfrac{\partial \hat{V}}{\partial t} + \hat{U}\dfrac{\partial \hat{V}}{\partial x} + \hat{V}\dfrac{\partial \hat{V}}{\partial y} + f\hat{U} = -g\dfrac{\partial \zeta}{\partial y} - \dfrac{C_D \hat{V}(\hat{U}^2 + \hat{V}^2)^{\frac{1}{2}}}{h + \zeta} + \nu_H\left(\dfrac{\partial^2 \hat{V}}{\partial x^2} + \dfrac{\partial^2 \hat{V}}{\partial y^2}\right) \end{array} \right\} \quad (17)$$

and

$$\dfrac{\partial \zeta}{\partial t} + \dfrac{\partial}{\partial x}\left\{(h + \zeta)\hat{U}\right\} + \dfrac{\partial}{\partial y}\left\{(h + \zeta)\hat{V}\right\} = 0 \quad (18)$$

$\hat{U}$ and $\hat{V}$ are now depth mean currents and in Equation (17) and (18) wind stress and atmospheric pressure gradient effects have been neglected.

It is a relatively simple matter to show that the equations of motion and continuity contain three sets of non-linear terms which generate tidal harmonics, M_4, M_6, M_8......etc. in the currents. These are:

$$\left. \begin{array}{l} \text{the advective terms} \quad \hat{U}\dfrac{\partial \hat{U}}{\partial x} \quad \text{etc} \\[1em] \text{the frictional terms} \quad \dfrac{C_D \hat{U}(\hat{U}^2 + \hat{V}^2)^{\frac{1}{2}}}{h + \zeta} \quad \text{etc} \\[1em] \text{the Shallow Water terms} \quad \dfrac{\partial}{\partial x}(h + \zeta)\hat{U} \quad \text{etc} \end{array} \right\} \quad (19)$$

In particular, in shallow shelf seas, the M_4 tidal component is likely to be large and to play an important role in determining the direction of sediment movement (see Pingree and Griffiths, 1979; Hunter, 1979).

An order of magnitude analysis of these terms, assuming a purely one-dimensional flow on the east side of the Bay (a region showing marked spatial accelerations) shows (see Table 11.2) that the friction terms is likely to be the most effective non-linear term in the equations of motion. These calculations were based on the co-tidal and co-range data shown in Fig. 8.1 and the M_2 and S_2 tidal current amplitudes shown in Fig. 11.5.

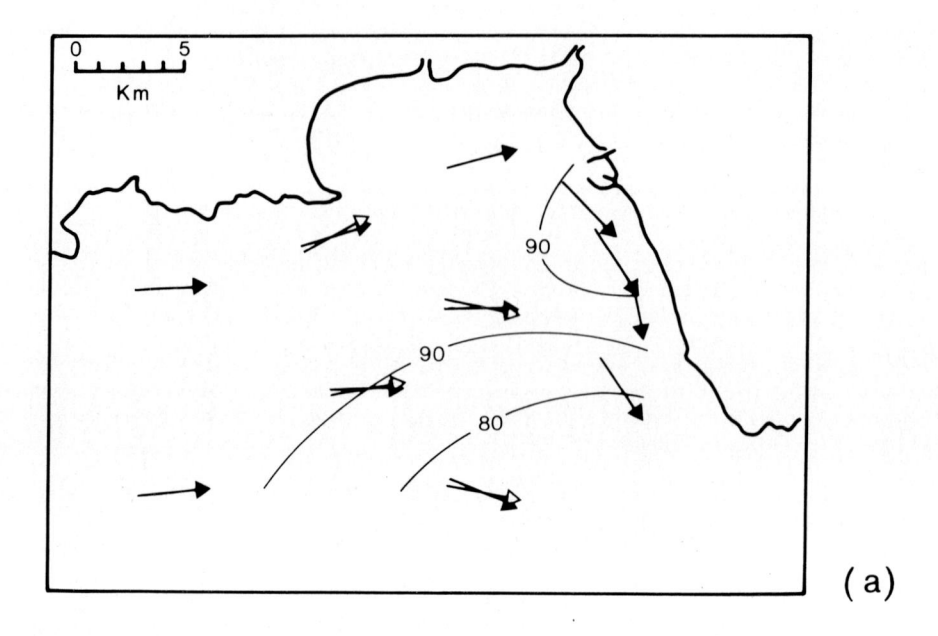

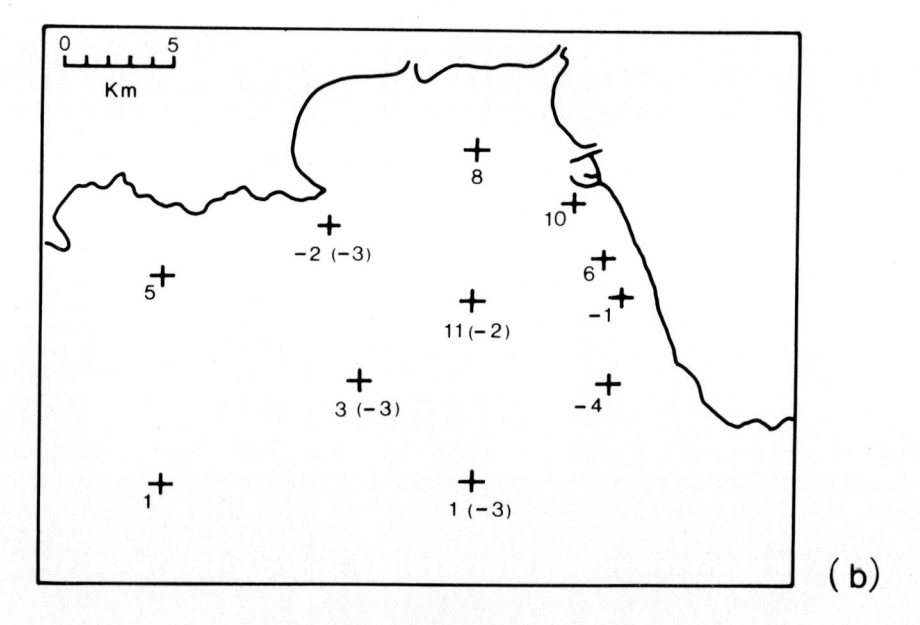

Figure 11.4. M_2 tidal current ellipse data: (a) orientation ϕ_σ and phase g_σ, (b) ellipticity as a percentage. Negative and positive values indicate clockwise and anti-clockwise rotations, respectively. Solid arrows indicate bottom currents and open arrows mid-depth currents.

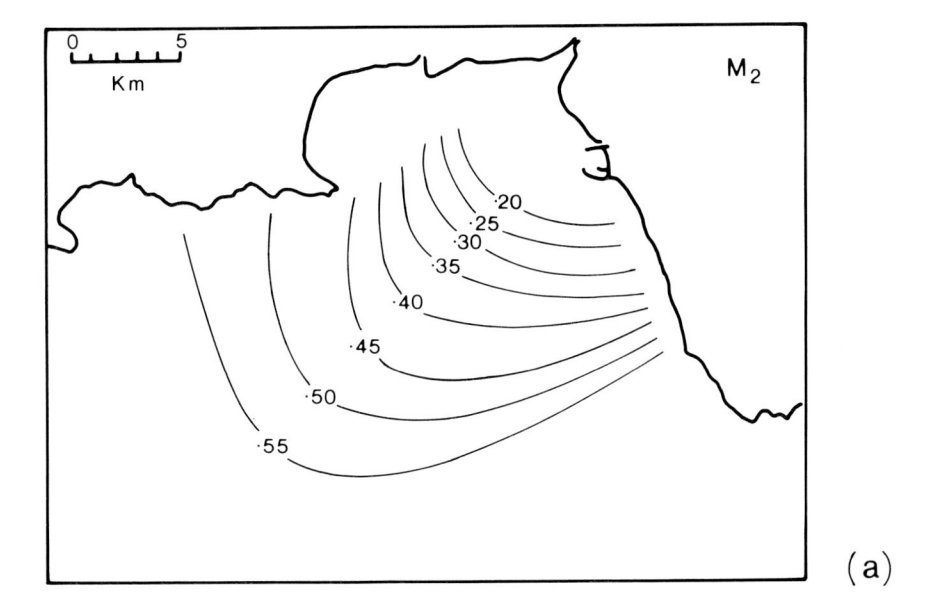

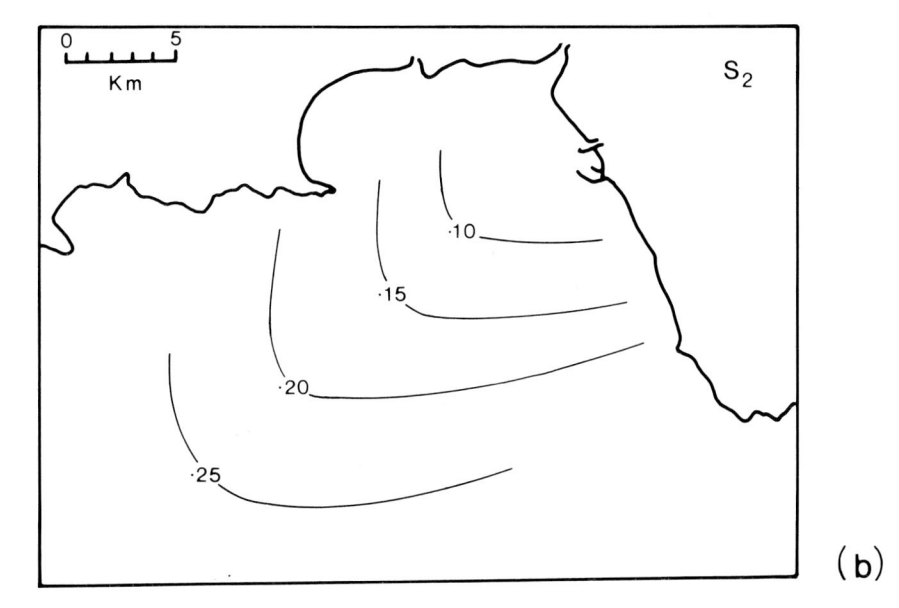

Figure 11.5. Distribution of (a) M₂ and (b) S₂ tidal stream amplitudes (semi-major axes of M₂ and S₂ ellipses) in m/s.

TABLE 11.2. Order of Magnitude Analysis of Non-Linear Terms in Equations of Motion in Swansea Bay.

Comparative Term (cgs units)	Non-linear terms (cgs units)
$O\left(\dfrac{\partial \hat{U}}{\partial t}\right) \simeq .007$	$O\left(\dfrac{\hat{U}\partial \hat{U}}{\partial x}\right) \simeq .004$
	$O\left(\dfrac{C_D \hat{U}(\hat{U}^2 + \hat{V}^2)^{\frac{1}{2}}}{h + \zeta}\right) \geqslant .004$

Calculated with h < 20m and a friction coefficient C_D = .0025 from data in Figures 8.1 and 11.5 on the east side of Swansea Bay.

The distribution of M_4 tidal currents is shown in Fig. 11.6 and shows that these are largest in areas where the advective or spatial acceleration terms and the friction terms are likely to be greatest. In general, Fig. 11.6 shows that the M_4/M_2 ratio in the currents increases to a maximum of about 0.15 in the shallower water nearer the coast. This is about an order of magnitude larger than the same ratio in the elevations which is about 0.017 (see Table 11.1 and Heathershaw and Hammond, 1979a). These differences serve to illustrate the importance of the non-linear terms in the flow of tidal currents near coasts, particularly in bays and in the vicinity of headlands.

From the tidal ellipse information we can also examine the distribution of currents over the Neap-Spring cycle. However, since sediment transport varies at high transport rates as U_*^3 and since tidal mixing varies as h/U_o^3 (see for example Robinson, 1979) where U_* is the friction velocity and U_o the tidal stream amplitude, it is instructive to look at the distributions of the currents as:

$$(M_2 - S_2)^3 \qquad \text{Neaps} \qquad (20)$$

$$(M_2 + S_2)^3 \qquad \text{Springs} \qquad (21)$$

In general, the M_2 and S_2 tidal ellipses have very nearly the same orientations and we therefore carry out an arithmetic addition of the M_2 and S_2 tidal currents. Fig. 11.7 shows that at any one location in the Bay we may expect tidal mixing or sediment transport to undergo an order of magnitude variation over the Neap-Spring cycle. Furthermore since the dissipation of tidal energy by friction is proportional to U_*^3 we may expect this to undergo a similar variation.

RESIDUAL CURRENTS

The tidally induced Langrangian residual velocity, $\bar{U}_L$ will consist of two components given (see Longuet-Higgins, 1969) by:

$$\bar{U}_L = \bar{U} + U_S \qquad (22)$$

where $\bar{U}$ is the Eulerian residual, i.e., the residual current which we measure at a fixed point, and U_S the Stokes velocity given by:

$$U_S = \overline{\int U dt \cdot \frac{\partial U}{\partial x}} \qquad (23)$$

where the integration is taken over a tidal period and the overbar denotes a time

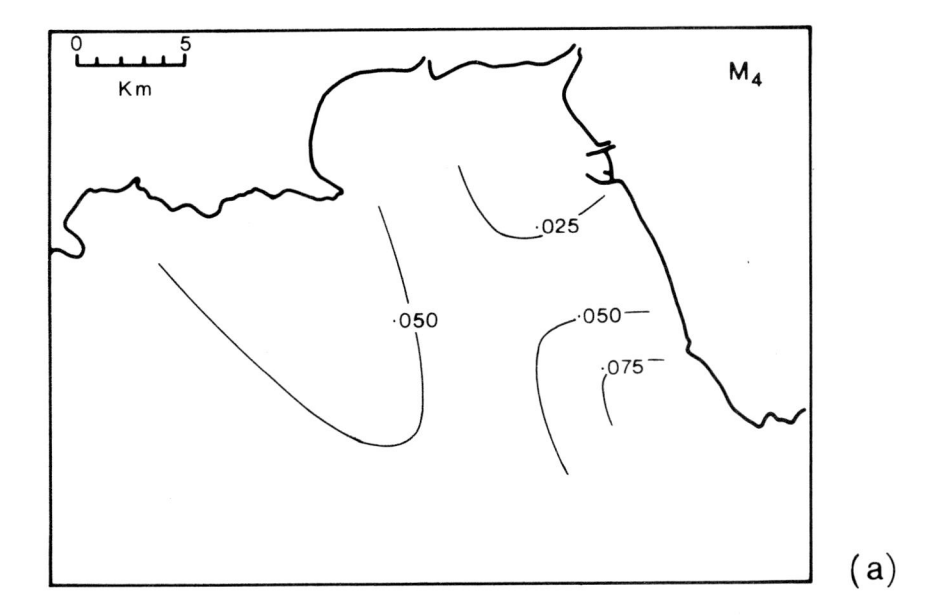

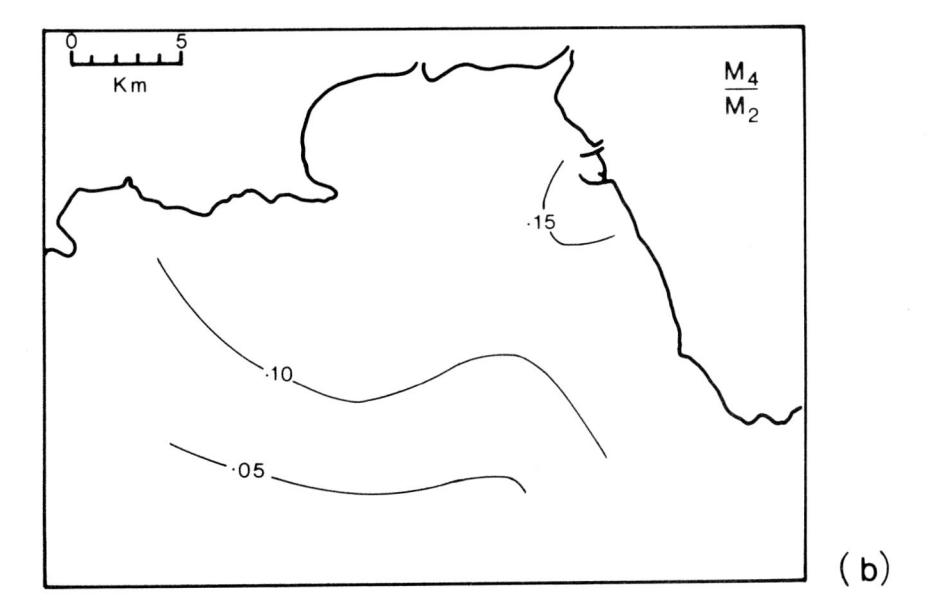

Figure 11.6. Distribution of (a) M₄ tidal stream amplitude and (b) ratio of M₄ to M₂ tidal stream amplitudes in m/s.

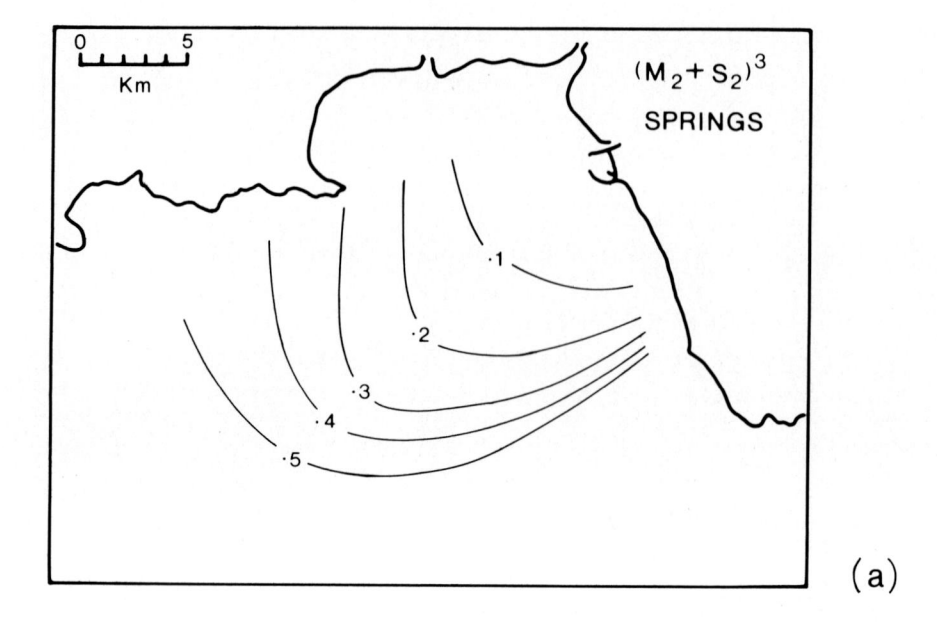

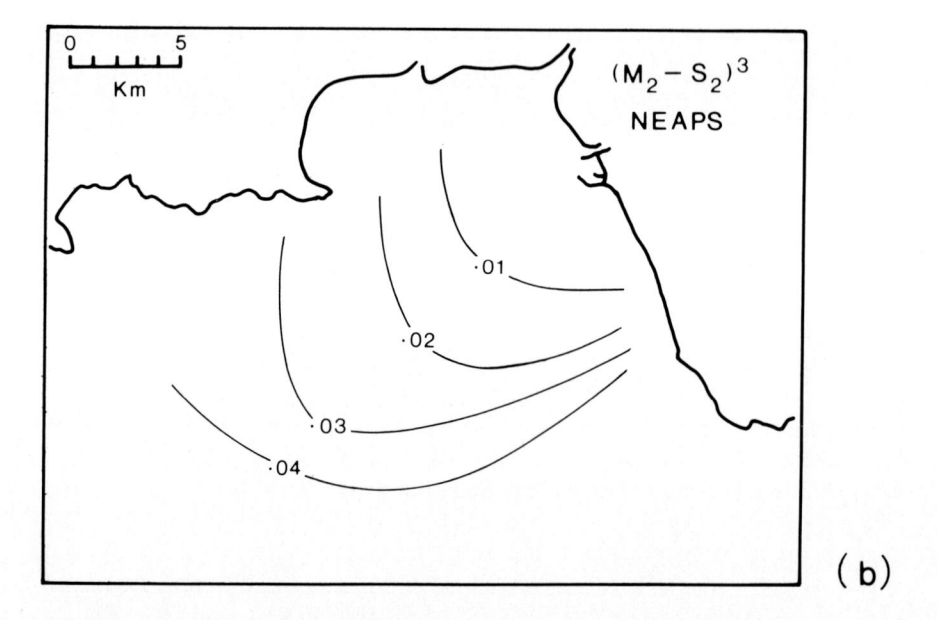

Figure 11.7. Distribution of (a) Spring tidal stream amplitude cubed and (b) Neap tidal stream amplitude cubed in m^3/s^3.

average over one or more tidal cycles.

Longuet-Higgins (1969) has shown that this term is of order $\bar{U}^2(T/L)$ where T and L are time and length scales associated with the current. By taking the time and distance between co-tidal lines in Fig. 8.1, it is possible to estimate T/L in the area of interest. Taking T = 600s and L = 15km gives $O(T/L) \simeq 0.0004$s/cm. Thus, with $U \simeq 50$cm/s, we have $O(U_S) \simeq .01$cm/s which as we shall see is generally much smaller than the measured Eulerian residuals. This result is confirmed by investigations of the residual circulation in this area using numerical models (Owen, 1979) which show little or no difference between the Eulerian and Langrangian residuals.

To obtain the Eulerian residuals we have applied a digital filter to the current meter data to eliminate the tidal currents. Doodson's X_0 filter was chosen for this purpose (see Heathershaw and Hammond, 1979a, for details). Vector time series of current speed and direction were resolved into E and N flowing components, U and V respectively, and the X_0 filter applied to hourly averages to yield filtered estimates every 24 hours, centred on 1200 GMT each day.

Examination of the progressive vector diagrams shown in Fig. 11.8 shows that at times there is considerable variability in the direction of the residual current. Consequently, following Ramster et al. (1978), we have calculated a steadiness factor B (ratio of vector mean to scalar mean expressed as a percentage) for each record. Where the residual flow is consistently in one direction B will be large and of the order of 100% (see Fig. 11.9). Residual flow data is presented in Fig. 11.10 in the manner suggested by Ramster et al. (1978). Full details of the residual flow estimates are given in Heathershaw and Hammond (1979a). Fig. 11.10 and Table 11.3 show that the measured residuals vary from about 8cm/s offshore to about .5cm/s close inshore.

Four interesting features emerge from the residual circulation pattern shown in Fig. 11.10, which have immediate relevance to the movement of sediment and pollutants in the area. These are:

(a) the area of low residual currents in the area between Port Talbot and the River Neath;
(b) the area of divergence in the residual velocity field between Port Talbot and Sker Point;
(c) the presence of a large clockwise eddy in the mean circulation over the Scarweather Sands (see Fig. 11.2), with near bottom convergence and mid-depth divergence to the north and south of the Bank; and
(d) the reversal with depth of the mean circulation near Mumbles Head which, as we shall see later, is possibly related to the presence of density currents.

SALINITY AND TEMPERATURE

Surface salinity distributions (data supplied by the Welsh National Water Development Authority)(see Figs. 11.11 and 11.12), indicate that there are appreciable horizontal gradients of salinity arising from the freshwater discharges into the Bay and these gradients persist throughout the tidal cycle and throughout the year. Furthermore, the summer and winter patterns are consistent with the seasonal variations in the outer Channel and Celtic Sea reported by Bowden (1955) and Hamilton (1973) which show an intrusion of the more saline and oceanic water into the Channel during the winter as a result of an increase in the wind driven currents. In fact, the 33°/oo isohaline is almost completely absent from the summer distributions shown in Fig. 11.11.

It is also apparent from the salinity and temperature data, that there is considerable vertical stratification at the head of the Bay which persists throughout the

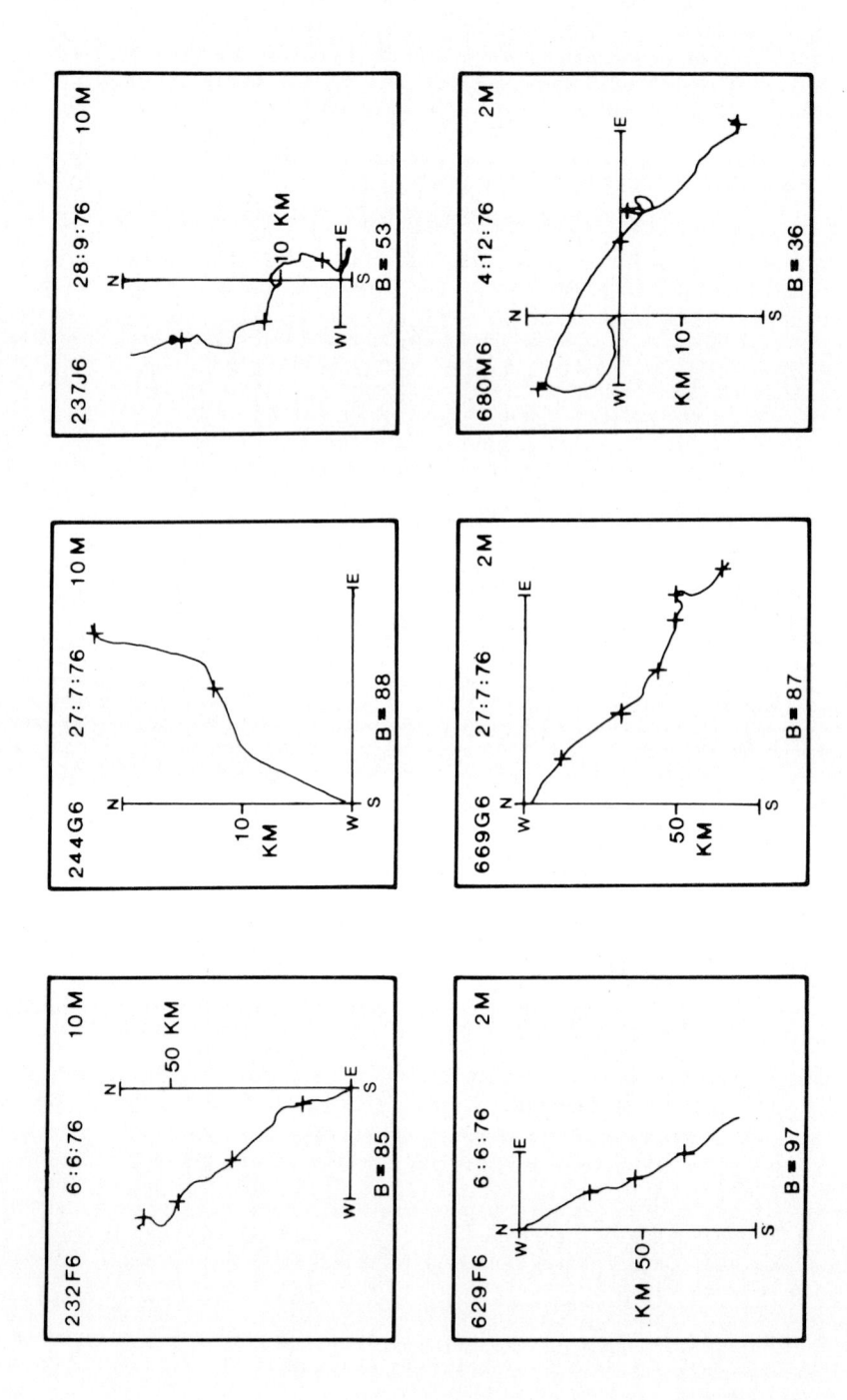

Figure 11.8. Progressive vector diagrams from near bottom (2m) and mid-depth (10m) simultaneous current measurements at Station A illustrating the quiescent flow state. Values of the steadiness factor B are indicated.

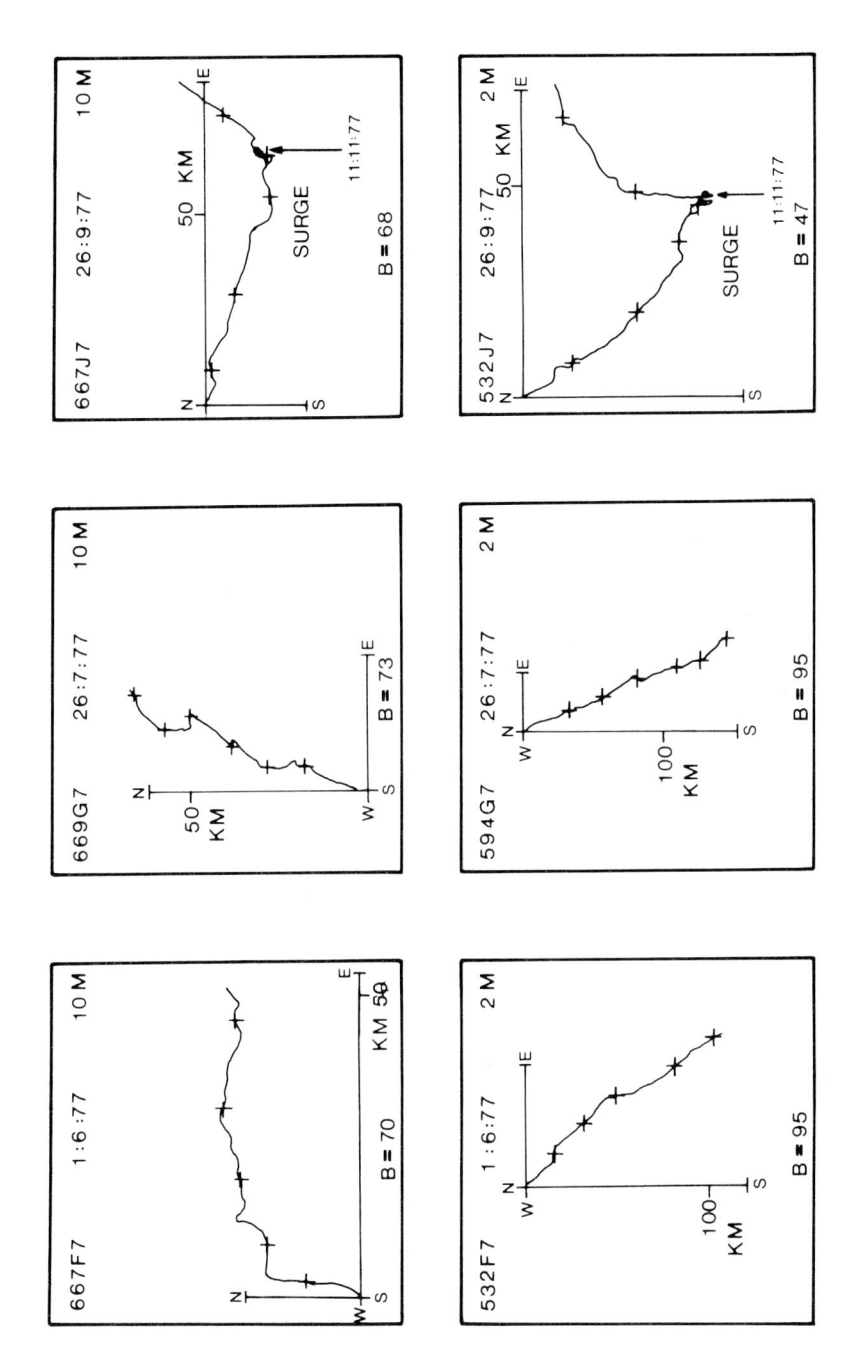

Figure 11.9. Progressive vector diagrams from near-bottom (2m) and mid-depth (10m) current measurements in 2-month period leading up to November 1977 storm surge.

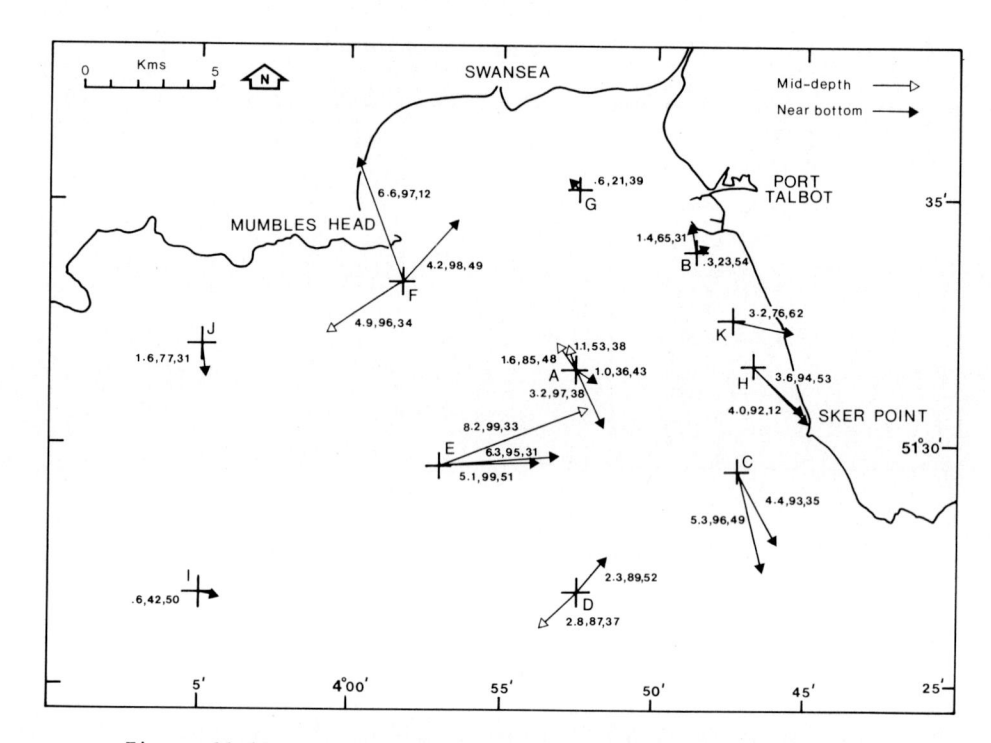

Figure 11.10. Summary of near-bottom (solid arrows) and mid-depth (open arrows) tidally induced residuals in Swansea Bay. Residual flow data has been presented in the manner suggested by Ramster *et al.* (1978) and consists of sets of three figures giving the residual flow in cm/s, the steadiness factor B as a percentage and the length of the record in days (in that order).

tidal cycle (maximum temperature differences between surface and bottom being of the order 0.5°C). Even at Station A, where the peak mid-depth tidal currents are of the order 50cm/s, there is still some evidence to suggest that weak vertical stratification persists over the tidal cycle (see Fig. 11.13).

On the basis of the salinity distributions shown in Figs. 11.11, 11.12 and 11.13, we would expect density currents to play some part in the non-tidal circulation of the Bay. To estimate their effect we have used the analytical solution obtained by Heaps (1972) to investigate density currents in Liverpool Bay and later by Hamilton (1973) to study the circulation in the Bristol Channel. Full details of our calculations are given in Heathershaw and Hammond (1979a).

In order to calculate the density currents, it is necessary to know:

(a) the isopycnal (lines of constant density) spacing;
(b) the freshwater discharges to the Bay.

Using the tidally and depth averaged data from Stations A, B and G (see Fig. 11.13), it is possible to estimate the isopycnal spacing and their approximate orientation. Fig. 11.14 shows that these are orientated towards the head of the Bay, that is towards the source of the freshwater discharge. However, we should note that these conditions do not appear to agree entirely with those implicit in the

TABLE 11.3. Summary of Measured Residual Currents from Station A (See Figure 11.2) to Illustrate use of Steadiness Factor.

Record	Elevation (m)	Residual current Speed (cm/s)	Direction (°T)	Steadiness (%)	Record length (days)
237K5 ⎤	10	0.91	54.97	64.78	8
238K5 ⎦	3	0.61	82.80	37.53	51
244A6 ⎤	10	1.93	16.80	58.87	16
238A6 ⎦	2	2.84	143.15	82.20	9
237D6 ⎤	10	2.14	297.11	95.74	3
560D6 ⎦	2	2.30	145.74	83.39	57
232F6 ⎤	10	1.62	323.58	84.64	48
629F6 ⎦	2	3.18	154.18	97.07	38
244G6 ⎤	10	1.55	30.34	87.89	20
669G6 ⎦	2	2.02	131.18	87.39	60
237J6	10	1.11	336.52	52.61	38
680M6	2	0.95	122.47	35.86	43
260B7	2	2.37	105.82	53.36	49
560D7	2	1.97	143.88	70.22	44
667F7 ⎤	10	1.21	70.22	70.28	54
532F7 ⎦	2	2.91	143.78	95.08	54
669G7 ⎤	10	1.28	23.60	73.01	61
594G7 ⎦	2	3.12	157.82	95.14	61
667J7 ⎤	10	1.83	85.99	68.08	53
532J7 ⎦	2	1.40	97.55	47.28	62

Bracketed records indicate simultaneous near-bottom and mid-depth measurements. The last three sets of records comprise the 90 day data set shown in Figure 11.17.

solution of the dynamical equations given by Heaps, which requires that the isopycnals be parallel to the coast and that there are no lateral constraints. However, we feel that the ispoycnal spacing gives a representative estimate of the density currents flowing on section X_1X_2 in Figs. 11.14 and 11.15.

The solution of the dynamical equations for a steady state (that is neglecting tides and all other variations with time), now taking U and V to be the density current components, gives:

$$U = \frac{g(h+\zeta)}{f} \cdot \frac{1}{\rho} \frac{\partial \rho}{\partial x} \cdot F_1 + \frac{fq}{C} \cdot F_2 \qquad (24)$$

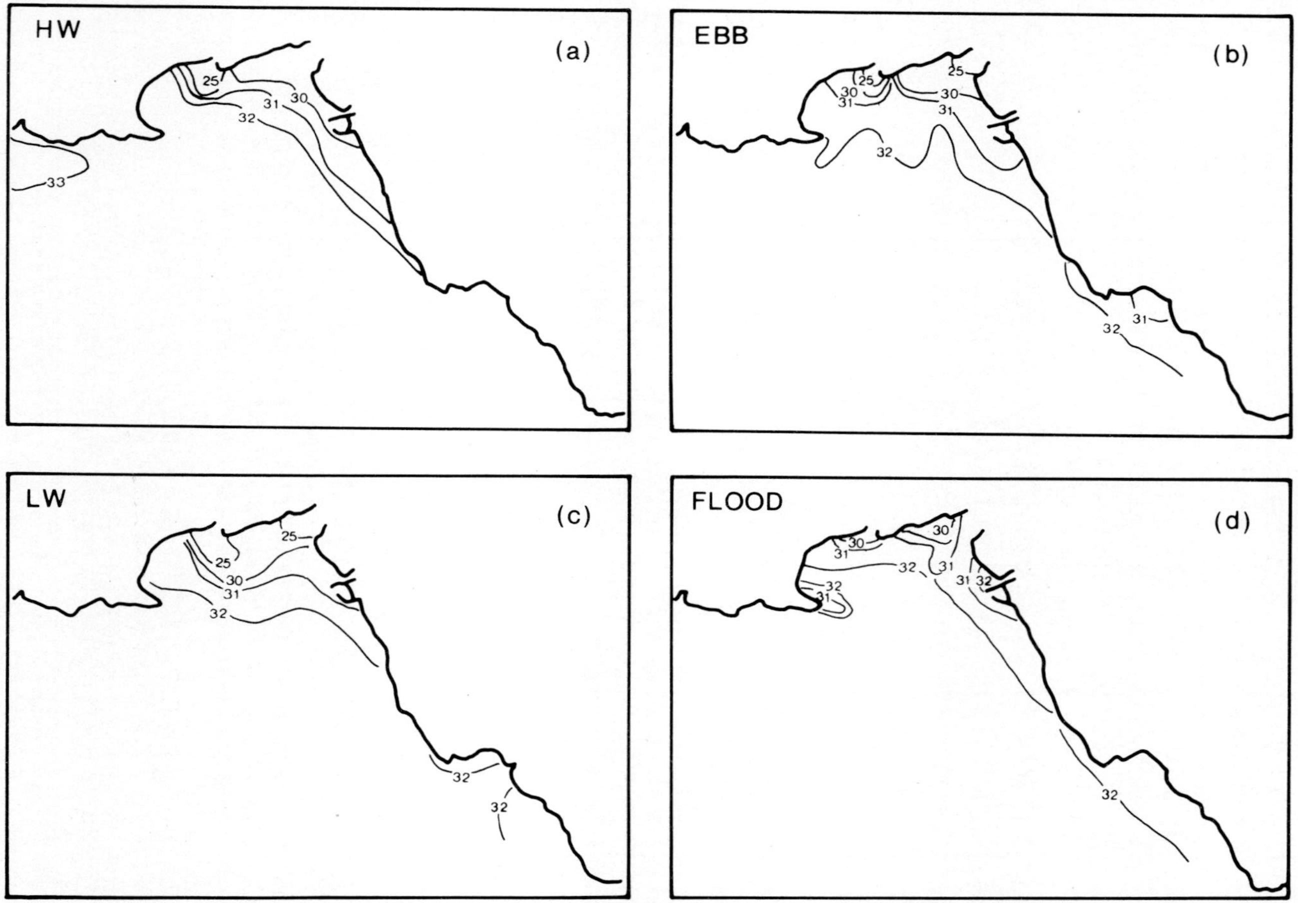

Figure 11.11. Summer surface salinity distributions (S°/oo) for (a) HW, (b) ebb, (c) LW and (d) flood stages of the tidal cycle, illustrating the effects of freshwater discharges in the head of the Bay.

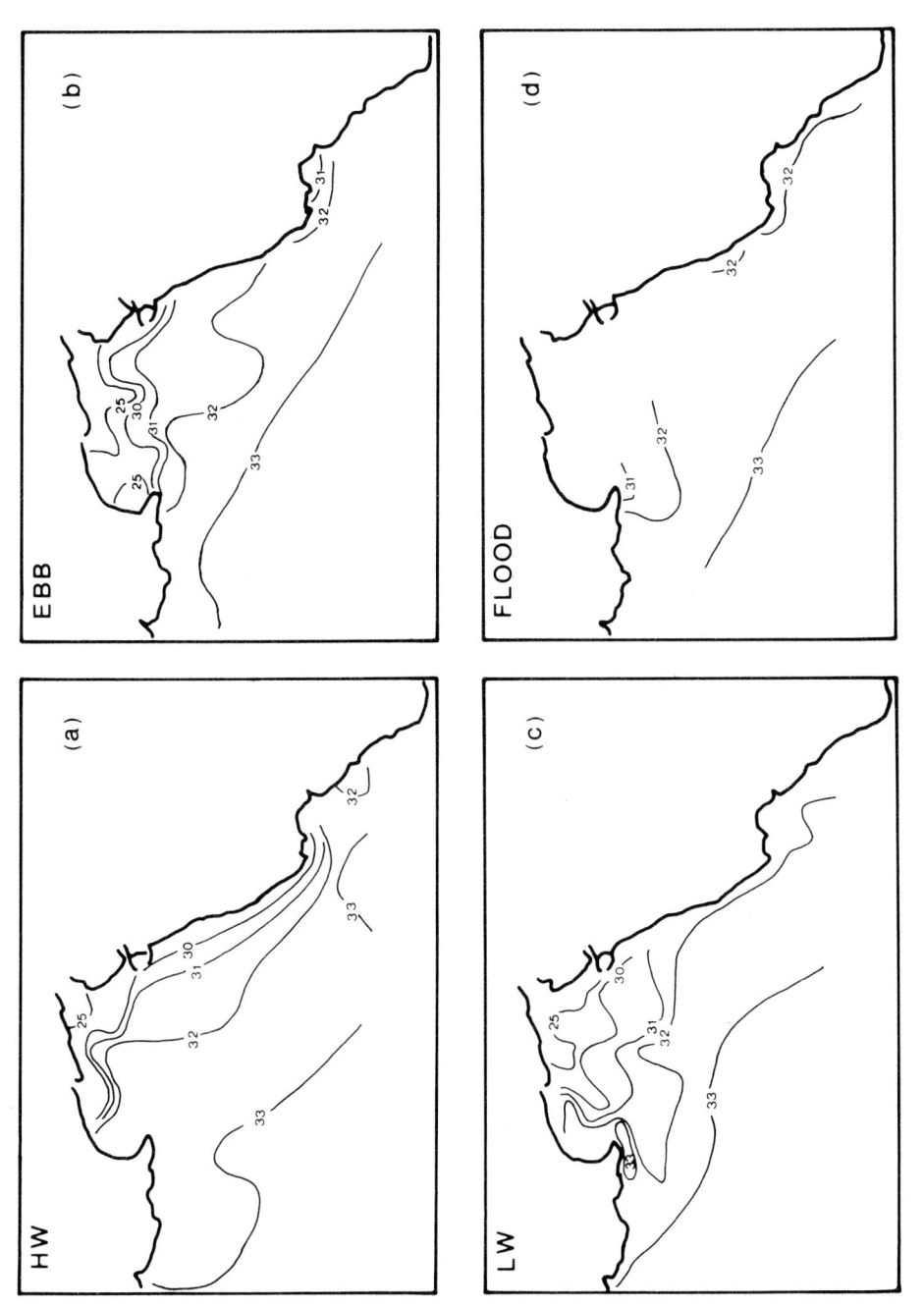

Figure 11.12. Winter surface salinity distributions (S°/oo) for (a) HW, (b) ebb, (c) LW and (d) flood stages of the tidal cycle illustrating the intrusion of more saline oceanic water (33°/oo isohaline) into the area.

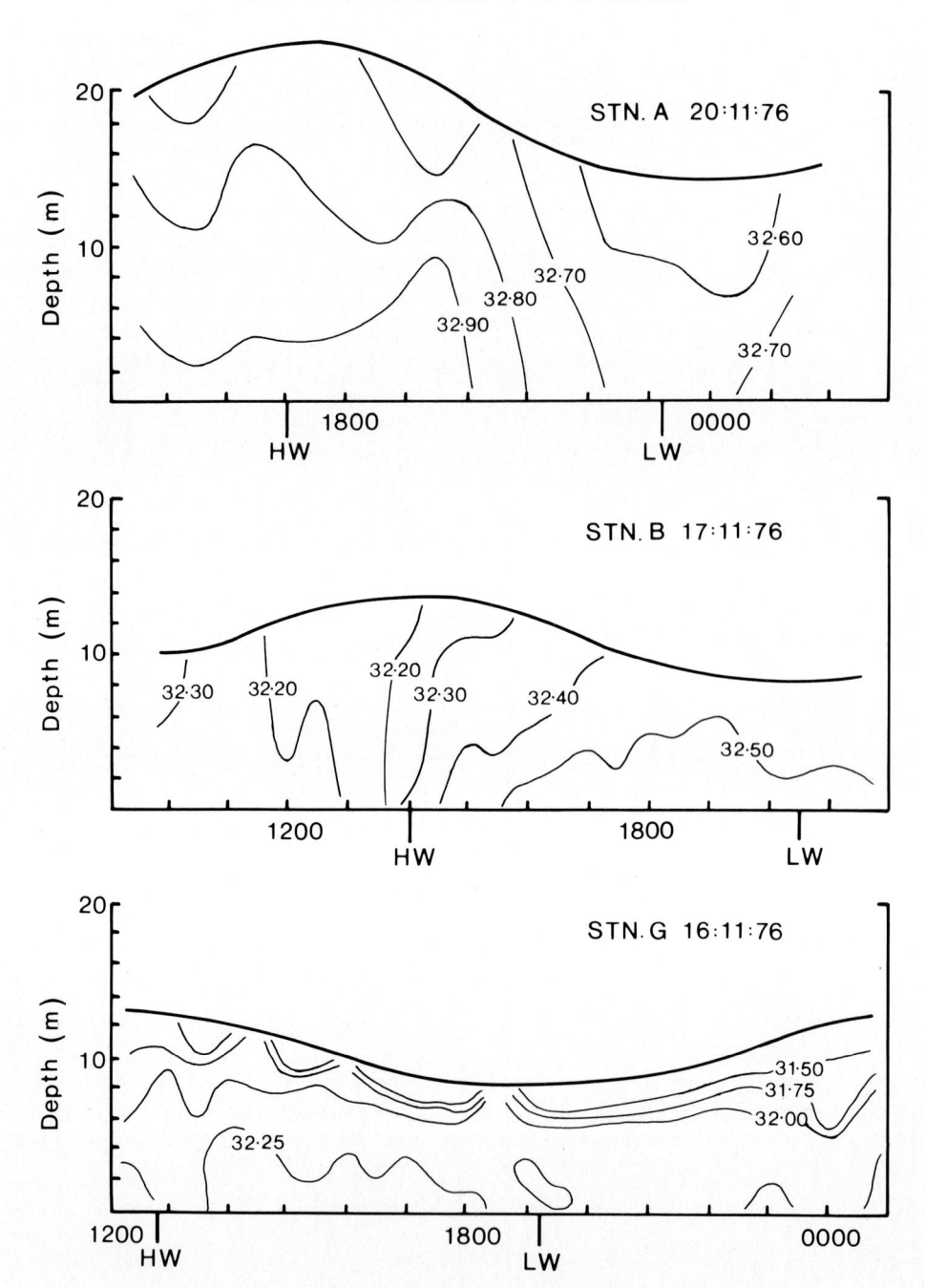

Figure 11.13. Salinity (S°/oo) time series at Stations A, B and G, illustrating both horizontal (a) and (b), and vertical (c) stratification effects.

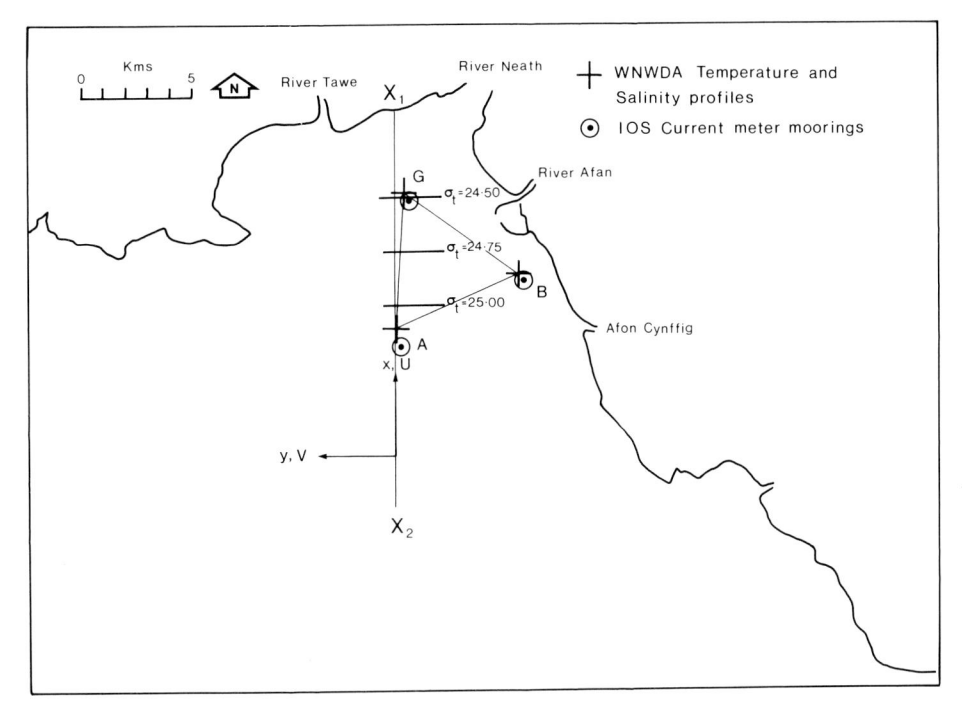

Figure 11.14. Isopycnal (σ_t) spacing and orientation, determined from salinity and temperature measurements at Stations A, B and G. X_1X_2 is the section along which the density currents U and V have been calculated. The location of the major river discharges are also shown.

$$V = \frac{g(h + \zeta)}{f} \cdot \frac{1}{\rho} \frac{\partial \rho}{\partial x} \cdot F_3 + \frac{fq}{C} \cdot F_4 \qquad (25)$$

F_1, F_2, F_3 and F_4 are all functions of depth Z, total depth h, the Coriolis parameter f, eddy viscosity N_Z and linear friction coefficient C as given by Heaps (1972). Here U and V are defined in a left handed system of co-ordinates with Z positive downwards (see Figs. 11.14 and 11.15), g is the acceleration due to gravity, ζ the displacement of the sea surface from its undisturbed level and ρ the fluid density, q is a river discharge parameter (see later).

Equations (24) and (25) thus contain two terms which influence the velocity field; these are:

$\frac{1}{\rho} \frac{\partial \rho}{\partial x}$ which represents the effects of the modified density field on the nearshore velocity field

$\frac{fq}{C}$ which represents the direct effect of the freshwater discharges on the nearshore velocity field.

$1/\rho \cdot (\partial \rho / \partial x)$ may be evaluated from the isopycnal spacing shown in Fig. 11.14. q is evaluated by dividing the freshwater discharge rate to the Bay by a representative length of coastline. Here we have looked at all the rivers discharging into the Bay from Mumbles Head to Sker Point. The bulk of the discharge (see Stoner, 1977) is provided by the Rivers Tawe, Neath and Afan which together discharge about 30m^3/s over a 20km length of coastline. Heathershaw and Hammond (1979a) have shown that

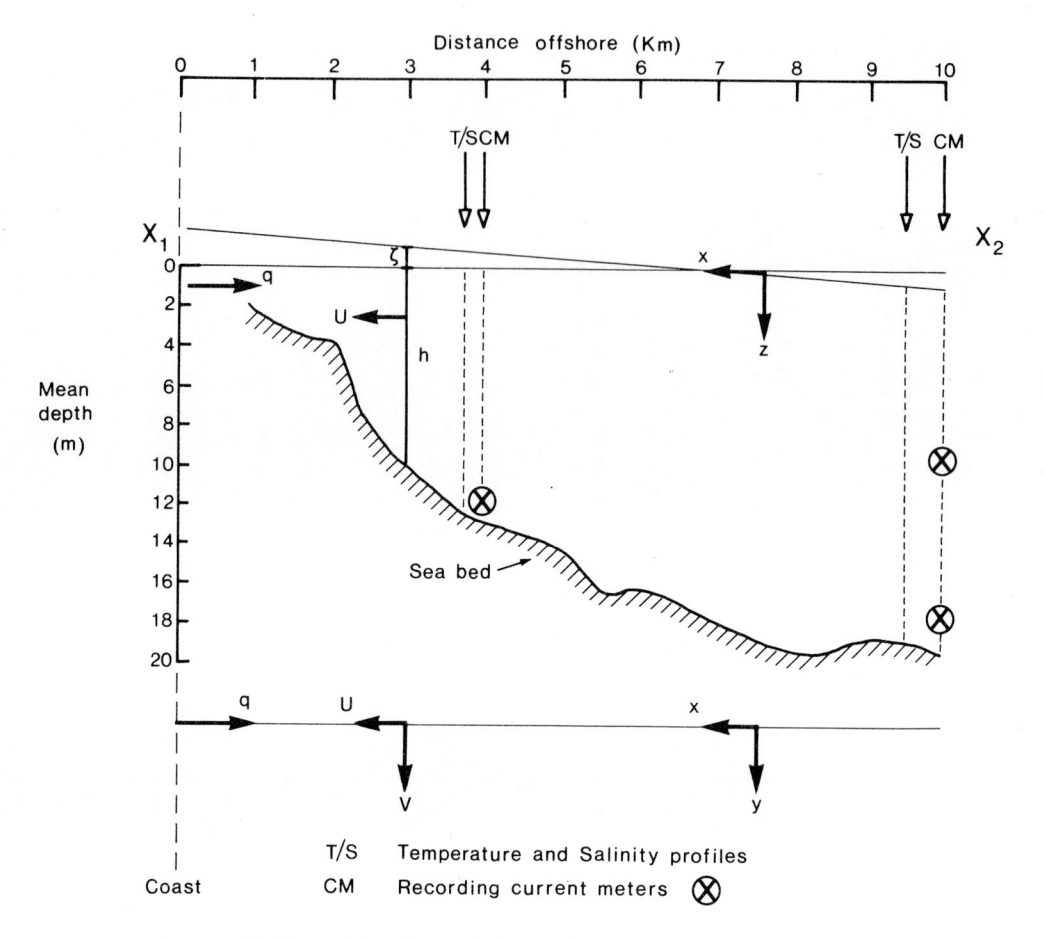

Figure 11.15. Details of the bathymetry along section X_1X_2 showing the positions of temperature and salinity measurements and current meter moorings. x, y, z, U and V are defined as shown. q is the river discharge parameter, h the mean depth and ζ the tidal elevation.

fq/C is small and of the order 10^{-2} cm/s, a value similar to that obtained by Heaps (1972) in Liverpool Bay.

In order to evaluate U and V from Equations (24) and (25) it is necessary to parameterize the variations of the eddy viscosity along the section X_1X_2 shown in Figs. 11.14 and 11.15. The procedure adopted by Heaps (1972), Hamilton (1973) and Heathershaw and Hammond (1979a) is to hold the ratio Ch/N_Z as a constant, that is:

$$n = Ch/N_Z \qquad (26)$$

where C is a linear friction coefficient.

This is not an unreasonable assumption in view of the evidence presented by Heaps (1972) which shows that the depth integrated and tidally averaged values of the eddy viscosity N_Z may be given on dimensional grounds by:

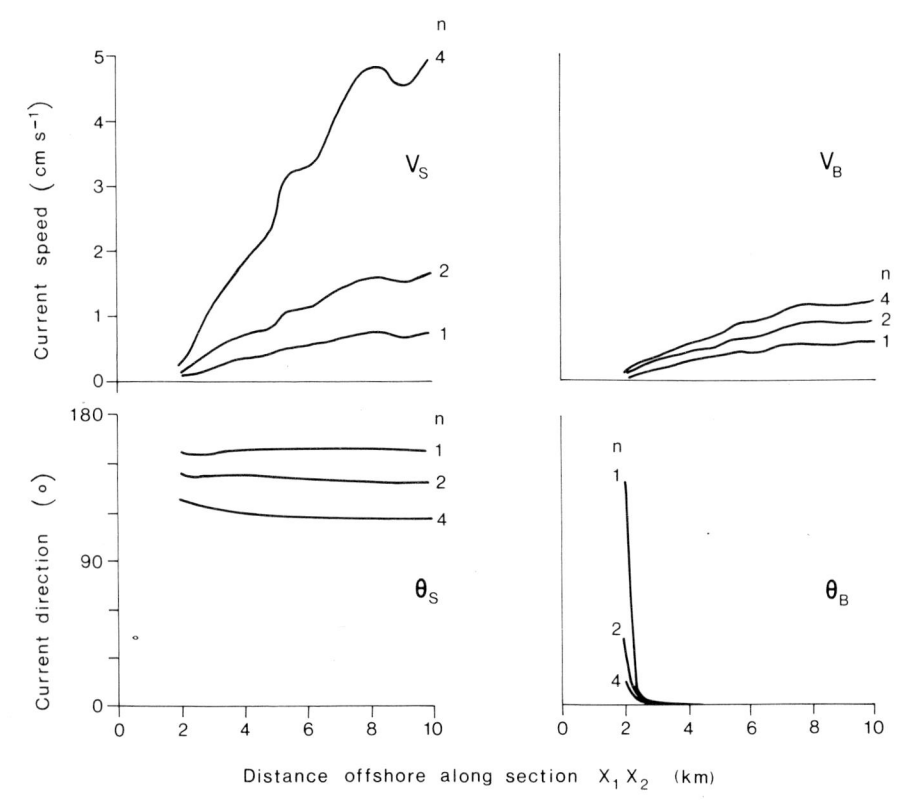

Figure 11.16. The variation of the resultant surface (V_S) and bottom (V_B) density currents along section X_1X_2 for values of n = 1, 2 and 4. The directions of the resultant currents θ_0 and θ_1, are measured anti-clockwise from the x axis in Fig. 11.15.

$$N_Z = MU_0 h \tag{27}$$

where M is a constant, U_0 is the tidal stream amplitude and h is the depth. Bowden et al. (1959) found that M varied between 1.49×10^{-3} and 2.83×10^{-3}. From current measurements at Stations A and G (see Fig. 11.15) a representative value of U_0 may be taken as 25cm/s and taking a mean value of $M = 2.16 \times 10^{-3}$ gives:

$$\dot{n} = \frac{Ch}{N_Z} = \frac{C}{MU_0} \tag{28}$$

which with C = 0.2cm/s gives n ≃ 4. Similarly to Heaps (1972) we have calculated U and V (see Heathershaw and Hammond, 1979a) for values of n = 1, 2 and 4. In a water depth of 20m and tidal stream amplitude of 50cm/s this gives N_Z values of 290, 195 and 98cm²/s respectively. Similarly to Heaps (1972), we find that this range of n values is realistic and probably accounts for the variation in tidally averaged N_Z values along the section.

Fig. 11.16 shows the speeds and directions of the surface and bottom currents, V_S and V_B respectively, along the section for different values of n and Fig. 11.17 shows the U and V profiles at a position midway along the section for a value of n = 4. The salient features of the density current field are:

Current speed (cm s^{-1})

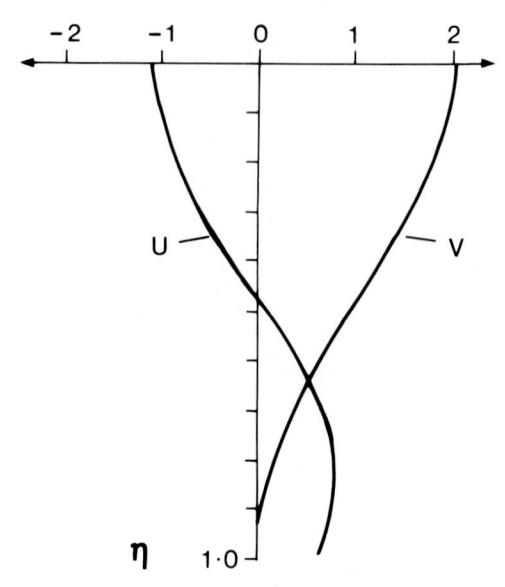

Figure 11.17. Density current profiles U and V for n = 4, mid-way along section X_1X_2 showing a shoreward flowing (U) bottom current of about 1cm/s and an alongshore current (V) flowing towards the west at about 2cm/s. η is the non-dimensional depth.

(1) the strong alongshore component of the surface current, towards the west (i.e., towards Mumbles Head), of order 2cm/s.
(2) the onshore component of the bottom current, towards the north (i.e., towards the coast) of order 1cm/s.

We can conclude from this analysis that the density currents are of the order 1-2cm/s and are thus comparable with the observed tidal residuals in the north of the Bay - particularly in the area bounded by a line between Port Talbot and Mumbles Head (see Fig. 11.2). To some extent this may explain the observed mean circulation in the vicinity of Mumbles Head (see Fig. 11.10) which shows a consistent (steadiness factor of 96%) surface flow to the southwest and a bottom flow which in general is directed into the Bay.

METEOROLOGICAL FORCING

The water circulation in shallow coastal waters is likely to be influenced by meteorological forcing, that is by the action of the wind on the sea's surface and by changes in atmospheric pressure.

The information that may be gained about these motions from shallow water current measurements is ostensibly limited by the uncertain response of conventional rotor-vane current meters to surface wave activity (see, for example, Hammond and Collins, 1979). However we will show later that this is not as serious a problem as it might appear at first sight, and that it is possible to make a number of general deductions from observation and theory which indicate how the circulation in this area might vary with differing meteorological inputs.

The action of a wind blowing towards a coast across shallow water is to pile up water against the coast (wind set-up). This will set up horizontal pressure gradients leading to a seaward flowing or slope current at or near the sea bed which, dependent upon the depth and the wind speed, will be in some kind of geostrophic balance. In the case of Swansea Bay, prevailing winds are from the southwest and we would thus anticipate a wind set-up effect during these periods. It is possible to determine the order of magnitude of the components in the resulting current system although precise estimates are made difficult by the uncertain nature of the eddy viscosity coefficient (N_Z) in the wind mixed surface layer and in the tidal current. Using Ekman's theory (described in Neumann and Pierson, 1966) we have estimated the wind driven surface currents and the slope currents for a typical wind speed of 5m/s and an extreme value of 20m/s (this value was exceeded during the November 1977 storm surge). These results are summarised in Table 11.4 and show that, for moderate wind speeds, the shoreward flowing surface currents are likely to be of order 2cm/s, with a seaward flowing slope current of about 0.4cm/s. This clearly does not allow continuity to be maintained and would suggest that the wind driven current turns alongshore where it impinges on the coast.

TABLE 11.4. Ratio of Water Depth (h) to Depth of Frictional Influence (D) for Various Wind Speeds (W). Also Shown are Maximum Values of the Surface and Slope Currents.

W (m/s)	N_Z (cm²/s)	h/D	Surface Current U (cm/s)	Surface Current V (cm/s)	Slope Current U (cm/s)	Slope Current V (cm/s)
2	100	7.61	.43	-.42	-.12	.25
4	103	2.69	1.79	-1.73	-.51	1.02
6	-	-	-	-	-	-
8	235	1.30	5.72	-3.35	-2.51	2.07
10	310	.33	7.73	-3.57	-3.58	2.22
12	400	.28	9.41	-3.45	-4.49	2.15
14	510	.24	10.60	-3.09	-5.15	1.93
16	650	.20	11.25	-2.60	-5.15	1.62
18	800	.18	11.81	-2.23	-5.84	1.39
20	950	.17	12.44	-1.98	-6.17	1.24

Eddy viscosity (N_Z) values have been based upon Thorade's (1914) relationship for the wind mixed surface layer and Bowden's (1953) dimensional relationship for the tidal currents. The depth h has been taken as 20m and here U and V are the shoreward and alongshore components of flow resulting from the wind blowing in a shoreward (U) direction. Full details of these calculations are given in Heathershaw and Hammond (1979a).

For a wind speed of 20m/s, the current system consists almost entirely of a shoreward flowing current of the order of 6cm/s which must turn along the coast, at the coast, to maintain continuity.

In a general way, we may also examine the effect of an applied wind stress at the sea-surface in terms of the ratio of the depth (h) to the thickness of the layer of frictional influence (D) which, notionally at least, is that depth below which the wind has little or no effect. D may be calculated from Ekman's theory (see Heathershaw and Hammond, 1979a for details). Table 11.4 shows how this ratio varies with wind speed (N_Z varying with wind speed also) and that for a water depth (h) of 20m (typical of the centre of the Bay), D is greater than h even at moderately low wind

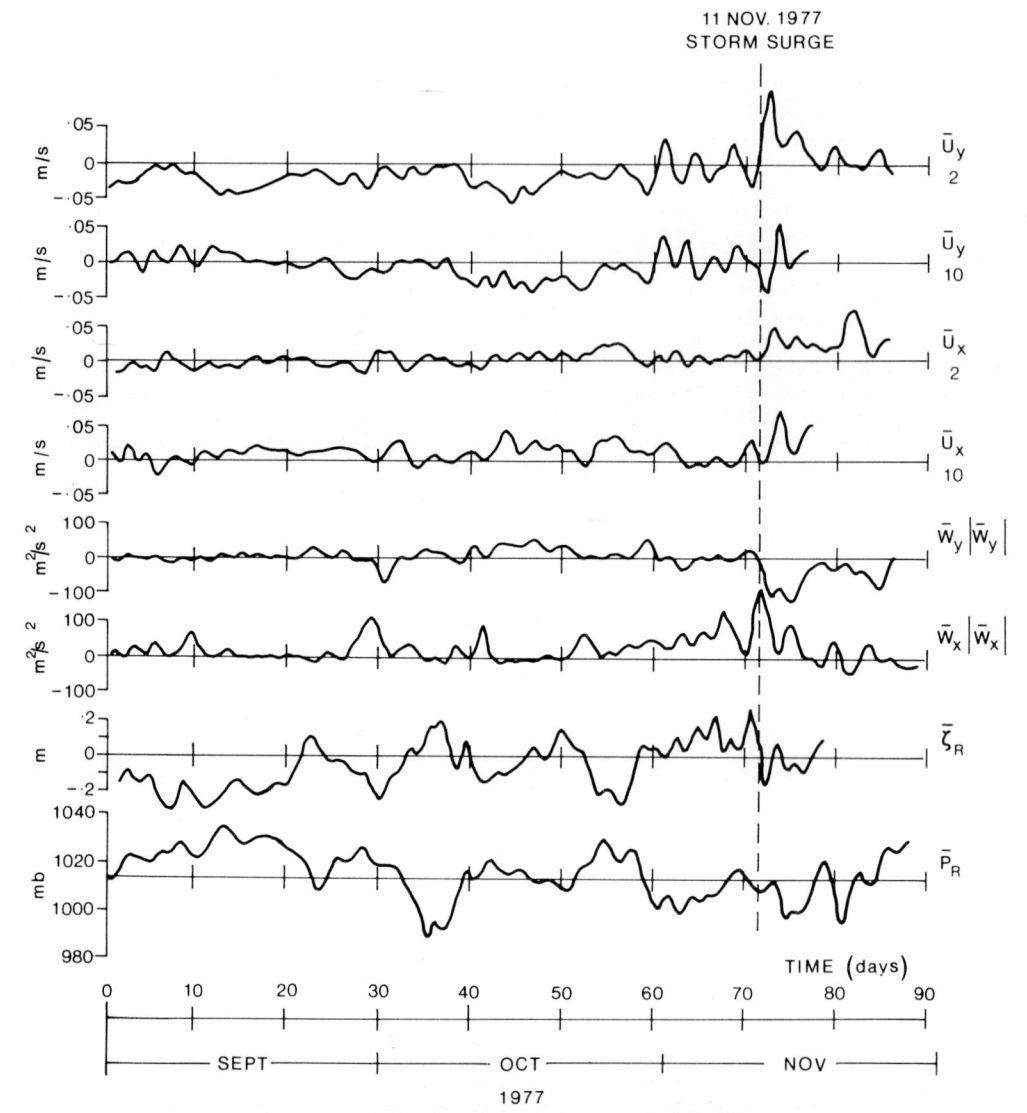

Figure 11.18. A 90-day data set illustrating the effects of meteorological forcing on the residual currents and tidal elevations in Swansea Bay and including the 1977 storm surge. The Figure shows the onshore-offshore (55°T) and alongshore (325°T) component of the residual flow, $\bar{U}_x$ and $\bar{U}_y$, and mean wind-speed squared as $\bar{W}_x|\bar{W}_x|$ and $\bar{W}_y|\bar{W}_y|$ the mean atmospheric pressure at Rhoose, $\bar{P}_R$ and mean tidal elevation residuals $\bar{\zeta}_R$ at Swansea.

speeds and that with increasing wind speed the ratio h/D falls off rapidly indicating that the wind's effect is increased throughout the water column.

However, observations show that the situation may be considerably more complex than this. During 1977, it was possible to make current measurements during a particularly severe storm surge (see also Chapter 9). Daily filtered residual flow estimates, obtained using a Doodson X_o filter, have been compared with daily mean wind speeds, residual tidal elevations and atmospheric pressure data. Fig. 11.18 shows a 90-day data set of these variables, wind speed ($\bar{W}$) having been plotted as $\bar{W}|\bar{W}|$ to parameterize wind stress. Current measurements and wind speed data have been resolved into a frame of reference giving alongshore and onshore-offshore components of the residual current and daily mean wind speed $\bar{U}_x$, $\bar{U}_y$, $\bar{W}_x$ and $\bar{W}_y$ respectively (see Heathershaw and Hammond, 1979a, for details). The storm surge of 11th November 1977 is clearly indicated. This followed the usual pattern for surges on the west coast of the British Isles (see Graff, 1978) leading to a 1.4m surge being recorded at Port Talbot (see also Figs. 9.2 and 9.3). Figure 11.18 shows that during the storm surge, and for the 10 days or so preceding it, there is a progressive change in the residual flow pattern culminating in a peak residual flow of the order of 10cm/s, at 2m above the sea-bed, which is nearly three times larger than the quiescent flow value. The peak occurs about one day later than the surge. In Fig. 11.17 it is worth noting the degree of correlation which exists between the same components of flow at the different depths.

The effect of the storm surge is perhaps best illustrated in the progressive vector diagrams for this period which are shown in Fig. 11.19 and which show a pronounced change in the direction of the residual flow, at both depths, at the time of the surge. The result is unusual in as much that the flow in this direction persists for some time after the surge. However, we should note that although the wind from the southwest gradually diminished after the surge, there was a relatively prolonged period of strong northwest winds following it, and we will show later that it is these which have the most pronounced effect on the circulation.

The 90-day data set shown in Fig. 11.18 was subjected to a multi-regression analysis. This has shown that the only significant correlation over the entire period occurs between the residual elevations ($\bar{\zeta}_R$) and atmospheric pressure ($\bar{P}_R$) which were significantly correlated at the 1% level with a negative correlation coefficient of -0.74. Fig. 11.18 illustrates this effect (the inverted barometer effect) clearly, with the observed tides being about 0.2m higher than predicted at timbs of low pressure and about 0.2m lower at times of high pressure (see also Chapter 9).

During periods of strong southwest winds, this response is likely to be complicated by the effects of wind set-up and Fig. 11.18 does indeed show that during the storm surge there is a much less clear correlation with atmospheric pressure and, in fact, during the 2-4 days following the surge the observed tides were lower than predicted even though the atmospheric pressure was low. This is due, we believe, to a wind induced set-down as a result of the prolonged period of northwest winds following the surge (see Fig. 11.18). In fact, the residual elevations shown in Fig. 11.18 indicate that a period of wind set-up is followed very rapidly by a period of set-down which appears to generate the large residual currents. Multi-regression analysis on the last 18 days' data (day 60 onwards), isolates this effect. These results are summarised in Table 11.5, which shows significant negative correlations between the residual currents and the wind stress and residual elevations. The presence of the negative correlations in Table 11.5 would suggest that the residual circulation in Swansea is influenced by wind set-up or set-down, but that following the storm surge of November 1977 the prolonged period of northwest winds lead to a set-down in the head of the Bay (this would to some extent explain the slight negative surge at Swansea and the positive surge at Port Talbot which have been reported by Graff (1978), which in turn would generate the strong shoreward flowing residuals shown in Fig. 11.17 and 11.18.

It is worth noting that no significant correlations were found between the residual currents and wave height, which was included as an independent variable in the multi-regression analysis to determine what effect, if any, the waves may have had on the residual flow estimates.

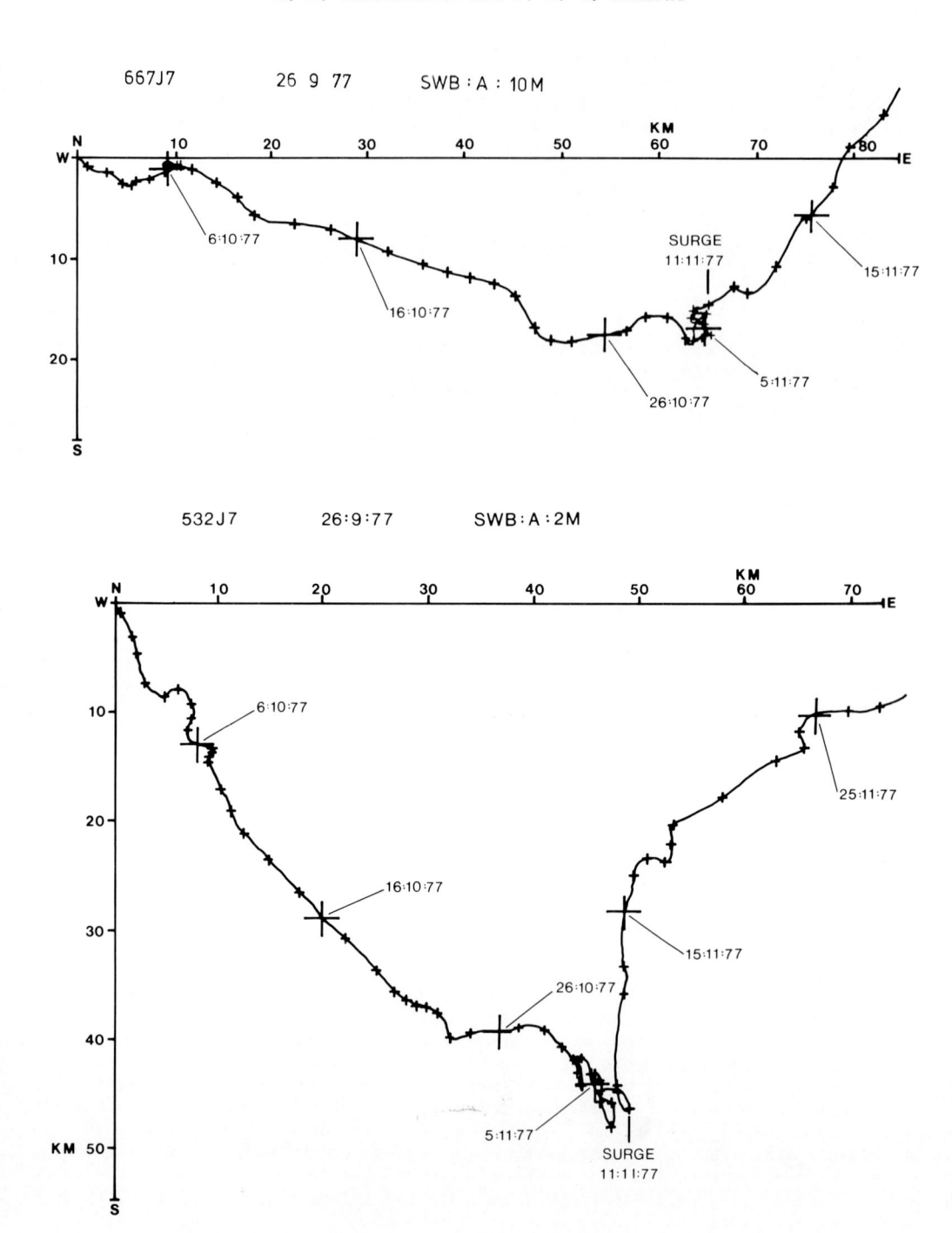

Figure 11.19. Progressive vector diagrams from simultaneous current measurements at heights of 10m (a) and 2m (b) above the sea-bed at Station A, showing the persistent northeast residual flow following the November 1977 storm surge.

TABLE 11.5. Meteorological Forcing; Multi-Regression Analysis of Data Shown in Fig. 11.17 (Full Details given in Heathershaw and Hammond, 1979a).

Data set	Correlated Variables	Correlation Coefficient (r) r	Significance levels 5%	1%
Days 1-78 inclusive	$\bar{\zeta}_R, \bar{P}_R$	-.74	.222	.287
Days 60-78 inclusive (Surge period)	$\bar{U}_{X_{10}}, \bar{W}_x\|\bar{W}_x\|$	-.58		
	$\bar{U}_{X_{10}}, \bar{\zeta}_R$	-.72		
	$\bar{U}_{X_2}, \bar{W}_y\|\bar{W}_y\|$	-.75	.468	.590
	$\bar{U}_{X_2}, \bar{\eta}_R$	-.69		
	$\bar{U}_{Y_2}, \bar{W}_y\|\bar{W}_y\|$	-.77		

$\bar{\zeta}_R$ daily mean residual elevations (at Swansea); $\bar{P}_R$ daily mean pressure (at Rhoose); $\bar{W}_x, \bar{W}_y$ daily mean wind speeds; $\bar{U}_x, \bar{U}_y$ daily residual flow estimates.
Note: x axis is positive shoreward in direction 055°T and y axis is positive alongshore in direction 325°T.

SUMMARY AND CONCLUSIONS

Observations of tidal and residual currents in Swansea Bay show that the area exhibits a diverse range of flow features. Foremost amongst these is the horizontal non-uniformity of the M₂ and S₂ tidal currents leading, via the non-linear terms in the equation of motion, to large quarter diurnal (M₄) currents, particularly in the vicinity of Porthcawl (see Fig. 11.6). These play a significant role in sediment transport (see Chapter 15). Furthermore, the area is characterized by an order of magnitude variation in tidal mixing and sediment transport over the Neap-Spring cycle.

Residual current observations, summarised in Fig. 11.10 and schematically in Fig. 11.20 confirm the presence of a large clockwise gyre situated over the Scarweather Sand and, associated with this, the presence of convergent flow near the sea-bed and divergent flow at mid-depth on the flanks of the sandbank.

The measured phases of the currents and elevations indicate a standing wave tidal oscillation with the M₂ tidal current phase being of the order of 90° within the Bay but showing a variation from south and north of about 10°: currents in the Bay apparently reach a maximum about 20 minutes later than those in the deeper flow of the Bristol Channel, to the south of the Scarweather Sands.

Theory and observation suggest that the circulation in the Bay is likely to be influenced by meteorological forcing, particularly during periods of storm surge activity. The response is complex, but the results indicate that wind set-up or set-down may be the most likely mechanism affecting the residual circulation. In particular, during a storm surge, wind-induced set-down would appear to have the greatest effect on the residual circulation. During these periods residual currents may reach speeds of about 10cm/s which is about five times the quiescent flow value. During these latter periods, residual tidal elevations show the expected inverse correlation with atmospheric pressure (inverted barometer effect) with the tides being over or under estimated by about 0.2m.

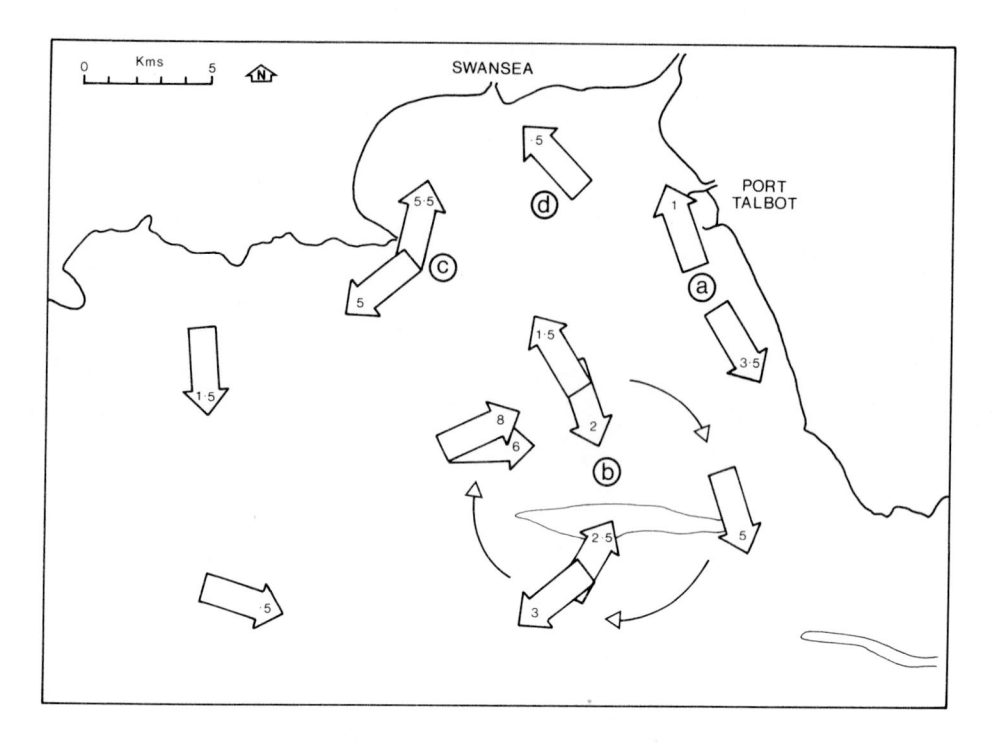

Figure 11.20. Schematic diagram showing the major features of the mean tidal or residual circulation in Swansea Bay and showing (a) an area of divergence to the south of Port Talbot; (b) an area of upwelling in a clockwise eddy over the Scarweather Sands; (c) an area of mean flow reversal off Mumbles Head; and (d) an area to the southwest of the River Neath, where the mean circulation may be influenced by density currents. Upper arrows indicate mid-depth residuals and lower arrows near-bottom residuals. The approximate strengths of the residuals (based on measured residuals in Fig. 11.10), in cm/s, are indicated by figures in the arrow heads.

In the shallow area to the north of the Bay, salinity and temperature measurements indicate that the freshwater discharges from the Rivers Neath, Tawe and Afan significantly modify the density field giving rise to density currents which are comparable with, if not greater than, the tidal residuals. It is not improbable that in the north of the Bay, the mean circulation is entirely controlled by the density field.

ACKNOWLEDGEMENTS

We would like to acknowledge the support and cooperation of our colleagues at the Institute of Oceanographic Sciences, Taunton. Salinity and temperature data were supplied by the Welsh National Water Development Authority, and Miss A.J. Wilding kindly made her tidal elevation data available. This work was supported financially by the Department of the Environment.

REFERENCES

Abdullah, M.I., Dunlop, H.M., and Gardner, D. (1973). Chemical and Hydrographic observations in the Bristol Channel during April and June, 1971. *J. Mar. Biol. Ass. UK., 53,* 299-319.

Bennett, A.F. (1975). Tides in the Bristol Channel. *Geophys. J.R. astr. Soc., 40,* 37-43.

Bowden, K.F. (1953). Note on wind drift in a channel in the presence of tidal currents. *Proc. R. Soc., A219,* 426-446.

Bowden, K.F. (1955). Physical Oceanography of the Irish Sea, *Fish. Invest., Lond., Ser. 2, 18,* 67pp.

Bowden, K.F., Fairbairn, L.A., and Hughes, P. (1959). The distribution of shearing stresses in a tidal current. *Geophys. J.R. astr. Soc., 2,* 288-305.

Cooper, L.H.N. (1967). The Physical Oceanography of the Celtic Sea. *Oceanogr. Mar. Biol. Ann. Rev., 5,* 99-110.

Defant, A. (1951). *Physical Oceanography,* Vol. 1. Pergamon Press, Oxford, 729pp.

Godin, G. (1972). *The Analysis of Tides.* Liverpool University Press, 264pp.

Gonella, J. (1972). A rotary-component method for analysing meteorological and oceanographic vector time series. *Deep Sea Res., 19,* 833-846.

Grace, S.F. (1936). Friction in the tidal currents of the Bristol Channel. *Mon. Not. R. astr. Soc. geophys. Suppl., 3,* 388-395.

Graff, J. (1978). Abnormal sea levels in the North West. *Dock Harb. Auth., 58,* 366-371.

Hamilton, P. (1973). The Circulation of the Bristol Channel. *Geophys. J.R. astr. Soc., 32,* 409-422.

Hammond, T.M., and Collins, M.B. (1979). Flume studies of the response of various current meter rotor/propellers to combinations of unidirectional and oscillatory flow. *Dt. Hydrog. Zeit., 32,* 39-58.

Heaps, N.S. (1968). Estimated effects of a barrage on tides in the Bristol Channel. *Proc. Inst. Civ. Engrs., 40,* 495-509.

Heaps, N.S. (1972). Estimation of density currents in the Liverpool Bay area of the Irish Sea. *Geophys. J.R. astr. Soc., 80,* 415-432.

Heaps, N.S. (1978). Linearized vertically-integrated equations for residual circulation in coastal seas. *Dt. Hydrog. Zeit., 31,* 147-169.

Heathershaw, A.D. (1977). Water Circulation in Swansea Bay. *I.O.S. Internal Document No. 18,* 11pp.(Unpublished manuscript).

Heathershaw, A.D., and Hammond, F.D.C. (1979a). Swansea Bay. Tidal currents: observed tidal and residual circulations and their response to meteorological conditions. I.O.S. Report (In preparation).

Hunt, J.N. (1964). Tidal Oscillations in estuaries. *Geophys. J.R. astr. Soc., 8,* 440-455.

Hunter, J.H. (1979). On the interaction of M_2 and M_2 tidal velocities in relation to Quadratic and Higher Power Laws. *Dt. Hydrog. Zeit., 32,* 145-153.

Longuet-Higgins, M.S. (1969). On the transport of mass by time-varying ocean currents. *Deep Sea Res., 16,* 431-447.

Maddock, L., and Pingree, R.D. (1978). Numerical simulation of the Portland Tidal Eddies. *Estuar. Coast. Mar. Sci., 6,* 353-363.

N.E.R.C. (1972). The Severn Estuary and Bristol Channel. Natural Environment Research Council Publications Series C. No. 9, 20pp.

Neumann, G., and Pierson, W.J. (1966). *Principles of Physical Oceanography,* Prentice Hall, Inc. Englewood Cliffs, N.S. 545pp.

Owen, A. (1979). The tidal regime of the Bristol Channel: a numerical modelling approach. (In preparation).

Pingree, R.D., and Griffiths, D.K. (1979). Sand transport paths around the British Isles resulting from M_2 and M_4 tidal interactions. *J. Mar. Biol. Ass. UK., 59,* 497-513.

Proudman, J. (1953). *Dynamical Oceanography.* Methuen, London, 409pp.

Pugh, D.T., Howarth, M.J., and Rossiter, J.R. (1971/72). An assessment of the knowledge of the Physical Oceanography of Liverpool Bay, the Severn Estuary and Bristol Channel. I.C.O.T. Internal Report No. 31, 20pp.

Ramster, J.W., Hughes, D.G., and Furnes, G.K. (1978). A 'Steadiness" Factor for estimating the variability residual drift in current meter records. *Dt. Hydrog.*

Zeit., *31*, 230-236.

Robinson, I.S. (1978). Tidal response of a wedge-shaped estuary to the installation of a power barrage: a simplified analytical approach. *Proc. Inst. Civ. Engrs.*, *65*, 773-790.

Robinson, I.S. (1979). The tidal dynamics of the Irish and Celtic Seas. *Geophys. J.R. astr. Soc.*, *56*, 159-197.

Stoner, J.H. (1977). A report on the first year of a programme to monitor inputs to Swansea Bay 1973-1974. *Welsh National Water Development Authority Report No. SS TW 77/2.* 24pp.

Taylor, G.I. (1921). Tides in the Bristol Channel. *Proc. Camb. Phil. Soc.*, *20*, 320-325.

Thorade, H. (1914). Die Geschuindigkeit von Triftstromungen und die Ekman'sche Theorie. *Ann. d. Hyd. u. Marit. Meteorolog.*, *42*, 379.

12. WAVES, CURRENTS AND LITTORAL DRIFT

R. H. Wilkinson

Institute of Oceanographic Sciences, Crossway, Taunton, Somerset TA1 2DW, U.K.

ABSTRACT

Measurements of the three velocity components and subsurface pressure in the nearshore zone were taken to monitor the wave and current conditions on Margam Beach, eastern Swansea Bay. Sediment tracer experiments were performed simultaneously.

The longshore currents are shown to be dominated by tidal influence, the tidal currents being shown to be little diminished by proximity to the shore. Any wave-induced longshore current will be confined to the breaker zone, which under normal conditions is about 25m wide. The width of the intertidal zone is about 400m. The size of both currents is shown to be of about the same order. The tracer experiments showed very little nett longshore movement of sediment even after six months. This is interpreted as the combined effect of the tide being a standing wave and in the majority of the wave energy approaching normal to the beach.

KEYWORDS

Longshore currents; Longshore transport; Wave-induced transport; Tidally-induced transport; Swansea Bay; Bristol Channel.

INTRODUCTION

This chapter is concerned with the longshore stability of the coastline in Swansea Bay, and in particular with the length of beach between Port Talbot and Sker Point, called Margam and Kenfig Sands (Fig. 12.1). The overall shape and orientation of the bay between the headlands at Mumbles and Sker Point is indicative of a long term longshore sediment transport equilibrium with the prevailing south westerly wave climate (King, 1972; Silvester, 1974; Komar, 1976 and others). Two observations support this suggestion, *viz*:

(i) there is no significant build up of sand on either side of Port Talbot Tidal Harbour; and
(ii) tracer placed on the beach by IOS Taunton during experiments in November 1976 was still very much in evidence when repeat experiments were attempted in May 1977.

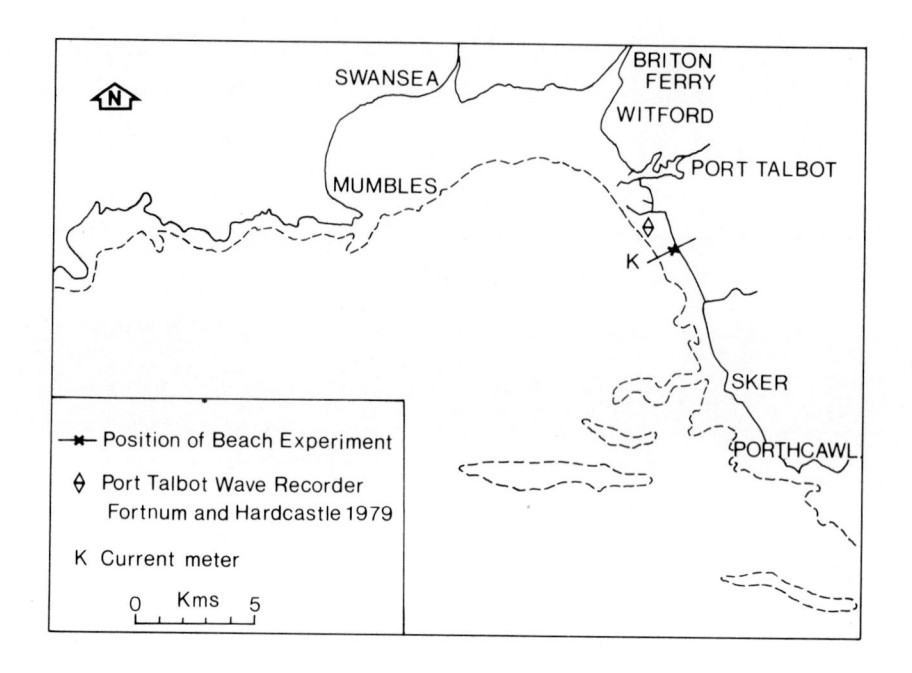

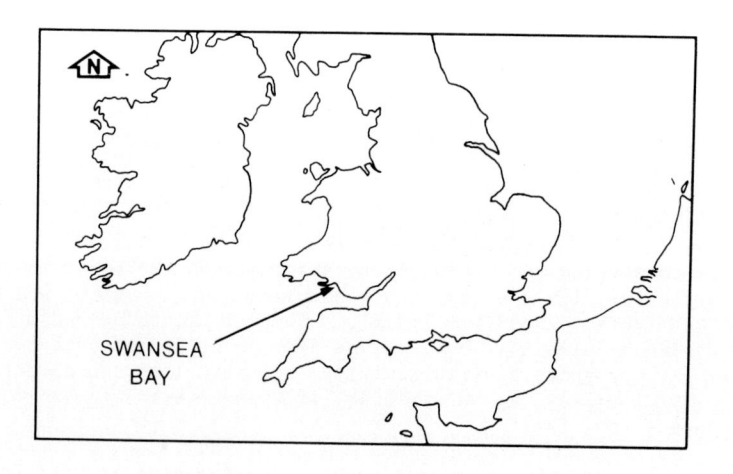

Figure 12.1. Location of Swansea Bay.

Waves, Currents and Littoral Drift

The longshore currents acting on the beach face and the waves incident on the beach were monitored whilst the littoral drift was investigated using separate tracer techniques. These experiments were intended to define the short term sediment movement and then compare the relative competence of waves and tides on such a beach.

EXPERIMENTAL TECHNIQUES

The three components of velocity in the nearshore zone were measured using two electromagnetic flowmeters orthogonally mounted 1m above the beach face (Fig. 12.2). Also visible on the rig in Fig. 12.2 were an FM wave pressure transducer and a prototype acoustic sediment movement detector. The location of this rig on the beach profile is shown in Fig. 12.3. Longshore current measurements were also available from a Plessey M021 self-recording current meter stationed 1km offshore (Station K on Fig. 12.1, see also Chapter 11, Fig. 11.2).

Electromagnetic flowmeter and pressure transducer records were obviously only available when the sensors were submerged, i.e., when the mean water level was at least above OD. During this period, it was possible to fit in an experimental run that was approximately 4 to 5 hours long. Twelve experimental runs were performed on tides ranging from springs to neaps, and the numbers used as plotting symbols in Figs. 12.4 and 12.5 refer to the numbers. The data was recorded on an analogue tape recorder, and digitized on return to the laboratory. The time-series so obtained were then statistically analysed using digital techniques. In this instance the relevant quantities are the 10 minute block means of the longshore horizontal velocity ($\bar{V}$) and the mean direction spectrum of the waves.

According to Galvin (1972), a wave breaks when its height is of the order of the water depth, and so, as the instruments are 1m above the beach face, the waves must be at least a metre high before any measurements could be obtained in the surf zone. This never happened during the experiment. The surf zone width (x_B) will be equal to breaker height/beach slope on a beach of uniform slope. The position of the instruments with respect to the water's edge obviously varies throughout the tidal cycle.

Estimates of the wave approach direction were available from radar observations made from the end of the southerly breakwater at Port Talbot Tidal Harbour (Heathershaw et al., 1979). These were taken from October 1976 to November 1977, and the apparatus achieved a success rate of 50%. This resulted in data not being available during the period of the beach experiment; however, the breakdowns were distributed throughout the year, and thus the results do give some idea of the angular wave climate.

The longshore sediment transport that occurs over a tidal cycle, from one low tide to the next, was assessed by the use of sediment tracer experiments that were performed simultaneously with the recording of data from the beach instrumentation rig. A fluorescent dyed sand of various colours and of similar grain size to the indigenous beach sand was used. Standard injection and sampling techniques were employed, and a full description and discussion of these can be found in Wilkinson (1980).

LONGSHORE CURRENTS

Comparison of the 10 minute block mean of the longshore component of velocity obtained from the beach rig with simultaneous tidal elevations at Port Talbot (kindly supplied by the British Transport Docks Board) is shown in Fig. 12.4. There is a large degree of scatter present between each curve that results from uncertainty in the absolute values of each axis. The longshore current zero is uncertain as a result of an unknown and variable DC offset on the electromagnetic flowmeters, and

Figure 12.2. Beach instrumentation rig, showing reference axes.

Waves, Currents and Littoral Drift 161

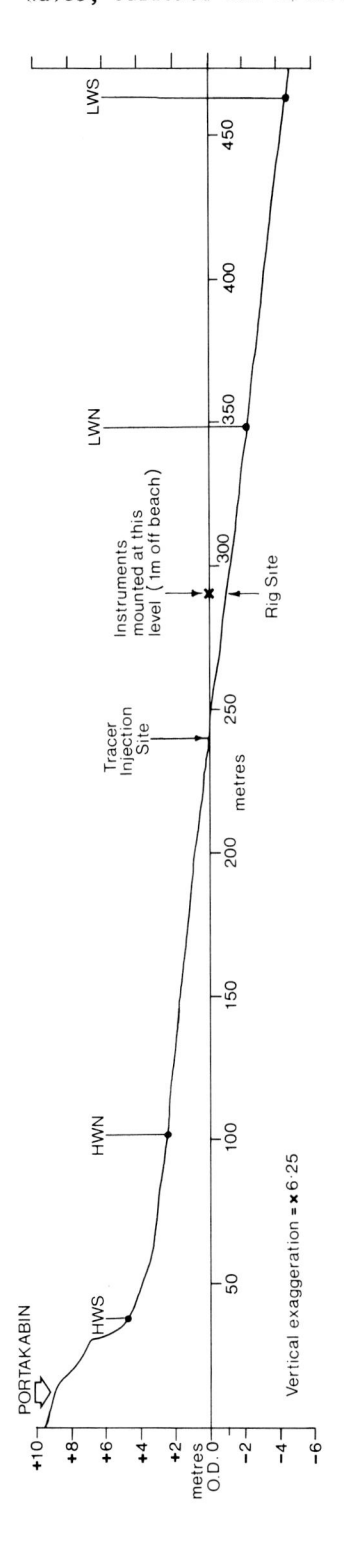

Figure 12.3. Position of instruments on beach cross-section.

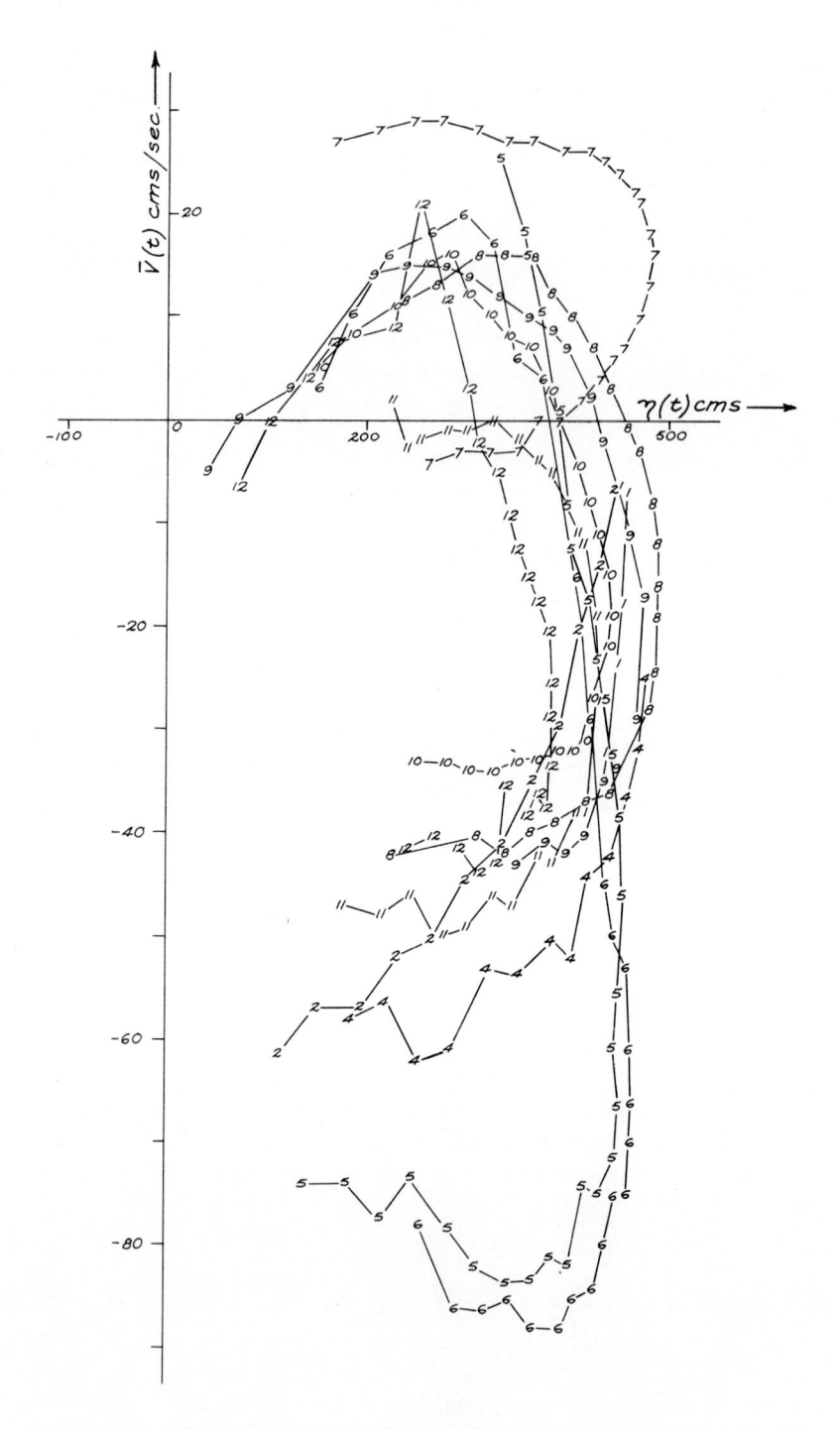

Figure 12.4. Surface elevation (η) against longshore velocity ($\bar{V}$).

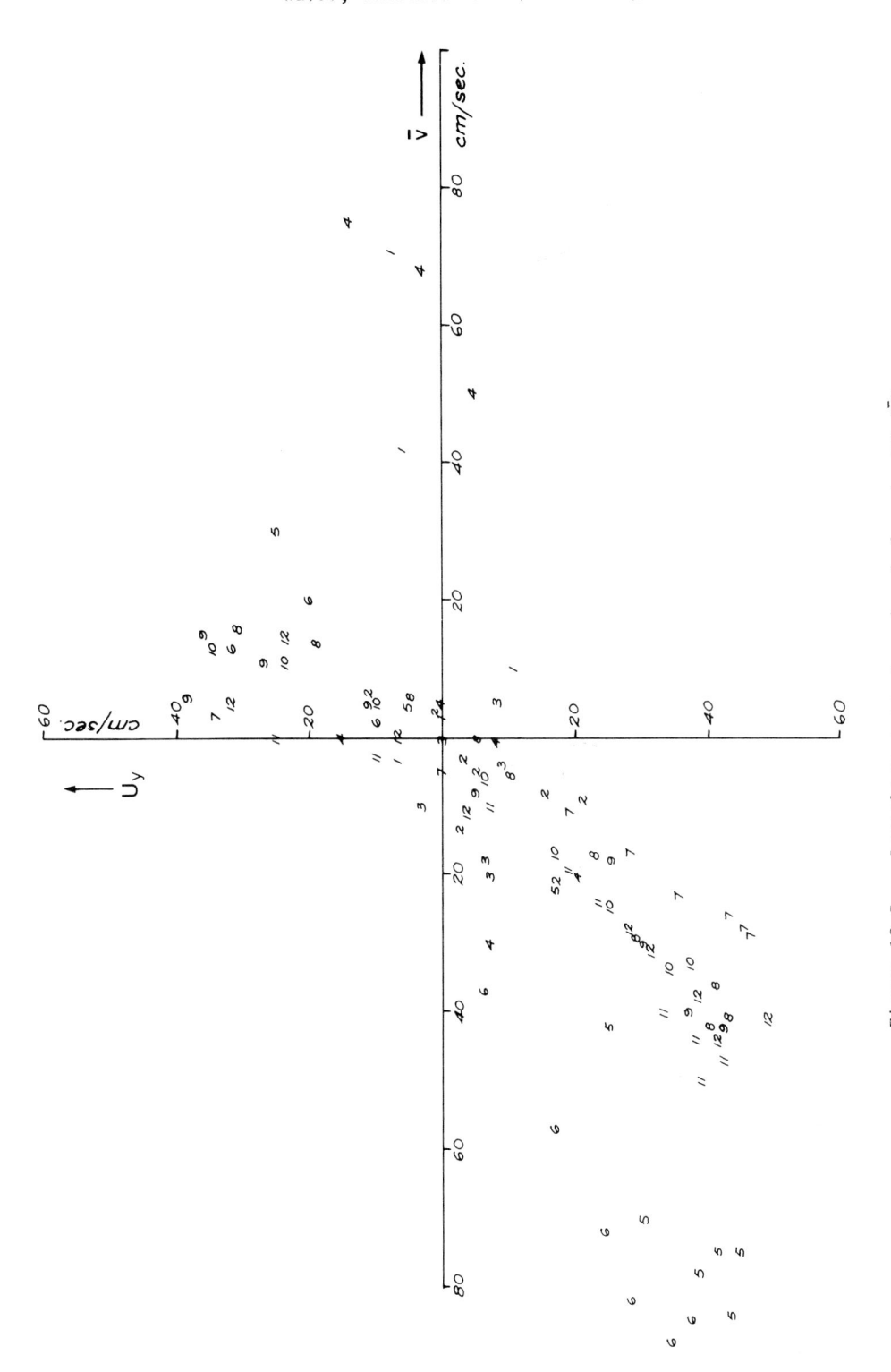

Figure 12.5. Longshore current on beach face by EM ($\bar{V}$) v. Longshore current from current meter K (u_y).

the tidal elevation, recorded in the tidal harbour, is uncorrected for wave set up on the beach (these topics are discussed more fully in Wilkinson (1980)). The shape of the curve in Fig. 12.4 indicates that the longshore current and tidal elevation are in quadrature, showing that the currents are the result of a tidal wave that is predominantly of a standing (wave) nature. Co-tidal data supplied by the Hydrographic Department (shown in Fig. 8.1) indicates that there is a point in the vicinity of the experiment where there is a "pure" standing tidal wave.

The longshore currents on the beach face ($\bar{V}$) were also compared with those measured 1km offshore by current meter K (u_y) in Figure 12.5. During 9 out of the 12 runs, $\bar{V}$ showed a good correspondence with u_y. The correlation coefficients of these 9 runs were all greater than 0.9, and the mean slope of the lines was 0.94. The comparison is even better away from the ends of the runs, which are times when the flowmeter may not be properly covered. The longshore velocity on the beach face ($\bar{V}$) is, of course, measured at a variable distance from the water's edge throughout the experimental run. The independence of the agreement between $\bar{V}$ and u_y from the distance from the water's edge suggests that the longshore velocity is approximately constant from 1km offshore to the seaward edge of the surf zone.

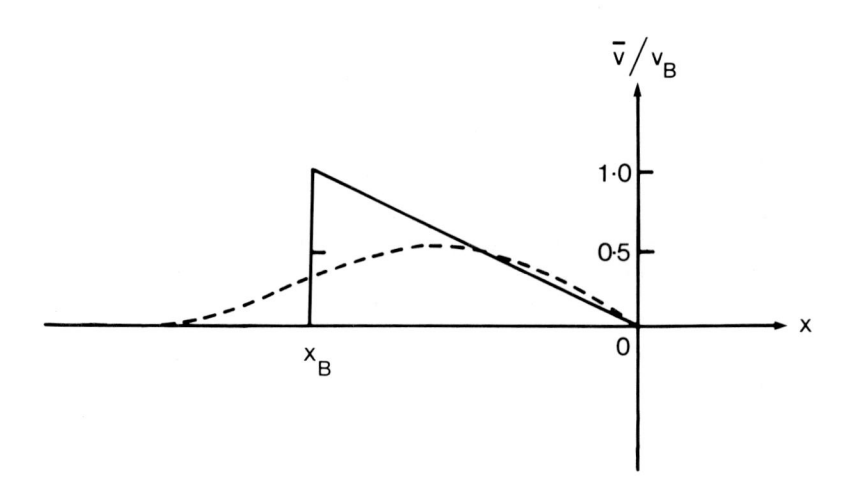

Figure 12.6. Theoretical wave-induced longshore current velocity profile with no lateral mixing, and with lateral mixing (dotted curve). From Longuet-Higgins (1972).

Wave-induced longshore currents are restricted to the vicinity of the surf zone (Longuet-Higgins, 1972) and, hence, we must rely on theoretical estimates. Longuet-Higgins showed the velocity distribution to be as in Fig. 12.6, with the velocity at the break point (V_B) given by:-

$$V_B = \frac{5\pi}{8} \frac{\alpha S}{C} g h_B \sin\theta_B$$

where C = Chezy friction coefficient (taken as 0.01).
α = ratio of wave amplitude:water depth at breaking (0.4).
S = beach slope (=0.2 at site).
g = 9.81m/s^2
h_B = water depth at breaker line.

Waves, Currents and Littoral Drift   165

θ_B = angle of wave incidence at breaker line

The curved profile, shown dotted, is that obtained when lateral mixing between water on either side of the breaker line is considered; a variable break point, as would occur with a real train of waves, would have a similar effect. The median of the monthly significant wave height found by Fortnum and Hardcastle (1979) at Port Talbot was 0.5m, giving a root mean square (RMS) value of 0.35m (Longuet-Higgins, 1952)(see also Chapters 14 and 37). Of the waves that were detected by the use of radar (Heathershaw et al., 1979), 75% were approaching in the sector between 230° and 240°, and 25% between 220° and 230°; the normal to the beach is at about 235°. These angular measurements are not related to the size of the waves; however, the limited wave approach angle for ocean, i.e. storm, waves can be seen by reference to the general orientation of the Bristol Channel (see, for example, Figs. 10.1 and 12.1). Also, all angular measurements of the wave energy distribution made during the tracer experiments showed that the vast majority of the energy was arriving normal to the beach during this period. Thus it is unlikely that the angle of wave incidence will ever exceed 5°, and so any wave-induced longshore current should be less than 0.3m/s.

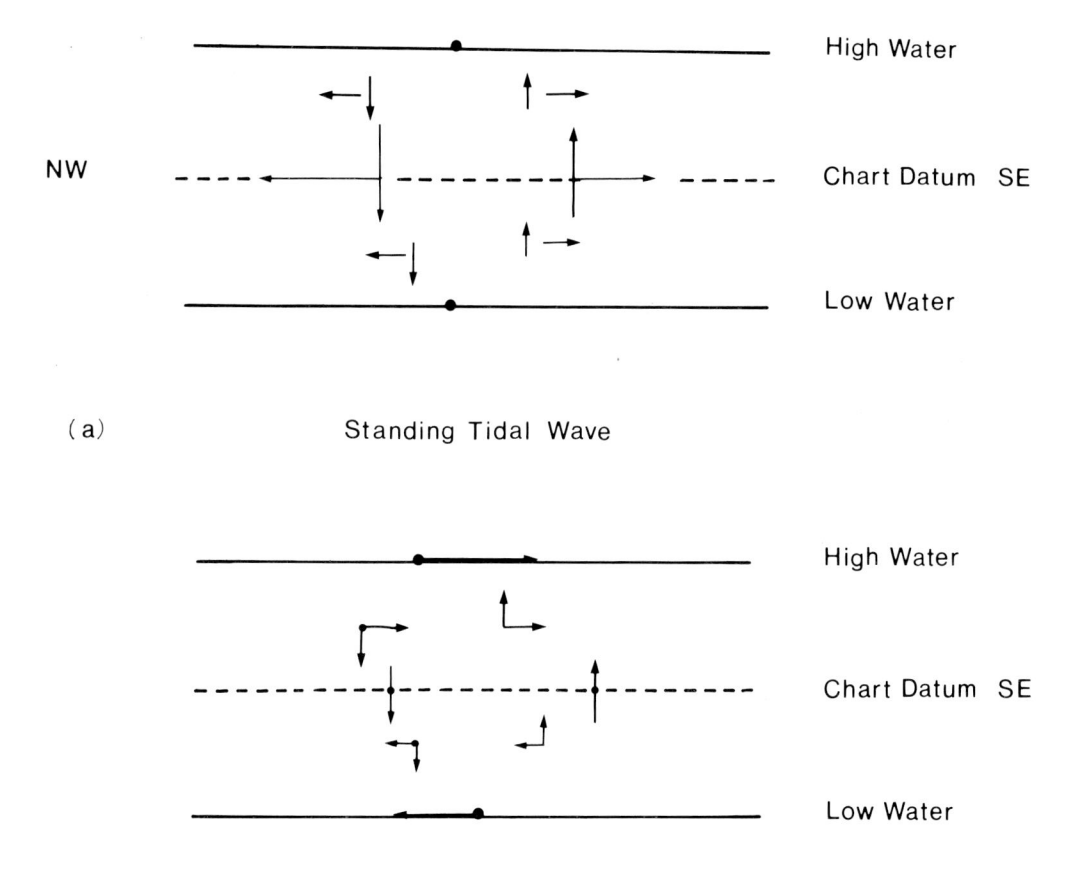

(a)   Standing Tidal Wave

(b)   Progressive Tidal Wave

Figure 12.7.   Action of longshore tidal current on beach face in relation to position of water's edge.

Thus, the wave-induced longshore currents that commonly occur on Margam/Kenfig beach are likely to be smaller than the longshore tidal currents. Their action on the beach face is restricted to the surf zone, which moves across the beach as the tide rises and falls, whereas the tidal current acts upon all the beach face that is below the instantaneous mean water level. The relation between the tidal current and the state of the tide is shown in Fig. 12.7(a). Each pair of arrows is drawn at the water's edge, the length of the horizontal arrow indicating the strength of the tidal current and the length of the vertical arrow indicating the rate at which the tide is rising. It can be seen that the action on the beach of the current under a standing tidal wave is symmetrical.

LONGSHORE SEDIMENT TRANSPORT

The position of the centroid of the tracer distribution was found at successive low tides and thus the amount of sand movement during successive tides could be assessed (Crickmore and Lean, 1962). The width of the beach face was taken to be 400m, and the depth of disturbance of the sand 2cm; hence the mass of sand moved since the previous tracer survey is:

$$\Sigma M = 14.31 \Delta \bar{y} \text{ tonnes}$$

where $\Delta \bar{y}$ is the change in the longshore position in metres of the centroid of the tracer cloud since the previous search. After an initial period during which the tracer may be coming into equilibrium with the indigenous sand, the movement of the centroid settled down to something mainly small ($\Delta \bar{y} \sim 1m$) and of random direction.

SEDIMENT BUDGET

The action of the tide on the beach has been seen to be symmetrical when the tidal wave is standing. Thus the amount of sand moved in one direction by the rising tide should be returned by the falling tide. Let us write the sediment budget for the longshore sand movement during a tidal cycle, and evaluate each term for the beach at Margam.

$$\Sigma M = M_{TL} + M_{TR} + 2M_W$$

where ΣM = Nett mass of sand moved during a tide (12.8hr).
M_{TL} = Mass moved by tide to the left.
M_{TR} = Mass moved by tide to the right.
M_W = Mass moved by waves in half a tide (6.4hr)
and $M_{TL} = -M_{TR}$

Wave-Induced Longshore Sand Movement

A generally accepted formula for wave-induced longshore sand transport in the surf zone is:

$$I_\ell = 0.77 (EC_h)_B \sin\theta_B \cos\theta_B \qquad \text{Komar (1976)}$$

where I_ℓ is the total load immersed weight transport rate in the whole surf zone, and $(EC_h)_B$ is the wave energy flux evaluated at the breaker line. This formula has its origins as an empirical correlation, but now has a theoretical derivation using radiation stress arguments and the principles of sediment movement energetics of Bagnold (1966)(Longuet-Higgins, 1972). The coefficient is however still found empirically. If the immersed weight flux is converted to a mass flux of sand, and evaluated over half a tidal cycle (6.4hr) for comparison with the tidal transport,

Waves, Currents and Littoral Drift

we obtain:

$$M_W = 6236 \, H^{5/2} \sin 2\theta_B \text{ tonnes}$$

where 'H' is the incident wave height in metres. This curve is plotted in Fig. 12.9.

Tidally Induced Longshore Sand Movement

The total load sediment transport rate on the beach face is found using the Ackers and White (1973) formula. As it is expected that the incoming waves will 'feel bottom' over the whole width of the beach face, the bottom stress used in the Ackers and White method (from logarithmic velocity distribution assumptions) must be modified to account for the waves. The method of Bijker (1967) was used for this; the use of this combination for longshore sediment movement calculations was evaluated by Swart (1976) and found to be the most satisfactory available.

It results in the longshore tidally induced sediment transport rate being written as:

$$Q_T = Q_T(V_{HT}, HT, Z_o, \text{Depth}, D_{35}, WHT, \lambda)$$

where
- V_{HT} = longshore current at height HT above bed ⎫
- Z_o = bed roughness (∼0.5cm)   ⎬ defines log velocity profile and hence bed shear stress
- Depth = depth of flow   ⎭
- D_{35} = 35 percentile grain size diameter
- WHT = wave height   ⎫ used to calculate wave orbital velocity at bed for
- λ = wave length ⎭ computation of Bijker stress magnification factor.

The mass of sand transported on the beach face to the right by the rising tide was then calculated from:

$$M_{TR} = \int_{\text{Low tide}}^{\text{High tide}} \int_{\text{Low Water}}^{\text{Water's edge}} Q_T \, dx \, dt$$

$$\approx \sum_{N=1}^{20} \left\{ \Delta t_N \sum_{i=1}^{N} Q_{Ti} \, \Delta x \right\}$$

The integral was evaluated numerically by replacing the smooth tidal elevation curve by 20 equal depth increases, as shown in Fig. 12.8(a). All parameters for calculating Q_T were taken as the time average over the variable time interval. As this is an order of magnitude calculation to investigate the competence of the tidal current to transport sand as compared with the wave induced current, an idealised form of the tidal curves was used.

$$V_{100}(t) = \hat{V}_{100} \sin \omega t$$
$$\zeta(t) = -\frac{TR}{2} \cos \omega t$$

and let $\hat{V}_{100} = TR/10$

where $V_{100}(t)$ = longshore tidal current 1m above seabed
TR = tidal range
$\zeta(t)$ = surface elevation

(as yet, any sediment transport calculation is of a speculative nature due to uncertainties in the transport rate formulae; highly accurate velocity data, etc., is

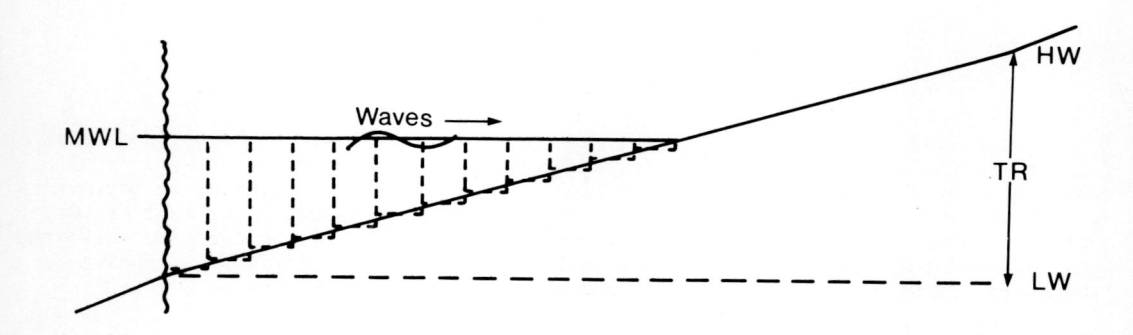

(a) Cross section of beach for tidal transport calculations

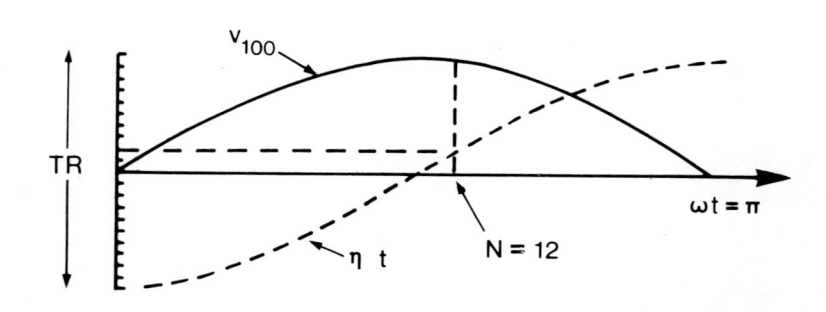

(b) Idealized behaviour of longshore tidal current (V_{100}) and surface elevation (η)

Figure 12.8.

inappropriate).

The calculations were performed for a series of tidal ranges and wave heights. The effect of varying wavelength of the incident wave was minimal, as under the conditions on the beach face, the waves were shallow water waves. The amount of tidal sediment transport on the beach face is proportional to its width, and thus for a given tidal range, it is proportional to the beach slope. The resulting set of curves are plotted in Fig. 12.9.

DISCUSSION

In Figure 12.9, a comparison can be easily made of the relative capabilities of wave induced and tidally induced mechanisms of mobilising sediment. (Compare with Chapter 14). The tidal standing wave in its idealised form used here cannot produce any nett transport over a full tidal cycle. The tidal range on this beach is between about 5m (neaps) and 10m (springs). The wave height climate of the area measured by Fortnum and Hardcastle (1979) gives a median monthly RMS wave height of 35cm (the RMS is more appropriate for calculating sediment transport rates on longshore current speeds, Komar, 1976). Thus much more sand is going to be moved to and fro on the beach face by the tides than is going to be moved by the available waves, so any nett movement will be as a result of small differences between the flood and ebb of the tide. In the offshore zone, Heathershaw and Hammond (Chapter 11) found residual tidal currents along the coast of up to 4cm/s, which results in sediment transport rates in the offshore zone of up to about 0.02 tonnes/m/day (see also Chapter 15). These sediment residuals are in the same direction as the tidal current residuals in this region, though of course, the non-linear nature of the transport formulae means that the two directions are not necessarily the same. Heathershaw and Hammond (*op.cit.*) find the current meter station K is at a divergence in the residual pattern of both tides and sediment transport, though both are weak.

All measurements of wave direction during the tracer experiment gave a mean direction spectrum indicating a normal wave approach for any frequencies containing a significant amount of energy. Thus, the small random tracer movements detected during the experiment can only have been the result of small random differences in the effects of the rising and falling tide.

If the tidal wave had been progressive, then nett sediment movement on the beach above mid-water is possible, as can be seen in Fig. 12.7(b). The tidal current is always in the same direction when this part of the beach is covered; i.e., the top half of the beach is only subjected to currents in the direction of propagation of the tidal wave. Non-linear effects of depth could also lead to nett sediment movement in this direction on the bottom half of the beach face.

CONCLUSIONS

The tidal currents are far more capable of moving sand on the beach face at Margam/Kenfig Beach than the waves, though the standing nature of the tidal wave means that any nett movement is small, being the result of small differences between the flood and ebb of the tide. The wave-induced mechanism is very ineffective in this region in that waves with large amounts of energy at significant angles to the shoreline are not available. A mechanism for the longshore drift of material on a beach face resulting from the action of a progressive tidal wave has been proposed.

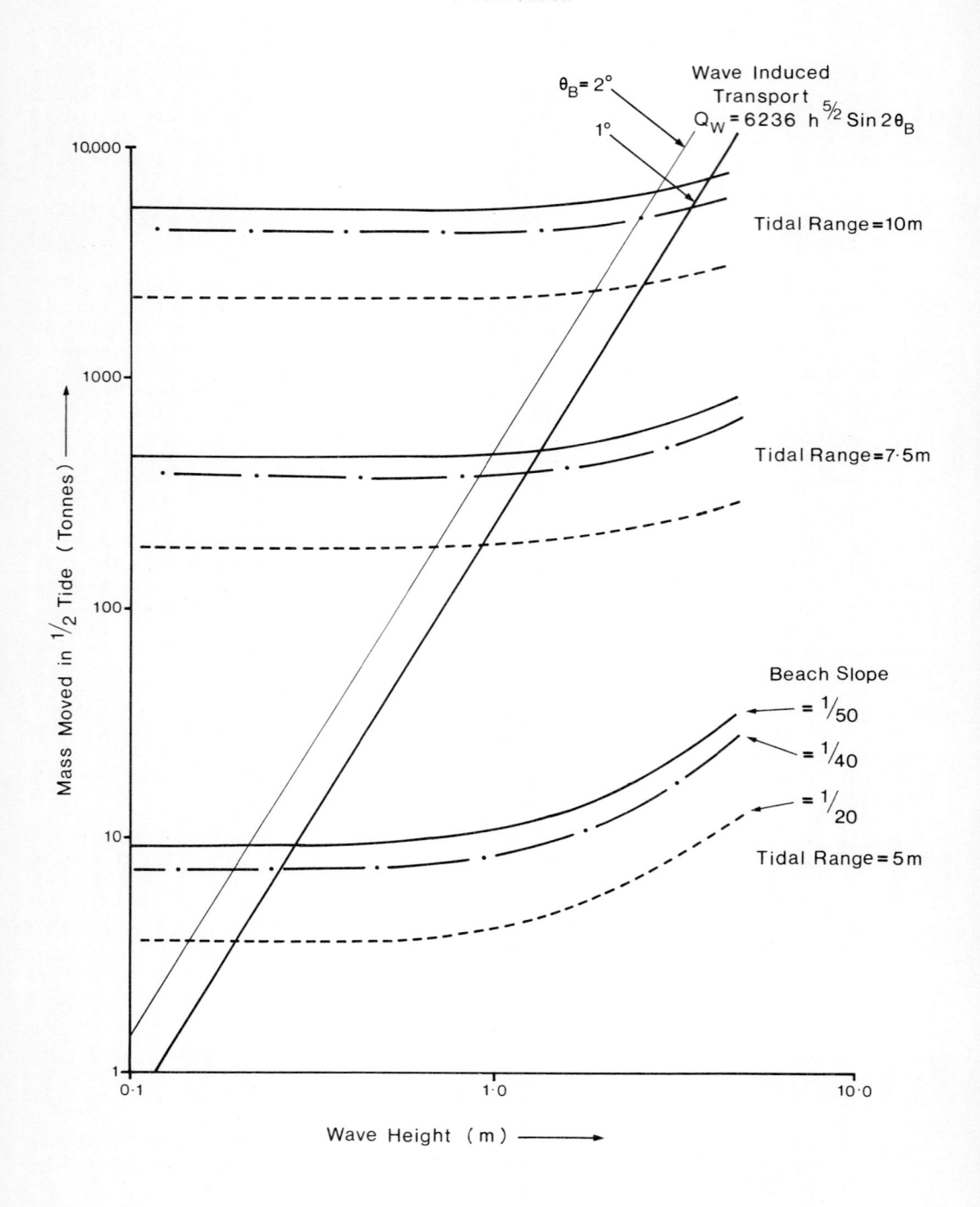

Figure 12.9.

ACKNOWLEDGEMENTS

The author is grateful to Drs. A.P. Carr and A.D. Heathershaw who organised and undertook the field experiments and whose advice has been invaluable in assisting in this interpretation of the results. The author is also grateful to D.J. Corns for assistance with the data analysis and computing, and Dr. K.R. Dyer for his many invaluable comments on the manuscript.

This work was financially supported by the Department of the Environment

REFERENCES

Ackers, P., and White, W.R. (1973). Sediment transport - new approach and analysis. *Proc. Am. Soc. Civ. Eng.*, Hy.11, *99*, 2041-2060.

Bagnold, R.A. (1966). An approach to the sediment transport problem from general physics. *U.S. Geol. Surv. Prof. Pap., 422-1.*, 37pp.

Bijker, E.W. (1966). The increase of bed shear in a current due to wave motion. *Proc. 10th Coastal Engrg. Conf.*, Tokyo, 1, 746-765.

Crickmore, M.J., and Lean, G.H. (1962). The measurement of sand transport by means of radioactive tracers. *Proc. Roy. Soc., A.266,* 402-421.

Fortnum, B.C.H., and Hardcastle, P.J. (1979). Waves recorded at Port Talbot on the south coast of Wales. Institute of Oceanographic Sciences, Internal Report No. 78. (Unpublished manuscript).

Galvin, C.J. (1972). Waves breaking in shallow water. *In:* Meyer, R.E. (Ed.). *Waves and Beaches and Resulting Sediment Transport,* Academic Press, 413-436.

Heathershaw, A.D., Blackley, M.W.L., and Hardcastle, P.J. (1979). Wave direction estimates in coastal waters using radar. Submitted to *Coastal Engineering*.

King, C.A.M. (1972). *Beaches and Coasts*. 2nd Ed. Edward Arnold.

Komar, P.D. (1976). *Beach Processes and Sedimentation*. Prentice Hall Inc.

Longuet-Higgins, M.S. (1952). On the statistical distribution of the heights of sea waves. *J. Mar. Res., 11*(3), 245-266.

Longuet-Higgins, M.S. (1972). Recent progress in the study of longshore currents. *In:* Meyer, R.E. (Ed.). *Waves and Beaches and Resulting Sediment Transport,* Academic Press, 203-249.

Silvester, R. (1974). *Coastal Engineering II,* Elsevier Scientific Pub. Co.

Swart, D.H. (1976). *Coastal Sediment Transport*. Delft Hydraulics Laboratory. Report No. R968, Delft, Holland, 61pp.

Wilkinson, R.H. (1980). Swansea Bay Project Topic Report No. 7, Institute of Oceanographic Sciences, Internal Report. (In preparation).

DISCUSSION II

CHAPTER 7:

Langdon: Can I ask Dr. Carr, I wondered how you worked out measurements of gradient change? Did you take HW and LW level and the distance between and calculate the changes compared with now? If you did, how do you know what the tide heights were then and that they were the same as the tide heights now?

Carr: In fact, there were a series of no less than four different surveys. Sometimes there were questions as to whether it was a complete revision, sometimes there were questions because the Ordnance Survey changed their methods of calculating their tide levels before and after 1868. Also, there's always the question that the LW marks are slightly less accurate because surveyed tide levels didn't follow predictions. The data showed, off the Neath area, that the beach had gone back progressively, in almost uniform steps between the different surveys; this comment can apply equally well in the area of the old Port Talbot Tidal docks, so there is a pretty consistent pattern. When Mike Blackley talks on the more recent changes in the beach (Chapter 17), you will see that the progressive steepening of the beach along the whole of the eastern coastline was relatively slow in the period between the 1850's and 1960's.

CHAPTERS 8 and 9:

Broadbent: Firstly, have you tried to get an offshore tide gauge record in this area? Secondly, have you done any work on any observed negative residuals?

Collins: In answer to the first part, we haven't installed any offshore tide gauges, but used tide gauges around the embayment. The stilling-well type gauges installed at Swansea and Port Talbot (by B.T.D.B.) were utilised and the accuracy of these has been determined from tests. Portable tide gauges were used elsewhere. We would have liked to install sea-bed gauges and it is one of the areas of research to be developed.

Williams (nee Wilding): In answer to the second part, the only large negative surge which did occur was that in January 1978; this was a stronge event, because of the marked semi-diurnal oscillations. As it didn't strictly come within my period of observations, I didn't in fact pursue the analysis any further; however, during 1976 and 1977, there was no negative surge greater than approximately 60cm.

Britton: Do you have any idea of the area of generation of the surges and, secondly, do you think that you should set up a warning service, similar to that on the east coast of the British Isles.

Williams: It is very difficult to say where they are coming from because of the limited observations to the west; indeed, in setting up a system, Lands End would be the furthest warning station. The construction of the Severn Barrage would obviously affect surges in the Bristol Channel, if not further to the west.

Collins: During the surge of November 1977, there certainly was extensive flooding on the flood plain of the Neath Valley.

Britton: I believe there was also a large surge in Avonmouth in 1940.

Collins: There was also some talk of extensive flooding in the Neath during the 1930's and 1940's. The really important factor is whether or not the surge coincides with high water. Other research being carried out in the Dept. of Oceanography (by J.K. Rigler) has been examining pressure within large-scale meteorological systems, using Scilly Isles data, to try to predict the surges. The derived regression equations, described certain surges, but others fell outside the general pattern. Certain industrial concerns located on flood plains along the west coast are undoubtedly under pressure from this flooding risk.

CHAPTER 11:

Collins: Could Dr. Heathershaw explain the southerly flow residuals for the westerly stations?

Heathershaw: I don't have any explanation. The residual flows give some sort of agreement with Uncle's (IMER) model, but the thing that spoils this is that we've found anomalous phases for the M_2 tidal constituents in the currents there.

Norton: We've done some measurements at the south dumping ground, which is one minute to east and three minutes to south of the southwesterly station of Dr. Heathershaw, and, although the periods of observation are only a couple of days, we have actually had a bottom residual which was east to northeast. I don't know whether that ties in or not? The other observation of interest, was that there was an asymmetry in the tidal movement where there was a significantly faster bottom flow on the ebb. Again, I wondered whether that tied in with your results?

Heathershaw: I would issue a word of caution about these diagrams (Figs. 11.10 and 11.20) because of the difficulty of presenting residual flow data. With a residual current of only 0.5cm/sec, one really has to ask oneself just how significant it is. In Swansea Bay, for example, it is apparent that the residual flows can change quite dramatically, with changes in the meteorological conditions.

CHAPTER 12:

Moran: Could Dr. Wilkinson explain the method of calculation of a mean wave height of 50cm. Our own observations in the Loughor Estuary, a very much more sheltered environment, have revealed mean height of 35cm?

Wilkinson: I was talking about median of the monthly significant wave heights. The extreme waves also approach the beach normally and they don't provide any longshore movement of sediment either.

Moran: Wouldn't a larger wave have a bigger effect than a smaller one?

Wilkinson: Yes, but they also approach the beach normally.

Britton: Do you have any information regarding the depth of disturbance of the sediment?

Carr: This was difficult, but we think that during the actual short-term tracer experiments, most of the movement has been in the top 2cm; it would be to a greater depth over a longer period. Depth of disturbance is one of the thorny problems of tracer work in general.

Britton: I've been impressed by so many calculations of methods of sediment transport. Did you consider taking direct measurements using a sediment trap?

Carr: No, we didn't.

Broadbent: What actual instrumentation was used and did you use other tracers (e.g. radioactive)?

Heathershaw: The three wave-induced velocity components were measured with two E/M current meters. In fact, 4 velocities were measured with the onshore velocity on two channels. On the beach we were restricted to the use of a fluorescent tracer because radioactive tracers, of the type used offshore, represents a potential health risk.

Allen: You mentioned that it took a day or two for tracer sand to settle down, and said that that was due to some difficulty with the material of the tracer; was its size distribution similar to that of the beach material?

Wilkinson: The size distribution of tracer never matches exactly natural sediment. The problem is that the top surface of the beach is obviously the most mobile and differences will occur unless the sediment is evently distributed to the "depth of *disturbance".*

<u>Carr</u>: *Offshore radioactive tracer experiments described by Dr. Heathershaw in Swansea Bay also showed much greater initial rates of transport than in the later stages. I think that one has got to watch the material until the movement settles down to something sensible; high rates of movement to start with are probably unrepresentative and I'm not certain if they can be overcome.*

<u>Collins</u>: *We have also installed some self-recording current meters on a scaffolding rig off Aberavon approximately at the "low water spring mark" the results from this experiment were very variable in a N/S direction along the beach. Some recent work suggests that this may just be the result of wave action on the impellors themselves. On one occasion we thought we had lost a meter but found it buried approximately 60cm down under the sand surface. Obviously, under severe conditions, there is a large depth of disturbance.*

<u>Wilkinson</u>: *Normally, I envisage the tide making quite a large amount of mobile sand.*

<u>Collins</u>: *How does the transport path indicated by the tracer experiments compare with indirect long-term indications of longshore transport, such as accumulation against groynes, harbour walls, etc? Also, how important is the longshore transport mode in terms of the overall pattern of sediment transport within the area?*

<u>Wilkinson</u>: *Two combined flow measurements and tracer experiments were carried out, one in November and one in May; in November, the electronic instrumentation didn't work very satisfactorily. In May, when we had hoped our original tracer to be out of the way, it became very obvious that much of the tracer we put down in November was still there. In terms of long-term accretion, and purely on personal observation, there does not appear to be any build up of sand on either side of Port Talbot Tidal Harbour.*

<u>Langdon</u>: *I used to stand on the breakwater at Port Talbot Tidal Harbour, when it was constructed over a beach; at that time, the beach was the same level on both sides, but you stand on it today and you'll find that the tide comes much further up the beach here than it does in the harbour. This difference seems to indicate, to me, that material comes into the harbour. Your thesis was that there is no littoral drift - if you look under the pier you'll find that there is. I know that you were talking about eastern Swansea Bay, but I recall when I first came to Swansea, how people used to say to me "what happened to the golden sands of Swansea? - There used to be a golden beach, where did it go, did it come back here?" Does anything you've seen give any ideas what is happening further round the Bay?*

<u>Wilkinson</u>: *The most convincing reason for no drift was the presence of the tracer on the beach after the winter period. I do not have any information on quantities of longshore transport elsewhere.*

<u>Carr</u>: *We calculated the centroid of the tracer which had been put down in November 1976 and which was still there during the injection in May 1977; it represented quite a sizeable quantity of the original tracer, something like 20 per cent. The centroid showed that the nett amount of movement of the labelled material was less than 50m towards the south during the 6 months winter period.*

<u>Flower</u>: *Mr. Langdon mentioned the difference in levels on the two sides of the Port Talbot Main Breakwater. I have also realised that and I am now organising the taking of levels on each side of the Breakwater. Therefore, in two or three years time, there will be some information available concerning the rate of change of these levels. The other point is that Mr. Jackson (Chapter 10) indicated that the waves came in from a seaward direction for some 3 or 4 thousand miles. My observation is that generally these waves come in at an angle of about 30° west of a line Normal to the Breakwater.*

<u>Wilkinson</u>: *The main angle measurements that I have analysed have come down normal*

to the beach, but we've also carried out some radar measurements of wave angle approach and perhaps Dr. Heathershaw could comment on those?

Heathershaw: The directions of wave approach that we get from the radar measurements at Port Talbot, are from a fairly narrow range of angles which deviate slightly from normal incidence. We had the radar set up on the end of the breakwater at Port Talbot, and unfortunately, during the storm surge of November, 1977, it was destroyed by large waves. However, even from these limited records there is a fairly narrow range of angles of wave approach and "normal" during the beach experiments means normal to within a degree or two. Over a longer period of time, it seems from the radar observations that directions of wave approach of $\pm\ 15°$ from the angle of the navigation channel would be in order.

13. SEDIMENTRY BED FORMS AND LINEAR BANKS

R. C. Britton[*] and S. R. Britton[**]

[*]*Department of Land Surveying, North East London Polytechnic*
[**]*B. P. Exploration Co. Ltd., Sunbury on Thames, Middlesex, U.K.*

ABSTRACT

The influence of the dynamic environment, primarily waves and tidal currents, on producing and maintaining sedimentary sea bed structures is examined. The main areas under consideration are the Nash, Scarweather and Helwick linear banks, and their associated sand wave fields.

It is concluded that the banks were originated during a period of lower sea level, the sand source being from glacial deposits, eroded mainly by waves. It is shown that the siting of the banks was not dependent on underlying structure and topography.

The present day influence of the strong, rectilinear, tidal currents around the banks, and the high energy wave environment on the banks is assessed, and the resulting variations in mobile sediment and lag deposits are described.

KEYWORDS

Linear banks; Sediment distribution; Sub-surface geology; Tidal currents; Waves; Sediment transport; Swansea Bay; Bristol Channel.

INTRODUCTION

This chapter is concerned with geographical areas near Swansea Bay in which the dominant sea bed sediment is non-cohesive sand sized material. In its response to present and past hydrodynamic environments, this material has been shaped into major sedimentary structures - linear banks and sand waves (see also Britton, 1977; Turner, 1976).

THE PRESENT DAY ENVIRONMENT

Sea Bed Morphology

Linear Banks: 'Linear bank' is synonymous with the term 'tidal current ridge',

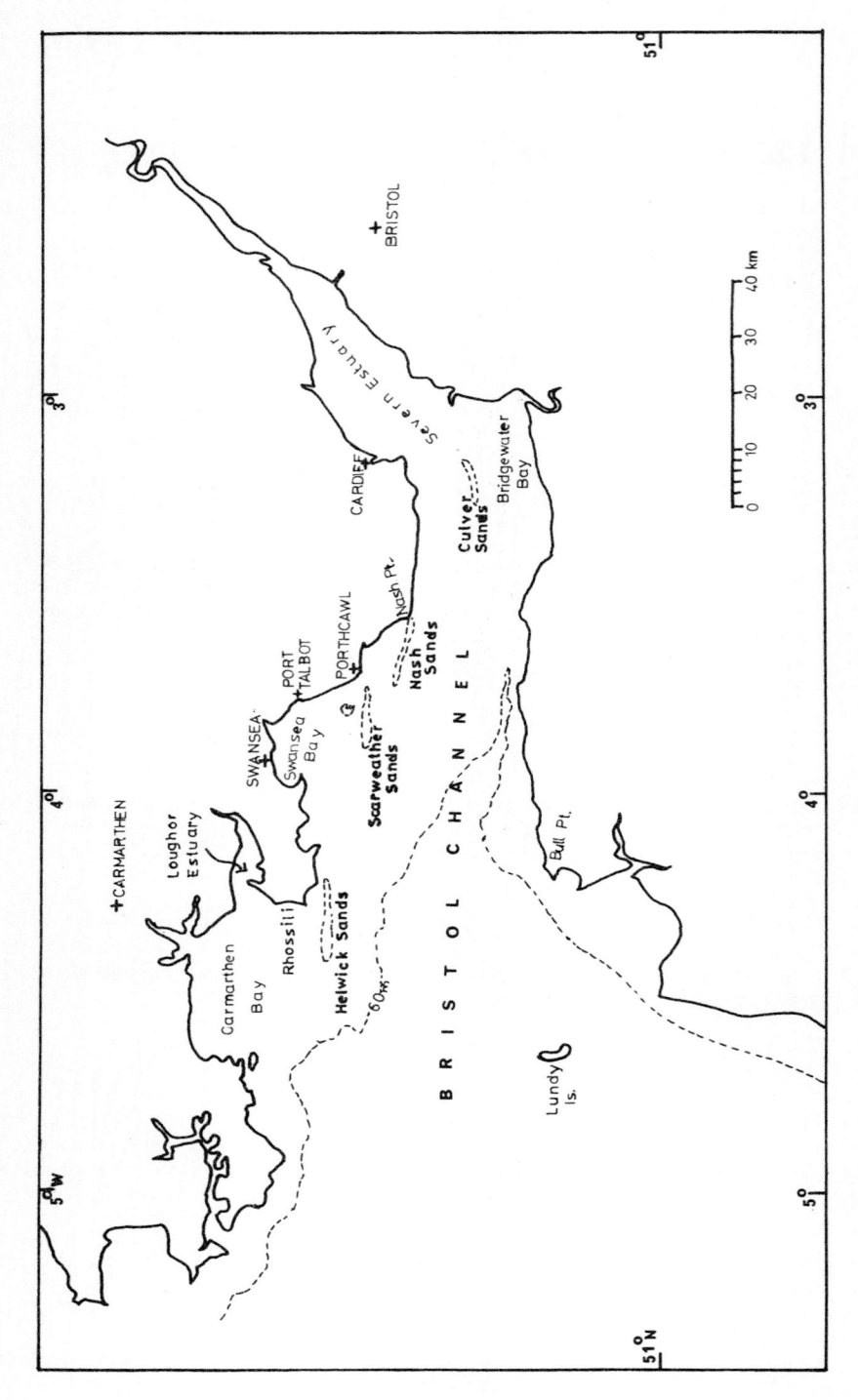

Figure 13.1. Regional Setting: Bristol Channel

first used by Off (1963), to describe linear sand bodies, on continental shelves, which are orientated with their long axes approximately parallel to tidal current cirections.

There are four major linear banks within the Bristol Channel (Fig. 13.1), of which three are sited in areas immediately peripheral to Swansea Bay: the Nash Sand, the Scarweather Sand, and the Helwick Sand. The fourth bank, the Culver Sand, has developed further to the east, between Barry and Bridgewater Bay, and will not be discussed here.

Some significant physical dimensions and characteristics of these banks are presented in Table 13.1. Linear banks are common features of many continental shelf seas,

TABLE 13.1. Dimensions of Some Linear Sand Banks

Bank/ Geographical Area	Length (km)	Maximum Width (km)	Maximum Height (m)	Typical Length/ Width Ratio	Mean Orientation (°, relative to North).
Helwick	13.5	2.7	30	5:1	082
Scarweather	9.6	1.6	20	6:1	100
Nash	13.7	1.2	17	11.4:1	105
Culver	9.7	0.9	12	10.8:1	078
Southern North Sea	12-52	0.9-2.2	24-42	23:1	-
East Coast U.S.A.	8-14	2.0	15-30	15:1	-
Great Bahama Bank	16-24	1.0-2.0	8	20:1	-
Arabian Gulf	8-80	0.8-3.2	3.7-16.5	25:1	-

and to set the Bristol Channel features in a wider context, information is also given from other geographical areas (Caston, 1972; Duane et al., 1972; Off, 1963 and Purdy, 1961). In terms of dimensional averages, the Bristol Channel banks are atypical, in being less linear than most features. They are also distinguished from the majority of banks in being isolated forms, rather than occurring in parallel or sub-parallel groups.

The orientations listed in Table 13.1 are average values, for, although the Bristol Channel banks have an approximately east-west trend, they are, to a greater or lesser extent, sinuous in plan. The banks rise from a predominantly flat sea bed, at a marked break in slope; they remain submerged at all states of the tide, except spring low waters, when their crests may be briefly exposed. In cross section the banks are usually asymmetrical, although the direction of asymmetry may vary along the length of an individual bank. The gradients of the flanks of the banks are between 0°30' and 3°30'. Examples of the cross sectional morphology are given in Fig. 13.2.

Sand Waves: Smaller sand bodies, termed sand waves, which form with their alignment transverse to the tidal current direction, are also common features of shelf seas; they are sometimes found in close association with linear banks, and this is the situation in the Bristol Channel. Sand waves are particularly well developed in the vicinity of the Helwick Sands, where they attain heights of up to 11m. Near the Nash and Scarweather Banks, sand waves are present, but rarely attain a height of more than 2-3m. Their areal extent around these three banks is shown in Fig. 13.3. The direction of cross-sectional asymmetry is also shown in Fig. 13.3, where appropriate. It is generally agreed that, for asymmetrical sand waves, a direction of sand transport may be inferred from their asymmetry (e.g. van Veen, 1935; Stride, 1963), the steeper slope being on the down-stream side of the transport path. Sand

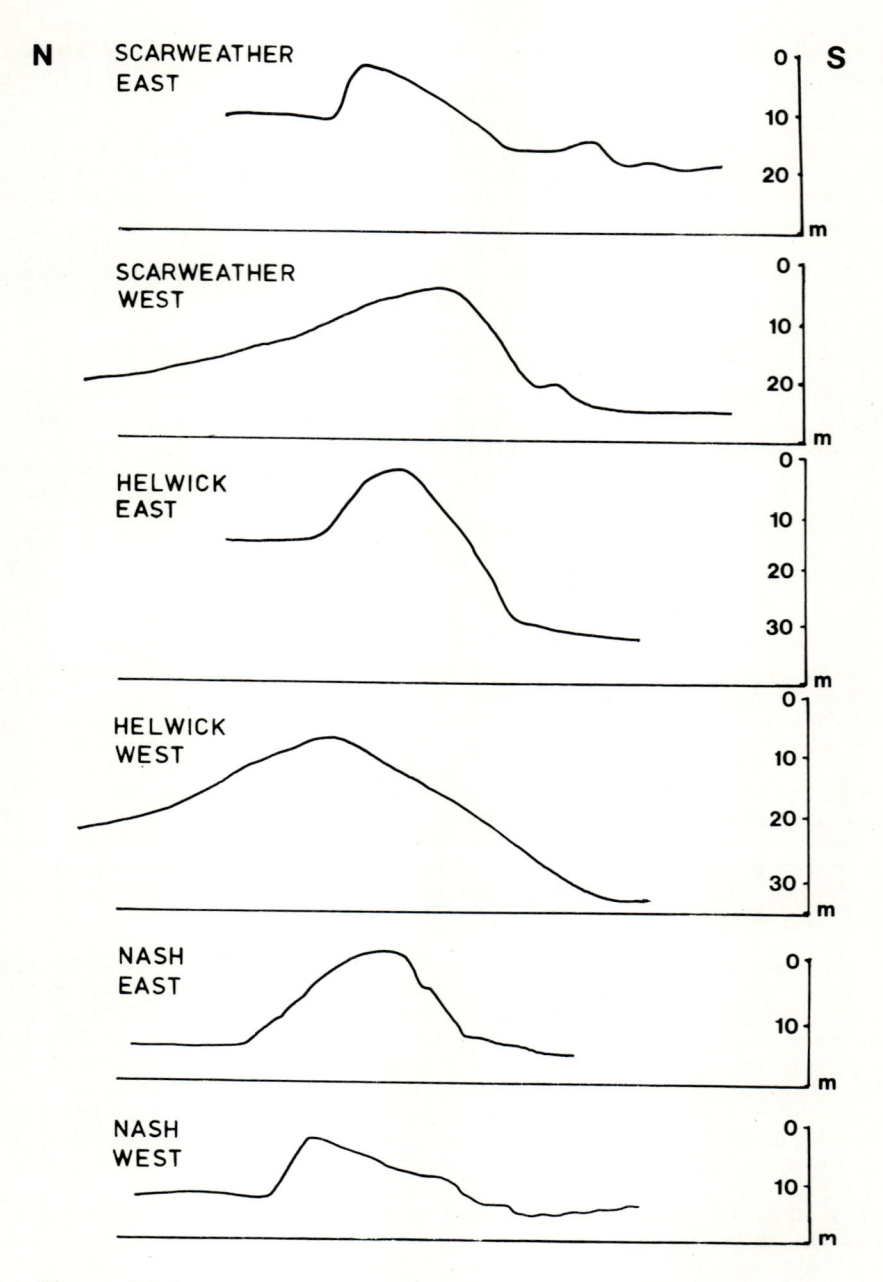

Figure 13.2. Cross sectional morphology of the linear banks. Depths below chart datums.

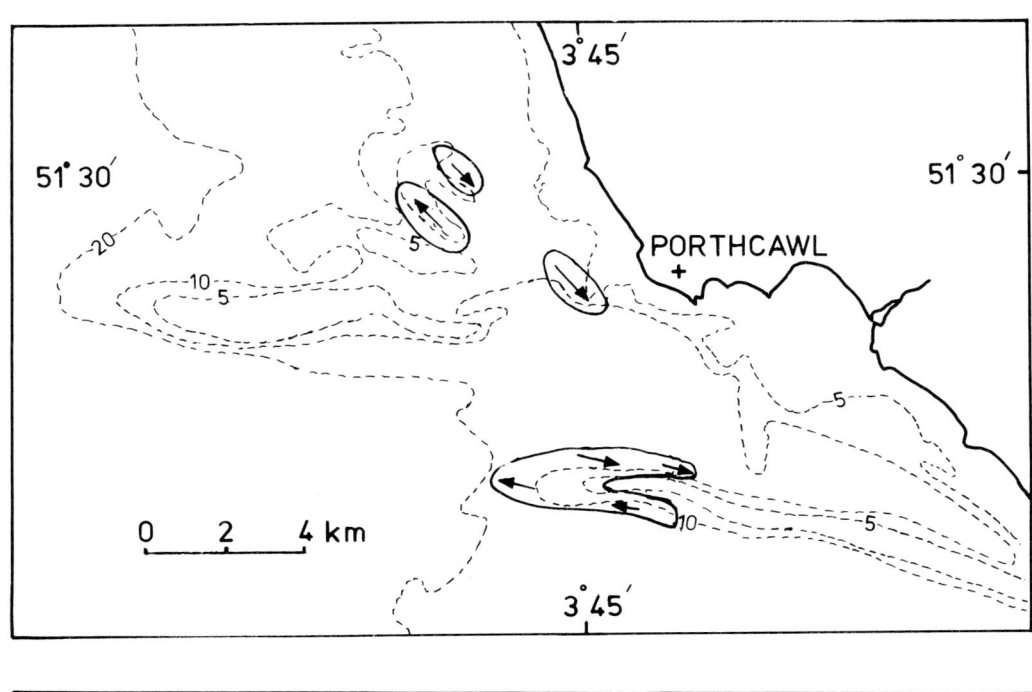

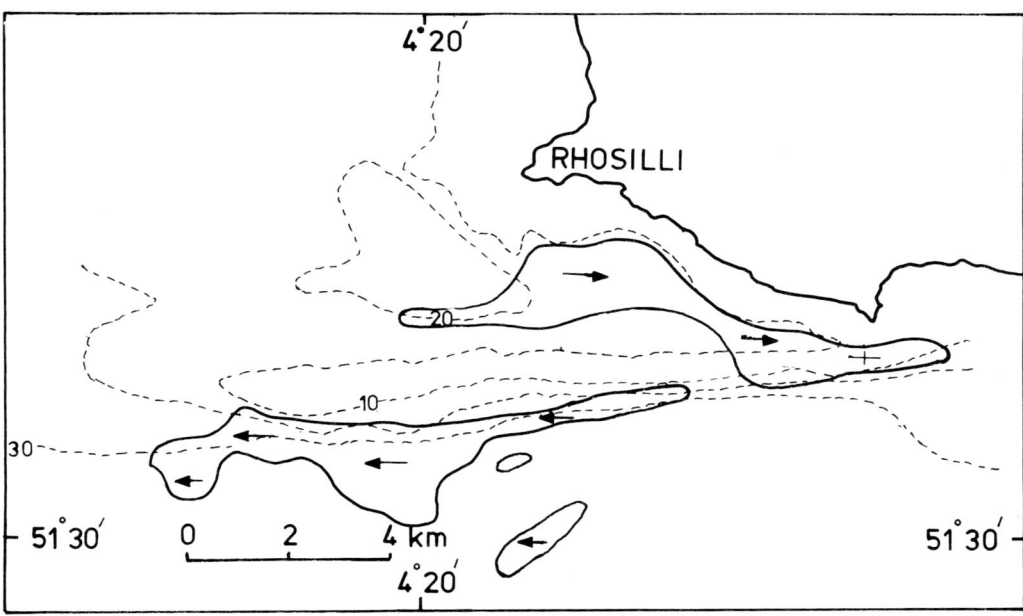

Figure 13.3. Areas and orientation of sandwaves.
Upper Figure: Nash and Scarweather Banks.
Lower Figure: Helwick Sands.
(Note: Bathymetry in metres).

wave crests are not necessarily straight and so these directions are only generally indicative, but they show an easterly movement to the north of the Nash and Helwick Banks, and a westerly movement to the south.

The Distribution of Surface Sediments.

The Overall Pattern: As stated in the Introduction, the dominant surface sediment is sand-sized material. There are however, variations both within the sand-sized bracket and in the presence of coarser and/or finer material, which significantly affect the nature and behaviour of the sediment.

The general pattern of surface sediment distribution is shown in Fig. 13.4. This information is based on the interpretation of acoustic sea-bed profiles and sonar scans, and underwater television imagery as well as a comprehensive grab sampling programme. Table 13.2 gives quantitative examples of typical surface sediments from representative areas (see also Chapter 34).

TABLE 13.2.   Sediment Characteristics.

Sediment Location	Mud Percentage	Sand Percentage	Gravel Percentage	Sand Fraction ($\emptyset$ Units) Mean Grain Size[1]	Sorting Coefficient[2]
Nash Sands	0	100	0	1.1-1.7	0.25-0.38
Helwick Sands	0	100	0	1.5-2.2	0.15-0.35
Scarweather Sands	0	100	0	2.2-2.6	0.15-0.30
North and South of Nash Sands	5	45	50	1.8-2.3	0.70-1.00
South of Helwick Sands	5	70	25	1.0-1.8	0.60-1.20
South of Scarweather Sands	5	45	50	1.5-1.9	0.90-1.20
Northwest of Scarweather Sands	25	75	0	2.6-2.9	0.40-0.60

[1] Mud: Finer than 63μm (4.0$\emptyset$); Sand: Coarser than 63μm (4.0$\emptyset$) and finer than 2.0mm (-1.0$\emptyset$).

[2] Calculated, following dry sieving at 0.5$\emptyset$ intervals, according to the following equations of McCammon (1962):

$$\text{Mean grain size} = \frac{\emptyset 10 + \emptyset 30 + \emptyset 50 + \emptyset 70 + \emptyset 90}{5}$$

$$\text{Sorting Coefficient} = \frac{\emptyset 85 + \emptyset 95 - \emptyset 5 - \emptyset 15}{5.4}$$

where $\emptyset n$ = phi value of the nth percentile, obtained from the cumulative curve of the grain size distribution.

The Linear Banks: The banks themselves are all sand covered, with the sand varying in grain size and sorting characteristics both from bank to bank and along the length and width of an individual bank. Generally, however, it is well sorted, consisting almost entirely of sub-angular to sub-rounded grains of quartz, with few carbonate or other mineral grains. The Nash Sands has the coarsest sand and the Scarweather Sands the finest sand.

Surface Sediment of the Surrounding Areas: The more mixed sediments tend to occur to the south of the banks, where there is a considerable coarse fraction present.

Bed Forms and Linear Banks

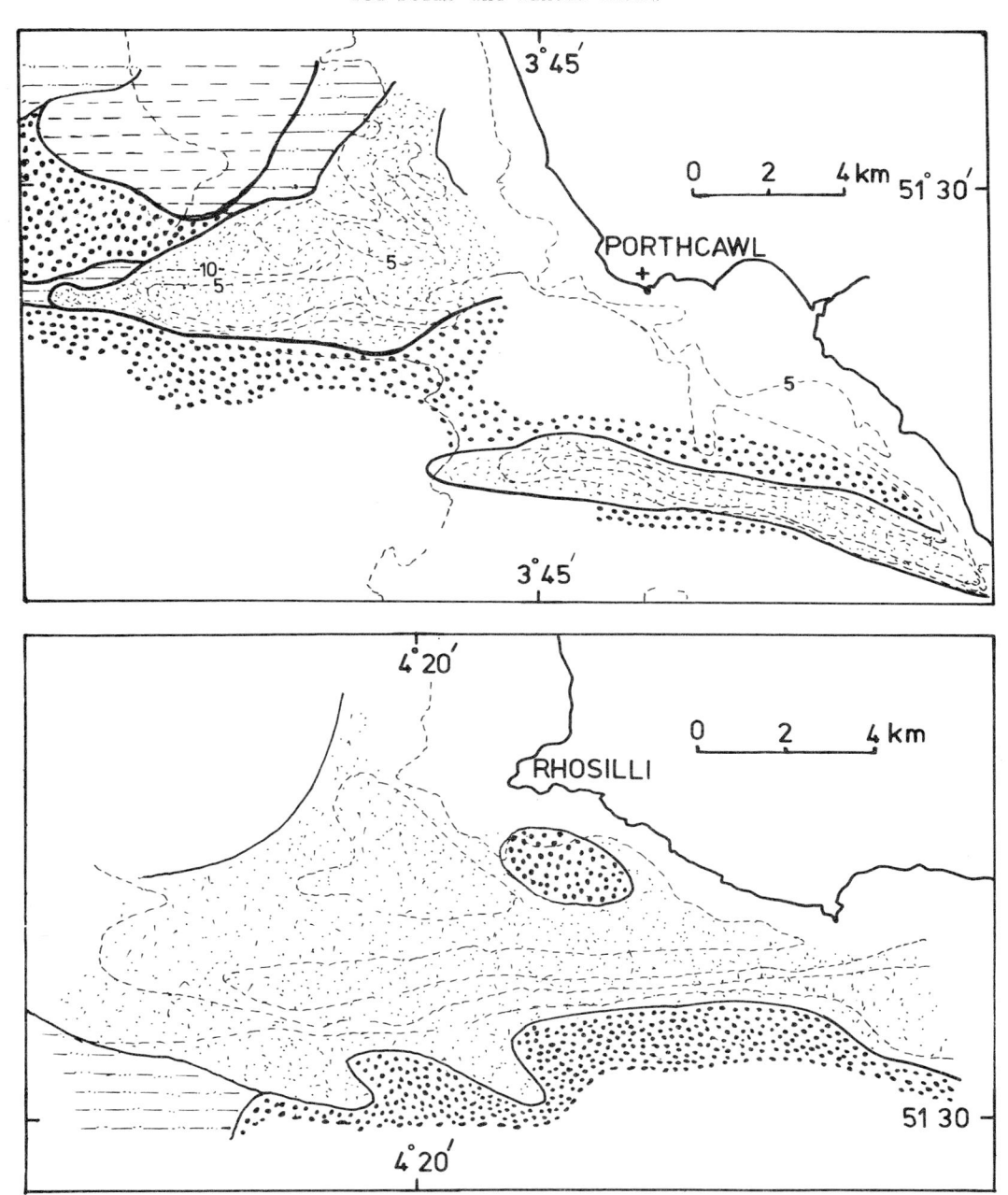

Figure 13.4. General pattern of surface sediment.
Upper Figure: Nash and Scarweather Banks.
Lower Figure: Helwick Sands.
(Note: Bathymetry in metres).
Key: Mud ≡ ; Mud + Sand ≡≡ ; Sand ∴ ; Gravel ∴ .

In areas where sand waves are not present (Fig. 13.3) the boundary between the bank(s) sand and the gravel is abrupt and is generally coincident with the break in slope.

Cobbles, up to 24cm in diameter, have been obtained from the gravels. Many pebbles have abundant epifauna, indicating that they are being rarely, if ever, transported.

Mud, up to 10% by weight (and typically nearer 5%), is present within these mixed sediments. Mud is also present in much larger quantities (up to 97%) in an area to the northwest of the Scarweather Sands (Fig. 13.4). Sediments from this area are composed typically of soft, sometimes nodular, dark grey mud and fine sand.

The Sub-Bank Topography and Thickness of the Sediment Horizon: Shallow seismic profiles obtained across the sand banks indicate that the interface, between the base of the sand and the top of the underlying horizon, has a low topography. Although acoustic penetration has not been achieved through the thickest sections of the banks, sub-bottom reflectors seen elsewhere beneath both flanks show no marked topography.

The coarser sediment exposed at the sea bed around the banks is interpreted as a lag deposit of Pleistocene glacial material (see Chapter 14). Pleistocene horizons are present beneath the sand banks resting over the bedrock surface. They are rarely thicker than 5m and often thinner than 1m, although around the Scarweather Sands they thicken to about 10m. To the north of the Scarweather Sands, there is a complex area of infilled channels cut into the Pleistocene deposits. These are up to 8m in depth (see also Chapter 3).

Tidal Currents

General Tidal Regime: Surface tidal current speeds over most of the Bristol Channel lie within the upper half of the range 50 to 250cm/s, which is the peak surface speeds for linear bank environments as stated by Off (1963).

Data from the present studies and those of Admiralty (Admiralty, 1945 and Admiralty Charts Numbers 1165 and 1179) confirm a strongly rectilinear tidal regime, with the major axes of the tidal ellipses being sub-parallel to the longitudinal axes of the linear banks. Fig. 13.5 shows the general flood and ebb directions of this rectilinear pattern. A strong similarity is evident around each of the banks.

Variations Within the Area: There are variations in current direction between the surface and near-bed water layers (see Chapter 11), the near-bed flows often tending to cut rather more obliquely across the banks, especially during the later stages of the flood tide. However, most of the significanct variations across the banks area are in the speed of the currents.

Considering the Nash and Scarweather Sands as one area and the Helwick Sands as another, there is a decrease from south-east to north-west across each area. For example, maximum rates at the entrance to Swansea Bay are about half those at the Scarweather Light Vessel at the western end of Scarweather Sands (Fig. 13.1). There is a further increase in current speeds towards Nash Point. Speeds around Helwick Sands are considerably higher than those to the north in Carmarthen Bay. Details of the actual rates are given in Fig. 13.5.

There are also variations in the duration of ebb and flood flows and the slack water period (defined here as flows <10cm/s). In the case of the Scarweather Bank, the flood stream starts to flow along the north-west of the bank about one hour before the predicted time of low water at Porthcawl, about 13km to the east. It is not

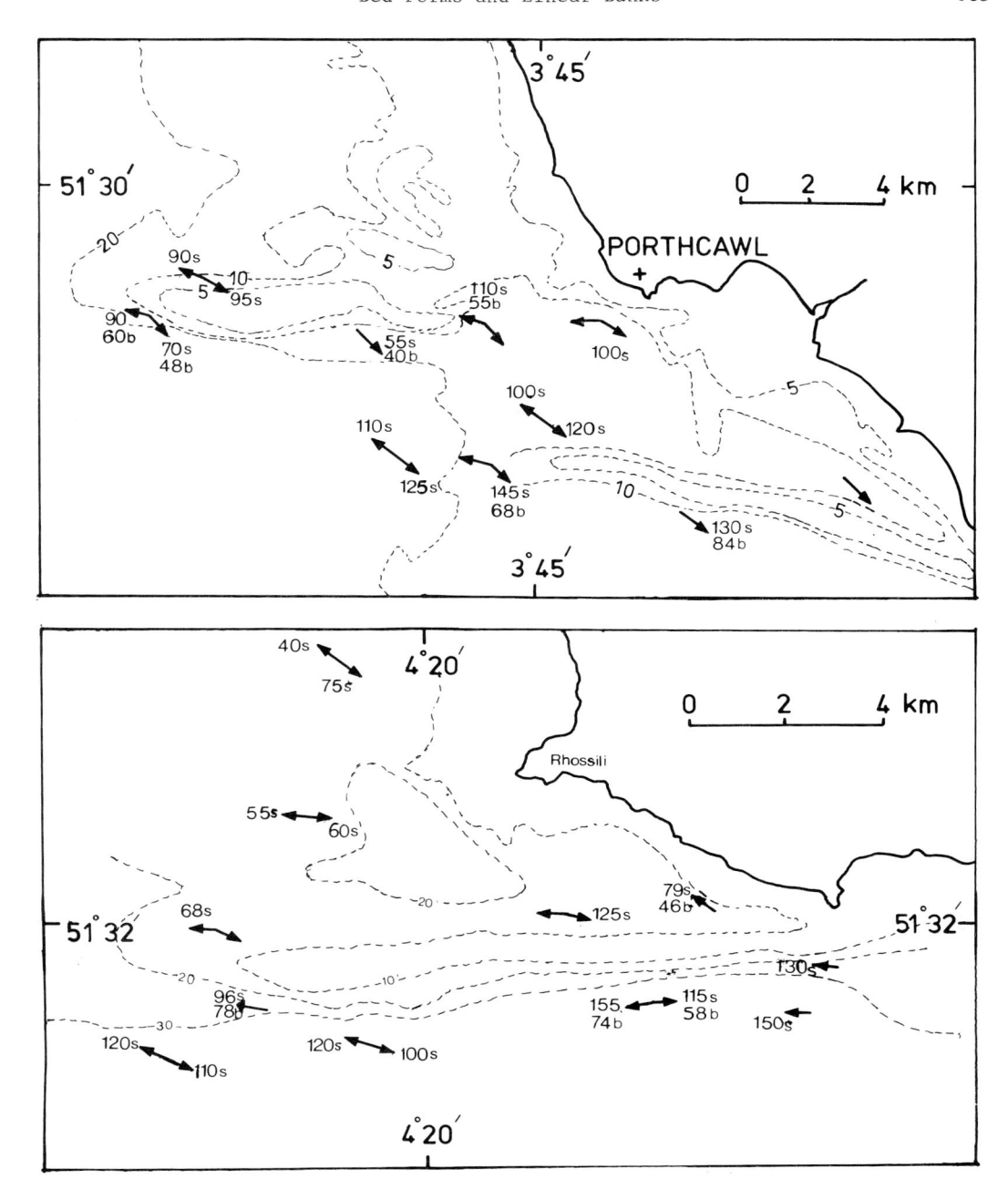

Figure 13.5. Tidal currents.
Upper Figure: Nash and Scarweather Banks.
Lower Figure: Helwick Sands.
Key: Bathymetry in metres; Speed: cm/s; Direction: degrees true.
s: near surface measurements; b: near bed measurements.

until about 2hr later that the flood becomes fully established to the south of the bank. The same is true of the Nash Sands, where the difference is most marked along the north-eastern flank of the bank, with the flood tide exceeding the ebb by about 2hr 30min. The main feature distinguishing flows north and south of the Helwick Bank is the long slack water period at the end of the ebb, to the north of the Bank. Here, and particularly north of the eastern part of the bank, speeds near the sea bed remain at or below 10cm/s for almost 2hr 30min before low water.

The combination of current speeds and duration of flows demonstrate that the flood or east-flowing stream is dominant to the north of each bank; conversely, the ebb or west-flowing stream is dominant to the south of each bank.

Threshold Velocities: When considering the influence of water flows on the sea-bed sediment, it is convenient to simplify the complex parameters of both the water movement and the natural sediment. It is then possible to consider what flow speed, measured 1m above the sea bed, will start to move sediment of particular mean grain sizes; this is referred to as the threshold velocity of the sediment.

Threshold velocity curves of Inman (1963) and Sternberg (1972) indicate that the threshold velocity of the sand banks' surface sediment is between 35-40cm/s. Taking the Helwick Sands as an example, Fig. 13.6 shows the variation in threshold velocities across the area.

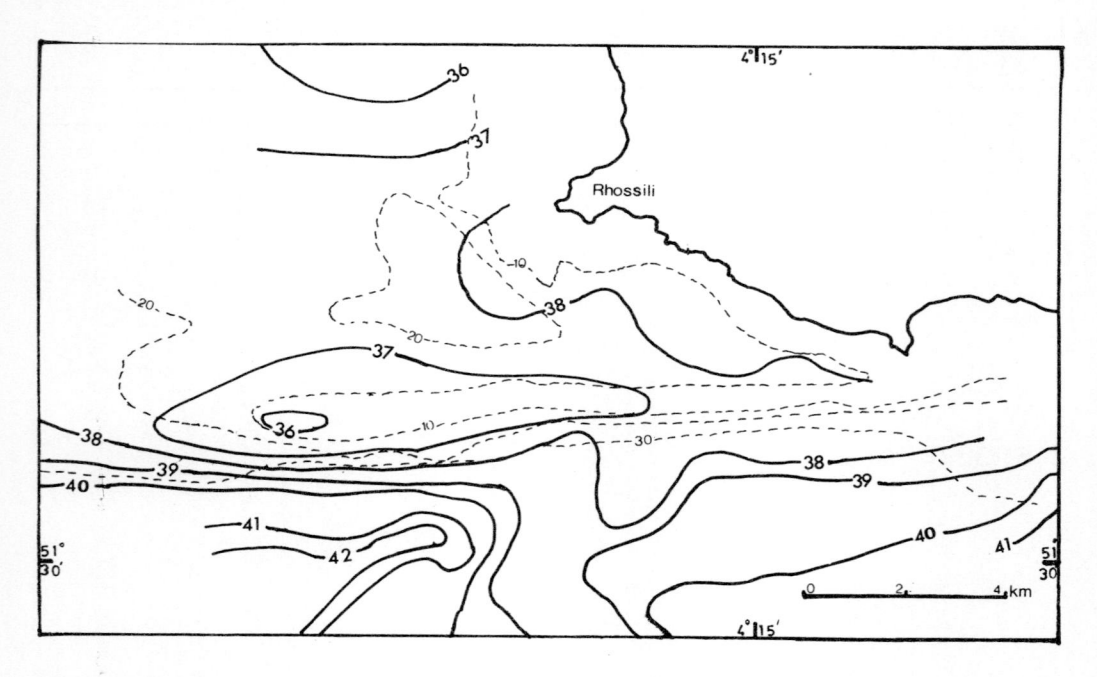

Figure 13.6. Threshold velocities (cm/s) of the sand fraction: Helwick Sands. (Bathymetry in metres).

It has been shown that tidal current speeds (Fig. 13.5) well exceed these values around the banks, and it will be shown that the water motion associated with the local water wave environment does so also. There are therefore the two major energy sources, tidal currents and waves, both capable of disturbing and transporting the sea bed sediment (see also Chapter 14).

Water Waves

Fetch and Wind Conditions: The area under consideration is exposed to the west and southwest to the Atlantic Ocean swell. It is therefore one of high wave energy - a factor which is very important in considerations of sediment transport and redistribution. The west and southwest are the directions of maximum fetch (3,500-4,000km); they are also those of the prevailing winds, although the strongest winds are from the northwest (McGarey et al., 1970). The maximum wave energy is received from the west-southwest (240°)(McMullen, 1970) although it must be noted that, in the area of the banks, the direction of maximum wave energy will vary from this due to refraction effects.

Wave characteristics: No field measurements of waves have been attempted by the authors, but some results have been published by Darbyshire (1963). These data were obtained from a recording gauge set up on the Helwick Light Vessel, situated off the western end of the Helwick Sands (Fig. 13.1), in a water depth of about 40m. Darbyshire described the waves as being "high for coastal waters" and as including swell from Atlantic storms. The maximum wave height recorded during a four-month winter period was 10.3m. The most frequent wave height was 2.1m, the average wave height 2.9m, and the significant wave height 4.6m. Characteristic wave periods were between 5-7 seconds.

Near-Bed Orbital Velocities: Calculations of near-bed orbital velocities, assuming the Airy wave theory (e.g. Inman, 1963), have shown that the motion associated with most unbroken waves of 3.0m or more in height is in excess of 40cm/s, for the wave periods and water depths encountered. If 40cm/s is taken as the approximate threshold velocity for the sand in the area (at least for unidirectional currents (see above)), then obviously these waves are significant in the transport and redistribution of sediment.

Breaking Waves: On the banks themselves, under storm conditions, waves break, and will behave as the swash moving up a gently shelving beach. This situation, when sediment movement may be exceptionally high, is more likely to occur at or around tidal low water. In this mode, waves are effectively acting as the limiting factor in the development of the height of the banks.

Sediment Transport

Introduction: The present morphology and surface sediment distribution of the banks and surrounding areas are a reflection of the balance between near-bed tidal currents and (currents induced by) water waves, together with a source of sediment.

The energy associated with both tidal currents and broken and unbroken waves in the area is sufficient to disturb and/or transport all but the coarsest sea-bed sedimentary material found in the area, at least periodically.

The threshold velocity needed to initiate sediment motion is exceeded in the area of the banks for at least 70% of all the semi-diurnal tidal cycles. The wave orbital motion superimposed on these currents may, of course, not be coincident with the tidal current vector.

Directions of Movement: The direct evidence of sand wave orientation and the indirect evidence of hydrological data, combine to give the net sediment transport patterns shown in Fig. 13.7.

It is apparent that there is a westerly movement along the southern edge of each bank, coincident with the general ebb current direction, and an easterly movement along the northern flanks, coincident with the general flood current direction. Per-

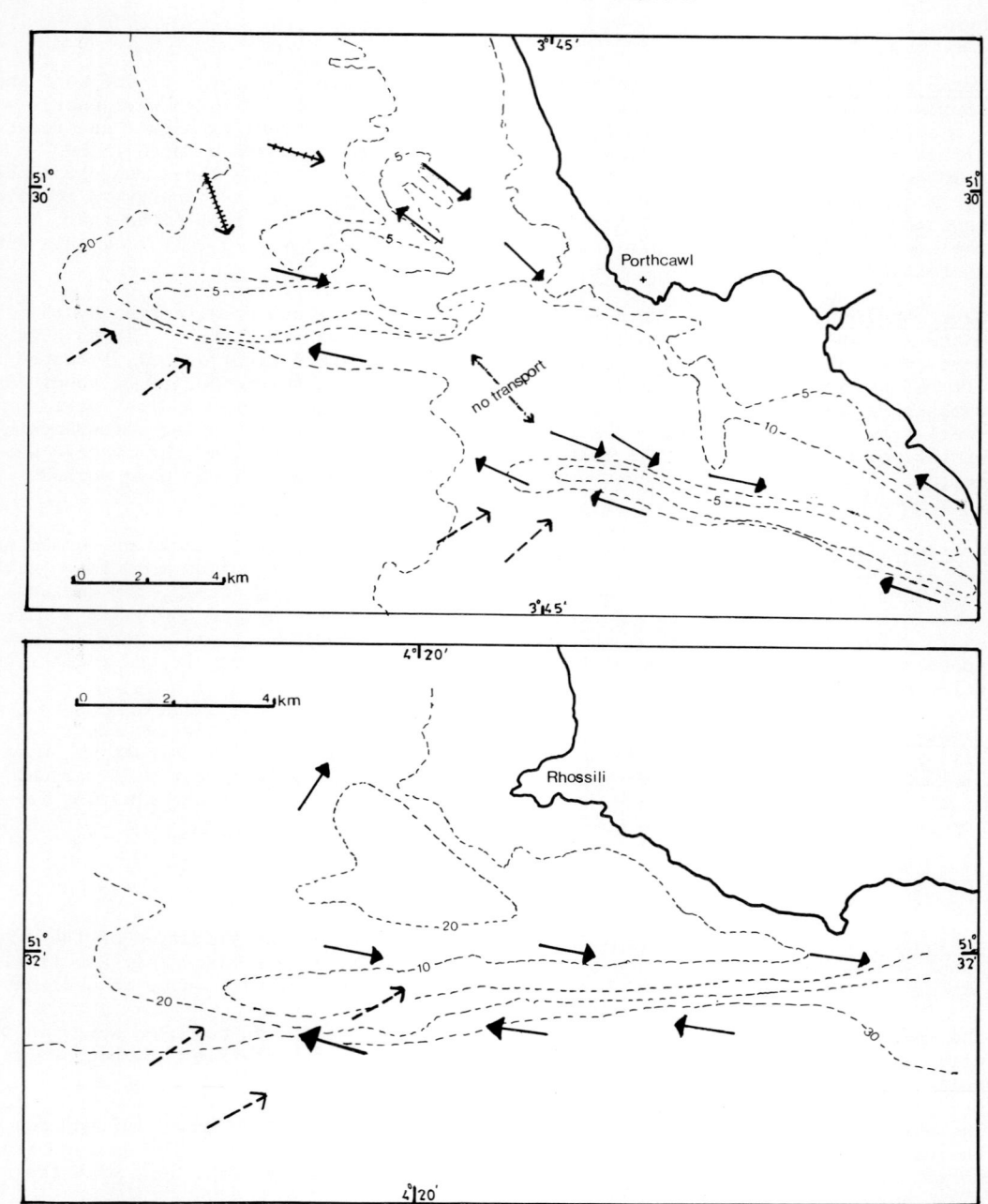

Figure 13.7. Net sediment transport patterns.
Upper Figure: Nash and Scarweather Banks.
Lower Figure: Helwick Sands.
Key: Bathymetry in metres; ⟶ Based on hydrological and sand wave data; ---> Based on wave orthogonals; ⧻> Mud pellet transport.

iodically, breaking waves will transport material towards the crests of the banks from a southwesterly direction.

There is no evidence to suggest that transport is occurring between the Nash and Scarweather Sands. No sand ribbons nor sand waves have been found between the two (Fig. 13.7 (upper)), and the sediment characteristics in terms of size and sorting are different (Fig. 13.4 (upper)).

There is evidence from the distribution of mud deposits that there is a transport from the northwest towards the northern side of the Scarweather Sands.

Hydrological data indicates that, from the western end of the Helwick Sands, there is a northeasterly movement into eastern Carmarthen Bay (Fig. 13.1).

THE ORIGIN AND DEVELOPMENT OF THE LINEAR BANKS

Initiation of the Banks

The Nash, Scarweather and Helwick Sands all occur in positions where the Bristol Channel suddenly widens to the west, each lying a short distance offshore from the associated change in coastline orientation (Fig. 13.1). They are orientated east-west as (westerly) continuations of the up-Channel coastline trend. It is concluded that the coastline configuration has played a key role in the siting and development of the banks. Tidal regimes are locally modified by the shape of the coastline, and at these locations, where the Bristol Channel suddenly widens, the tidal currents decelerate. It is at these points that deposition of sedimentary material will be concentrated (see also Ferentinos and Collins, 1979).

During the Quaternary era, many sea level changes took place, the last of which, in this area, was the post-glacial Flandrian transgression (See Chapter 4). During this transgression, the areas now occupied by the banks would have been subjected to the strongly erosive effects of an advancing surf-zone environment. A great deal of erosion of the poorly consolidated glacial deposits would have taken place at this time. The finest sediment would have been carried out of the area, presumably westwards, by tidal currents, while the coarsest material remained as the present lag deposit. The sand-sized fraction became a mobile surface sediment layer. Some of this eroded material would have been carried by waves on to the beaches of the advancing coatline. Extensive coastal dunes that are found today around eastern Carmarthen Bay and the Kenfig area (see also Chapter 7 and 17) were probably initiated from this material. However, a proportion of the wave-eroded sand remained in the offshore zone to be transported by and deposited from tidal currents.

It could be suggested that the banks owe their position to an origin as coastal spits, formed by longshore drift during a period of lowered sea level. This would imply longshore drift in a westerly direction. However, the direction of maximum fetch during Flandrian times would have been as now, i.e. from the west and southwest. These two facts are clearly incompatible, and it is therefore not feasible that the banks could have been formed in this way.

Whatever the exact origin of the banks, there is no evidence that their siting was controlled or influenced by any existing geological structure or topographic feature.

Growth and Movement of the Banks

Movement: Within the recent past, the surveys conducted by the authors between 1970-1973, and those of the Admiralty published in 1948, show no movements or changes in length of the banks that are within the accepted accuracy of the position fixing system employed (see Chapter 7) - the Decca Navigator main chain system. This apparent stability is consistent with the findings of authors working on similar features in other areas. In the southern North Sea, Houbolt (1968) found a maximum value of shift to be 1.6km, in about 70 years and this is considered by Caston (1972) to be exceptionally rapid.

Any movement of the banks which does occur may be reflected in their cross sectional asymmetry (Caston, 1972; Houbolt, 1968). In the case of Nash Sands, the asymmetry is associated with sinuousity of the Bank, with the steeper flank occurring on the outside of the curves (i.e. the convex flank in plan view). This would indicate that, if the process continues, the bank will become increasingly sinuous. The same process seems to be happening at Scarweather Sands, where a marked shift in the crestline orientation is coincident with a marked change in the asymmetry of the bank. The western, larger part, is strongly asymmetrical to the south, and the smaller eastern section is asymmetrical to the north. This could indicate that these two sections are moving in opposite directions. In the case of the Helwick Sands, which are generally asymmetrical to the south, this may be a reflection of a southerly slope of the underlying surface upon which the bank rests.

<u>Growth</u>: As has been mentioned above, there is no evidence of significant changes in the length of the banks since the Second World War. It would seem unlikely that the banks will grow any further to the east, as they are effectively constrained by the coastline configuration. There is some indirect evidence of the westwards growth of the Helwick Sands over the last 200 years. In a hydrographic survey conducted by Murdoch Mackenzie Junior in 1771, and more recently reproduced by Robinson (1962); the Helwick Sands are shown to be approximately half their present day length of 13.5km. While the methods of survey and position fixing at this time would obviously leave a great deal to be desired, some significance may be attached to it because of the presence of a "leading line open" just to the west of Worms Head for vessels approaching the Loughor Estuary (Fig. 13.1). This line indicates a safe navigational passage across what is now the shoalest part of the Helwick Sands.

SUMMARY OF CONCLUSIONS

1. The linear sand banks originated during the Flandrian transgression, when glacial deposits were eroded by an advancing surf zone.
2. Following an initial erosive phase, the sediments were distributed by waves and tidal currents. Much of the fine material was removed from the area in suspension, while sand was deposited at points where the Bristol Channel widens.
3. The maximum height of the banks is limited by breaking waves.
4. There is a characteristic tidal current pattern around the three banks, in that the east flowing flood dominates along the northern flanks, whereas the west flowing ebb dominates along the south. This results in a clockwise net sediment circulation.

REFERENCES

Admiralty. (1945). *Tidal streams of the waters surrounding the British Isles and off the west and north coasts of Europe. Gibraltar to Yugorski Strait. Part I.* Hydrographic Dept., Admiralty (London), 599pp.

Britton, R.C. (1977). *Structure of some marine sedimentary bodies and their dynamic environments.* Unpub. Ph.D. Thesis, University of Wales, 255pp.

Caston, V.N.D- (1972). Linear sand banks in the southern North Sea. *Sedimentology, 18,* 63-78.

Darbyshire, M. (1963). Wave measurements made by the N.I.O. *In:* Bretschneider, C.L. (Ed.). *Ocean Wave Spectra.* Prentice Hall, London, 285-291.

Duane, D.B., Field, M.E., Meisburger, E.P., Swift, D.J.P., and Williams, S.J. (1972). Linear shoals on the Atlantic inner continental shelf, Florida to Long Island. *In:* Swift, D.J.P., Duane, D.B., and Pilkey, O.H. (Eds.) *Shelf Sediment Transport - Process and Pattern.* Dowden, Hutchinson and Ross, 656pp.

Ferentinos, G., and Collins, M.B. (1979). Tidally induced secondary circulations and their associated sedimentation processes. *J. Oceanograph. Soc. Japan, 35,* 65-74.

Houbolt, J.J.H.C. (1968). Recent sediments in the Southern Bight of the North Sea. *Geologie Mijnb., 47,* 245-273.

Inman, D.L. (1963). Ocean waves and associated currents. *In:* Sheppard, F.P. (Ed.) *Submarine Geology,* 2nd Edition, 49-81. Harper and Row, New York, 557pp.

McCammon, R.B. (1962). Efficiencies of percentile measures for describing the mean size and sorting of sedimentary particles. *J. Geol., 70,* 453-465.

McGarey, D.G., Fraenkel, P.M., Ridgeway, R.J., Kier, M., Hill, L.P., Low, D.W., Dale, R.N., and Mason, D.F. (1970). Port Talbot harbour - discussion. *Proc. Instn. civ. Engrs., 48,* 527-561.

McMullen, C. (1971). *In:* Port Talbot harbour - discussion. McGarey, D.G., *et al. Proc. Instn. civ. Engrs., 48,* 527-561.

Off, T. (1963). Rhythmic linear sand bodies caused by tidal currents. *Am. Ass. Pet. Geol. Bull., 47,* 324-241.

Purdy, E.G. (1961). Bahamian oolite shoals. *In:* Peterson, J.A., and Osmond, J.C. (Eds.). *Geometry of Sand stone Bodies,* 53-62. American Association of Petroleum Geologists, Symposium. 45th Annual Meeting, 1960, 240pp.

Robinson, A.H.W. (1962). *Marine Cartography in Britain.* Leicester Univ. Press. 222pp.

Sternberg, R.W. (1972). Predicting initial motion and bedload transport of sediment particles in the shallow marine environment. *In:* Swift, D.J.P., Duane, D.B., and Pilkey, O.H. (Eds.). *Shelf Sediment Transport - Process and Pattern.* Dowden, Hutchinson and Ross, 656pp.

Stride, A.H. (1963). Current swept sea floors near the southern half of Great Britain. *Q. Jl. geol. Soc. Lond., 119,* 175-199.

Turner, S.R. (1976). *Some aspects of sedimentary bodies in parts of the Bristol Channel.* Unpub. Ph.D. Thesis, University of Wales, 235pp.

van Veen, J. (1935). Ondulations de sable dans la Mer du Nord. *Hydrogr. Rev., 12,* 21-29.

14. THE SUPPLY OF SAND TO SWANSEA BAY

M. B. Collins[*], C. B. Pattiaratchi[*], F. T. Banner[*] and G. K. Ferentinos[**]

[*]Department of Oceanography, University College of Swansea, U.K.
[**]Department of Geology (Tay Estuary Research Centre), University of Dundee, U.K.

ABSTRACT

The distribution of sediment types on the seabed of greater Swansea Bay is briefly described. The distribution of sedimentary bedforms (sandwaves, etc.) is also described and their significance as indicators of pathways of sediment transport in bedload is discussed. From the tidal and wave regimes, the predictable interactions between tidal currents and the seabed, and between waves and the seabed are discussed, and the percentage exceedance of the thresholds of movement for the non-cohesive sediments is postulated. The likely paths, directions and rates of non-cohesive sediment bedload transport under unidirectional (tidal) currents and under the combined action of unidirectional and oscillatory (wave-induced) currents are compared. It is concluded that the supply of sand to the Bay is sporadic, but that it plays an important part not only in beach development in the Bay but also to the sediment-circulation regime of the adjacent Bristol Channel.

KEYWORDS

Sediment supply; Sediment transport; Tidal currents; Wave-induced oscillatory-currents; Swansea Bay; Bristol Channel.

INTRODUCTION

Earlier chapters (3, 4 and 6) have described how Swansea Bay is floored largely by areas of relict sediments which are immobile, but that some facies (facies 4 and 6 of Chapter 4) are presently being transported within the Bay. These mobile sediments build the beaches, which experience loss by aeolian transport to the sand-dunes which fringe the north and eastern coasts of the Bay (see Plates 14.1, 14.2 and 14.3 and Chapter 7). The central Bristol Channel, in the approaches to and south of the Bay, has been shown (Chapter 5) to comprise broad areas of scoured seabed to the south and southeast, where bedrock is exposed and no mobile sediment is present, and even broader areas to the south and southwest, which are covered by relict Quaternary deposits and mobile, palimpsest sediments which are derived from them (Chapters 4, 5; see also Chapter 16). The scoured area of bedrock in the central Bristol Channel has been suggested to be a zone of "bedload parting" (Stride, 1963, Belderson et al., 1971; Kenyon and Stride, 1970; Hamilton, 1979) from which sand in bedload is continually being removed by tidal currents, in both up-channel

PLATE 14.1. Evidence of intense onshore aeolian transport on the backshore, in northwest Swansea Bay (viewed towards the south, with Mumbles Head in the background). Wind and (sharp-crested) wave approach is from the southeast.

and down-channel directions. Certainly, the zone of scour is closely comparable to the region where there is maximum mean bottom-stress due to tidal currents, even when only the M_2 tide is predicted over a tidal cycle (Fig. 14.1, derived by the method of Pingree and Maddock, 1977, from a numerical model (Wilding, 1979) of M_2 tidal streams). It has already been pointed out elsewhere (Banner, 1979; Collins and Banner, 1980) that this major bed-load transport path must be bypassed, in order to replenish the scoured zone as a source area and to prevent infilling of the up-channel regions of the Bristol Channel-Severn Estuary.

Because the supply of modern sediment to the Bay from fluvial discharges is negligible (Chapters 19 and 27) and because that from coastal erosion is nil (witness the permanency of the cliff lines of the Bay and nearby coast, see Chapter 2), the sand and silt which is moving within the Bay must have entered from outside it, i.e., from the Bristol Channel itself. The possibility immediately arises that Swansea Bay, and adjacent coastal or inshore zones, may form part of this sediment bypass.

The Bay itself is likely to have filled with deposits to the maximum possible level at, or soon after, the attainment of modern sea-levels (Chapter 6) and it is probable that further introduction of sediment cannot lead to its permanent deposition there: "effectively, the Bay has filled with sediment to its capacity under the prevailing, stationary hydrodynamic regime" (Culver and Banner, 1978). Mobile sand, in the greater Swansea Bay area, must be transitory (Collins, Ferentinos and Banner,

The Supply of Sand

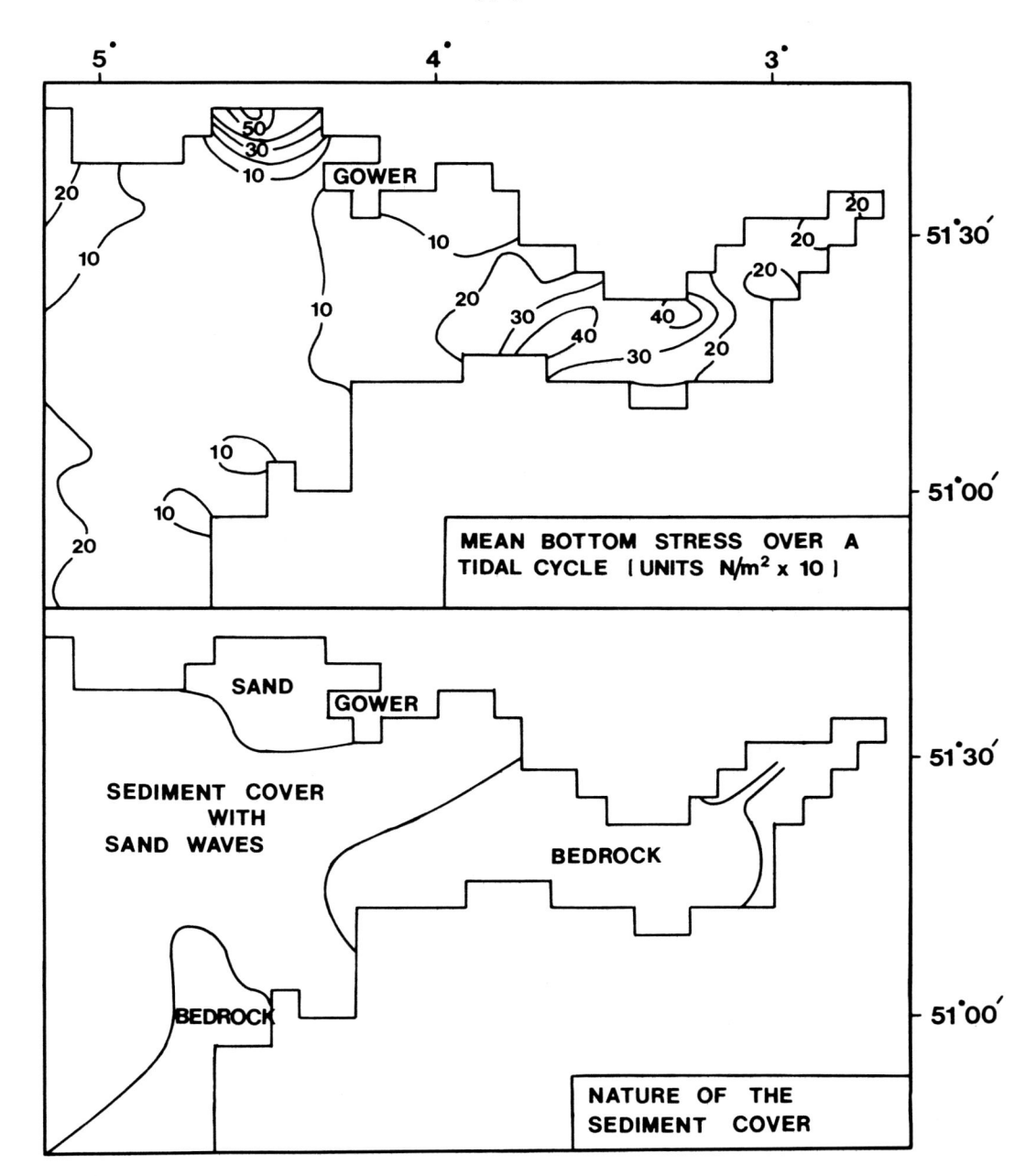

Figure 14.1. Results derived from a two-dimensional numerical model of the Bristol Channel - mean bottom stress - compared with the nature of the sediment cover (from various sources, see Wilding, 1979).

1979).

This transitory, mobile sand can be moved by tidal currents or by wave action, separately or in conjunction.   This chapter seeks to suggest how combinations of these mechanisms (both in "average" and in extreme climatic conditions) suggest sources for the sediment moving in the Bay and also explain the role of the Bay in the sediment transport pattern of the central Bristol Channel as a whole.   The evidence is examined systematically.

SEDIMENT AND SEDIMENT-BEDFORM DISTRIBUTION

Within Swansea Bay, north and east of the "areas of nil net deposition" (Figure 4.3), where no mobile sediments occur, are areas of mobile sand (facies 4 of Figure 4.2)and sandy mud or muddy sand (facies 6 of Figure 4.2);the former sediment is dominant on the beaches and the immediate sublittoral, while the latter occurs in a southwest-northeast aligned zone between the Green Grounds and the Kenfig Patches. Collins et al. (1979) have noted that the sandy areas of "facies 4" include the sand veneer on the beaches of western Swansea Bay (where the sands move as intertidal, reniform sand-bars, across the beach substrata of facies 3, Flandrian muds and peats, as shown by Banner and Collins, 1975, Pl. 1 and Fig. 2), the littoral accumulation of the "Neath delta" in the northeast, and mobile sand, in transit over relict gravels and other mobile (or very rarely mobile) deposits in the sublittoral of the western half of the Bay.   It is this sand which supports a modified *Spisula* community (Chapter 34) but which yields (littorally and sublittorally), especially in the western side of the Bay, heavy (but fresh) dead shells of *Arctica islandica* and *Ostrea edulis*, species which no longer live within the Bay but which must have been transported there from habitats in the waters of the Bristol Channel near the White Oyster Ledge to the southwest (Fig. 14.2) or from even further in that direction (compare Chapter 35).   Comparison with Figure 16.3 also shows the littoral sands of Western Swansea Bay to have mineralogical affinity with the littoral and inshore-sublittoral sands of the immediate southwest (beyond the Mumbles), as all belong to the tourmaline-amphibole-epidote "province".   The littoral sands of the north and east of the Bay have heavy minerals of higher specific gravity, but which are still in "entrainment equivalence" (Chapter 16); some of the highest proven concentrates of zircon occur sporadically on the westward-facing beach (1100 ppm zirconium) south of Aberavon (Hill and Parker, 1970).   These beaches of the east of the Bay are described in Chapters 12 and 17; they have steeper beach gradients than the western beaches and lack reniform inter-tidal sandbars; in other respects (e.g., consisting of a mobile sand veneer over relict Flandrian substrata),they are similar.

The muddy sand/sandy mud (supporting the *Abra* community, see Chapter 33) of "facies 6" is believed (Chapter 4) to consist largely of dredged Flandrian material which is constantly being hydrodynamically redistributed; its possession of chlorite, zircon and rutile suggests partial provenance in Flandrian and fluviatile (Neath River) sources (Chapter 16).   Its area grades southwestwards into "facies 4" sands (Fig. 14.2) of the "zircon-rutile province" (Fig. 16.3) which extends offshore to the west and southwest, an area of sand cover which becomes continuous south of the latitude of the Scarweather Sand (Fig. 14.2).

The scoured area of the central Bristol Channel seabed extends north to approximately 51°23'N (at around the 30m bcd isobath south of Swansea Bay), north of which the relict Quaternary deposits (see Evans and Thompson, 1979, p.10 and Figure 5.1) cover the bedrock and which are themselves partly or wholly covered by mobile sediments up to 2m in thickness.   Figure 14.2 indicates the area, southwest of Swansea Bay, in which sandwave fields are well developed; the observed orientation of the crestlines approximates to N-S and their steeper slopes face west, suggesting a clear dominance of westward, downchannel sand-transport in this area.   In this area, sandwave heights range from 1 to 4m, and wavelengths from 25 to 70m.   The sandwaves are accompanied by megaripples (which are also crestally aligned N-S), but which have a wavelength ranging from 5 to 10m and height less than 40cm.   Northwards, the sand cover becomes thinner (0.2m or less) and discontinuous; sand-ribbons develop, with

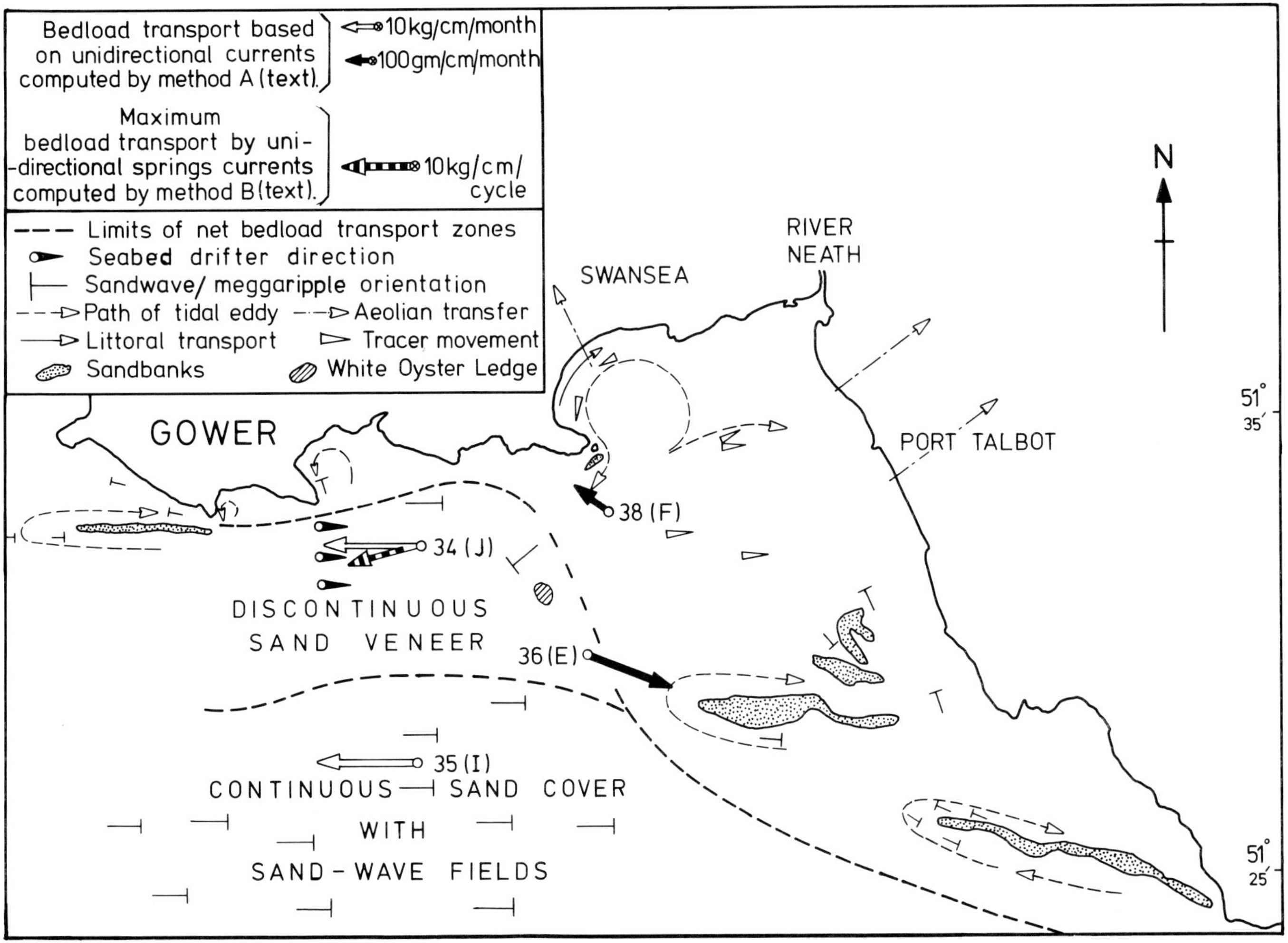

The Supply of Sand

Figure 14.2. Schematic diagram showing sediment transport paths in Swansea Bay, based on evidence from a variety of direct observations and indirect interpretations (See Key).

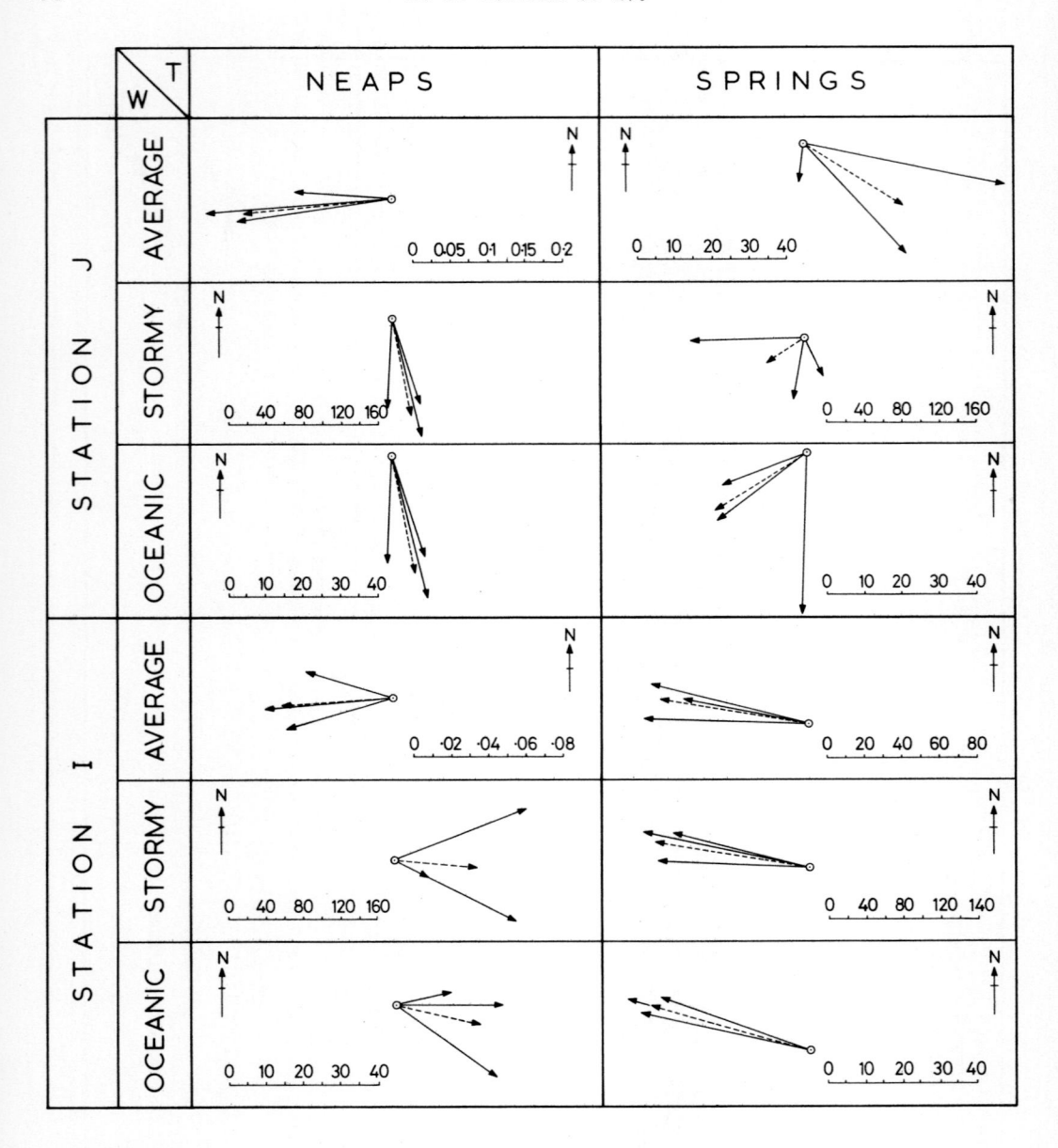

Figure 14.3. Sediment transport vectors for transport under the combined influence of waves and currents at Stations I and J (see Fig. 14.2): continuous lines represent individual tidal cycles; dashed lines represent "mean" vectors. Different tidal phases (T) and wave conditions (W) are represented (see text and, in particular, Table 14.4).

E-W orientation again suggesting sand transport along an E-W axis. Sandribbons can occur between trains of sandwaves. The sands of this area are of medium to coarse grainsize (1.5 to 1.0ϕ) and well (to moderately well) sorted (sorting coefficients

0.3 to 0.7). Mineralogically, these sands are characterised by the dominance of garnet in the heavy mineral assemblage, the garnet concentration reaching a maximum (>20%) between the 20m and 35m isobaths (Barrie, 1978).

North of the latitude of the Scarweather Sand, the zircon-rutile-assemblage (Figure 16.3) again characterises the sands, which become a discontinuous veneer (Figure 14.2); these sands (which form part of textural provinces 6, gravelly sand, and 7, sandy gravel and gravel, see Collins et al., 1979, Figure 10, and Figure 5.2, this book) form a poorly sorted, coarse grained (0.5 to 1.0ϕ) veneer upon which thicker patches (up to 1m thick, made of well-sorted, medium grainsize sand, 1.1 to 1.3ϕ) exist. The sand patches are megarippled, with crestal orientation NW-SE, wavelengths from 5 to 10m, and heights less than 40cm. Megaripples occur widely in this area, those more offshore indicating transport to the NE, but those more inshore being variable in their orientation, some, again, indicating westward transport (Figure 14.2) but others suggesting eastwards or even southwards sand movement. Thus, these "facies 4" sands give clear suggestions of westward transport south of 51°28' (i.e., that area which is generally below the 20m isobath, see Figures 5.1 and 5.2) but, in generally shallower, more inshore areas, they become not only discontinuous but suggest varying bedload transport directions, some being northeastwards, and, mineralogically, belong to the same province as that within the south and west of the Bay.

The sediments of the linear sandbanks are described in Chapters 13 and 34. The Mixon Shoal (Figure 5.3), has mineralogy resulting from hydrodynamic equivalence which matches that of the other banks (Figure 16.3).

EVIDENCE FROM TRACERS AND DRIFTERS

The northeastward movement of littoral sand in the berm of the western part of the Bay is evidenced by accumulations there behind groynes and discharge pipes (Banner and Collins, 1975, Fig. 2); whereas northerly (aeolian) transport of material, across the dunes (Fig. 14.2), is evidenced by the aperiodic transfer of material onto the main coastal road (Plates 14.1, 14.2 and 14.3). Southward movement on the low-tide terrace of the same area is indicated by fluorescent tracer (Collins et al., 1979). No littoral longshore transport has been indicated in the tracer-studies of the eastern beaches carried out by IOS (see Chapters 12 and 17). The injections of tracer into the sublittoral, central part of the Bay itself has indicated net eastwards (or to ENE) movement there (Collins et al., 1979 and see Chapter 37). These transport directions are shown in Figure 14.2 and should be supplemented by the distribution of shells of *Arctica* and *Ostrea* mentioned above. These latter are a kind of natural "bottom drifter". Woodhead seabed drifters were released outside the Bay, south of Oxwich Point (Figure 14.2). The results have been described in detail by Ferentinos & Collins (1978 MS) and summarised by Collins and Banner (1980). 20 to 27% of the recoveries came from the littoral of western Swansea Bay, and 54 to 67% were found on the eastern side of the Bay, between Port Talbot and Porthcawl. They showed a very clear drifter-transport eastwards. This may indicate an eastward drift of silt-sized material from the area of the drifter-release sites.

TIDAL AND WAVE ENERGIES

The essentially rectilinear tidal currents of the Bristol Channel (which are modified in the Bay by shallow-water effects and bathymetry, see Chapter 11) have been recorded at near-bed stations (approximately 2m above the bed) marked 34(J) and 35(I) on Figure 14.2. Max speeds recorded at Springs tides are about 85cm/s, and at Neaps 45cm/s. The duration of the ebb (westward-flowing) current is shorter than that of the flood, but the ebb currents are faster. Six weeks' data from each station were

PLATE 14.2. An example of the result of onshore aeolian transport, by southeasterly winds, in the area to the west of Swansea (April, 1975). In the foreground, sand has been deposited on the Mumbles Road: in the background, wind action can be seen transporting sand across the grass verge adjacent to the road. Such sand deposits, on the main road, are subsequently removed by Swansea City Council.

analysed and the velocities (compare Figure 14.1) were compared to the threshold velocities applicable (Miller et al., 1977) to the surface sediment in the area of the stations (medium to coarse sand). It was found that the thresholds were exceeded by these unidirectional currents for between 34% and 52% of the time (see Table 14.1).

TABLE 14.1. Exceedance of Threshold

Mechanism:		Tidal	Wave
STATION 34 (J)	Medium Sand	52%	10%
	Coarse Sand	34%	2%
STATION 35 (I)	Medium Sand	52%	0.01%
	Coarse Sand	34%	3%

Data from a wave-rider buoy stationed just to the west of the Scarweather Sand were collected over a 12-month period and were used to calculate near-bed wave-induced (orbital) velocities. These were compared to the sedimentary threshold velocities for waves (Komar and Miller, 1973), and exceedance values are again shown in Table 14.1. Exceedance was, of course, more frequent at the shallower, more inshore station.

From this, if wave and current kinetic energies are considered separately, it would appear that the latter are dominant.

SAND TRANSPORT BY TIDAL CURRENTS

The data from current meter stations 34(J) and 35(I) were originally analysed (Method A; Ferentinos and Collins, 1978) by using a 30-day period and the method described by Sternberg (1972); the calculated bedload transports were averaged for the 30-day periods, with an assumed logarithmic distribution of near-bed velocities, an average Z_0 value (roughness length) of 0.02cm, and a Karman constant of 0.4. The assumption, that bedload transport occurs, was substantiated by the calculation of shear stress values (τ_0) below those needed for sand transport in suspension (Bagnold, 1966). The resulting vectors for calculated sand transport, from this unidirectional current data, are shown on Figure 14.2; it also shows that the vectors for 34(J) and 35(I) are thus calculated to be two orders of magnitude greater than for stations 36(E) and 38(F).

A more detailed analysis (Method B; Pattiaratchi, 1979) of some sections of the data (three Springs and three Neap tides) from Stations 34(J) and 35(I)(see Table 14.2) yielded different results for sediment transport. Method B differed from Method A by examining the tidal cycles separately, rather than averaging them, and by applying different values to Z_0, based on tidal state. The results given in Table 14.2 use Z_0 = 0.08cm (for the decelerating phase of the tide) and Z_0 = 0.16cm (for the accelerating phase), based on field measurements in the sublittoral of Oxwich Bay (C.G. Ruck, pers. comm; these values agree with those given by Harvey and Vincent (1976) for the southern North Sea). Different Z_0 values used on the same data did not alter the direction of the calculated resultant vector, but the magnitude of that vector varied (within an order of magnitude). The same order of difference

TABLE 14.2. Sediment Transport under Unidirectional Currents (Method B).

		Cycle	Resultant kg/cm/cycle	Direction	Mean Resultant kg/cm/cycle	Mean Direction	Dates	LW-HW Range(m)
STATION 35 (I)	Neaps	1	0.059	264	0.083	271	21-22/6/76	4.5
		2	0.076	287				4.2
		3	0.12	265				4.4
	Springs	1	3.18	266	4.62	272	12-13/6/76	8.4
		2	4.18	268				8.6
		3	5.92	277				8.7
STATION 34 (J)	Neaps	1	0.25	263	0.21	265	21-22/6/76	4.5
		2	0.13	265				4.2
		3	0.26	267				4.4
	Springs	1	7.96	240	9.85	257	12-13/6/76	8.4
		2	14.34	265				8.6
		3	7.74	260				8.7

has been found by Gadd et al. (1978) between predictions (using four methods!) and actual transport (using radioactive tracers) in the New York Bight; Gadd et al. (cit) found that real transport was the same or (an order of magnitude) less than that calculated using Bagnold's (1966) method. Heathershaw & Hammond (Chapter 15) also conclude that estimates (using Gadd et al.'s modification of Bagnold's 1966 method) give results from a quarter to twice that of the measured rates.

The resultants given by Method B in Table 14.2 show a dramatic change from Neaps to Springs, even allowing for unpredictable increases (e.g., cycle 2 of the Springs tide at Station 34(J)) due to non-tidal effects (compare Chapters 8 and 9). Even allowing for these variations between cycles, and for the limitations of the interpretative technique, the results are significant in that the resultants all are directed westwards.

SAND TRANSPORT BY WAVES

Typical distribution of near-bed wave orbital velocities within Swansea Bay have already been published (Collins et al., 1979, Fig. 8). Both in the immediate approaches to Swansea Bay, and in the adjacent areas of the Bristol Channel, the fetch to the west and west-south-west is great (extending, in effect, to the Caribbean). Therefore, the longest period waves (of high kinetic energy but, until shoaling and retardation, not necessarily of high potential energy or height) must enter the area from the W and WSW, often arising from storms in the Atlantic Ocean and Celtic Sea. More locally developed storm centres can create wave trains which, though of lesser period and wavelength, can be of greater heights, and, therefore of at least equal energies and, as shown below, often of greater effect on bedload transport. Such storm-generated waves can develop with adequate duration of exposure to atmospheric energy, if the storm centres create waves entering the Bay from the west through to the southeast.

In the calculations made here, wave data recorded near the Scarweather Lightship have been used; a wave-rider buoy installed here between October, 1974, and September 1975, recorded wave periods from 4 to 15 secs and heights from 0 to 5m (Carr et al., 1976). We believe that these heights can, on occasion, be exceeded and that 10m-high waves can occur, although rarely. Data recorded at the Helwick Light Vessel (Darbyshire, 1962, 1963) gives heights up to 7m there (periods from 3 to 11 secs) between January and December, 1962.

In Table 14.3, estimates are given of the transport of medium sand due to waves alone. The method of calculation, for particular depths, wave periods and significant wave heights (Hsig), was that used by Madsen and Grant (1976). Waves of greater period but smaller height ("oceanic") give lower calculated sand transport rates than those of shorter period (e.g., "stormy") but greater heights. This demonstrates the importance of wave height (as compared to the importance of wave period) when predicting sand transport rates.

TABLE 14.3. Wave-induced Sediment Transport Rates (kg/cm/tidal cycle).

Water Depth	"Average" States	"Stormy" States	"Oceanic" States
20m	7.04×10^{-6}	10.92	9.12
30m	7.48×10^{-8}	9.12	7.20×10^{-3}
40m	8.08×10^{-10}	4.12×10^{-2}	4.92×10^{-4}

"Average" - wave period = 7.5 secs, Hsig = 0.5m

"Stormy" - wave period = 8.5 secs, Hsig = 2.7m

"Oceanic" - wave period = 12.5 secs, Hsig = 2.3m.

At current meter station 35(I), the water depth ranges over the Springs tidal cycle from 36m to 46m; by comparing Tables 14.2 and 14.3, the calculated tidal-current transport (alone) would give sand transport rates at neap tides similar to under "stormy weather" waves (alone), at least to within the same order of magnitude. However, under all other wave conditions and under all other tides, unidirectional current transport (alone) would exceed that due to waves (alone) by many orders of magnitude.

At current-meter station 34(J), the water-depth ranges from 20 to 30m. A similar comparison suggests that (a) in "stormy" waves, the transport equals that of springs tidal currents both at high and at low water, and (b) in "oceanic" waves, the same equality of transport would occur at low water only. As maximum tidal current transport would be expected to occur near mid flood and mid ebb (i.e., in water depth about 25m), then again it can be predicted that the transport from this current would equate only to that produced by the "stormy" waves.

SAND TRANSPORT BY THE COMBINED ACTION OF WAVES AND TIDAL CURRENTS.

Only in the rarest of cases can tidal currents act in the absence of waves, and only for short periods, at slack water, can waves act in the absence of effective currents. Therefore, computations which assume the isolation of these mechanisms, one from the other, have a degree of unreality, except when one or other of the mechanisms acts unidirectionally and with extreme energies. An example could be the development of trains of abnormally high storm waves crossing the area during tidal slack water. Of course, if such wave trains were to be moving in a direction close to that taken by the ebb or flood currents, then the kinetic energies of each would complement the other.

Because of the practical impossibility of measuring extreme wave conditions, especially when wave trains of the theoretically highest possible energies are combined with maximum possible tidal currents, field monitoring can do no more than provide data for relatively quiescent periods. The data cannot take into account the rarer, but extreme and very effective, event. Consequently, wave activity, and especially the combined activity of waves and currents must be subjected to theoretical prediction.

The combined transport due to waves and currents may be predicted by the combined use of two equations. One is that originally given by Sternberg (1972), noted above, which is based on the analysis of unidirectional currents alone. The other is based on the work by Bagnold (1963) on the combined action of waves and currents; this was used in laboratory studies by Inman and Bowen (1963). The latter equation gives the transport rate J_1 (due to mobilisation by waves and subsequent transport by unidirectional current) as:

$$J_1 = \frac{K_1 W U_2}{U_m} \frac{\rho_S}{\rho_S - \rho} g$$

where K_1 = coefficient of proportionality, depended in part on grain-size (lying between 0.01 and 0.1, according to Inman (1963); assumed here to equate to 0.05).

- W = decrement in transmitted power of the waves due to bed-drag (varying according to wave group velocity, wave attenuation and kinetic fluid viscosity, calculated according to the method of Inman and Bowen, 1963).
- U_2 = unidirectional current velocity at 2cm above the bed
- U_m = maximum wave-induced orbital velocity at 2cm above the bed
- ρ_S = density of solid particle (2.65 for quartz)
- ρ = density of seawater
- g = gravitational acceleration

(The U_2 and U_m values at 2cm above the bed were selected for comparison with experimental studies of the combined action of currents and waves on the threshold of movement of sand particles (Hammond and Collins, 1979)).

The former equation (that of Sternberg) gives a **transport rate**, J_2, as:

$$J_2 = K_2 \rho U_*^3 \frac{\rho_S}{\rho_S - \rho} g$$

where K_2 = coefficient varying in proportion to excess shear stress (which, of course, is proportional, in part, to sand grain size).
and U_* = friction velocity (assuming a logarithmic velocity profile).

The sum of both J_1 and J_2 can give "a prediction" of the total transport rate. In this model, it is assumed that the effect of waves is simply to mobilise sedimentary material: as noted in the previous section, sediment transport due to the progression of wave trains is negligible compared to that resulting from tidal currents, and in this model it is neglected. Therefore, the model assumes mobilisation of the sand by the combined action of waves and currents, but transport by unidirectional currents alone. Any transport by wave trains (e.g., in extreme storm) would be additional to that predicted here.

The quantitative results for stations 34(J) and 35(I), predictable from these equations, are given in Table 14.4. They assume, of course, that there is an adequate supply of medium-grain sand for mobilisation and transportation in the rates which are predictable. The values derived result from input of the same data-sets as were used in previous sections (for unidirectional current transport and for wave-transport, considered separately). In agreement with the values obtained when wave-induced transport alone was considered (Table 14.3), Table 14.4 shows that maximum transport rates occur when the waves are high (i.e., "stormy" states), but not necessarily when the wavelength and period are greatest (i.e., "oceanic"). In these conditions, the transport due to the combined action of waves and currents is greater than that calculated for transport by waves alone: e.g., the maximum rate on Table 14.3 for "stormy" states is 10.92 kg/cm/cycle, at 20m water depth, whereas in Table 14.3, a comparable wave state produces from 53.8 to 109.68 kg/cm/cycle at Station 34(J) and even more (up to 167.56 kg/cm/cycle) at the deeper station 35(I). Compared to transport rates computed for unidirectional currents acting alone (Table 14.2), the minimum values predicted by the combined wave-current model are similar (i.e., of the order of 0.1 kg/cm/cycle) but the maximum values are much greater (e.g., springs tides at station 34(J) give 9.85 kg/cm/cycle by currents alone, 29.5 to 53.8 kg/cm/cycle by combined wave action and current transport). The direction of transport in each tidal cycle is greatly affected by the wave activity. When tidal currents alone are considered (Table 14.2), the predicted transport directions all fall within the sector 240°-287°, with the means falling within the 257°-272° sector (see also Figure 14.2). However, the combined action of waves and currents strongly modifies these resultants and can even lead to reversal of the direction predicted from tidal current directions alone. The vectors of both individual cycles and the mean are shown in Figure 14.3 (derived from Table 14.4).

Therefore, it is not only possible but probable that when "stormy" waves (3m high or so) are present at neaps tides, that quantities of sand will be moved from the southwest into the Bay, from the vicinity of Station 35(I) (i.e., the area where there already exists continuous available sand cover).

It must be emphasised that these computed transport rates:
   (a) assume that adequate quantities of sand are available for such transport; this would imply transport from a source area in the vicinity of Station 35(I) rather than from near Station 34(J);
   (b) take into account only tidal-current transport after wave action has put sand into motion, and do not include transport rates due to wave-induced currents; the latter would be an additional transport mechanism, especially when storm waves superimpose upon swell from the southwest and west;
   (c) apply to stormy sea states (5 to 7) which occur frequently in each year (see below), but not to the extreme event of a whole gale, which is rarer but which would be even more effective in the transfer of energy from the atmosphere to the seabed (for example, Draper (1980) gives, for the Bristol Channel, a once in 50 years extreme fully developed wave height (for fully developed storms lasting 12 hrs) of 18m (Fig. 10.10)).

Figures 5.1 and 5.2 show how topographic barriers may exist to such bedload transport between much of the distance between Mumbles and the White Oyster Ledge; however there is a narrow channel just north of the White Oyster Ledge and a broad one southeast of it, in the southerly approach to the Bay west of the Scarweather Sand.

TABLE 14.4

	Weather	Cycle	Resultant kg/cm/cycle	Resultant Direction Degrees from North	Mean Resultant kg/cm/cycle	Mean Direction
STATION 35 (I), NEAPS	Average	1	0.10	253°		
	Average	2	0.08	288°	0.096	266°
	Average	3	0.12	265°		
	Stormy	1	133.00	118°		
	Stormy	2	130.11	68°	91.28	96°
	Stormy	3	38.06	119°		
	Oceanic	1	32.98	126°		
	Oceanic	2	28.71	90°	23.03	104°
	Oceanic	3	13.69	75°		
STATION 35 (I), SPRINGS	Average	1	88.36	272°		
	Average	2	68.32	282°	81.12	280°
	Average	3	87.85	285°		
	Stormy	1	163.31	273°		
	Stormy	2	188.46	283°	167.56	280°
	Stormy	3	153.00	285°		
	Oceanic	1	46.87	283°		
	Oceanic	2	51.26	286°	43.37	286°
	Oceanic	3	42.22	290°		
STATION 34 (J), NEAPS	Average	1	0.25	266°		
	Average	2	0.13	275°	0.198	265°
	Average	3	0.21	262°		
	Stormy	1	97.88	163°		
	Stormy	2	135.02	167°	109.68	170°
	Stormy	3	99.41	183°		
	Oceanic	1	29.27	163°		
	Oceanic	2	40.45	167°	32.83	170°
	Oceanic	3	29.76	183°		
STATION 34 (J), SPRINGS	Average	1	40.89	138°		
	Average	2	54.43	102°	31.66	123°
	Average	3	10.59	187°		
	Stormy	1	67.97	191°		
	Stormy	2	122.67	269	53.80	226°
	Stormy	3	47.44	156°		
	Oceanic	1	24.07	249°		
	Oceanic	2	46.33	182°	29.50	237°
	Oceanic	3	31.15	232°		

The Supply of Sand

The combined breadths of these entrance channels is about 5.6km.

There are about 100 days in each year when neaps tides are comparable to those used in the calculations in Table 14.4; i.e., in each year, there are 200 cycles which would allow E to ENE bedload transport if the waves can attain 3m height. Wave records from the Helwick Light Vessel (Darbyshire, 1962, 1963) show that wave heights of 3m are reached or exceeded there for 22% of the year. Local wave trains will achieve 3m height in windspeeds of 12m/sec or more, and such speeds are reached or exceeded at Mumbles for 18% of the year (Oliver, 1971). It is reasonable to assume that waves of 3m or more in height occur at and near Station 35(I) for about 20% of the year. It is possible, therefore, that during 40 of the annual neap cycles, on average, bedload transport will be in E - ENE directions, towards the Bay.

If the computed transport of 91 kg/cm/cycle operates for 40 cycles, annually, across the 5.6km breadth of channel, then 2×10^6 tonnes of sand will be transported annually, by this mechanism alone, into the Bay.

It has been shown above (Chapter 4) that many areas of the Bay experience no net deposition (Figure 4.3) and that, in the others, the mobile sediment is very thin. However, maintenance dredging in the approach channels to Swansea and Port Talbot harbours amounts to 1.2×10^6 tonnes annually (British Transport Docks Board, 1970): this is discussed further in Chapters 36 and 37. It may be emphasised that once sand has entered the Bay from the Channel, the only mechanisms for its removal are (a) tidal currents leaving the Bay at ebb as a corner current around Mumbles (Figure 14.5), where maximum recorded speeds vary from 0.5m/s (neaps) to 1m/s (springs) (Collins et al., 1979; see also Ferentinos and Collins, 1979); (b) tidal currents through the Nash Passage at flood (Figure 14.5), (c) aeolian transport from the beach to the supralittoral dunes (see Chapters 7 and 17), and (d) dredging.

As noted above, these computations for sediment transfer apply to "Stormy" sea states which can be expected to occur for about 20% of each year. However, there are rarer, much more extreme events (Draper, 1980) which may have very considerable (even spectacular) effects upon sand transport. Whole gales (25m/s, or more, windspeed) are rare but can occur (50 year extreme windspeeds of 32-34m/s at 10m above sea level for the Bristol Channel (Draper, 1980, Fig. 10.2)), especially from the W-SE sector. If waves of 7m height (assuming 10sec period still dominant in the mixed sea) are induced, then, at Station 35(I) the transport rates for medium sand will rise (at neaps tides) to 145.4 kg/cm/tidal cycle, in a direction of 097°. 207.7 kg/cm/cycle, in the same direction, would be induced by 10m-high waves. These values are about twice those estimated for "stormy" states in Table 14.4. If the dominant wave period were to be less than 10secs (e.g., 8secs, as at the Helwick Light Vessel, where such waves of 10m have been recorded (Darbyshire, 1962) for 0.4% of the time), then the transport rates would be virtually doubled yet again.

The 10-sec period, 7m-high waves could, therefore, result in a mass transfer of medium sand, across the 5.6km-broad entrance to the Bay, of 80,800 tonnes during one neaps tidal cycle. Similar waves of 10m height could result in a transfer of 115,400 tonnes in one cycle. Again, 8sec period waves could double these values. Sudden influxes of sediment into the Bay do occur during gales. In January, 1975, about $2 \times 10^6 m^3$ of sediment (mud, silt and fine sand) accumulated within Port Talbot Tidal Harbour within days (Collins and Banner, 1980; see also Chapter 37). The harbour had been dredged to 32.5 feet (9.9m) below datum in September, 1974, but had accreted to 27.5 feet b.d. (8.4m) in early January, 1975 in its southern part, and 29.6 feet b.d. (9.0m) in its inner channel. This required about five times the annual dredging rate (i.e., 5.8×10^6 hopper cubic yards), as immediate contract dredging, in order to restore harbour depth. As the threshold velocities needed to move fine sand are less than those required for medium sand, the transport rates for the fine sand which was transferred into the harbour are likely to be much greater than those computed above for the medium-sand sedimentary fraction. Therefore, it can be concluded that such an influx of sediment into Swansea Bay can be accounted for by the combined action of wave and tidal current action in its southwest approaches.

DISCUSSION AND CONCLUSIONS

Figure 14.4 shows the vectors for bedload net transport of medium sand, due to the combined action of waves and of tidal currents at five stations in the approaches to Swansea Bay (see also Figure 14.2).

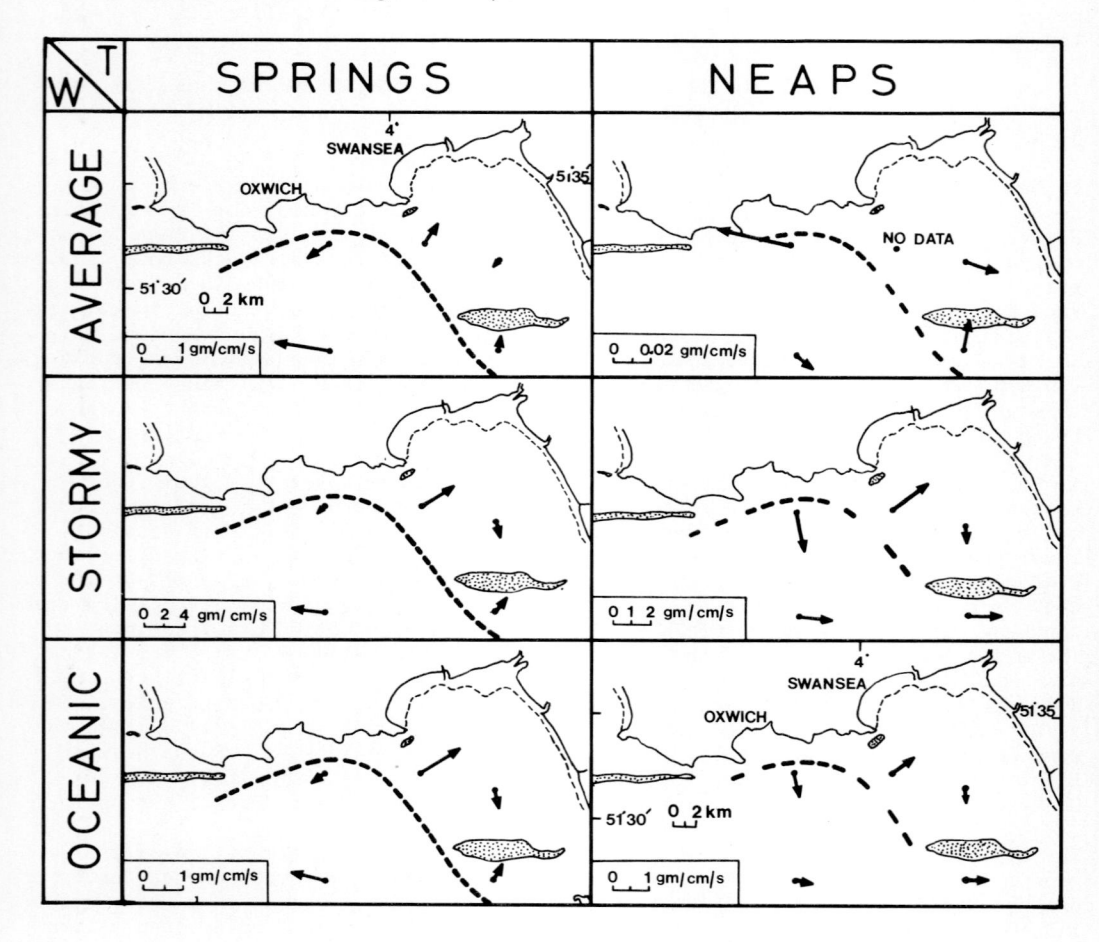

Figure 14.4. Sediment transport vectors for bed load transport, under the combined influence of waves and currents, at 5 stations in the area under investigation. Differing tidal phases (T) and wave conditions (W) are represented (see text).

The southerly-directed vector-resultant at Station 34(J), for neaps tides under "stormy" and "oceanic" wave activity, agrees with that deduced for the residual near-bed currents described in Chapter 11. It is of particular interest in that the implied offshore sand transport could explain, in part at least, the discontin-

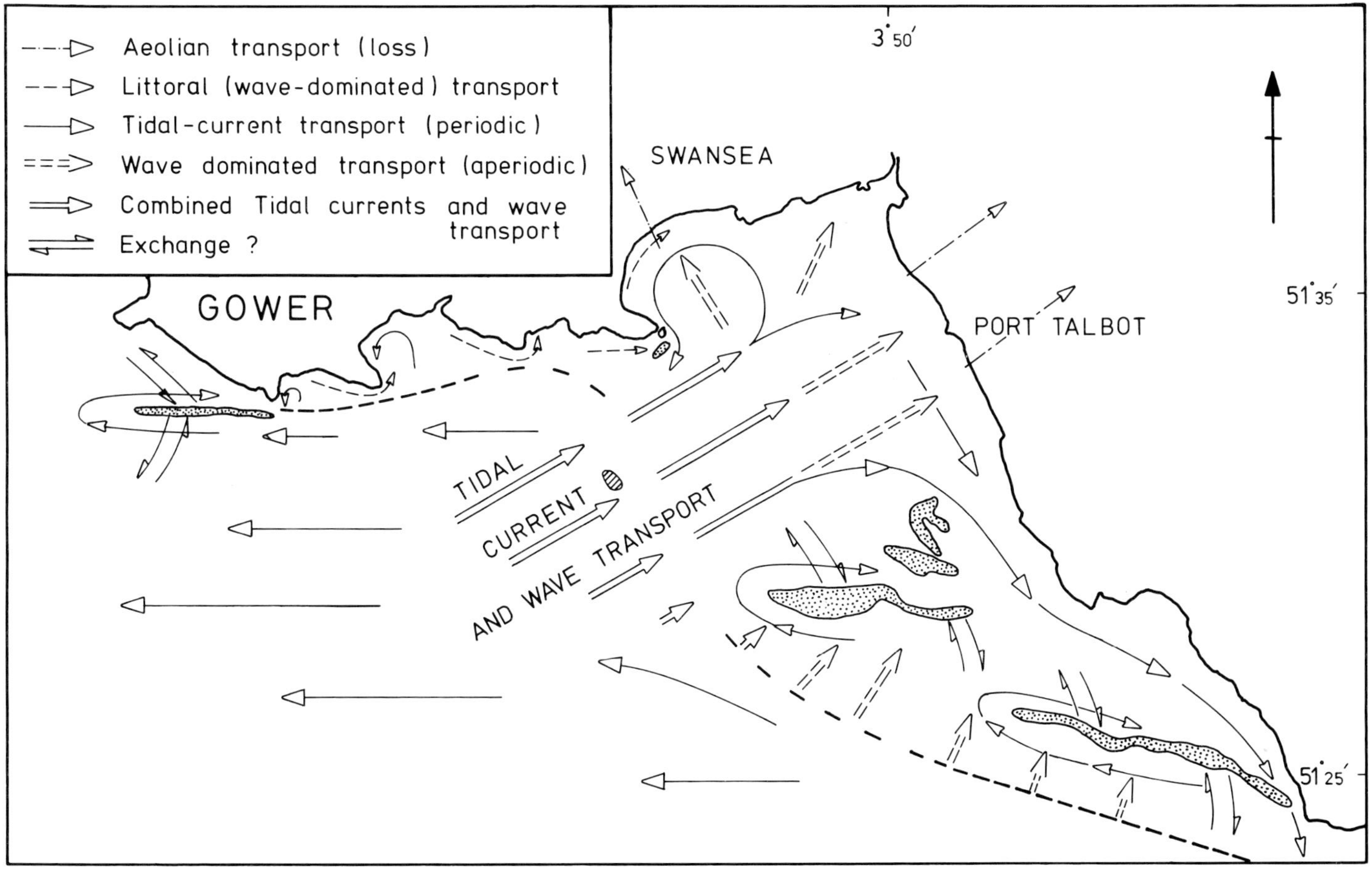

Figure 14.5. Postulated sand transport directions in Swansea Bay.

PLATE 14.3. An example of the transport and build up of material, by southeasterly storm wind action, in northern Swansea Bay during October 1979 (Photos: J.K. Rigler). (a) Rippled bedforms in the sand deposited on the central reservation of the dual carriageway; (b) View looking east, towards Swansea Docks, showing accumulation of sand and subsequent "replacement" of sand by council employee.

uousness of the sand cover in that region (Figure 14.2). It also suggests the existence of a bedload parting between this offshore transport and a (wave-dominated) shorewards, inshore transport; the latter being responsible for beach accretion. The parting zone is indicated by the dashed line immediately south of Gower on Figures 14.2 and 14.5.

Current meter stations N and NW of the Scarweather Sand also are represented by vectors showing similar computed bedload transport. Those for station 38(F) (see Figure 14.2 for identification), when computed for "average", "stormy" and "oceanic" waves at springs tides, and for "stormy" and "oceanic" waves at neaps ("average" waves at neaps are not yet computed), all show bedload transport occurring in a northeasterly direction, i.e., into the Bay. As discussed in the previous section, the maximum rates of transport would be doubled for waves of 7m height and quadrupled for 10m-high waves. This station 38(F) is in an area of nil net deposition (compare Figure 4.3) which has only thin and transitory sand cover. Therefore, sand moving to station 38(F) does not remain there but must move further northeast, into the area occupied by mobile sediments of facies 4 and 5 (Figure 4.2), i.e., Province 4 of Collins et al., 1979 (see Figure 5.2.). Moreover, the clay and consolidated-mud lumps, which have been found in the aperiodic infill of Port Talbot Tidal Harbour, are lithologically and microfaunally of Flandrian origin (facies 3 of Chapter 4), and indicate that erosion of the seabed of Swansea Bay must occur at such times of high wave activity.

The station immediately north of the Scarweather (Figure 14.4) has weak and rotatory bedload transport vectors, according to this mode of computation. This station lies in Province 1 (see Figure 5.2), the area of sandy mud and muddy sand (Collins et al., 1979), of the *Abra* community (Chapter 33), which has facies 6 (mobile sandy mud of palimpsest origin)(Chapter 4) moving below the broad zone of flood current divergence (Figure 14.5). This NE-SW orientated zone of muddy sand is aligned from Port Talbot towards the southwest approaches to the Bay, where it faces no topographic barrier.

The postulated sand transport directions are summarised on Figure 14.5. The complex pattern results from interplay of topography (coastline configuration and bathymetry), wave-action and tidal-currents. It appears that sand transport into the Bay occurs during stormy (and even more extreme weather conditions) during neaps tides, and that very large quantities of sand can be carried into the Bay during exceptionally severe weather. Once in the Bay, the sand is available for redistribution (Plate 14.1), producing the beaches (and, thence, by aeolian transport, the dune deposits and landward transfer (Plates 14.2 and 14.3) and accumulations which must be dredged. Some may form part, at least, of the Mixon Shoal sandbank, and a residual, well-sorted fraction (of reduced heavy mineral content, Chapter 16) may contribute to an exchange with the linear sandbanks to the southeast.

ACKNOWLEDGEMENT

The authors gratefully acknowledge preparation of the Figures by Mr. K. Naylor.

REFERENCES

Bagnold, R.A. (1963). Sedimentation: beach and nearshore processes. Chapter 21 In: Hill, M.N. (Ed.), *The Sea*, Wiley Interscience, 3, 507-528.

Bagnold, R.A. (1966). An approach to the sediment transport problem from general physics. *U.S. Geol. Surv. Profess. Paper 422-J*.

Banner, F.T. (1979). Sediments of the north-west European shelf. In: Banner, F.T. Collins, M.B., and Massie, K.S. (Eds.). *The North-west European Shelf Seas: the seabed and the sea in motion. 1. Geology and Sedimentology*. Elsevier Oceanographic Series *24A,* 271-300.

Banner, F.T., and Collins, M.B. (1975). Field meeting: "Introduction to Oceanography" at University College of Swansea. *Proc. Geol. Ass., 86,* 87-94.

Barrie, J.V. (1978). *Heavy mineral distribution in bottom sediments of the Bristol Channel.* Unpub. M.Sc. thesis, University of Wales.

Belderson, R.H., Kenyon, N.H. and Stride, A.H. (1971). Holocene sediments on the continental shelf west of the British Isles. *In:* Delany, S.M. (Ed.). *The Geology of the East Atlantic Continental Margin, Pt. 2: Europe.* S.C.O.R. Symp. Cambridge, 1970, Inst. Geol. Sci., Rep., *70/14,* 157-170.

British Transport Docks Board (1970). The Severn Estuary, *Report on Research 1969,* 16-17.

British Transport Docks Board (1978). *Port Talbot Accretion Final Report.* B.T.D.B. Southall, Report *270.*

Carr, A.P., Heathershaw, A.D., and Blackley, M.W.L. (1976). *Swansea Bay (Sker) Project: Progress Report for the period August 1975 to July, 1976.* IOS (Taunton) Report *26* (Unpub.), 1-19.

Collins, M.B., Ferentinos, G., and Banner, F.T. (1979). The hydrodynamics and sedimentology of a high (tidal and wave) energy embayment (Swansea Bay, Bristol Channel). *Estuar. and Coast. Mar. Sci., 8,* 49-74.

Collins, M.B., and Banner, F.T. (1980). Sediment transport by waves and tides: exemplified by a study of Swansea Bay, Bristol Channel. *In:* Banner, F.T., Collins, M.B., and Massie, K.S. (Eds.). *The North-west European Shelf Seas: the seabed and the sea in motion. 2.* Elsevier Oceanographic Series, *24B*(Chapter 11).

Culver, S.J., and Banner, F.T. (1978). Foraminiferal assemblages as Flandrian palaeoenvironmental indicators. *Palaeogeo., Palaeoclimatol., Palaeoecol., 24,* 53-72.

Darbyshire, M. (1962). Wave measurements made by the National Institute of Oceanography. *Mar. Observer,* Jan. 1962, 32-40.

Darbyshire, M. (1963). Wave measurements made by the National Institute of Oceanography. *Proc. Conf. Ocean Wave Spectra,* 285-291.

Draper, L.R. (1980). Wave climatology of the U.K. Continental Shelf. *In:* Banner, F.T., Collins, M.B., and Massie, K.S. (Eds.). *The North-west European Shelf Seas: the seabed and the sea in motion. 2.* Elsevier Oceanographic Series, *24B* (Chapter 10).

Evans, D.J., and Thompson, M.S. (1979). The geology of the central Bristol Channel and the Lundy area, Southwestern Approaches, British Isles. *Proc. Geol. Ass., 90,* 1-14.

Ferentinos, G., and Collins, M.B. (1978). *Sediment transport through the area south of eastern Gower, as related to the sediment budget of Swansea Bay.* Final Report to I.O.S. Taunton (N.E.R.C. Contract), *1,* (Unpub.).

Ferentinos, G., and Collins, M.B., (1979). Tidally induced secondary circulations and their associated sedimentation processes. *J. Oceanograph. Soc. Japan, 35,* 65-74.

Gadd, P.E., Lavelle, J.W., and Swift, D.J.P. (1978). Estimates of sand transport on the New York Shelf using near-bottom current-meter observations. *Jour. Sedim. Petrol., 48,* 239-252.

Hamilton, D. (1979). The Geology of the English Channel, South Celtic Sea and Continental Margin, South Western Approaches. *In:* Banner, F.T., Collins, M.B., and Massie, K.S., (Eds.). *The North-west European Shelf Seas: the seabed and the sea in motion. 1. Geology and Sedimentology.* Elsevier Oceanographic Series, *24A,* 61-88.

Hammond, T., and Collins, M.B. (1979). On the threshold of sand-sized sediment under the combined influence of unidirectional and oscillatory flow. *Sedimentology,* (In press).

Hammond, T., and Collins, M.B. (In press). The design and use of an oscillating trolley wave-simulator, for installation in unidirectional-flow flumes. *Estuar. and Coast. Mar. Sci.*

Harvey, J.G., and Vincent, C.E. (1976). Observations of shear in near-bed currents in the southern North Sea. *Estuar. and Coast. Mar. Sci., 5,* 715-731.

Hill, P.A., and Parker, A. (1970). Tin and zirconium in the sediments around the British Isles: a preliminary reconnaissance. *Econ. Geol., 65,* 409-416.

Inman, D.L. (1963). Sediments: physical properties and mechanics of sedimentation. *In:* Shepard, F.P. (Ed.). *Submarine Geology,* (2nd Ed.), Harper and Row, 49-81, 101-147.

Inman, D.L., and Bowen, A.J. (1963). Flume experiments on sand transport by waves and currents. *Proc. 8th Coastal Eng. Conf.,* 137-150.

Kenyon, N.M., and Stride, A.M. (1970). The tide swept continental shelf sediments between the Shetland Isles and France. *Sedimentology, 14,* 159-173.

Komar, P., and Miller, M. (1973). The threshold of sediment movement under oscillatory water waves. *Jour. Sedim. Petrol., 43,* 1101-1110.

Madsen, O.S., and Grant, W.D. (1976). Quantitative description of sediment transport by waves. *Proc. 15th Coastal Eng. Conf. (2),* 1093-1112.

Miller, M.C., McCave, I.N., and Komar, P.D. (1977). Thresholds of sediment motion under unidirectional currents. *Sedimentology, 24,* 507-527.

Oliver, J. (1971). Climatology. *In:* Balchin, W.G.V. (Ed.). *Swansea and its region.* University College of Swansea and British Association for Advancement of Science, 41-58.

Pattiaratchi, C.B. (1979). *Estimates of sediment transport through the area south of eastern Gower due to unidirectional and oscillatory flow.* Unpub. B.Sc. thesis, University College of Swansea, Dept. of Oceanography.

Sternberg, R.W. (1972). Predicting initial motion and bedload transport of sediment particles in the shallow marine environment. *In:* Swift, D.J.P., Duane, D.B., and Pilkey, O.H. (Eds.). *Shelf Sediment Transport: Process and Pattern.* Dowden, Hutchinson & Ross, Pa., 61-82.

Stride, A.H. (1963). Current swept sea floors near the southern half of Great Britain. *Qt. Jl. Geol. Soc. London, 119,* 175-200.

Wilding, A.J. (1979). *Numerical Studies of Tides, Free Oscillations and Surges in Swansea Bay.* Unpub. Ph.D. thesis, Unversity of Wales, 184pp.

15. TRANSPORT AND DEPOSITION OF NON-COHESIVE SEDIMENTS IN SWANSEA BAY

A. D. Heathershaw and F. D. C. Hammond

Institute of Oceanographic Sciences, Taunton, Somerset, U.K.

ABSTRACT

Observed and predicted sediment transport rates and directions have been used to determine the sedimentary regime in Swansea Bay and the relative magnitudes of the bed load and suspended load modes of transport.

The observed sediment distributions reflect strongly the tidal dynamics of the area, with a region of possible net deposition and muddy silty sands occurring within the Bay in an area of low tidal energy. Correspondingly, areas of high tidal energy are characterized by coarse grained deposits and erosional bedforms.

It is shown that suspended load transport rates for sand size material (median diameter $d_{50} \simeq 170 \mu m$) are, on average, a factor of 6 times lower than bed load transport of the same size material. Net or tidally-averaged bed load transport rates show a shoreward decrease of nearly two orders of magnitude from about 2 tonnes/m/day in the vicinity of the offshore sand banks to about .02 tonnes/m/day in the Bay head.

Nevertheless, suspended sediment concentrations have been found to be sufficiently large to modify the turbulent and mean flow structure of the bottom boundary layer, leading to modified equilibrium velocity and concentration profiles. It is shown that fitting of conventional logarithmic velocity profiles under these circumstances may lead to over-estimates of the roughness length (Z_o) and friction velocity (U_*).

The available evidence suggests that the sedimentary system in Swansea Bay is essentially 'by-passed' by a strong westward movement of sediment along the north coast of the Bristol Channel with only a weak and sporadic transfer of material into the Bay, possibly as a result of wave activity during strong southwest winds.

KEYWORDS

Sediment distribution; Bed load transport; Suspended load transport; Wave effects; Swansea Bay; Bristol Channel.

INTRODUCTION

This chapter describes measurements of sediment transport rates and the sediment circulation pattern in Swansea Bay.

Observed and predicted transport rates have been used to determine the relative magnitudes of suspended and bed load transport rates, principally under tidal currents, and finally in the selection of a suitable sediment transport formula for the prediction of sediment transport paths in the area. The role of surface wave activity in modifying the sediment transport processes is also briefly considered.

Previous studies of sediment transport processes in Swansea Bay (e.g., Davies, 1974, 1975; Ferentinos and Collins, 1978; Collins et al., 1979) have concentrated largely on a fundamental description of the origins, transport and deposition of both non-cohesive and the cohesive sediments in the area. Sediment transport paths have been inferred from grain size distributions and the asymmetry of large amplitude bedforms; current measurements have also been used to describe the various hydrodynamic regimes.

In this chapter, we examine the previous and largely sedimentological interpretations of the area and show that in general these are consistent with the observed fluid dynamical processes and predictions from sediment transport theory. However, there are some important differences.

DYNAMICS OF SEDIMENT TRANSPORT

Sediment may be moved on or above the sea bed in two modes:

(a) bed load, in which grains roll or saltate along the sea bed perhaps at heights of up to a few grain diameters;
(b) suspended load in which grains are transported within the body of the fluid at some distance (many grain diameters) from the boundary.

Under tidal currents the motile agencies for these modes consist, respectively, of:

(c) the action of an applied stress at the sea bed by the action of the tidal current flowing above it;
(b) the production of turbulent kinetic energy by shear in the bottom boundary layer.

In some cases, (c) and (d) will be modified by the effects of wave activity.

The principal difficulty involved in measuring and predicting sediment transport is its extreme non-linearity. From a dynamic point of view bed load transport q_{sb} is related to the friction velocity U_* times the excess shear stress $(\tau - \tau_{cr})$, at high transport rates, and to U_* times the excess shear stress squared $(\tau - \tau_{cr})^2$, at low transport rates. Suspended sediment transport (q_{ss}) is dynamically related to the friction velocity U_* to a power greater than unity, times the excess shear stress. Here τ is the shear stress exerted on the sea bed and τ_{cr} is a critical value of τ related to the threshold of movement of material as bed load or in suspension.

Thus to summarise:

$$q_{sb} \alpha \begin{cases} U_*(\tau - \tau_{cr}) \alpha\, U_*^3 & \text{at high transport rates} \\ U_*(\tau - \tau_{cr})^2 \alpha U_*^5 & \text{at low transport rates} \end{cases}$$

and

$$q_{ss} \alpha\; U_*^n (\tau - \tau_{cr}) \alpha U_*^{n+2}$$

where n = 1 at least.

Further difficulties arise in computing bed load transport on rippled beds due to the uncertainty in partitioning the bed shear stress into that part which overcomes form drag and that part which is due solely to skin friction (see, for example, Smith, 1977; Smith and McLean, 1977).

Whereas it is possible to calculate bed load transport from a knowledge of the sediment and flow characteristics alone, calculation of suspended load transport also requires a knowledge of the concentration at a specific height above the sea bed. This information, which requires special measuring techniques, is frequently not available and successful suspended load prediction, particularly on the continental shelf, is one of the major difficulties presently confronting sedimentologists, geologists and oceanographers.

DISTRIBUTION OF SEDIMENTS

The range and diversity of sediments in Swansea Bay is considerable; this, in itself, makes the prediction of sediment transport rates difficult. Fig. 15.1 shows the range of sediment types observed on the east side of the Bay and illustrates a five-fold variation in grain size from the fine silty material of about 50μm grain size, in the area off Port Talbot, to the coarse 250μm grain size material in the vicinity of Sker Point. This distribution reflects closely the variation in tidal current amplitude in the area and the residual water movements (see Figs. 11.5 and 11.10).

In the present study, we have been concerned primarily with the movement of material having a median (d_{50}) grain size of about 170μm, which corresponds approximately to the size of material found on the foreshore on the east side of the Bay. The manner in which this size of material moves through the population of grain sizes found in the area is by no means clear; in particular, the way in which non-cohesive sand size material moves across cohesive material of the type found off Port Talbot is not known and this is clearly one of the major difficulties in predicting the movement of a coarse grained material.

BED LOAD TRANSPORT

Measurements of the near-bottom velocity field ($\bar{U}_{200}$) have been used to predict sediment transport rates and directions in the area. In order to do this, however, it has been necessary to select a suitable sediment transport formula. This has been achieved by comparing bed load transport estimates from two radioactive tracer experiments, at positions T1 and T2 in Fig. 15.2, with predicted transport rates using current measurements from Stations A and C. Full details of the tracer experiment and comparisons of sediment transport formulae are given in Heathershaw and Hammond (1979b). Examples of tracer dispersion patterns are given in Fig. 15.3 and it should be noted that these reflect strongly the phase of the tide following the release of the tracer (i.e., ebb at T1 and flood at T2) and cannot be used to infer directions of net sediment movement until the tracer has come into equilibrium with the sea bed. Heathershaw and Carr (1977) have found that this may take as long as 10 - 20 days.

To obtain friction velocity (U_*) estimates from our measurements of the near bottom velocity field ($\bar{U}_{200}$), it is necessary to assume some form for the vertical velocity distribution in the bottom boundary layer. It is usual to assume that this is logarithmic and of the form:

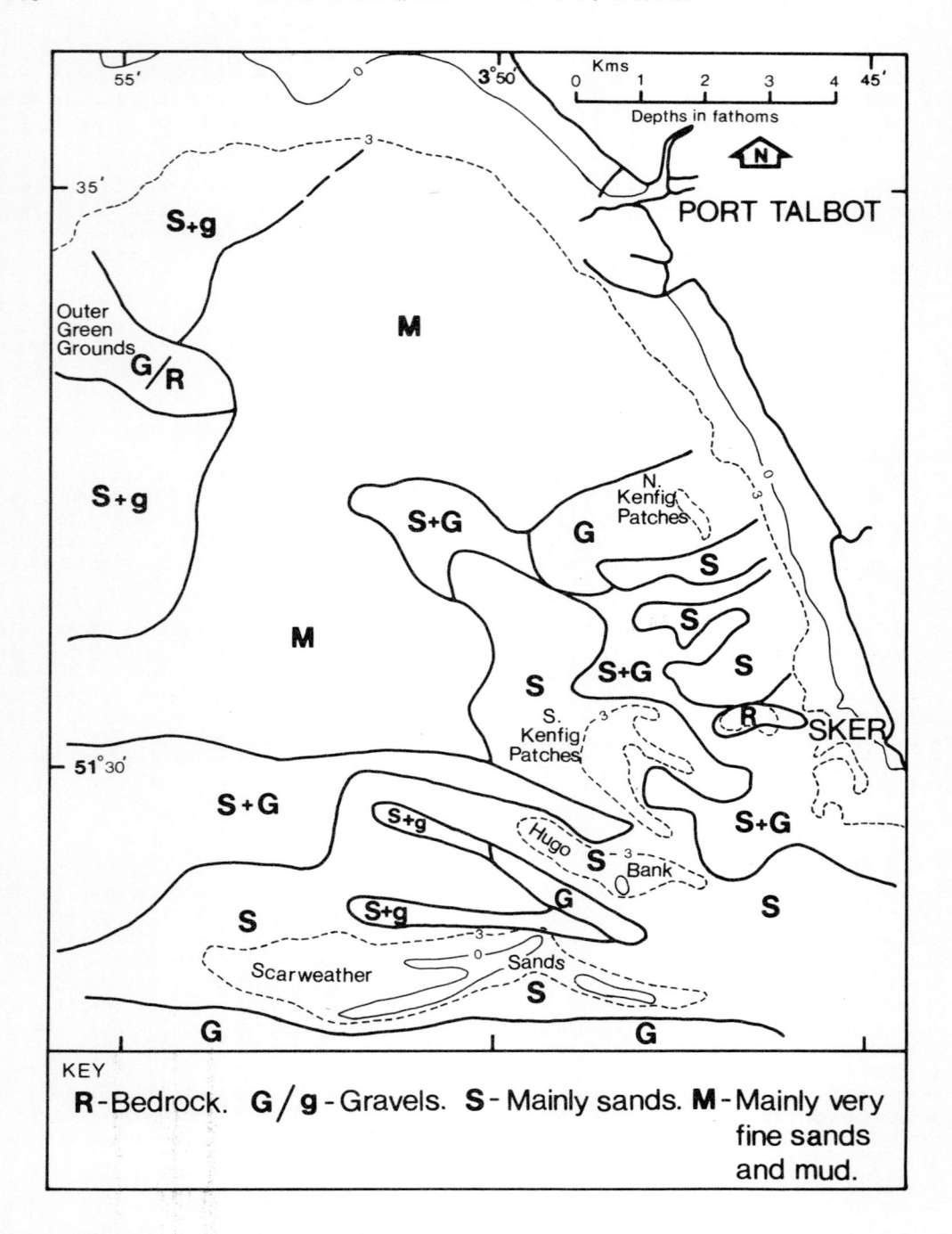

Figure 15.1. Sediment distribution on the east side of Swansea Bay.

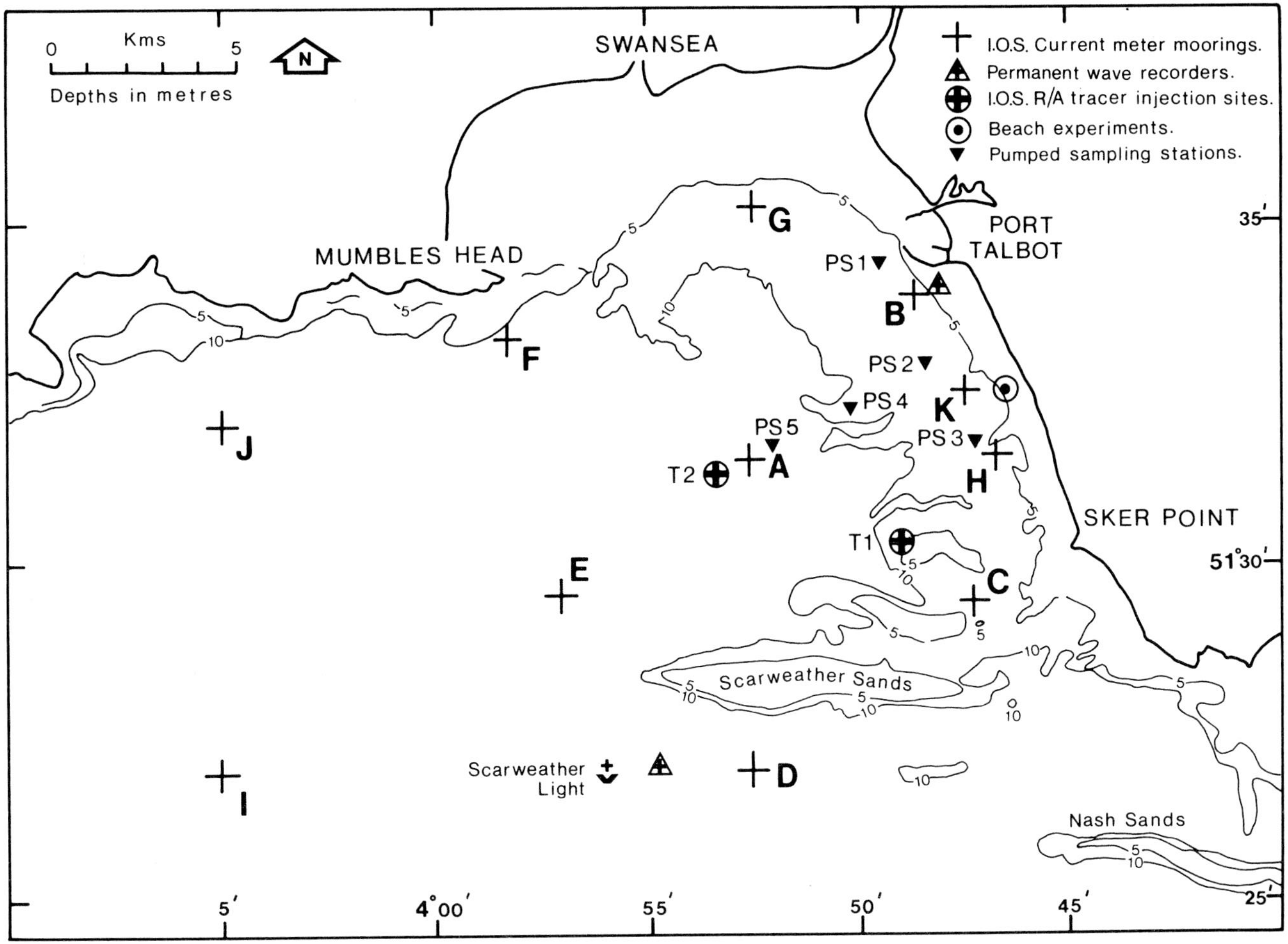

Figure 15.2. Location of recording current meter moorings and positions at which near bottom velocity profile and suspended sediment measurements were made. The locations of radioactive tracer experiments (T1 and T2) are also indicated.

$$\bar{U}(Z) = \frac{U_*}{\kappa} \ln\frac{Z}{Z_o} \tag{1}$$

where $\bar{U}$ is the mean flow at a height Z above the sea bed, Z_o is the roughness length and κ is von Karman's constant, usually taken as 0.4 for suspension-free flows. However, it should be noted that logarithmic velocity profiles may not be applicable at all times throughout the tidal cycle (e.g., Sternberg, 1968, 1972) and we will show later that the form of the profile may be influenced by vertical stratification effects of the type reported by Smith and McLean (1977) and Taylor and Dyer (1977).

The use of a logarithmic velocity distribution (Equation 1) in predicting sediment transport rates on the continental shelf presents a major difficulty since in the majority of cases Z_o is not known. Heathershaw and Hammond (1979b) have found that reported Z_o values fall roughly into four categories according to the sediment types most frequently encountered on the continental shelf. These are summarised in Table 15.1 and it should be noted that these values are quite independent of any changes which may occur over the tidal cycle.

TABLE 15.1. Roughness Length Z_o Values Used in Calculating Bed Load Transport Rates in Swansea Bay.

Sediment	Bedform	Roughness Length Z_o (cm)
Sand or Gravel	Rippled) Irregular)	.5
Sand/gravel or Gravel/sand	Irregular) Irregular)	.1
Muddy sand or sandy mud	Planar) Planar)	.05
Mud	Planar	.01

Heathershaw and Hammond (1979b) have found a two order of magnitude variation in the predicted net bed load transports using the five formulae listed in Table 15.2 Fig. 15.4 summarises the comparisons of predicted and observed net or tidally averaged transport rates at Stations A and C using the 5 different formulae and from the tracer experiments at T1 and T2.

Best estimates of the net bed load transport appear to be given by Bagnold's (1963) formula, in a modified form due to Gadd et al. (1978), which gives estimates which are within a factor of 0.5 - 2 of the measured rates (See Figure 15.4) (and see also Chapter 14). Bagnold's original formula expressed the bed load transport rate q_{sb} in terms of the stream power ω and an efficiency factor K, that is

$$q_{sb} = \frac{\rho_s}{\rho_s - \rho} \cdot K\omega \tag{2}$$

where ρ_s is the sediment density, ρ is the density of sea water and ω is the stream power given by the product of the bed stress τ and the friction velocity U_*. The application of this formula requires specification of the efficiency factor K which has been shown (e.g., Sternberg, 1972) to be a function not only of grain size but also of bed form amplitude. This dependence has been removed by Gadd et al. (1978), who, using the flume data of Guy et al. (1966), have expressed (2) in terms of the current at 100cm above the sea bed, $\bar{U}_{100}$, and a threshold velocity $\bar{U}_{cr}$. (Note that

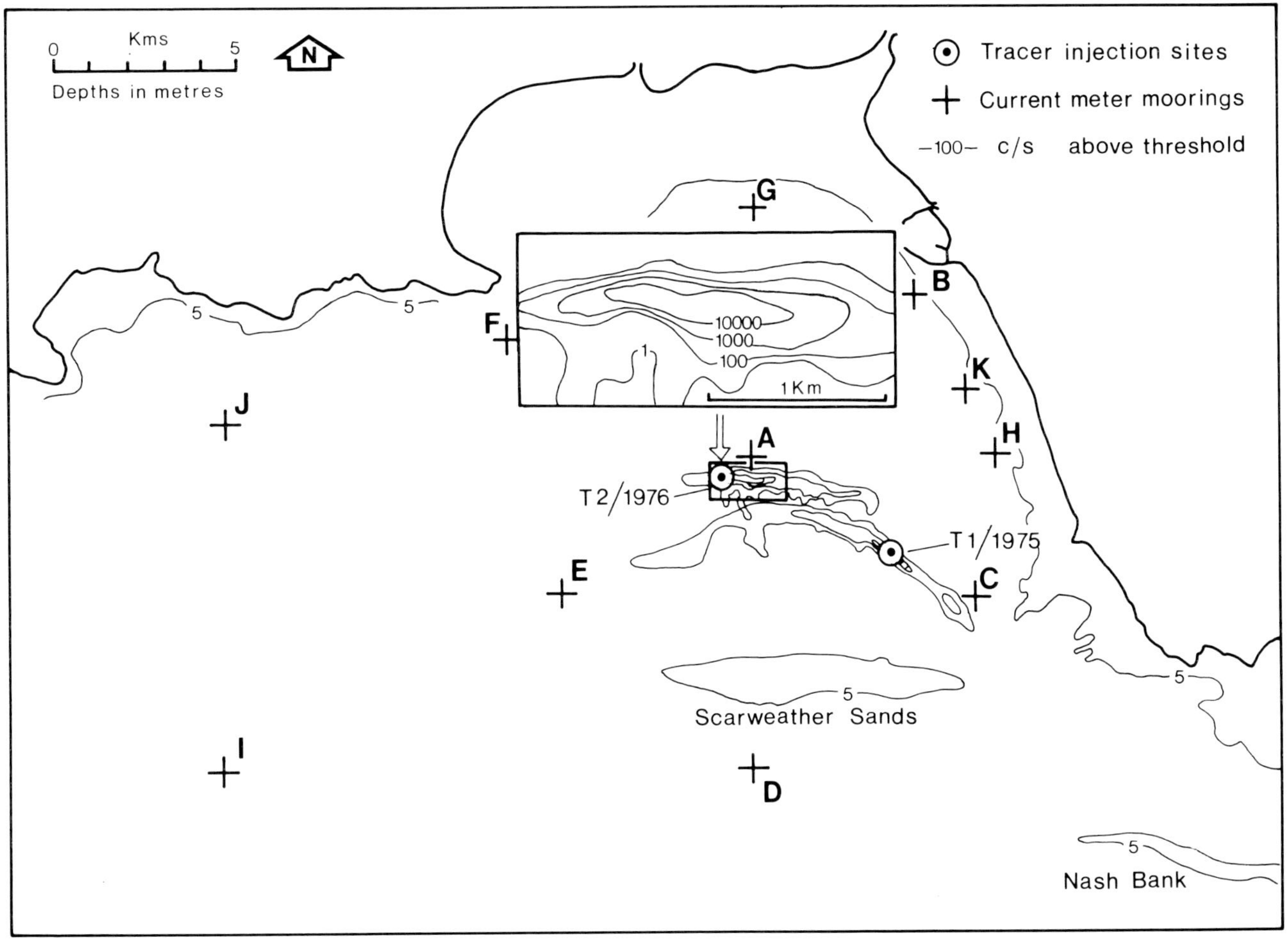

Figure 15.3. Tracer dispersion patterns at T1 and T2 approximately 2-3 days after injection. The initial dispersions reflect the phase of the tide following injection rather than the long term sediment drift which can only be established 10-12 days after the release of the tracer.

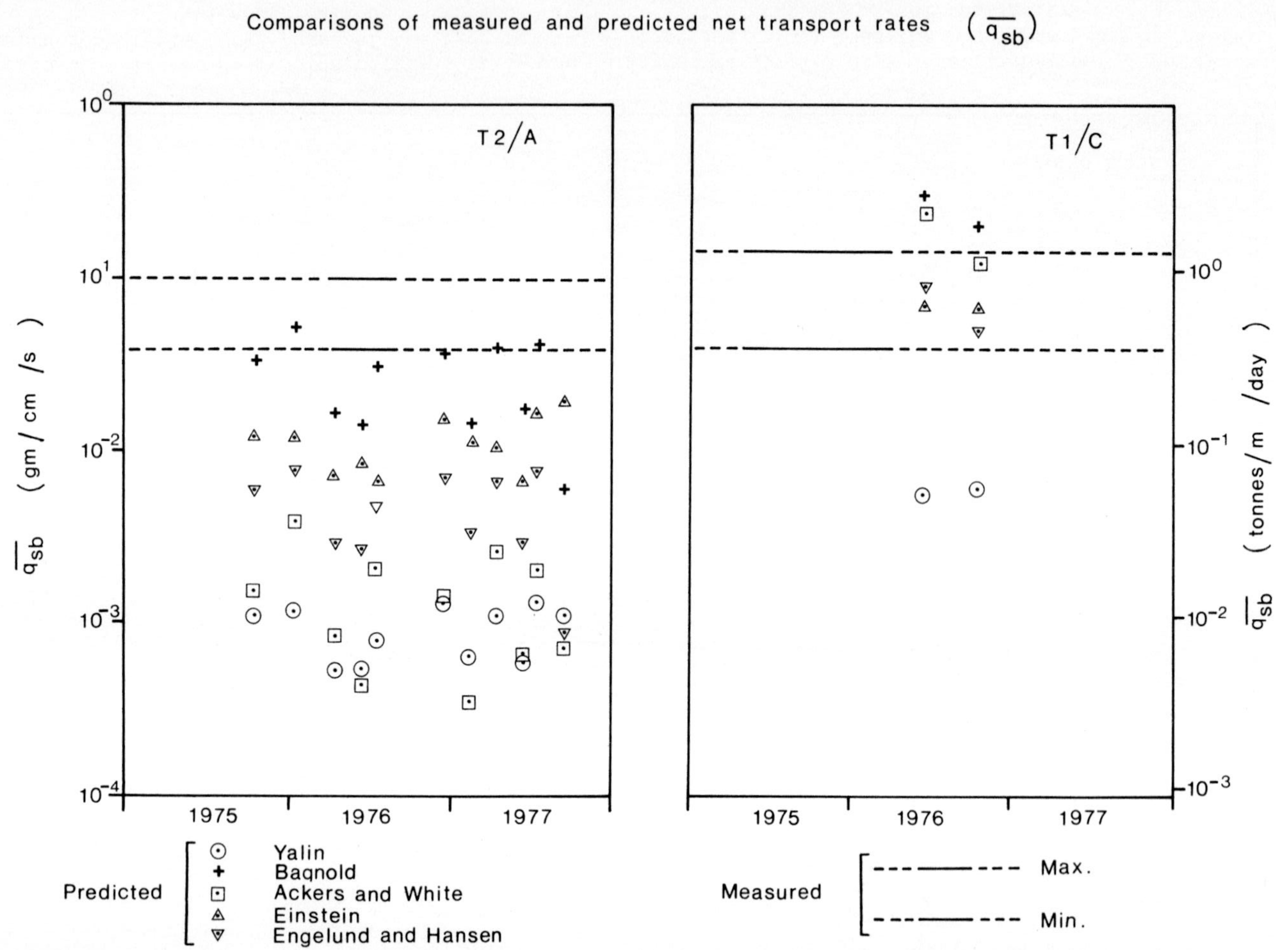

Figure 15.4. Comparisons of observed and predicted net bed load transport rates ($\bar{q}_{sb}$). The maximum and minimum measured rates are derived from radioactive tracer experiments at T1 and T2.

Bagnold's original formula - Equation 2 - predicts sediment transport at all flow speeds). Thus:

$$q_{sb} = \alpha(\bar{U}_{100} - U_{cr})^3 \quad (3)$$

where α is a coefficient, having the dimensions of $gm/cm^4/s^2$, which was obtained from flume data. For this study Equation (3) has been written in terms of the measured currents at a height of 200cm above the sea-bed ($\bar{U}_{200}$) by assuming a logarithmic velocity profile and by taking an appropriate roughness length Z_0 (see Table 15.1). The value of the coefficient α varies according to grain size and Gadd et al. (1978) give values of α for median (d_{50}) grain sizes of 180μm and 450μm. In this investigation, we have been particularly concerned with the prediction of sediment transport rates and directions for the size of material found on the foreshore on the east side of the Bay and on the sand banks, to the south of the area. Box core and grab samples (see Heathershaw and Hammond, 1979b; Blackley, 1978) indicate a median (d_{50}) grain size of about 170μm. This corresponds fairly closely to the mean tracer particle sizes which were of the order 160-170μm ± 20μm. We have thus taken a value of α of 7.55×10^{-5} $gm/cm^4/s^2$ which corresponds in Gadd et al's calibration of Equation 3 to a median grain size of 180μm and is therefore considered a suitable value.

TABLE 15.2. Sediment Transport Formulae used in Comparisons of Observed and Predicted Sediment Transport Rates in Swansea Bay.

Originators		Date	Type	Mode
Bagnold	a	1963	Deterministic	Bed load
Yalin	a	1963	Deterministic	Bed load
Einstein	a	1950	Stochastic	Bed load
Ackers and White	b,c	1973	Deterministic	Total load
Engelund and Hansen	b,c	1967	Deterministic	Total load

Used recently by (a) Gadd et al. 1978; (b) Swart, 1976; (c) Flemming and Hunt, 1976.

Values of the critical velocity (U_{cr}) have been calculated using a logarithmic velocity profile (Equation 1) and a critical velocity (U_{*cr}) obtained from Yalin's (1972) modified Shields' curve (see Heathershaw and Hammond, 1979b, for details). Thus, for each location, a roughness length Z_0 and critical friction velocity U_{cr} were specified and net bed load transport rates calculated using Bagnold's (1963) formula in the modified form shown in Equation (3).

Bagnold's formula is one of the simplest expressions currently in use by oceanographers and engineers and is based on the physics of the stream power concept. Indeed, its success in this particular application may owe much to this simplicity. The more sophisticated techniques, e.g., Ackers and White's (1973) formula, tend to yield lower estimates (See Fig. 15.4). However, it is worth noting that in the absence of a tracer estimate and in terms of their median performance we might equally well have chosen Engelund and Hansen's (1967) or Einstein's (1950) formulae.

SUSPENDED LOAD TRANSPORT

It is not possible to predict directly suspended sediment transport rates from a knowledge of the near-bottom velocity field and the sediment characteristics alone. The solution of the steady state diffusion equations (see Yalin, 1972) gives the mass concentration at a height Z above the sea bed, C(Z), in terms of a reference

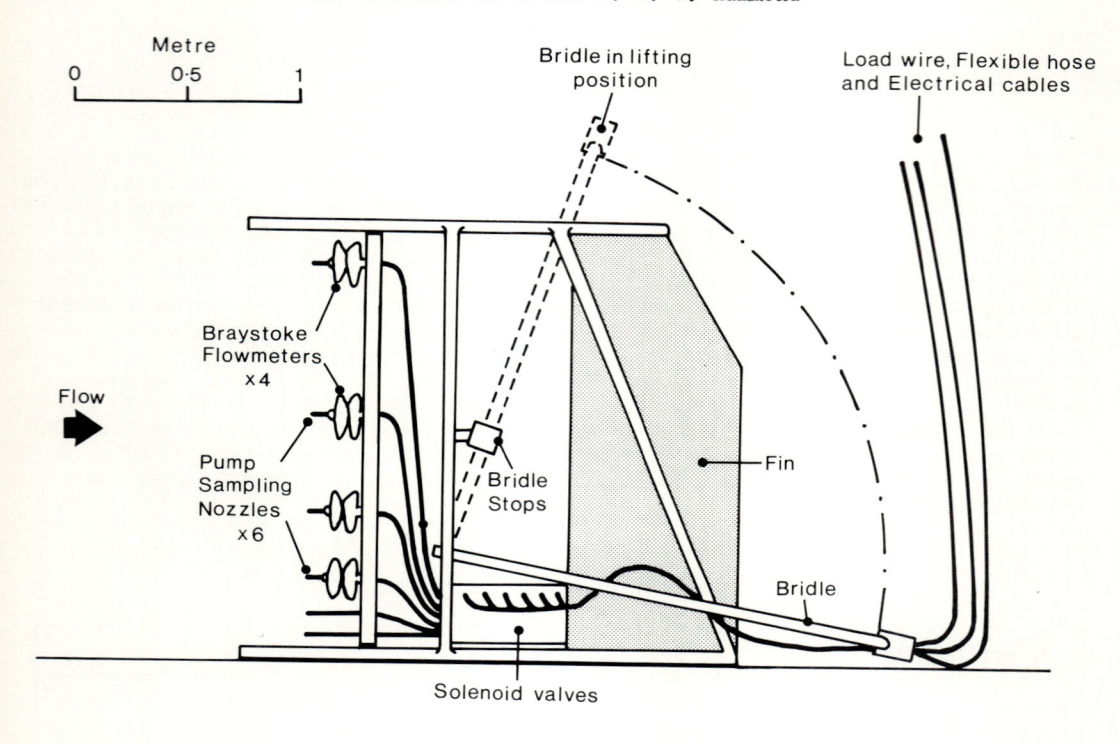

Figure 15.5. Equipment used to measure near-bottom velocity profiles and suspended sediment concentrations, showing the 4 Braystoke rotors and 6 pump sampling nozzles which are connected by electrically operated solenoid valves to a single hose. The probe is aligned with the mean flow by a large fin as it is lowered to the sea-bed.

concentration C(a) measured at a height a. The resultant profile, known as the Rouse concentration profile, is:

$$\frac{C(Z)}{C(a)} = \left(\frac{h-Z}{h-a} \cdot \frac{a}{Z}\right)^{\frac{W_S}{\kappa U_*}} \quad (4)$$

where h is the total flow depth and W_S the settling velocity. However, various attempts have been made to relate C(a) to a near bed concentration which might in turn be related to the bed-load. In particular, Smith (1977) and Smith and McLean (1977) have suggested that the reference concentration C(a) may be expressed in terms of the bed load concentration at a height equal to the roughness length. Thus C(a) may be written as:

$$C(a) = C(o)\gamma_o s/(1 + \gamma_o s) \quad (5)$$

where s is the normalised excess shear stress given by:

$$s = \tau - \tau_{cr}/\tau_{cr}$$

and γ_o is an empirically determined constant of order 10^{-3}, provided a is taken as approximately equal to Z_o. C(o) is, notionally at least, the maximum permissible concentration at the bed and for $S \to \infty$, i.e., large excess shear stresses, C(a)→C(o).

For low excess shear stresses Smith (1977) has shown that:

$$C(a) = \gamma_1 \rho_s S \qquad (6)$$

for $a \simeq Z_0$. For material having a grain size of approximately 180μm, Smith and McLean (1977) have found $\gamma_0 = 2.4 \times 10^{-3}$ and $\gamma_1 = 1.24 \times 10^{-3}$. However, Dyer (1979) measuring on a rippled sand bed having a mean grain size of 250μm has found a value of γ_1 significantly different from that reported by Smith and McLean (1977) and about an order of magnitude lower.

The methods outlined above may provide a means of predicting suspended sediment transport rates from a knowledge of the velocity field and sediment characteristics alone. However, as we have seen, considerable uncertainty still surrounds the values of the empirical coefficients γ_0 and γ_1.

Suspended sediment measurements in Swansea Bay at locations PS2, PS4 and PS5 (see Fig. 15.2), using the pumped sampling equipment shown in Fig. 15.5, have revealed a complex pattern of behaviour. Grain size analysis (see Fig. 15.6) of pumped suspended sediment and sea bed samples at PS2 show that the median grain sizes of the material in suspension and on the sea-bed are broadly similar with $d_{50} \simeq 70\mu m$. However at PS5 (see Heathershaw and Hammond, 1979b), there is considerably more variation with the sea-bed samples being up to a factor of 2 times coarser than the material in suspension. It is also interesting to note that there is little systematic variation of mean grain size with height above the sea bed.

Logarithmic velocity profiles (Equation 1) were fitted to velocity measurements in the bottom boundary layer, averaged over a period of 10 minutes, using a least squares regression technique to give the friction velocity U_* and roughness length Z_0. Only 45% of the velocity profiles could be fitted at the 95% confidence level and nearly all profiles showed a tendency to be concave downwards, even at the 99% confidence level, indicating possible stratification effects (see later discussion).

Concentration measurements were made at heights of 10, 15, 25, 40, 80 and 180cm above the sea-bed, to give one profile approximately every half hour throughout the tidal cycle. Profile measurements were considered important at this stage to determine the validity of Equation (4).

Examples of velocity and concentration profiles are shown in Figs. 15.7, 15.8 and 15.9, while Figs. 15.10 and 15.11 show the variation of U_*, $\bar{U}_{100}$ and the concentrations at different heights above the sea bed, through the tidal cycle at PS2 and PS4. The variations of Z_0 with U_*, at PS2 and PS4, are shown in Figs. 15.12 and 15.13 and indicate an order of magnitude variation in Z_0 over the tidal cycle with, on Springs, flood values being higher than ebb values. At PS2, on Springs, the situation appears to be similar. However, with the exception of the ebb values which lie in the range .1 to .5cm, the observed roughness lengths are, in general, higher than would be expected given the flow conditions and sediment characteristics for the area. This behaviour may be due in part to the presence of ripples on the sea-bed and the way in which their amplitudes vary over the tidal cycle. Alternatively, it may be due to high suspended sediment concentrations, particularly near the bed, where the presence of a moving layer of grains may modify the velocity profile and provide an effective bed roughness which is related to the thickness of the moving, or saltating, layer, and which in turn is related to the excess shear stress. Under these circumstances Z_0 is given (see Smith, 1977) by:

$$Z_0 = \frac{\delta(\tau - \tau_{cr})}{(\rho_s - \rho)g} + Z_N \qquad (7)$$

where Z_N is the flat bed roughness related to the grain size d, by $Z_N = d/30$ (Yalin, 1972). However, analysis of our data does not reveal any obvious correlations of

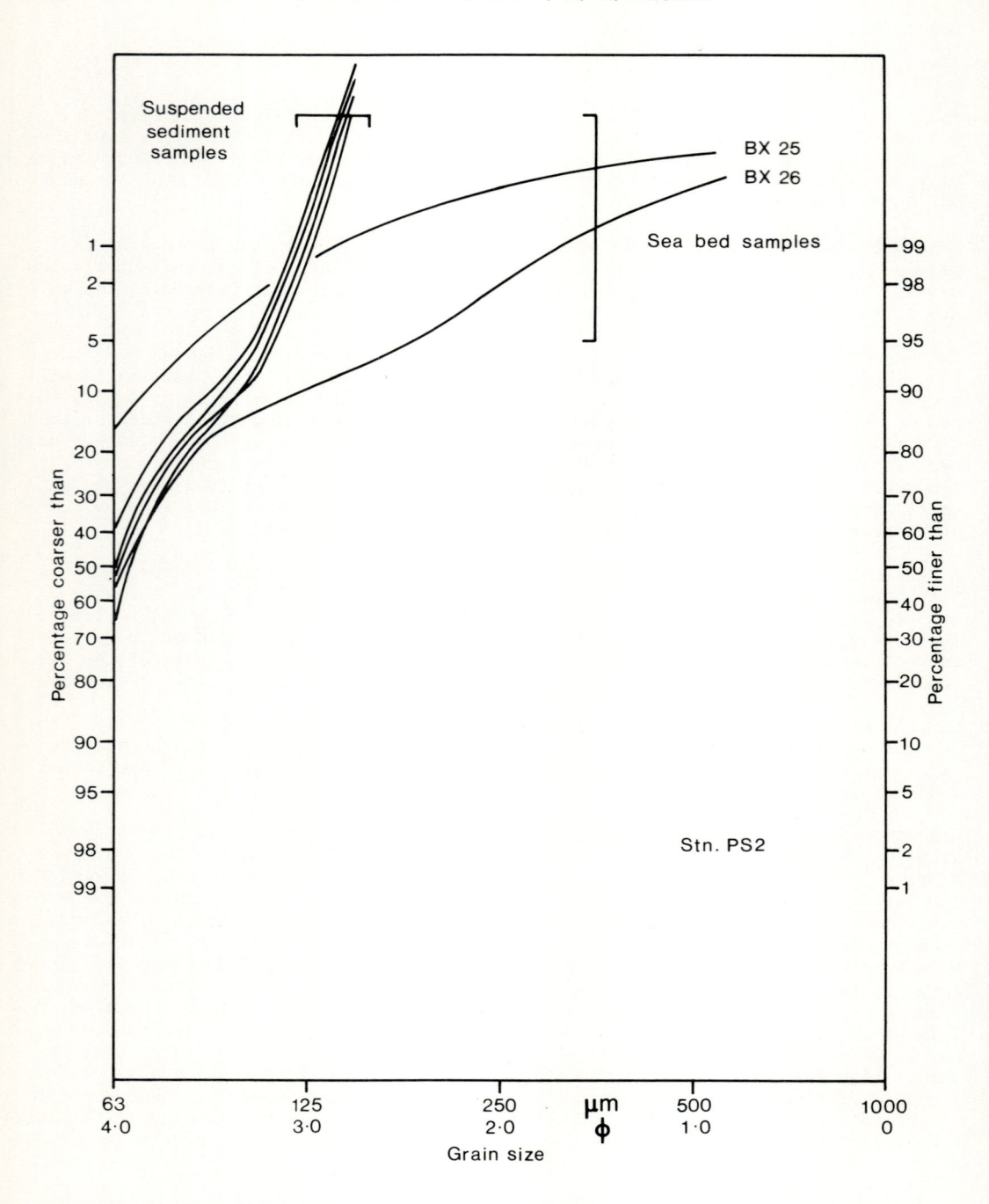

Figure 15.6. Grain size analyses of sea-bed and suspended sediment samples in the vicinity of Station PS2 (see Fig. 15.2) showing a median grain size for material in suspension and on the sea bed of about 70μm.

Non-Cohesive Sediment Transport

PS2/29:3:77 Neaps

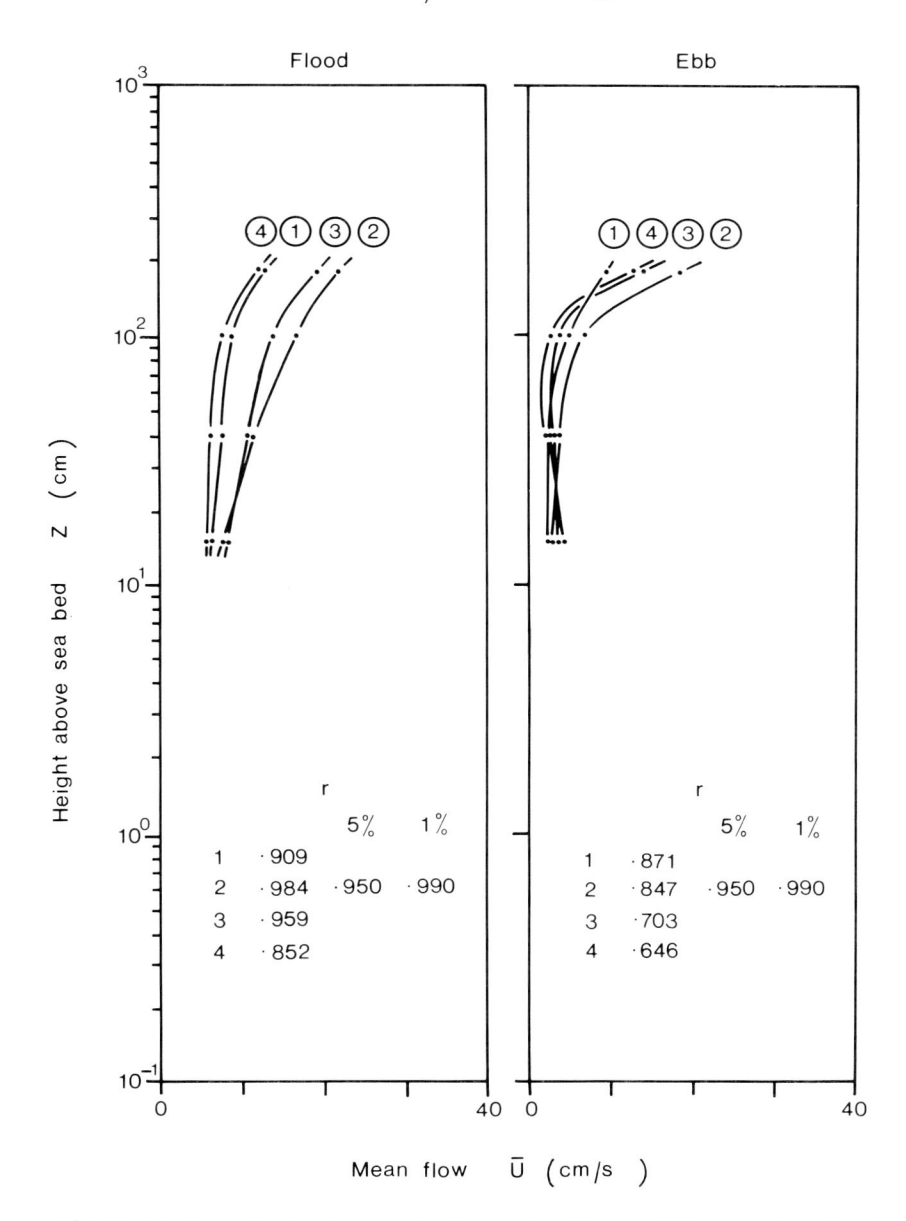

Flood | Ebb

Height above sea bed Z (cm)

	r	5%	1%
1	·909		
2	·984	·950	·990
3	·959		
4	·852		

	r	5%	1%
1	·871		
2	·847	·950	·990
3	·703		
4	·646		

Mean flow $\bar{U}$ (cm/s)

Figure 15.9. Typical near bottom velocity profiles at Station PS2 measured over a period of about 4 hours on the Ebb and Flood stages of a Neap tidal cycle. Values of the correlation coefficient (r) obtained by fitting a logarithmic velocity profile (Equation 1) to these data are also shown.

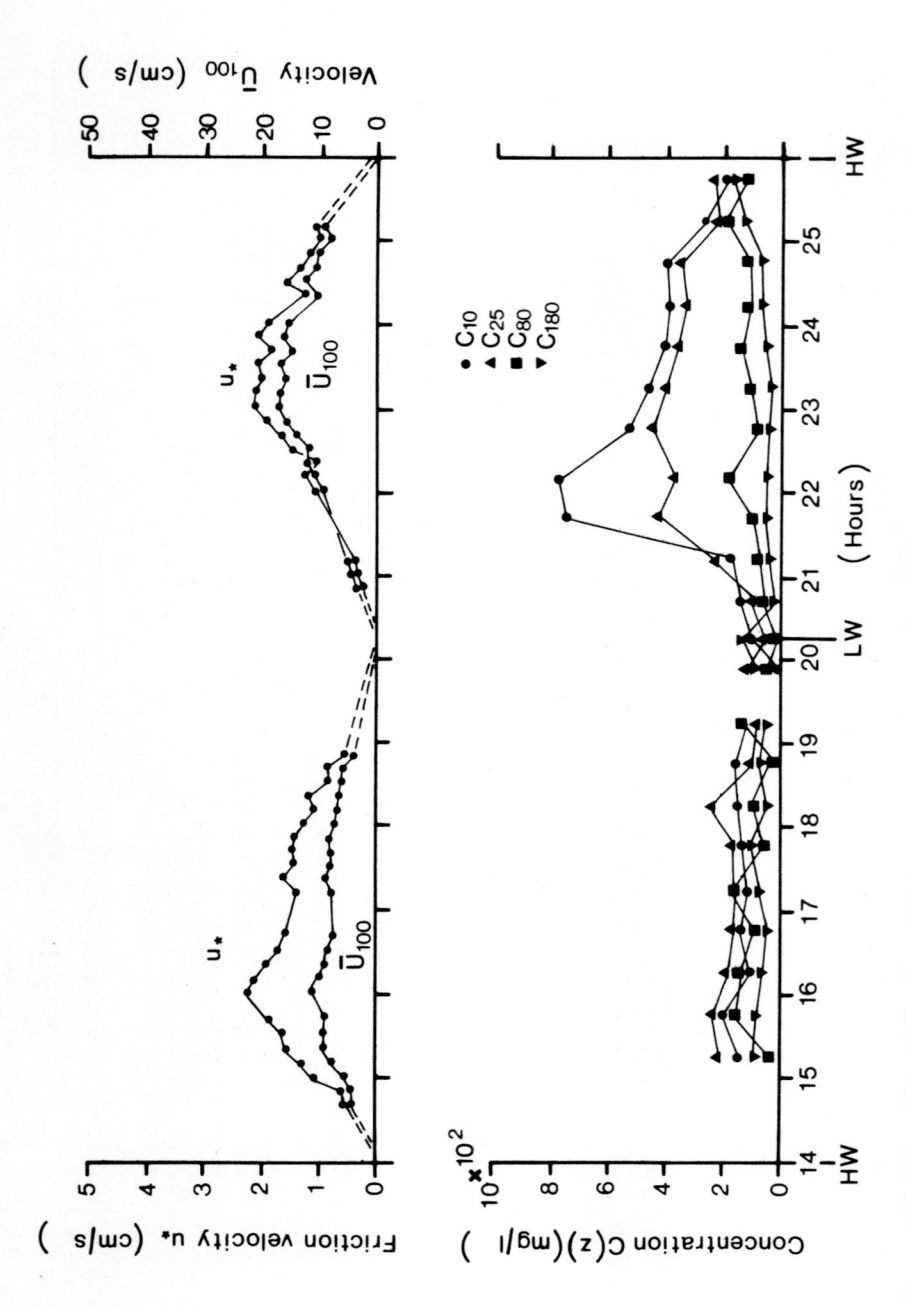

Figure 15.10. The variation of the suspended sediment concentrations (C) at heights of 10, 25, 80 and 180 cm above the sea-bed at Station PS2 (Neaps), with U_* and $\bar{U}_{100}$.

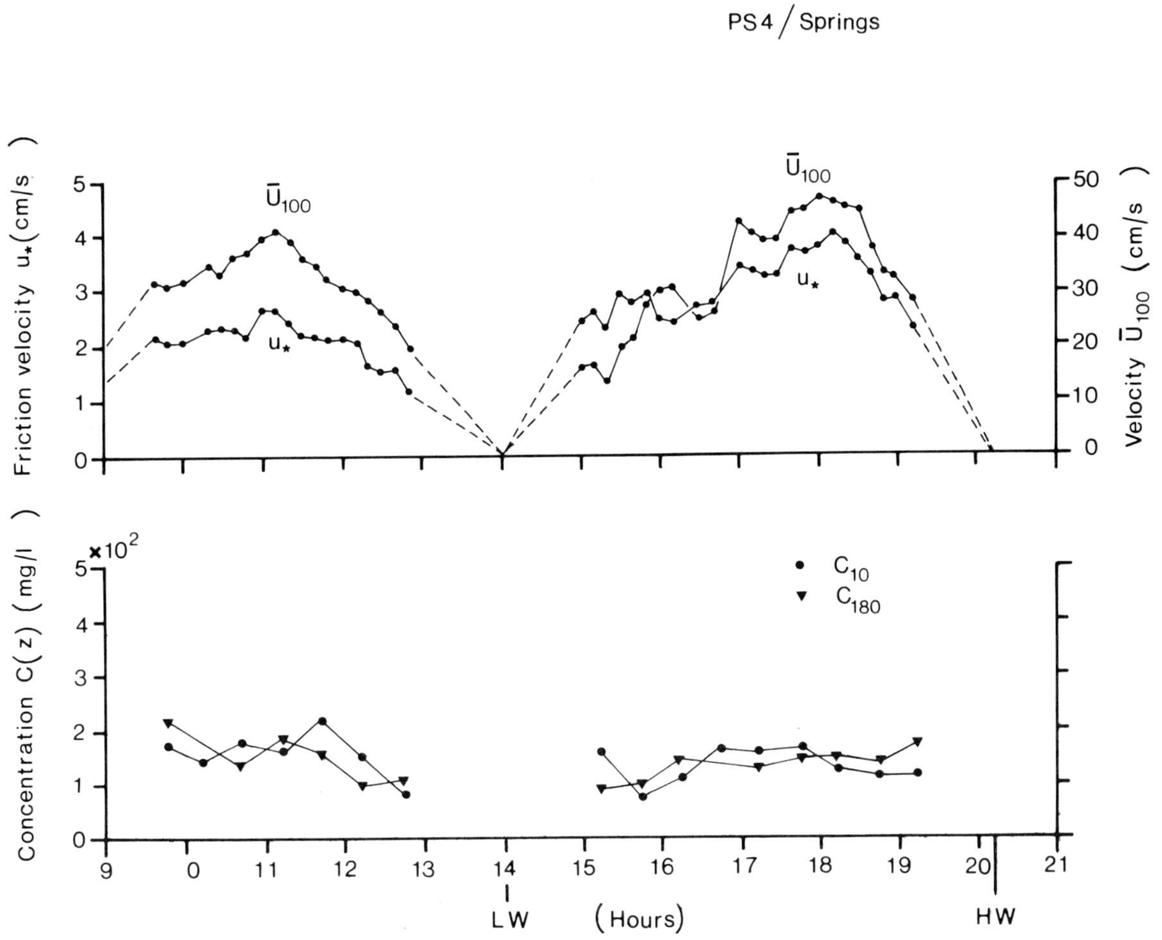

Figure 15.11. The variation of the suspended sediment concentration (C), at heights of 10 and 80cm above the sea-bed at Station PS4 (Springs) with U_* and $\bar{U}_{100}$.

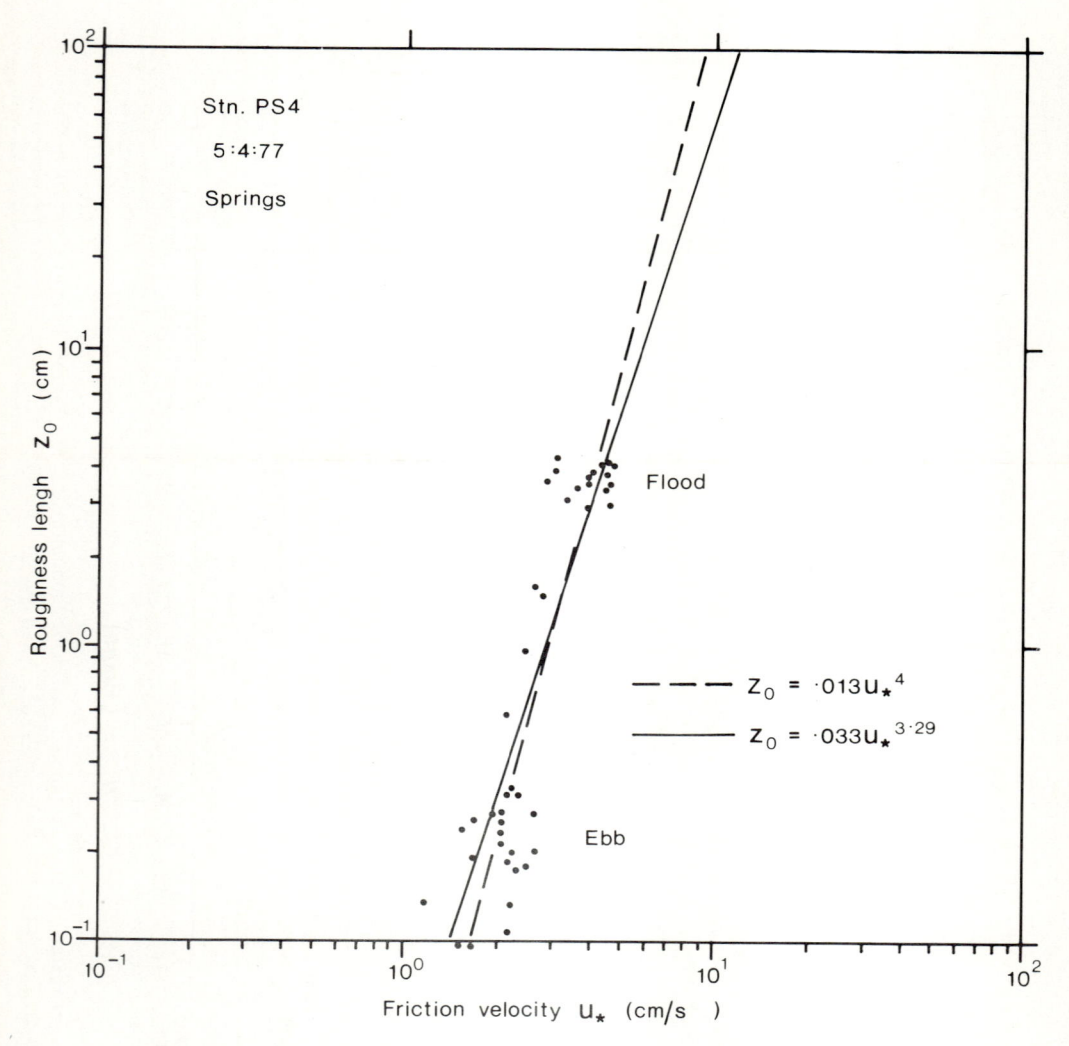

Figure 15.12. The variation of roughness length (Z_0) with friction velocity (U_*) at Station PS2 (Springs) showing an order of magnitude variation in Z_0. The broken line indicates a trend of $Z_0 \alpha U_*^4$ whereas the solid line indicates a significant correlation between Z_0 and U_* of the form $Z_0 = .033 \, U_*^{3.29}$.

the form shown in Equation (7), although Figures 15.12 and 15.13 do suggest that Z_0 may be proportional to U_*^4, which is a similar result to that of Dyer (1979), and it seems more likely to us that the complex pattern of behaviour observed in the measured Z_0 values is a consequence of the stabilising effect of suspensions in the boundary layer. This will lead to modified forms of the equilibrium velocity and concentration profiles in a constant stress layer. The effect of a density gradient may be expressed in terms of the Monin-Obukhov length L (see Taylor and Dyer, 1977, for discussion) defined by:

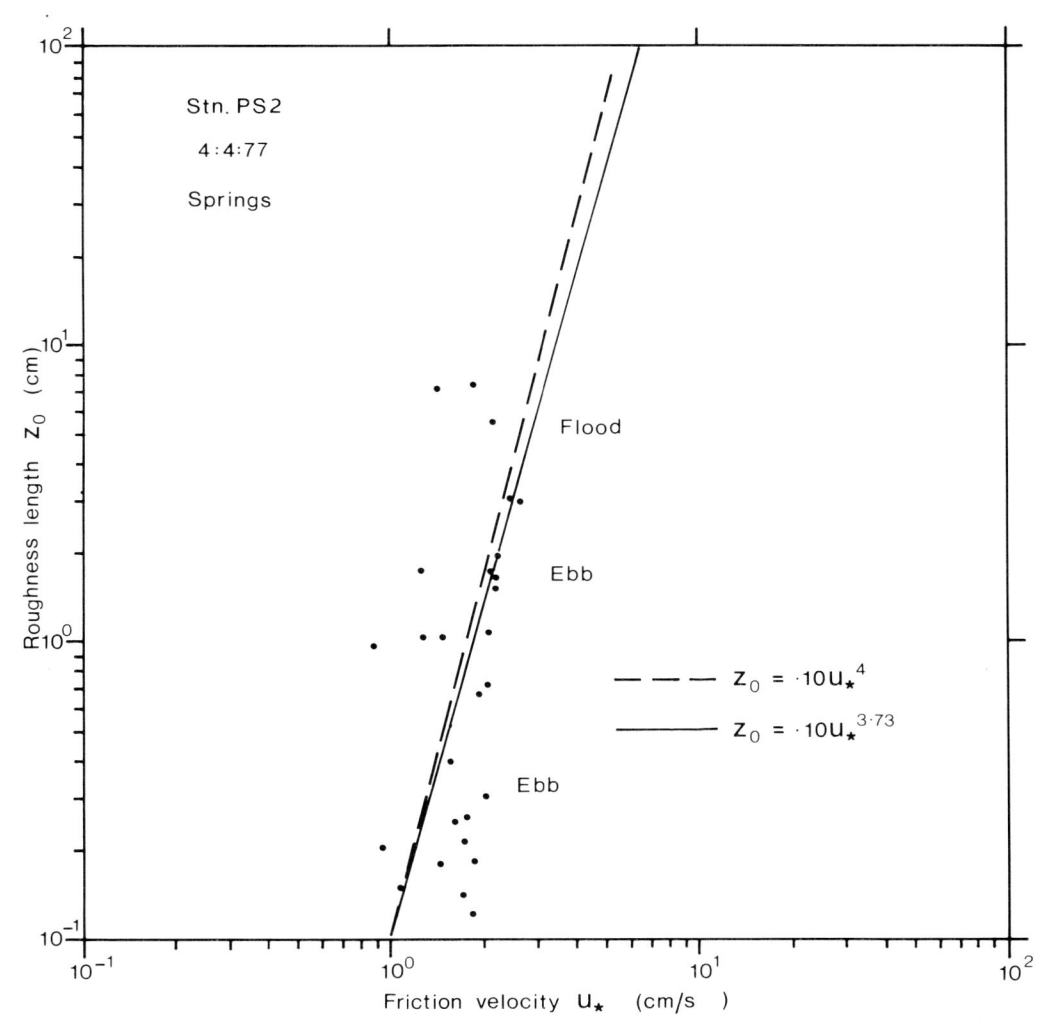

Figure 15.13. The variation of roughness length (Z_0) with friction velocity (U_*) at Station PS4 (Springs) showing a similar variation to that in Fig. 15.12 and illustrating flood Z_0 values higher than those observed during the ebb stage of the tidal cycle. The broken line indicates a trend of $Z_0 \alpha U_*^4$ and the solid line a significant correlation of the form $Z_0 = .10 \, U_*^{3.73}$.

$$L = \frac{\bar{\rho} U_*^3}{\kappa g \overline{\rho' w'}} \tag{8}$$

where ρ' and w' are the fluctuating parts of the density and vertical velocity fields, $\bar{\rho}$ is the mean density and $\overline{\rho' w'}$ represents a density or buoyancy flux.

The velocity profile (1) may now be written as:

$$\bar{U} = \frac{U_*}{\kappa}\left(\ln\frac{Z + Z_0}{Z_0} + \frac{\beta Z}{L}\right) \qquad (9)$$

(the $\ln\frac{Z + Z_0}{Z_0}$ form is used for computational ease at this stage) where β is an empirically determined constant which from atmospheric boundary layer experiments (Businger et al., 1971) has been found to be 4.7 ± 0.5.

Taylor and Dyer (1977), using the results of Barenblatt (1953, 1955) have shown that (9) may be expressed in terms of the suspended sediment concentrations and settling velocity as:

$$\bar{U} = \frac{U_*}{\kappa}\left[\zeta + \frac{1}{B}\ln\left\{1 + \frac{AB}{(1-B)} \cdot (e^{(1-B)\zeta} - 1)\right\}\right] \qquad (10)$$

where
$$\zeta = \ln[(Z + Z_0)/Z_0] \qquad (11)$$

A and B are given by:

$$A = \frac{\beta W_S \kappa g \gamma C_0 Z_0}{U_*^3} \quad \text{and} \quad B = \frac{W_S}{\kappa U_*} \qquad (12)$$

where, C_0 is now the 'surface concentrations' of sediment which is analogous in some respects to $C(0)$ in Equation (5) and $\gamma = (\rho_s - \rho)/\rho$, where ρ_s is the sediment particle density. The concentration profile corresponding to (10) is of the form:

$$\ln\frac{C(Z)}{C_0} = -B\zeta - \ln\left[1 + \frac{AB}{(1-B)} \cdot (e^{(1-B)\zeta} - 1)\right] \qquad (13)$$

Figs. 15.14 and 15.15 show velocity and concentration profiles of the form predicted by Equations (10) and (13) where values of A and B have been calculated using the observed total concentration of suspended sediment (d>0) at $Z = 10$cm (see Heathershaw and Hammond, 1979b for details).

As a result of fitting logarithmic velocity profiles of the form

$$\bar{U} = \frac{U_*}{\kappa}\ln\frac{Z}{Z_0}$$

to a velocity distribution of the type given in Equation (10), the roughness length (Z_0) and friction velocity (U_*) will be systematically overestimated. This is clear from Fig. 15.14 where, in order to fit Equation (10) to the data, it has been necessary to take a Z_0 value of .5cm and a friction velocity estimate, U_*, of 2.5cm/s which may be compared with the measured values of $Z_0 = 1.07$cm and $U_* = 3.42$cm/s. A Z_0 value of .5cm would still be considered high for the area (see Table 15.1). However, the theory does serve to illustrate that even quite moderate concentrations of the order of 200mg/l (at $Z = 10$cm) may modify the turbulent and mean flow characteristics of the bottom boundary layer, leading to the concave downwards form of the measured velocity profiles shown in Figs. 15.8, 15.9 and 15.14, and lead to overestimates of friction velocity U_* and roughness length Z_0.

Fig. 15.15 shows measured and predicted concentrations of the form given in Equations (4) and (13). Here, the agreement between the measured values and those predicted by the Monin-Obukhov theory is not so good except perhaps nearer the bed where there is some evidence to suggest the measured values may follow Equation (13). Since we have attempted to fit Equation (10) to the measured velocity profile, the concentration profile given by Equation (13) will not necessarily pass through the measured concentration values.

PS5 / 3:4:77 Springs

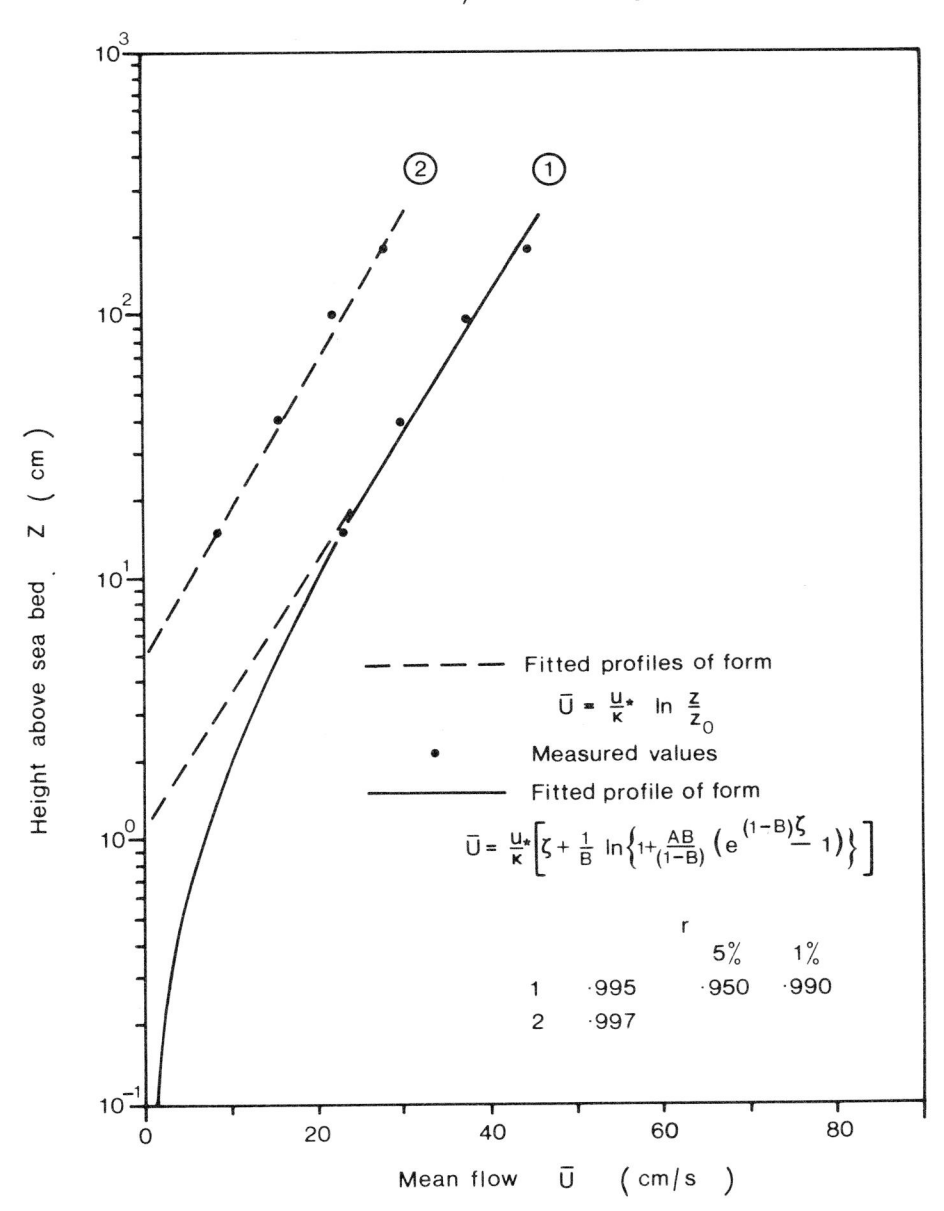

Figure 15.14. Velocity profile measurements (•) at Station PS5 (Springs). The broken lines show fitted logarithmic velocity profiles of the form given in Equation (1). The solid curve represents a velocity profile modified by the effects of suspended sediment and of the form given in Equation (10). Values of the correlation coefficient (r) obtained by fitting (1) to the measured currents are also indicated together with 5% and 1% significance levels.

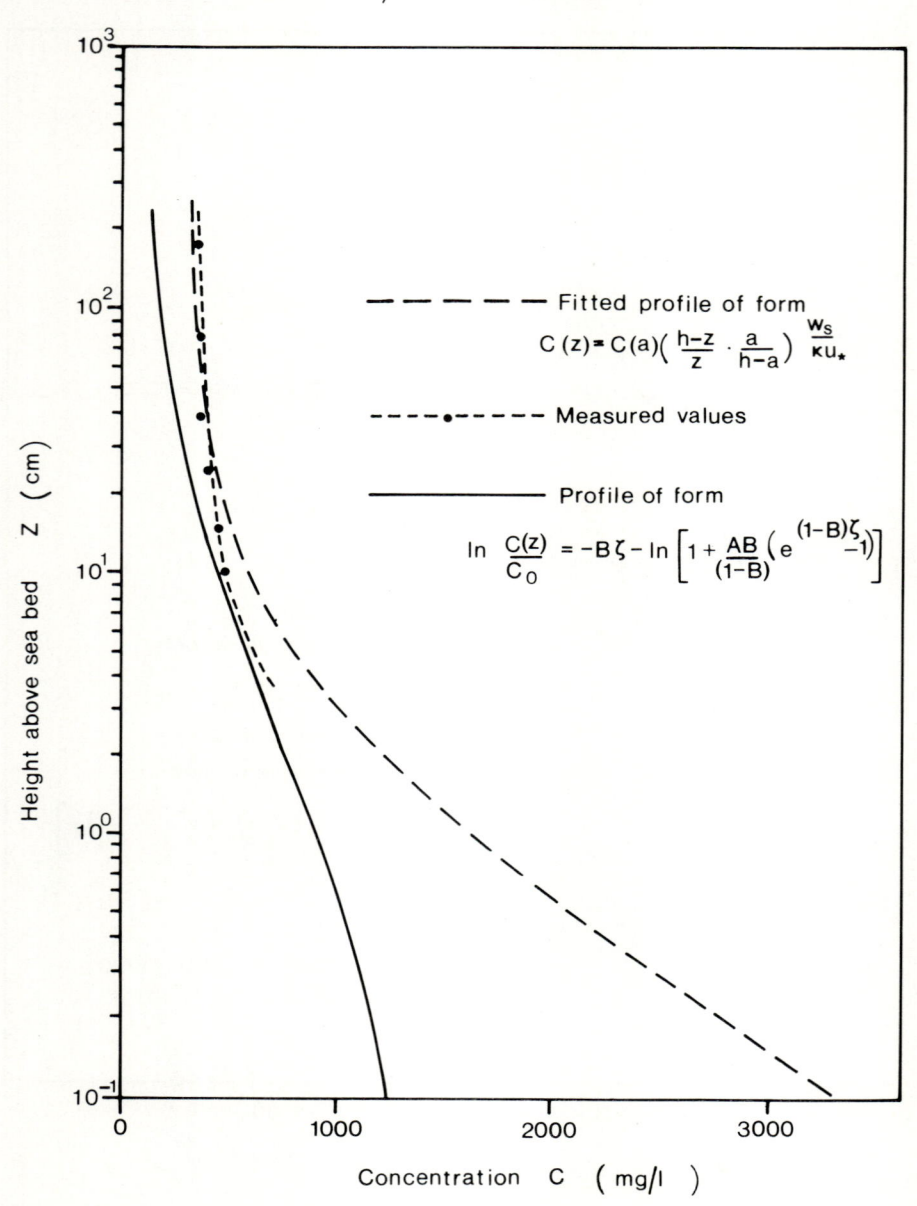

Figure 15.15. Suspended sediment concentration measurements (•), compared with profiles of the form given in Equation (4) (broken line - large dashes) and Equation (10) (solid line) The solid line is the modified concentration profile corresponding to velocity profile (1) in Fig. 15.14, which has been fitted by iterating in U_* and Z_0 only. Thus the concentration profile will not necessarily pass through the measured values.

Despite the fact that velocity and concentration profiles may not be of the usual form, suspended sediment transport rates have been calculated by numerically integrating the product of Equations (1) and (4) over the entire flow depth, that is:

$$q_{ss} = \int_{Z_o}^{h} C(Z) \frac{U_*}{\kappa} \ln \frac{Z}{Z_o} \cdot dZ \qquad (14)$$

where Z_o is the measured roughness length and h the total flow depth. In Equation (4) the settling velocity W_s has been taken as .32cm/s, corresponding to a mean particle size for the suspension, which shows no systematic variation with height, of about 70µm (see Fig. 15.6). A value of 70µm has also been taken for the median grain size (d_{50}) of the suspension. κ has been taken as .4 and U_* calculated from the measured velocity profiles. The depth increment dZ was taken as .1cm and Table 15.3 shows suspended sediment transport rates, for d>0, obtained from Rouse profiles (Equation 4) fitted by a least squares regression to the measurements at PS2, PS4 and PS5 significant at the 95% confidence level. It is important to note, however, that only 42% of concentration profiles could be fitted at the 95% level (this may be compared with 45% for the velocity profiles).

TABLE 15.3. Comparisons of Instantaneous Suspended and Bed Load Transport Rates.

Location (Profile No.)		U_* (cm/s)	q_{ss} d>0 (gm/cm/s)	q_{ss} d>40µm	q_{sb} (gm/cm/s)	U_{100} (cm/s)
Springs	PS2/64	2.05	3.54	.071	.20	38.95
Springs	PS4/83	2.27	4.08	.082	.44	43.14
Springs	PS5/62	2.94	10.50	.21	2.15	55.87
Neaps	PS2/25	1.88	0.95	.019	.092	35.72

The bulk of the suspended sediment data indicate that the ratio of material coarser than 40µm is about 1/50 of the total concentration of all sizes. Thus, the transport rates for coarse material, shown in Table 15.3 have been derived using this ratio. Also shown are bed load transport rates, calculated using Bagnold's formula (Equation (3)). Table 15.3 shows that, while total suspended load transport rates are on average a factor of 10 times larger than the bed load transport, suspended load transport of material coarser than 40µm is a factor of 6 times lower than the bed load transport.

A conspicuous feature of the concentration profiles shown in Fig. 15.7 is the almost uniform concentration, with depth, in the lower 2m of the flow. Furthermore, Figs. 15.10 and 15.11 show little systematic variation in concentration over the tidal cycle and suggest that in general the suspension behaves as 'washload'. This situation occurs when the settling velocity (W_s) is small compared with the friction velocity U_*. Fitting profiles of the form given in Equation (4) to the measured concentrations yields depth mean concentrations for the area of about 90mg/l. This figure is lower than the surface and near-bed concentrations reported by Davies (1974), which were of the order of 100 and 400mg/l respectively, but higher than the values given by Ferentinos and Collins (1978) which lie typically in the range 6 - 60mg/l near the bed. However, it is interesting to note that our figures for concentrations of material coarser than 40µm (d>40µm) are similar to those given by Ferentinos and Collins.

Taking the area of Swansea Bay bounded by a line of longitude (3°58.6'W) running south through Mumbles Head, a line of latitude 57°30'N and the coast (see Figure 15.16) gives an area of approximately $1.77 \times 10^8 m^2$. This also corresponds to the area bounded by the topographically high features in the area, namely the White Oyster Ledge in the west (shown in Fig. 14.2; see also Chapter 5) and the Scarweather Sands in the south. Taking the mean depth over the area as 15m gives a mean tidal volume of $2.66 \times 10^9 m^3$. Thus, taking a depth mean concentration of the order of 90mg/l yields a total of about 2.4×10^5 tonnes of sand and silt in suspension. This figure may be compared with the natural and artificial inputs of suspended sediment to the area given by Collins et al. (1979); suspended sediment from rivers contributes about 200 tonnes/day and maintenance dredging of Port Talbot and Swansea harbours contributes about 1.2×10^6 tonnes of sand and silt annually. Approximately 9×10^6 tonnes of fine sand, silt and gravel were deposited on spoil grounds, within the area being considered from capital dredging at Port Talbot (Davies, 1975).

SEDIMENT TRANSPORT PATHS

The principal objectives of this study (see Carr, 1975; Carr et al., 1976, 1977; Heathershaw et al., 1978) have been to examine the supply of sand to Swansea Bay, particularly the foreshore on the east side of the Bay, to the south of Port Talbot. Comparisons of suspended and bed load transport rates (see Tables 15.3 and 15.4) have established that for material coarser than 40μm, the principal mode of transport is likely to be bed load. Table 15.3 shows that bed load transport of this size of material is, on average, about 6 times larger than the corresponding suspended load transport rate. Thus, we are only concerned here with bed load transport paths and, using Bagnold's formula (Equation (3)) and near-bottom current measurements, we have predicted sediment transport rates and directions for the area as shown in Fig. 15.16. The directions give general agreement with previously published transport paths for the area (Ferentinos and Collins, 1978; Collins et al., 1979) and with geophysical evidence (e.g., sand wave alignment and asymmetry, sand ribbon orientation) presented by Collins et al. (1979). Fig. 15.16, which should be compared with the residual water circulation pattern shown in Fig. 11.10, suggests that in terms of the transport rates, the sediment circulation system consists of a strong westward flowing stream of sand by-passing the Bay, with transport rates in the Bay being nearly two orders of magnitude lower than those in the offshore area. Furthermore, Fig. 15.16 indicates that, in general, there are no major sediment transport paths into the area and that such transport as occurs from the westward flowing stream is likely to be due to second order effect, e.g., wave-induced transport during storms (see Chapter 14, Fig. 14.5). In particular we note that there is unlikely to be a transport of material into the area from the east in the vicinity of Sker Point, where transport is to the south, and that the only inputs of material into the Bay from the west appear to be a weak and variable transport near Mumbles Head and a strong eastward movement of material at the east end of the Scarweather Sands, which is almost certainly associated with those processes maintaining the sand banks in the area in equilibrium (see Heathershaw and Hammond, 1979b).

The calculated directions of sediment movement do, in fact, indicate three major features of sedimentological significance. These are:

(a) An area of divergence in net sediment transport in the area to the south of Port Talbot characterised by low transport rates of the order of .02 tonnes/m/day, but which increase in a southerly direction along the coast;
(b) an area of convergence in net sediment transport in the vicinity of the Scarweather Sands;
(c) the presence of a strong westward transport of sediment outside the Bay of the order of 2 tonnes/m/day.

The observed water and sediment circulations in the vicinity of the Scarweather Sands

TABLE 15.4. Comparisons of Net Bed-Load Transport Rates ($\bar{q}_{sb}$).

	Location	Transport Rates (gm/cm/s/tonnes/m/day) min.	max.
Measured			
(Heathershaw and Carr, 1977)	T1	.039/.34	.14/1.21
	T2	.037/.32	.097/.84
Predicted			
(Bagnolds' (1963) formula)	C	.2/1.73	.3/2.59
	A	.014/.12	.059/.51

Predicted sediment transport rates were calculated using Bagnolds' (1963) formula in a modified form due to Gadd et al. (1978)(See Equation 3).

are consistent with the mechanisms of sand bank formation proposed by Pingree (1978) and Pingree and Maddock (1979). The results of these observations are described elsewhere (Heathershaw and Hammond, 1979b) and show that vorticity generated by tidal streaming at a point of abrupt change in the coastal geometry (this occurs in the Porthcawl area) leads to secondary circulation effects giving rise to a near-bottom convergence and mid-depth divergence in the mean circulation on the flanks of the sand bank.

THE EFFECTS OF WAVES

The theory of wave/current ineraction is still poorly understood, although recent theoretical developments (e.g., Grant and Madsen, 1979) go some way towards improving our understanding of the physical processes involved. The effect of this interaction on sediment transport is still more tenuous since sediment transport theories, as we have seen, can in themselves give widely differing estimates. Present approaches are largely empirical (e.g., Owen and Thorn, 1978) and it is likely to be some time before theories are available which are capable of dealing with the wide range of conditions encountered on the continental shelf.

One approach which has been used is that developed by Bijker (1967) which although semi-empirical does attempt to deal with the physical interaction of the waves and the currents. The theory consists of making a vector addition of the orbital velocity (U_o) of the wave and the velocity due to the tidal current alone at a height above the sea bed equivalent to the thickness of the viscous sublayer. The resultant velocity is converted to a bed shear stress using Prandtl mixing length theory, in which the bed shear stress is given by:

$$\tau = \rho l^2 \left[\frac{\partial U(Z)}{\partial Z} \right]^2_{Z \to 0} \qquad (15)$$

where $U(Z)$ is the combined velocity at a height Z above the bed, ρ is the density, τ is the bed shear stress and l is the mixing length given by $l = \kappa Z$ for small values of Z.

Thus, according to Bijker's theory, the maximum enhancement of the bed shear stress is given by:

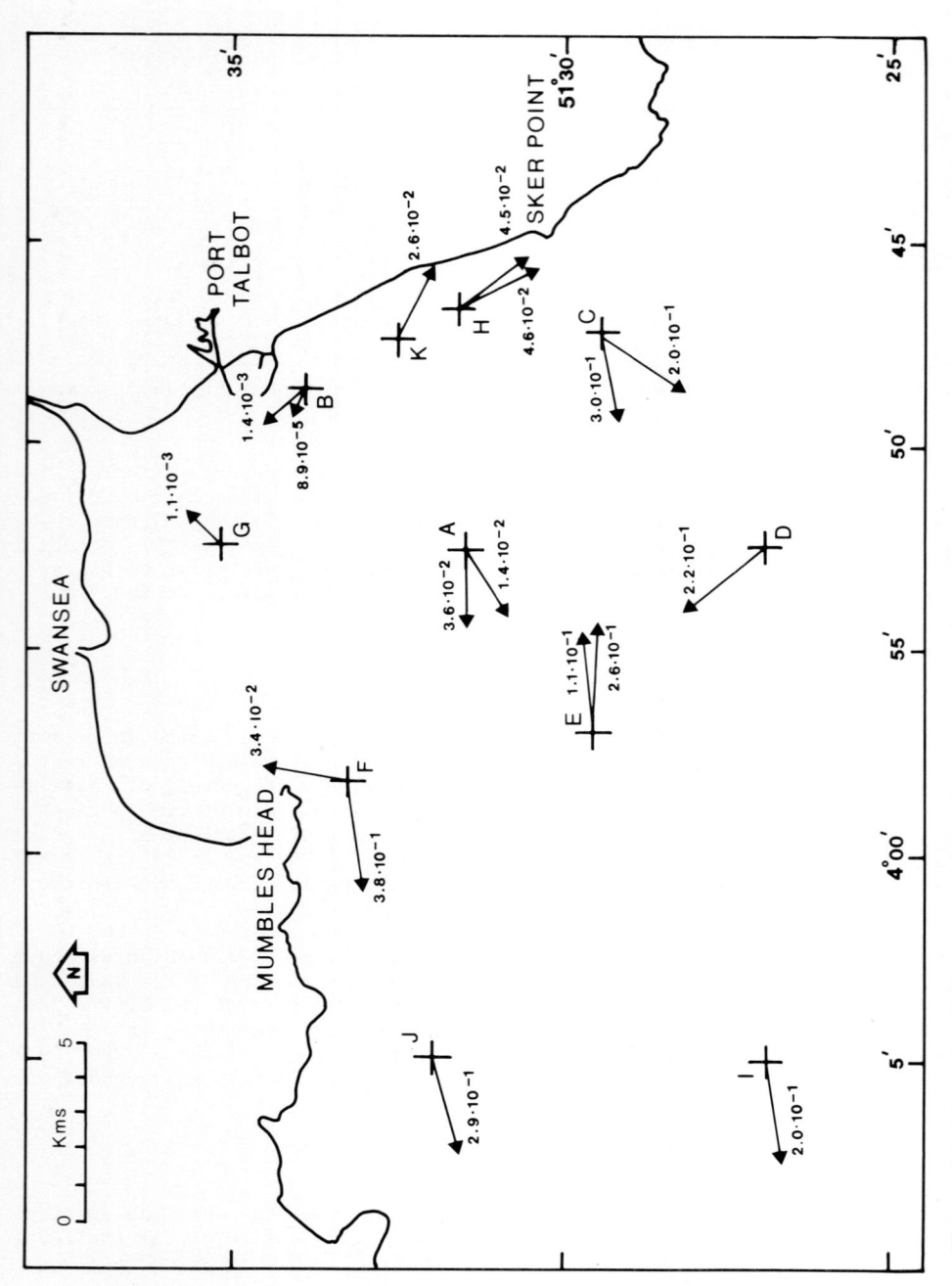

Figure 15.16. Predicted net bed load transport rates ($\bar{q}_{sb}$) and directions for area calculated using a modified form of Bagnold's (1963) sediment transport formulae. Transport rates are given in gm/cm/s.

$$\psi = \frac{\tau_{wc}}{\tau_c} = 1 + \frac{1}{2}\left(\xi \frac{U_0}{\hat{U}}\right)^2 \qquad (16)$$

where τ_{wc} is now the resultant bed shear stress due to waves and currents, τ_c is the bed shear stress due to currents alone, ξ is given (see Heathershaw and Hammond, 1979b) by $\xi = p\ln(\psi e Z_0)$, h is the mean depth, p is an empirically determined constant which Bijker (1967) found equal to 0.45 and $\hat{U}$ is the steady depth mean current. In this paper, ψ is referred to as the Bijker magnification factor.

To obtain an upper limit to the enhancement of the bed shear stress due to wave activity, Equation (16) has been evaluated for typical and extreme wave conditions. ξ has been calculated with a roughness length Z_0 of .05cm and the depth-mean current in (16) has been calculated in terms of the current at a height of 1m above the sea bed by integrating the logarithmic velocity profile (1) over the entire flow depth. The variation of ξ with wave height H for a wave period of 8s (typical for the area) and water depth of 20m is plotted in Fig. 15.17. This shows, for example, that even moderate wave conditions (H = 1m) increase sediment transport rates (calculated using Bagnold's formula) by a factor of 5 say at peak tidal flows (i.e., $\hat{U}_{100}$ = 50 cm/s) with the effect becoming more pronounced as the steady current $\hat{U}_{100}$ decreases in strength. However, it should be borne in mind that sediment particles which are suspended by the enhanced bed shear stresses due to waves are likely to move in a direction which is governed principally by the tidal currents. Furthermore, the waves are not a persistent feature of the near-bed water movements. This is illustrated in Fig. 15.18, which shows exceedance curves for wave induced and tidal currents. Typical current threshold values are also indicated, that for the waves having been calculated using Komar and Miller's (1974) threshold criterion:

$$\frac{\rho}{\rho_s - \rho} \cdot \frac{U_{0cr}^2}{gd} = 0.21\left(\frac{U_{0cr}T}{\pi d}\right)^{\frac{1}{2}} \qquad (17)$$

where U_{0cr} is the critical near bed orbital velocity and T the wave period, a typical value for the area having been taken as T = 8s. The grain size d has been taken as the median grain size of 170μm and the steady current threshold, U_{cr}, calculated from Shields' curve and a roughness length of Z_0 = .05cm assumed in calculating the corresponding current at 2m above the sea bed from the logarithmic velocity profile (1).

These results suggest that in the offshore areas (h ≃ 20m) the threshold due to waves is on average exceeded for only 25% of the time and that if waves were capable of directly influencing sediment movement then the effect would be minimal (compare with Table 14.1). This observation is corroborated to some extent by the apparent lack of movement of tracer towards the coast from site T2 in Fig. 15.3. However, this may occur in shallower water and as reported by Heathershaw and Carr (1977), some movement of tracer towards the coast at T1 may have occurred due to a wave-induced mass transport effect (see later discussion). The figure of 25% for the threshold of movement under waves may be compared with exceedance levels of 65-85% for the threshold of sediment transport in a unidirectional flow (see Fig. 15.18; also compare with Table 14.1).

From observation and theory, it appears that, on average, the direction of sediment movement is controlled by the tidal currents with perhaps some intensification of transport by wave activity. It is interesting to note that in Fig. 15.4 the observed transport rates are consistently higher than those predicted by most of the theories examined. This may be due to an enhanced transport in the tidal current direction by waves.

The mass transport effect arises from the fact that the wave particle orbits are not closed, giving rise to a steady movement of the water particle at the surface

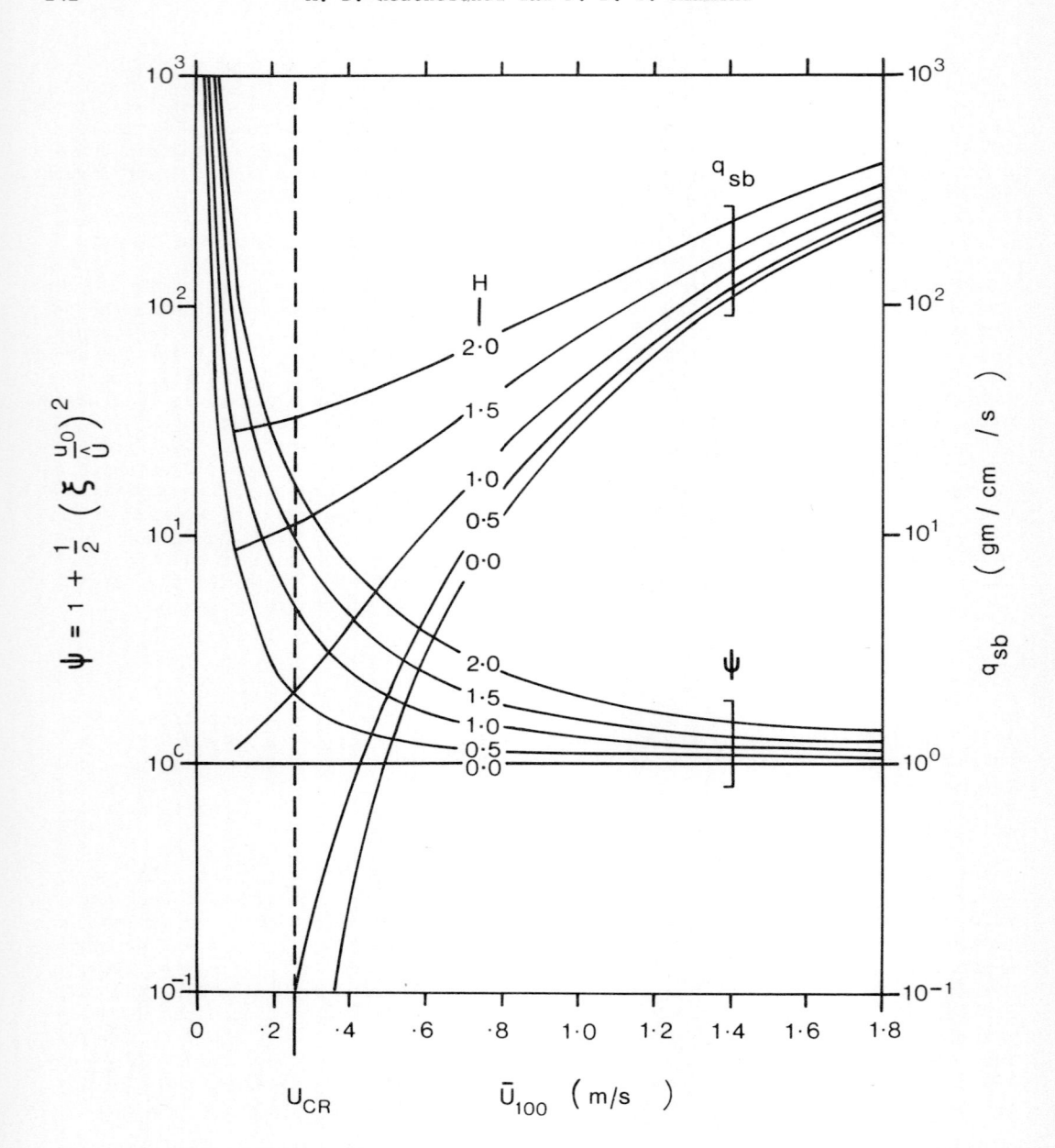

Figure 15.17. The effect of waves on sediment transport. Bijker's (1967) magnification factor (ψ) illustrating the effecting of increasing wave height (H) on bed load transport rates (q_{sb}) as a function of the current at a height of 100cm above the bed ($\bar{U}_{100}$). These calculations have been carried out for a wave of 8s period and a water depth of 20m with a roughness length (Z_0) of .05cm (typical for the Swansea Bay area).

Non-Cohesive Sediment Transport

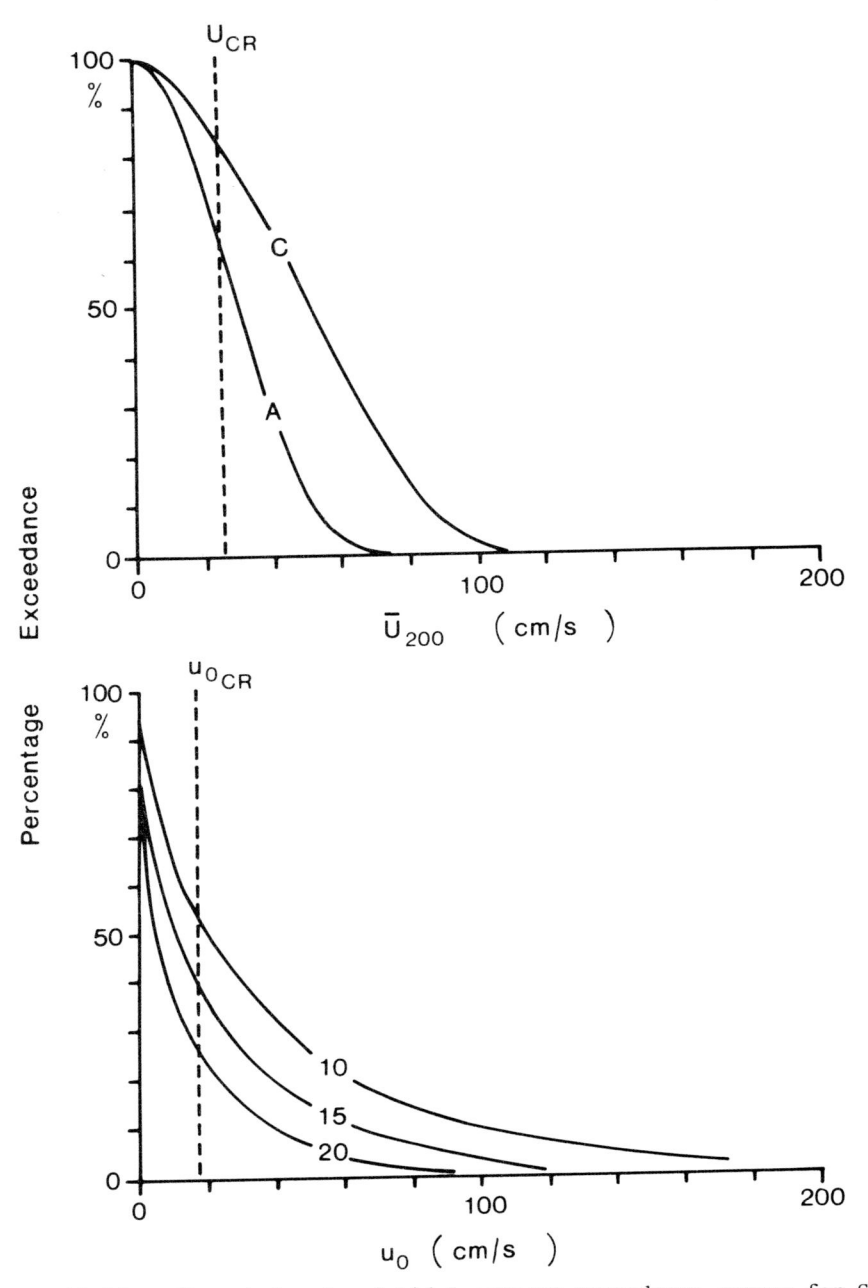

Figure 15.18. Wave induced and tidal current exceedance curves for Swansea Bay. These are based on near-bottom ($\bar{U}_{200}$) current measurements at Stations A and C and wave measurements near the Scarweather Light Vessel (see Fig. 15.2). The threshold values of sediment transport under waves and currents, $U_{o_{cr}}$ and U_{cr} are indicated. $U_{o_{cr}}$ has been calculated from Equation (17). A typical wave period of 8s has been used in calculating $U_{o_{cr}}$.

and near the bed in the direction of wave propagation. Heathershaw and Hammond (1979b) have examined the Stokes drift (U_S) at different depths using Longuet-Higgins' (1953) solution for flow in the interior of the fluid which at the bed gives the well known expression:

$$U_S = \frac{5}{4} \cdot \frac{a^2 \sigma k}{\sinh^2 kh} \qquad (18)$$

where a is the wave amplitude, σ its angular frequency, k its wave number equal to $2\pi/\lambda$ where λ is the wavelength and h the total depth. Equation (18) which strictly speaking is only valid for laminar flow, but which Longuet-Higgins (1957), in an appendix to the paper by Russell and Osorio (1957) has shown may also apply to turbulent flow, predicts a steady forward mass transport at the sea-bed.

We must conclude therefore that during periods of prevailing southwest wave activity there is likely to be a steady shoreward drift at the bed and for an extreme wave height of 2m, wave period of 8s and water depth of 20m, Equation (18) predicts that this will be of the order of 2cm/s.

SUMMARY AND CONCLUSIONS

Observed and predicted transport rates have indicated that for sand size material ($d_{50} \simeq 170\mu m$) bed load is likely to be the dominant mode of transport in the area. However, it is necessary to look at this process against a background of high concentrations of fine particulate matter ($d < 40\mu m$). Although the mean particle size of the suspension is about 70μm with a settling velocity of .32cm/s, the finer particulate matter will have considerably lower settling velocities and we would thus anticipate little variation in the concentrations over the tidal cycle (see Figs. 15.10 and 15.11). In fact, a depth-mean concentration of the order of 90mg/l would appear to be present for most of the time as 'washload'. However, this work has shown that these concentrations are sufficiently high to modify the turbulent structure of the bottom boundary by inducing density gradients near the sea-bed leading to equilibrium velocity profiles (Fig. 15.14) of the form predicted by Monin-Obukhov similarity arguments (e.g., see Taylor and Dyer, 1977). These profiles may lead to overestimates of the roughness length Z_0 and friction velocity U_* derived from fitted logarithmic velocity profiles of the form given in Equation (1). The variations of Z_0 with U_* as shown in Figs. 15.12 and 15.13 may also suggest a more complex pattern of behaviour in which Z_0 varies with both thickness of the bed load layer and changes in amplitude of bed forms on the sea-bed (see Dyer, 1979).

Suspended sediment measurements have not indicated any systematic variations of depth-mean concentration in moving from the weaker nearshore tidal flows to the higher energy environment further offshore. The observed depth-mean concentrations are, in general higher, than those reported by Ferentinos and Collins (1978) and for the area on the east side of the Bay we have found these to be, on average, of the order 90mg/l. However at peak tidal flow rates, near-bed concentrations of 200-500mg/l have been observed (see Figs. 15.7, 15.10 and 15.11) at Stations PS2, PS4 and PS5.

Bed load transport rates have been predicted using a modified form (Equation (3)) of Bagnold's (1963) formula. Comparisons with radioactive tracer estimates have shown (see Heathershaw and Hammond, 1979b), that this formula gives the best predictions (within a factor of 0.5 - 2) of the observed transport rates, although the net transport rates predicted by the various formulae may vary by as much as 2 orders of magnitude. However, the formulae all predict similar directions of sediment movement.

Predicted bed load transport paths for the area are presented schematically in Fig.

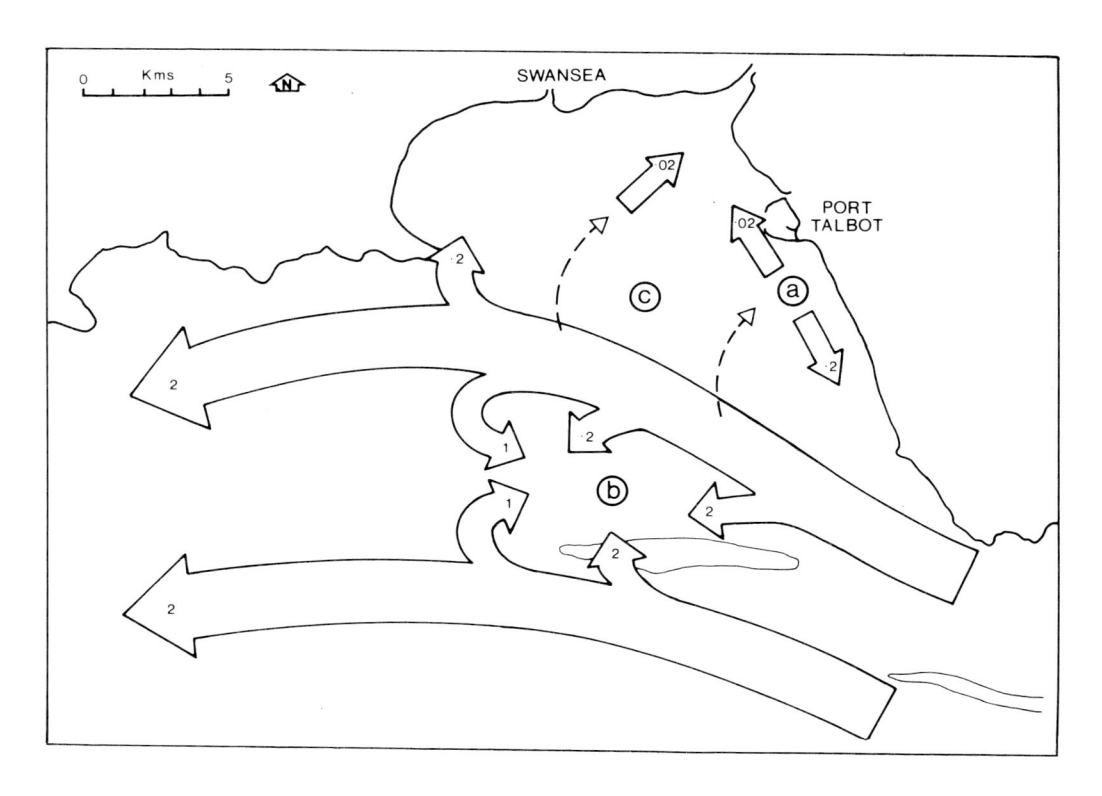

Figure 15.19. A schematic summary of sediment transport paths based upon the information presented in Fig. 15.16, and the orientation of bedforms given by Collins et al. (1979). The figure shows a two order of magnitude variation in bed-load transport rates from about 2 tonnes/m/day (figures in arrowheads) in the offshore areas to about .02 tonnes/m/day in the vicinity of Port Talbot and Swansea. Important features are (a) the area of bed-load divergence to the south of Port Talbot and (b) the area of bed-load convergence in the vicinity of the Scarweather Sands. The broken arrows (c) indicate a possible wave induced transfer of material from the westward movement of sediment into the Bay.

15.19 (compare with Fig. 14.5). These give general agreement with geophysical evidence and indicate a westward movement of sediment close to the coast south of Porthcawl, and across the southern extremity of the Bay through the sand bank system comprising the Nash Bank and Scarweather Sands, towards the Gower coast and westward through the Helwick Bank. The rate of movement of material in this area is estimated to be of the order of 2.10^{-1} gm/cm/s, that is about 2 tonnes/m/day. Moving inshore there is a general decrease in transport, reflecting the diminishing tidal energy until in the vicinity of Port Talbot and the River Neath transport rates two orders of magnitude lower and equal to about .02 tonnes/m/day are observed (compare with Table 14.2).

These differences suggest that the Bay is effectively by-passed by the offshore westward movement of sediment. In fact, the only predicted movements of sand size material into the Bay from the west occur in the vicinity of Mumbles Head and at the western extremity of the Scarweather Sands, the latter probably being associated with bank forming processes. The observed transport pattern suggests that if movement of material into the Bay does occur it can only occur by a transfer of material from the west flowing stream in the area between Mumbles Head and the south extremity of the White Oyster Ledge. We should note here that radioactive tracer experiments carried out in this area and referred to by Collins et al. (1979) have indicated an easterly movement of material into the Bay. However in one case tracer having a mean size of 15µm was used and would thus have simulated suspended load transport and in the other case, although a coarser material was used (mean grain size of 140µm) the material was released at the surface on a flooding tide and the observed dispersion patterns are likely to be biased in an easterly direction. The interpretation presented in Fig. 15.19 is in general agreement with the conjectural sediment circulation patterns given by Ferentinos and Collins (1978) and Collins et al. (1979), except that transport into the Bay by tidal currents seems unlikely and it is possible that a wave-induced transport, particularly during periods of strong southwest winds is the most likely mechanism although we have no direct evidence of its occurrence (see Chapter 14). However, against this hypothesis must be balanced the finding that wave-induced mass transport effects in the area are small and of the order 2cm/s at the bed and that tracer studies do not indicate any appreciable shoreward movement of material (see Fig. 15.3) even over long periods of time when appreciable wave activity is known to have occurred. Furthermore, despite the presence of the west flowing sand stream close to the Gower coast, we should not discount the possibility, as suggested by Collins et al., 1979, of an easterly transport very close inshore, probably by wave activity.

ACKNOWLEDGEMENTS

We would like to acknowledge the support and co-operation of our colleagues at the Institute of Oceanographic Sciences, Taunton. This work was supported financially by the Department of the Environment.

REFERENCES

Ackers, P., and White, W.R. (1973). Sediment transport: New approach and analysis. Proc. ASCE, J. Hyd. Div. HY 11, 2041-2060.
Bagnold, R.A. (1966). Mechanics of marine sedimentation. In: Hill, M.N., (Ed.). The Sea. Interscience Publ., New York, 507-582.
Barenblatt, G.F. (1953). On the motion of suspended particles in a turbulent stream. Prikl. Matem. Mekh., 17, 261-274, (Engl. Trans.).
Barenblatt, G.F. (1955). Concerning the motion of suspended particles in turbulent flow occupying a half-space, or flat open channel of finite depth. Prikl. Matem. Mekh., 19, 61-68, (Engl. Trans.).
Bijker, E.W. (1967). Some considerations about scales for coastal models with movable beds. Delft Hydraulics Laboratory, Report No. 50, 142pp.
Blackley, M.W.L. (1978). Swansea Bay (Sker) Project Topic Report: 3. Geophysical Interpretation and sediment characteristics of the offshore and foreshore areas, I.O.S. Report No. 60/78, (Unpublished manuscript), 42pp.
Businger, J.A., Wyngaard, J.C., Izumi, I., and Gradley, E.F. (1971). Flux-profile relationships in the atmospheric surface layer. J. Atmos. Sci., 281, 181-189.
Carr, A.P. (1975). Swansea Bay (Sker) Project. Progress Report for the period to March 1975 and subsequent developments. I.O.S. Report No. 20/75, (Unpublished manuscript), 17pp.
Carr, A.P., Heathershaw, A.D., and Blackley, M.W.L. (1976). Swansea Bay (Sker) Project. Progress Report for the period August 1975 to July 1976. I.O.S. Report No. 26/76, (Unpublished manuscript), 28pp.

Non-Cohesive Sediment Transport

Carr, A.P., Heathershaw, A.D., and Blackley, M.W.L. (1977). Swansea Bay (Sker) Project. Progress Report for the period August 1976 to July 1977, I.O.S. Report No. 48/77, (Unpublished manuscript), 63pp.

Collins, M.B., Ferentinos, G., and Banner, F.T. (1979). The Hydrodynamics and Sedimentology of a High (Tidal and Wave) Energy Embayment (Swansea Bay, Northern Bristol Channel). *Estuar. Coast. Mar. Sci.*, **8**, 49-74.

Davies, C.M. (1974). Variability of suspended sediment in rotary currents, Swansea Bay (Bristol Channel), Great Britain. *Mar. Geol.*, **16**, M31-M38.

Davies, C.M. (1975). Paths of suspended sediment transport in Swansea Bay. *Proc. Challenger Soc.*, **4**, 259-260.

Dyer, K.R. (1979). Velocity profiles over a rippled bed and the threshold of movement of sand. *Estuar. Coast. Mar. Sci.*, (In press).

Einstein, H.A. (1950). The bed load function for sediment transportation in open channel flows. *Soil Conserv. Serv. Tech. Bull.*, US. Dept. Agric., No. 1026.

Englund, F., and Hansen, E. (1967). *A monograph on sediment transport in alluvial streams*. Teknisk Vorlag, Copenhagen.

Ferentinos, G., and Collins, M.B. (1978). Sediment transport through the area to the south of Eastern Gower, as related to the sediment budget of Swansea Bay. *University College of Swansea, Final Report to I.O.S. Taunton*. (Unpublished manuscript), 120pp.

Flemming, C.A., and Hunt, J.N. (1976). A mathematical sediment transport model for unidirectional flow. *Proc. Inst. Civ. Engrs.*, **61**, 297-310.

Gadd, P.E., Lavelle, J.W., and Swift, D.J.P. (1978). Estimates of sand transport on the New York Shelf using near-bottom current meter observations. *J. Sed. Pet.*, **48**, 239-252.

Guy, H.P., Simons, D.B., and Richardson, E.V. (1966). Summary of alluvial channel data from flume experiments 1955-1961. *US. Geol. Surv. Prof. Paper*, **462I**, 96pp.

Grand, W.D., and Madsen, O.S. (1979). Combined wave and current interaction with a rough bottom. *J. Geophys. Res.*, **84**, No.C4, 1797-1808.

Heathershaw, A.D., and Carr, A.P. (1977). Measurements of sediment transport rates using radioactive tracers. *ASCE Proc. Coastal Sediments '77*, Charleston, S.C., U.S.A., 20pp.

Heathershaw, A.D., Carr, A.P., Blackley, M.W.L., and Hammond, F.D.C. (1978). Swansea Bay (Sker) Project. Progress Report for the period August 1977 to July 1978, I.O.S. Report No. 74/78, (Unpublished manuscript), 47pp.

Heathershaw, A.D., and Hammond, F.D.C. (1979a). Swansea Bay: Tidal currents: observed tidal and residual circulations and their response to meteorological conditions. I.O.S. Report, (In preparation).

Heathershaw, A.D., and Hammond, F.D.C. (1979b). Swansea Bay: Offshore sediment movement and its relation to observed tidal current and wave data. I.O.S. Report, (In preparation).

Komar, P.D., and Miller, M.C. (1974). Sediment threshold under oscillatory waves. *Proc. 14th Coastal Eng. Conf.*, Copenhagen, 756-775.

Longuet-Higgins, M.S. (1953). Mass transport in water waves. *Phil. Trans. Roy. Soc. London, Ser. A.*, **245**, 535-581.

Longuet-Higgins, M.S. (1957). The mechanics of the boundary-layer near the bottom in a progressive water wave. Appendix to Russell and Osorio, (1957).

Owen, M.W., and Thorn, M.F.C. (1978). Effect of waves on sand transport by currents. *Proc. 16th Conf. on Coastal Eng.*, Hamburg (In press).

Pingree, R.D. (1978). The formation of the Shambles and other banks by tidal stirring of the seas. *J. Mar. Biol. Ass. UK.*, **58**, 211-226.

Pingree, R.D. and Maddock, L. (1979). The tidal physics of headland flows and offshore tidal bank formation. *Mar. Geol.*, **32**, 269-289.

Russell, R.C.H., and Osorio, J.D.C. (1957). An experimental investigation of drift profiles in a closed channel. *Proc. 6th Conf. on Coastal Eng.*, Miami, 171-193.

Smith, J.D. (1977). Modelling of sediment transport on continental shelves. In: Goldberg, E.D., McCave, I.N., O'Brien, J.J., and Steele, J.H. (Eds.). *The Sea*, **6**, Wiley Interscience, New York, 539-577.

Smith, J.D., and McLean, S.R. (1977). Spatially averaged flow over a wavy surface. J. Geophys. Res., 82, 1735-1746.

Sternberg, R.W. (1968). Friction factors in tidal channels with differing bed roughness. Mar. Geol., 6, 243-260.

Sternberg, R.W. (1972). Predicting initial motion and bedload transport of sediment particles in the shallow marine environment. In: Swift, D.J.P., Duane, D.B., and Pilkey, O.H. (Eds.). Shelf sediment transport: Process and Pattern. Dowden, Hutchinson and Ross, Stroudsberg, 61-81.

Swart, D.H. (1976). Coastal sediment transport. Delft Hydraulics Laboratory Report No. R968, 61pp.

Taylor, P.A., and Dyer, K.R. (1977). Theoretical models of flow near the bed and their implications for sediment transport. In: Goldberg, E.D., McCave, I.N., O'Brien, J.J., and Steele, J.H. (Eds.). The Sea, 6, Wiley Interscience, New York. 579-601.

Yalin, M.S. (1963). An expression for bed load transportation. Proc. ASCE, J. Hyd. Div., 221-250.

Yalin, M.S. (1972). Mechanics of Sediment Transport. Pergamon Press, Oxford, 290pp.

16. MINERALOGY OF NONCOHESIVE SEDIMENTARY DEPOSITS

J. V. Barrie

Department of Oceanography*, University College of Swansea, Swansea, U.K.
*Present address: Centre for Cold Ocean Resources Engineering (C-CORE), Memorial University of Newfoundland, St. John's, Newfoundland, Canada

ABSTRACT

Heavy and light mineral associations, from 'recent' bottom sediments of Swansea Bay and the northern Bristol Channel, demonstrate hydraulically equivalent/inequivalent relationships. Hydraulic inequivalence is a result of (1) preferential mineral size of certain minerals from source, which controls the mineral suite changes, created by, (2) differential entrainment of minerals by density and size. Defined from variations in hydraulic equivalence and delimited by heavy mineral concentrations, four mineral assemblages are described. These reflect sediment response to the superimposition of both modern hydrodynamics and recent sedimentation.

KEYWORDS

Sediments; Mineralogy; Heavy minerals; Hydraulic equivalence; Mineral assemblages; Swansea Bay; Bristol Channel

INTRODUCTION

Mineralogy of non-cohesive sediments is normally classified on the basis of mineral density within the sand size fraction. Heavy minerals are defined as those minerals of specific gravity generally greater than 2.90. The bulk of the mineral grains are less than 2.90 and are simply noted as the light minerals (lights). The lights can be further divided into two major categories; (1) quartz and feldspar minerals (specific gravity 2.65) and (2) the calcitic, biogenic material where particle shape is a major factor.

Hydraulic equivalence, fostered by Rubey (1933), states that mineral grains of different densities should have the same settling velocities. In other words, the hydraulic conditions which would permit the deposition of a particular quartz grain is inversely proportional to the power of its density. Subsequent studies (van Andel, 1959; Briggs, 1965; Hand, 1964; Lowright et al., 1972; Slingerland, 1977) have revealed that standard hydraulic equilibrium, as defined by Rubey, is inapplicable to most natural non-cohesive sands. Recent investigations have defined two possible explanations for the divergence, as outlined by Lowright et al. (1972). The first concerns the individual preferential size in both light and heavy minerals.

250   J. V. Barrie

as inherited from the source rock or till; the second, the hydraulic "inequivalence" is the result of differential transport of the various minerals in a sand, causing selective sorting by size, density, and shape.

The development of the concept of selective deposition and transport of heavy mineral grains has given rise to explanations for the thin laminae of heavy mineral placers commonly found on marine beaches (Everts, 1972). Stapor (1973) describes two mechanisms that create such deposits; operative on beaches subjected to both high and low wave energy inputs of the northeastern Gulf of Mexico. On the beaches open to the greater input of energy, the process resulted in the removal of coarser grains from the initial population, all proportional to decreasing density. On sheltered beaches the process is reversed, with the removal of the finer grains leaving a coarse deposit. May (1973) proposed a model which described the variation in the distribution of bottom fluid velocities, resulting in sediment being transported shorewards in relation to it's density and grain size. Conditions which are favourable for the shoreward movement of fine heavy minerals (i.e., depth/wavelength ratio), but not seaward, under shoaling waves relative to coarse quartz, will leave an above-average concentration of heavies on the beach. Woolsey et al. (1975), in addition to these factors, advocates winnowing processes by eolian transport conjointly with variations in wave energy, as seen on Sapelo Island, Georgia.

THE PHYSICAL ENVIRONMENT

The Holocene period saw a transgressing sea inundate the Swansea Bay, northern Bristol Channel region (Fig. 16.1), depositing Flandrian peats and silts (North, 1955). At the inception of these conditions a rapid redistribution of the existing Quaternary deposits, into something approaching the present day pattern was accomplished covering previously exposed Palaeozoic outcrops (Culver and Banner, 1979; see also Chapters 2, 3 and 4).

The Quaternary sediments were derived from both the Wolstonian and Devensian glacial advances. The mineral suites defining the sediments are direct results of the paths followed by each. Griffiths (1939) defined the line of contact, between the Irish and Welsh Drifts of the Wolstonian, by examining the mineralogical differences between the respective drift deposits. This investigation revealed that the minerals epidote (green), amphibole (blue-green), staurolite, kyanite and andalusite were common in Irish Sea glacial material but non-existant in material derived from the Welsh ice-sheet. All other minerals found were common to both glacial sediments. The succeeding Devensian glaciation deposited a Welsh Drift mineral assemblage only. The extent of the Welsh ice-sheet was very close to the limit of the Wolstonian advance (Bowen, 1970; Griffiths, 1939), although some overlap of the older Irish Sea Drift occurred.

It was, then, in the late Flandrian that the modern hydrodynamic regime of the Bristol Channel was attained. The resultant tidal current pattern is essentially rectilinear, along the axis of the Channel, with a large vertical range and associated high current velocities. Within the embayments, of the north coast, the simple rectilinear tidal situation is modified. 'Eddies' within the embayments of Oxwich, Port Eynon and Swansea (Rees, 1940; Collins et al., 1979) have been suggested. Recent investigations in Swansea Bay (Collins et al., op.cit.) has confirmed that a quasi-permanent tidal gyre (eddy) exists on the western side of the embayment, causing a flow past Mumbles Head (Fig. 16.1) for approximately 9 hr. As the current passes the Mumbles promontory, it is deflected by the main rectilinear Channel stream; the deflection is to seawards during ebb, and it is returned to the anticlockwise eddy system during flood. This pattern causes reinforcement of the tidal currents around Mumbles Head. The restricted entrance and configuration of the Loughor Estuary also gives rise to reinforced tidal currents increasing to the Loughor River. Swell direction is predominantly from the southwest (Barrie, 1979b) and as it is this

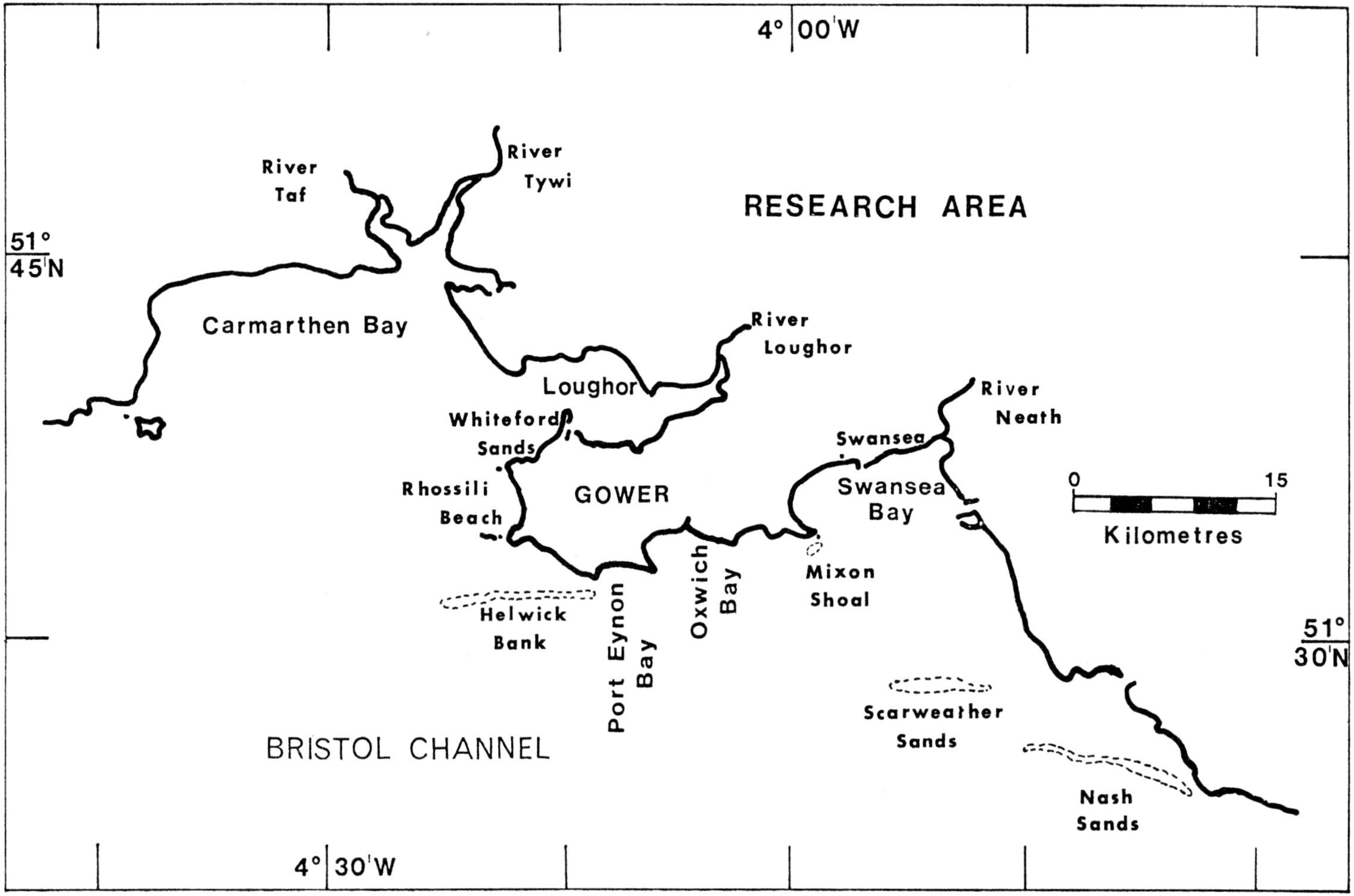

Figure 16.1. Area of research.

252   J. V. Barrie

direction which is that of the longest fetch, wave energy (acting upon the 'mobile' sediment cover) is considered to be most effective from the southwest. The Mumbles tidal eddy and the Loughor Estuary, therefore, are protected areas from the dominant swell.

MINERALOGY

Quartz makes up the majority of sediment (90%) in the northern Bristol Channel and Swansea Bay. Though not surprising, one feature of the nature in which it is found is anomalous. Examination of the beach and offshore samples has shown that hematitic staining on quartz was a dominant feature varying in intensity. Stuart (1924), similarly, noticed such staining in the dune sands of the South Wales beaches. Griffiths (1939) conversely, noted the absence of hematitic staining on the mineral grains from glacial, Pleistocene, deposits adjacent to the area under investigation.

The origin of the iron staining has been a much disputed topic among geologists for many decades, due to the general lack of understanding of the mode of formation of hematitic stain in modern sediments. From investigations carried out on Sable Island, Nova Scotia, and its surrounding offshore bank, James and Stanley (1967; 1968) concluded that the staining originated under subaerial conditions during low sea level stands; this is a hypothesis which correlates well with results of the area under present investigation. The intense staining found in offshore sediments of the northern Bristol Channel can be considered evidence of the materials original relict origin.

The remainder of the light minerals include minor amounts of feldspar (mainly orthoclase), coal, dolomite and various micas. The predominant form of calcite was as biogenic material. In most cases this made up a small percentage of the total sediment sample.

Quantitative heavy mineral separations (Barrie, 1979a) have revealed that the sediment samples are composed of between 0.1% to greater than 3.0% (average 1.75%) of mineral concentrations with a density in excess of 2.92. The opaque fraction (mainly ilmenite, hematite, magnetite) remain, reasonably consistently, at approximately 75% of this fraction. More than 30 non-opaque heavy minerals have been identified from the remaining 25%. Seven of these minerals (tourmaline, garnet, chlorite, zircon, rutile, epidote, amphibole) comprise a (percentage) mean of over 5.0% of the total fraction. Some ten of these minerals (siderite, apatite, staurolite, andalusite, clinopyroxenes, orthopyroxenes, topaz, cassiterite, flourite, kyanite) have a mean percentage in excess of 1.0%.

DISCUSSION

Three of the seven major minerals found in the Swansea Bay, northern Bristol Channel region show preferential size characteristics in both onshore Pleistocene deposits and offshore sediments. Zircon and rutile, both of high specific gravity, occur in a narrow fine size range in glacial tills (Griffiths, 1939), as with offshore occurrences. Zircon is found predominately around 0.075mm (Fig. 16.2) while rutile is slightly coarser with a dominant mean of 0.10mm (Fig. 16.2). Griffiths (1939) quotes that the average grain size of the amphibole in South Wales glacial tills is between 0.15mm and 0.20mm while the present investigation has shown a mean restricted grain size of 0.15mm (Fig. 16.2) for amphibole. Amphibole, like tourmaline and epidote, have specific gravities that range in the light end of the heavy mineral range. Considering hydraulic equivalence, it would be expected that changes in mean grain size will alter either the state of hydraulic equivalence (i.e. hydraulic inequivalence) or the mineral abundances.

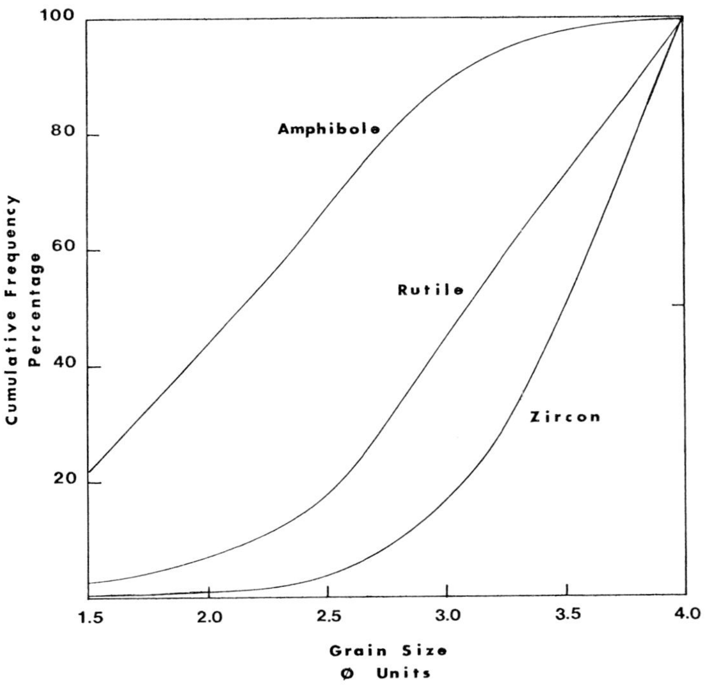

Mineralogy of Noncohesive Sediments

The heavy mineral distribution reflects conditions of hydraulic equivalence/inequivalence in the northern Bristol Channel. However, preferential mineral size of three minerals is not adequate to explain totally the results but is only sufficient to create some significant mineral changes, determined by hydrodynamic sedimentary selection. Also, the supply of material from land drainage, though relatively small, is significant in the present distribution of chlorite and magnetite within the embayments. These factors are best demonstrated by four mineral assemblage groups that make up the northern Bristol Channel and Swansea Bay region.

From a depth range of 20 to 25m (below chart datum) offshore concentration of zircon and rutile dominate into nearshore regions often extending as far as the intertidal zone (Fig. 16.3). The area which corresponds to this mineral assemblage is one of predominately medium sands (Barrie, 1979a) which are poorly sorted; the sediments fining into better sorted material in the shallower areas. Apparent hydraulic inequivalence exists with the heavy minerals being almost four times smaller than would be expected by hydraulic equivalence. Within this mineral assemblage area the hydraulic preference for the smaller size ranges and greater densities accomodates the very fine grained and dense zircon and rutile. Only in the samples which correspond to the very shallow end of this group, where sediment grain size becomes finer, is the hydraulic inequivalence reduced.

Distinct from this mineral assemblage distribution is that of the shoaling sand banks (Nash, Scarweather, Mixon, Helwick) and the bathymetric slope off the coast of South Gower (Fig. 16.3). These areas of greatest wave and tidal action are defined by a

Figure 16.2. Mean size distribution of zircon, rutile and amphibole in bottom sediments of Swansea Bay and the northern Bristol Channel.

253

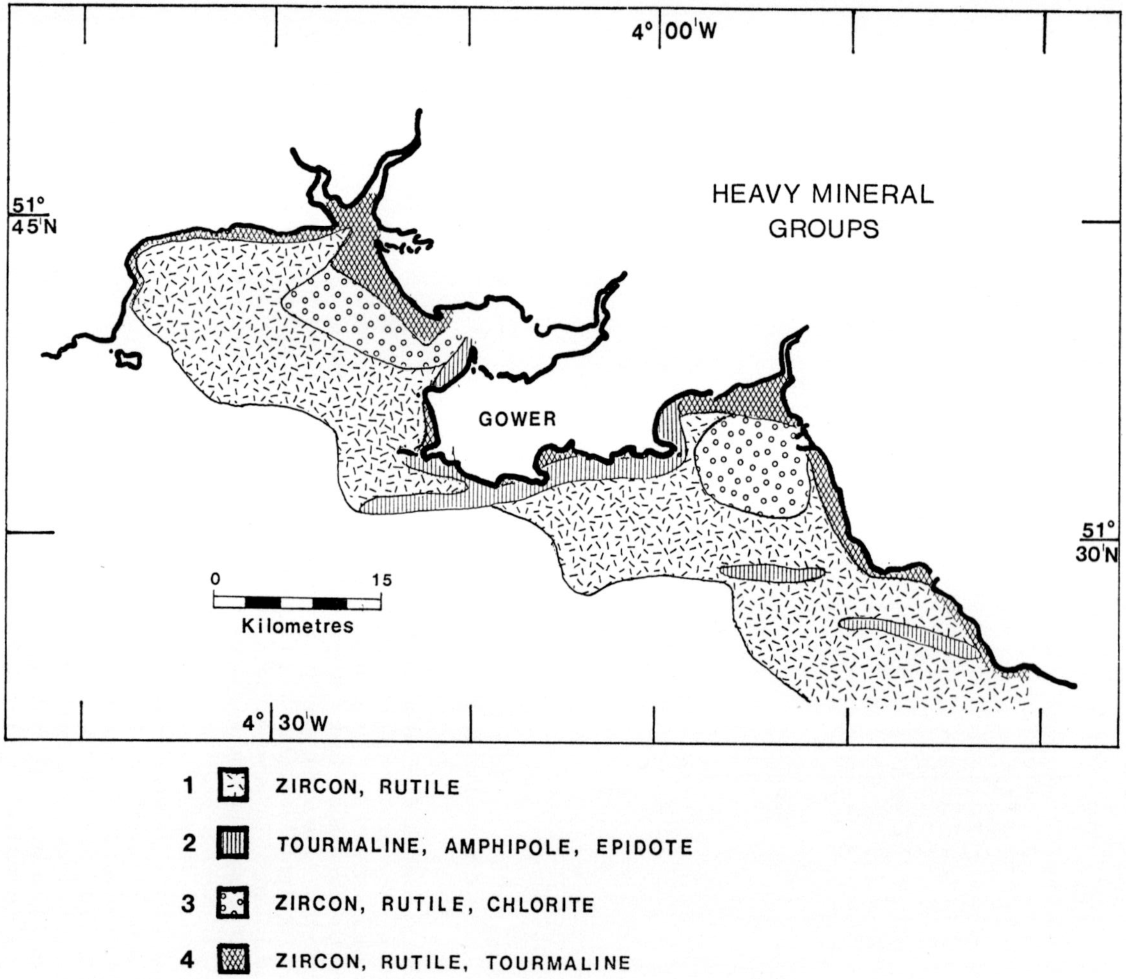

Figure 16.3. Distribution of heavy mineral assemblages.

Mineralogy of Noncohesive Sediments

tourmaline, epidote, amphibole mineral suite.

This assemblage could be predicted with reference to the average mean grain size of medium sand (Barrie, 1979a) and standard hydraulic equivalence. Zircon and rutile are both denser and size restricted while garnet is ubiquitous throughout the region due to it's greater density and non-restricted size. The well sorted sands are truly in entrainment equivalence and therefore hydraulic equivalence.

The east central areas of Carmarthen and Swansea Bays demonstrate a heavy mineral assemblage of chlorite, zircon and rutile (Fig. 16.3). This assemblage group is well defined in Swansea Bay, where sampling was extensive (Barrie, 1979a). Banner (1979) describes the sediments from this area as dredged and dumped fine sand and mud of glacial and Flandrian origin (see also Chapter 4). If this interpretation is correct, then the glacial and (presumably) the majority of Flandrian sediments are of Welsh Drift origin. The noticeable absence of epidote, amphibole, andalusite and staurolite in the samples supports this hypothesis. As previously mentioned chlorite, discharged from the Neath River in Swansea Bay and the Taff and Tywi Rivers in Carmarthen Bay, concentrates in the east central portions of both embayments.

On the sediment within the eastern central zones of Carmarthen and Swansea Bays, the tidal current influence is very much reduced (Ferentinos, 1979). Wave energy is sufficient to control sediment distribution but is only intermittent in relation to the influence of strong south to southwesterly swell wave action. Consequently, the irregular hydraulically rough to smooth boundary conditions (together with the artificial dredging input into Swansea Bay) will result in sediment being supplied and subsequently deposited out of suspension. This ideal condition for hydraulic equivalence would select only those heavy minerals abundant in the very fine grain sizes (zircon, rutile, chlorite). The mineral assemblage can be considered to be controlled by both source and location; the latter reflecting an area of hydrodynamic characteristics which are different to those of other mineral groups.

Zircon and rutile, with the major addition of tourmaline, make up the sands of the intertidal beach environment (Fig. 16.3). The influence of discharge from major rivers within the embayments alter the mineral concentrations of each samples. For example, the samples adjacent to the Neath River are totally devoid of epidote, amphibole and andalusite but contain greater concentrations of chlorite; this is a direct result of the supply of Welsh Drift minerals from the River Neath.

Within the intertidal beach environment, the actual position of the individual beach samples will dictate the average amount and form of energy input. This, in turn, influences the variation in hydraulic equivalence. The samples analysed in this study were taken from the seaward end of the waves will be superimposed on the bed with high turbulence levels. Hydraulic inequivalence, caused by variation in entrainment values in response to differences in mean wave-induced oscillatory velocities, is most evident on those beaches exposed to the predominant southwesterly swell (see also Chapter 12). On the upper sections of the berms of the southwesterly facing open beaches (especially Rhossili Beach in Carmarthen Bay), there are thin laminae of fine heavy mineral concentrations in inequivalence with quartz (light minerals). This is the final result of the differential entrainment created by wave surge on the beach shelf. The greater concentration of zircon and rutile on the southwest facing beach sands, described by Hill and Parker (1970) and by the present author, can then be explained.

The inequivalence becomes less apparent in the protected zones of the embayments, until equivalence is reached in the totally protected areas, where tidal currents (enhanced by recirculatory flow) become the dominant hydraulic factor in the selective control of the sediment. In these areas of reinforced tidal currents, the em-

255

256   J. V. Barrie

bayment side of Mumbles Head of Swansea Bay, Whiteford Sands in Carmarthen Bay and the embayment sides of Oxwich Point and Port Eynon Point, heavy mineral concentrations are enriched and a completely different mineral assemblage exists. Like the shoaling banks and South Gower coastline a tourmaline, epidote, amphibole assemblage, in hydraulic equivalence, corresponds to the medium grain size, well sorted, sediment (Barrie, 1979a) that has been selected for under a reinforced tidal regime.

SUMMARY

Four mineralogical provinces in Swansea Bay and the northern Bristol Channel have been delimited based on the major non-opaque heavy minerals. The mineralogical assemblages are a result of source control (imposed by the original relict sediment), recent river input and the superimposition of the Bristol Channel hydrodynamics on a seabed of a certain roughness. Size control from source and the differential entrainment values for individual minerals, depending on size, shape and specific gravity, create light/heavy mineral associations that are both in equivalence and in inequivalence, with the heavy minerals being much smaller than would be predicted.

REFERENCES

Banner, F.T. (1979). Sediments of the Northwest European continental shelf. In: Banner, F.T., Collins, M.B., and Massie, K.S. (Eds.). The Northwest European Shelf Seas: The Seabed and the sea in motion. Elsevier, Amsterdam 271-300.

Barrie,J.V. (1979a). Heavy mineral distribution in bottom sediments of the Bristol Channel, U.K. Estuarine and Coastal Marine Science (in press).

Barrie,J.V. (1979b). Hydrodynamic factors controlling the distribution of heavy minerals (Bristol Channel). Estuarine and Coastal Marine Science (in press).

Bowen, D.Q. (1970). South-east and central Wales. In: Lewis, C.A. (Ed.). The Glaciations of Wales and Adjoining Regions. Longmans, London, 378pp.

Briggs, L.I. (1965). Heavy mineral correlations and provenances. Jl. Sedim. Petrol., 35, 939-955.

Collins, M.B., Ferentinos, G., and Banner, F.T. (1979). The hydrodynamics and sedimentology of a high (tidal and wave) energy embayment (Swansea Bay), northern Bristol Channel). Estuarine and Coastal. Mar. Sci., 8, 49-74.

Culver, S.J., and Banner, F.T. (1979). The significance of derived pre-Quaternary foraminifera in Holocene sediments of the north-central Bristol Channel. Mar. Geol., 29, 187-207.

Everts, C.H. (1972). Exploration for high energy marine placer sites. Univ. Wisconsin Sea Grant Technical Report, 10, 179pp.

Ferentinos, G. (1978). Hydrodynamic and Sedimentation Processes in Swansea Bay and along the central Northern Bristol Channel coastline. Unpub. Ph.D. Thesis, University of Wales.

Griffiths, J.C. (1939). The mineralogy of the glacial deposits of the region between the Rivers Neath and Tawe, South Wales. Proc. Geol. Ass., 50, 433-462.

Hand, B.M. (1964). Hydrodynamics of Beach and Dune Sedimentation. Unpub. Ph.D. Thesis, Pennsylvania State University.

Hill, P.A., and Parker, A. (1970). Tin and zirconium in the sediments around the British Isles: A preliminary reconnaissance. Econ. Geol., 65, 409-416.

James, N.P., and Stanley, D.J. (1967). Sediment transport on Sable Island, Nova Scotia. Smithsonian Misc. Paper 4727, 152, 33pp.

James, N.P., and Stanley, D.J. (1968). Sable Island Bank of Nova Scotia: Sediment dispersal and recent history. Amer. Assoc. Petrol. Geol. Bull., 52, 2208-2230.

Lowright, R., Williams, E.G., and Dachille, F. (1972). An analysis of factors controlling deviations in hydraulic equivalence in some modern sands. Jl. Sedim. Petrol., 42, 635-645.

May, J.P. (1973). Selective transport of heavy minerals by shoaling waves. Sedimentology, 20, 203-211.

Mineralogy of Noncohesive Sediments

North, F.J. (1955). *The Evolution of the Bristol Channel.* National Museum of Wales, Cardiff.

Rees, T.K. (1940). Algal colonization at Mumbles Head. *J. Ecol.*, **28**, 403-411.

Rubey, W.W. (1933). The size-distribution of heavy minerals within a water-laid sandstone. *J. Sedim. Petrol.*, **3**, 3-29.

Slingerland, R.L. (1977). The effects of entrainment on the hydraulic equivalence relationships of light and heavy minerals in sands. *J. Sedim. Petrol.*, **47**, 753-770.

Stapor, F.W., Jr. (1973). Heavy mineral concentrating processes and density/size equilibrium in the marine and coastal dune sands of the Apalachicola, Florida, region. *J. Sedim. Petrol.*, **43**, 396-407.

Stuart, A. (1924). The petrology of the dune sands of South Wales. *Proc. Geol. Assoc.*, **35**, 316-331.

van Andel, T. (1959). Reflections on the interpretation of heavy mineral analysis. *J. Sedim. Petrol.*, **29**, 153-163.

Woolsey, J.R., Vernon, J.H., and Hunt, J.L. (1975). Backshore heavy-mineral concentration on Sapelo Island, Georgia. *J. Sedim. Petrol.*, **45**, 280-284.

17. SWANSEA BAY: BEACHES AND SUPRALITTORAL DEPOSITS

M. W. L. Blackley and A. P. Carr

Institute of Oceanographic Sciences, Taunton, Somerset, U.K.

ABSTRACT

The paper describes the features of the beaches along the east side of Swansea Bay and the methods used to record changes in beach characteristics over time.

Evidence from photogrammetry (1968-75) shows that the beach level fell by the equivalent of 0.4m overall. This led to increased exposure of peat and clay on Margam and Kenfig beaches.

Surveyed profiles (mainly 1975-77) indicate that, although there is a tendency for sections to be lower during the winter storm period than in the summer, it is the short term (i.e. monthly) fluctuations in height which are the principal feature. On any specific survey date, there is no consistent erosional or accretional trend operating along the beaches as a whole. However, taking the entire 18 month intensive survey period gives a more significant result: variations in beach level increase towards the south.

Volume changes over a complete 2-year period were rather small except where due to human interference. Measurements along a specific profile at Morfa Beach indicate that minimum change occurred at mid-tide level. At Kenfig Beach dune face recession was shown to be at a rate of up to about 2.5m per year over 4 years.

Sediment sampling results were largely inconclusive although the finest material was always found at low water level.

KEYWORDS

Beaches; Photogrammetry; Surveying; Sedimentation; Erosion; Wales coast; Swansea Bay; Bristol Channel.

INTRODUCTION

Chapter 7 describes some of the documentary evidence for the long-term changes which have taken place on the eastern side of Swansea Bay. It has been shown that the area has tended to recede landwards over historical time and that this trend increased during the nineteenth century, at least in the neighbourhood of coastal engineering works.

This chapter concentrates on the nature of the changes currently taking place on the beaches which extend along the east side of Swansea Bay although some consideration is given to the dune systems lying to landward. Techniques have included photogrammetry, topographic surveying, sediment sampling and beach experiments, but the latter are only referred to here in passing.

Description of the Beach

The three beaches which form the subject of this paper run from the mouth of the River Neath in the north to Sker Point in the south, a distance of approximately 12.5km. They are the Aberafan Beach, here defined as extending from Witford Point to the Port Talbot tidal harbour; the Morfa Mawr and Margam Beaches, whose limit is the tidal harbour in the north and the River Kenfig in the south; and, finally, the Kenfig Beach bounded by the River Kenfig and Sker Point. (All places referred to in the text are shown in Figure 17.1). The Port Talbot tidal harbour and associated deep water channel appear to separate Aberafan Beach from those further to the south. The Margam and Kenfig Beaches are similarly, but less effectively, divided by the River Kenfig. The latter is only poorly defined as it passes across the beach face, consisting as it does of a series of separate shallow braided streams. Additionally a buried outfall pipe and a further buried outfall pipe plus factory effluent from a culvert, traverse the Margam Beach 0.2km and 1.5km south of the southern breakwater of the tidal harbour, respectively.

At one time, all three beaches were backed by sand dunes but today only Kenfig Burrows remains in a largely natural state. Further north, the dunes have been used as a source of building sand and the levelled areas either then built upon or used to deposit slag or other waste materials. Until 1973, sand was also won from the foreshore along parts of the Margam and Kenfig beaches (Carr and Blackley, 1977). South of Section N, a thin belt of dunes has been left to landwards of Margam Beach. To some degree this acts as a protective barrier. Elsewhere, from the breakwater of the tidal harbour to Section N, the beach abuts an artificial cliff of slag waste, rising some 10-12m above high water mark. This, too, has protective value.

North of Port Talbot tidal harbour, a sea wall and promenade extend some 2.3km towards the River Neath. Thereafter, remnants of dunes occur.

The large tidal range ($\sim$9.2m on normal spring tides), a potentially easily erodible coastline, and the dominance of fine sand grade material (mostly within the range 2.12 $\pm$ 0.25$\emptyset$, where phi ($\emptyset$) = -log$_2$ diameter in millimetres) are all factors which have contributed towards the formation of wide, generally planar, beaches with 450m or more occasionally exposed between high and low water spring tide levels. Smooth profiles are widely regarded as characteristic of large tidal range, exposed sites and limited sediment supply (e.g. King, 1972). Although the gradients remain relatively gentle, the documentary evidence (see Chapter 7) suggests that, at one time, they were still more so. At the present time, slopes at mid-tide level are of the order of 1:50 at the northern end of Aberafan Beach. Gradients increase to between 1:40 and 1:45 towards the tidal harbour, possibly because of the restricting influence of the sea wall which extends along the back of the beach in that area and the effects of the northern tidal harbour breakwater.

To the south of the Port Talbot tidal harbour, the gradients are more variable with mean mid-tide values ranging between 1:48 and 1:61. This variability may be attributed, at least in part, to the diversity of sediment types present on Margam and Kenfig beaches, as compared with Aberafan's uniform sand beach. Bagnold (1940) considered, as a result of laboratory experiments, that beach slope is dependent only on the grain size. Bascom (1951) believed that there was a clear correlation

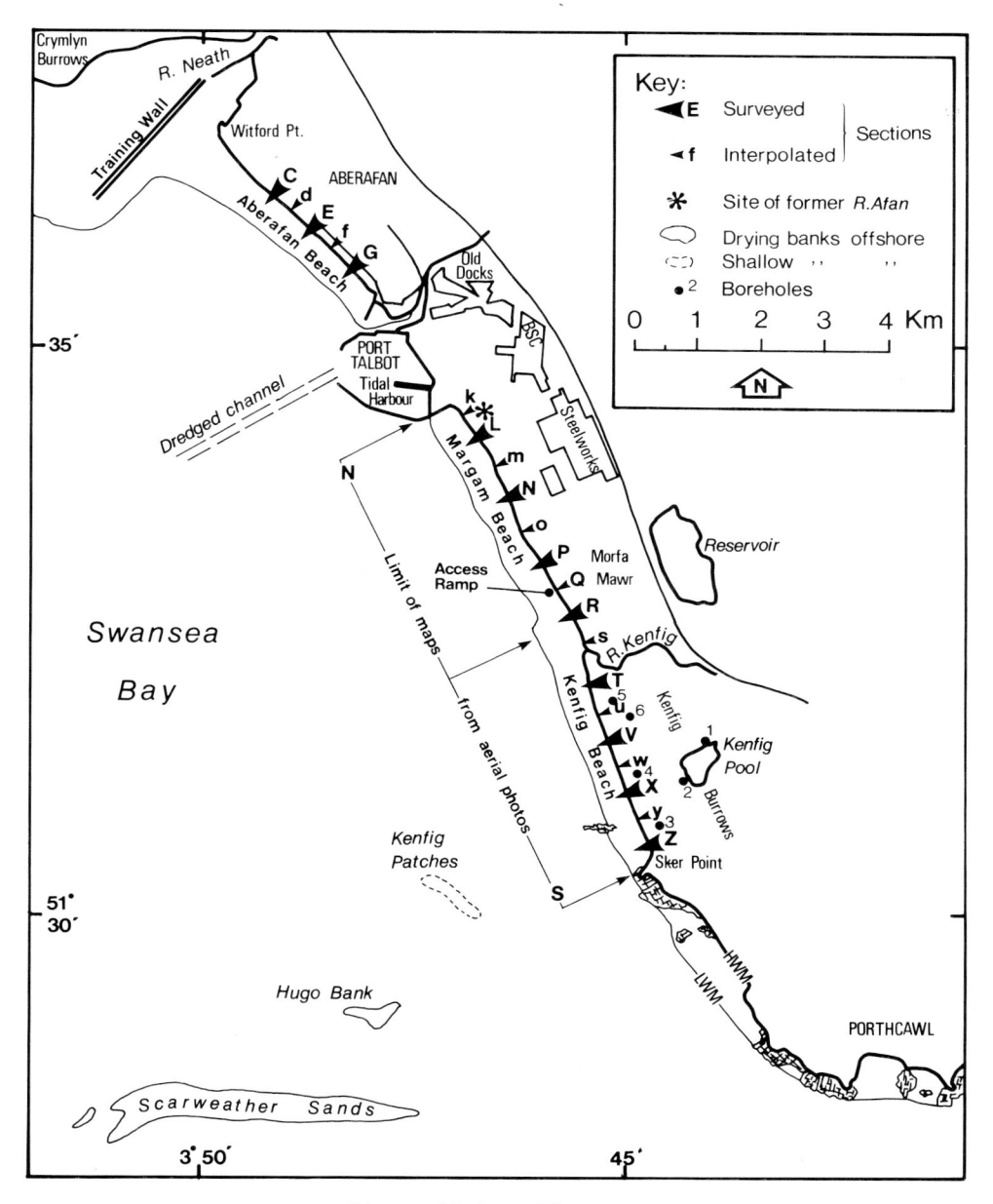

Figure 17.1. Site map.

between minimum slope and grain size. However King (1972), showed that wave length and wave steepness were also relevant.

Throughout almost the entire length of Margam and Kenfig beaches a scatter of coarse material - generally within the pebble size range - is found at about high water mark, while above high tide level there is a well-developed, but intermittent, cobble storm beach which is subject to short-term, mainly random, topographic changes.

This storm beach is virtually absent both immediately south of the tidal harbour and south of the River Kenfig. In consequence, in the latter area the sand dunes are less effectively protected and undergo periodic erosion through wave attack.

Deposits of Flandrian age are exposed along the Margam and Kenfig foreshore (see also Chapter 4); they range from blue clastic clays and sandy clays to sandy peats and pure peats. *Scrobicularia* shells are found in some of the blue clays, whilst certain of the peat exposures contain quite large roots amongst the fibrous material. In general, the peat is fairly resistant to erosion and tends to form a protective capping over the softer clays. The result is the formation of horizontal peat ledges. Where erosion is at an advanced stage, isolated peat blocks are left standing by as much as 60cm above the surrounding beach level. Protruding clays tend to be eroded into deep gulleys running parallel to the slope of the beach. It is possible that these fissured outcrops are eventually planed down to beach level, but the wide, flat expanses of clay at (or just below) the beach surface may equally well reflect the original level of the geological discontinuity.

Margam, and especially Kenfig, beaches include a number of areas covered with large rounded cobbles and boulders. Such deposits are most prevalent towards the southern end of Kenfig Beach (for example, on Section X, Fig, 17.1) and appear to represent a lag deposit following recession of the beach. The cobbles and boulders tend to occupy depressions in the beach or the site of previously eroded clay outcrops. Their distribution appears reasonably constant for months at a time, only being subject to intermittent covering by sand. Nevertheless, some movement is apparent over longer periods of time.

Kenfig Burrows is a dune area roughly of equilateral triangular shape with an apex to the south. The sides are approximately 3km long. Many of the ridges reach a crest height of some 15m although this is exceeded along the landward margins of the system, where the dunes abut hummocky Boulder Clay. Unlike some other systems only the seawards ridge, parallel to the coastline, is well defined. Kenfig Pool is a conspicuous element of the landscape along the landward margin, and other areas of standing water, as well as dune slacks, occur from time to time. Boreholes (Carr and Blackley, 1977; Blackley, 1978) have proved that at least the seaward dunes are underlain by extensive thicknesses of cobbles and pebbles. One peat sample from approximately -3.3m OD (Ordnance Datum) from Borehole 4 was dated by the radiocarbon (^{14}C) method and gave a figure of 5686 $\pm$ 45 years BP. Using the borehole and other geological and geophysical data it appears likely that Kenfig Burrows contains about 4×10^7 tonnes of sand. This is perhaps one third of the original amount in the dune systems along the east side of the Bay and this radiocarbon date together with others (Godwin and Willis, 1961) suggest that the present dune systems are likely to have been laid down within the last 6000 years or so (see also Chapter 4).

TECHNIQUES

Maps Derived from Aerial Surveys

A total of 4 flights along the coast were carried out by Meridian Airmaps Ltd., in 1966, 1968, 1970 and 1975, for the British Transport Docks Board; three of these aerial surveys have been used by the Institute of Oceanographic Sciences to produce comparative maps of the beach south of the tidal harbour. All the relevant photography was flown to give a nominal scale of 1:6000 during the summer half of the year when conditions are generally more stable. The 1968 flight corresponds with the beginning of construction of the new harbour at Port Talbot; 1970 with its completion; and that of 1975 some 5 years after completion.

At the scale of the photography, heights can be plotted to an accuracy of $\pm$ 0.15m.

Beaches and Supralittoral Deposits 263

All 3 derived maps were produced using a Kern PG2 photogrammetric plotter. Contours were drawn at 1m intervals and other detail, notably the exposures of clay, peat and cobbles and boulders, were recorded. Comparisons were then made as to the displacement of the contours, the computed volume changes between the 3 flights and the areas of peat and clay exposed on each occasion. Exposures of peat and clay had also been mapped by the Geological Survey in 1952.

Beach Sections and Sampling

The changes of beach topography were measured on a monthly basis between October 1975 and April/May 1977, with one further survey in October 1977. Eleven sections, each approximately 1km apart, were laid out at right angles to the beach: C, E and G on Aberafan Beach; L, N, P, R and T, V, X and Z on Margam and Kenfig beaches, respectively (see Fig. 17.1). Fuller details are given in Blackley and Carr (1977). On each occasion, the sections were surveyed on spring tides, profiles being effectively made within 1½ hours of the time of low water. The average length of the beach sections was 420m from the seawards bench mark, but they could vary between 320m and 520m reflecting geographical location, time of survey and the particular spring tide range. The sections on Aberafan Beach and L, T and V were all virtually free from peat and clay outcrops. All breaks of slope and changes of lithology were recorded, together with some additional points on apparently extensive uniform stretches of beach.

Because monthly changes were, for the most part, small, a simple computer program was written which used the surveyed heights at known, but irregularly spaced, distances to interpolate heights at a fixed interval (20m) over a standard length profile. The program then compared the profiles in successive months and calculated the difference in area between them. From these data, calculations were made of changes of the volume of beach material on the basis that the adjacent beach followed the trends shown by the profile. This method has been adopted elsewhere (e.g. Bruun, 1954).

In addition, some supplementary survey work was undertaken. One specific profile was located in the area of the maximum peat outcrop (about 260m N of Section P, Fig. 17.1). More significant, however, was that along the line of 'Q' which was the location utilised for 2 beach experiments in November 1976 and April/May 1977 (See also Chapter 12).

Although, initially (December 1974) the sediment of the foreshore zone was closely sampled between Witford Point and Porthcawl, at positions corresponding to high, mid, and low water, subsequent sampling was restricted to bimonthly intervals along the 11 sections surveyed topographically. Samples were taken between October 1975 and April 1977, but because the variability was so small, only the specimens from December 1974, October and December 1975 and February, April and August 1976 were analysed. These were sieved at $\frac{1}{4}\emptyset$ intervals. Furthermore, analysis by conventional statistical moment measures was rapidly abandoned as being of only limited value in the particular context.

RESULTS AND DISCUSSION

Evidence from Photogrammetry (1968 - 1975).

Peat and Clay Exposure: Clay has been exposed on the beaches south of Port Talbot harbour since at least the late 1930's (Table 17.1). It was estimated, in 1940, that about 4000m² of clay was exposed just north of the Access Ramp. In 1952 the Geological Survey mapped these exposures (as "Submerged Forest Beds") on both Margam and Kenfig beaches. Their survey showed that 81,000m² of peat and clay were exposed on the Margam Beach whilst the Kenfig Beach was free from any exposures. The total figure was made up of 23,000m² in an area now covered by the Port Talbot tidal harbour, 29,000m² just north of the River Kenfig and a similar figure, 29,000m² in the intervening area.

Figures for 1973 are in dispute, ranging from 17,300m² to 37,600m² (Beynon; evidence to 1973 Public Enquiry) and 180,000m² (Kelling, Consultancy Report). Kelling did, however, include peat or clay within 8cm of the surface as well as actual exposures.

The values obtained from using photogrammetric techniques are likely to be minimum ones because scattered areas of clay eroded level with the beach are very difficult to differentiate from the rest of the sand cover, while clay covered with a thin veneer of sand would be interpreted as sand. Neither during the 1968, 1970 nor 1975 aerial surveys, nor during the 1975-1977 beach survey work, were peat or clay outcrops encountered in two areas. These were from the tidal harbour to approximately the British Steel Corporation culvert, 1.5km south of the southern breakwater; and south of the River Kenfig, towards Section V (Fig. 17.1). Absence of such deposits may be explained by the fact that the River Afan once flowed across the first area mentioned, before it was diverted during the construction of the original Port Talbot Docks. Similarly, meandering of the course of the River Kenfig may have eroded away any peat and clay exposures in the second area at an early date. North of the River Kenfig, in 1968, the exposures were rather scattered. They occurred at levels of between -2 and +2m OD between Sections N and P, while just south of the Access Ramp they were between +2 and +3m OD. By 1970, by far the largest area of peat and clay lay on Section N at between low water (∿ -4m OD) and +1m OD. A new exposure was apparent at low water just south of Section P. The highest outcrops were no longer visible. Five years later the areas of the exposures had increased and were higher up the beach.

TABLE 17.1. Areas of Peat and Clay (in m²) Exposed Along the Foreshore Between Port Talbot and Sker Point 1940-1975.

Date	Source of Data	Port Talbot-River Kenfig	S of River Kenfig-Sker Point
1940	1973 Public Enquiry	4,000	-
1952	Geological Survey	81,000 (29,000 (29,000 (a) (23,000 (b)	None mapped
1968 April	Aerial Photography	32,000	None visible
1970 June	Aerial Photography	35,000	3,500
1973 March	Public Enquiry	180,000 (c)	Not surveyed
1973 March	Public Enquiry	37,600	Not surveyed
1973 Dec.	Public Enquiry	17,300	Not surveyed
1975 Oct.	Aerial Photography	44,500	28,000

(a) Area now within Tidal Harbour.
(b) Area in vicinity of River Kenfig.
(c) Peat and clay covered by less than 8cm of sand.

While there is a seasonal element that has to be taken into account because exposures are more likely to be greater in the winter than in the summer, when the beach tends to accrete, Table 17.1 nevertheless shows that, since 1940, there has been a steady increase in the area of peat and clay exposed on the foreshore. Only Kelling's 1973 figure is anomalous and is, as noted above, based on different criteria.

South of the River Kenfig, no clay or peat exposures were apparent in the 1968 survey whilst by 1970 only a small exposure was noted just south of Section X at a level of between -3 and -2m OD. By 1975, this area had greatly increased, and extended northwards towards Section V at between -3 and zero m OD. In a similar fashion, the cobble exposures somewhat nearer high water mark (assumed to be lag) had also become more extensive.

The rate of erosion on Kenfig Beach has been very striking, the peat and clay exposures increasing from a few thousand m^2 in 1970 to over 28,000m^2 in 1975.

From the aerial distribution of the outcrops, relative to Ordnance Datum, it seems that within the Flandrian sediments exposed over the beach face there are three zones of more resistant material (peat): the first is around +3m OD; the second +2 to zero m OD; and the third -1 to -2m OD. The peat ledge at around +3m OD is very narrow and appears to be protected by the storm beach, only being revealed when this feature is pushed back.

Comparison of Beach Contours: The positions of the contours obtained from the three flights in 1968, 1970 and 1975 were compared one with another. For this purpose the 8 sections on Margam and Kenfig beaches used for the topographic surveys were supplemented by a further 8 lines, one to the north of the levelled sections and the remainder intermediate to them. Between 1968 and 1970 the Margam Beach remained fairly static, apart from some limited accretion at about mean tide level along Sections K, M, N and O. Margam and Kenfig beaches are separated by the River Kenfig, the river area being best described by Section S although R and T are also peripheral to it. Erosion was marked on Section S, notably immediately above and below zero OD. This reflects changes in the course of the river across the beach surface. Some of these changes may be man-induced as a result of sand winning in the area.

Between 1968 and 1970, the rest of Kenfig Beach became steeper; i.e. there was greater retreat of the contours at the seaward edge of the beach as compared with the landward edge. On Section X the beach gradient, between +4m OD and -3m OD, increased from approximately 1:53 to 1:44 while a marked area of erosion occurred between -1 and -3m OD across both Sections V and X. By 1975, the areas of erosion had moved further landward ranging from approximately zero to +3m OD on both Margam and Kenfig beaches and, like that around the River Kenfig between 1968 and 1970, may be partially man-induced especially as far as lines 'N' to 'R' are concerned. The erosion had the effect of increasing the exposures of peat and clay over much of the area of the two beaches.

Accretion is apparent over much of Section S (River Kenfig, Fig. 17.1) and over nearly all the sections from N to Z at or near low water mark.

The net result of the changes between 1968 and 1975 (Fig. 17.2) indicates that, in spite of some build-up of the beaches between 1970 and 1975 below mid-tide level, the beaches have suffered erosion.

In addition to the foregoing comparison, the height information was used to estimate the net change in volume of material over the period 1968-75, along similar lines to those decided for the 1975-77 beach levelling data (see below). It suggests a net loss of approximately 2.8×10^6 tonnes of material, equivalent to an overall fall in beach level of 0.40m between Port Talbot Tidal Harbour and Sker Point over the 7-year period. This is greater than the potential error of the survey (Table 17.2). The plotting height error for surveys based on 1:6000 scale aerial photography is $\pm$0.15m. The least amount by which the beach could have changed between 1968-75 was then calculated by assuming the maximum potential plotting error. This gave a figure of approximately 800,000 tonnes which was equivalent to a drop of 0.11m in beach level if the loss of the material were spread evenly over

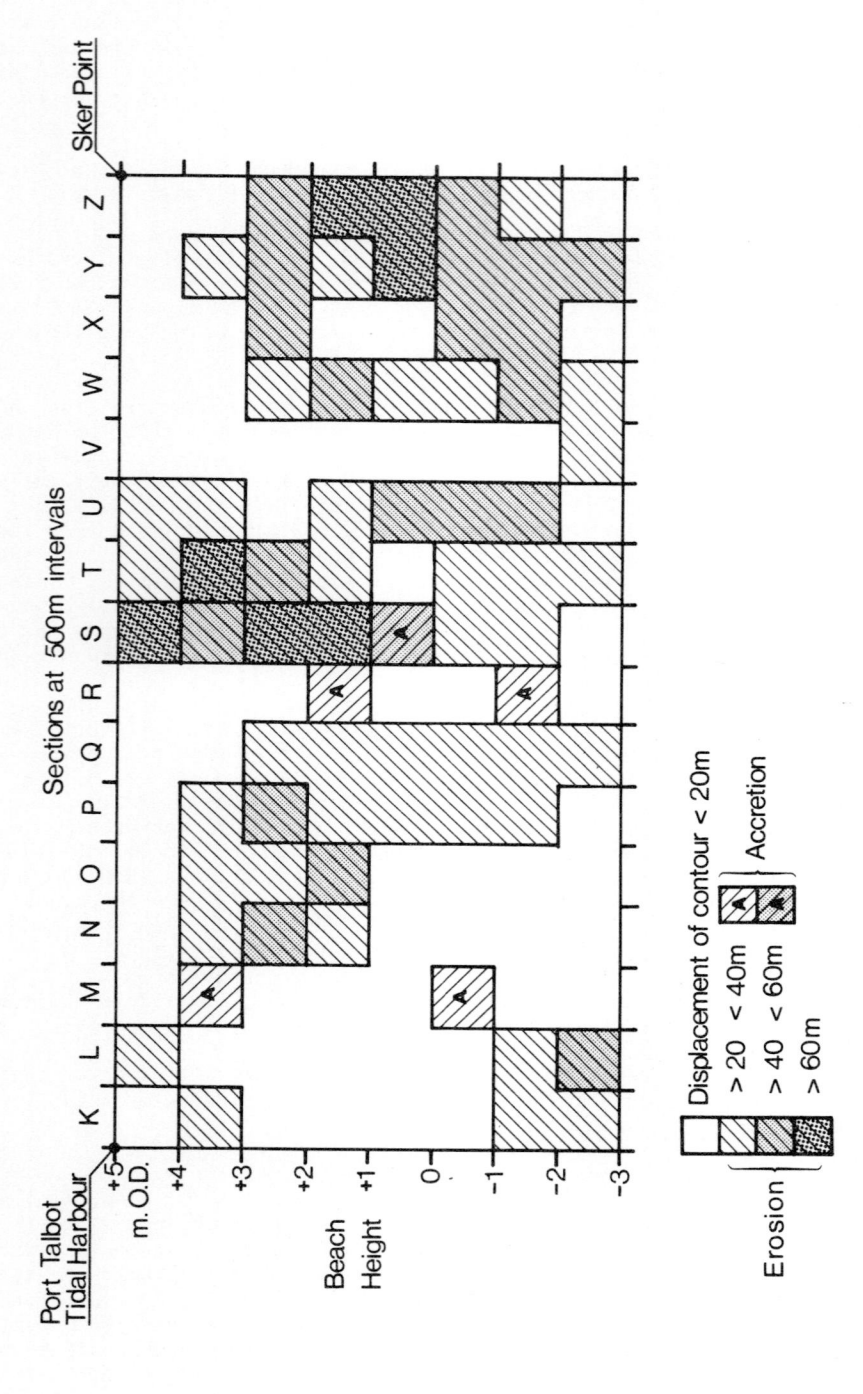

Figure 17.2. Schematic plan showing change in position of beach contours 1968-75, based on aerial surveys.

TABLE 17.2. Summary of Calculations Regarding Beach Level Between Port Talbot Harbour and Sker Point.

	Beach Overall	Port Talbot-River Kenfig	River Kenfig-Sker Point
(a) Beach level fall attributable to sand-winning (m)+			
Pre-1964 known extraction	0.05	0.06*	0.04*
estimated extraction	0.09	0.12*	0.08*
1964-73 known extraction	0.13	0.19*	0.10*
estimated extraction	0.16	0.24*	0.10*
Total period known extraction	0.18	0.21*	0.15*
estimated extraction	0.25	0.31*	0.18*
+ See Carr and Blackley (1977)			
* Assumes no longshore transfer north and south of River Kenfig.			
(b) Beach level fall calculated from aerial photographs (m).			
1968-75 calculated	0.40	0.33	0.53
calculated less maximum potential plotting error for scale of map	0.11	0.09	0.15
(c) Beach fall calculated from surveyed profiles (m).			
October 1975 to April 1977	0.02	<0.01	0.06
October 1975 to October 1977	<0.01	0.04	0.00

Note: The beach width and length used for these calculations varies slightly: (a) uses a mean low tide width of 350m and a distance from the Port Talbot Docks breakwater; (b) and (c) are observed distances down beach with a longshore distance calculated from the new Port Talbot Tidal Harbour southern breakwater.

the whole area.

In sum, the 7-year timespan covered by the photogrammetric surveys showed a continuation of the trends indicated in the cartographic evidence dating from the mid-nineteenth century (see Chapter 7). However, the rates of change were much greater.

Evidence from Beach Profiles (1975-1979).

Profile Changes: Fig. 17.3 shows comparative profiles for 6 of the 11 Sections surveyed monthly between September/October 1975 and April/May 1977. Each pair of profiles correspond to the maximum volume change for that section during the 18-month period (see below). This is not the same as the conventional 'sweep zone' because not all parts of the profile represent maximum or minimum values. The seven calendar months October to April account for 19 out of 22 of such profiles and suggest that severe winter storms were the most likely cause of these changes. Owens (1977), describing the 'storm coast' environment of the Magdalen Islands in the Gulf of St. Lawrence, noted a similar phenomenon. He wrote: 'Comparison of the summer and winter sweep zone profiles showed that during the winter there was a very significant increase in the variation within the sweep zone. The overall elevation of the profiles tended to be lower during the winter but the major difference between

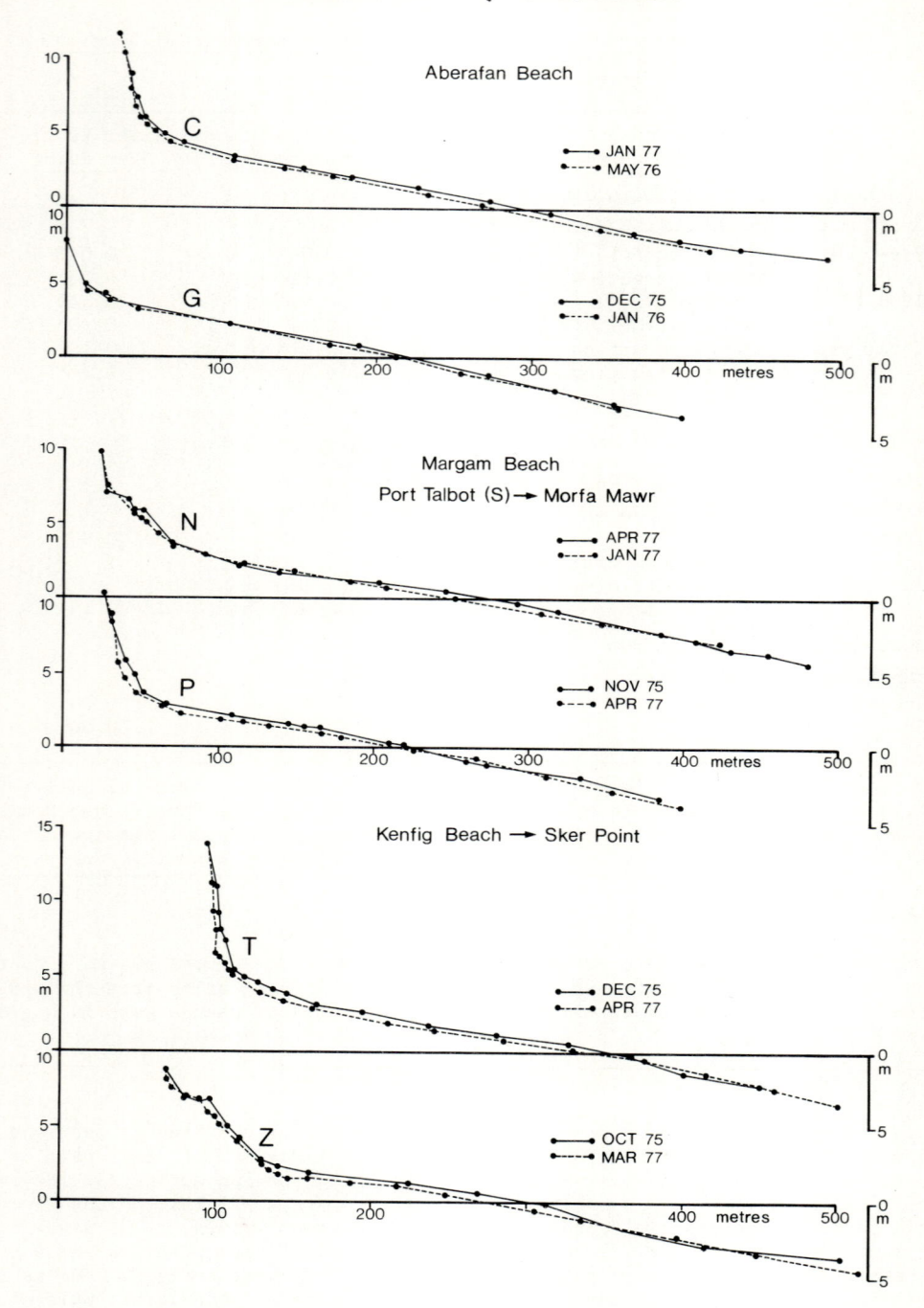

Figure 17.3. Profiles showing maximum range during period Oct 1975-Apr 1977.

Beaches and Supralittoral Deposits

the two sets of profiles is the degree of variation. This resulted from the greater frequency and intensity of storm wave action during the winter'.

It is interesting to note that for Swansea Bay, with the exception of April 1977 (5 instances), no month is represented by more than 2 extreme records. There is thus little tendency for consistent erosion or accretion of the beaches overall, as the April 1977 data for the adjacent Sections 'N' and 'P' demonstrate (Fig. 17.3). In the case of Section N, this month had the maximum volume of sediment, yet Section P (only 1km to the south) had its minimum quantity. The recession of the sand dunes on the line of Section T (and Z) can also be clearly seen in Fig. 17.3. Between September 1975 and October 1977, this resulted in dune retreat of about 5m; from the latter date up to June 1979, a further 4m was eroded.

Figure 17.4 depicts the results of a number of surveys along line 'Q' from November 1976 to June 1979, on a somewhat different basis. Height readings were taken at a series of standard positions and a mean profile calculated, together with range and standard deviations. The beach zone showing the least change (approximately 9.5cm) is at about mid-tide level and thus subject to the shortest duration of wave attack. The relative stability of beaches at or just above mid-tide level has been commented upon by Bascom (1951). This part of Section Q is also the most resistant area in cone penetrometer tests. Comparisons between height range and Cone Index (Davidson, 1967) give correlation coefficients of 0.88 and 0.867 and a confidence level better than .99 (i.e. 1 possibility in 100 of the result occurring by chance)(Blackley and Carr, 1977).

Maximum variation in height for 'Q' was near the top of the sand beach and equalled 63cm in 3 months, with successive falls being 13.5, 6.0, 27.0, and 16.5cm. The first and last values of this group are over fortnightly intervals, while the others are changes over a one-month period. Weekly changes reported by King (1972) ranged between 100cm for Marsden Beach, County Durham (median size range 1.47$\emptyset$) and 2 to 5cm for Rhossili Beach, South Wales (median size range 2.12$\emptyset$, i.e. identical with this beach).

Because the monthly changes were usually very small (<50cm) the vertical scale on the profiles has had to be exaggerated in order to show differences between surveys. Sections C, G, N, P, T and Z (Fig. 17.3) all have a vertical exaggeration of x10 and Section Q (Fig. 17.4) one of x25. This change in proportions disguises the comparatively flat nature of the prototype beach over most of its length.

Table 17.3 records the maximum change in elevation for each section during the 18-month period within the ranges +3m to zero m OD and zero to -4m OD. The +3m value is approximately mean high water level. It was preferred to use this level rather than the level of high water spring tides because, under calm conditions, the complicating effect of the pebble and cobble component at the back of certain sections along the beach is effectively eliminated. Comparisons are therefore restricted to the sand beach alone.

Table 17.3 suggests that the beaches become progressively less stable from north to south, from Section C at least as far as Section V and probably as far as Z (which has suffered the maximum overall loss). Although one atypical value for Section P, at low water level, proves a marked exception to this observation; other discrepancies are very minor. Correlations between maximum height range per section (x-axis) against distance from C (y-axis), for example, give a confidence level of .99.

Table 17.3 also shows that, for certain specified wave directions and wave characteristics, there is a clear correlation between computed wave energy reaching the beach and the overall height range per section. However, this correlation is restricted to that stretch of the beach (Sections C to T) where the alignment of the foreshore is at right angles to the direction of wave approach. Further south

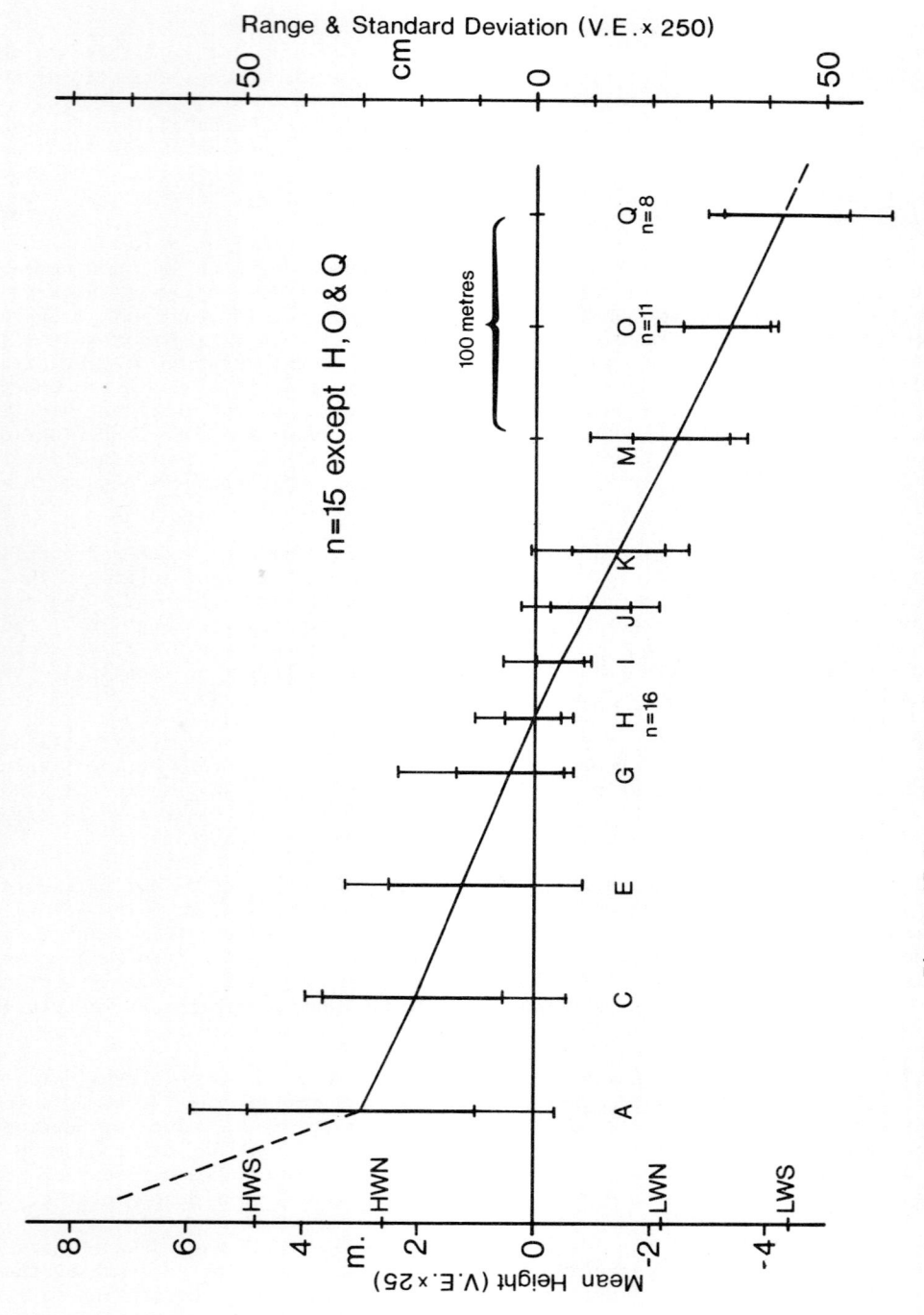

Figure 17.4. Section Q. Changes Nov 1976 to June 1979.

TABLE 17.3. Beach Sections: Maximum Change in Height (m) at any Point, Between Sept/Oct 1975 and April/May 1977.

	Section	Between Mean high water (~+3) and 0m OD	0m to low water spring tides (~-4m OD)	Overall Average	Max
Aberafan Beach	C	0.4	0.4	0.4	0.4
	E	0.45	0.55	0.5	0.55
	G	0.4	0.55	0.475	0.55
Margam Beach	L	0.6	0.45	0.525	0.6
	N	0.6	0.55	0.575	0.6
	P	0.6	1.1	0.85	1.1
	R	0.4	0.65	0.525	0.65
Kenfig Beach	T	0.7	0.7	0.7	0.7
	V	1.1	0.9	1.0	1.1
	X	0.7	0.95	0.825	0.95
	Z	0.8	0.8	0.8	0.8
Significance Level: (Height range v distance from Section C)	C→Z	.99	.98	.99	.99
	C→V	.95	.95	.99	.98
(Height range v computed wave energy)	C→T	.90	.999	.999	-
	C→Z	N.S.	N.S.	N.S.	-

For computed wave energy, the following were used: an offshore wave direction of 270°; T_z = 8s and H_s = 1m. Significance levels are somewhat lower with approach directions of 260° and 250°. (N.S. = Not Significant at any level).

(Sections V to Z), such a relationship between beach orientation and wave direction does not hold; neither, then, does the relation between beach profile variability and computed wave energy reaching the shoreline.

The Ogwr Borough Council have records of surveys taken by consultants (W.S. Atkins and Partners), their predecessors (Penybont RDC) and themselves on Kenfig Beach. These date from 1958 onwards and were carried out at varying time intervals. A series of 3 sections falls within a strip of beach 200m either side of Section V. These sections run from a point above high water mark to approximately mid-tide position and suggest that between October 1959 and April 1977 the beach level dropped by at least 3m over this length with a maximum fall of 4.5m. The maximum change recorded on Section V by IOS between September 1975 and April 1977 was rather less than 1m.

Calculations of Changes in Quantity of Beach Material: The overall changes in area between each survey for the Aberafan, Margam and Kenfig beach profiles can be seen in Figure 17.5. Each section was split into two taking the midwater position (approximately zero OD). This enabled any differences in response between the upper and lower beaches to be seen. For most of the months a change in the area of the lower part of the beach was reflected by a change in the same direction of the upper beach. During the two winter periods, although there were extremes of accre-

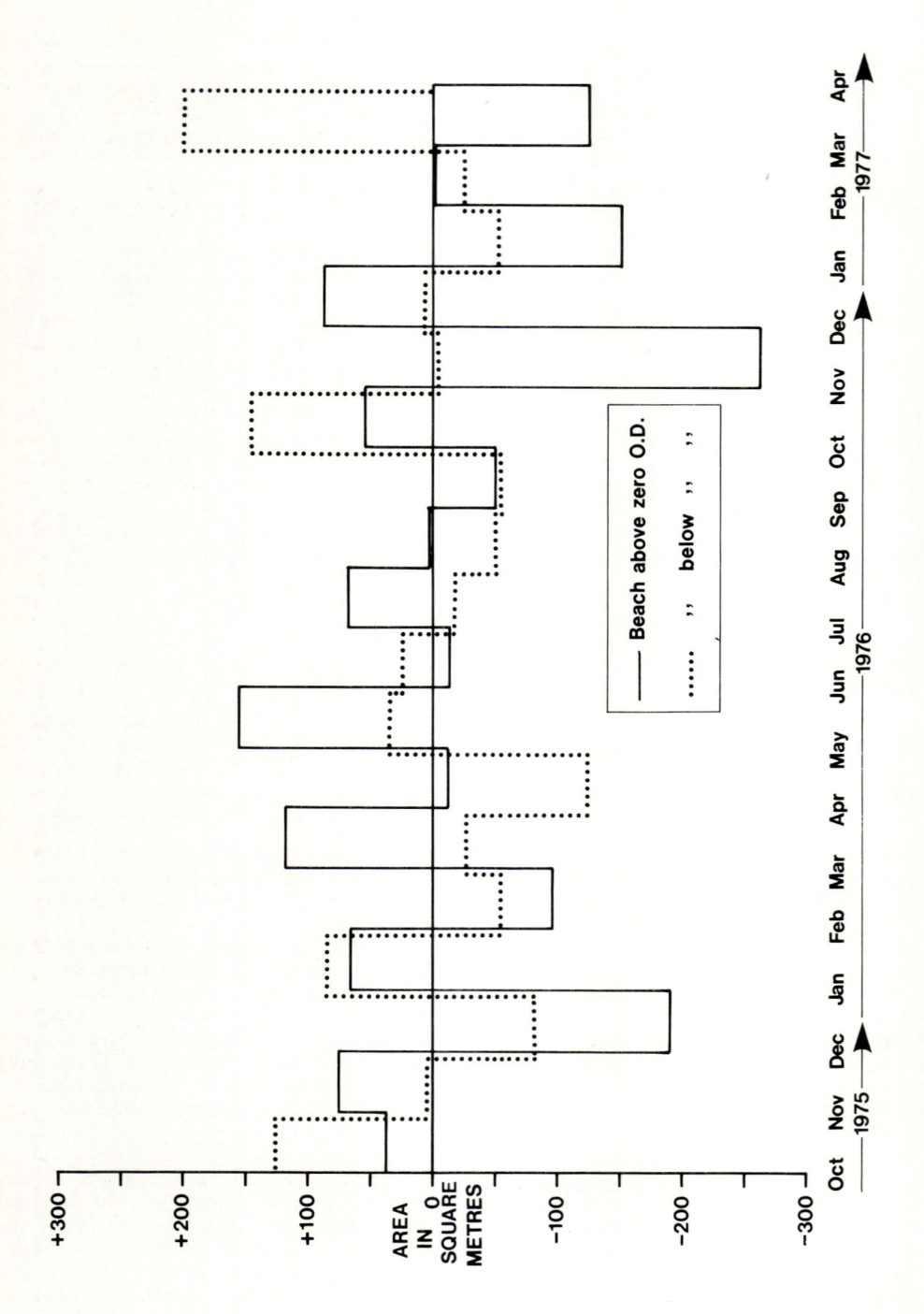

Figure 17.5. Overall change in area along Sections between successive months. Upper and lower halves (above and below zero O.D.).

tion and erosion, the net effect was one of erosion. For the intervening summer period the extremes were not nearly so evident, the net effect during this time being accretion. These results support observations on other beaches (e.g. Shepard, 1950; Fox and Davis, 1978) that the higher energy waves of the winter tend to comb down the beach and remove the material while the smaller waves during the summer have a more constructive effect. Interestingly however, Sonu and Russell (1967) found so-called 'summer' and 'winter' profiles within a few hundred metres of each other at the same time. As noted above, variations in trend between adjacent sections are also found in Swansea Bay.

More information can be gained from comparing the total areal change in material on each specific section over the 18-month period. Although for an individual section the monthly gains and losses were appreciable, the resulting net imbalance was relatively small. On most sections, the major loss of material took place between the backshore and the mid-tide mark. Although there was some gain in material between midwater and low water, thus making the sections shelve more gently over the period autumn 1975 to spring 1977, and so contrasting with the steepening shown by the long-term cartographic evidence, it accounted for under half the material lost higher up the beach. More specifically, on the Aberafan Beach the two end sections remained fairly constant (with some net gain on G) whilst the centre one underwent some erosion. The amount of change on Margam Beach was greater than Aberafan but there was no consistent pattern between one section and another, erosion on one section apparently being balanced by accretion on the next. On Kenfig Beach, the one notable feature was the consistent losses on Section Z, amounting to an average fall in height of 21cm over its entire length. It is here where computed wave approach and beach alignment are most discordant.

It is possible, if the results are treated with caution, to arrive at an order of magnitude for the amount of sand gained or lost from the beaches during the 18-month period. The assumption has to be made that the beach 500m either side of a line of section responds in the same way as the section itself. The results (converted into tonnes, where 2.08 tonnes = m^3 (Terzaghi and Peck, 1968)) are as follows:

Aberafan Beach	8,320 tonnes loss
Margam Beach	31,200 tonnes loss
Kenfig Beach	166,920 tonnes loss

In order to eliminate seasonal effects, all the beach sections were resurveyed in October 1977 (i.e. after two complete years). The net results for the whole period are:

Aberafan Beach	+ 22,880 tonnes gain	
Margam Beach	-166,400 tonnes loss	(all due to changes during the construction of a new outfall).
Kenfig Beach	+ 9,360 tonnes gain	

For Kenfig Beach, the continuing losses on Section Z (which, by October 1977 was equal to 29cm) were outweighed by gains around the River Kenfig during the 1977 summer season. A proportion of the latter is likely to have been directly derived from the eroded dune face nearby (see Section T in Fig. 17.3).

It will be noted that the 2-year net total quoted above is under 6% of the value obtained from the photogrammetry for 1968-75. Taking all 3 of the beaches together, the net change between October 1975 and April 1977 is equivalent to an overall fall in height of 0.021m and, that between April and October 1977 to an overall gain of 0.007m. Such accuracy is outside that attainable in surveying profiles in an intertidal environment.

The 1975-77 data show a relative stability not found in the photogrammetric evidence for the 7-year period immediately previous.

Particle Size Analyses

As noted above, samples were taken bimonthly from high, mid and low water lines on the 11 surveyed sections. The mean and standard deviations of the sand fraction can be seen in Table 17.4 and Figure 17.6. From Figure 17.6 it can be seen that

TABLE 17.4. Mean Grain Size and Standard Deviation in Ø Units for Samples Collected along the Eleven Survey Sections on Aberafan, Margam and Kenfig Beaches at HW, MW and LW. (n=6) For Location see Figure 17.1.

Section	HW Mean Ø	HW Std Dev	MW Mean Ø	MW Std Dev	LW Mean Ø	LW Std Dev
C	2.12	0.44	2.09	0.70	2.53	0.89
E	2.26	0.29	2.16	0.47	2.89	0.52
G	2.08	0.32	1.97	0.44	2.52	0.70
L	2.05	0.38	1.76	0.73	2.38	0.62
N	2.03	0.46	1.98	0.58	2.04	0.61
P	2.19	0.40	2.07	0.45	2.22	0.58
R	2.25	0.42	2.25	0.53	2.31	0.70
T	2.00	0.39	1.85	0.72	2.20	0.67
V	1.61	0.74	1.74	0.86	2.26	0.84
X	2.02	0.58	2.05	0.76	2.32	0.58
Z	2.00	0.69	2.14	1.00	2.50	0.69

the finest sand material was always at low water mark. Bruun (1954) regarded a decrease in grain size from the shore towards the sea as a sign of profile maturity. The concentration of fine material on Aberafan Beach may be due to the close proximity of the River Neath. The MW samples were coarser than the HW samples on Aberafan and Margam Beaches, but this situation was reversed for the last three sections (V, X and Z) on the Kenfig Beach. It is possible that this is due to the fact that, although the beaches are generally wet, samples collected at high water on Margam and especially Aberafan beaches tend to contain a higher proportion of fine windblown sand. This theory is supported if the sorting coefficients are compared, the material in the Aberafan and Margam HW samples being better sorted than any of the others.

Along the foreshore, there was a tendency for the material to become finer towards the centre of Aberafan Beach, where the finest sample had a mean grain size of 2.89 Ø; towards Sker Point and, unlike Kelling's observations (Kelling, 1973), towards the River Kenfig.

However, individual results were somewhat variable from survey to survey. The results tended to be inconclusive and, in general, the use of moment measures and particle sizes were not considered to be particularly helpful in the elucidation of sediment transport processes and patterns. Because of the local irregularities and temporal changes, it has proved impossible to make the extended correlations reached by such workers as McCave (1978) for East Anglia or even by Kelling (1973) for the beaches described here. Fluorescent tracer experiments have indicated that net longshore transport is extremely slow (see Chapter 12) when compared with that described by Davis (1978) for apparently lower energy beaches in the Gulf of Mexico. Similarly, while sedimentary structures such as the linguoid ripples described by Kelling (1973) do occur from time to time, they are atypical, and such directions

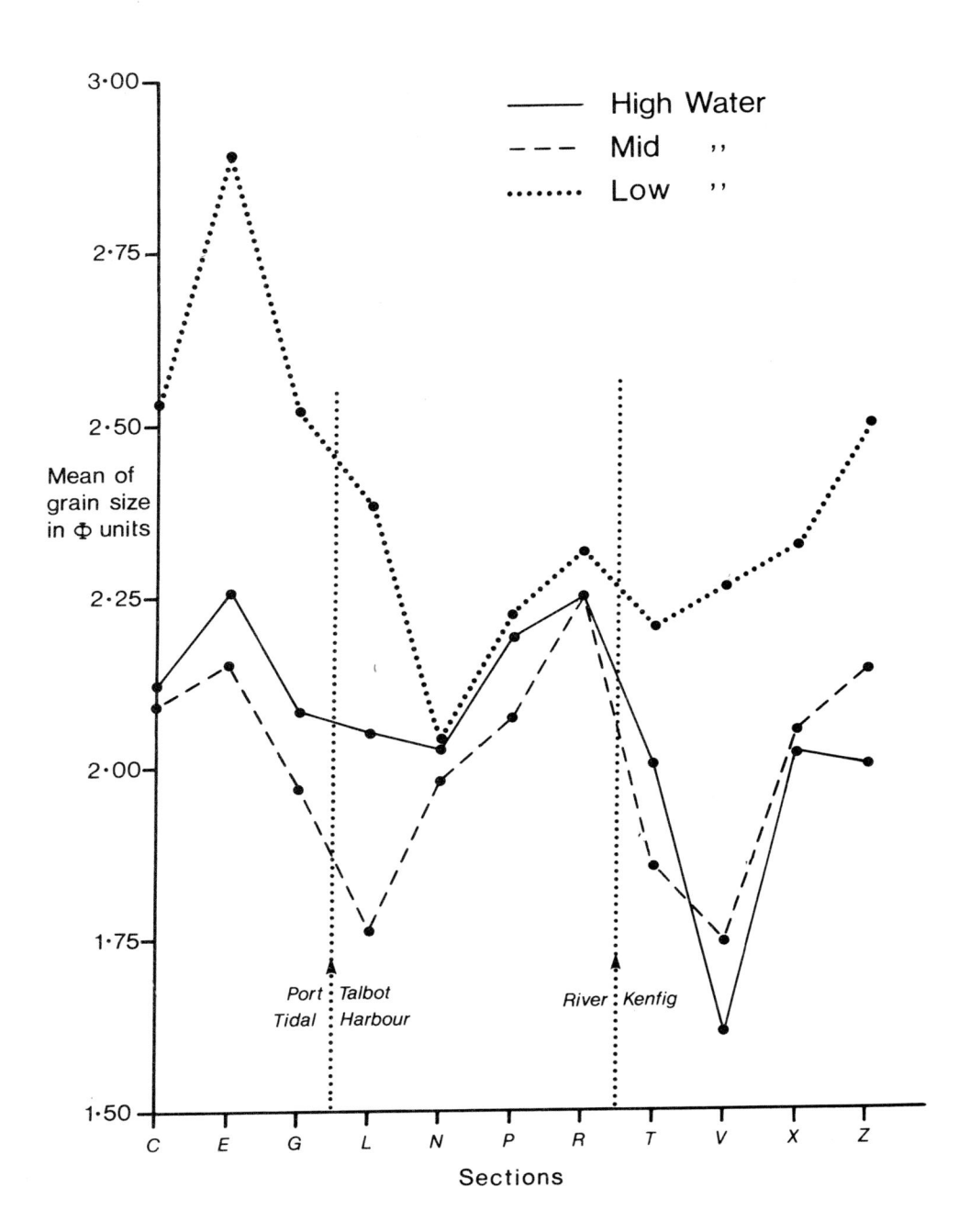

Figure 17.6. Plots of mean phi size of samples collected at HW, MW, and LW against appropriate survey section along Aberafan, Margam and Kenfig beaches. (n=6).

of transport as they indicate may well be unrepresentative.

CONCLUSIONS

The topographical surveys carried out during the period October 1975 to October 1977 demonstrated the susceptibility of the beaches along the eastern shore of Swansea Bay to change. However such changes were variable both in respect of time and location. Except at Section Z, the most southerly of all the sections, where continual losses of sediment occurred, no consistent trends emerged over the two-year period. Taking the beaches as a whole, the net imbalance of sediment was small.

The absence of well-defined trends made the period 1975-77 very distinct from that of 1968-75 which was covered by photogrammetry. The photogrammetric analysis showed an appreciable fall in beach level, possibly as much as 0.4m overall. Calculations indicate that the volume of sediment 'lost' to the system was very similar to that removed from the beaches by sand and gravel winning up to its prohibition in 1973 (Table 17.2).

Nevertheless, the seven-year period 1968-75 merely seems to have shown, in an extreme form, the recession of the beach that had already been indicated in the longer-term historical evidence. The timespan 1975-77 may well have been too short to demonstrate any but the most obvious trends and, in any event, was probably complicated by adjustments of beach level as a response to the earlier phase of sand extraction

ACKNOWLEDGEMENTS

The work described in this paper was supported financially by the Department of the Environment. The authors would also like to express their appreciation of help from the Hydrographic Department (MOD) regarding source material, and to the Scottish Reactor Centre for radiocarbon dating under their reference SRR-967.

REFERENCES

Bagnold, R.A. (1940). Beach formation by waves: some model experiments in a wave tank. *J. Instn. Civ. Engrs.*, 15, 27-52.

Bascom, W.N. (1951). The relationship between sand size and beach face slope. *Trans. Am. Geophys. Un.*, 32, 866-74.

Blackley, M.W.L. (1978). Swansea Bay (Sker) Project Topic Report. 3. Geophysical interpretation and sediment characteristics of the offshore and foreshore areas. *Inst. Oceanographic Sciences, Report* 60/78, 42pp. Unpublished Manuscript.

Blackley, M.W.L., and Carr, A.P. (1977). Swansea Bay (Sker) Project Topic Report. 2. Evidence for beach stability. Photographic and topographic measurements. *Inst. Oceanographic Sciences Report* 51/77, 45pp. Unpublished Manuscript.

Bruun, P. (1954). Coast erosion and the development of beach profiles. *US Beach Erosion Board., Tech. Mem.*, 44, 79pp and Appendix.

Carr, A.P., and Blackley, M.W.L. (1977). Swansea Bay (Sker) Project Topic Report 1(a) Introduction. (b) Long term changes in the coastline. *Inst. Oceanographic Sciences, Report* 42/77, 63pp. Unpublished Manuscript.

Davidson, D.T. (1965). Penetrometer measurements. In: Black, C.A. (Ed.). *Methods of Soil Analysis*, Part 1. Amer. Soc. Agronomy, Madison, Wisconsin, U.S.A.

Davis, R.A. (1978). Beach sedimentology of Mustang and Padre Islands. A time-series approach. *J. Geol.*, 86, 35-46.

Fox, W.T., and Davis, R.A. (1978). Seasonal variation in beach erosion and sedim-

entation on the Oregon coast. *Geol. Soc. Am. Bull.*, *89*, 1541-1549.
Godwin, H., and Willis, J. (1961). Cambridge University Natural Radiocarbon Measurements. *Radiocarbon*, *3*, 60-76.
Kelling, G. (1973). Morfa Mawr beach - a preliminary evaluation of the effects of sand and gravel extraction. Unpublished Report to the Council of the Borough of Port Talbot. 17pp.
King, C.A.M. (1972). *Beaches and Coasts*. 2nd Ed., Edward Arnold, London, 570pp.
McCave, I.N. (1978). Grain-size trends and transport along beaches. Example from eastern England. *Mar. Geol.*, *28*, M43-51.
Owens, E.H. (1977). Temporal variations in beach and nearshore dynamics. *J. Sedim. Petrol.*, *47*, 168-190.
Shepard, F.P. (1950). Longshore bars and longshore troughs. *U.S. Beach Erosion Board, Tech. Mem.*, *15*, 32pp.
Sonu, C.J., and Russell, R.J. (1967). Topographic changes in the surf zone profile. *10th Conf. on Coast. Eng., Tokyo, 1966*. 502-524.
Terzaghi, K., and Peck, R.B. (1968). *Soil Mechanics in Engineering Practice*. 2nd. Ed. Wiley, New York, 729pp.

18. RHEOLOGY OF COHESIVE SUSPENSIONS

R. Bryant[*], A. E. James[**] and D. J. A. Williams[*]

[*]Department of Chemical Engineering
[**]Department of Oceanography, University College, Swansea, U.K.

ABSTRACT

Model and natural cohesive suspensions behave as pseudoplastic fluids. The rheological properties of model suspensions of kaolinite and quartz are interpreted in terms of inter-particle forces and the specific modes of interaction between the constituent minerals. This provides a rational basis for the interpretation of the rheology of the more complex natural cohesive sediments.

KEYWORDS

Rheology; Cohesive sediments; Flocculation; Kaolinite/Quartz suspensions; Estuarine muds; Bristol Channel.

INTRODUCTION

The rheological properties of cohesive suspensions are of theoretical and practical interest in the analysis of engineering problems, such as the erosion and transport of natural cohesive sediments like mud (Krone, 1963, 1972; Migniot, 1968; Peirce et al., 1976). An understanding of the flow behaviour of cohesive sediments is also important in the analysis of environmental problems (Kirby and Parker, 1977).

Interpretation of the rheological behaviour of cohesive sediments requires a full understanding of the physico-chemical hydrodynamics involved. Clearly this is a formidable task in the case of mud suspensions from estuaries due to the complex nature of their particle size distributions (mainly in the colloidal range), mineralogy, chemical properties of the suspending medium and sometimes their biology (Neiheisel, 1966; Krone, 1972; Schubel, 1978). Satisfactory in situ measurements of the physical variables of importance, such as the temporal and spatial variation in particle concentration and fluid velocity is problematical, particularly in high-energy, high-turbidity environments such as the Bristol Channel (Kirby and Parker, 1977; Bryant et al., 1980).

The complexity of the natural environment has prompted laboratory work on model cohesive sediments thereby allowing a measure of control over the physico-chemical variables involved (see e.g., Einsele et al., 1974).

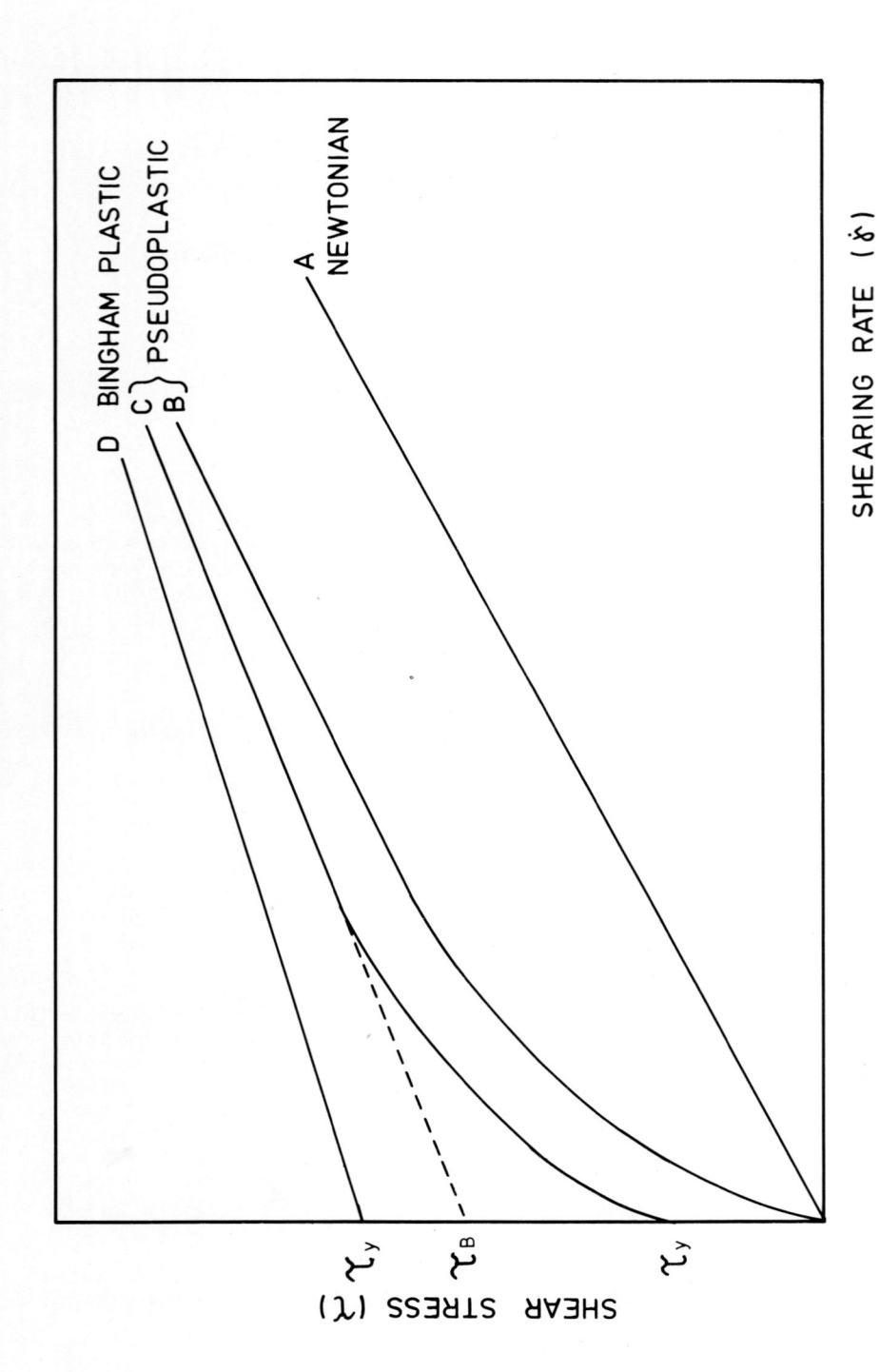

Figure 18.1. Rheological models.

In this chapter, various aspects of the experimental and theoretical work on the rheology of model and natural cohesive suspensions being done in the writers' laboratory are reviewed.

EXPERIMENTAL

The apparatus used for rheological measurements in the writers' laboratory is the Weissenberg Rheogoniometer (Sangamo Ltd., Bognor Regis, U.K.) fitted with a stainless steel coni-cylindrical cell (Mooney and Ewart, 1934) of the following dimensions:

Outer radius (R_o)	45.1mm
Inner radius (R_i)	44.2mm
Cylinder height	46.4mm
Cone angle	0.97°

The errors involved in the assumption of constant shear rate in the couette and cone and plate sections of the Mooney cell may be calculated (Fredrickson, 1964). Thus for the couette section the relative difference in shear stress between inner and outer cylinders ($R_o/R_i \simeq 1.02$) is 3.9%, while that for the cone and plate geometry is 0.029%. Modifications to this apparatus to control the suspension temperature and pH within the Mooney cell are described by Williams (1976). It is necessary to do rheological measurements not only over the range of shearing rates ($\dot{\gamma}$) typical of the benthic boundary layer ($0 \simeq \dot{\gamma} \leqslant 20 s^{-1}$) but also over as wide a range as possible so that an accurate description of the rheological behaviour of a cohesive suspension is obtained. Further, if measurements are to be used with any confidence in quantitative analysis, then the rheometer must be capable of providing absolute values of shear stress (T) as a function of shear rate. Preferably, there should be constant shear rate throughout the sample under test. In these respects, the Weissenberg Rheogoniometer and Mooney cell largely avoids the practical and theoretical limitations of the rheometers used by Krone (1963) and Migniot (1964).

Model cohesive sediments

The rheology of model cohesive suspensions consisting of kaolinite-quartz mixtures has been investigated by Williams and James (1980), under environmental conditions approximating those of an estuary, namely pH 6-8 and salt concentration $\leqslant 10^{-1}$M NaCl. The preparation and characterisation of kaolinite as homoionic substituted sodium kaolinite is described elsewhere (Williams and Williams, 1978); the characterisation of colloidal quartz (size, shape, specific surface area and elemental analysis) is given by Michael (1978). Kaolinite-quartz suspensions (volumetric concentration of solids C = 0.02) behave as pseudoplastic materials exhibiting non-Newtonian behaviour at low shear rates ($\leqslant 100 s^{-1}$) and become Newtonian at high rates of shear ($100 s^{-1} < \dot{\gamma} < 1673 s^{-1}$)(see Fig. 18.1). Rheograms for 100% quartz suspensions were Newtonian (curve A- Fig. 18.1) for all experimental conditions; evidently the secondary minimum flocculation possible in these chemical environments is unable to withstand even low rates of shear ($\dot{\gamma} \to 0$)(Michael, 1978).

Estuarine mud suspensions

The flow behaviour of mud suspensions from Rotterdam and Brisbane has been examined (Williams and James, 1979); typical rheograms are shown in Fig. 18.2. Both muds exhibited increasing pseudoplasticity with increased volumetric solids concentration in the range $0.0116 \leqslant C \leqslant 0.124$ for Brisbane mud and $0.0118 \leqslant C \leqslant 0.126$ for Rotterdam mud. Mud suspensions at C = 0.0039 behaved as Newtonian fluids throughout the experimental range of shear rates $0.0167 s^{-1} \leqslant \dot{\gamma} \leqslant 1673 s^{-1}$. This pseudoplastic behaviour is to be contrasted with the assumption of a Bingham plastic model for

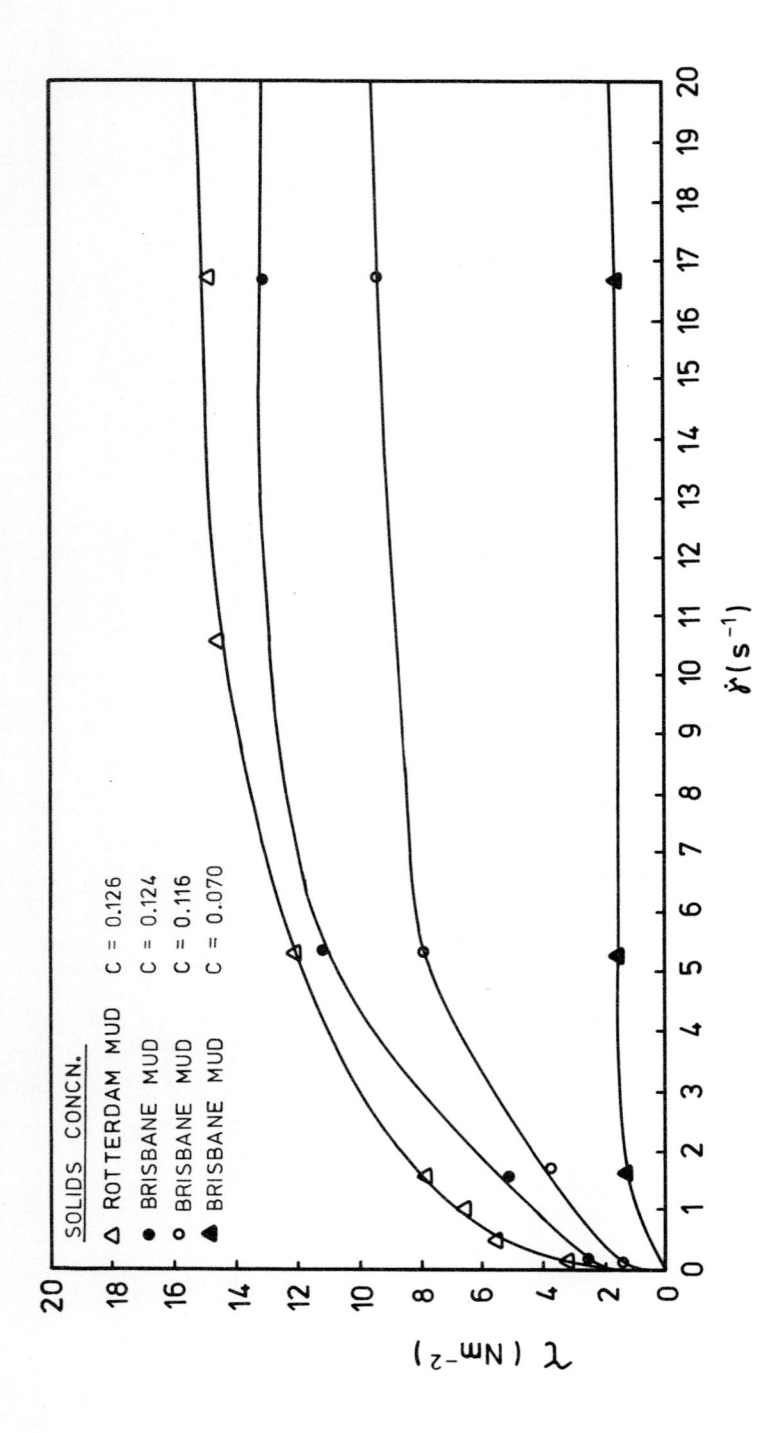

Figure 18.2. Rheogram for mud suspensions, pH of Brisbane mud = 7.7; pH of Rotterdam mud = 7.1. Salinity = 30°/oo.

highly concentrated estuarine muds (Krone, 1963; Migniot, 1968)(Fig. 18.1, curve D). There is no clear evidence for the existence of a lower critical yield stress T_y (Fig. 18.1, curve C) in these muds, however its presence may well depend on solids concentration.

DISCUSSION

The pseudoplastic (shear thinning) behaviour of model suspensions and muds suggests that flocculation is an important factor influencing the flow behaviour of cohesive sediments. In these suspensions floc structure is progressively broken down with increasing shear rate. An analysis of the flocculation process and the manner in which flocculation affects rheological behaviour is a complex problem, but it is clear that interparticle forces are of major importance. These forces are:

(a)   van der Waals' attractive forces;
(b)   coulombic (electrostatic) forces which may be attractive or repulsive, and
(c)   forces which involve the behaviour of organic molecules adsorbed on the particle surface.

In the absence of (c) flocculation is largely the result of van der Waals' forces, whereas stability against flocculation is attributable to repulsion between similarly charged electrical double layers. Stability is commonly assessed with the aid of a potential energy diagram in which the free energy of interaction V_T, the sum of the van der Waals' attraction energy V_A and the electrical repulsion energy V_R is plotted as a function of the distance of separation between two particles (Ottewill, 1973). However, in the presence of a velocity gradient (orthokinesis), stability analysis requires simultaneous consideration of interparticle and hydrodynamic forces. Such an analysis has presently been done only for the relative motion of two equi-sized, uniformly charged spheres in a laminar velocity gradient (Zeichner and Schowalter, 1977). However, the suspensions of interest contain dissimilarly charged particles of non-uniform shape at relatively high solids concentration and as such, present an intractable problem in terms of the Zeichner and Schowalter analysis. Accordingly, we are restricted to an examination of the flocculation process and its influence on rheology, in terms of interparticle energies at equilibrium, as a function of chemical environment. Such an analysis will provide, on energetic grounds, an indication of the most likely mode of interaction between particles.

Calculation of V_T for two particles requires specification of the following (see Flegmann *et al.* (1969); Williams (1976):

(a)   particle shape;
(b)   mode of interaction of particles, and
(c)   zeta potential (ζ).

In our analysis we approximate the face and edge of a kaolinite particle by a plate and cylinder respectively, and the quartz particle by a sphere. In a kaolinite-quartz mixture, various interactions between particles must be considered, e.g., kaolinite particles may interact in the following modes: face-face, face-edge and edge-edge. Additional interactions are quartz-kaolinite face, quartz-kaolinite edge and quartz-quartz. Calculation of zeta potential for kaolinite is not a simple matter, since the particle has two dissimilar electrical double layers. Estimates of ζ for the face and edge for salt concentrations in the range 10^{-4}M to 10^{-1}M NaCl and pH 6-8 are obtained from electrophoretic mobility data by the method of Williams and Williams (1978).

The variation of V_T with separation distance for the various interaction modes indicates that for kaolinite particles, the face-edge mode is the most likely, leading

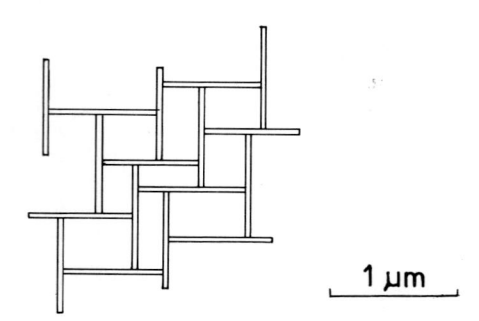

(a) Card-House.

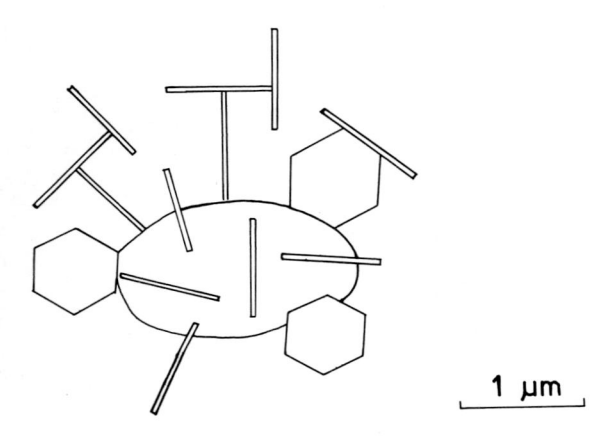

(b) 'Pin-cushion'.

Figure 18.3(a) and (b)   Floc Structures.

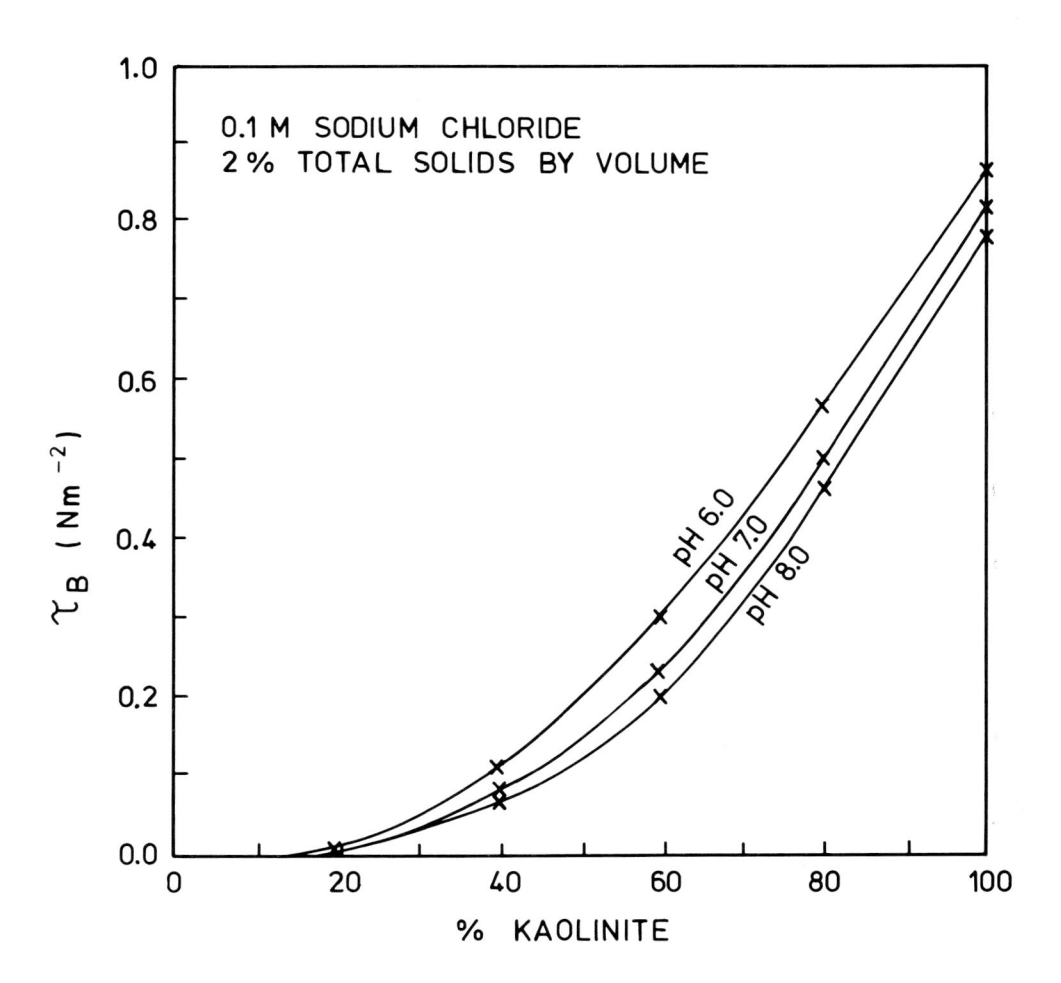

Figure 18.4. Upper Bingham yield stress (T_B) as a function of the % of kaolinite in a kaolinite/quartz mixture.

to 'card-house' flocs (Fig. 18.3a), while in kaolinite-quartz suspensions, the dominant interactions will occur between kaolinite edges and quartz particles giving rise to a 'pin-cushion' floc structure (Fig. 18.3b)(Williams and James, 1980).

The upper Bingham yield stress T_B (Fig. 18.1) may be regarded as a measure of the work done in disrupting the floc structure in a cohesive suspension. The reduction in T_B with increase in quartz % (Fig. 18.4) is readily explained in terms of interparticle forces: in wholly kaolinite suspensions 'card-house' flocs by their very nature will exhibit strong floc-floc linkages while 'pin-cushion' flocs in a mixture will show less interlinking and hence a low resistance to shear. For mud suspensions T_B varied in a non-linear manner with C (Williams and James, 1979).

In estuarine sediments, particularly heavily contaminated ones of industrial estuaries, the effects of specific interactions noted in model systems may be masked by the adsorption of organic molecules on particles. The precise effect of such molecules on the electrokinetic properties and stability against flocculation of colloidal particles such as clay minerals and quartz in estuary and coastal waters is poorly understood (Neihof and Loeb (1974); Hunter and Liss (1979)). It is clear however that in the benthic boundary layer, with its velocity distribution, that in addition to surface charge considerations, it is necessary to consider orthokinesis. The significance of orthokinetic flocculation in the benthic boundary layer has been discussed by Krone (1972). Edzwald et al. (1974) have shown that differences in orthokinetic flocculation characteristics of the minerals kaolinite and illite satisfactorily accounts for the spatial distribution of these minerals in the Pamlico River estuary, North Carolina, U.S.A.

CONCLUSIONS

The rheological behaviour of model cohesive suspensions is strongly influenced by physico-chemical factors, such as pH, salt concentration and mineralogical composition. This influence is largely reflected in the way in which these factors affect the flocculation process: we anticipate a similar influence on the rheological behaviour of cohesive suspensions in estuarine and coastal waters.

REFERENCES

Bryant, R., Williams, D.J.A., and James, A.E. (1980). A sampler for cohesive suspended sediment in the benthic boundary layer. *Limnol. and Oceanogr.* (In press).
Edzwald, J.K., Upchurch, J.B., and O'Melia, C.R. (1974). Coagulation in estuaries. *Environ. Sci. and Tech., 8,* 38.
Einsele, G., Overbeek, R., Scharz, M.U., and Unsold, G. (1974). Mass physical properties, sliding and erodibility of experimentally deposited and differently consolidated clayey muds. *Sedimentol., 21,* 339-372.
Flegmann, A.W., Goodwin, J.W., and Ottewill, R.M. (1969). Rheological studies on kaolinite suspensions. *Proc. Biol. Ceramic Soc.,* No. 13, 31-45.
Fredrickson, A.G. (1964). *Principles and Applications of Rheology.* Prentice Hall.
Hunter, K.A., and Liss, P.S. (1979). The surface charge of suspended particles in estuarine and coastal waters. *Nature, 282,* 823-825.
Kirby, R.R., and Parker, W.R. (1977). The physical characteristics and environmental significance of fine-sediment suspensions in estuaries. In: *Studies in Geophysics, Estuaries, Geophysics and the Environment.* National Academy of Sciences, Washington, D.C., U.S.A., 110-120.
Krone, R.B. (1963). A study of rheologic properties of estuarial sediments. *Hyd. Eng. Lab., SERL. Ref. No. 63-8.* University of California, Berkley.
Krone, R.B. (1972). A field study of flocculation as a factor in estuarial shoaling processes. *U.S. Army, Corps of Eng., Comm. Tidal Hydraul., Tech. Bull. No.19.*
Migniot, C. (1968). A study of the physical properties of various forms of very

fine sediments and their behaviour under hydrodynamic action. *La Houille Blanche, No.7*, 591-622.
Michael, H. Ll. (1978). *Colloidal and surface properties of quartz* . Ph.D. Thesis, University of Wales (Unpub. MS), Chapter 2.
Mooney, M., and Ewart, R.H. (1934). A conicylindrical viscometer. *Physics, 5*, 350.
Neiheisel, J. (1966). Significance of clay minerals in shoaling problems. *U.S. Army, Corps of Eng., Comm. Tidal Hydraul., Tech. Bull. No. 10.*
Ottewill, R.H. (1973). Particulate dispersions. *In: Colloid Science 2*, The Chemical Society, London, 173-219.
Peirce, T.J., Jarman, R.T., and Le Turville, C.M. (1970). An experimental study of silt scouring. *Proc. Instn. Civ. Engrs., 45*, 231-243.
Schubel, J.R., Wilson, R.E., and Okubo, A. (1978). Vertical transport of suspended sediment in Upper Chesapeake Bay. *In:* Kjerfve, B. (Ed.)., *Estuarine Transport Processes*. Belle W. Branch Library in Marine Science, No. 7, University of South Carolina Press, Columbia, U.S.A., 161-175.
Williams, D.J.A., and James, A.E. (1979). Rheology of Brisbane and Rotterdam mud. *Report to Hydraulics Research Station, Wallingford, U.K.* Department of Chemical Engineering, University College of Swansea, U.K.
Williams, D.J.A., and James, A.E. (1980). Rheology of kaolinite-quartz suspensions (In preparation).
Williams, D.J.A., and Williams, K.P.W. (1978). Electrophoresis and zeta potential of kaolinite. *J. Coll. Int. Sci., 65*, 79-87.
Williams, K.P.W. (1976). *Microelectrophoresis of Mineral Suspensions*. Ph.D. Thesis, University of Wales (Unpub. MS), Chapter 2.
Zeichner, G.R., and Schowalter, W.R. (1977). Use of trajectory analysis to study stability of colloidal dispersions in flow fields. *A.I. Chem. E.J., 23*, 243.

19. SUSPENDED SEDIMENT DISTRIBUTIONS IN NORTHERN SWANSEA BAY

C. M. Davies

Dept. of Maritime Studies, University of Wales Institute of Science and Technology, Cardiff, U.K.

ABSTRACT

Examination of the rotatory current system in northern Swansea Bay indicates distinct phases of rotation. Suspended sediment flux at certain phases markedly influences the residual flux, particularly the sustained direction of bed currents on the flood tide. Flux differences either side of Swansea Channel indicate that some near-bed suspended load is retained in Swansea Channel during cross-channel transport, probably contributing to anomalous mud sedimentation in an area comprising generally coarser sediments.

KEYWORDS

Suspended sediment flux; Near-bed suspended sediment; Mud; Tidal currents; Swansea Bay; Bristol Channel.

INTRODUCTION

Initial research into mud sedimentation in Swansea Bay (Davies, 1972) was motivated by noticeable changes in sedimentation patterns on the western intertidal zone in the late 1960's (Davies, 1971), determined from comparative analyses of aerial photographs obtained in May 1966, April 1968 and June 1970 (by Meridian Airways, for B.T.D.B.).

Reconnaissance surveys, in 1970, by the present author found that surface suspended sediment existed in relatively high concentrations in the vicinity of the Inner Spoil Ground and around Swansea Channel (Fig. 19.1). Surveys of the Tawe estuary by B.T.D.B. in 1968 found that "silt coming into the estuary from upstream sources is relatively small and probably accounts for not much over 10% of the annual dredging in the estuary.....and silt enters the estuary from Swansea Bay" (B.T.D.B. , 1971).

The need arose, therefore, for baseline data on suspended sediment distributions in the northern part of the embayment to elucidate:(1) why suspended sediment levels should be relatively high in this region; (2) their transport paths; and (3) their relationship to Swansea Channel and its maintenance.

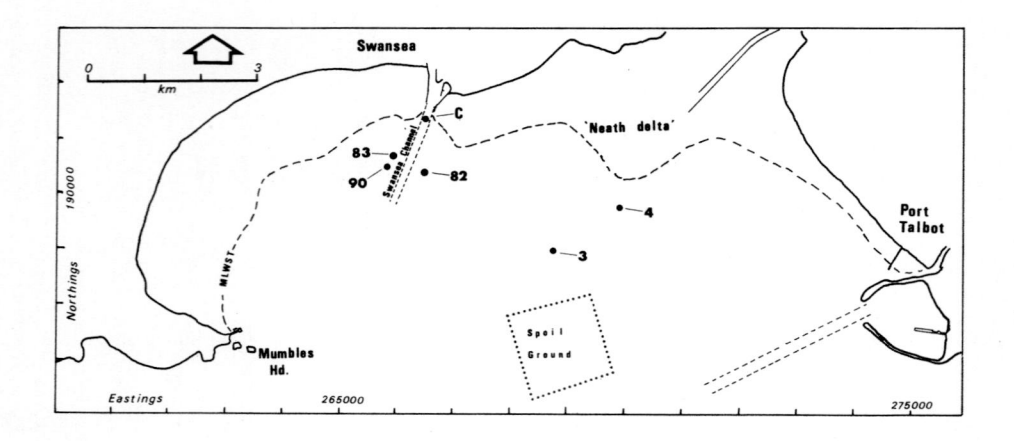

Figure 19.1. Swansea Bay: location of current meter stations, from Davies (1972) and BTDB (1971). Stations 3 and 4 were Plessey M021 current meters mounted 1m above the bed; all other stations used direct-reading current meters.

With continued studies of the hydrodynamics and sedimentology of Swansea Bay throughout the 1970's by other researchers, this symposium provides a convenient opportunity to review data on mud suspensions obtained during 1969-72 (Davies, 1972).

SURVEY DETAILS

Details of survey techniques and equipment performance have been described elsewhere (Davies, *op.cit.*). However, in summary, the main surveys were undertaken in March, April, July, August and September 1971, particularly on days when wind, represented by Beaufort Numbers, were 0 or 1, thereby minimizing meteorological effects. A launch, *Silurian,* was kindly provided by BTDB for the surveys and usually kept station with anchors fore and aft, the vessel's location being monitored from the Decca Hifix chain.

Measurements of current velocity and direction, suspended sediment concentration, salinity and water temperature were obtained at $\frac{1}{4}$ hr frequency at 1m intervals in vertical profile, using direct-reading instruments, each data point being monitored for 30-40s.

The data set herewith is primarily a review of data from 3 tide cycle stations in Davies *(op.cit.)*: 82, 83 and 90. Stations 82 and 83 are almost equidistant either side of Swansea Channel and recorded on consecutive days on medium/spring tides, during which time the channel was dredged; Station 90 was recorded on a spring tide in the absence of dredging. Maintenance dredging operations normally occupied the period HW- $3\frac{1}{2}$hr to HW+ $2\frac{1}{2}$hr.

SWANSEA CHANNEL

In 1971, Swansea Channel was about 2700m in length, approximately 120m wide, and 0-4m below the adjacent embayment floor. It was nominally maintained at 8.01m below OD, Newlyn, which is also the present (1979) level (from Admiralty Chart 1161); however, for a number of years in the intervening period, the Channel was maintained at 9.00m below OD.

Unpublished data from periodic BTDB hydrographic surveys in the late 1960's and early 1970's showed that over most of its length, the Channel was maintained with a slight seaward gradient; however, near the Inner Fairway Buoy, there was persistent shoaling with deeper water upchannel where dense mud suspensions have been observed (Davies, 1972, Fig. 5.6). Channel maintenance was undertaken mainly by the trailer suction dredger *Baglan*, and in 1971, 668835m^3 (874,294yds^3) of sediment was dredged from the Channel and 98135m^3 (128,281yds^3) was dredged from the ferryport and catchpit (data courtesy of Chief Docks Engineer's Office, South Wales, 1972). This approximate 1m tonnes of sediment was deposited at the Inner Spoil Ground (Fig. 19.1).

Assuming continuity of borehole information from near the west breakwater (kindly provided by Swansea Dock Engineer, 1979, in compilation of an unpublished report (Davies, 1970)) to the inner part of the channel, virgin material likely to have been encountered in the inner channel would have consisted of:(1) very dense black silty sandy GRAVEL with cobbles, down to about 6.40m below OD, (2) medium dense silty sandy coarse GRAVEL, down to about 8.50m below OD; and (3) loose grey clayey SAND with peat, down to about 11.10m below OD.

The sediments of the adjacent embayment floor have been described by Collins et al. (1979) and comprise gravelly SAND and SAND, of late Holocene age. Near the seaward end of Swansea Channel, unpublished grab sample data, obtained by the present author in 1969-70, showed the sand to be well sorted, having mean sizes of 2.45ϕ - 2.50ϕ. High concentrations of suspended sediment occurred near to the floor in the inner part of the channel, measurements varying from 1.00 to over 5.00kg/m^3 (i.e. beyond the range of the Instanter siltmeter used in the surveys); these suspensions occasionally being observed on echo-sounder records. Vertical profiles measured in the channel after the passage of a large vessel indicated that propeller wake was sufficiently strong to entrain near-bed suspensions well up into the water column (Davies, 1972, Fig. 5.5).

RESULTS

Tidal Currents

In summary, the data indicated that in the Bay's north region, at least on medium and spring tides, tidal currents followed an anticlockwise rotatory system, though continual rotation was not sustained throughout the tide cycle. Velocity maxima occurred at approximately HW- 4hr (4 hours before High Water) and HW+ 2hr on all ranges monitored, but surface velocities rarely exceeded 0.60m/s on spring tides. Therefore, aperiodic wave-induced and inertia currents are likely to influence significantly water mass movements in the area.

Basic data for velocity and direction are presented in Fig. 19.2 and Fig. 19.3, respectively,for Stations 82, 83 and 90, illustrating values recorded at the bed (approx. 5cm above), 2m below the water surface, and the depth-integrated mean. The data are related in seconds to the time of high water preceding the start of each survey.

Current velocities: Two orders of oscillation are readily evident in the velocity data (Fig. 19.2): a 1st oscillation with a frequency of about 4.3 x 10^{-5}Hz (23000s), representing the cycle between the maxima (or minima) of the flood and ebb phases, and a superimposed, 2nd order oscillation varying between 5.6 x 10^{-4}Hz and 3.3 x 10^{-4}Hz (1800-3000s), representing free oscillations of the water mass. The latter frequency is also evident in the current direction and suspended sediment data.

To filter the effects of the 2nd order oscillation and elucidate the trend of the semi-diurnal tide, a curve was fitted through the mean velocity data using a polynomial regression program on a HP 9821A calculate/9861A plotter. The resulting trend showed that the ebb velocity maximum, low-tide slack water, flood velocity maximum, and high-tide slack water occurred approximately one hour in advance of mid-ebb, low water, mid-flood, and high water, respectively. For Stations 82, 83 and 90 (i.e., medium/spring tides), the ebb maxima are 0.50 - 0.60m/s near the water surface, some 0.10 - 0.15m/s faster than the flood maxima. Except for high-tide slack water at Station 83, surface and depth-mean velocities reached a minima of about 0.10m/s. At Station 82, but to a lesser extent at Stations 83 and 90, it is difficult to recognize the tide-cycle trend in bed velocities owing to the amplitude of the free oscillations being comparable, if not exceeding, the semi-diurnal maxima-minima range.

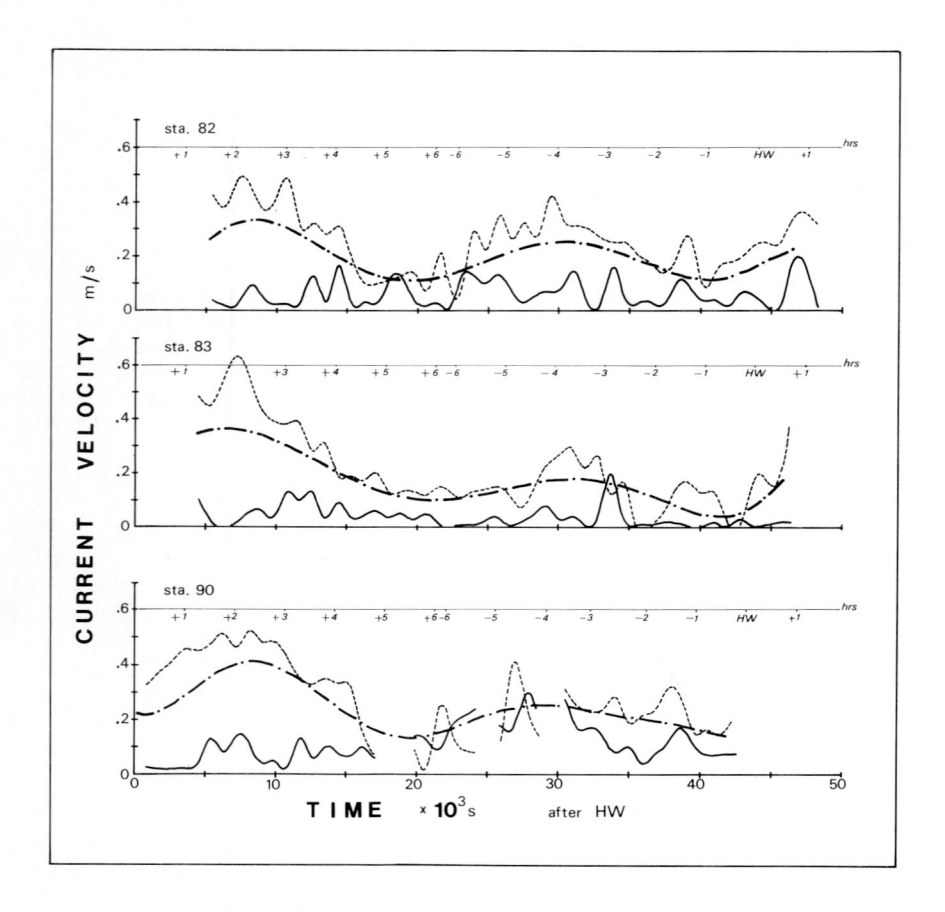

Figure 19.2. Current velocities at Stations 82, 83 and 90: solid line = bed currents, dashed line = currents 2m below water surface, dot/dash line = depth integrated mean currents. Curves through (1) surface and bed currents data fitted by a third-degree natural spline function, and (2) mean current data by a polynomial regression, using a HP 9821A calculator/9861A plotter.

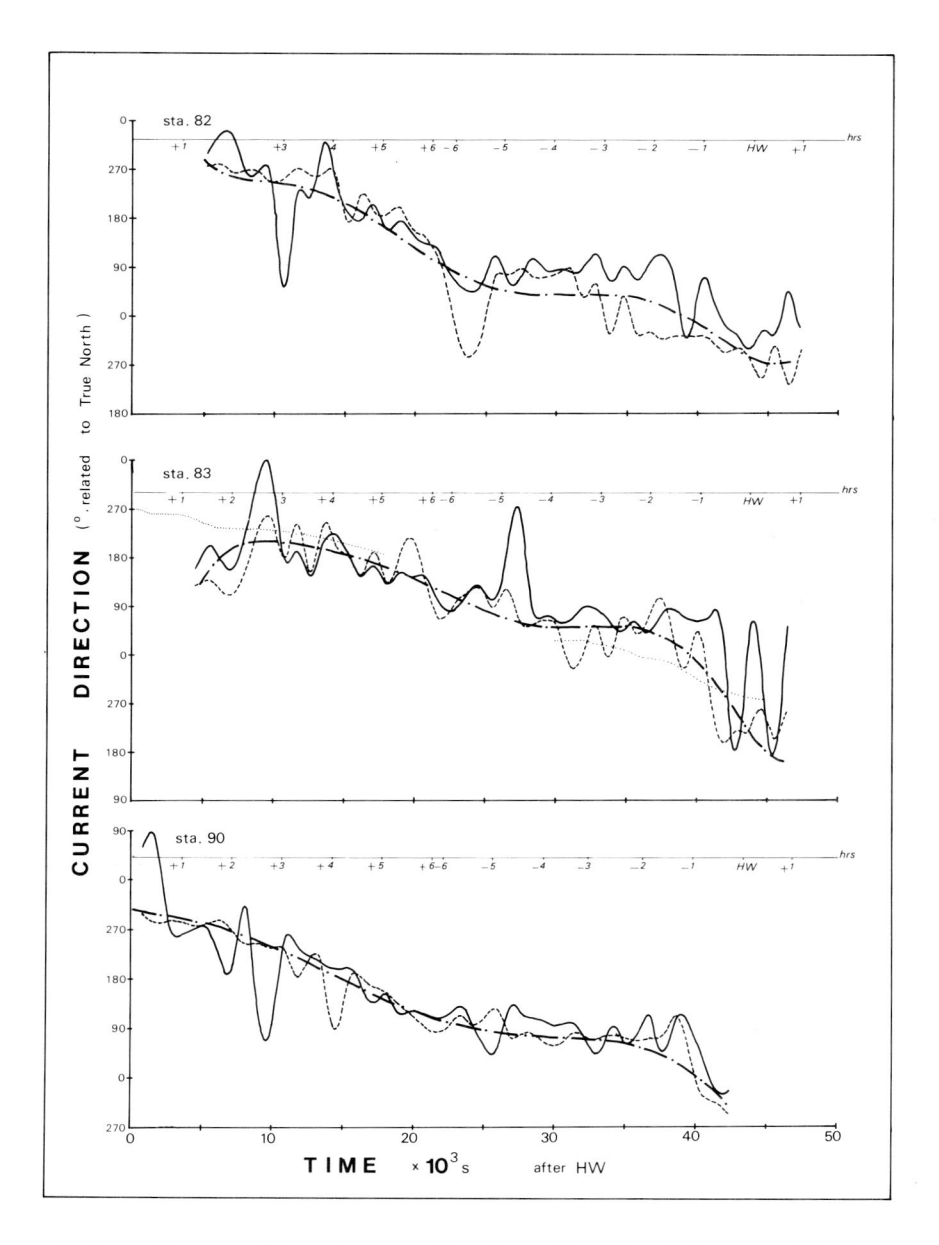

Figure 19.3. Current directions at Stations 82, 83 and 90: solid line = bed currents, dashed line = currents 2m below water surface, dot/dashed line = depth integrated mean currents. Dotted line in Station 83 = data transposed for Station 9 of Collins et al. (1979, Fig. 7). Curve fitting as described in Fig. 1972.

In considering the likely velocity field at neap tides, a comparison of similar time points in the tide cycle at Stations 79 (range 3.8m) and 80 (range 4.5m) with nearby Station 90 (range 8.0m), and Stations 74 (range 5.0m) and 78 (range 3.6m) with nearby Station 83 (range 7.0m) in data in Davies (1972) suggest that spring tide velocities were 2 to 3 times neap tide values.

The Rotatory System: A filtering technique similar to that used on the velocity data was applied to the depth-mean directions, determining the tide-cycle trend, and the resulting curves are broadly similar for Stations 82, 83 and 90 (Fig. 19.3). The data indicated that the 360° semi-diurnal rotation consisted of 3, probably 4, phases, with breaks at about HW+ 2½hr, HW- 5hr, HW- 2½hr, and probably HW.

Ebb Tide: Ebb-tide currents followed a simple pattern, in contrast to those of the flood tide. At the velocity maximum (approx. HW+ 2hr), mean directions are 250°, 205° and 260° (true) at Stations 82, 83 and 90, respectively. Prior to the velocity maximum, the apparent angular velocity of the currents averages 8.5×10^{-5} rad/s (17°/hr); at Station 83, however, the data set commenced at HW+ 1hr, when mean direction was 130°, rotating clockwise to 205° by the velocity maximum.

After the velocity maximum, anticlockwise rotation increased in speed, reaching a peak of 2.9×10^{-4} rad/s (60°/hr) at Station 82 and 2.2×10^{-4} rad/s (45°/hr), occurring at HW+ 3½hr (Station 90) and HW+ 5½hr (Stations 82 and 83), so that by Low Water, currents were aligned eastwards (90 - 115°).

Throughout most of the ebb tide, angular variation between surface mean, and bed vectors was generally less than 50°. However, one anomaly common to the three data sets occurred at about HW+ 2hr: at Stations 82 and 90, bed currents rotated anticlockwise to 60 - 70° true, sustaining this direction for about ½hr, and at Station 83, bed currents rotated clockwise to 010° true. At Stations 82 and 90, this anomaly was coincident with very low velocities (Fig. 19.2), and the phenomenon probably represented minor eddying.

Flood Tide: Minor eddying was also evident at Station 82 at HW- 5hr during a period of low velocity, when surface currents rotated anticlockwise some 150° to about 290° true. Also a similar feature occurred at Station 83 at about HW- 4hr near to the bed, with clockwise rotation to 270° true. Apart from minor eddying, the easterly current direction was sustained in the early/mid-flood period, i.e. there is no rotation during the flood velocity maximum. Mean directions were 040°, 050° and 075° true at Stations 82, 83 and 90, respectively, from about HW- 5½hr to HW- 2hr. However, by mid-flood, there was increasing variance in surface and bed vectors about the mean.

For example, from HW- 5hr to HW- 3hr at Station 82, surface and bed vectors were coincident in direction, at about 090° true, but at HW- 3hr, surface currents rotated anticlockwise at about 3.1×10^{-4} rad/s (65°/hr) reaching 325° true by HW- 3hr, at which time the bed currents were still flowing at 090° true. Davies (1972) referred to this feature as an *ebb direction advance*. From HW- 2hr to HW- 1hr, the surface currents remained aligned at about 320° true while the bed currents rotated anticlockwise. The mean direction rotated from about HW- 2½hr, reaching an angular velocity of 2.9×10^{-4} rad/s (60°/hr) which before High Water reduced to about 8.5×10^{-5} rad/s (17°/hr), representing the 4th phase break in rotation.

The ebb direction advance: was evident also at Stations 83 and 90, but here it occurred later: at Station 83, surface currents recommenced rotation at HW- 2hr followed by bed currents at HW- 1hr, whereas at Station 90, surface and bed vectors rotated simultaneously, at HW- 1hr.

The data suggests that the ebb direction advance occurs initially to the east of Swansea Channel, gradually progressing westward, or possibly southwestward, representing a surface current which initially flows over but eventually suppresses the eastward bed flood current. By High Water, currents were flowing between 270 - 300° true at the three stations, with surface velocities approaching 0.20 - 0.30m/s.

Suspended Sediment Distributions

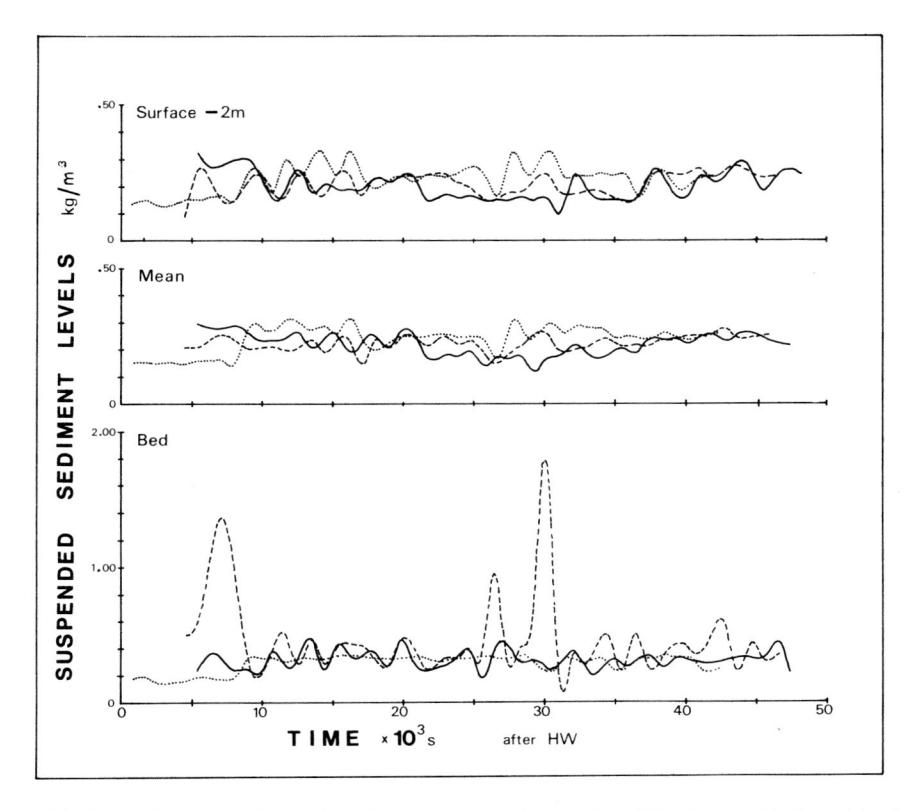

Figure 19.4. Suspended sediment concentrations for Stations 82 (solid line), 83 (dashed line), and 90 (dotted). Data points connected by a spline function.

Suspended Sediment Concentrations

Suspended sediment measurements (Fig. 19.4) are also affected by 2nd order oscillations. Initially a polynomial regression was attempted in filtering the data, but produced insignificant results mainly because the amplitude of the oscillations is almost comparable with longer period variations. Subsequently, the data were filtered by a 5-point smoothing routine (Fig. 19.5).

In isolation, the unprocessed data (Fig. 19.4) contribute little to an interpretation of suspended sediment distributions, except to indicate that (1) surface and depth-mean data vary within 0.15 - 0.30kg/m³, which is almost the range of the 2nd order oscillation, and (2) bed data vary within 0.20 - 0.50kg/m³, with two surges over 1.00kg/m³ at Station 83 coincident with velocity maxima.

At Station 82 (Fig, 19.5) surface and mean data vary in a cycle the period of the semi-diurnal tide, their minima (∿0.15kgm/³) occurring at about HW- 4½hr (dir.∿060°) and maxima occurring just after High Water. The precise time of the maxima was difficult to evaluate, due to truncation of the data set by the smoothing routine; however, it is estimated at HW+ 1hr (dir. ∿270°). Within this cycle, there is a subordinate peak of 0.22 - 0.24kg/m³ at HW+ 5hr (dir. ∿160°). Bed concentrations do not conform to the same pattern, having 2 (probably 3) maxima per tide cycle: 0.32

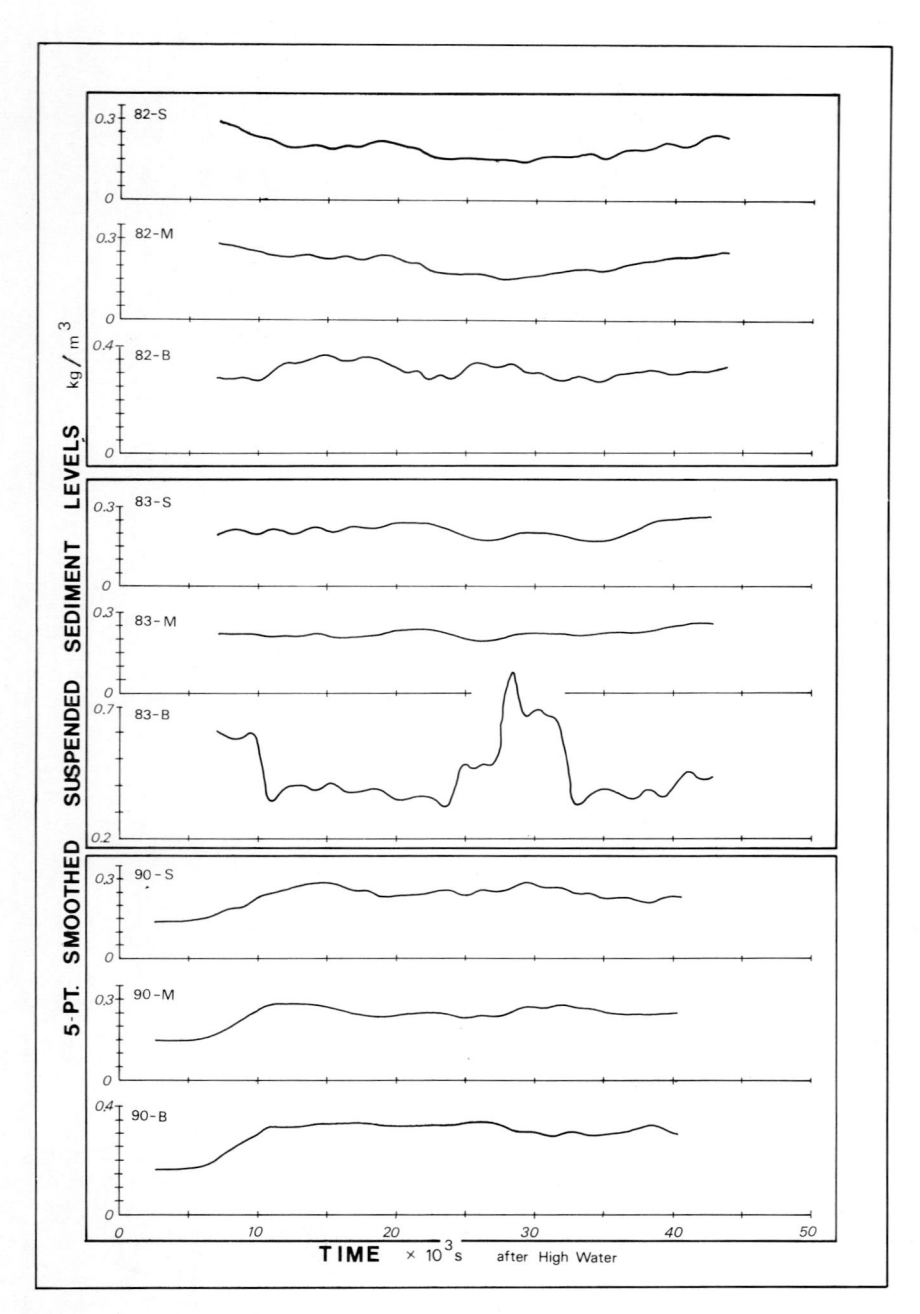

Figure 19.5. Five-point smoothing of suspended sediment data to filter the effects of free oscillations.

- 0.37kg/m³ at about HW+ 4½hr (dir. ∿180°), HW- 5hr (dir. ∿055°), and probably High Water (dir. ∿330°).

At Station 83, the surface concentrations exhibited maxima of ∼0.25kg/m³ at HW+ 6hr (dir. ∼090°) and HW- 1hr (dir. ∼300°) with a subordinate maximum of 0.20kg/m³ at HW- 4hr (dir. ∼050°). The mean concentrations showed a similar distribution. Although the surges of 1.37 and 1.80kg/m³ (Fig. 19.4) contributed significantly to the smoothed bed maxima configuration, several data points near the surges exceed 0.50kg/m³ (Fig. 19.4) and,therefore,the smoothed maxima were considered to have represented overall increases in bed concentrations at these times. In the unprocessed data, the surges occur at HW+ 2hr (dir. ∼160°) and HW- 4hr (dir. ∼065°), coincident with the velocity maxima, and the latter being preceded by a surge of 0.96kg/m³ at HW- 5hr (dir. ∼180°).

At Station 90, there was a broad similarity between the distributions of surface, mean and bed concentrations. From High Water to about HW+ 1hr, concentrations were relatively low, 0.14 - 0.16kg/m³, but gradually increased thereafter. Bed concentrations were almost constant at about 0.33kg/m³ for the remainder of the tide cycle, whereas surface concentrations showed a series of maxima and minima, though the range was low, less than 0.60kg/m³.

Residual Currents and Residual Suspended Sediment Fluxes.

For Stations 82, 83 and 90, measured velocity and direction data were converted to co-ordinates U_N and U_E, being the velocity components in northing and easting directions, and C_N and C_E, the suspended sediment fluxes, were obtained subsequently from the products of suspended sediment concentration with U_N and U_E, respectively. The co-ordinates were averaged over 50 data points, giving a tide period of 12.50 hours, the computations being reconverted to residual currents in m/s related to true north and residual suspended sediment fluxes in kg/m²/s related to true north (Fig. 19.6). Breaks in each data set were interpolated from a polynomial equation used to curve-fit data linking either side of the break.

Except for surface and depth-mean values at Station 90, residual suspended sediment fluxes were coincident with the residual currents. Near the bed, residuals were generally easterly (ENE to SE), whereas surface and mean residuals were westerly (NW to SW), except at Station 83, where the latter residuals were southeasterly.

DISCUSSION

Tidal Currents

There have been several published outlines of the tidal current circulation of Swansea Bay (Admiralty, 1945; Davies, 1974a; Collins et al., 1979)(See also Chapter 11). Because suspended sediment transport is dependent primarily on the circulation pattern, the significance of the tidal current data herewith is assessed with respect to tidal circulation within the whole embayment.

Davies (1974a, Fig. 1) presented a synthesis of tidal circulation within Swansea Bay, depicting two current systems, one in the Bay's northern region and one offshore, separated by divergent and convergent singularities on the flood and ebb phases, respectively. However, subsequent research in the mid 1970's by the Dept. of Oceanography, U.C. Swansea disproved the circulation pattern suggested for the western foreshore (Davies, op.cit.), by demonstrating that (1) currents northeast of Mumbles Head flowed in southerly and southeasterly directions for about 9hr of the tide cycle, and (2) currents over the western intertidal area flowed from west to south during submergence (Collins et al., 1979, Fig. 3).

The results of the U.C. Swansea research are summarized largely in Collins et al.

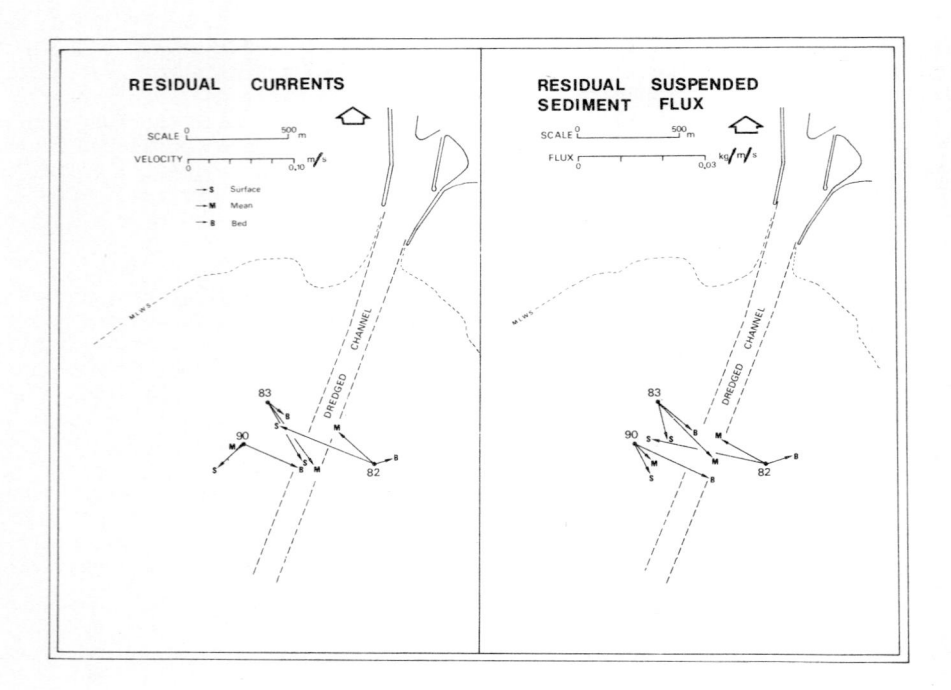

Figure 19.6. Residual currents and residual suspended sediment fluxes for stations adjacent to Swansea Channel.

(1979), including a schematic presentation of tidal current circulation. However, in comparison with the data herewith, there are a number of points requiring further consideration:

(1) that there is a "dominant southwesterly water movement (anticlockwise eddy) throughout 9hr of the tide cycle between Swansea Docks and Oystermouth" (Collins et al., p.58).
(2) whether the mid/late-flood anticlockwise gyre northeast of Mumbles Head is sufficiently expansive to influence circulation in the Bay's northern region (Collins et al., Fig. 11), and
(3) whether Swansea Channel has any major local effect upon tidal currents at the bay head.

The present data would seem to confirm a residual southwesterly flow between Swansea Docks and Oystermouth, *however* (1) this dominance applies to surface and mean currents but not bed currents, (Fig. 19.6), and (2) water movement (surface or bed) in the study area is not southwesterly for a *9hr period* of the tide cycle (Fig. 19.3). Surface and mean currents at Station 83 did not conform to this pattern, having southeasterly residuals, induced primarily by southerly flow (Fig. 19.3) during the ebb velocity maximum. Residual bed currents (Fig. 19.6) were generally easterly (ENE to SE), due to the bed velocity maximum being greater, or sustained longer, on the flood phase than on the ebb phase (Fig. 19.2).

It is unlikely that the mid/late-flood anticlockwise gyre northeast of Mumbles Head is sufficiently expansive to influence tidal circulation at the bay head, as suggested by Collins et al., (Fig. 11), the gyre being unperceived in the data herewith and in that of BTDB (1971, Station C).

Flow on the ebb phase indicated by the present data (Fig. 19.7) is broadly in agreement with that described by Collins et al. for the bay head, but not flow on the flood phase. In Fig. 19.3, current direction data of Station 9 of Collins et al. (their Fig. 7) has been transposed upon the approximate geographically coincident Station 83 of the data herewith. Although it is not specified to which part of the water column Station 9 data relates, the data can be incorporated largely within the current rotation of Station 83 defined by the limits of the free oscillations. However, the published Station 9 data do not incorporate information on the early flood phase (i.e., during much of the flood velocity maximum), the importance of this period being considered below.

Off the Tawe Estuary (BTDB, 1971, Station C), surface and bed currents were easterly for almost the complete flood phase. In the Bay's northern region, at least on medium and spring tides, (Davies, 1974a, Fig. 2) showed that the flood phase consisted of two flow components: (1) an initial period of ENE to NE flow, in which surface and bed vectors were aligned in similar directions, followed by (2) a period when northeasterly surface currents overrode and eventually suppressed easterly bed currents. It is unlikely that the northwesterly surface currents represent the Mumbles Head gyre because these currents originated on the east side of Swansea Channel at about HW- 4hr (Fig. 19.3, Station 82) but not on the west side until between HW- 2hr and HW- 1hr (Fig. 19.3, Stations 83 and 90). Therefore, the cause of the northwesterly surface currents lies generally eastward of Swansea Channel not southwestward. Davies (1974a, Fig. 1) attributed the cause to deviation of tidal currents on the southwest of the 'Neath Delta' (Fig. 19.1), which may also explain why, on medium and neap tides, near-bed currents at the Plessey current meter station nearer the delta (Station 4) rotated anticlockwise one hour or so in advance of Station 3 (Davies (1972), Fig. 4.5 and Fig. 4.6; Collins et al. (1979) Fig. 6).

As the tidal currents in the Bay's northern region are relatively weak (<0.50m/s), bathymetry is a relatively important control on current directions. The direction data of the bed currents (Fig. 19.3) were often aligned parallel to bathymetric contours of the embayment floor, particularly on the flood phase, but showed no variation which could be attributed to the influence of Swansea Channel. Therefore, if the Channel morphology has any affect upon tidal currents, this influence would seem to be contained to the Channel margins. However, at Station C (BTDB, 1971) on the early ebb tide (Fig. 19.7), the freshwater outflow of the Tawe Estuary was aligned parallel to Swansea Channel. Further into the embayment, this flow was probably deflected southwestward by the coastal currents running westward across the Channel at that time. This might contribute to the southward flow at Station 83 at HW+ 2hr (Fig. 19.7), but whereas salinity stratification was evident at Station C (BTDB, op.cit.), none was observed at Station 83.

A further consequence of tidal currents in Swansea Bay being weak is the likely importance of modification by wind-drift and inertia currents. In the absence of observational data from within Swansea Bay, Collins et al. (1979, Fig. 6) have presented a theoretical review of the effect of a southwesterly swell (the dominant swell direction) and a southeasterly sea (the Bay's most exposed aspect). This review suggests that (1) from a strong southwesterly swell, tidal circulation in the Bay's northern region is likely to be modified to a greater extent than off Oystermouth, and (2) a strong southeasterly sea is likely to modify tidal circulation within the entire embayment.

Suspended Sediment Transport

From a network of stations comprising Eulerian measurements of suspended sediment levels, it is not possible to backtrack outside the network and identify conclusively sediment sources. However, it is possible to indicate (1) where large volumes

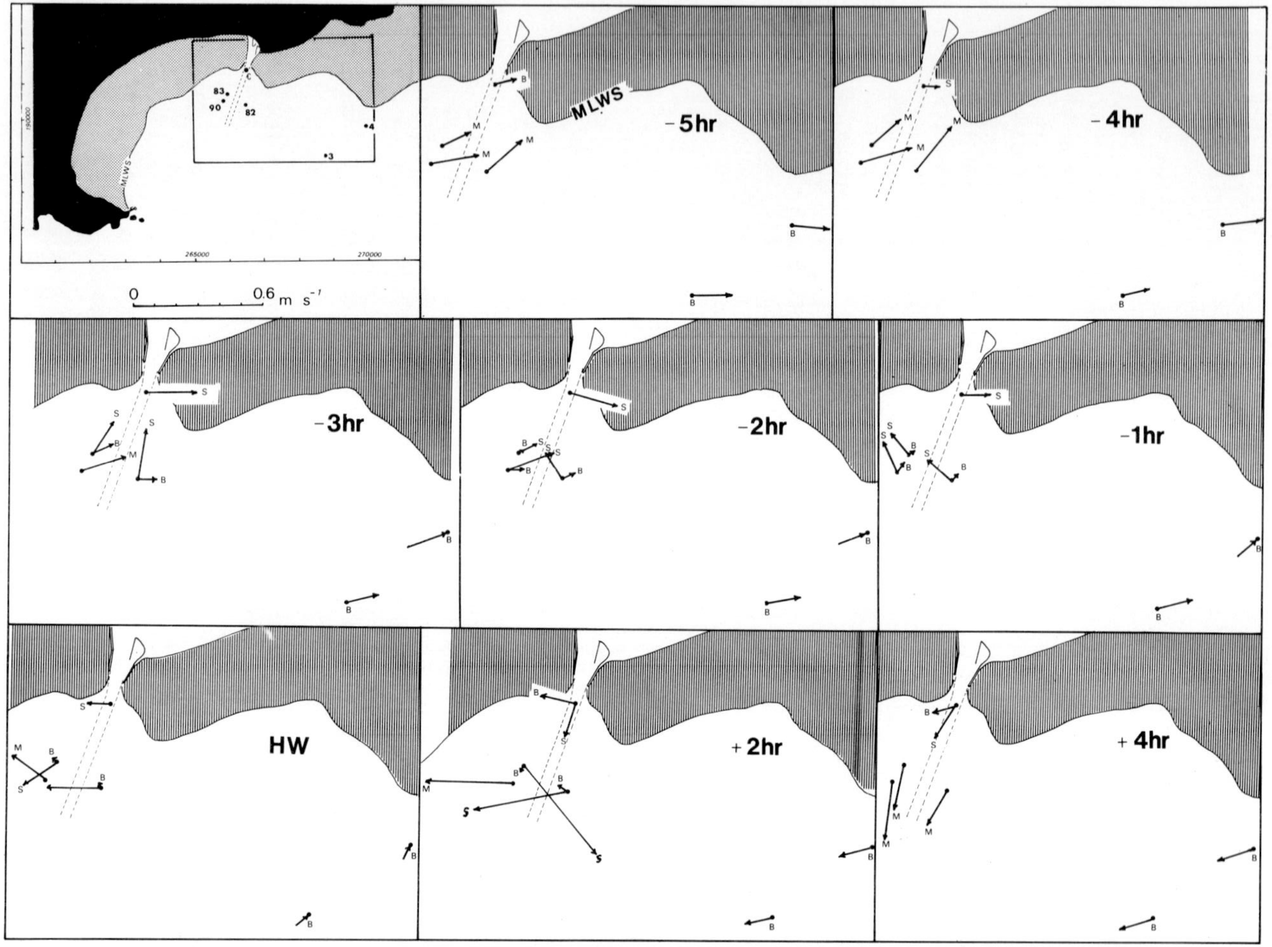

Figure 19.7. Schematic presentation of current vectors in northern Swansea Bay at different periods of a medium/spring tide cycle.

of sediment enter the network, (2) transport patterns within the network, and (3) the possible occurrence of dredging-induced processes.

Davies (1972) reviewed possible sources of suspended sediment, and later concluded (Davies, 1974b) that the most significant source could be reworking and recycling of spoil deposited at two active (1971) grounds. Collins et al. (1979, Fig. 12) considered that spoil was transported (and deposited) over a large muddy SAND/sandy MUD province in the northeast of the Bay, over which early ebb currents flow into the Bay's northern region. It is suggested that the latter flow is a major transport path of suspended sediment into the bay head because (1) ebb currents recorded at the Plessey current meter stations southwest of the 'Neath Delta' were orientated more towards the Bay's northern region on neap tides than on spring tides (Davies, 1972, Fig. 4.5 and Fig. 4.6), coincident with (2) mean suspended sediment levels at equivalent periods in the tide cycle being greater on neap tides than on spring tides (Davies, 1974b).

Although suspended sediment levels are relatively high in the Bay's northern region, the seabed material has virtually no mud content, except in Swansea Channel, where mud content increases upchannel with ephemeral dense suspensions near the inner fairway buoy.

The present data provide an explanation of mud sedimentation in Swansea Channel. Discounting surges (which endorse the following outline), the overall concentration of near-bed suspensions was higher on the west side (Station 83) than on the east side of Swansea Channel (Station 82), particularly on the flood phase (Fig. 19.4) and as the eastward residual flux of suspended sediment was greater on the west side also (Fig. 19.6), this suggests that some near-bed suspended sediment was retained in Swansea Channel during cross-channel transport, particularly on the early/mid-flood phase. In the inner channel area, near bed velocities are probably, for a given tide, than near the adjacent embayment floor (e.g. compare Station C of BTDB (1971) with the present data), and although ephemeral dense suspensions occur, sedimentation is probably disrupted to a certain extent because of the effect of propeller wake from vessels in the Channel.

There are two local sources which possibly contribute to the relatively high near-bed suspended load on the west side of the Channel. In the Bay's northern region, there is a considerable northwesterly (becoming southwesterly) flux of suspended sediment in surface currents on the late flood and ebb phases; this material is probably transported in an anticlockwise curvature with the remaining ebb and, considering the velocity field, it is unlikely that this load would be flushed from the Bay on one tide; therefore, following a decrease in water level on the ebb, some of this sediment could be returned by northeast bed currents on the flood phase.

Another source could arise from dredging in Swansea Channel. Studies in the operation of trailer suction dredgers in some areas (CMT, 1970) suggested that for 1 unit volume of sediment retained in the hopper, 2 unit volumes would be entrained by the draghead or through overspill in filling the hopper. Studies in the Usk Estuary (Davies, 1978) showed that overspill suspended load sand relatively quickly to near the channel floor. As tidal currents run generally westward for at least 60% of the dredging period at Swansea Channel, overspill could contribute to the relatively high near-bed suspensions.

CONCLUSIONS

Reviewed in light of subsequent research, the 1971 data herewith concur with the interpretation of tidal circulation in Collins et al. (1979) *except* for the flood phase in the Bay's northern region. Here flood currents comprised two components: an initial period of ENE to NE flow in which surface and bed vectors were aligned in similar directions, followed by a period when northwesterly surface currents overrode and eventually suppressed easterly bed currents. Further, it is unlikely that the northwesterly currents represent the anticlockwise gyre extending from Mumbles Head because the surface currents progressed from the east.

Suspended sediment distributions in northern Swansea Bay appear to be influenced by two components: a large generally westward residual flux in surface waters; and a less intense eastward residual flux in bed currents which contributes to anomalous mud sedimentation (in Swansea Channel) within an area of the embayment floored by coarser sediments.

REFERENCES

Admiralty (1945). *Tidal Streams of the Waters Surrounding the British Islands and off the West and North Coasts of Europe.* Part 1. Hydrographic Department, Taunton, U.K.
B.T.D.B. (1971). *Swansea Docks - preliminary study of the Tawe Estuary.* British Transport Docks Board. Report R225.
C.M.T. (1970). *Report on a Survey of Dredging Technology.* Report prepared by the National Ports Council for the Committee of Marine Technology, London, 74pp.
Collins, M., Ferentinos, G., and Banner, F.T. (1979). The Hydrodynamics and Sedimentology of a High (Tidal and Wave) Energy Embayment (Swansea Bay, Northern Bristol Channel). *Estuar. Coast. Mar. Sci., 8,* 49-74.
Davies, C.M. (1970). A High Resolution Continuous Seismic Survey of Swansea Bay. Unpub. Report to Swansea Dock Engineer, B.T.D.B., 24pp.
Davies, C.M. (1971). Some sedimentary processes occurring in Swansea Bay. *Proc. Geol. Soc. London, 1664,* 296-297.
Davies, C.M. (1972). *Aspects of suspended sediment transport in Swansea Bay.* Unpub. Ph.D. Thesis, University of Wales, 241pp.
Davies, C.M. (1974a). Variability of sediment suspended in rotary currents, Swansea Bay (Bristol Channel), Great Britain. *Mar. Geol., 16,* M31-M38.
Davies, C.M. (1974b). Paths of suspended sediment transport in Swansea Bay. *Proc. Challenger Soc., IV,* 259-260.
Davies, C.M. (1978). Interrelations between Sedimentary Processes and Dredging in Estuaries and Coastal Waters. *The Hydrographic Journal, 12,* 5-12.

DISCUSSION III

Heathershaw: I wonder whether (Woodhead) drifters do, in fact, indicate sediment transport paths very well, because both sediment transport and drifters respond in a non-linear way. We've seen that sediment has a very high power law dependence and I should think that drifters have a square law dependence. Perhaps it's not surprising that drifters appear to go in the wrong direction, as they are more influenced by waves than they are by tidal currents.

Collins: Yes, I think they do indicate some form of sediment transport path. We had doubts about our own interpretation, because we had totally contradictory results (See Fig. 14.2). So we tested the drifters in a flume, under combined oscillatory motion and unidirectional flow; these tests showed that they were very susceptible to wave action. This still needn't negate the argument of west to east transport - there could still be a transfer of sand in that direction. Drifters might "over-respond" to wave action, but the effect could still be in that direction. The other thing we are worried about in our interpretation of transport paths was the response of the current meter impellers in such a shallow-water environment and we actually tested the impellers, as well, under the combined action of waves and currents, because we felt that the vectors we were getting might be "over-reading" on the current meters, due simply to wave action. However, at the time when we recorded the readings presented here, conditions were relatively calm and it was undoubtedly responding mainly to tidal currents.

Mantoura: What is the average depth of disturbance and what is the approximate residence time for material in Swansea Bay?

Heathershaw: In fact, we have determined the depth of burial of sediment particles in the radioactive tracer experiments and found it to be about 10cm in the Outer Bay but larger on the Kenfig Patches, because there you have megaripples and it is the bedforms, in a way, that determine the depth of burial. I've not calculated the residence time of a sediment particle.

Norton: We did some side-scan sonar observations in the central Bristol Channel and, although they were centred on the dumping ground, they did overlap with the areas covered in the Collins (et al.) paper (Chapter 14) and by Heathershaw and Hammond (Chapter 15). Looking at the orientation of the bedform, we found a predominantly westward movement throughout the survey area; but towards the west, to the south of Oxwich Point, there were some indications that the west extremities of those bedforms were stopping moving west and starting moving east. I wonder if that is just a local anomaly we found, and whether there is any support for that in Dr. Heathershaw's experience?

Another matter is the observed conflict between residual water movements, and apparent residual bed movements which we observed at the dumping ground. Near here, there was a coarse/medium sand grain population, with bedforms going west and our limited observations there had an east-northeast component in the water column above the sea bed. This could be rationalised when you look at the detailed tidal wave pattern, because it was asymmetric and there were faster flows on the ebb (towards the west) than on the flood (towards the east). Therefore, it wasn't necessary in that case, to invoke wave motion to explain the disagreement between water column residuals and the actual direction of the coarse/medium sand bedforms. Again, is that found in other parts of the area?

Heathershaw: In answer to the first part of your question, I think there is probably still a lot of controversy about sand waves, their asymmetry and what it means in terms of sediment transport paths. The paths I showed indicated a net transport of material through the area on a large scale. Now, what actually happens locally, is another story altogether, because as we have already seen from Dr. Britton's paper (Chapter 13) it is possible to have sand waves oriented in opposite directions on either side of a sand bank and, thus, the transport paths I showed were really an attempt to show what happens in general through the area and I'm prepared to accept that there must be some local variations on that scheme.

In answer to the second part of the question, it is quite clear that you can have residual sediment movements which are, or can be, opposite in direction to residual water movements; these can be explained in terms of the non-linear terms in the equations of motion and the way they generate higher harmonics, in particular the M_4 tidal currents. It is the phase relationship between the M_4 and M_2 tidal currents which determines the ebb/flood asymmetry, although that, in itself, isn't enough to explain the observed directions of sediment movement because you have to bear in mind that sediment transport is also non-linear. By the time all these factors have been taken into account, it isn't at all surprising that sediment movements and residual water movements are not always comparable.

Norton: Is the asymmetry of the water flow at your stations sufficient to explain sediment movement, or did you still have to invoke the combined wave and tidal flows that were suggested earlier?

Heathershaw: No, you can explain them in terms of the tidal currents alone.

Collins: A number of papers have been presented by IOS (Taunton) now and they've dealt with the stability of the banks, the changing beach profiles and the offshore sediment transport. Accepting the fact that we don't know where the westerly sand stream may be coming from, is there any evidence now, of any interconnection between changes in the onshore and offshore deposits and sediment transport?

Heathershaw: If I understand you correctly, you're asking is there any evidence of a transfer of material from the east-west movement, into the Bay.

Collins: Not exactly, both a transfer and the overall balance in the area generally For example, is there any evidence for the changes in the beaches from the connection between offshore currents, sediment transport and beach movements?

Heathershaw: I don't think we really know enough about the sediment transfer processes. For example, you'd have to know much more about rates of sediment movement over mud than we can establish from our measurements. These difficulties apart, this is one area where, sometime in the future, numerical models might have a role to play. If sediment transport equations can be coupled to a numerical model for water circulation, it should be possible to simulate changes, say in the offshore area, and determine the effect they have on the inshore region; however, at the moment, I don't think it's feasible, given the sort of data you or I have - we just don't have the right sort of information with which to make that kind of prediction. There might be something coming from a study we've made on the East Coast, which suggests a tentative relation between changes in offshore banks and changes in the coastline, but we've no evidence to suggest that there's that sort of coupling in Swansea Bay.

Britton: In the west of the area, I would certainly consider that sediment is moving from the western end of the Helwick Sands into eastern Carmarthen Bay - moving into the Loughor Estuary and towards Cefn Sidan, but I wouldn't like to speak for Swansea Bay.

Heathershaw: However, you think there is evidence that material is moving down the coast towards the end of the Scarweather Sands.

Langdon: As a listener and not a contributor, I felt rather cheated when Dr. Collins was talking. I wrote down "If the transport is to the west where's the source of the sand" and then Dr. Heathershaw, when he was talking, said he didn't know where it was coming from. Then, Dr. Britton gave some sort of explanation that I thought was quite interesting and probably the answer.

Price: We've got I think, five different versions of a sediment distribution map for Swansea Bay Area and, as far as my mapping is concerned, most of them are admissable in terms of the relict sediments of the Bay. An exception to this generalisation is the province which everybody, has mapped on the eastern side of Swansea Bay variously labelled, muddy sand or sandy mud. I'd just like to ask whether either Dr. Heathershaw or Dr. Collins would like to say where that has come from? It is not explicable in terms of the relict sediment.

<u>Collins</u>: This is our interpretation of that deposit. Firstly, in terms of the physical environment, it does seem to exist where there is a tidal current divergence. Secondly, if you are considering waves, certainly you would expect a fining offshore from the southwesterly swell, so that two factors show there could be naturally-induced deposition in that area. Now, in addition, we have the problem of material dredged and dumped out in the Bay and I myself would like to ask Dr. Davies whether, in fact, the existence of the sandy mud/muddy sand deposit could be partially due at least to the dumped material in the Bay and whether there is any correlation between the increase in mud and the dredging activity? The other characteristic about the deposit is that the sand within often occurs in laminations. It could well be that during periods of severe storms, sand is moved into the area and deposited as laminations within that muddy/sandy mud deposit (see also Chapter 37). Now, whether that prevents material actually traversing the Bay and getting across to the eastern side, I don't know. So, Dr. Davies, was there any increase in the mud, both littoral and sublittoral when there were incidences of dredging?

<u>Davies</u>: I can't really answer, because my observations were subsequent to a period of intense capital dredging within the embayment. Approximately 9 million tonnes of sediment were dredged in the construction of Port Talbot tidal harbour and deposited at a site where the spoil was probably in disequilibrium with hydrodynamic conditions. Also, at that time, about 2 million tonnes of spoil per annum, from maintenance dredging, was deposited at another embayment site closer to Swansea. One interesting thing to do now would be to remeasure suspended sediment levels in the same area, to see whether the overall amount of material in suspension in the early 1970's was greater than normal, due to the effect of dredging, unfortunately, this doesn't really answer your question.

<u>Langdon</u>: If I could just add one point. The spoil ground noted on the charts was licensed in 1947 and, just about the time that Dr. Davies was carrying out his investigation (early 1970's) we (B.T.D.B.) surveyed it and found there was nothing there, i.e., it was still at the same level that it was in 1947. During that time, about 23 million tons of dredgings had been deposited and, of course, spread throughout the Bay. This would imply then, that it is quite the wrong place to put it, wouldn't it?

<u>Price</u>: I think then, that what all this means is, that the consensus of opinion is that this deposit is largely of artificial origin, which is what I wanted to confirm.

(Editor's Comment: See also Discussion following Chapter 37).

20. INPUTS TO SWANSEA BAY

C. J. Chubb, R. P. Dale and J. H. Stoner

Welsh Water Authority, Cambrian Way, Brecon, Powys, U.K.

ABSTRACT

The First Report of the Working Party on Possible Pollution in Swansea Bay (Welsh Office, 1974a, b) highlighted the lack of knowledge on the composition and dispersion of discharges to the Bay and recommended that the former River Authorities and industries concerned understood the sampling, flow gauging and analytical work required to establish the mass input of toxic substances to Swansea Bay. As a result the fifty significant inputs to the Bay were monitored intensively over a one year period (December 1973 - December 1974).

The Severn Estuary Joint Committee Technical Working Party (Welsh Water Authority, 1977) identified sixteen major inputs to the Bay as being significant within the wider context of the Severn Estuary and Bristol Channel, and these inputs have been monitored during 1978 and 1979 in order to quantify the mass input of materials from these sources more accurately.

The present chapter summarises the findings of the latter monitoring programme and describes input budgets for organic matter, nutrients, dissolved and particulate metals and organochlorine pesticides.

KEYWORDS

Coastal water inputs; Trace metals; Nutrients; Organochlorines; Pollution; Swansea Bay; Bristol Channel.

INTRODUCTION

The study area comprises an 80km stretch of coastline and associated nearshore waters between Nash Point in the east and Worms Head in the west together with the adjacent sea area shown in Fig. 20.1.

The catchment area draining to Swansea Bay accommodates a population of approximately half a million people and a wide variety of industries. Approximately two thirds of the fresh water run-off to the Bay is derived from the Rivers Neath and Tawe. These rivers receive discharges from opencast mining operations, collieries, disused mines, treated sewage and various trade wastes. In addition the Tawe and

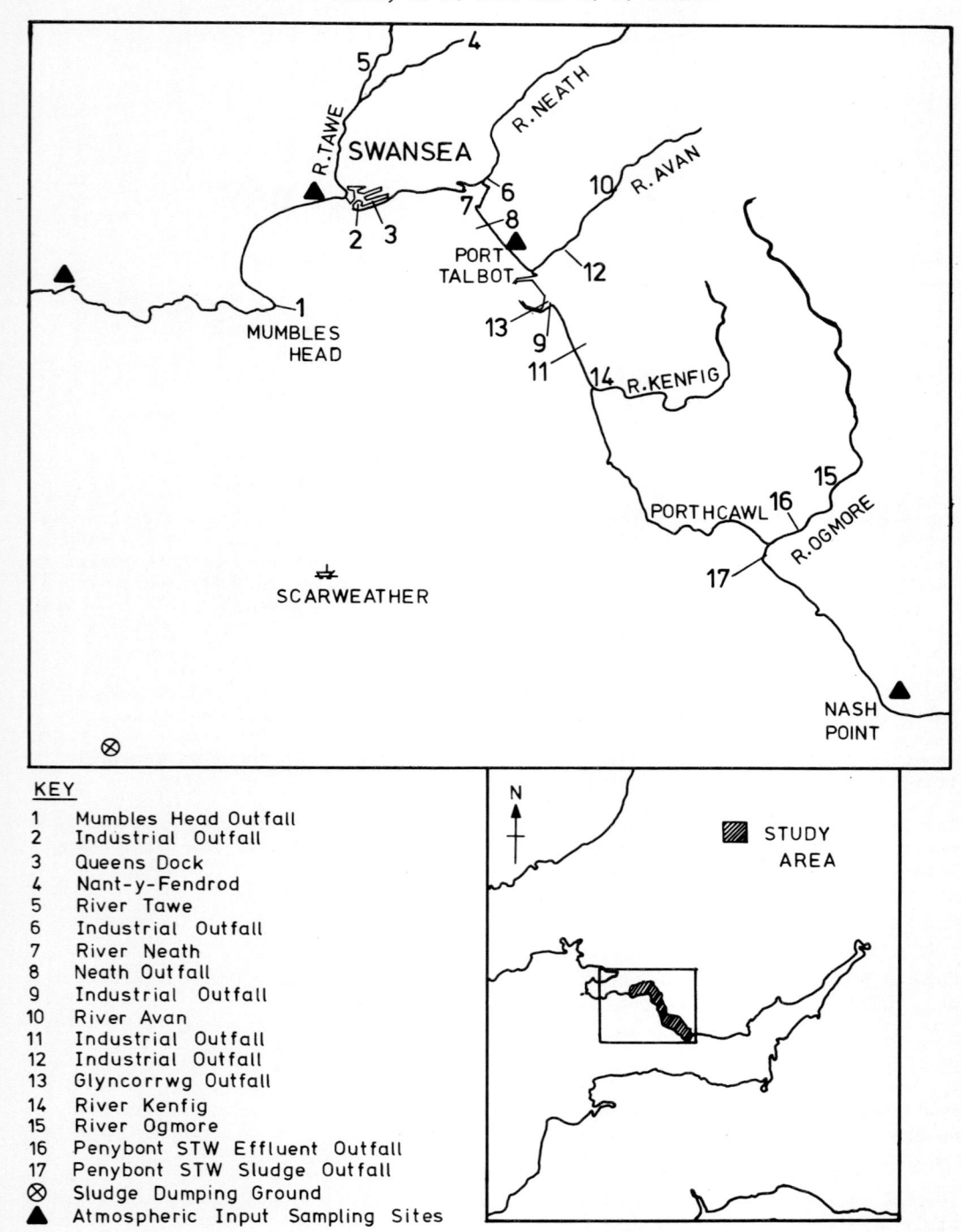

Figure 20.1. Inputs to Swansea Bay.

its tributary the Nant-y-Fendrod are polluted by present and past industrial metal processing activities.

Thirty-four of the forty-one effluents discharging either directly to Swansea Bay or to estuaries entering the Bay consist predominantly of domestic sewage, the other seven are mainly industrial waste.

Thirty of the domestic discharges are discharged without any form of treatment and where these are made either to estuaries or through inadequate outfalls to the Bay itself they often result in bacteriological and aesthetic pollution of the foreshore. The only discharges of fully treated domestic effluent are those from the treatment works at Bishopston and Penybont, whilst the larger Mumbles Head outfall discharges screened and comminuted sewage at favourable states of the tide.

There are only seven industrial outfalls discharging directly to the Bay, although large quantities of industrial effluent enter indirectly via domestic sewers or rivers.

The First Report of the Working Party on possible pollution in Swansea Bay (Welsh Office, 1974a, b) highlighted the lack of knowledge on the composition and dispersion of discharges to the Bay. There was a lack of regular, systematic analysis of inputs and flow rate measurement was often not synchronised with the sampling of inputs, thus making the calculation of mass inputs of substances highly speculative. The Working Party recommended that the former River Authorities and industries concerned, undertake the flow gauging, sampling and analytical work required to establish the mass input of toxic substances to Swansea Bay.

As a result, fifty significant inputs to the Bay were identified and monitored during 1973-74. On the basis of the data obtained and additional information gathered by the Severn Estuary Joint Committee (Stoner, 1977; Welsh Water Authority, 1977) sixteen major inputs, which together account for more than 90% of the input of all materials to the Bay, were selected for further investigation.

The present chapter summarises the findings of an intensive monitoring programme carried out between October 1977 and March 1979. (See also Chapters 21 and 27).

In addition to the above discharges inputs via the atmosphere and licensed sludge dumping at the dumping ground south of the Gower coast (see Fig. 20.1) are considered.

IMPLEMENTATION OF MONITORING PROGRAMME

Sampling Programme

The sixteen inputs monitored are shown in Fig. 20.1 and the sampling frequency is shown in Table 20.1

TABLE 20.1. Sampling Frequency

Discharge Type	Sampling Frequency
Major Rivers	Fortnightly
Minor Rivers	Monthly
Domestic Outfalls	Six twenty-four hour surveys*
Industrial Effluents	Monthly twenty-four hour surveys*

*24 hour surveys involved the collection of 24 hourly samples which were then bulked on a flow proportional basis to give 6 composite samples for analysis.

Measurement of River Flow

In order that inputs from the rivers could be compared, it was decided to consider samples during a common period, namely 1 November 1977 to 31 December 1978. During this period, mean river flows were generally close to average (See Table 20.2).

Measurement of river flow is an established technique and the accuracy of these measurements is expected to be within ± 15%.

TABLE 20.2.   River Inputs to Swansea Bay.

River	AIF[1]	ADF[2]	NWC Water Quality Class*
Nant y Fendrod	0.49	0.38	3
Tawe	12.7	11.1	2
Neath	12.6	12.1	2
Afan	3.5	4.4	1A
Kenfig**	0.48	0.88	3
Ogmore	5.7	6.0	1B

[1]Average instantaneous flow m^3/sec. Average of the instantaneous flows measured at the time of sampling. [2]Average daily flow m^3/sec. Long term average daily flow of the river. **Discharge not continuous due to abstraction for industrial use. *National Water Council (1978).

Flow Measurement of Domestic and Industrial Discharges

In general, the measurement of flows from domestic and industrial discharges posed the major problems for flow measurement. Most of these discharges had never been measured prior to this study especially the domestic discharges. Typically the problems were lack of access, intermittent discharges, tide locking and backwater effects. The difficulties were overcome by current meter gaugings in sewers, the calibration of storage chambers, the evaluation of pump characteristics and the application of theoretical hydraulic formulae for regular channels. Dilution gauging using lithium chloride was used in calibration exercises but was not used on a regular basis during the survey.

Sample Analysis

In order to obtain meaningful mass inputs data it was essential to ensure that the analytical data produced by the collaborating laboratories was comparable. A comprehensive series of inter-laboratory calibration exercises were carried out. The detection limits are listed in Table 20.3 and the precision and accuracy of the analytical methods employed for each determinand are reported in the second Report of the Severn Estuary Survey and Systems Panel (Welsh Water Authority, in press). Samples collected during the programme were routinely analysed for all of the determinands listed with the exception of mercury and the organochlorine pesticides which were only determined on a limited number of samples.

Other Inputs

In addition to the inputs entering Swansea Bay via rivers and discharges, efforts

TABLE 20.3. Analytical Detection Limits of Participating Laboratories.

DETERMINAND	GLAMORGAN RIVER DIVISION	SOUTH WEST WALES RIVER DIVISION	WELSH W.A. MARINE LABORATORY
1. Sediments (μg litre^{-1})			
Suspended Solids (105°C)	400.0	1000.0	–
Suspended Solids (500°C)	400.0	1000.0	–
2. Nutrients (μg litre^{-1})			
Ammoniacal nitrogen	10.0	10.0	–
Total oxidised nitrogen	10.0	50.0	–
Ortho phosphate	10.0	10.0	–
Silicate	20.0	50.0	–
3. Metals (μg litre^{-1})			
Cadmium dissolved and total	0.5(a) 0.1(b)	0.13	0.03(e)
Chromium "	0.8(a) 0.5(b)	0.56	–(e)
Copper "	0.7(a) 0.3(b)	0.35	0.2(e)
Iron "	1.0(a) 1.0(b)	0.52	–(e)
Lead "	5.0(a) 1.0(b)	0.53	0.2(e)
Manganese "	0.5(a) 0.25(b)	0.24	0.2(e)
Nickel "	1.3(a) 0.5(b)	0.49	0.1(e)
Zinc "	0.3(a) 0.1(b)	0.23	0.2(e)
Mercury (Total)	0.5(c) 0.01(d)	–	0.05(e)
4. Organochlorines (gramme litre^{-1})			
α - H.C.H.	20×10^{-9}	–	0.8×10^{-9}
β - H.C.H.	20×10^{-9}	–	0.8×10^{-9}
γ - H.C.H.	20×10^{-9}	–	0.8×10^{-9}
δ - H.C.H.	20×10^{-9}	–	0.8×10^{-9}
Aldrin	20×10^{-9}	–	0.3×10^{-9}
Dieldrin	50×10^{-9}	–	0.5×10^{-9}
Endrin	50×10^{-9}	–	1.6×10^{-9}
Heptachlor	20×10^{-9}	–	3×10^{-9}
Heptachlor epoxide	20×10^{-9}	–	0.8×10^{-9}
Endosulfan A	–	–	0.8×10^{-4}
Endosulfan B	–	–	0.8×10^{-4}
p,p - D.D.E.	50×10^{-9}	–	0.8×10^{-9}
o,p - D.D.E.	50×10^{-9}	–	0.8×10^{-9}
p,p - D.D.T.	50×10^{-9}	–	4.8×10^{-9}
o,p - D.D.T.	50×10^{-9}	–	1.6×10^{-9}
p,p - T.D.E.	50×10^{-9}	–	1.6×10^{-9}
o,p - T.D.E.	50×10^{-9}	–	1.6×10^{-9}
Chlordane	–	–	1.0×10^{-9}

(a) Limits of detection to 12.7.78
(b)   "   "   "   from 13.7.78
(c)   "   "   "   to 13.12.78
(d)   "   "   "   from 14.12.78
(e) Dissolved metals only

have been made to quantify the mass inputs via the atmosphere and sludge dumping.

Data on sludge dumping during 1978 was provided by the Ministry of Agriculture, Fisheries and Food. The estimated inputs to the study area via the atmosphere were calculated by the Atomic Energy Research Establishment, Harwell (Cambray, R., *pers. comm.*) on the basis of deposition data from four sites around the Bay (see Figure 20.1) for the period October 1978 - July 1979. A detailed account of this study which was supported by the Welsh Office, is given in the Second Report of the Severn Estuary Joint Committee's Systems and Survey Panel (Welsh Water Authority, in press).

Data Manipulation and Presentation

Mass inputs were calculated for each sample as the product of the associated flow and concentration data. The arithmetic mean of the individual mass inputs was calculated to give an average mass input for each determinand from each source. Where a determinand occurred at a concentration below the detection limit of the analytical technique employed, the mass input was calculated as the product of the flow and the appropriate detection limit. The detection limits of the various laboratories and the incidence of "less than" concentrations are listed in Tables 20.3 and 20.4. As indicated in Table 20.4, the majority of determinands were detected in >80% of all sample categories, with the exception of organochlorine pesticides.

The use of detection limits to calculate the mass inputs of mercury, chromium, cadmium and lead for some discharges (8% - 30% of data) is unlikely to significantly affect the budget for these determinands, since the associated flows were relatively small.

RESULTS

Details of the concentration and mass input data obtained for each discharge are tabulated in Tables 20.5 and 20.6 and the five major inputs for each determinand are identified in Table 20.7, to be found at the end of the text.

In order to present the survey results in a simple and comprehensible format, the averaged data has been summarised according to the following discharge types: (i) rivers and streams, (ii) industrial discharges and (iii) domestic sewage. Whilst this classification is an over simplification and does not isolate either industrial effluents discharged to domestic sewers or discharges to rivers above the tidal limit, it does allow the quantification of direct industrial and domestic inputs and their comparison with "background" inputs from fresh water run-off. The results, together with the estimated inputs from sludge dumping and the atmosphere are tabulated in Table 20.8 and summarised diagrammatically in Fig. 20.2 (after Tables 20.5-20.8).

Flow

During the programme the mean measured volumetric input to the Bay from rivers and discharges was 37.9m^3/sec. Rivers and streams accounted for 93.6% of this flow and the two major rivers, the Tawe and the Neath together contributed 66.8% of the total.

Suspended Solids

Rivers and streams were the major source of suspended solids discharged to the Bay and the survey results give an estimated input of 111 tonnes per day. This estimate must be considered to be approximate, since it represents the arithmetic mean of

TABLE 20.4. Percentage of Samples Below Detection Limits for Analytical Techniques Employed.

Determinand	No. of Samples Analysed	% "Less Than" Values
1. Sediments		
Suspended Solids (105°C)	898	0
Suspended Solids (500°C)	710	1
2. Nutrients		
Ammoniacal Nitrogen	893	2
Total Oxidised Nitrogen	818	3
Ortho Phosphate	747	8
Silicate	803	0
3. Metals		
Cadmium Diss.	561	45
Cadmium Part.	63	0
Cadmium Total	624	22
Chromium Diss.	474	38
Chromium Part.	63	25
Chromium Total	615	11
Copper Diss.	556	1
Copper Part.	63	3
Copper Total	622	0
Iron Diss.	459	1
Iron Part.	63	0
Iron Total	622	0
Lead Diss.	339	34
Lead Part.	63	24
Lead Total	330	8
Manganese Diss.	550	0
Manganese Part.	63	0
Manganese Total	620	0
Nickel Diss.	562	12
Nickel Part.	41	10
Nickel Total	197	2
Zinc Diss.	559	0
Zinc Part.	63	0
Zinc Total	621	0
Mercury Total	610	30
4. Organochlorines		
α - H.C.H.	382	100
β - H.C.H.	382	100
γ - H.C.H.	382	66
δ - H.C.H.	382	100
Aldrin	382	100
Dieldrin	382	85
Endrin	382	100
Heptachlor	382	100
Heptachlor epoxide	382	100
Endosulfan A	382	100
Endosulfan B	382	100
p,p - D.D.E.	382	100
o,p - D.D.E.	382	100

p,p - D.D.T.	382	100
o,p - D.D.T.	382	100
p,p - T.D.E.	382	100
o,p - T.D.E.	382	100
Chlordane	382	100

a relatively small number of spot samples. The largest input of suspended solids arising from effluents was from discharge number 11 which discharged 17.1 tonnes per day and accounted for 9.5% of the total input (See Fig. 20.2a).

Organic Matter

Attempts have been made to estimate the input of organic matter to the Bay using the following techniques:-

Biochemical Oxygen Demand: The best available Biochemical Oxygen Demand (BOD) data based on historic data for discharges and routine river monitoring data. The total BOD input to the Bay was 49.6 tonnes per day of which sludge dumping accounted for 51.0% and domestic sewage a further 27.2%. The nature of the industrial discharges Nos. 8, 9, 11 and 12 precluded an assessment of the BOD input from these sources. The largest individual input from a land based discharge was 6.5 tonnes from the Mumbles trunk sewer and this contributed 13.1% of the total input (See Fig. 20.2c).

Particulate Organic Matter: An estimate of particulate organic matter (POM) was made by subtracting the ashed solids input from the total solids input. The POM input derived in this way was 61.9 tonnes per day. Sludge dumping contributed 27.4% of the total, thus confirming it as the major source of organic material. The organic input from the industrial discharges was higher (15.8%) than might be inferred from the BOD data discussed above due to the inhibition of the BOD test when applied to some industrial effluents. It should be noted that the POM estimates do not differentiate between biologically available organic matter and relatively inert mineral forms such as coal. The River Tawe was the second largest source of POM contributing 22.7% of the total input, although much of this may have been biologically unavailable (See Fig. 20.2d).

Nutrients

Nitrogen: Nitrogen is present in relatively high concentrations in domestic sewage in both organic and inorganic forms. The inorganic fraction exists largely as free and saline ammonia. During treatment, or after dispersion in well oxygenated waters, the ammonia is converted to its oxide forms, the ultimate oxidation product being nitrate. In good quality rivers, nitrogen is present predominantly in the form of nitrate, whilst industrial effluents can contain nitrogen in any of its forms. Because of the variety of sources and, therefore, forms in which nitrogen is introduced to Swansea Bay, the ammonia and total oxidised nitrogen data have been combined to give the input of total inorganic nitrogen (TIN). The total input of inorganic nitrogen to the Bay during the survey period was 10,600kg per day and the two major inputs were industrial discharges, Nos. 9 and 11, which comprised 42.0%. Sludge dumping (8.4%) and the Mumbles Trunk Sewer (10.4%) were the other major contributors of TIN to the Bay (See Figs. 20.2b,e and f).

Phosphorus: Phosphorus occurs in both particulate and soluble phases in natural waters and in the soluble form it can exist either organically bound or in the fully oxidised form as orthophosphate. The analytical techniques used in this study determined only the orthophosphate fraction and, therefore, only this form of phosphorus was considered. Rivers and streams accounted for 35.0% of the total orthophosphate input of 1,140kg per day. The largest individual discharge of orthophosphate was the Mumbles Trunk Sewer (25.3%) and sludge dumping accounted for a further 36.5% (See Fig. 20.2h).

Silicate: The major proportion of silica entering the Bay did so via rivers and streams as a result of natural weathering processes. Rivers and streams accounted for 86.7% of the total input of 13,100kg per day. Approximately half of the total input entered the Bay via the Rivers Neath and Tawe (See Fig. 20.2g).

Metals

Cadmium: The total input of cadmium was 5.83kg per day of which the Nant-y-Fendrod contributed 2.5kg per day. Previous work undertaken by the Welsh Water Authority during 1973/4 indicated a mass input of 5.8kg per day from this source. This reduction can be attributed to the closure of a sulphuric acid plant in the catchment and the reculverting of a tributary stream which was grossly polluted with heavy metals from tip leachate. The removal and levelling of these tips has also contributed to the improvement in water quality. The Rivers Tawe and Neath together contribute 17.2% of the total cadmium input to the Bay, however, this is due mainly to the large volume discharged by these rivers rather than significantly elevated levels of cadmium in the river waters.

Sludge dumping is the second largest point source of cadmium accounting for 14.1% of the total input whilst input via the atmosphere over the study area (See Fig. 20.1) was estimated at 13.7% of the total (See Fig. 20.2i).

Chromium: Two discrete sources contribute 80.0% of the total chromium input to the Bay of 119kg. The Neath outfall was the largest source discharging 61.8kg per day of which 88% was in the soluble form and, therefore, potentially biologically available. Sludge was the other major input, accounting for 33.4kg per day (See Fig. 20.2k).

Copper: The total copper input to the Bay was 180kg per day, the major sources being discharge Number 12 and the River Tawe which jointly contributed 60.7% of the total. The proportion of soluble copper from the former source was 40% whilst only 10.5% of the copper input from the River Tawe was in the soluble phase. There were also significant inputs of copper from sludge dumping and via the atmosphere which together contributed 15.6% of the total input to the study area (See Fig. 20.2ℓ).

Iron: Industrial discharges Nos. 9 and 11 together discharged 8,012kg of iron per day which comprised 72.1% of the total input to the Bay, 83% of which was in the particulate form. The combined input from the Rivers Neath and Tawe was 1,808kg, 91% of which was in particulate form. The large proportion of particulate iron in the rivers arose partly from the geochemical abundance of iron and partly from industrial discharges to the rivers (See Fig. 20.2q).

Lead: The total lead input to the Bay was 153kg per day of which 47.9% was contributed by industrial discharges Nos. 9, 11 and 12. The input from these three discharges was 73.4kg per day of which 90.3% was in the particulate form. The two other major inputs of lead resulted from sludge dumping and deposition from the atmosphere, which accounted for 14.1% and 22.2% respectively of the total lead input to the study area (See Fig. 20.2m).

Manganese: Rivers and streams accounted for 67.7% of the total manganese input of 524kg per day, the majority of which was in the dissolved form (65%). The River Tawe, which comprised 33.4% of total input, was the major source of this metal (See Fig. 20.2o).

Nickel: The River Tawe contributed 71.6% of the total input of nickel to the Bay (211kg per day) and this resulted largely from metal processing activity in the catchment. The average concentration of dissolved nickel in the River Tawe during the survey period was 105µg per litre. The only other significant sources of nickel were the River Neath and deposition from the atmosphere. The input from the River Neath was 11.3% (23.9kg per day) of the total input and had an average dissolved nickel content of 10.2µg per litre. The atmospheric input was 15.0kg per day (See Fig. 20.2p).

Zinc: The Nant-y-Fendrod was the largest single source of zinc and represented 24.9% of the total input to the Bay. Contamination by leachate from tips of metal refining waste in the Lower Swansea Valley resulted in the combined Tawe and Nant-y-Fendrod discharge contributing 39% of the total input. The other major source was deposition from the atmosphere which contributed 18%. Industrial discharges Nos. 9 and 11 jointly contributed 26.8% of the total zinc input; 70% of the input from these two discharges was in the particulate form (See Fig. 20.2n).

Mercury: Outfall Number 8 discharged 6.0kg per day during the survey period and although estimates for the input of mercury from atmospheric input could not be quantified, this outfall was clearly the major source probably comprising more than 75% of the total input to the Bay. The River Tawe, Neath and Ogmore together comprised 9.2% of the total mercury input from land based sources, although the average total mercury concentrations in these rivers was less than 0.3µg per litre (See Fig. 20.2j).

Organochlorines

A limited number of samples from the inputs investigated were analysed for their organochlorine content. The organochlorines investigated and the detection limits of the methods used are listed in Table 20.3.

The vast majority of the samples analysed did not contain detectable quantities of organochlorines (see Table 20.4). Gamma HCH and Dieldrin were the only commonly detected pesticides and the results are discussed below. Aldrin was detected in one sample from discharge Number 16 (0.03µg/litre) and p.p. D.D.E. was frequently detected in discharge Nos. 1 and 3, average concentrations being 22.0µg/litre and and 18.0µg/litre respectively.

Gamma HCH: Gamma HCH was found in all rivers. The mean detected concentrations varied between 5.17µg/l and 18.67µg/l. These figures represent a positive data return of between 15% and 43% for all river samples. None of the domestic sewage or industrial discharges contained significant quantities of Gamma HCH.

Dieldrin: Dieldrin was also found in the rivers in a limited number of samples for which the mean concentration range was between 1.1 to 2.74µg/l. Occasional positive results were also found in samples taken at Mumbles outfall and the Queens Dock Outfall, mean concentrations (when detected) being 12.83µg/l for the former and 6.00µg/l for the latter discharge.

CONCLUSIONS

(1) An attempt has been made to produce a comprehensive inputs budget for the study area (see Figure 20.1). It must be recognised, however, that whilst the data from land based sources was reliable, the input via the atmosphere can only be considered to be an approximation since it relied on an extrapolation of data obtained from land based sampling stations.

The estimated input from sludge dumping was reliable since it was monitored by MAFF.

However, not all of the sludge dumped would remain in the survey area for any significant time.

The budget also excluded any input of materials from the seaward boundaries of the study area since this was not practical and the scale of effort required to quantify these inputs could not be justified.

(2) Rivers and streams accounted for the major proportion of the volume (94%) and the weight of solids (61%) discharged from the Bay.

(3) Sludge dumping was the major source of organic matter and accounted for 51% of the BOD and 27.4% of the POM input. Domestic sewage was the major land based contributor of BOD (27.2%) whilst rivers and streams were the major source of POM (40.2%). It must be noted that the POM content of rivers included organic material which was biologically unavailable.

(4) Industrial and domestic discharges contributed two-thirds of the TIN input and approximately one third of the orthophosphate input to the Bay. Rivers and streams were the major source of silicate entering the Bay (86.7%) and also contributed approximately a quarter of the TIN and orthophosphate inputs.

(5) Sludge dumping represented a significant proportion of the total inputs of all the metals for which data was available. The contributions to the total input of chromium (28.1%) lead (25.5%) and cadmium (14.1%) were particularly notable.

Atmospheric metal inputs were also significant particularly for the metals zinc (18.4%), lead (19.3%) and cadmium (13.7%).

Metal levels were elevated in the River Tawe and Nant-y-Fendrod as a result of past and present mining and industrial metal processing activities (See also Chapter 21). The River Tawe was a major source of nickel (71.6%), manganese (33.4%), copper (23.4%), zinc (14.2%) and cadmium (10.8%). The Nant-y-Fendrod was the largest individual source of cadmium (42.9%) and zinc (24.9%).

The largest individual sources of the metals chromium, copper, iron and mercury were sewage and direct industrial discharges in the vicinity of the towns of Neath and Port Talbot.

The metals copper, iron, lead and nickel were predominantly discharged in particulate form whilst the metals cadmium, chromium, manganese and zinc were in dissolved phase.

(6) The majority of samples analysed for organochlorines did not contain detectable quantities. The only compounds which were frequently detected were Gamma HCH and Dieldrin, both of which occurred at very low concentrations.

TABLE 20.5. Average Concentration for each Determinand for each Input
(D = dissolved; P = particulate; T = total).

Determinand		1	2	3	4	5	6	7	8	9	10	11	12	13	14	15	16	17
P.O.M. (mg/l)		146.5	40.5	66.3	1.4	2.9	43.7	3.20	61.0	85.0		92	105	48.8	3.7	3.4	12.5	
B.O.D. (mg/l)		134	147	106			160	1.80			1.40			59.0	3.70	3.70	161	4320
S. Solids (105℃)(mg/l)		173	60.4	96.8	26.8	12.0	104	23.0	151	262	6.33	335	444	71.0	10.5	15.6	15.4	6959
S. Solids (500℃)(mg/l)		26.5	19.9	30.5			60.3	19.8	90.0	177	9.40	243	339	22.2	6.80	12.2	2.94	
NH_3 - N (mg/l)		19.5	219	5.00	18.5	53.1	7.59	68	2.33	97.5	12.7	24.9	0.71	57.6	13.9	31.0	10.8	29.375
T.O.N. (mg/l)		3.43	1.38	2.51	1.01	0.71	1.08	0.71	2.19	1.52	0.62	1.52	147	1.36	2.47	1.32	0.53	3.46
Diss. SiO_2 (mg/l)		10.9	5.32	11.4	8.05	3.14	5.79	3.61	5.89	8.65	5.23	5.59	5.04	7.83	6.75	5.77	8.77	6.45
O - Phosphate (mg/l)		5.76	0.93	0.97	0.03	0.03	0.09	0.09	0.19	0.09	0.01	0.03	1.30	1.28	0.44	0.17	3.01	60.9
Total Hg (µg/l)		0.34	0.40	0.30	0.30	0.30	0.50	0.18	269	0.52	0.11	0.43	1.20	0.50	0.25	0.13	0.83	
Cadmium (µg/l)	D. P. T.		0.32	0.63	61.5	0.36	0.41	0.19	0.41	0.51	0.22 0.11	0.40	120	0.30	0.13 0.15	0.10 0.11	0.30	
Chromium (µg/l)	D. P. T.	1.90	1.47	1.88	97.7	0.43	0.62	0.42	1.00	3.62		2.72	81.1	0.69			0.42	0.243
	D. P. T.	4.29	27.5	4.38	0.63	0.76	0.83	- 0.78	2340	0.88	0.52	18.9	56.9	41.8	0.73	0.67	18.7	4.32
Copper (µg/l)	D. P. T.		71.9	4.80	1.04	24.9	1.82		2670	6.68		94.4	69.9	62.7			21.6	
	D. P. T.	53.9	29.8	4.03	3.48	3.56	14.6	5.00 7.11	24.1	45.5	1.30 2.78	22.6	46200	23.0	2.98 7.51	2.71 6.49	14.1	6.20
Iron (µg/l)	D. P. T.		262	30.4	23.1	22.1	70.3		346	112		80.1	97800	38.4			36.2	
	D. P. T.	1480	499	691	389	139	584	1550	111	1340	237	28300	529	335	563	358	92.5	
Lead (µg/l)	D. P. T.		2080	4120	3040	971	3310		2010	28600		139000	3750	1370			159	
	D. P. T.	65.7	4.25	1.00	8.12	1.1	10.2	1.23 2.85	8.14	10.7	0.91 0.80	6.37	9350	4.24	0.68 2.01	1.20 4.4	4.58	0.87
Manganese (µg/l)	D. P. T.		26.4	31.1	149	3.6	24.3		38.2	1064		198	34400	21.4			7.44	
	D. P. T.	231	31.0	853 650	1970	94.4	80.3	138 33.1	9.28	185	65.0 6.22	460	12800	148	209 13.9	28.6 19.6	65.0	
Nickel (µg/l)	D. P. T.		72.4		2030	121	279		160	862		1160	36000	200			74.2	
	D. P. T.	6.33	60.8	4.38	20.2	105	4.79	10.2 27.9	1.38	7.77	4.48 1.10	14.2	78.3	2.86	7.56 1.66	2.76 1.56	70.5	2.88
Zinc (µg/l)	D. P. T.		184	4.75	33.4		13.1		18.8	13.3		45.5	161	4.95			64.7	
	D. P. T.	264	62.5 199	1370 984	8430 8910	57.0 66.8	76.7 258	10.2 19.5	52.3 800	115 3940	13.1 6.72	228 2450	1010 1550	74.3 285	14.1 10.4	6.86 9.27	57.6 73.5	4.69

Coastal Water

TABLE 20.6. Average Mass Input (kg/day). (D = dissolved; P = particulate; T = total; Loadings Derived from Ratios Obtained from SEJC Phase II Inputs Programme).
*

Determinand	Discharge No.	1 *	2	3 *	4	5	6	7	8	9	10	11	12	13	14	15	16	17
P.O.M.		6594	30.5	463	726 *	14,100 *	479	7310 *	1412	2666	564 *	5097	85	559	246	1911	309	2320 *
B.O.D.		6520	221	1100	164	2010	4380	1460	NA	NA	592	NA	NA	3500	332	1640	167	2216
S. Solids (105°C)		7683	45.4	861	2006	41605	1122	51860	3474	8224	2085	17112	374	813	674	12781	380	3570
S. Solids (500°C)		1089	14.9	398	1280	27500 *	643	44550	2062	5558	1521	12015	289	254	428	10870	71.0	
NH₃ – N		854	164	14.7	18.5	53.1	78.4	68.0	52.5	3053	12.7	1277	0.52	665	13.9	31.0	244	15.06
T.O.N.		244	1.09	74.2	79.0	741	11.4	673	50.0	48.0	225	74.3	117	15.8	110	637	21.8	1.77
T.I.N.		1098	165	88.9	97.5	754	89.8	741	102	3101	238	1351	118	681	124	668	266	16.8
Diss. Silicate		616	4.29	87.0	304	3102	61.2	3632	136	270	1739	289	3.26	90.5	224	2358	220	3.3
O-Phosphate		288	0.69	2.38	1.11	17.4	1.03	185	4.18	2.88	5.15	1.41	0.82	14.7	10.9	99.0	61.1	31.2
Total Hg.		0.01	0.0003	0.001	0.03	0.35	0.006	0.27	6.00	0.02	0.03	0.02	0.001	0.006	0.01	0.06	0.02	
Cadmium D.		0.05	0.0003	0.002	1.77	0.55	0.0044	0.30	0.01	0.02	0.11	0.02	0.02	0.007	0.003	0.06	0.008	0.012
P.		0.04	0.0008	0.01	0.73	0.09	0.002	0.10	0.01	0.10	0.01	0.11	0.02	0.0007	0.002	0.05	0.003	
T.		0.09	0.001	0.01	2.50	0.63	0.01	0.37	0.02	0.11	0.12	0.13	0.04	0.008	0.005	0.11	0.01	
Chromium D.		0.07	0.26	0.02	0.02	0.78	0.01	0.55	54.2	0.03	0.06	0.77	0.03	0.48	0.01	0.37	0.61	2.22
P.		0.14	0.03	0.03	0.02	8.25	0.01	0.42	7.58	0.18	0.05	3.86	0.01	0.24	0.01	0.28	0.07	
T.		0.20	0.05	0.04	0.05	9.03	0.02	0.97	61.8	0.21	0.11	4.64	0.04	0.72	0.02	0.65	0.68	
Copper D.		1.07	0.03	0.01	0.26	4.44	0.15	6.86	0.54	1.39	0.54	1.20	27.0	0.27	0.05	1.28	0.43	3.18
P.		1.31	0.16	0.25	0.86	37.7	0.59	3.80	6.91	2.01	0.32	2.96	40.2	0.18	0.07	4.64	0.85	
T.		2.38	0.19	0.27	1.12	42.2	0.75	10.7	7.44	3.40	0.86	4.12	67.2	0.44	0.13	5.91	1.28	
Iron D.		54.1	0.48	2.28	16.6	130	6.43	38.3	2.66	40.5	1.52	1310	0.30	3.89	0.45	9.12	2.79	
P.		14.4	1.02	31.7	106	783	30.5	858	42.9	851	34.1	5810	2.65	11.9	10.0	204	1.91	
T.		68.5	1.51	34.0	123	912	37.0	896	45.6	892	35.7	7120	2.96	15.8	10.4	213	4.70	
Lead D.		0.58	0.004	0.003	0.27	1.39	0.11	1.77	0.17	0.32	0.31	0.36	6.58	0.05	0.01	0.73	0.14	0.447
P.		2.85	0.02	0.47	3.89	5.12	0.16	1.86	0.68	34.2	0.10	10.6	21.5	0.20	0.02	2.67	0.14	
T.		3.44	0.02	0.05	4.16	6.51	0.30	3.63	0.85	34.5	0.41	10.9	28.0	0.25	0.03	3.40	0.28	
Mn D.		8.22	0.03	2.61	42.0	87.2	0.85	65.8	0.21	5.70	18.7	20.1	9.58	1.72	3.92	13.4	1.36	
P.		1.93	0.03	3.22	4.30	87.7	2.19	21.4	3.48	21.2	0.44	34.4	16.5	0.59	2.22	10.2	0.29	
T.		10.1	0.06	5.83	46.3	175	3.04	87.1	3.69	26.9	19.1	54.4	26.1	2.31	4.14	23.6	1.65	
Nickel D.		0.23	0.06	0.01	0.86	73.6	0.05	6.28	0.03	0.25	1.52	0.66	0.05	0.03	0.22	1.27	1.72	1.48
P.		0.13	0.10	0.001	1.16	77.6	0.10	17.6	0.38	0.18	0.10	1.94	0.08	0.02	0.02	0.63	0.37	
T.		0.36	0.15	0.01	2.01	151.0	0.15	23.9	0.41	0.43	1.61	2.61	0.12	0.05	0.24	1.90	2.10	
Zinc D.		7.61	0.06	4.16	214	115	0.83	20.7	1.17	3.55	6.66	9.83	0.58	0.86	0.37	4.73	1.49	2.40
P.		4.47	0.09	2.79	15.8	16.6	1.99	13.0	17.4	121	0.76	112	0.47	2.40	0.16	4.45	0.35	
T.		12.1	0.15	6.95	230	131	2.82	33.6	18.6	124	7.42	122	1.05	3.26	0.53	9.18	1.83	
Flow (M³/SEC)		0.571	0.009	0.104	0.493	12.7	0.125	12.6	0.270	0.363	3.49	0.562	0.008	0.132	0.476	5.67	0.279	0.006

TABLE 20.7. The Five Major Inputs of Each Substance as a Proportion of the Total Input of that Substance (%).

	DISCHARGE	FLOW	SUS-PENDED SOLIDS	B.O.D.	P.O.M.	T.I.N.	DISS. SILICATE	ORTHO-PHOSPHATE	CADMIUM	CHROMIUM	COPPER	IRON	LEAD	MAN-GANESE	NICKEL	ZINC	MERCURY
1.	Mumbles Trunk Sewer	1.5		13.1	10.6	10.4	4.7	25.3									
2.	Industrial																
3.	Queens Dock																
4.	Nant-y-Fendrod								42.9					8.8		24.9	
5.	River Tawe	33.5	23.0		22.7	7.5	23.7		10.8	7.6	23.4	8.2		33.4	71.6	14.2	5·0
6.	Industrial			8.8													
7.	River Neath	33.3	28.7		11.8		27.7	16.2	6.4		5.9	8.1		16.6	11.3		3·9
8.	Neath Outfall									51.9							85·7
9.	Industrial					29.3						8.0	22·5			13.4	
10.	River Afan	9.2					13.3										
11.	Industrial		9.5		8.2	12.7				3.9		64.1	7·1	10.4	1.2	13.2	
12.	Industrial										37.3		18·3				
13.	Glyncorrwg			7.0													
14.	River Kenfig																
15.	River Ogmore	15.0	7.1				18.0	8.7									0·9
16.	Penybont STW Effluent			4.5				5.4									
17.	Penybont STW Sludge																
18.	Sludge Dumping		14.4	51.0	27.4	8.4		36.5	14.1	28.1	8.4	5.9	14·1	6.7	3.5	18.4	2·3
19.	Atmospheric Inputs								13.7	3.4	7.2		22·2		7.1		
	CONTRIBUTION TO TOTAL INPUT FROM FIVE MAJOR SOURCES ITEMISED (%)	92.5	82.7	84.4	80.7	68.3	87.4	92.1	87.9	94.9	82.2	94.3	84·2	75.9	94.7	84.1	97·8

TABLE 20.8. Inputs to Swansea Bay by Discharge Type.
(D = Dissolved; P = Particulate; T = Total)

AVERAGE MASS INPUT (kg/day)

CATEGORY	DETERMINAND		DOMESTIC SEWAGE	INDUSTRIAL EFFLUENT	RIVERS & STREAMS	SLUDGE DUMPING TO SEA	ATMOSPHERIC INPUTS	TOTAL
ORGANIC MATTER	B.O.D.		13,500	4,600	6,200	25,300	-	49,600
	P.O.M.		10,215	9,770	24,900	17,000 *	-	61,900
SEDIMENTS	SUSPENDED SOLIDS		13,300	30,400	111,000	26,100	-	181,000
NUTRIENTS	AMMONIACAL NITROGEN		1,790	4,630	197	-	-	6,620
	TOTAL OXIDISED NITROGEN		358	302	2,466	-	-	3,130
	TOTAL INORGANIC NITROGEN		2,150	4,930	2,660	899	-	10,600
	ORTHO PHOSPHATE		399	12	318	416	-	1,140
	DISS. SILICATE		1,015	762	11,358	-	-	13,100
METALS	CADMIUM	D	0.067	0.075	2.79	-	-	2.93
		P	0.057	0.243	0.982	-	-	1.28
		T	0.12	0.311	3.77	0.82	0.8 **	5.83
	CHROMIUM	D	1.18	55.3	1.79	-	-	58.2
		P	0.48	11.7	9.03	-	-	21.2
		T	3.85	66.8	10.8	37.4	4	119.0
	COPPER	D	1.78	30.3	13.4	-	-	45.5
		P	2.59	52.8	47.4	-	-	103.0
		T	7.55	83.1	61.1	15.1	13	180.0
	IRON	D	62.1	1360	196	-	-	1,619
		P	59.9	6738	1995	-	-	8,793
		T	123	8098	2190	-	650	11,100
	LEAD	D	0.76	7.54	4.48	-	-	12.8
		P	3.66	67.2	13.66	-	-	84.5
		T	4.17	74.7	18.14	21.6	34	**153.0**
	MANGANESE	D	13.9	36.5	231	-	-	281.0
		P	6.03	77.8	124	-	-	208.0
		T	19.9	114.0	355	-	35	**524**.0
	NICKEL	D	1.99	1.10	83.8	-	-	86.9
		P	0.52	2.78	97.1	-	-	100.0
		T	4.0	3.88	181.0	7.4	15.0	211.0
	ZINC	D	14.1	16.0	361.0	-	-	391.0
		P	10.0	253.0	50.8	-	-	314.0
		T	26.5	269.0	412.0	45.8	170.0	923.0
	MERCURY	T	0.04	6.05	0.75	0.16	-	**7.0**

* Assuming 65% POM in sewage sludge. ** Probably an overestimate due to inclusion of "less than" data.

322   C. J. Chubb, R. P. Dale and J. H. Stoner

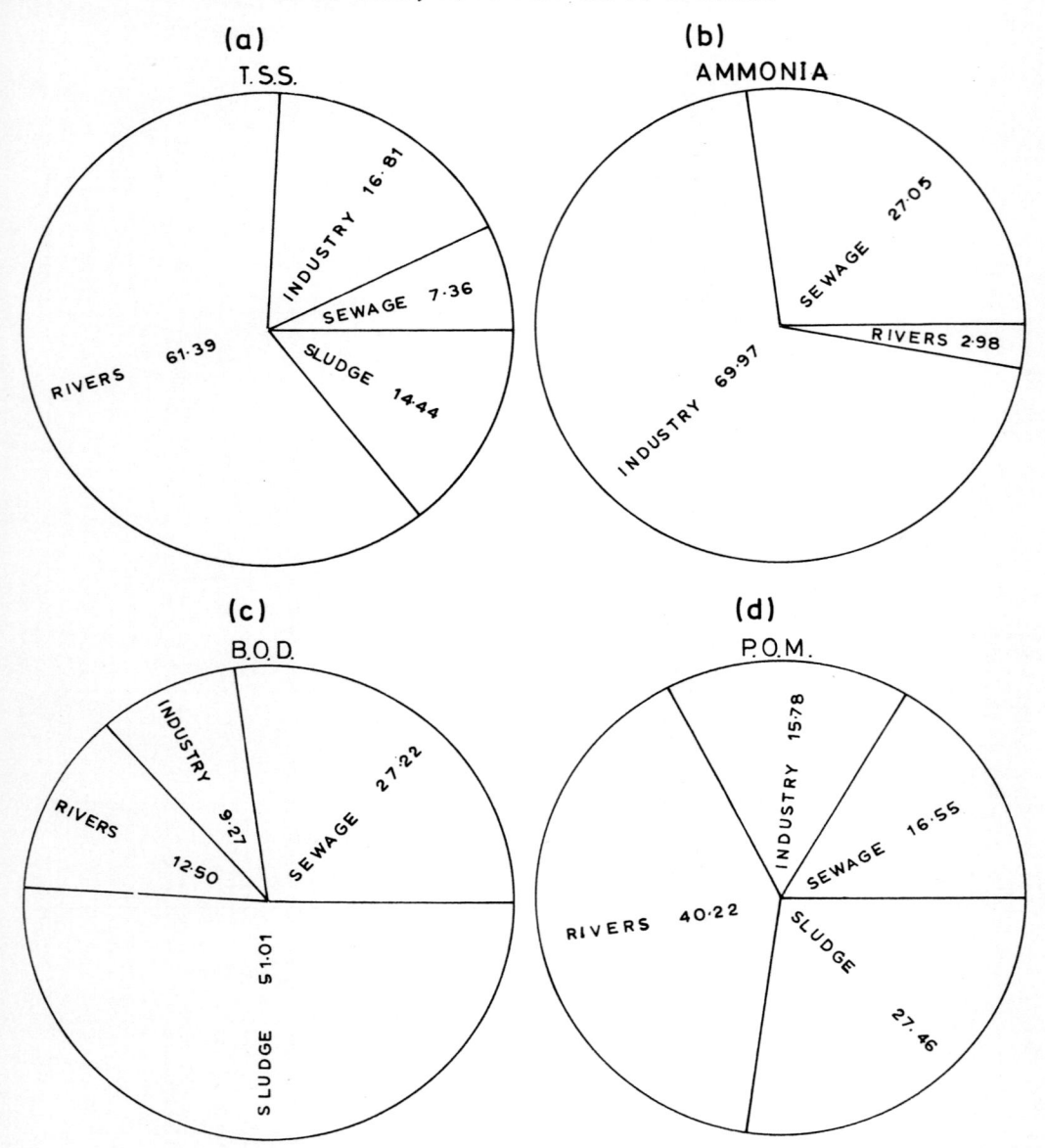

(a) T.S.S.
- RIVERS 61.39
- INDUSTRY 16.81
- SEWAGE 7.36
- SLUDGE 14.44

(b) AMMONIA
- INDUSTRY 69.97
- SEWAGE 27.05
- RIVERS 2.98

(c) B.O.D.
- RIVERS 12.50
- INDUSTRY 9.27
- SEWAGE 27.22
- SLUDGE 51.01

(d) P.O.M.
- RIVERS 40.22
- INDUSTRY 15.78
- SEWAGE 16.55
- SLUDGE 27.46

Figure 20.2a-q. Percentage of mass input derived from (i) rivers and streams, (ii) industrial discharges, (iii) domestic sewage, (iv) sludge dumping and (v) atmospheric deposition for various components.
(a) TSS, (b) Ammonia, (c) BOD, (d) POM.

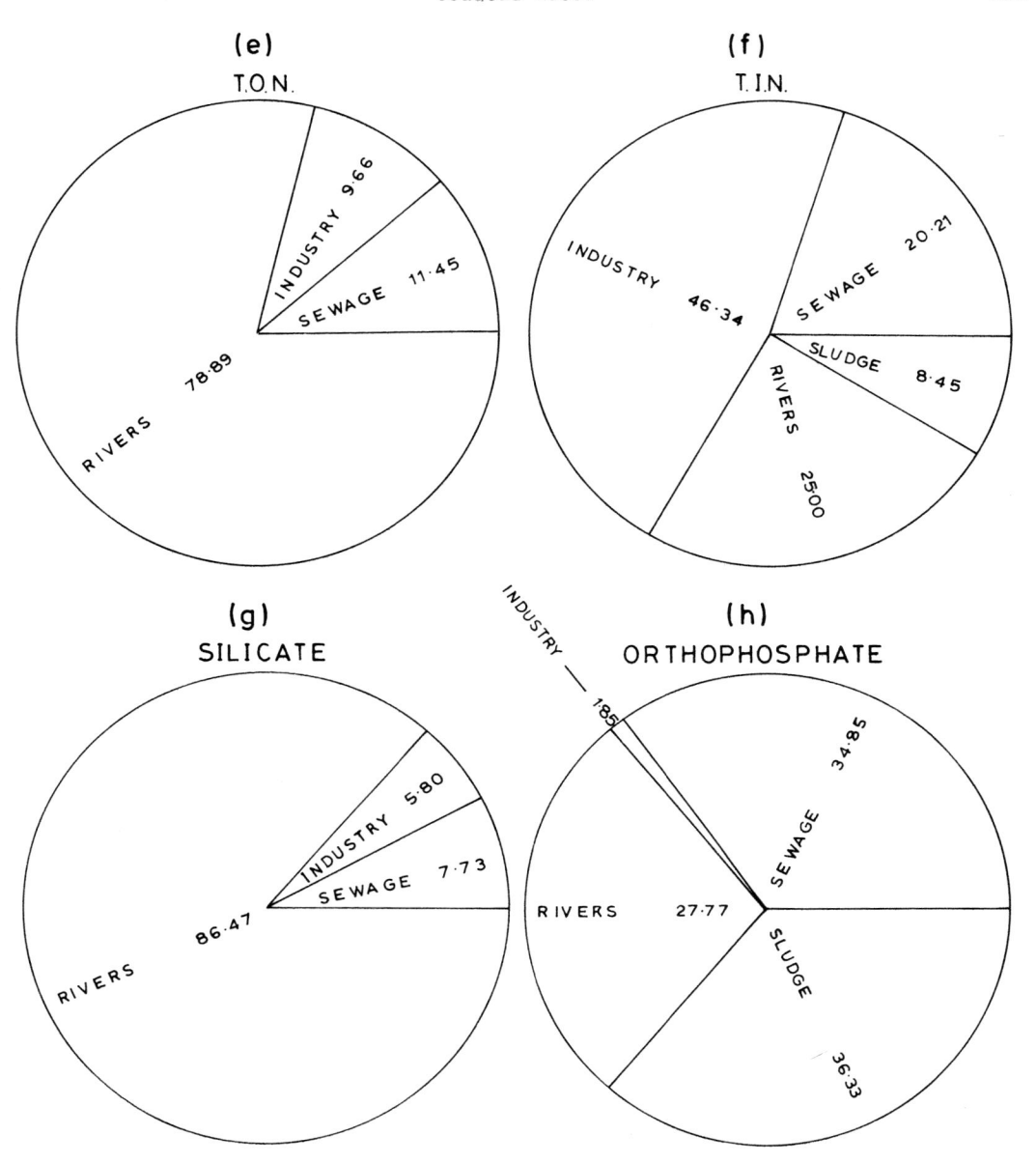

Figure 20.2e-h.
(e) TON, (f) TIN, (g) Silicate, (h) Orthophosphate.

(i)
TOTAL CADIUM

- RIVERS 64·65
- INDUSTRY 5·33
- SEWAGE 2·23
- ATMOS. 13·72
- SLUDGE 14·06

(j)
TOTAL MERCURY

- INDUSTRY 86·43
- RIVERS 10·71
- SLUDGE 2·29
- SEWAGE

(k)
TOTAL CHROMIUM

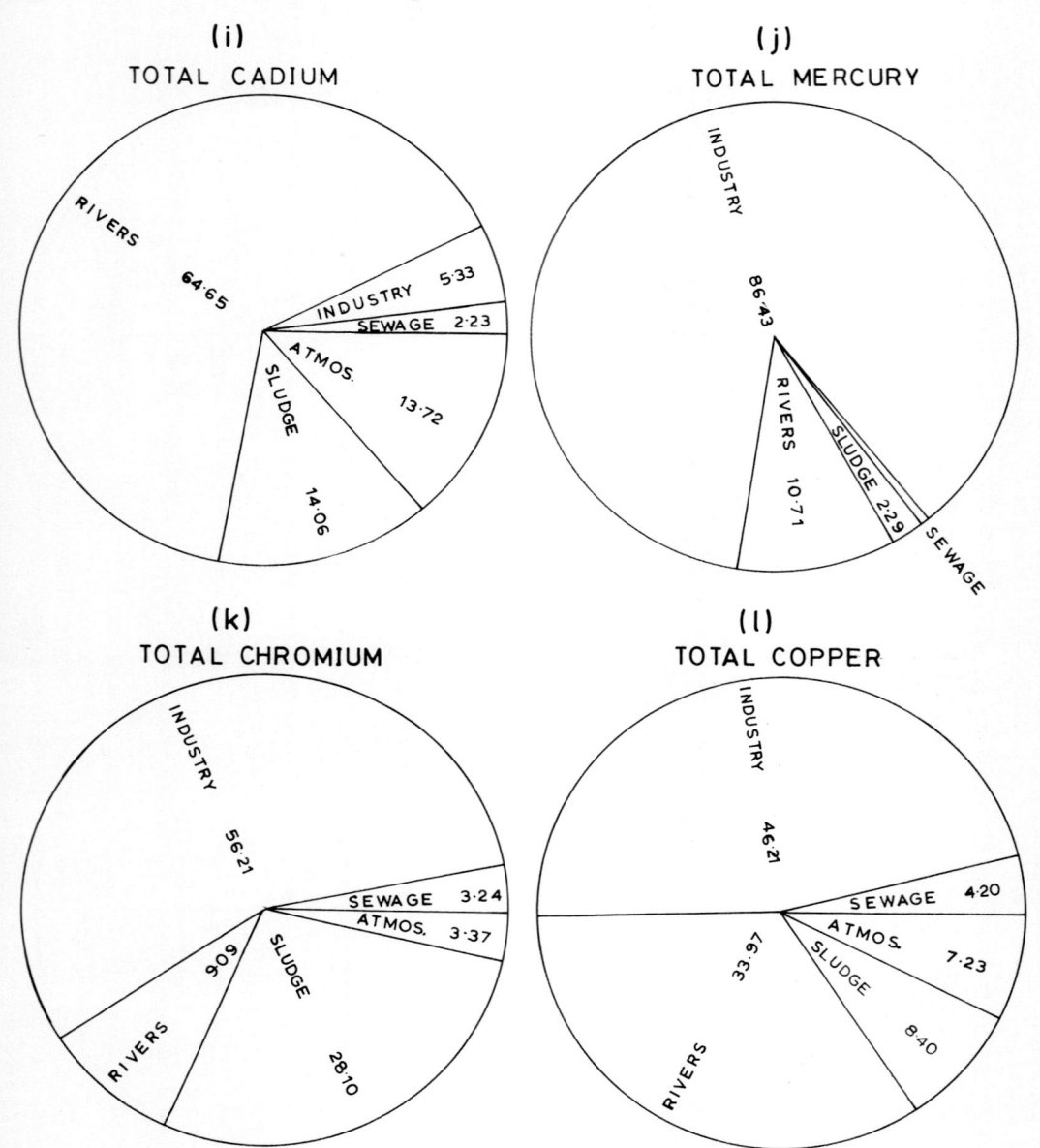

- INDUSTRY 56·21
- SEWAGE 3·24
- ATMOS. 3·37
- RIVERS 9·09
- SLUDGE 28·10

(l)
TOTAL COPPER

- INDUSTRY 46·21
- SEWAGE 4·20
- ATMOS. 7·23
- SLUDGE 8·40
- RIVERS 33·97

Figure 20.2i-1.
(i) Total Cadmium, (j) Total Mercury, (k) Total Chromium, (l) Total Copper.

Coastal Water

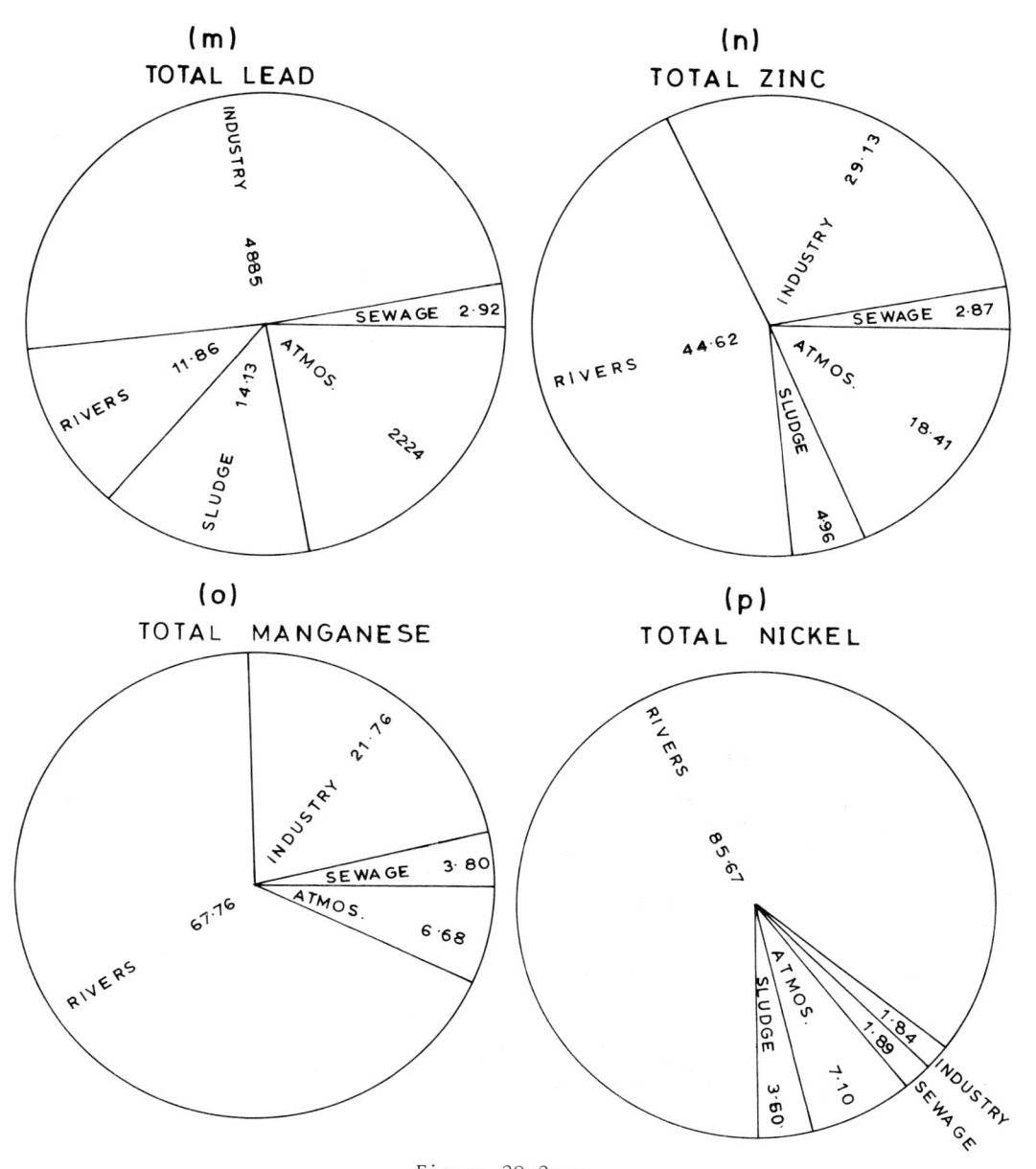

(m) TOTAL LEAD
- INDUSTRY 48.85
- SEWAGE 2.92
- ATMOS. 22.24
- SLUDGE 14.13
- RIVERS 11.86

(n) TOTAL ZINC
- INDUSTRY 29.13
- SEWAGE 2.87
- ATMOS. 18.41
- SLUDGE 4.96
- RIVERS 44.62

(o) TOTAL MANGANESE
- INDUSTRY 21.76
- SEWAGE 3.80
- ATMOS. 6.68
- RIVERS 67.76

(p) TOTAL NICKEL
- RIVERS 85.67
- ATMOS. 7.10
- SLUDGE 3.60
- INDUSTRY 1.84
- SEWAGE 1.89

Figure 20.2m-p.
(m) Total Lead, (n) Total Zinc, (o) Total Manganese, (p) Total Nickel.

(q)
TOTAL IRON

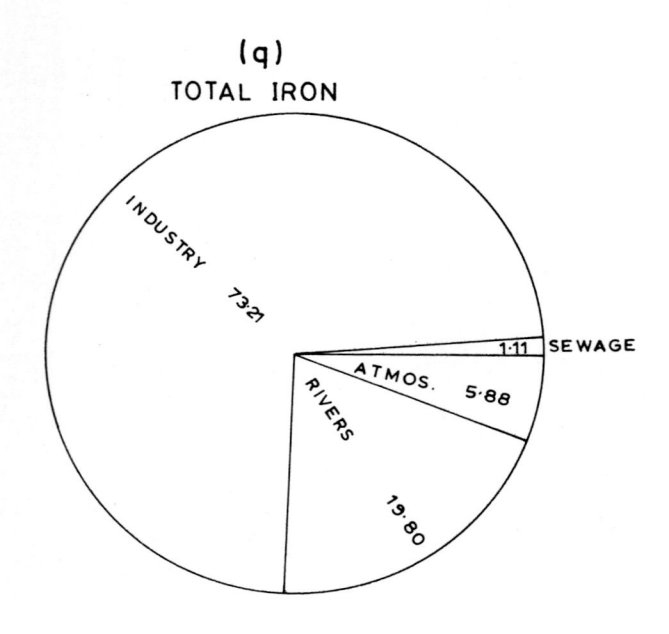

INDUSTRY 73.21

SEWAGE 1.11

ATMOS. 5.88

RIVERS 19.80

Figure 20.2q.   Total Iron.

REFERENCES

National Water Council. (1978). *River Water Quality - The Next Stage: Review of Discharge Consent Conditions.* National Water Council.

Stoner, J.H. (1977).   *A Report on the First Year of a Programme to Monitor Inputs to Swansea Bay. 1973-1974.* Welsh Water Authority Tidal Waters Report 77/2, 66pp.

Welsh Office. (1974a).   *Report of the Working Party on Possible Pollution in Swansea Bay.* Vol. I, Welsh Office, 33pp.

Welsh Office (1974b).   *Report of the Working Party on Possible Pollution in Swansea Bay.* Vol. II, Welsh Office, 110pp.

Welsh Water Authority (1977).   *First Report* (Severn Estuary Survey and Systems Panel) *to the Technical Working Party of the Severn Estuary Joint Committee (May 1977)* Welsh Water Authority Tidal Waters Report 77/1, 125pp.

Welsh Water Authority (In press).   *Second Report* (Severn Estuary Survey and Systems Panel) *to the Technical Working Party of the Severn Estuary Joint Committee (October, 1979).* Welsh Water Authority Tidal Waters Report 79/5.

DISCUSSION IV

Nelson: I did not understand how you calculated input when the component is below the detection limit?

Stoner: The mass input was obtained by multiplying the detection limit by the flow to provide a (maximum) input value; it wasn't used very often, since, as you'll see in the full paper, the nutrients, organics and most of the metals were detected in the vast majority of samples.

Nelson: How did you do your metal determination?

Stoner: Metals in effluents were determined by pre-concentration by evaporation, followed by AAS; for the rivers and streams we used Chelex ion exchange resin to pre-concentrate.

Norton: I'm intrigued by the apparent assumption in your paper of dumping as an input into Swansea Bay. I'm not sure that view is shared entirely by the authorities. I have (actual) figures for this dumping, which are distinctly lower than the licenced level which the Water Authority may have used.

Stoner: The dumping figures used were provided by Dr. Norton's Department and, since the dumping ground is within the study area, the figures were included; they obviously represent a maximum possible input from sludge dumping.

Webber: Information point. I've some data for water quality from one side of Swansea Bay, which shows a large seasonal variation in coliform levels; also my coliform levels were considerably higher than stated.

Chubb: It wouldn't surprise me to find seasonal variation and we said in fact, that the overall distribution pattern in the Bay can be shown to be seasonal, at particular locations.

Grant: You mention that tidal currents were the main influence on the direction of movement. Our work (in Aberdeen Bay), while agreeing with this, has shown that wind can influence the extent of water mass spread. When you have an offshore wind, the water might move out of Swansea Bay, but when you have an onshore wind, water spread is restricted, the water becoming concentration within the Bay. For example, in Aberdeen Bay, we find very marked frontal systems forming under onshore winds, as polluted river waters become concentrated within the Bay; this can have quite a marked effect on water quality.

Stoner: I agree that meteorological conditions can be very important and, hence, one must remember that the results presented represent surface water quality under the tidal and meteorological conditions prevailing at the time of the survey.

21. TRACE METAL STUDIES IN THE RIVER TAWE AND SWANSEA BAY

C. M. G. Vivian

Lancashire and Western Sea Fisheries Joint Committee, University of Lancaster, Bailrigg, Lancaster LA1 4XY, U.K.

ABSTRACT

The River Tawe drains the Lower Swansea Valley, an area severely contaminated by smelting and other industries over the last 250 years, not least by the 5 million tons of waste material left in the Valley. The concentrations and distribution of cadmium, copper, nickel, lead and zinc have been studied in waters and sediments from the River Tawe and its estuary and in Swansea Bay sediments. The trace metals were determined by atomic absorption spectrophotometry; in waters, after pre-concentration by chelating ion-exchange resin and in sediments, after acid digestion by refluxing for 3 hours with concentrated nitric and perchloric acids (3:1 by volume). The high trace metal levels found in River Tawe water and in sediments from the river, its estuary and in Swansea Bay, result from the weathering and erosion of the waste material left in the Lower Swansea Valley. As a result, the River Tawe appears to be a major source of certain trace metals to coastal waters of the Northern Bristol Channel.

KEYWORDS

Trace metals; Mining waste; River sediments; River run-off; Sub-littoral sediments; Swansea Bay; Bristol Channel.

INTRODUCTION

The trace metal content of river waters and sediments is normally controlled by the abundance of metals in the rocks and soils of the river's catchment area, and by their geochemical mobility. Thus, a catchment area containing mineralized rocks will usually have elevated metal levels in the waters and sediments of the rivers draining it (Abdullah and Royle, 1972; Aston et al., 1974; Elderfield et al., 1971). However, very high levels in rivers are normally associated with polluting discharges and/or metalliferous mining and smelting activities (Abdullah and Royle, 1972; Fuge, 1973; Ireland, 1973; Pasternak, 1973, 1974a, 1974b; Thornton et al., 1975). Because of run-off over waste tips and through mines, the pollution may continue for many years after the mining and/or smelting activities have ceased (Carpenter, 1924, 1925; Jones, 1940a, 1940b, 1958; Jones and Howells, 1969, 1975; Laurie and Jones, 1938; Newton, 1944). Estuarine and coastal waters and sediments are influenced likewise, although usually to a lesser extent due to dilution with 'clean' sea

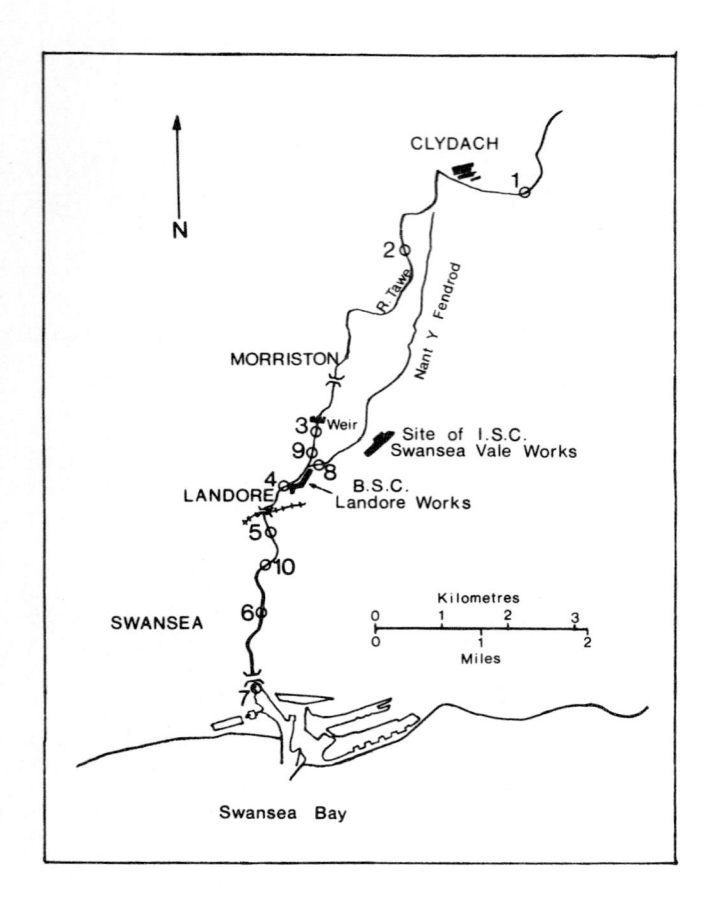

Figure 21.1. River Tawe sample stations.

sea water and marine sediments.

REGIONAL SETTING

The geology of the River Tawe's catchment area comprises predominantly sandstones, limestones, grits and shales of the Old Red Sandstone and Carboniferous series (Harding, 1971; See also Chapters 2 and 3) and no mineralization is known to occur in the area (Bloxam et al., 1972). The area was glaciated and the Lower Swansea Valley is floored with a considerable thickness of alluvium. The river is 'flashy', with an average flow of 10-11m^3/s and a range of 1-310m^3/s (Harding, 1971; Ledger, 1967). The absolute limit of tidal penetration is the weir just below Morriston road bridge (Fig. 21.1) but salt water seldom penetrates further upstream than the obstruction provided by the foundations of the Landore railway bridge (Williams, 1970).

In the Lower Swansea Valley coal has been mined since the fourteenth century, providing the basis for smelting and other industries. Metals extracted or worked in the Valley included gold, silver, lead, tin, nickel, cobalt, arsenic, iron, copper and zinc, the last two being by far the most important (Hilton, 1967). Smelting of copper started in 1717 and of zinc and other metals in the 1850's, with the Valley being the centre of the British copper and zinc smelting industries in the latter part of the nineteenth century (Hilton, 1967). The last copper smelter closed in 1920 and the last zinc smelter in 1971. The only remaining metal extraction plant in the Valley is a nickel refinery at Clydach. Approximately 5 million tons of industrial waste was dumped in the Lower Swansea Valley (Holt, 1964) and this waste has been found to be highly variable in chemical composition, even within a single tip (Gadgil, 1964). Trace metal concentrations in the waste material are very high; up to 1% copper, 9.7% lead, 11.3% zinc and 0.4% uranium have been found (Bloxam, 1971; Gadgil, 1964; Street and Goodman, 1967). Ponds receiving drainage from the tips have been found to have high trace metal levels in their waters, e.g. 20.5mg/l zinc and 10.1mg/l cadmium (Street and Goodman, 1967). In addition, very high levels of cadmium (11mg/l), lead (37mg/l) and zinc (38mg/l) have been reported in the waters of the Nant-y-Fendrod, a small tributary joining the Tawe just above Landore (South West Wales River Authority, Annual Reports, 1965-74). The Nant-y-Fendrod drains the site of the zinc smelter referred to previously which also included a sulphuric acid plant up until 1974.

Strong tidal currents occur in Swansea Bay (0.8m/s has been recorded at Mumbles Head (I. Borthwick, *pers. comm.*)) due to the large tidal range of 8.6m at spring tides experienced at Swansea Docks. The eastern side of the Bay is directly exposed to the prevailing south-westerly winds and Atlantic swell and thus considerable turbulence occurs. The Bay is therefore generally well mixed and very turbid. The high energy environment causes considerable sediment mobility in the Bay (Collins *et al.*, 1979) as is shown by the extensive and continued dredging necessary to maintain the Swansea and Port Talbot shipping channels at the required depth.

METHODS

River water and sediment samples were collected from the freshwater and estuarine mixing regions of the River Tawe at the stations shown in Fig. 21.1. In addition, sub-littoral surficial marine sediments were collected from an area of approximately 100km^2 in Swansea Bay at the stations shown in Fig. 21.2, using a Shipek grab from the R.V. *Ocean Crest*. In sampling the Swansea Bay sediments, care was taken to sample the surface oxidized layer (1-3cm thick) away from the side of the Shipek bucket.

River water samples were filtered within 1½ hours of collection using GF/C filter papers and analysed for trace metals by atomic absorption spectrophotometry, after preconcentration using Chelex-100 resin (Riley and Taylor, 1968) with an overall precision of ± 10% or better. Sediments were collected in polythene bags, frozen, freeze-dried, disaggregated gently in a pestle and mortar and the 2mm fraction stored in plastic containers for subsequent analysis. Each sediment sample was analysed for grain-size by sieving, for organic carbon by the wet oxidation method of Gaudette *et al.* (1974) and for carbonate by the titration method of Grimaldi *et al.* (1966). The sediment samples were subjected to two digestion procedures:(a) boiling under reflux for 3 hours with concentrated nitric and perchloric acids (3:1 by volume) and (b) standing for 12-14 hours at room temperature in 25% v/v acetic acid after an initial 60 second period of ultrasonic disaggregation. Only the results of the nitric/perchloric acid digestions are reported for the Swansea Bay sediments. The acid digests were analysed for trace metals by atomic absorption spectrophotometry. Replicate analyses of representative sediment samples gave an overall precision for both extraction methods, of ± 5% or better for all 5 elements determined.

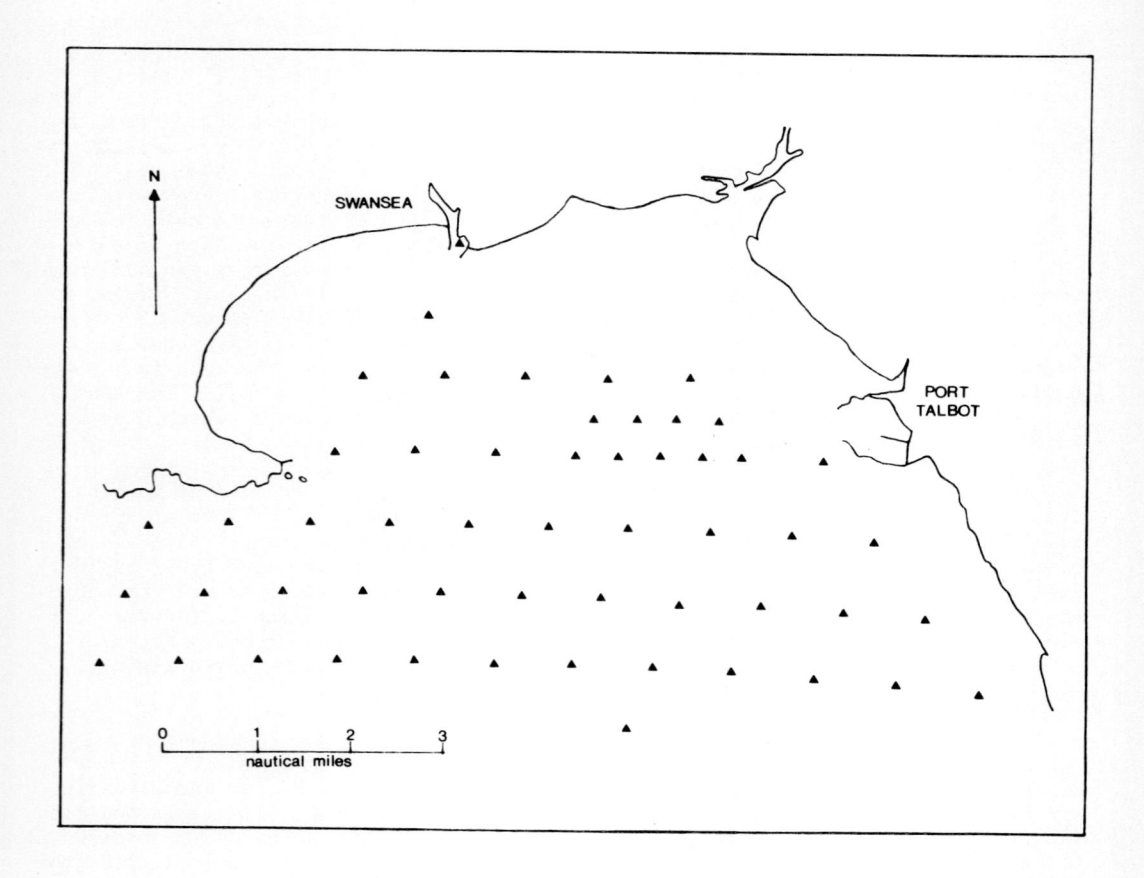

Figure 21.2. Swansea Bay sample stations.

RESULTS AND DISCUSSION

River and Estuarine Waters

A summary of the river and estuarine dissolved trace metal results is shown in Table 21.1. Many of these can be seen to be anomalously high compared with the average values shown at the foot of the table. Several features are evident in the results from Table 21.1.

1. Between Stations 1 and 2 there were large increases in nickel concentrations and small increases in copper concentrations which were probably due to an input from the nickel refinery at Clydach.
2. Between Stations 3 and 4 there were large increases in cadmium and zinc concentrations and smaller increases in copper and lead concentrations. These resulted from the inflow of the Nant-y-Fendrod, which was found to have very high dissolved trace metal concentrations - Station 8 in Table 21.1.
3. On one occasion there was a large increase in zinc concentration and a smaller increase in cadmium and copper concentrations between Stations 4 and 5 which does effect the averages concerned in Table 21.1, as one can see. This may have been due to effluent from the British Steel Corporation's Landore works, where occasional

TABLE 21.1. River Tawe Dissolved Trace Metal Results and Average River Water Trace Metal Concentrations - µg/l.

Station	Cd	Cu	Ni	Pb	Zn	No. of Samples
1	1.2 1.1-1.2	3.1 3.0-3.1	5.2 5.0-5.3	4.8 4.1-5.5	17 16-17	2
2	1.3 1.2-1.3	4.6 4.1-5.1	153 150-155	4.8 4.1-5.5	17 15-18	2
3	1.3 0.9-1.6	3.6 1.9-6.7	137 74-171	5.6 4.1-6.3	21 12-39	12
4	6.6 5.0-8.0	3.9 3.4-4.6	148 113-167	6.6 5.0-7.5	443 333-595	4
5	6.2 4.7-7.4	5.4 4.0-9.7	115 66-167	6.9 5.3-8.5	764 435-1430	5
6	4.4 2.4-6.3	2.5 2.1-2.9	88 19-156	7.2 6.8-7.5	312 93-530	2
7	3.6 2.5-5.9	2.5 2.2-3.0	56 30-137	6.3 5.0-7.5	169 19-435	4
8	125 90-160	40[a] -	60[b] 50-70	61 15-150	7620[c] 5600-8800	4
Average river water concentrations:						
Bowen (1966)	0.08	10	10	5	10	
Riley & Chester (1971)	-	5	0.3	3	10	
Turekian (1971)	-	7	0.3	3	20	
Wilson (1976)	1	7	10	5	25	

- No data.
[a] One sample.
[b] Two samples
[c] Five samples

discharges of zinc have been reported (South West Wales River Authority, Annual Reports, 1965-1974).
4. Seawards from Station 5, levels of all metals decreased as the river water was diluted by sea water with much lower trace metal concentrations.

Abdullah and Royle (1974) and Abdullah et al. (1972) reported high concentrations of dissolved cadmium, copper, nickel, lead and zinc in Swansea Bay waters. These were not accounted for by the trace metal concentrations found by the former authors in rivers flowing into the Bay, with the exception of nickel in the Tawe. The levels they found indicate that they probably sampled the River Tawe above the confluence with the Nant-y-Fendrod and below Clydach and thus did not detect a major source of metals to Swansea Bay. Trace metal concentrations in other rivers flowing into the northern Bristol Channel between Caldy Island and Porthcawl have been found to be relatively low (Abdullah and Royle, 1974; Vivian and Massie, 1977).

River and Estuarine Sediments

The results of trace metal analyses of sediments from the River Tawe are shown in Table 21.2 and it can be seen that very high concentrations were found. The lowest trace metal concentrations were found at Station 3, which is above the confluence of the Tawe and the Nant-y-Fendrod, the latter having extremely high sediment trace metal concentrations (Station 8 in Table 21.2) probably derived from waste material on the site of the zinc smelter. Very high zinc concentrations were found at Station 5, below the confluence of the Tawe with the Nant-y-Fendrod and just in the saline part of the river, and this may be due to the precipitation/adsorption reactions of the metals with suspended matter on entering the estuary. The occasional discharges of zinc from the British Steel Corporation's Landore works already referred to might also explain the very high zinc concentrations at Station 5. The highest concentrations of cadmium, nickel and lead in Tawe sediments were found at Station 7, where considerable flocculation and deposition of suspended matter could be seen to be taking place. Thus, the high trace metal concentrations in sediments there were probably due to deposition of suspended matter that had adsorbed large amounts of trace metals further upstream. In a core taken at station 7, there was a tendency for trace metal concentrations to increase with depth, indicating higher levels of contamination in the past. A large proportion of the total trace metal content (nitric/perchloric acid digestion) in Tawe sediments was extracted by 25% acetic acid, thus indicating that it could be released into the overlying waters if the physico-chemical conditions varied, e.g. pH. The variability of the trace metal concentrations in the Tawe sediments with time and location

TABLE 21.2. River Tawe Sediment Results - µg/g.

Station	Date	Depth cm	Nitric/perchloric digestions Cd	Cu	Ni	Pb	Zn	Acetic digestions Cd	Cu	Ni	Pb	Zn
3	27.11.72	0	2	34	91	69	306	1	2	35	17	86
3	27.11.72	10	3	109	365	173	556	2	20	150	48	20
3	27.11.72	20	2	36	89	63	306	1	17	31	18	86
4	27.11.72	0	11	112	168	415	1133	7	37	96	105	639
5	27.11.72	0	15	216	159	669	5496	7	32	67	150	3299
6	27.11.72	0	3	51	91	225	636	3	27	44	91	324
7	27.11.72	0	21	75	165	533	1016	17	21	48	99	641
7	27.11.72	10	35	94	269	693	1456	23	6	120	223	639
7	27.11.72	20	45	83	190	1193	1116	26	7	65	258	588
7	27.11.72	30	51	145	310	1313	1166	40	51	93	180	768
7	27.11.72	40	53	169	341	913	1296	20	5	106	180	499
3	14. 4.73	0	3	89	144	143	516	2	35	64	41	212
4	14. 4.73	0	12	196	169	573	2526	5	9	126	285	1409
5	14. 4.73	0	70	916	3109	97	10596	20	26	1030	105	3749
6	14. 4.73	0	8	91	257	393	876	6	29	152	135	579
7	14. 4.73	0	14	78	190	319	896	10	10	108	135	509
9	14. 4.73	0	8	91	230	1529	2006	5	40	140	680	1309
10A	14. 4.73	0	4	92	177	261	1556	3	35	75	105	862
10B	14. 4.73	0	14	272	699	387	2116	13	40	505	125	1419
7	13. 3.74	0	12	110	99	229	5036	4	10	30	115	419
8A	11. 8.73	0	28	142	89	923	2716	26	12	17	885	6149
8B	11. 8.73	0	335	976	331	6993	13596	312	334	812	8900	31199
8C	11. 8.73	0	107	2000	64	903	35796	14	40	13	275	1204

was very probably due to the very variable composition of the waste material in the Valley which makes up a large proportion of the sediment in many places. High trace metal concentrations have also been found in River Neath sediments (Vivian and Massie, 1977) although they are not nearly as high as those found in the Tawe, as much more extensive smelting and other industrial activities took place in the Lower Swansea Valley than in the Neath Valley.

The only published sediment trace metal data for the Tawe are those of Bloxam et al. (1972) who reported high concentrations of cadmium, copper, lead, silver and zinc. Their results tended to be higher than the results reported here but the differences are probably due to the different analytical method used (X-Ray Fluorescence), to different sample sites and to the variability of sediment composition already mentioned. In comparison with sediment trace metal data from other rivers and estuaries, Tawe sediments have exceptionally high trace metal concentrations and it is only in sediments from severely contaminated areas that concentrations reach those found in Tawe sediments (Banat et al., 1972; Bryan and Hummerstone, 1971, 1973; Elderfield et al., 1971; Kronfield and Navrot, 1974; Thornton et al., 1975). Since some authors' data is based upon the analysis of smaller particle size fractions than those used in this study, the Tawe sediment trace metal results may be more exceptional than is at first apparent.

Swansea Bay Sediments

A summary of the trace metal analyses of Swansea Bay sediments is shown in Table 21.3.

TABLE 21.3. Summary of Swansea Bay Sediment Trace Metal Results µg/g.

	No.		Cd	Cu	Ni	Pb	Zn
All Sediments	54	Mean Range	2.8 0.7-9.3	16.0 2.0-45.0	23 6-65	65 13-154	145 32-446
Sands	15	Mean Range	2.2 0.7-4.1	8.0 2.0-32.0	15 6-36	41 13-139	84 32-266
Muddy Sands	17	Mean Range	2.4 1.5-3.7	10.0 5.0-16.5	18 13-28	50 26-75	116 70-196
Sandy Muds	19	Mean Range	3.6 1.5-9.3	24.5 12.0-45.0	32 19-65	92 57-154	218 116-446
Muds	3	Mean Range	3.6 3.3-4.1	35.5 34.0-38.0	37 34-40	99 94-106	198 144-260

Geographical variations: There are a great variety of sediment types found within Swansea Bay (Collins et al., 1979). The general pattern is of coarser grained gravels and sands with bare rock outcrops in the west and muddy sands and muds to the east (See Chapter 4). Fluid mud has been reported in the dredged channel approaches to Swansea and Port Talbot Docks (Davies, 1972 and Chapter 19; Kirby and Parker, 1973). Culver (1976) reported "inliers" of Pleistocene material appearing through the recent sediments and he interpreted the muddy sand on the eastern side of the Bay as material dredged from the Tawe, Neath and Port Talbot channels and docks, removed and redistributed from the spoil grounds by subsequent wave and tidal current action. As would be expected from the great variability of sediment type and distribution discussed above, there was no obvious regional trend in trace metal levels other than those resulting from variations in sediment grain-size by cluster analysis. The highest trace metal concentrations were found at two stations near the mouth of the River Tawe, in which high sediment trace metal concentrations have been found as already mentioned. Also, these stations are in the area of fluid mud reported by Davies (1972) and such muds are known to often have high trace metal concentrations (Kirby and Parker, 1973). Waste materials from the Lower Swansea Valley have provided considerable quantities of certain metals in dissolved and particulate forms to the River Tawe and thence to Swansea Bay (Vivian and Massie, 1977) but it is unlikely that any pattern due to this localized input will persist in Swansea Bay sediments as these are extensively reworked, both naturally by wave and tidal currents and artificially by dredging. Also, there are inputs from other sources, notably the discharges from the Port Talbot and Baglan Bay industrial complexes, and the sewage discharges from the Neath and Mumbles outfalls.

Mercury was determined in Swansea Bay sediments by Clifton and Vivian (1975) who found concentrations ranging from 20-1600mg/g. Slightly higher mercury levels, relative to the organic carbon content, were found within a 2km radius of the outfall from the Baglan Bay petrochemical complex which has a chlor-alkali plant.

Metal/Sediment property correlations: All the sediment parameters measured, together with the trace metal results obtained were subjected to linear regression analysis, and the resulting matrix is presented in Table 21.4. Significant positive

TABLE 21.4. Correlation Matrix.

	Cd	Cu	Ni	Pb	Zn	CSD	MSD	FSD	MUD	ORG	CRB
Cd	1.000	0.696	0.753	0.684	0.697	0.031	-0.184	-0.554	0.483	0.573	0.139
Cu		1.000	0.885	0.689	0.806	-0.228	-0.422	-0.619	0.742	0.778	-0.184
Ni			1.000	0.876	0.899	-0.151	-0.367	-0.695	0.741	0.814	-0.041
Pb				1.000	0.915	-0.089	-0.430	-0.633	0.702	0.773	-0.072
Zn					1.000	-0.127	-0.415	-0.609	0.691	0.806	-0.067
CSD						1.000	0.611	-0.286	-0.450	-0.350	0.643
MSD							1.000	0.053	-0.737	-0.633	0.220
FSD								1.000	-0.657	-0.657	-0.376
MUD									1.000	0.912	-0.065
ORG										1.000	-0.050
CRB											1.000

CSD = Coarse Sand (500-2000μm); MSD = Medium Sand (250-500μm); FSD = Fine Sand (63-250μm); MUD = Mud (<63μm); ORG = Organic Carbon; CRB = Carbonate.
Underlined coefficients are significant at the 0.1% level.

correlations were found between all the trace metals studied, suggesting a common source or sources of the trace metals, although they may not occur in the same forms/phases in the sediments. As one would expect, the organic carbon and the mud contents of the sediments showed a high positive correlation, while the carbonate content showed a positive correlation only with the coarse sand fraction. All the trace metals studied showed significant positive correlations with both the mud and the organic carbon contents, and negative correlations with the other sediment properties. Clifton and Vivian (1975) also found strong positive correlations between the mercury, organic carbon and mud contents of Swansea Bay sediments. In coastal marine sediments, significant positive correlations have been found between trace metal levels and mud and/or organic carbon contents by many workers (Armstrong et al., 1976; Jaffe and Walters, 1977; Jones, 1973; Kwiecinski et al., 1973; Mackay et al., 1972; Perkins et al., 1973; Winter and Barrett, 1972). The correlation of metal levels with organic carbon and mud contents implies, but does not prove, a causal relationship, though this is tacitly assumed by most authors. In this work, trace metals correlated better with organic carbon than with mud, suggesting that the former was more important in controlling trace metal contents of coastal marine sediments, as suggested by Loring (1975) for mercury in sediments of the Gulf of St. Lawrence. The mud size fraction will contain clay minerals, which have been shown to be effective adsorbers of trace metals (Carritt and Goodgal, 1954; Chester, 1965; Krauskopf, 1956; Rickard, 1971). However, clay particles in coastal sediments have been shown to be extensively incorporated in organic/mineral aggregates (Johnson, 1974) and this can considerably reduce if not stop the direct adsorption of trace metals by clay minerals (Meyers and Quinn, 1974) and probably will have the same effect on hydrous manganese and iron oxides in the sediments. This may be partly due to a reduction in surface area caused by the aggregation of the particles by the organic material (Weiler and Mills, 1965).

CONCLUSIONS

The high dissolved trace metal levels found in the Tawe were principally the result of run-off over and through the waste material left by smelting and other industries in the Lower Swansea Valley over the last 250 years. With the closure of the zinc smelter and the sulphuric acid works, the dissolved trace metal concentrations in the Nant-y-Fendrod and thus the lower Tawe should be lower than those found previously. However, the experience in other areas of mining and/or smelting contamination suggests the problem is likely to continue for many years albeit at a gradually decreasing level. The Tawe and in particular the Nant-y-Fendrod, appear to be a major source of trace metals to the coastal waters of the Northern Bristol Channel between Caldy Island and Porthcawl, being the source of the elevated dissolved trace metal concentrations in Swansea Bay sea water reported by Abdullah and Royle (1974) and Abdullah et al. (1972).

Sediments from the Tawe have been shown to contain extremely high trace metal concentrations, comparable with those found in areas of mining and/or smelting contamination. This is the result of weathering and erosion of waste material dumped by the smelting and other industries in the Lower Swansea Valley over the last 250 years. Trace metal concentrations found in Swansea Bay sediments were very high compared to concentrations reported from elsewhere around the coast of Britain particularly when the particle size analysed by various authors is taken into account. Comparable or higher concentrations have only been reported from heavily polluted areas such as the Firth of Clyde, Liverpool Bay and the Bristol Channel (Table 21.5).

ACKNOWLEDGEMENTS

This work was supported by an N.E.R.C. Research Studentship to the author while at the Department of Oceanography, University College of Swansea. I thank Professor F.T. Banner for the use of departmental facilities and equipment.

TABLE 21.5. Trace Metal Concentrations in British Coastal Sediments, µg/g.

No.	Location	Cd	Cu	Ni	Pb	Zn
1	Swansea Bay	2.8 0.7 - 9.3	16 2 - 45	23 6 - 65	65 13 - 154	145 32 - 446
2	Loughor Estuary	-	32	18	22	126
3	Bristol Channel	-	38	36	119	280
4	Bristol Channel	2.5	44	-	133	345
5	S. Cardigan Bay	1.1 0.2 - 3.4	11 3 - 43	- -	25 5 - 240	36 15 - 144
6	N. Cardigan Bay	1	13 2 - 72	20 4 - 93	19 10 - 145	- -
7	Conway	-	9 5 - 16	27 20 - 30	55 30 - 85	265 200 - 400
8	Liverpool Bay	-	8 1 - 104	-	-	70 22 - 651
9	Liverpool Bay	1.4 0.8 - 2.8	8 2 - 49	-	38 10 - 230	59 18 - 340
10	Liverpool Bay	0.4 0.2 - 1.2	87 37 - 210	-	133 55 - 270	318 140 - 590
11	N.E. Irish Sea	-	7	18	-	44
12	Solway Firth	1 ND - 2.4	10 5 - 19	38 20 - 85	37 ND - 72	63 24 - 105
13	Firth of Clyde	6 3 - 7	99 38 - 208	50 34 - 70	182 77 - 320	354 136 - 826
14	Firth of Clyde	3.4	37 22 - 77	50 19 - 62	86 48 - 134	165 70 - 244
15	Off N.E. Coast	0.2 0.1 - 0.8	8 2 - 49	10 7 - 22	45 17 - 238	74 20 - 198
16	Torbay	0.4 0.2 - 7.6	4.2 2.6 - 7.6	7.2 4.2 - 15	31 21 - 66	25 17 - 42
17	Crustal Average	0.2	55	75	13	76

		Size Fraction Analysed µm
1.	This Work,	< 2000 m
2.	Wright, Stoner and Chester (1976),	< 61
3.	Chester and Stoner (1975),	< 61
4.	Kirby and Parker (1973),	Total ?
5.	Jones (1973),	Total
6.	Moore (1963),	Total
7.	Elderfield, Thornton and Webb (1971),	< 204
8.	Winter and Barrett (1972),	< 1000
9.	Wood, Rolfe and Kirkwood (1976), first survey,	Total
10.	Wood, Rolfe and Kirkwood (1976) - second survey,	< 63
11.	Cronan (1970),	< 2000
12.	Perkins and others (1973),	< 204
13.	Mackay, Halcrow and Thornton (1972) - dumping area.	< 204
14.	Mackay, Halcrow and Thornton (1972) - background area,	< 204
15.	Taylor (1979),	Total
16.	Taylor (1974),	Total
17.	Mason (1966).	-

REFERENCES

Abdullah, M.I. and Royle, L.G. (1972). Heavy metal content of some rivers and lakes in Wales. *Nature, 238,* 329-330.

Abdullah, M.I., and Royle, L.G. (1974). A study of the dissolved and particulate trace elements in the Bristol Channel. *J. mar. biol. Ass. UK., 54,* 581-597.

Abdullah, M.I., Royle, L.G., and Morris, A.W. (1972). Heavy metal concentrations in coastal waters. *Nature, 235,* 158-160.

Armstrong, P.B., Hanson, G.M., and Gaudette, H.E. (1976). Minor elements in sediments of Great Bay Estuary, New Hampshire. *Environ. Geol., 1,* 207-214.

Aston, S.R., Thornton, I., Webb, J.S., Purves, J.B., and Milford, B.L. (1974). Stream sediment composition. An aid to water quality assessment. *Wat. Air. Soil Pollut., 3,* 321-325.

Banat, K., Foerstner, U., and Muller, G. (1972). Heavy metals in the sediments of the rivers Danube, Rhine, Ems, Weser and Elbe in the area of the Federal Republic of Germany. *Naturwissenschaften, 59,* 525-528.

Bloxam, T.W. (1971). Uraniferous slag tips near Swansea, South Wales. *Min. Exploit. Econ. Geol., Univ. Wales Inter-coll. Colloq., Gregynog,* 1970, p.48.

Bloxam, T.W., Aurora, S.N., Leach, L. and Rees, T.R. (1972). Heavy metals in some river and bay sediments near Swansea. *Nature phys. Sci., 239,* 158-159.

Bowen, H.J.M. (1966). *Trace elements in biochemistry.* Academic Press, London.

Bryan, G.W., and Hummerstone, L.G. (1971). Adaption of the polychaete *Nereis diversicolor* to estuarine sediments containing high concentrations of heavy metals. I. General observations and adaption to copper. *J. mar. biol. Ass. UK., 51,* 845-863.

Bryan, G.W., and Hummerstone, L.G. (1973). Adaption of the polychaete *Nereis diversicolor* to estuarine sediments containing high concentrations of zinc and cadmium. *J. mar. biol. Ass. UK., 53,* 839-857.

Carpenter, K.E. (1924). A study of rivers polluted by lead mining in the Aberystwyth district of Cardiganshire. *Ann. Appl. Biol., 11,* 1-23.

Carpenter, K.E. (1925). On the biological factors involved in the destruction of river-fisheries by pollution due to lead mining. *Ann. Appl. Biol., 12,* 1-23.

Carritt, D.E., and Goodgal, S. (1954). Sorption reactions and some ecological implications. *Deep Sea Res., 1,* 224-243.

Chester, R. (1965). Adsorption of zinc and cobalt on Illite in seawater. *Nature, 206,* 884-886.

Chester, R., and Stoner, J.H. (1975). Trace elements in sediments from the Lower Severn Estuary and Bristol Channel. *Mar. Pollut. Bull., 6,* 92-95.

Clifton, A.P., and Vivian, C.M.G. (1975). Retention of Mercury from an industrial source in Swansea Bay sediments. *Nature, 253,* 621-622.

Collins, M., Ferentinos, G., and Banner, F.T. (1979). The hydrodynamics and sedimentology of a high (Tidal and Wave) energy embayment (Swansea Bay, Northern Bristol Channel). *Estuar. Coast. Mar. Sci., 8,* 49-74.

Cronan, D.S. (1970). Geochemistry of recent sediments from the central northeastern Irish Sea. *Institute of Geological Sciences,* Report No. 70/17, 40pp.

Culver, S.J. (1976). *A study of the post-glacial Foraminiferida of Swansea Bay, South Wales.* Unpub. Ph.D. Thesis, University of Wales.

Davies, C.M. (1972). *Aspects of Suspended Sediment Transport in Swansea Bay.* Unpub. Ph.D. Thesis, University of Wales.

Elderfield, H., Thornton, I., and Webb, J.S. (1971). Heavy metals and oyster culture in Wales. *Mar. Pollut. Bull., 2,* 44-47.

Fuge, R. (1973). The chemistry of some mine water in Cardiganshire. *Min. Exploit. Econ. Geol., Univ. Wales Inter-coll. Colloq., Gregynog,* 1970, 16-20.

Gadgil, R.L. (1964). Plant ecology of the Lower Swansea Valley (a) Vegetation trials. *Lower Swansea Valley Project Report,* No. 9.

Gaudette, H.E., Flight, W.R., Toner, L., and Folger, D.W. (1974). An inexpensive titration method for the determination of organic carbon in recent sediments. *J. sedim. Petrol., 44,* 249-253.

Grimaldi, F.S., Shapiro, L., and Schrepfe, M. (1966). Determination of carbon dioxide in limestone and dolomite by acid-base titration. *U.S. Geol. Surv. Prof. Pap.*, No. 550-B, 186-188.

Harding, D.M. (1971). Hydrology. In: Balchin, W.G.V. (Ed.). *Swansea and its region*. University College of Swansea, Swansea, 59-77.

Hilton, K.J. (1967). An outline of the industrial history of the Lower Swansea Valley. In: Hilton, K.J. (Ed.). *The Lower Swansea Valley Project*. Longmans, London, 15-37.

Holt, G. (1964). Tips and tip working in the Lower Swansea Valley. *Lower Swansea Valley Project Report*, No. 12.

Ireland, M.P. (1973). Result of fluvial zinc pollution on the zinc content of littoral and sub-littoral organisms in Cardigan Bay, Wales. *Environ. Pollut.*, 4, 27-35.

Jaffe, D., and Walter, J.K. (1977). Inter-tidal trace metal concentrations in some sediments from the Humber Estuary. *Sci. Total Environ.*, 7, 1-15.

Johnson, R.G. (1974). Particulate matter at the sediment-water interface in coastal environments. *J. mar. Res.*, 32, 313-330.

Jones, A.N., and Howells, W.R. (1969). Recovery of the River Rheidol. *Effl. Wat. Treat. J.*, 11, 605-610.

Jones, A.N., and Howells, W.R. (1975). The partial recovery of the metal-polluted River Rheidol. *Brit. Ecol. Soc. Symp.*, 15, 443-459.

Jones, A.S.G. (1973). The concentration of copper, lead, zinc and cadmium in shallow water sediments, Cardigan Bay, Wales. *Mar. Geol.*, 14, 171-179.

Jones, J.R.E. (1940a). A study of the zinc-polluted River Ystwyth in North Cardiganshire, Wales. *Ann. appl. Biol.*, 27, 368-378.

Jones, J.R.E. (1940b). The fauna of the River Melindwr, a lead-polluted tributary of the River Rheidol in North Cardiganshire, Wales. *J. Anim. Ecol.*, 9, 188-201.

Jones, J.R.E. (1958). A further study of the zinc-polluted River Ystwyth. *J. Anim. Ecol.*, 27, 1-14.

Kirby, R., and Parker, W.R. (1973). Fluid mud in the Severn Estuary and the Bristol Channel and its relevance to pollution studies. *Preprints, Institute of Chemical Engineers, Graduates and Students Section, Annual Symposium, Exeter, 27th-28th September 1973, Estuarine and Coastal Pollution*. Paper No. A4.

Krauskopf, K.B. (1956). Factors controlling the concentrations of thirteen rare metals in sea water. *Geochim. cosmochim. Acta.*, 9, 1-328.

Kronfeld, J., and Navrot, J. (1974). Transition metal contamination in the Qishon River system, Israel. *Environ. Pollut.*, 6, 281-288.

Kwiecinski, B., Acedo, M., and Guillen, A. (1973). Organic material and trace element distribution in the sediments of the Gulf of Panama. *Geol. For. Stockh. Forh.*, 95, 381-393.

Laurie, R.D., and Jones, J.R.E. (1938). The faunistic recovery of a lead-polluted river in North Cardiganshire, Wales. *J. Anim. Ecol.*, 7, 272-286.

Ledger, D.C. (1967). The River Tawe. In: Hilton, K.J. (Ed.). *The Lower Swansea Valley Project*. Longmans, London, 111-122.

Loring, D.H. (1975). Mercury in the sediments of the Gulf of St. Lawrence. *Can. J. Earth Sci.*, 12, 1219-1237.

Mackay, D.W., Halcrow, W., and Thornton, I. (1972). Sludge dumping in the Firth of Clyde. *Mar. Pollut. Bull.*, 3, 7-10.

Mason, B. (1966). *Principles of Geochemistry*, 3rd. Ed. John Wiley, London.

Meyers, P.A., and Quinn, J.G. (1974). Organic matter on clay minerals and marine sediments - effect on adsorption of dissolved copper, phosphate and lipids from saline solutions. *Chem. Geol.*, 13, 63-68.

Moore, J.R. (1968). Recent sedimentation in northern Cardigan Bay, Wales. *Bull. Br. Mus. nat. Hist., C. Mineral.*, 2(2), 19-131.

Newton, L. (1944). Pollution of the rivers of West Wales by lead and zinc mine effluent. *Ann. appl. Biol.*, 31, 1-11.

Pasternak, K. (1973). The spreading of heavy metals in flowing waters in the region of occurrence of natural deposits and of the zinc and lead industry. *Acta. Hydrobiol., Krakow*, 15, 145-166.

Pasternak, K. (1974a). The accumulation of heavy metals in the bottom sediments of the River Biala Przemsza as an indicator of their spreading by water courses from the centre of the zinc and lead mining and smelting industries. *Acta. Hydrobiol., Krakow, 16,* 51-63.

Pasternak, K. (1974b). The influence of the pollution of a zinc plant at Miasteczko Slaskie on the content of micro-elements in the environment of surface waters. *Acta. Hydrobiol., Krakow, 16,* 273-297.

Perkins, E.J., Gilchrist, J.R.S., Abbott, O.J., and Halcrow, W. (1973). Trace metals in Solway Firth sediments. *Mar. Pollut. Bull., 4,* 59-61.

Rickard, D.T. (1971). The chemistry of copper in natural aqueous solutions. *Stockh. Contr. Geol., 23,* 1-64.

Riley, J.P., and Chester, R. (1971). *Introduction to marine chemistry*. Academic Press, London.

Riley, J.P., and Taylor, D. (1968). Chelating resins for the concentration of trace elements from sea water and their analytical use in conjunction with atomic absorption spectrophotometry. *Analytica chim. Acta., 40,* 479-485.

Street, H.E., and Goodman, G.T. (1967). Revegetation techniques in the Lower Swansea Valley. In: Hilton, K.J. (Ed.). *The Lower Swansea Valley Project*. Longmans, London, 71-110.

Taylor, D. (1974). Natural distribution of trace metals in sediments from a coastal environment, Tor Bay, England. *Estuar. & Coast. Mar. Sci., 2,* 417-424.

Taylor, D. (1979). The effect of discharges from three industrialized estuaries on the distribution of heavy metals in the coastal sediments of the North Sea. *Estuar. & Coast. Mar. Sci., 8,* 387-393.

Thornton, I., Watling, H., and Darracott, A. (1975). Geochemical studies in several rivers and estuaries used for oyster rearing. *Sci. Total Environ., 4,* 325-345.

Turekian, K.K. (1971). Rivers, tributaries and estuaries. In: Hood, D.W. (Ed.). *Impingement of man on the oceans*. Wiley-Interscience, London, 9-73.

Vivian, C.M.G., and Massie, K.S. (1977). Trace metals in waters and sediments of the River Tawe, South Wales, in relation to local sources. *Environ. Pollut., 14,* 47-61.

Weiler, R.R., and Mills, A.A. (1965). Surface properties and pore structures of marine sediments. *Deep Sea Res., 12,* 511-529.

Williams, J.K. (1970). *Salinity measurements in the River Tawe*. Unpub. B.Sc. Dissertation, Dept. Oceanography, U.C. Swansea.

Wilson, A.L. (1976). Concentrations of trace metals in river waters: A review. *Water Research Centre Technical Report*, No. TR 16.

Winter, A., and Barrett, M.J. (1972). Bed sediments: Chemical examination. In: *Out of Sight, Out of Mind, Report of a working party on the disposal of sludge in Liverpool Bay*. Dept. of Environment, H.M.S.O., 2, 287-295.

Wood, P.C., Rolfe, M.S., and Kirkwood, D.S. (1976). Chemical analysis of sediments from Liverpool Bay: 1973/1974. In: *Out of Sight, Out of Mind, Report of a working party on the disposal of sludge in Liverpool Bay*. Dept. of Environment, H.M.S.O., 4, 57-67.

Wright, D., Stoner, J.H., and Chester, R. (1977). Some preliminary results of trace metal studies in the Loughor Estuary and Burry Inlet. In: Nelson-Smith, A., and Bridges, E.M. (Eds.). *Problems of a small Estuary. Proceedings of a Symposium on the Burry Inlet (South Wales)*. 13-15th September, 1976 at University College of Swansea. Quadrant Press Ltd., Swansea. Session 4, Paper 3, 21pp.

22. OCCURRENCE AND SURVIVAL OF VIRUSES IN SEAWATER

J. M. Tyler

Welsh Water Authority, Virology Laboratory, Gowerton, Swansea, U.K.

ABSTRACT

Viruses have been detected in samples of seawater collected from Swansea Bay and the Severn Estuary. Those viruses which are of major interest today are those which are pathogenic to man and other animals. The primary sources of these viruses in coastal waters are discharges of treated and untreated sewage effluents.

Laboratory experiments have shown that survival of viruses in seawater is influenced by particulate matter suspended in the seawater. It is suggested that viruses may accumulate in sediments and could be released into the water column by means of agitation. Virus accumulation may be favoured in sediments which contain a high proportion of clay minerals.

KEYWORDS

Virus; Sewage effluent; Seawater; Suspended sediment; Adsorption/Desorption; Swansea Bay; Bristol Channel.

INTRODUCTION

Sewage is discharged into the waters of Swansea Bay (i.e. the area to the northeast of a line joining Worms Head and Nash Point). Approximately 30% is fully treated before discharge, a further 30% is screened and discharged after tidal storage and about 40% is discharged crude (Stickler, 1974). A number of the crude effluents are discharged from short coastal outfalls at or just below the low water mark.

Various enteric viruses are excreted in large numbers in human faeces and urine during infection and may be found in raw domestic sewage. The use of secondary treatment processes such as trickling filtration, activated sludge and oxidation ponds can reduce the infectious virus titres by varying degrees. The removal of infectious viruses by these processes is not complete, however, and each process appears to give variable results. Even chlorination of the secondary effluents may not disinfect the waste waters. This effluent, discharged into receiving waters introduces enteric viruses to these waters, the fate of which is not completely understood.

The enteric viruses found in faeces, sewage and polluted waters include the enteroviruses (polio, coxsackie and ECHO), infectious hepatitis virus, adenoviruses and reoviruses. Other viruses may be ingested by humans and subsequently isolated in faeces, but are not particularly significant in the transfer of disease by contaminated water (Scarpino, 1975). Viruses are not part of the normal flora of the human intestinal tract and are excreted only by infected individuals. Clarke *et al.* (1962) pointed out that while essentially everyone discharges coliforms and streptococci, the excretion of enteric viruses in faeces by apparently healthy individuals is largely confined to children under the age of 15 years. It should be remembered that the term "infected" does not necessarily imply the presence of a disease syndrome. Individuals may be infected with a virus, and hence be excreting virus particles without showing overt signs of disease. The concentration of virus in sewage varies widely, influenced by viral infection rates in the community, the time of the day, the season of the year, the ratio of industrial to domestic waste, and the extent of sewage dilution from seepage or surface run-off into the sewerage system. Enteroviruses cause a variety of illnesses, most of which are very mild. However, they can, on occasion, cause severe illness and death. The majority of persons, usually children, who are infected with these viruses never realise that they are infected; such infections result in no obvious symptoms and the individual is not ill.

Infectious viruses can be carried in water to points distant from their origin in sewage. Reports indicate that it is not uncommon for fresh and estuarine waters to carry detectable virus for several miles (Grinstein *et al.*, 1970; Lamb *et al.*, 1964; Metcalf and Stiles, 1968; Shuval *et al.*, 1971; Theios *et al.*, 1967). The importance of enteric viruses in water is related to their infectivity and their resistance to the aquatic environment, rather than to their numbers. Enteric viruses can survive for long periods in natural waters (Akin *et al.*, 1971). Domestic sewage and naturally occurring organic materials may prolong virus survival in natural waters (Berger *et al.*, 1970; Clarke *et al.*, 1961; Joyce and Weiser, 1967). Shuval *et al.* (1971) reported that enteroviruses showed little or no die-away in the sea from the time of discharge until being carried to a bathing beach many hours later where they were detected. During the same period the coliform count was reduced by 3 orders of magnitude by die-away alone. This suggests that enteroviruses are more resistant to natural inactivation factors in seawater than coliforms, and shows the limitation of depending on these bacteria as a pollution indicator organism, at least as far as viruses are concerned. Viruses adsorb to clay and soil particles in water. The association of viruses with suspended materials in natural waters may alter the virus survival patterns.

The present study was designed to examine (a) the occurrence of enteroviruses in Swansea Bay and (b) the survival under laboratory conditions of virus in seawater, and especially the influence of sediments on their survival. The work includes laboratory studies which utilized natural seawater and sediments from Swansea Bay rather than pure clays and artificial seawater which have been used in previous investigations.

MATERIALS AND METHODS

Isolation of Viruses from Field Samples.

Sampling Sites: Seven sites (A - G) situated in Swansea Bay were sampled 5 times between January and July 1979 for enteroviruses (Fig. 22.1). An additional sample site (Station H) was sampled at monthly intervals between August 1978 and July 1979 for enteroviruses. All virus samples were obtained from surface water at distances up to 1.5km from low water mark. The samples were collected in sterile plastic containers and were transported to the laboratory for concentration and virus assay within 6 hours of collection. Samples of water were also collected from a

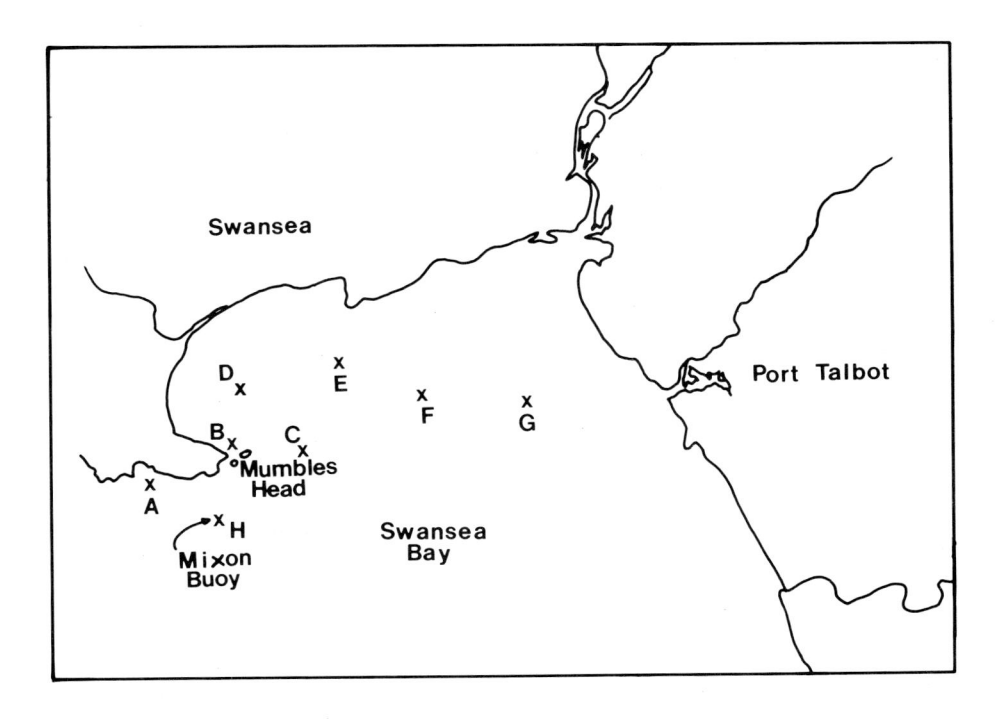

Figure 22.1. Position of sampling sites in Swansea Bay.

number of sites at low water from the main channel of the Severn Estuary on two occasions.

Concentration of Samples for Isolation of Enteroviruses: Viruses in 20 litre samples of sea water were concentrated by adsorption to and elution from 293mm diameter cellulose nitrate filters (0.45µm pore size; Sartorius Ltd.). Samples which contained large amounts of particulate matter were passed through a prefilter (Whatman GF/F) in series with the cellulose nitrate membrane. The water samples were adjusted to pH 3.5 with HCl prior to passage through the filters under pressure. Viruses adsorbed to the filters were eluted with 400 ml 3% beef broth at pH 9.0 (Lab. lemco Broth; Oxoid Ltd.). The beef broth was then acidified to pH 3.5 and incubated at 4°C for 30 minutes until a precipitate had formed. The beef broth was then centrifuged at 5,000 rpm for 15 minutes and the resulting pellet, which contained the viruses, resuspended in 10ml 2% Na_2HPO_4 buffer at pH 7.5. The concentrated virus suspension was then stored at -20°C until these samples could be assayed for viruses.

Assay of Concentrated Samples for Enteroviruses: Virus assays were performed by the plaque forming unit (PFU) method (Wallis & Melnick, 1967) using the BGM cell line which was passaged, grown and maintained as described by Melnick and Wenner (1969). The sampling procedures and sampling methodologies are optimized and largely selective for the detection of enteroviruses (Farrah et al., 1977; Melnick and Wenner, 1969; Payment et al., 1976). Thus the enteric viruses isolated are referred to as enteroviruses even though this was not confirmed by neutralization with specific antisera. The concentrated samples were placed on cell monolayers (2ml per 75cm^2 cell surface area) for 60 minutes to allow for viral adsorption. The cell monolayers were then overlaid with a nutrient agar medium (Double strength MEM supplemented by 5% FCS and 50% purified agar) and incubated at 37°C. The overlaid cell cultures were examined daily for 10-14 days for the presence of plaques. The results are reported as PFU per 10 litre of seawater.

Growth and Preparation of Bacteriophage Stocks: Bacteriophage MS2 was obtained from the American Type culture collection (ATCC 15597-B). The host bacteria used for detection viable phage particles was *Escherichia coli* strain HfrR1, kindly provided by Professor W. Hayes, Edinburgh University.

Seawater samples containing bacteriophage were assayed by the double agar layer technique (Adams, 1959).

Laboratory Experiments

Laboratory studies were performed using MS2 bacteriophage as an enterovirus model.

Experimental Inactivation of Bacteriophage MS2 in Seawater: (i) Four sets of flasks were set up, each containing 100ml of medium-fresh seawater, aged seawater, filtered seawater and artificial seawater. The flasks were maintained static at room temperature (20 $\pm$ 3°C) throughout the experiment. Fresh seawater was collected from sublittoral areas around Swansea and the Gower Peninsula, and used within 24 hours of collection. It contained organic particulate matter, some of which originated from plankton and bacteria, and also a small amount of sediment. "Aged Seawater" was seawater collected and stored in dark bottles at 4°C for 6 months before use. Filtered seawater was fresh seawater which had been passed through Grade 1 Whatman filter paper to remove coarse debris, then filtered twice through Millipore 0.45µm filters (Millipore HAWP, Millipore Corp. Ltd.). Artificial seawater was prepared according to the method of Barnes (1954). The filtered and the artificial seawater were assumed to contain little or no particulate matter, although it has been reported (Gerba and Schaiberger, 1975) that particulate matter may be present in artificial seawater solutions. This particulate matter was said to have originated from dust particles or bacterial debris in the salt, the flasks, or the distilled water used in preparation of the artificial seawater.

Virus was added to each flask to give a concentration of 10^3 PFU/ml and samples were removed for assay of surviving virus at approximately 24 hour intervals. As this method did not measure the true irreversible inactivation of virus in seawater containing sediment, but only the decrease in numbers of PFU which includes the decline in PFU due to loss of those phage which were reversibly attached to sediment and particulate matter, the experimental procedure was modified:-

(ii) Adsorption of MS2 to particulate matter: three sets of 5 litre flasks were set up in duplicate containing 3 litre filtered seawater. Two sets of flasks (a) and (b) contained 500g sediment and organic particulate matter. The other flasks (c) contained no particulate matter. To each flask was added virus to give a concentration of 10^8 PFU/ml. All flasks were incubated at 10°C in an orbital incubator shaking at 40 revs/min to simulate gentle wave action. Samples were taken from flasks (a) and (c) without disturbing the flasks. Before samples were taken from flasks (b) the contents were thoroughly shaken to distribute the sediment throughout the seawater and possibly to dislodge any reversibly bound virus particles from the particulate matter. All samples were assayed as described previously.

RESULTS

Viruses in Seawater

Analysis of Field Samples

The results are presented in Tables 22.1, 22.2 and 22.3.

TABLE 22.1. Results of Virus Assays from Swansea Bay.

Date Sampled	A	B	C	D	E	F	G
15th Jan.	0	1	0	16	0	0	1
20th Feb.	0	10	2	0	8	0	4
19th Mar.	0	2	0	0	0	2	0
14th May	0	0	0	1	0	0	6
10th July	0	0	4	1	0	0	2

Numbers given are numbers of PFU per 10 litre seawater.

TABLE 22.2   Results of Monthly Sampling at Station H (Mixon Buoy).

Sample Date	PFU/10 litre Seawater
17th August	4
8th September	2
12th October	1
1st December	2
20th December	0
25th January	8
23rd February	10
19th March	2
23rd April	0
7th June	20
26th July	12

TABLE 22.3. Numbers of Enteroviruses in Samples of Water Collected from Sites in Mid-Channel of the Severn Estuary.

Sample Date	1	2	3	4	5	6	7
9th January	2	6	2	<1	2	0	2
6th February	4	10	10	0	8	8	0

Numbers given are numbers of plaque-forming units (PFU) per 10 litre sample.

Assay of Samples for Enteroviruses: At Station A, no viruses were isolated from the seawater samples at any time during the course of this study. At Stations E and F only one of the seasonal samples at each station proved positive for enteroviruses (2-8 PFU/10 litre). At the other stations in Swansea Bay enteroviruses were found in at least 2 of the 5 seasonal samples at each of the Stations (B, C, D, G). The maximum recorded virus concentration was 16 PFU/10 litre in the sample from Station D on 15th January. All other samples with the exception of that from Station B on 20th February had less than 6 PFU per 10 litre seawater.

From the samples taken at Station H (Mixon Buoy) a maximum of 20 PFU/10 litre seawater was found.

Experimental Inactivation of Bacteriophage MS2 in Seawater: (i) The results are shown in Fig. 22.2. The highest rate of inactivation was in fresh seawater where

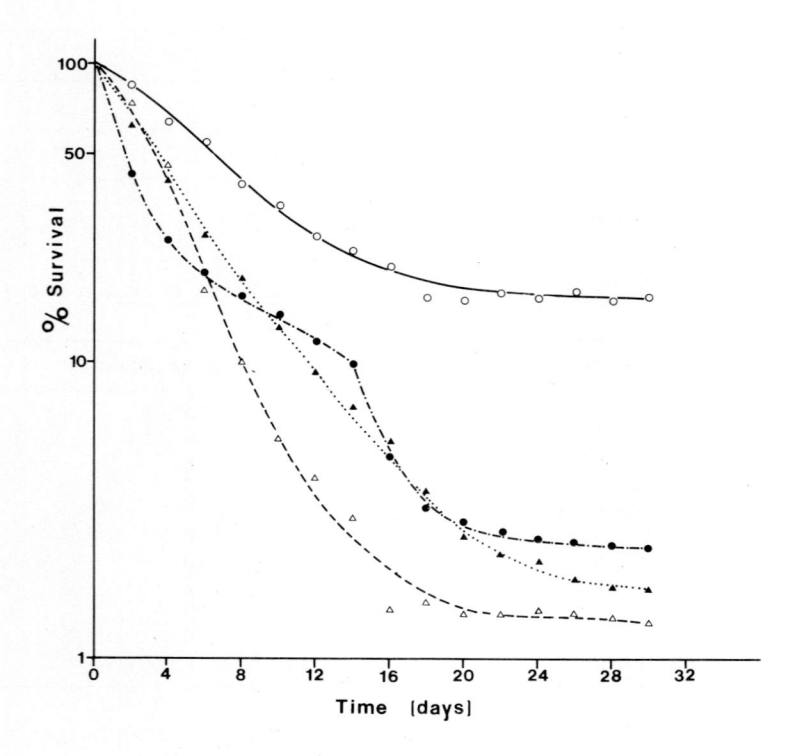

Figure 22.2. Inactivation of MS2 in seawater: the effect of particulate matter.
MS2 (100ml suspensions, at 10^3 PFU/ml in 250ml Erlenmeyer flasks) were incubated at room temperature (20 + 3°C) in :- Artificial Seawater o——o ; Aged Seawater •—·—• ; Filtered Seawater ▲········▲ ; Fresh Seawater ∆---∆ .

98.6% of the virus had been inactivated in 30 days. Filtered seawater gave a slightly lower rate with 98.3% inactivation in 30 days, and artificial seawater produced only 83% inactivation in the same time period. Aged seawater gave a final rate of 97.7% inactivation in 30 days.

(ii) Adsorption of MS2 to particulate matter: the results are shown in Fig. 22.3. The maximum inactivation (98% in 32 days) of MS2 occurred in filtered seawater. Inactivation of virus in seawater-plus-sediment occurred at a steady rate and reached 95% inactivation after 32 days. Inactivation of virus in seawater-plus-sediment which was shaken at 4 day intervals also reached 95%, but after each period of shaking there was an increase in the phage titre, followed by a relatively rapid decrease in titre and an increase in the rate of inactivation.

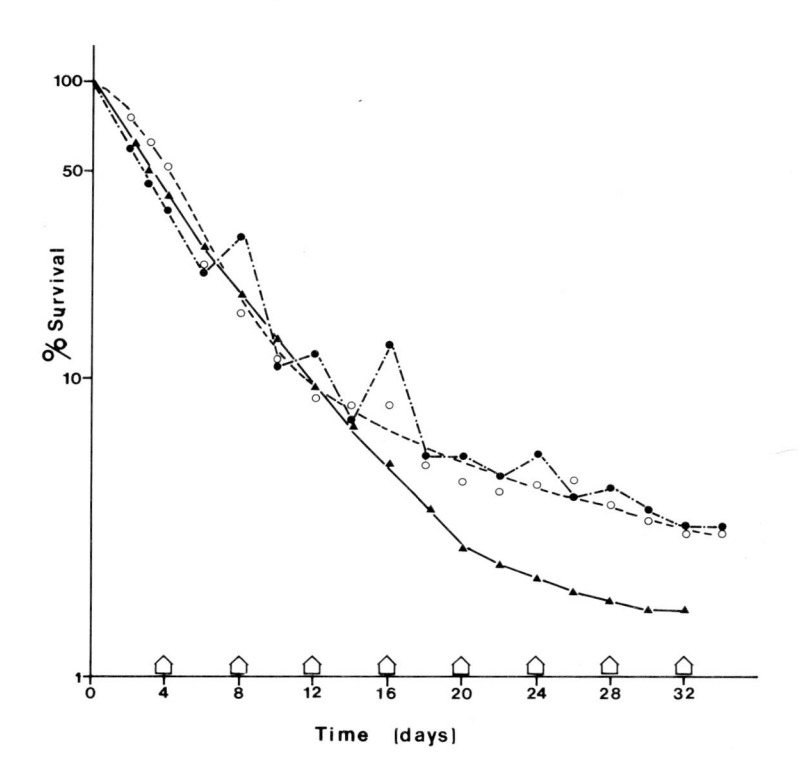

Figure 22.3. Adsorption of MS2 to particulate matter in seawater.
MS2 (3 litre suspension, at 10^8 PFU/ml in 5 litre flasks) were incubated at 10°C in:
  Flask (a) Static: Seawater plus sediment   o----o
  Flask (b) Shaken: Seawater plus sediment   •—·—•
  Flask (c) Shaken: Filtered seawater.   ▲——▲

⌂ Denotes that Flasks (b) and (c) were shaken before samples were removed.

DISCUSSION

It has been shown that viruses can be isolated from the waters of Swansea Bay and the Severn Estuary. However, the numbers of these potentially pathogenic particles which have been detected have been very low. Although these small numbers of viruses are not acceptable in terms of the Standards for virus quality of bathing waters put forward by the E.E.C., which state that there should be no enteroviruses in a 10 litre sample of bathing water, it must be stressed that it cannot be stated that there is a risk to health in bathing in waters that fail to meet these Standards. There is in fact very little evidence to support a risk to health. In Britain a detailed investigation of the medical and bacteriological aspects of the contamination of bathing beaches by sewage was carried out by a Committee set up by the Public Health Laboratory Service. In this report (MRC. 1959) they concluded that a serious risk of contracting disease through bathing in sewage-polluted water is probably not incurred unless the water is so fouled as to be aesthetically revolting. The Environmental Protection Agency of the U.S.A. suggest that standards for bathing water should relate to the amount of water ingested by a bather and the infective dose of the pathogenic microorganism. A minimum acceptable level for viruses in natural waters is difficult to define because an infective dose will vary between virus strains and between individual bathers and will be influenced by factors such as the age and state of health of the recipient and also by immunity acquired by previous exposure or vaccination.

Viruses that are present in sewage may exist in several physical states; suspended as individual virions, aggregated in viral clumps, or associated with suspended solids. Although viruses are known to form complexes with suspended particulates, little research has been done to determine what fraction of the total virus population might be associated with solids, what is the nature of the virus-solids complex, or how the survival of viruses in seawater might be affected by such solids-associated viruses. Stagg et al. (1978) showed that viruses readily become adsorbed to the surface of sewage solids. Adsorption of viruses to organic and mineral particulates is a reversible process, and the point of dynamic equilibrium between adsorbed and desorbed virus is dependent upon such factors as the ionic strength of the suspending medium, pH of the medium, and the presence of organic molecules which compete with the viruses for adsorption sites on the particulates (Gerba and Schaiberger, 1975; Moore et al., 1975; Schaub and Sagik, 1975).

The association of viruses with solids has been demonstrated to impart a protective effect (Stagg et al., 1978) resulting in enhanced survival in natural waters.

The experiments described above seem to indicate that although virus levels might be shown to decline with time in natural bodies of water, this may not be a true picture of the amount of infectious virus which may be present in an area. The laboratory experiments demonstrate that the rate of inactivation of viruses is influenced by the particulate matter in the seawater. There was a progressive increase in the rate of decline of detectable MS2 phage in media with increased amounts of organic and inorganic particulate matter in suspension. However, this decrease in numbers of detectable phage is only partly due to true inactivation of the virus in seawater. Adsorption onto particulate matter may in fact be masking the true rate of inactivation of the viruses. Most natural environments such as lakes, ponds, soils and seawater contain colloidal particles which offer a large surface area on which microorganisms are adsorbed and which may protect them from inactivation in natural seawater. Swansea Bay consists largely of reworked glacial deposits and Flandrian clays (see Chapter 4). Suspended inorganic material in the water column consists mainly of montmorillonite (F.T. Banner, pers. comm.). Because of their colloidal nature, clay minerals are closely associated with microorganisms in soils and various water bodies.

Bitton and Mitchell (1974) examined the effect on montmorillonite on survival of bacteriophages in seawater. They found that montmorillonite had a strong protective effect but that the survival did not increase significantly when the clay concentration of the seawater was above 200µg/ml. Biocolloids such as bacterial cells have also been shown to have a significant protective effect in seawater (Bitton and Mitchell, 1974). The protective effect is probably a result of the adsorption of virus onto the surfaces of these colloids. Sorption of the virus on the particulate matter is reversible and does not affect its infective ability (Cookson and North, 1967). Clay minerals may also protect the virus from inactivation by absorbing the lytic enzymes or anti-viral toxins which might be produced by an antagonistic microflora.

These investigations suggest that viruses may accumulate in sediments and slimy deposits on the sea bottom near the shore and could easily be released into water by means of agitation. Virus accumulation may be favoured in types of sediments which contain a high proportion of clay minerals rather than more coarse sandy sediments.

Thus sediments could represent a transient reservoir of viruses, and infectious virus particles could be mechanically returned to seawater. Wave motions and bottom currents in shallow waters could be responsible for the release of viruses from sediments under natural conditions.

Samples which contained a heavy load of suspended sediment proved very difficult to process by the normal virus concentration techniques and viruses were not specifically eluted from the sediments in these samples. The reslatively low counts of enteroviruses may merely reflect a situation in which most of the viruses present in a sample were reversibly bound to sediments and were, therefore, not detected by the virus assay techniques used. In conclusion, the public health significance of enteric viruses in marine sediments, as well as seawater cannot alone be evaluated from statistical and epidemiological data because the release into nearshore waters of viruses deposited in marine sediments should also be considered.

The enterovirus work described above is part of a project initiated and supported by the Welsh Office and the Welsh Water Authority. The laboratory experiments were undertaken whilst the author was in receipt of an S.R.C. Studentship.

The views expressed in this paper are those of the author and do not necessarily represent the views of the Welsh Office or the Welsh Water Authority.

REFERENCES

Adams, M.H. (1959). *Bacteriophages*. Interscience Publishers Inc., New York.
Akin, R.W., Benton, W.H., and Hill, W.F. (1971). Enteric Viruses in ground and surface waters: a review of their occurrence and survival. Proc. 13th. Wat. Qual. Conf., University of Illinois, Urbana, p.59.
Barnes, H. (1954). Some tables for the Ionic composition of seawater. *J. Exp. Biol.*, *31*, 582-588.
Berger, B.B. et al. (1970). Engineering evaluation of virus hazard in water. *J. Sanit.Engng. Div. Am. Soc. civ. Engrs.*, *96*, 111-161.
Bitton, G., and Mitchell, R. (1974). Effect of Colloids on the survival of bacteriophages in seawater. *Water Res.*, *8*, 227-229.
Clarke, N.A., Berg, G., Kabler, P.W., Chang, S.L. (1964). Human enteric viruses in water: source, survival and removeability. In: Proc. 1st. Intl. Conf. Wat. Pollut. Res. London (1962), 2, *Advances in Water Pollution Research*. Vol. 2, Pergamon, London, 523-536.
Clarke, N.A., Stevenson, R.E., Chang, S.L., and Kabler, P.W. (1961). Removal of enteric viruses from sewage by activated sludge treatment. *Am. J. Publ. Hlth.*, *51*, 1118-1129.
Cookson, J.T., and North, W.J. (1967). Adsorption of viruses on activated carbon, equilibria and kinetics of the attachment of phage T_4 on activated carbon. *Environ. Sci. Tech.*, *1*, 46.
Farrah, S.R., Goyal, S.M., Gerba, C.P., Wallis, C., and Melnick, J.L. (1977). Concentration of enteroviruses from estuarine water. *Appl. Environ. Microbiol.*, *33*, 1192-1196.
Gerba, C.P., and Schaiberger, G.E. (1975). Effect of particulates on virus survival in seawater. *J. Wat. Pollut. Control. Fed.*, *47*, 93-103.
Grinstein, S., Melnick, J.L., Wallis, C. (1970). Virus isolations from sewages and from a stream receiving effluents of sewage treatment plants. *Bull. W.H.O.*, *42*, 291-296.

Joyce, C., and Weiser, H.H. (1967). Survival of enteroviruses and bacteriophage in farm pond waters. *J. Am. Wat. Wks. Ass.*, *59*, 491.

Lamb, G.A., Chin, T.D.Y., and Scarce, L.E. (1964). Isolations of enteric viruses from sewage and river water in a metropolitan area. *Am. J. Hyg.*, *80*, 320-327.

Medical Research Council. (1959). *Sewage contamination of bathing beaches in England and Wales*. H.M. Stationery Office, London, p.23.

Melnick, J.L., and Wenner, H.A. (1969). Enteroviruses. *In:* Lennette, E.H., and Schmidt, N.J. (Eds.). *Diagnostic procedures for viral and Rickettsial infections*. Am. Publ. Health Assoc., Washington, D.C., p.529.

Metcalf, T.G., and Stiles, W.C. (1968). Viral pollution of shellfish in estuary waters. *J. Sanit. Engng. Div. Am. Soc. civ. Engrs.*, *94*, 595.

Moore, B.E., Sagik, B.P., and Malina, J.F. (1975). Viral association with suspended solids. *Water Res.*, *94*, 197-203.

Payment, P., Gerba, C.P., Wallis, C., and Melnick, J.L. (1976). Methods for concentrating virus from large volumes of estuarine water on pleated membranes. *Water Res.*, *10*, 893-896.

Scarpino, P.V., (1975). Human enteric viruses and bacteriophages as Indicators of sewage pollution. *In:* Gameson, A.L.H. (Ed.). *Supplement to Progress in Water Technology: Discharge of sewage from sea outfalls*. Proc. Int. Symp. Pergamon Press, Oxford, England, 49-61.

Schaub, S.A., Sagik, B.P. (1975). Association of enteroviruses with natural and artificially introduced colloidal solids in water and infectivity of solids associated virious. *Appl. Microbiol.*, *30*, 212-222.

Shuval, H.F., Thompson, A., Fattal, B., Cymbalista, S., and Wiener, Y. (1971). Natural virus inactivation processes in seawater. *J. Sanit. Engng. Div. Am. Soc. civ. Engrs.*, *97*, 587-600.

Stagg, C.H., Wallis, C., Ward, C.H., and Gerba, C.P. (1978). Chlorination of solids - associated coliphages. *Progress Wat. Technol.*, *10*, 381-387.

Stickler, D.T., (1974).*In:*Report of the working group on possible pollution in Swansea Bay. Vol.II. Welsh Office, Cardiff, 110pp.

Theios, E.P., Morris, J.C., Rosenbaum, M.H., and Baker, A.G. (1967). Effect of sewage treatment on recovery of poliovirus following mass oral immunization. *Am. J. Public Hlth.*, *57*, 295-300.

Wallis, C., and Melnick, J.L. (1967). Concentration of viruses on membrane filters. *J. Virol.*, *1*, 472-477.

23. THE DISCHARGE OF MEDICAL RADIONUCLIDES FROM A NEARSHORE OUTFALL, MUMBLES, WESTERN SWANSEA BAY

J. L. Birks

Department of Medical Physics, Singleton Hospital, Swansea, U.K.

ABSTRACT

The use of radionuclides in medicine has greatly increased over the past few years and possible environmental consequences of the release of Iodine-131 and Technetium-99m from a large hospital into the Swansea municipal sewers have been investigated. Liquid wastes are discharged into the sea from the Mumbles outfall and seaweed provides a convenient indicator of the presence of these radionuclides.

The assessment of radioactivity in seaweed samples collected at low water mark enabled the area of beach showing the highest level of radioactivity to be located. Thereafter the monitoring of samples from this site over a period of several months enabled the levels occurring to be related to hospital discharges.

Technetium-99m cannot be detected in seaweed at its present level of usage, but the radioiodine content may reach 1 nCi/kg after the hospital treatment of a patient for metastatic thyroid cancer. Although this presents no significant health hazard to the general public the prevention of such contamination for aesthetic reasons is suggested

KEYWORDS

Iodine-131; Technetium-99m; Radioactive discharge; Radioactivity uptake by seaweed; Swansea Bay; Bristol Channel.

INTRODUCTION

Chapter 21 relates to Swansea's legacy of long-lived environmental heavy metal contamination from the technology of earlier times. This chapter has to do with radioactive contamination that might arise due to more recent technology. The problem of safe disposal of the short-lived medical radioactive wastes is nothing like so serious as the heavy-metal problem; nevertheless care has to be taken so that the benefits of this modern technology are not diminished by some accompanying detriment.

The use of radionuclides in medicine has greatly increased over the past decade as their usefulness in gaining quantitative diagnostic information relating to the structure and function of various organs of the body has been realised. There are also important therapeutic measures which involve the administration of substantial

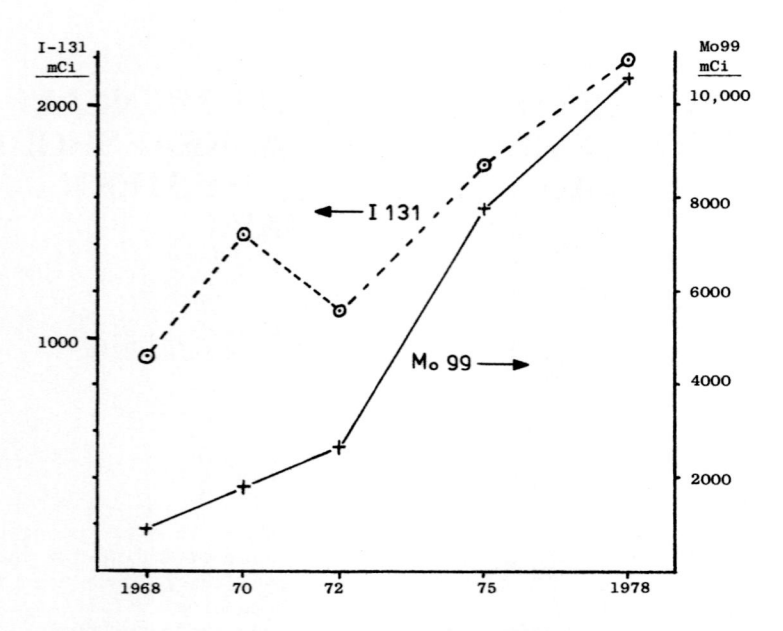

Figure 23.1. Increase in use of I-131 and Tc-99m (1968-1978).

quantities of radioactivity to patients.

Figure 23.1 shows the increasing use of two particular radionuclides at Singleton Hospital, Swansea during the years 1968-1978. Iodine-131 is a nuclide with an 8-day half-life and its usage rose in fact from just under 500 mCi in 1967 to 2,200 mCi in 1978. Much of the increase in use of Iodine-131 is due to the treatment of metastatic thyroid cancer, where excretion of a substantial proportion of the radioactivity in urine follows very soon after its administration. (Measurements on several patients have shown that on average 63% of the given radioactivity is excreted within 24 hours).

The other radionuclide, Technetium-99m, (which is shown here in terms of the activity of its parent Molybdenum-99) has shown an even greater increase in usage. This nuclide has a half-life of only 6 hours and is used for diagnostic investigations. Various compounds incorporating the nuclide are used, and many of these are again largely excreted in urine within perhaps 1 hour of administration. (In bone scanning for example, some 40% of a 15 mCi dose of Tc-99m-methylene-diphosphonate may be excreted within 1 hour).

As far back as 1970, in the United States, C.E. Moss found readily detectable levels of Iodine-131 and Technetium-99m at the outfall of a sewage treatment works in Allegheny County, Pennsylvania, which drains into the Ohio River. Other workers have since then measured concentrations of these radionuclides which are less than the maximum permissible concentrations in water, but which indicate that some concern is justified if their use in the medical field continues to increase.

When estimating the maximum permissible quantities of radioactivity for disposal into municipal sewers, it is common for the authorities to base the allowed disposal on the assumption that radioactive liquid waste is mixed with the total liquid effluent from an institution. However, when test disposals were made from a ward in

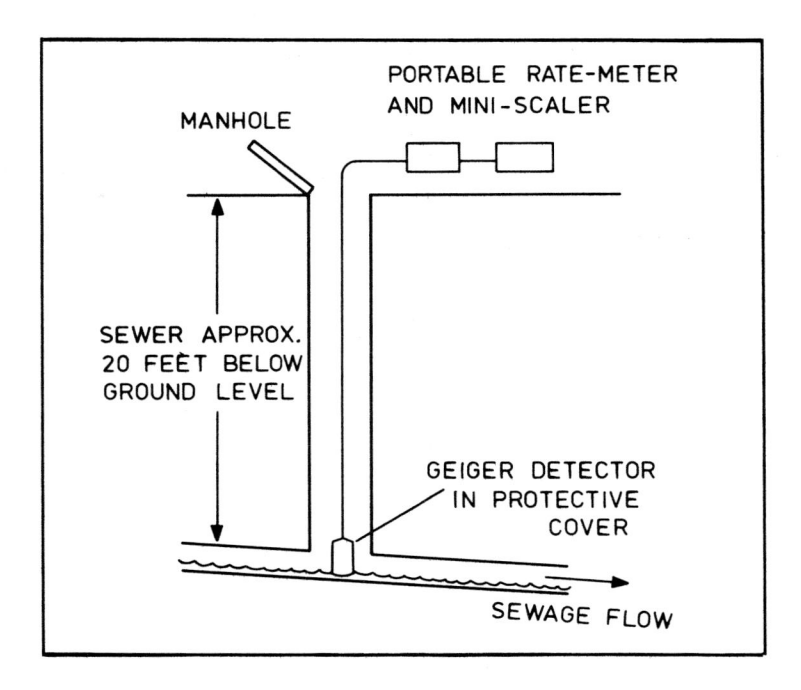

Figure 23.2. Investigation into flow of liquid waste from hospital ward.

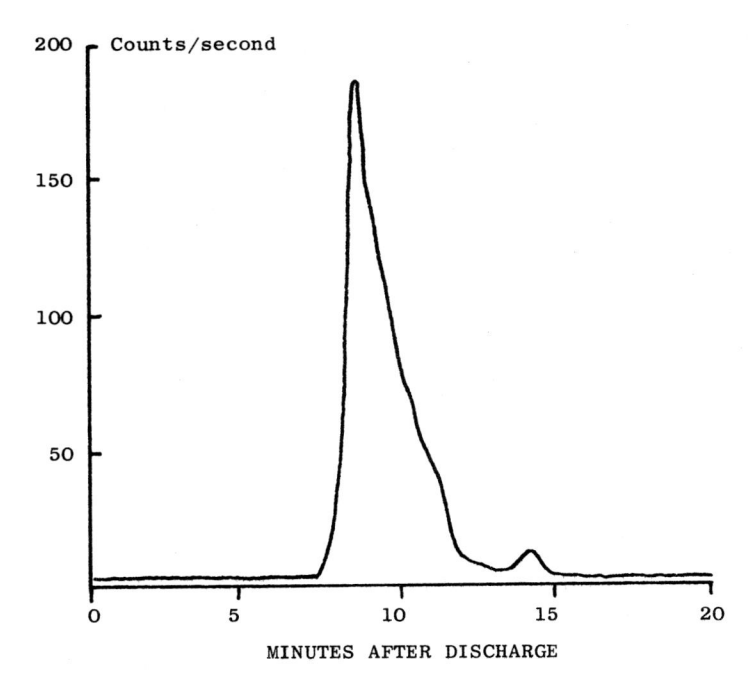

Figure 23.3. 'Pulse' of radioactivity in main sewer.

Singleton Hospital, it was shown that mixing is in fact far from complete. These tests, assessed using a Geiger counter lowered into a manhole at a monitoring point situated just before the hospital effluent enters the municipal sewage system (Fig. 23.2), indicate that some eight minutes elapse before the first appearance of radioactivity at the monitoring point. A rise to peak concentration then occurs within one minute (Fig. 23.3), followed by a more gradual fall, so that in another four minutes, the activity registered returns to near background level again.

No chemical or biological treatment of the sewage effluent takes place in Swansea, though delay tanks are in use at certain times relative to high tide. We may imagine therefore that this bolus of radioactivity will be carried along without too great a dilution by other sewage inflows until it is discharged into the sea from the outfall near Mumbles Head. It might be supposed that after it enters the sea, a small 'cloud' of radioactivity will form which is likely to remain close to the surface due to the higher temperature and lower density of sewage effluent relative to seawater. This cloud will be borne along under the influence of wind and tide until it is finally dispersed. It might be possible for radioactivity to be driven inshore by the prevailing south-westerly winds and on an incoming tide if dilution and dispersion in the sea is not very rapid. Could these two radionuclides therefore, used so largely in the medical field, be detected in the seashore environment?

SEAWEED AS AN INDICATOR

In view of their short half-lives, any material which might concentrate the radionuclides must have rapid uptake and high concentrating ability. A survey of published concentration factors for iodine showed that seaweeds might be of interest in this regard, since 1g of seaweed may contain 10^4 times more iodine than 1g of the seawater around it. No concentration factors for technetium could be found in mid-1974, but figures of 10^5 to 10^6 for bladder-wrack *(Fucus vesiculosis)* and possibly 10^3 for laverweed *(Porphyra)* have been suggested (Jefferies, 1974). Laboratory experiments were therefore carried out on four species of seaweed, measuring the concentration factor (i.e. the ratio of the radioactivity per g of seaweed to the activity per g of seawater) for a few hours after the radionuclide was introduced (in the form of sodium-iodide or pertechnetate). Some results are shown in Figs. 23.4 and 23.5. Figure 23.4 gives the uptake of radioiodine by a specimen of *Fucus serrata*. The concentration factor rises to 140 after about 4 hours. Fig. 23.5 shows a radioiodine concentration factor of only 17 after 3 hours by the seaweed *Ulva lactuca*.

The results of such tests were somewhat variable, and the uptake may be affected by:
a. the specific activity and chemical and physical state of the radionuclide,
b. the age of the particular part of the seaweed plant.
c. the intensity of ambient light,
d. water temperature,
e. the presence of suspended sediment or plankton in the seawater.

There are still questions to be asked regarding the accumulation of both radionuclides by various species of seaweed, but as biological indicators of seashore contamination they seem very suitable.

i. They are abundant along the rocky shore-line in this area.
ii. They are fixed geographically and therefore indicate contamination at the site of collection.
iii. They are easily collected in fairly large sample volumes without any fear of reducing the local population of a species.
iv. *Porphyra umbilicalis* is gathered locally and eaten as the Welsh delicacy 'Laver-

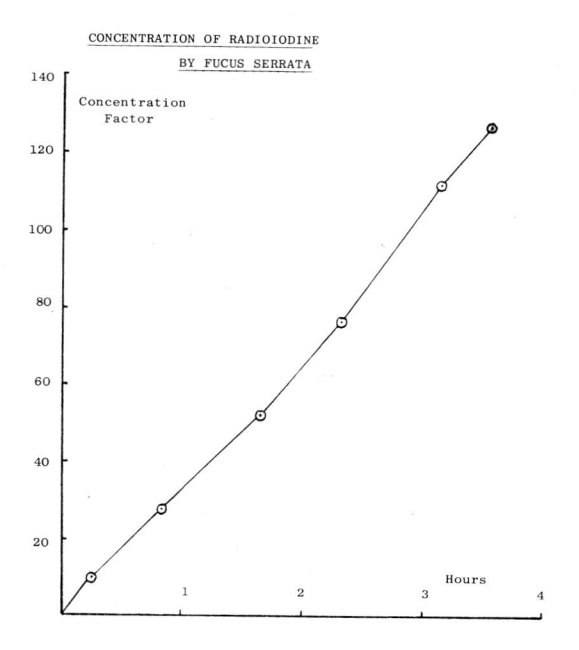

Figure 23.4. Concentration of radioiodine by *Fucus serrata*

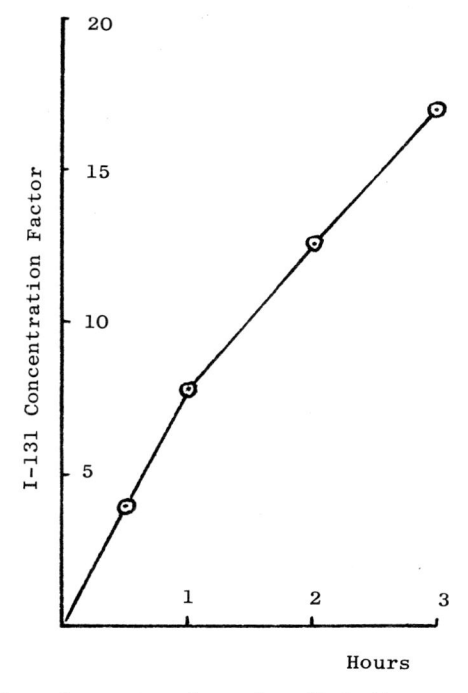

Figure 23.5. Concentration of radioiodine by *Ulva lactuca*.

Bread' - making measurements of its radioactivity of added interest.

ENVIRONMENTAL SURVEY

Geographical

An environmental survey of four different species of seaweed was first made at various sites within 1500 metres of the outfall at Mumbles Head (Fig. 23.6). The seaweed was collected at low tide, cut into small pieces and packed into ½-litre plastic containers whilst on the beach to avoid any possible laboratory contamination. Radioactivity measurements were performed using a 5" diameter by 3" thick

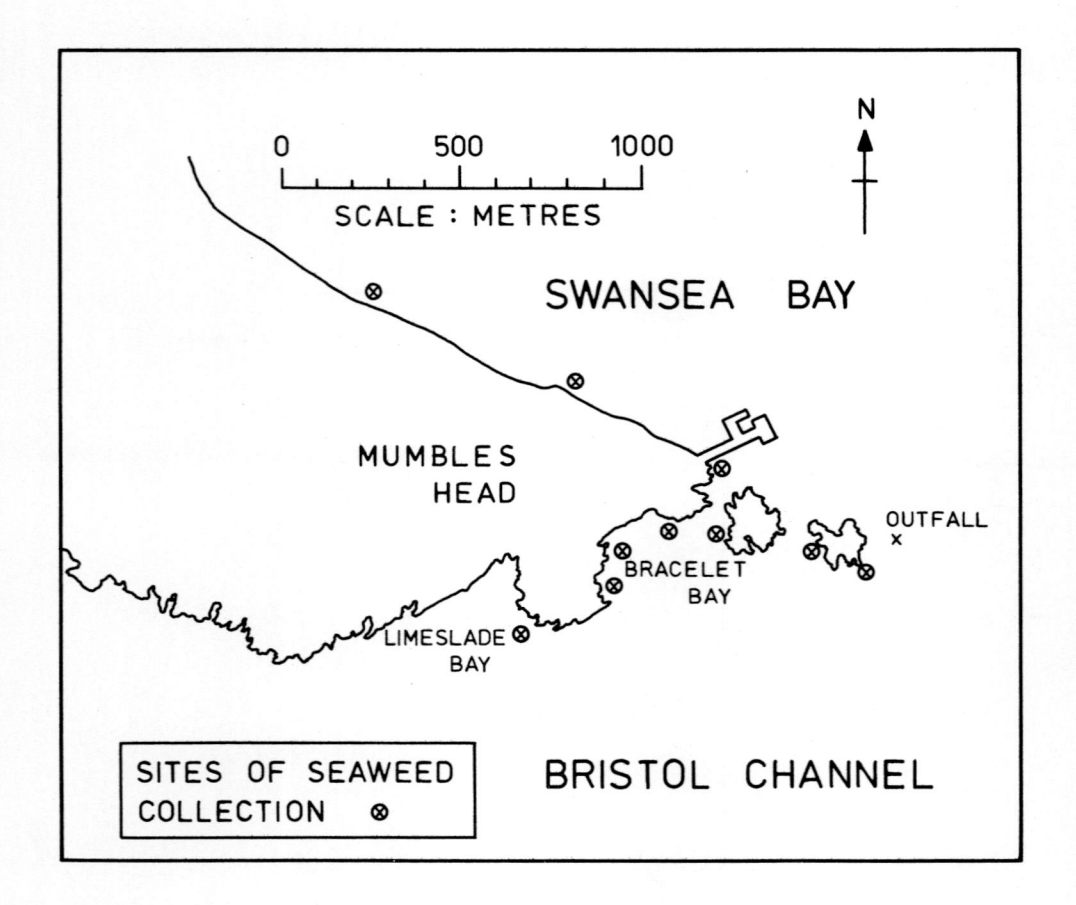

Figure 23.6. Sketch map showing the sites of seaweed collection for the environmental survey.

sodium iodide crystal scintillation detector, counting each sample for 10^4s (about $2\frac{3}{4}$ hours). The results seemed to indicate highest counts in an Iodine-131 window for an area of beach in Bracelet Bay, approximately 600 metres west of the outfall. Areas nearer the actual outfall, which is covered by seawater at all states of the tide, showed less radioactivity.

Radioiodine monitoring

Periodic monitoring of the radioiodine content of seaweed taken from this particular area of beach was then undertaken, especially at times when large therapeutic doses of Iodine-131 were administered. It was found that when only relatively small quantities of radioiodine were used, to treat perhaps 3 or 4 thyrotoxic patients per week with around 5 mCi for each patient, the level of Iodine-131 in the seaweed was generally undetectable against the natural background level that had been determined from samples taken off remote beaches or samples that had been stored for radioactive decay over several weeks. (The background level was chosen so that there was less then 5% chance that uncontaminated seaweed would be considered as having a positive radioiodine content).

When the activity seemed definitely higher than background the sample was stored for some two weeks and the measurement repeated to see if reduction in activity compatible with the 8-day half-life of Iodine-131 had occurred. As a further confirmation that it really was Iodine-131 that was present, two samples were sent to Dr. Clive Biggin of Sheffield Polytechnic who kindly carried out gamma spectrometry using a Lithium-drifted Germanium detector. He showed that a small but definite 364 keV peak, characteristic of Iodine-131, was present.

When very large doses of Iodine-131 were used to treat cases of thyroid cancer, sampling was done consistently and the pattern of concentration and loss of radioiodine by the seaweed was followed. Figure 23.7 shows the activity present in the seaweed *Fucus serrata* rising to nearly 600 pCi/kg after a 150 mCi dose. A single sample of *Porphyra* showed rather less radioiodine than the *Fucus* seaweed.

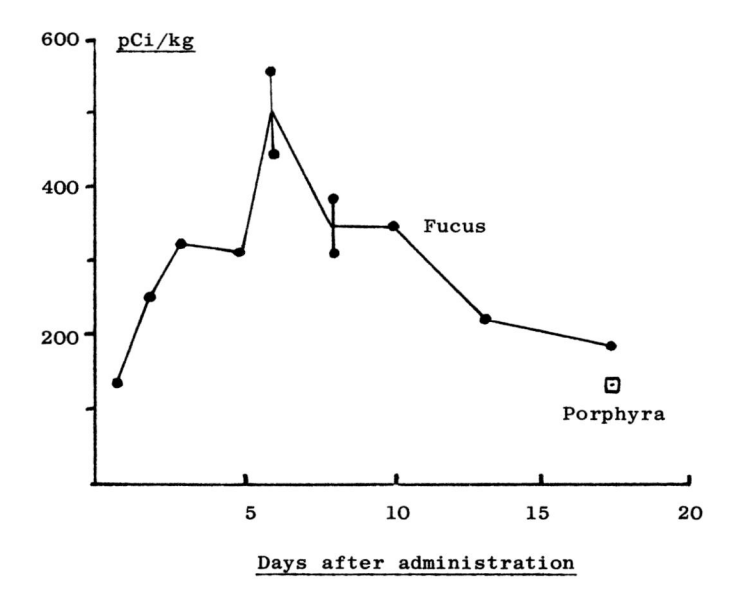

Figure 23.7. Radioiodine in seaweed after 150mCi dose used in hospital.

Another set of results is shown in Fig. 23.8 where the concentration in *Fucus serrata* rose to a maximum of around 1 nCi/kg some 3 to 4 days after 200 mCi of Iodine-

360   J. L. Birks

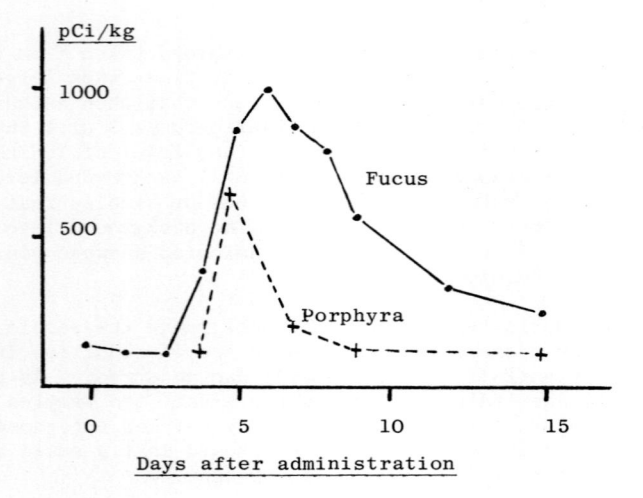

Figure 23.8.   Radioiodine in seaweed after 200mCi dose used in hospital.

131 were used.   *Porphyra* (the seaweed which is eaten as Laverbread) showed around 600 pCi/kg.

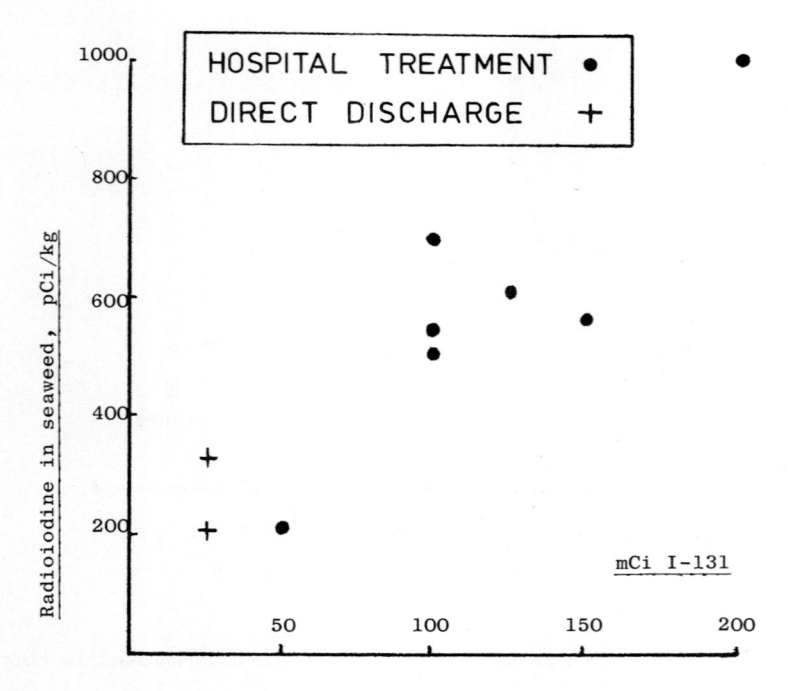

Figure 23.9.   Radioiodine contamination related to hospital discharges.

Discharge of Medical Radionuclides

In Fig. 23.9, the maximum levels of radioiodine found in *Fucus serrata* are plotted against the doses of Iodine-131 used at the hospital, demonstrating the rough correlation that exists. Two points on this graph show the radioiodine detected in two seaweed samples after 25 mCi had been discharged directly through the outfall pipe - an experiment performed through the kind co-operation of Mr. Ian Borthwick and Dr. Michael Collins of the Department of Oceanography, University College, Swansea.

Later in the course of this work a Ge-Li detector became available in Swansea. Fig. 23.10 shows the gamma spectrum of a *Fucus serrata* sample after background had been subtracted. The 364 keV photons from Iodine-131 were readily detected, together with associated 284 and 637 keV emissions of less abundance. Radionuclides of the naturally occurring Radium-226 and Thorium-232 series were also present.

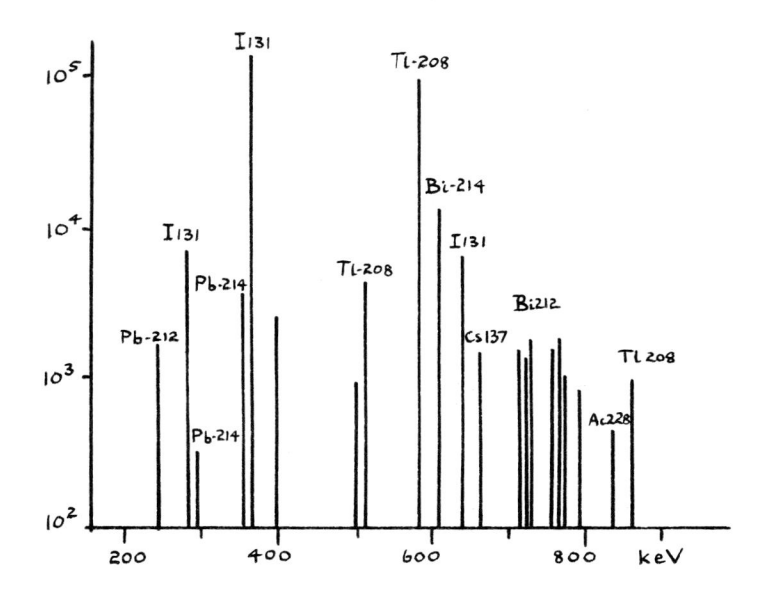

Figure 23.10. Ge(Li) spectrum of seaweed (background subtracted).

Monitoring of Technetium-99m

In the search for possible Technetium-99m accumulation in seaweed, samples were counted twice with an interval of at least 3 days in between so that any reduction in count-rate would be due to the 6-hour half-life. Such measurements failed to show the presence of any Technetium-99m contamination during the routine use of about 50 mCi of this radionuclide per day. In order to find out if uptake would occur in seaweed and what its level would be after the discharge of a known quantity of the radionuclide, a few special large releases were made from the hospital.

The resulting seaweed samples were counted using the 5" x 3" sodium iodide crystal for 50,000s (around 14 hours). A multi-channel analyser stored the gamma spectrum. After 3 days the sample was re-counted when any Technetium-99m present initially would have decayed through 12 half-lives. Thus any reduction in counts over the channels corresponding to the technetium photo-peak would be due to decay from the initial level. By subtraction of the second record from the first, the net Technetium-99m activity could be obtained.

The results of three tests are summarised in Table 23.1. In Test A, 400 mCi of the isotope were discharged from the hospital 8¾hr before high water, and *Fucus serrata* was collected 26 hours later. A technetium concentration of 147 pCi/kg was found, calculated for the time of sample collection.

In Test B, 300 mCi were discharged 7½ hours before high water and seaweed was collected after 25 hours. The measurement was 118 pCi/kg. If allowance is made for the different activities discharged, the correlation between the results of tests A and B is very good as shown by the last column of Table 23.1.

In Test C, 200 mCi were discharged 3½hr before high water and seaweed was collected after 9½hrs. There was no significant radioactivity in the sample this time. I have attempted to explain these results in terms of the tidal flows around Mumbles Head.

In Test A and B is seems possible that the radioactive liquid would reach the out-

TABLE 23.1.   Technetium-99m Levels in Seaweed Following Hospital Discharges.

Test	Discharge mCi	Seaweed Tc pCi/kg at Time of Collection	Interval hr	pCi/kg per mCi Tc Discharged
A	400	147	26	0.368
B	300	118	25	0.393
C	200	-	10	-

fall and be discharged into the sea before high water. Under these circumstances the 'cloud' of radioactivity in the sea would probably stay near the surface and in the vicinity of Mumbles Head initially. Later there would be a westerly drift on the outgoing tide before the radioactivity was brought inshore by the next in-flowing tide. The seaweed had then perhaps 8 hours or so in which to concentrate the isotope before samples were collected at the following low tide.

In Test C however, the release of the radionuclide took place nearer the time of high water and discharge from the outfall was probably into an ebbing tide. This radioactivity would not have been brought into the vicinity of Bracelet Bay by the time the seaweed sample was collected, and this seems to explain why the seaweed in Test C showed no uptake.

DISCUSSION

A consideration of the hazards to health from the levels of radioiodine detected has shown that both the external radiation hazard and the ingestion hazard to a person who consumes large quantities of locally gathered laverbread are minimal. However, even this small amount of radioiodine could be regarded as unwelcome and it would be preferable to reduce the environmental contamination to an undetectable level. The preservation of a 'clean' environment, free from all artificial radioactivity, is desirable anywhere and is especially important in an area such as Bracelet Bay which is used for recreational purposes by a large number of people.

At present, the disposal of this sort of radioactive liquid waste is based upon the philosophy of dilution and dispersion into a very large volume of water. The likelihood of insufficient mixing, even when the volume of water available is extremely large, plus the possibility of concentration by organic or inorganic materials, may result in less than the expected degree of dispersion when this philosophy is applied in practice. The alternative philosophy is one of concentration and shielded storage of the radioactivity until decay has sufficiently reduced the hazard.

This alternative appears to be quite possible if ion-exchange resin is used to absorb the radioiodine from urine, using a disposal unit similar to that shown in Fig. 23.11.

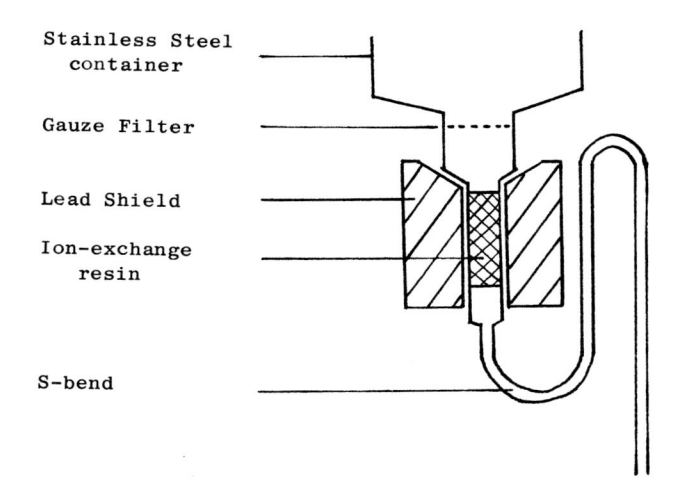

Figure 23.11. Ward unit for removal of I-131 from urine.

Experimental tests have shown that over 99% of the radioiodine can be removed from urine which is passed through a column 2 cm. in diameter and 8 cm. long containing 'Amberlite' IRA 410 resin. The use of such a unit would replace a large, unmanageable volume of liquid waste with a compact volume of solid waste, namely the ion-exchange column. This could be stored in a lead-shielded enclosure to allow for radioactive decay or possibly it could be buried immediately on a suitable municipal dump under 2m or so of overburden. If it were thought desirable to avoid the discharge of radioiodine from a hospital into the municipal sewers then the use of a disposal unit based on the ion-exchange process would provide a practical way of accomplishing this. The reasons for doing so would however be aesthetic rather than the avoidance of a significant radiation hazard.

ACKNOWLEDGEMENTS

This work formed part of a thesis for the Ph.D. degree and I would like to record my thanks to Professor G.F. Elliott and Dr. E.A. Bowers of the Open University for their interest and encouragement, and also to Dr. M.R. Hopkins of the Department of Physics at University College, Swansea, for his helpful advice.

My colleagues at Singleton Hospital provided helpful and stimulating discussions during the course of this work and in particular I must record my gratitude to Mr.

A. Sivyer and Dr. W.D. Morgan. Thanks are also due to the Swansea County Borough Engineer's Department and to members of the Oceanography Department at University College, Swansea, who provided useful background information on certain aspects, and to Mrs. S.A. Thomas who performed valuable work on the illustrations and typing the script.

REFERENCES

Moss, C.E. (1973). Control of radioisotope releases to the environment from diagnostic isotope procedures. *Health Physics, 25,* 197-198.
Jefferies, D.F. (1974). Personal communication.

DISCUSSION V

James: I'd like to ask Dr. Tyler if she'd like to speculate on the mechanism of adsorption of the viruses onto the clay particles.

Tyler, J: It is believed to be an electrostatic attraction, but I do not know why and how long it lasts.

James: I was interested in the fact that you said once you'd subjected it to some agitation, you were able to split the viruses off the clay particles, which suggests that it's not a specific type of adsorption.

Tyler, J: All I can really say is not that we are able to split it off the particles, but that we are able to detect an increased amount.

Birks: I believe there are cases of seaside resorts where children are suspected of having contracted polio. I wonder if there is any work done on the number of viruses per 10 litres of seawater, to arrive at some maximum permissible or safe level?

Tyler, J: Firstly, there has been a little work done, but it's difficult to isolate particular viruses in seawater. Secondly, I don't think there's any evidence at all that polio has been caught by bathing in any waters in Great Britain. Although it might be possible, as you say, that polio has been contracted in places where there has been a number of people present, we wouldn't know whether it's been contracted by bathing, or whether by person to person transmission, which is quite feasible. Trying to sort out between disease transmission, whether person to person, or from bathing in the water is very difficult.

Waters: Would Dr. Tyler agree that the incidence of people being ill associated with eating shellfish has decreased since 1962, when fishery procedures in cleaning were improved?

Tyler, J: Yes.

Dale: Have the local shellfish ever been monitored for radio-iodine?

Birks: No, seaweed is much easier to collect in the large volumes I required for my monitoring studies.

Tait: My own limited observations on the take up of radio-iodine by *Fucus* suggests that the iodine is most actively concentrated in the parts of the thallus that are most actively growing. As rate of growth varies seasonally, it would appear that the seaweeds vary in their sensitivity to radio-iodine, and therefore in their sensitivity as indicators of pollution.

Banner: Some years ago, I was contacted by a Consultant at Bridgend General Hospital who was investigating the occurrence of "Puppet Syndrome" in babies in the area. This is a general neural disorder. Babies jerk as if they are puppets and this is probably congenital, caused by mercury ingested by the mothers. He had recognised a particularly high number of cases of this syndrome in the area between Bridgend and Llanelli, which corresponds to the lava bread eating belt. He suspected that it could be due to mercury ingested with the *Porphyra* alga as lava bread. I wondered whether anyone had followed this up? I know that his own work, like ours at Swansea, was hampered by lack of resources.

Birks: I know nothing about this "Puppet Syndrome" I'm sorry to say, nor do I really know about mercury concentrations in the *Porphyra* seaweed. I might say though that the majority of the lava bread eaten locally is not from the Swansea area, but brought from the Lake District and the Northern Irish Sea.

24. DIFFUSION AND DISPERSION CHARACTERISTICS IN SWANSEA BAY: SOME PRELIMINARY RESULTS

I. Borthwick*

Department of Oceanography, University College, Swansea, U.K.
*Present Address: Department of Biology, Memorial University, St. Johns, Newfoundland, Canada

ABSTRACT

Dye diffusion experiments were carried out in Swansea Bay to determine the characteristics and nature of horizontal diffusion processes prevalent in the area. Sixteen were instantaneous point releases, and four may be described as "far-field" releases, where dye was introduced at some point remote from the receiving area.

Results from the "far-field" experiments demonstrate a decay of maximum concentration with with time varying from $t^{-1.57}$ to $t^{-4.81}$. This suggests the importance of shear diffusion processes in dispersing the dye patch.

Results from the instantaneous point releases demonstrated dye plumes elongated in the mean direction of flow, and a two-dimensional horizontal analysis was conducted. Values were computed for the horizontal variance (σ_{xy}^2) and horizontal diffusion coefficient (K_{xy}), and these results were compared with a rotationally symmetrical analysis proposed by other authors.

The results indicate that the rotationally symmetrical analysis is not valid for the present investigations, and that the horizontal variance σ_{xy}^2 is proportional to $t^{2.11}$. The horizontal diffusion coefficient is related to the patch scale to the power of 1.19. These results are directly comparable to other published data, and suggest that the turbulence processes acting in Swansea Bay are anisotropic and non-homogeneous.

KEYWORDS

Horizontal diffusion; Dispersion; Effluent dispersal; Tracers; Swansea Bay; Bristol Channel.

INTRODUCTION

Sixteen instantaneous point-source dye releases and four "far-field" releases were carried out in Swansea Bay between 1975 and 1977. These were of a short duration, spanning half a tidal cycle, with a maximum diffusion time of 6.3 hours occurring during the River Neath investigation. The experiments were initiated to examine the horizontal diffusion characteristics of the Bay at two depth intervals (1m and

5m below the surface).

The former experiments involved the introduction of a slug of Rhodamine-WT dye, released as an instantaneous point source, in the surface layer. The latter consisted of a release of dye, over a longer period of time, at a location geographically remote from the prime receiving area; in the case of the Mumbles experiments through an existing submarine outfall, and the Tawe and Neath releases at some distance upstream from the river mouth.

By utilizing a source remote from the receiving area the overall dispersion characteristics may be observed, that is the mixing processes occurring within the pipeline or the river system and the subsequent dispersion in the receiving area. In the case of the instantaneous point-releases, dye was discharged directly into the water column at a known point in space and time, and the diffusion characteristics of the particular receiving area under consideration were assessed directly. The former demonstrate the efficiency of an existing system to disperse effluent, whilst the latter show the potential dispersion characteristics of a given area.

The instantaneous slug releases were carried out in the offshore environments as shown in Fig. 24.1 (at Stations B,C,D, E and F). "Far-field" experiments were conducted off Mumbles Head, at Station A,and upstream in the Tawe and Neath estuaries. Also shown in this figure are the net drift of the dye patches, as indicated by the movement of the centre of mass of the dye, and by surface drogues. The overall extent, at low tide, of freshwater in the Bay from the two major river systems is also shown. Additional data are available on the water masses in the Bay, as shown by the surface salinity distribution, which further demonstrate the dominant influence of fresh water in the Western and Central portions of the inner Bay at low water (See also Figs. 11.11 and 11.12).

The geographical location and hydrodynamic regime of the area are the subject of other papers in this symposium, and it is unnecessary to go into detail here. However, it should be noted that local conditions prevalent during the dye experiments will undoubtedly affect the small-scale diffusion processes under consideration. Consequently it is necessary to consider the hydrodynamic characteristics and topography of the area in the vicinity of the dye plume rather than a general overview of the situation. Thus supplementary information on currents, stability, vertical shear parameters, and local environmental conditions are also available, but will not be included here

METHODS

The preliminary investigations carried out in 1975 in Mumbles utilized a discrete sampling method and subsequent laboratory analysis on an Aminco fluorometer. During the 1976-1977 field seasons, two Turner Model 110 fluorometers (G.K. Turner Associates, Palo Alto, California) with continuous flow cells were used, and continuous *in situ* monitoring of the dye patch was possible. Water was pumped from two depths (1m and 5m) by means of separate tubing systems fixed to a rigid boom and weighted buoy arrangement, and then delivered to a specific fluorometer on board the vessel. The lag time and capacity of the two separate pump systems were calibrated and accounted for. Initially,temperature was continuously recorded using a Robertson's Research temperature probe, but since there was no significant variation (maximum 1.5°C) over the period of each experiment, these measurements were discontinued and temperature was recorded at half-hourly intervals.

Each fluorometer was calibrated, using the flow cells, with standard concentrations of dye, and calibration curves of fluorescent intensity against concentration were plotted. The calibrations were repeated at regular invervals throughout the field studies, and a computer programme was developed to convert fluorescence values to

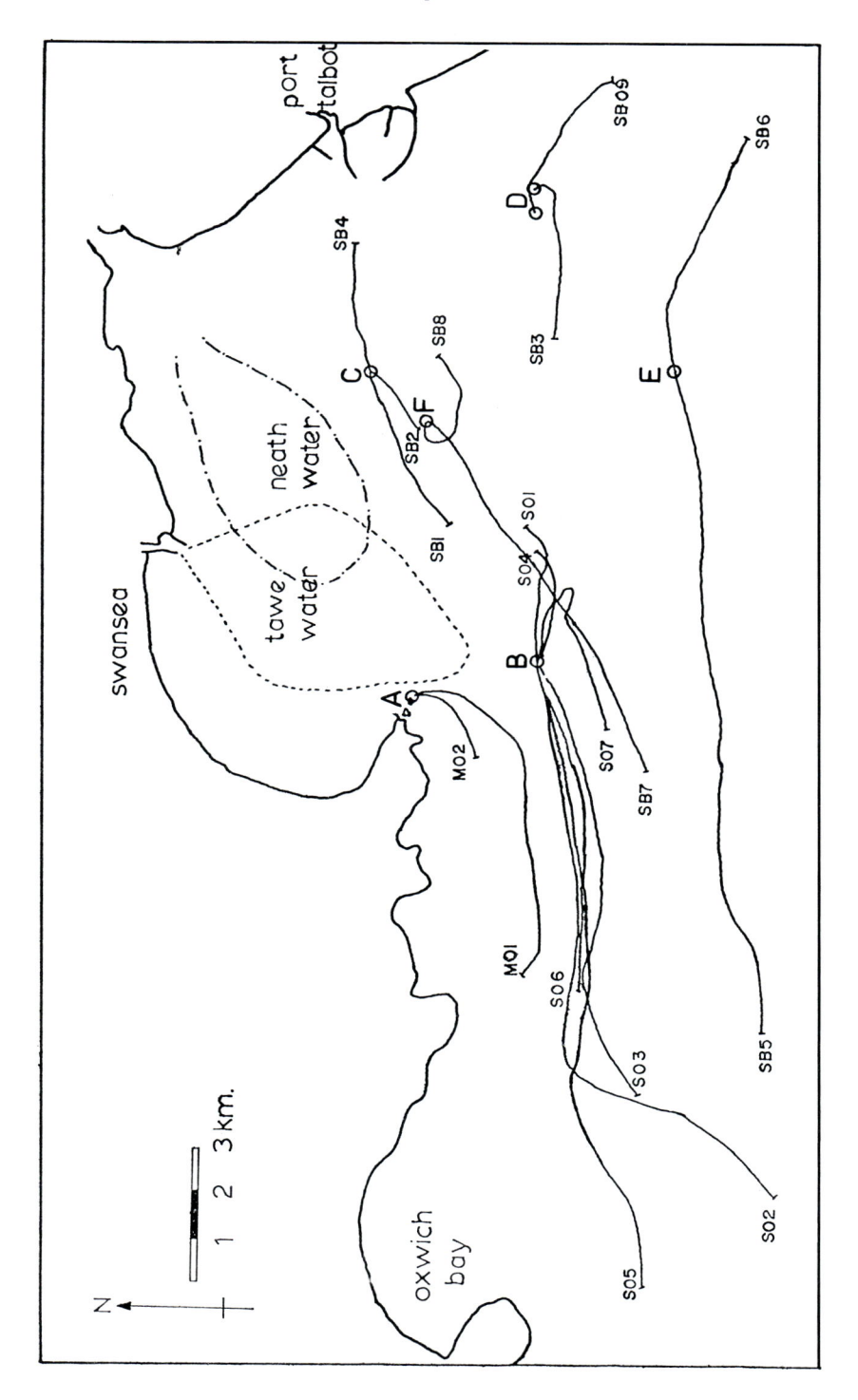

Figure 24.1. Movement of dye plumes.

concentration. Included in this programme was a temperature correction factor, which accounted for temperature variation from experiment to experiment.

The output signals from the fluorometers were recorded on a Racal "Store-Four" tape recorder, and relayed to a dual channel chart recorder for an immediate confirmation of recording status. The chart record gave an *in situ* indication as to the presence or absence and relative concentrations of the dye. The tape record of fluorescence was subsequently filtered to remove background noise, digitized for computer input, and reduced to concentration values by the programme mentioned above; the datum interval being one second. Thus, a five minute track across the dye plume produced 300 data points.

The technique used for tracking the dye was consistent throughout the 1976-1977 studies and followed the normal practice for dye tracing. To ensure reproducibility of results the same mass of dye (1.2kg) was released at all the offshore locations (giving an original concentration of 3×10^{-2} gm/cm³), however, the Tawe and Neath releases utilized twice this amount. The density of the dye was adjusted to that of the receiving area, except in the case of the river releases, where the impact of freshwater was of prime consideration, and here it was adjusted to a density of 1 gm/cm³.

Drogues were released at the outset of the experiment and at subsequent intervals to facilitate location of the patch. Tracks were run across the plume in order to fully describe the dye distribution at a certain time interval from the initial release. This time interval is referred to as the diffusion time. Position fixing was by the Decca Navigator system. 'Motorola' mini-ranger electronic positioning system, or by land-based theodolite angles.

ANALYSIS AND RESULTS

"Far-field" Experiments

The objective of the "far-field" studies was to gauge the impact of remote sources entering the Bay, by monitoring the dispersion of the introduced dye patch both qualitatively and quantitatively. The former was carried out by observing the size and distribution of the patch in space and time, and the latter by relating the maximum concentration to time from release and distance from the source.

Two releases were carried out at Mumbles, at 2 hours before and 2½ hours after high water and, on both occasions, the complex nature of the circulation system and diffusion processes were apparent. The sampling method and the rate at which the dye dispersed was such that a full analysis of the patch distribution in time was impossible, and so the quantitative evaluation was restricted to the behaviour of the maximum concentration (C max) with the time (t) and distance (x) from the source.

The dye patch in both surveys split in two, forming an inshore and offshore plume, and Fig. 24.2 shows the dye distribution for the HW +2½ hours release; A1-A4 representing the inshore maxima, and B1-B6 the offshore maxima. The transverse lines across the patches indicate where crossplume distributions were measured. Plots of Cmax v.t are shown in Fig. 24.3, where M01 refers to the high water +2½ hours release and M02 the high water -2½ hours release. (Note in Fig. 24.2, A and B merely relate to "inshore" and "offshore" plumes.)
Regression analyses on the results show the decay rates of maximum concentrations with time, and with distance from the source; these are summarised in Table 24.1 for both the mbles and the Tawe and Neath releases. The relationships are of the general form:

$$C_{max} = at^b$$ where b = time rate of decay factor

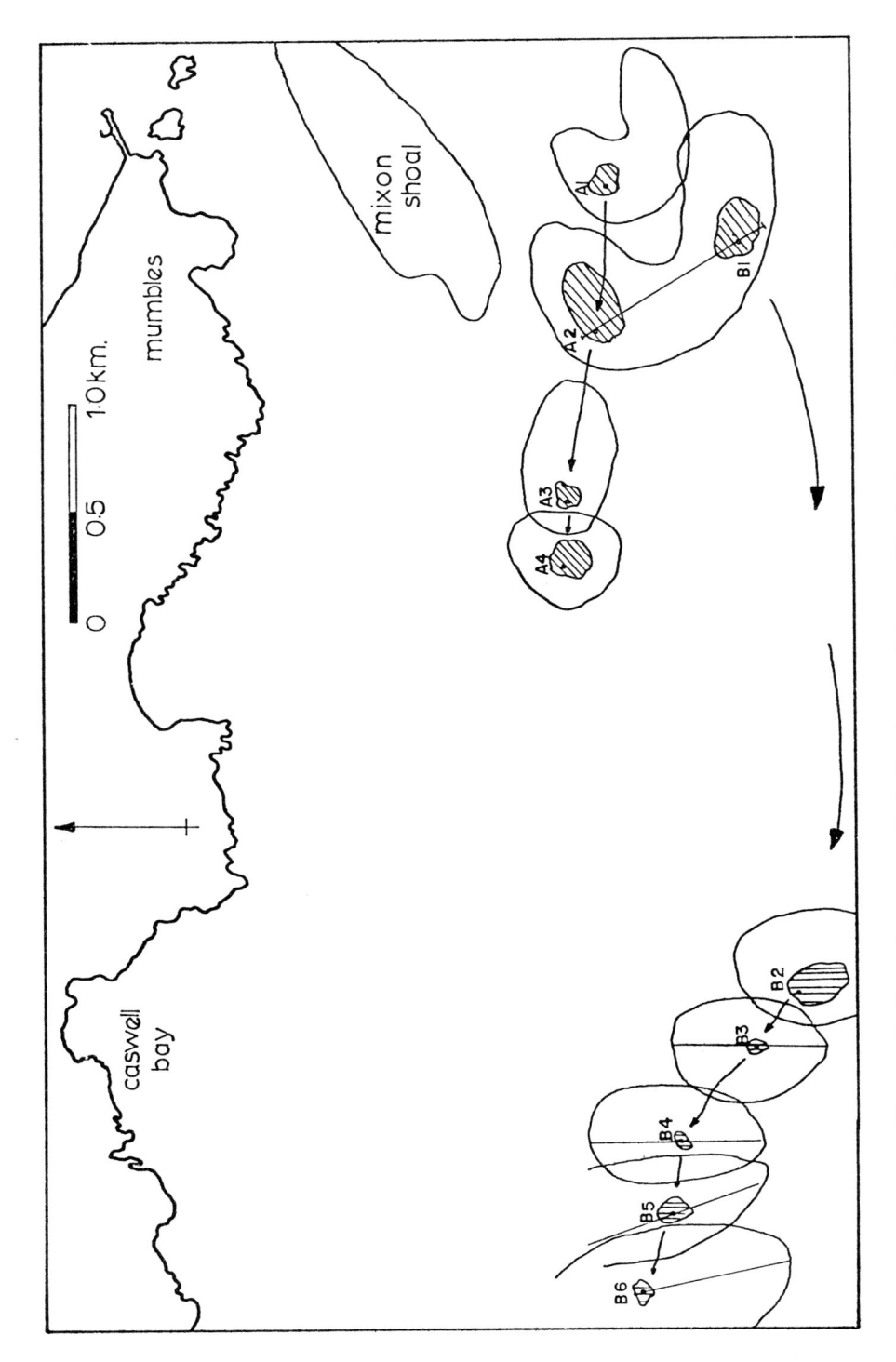

Figure 24.2. Rhodamine Distribution. Release HW +2½ hours at Mumbles Head.

TABLE 24.1. "Far Field" Dye Results.

EXPERIMENT		TIME RATES OF DECAY (b) C_{max} vs t	CORRELATION COEFFICIENT	DISTANCE RATES OF DECAY (d) C_{max} vs x	CORRELATION COEFFICIENT
MO1 (HW+2½)	inshore	-2.56	0.94	-1.79	0.93
	offshore	-2.04	0.97	-1.44	0.92
MO2 (HW-2)	inshore	-4.81	0.99	-2.38	0.92
	offshore	-3.54	0.96	-2.56	0.95
Neath	(HW+1)	-1.57	0.98	-2.79	0.95
Tawe	(HW+1)	-1.80	0.95	-1.87	0.94

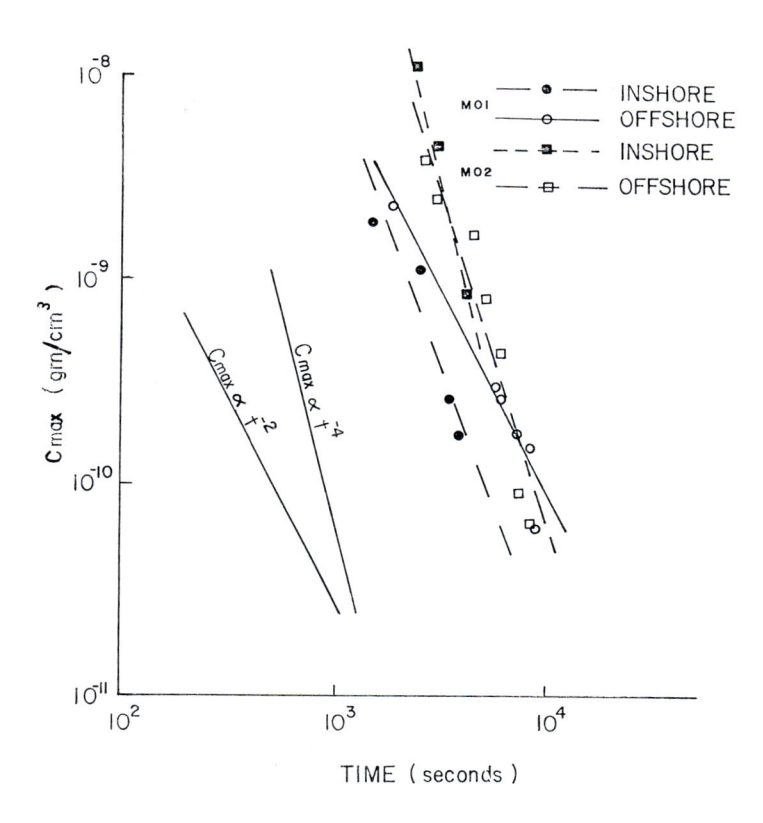

Figure 24.3. Mumbles dye experiments.

$C_{max} = Cx^d$ where d = distance rate of decay factor

Instantaneous Point Releases

In these experiments the initial condition of the patch is known and controlled in time and space; the subsequent diffusion of the plume can thus be carefully monitored, and the dye distribution can be fully described for given diffusion times.

Figure 24.4 shows typical dye distributions after a release (HW +1hr) at Station C in Eastern Swansea Bay; 24.4(a) depicts the distribution 1 hour after release and 24.4(b) 1.5 hours after. The contour maps are constructed using the SYMAP computer contouring programme (Harvard School of Computer Graphics), which analyses the distribution of dye concentration along the ship's track (dashed lines in the figure) and constructs contour lines at designated intervals. Axes are constructed through the centroid of the distribution, with the x-axis being taken in the direction of the mean current by which the centre of mass of the patch is being advected.

Due to the general characteristics of elongation of the patches throughout the ex-

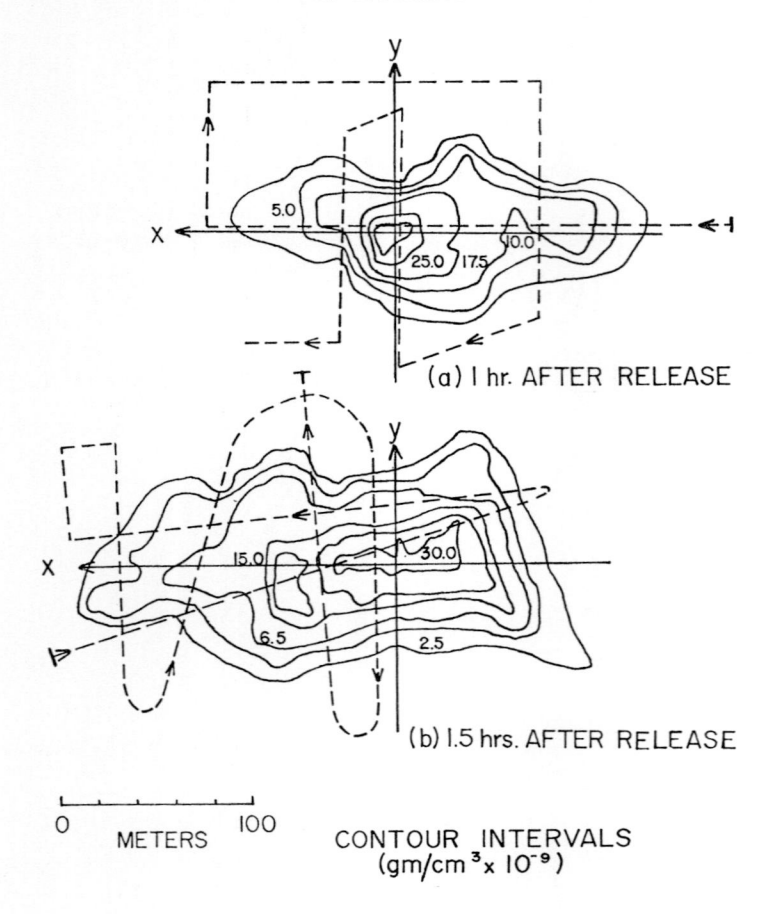

Figure 24.4. Rhodamine-WT distribution after a release in Eastern Swansea Bay (SBOI 29/10/76).

periments, it is assumed that radial symmetry does not exist and that diffusion occurs at different rates in the x and y directions. This suggests that the similarity theory is not valid and that horizontal turbulence is anisotropic.

Moments are taken about the centre of mass of the dye patch and the longitudinal variance σ_x^2 is given by:

$$\sigma_x^2 = C(x,y)x^2 dxdy \qquad C(x,y)dxdy \qquad (1)$$

with a similar equation for the lateral variance σ_y^2.

The computed values of σ_x^2 for a series of experiments from Eastern Swansea Bay are presented in Table 24.2. In order to simplify the discussion and allow a comparison to be made with other authors, the horizontal variance (σ_{xy}^2) has been calculated, and may be described as follows:

$$\sigma_{xy}^2 = \sigma_x^2 + \sigma_y^2 \qquad (2)$$

TABLE 24.2. Observed Horizontal Variances at 1m and 5m Depths.

RELEASE (TIDE STATE)	Diff. time (sec) x10⁴	σ_x^2 (cm²) x 10⁷	σ_y^2 (cm²) x 10⁷	σ_{xy}^2	σ_y/σ_x (e)	σ_r^2* (cm²) x 10⁷	σ_{rt}^2** (cm²) x 10⁷
SB01 HW+1hr 29.10.76	0.36	1.41 (2.01) 1.99 (0.99) 10.50 (9.19)	0.31 (0.49) 0.49 (0.34) 1.32 (0.92)	1.72 (2.50) 2.48 (1.33) 11.82 (10.11)	0.46 (0.49) 0.50 (0.59) 0.35 (0.32)	0.66 (0.99) 0.99 (0.58) 3.72 (2.91)	1.32 (1.98) 1.98 (1.16) 7.44 (5.82)
	0.54						
	0.72						
SB03 HW-½hr 30.10.76	0.24	0.56 (0.90) 2.90 (5.92) 13.19 (9.04) 20.12 (24.92)	0.08 (0.09) 0.18 (0.13) 0.34 (0.42) 0.80 (0.82)	0.64 (0.99) 3.08 (6.05) 13.53 (9.46) 20.92 (25.74)	0.37 (0.31) 0.25 (0.14) 0.16 (0.21) 0.06 (0.18)	0.21 (0.23) 0.72 (0.88) 2.12 (1.95) 4.01 (4.52)	0.42 (0.56) 1.44 (1.76) 4.24 (3.90) 8.02 (9.04)
	0.36						
	0.63						
	0.90						
SB04 LW+½hr 31.10.76	0.54	1.85 (2.51) 7.42 (7.93) 11.40 (15.66) 37.16 (36.87)	0.42 (1.70) 0.82 (0.76) 4.76 (4.26) 7.71 (6.49)	2.27 (4.21) 8.69 (8.80) 16.16 (19.92) 44.87 (43.36)	0.47 (0.82) 0.33 (0.31) 0.65 (0.52) 0.46 (0.42)	0.83 (2.07) 2.47 (2.46) 7.37 (8.17) 16.93 (15.47)	1.76 (4.14) 4.94 (4.92) 14.74 (16.34) 33.86 (30.94)
	0.81						
	1.26						
	1.62						

figures in brackets indicate 5m values
*After Kullenberg 1974
**After Bowden 1972

assuming the distribution is Gaussian. Bowden (1972) and Kullenberg (1974) have proposed relationships whereby the longitudinal and latitudinal variances may be related to the rotationally symmetrical variances as follows:

$$\sigma_{rc}^2 = 2\,\sigma_x \cdot \sigma_y \qquad \text{Bowden (1972)} \qquad (3)$$

$$\sigma_r^2 = \sigma_x \cdot \sigma_y \qquad \text{Kullenberg (1974)} \qquad (4)$$

It is obvious that there is some discrepancy between these relationships and, in order to test their validity, both methods have been applied. The results are shown in Table 24.2 and discussed in the "conclusions" section. These methods assume that the areas enclosed by the corresponding isolines in the elliptical and rotationally symmetrical distributions, respectively, are equal. This is a reasonable assumption in some cases, but cannot always be used and the degree of "elongation" (e) of the patch, which is described by the ratio σ_y/σ_x may be used to indicate the applicability of the rotationally asymmetrical approach to the data (see Instantaneous Release section).

From the values of the cross plume variances the diffusion characteristics may be calculated:

Longitudinal Diffusion Coefficient.

$$K_x = \frac{\sigma_x^2}{2t} \qquad (5)$$

Lateral Diffusion Coefficient

$$K_y = \frac{\sigma_y^2}{2t} \qquad (6)$$

Horizontal Diffusion Coefficient

$$K_{xy} = \frac{\sigma_{xy}^2}{4t} \qquad (7)$$

"Apparent" Horizontal Diffusion Coefficient

$$K_b = \frac{\sigma_{rc}^2}{4t} \qquad \text{(Bowden 1972)} \qquad (8)$$

Horizontal Diffusion Coefficient

$$K_a = \frac{\sigma_r^2}{4t} \qquad \text{(Kullenberg 1974)} \qquad (9)$$

where t = diffusion time

The "SCALE" of diffusion is defined as:

$$L_{xy} = 3.6_{xy} \qquad (10)$$

$$L_b = 3.6_{rc} \qquad \text{(Bowden 1972)} \qquad (11)$$

$$L_a = 3.6_r \quad \text{(Kullenberg 1974)} \quad (12)$$

The data for the diffusion coefficients and their respective patch scales are shown in Table 24.3.

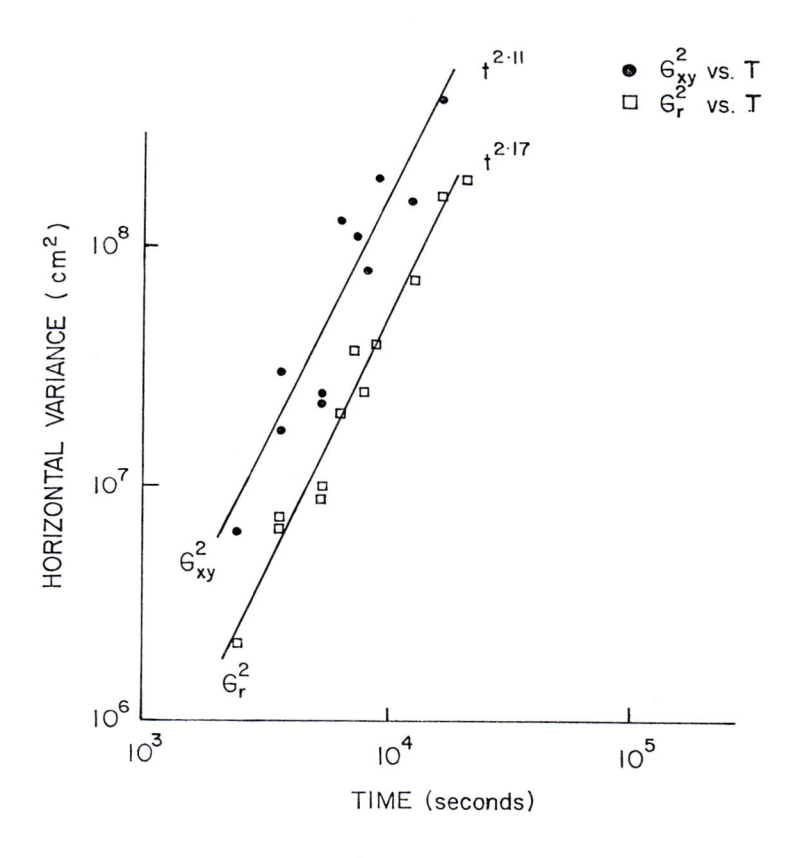

Figure 24.5. Horizontal variance vs time for 1m depth.

Figure 24.5 shows a plot of horizontal (σ_{xy}^2) and rotationally symmetrical variances (σ_r^2) after Kullenberg (1974), against time at 1m depth, for all the Eastern Swansea Bay experiments. The plot derived from Bowden's relationship (Equation (3)) has been omitted for sake of clarity. Regression analyses were applied to each set of data and gave the following relationships (correlation coefficients (r) are shown in brackets):

1m Depth.

2 Dimensional	$\sigma_{xy}^2 = 0.58\ t^{2.11}$	(r=0.93)	(13)
Bowden	$\sigma_{rc}^2 = 0.21\ t^{2.17}$	(r=0.98)	(14)
Kullenberg	$\sigma_r^2 = 0.11\ t^{2.17}$	(r=0.98)	(15)

TABLE 24.3. Observed Diffusion Characteristics at 1m and 5m Depth.

RELEASE	t (sec) x10⁴	K_{xy}	K_a*	K_b**	L_{xy}	L_a*	L_b**
		\multicolumn{3}{c	}{(cm²sec⁻¹) x10³}	\multicolumn{3}{c	}{(cm) x10³}
SB01 HW+1hr	0.36	1.19 (1.74)	0.46 (0.69)	0.92 (1.38)	12.44 (15.00)	7.71 (9.45)	10.90 (13.35)
	0.54	1.15 (0.62)	0.46 (0.27)	0.92 (0.54)	14.94 (10.94)	9.42 (7.22)	13.32 (10.21)
29.10.76	0.72	4.10 (3.51)	1.29 (1.01)	2.58 (2.02)	32.62 (30.16)	18.30 (16.18)	25.88 (22.88)
SB03 HW-½hr	0.24	0.67 (1.03)	0.22 (0.30)	0.44 (0.60)	7.60 (9.44)	4.37 (5.06)	6.18 (7.16)
	0.36	2.14 (4.20)	0.50 (0.61)	1.00 (1.22)	16.65 (23.33)	8.06 (8.88)	11.40 (12.56)
30.10.76	0.63	5.37 (3.75)	0.84 (0.77)	1.68 (1.54)	34.90 (29.13)	13.81 (13.24)	19.53 (18.72)
	0.90	5.81 (7.15)	1.14 (1.26)	2.28 (2.52)	43.39 (43.18)	19.00 (20.17)	26.87 (28.52)
SB04 LW+½hr	0.54	1.05 (1.95)	0.41 (0.96)	0.82 (1.92)	14.92 (19.47)	8.90 (13.64)	12.59 (19.29)
	0.81	2.54 (2.68)	0.76 (0.76)	1.52 (1.52)	27.23 (27.97)	14.90 (14.86)	21.07 (21.01)
31.10.76	1.26	3.21 (3.59)	1.46 (1.62)	2.92 (3.24)	38.14 (42.34)	25.75 (27.11)	36.41 (38.34)
	1.62	6.92 (6.69)	2.61 (2.39)	5.22 (4.78)	63.55 (62.47)	39.03 (37.31)	55.20 (52.76)

figures in brackets indicate 5m values

*Kullenberg (1974)
**Bowden (1972)

5m Depth

2 Dimensional	$\sigma_{xy}^2 = 9.37\ t^{1.80}$	(r=0.86)	(16)
Bowden	$\sigma_{rc}^2 = 1.48\ t^{1.95}$	(r=0.95)	(17)
Kullenberg	$\sigma_r^2 = 0.74\ t^{1.96}$	(r=0.95)	(18)

Figure 24.6 presents a plot of diffusion coefficients (K_{xy} and K_a) against the corresponding patch scales (L_x and L_a) for the Eastern Swansea Bay experiments. Again, the plot derived from Bowden's relationship has been omitted for clarity. Regression analyses yielded the following:

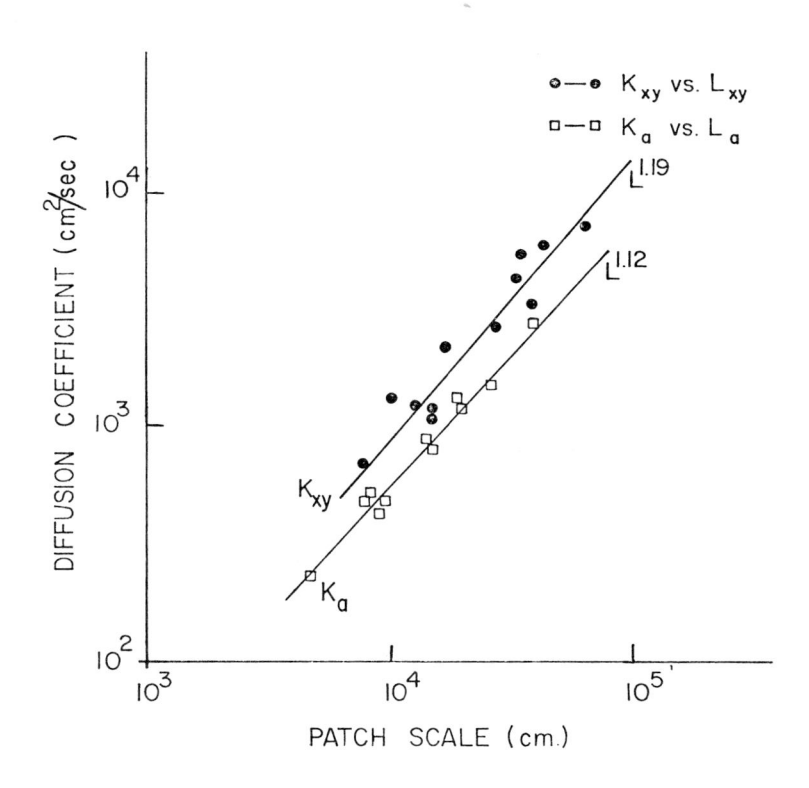

Figure 24.6. Diffusion coefficient vs patch scale for 1m depth.

1m Depth.

2 Dimensional	$K_{xy} = 15.11 \times 10^{-3} L^{1.19}$	(r=0.96)	(19)
Bowden	$K_b = 25.68 \times 10^{-3} L^{1.12}$	(r=0.99)	(20)
Kullenberg	$K_a = 18.91 \times 10^{-3} L^{1.12}$	(r=0.99)	(21)

5m Depth.

2 Dimensional	$K_{xy} = 21.48 \times 10^{-3} L^{1.16}$	(r=0.92)	(22)
Bowden	$K_b = 40.17 \times 10^{-3} L^{1.07}$	(r=0.96)	(23)
Kullenberg	$K_a = 29.18 \times 10^{-3} L^{1.08}$	(r=0.96)	(24)

CONCLUSIONS

"Far-field" Experiments

In both of the Mumbles releases the dye patch divided into an inshore and offshore plume, undoubtedly caused by velocity shears due to the complex flow configuration around Mumbles Head and the Mixon Shoal Sand Bank. In both cases (see Table 24.1 and Fig. 24.3) the rate of decay of the concentration maximum was more rapid in the inshore area than the offshore, where variable bottom topography and current shears would act to enhance diffusion.

The importance of shear diffusion is further indicated by the different rates of decay between experiments MO1 and MO2 (Table 24.1 and Fig. 24.3), the decay rate increasing approximately as $t^{1.7}$ for both inshore and offshore zones. This increase may be accounted for by the difference in the vertical shear regime on each experiment. The former release (MO1) occurred at 2½ hours after high water during maximum tidal current velocities, which essentially were constant with depth, thus vertical shear was at a minimum. The net result being that the patch was advected and small scale diffusion was apparently reduced. The latter release at effectively slack high water, was subjected to a rapidly changing spectrum of turbulence due to the variability in current speed and direction, and instead of the patch being advected, small scale turbulence dispersed the dye plume.

The Neath and Tawe results (Table 24.1) show markedly reduced rates of decay, $t^{-1.57}$ and $t^{-1.80}$ respectively, compared to the Mumbles area. The flow patterns in the estuaries are characteristically uniform and unidirectional, and the dye patch, due to it's small size, is initially advected into the embayment, where a more varied spectrum of turbulent eddies cause the subsequent dispersion.

In a two dimensional system with constant diffusion coefficients, the solution of the diffusion equation predicts a decay of maximum concentration as t^{-1}. It is obvious from the results presented that the time dependence of the maximum concentration is much stronger than this, suggesting the importance of shear diffusion in these cases.

Instantaneous Release

From Table 24.2 it is obvious that there is a considerable degree of variation in the computed values of σ_{xy}^2; σ_r^2 and σ_{rc}^2. It can be seen that the values calculated by Bowden's method (σ_{rc}^2) more closely follow those of the 2 dimensional analysis (σ_{xy}^2) than do the results after Kullenberg's method. A similar pattern can be observed in Table 24.3 when dealing with the diffusion coefficients, thus if the rotationally symmetric approach is to be used, then Bowden's relationships (Equations (3), (8) and (11)) should be applied. It should be noted that always σ_r^2, σ_{rc}^2 and σ_{xy}^2, and from the results in Table 24.3 the degree of variation, is dependent on the amount of 'elongation' (e) of the patch. If the elongation is significant then the rotationally symmetrical analysis should not be used, since a substantial error in the diffusion parameters will occur.

It can be seen from the derived relationships (Equations (13) to (24)) that there is a significant difference between the 2 dimensional analysis and the rotationally symmetrical approach. Since the elongation parameter for the majority of the releases was 0.50 it is suggested that the 2 dimensional approach is more suitable. It should also be noted that the difference in the two rotationally symmetrical approaches (Bowden and Kullenberg) is restricted to the constant term in the relationships, and that the power functions are similar. The rate of diffusion is shown to be more rapid in the surface layer than at the 5m depth.

According to the similarity theory of turbulence, variance increases as the third power of time and diffusion coefficient as the 4/3 power of scale. It is obvious from the relationships shown in Equations (13) and (16) that the observations conform more closely to $\sigma^2 = t^2$. This was demonstrated by Kullenberg (1974) using his own data and that of Meerburg (1971) and the RHENO-experiment. Similarly, Talbot (1974) showed that the variance is more nearly dependent on the relation:

$$\sigma_{rc}^2 = 0.47 \, t^{2.05} \tag{25}$$

and that if the results are grouped for different sea areas (Talbot, 1976) then for shallow tidal seas the equation becomes:

$$\sigma_{rc}^2 = 2.13 \cdot 10^5 t^{0.96} \tag{26}$$

and for open sea areas:

$$\sigma_{rc}^2 = 1.4 \cdot 10^{-3} t^{2.48} \tag{27}$$

Talbot suggests that in shallow tidal areas there is little variation in the diffusion coefficient as the patch spreads, whereas in the open sea it increases approximately as $t^{1.5}$. In the present investigations it appears that the diffusion coefficient increases with time in approximately the same manner, thus accounting for a more rapid spread of the patch than is predicted by Equation (26).

Okubo (1968) obtained the relation:

$$\sigma_{rc}^2 = 0.0108 t^{2.34} \tag{28}$$

for a wide scale of time periods.

In conclusion, it is suggested that the variances computed from the present investigations are realistic and can be regarded as inter-comparable with the results of other authors.

Equations (19) and (22) demonstrate that the diffusion coefficient is related to the scale to the power 1.19 for 1m depth and 1.16 for 5m depth. These results are directly comparable to those presented by Okubo (1968, 1971) who gives the value as 1.15. However, since the scales covered by the present experiment are small, it is rather pertinent to compare the results with larger scale experiments. It should be noted that the results differ somewhat from those predicted by the similarity theory and the 4/3 power law, suggesting that the eddies responsible for the horizontal spread of the dye are in fact anisotropic and non-homogeneous.

The purpose of this chapter is to present some preliminary data from some small-scale, short period dye diffusion experiments. The results demonstrate that they are directly comparable with other investigations and also indicate that some further analyses are necessary, particularly in the application of shear diffusion models.

It is regarded that Equations (13), (16), (19) and (22) are satisfactory for estimating values of eddy diffusion in Eastern Swansea Bay at 1m and 5m depths.

REFERENCES

Bowden, K.F. (1972). Measurements of diffusion in the sea. *Mem. Soc. r. Sci. Liege,* 6^e serie, 79-89.

Kullenberg, G. (1974). An experimental and theoretical investigation of the turbulent diffusion in the upper layer of the sea. *Rep. Inst. Phys. Oceanogr.,* Univ. Copenh., 25pp.

Meerburg, A.J. (1971). A diffusion experiment near an amphidromic current point in the North Sea. *Wetensch. Rapp. W.R.* 71 (1)(De Blit: Koninkl. Nederl. Meteorol. Inst).

Okubo, A. (1968). A new set of oceanic diffusion diagrams. Chesapeake Bay Inst., *The John Hopkins Univ. Tech. Rep. No. 38,* 52pp.

Okubo, A. (1971). Oceanic diffusion diagrams. *Deep Sea Res., 18(8),* 789-802.

Talbot, J.W. (1974). Interpretation of diffusion data. Paper 32 *In: Proc. Int. Symp. Discharge of Sewage from Sea Outfalls,* London, September 1974, 321-331.

Talbot, J.W. (1976). Diffusion Data, *Fisheries Research Tech., Rep. No. 28,* M.A.F.F., Lowestoft.

25. ENVIRONMENTAL HYDRODYNAMIC MODELLING PROBLEM IDENTIFICATION AND A STRATEGY TO MODEL ASSESSMENT

G. D. Tong

Department of Civil Engineering, University College of Swansea, Swansea SA2 8PP, U.K.
Formerly of the International Institute for Hydraulic and Environmental Engineering, Delft, The Netherlands

ABSTRACT

Fundamental problems of expressing the governing physics and computing numerical solutions in the field of environmental fluid mechanics are identified. Attention is drawn by example to the mandatory requirement of assessing the performance of a numerical method in as much as it could unknowingly be destroying carefully formulated physics.

KEYWORDS

Continuum description; Turbulence; Short-waves; Discrete systems; Steep gradients; Oscillations; Truncation error; Numerical diffusion; Numerical dispersion, Optimal upwinding parameter; Eigenvalue analysis; Operator spectrum; Amplification; Phase error.

INTRODUCTION

The mathematical modelling of the dynamics of a large water mass is a complex and difficult exercise for a number of reasons. An interested layman's imaginative list of the important physical features to be considered would be largely correct and probably fairly complete.

Fortunately, for the dynamical description of estuarine and coastal waters, an appropriate set of equations governing shallow water motion on the earth's surface can be derived from the Navier-Stokes equations of the parent subject Fluid Mechanics. These equations provide a firm basis from which the physics of the problem can be approached.

The differential equation set describes the behaviour of the water mass as a continuum and, for its solution, calls for an information input such as the geometry and surface roughness characteristics of the basin, atmospheric conditions, the rotation of the earth and fluid properties. As well, the mathematical statement of the problem points to the need for a set of initial conditions over the domain of interest and a set of boundary conditions around the boundary of the given domain. From such an input, the solution of the equation set is obtained as an evolving picture of the domain's behavioural response.

It is important to remember that the differential equation set description is one of a continuum and stands as an accurate, infinitely resolving description of the physics. But unfortunately, these multi-dimensional, non-linear equations have so far defied analytical solution techniques and, since the advent of the digital computer, recourse has been made to numerical techniques. Even so, a number of simplifications are still invoked in the usual derivation of a working set of equations governing shallow water motion and each of these introduces an attendant loss of resolution.

The first is the loss of the turbulent structure of the motion through a time ensembled (Reynold's) averaging. Second is the elimination of the vertical space dimension by the introduction of an assumed hydrostatic pressure distribution and an integration over the water column. This renders the vertical velocity profile uniform and so eliminates any further dispersive effects as would have occurred with a non-uniform profile of time-averaged velocities. Through the limits of the integration an opportunity presents itself to introduce compensating information in the form of an empirical bottom friction law representing the bottom shear stress and its effect and an empirical free surface law representing, for example, wind shear.

The simplifications defined so far provide the two-dimensional equations given in conservation form in next Section. These are the basis of the currently widely researched area of two-dimensional environmental hydrodynamics. Above the so-called "two-dimensional" models, considerable attention is now being given to the solution of the full three-dimensional equations or a pseudo three-dimensional variant of the two-dimensional equations using, for example, a spectral representation in the third (vertical) direction. See for example (Cooper and Pearce, 1977; Heaps, 1974). Below the two-dimensional formulation lie the one-dimensional models which assume a uni-directional motion and which have received a huge amount of research effort in the last one and a half decades.

In the assessment of a modelling performance, one would look carefully at the points mentioned thus far. It is not so conceptually difficult to spot where a representation of the physics might be inadequate but the corrective action required could involve a lengthy and costly field program and probably a commensurate lengthy and costly code development.

It is in taking up this subject of model assessment at the next stage that problems, rather less readily perceived, are met. Let us assume that we have an adequate representation of the physical situation and let us further assume that a numerical model has been coded, debugged and run, for example, in a situation of steady flow past a breakwater. [The detailed modelling of such a flow situation is a very complex problem necessitating an investigation of vorticity shedding from the breakwater tip, momentum transfer by two and three-dimensional turbulence mechanisms and three-dimensional secondary flow effects. See for example (Flokstra, 1977; Lean and Weare, 1979)]

Now even for the vastly simplified flow condition as characterised by a uniform eddy viscosity field, the velocity vector plot, Fig. 25.1a, serves to illustrate what might be considered as a somewhat disappointing result but very much a typical one. Attention is focussed on the oscillating flow pattern upstream of the breakwater tip. What has gone wrong? The phenomenon of oscillating solutions is found in the results of many numerical tests and can arise from a number of sources. Strong motivation therefore exists for a fundamental understanding of the root cause of the phenomenon and thus to enable subsequent action for its diminishment to be aimed at prevention rather than cure.

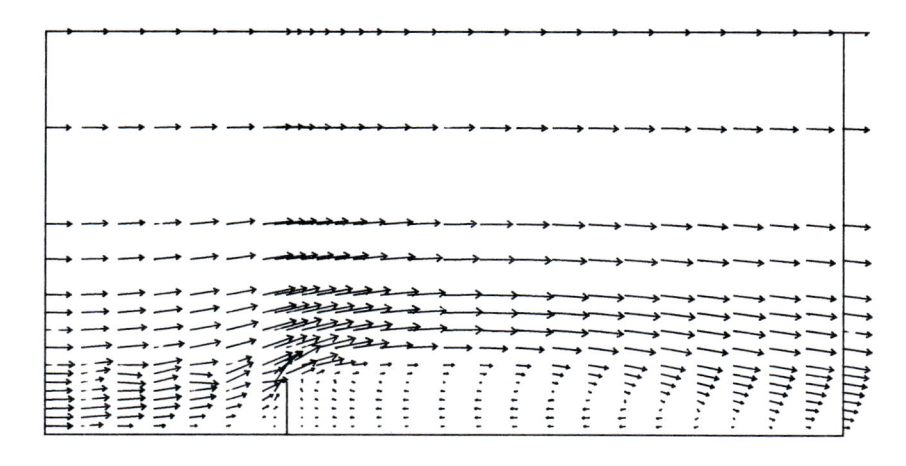

Figure 25.1a. Flow past a breakwater, $\nu_t = 0.005 \text{m}^2/\text{s}$.

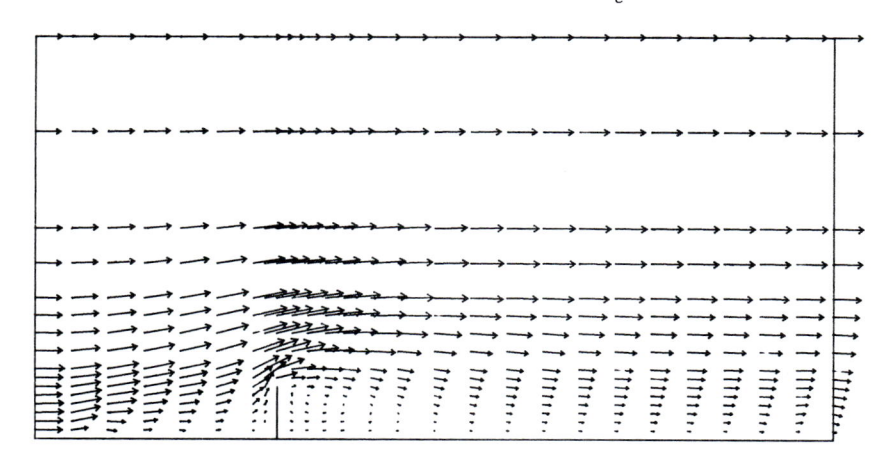

Figure 25.1b. Flow past a breakwater, $\nu_t = 0.05 \text{m}^2/\text{s}$.

CONSERVATION FORM OF THE TWO-DIMENSIONAL DEPTH-AVERAGED REYNOLD'S EQUATIONS FOR GEOPHYSICAL FLOWS.

These governing hydrodynamic equations are here assembled for completeness

Momentum x.

$$\frac{\partial p}{\partial t} + \frac{\partial}{\partial x}\frac{p^2}{(\eta + H)} + \frac{\partial}{\partial y}\frac{p^2}{(\eta + H)} - \Omega q + g(\eta + H)\frac{\partial \eta}{\partial x}$$

$$-\frac{1}{\rho}\left[\tau_x^{wind} - \tau_x^{friction}\right] = 2\frac{\partial}{\partial x}\left(\nu_t \frac{\partial p}{\partial x}\right) + \frac{\partial}{\partial y}\left(\nu_t\left(\frac{\partial p}{\partial y} + \frac{\partial q}{\partial x}\right)\right)$$

Mass.

$$\frac{\partial \eta}{\partial t} + \frac{\partial p}{\partial x} + \frac{\partial q}{\partial y} = 0$$

Momentum y.

$$\frac{\partial q}{\partial t} + \frac{\partial}{\partial x}\frac{qp}{(\eta + H)} + \frac{\partial}{\partial y}\frac{q^2}{(\eta + H)} + \Omega p + g(\eta + H)\frac{\partial \eta}{\partial y}$$

$$-\frac{1}{\rho}\left[\tau_{y_{wind}} - \tau_{y_{friction}}\right] = 2\frac{\partial}{\partial y}\left(\nu_t \frac{\partial q}{\partial y}\right) + \frac{\partial}{\partial x}\left(\nu_t\left(\frac{\partial p}{\partial y} + \frac{\partial q}{\partial x}\right)\right)$$

where x, y, t is a standard co-ordinate system
  g is the acceleration due to gravity
  Ω is the Coriolis parameter for the accelerating frame of reference (rotating earth). $\Omega = 2\omega\sin\phi$ where $\omega = 0.26$ rad.hr^{-1} and ϕ is the latitude in degrees.
  ρ is the density of the fluid, assumed constant in the above
  ν_t is the turbulent eddy viscosity.
  η is the surface elevation about a mean water level (datum)
  H is the bottom level with respect to datum

$$p = U(\eta + H) \text{ where } U = \frac{1}{(\eta + H)}\int_{-H}^{\eta} \bar{u}\, dz$$

$$q = V(\eta + H) \text{ where } V = \frac{1}{(\eta + H)}\int_{-H}^{\eta} \bar{v}\, dz$$

and the following main assumptions have been used in moving from the Navier-Stokes Equations to the equations here presented.

1. The Reynold's proposal (Lamb, 1932) of decomposing an instantaneous velocity into a mean and fluctuating component, $u_i = \bar{u}_i + u'_i$, and time averaging.
2. The assumption that the dominant shearing mechanism is by the fluctuating component correlations, the Reynold's Stresses $\tau_{ij} = \overline{-\rho u'_i u'_j}$. Viscous stresses and an extra effective stress arising from the depth averaging have been neglected.
3. The Boussinesq assumption (Launder and Spalding, 1972) that the shear stresses can be written in terms of the gradients of the component mean velocities. This is the equation closure by analogy with a Newtonian fluid in laminar motion,

$$\tau_{ij} = \rho\nu_t\left(\frac{\partial \bar{u}_i}{\partial x_j} + \frac{\partial \bar{u}_j}{\partial x_i}\right)$$

4. Bottom friction and wind stress are incorporated by empirical laws, e.g.,

$$\tau_{x_{friction}} = \frac{\rho g p\sqrt{p^2 + q^2}}{C^2(\eta + H)^2}$$

where C is the Chezy friction coefficient.

STEEP GRADIENTS AND THE DISCRETE VERSUS THE CONTINUUM

To answer the question posed at the end of the Introduction, we appeal to the common-sense notion that the numerical or discrete analogue of the continuum system suffers a further loss in resolution in that primary information, for example, the value of a field variable, is defined in the first instance at discrete points (It is quite apparent that a solution surface can be interpolated between these nodal points and, unlike finite difference methodology, it is an integral part of the finite element method to do this).

Having introduced a discretised domain we further follow common-sense and ask the natural question of how such a discrete system will allow representation of high rates of change, i.e., large gradients. If we consider a solution surface as being made up of the superposition of component modes then our common-sense notion will tell us to watch carefully the high frequency component of such a spectrum. In the Section on Wave Deformation Analysis, the results of the decomposition of a solution variable field, for a simple advective equation, into component harmonic modes are given. This Fourier decomposition demonstrates the value of getting some quantification on the characteristics of the discrete operator spectrum.

Although this discussion cannot touch on all potential sources of computational difficulty leading to unsatisfactory results, it is contended that such difficult computational areas can be largely understood and adequately handled if they are first of all seen generally in terms of the stimulation of high frequency components. Some classic cases are:

(a) shock wave propagation with the usual attendant wiggles fore and aft.
(b) the boundary condition requirement for the diffusive part of the advection-diffusion equation which gives rise to high rates of change near to boundaries, or in a more general context,
(c) steep gradients set up by boundary conditions being significantly different to an existing internal flow field
(d) non-linear terms, which, if not checked by physical diffusion or other means, breed ever higher frequency components
(e) source dominated situations where steep gradients can appear anywhere in the flow field as a function of the source.

In the Section on Truncation Error Analysis, an example of another standard analysis is given, a Taylor Series analysis. It seems to be an increasingly common view that identification of the formal accuracy of a discretisation scheme by a Taylor Series Expansion has quite restricted interpretation. Again, it is contended that this simple analysis offers considerable insight if interpreted more completely than is often the case. Particular attention is drawn to the even and odd order derivatives which make up the error series and which lead to the quite different numerical effects of diffusion and dispersion respectively. Frequently only the diffusive or dissipative properties are discussed in reference to damped solutions. It is only when dispersive characteristics are also examined that the full value of a Taylor Series Analysis becomes evident. Indeed, the classic problem cases mentioned above can largely be attributed to the numerical dispersion of high frequency components.

Finally, it is emphasised that both numerical diffusion and dispersion should be recognised separately, examined together and both in terms of wave number space.

TRUNCATION ERROR ANALYSIS

It is appropriate now to discuss the foregoing ideas quantitatively. In principle the analyses in this and the following Section can be carried out on a linearised form of the two-dimensional equations in the second Section. The algebra is certainly prohibitive here and so analysis will be restricted to that of the one-dimensional linearised advection equation $u_t + \bar{u}u_x = 0$, $\bar{u} > 0$.

A simple difference scheme, first order accurate in space and time, is chosen to illustrate the analysis (Fig. 25.2).

The resulting difference equation takes the form:

$$u_j^{n+1} = (1 - C_r) u_j^n + C_r \cdot u_{j-1}^n \quad \text{where} \quad C_r = \frac{\bar{u} \Delta t}{\Delta x}$$

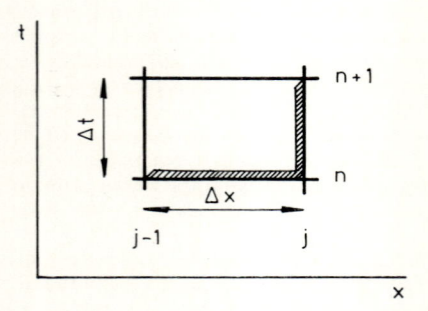

Figure 25.2. A first order "upstream" difference scheme.

Expanding in Taylor Series about the point (j,n) and grouping terms, we find we are returned with the following equation:

$$u_t + \bar{u}u_x + \frac{\Delta t}{2!} u_{tt} - \bar{u}\frac{\Delta x}{2!} u_{xx} + \frac{\Delta t^2}{3!} u_{ttt} + \bar{u}\frac{\Delta x^2}{3!} u_{xxx} + ..H.O.T.. = 0$$

where the additional terms are collectively termed "truncation error" (principal part thereof shown) and identified as diffusive and dispersive components. (In an assumed harmonic solution only odd order derivatives yield an imaginary component and hence contribute to a phase or dispersive error).

By invoking the original differential equation the returned equation can be written:

$$u_t + \bar{u}u_x = \left\{ \bar{u}\frac{\Delta x}{2!} - \bar{u}^2 \frac{\Delta t}{2!} \right\} u_{xx} + \left\{ -\bar{u}\frac{\Delta x^2}{3!} + \bar{u}^3 \frac{\Delta t^2}{3!} \right\} u_{xxx} + H.O.T.$$

or

$$u_t + \bar{u}u_x = \nu_N \cdot u_{xx} + D_N \cdot u_{xxx}$$

clearly showing the numerical diffusion (ν_N) and the numerical dispersion (D_N).

It is precisely these truncation error terms that cause unsatisfactory numerical results and, having identified them and their diffusive and dispersive roles, a further step (see next Section), can now be taken to consider them in terms of degree of resolution or wave number space.

In passing we note that both ν_N and D_N vanish for C_r, the Courant Number, equal to unity. Clearly this is a difficult condition to ensure for a non-linear system and is the basis behind Lagrangian or adaptive grid techniques such as the method of characteristics (on a network of characteristics) for purely advective (hyperbolic) problems. In the more usual Eulerian (stationary grid) discrete systems the procedure is to accept the presence of error terms initially and to eradicate them or reduce them to an acceptable level. Grid refinement is an obvious means of error reduction. Identification followed by direct subtraction of the error terms as part of the differential equation to be discretised is the most logical and appealing approach and the one on which the best but few difference schemes are based. Regrettably it seldom reaches the literature and appears to be passed over when it does. It does of course require the facility for higher order interpolation and motivates the promising research area of compact Hermitian operators.

The concept of identifying an "optimal upwinding parameter", in direct contrast with upwinding, has received some attention. See for example (Christie and co-workers, 1976). This is just another, more indirect way of *removing* discretisation error. The tacit underlying rationale is to allow just that amount of numerical diffusion and dispersion to *formally* exist by the use of a weighting function (to give an upwind bias) such that, by virtue of the original differential equation, say an advection-diffusion equation, and only by virtue of the equation form, derivative types are inherently transformed in the solution process from one form to another (i.e., odds to evens or *vice versa*) allowing the *different* error types to exactly or almost exactly cancel each other. Clearly the method has to be proved in transient, multidimensional non-linear problems before it can be put forth as a general technique. It is not readily apparent that it can be made to work in a purely hyperbolic situation.

WAVE DEFORMATION ANALYSIS

Finally the ideas in the foregoing Sections are brought together in an analysis of the deformation of a wave form as it is computationally propagated. The analysis is based on a von Neumann eigenvalue analysis and is extended to include phase error by defining a complex propagation factor as introduced by Leendertse (1967) and further discussed by Abbott (1979, 162-164).

After a spatial Fourier decomposition of the discrete system the transformation (or amplification) matrix, which maps a solution from one time level (n) to the next (n + 1) is obtained and its eigenvalues extracted. In addition to amplification properties (modulus of the eigenvalues), the complex propagation factor essentially allows a relative celerity (the ratio of the numerical speed of propagation and the physical speed of propagation as a function of wave number) to be defined in terms of the real and imaginary parts of the eigenvalues.

Again for the difference equation of the previous Section, a single equation system, a Fourier decomposition $u_j = \sum_K \zeta_u e^{ikmx}$ yields:

$$A_k = g = (1 - C_r) + C_r \cdot e^{-ikm\Delta x}$$
$$= 1 - C_r \cdot (1 - \cos\frac{2\pi}{N}) - i \cdot C_r \cdot \sin\frac{2\pi}{N}$$

where k is the wave number

$m = \dfrac{2\pi}{2\ell}$

2ℓ is the total reach length

and $N = \dfrac{2\ell}{k\Delta x}$, the number of grid points per wavelength.

A_k can of course be represented on an Argand diagram but it is more conveniently represented as an amplification and a phase portrait, respective plots of $|A_k|$ and Q against N where:

$$Q = \frac{\text{artan}\left[\frac{-\text{Im}(g)}{\text{Re}(g)}\right]}{\frac{2\pi}{N} \cdot C_r}, \text{ the relative celerity. See Abbott (1979).}$$

Portraits for the simple first order explicit operator and the well known 4-point implicit operator (fully centered) are given in Fig. 25.3. These portraits are the "performance" curves of a discretisation and can be reasonably expected as the minimum specification sheet for a numerical discretisation before entering it into engineering practice. Not forgetting that the analysis is linear, they convey much in regard to the expected behaviour of the model.

1. Their asymptotic behaviour indicates that a dominantly long wave situation (N large) is not too demanding on a numerical discretisation.

2. In the more severe situation of steep gradients where the high frequency (N small) part of the spectrum is dominant a more interesting situation exists.
(i) For a low accuracy (first order scheme) the phase portrait indicates that dispersive error can be expected. Glancing up at the amplification portrait, we predict the classic situation, elucidated in the paper by Holly and Cunge (1975), of numerical diffusion damping out or at least partially masking numerical dispersion.
(ii) For the higher accurate (second order scheme) it is seen that for any Courant Number other than unity dispersive error can again be expected. The amplification portrait says that no damping of any mode exists for any Courant Number, precisely the formula for observing wiggles (the spreading in space or dispersion of component modes).

Is damping dangerous? In returning to the original problem of flow past a breakwater, let us increase the eddy viscosity (diffusion coefficient) by an order of magnitude. (It is now an order of magnitude larger than physically reasonable through the important shear layer and at least two orders of magnitude larger than physically reasonable in the far field). The result is obvious. See Fig. 25.1b. Certainly the solution has been rid of the oscillations, but it is the overall dimensions of the resulting eddy that is to be noted. If the flushing characteristics of a pollutant were important then the answer is very definitely yes, unless the damping is carefully monitored and controlled with a fundamental understanding of the numerics and a constant regard for the demands of the physics.

Recently, a similar breakwater calculation has been given by Abbott (1979, 258-259), and the more appropriate way to tackle the problem is demonstrated. Elimination by direct differencing out of the troublesome higher order dispersive terms gets rid of the oscillations without recourse to artificial damping.

CONCLUDING REMARKS

The major problems in the computation of environmental flows have been identified. They are the same as those of the general area computational fluid mechanics and have been seen to fall into two main categories. First, the problem of expressing the governing physics and second, the problems caused by a necessity to discretise a continuum description.

Further identification of discretisation error reveals it to be of such a form as to have a strong likelihood of being confused with the physical processes being expressed. For example diffusive error and the modelling of turbulence or dispersive error and the modelling of short waves using a third derivative Boussinesq term formulation. [See the lead work of Abbott, Petersen and Skovgaard (1978), for an enlightening discussion of numerical short wave modelling].

This dangerous situation identifies that aspect of modelling which can be conveniently considered as physics/numerics interaction. The message is clear. The modeller must, in the first instance, have a detailed understanding and a good degree of intuition for the physical processes he is attempting to model. Second, he must be able to choose or devise a numerical technique which is commensurate in accuracy with the demands of the physics. Numerical methods by itself is insufficient and the modeller should have at his disposal some tools for the analysis of the methods employed.

Attention has been drawn to the two main types of numerical error encountered in computational fluid mechanics, numerical diffusion (damping) and numerical dispersion (phase error). The value of identifying them separately, considering them together and both in terms of wave number space or degree of resolution has been demonstrated.

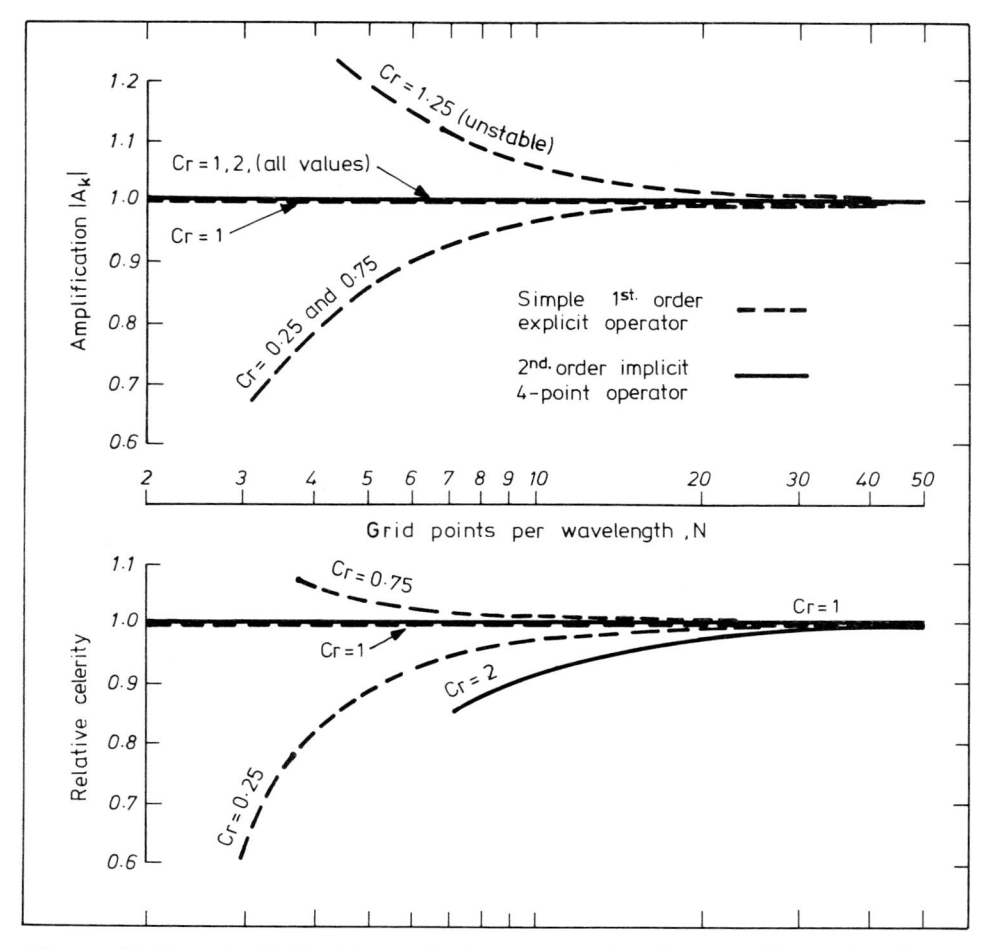

Figure 25.3. Amplification and phase portraits for two discretisations of the advection equation $u_t + \bar{u}u_x = 0$.

Any numerical technique must pay heed to these aspects which common-sense says will be severe where gradients are steep. Finally, a practical criterion for the comparison of the finite difference and the finite element method as are commonly practised is offered. In finite differences on a regular grid the truncation error can be identified in a linearised sense (if one perseveres with the algebra) and the leading error terms can be differenced out. In the finite element method, usually on an irregular mesh, the discretisation error will vary as a function of the mesh but then the error can be reduced by the very facility of an irregular mesh allowing refinement in regions of steep gradients.

REFERENCES

Abbott, M.B. (1979). *Computational Hydraulics*. Pitman, London.
Abbott, M.B., Petersen, H.M., and Skovgaard, O. (1978). On the numerical modelling of short waves in shallow water. *I.A.H.R. Jl. Hydraulic Res.*, 16(3), 173-204.

Christie, I., Griffiths, D.F., Mitchell, A.R., and Zienkiewicz, O.C. (1976). Finite element methods for second order differential equations with significant first derivatives. *Int. Jl. Num. Meth. Engng., 10,* 1389-1396.

Cooper, C.K., and Pearce, B.R. (1977). Development of a simple numerical model to calculate the 3-D structure of currents in coastal areas using a depth varying eddy viscosity. *In: Proc. 17th I.A.H.R. Cong., 2,* 141-148.

Flokstra, C. (1977). The closure problem for depth-averaged two-dimensional flow. *In: Proc. 17th I.A.H.R. Cong., 2,* 247-256.

Heaps, N.S. (1974). Development of a three-dimensional numerical model of the Irish Sea. *Rapp. P.-v. Reun. Cons. int. Explor. Mer., 167,* 147-162. December, 1974.

Holly, F.M., and Cunge, J.A. (1975). Time-dependent mass dispersion in natural streams. *Symposium on Modelling Techniques, A.S.C.E., New York,* 1121-1137.

Lamb, H. (1932). *Hydrodynamics, 6th Edition,* Section 369, Cambridge University Press, 674-678.

Launder, B.E., and Spalding, D.B. (1972). *Mathematical Models of Turbulence.* Academic Press, 3.

Lean, G.H., and Weare, T.J. (1979). Modelling two-dimensional circulating flow. *A.S.C.E. Jl. Hyd. Div., 105,* 17-26, January 1979.

Leendertse, J.J. (1967). Aspects of a computational model for long period water wave propagation. *RAND Memorandum RM-5294-PR,* Santa Monica, California.

26. NUMERICAL MODELLING OF DISPERSION IN TIDAL AREAS

C. Taylor

Department of Civil Engineering, University College, Swansea, Singleton Park, Swansea SA2 8PP, U.K.

ABSTRACT

The Finite Element Numerical Method is used to formulate, in matrix form, the equations governing the dispersion of effluent within a bounded tidal domain. The relevant equations are those depicting conservation of momentum and mass and the advective diffusion equation for each effluent species. Each equation is assembled in matrix form and subsequently solved, either coupled or uncoupled, using appropriate iterative implicit techniques.

The applicability of the technique is tested by comparison with known analytic solutions and other physical or numerical models.

KEYWORDS

Tidal domain; Hydrodynamics; Advective diffusion; Numerical solution; Implicit technique; Finite element; Coastal waters.

INTRODUCTION

A simulation of the mode of effluent dispersion and decay within a particular tidal system is obviously a necessary pre-requisite to an effective design of outfalls and subsequent system management. An effective design, in the present context, is defined as that which imparts a required or tolerable, but both retrievable, effect on the tidal environment.

Most systems of the type considered here are physically complex. When this is coupled with the possible biological or chemical complexities of each effluent species, either singly or collectively, the task of simulation becomes formidable. Although complete generalisation is obviously beyond the scope of any analysis a significant contribution to such studies, with measurable benefit, can be made by using physical (Ippen, 1966; Holley *et al.*, 1970) or numerical models (Kent, 1960; Leendertse, 1967, 1968). The main objective of the present chapter is to formulate and test one such model, based on the Finite Element Method, for predicting the dispersion of effluents in a tidal domain. A domain, for present purposes, refers to a river, an estuary or a sea.

In order to achieve a meaningful analysis the numerical model should simulate the prototype current velocity, water-depth and effluent dispersion, both spatially and temporally, during a tidal cycle. In addition, to complete the model, any biological, chemical and decay processes should be coupled to the physical dispersive mechanism. The relevant equations of continuity, momentum and dispersion can be combined to set up a numerical model of the physical dispersion for a particular domain of known geometry. The validity of the model should, however, be checked by comparison with prototype measurements before any extrapolation, or indeed interpolation, of known data can be made.

A quantitative measure of the distribution of both water velocity and depth is, owing to the temporal nature of the required parameters, particularly difficult under prototype conditions. However, postulations relating to a 'typical' tide can be made with reasonable accuracy. Once the model has been checked, extreme values such as the coincidence of maximum effluent input and low tidal range, is then simply a particular example. The magnitude of dispersion coefficients, obtained by using suitable tracers in either the prototype or a physical model, are again both spatial and temporal, and typical values are calculated.

The most difficult to quantify, at the present time, are any biological or chemical processes associated with a particular effluent when either considered in isolation or in association with other effluents within the domain. For instance the decomposition of sewage, measurable by the B.O.D., is a temporal function of effluent concentration, ambient conditions, bacterial population, the toxic levels of other effluents to bacterial metabolism, generation and growth. These highly complex interrelationships are currently the subject of a considerable amount of fundamental research. However the availability of quantitative information is noticeably lacking.

Obviously the introduction of such complexities into even a problem of simple geometry would lead to analytically intractible equations. Therefore, recourse has usually been made to either numerical techniques or physical model studies in an attempt to obtain a rational basis for design. Due to the advent of large capacity digital computers it has been possible to achieve both reasonable accuracy and economy by utilising numerical models. A distinct advantage of such models is the speed with which an analysis can be conducted for any known change in input or sanitary conditions. This means that for a maintained effluent outfall distribution, into a tidal domain, the immediate and long term effects of any undesirable overload can be quickly analysed. The model is, therefore, a particularly useful tool for system management and control.

The author presents one such numerical model, based on the Finite Element Method, and tests its validity against values obtained from known analytical and other numerical solutions.

BASIC MATHEMATICAL CONCEPTS

The three concepts which combine to form a mathematical definition of the tidal and dispersive processes currently under investigation are:

(i) Momentum and mass transfer associated with tidal hydraulics;
(ii) Dispersive processes depicting spatial and timewise variation in effluent concentration;
(iii) Quantification of the decay processes associated with a particular effluent species.

Hydrodynamic Equations

The physical processes depicting variations in both tidal elevation and velocity distribution are generally adequately described using the vertically integrated form of the momentum and continuity equations for an incompressible constant density fluid (Leendertse, 1967, 1970), i.e.

Momentum:

$$\frac{\partial u}{\partial t} + u\frac{\partial u}{\partial x} + v\frac{\partial u}{\partial y} - \Omega v + g\frac{\partial \eta}{\partial x} + g\frac{uV}{C_h^2 H} - \frac{W_x}{H} = 0 \quad (1)$$

$$\frac{\partial v}{\partial t} + u\frac{\partial v}{\partial x} + v\frac{\partial v}{\partial y} + \Omega u + g\frac{\partial \eta}{\partial y} + g\frac{vV}{C_h^2 H} - \frac{W_y}{H} = 0 \quad (2)$$

and

Continuity:

$$\frac{\partial \eta}{\partial t} + \frac{\partial}{\partial x}(Hu) + \frac{\partial}{\partial y}(Hv) = 0 \quad (3)$$

in which u, v are the vertically averaged velocities in an xy orthogonal coordinate horizontal plane, η the fluid surface location measured from the datum mean sea level (Fig. 26.1), Ω the Coriolis parameter, g the acceleration due to gravity, C_h the Chezy coefficient, and W_x, W_y the water surface stress due to wind in the x,y coordinate directions, respectively.

Further,

$H = (h+\eta)$ where h is the depth to the sea bed measured from the M.W.L.

$$V = (u^2 + v^2)^{\frac{1}{2}}$$

$$u = \frac{1}{H}\int_{-h}^{\eta} U \, dz$$

$$v = \frac{1}{H}\int_{-h}^{\eta} V \, dz$$

where U and V are, locally, the actual velocities of the fluid particles.

The basic assumptions invoked in the derivation of the above equations are:

(i) pressures are hydrostatic
(ii) shear stresses on vertical planes are negligible

(iii) mass density is independent of effluent concentration
(iv) $p_\eta = 0$

and $\quad W_\eta = U_\eta \frac{\partial \eta}{\partial x} + V_\eta \frac{\partial \eta}{\partial y} + \frac{\partial \eta}{\partial t}$

on the free surface, and

(v) $\quad W_{-h} = U_{-h} \frac{\partial h}{\partial x} + V_{-h} \frac{\partial h}{\partial y}$

on the sea bed where the suffices denote the locations at which the variables are measured.

Boundary and Initial Conditions - Hydrodynamic Equations

The usual boundary conditions which can be imposed when solving the hydrodynamic equations are (Fig. 26.2),

$$u(x,y,t = \tau) = u \text{ on } \Gamma_1$$

$$v(x,y,t = \tau) = v \text{ on } \Gamma_1$$

$$\eta(x,y,t = \tau) = \eta \text{ on } \Gamma_2$$

$u = v = 0$ for $t \geq 0$ on Γ_3 which corresponds to a no-slip boundary condition, or:

$$(u\ell_x + v\ell_y) = 0 \text{ on } \Gamma_3 \text{ which allows tangential slip}$$

and

$$(u\ell_x + v\ell_y)^{(t=\tau)} = V_n^{(t=\tau)} \text{ on part } \Gamma_4 \text{ where } \ell_x \text{ and } \ell_y \text{ are}$$

the direction cosines of the outward normal to the boundary. The required initial conditions are,

$$\eta, h(x,y,t = 0) = \eta_0, h_0(x,y)$$

$$u(x,y,t = 0) = u_0(x,y)$$

$$v(x,y,t = 0) = v_0(x,y)$$

If such conditions are now known, then the equations are solved for a few tidal cycles until each cycle is identical to that evaluated previously.

Convective-Diffusion Equation

A time averaged vertically integrated form of the convective-diffusion equation for a well mixed estuary can be written:

$$\frac{\partial c^i}{\partial t} + u \frac{\partial c^i}{\partial x} + v \frac{\partial c^i}{\partial y} = \frac{1}{H} \left\{ \frac{\partial}{\partial x} \left(H D_x^i \frac{\partial c^i}{\partial x} \right) + \frac{\partial}{\partial y} \left(H D_y^i \frac{\partial c^i}{\partial y} \right) \right\}$$

$$+ Q^i + S^i c^i \tag{4}$$

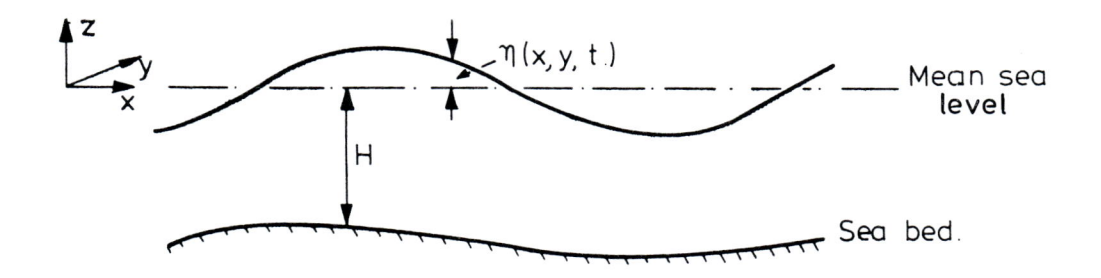

Figure 26.1. Vertical section showing free surface.

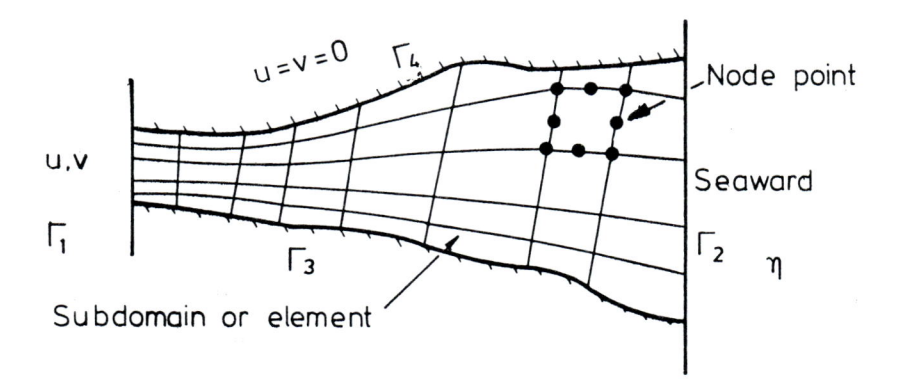

Figure 26.2. Typical subdivision of an estuary into finite elements.

in which C^i represents the local concentration of the ith species, D_x^i, D_y^i represent the dispersion coefficients of the x,y orthogonal coordinate directions, respectively, Q is a source/sink term and S^i a decay coefficient. Again, following the vertically integrated procedure,

$$C^i = \frac{1}{H} \int_{-h}^{\eta} \bar{C}^i \, dz$$

where $\bar{C}^i$ is the local concentration value of the ith species, is adopted.

Boundary and Initial Conditions - Convective-Diffusion Equation.

Either natural or forced boundary conditions can again be imposed, for instance:

$$C' = C_5' \text{ on } \Gamma_5$$

and

$$D_x^i \frac{\partial C^i}{\partial x} \cdot \ell_x + D_y^i \frac{\partial C^i}{\partial y} \ell_y + \bar{q} = 0 \text{ on } \Gamma_6$$

where q represents an outward flux per unit area of the Γ_6 part of the boundary.

The initial conditions take the form:

$$C^i (x,y, t = 0) = C_o^i (x,y)$$

It is not usual to have an accurate distribution of initial values of C^i and, particularly when the species is non-conservative, a timewise evaluation of local concentration of the pollutant is the only means of proceeding with the calculations. In this case:

$$C^i (x,y\ t = 0) = 0$$

and the distribution associated with each tidal cycle is evolved from this basic premise.

A solution technique is now required in which equations (1) - (4) can be solved simultaneously to provide a temporal and spatial distribution of the basic variables u,v,η and C^i. The particular technique employed by the author is the Finite Element Method (Hinton and Owen, 1979) wherein the physical domain of interest can be represented as a series of subdomains or elements (Fig. 26.2). The method leads to a matrix equation which can be solved for the variable values at discrete points or nodes within the domain. Irrespective of which solution technique is employed, the success of such a mathematical approach is, however, highly dependent on the parameters and coefficients utilised in the equations. The more pertinent of these are:

(i)   Chezy coefficient
(ii) Dispersion coefficients, and
(iii) Decay coefficients

the first of which can markedly affect the accuracy of hydrodynamic predictions and the other two the local values of species concentration.

The Chezy coefficient is not unduly difficult to rationalise and fairly accurate predictions can be made from a limited number of experiments. However, the dispersion coefficients are particularly difficult to obtain. These can usually be approximated from field observations where, by trial and error, values can be obtained by comparing experimental and numerical results. The decay coefficients are in the same category as the dispersion coefficients and extensive experimentation is usually required in order to obtain meaningful values.

FINITE ELEMENT FORMULATION

Although the F.E.M. has been developed quite extensively in recent years and recorded in a number of texts (Hinton and Owen, 1977, 1979; Taylor and Morgan, 1978), a brief resume of the technique will be included.

In general, a solution is sought to equations of the form:

$$D(\phi) = 0 \qquad (5)$$

where D is a differential operator, c.f. equations (1) - (4), and subject to known initial and boundary conditions.

Following the Galerkin Method of Weighted Residuals (Taylor and Davis, 1974), equation (5) becomes:

$$\iint_A W_j \ [D(\phi_a)] \ dA = 0 \qquad j = 1....m \qquad (6)$$

where A is the area of the domain, W_j a weighting function (as yet undefined) and ϕ_a a set of trial functions.

If within a single subdomain or element the trial functions can be associated with discrete nodal values of the variable ϕ and a chosen shape function, N, such that the variable can be represented by:

$$\phi_a = \sum_{k=1}^{n} N_k \ (x,y) \ \phi_k \qquad (7)$$

n = number of nodes in a subdomain
where N is a function of x and y only and ϕ_k is the discrete value of ϕ at node k. The general weighted, integrated differential equation (6) can now be re-written:

$$\sum_{e=1}^{n_e} \left[\iint_{A_e} W_j \ D(\sum_{k=1}^{n} N_k \ \phi_k) \ dA_e \right] = 0 \qquad (8)$$

where A_e now represents the subdomain area and the summation is over all elements n_e. In the Galerkin technique $W_j = N_j$ and equation (8) becomes:

$$\sum_{e=1}^{n_e} \left[\iint_{A_e} N_j \ \bigg| D(\sum_{k=1}^{n} N_k \ \phi_k) \ dA_e \right] = 0 \qquad (9)$$

The particular form taken by N, in a local coordinate system, is outlined in the

Appendix. It is sufficient to state at this juncture that (9) can be formulated quite readily for the most complex field equations resulting in a matrix equation of the form:

$$M \{\phi\} = 0 \qquad (10)$$

which, with a suitable algorithm, can be solved for given initial and boundary conditions. The method of matrix assembly will now be evolved for one equation, say the diffusion equation, and the interested reader can repeat the process for the other equations.

Matrix Equation Assembly

Defining the pertinent variables in terms of discrete nodal values:

$$\beta_a = \sum_{k=1}^{n} N_k \beta_k \qquad (11)$$

where

$$\beta_a = \begin{Bmatrix} C_a^i \\ u_a \\ v_a \\ h_a \\ \eta_a \\ D_a \\ Q_a \\ S_a \end{Bmatrix} \qquad (12)$$

equation (4) can be written, upon application of the Galerkin technique,

$$\sum_{e=1}^{n_e} \iint_{A_e} N_j \left\{ \frac{\partial C_a^i}{\partial t} + u_a \frac{\partial C_a^i}{\partial x} + v_a \frac{\partial C_a^i}{\partial y} - Q_a^i - S_a^i C_a^i \right.$$

$$\left. - \frac{1}{H_a} \left[\frac{\partial}{\partial x} \left(H_a D_{xa}^i \frac{\partial C_a^i}{\partial x} \right) + \frac{\partial}{\partial y} \left(H_a D_{ya}^i \frac{\partial C_a^i}{\partial y} \right) \right] \right\} dA_e = 0 \qquad (13)$$

Utilising Green's theorem to reduce second order differential terms results in

$$\sum_{e=1}^{n_e} \iint_{A_e} \left[N_j \left\{ \frac{\partial C_a^i}{\partial t} + u_a \frac{\partial C_a^i}{\partial x} + v_a \frac{\partial C_a^i}{\partial y} - Q_a^i - S_a^i C_a^i \right. \right.$$

$$\left. + \frac{\partial N_j}{\partial x} D_{xa}^i \frac{\partial C_a^i}{\partial x} + \frac{N_j}{H_a} D_{xa}^i \frac{\partial H_a}{\partial x} \frac{\partial C_a^i}{\partial x} + \frac{\partial N_j}{\partial y} D_{ya}^i \frac{\partial C_a^i}{\partial y} \right.$$

$$+ \frac{N_j}{H_a} D_{ya}^i \frac{\partial H_a}{\partial y}\Bigg\} dA_e - \int_{\Gamma_6} N_j \left[D_{xa}^i \ell_x \frac{\partial C_a^i}{\partial x} + D_{ya}^i \ell_y \frac{\partial C_a^i}{\partial y} \right] d\Gamma = 0 \quad (14)$$

which, upon assembly, can be written in the matrix form

$$[M^1] \{C^i\}_t + \{F^1\}_t = 0 \qquad (15)$$

in which

$$m_{jk}^1 = \sum_{e=1}^{n_e} \iint_{A_e} N_j N_k \, dA_e$$

$$f_j^1 = \sum_{e=1}^{n_e} \iint_{A_e} \Bigg[N_j \{ u_a \frac{\partial C_a^i}{\partial x} + v_a \frac{\partial C_a^i}{\partial y} - Q_a^i - S_a^i C_a^i \}$$

$$+ \{ \frac{\partial N_j}{\partial x} D_{xa}^i \frac{\partial C_a^i}{\partial x} + \frac{N_j}{H_a} D_{xa}^i \frac{\partial H_a}{\partial x} \frac{\partial C_a^i}{\partial x} + \frac{\partial N_j}{\partial y} D_{ya}^i \frac{\partial C_a^i}{\partial y}$$

$$+ \frac{N_j}{H_a} D_{ya}^i \frac{\partial H_a}{\partial y} \} \Bigg] dA_e - \int_{\Gamma_6} N_j (-\bar{q}) \, d\Gamma \qquad (16)$$

$$j = 1,2,\ldots n$$
$$k = 1,2,\ldots n$$

and $\dot{C}^i = \dfrac{C_a^i}{t}$

Each of the governing equations can be treated in exactly the same manner leading to an uncoupled set of equations,

$$\left.\begin{array}{l} [M^I] \{\dot{c}\}_t + \{F^I\}_t = 0 \\[6pt] [M^{II}] \{\dot{u}\}_t + \{F^{II}\}_t = 0 \\[6pt] [M^{III}] \{\dot{v}\}_t + \{F^{III}\}_t = 0 \\[6pt] [M^{IV}] \{\dot{\eta}\}_t + \{F^{IV}\}_t = 0 \end{array}\right\} \qquad (17)$$

or, assembled in a coupled form:

$$[M] \{\dot{\beta}_1\}_t + \{F\}_t = 0 \tag{18}$$

where

$$\{\dot{\beta}_1\} = \begin{Bmatrix} \dot{c}^i \\ \dot{u} \\ \dot{v} \\ \dot{\eta} \end{Bmatrix}$$

Equation (18) can be solved quite readily for known initial and boundary equations using standard elimination techniques (Owen and Minton, 1979).

Time Integration

The time integration scheme adopted by the author is the Adams Moulton fourth degree predictor corrector scheme. The predictor formula, given in terms of β_1, is:

$$\{\beta_1\}_{t+4\Delta t} = \{\beta_1\}_{t+3\Delta t} + \frac{\Delta t}{24} \{55 \{\dot{\beta}_1\}_{t+3\Delta t} - 59\{\dot{\beta}_1\}_{t+2\Delta t}$$

$$+ 37 \{\dot{\beta}_1\}_{t+\Delta t} - 9 \{\dot{q}\}_t \} \tag{19}$$

and the corrector,

$$\{\beta_1\}_{t+4\Delta t} = \{\beta_1\}_{t+3\Delta t} + \frac{\Delta t}{24} \{9 \{\dot{\beta}_1\}_{t+4\Delta t} + 19 \{\dot{\beta}_1\}_{t+3\Delta t} - 5 \{\dot{\beta}_1\}$$

$$+ \{\dot{\beta}_1\}_{t+\Delta t} \} \tag{20}$$

in which t represents the initial time level and Δt a specified time interval. Using the Runge Kutta fourth degree equations to provide the necessary derivatives for (19):

$$\{\beta_1\}_{t+\Delta t} = \{\beta\}_t + \frac{\Delta t}{6} \{K_0\} + 2\{K_1\} + \{K_3\} \tag{21}$$

where $\{K_0\} = f(t, u_t, \eta_t, v_t)$

$$\{K_1\} = f(t + \frac{\Delta t}{2}, u_t + \frac{\Delta t}{2} \{K_0\}, v_t + \frac{\Delta t}{2} \{K_0\}, h_t + \frac{\Delta t}{2} \{K_0\})$$

$$\{K_2\} = f(t + \frac{\Delta t}{2}, u_t + \frac{\Delta t}{2} \{K_1\}, v_t + \frac{\Delta t}{2} \{K_1\}, h_t + \frac{\Delta t}{2} \{K_1\})$$

$$\{K_3\} = f(t + \Delta t, u_t + \Delta t \{K_2\}, v_t + \Delta t \{K_2\}, h_t + \Delta t \{K_2\}) \tag{22}$$

and the updated time derivative required for equation (20) is found using:

$$\{\dot{\beta}_1\} = f(u,v,h,t) \tag{23}$$

The updated derivative at $(t+4\Delta t)$ required for the corrector is found from equation (23) and the corrector value $\{q\}_{t+4\Delta t}$ evaluated.

If this is sufficiently close to the predicted value, the process continues by predicting an updated value for $\{q\}_{t+5\Delta t}$. If, however, the convergence criterion is not satisfied, then a further solution is obtained to equation (23) using the unconverged corrector value to form the right hand side. The corrector formula is again used and this latter process repeated until the required tolerance is achieved.

APPLICATIONS

The first example illustrates the pick-up of sediment from a channel bed (Fig. 26.3), where a uniformly flowing stream passes over a stable bed and picks up sediment from an unstable bed downstream. The steady state contours of equal concentration are as shown on Fig. 26.4. This illustrates that for known diffusion and well defined geometry, the finite element method can be readily employed to simulate such phenomenon.

The second example considered is that of the concentration of an effluent in a well mixed estuary where the tidal component at the seaward end is simulated by:

$$\eta_1 = \sin(1.405 \times 10^{-4} \, xt)$$

A fresh water discharge of $2000 m^3/s$ provides the upstream boundary condition on velocity distribution.

The estuary is 15,000 metres long and initial depth conditions vary from 20m upstream to 80m downstream. For tidal propagation a constant Chezy coefficient of $Ch = 50m^{\frac{1}{2}}/sec$ is used. A point conservative source maintained at a non-dimensionalised concentration of 1.0 simulates the input of a species of effluent with $D_x = 1000 m^2/s$ and $D_y = 800 m^2/s$.

A contour plot showing the concentration distribution at 7.5hrs after low water is shown on Fig. 26.5.

CONCLUSIONS

The temporal and spatial distribution of tidal elevations, currents and dispersion of effluent can be simulated using the Finite Element Approach. The ease with which complex geometries and natural boundary conditions can be accommodated has also been shown.

If the physical and biological coefficients can be defined then the numerical model outlined can be utilised to effect. However, considerable effort is necessary before such data can be made available and used with confidence.

APPENDIX

Of the many different types of elements one of the most useful for the present class of problems is the eight noded isoparametric element (Fig. 26.6). A local ξ, η curv-

404   C. Taylor

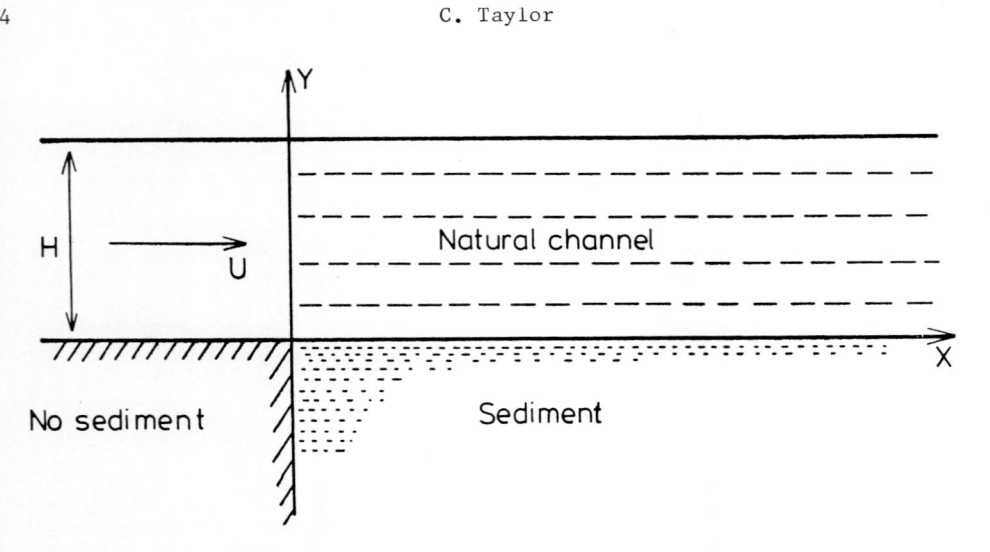

Figure 26.3.   Flow over an unstable bed

ilinear coordinate system is used where the value of both ξ and η are $\leq \pm 1$.

Utilising the local coordinate system, the local value for the pertinent variables can be defined:

$$\beta_a = \sum_{i=1}^{8} N_i (\xi,\eta) \beta_i$$

in which

$$N_1(\xi,\eta) = -\frac{1}{4}(1-\xi)(1-\eta)(1+\xi+\eta)$$

$$N_2(\xi,\eta) = \frac{1}{2}(1-\xi^2)(1-\eta)$$

$$N_3(\xi,\eta) = \frac{1}{4}(1+\xi)(1-\eta)(\xi-\eta-1)$$

$$N_4(\xi,\eta) = \frac{1}{2}(1+\xi)(1-\eta^2)$$

$$N_5(\xi,\eta) = \frac{1}{4}(1+\xi)(1+\eta)(\xi+\eta-1)$$

$$N_6(\xi,\eta) = \frac{1}{2}(1-\xi^2)(1+\eta)$$

$$N_7(\xi,\eta) = \frac{1}{4}(1-\xi)(1+\eta)(-\xi+\eta-1)$$

$$N_8(\xi,\eta) = \frac{1}{2}(1-\xi)(1-\eta^2)$$

and β_i is the discrete value of the variables at the ith node.

Since integrations are conducted with respect to x and y it is necessary to define a relationship between local and global coordinates. This is accomplished in exactly the same manner as above such that:

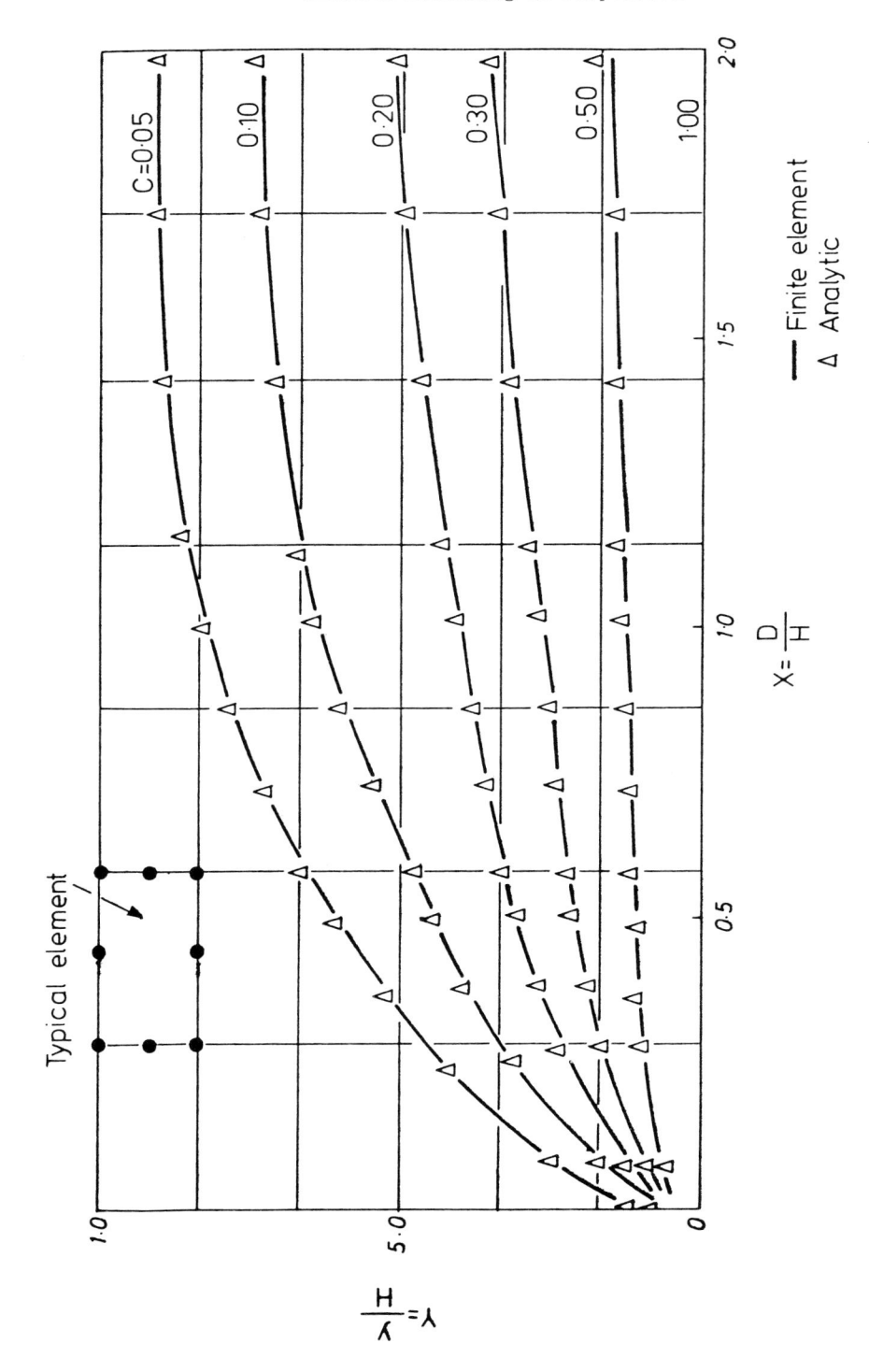

Figure 26.4. Curves of constant concentration.

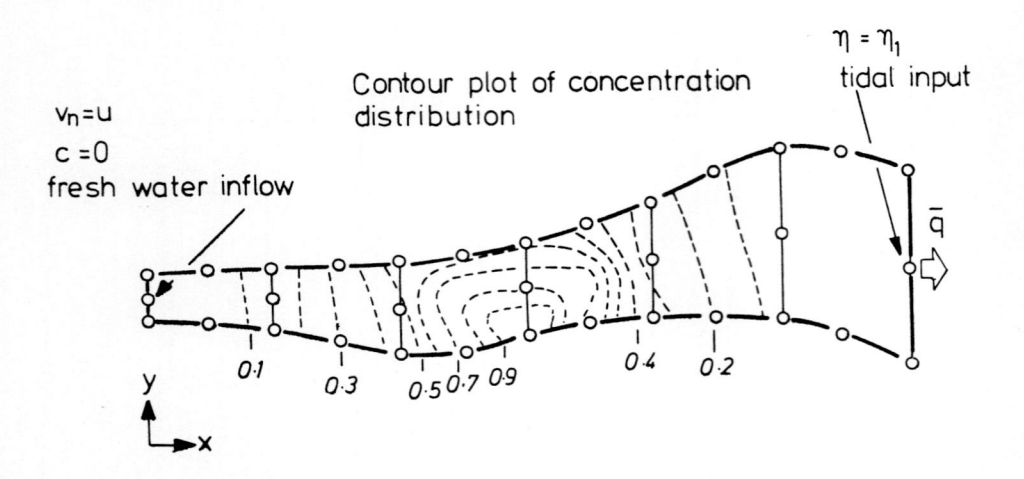

Figure 26.5. Well mixed estuary.

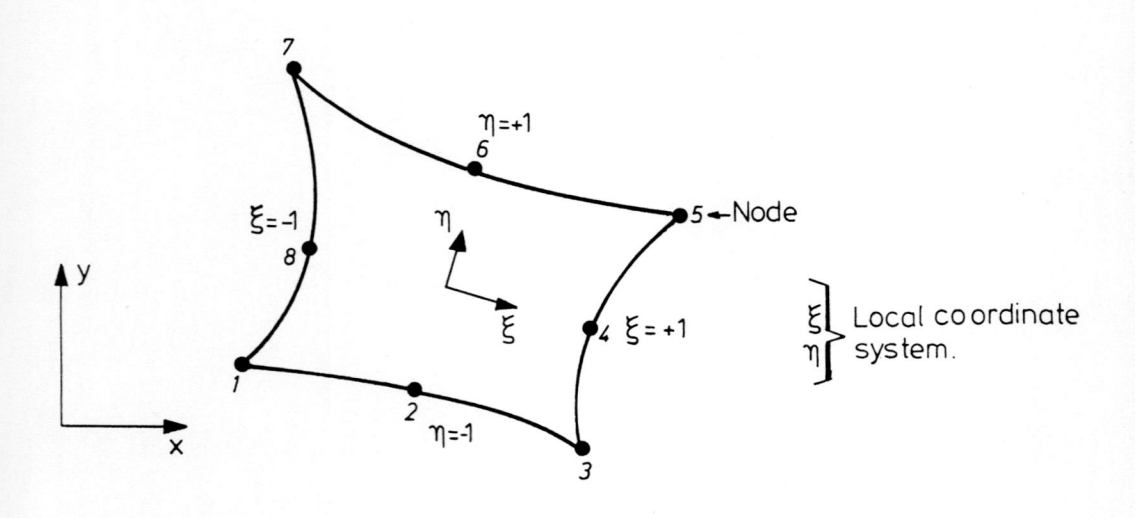

Figure 26.6. Eight noded isoparametric element.

$$x = \sum_{i=1}^{8} N_i(\xi,\eta)\, x_i$$

$$y = \sum_{i=1}^{8} N_i(\xi,\eta)\, y_i$$

where x_i, y_i is coordinate location of the ith node.

Further details of equation assembly and solution techniques can be found in Taylor and Davis (1974), Hinton and Owen (1977), Taylor and Morgan (1978), Hinton and Owen (1979) and Owen and Hinton (1979).

REFERENCES

Hinton, E., and Owen, D.R.J. (1977). *Finite Element Programming*. Academic Press.

Hinton, E., and Owen, D.R.J. (1979). *An Introduction to Finite Element Computations,* Pineridge Press.

Holley, E.R., Marleman, D.R.F. and Fischer, M.B. (1970). Dispersion in homogeneous estuary flow. *J. Hyd. Div., Proc. A.S.C.E., 96.*

Ippen, A.T. (1966). *Estuary and Coastline Hydrodynamics.* McGraw-Hill, New York.

Kent, R. (1960). Diffusion in a sectionally homogeneous estuary. *J. Sanit. Eng. Div. Proc. A.S.C.E., 86.*

Leendertse, J.J. (1967). *Aspects of a Computational Model for Long-Period Wave Propagation.* Rand Memorandum, RM-5294-PR.

Leendertse, J.J. (1970). *A Water Quality Simulation Model for Well Mixed Estuaries and Coastal Areas.* Vol. 1. Principles and Computation, Rand Memorandum, RM-6230-RG.

Owen, D.R.J., and Hinton, E. (1979). *Simple Guide to Finite Elements,* Pineridge Press.

Taylor, C., and Davis, J. (1974). Tidal and long wave propagation - a Finite Element Approach. *Computers and Fluids, 1.*

Taylor, C., and Morgan, K. (1978). *Numerical Methods in Laminar and Turbulent Flow.* Proc. Int. Conf. on Numerical Methods in Laminar and Turbulent Flow, University College of Swansea, Pentech Press.

27. WATER QUALITY STUDIES IN SWANSEA BAY

N. C. Humphrey, C. Pattinson and J. H. Stoner

Welsh Water Authority, Cambrian Way, Brecon, Powys, U.K.

ABSTRACT

Swansea Bay receives substantial discharges of domestic and industrial effluent and the Welsh Water Authority has undertaken extensive investigations to establish the impact of these discharges on water quality in the Bay.

Factors affecting surf zone water quality in the Bay are discussed using bacteriological data from surveys conducted by the Authority and others. Changes in water quality at the surf zone resulting from improved effluent disposal techniques are outlined.

Extensive water quality information was also collected offshore at various tidal states throughout one year: determinands reported include salinity, suspended load, numbers of presumptive *Escherichia coli*, total oxidized nitrogen, ammonia, orthophosphate, silicate and dissolved copper, lead, cadmium, nickel, zinc, iron and manganese. The relative importance of seasonal influences, prevailing hydrography and natural and anthropogenic discharges on the observed distribution of these determinands are discussed and the ambient levels compared to those in other coastal regimes. Factors influencing the mortality of *Escherichia coli* in Swansea Bay are outlined.

KEYWORDS

Water quality; Coastal waters; Coliforms; Nutrients; Trace metals; Swansea Bay; Bristol Channel.

INTRODUCTION

Swansea Bay receives substantial inputs of material from several major rivers and industrial and domestic discharges. There are also inputs from the sludge dumping grounds at the seaward limit of the study area and from atmospheric deposition. These inputs have been quantified by Chubb, Dale and Stoner (Chapter 20).

Elevated levels of some trace metals have been found in sediments from the Bay (Bloxom and Aurora, 1972; Chester and Stoner, 1975; Clifton and Vivian, 1975) and in *Fucus vesiculosus* collected in the vicinity of Mumbles Head (Fuge and James, 1974). There has been little water quality information published to date, although Morris and Bale (1975) compared levels of copper, cadmium, zinc and manganese in *Fucus vesiculosus* and waters from the Bay whilst Abdullah et al. (1973, 1974) reported nutrient and trace metal levels at a limited number of stations in the Bay. The bacteriological quality of the surf zone was investigated by Stickler (1974).

Due to the paucity of comprehensive published information, a programme was undertaken to establish water quality in Swansea Bay and, in conjunction with other studies presented at this Symposium (see especially Chapters 15, 20, 22, 24 and 34), should provide a rational basis for pollution control in the area.

SAMPLING PROGRAMME

Offshore Grid

A grid of 70 stations was initially established in Swansea Bay between Nash Point and Oxwich Point (Fig. 27.1.1). Samples for the determination of salinity, numbers of presumptive *Escherichia coli*, total suspended solids and a range of inorganic nutrients and trace metals were collected in 51 acid-washed polypropylene bottles on three occasions during October and November 1976 (Surveys 1-3), at times approximating to high water, low water and mid ebb respectively. The grid was extended to 94 stations during surveys 4-20 to provide greater coverage of the nearshore regime (Fig. 27.1.2). Water samples were again collected at high water, low water, mid ebb and mid flood on five occasions during 1977. Each grid took approximately two hours to complete. The survey programme is summarised in Table 27.1.

TABLE 27.1. Survey Programme in Offshore Swansea Bay.

Survey Number	Date	Tidal state with respect to high water (hr)	Tidal Range at Swansea (m)
1	28.10.76.	HW	7.1
2	3.11.76.	HW + 6	6.3
3	9.11.76.	HW + 3	7.4
4	22.3.77.	HW + 2	8.3
5	22.3.77.	HW - 6	8.3
6	24.3.77.	HW - 1	7.3
7	24.3.77.	HW + 3	7.3
8	10.5.77.	HW - 3	4.8
9	10.5.77.	HW + 3	4.8
10	12.5.77.	HW - 5	4.8
11	12.5.77.	HW - 1	4.8
12	12.7.77.	HW - 6	5.1
13	12.7.77.	HW	5.1
14	14.7.77.	HW + 3	6.3
15	14.7.77.	HW - 3	6.3
16	13.9.77.	HW + 3	8.7

17	13.9.77.	HW - 3	8.7
18	15.9.77.	HW	9.4
19	15.9.77.	HW - 6	9.4
20	8.11.77.	HW - 6	7.0
21	8.11.77.	HW	7.0
22	10.11.77.	HW + 3	9.1
23	10.11.77.	HW - 3	9.1

Surf Zone

Since 1973 a selection of sites in the surf zone of Swansea Bay have been examined for the presence of the Coliform group of sewage indicator bacteria (Fig. 27.2). Samples were collected at a depth of approximately 30cm between June and September of 1973, 1975, 1977 and 1978, although only a few sites were monitored in all years.

SAMPLE TREATMENT AND ANALYSIS

Salinity

Salinity was determined on unfiltered water samples using a Plessey 6230N inductive salinometer, previously standardised with I.A.P.S.O. Standard Sea Water.

Suspended Load

A 500ml aliquot was filtered through a weighed GF/C glass fibre filter paper which had previously been ignited at 500°C. The paper was soaked with distilled water immediately prior to use to minimise retention of dissolved salts and any adsorbed salts were subsequently removed by washing the used paper with 3 x 5ml aliquots of distilled water. Suspended load was determined after drying the used paper at 105°C.

Escherichia coli and Total Presumptive Coliforms

Samples for the estimation of total presumptive Coliforms in the surf zone were collected directly in sterile bottles whilst samples collected during the grid surveys for the estimation of *E. coli* were decanted into sterile glass bottles immediately after collection as previously described. Tests confirmed that the latter method of collection did not significantly contaminate samples. Samples were stored in the dark at 5°C and analysis commenced within three hours.

Numbers of presumptive *E. coli* were determined by a membrane filtration method using 0.4% Teepol broth and incubation at 30°C and 44°C (Department of Health and Social Security *et al.*, 1969); numbers of presumptive Coliforms were determined in an identical manner using an incubation temperature of 37°C.

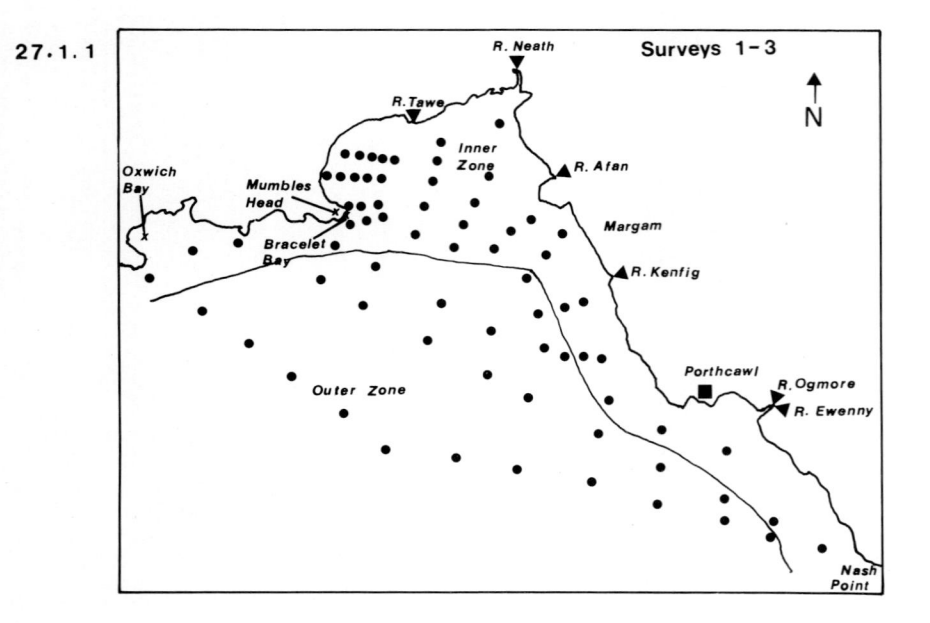

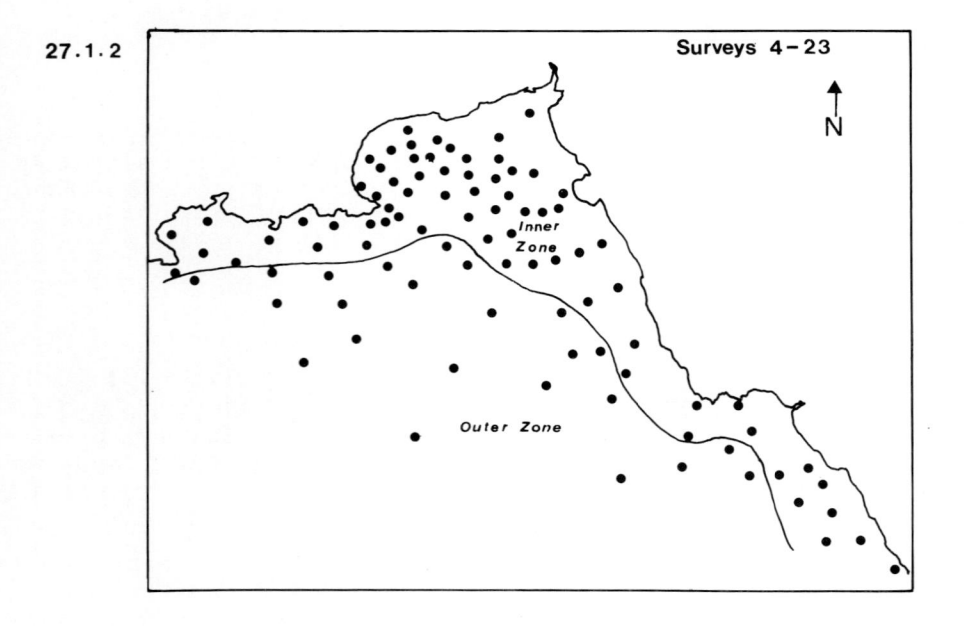

Figure 27.1. Sampling stations in Swansea Bay.

Water Quality Studies 413

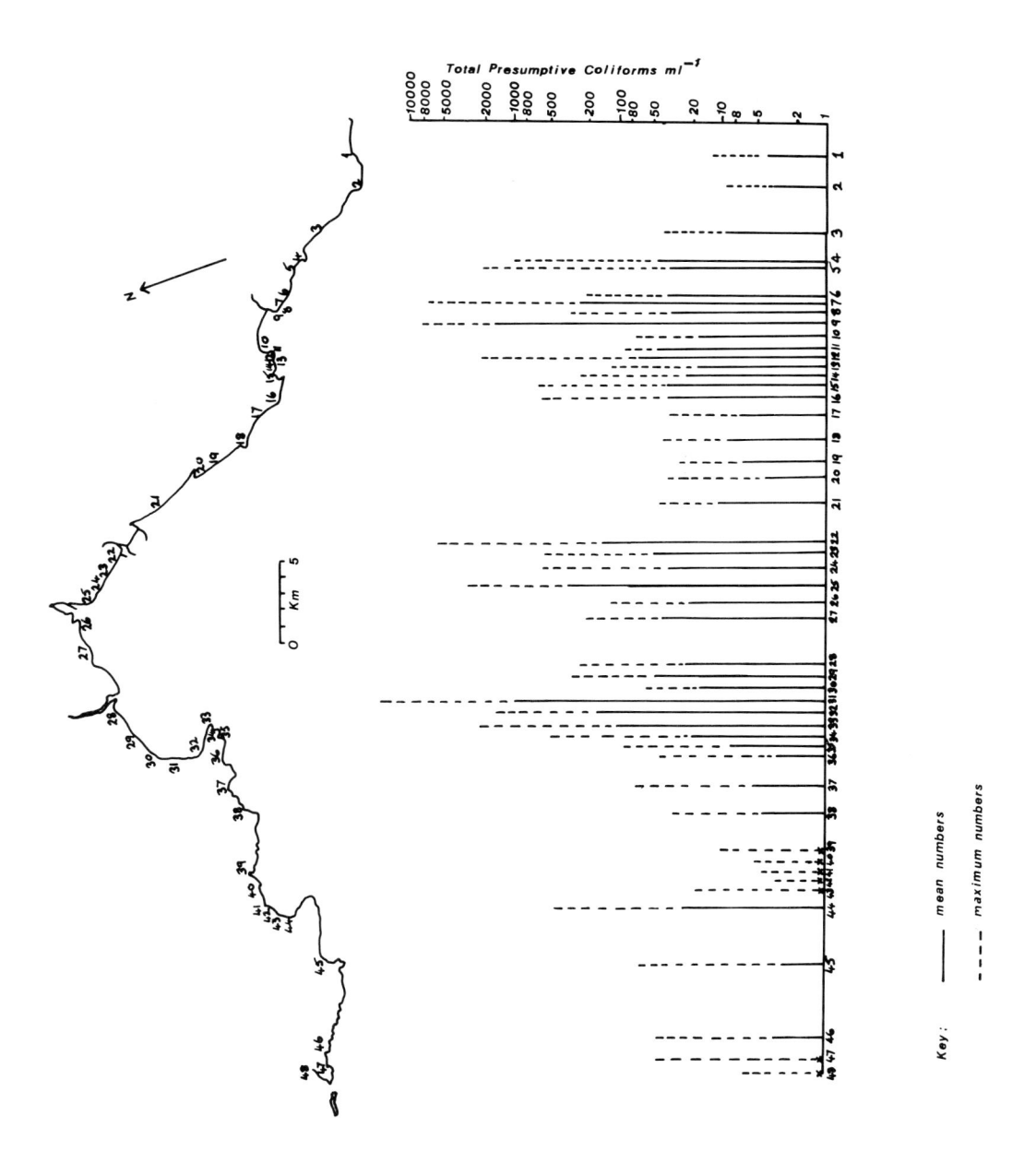

Figure 27.2. Mean and maximum numbers of coliforms recorded in the surf zone of Swansea Bay.

Dissolved Nutrients

Nutrient samples were filtered within two hours of collection through 0.45µm membrane filters; orthophosphate samples were stored in glass bottles whilst silicate, total oxidised nitrogen and ammonia samples were stored in polypropylene bottles (Riley, 1975). Filtered samples were immediately frozen and stored at -20°C until required for analysis (Riley, 1975).

Nutrients were determined using a three-channel Technicon Autoanalyser II system. Total oxidised nitrogen was determined by the method of Strickland and Parsons (1972) following quantitative reduction of nitrate to nitrite by a copper-cadmium amalgam whilst ammonia was determined by a modified Berthelot reacion (Grasshoff, 1970). Orthophosphate and silicate were determined by the methods of Chan and Riley (1966) and Brewer and Riley (1966) respectively.

Dissolved Trace Metals

Water samples for trace metal analysis were filtered through 0.45µm membrane filters within a few hours of collection. Dissolved levels of copper, lead, cadmium, nickel, zinc, iron and manganese were determined using a single-beam Varian AA6 Atomic Absorption Spectrophotometer equipped with hydrogen background correction, after preconcentration of these metals from a 2l. filtered aliquot on "Chelex-100" resin using a modification of the method of Riley and Taylor (1968).

RESULTS AND DISCUSSION: SURF ZONE

Figure 27.2 summarises the mean and maximum number of Coliforms (expressed as numbers of presumptive Coliforms) recorded in the surf zone of Swansea Bay during the period 1973-1978; this data was compiled from a number of sources, including previously published data (Steen and Stickler, 1976; Stickler, 1974) and internal Water Authority surveys.

Stickler (1974) found that his results were highly correlated with proximity to Nash Point: the further west from Nash Point, the lower the number of Coliforms to be expected at beach sites. A similar observation was made by Steen and Stickler (1976) who reported that numbers of Coliform bacteria in the surf zone increased with distance eastward. With the availability of more data, it is now possible to suggest that this is not necessarily valid for Swansea Bay. The probability of elevated numbers of Coliforms appears to be increased by proximity to specific discharges. For example, elevated numbers were encountered near Ogmore, Aberafan and the River Neath and at Mumbles. Similarly, low numbers of Coliforms were recorded where discharges were absent or only minor, irrespective of geographical position. Thus, three areas of relatively low Coliform numbers were identified:

Gower Peninsula. With the possible exception of one site in Oxwich Bay, all sites examined to the west of Bracelet Bay had relatively low numbers of Coliforms. Both mean and maximum Coliform numbers were the lowest observed in Swansea Bay.

Margam to Porthcawl. This long stretch of sandy beach was surveyed extensively by Stickler (1974) and comparatively little more recent information is available. However, all available data suggests that low Coliform numbers occurred throughout this area, except possibly near the efflux of the River Kenfig.

Southerndown to Cold Knap. Although many of these sites lie outside the accepted boundary of Swansea Bay (Nash Point), they serve to illustrate the point at issue. Many of these sites returned numbers of Coliforms as low as sites on the Gower Peninsula and elevated numbers were only encountered at one site near a local discharge.

Surf zone water quality assessed in terms of the size of the Coliform population is very variable, even at a site near which any discharges remain unchanged. Apart from any variability inherent in sampling and analytical methods (see for example Stickler, 1974), a number of external influences can be identified.

Extensive surf zone bacteriological data collected throughout Wales over the past six years suggests that climatic conditions are a major influence on water quality; when land runoff is increased by excessive rainfall, Coliform numbers can be substantially elevated even at relatively unpolluted sites. This effect is illustrated by a comparison of five sites in Swansea Bay (Table 27.2). The mean number of Coliform bacteria was significantly elevated at each site during the summer of 1978, when the weather was wet and cold, compared to the dry summer of 1973.

TABLE 27.2. A Comparison of the Mean Numbers of Presumptive Coliform Bacteria at Sites in Swansea Bay, in 1973 and 1978.

Site	Mean Coliforms ml^{-1} 1973	Mean Coliforms ml^{-1} 1978	Significance of difference between mean % *
Southerndown	3.73	15.37	0.02
Sandy Bay, Porthcawl	7.50	16.83	0.05
Aberafan, slip	4.56	18.17	0.02
Bracelet Bay	3.30	11.69	< 0.001
Oxwich Bay	0.214	1.03	0.01

* means compared by deriving Student t statistic, with log$_{10}$ transformed data

It is apparent that enlightened management of those discharges which are controllable can minimise the effect on surf zone water quality. This can be illustrated with the results of a survey to examine the effect of altering the discharge regime of the Mumbles Head sewer outfall pipes. By allowing sewage discharge only on the ebb tide instead of beginning to discharge on the flood tide, significant surf zone water quality improvements resulted (Table 27.3). At each site numbers of *E. coli* (a more specific faecal indicator bacterium) were monitored over a tidal cycle, on neap and spring tides, both before and after altering the discharge regime. At each site the mean number of *E. coli* was significantly reduced.

The state of tide (high or low) and the position of the lunar cycle (spring or neap) can significantly effect the numbers of bacteria in the surf zone. Stickler (1974) found a significant correlation between tidal state and number of Coliforms at a relatively small number of the sites he examined. However, there was no apparent correlation with tidal state at the majority of sites despite considerable variation in numbers. This is demonstrated by histograms of *E. coli* against time, for two sites used in the Mumbles Head Sewer outfall investigation (Fig. 27.3); no definite tidally associated behaviour was apparent although considerable variations in numbers were encountered both before and after altering the discharge regime.

TABLE 27.3. A Comparison of the Mean Number of *E. coli* at Four Sites Near Mumbles Head, Before and After Alteration of the Outfall Discharge Regime.

SITE OR TRANSECT	old regime mean number 100 ml^{-1}	old regime 95 percentile 100 ml^{-1}	new regime mean number 100 ml^{-1}	new regime 95 percentile 100 ml^{-1}	Significance of difference mean nos. % *
Blackpill	1866	10000	407	3102	0.1
West Cross	1125	10000	491	6954	1.0
Mumbles	853	6327	226	2320	0.1
Bracelet Bay	502	1380	147	1038	0.1

* assessed by Student t statistic on $\log_{10}$ transformed data.

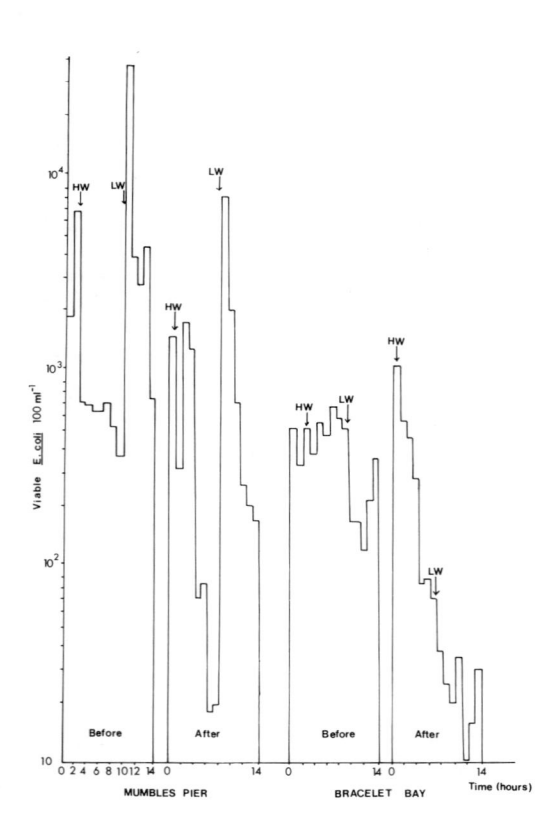

Figure 27.3. The variation of viable *E. coli* numbers over a tidal cycle on spring tides of similar tidal range before and after change of discharge regime.

RESULTS AND DISCUSSION: OFFSHORE

Salinity

The hydrography of Swansea Bay has been described by Collins et al. (1979) who concluded that it had a variable hydrodynamic regime as a result of the interaction between the Bay's bathymetry and the adjacent rectilinear tidal system in the Bristol Channel.

Surface salinity distributions in the Bay from surveys at different tidal states are shown in Fig. 27.4. The isohalines indicate that fresh water from the Rivers Neath and Tawe dispersed in a southerly/southwesterly direction on the ebb tide and tended to be entrained in the western half of the Bay on flood tides. This supports the observations of Collins et al. (1979) that there is an anticlockwise gyre in the western part of the Bay and a zone of divergence in the east. However, it should be noted that there were considerable variations in the position of isohalines between surveys which suggests that circulation varied considerably with fresh water runoff, tidal range and meteorological conditions. These variations were also encountered in the distribution of other water quality parameters considered below and the selection of figures presented should not be taken as definitive but merely representative of conditions prevailing at the time of a particular survey.

E. coli

Figure 27.5 illustrates typical examples of the distribution of E. coli in Swansea Bay during periods of relatively high runoff. These indicate that most of the surface water in the Bay contained relatively low numbers of E. coli and for these particular examples more than 70% of sites had E. coli concentrations of less than 500 per 100ml, even in worst conditions (Table 27.4).

TABLE 27.4. Variations in the Spatial Distribution of Viable E. coli Numbers at Four Tidal States in Swansea Bay.

TIDAL STATE hours relative to high water*	Percentage of sites with numbers of E. coli 100 ml^{-1} in the contour bands			
	<100	100 - 500	500 - 2000	>2000
+5.2	37.2	38.4	15.0	9.4
-1.0	37.6	33.3	22.6	6.5
+1.8	46.8	35.1	11.7	6.4
+3.0	62.4	32.3	1.1	4.2

* predicted for Swansea

Most E. coli were contributed from a small number of sources, confirming the conclusions reached from the surf zone results. The highest concentrations of E. coli, irrespective of time of year, were found in the vicinity of the Mumbles Head outfall, the Rivers Tawe, Neath and Afan and occasionally around the mouth of the River Kenfig.

No seasonal trends were apparent in the distribution of E. coli although the impact

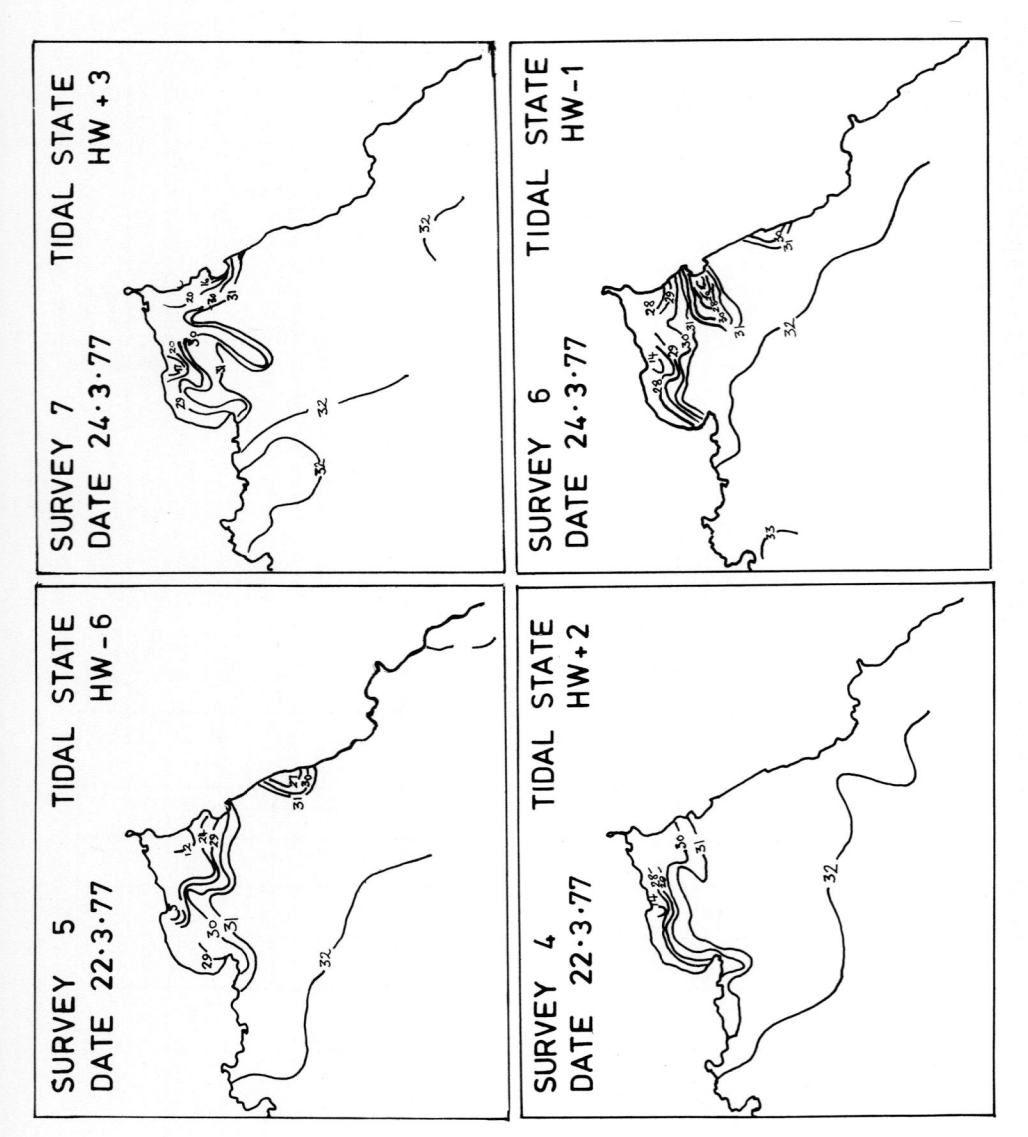

Figure 27.4. Distribution of salinity in Swansea Bay. (Units °/oo).

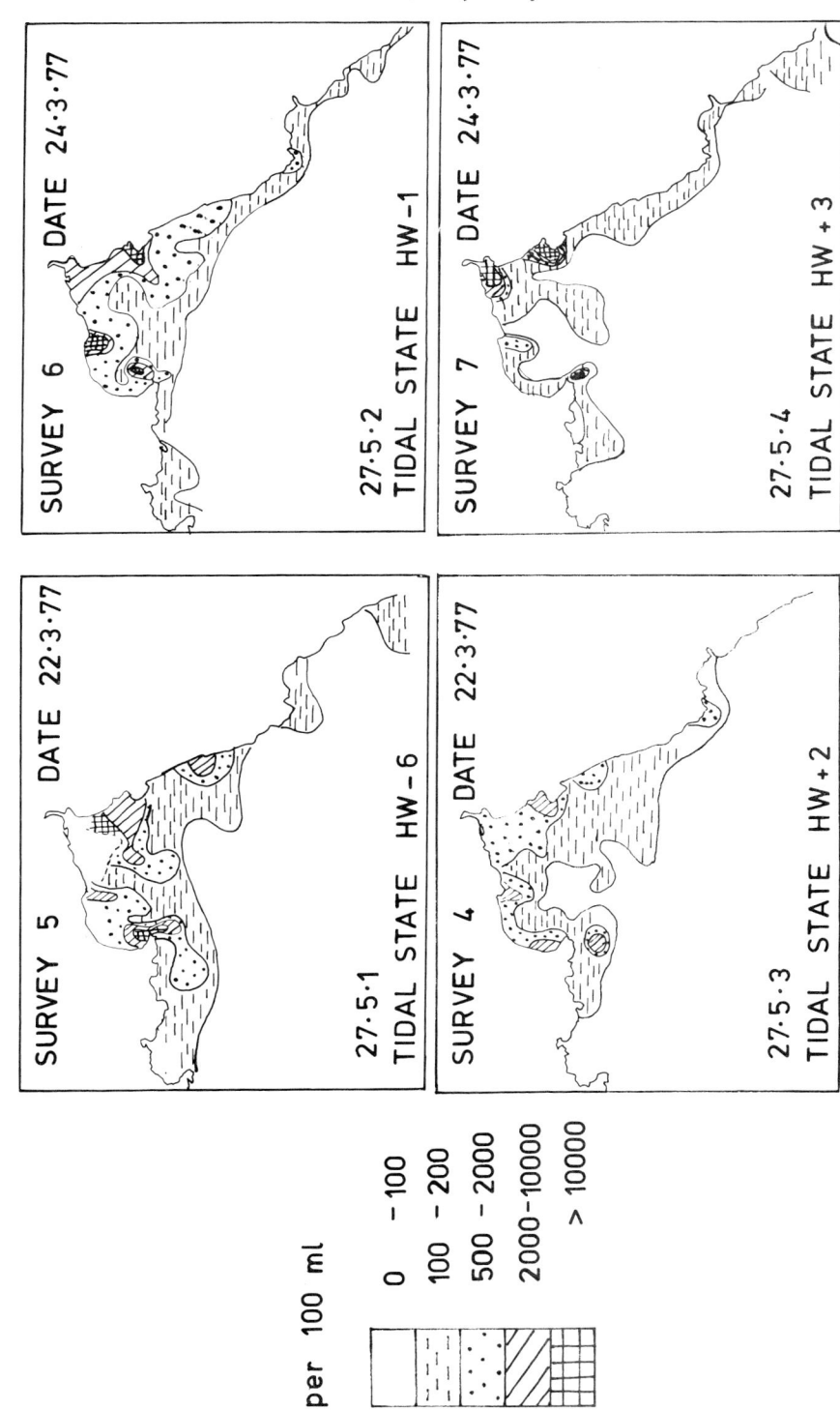

Figure 27.5. Distribution of presumptive *E. coli* in Swansea Bay.

of the major discharges was clearer at times of high runoff, especially in Spring. The major influence on pattern and extent of distribution appeared to be tidal.

At or near low water, when the highest number of sites had high $E.\ coli$ levels (Table 27.4), the effects of discharges from the Mumbles outfall and the Rivers Tawe, Neath and Afan were most noticeable, with a maximum excursion to seaward. However, at the same time relatively $E.\ coli$-free water penetrated quite extensively into the inner bay (Fig. 27.5.1), especially east of the River Tawe.

As the tide began to flood (Fig. 27.5.2) relatively $E.\ coli$-free water appeared to move clockwise into the inner bay which, although inhibiting the seaward excursion of the major inputs, induced coastal streaming especially in the northern and eastern areas. From just after high water (Fig. 27.5.3) the anticlockwise circulation noted earlier tended to minimise the effects of the discharges by transporting $E.\ coli$-free water into the inner bay; at mid ebb (Fig. 27.5.4), over 90% of sites examined had $E.\ coli$ concentrations of less than 500 per 100ml (Table 27.4), although the effects of the major discharges was still apparent. The most significant dilution of these discharges therefore occurred on the ebb tide.

There was little evidence to suggest that much of the significant quantity of $E.\ coli$ discharged into the inner Swansea Bay was transported to the Gower. The data suggest that, although water containing high concentrations of $E.\ coli$ did stream towards Oxwich Bay at the end of the ebb tide, insignificant quantities found their way ashore. This confirmed the conclusions derived from the surf zone data.

A major influence on the fate of $E.\ coli$ in the sea apart from physical dilution and dispersion is the concentration of suspended solids. $E.\ coli$ in sewage diluted with sea water containing 2000mg/l of suspended solids will die-off at approximately half the rate of organisms in sea water containing 20mg/l of suspended solids (unpublished results). The major mechanism resulting in $E.\ coli$ die-off $in\ situ$ is irradiation with sunlight, especially at frequencies between 300 and 400nm (Gameson and Gould, 1975). The major effect of suspended solids on $E.\ coli$ mortality is therefore in blocking or absorbing sunlight, although some experimental data suggests they may play another direct role which is not as yet understood. At certain times of year, apparently during periods of elevated irradiation, $E.\ coli$ die-off can be enhanced by increased salinity; this is obviously especially noticeable in water containing low suspended solids. These conditions are generally obtained throughout most of Swansea Bay (Fig. 27.6) and suggest that die-off rates were very high during summer periods. However, the opposite conditions obtained in some areas; high suspended loads and low salinities occurred towards the surf zone in the area between Mumbles Head and the River Tawe and the area between the River Neath and Margam at low water. These areas contained high levels of $E.\ coli$ and die-off rates in these regions could be expected to be much lower than elsewhere in Swansea Bay.

Inorganic Nutrients

The nutrient concentrations recorded in the inner and outer zones of Swansea Bay throughout the survey programme are summarised in Table 27.5 where they are compared to nutrient levels found in other coastal regimes; the region covered by the outer zone is illustrated in Fig. 27.1 and represents that area where the direct influence of natural and anthropogenic discharges was not generally apparent. The significant seasonal trends apparent in the distribution of several nutrients in both the inner and outer zones of Swansea Bay are illustrated in Fig. 27.7 whilst selected examples of spatial nutrient distributions are shown in Figs. 27.8-27.11, which also includes the five major discharges for each determinand designated A-E in decreasing order of importance.

Water Quality Studies 421

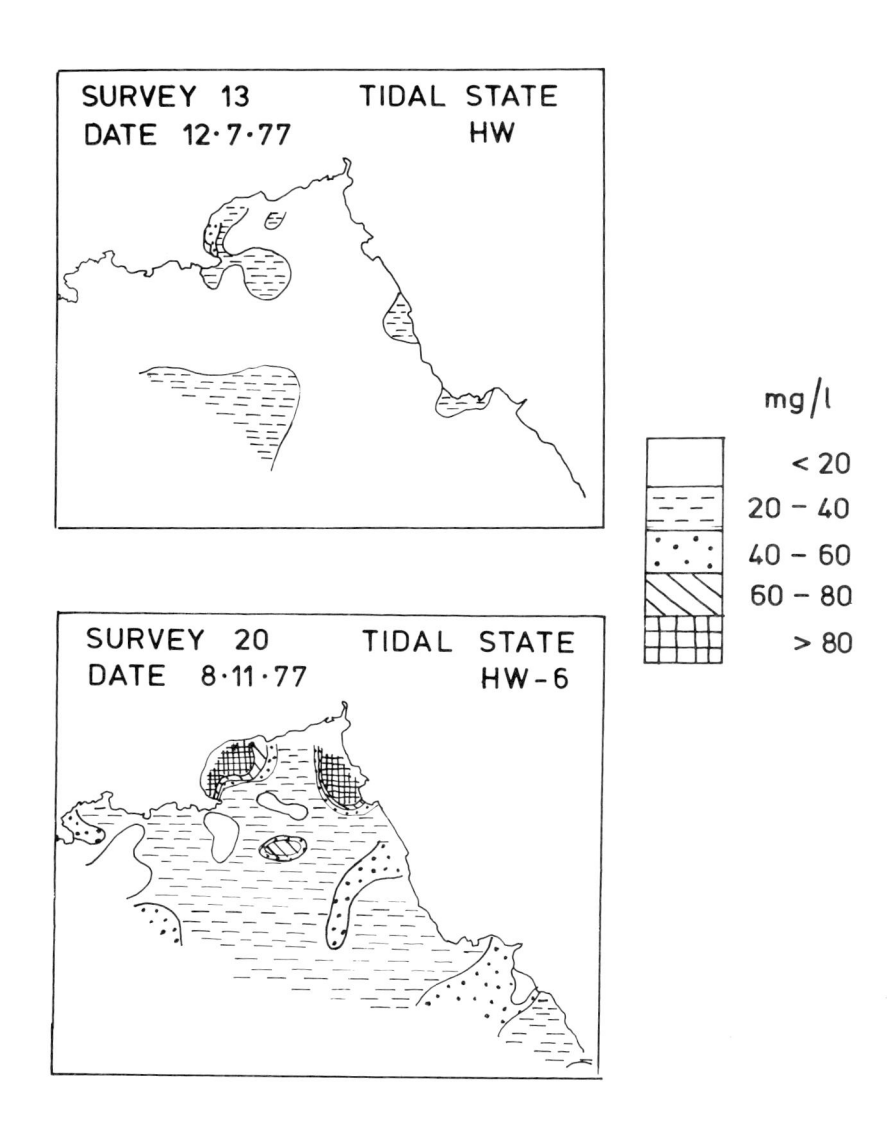

Figure 27.6. Distribution of total suspended solids in Swansea Bay.

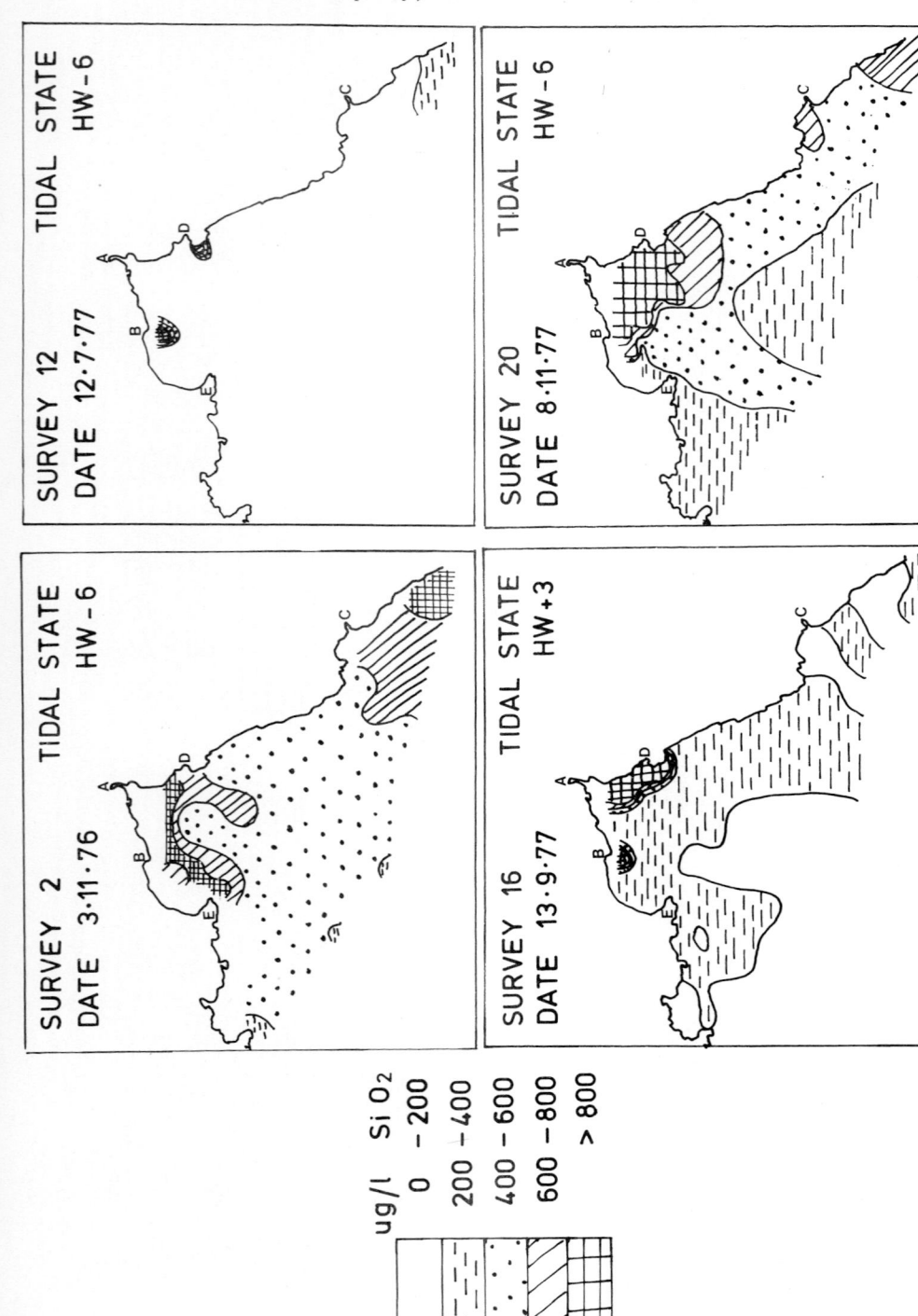

Figure 27.8. Distribution of dissolved reactive silica in Swansea Bay. (A-E: major discharges of silicate).

Water Quality Studies

TABLE 27.5. A Comparison of Mean Nutrient Levels in Swansea Bay With Those from Other Sea Areas (Conc. µg/l).
(Maximum and minimum levels recorded are given in parentheses).

	TON - N	NH_3 - N	PO_4 - P	SiO_2
Present Work				
Nov. 1976; Inshore	496(4-1093)	56(17-159)	44(13-79)	808(342-2015)
Offshore	473(0.5-1643)	36(0-126)	48(0-76)	635(0 -635)
Mar. 1977; Inshore	596(170-1100)	16(0-200)	29(0-92)	956(75-3000)
Offshore	555(360-790)	6(0 -18)	25(0 -49)	823(79-1629)
May 1977; Inshore	442(150-720)	64(0 -1950)	35(0 -173)	575(100-984)
Offshore	453(43-630)	21(4-89)	33(14 -60)	559(102-963)
July 1977; Inshore	195(0 -580)	19(1 -285)	9(0-227)	70(0-878)
Offshore	189(20-360)	12(1 - 56)	9(0-79)	44(21-128)
Sep. 1977; Inshore	357(13-1610)	53(7-1000)	28(0-100)	321(26-2844)
Offshore	335(17-870)	35(9 -211)	26(1 -80)	231(150-385)
Nov. 1977; Inshore	449(10-980)	61(4 -1365)	27(2 -177)	552(149-2780)
Offshore	413(150-610)	112(1 -1365)	31(7 -235)	340(171-748)
Eastern Irish Sea [1]	(84 -490)		(18.6-43.4)	
Dec. 1977; Liverpool Bay [2]	(105-420)			
Jan. 1975; Liverpool Bay [3]		75.6(0-770)		
Dec. 1975; Liverpool Bay [3]		1088(168-4970)		

1. Jones, P.G.W., and A.R. Folkard (1971); 2. Abdullah, M.I., and L.G. Royle (1973); 3. Foster, P., K.B. Pugh and D.T.E. Hunt (1978).

Silicate: Mean silicate levels in both the inner and outer zones of Swansea Bay exhibited a well-defined seasonal variation, with the lowest concentrations being recorded during July (surveys 12-15) in both areas (Fig. 27.8). There was no evidence of a depletion of silicate during the anticipated period of the spring diatom bloom (Spencer, 1975).

The extent of biological utilisation of silicate during July was seen in the uniformly low concentrations recorded throughout the Bay on this occasion and the minimal impact discharges exerted on these distributions. In contrast, dilution of fresh water runoff by sea water was the dominant mechanism controlling the silicate distribution on every other occasion; high silicate levels were consistently recorded in the vicinity of the Rivers Tawe, Neath, Afan and Ogmore at all tidal states. The absence of any simple inverse relationship between silicate concentration and salinity during any survey can be attributed to the multitude of potential fresh water end members in the river water-sea water mixing series. Anthropogenic discharges exerted no discernible influence at any time. The higher silicate levels recorded offshore during survey 1 and around Nash Point during surveys 2 and 20 probably reflect the influence of freshwater discharges located further upstream.

Orthophosphate: Biological utilisation was again the dominant factor controlling the distribution of phosphate during July 1977 (surveys 12-15) when phosphate levels

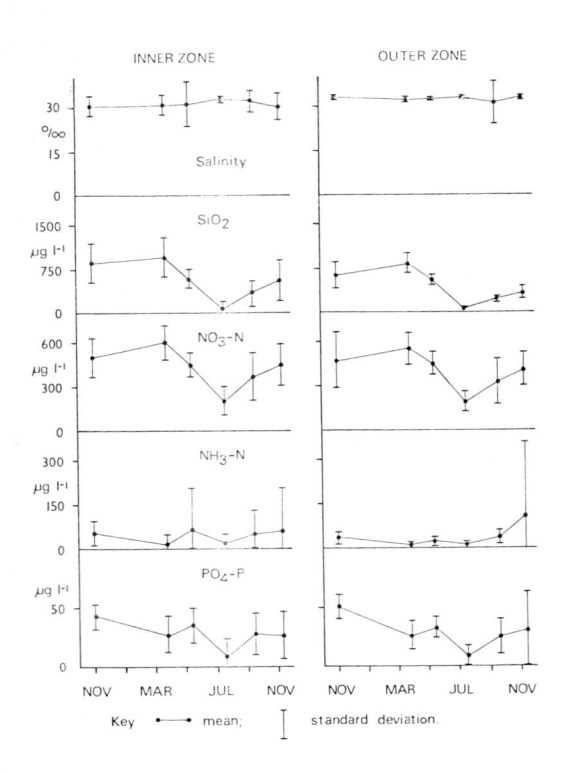

Figure 27.7. Seasonal changes in nutrient levels from Swansea Bay.

of less than 15µg/l PO_4-P were recorded throughout the Bay.

However, the distribution of phosphate was generally extremely complex and few consistent trends emerged (Fig. 27.9). Elevated phosphate levels were sometimes recorded in the vicinity of the major phosphate discharges from the Mumbles Head outfall, River Ogmore and Penybont Sewage Treatment Works (S.T.W.) although they never formed well-defined plumes. Occasionally, high phosphate levels were recorded near the Tawe Estuary although low levels were usually found near the efflux of the Rivers Tawe and Neath. The phosphate-rich plume frequently recorded in the vicinity of the River Afan could not be attributed to any known discharge in this area. Nevertheless, mean phosphate concentrations in Swansea Bay under conditions of minimal biological activity generally conformed well with those recorded in other coastal regimes subject to anthropogenic influences.

<u>Total Oxidised Nitrogen</u>: Clearly defined plumes containing high nitrate concentrations were associated with major discharges of total oxidised nitrogen throughout the programme (Fig. 27.10). High concentrations were consistently recorded near the mouths of the Rivers Tawe, Neath and Afan whilst the impact of the River Kenfig was also discernible on several occasions. However, in contrast, lower nitrate concentrations were recorded around the mouth of the River Afan during survey 6. This suggests that the high nitrate concentrations otherwise recorded along the north eastern coast on this and other occasions primarily originated from nitrification of the considerable ammoniacal discharge from the two major industrial discharges situated between the Rivers Afan and Kenfig, rather than from fresh water runoff.

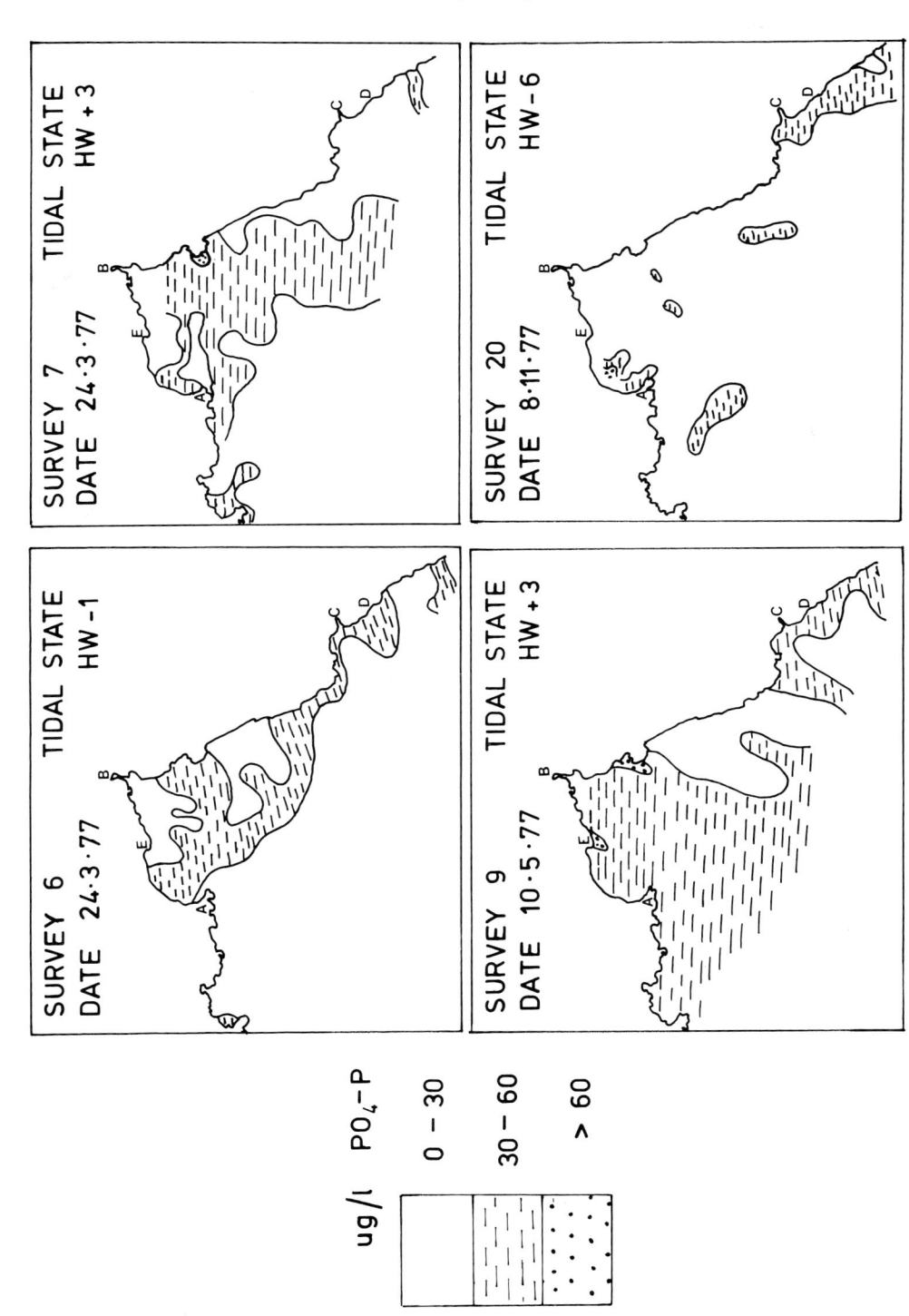

Figure 27.9. Distribution of dissolved orthophosphate in Swansea Bay. (A-E: major discharges of orthophosphate).

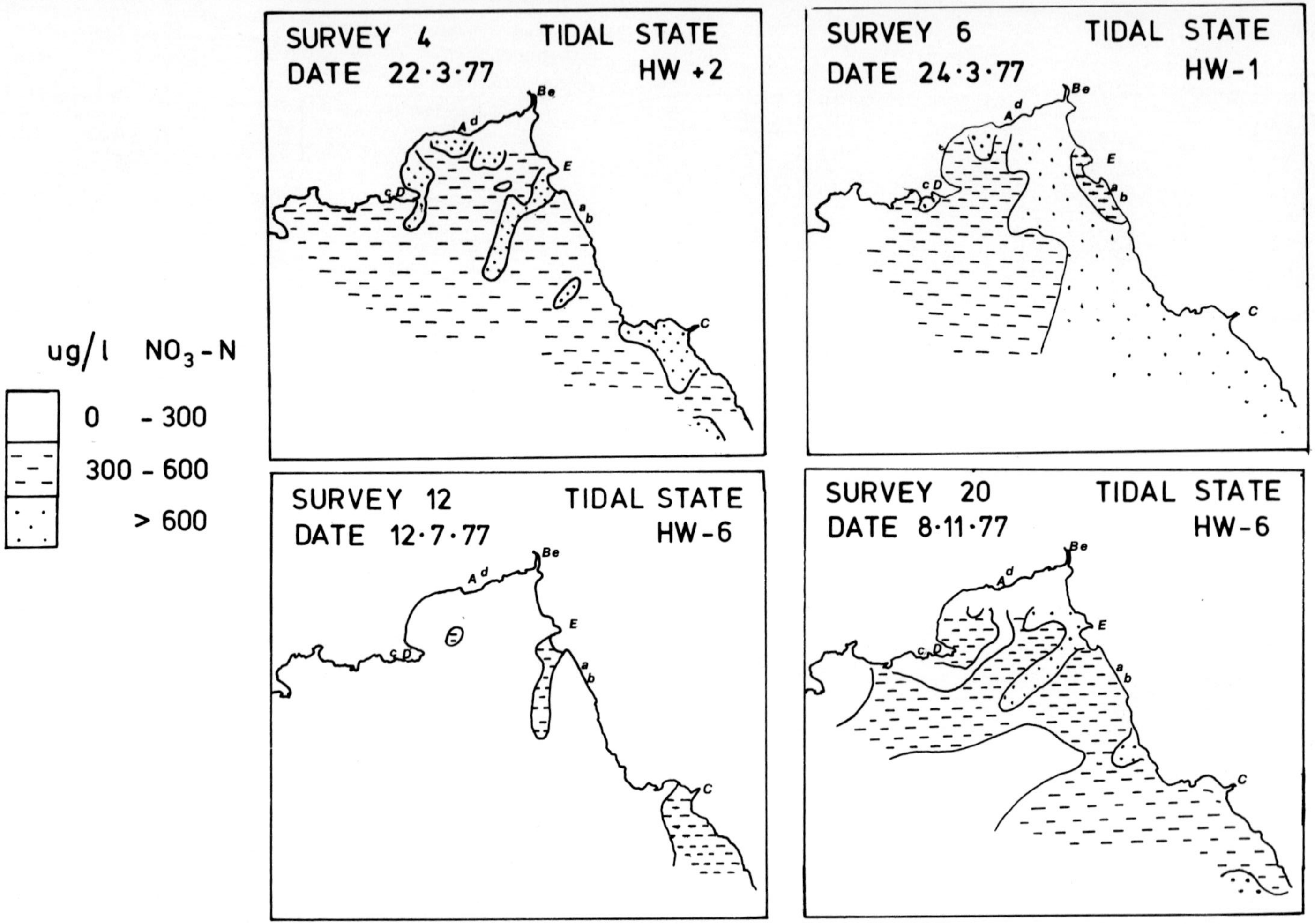

Figure 27.10. Distribution of total oxidised nitrogen in Swansea Bay. (A-E: major discharges of total oxidised nitrogen; a-e: major discharges of total inorganic nitrogen).

Water Quality Studies   427

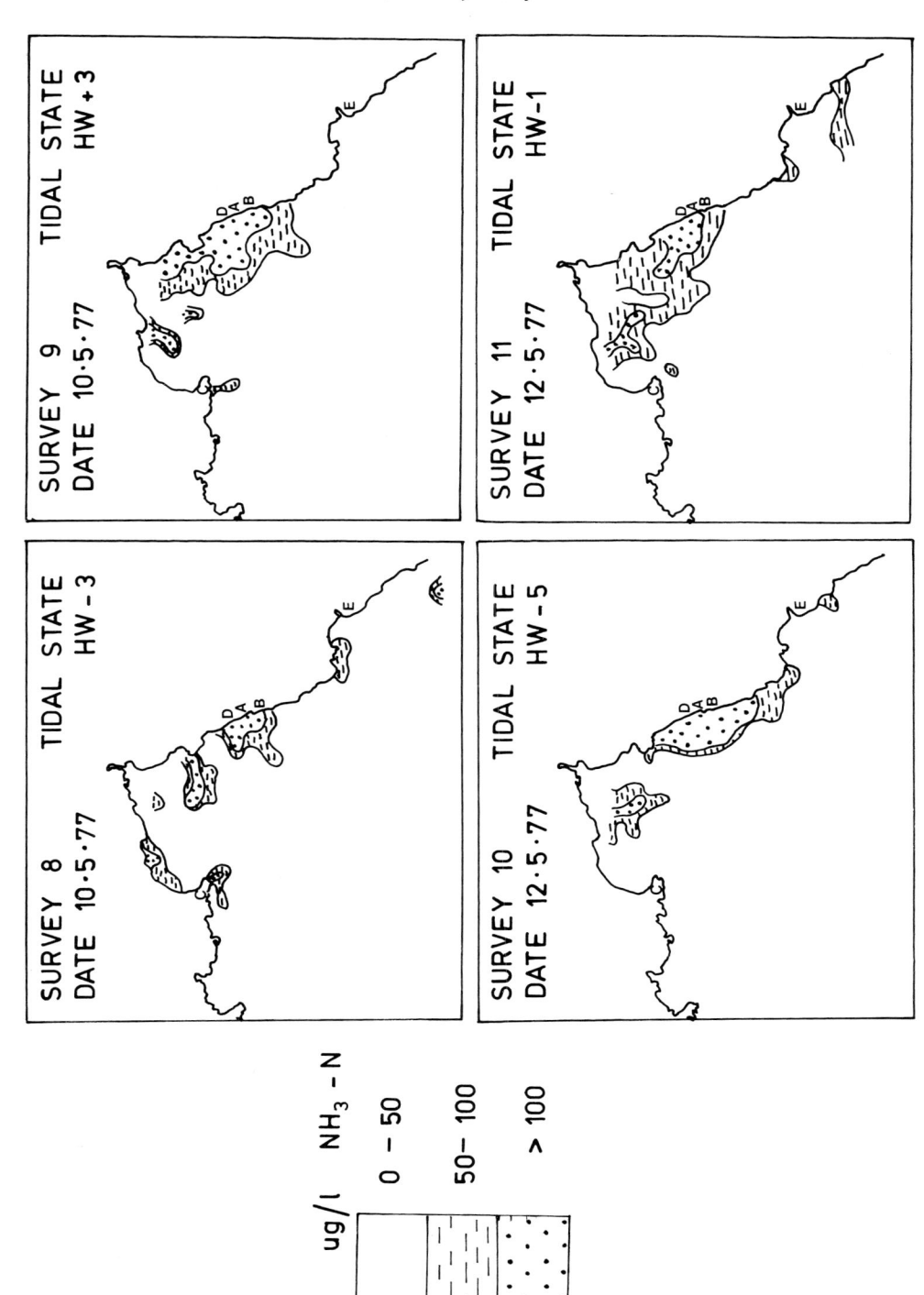

Figure 27.11. Distribution of ammoniacal nitrogen in Swansea Bay. (A-E: major discharges of ammoniacal nitrogen).

These two industrial discharges contributed 42% of the total inorganic nitrogen entering Swansea Bay from terrestrial sources, despite their being relatively minor sources of total oxidised nitrogen (See Chapter 20). Figure 27.10 includes the five major discharges of total inorganic nitrogen in addition to those for total oxidised nitrogen. The effect of all these nitrogen-rich discharges was still apparent during surveys 12-15, despite the extensive biological utilisation occurring on these occasions. The high nitrate levels frequently encountered near Nash Point presumably again originated from discharges upstream.

The importance of these discharges in determining ambient total oxidised nitrogen levels in Swansea Bay was readily apparent as much higher levels were recorded in this area during periods of minimal biological activity than were found in other coastal regimes.

Ammonia: Anthropogenic discharges exerted a considerable localised influence on the distribution of ammonia in Swansea Bay on all occasions, including periods of high biological activity. The major industrial discharges situated between the Rivers Afan and Kenfig were the dominant factor producing high ammonia levels along the north eastern coast of the Bay at all tidal states. In contrast, high ammonia concentrations were only occasionally recorded in the vicinity of the Mumbles Head outfall and the discharge from Penybont S.T.W. although both were also major sources of ammoniacal nitrogen. The effects of other smaller anthropogenic discharges were also apparent during some surveys: enhanced ammonia levels were recorded next to the Neath outfall during survey 6 and near the minor crude sewage discharge at Iron Gate Point during surveys 6, 8, 11 and 17.

The River Tawe was the only natural discharge which produced a clearly-defined plume of elevated ammonia concentrations at most tidal states (Fig. 27.11) although it seems certain that the ammoniacal nitrogen originated primarily from the industrial discharges associated with this river. The River Neath and associated discharges occasionally produced high ammonia concentrations although lower concentrations were generally recorded around this discharge. The origin of the high ammonia levels recorded around the mouth of the River Afan on several occasions is again uncertain as the discharges in this vicinity made a negligible contribution to the ammonia budget of Swansea Bay.

The high ammonia concentrations occasionally recorded off Nash Point presumably again originated from discharges situated upstream. The origin of the high levels found infrequently in Oxwich Bay is unknown as no discharges were recorded in this area of Swansea Bay.

The extent to which anthropogenic discharges control ammonia concentrations in Swansea Bay, even during periods of high nutrient utilisation, generally obscured any significant seasonal trends although there was a tendency towards higher levels during winter months, as suggested by Spencer (1975). Mean ammonia levels in both the inner and outer zones of Swansea Bay during periods of minimal biological utilisation were similar to those recorded in Liverpool Bay on one occasion (Foster *et al.*, 1978), although they were much lower than those obtained in this coastal regime one month later.

Dissolved Trace Metals

No seasonal trends were apparent in the metal levels recorded in Swansea Bay. Table 27.6 compares the metal levels found in the inner and outer zones defined previously with those recorded in other coastal and oceanic regimes using similar analytical techniques. Selected examples of spatial dissolved metal distributions are illustrated in Figs.27.12-15, which again incorporates the five major discharges designated A-E in decreasing order of importance. (See also Chapters 20 and 21 for further

TABLE 27.6. A Comparison of Mean Dissolved Metal Levels in Swansea Bay With Those from Other Sea Areas (Conc. µg/l).

		Cu	Pb	Cd	Ni	Zn	Fe	Mn
Present Work								
Nov. 1976	Inshore	1.4	0.8	0.7	4.3	19.7	3.2	10.0
	Offshore	1.5	0.8	0.7	2.6	13.4	1.7	1.8
Mar. 1977	Inshore	2.4	0.8	0.8	6.4	40.1	1.7	14.1
	Offshore	2.0	0.7	0.9	2.3	12.7	1.5	3.6
May 1977	Inshore	2.5	0.8	0.6	4.9	16.4	2.1	8.1
	Offshore	3.0	0.7	0.5	2.2	13.0	2.0	1.1
Jul. 1977	Inshore	2.1	0.7	0.6	2.4	15.0	1.4	6.2
	Offshore	3.0	0.8	0.5	1.6	15.2	1.3	2.0
Sep. 1977	Inshore	2.3	1.4	0.6	2.9	18.1	2.5	3.8
	Offshore	2.1	0.6	0.5	1.4	16.9	2.5	0.8
Nov. 1977	Inshore	4.2	0.7	0.7	3.2	24.6	2.3	5.5
	Offshore	4.4	0.8	0.6	2.0	19.1	3.6	1.1
World Ocean:	Nearshore[1]	0.90	-	0.09	1.80	2.40	1.20	0.37
	Offshore	0.80	-	0.07	1.20	1.40	1.40	0.22
Liverpool Bay[2]		1.45	1.74	0.27	-	11.8	-	-
Bristol Channel[3]		2.24	1.38	1.94	1.11	8.13	2.28	1.90
Swansea Bay[3]		2.09	1.93	3.10	1.03	9.77	-	2.84
Swansea Bay[4]		2.3	3.4	1.4	3.8	15	-	-

1. Chester, R., and J.H. Stoner (1974); 2. Abdullah, M.I., L.G. Royle and A.W. Morris (1972); 3. Abdullah, M.I., and L.G. Royle (1974); 4. Vivian, C.M.G., (1975).

information on dissolved trace metals in this area).

Copper: Few discharges exerted any influence on the distribution of copper in Swansea Bay throughout most of the programme and levels were generally less than 1µg/l. Nevertheless, mean concentrations in the Bay were much higher than those found in oceanic systems and were also higher than those recorded in Swansea Bay and the Bristol Channel by other workers.

The large industrial discharge into the River Afan was the major influence on the distribution of copper and the impact of other significant copper discharges was only apparent during survey 1 (Fig. 27.12). The elevated copper levels recorded between the Rivers Afan and Kenfig on this occasion were not associated with any known major terrestrial copper discharges and could represent a significant local-

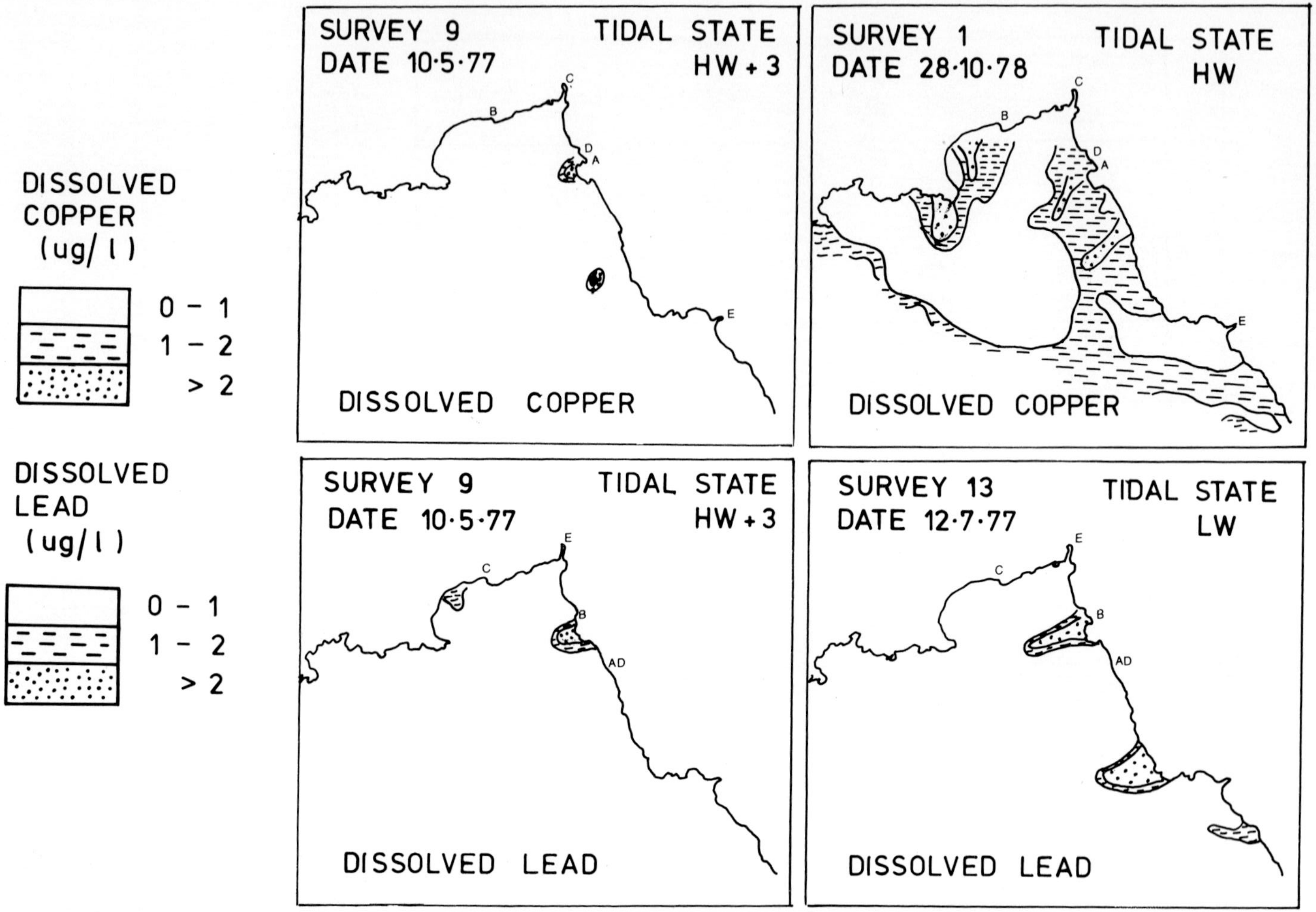

Figure 27.12. Distribution of some trace metals in Swansea Bay: Copper, Lead. (A-E: major discharges of trace metals)

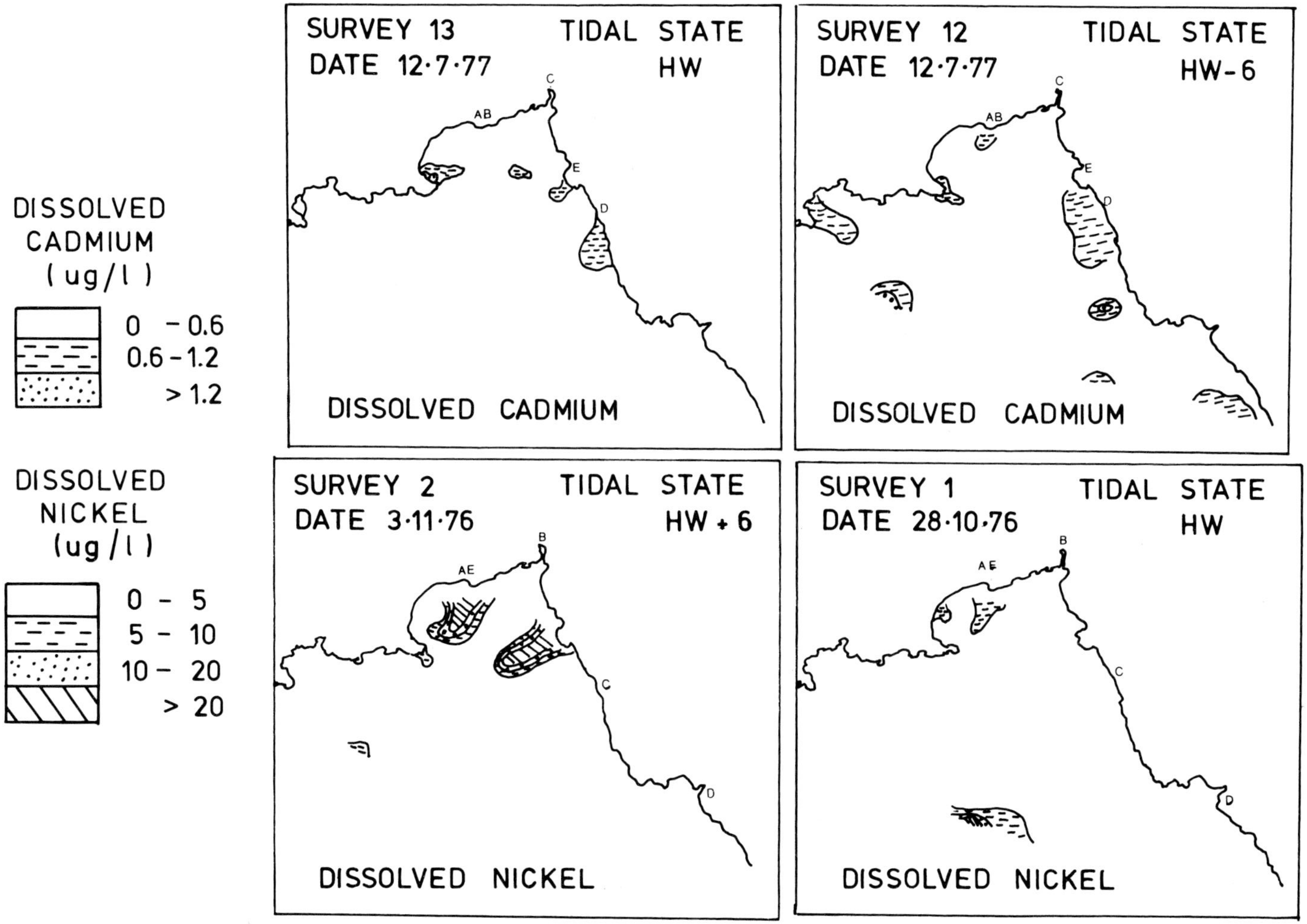

Figure 27.13. Distribution of some trace metals in Swansea Bay: Cadmium, Nickel. (A-E: major discharges of trace metals).

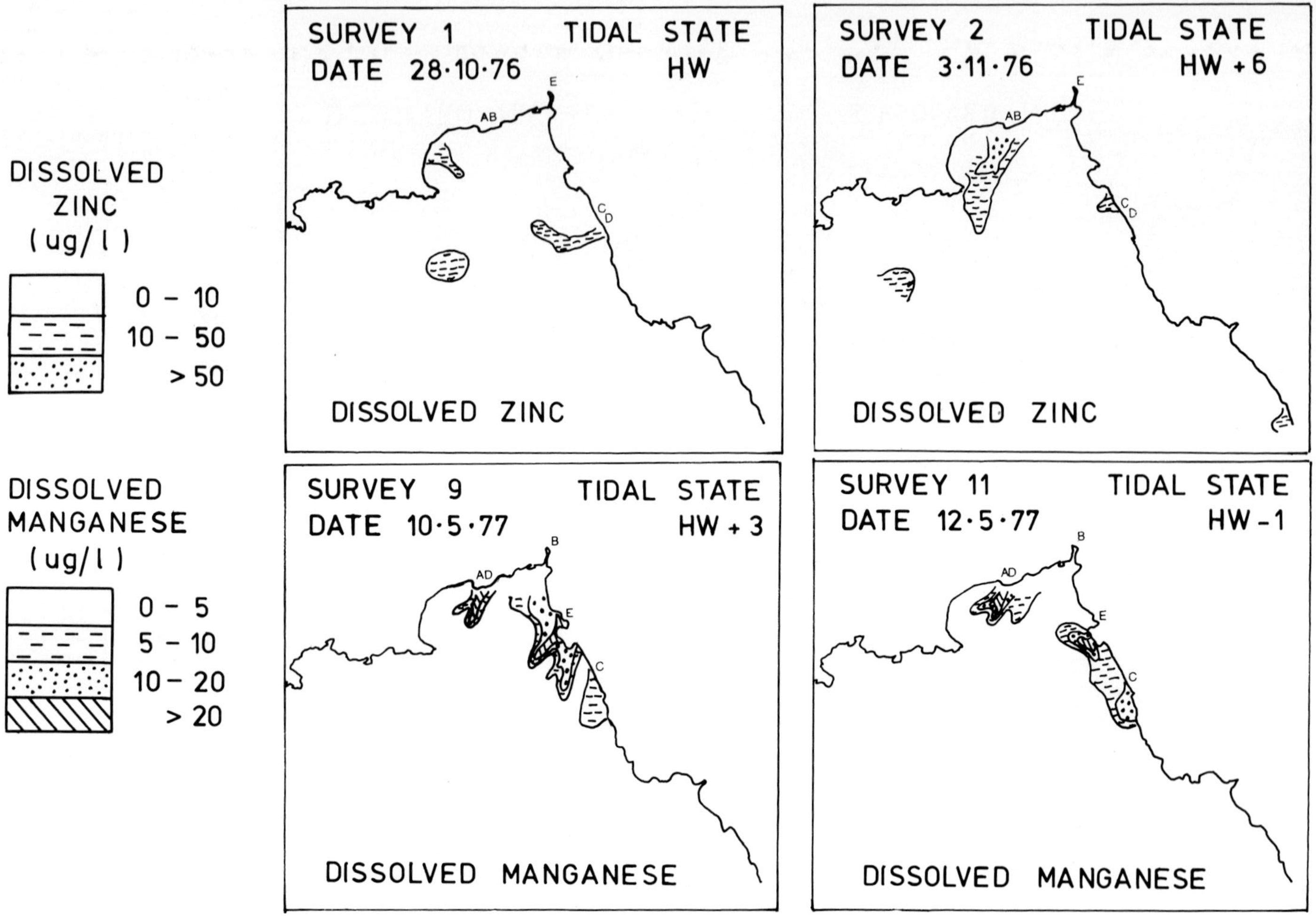

Figure 27.14. Distribution of some trace metals in Swansea Bay: Zinc, Manganese. (A-E: major discharges of trace metals).

ised aerial contribution from the adjacent industrial areas. Similarly, the origin of the high copper concentrations found to the west of Mumbles Head could not be identified.

The River Tawe during survey 1 was the only natural discharge to exert any discernible influence and the shape of the distribution on this occasion confirmed that the discharge flowed westward along the coast.

Lead: Lead levels were generally less than 1µg/l (Fig. 27.12) although the mean concentrations were lower than those found in this area by other workers.

The large industrial discharge into the River Afan again exerted the largest influence on the lead distribution although the significant industrial discharges between the Rivers Afan and Kenfig produced enhanced lead levels on several occasions. The high lead concentrations in the Nant-y-Fendrod were only occasionally reflected in the lead distribution downstream of the River Tawe. No consistent pattern emerged from the enhanced lead concentrations occasionally found to the west of Mumbles Head and they were not associated with any known major lead discharges.

Cadmium: Cadmium concentrations in Swansea Bay (Fig. 27.13) were much higher than those found in oceanic waters although, again, the mean values were lower than those recorded in the same area by other workers.

High cadmium concentrations were frequently recorded in the vicinity of the Rivers Tawe and Nant-y-Fendrod which were the major cadmium discharges to the Bay. Cadmium in these rivers originated from anthropogenic influences upstream. In addition, enhanced cadmium levels were also consistently found near the Mumbles Head outfall and the major industrial discharges located in and around the River Afan although none of these discharges were major sources of cadmium. The high levels in the latter area could again, in part, be the product of a significant aerial cadmium input to the Bay. The relatively high cadmium concentrations consistently encountered to the west of Mumbles Head were not associated with known discharges and their origin is unknown.

Nickel: Dissolved nickel concentrations in the outer zone of Swansea Bay were generally typical of those found in other coastal and oceanic regimes although significantly higher levels were encountered inshore (Fig. 27.13).

Runoff from the River Tawe was the major factor controlling the nickel distribution in Swansea Bay at all tidal states which reflects the dominance of this discharge in the supply of nickel to the Bay; the streaming of the discharge from this river westward along the coast was readily apparent on numerous occasions. In contrast, the River Neath exerted no discernible influence despite being the second largest terrestrial source of nickel. Higher nickel concentrations were often encountered near the Mumbles Head outfall although this discharge was only a minor source of nickel to the Bay. Similarly, there were no major nickel discharges reported in the vicinity of the high nickel levels found around the mouth of the River Afan.

Zinc: Mean zinc levels in Swansea Bay (Fig. 27.14) were much higher than those reported for oceanic waters and were significantly higher than those recorded by other workers in both the same area and other coastal regimes.

The areas containing high zinc concentrations in the nearshore zone were all associated with known major zinc discharges. The dominant discharges at most tidal states were the combined runoff from the Rivers Tawe and Nant-y-Fendrod and numerous major industrial discharges in the vicinity of the River Afan.

Manganese: The high manganese concentrations encountered in three distinct areas of Swansea Bay at most tidal states (Fig. 27.14) were all associated with known

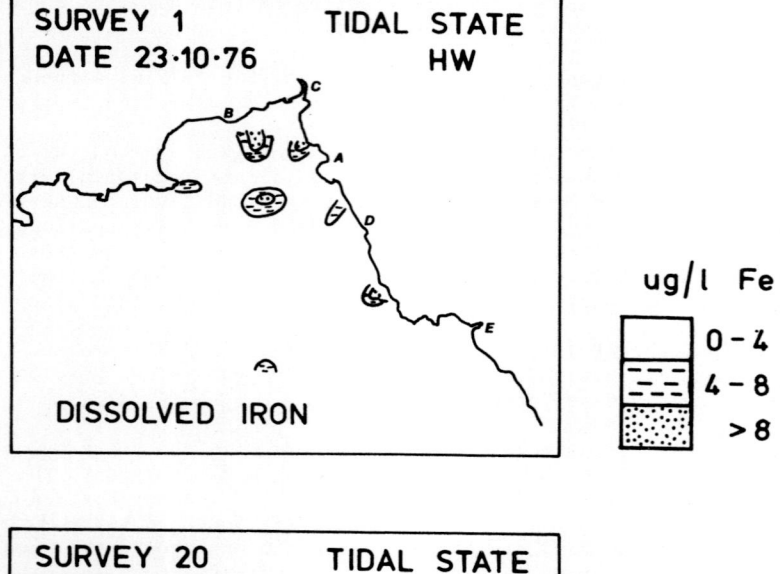

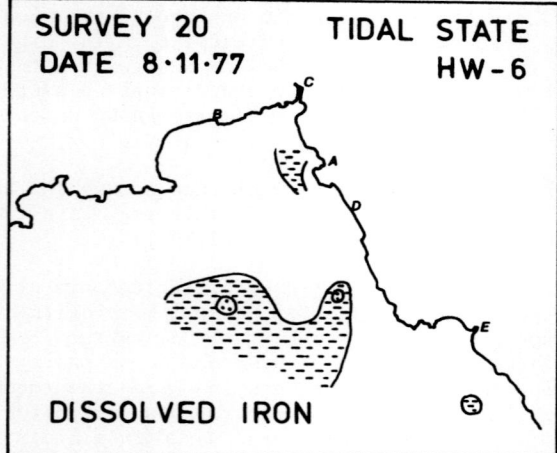

Figure 27.15. Distribution of some trace metals in Swansea Bay: Iron. (A-E: major discharges of trace metals).

major manganese discharges: the industrial discharges between the Rivers Afan and Kenfig, River Afan and associated industrial discharges and the combined runoff from the Rivers Tawe and Nant-y-Fendrod. The effect of the River Neath was also clearly discernible on several occasions. In contrast, the Mumbles Head outfall and the discharge from Penybont S.T.W. only occasionally produced enhanced manganese levels. The high manganese concentrations recorded offshore and in the vicinity of Nash Point could be attributed to discharges situated to the east of the Bay. The origin of the elevated manganese concentrations found in Oxwich Bay during survey 1 is again unknown.

These discharges produced much higher mean manganese levels in the inner zone of Swansea Bay compared to either the outer zone or other coastal regimes. In contrast, manganese concentrations in the outer area were typical of those found in other coastal waters of Britain although they were still much higher than typical oceanic values.

Iron: Few consistent trends emerged from the distribution of iron and concentrations of less than 2μg/l were generally encountered throughout Swansea Bay (Fig. 27.15). Dissolved iron levels in the outer area were comparable with those recorded in other oceanic and coastal regimes on most occasions whilst mean inshore values were slightly higher. The minimal effect exerted by discharges on dissolved iron concentrations can probably be mainly attributed to the extreme reactivity of this species in the marine environment: any dissolved or colloidal iron species present in discharges would tend to flocculate immediately on entering a saline regime.

Discharges exerted their greatest influence during survey 1 when high iron concentrations were recorded next to the Rivers Tawe, Neath and Kenfig, the Mumbles Head outfall and the industrial discharges situated between the Rivers Afan and Kenfig. The effects of the Rivers Tawe, Afan and Neath were occasionally apparent during the remainder of the programme. The origin of the considerable area of high iron concentrations recorded offshore during survey 20 is unknown and they were not associated with increased levels of any other determinands.

SUMMARY AND CONCLUSIONS

Salinity observations confirmed that there was an anticlockwise gyre in the western area of the Bay and an area of divergence in the east although the pattern of circulation in the Bay clearly varied considerably, depending on tidal range, freshwater runoff and meteorological conditions.

Bacteriological quality of the surf zone was excellent on the Gower and east of the River Ogmore due to the absence of significant freshwater and domestic sewage discharges. Elevated numbers of presumptive Coliforms were recorded in the western part of the Bay due to the effects of sewage, storm water and polluted river water although these could be reduced by the new method of operating the Mumbles discharge. Beaches in the vicinity of the Rivers Neath and Afan were polluted by freshwater runoff and crude sewage discharges whilst the mouth of the River Ogmore was still bacteriologically contaminated by the river discharge and effluent from Penybont S.T.W. The proposal to re-route sewage from Porthcawl to Penybont S.T.W. should bring about a dramatic improvement in surf zone water quality in Sandy and Trecco Bays.

The offshore distribution of *E. coli* could be readily explained by established natural and anthropogenic discharges although the hydrography of the Bay exerted a major influence at all tidal states. The die-off rate of *E. coli* could be expected to be very high throughout much of Swansea Bay during summer months although this would be inhibited by the high suspended loads recorded off some rivers and discharges.

Significant seasonal trends were apparent in the distribution of silicate, orthophosphate and total oxidised nitrogen in the Bay although the effects of discharges were apparent in most instances. The distribution of silicate was controlled by natural discharges throughout most of the year whilst, in contrast, anthropogenic discharges controlled the distribution of ammonia in the Bay. No consistent trends emerged from the distribution of orthophosphate. High total oxidised nitrogen levels were recorded in the vicinity of major natural and anthropogenic discharges although there was evidence that nitrification of the significant industrial discharge of ammonia into the north eastern area of Swansea Bay was the dominant factor in determining ambient total oxidised nitrogen levels.

Trace metal levels could generally be explained by known discharges to the Bay. The distribution of copper and lead was primarily controlled by direct anthropogenic discharges whilst in contrast, natural discharges affected by anthropogenic influences upstream were the dominant factor affecting the distribution of cadmium and nickel. Natural and anthropogenic discharges both exerted a significant influence on the zinc and manganese levels in the Bay. In addition, there was some evidence of the atmospheric deposition of copper and cadmium along the north eastern coast. The reactivity of iron on entering a saline regime generally minimised the observed effects of discharges on the distribution of this metal.

Therefore, water quality in Swansea Bay is readily explained by a combination of the hydrography of the region and known discharges to the Bay. Moreover, whilst concentrations of many of the determinands investigated were considerably elevated in waters in the immediate vicinity of major natural and/or anthropogenic discharges, the levels of these determinands throughout the Bay were generally similar to those reported for other coastal regimes around the United Kingdom.

REFERENCES

Abdullah, M.I., Dunlop, H.M., and Gardner, D. (1973). Chemical and hydrographic observations in the Bristol Channel during April and June, 1971. *J. mar. biol. Ass. UK., 53,* 299-319.

Abdullah, M.I., and Royle, L.G. (1973). Chemical evidence for the dispersal of River Mersey runoff in Liverpool Bay. *Estuar. Coast. Mar. Sci., 1,* 401-409.

Abdullah, M.I., and Royle, L.G. (1974). A study of the dissolved and particulate trace elements in the Bristol Channel. *J. mar. biol. Ass. UK., 54,* 581-597.

Bloxam, S., and Aurora, N. (1972). Heavy metals in river and bay sediments near Swansea. *Nature, 239,* 158-159.

Brewer, P.G., and Riley, J.P. (1966). The automatic determination of silicate - silicon in natural waters with special reference to sea water. *Analyt. chim. Acta., 35,* 514-519.

Chan, K.M., and Riley, J.P. (1966). The automatic determination of phosphate in sea water. *Deep Sea Res., 3,* 467-471.

Chester, R., and Stoner, J.H. (1975). Trace elements in sediments from the lower Severn Estuary and Bristol Channel. *Mar. Pollut. Bull., 6,* 92-95.

Clifton, A.P., and Vivian, C.M.G. (1975). Retention of mercury from an industrial source in Swansea Bay sediments. *Nature, 253,* 621-622.

Collins, M., Ferentinos, G., and Banner, F.T. (1979). The hydrodynamics and sedimentology of a high (tidal and wave) energy embayment (Swansea Bay, Northern Bristol Channel). *Estuar. Coast. Mar. Sci., 8,* 49-74.

Department of Health and Social Security, Welsh Office, and Ministry of Housing and Local Government. (1969). *Report 71. The Bacteriological Examination of Water Supplies,* 4th Ed. H.M.S.O., London.

Foster, P., Pugh, K.B., and Hunt, D.T.G. (1978). Ammonia Distributions in the surface waters of Liverpool Bay. *Estuar. Coast. Mar. Sci., 7,* 71-78.

Fuge, R., and James, K.H. (1974). Trace metal concentrations in *Fucus* from the Bristol Channel. *Mar. Pollut. Bull., 5,* 9-12.

Gameson, A.L.H., and Gould, D.J. (1975). Effects of solar radiation on the mortality of some terrestrial bacteria. *In:* Gameson, A.L.H. (Ed.). *Discharge of Sewage from Sea Outfalls*. Pergamon Press, Oxford, 209-219.

Grasshoff, K. (1970). *Advances in Automated Analysis,* Vol. 2. Mediad, White Plains.

Jones, P.G.W., and Folkard, A.R. (1971). Hydrographic observations in the eastern Irish Sea with particular reference to the distribution of nutrient salts. *J. mar. biol. Ass. UK., 51,* 159-182.

Morris, A.W., and Bale, A.J. (1975). The accumulation of cadmium, copper, manganese and zinc by *Fucus vesiculosus* in the Bristol Channel. *Estuar. Coast. Mar. Sci., 3,* 153-163.

Riley, J.P. (1975). Analytical Chemistry of Sea Water. *In:* Riley, J.P., and Skirrow, G. (Eds.)., *Chemical Oceanography,* Vol. 3, 2nd Ed. Academic Press, London, 193-514.

Riley, J.P., and Taylor, D. (1968). Chelating resins for the concentration of trace elements from seawater and their analytical use in conjunction with atomic absorption spectroscopy. *Analyt. chim. Acta., 40,* 479-485.

Spencer, C.P. (1975). The Micronutrient Elements. *In:* Riley, J.P., and Skirrow, G. (Eds.). *Chemical Oceanography,* Vol. 2, 2nd Ed., Academic Press, London, 245-300.

Steen, P.J., and Stickler, D.J. (1976). *A Sewage Pollution Study of Beaches from Cardiff to Ogmore*. The University of Wales, Institute of Science and Technology.

Stickler, D.J. (1974). *Report of the Working Party on Possible Pollution in Swansea Bay*. The Welsh Office, Cardiff.

Strickland, J.D.H., and Parsons, T.R. (1972). *A Practical Handbook of Seawater Analysis*. 2nd Ed., Fish. Res. Bd. Can. Bull., 167, 310pp.

Vivian, C.M.G. (1975). *Distribution of certain trace elements in seawater and sediments in relation to local sources, Swansea Bay and adjacent parts of the Bristol Channel*. Ph.D. Thesis, University of Wales, (Unpub.), 212pp.

28. CHEMISTRY OF SWANSEA BAY: I. GENERAL DESCRIPTION

A. W. Morris and R. F. C. Mantoura

Natural Environment Research Council, Institute for Marine Environmental Research, Prospect Place, The Hoe, Plymouth PL1 3DH, Devon, U.K.

ABSTRACT

The influence of Swansea Bay on the regional chemistry of the Bristol Channel has been investigated during five cruises to the outer Bay area between February 1977 and January 1978. Salinity, temperature, turbidity, nitrate, nitrite, phosphate, silicate, chlorophyll a, phaeopigment and dissolved organic carbon were measured. Comparisons of this outer Bay data with data for equivalent salinity waters of the central Bristol Channel shows that the outer Bay region is affected only to a limited extent by natural, industrial and domestic run-off into the Bay; this is probably attributable to the eddy circulation pattern within the inner Bay. Nutrient levels are therefore mainly determined by seasonal production processes. Enhanced summer silicate depletion was found in parts of the outer Bay yielding undetectable concentrations (<0.05µg - at Si/l) whereas nitrate and phosphate were always present in significant amounts

KEYWORDS

Coastal waters; Salinity; Temperature; Nutrients; Primary production; Seasonal variations; Swansea Bay; Bristol Channel.

INTRODUCTION

Irregularities in the shoreline of estuaries and coastal regions, by their influence on transport and mixing processes, can produce localised physical, chemical and biological water characteristics which differ appreciably from those prevalent in the adjacent waters. These differences are particularly accentuated where local fresh water contributions are significant. This situation is evident in the Bristol Channel, where regional variations in the ecology of the region which are induced by major coastal embayments are under investigation by the Institute for Marine Environmental Research. This programme has included a series of investigations of the outer Swansea Bay area. Chemical data obtained during this work demonstrate the considerable temporal and spatial variability of the waters of this region. In this Chapter, the general features of this variability are discussed. Further contributions to this Symposium, by Mantoura and Morris (this Chapter, Part II) and by Joint (Chapter 29), provide detailed discussions of the principal chemical and biological processes involved.

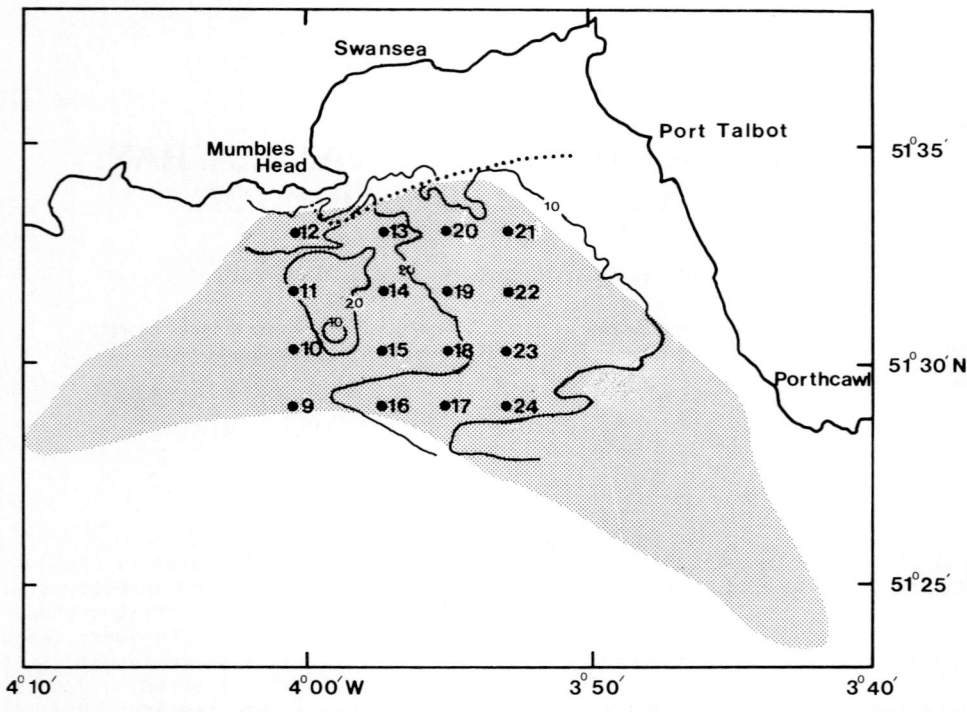

Figure 28.1. Sketch chart showing the position of the sixteen stations (numbered 9 to 24) comprising the outer Swansea Bay grid. The broken line marks the boundary between the outer Bay region of rectilinear tidal currents running parallel to the coast from the inner Bay region of anticlockwise eddy circulation (after Collins et al., 1979). The shaded area encloses the extrapolated nearest high and low water positions of all samples taken throughout this programme. Depth contours (m) within the grid region are shown.

TABLE 28.1. Positions of the Sixteen Stations Comprising the Outer Swansea Bay Grid.

Station No.	Latitude N	Longitude W	Station No.	Latitude N	Longitude W
9	51°29′	04°00.5′	17	51°29′	03°55.2′
10	51°30.3′	04°00.5′	18	51°30.3′	03°55.2′
11	51°31.7′	04°00.5′	19	51°31.6′	03°55.2′
12	51°33′	04°00.5′	20	51°33′	03°55.2′
13	51°33′	03°57.3′	21	51°33′	03°53′
14	51°31.7′	03°57.3′	22	51°31.7′	03°53′
15	51°30.3′	03°57.3′	23	51°30.3′	03°53′
16	51°29′	03°57.3′	24	51°29′	03°53′

EXPERIMENTAL

Sixteen regularly spaced stations, numbered 9 to 24 in Figure 28.1, encompassing a rectangular area of approximately 60km^2 of the outer Swansea Bay area were selected and used throughout this investigation; the nominal positions of these stations are listed in Table 28.1. The northwest corner of this grid of stations reaches within 2km of the coastline west of Mumbles Head; from there, the northern boundary of the grid runs eastward for 8.3km, and the grid extends 7.2km south of this boundary. Although the detailed submarine topography of the grid region is quite rugged, particularly in the region south of Mumbles Head (Collins et al., 1979), tidally averaged water depths within the area generally increase from east to west and are predominantly in the range 15 to 25m.

The selected grid of stations falls entirely within the main Bristol Channel tidal system of rectilinear tidal currents generally running parallel to the coastline. However, the northern boundary of the grid closely approaches the area of divergence which separates the southerly field of rectilinear tidal streams from the northerly region of localised anticlockwise eddy system of tidal currents within Swansea Bay (Collins et al., 1979). The position of this boundary has been marked in Fig. 28.1.

The stations of the outer Swansea Bay grid were sampled during five cruises between February, 1977 and January, 1978 (Table 28.2). On all but one cruise (B9/77) the sampling was repeated after an interval of 4 or 5 days. Each of the transects followed the numerical order of station designation, apart from the second grid of Cruise B2/77, when the direction was reversed. A complete transect was generally completed in about 3½ hours. Extensive sampling of the central Bristol Channel region was also undertaken during these cruises, and additional data for the Swansea Bay grid and the central Bristol Channel region have been obtained from other IMER cruises which fell within the time span of this study.

TABLE 28.2. Date, Timing and Tidal Conditions For Each Transect of the Outer Swansea Bay Grid. Figures under Tidal Conditions Denote the Time (Hours and Minutes) of Commencement of the Grid Transect Relative to the Time of High Water at Swansea.

Cruise and Grid	Date	Time	Tidal Conditions
B2 77 1	14 FEB 1977	1040-1529	-4.48 : NEAPS +1DAY
B2 77 2	18 FEB 1977	1814-2136	-1.00 : SPRINGS -1DAY
B4 77 1	09 MAY 1977	1734-2057	-6.34 : SPRINGS +4DAYS
B4 77 2	13 MAY 1977	2027-2344	+4.07 : NEAPS +2DAYS
B7 77 1	07 AUG 1977	1808-2148	-5.44 : NEAPS -3DAYS
B7 77 2	12 AUG 1977	1036-1353	-6.23 : NEAPS +2DAYS
B9 77 1	04 NOV 1977	1745-2032	-5.33 : NEAPS -2DAYS
B1 78 1	20 JAN 1978	0709-1037	+3.47 : NEAPS +2DAYS
B1 78 2	24 JAN 1978	1225-1534	-6.27 : SPRINGS -2DAYS

The dates, timing and tidal conditions appropriate to each traverse of the grid are listed in Table 28.2. The timing was mainly determined by overall cruise logistics and no attempt was made to sample under selected tidal conditions. The tidal excursion for points within the grid is of the order of twice the grid width. In accordance with the tidal streams, these tidal excursions are predominantly east to west orientated within the grid area, but outside the area they tend to curve in parallel with the general coastline trend, particularly to the east. For every sampling incident throughout this investigation, the positions occupied by the sampled water at the times of nearest high and low water have been determined. The envelope embracing all such points is included in Fig. 28.1.

Near surface water, obtained from a depth of 2m using a submersible pump, was used for all determinations. Continuous records of the salinity and temperature of this pumped water throughout each traverse of the grid were obtained using a Plessey Thermosalinograph Model No. 6600T. Chlorophyll fluorescence (Turner Model III Fluorometer) and turbidity (Partech Electronics Ltd., Model HP-LP) were also measured continuously along the cruise track. No attempts were made to calibrate accurately the fluorometer output or to correct for interferences due to the presence of suspended particles, so that only a relative, and necessarily arbitrary, measure of chlorophyll concentration for comparative purposes was obtained. The turbidimeter was calibrated according to the manufacturer's recommendations. Accurate chlorophyll a and phaeopigment concentrations were obtained for discrete samples, collected at each of the sixteen grid stations, using the procedure recommended by Strickland and Parsons (1972). Generally, the fluorometer output agreed in a qualitative way with the discrete chlorophyll a measurements.

Dissolved organic carbon was determined, in triplicate, with discrete samples collected at the sixteen grid stations. After filtration through a previously ashed (450°C) Whatman GF/C glass fibre paper, a modified seagoing version of an automated photochemical analyser (Collins and Williams, 1977) was used for the analysis. The determinations were calibrated by the method of standard additions.

A subsidiary stream, tapped from the main pumped supply, was filtered through a 0.45μm pore-sized membrane filter prior to nutrient analysis using a Technicon II Auto Analyser (Morris et al., 1978). Nitrate + nitrite was determined after reduction of nitrate to nitrite according to the method of Brewer and Riley (1965), but using the reductor described by Stainton (1974). Nitrite concentrations were obtained by omitting the reduction step. Phosphate determinations followed the method of Chan and Riley (1965) and the Technicon Method No. 186-72W was used for silicate analysis. Nutrient concentrations were recorded during each traverse of the grid at a rate of 30 samples per hour; the pumped sample water was interspersed with a deionised water wash using a sample to wash ratio of 1:1. Calibration of the nutrient assays was achieved using the method of standard additions. Results were corrected, as appropriate, for refractive index errors according to the procedure recommended by Froelich and Pilson (1978).

RESULTS

Continuously recording techniques deployed in estuarine and coastal waters usually reveal small-scale (10-500m) heterogeneities in the horizontal plane consistent with the turbulent nature of the mixing processes involved. Such variability was evident in the present study. This discussion, however, is predominantly focussed on seasonal variability of grid conditions in comparison with the adjacent offshore waters: within grid variability is discussed elsewhere (Mantoura and Morris, this Chapter, Part II). A few vertical profiles, at various points within the grid, have been investigated. However, the waters have been found to approximate to well-mixed conditions so that near surface properties can generally be assumed to be characteristic of the entire water column.

Salinity and Temperature

The ranges, means and standard deviations of salinity and temperature values at the sixteen grid points for each transect are listed in Table 28.3.

TABLE 28.3. Range, Mean and Standard Deviation About the Mean of Salinity and Temperature at the Sixteen Outer Swansea Bay Stations for Each Grid Transect.

CRUISE AND GRID			SALINITY ‰			TEMPERATURE °C		
			range	mean	s.d.	range	mean	s.d.
B2	77	1	29.97-31.70	30.72	0.57	6.70-7.00	6.85	0.08
B2	77	2	30.70-31.85	31.41	0.35	6.75-6.98	6.87	0.07
B4	77	1	32.28-32.63	32.52	0.12	10.05-10.35	10.14	0.09
B4	77	2	31.80-32.66	32.24	0.24	10.29-10.77	10.53	0.12
B7	77	1	32.78-33.12	32.96	0.11	17.23-18.25	17.64	0.30
B7	77	2	32.92-33.08	33.01	0.06	17.68-18.70	18.16	0.31
B9	77	1	31.98-33.16	32.59	0.35	12.53-13.20	12.80	0.19
B1	78	1	32.14-32.93	32.58	0.23	5.45-6.50	5.96	0.31
B1	78	2	31.53-32.59	32.02	0.39	5.90-6.49	6.06	0.20

During each individual traverse of the grid, the overall range of salinity encountered was quite restricted, varying from as little as 0.16°/oo during the second grid of cruise B7/77 to, at most, 1.73°/oo for the first grid of Cruise B2/77. These ranges correspond to coefficients of variation of ± 0.18% and ± 1.85%, respectively. Furthermore, when the data from all surveys are considered, salinities are always relatively high and the difference between the overall maximum (33.16°/oo) and minimum (29.97°/oo) is only 3.19°/oo. Accordingly, seasonal salinity trends are not pronounced, although the lower salinities, and the greater ranges of salinity within the grid, tend to occur in the winter period, as shown in Fig. 28.2. It follows, therefore, that the waters of the investigated region represent only the later stages of the mixing of inshore water of the Swansea Bay region with the central Bristol Channel waters.

Mean temperatures for the grid exhibit a pronounced seasonal cycling typical of temperate coastal waters, but, in accordance with the restricted salinity ranges, variations within the grid on each sampling occasion were relatively small (see Table 28.3). The seasonal changes in mean temperature of the grid water are shown in Fig. 28.3 and are compared with those found for waters of the same salinity within the central Bristol Channel as the temperature difference $\overline{\Delta T}$. This illustrates clearly the less regulated temperature of water nearer to the coast. More rapid heating of this water, particularly during May, gives rise to a maximum difference of nearly +1.3°C in June, whereas differential cooling during the autumn and winter leads to a maximum winter difference of -0.9°C in January.

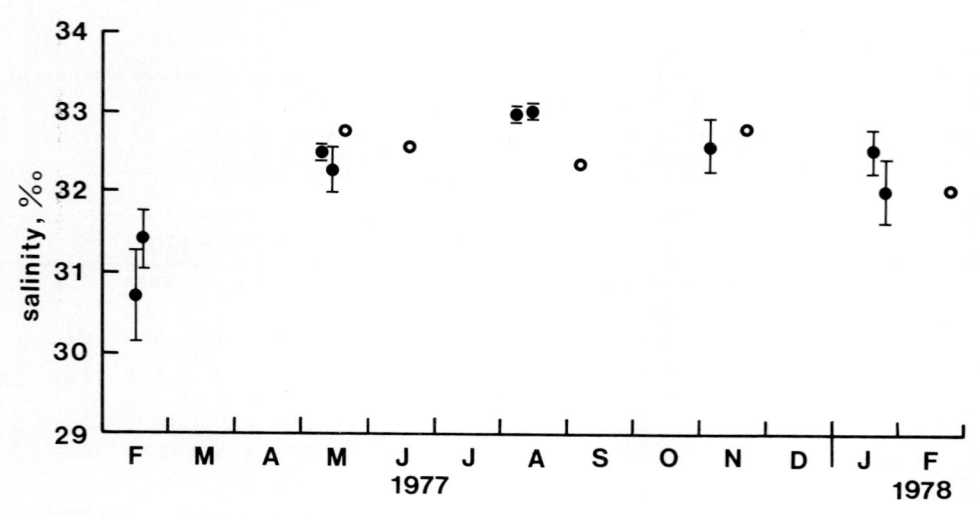

Figure 28.2. The seasonal variation of the mean salinity within the outer Swansea Bay grid. Closed dots are data collected in the basic programme of sampling and open dots are data from other IMER Cruises within the region. Bars show the range corresponding to ± 1 standard deviation about the mean.

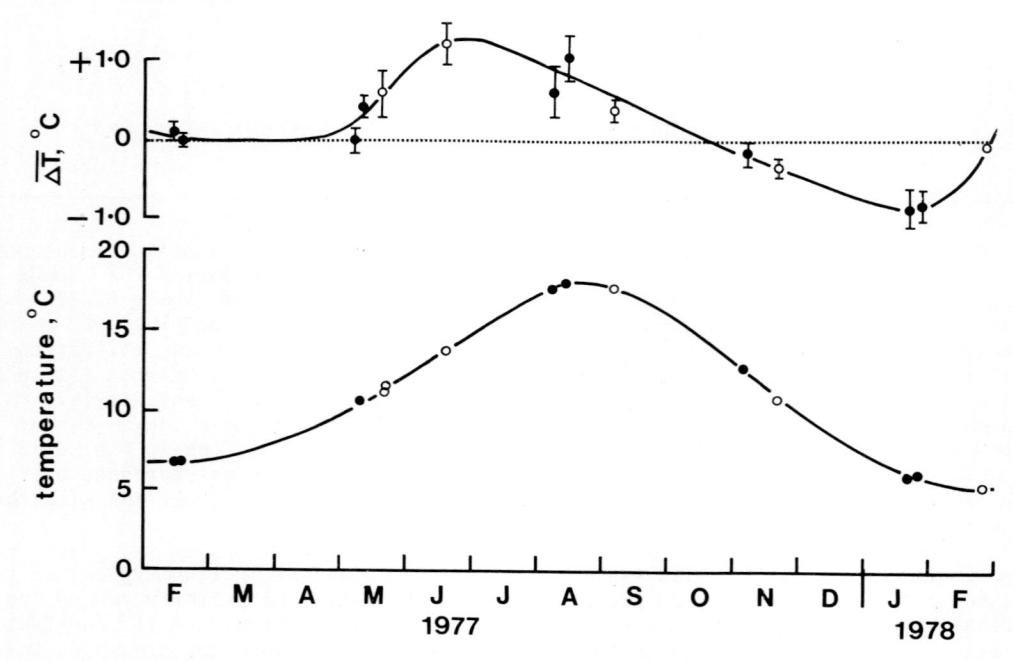

Figure 28.3. The seasonal variation of mean temperature within the outer Swansea Bay grid. $\overline{\Delta T}$ values are the difference between the mean temperature within the grid and the simultaneous mean temperature of water of equivalent salinity in the Central Bristol Channel region, error bars (± 1 standard deviation) are included. Closed dots are data collected in the basic programme of sampling and open dots are data from other IMER Cruises within the region.

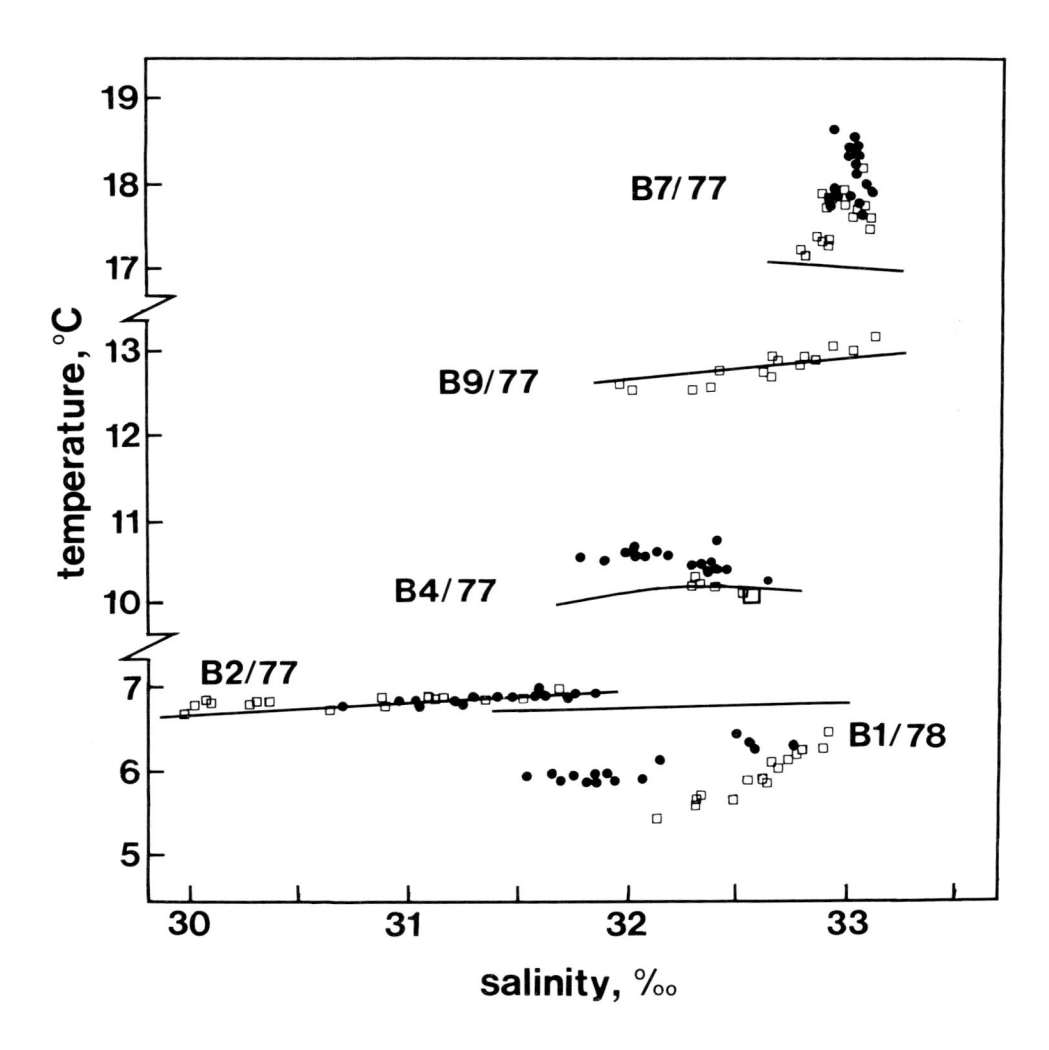

Figure 28.4. Temperature-salinity relationships measured during the first (open squares) and second (closed dots) samplings of the outer Swansea Bay grid during each cruise. The lines define the temperature-salinity characteristics of Central Bristol Channel water at the same time. The larger open square in the figure for the first grid of Cruise B4/77 encloses eleven data points.

Temperature-salinity (T-S) relationships for each grid sampling are illustrated in Fig. 28.4 and compared in each case with the T-S relationships observed at the same time for bulk Bristol Channel water. The temperature differences $\overline{\Delta T}$ noted above must result mainly from an accentuated heat exchange with the atmosphere through tidal substrate exposure within waters whose temperature is relatively poorly buffered by the restricted depths. Hence temperature cannot be considered conservative in the conventional oceanic sense. Nevertheless T-S relationships can, with due interpretive caution, be used as indicators of coastal "water-types".

During Cruise B7/77 in August, temperatures throughout the grid on both sampling occasions were considerably higher than in central Bristol Channel waters of corresponding salinity, and relatively large ranges of temperature were encountered. Clearly, localised solar heating was exerting a dominant control over the temperature structure at this time. Mean temperature within the grid rose by more than 0.5°C over the 5 day interval between samplings, whereas the mean salinities for the two samplings agreed closely, and the overall salinity ranges encountered on each occasion were very restricted. Localised heating relative to central Bristol Channel water is also indicated by the data from the second grid sampling during Cruise B4/77. The very consistent temperature and salinity values measured for the majority of samples collected during the first grid sampling of this cruise were due mainly to traversing the grid in a predominantly eastward direction during the flood tide.

The single grid coverage of Cruise B9/77 and the duplicate coverage of Cruise B2/77 yielded T-S relationships which were linear and corresponded closely to those characteristic of bulk Bristol Channel water at the respective times of sampling. The close correspondence of both grids of Cruise B2/77, covering somewhat different salinity ranges, suggests that the comparatively extended ranges of salinities, and the comparatively low values encountered, could be a consequence of seasonal changes in the hydrodynamics of the Bristol Channel rather than a reflection of enhanced winter run-off into the local Swansea Bay region.

The T-S relationships for both surveys of Cruise B1/78 are non-linear and lie well below that characteristic of the central Bristol Channel, due to enhanced inshore winter cooling. However, there is also a marked disparity between the T-S relationships recorded for the two surveys only 4 days apart. This suggests that differing "water-types" may have been encountered. Although this conclusion is not unequivocable, it is noticeable that the second grid of this cruise sampled waters whose extrapolated high water positions extended further to the southeast than for any other sampling

Nutrients

Nutrient data obtained during this investigation are summarised in Table 28.4 as ranges, means and standard deviations of nitrate, phosphate and silicate measured during each grid transect. All three nutrients undergo pronounced seasonal changes in concentration: minimum concentrations were encountered in August (Cruise B7/77), with considerably higher concentrations at other times (see Fig. 28.5). The mean values of each nutrient within the grid were quite similar for the May Cruise B4/77 to those found in winter (Cruise B1/78) when the mean salinities were also comparable. It appears therefore that the pronounced summer depletion of nutrients, presumably initiated by the spring phytoplankton outburst, occurred after the May investigation.

For salinities less than 28°/oo within the main Bristol Channel/Severn Estuary system, nutrient concentrations are high and determined predominantly by source concentrations and mixing processes (Abdullah et al., 1973; A.W. Morris, unpublished data). Primary production within this region is always severely restricted by high turbidity and the low rates of production achieved do not affect substantially the distributions of nutrients. At higher salinities, away from the immediate coastline, although the nutrient concentrations are determined primarily by mixing between the high nutrient waters emanating from the Severn Estuary and low nutrient-high salinity waters entering the Channel from the seaward end, they are modified by production processes occurring therein. Figure 28.6 compares the nutrient-salinity relationships in these central Bristol Channel waters determined during Cruises B7/77 and B1/78, which are typical of summer and winter conditions, respectively. Nitrate, phosphate and silicate concentrations in the winter (Cruise B1/78) vary

Chemistry: General Description 447

TABLE 28.4. Range, Mean and Standard Deviation About the Mean of Nitrate, Phosphate and Silicate Concentrations at the Sixteen Outer Swansea Bay Stations for Each Grid Transect.

CRUISE AND GRID			NITRATE-N			PHOSPHATE-P			SILICATE-Si		
						µg at. per litre					
			range	mean	s.d.	range	mean	s.d.	range	mean	s.d.
B2	77	1									
B2	77	2	47.9-55.5	51.7	2.7						
B4	77	1	37.1-43.0	41.0	1.9	1.10-1.25	1.18	0.05	10.1-10.8	10.4	0.22
B4	77	2	33.3-38.8	36.8	1.5	1.50-1.69	1.61	0.06	8.50-10.8	9.94	0.79
B7	77	1	8.9-21.3	16.8	3.7	0.38-0.66	0.56	0.08	<0.05-0.49	0.26	0.13
B7	77	2	7.4-17.3	13.5	2.6	0.28-0.69	0.56	0.11	<0.05-0.59	0.41	0.18
B9	77	1	28.4-32.5	30.1	1.3	1.24-1.33	1.28	0.03	4.56-8.43	5.96	0.98
B1	78	1	33.1-43.7	40.1	2.5	0.79-1.39	1.08	0.21	5.70-10.5	8.89	1.21
B1	78	2	31.6-40.4	35.8	2.7	1.16-1.76	1.42	0.17	7.08-14.6	11.7	2.47

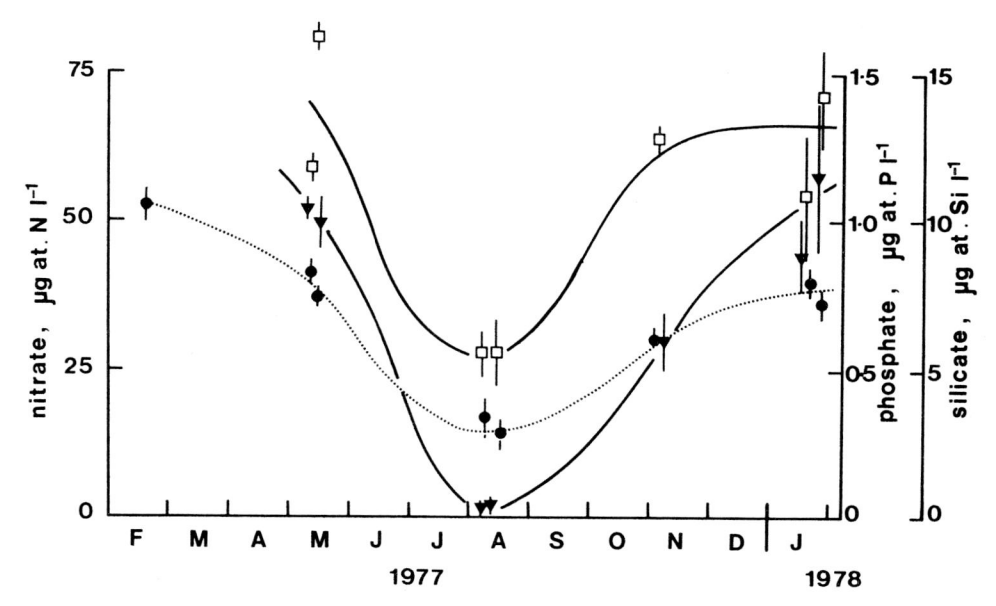

Figure 28.5. Mean concentrations of nitrate (closed dots), phosphate (open squares) and silicate (closed triangles) in the outer Swansea Bay grid. Bars correspond to ± 1 standard deviation about the mean.

linearly with salinity within the salinity range 25-35°/oo. These relationships are indicative of conservative, mixing-dominated behaviour. In August (Cruise B7/77), however, the three nutrient-salinity relationships display pronounced curvature indicative of *in situ* removal during primary production. The salinity range corresponding to values found within the grid is indicated in Fig. 28.6. It can be seen that the Bristol Channel waters contributing to the grid are intermediate between the estuarine waters consistently showing apparent conservative nutrient behaviour and coastal waters in which seasonal nutrient cycling is dominant. With the maintenance of relatively high nitrate and phosphate concentrations throughout

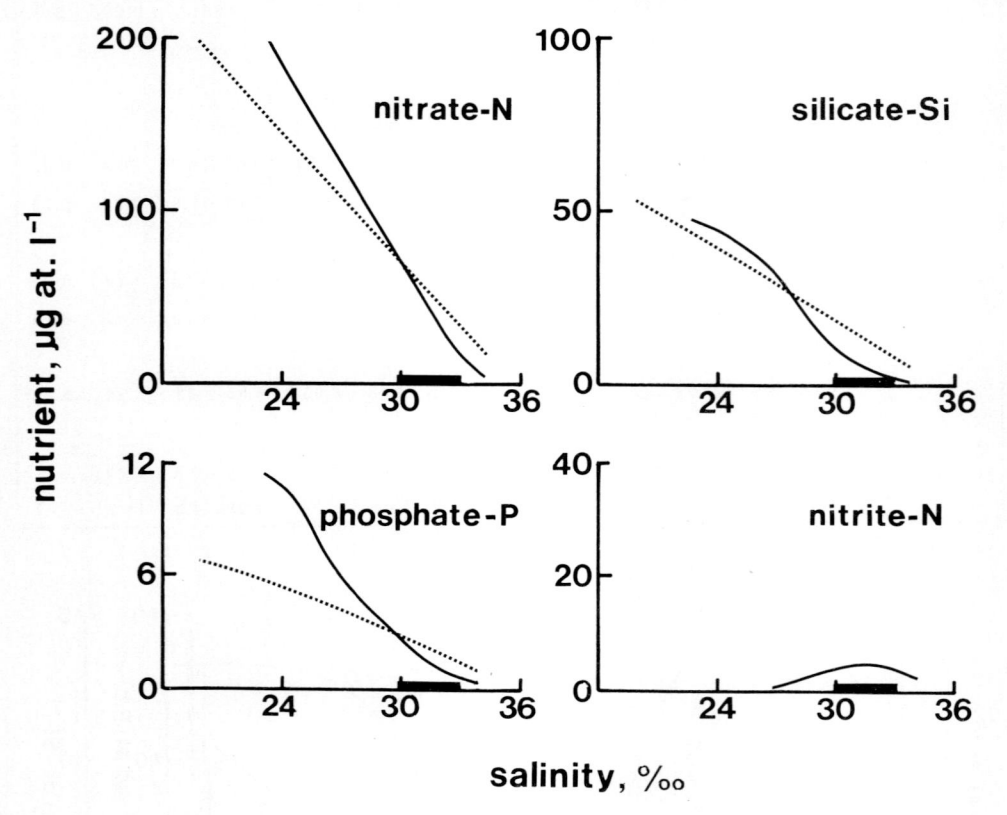

Figure 28.6. Nutrient-salinity relationships in the Central Bristol Channel region during the summer cruise B7/77 (full lines) and winter cruise B1/78 (broken lines). The bars on the salinity scale define the range of salinities encountered within the outer Swansea Bay grid throughout this investigation.

the summer, this intermediate region appears to be potentially the most productive zone of the Bristol Channel/Severn Estuary system.

Within the outer Swansea Bay grid, nutrient concentrations will be determined by inputs both from the central Bristol Channel waters and from the local coastal zone, and modified by *in situ* processes therein. However, prior nutrient utilisation in the offshore waters contributing to the grid must account for an appreciable part of the total summer depletion of nutrient levels within the grid shown by Fig. 28.5. The proportionately greater summer depletion of silicate relative to nitrate and phosphate in the central Bristol Channel waters is reflected in the concentrations during Cruise B7/77, when silicate was generally very low and undetectable (<0.05 µg-at Si/l) at a few stations. Thus silicate depletion approached 100%, whereas nitrate and phosphate were reduced to some 30-40% of their winter concentrations.

Appreciable short-term changes in mean nutrient concentrations within the grid are sometimes apparent when comparing results obtained for transects only 4 or 5 days apart. Particularly noticeable is the increase in mean phosphate concentration from 1.18 to 1.61µg-at P/l between the two transects of Cruise B4/77, when the mean nitrate and silicate concentrations remained in close correspondence. The mean phosphate and silicate concentrations were significantly higher for the second transects of the grid during Cruise B1/78; in contrast, the mean nitrate concentration was slightly lower. These differences are not accountable for by the corresponding changes in mean salinity, if it is assumed that linear nutrient - salinity relationships exist. It appears therefore that localised "water-types", differing in their degree of localised coastal influence, are prevalent in the region and are responsible, to some extent, for the within-grid variability noted above. The T-S relationships encountered during Cruise B1/78 support this conclusion.

The variability of nutrient concentrations within the grid is at most times, but particularly during low-nutrient summer conditions, greater than is deducible from a consideration of the salinity range encountered within the grid and the variability in the concentrations of nutrients in central Bristol Channel waters of that salinity range. For example, coefficients of variation of the concentrations of nitrate, phosphate and silicate for the second grid of Cruise B7/77 were 19%, 20% and 44%, respectively. This within grid variability is considered in detail elsewhere (Mantoura and Morris, this Chapter, Part II; Joint, Chapter 29).

Nitrite, which was below detection level (<0.1µg-at N/l) during winter in the central Bristol Channel and grid regions, was detectable in these regions during the August Cruise B7/77, and was presumably being produced by excretion during nitrate assimilation and/or by oxidative regeneration of reduced nitrogen compounds. During this summer cruise, nitrite and ammonia represented an appreciable proportion of the inorganic nitrogen pool. Within the grid 0.5-1.1µg-at N/l of nitrite were found, compared with 7-21µg-at N/l present as nitrate. Ammonia was not determined during this investigation but we have since measured 0.2-0.8µg-at N/l of ammonia in the eastern part of the grid in August, 1979.

Chlorophyll a, Phaeopigment and Dissolved Organic Carbon

Data for chlorophyll a, phaeopigment and dissolved organic carbon are summarised in Table 28.5.

Apart from the summer Cruise B7/77, the ranges of chlorophyll a concentrations encountered within the grid on each occasion are quite similar although the mean values clearly demonstrate a seasonal variation in standing crop of photosynthetic organisms. The considerably higher levels, and greatest overall range, found during Cruise B7/77 coincided with the lowest nutrient levels. When data from other IMER cruises are included, it becomes apparent that chlorophyll a concentrations increased sharply during May/June (after Cruise B4/77 was completed) to elevated but variable concentrations (0.7 to >7µg/l) showing considerable spatial heterogeneity throughout the summer, and reduced to characteristic winter levels (0.5 - 1.0µg/l) during October. Generally, phaeopigment concentrations varied inversely with chlorophyll a. Mean winter concentrations within the grid were close to 1µg/l but were reduced by about half during the productive summer period, May to October.

Dissolved organic carbon concentrations within the grid were quite variable, ranging overall from 0.59mgC/l to greater than 4.4mgC/l, although concentrations greater than 1.4mgC/l were only rarely encountered. The abnormally high values (>4.4

TABLE 28.5. Range, Mean and Standard Deviation about the Mean of Dissolved Organic Carbon, Phaeopigment and Chlorophyll a Concentrations at the Sixteen Outer Swansea Bay Stations for Each Grid Transect.

CRUISE AND GRID		DISSOLVED ORGANIC CARBON mg per litre			PHAEOPIGMENT µg per litre			CHLOROPHYLL a µg per litre		
		range	mean	s.d.	range	mean	s.d.	range	mean	s.d.
B2 77	1	0.59-1.15	0.69	0.17						
B2 77	2	0.62-1.15	0.85	0.19						
B4 77	1	0.87-1.32	0.96	0.13	0.4-1.5	1.03	0.36	0.7-1.5	0.97	0.22
B4 77	2	0.79-1.25	1.03	0.12	0.3-2.0	1.08	0.47	0.2-0.7	0.42	0.14
B7 77	1	1.08-1.49	1.22	0.12	0.3-1.1	0.62	0.23	0.7-1.7	1.09	0.32
B7 77	2	0.88-1.38	1.09	0.13	0.1-1.5	0.45	0.36	1.2-7.2	2.17	1.50
B9 77	1	1.06-1.95	1.29	0.27	0.6-1.2	0.86	0.18	0.6-1.0	0.70	0.13
B1 78	1	0.93->4.4	1.65	1.09	0.5-1.9	1.09	0.47	0.2-0.8	0.52	0.25
B1 78	2	0.72-1.41	1.03	0.17	0.7-2.1	1.14	0.42	0.4-1.5	0.74	0.29

mgC/l) were determined on only one occasion, at a few stations of the first grid of the winter Cruise B1/78. Levels elsewhere during that transect were not abnormally high and elevated concentrations were not encountered during the second grid, sampled after an interval of 4 days. A sporadic pollution incident appears to be the most plausible explanation. Apart from these unusual results, dissolved organic carbon levels indicate a small but significant seasonal variability. Mean grid values varied between 0.69 and 1.03mgC/l during the winter cruises, whereas means of 1.22 and 1.09mgC/l were found during the summer Cruise B7/77. These results are in general agreement with those of Mantoura and Mann (1977) who recorded 0.8 to 1.5mgC/l, during an extensive study of the central Bristol Channel region in July 1976, for salinities comparable to those prevalent in the grid. Higher concentrations in this range were attributed to exudation by phytoplankton and the results of zooplankton grazing, although elevated concentrations of dissolved organic carbon detected in the Swansea Bay region appeared to arise from shoreline emission.

Turbidity

Suspended solid concentrations within the grid showed a marked seasonal variability: a range of 10-100mg/l with a mean of 25mg/l was measured during the winter Cruise B2/77, whereas a range of 3-18mg/l with a mean of 7mg/l was found during the August Cruise B7/77. Generally, these levels are similar to those in the central Bristol Channel waters of the same salinity range, although higher levels within the grid, apparently arising from local sources, particularly to the southeast, were sometimes evident.

DISCUSSION

It is evident, from the high levels and restricted ranges of salinity encountered during this seasonal investigation, that the water within the grid represents only the later stages of the mixing between coastal waters of the Swansea Bay region with offshore central Bristol Channel water. Riverine and industrial inputs to the Bay appear to be extensively dissipated within the Bay by an anticlockwise eddy circulation of tidal currents. Consequently, the quality of the grid waters is to a large extent determined by processes characteristic of the bulk of the Bristol Channel. However, coastal influences can be discerned by a detailed comparison of water quality within the grid with that of Bristol Channel waters of equivalent salinity. For example, T-S relationships within the grid differ from those characteristic of the central Bristol Channel due mainly to the differential heating and cooling of inshore waters.

Mean nutrient concentrations within the grid show seasonal fluctuations similar to those evident for the central Bristol Channel, thereby largely reflecting their common source together with the absence of pronounced coastal influences. However, local influences are evident in the considerable variability of nutrient concentrations within the grid, relative to the simultaneous salinity variations, which is most noticeable during low-nutrient summer conditions. This heterogeneity is indicative of incomplete mixing of localised "water-types" and/or heterogeneity in the propagation of *in situ* processes within the grid. Primary production processes, both within and external to the grid appears to be the dominant seasonal controlling factor. Apart from silicate, inorganic nutrients are maintained in relative abundance within the grid at all times, indicating a potential for continuous high productivity during the spring and summer months. During the summer (Cruise B7/77), extensive silicate depletion occurred over part of the grid whereas silicate was present in appreciable quantities throughout the central Bristol Channel waters. Such conditions can be expected to induce spatial heterogeneity in the phytoplankton species composition of the region.

Primary production rates of 1.0 and 1.0, 4.7 and 5.3 and 34.3 and 28.6μgC/m^2/hr were measured at the mid-point of the grid during the first and second traverses of Cruises B2/77 (January), B2/77 (May) and B7/77 (August), respectively. Mean levels of chlorophyll *a*, phaeopigment and dissolved organic carbon within the grid all vary seasonally in general accord with these production rates and the mean nutrient data although, as for the nutrients, within-grid variability is high, particularly during summer.

It is evident from these results, that any pronounced effects of natural, industrial and domestic inputs to Swansea Bay must be mainly confined within the inner Bay region characterised by the distinctive eddy circulation patterns. In the outer Bay, mean water quality characteristics differ only to a small extent from those prevalent in waters of equivalent salinity present in the central Bristol Channel, although small-scale heterogeneity in water quality is enhanced. This within-grid variability, and its causes, are considered in detail elsewhere (Mantoura and Morris, this Chapter, Part II).

ACKNOWLEDGEMENTS

Although we are indebted to many of our colleagues at IMER for help with the collection and analysis of samples during this work, the assistance given by A.J. Bale and R.J.M. Howland warrants individual credit. This work forms part of the Estuarine Ecology Programme of the NERC and was partly supported by the Department of the

Environment under Contract No. DGR 480/48.

REFERENCES

Abdullah, M.I., Dunlop, H.M., and Gardner, D. (1973). Chemical and hydrographic observations in the Bristol Channel during April and June, 1971. *J. mar. biol. Ass., U.K., 53,* 299-319.

Brewer, P.G., and Riley, J.P. (1965). The automatic determination of nitrate in seawater. *Deep-Sea Res., 12,* 765-772.

Chan, K.M., and Riley, J.P. (1965). The automatic determination of phosphate in seawater. *Deep-Sea Res., 13,* 467-471.

Collins, K.J., and Williams, P.J. Le B. (1977). An automated photochemical method for the determination of dissolved organic carbon in sea and estuarine waters. *Mar. Chem., 5,* 123-141.

Collins, M., Ferentinos, G., and Banner, F.T. (1979). The hydrodynamics and sedimentology of a high (tidal and wave) energy embayment (Swansea Bay, Northern Bristol Channel). *Estuar. & Coast. Mar. Sci., 8,* 49-74.

Froelich, P.N., and Pilson, M.E.Q. (1978). Systematic absorbance errors with Technicon Autoanalyser II colorimeters. *Water Res., 12,* 599-603.

Mantoura, R.F.C., and Mann, S.V. (1979). Dissolved organic carbon in estuaries. *In:* Severn, R.T., Dinely, D., and Hawker, L.E. (Eds.). *30th Symposium of the Colson Research Society, Bristol, 1978.* Scientechnica, Bristol, 279-286.

Morris, A.W., Howland, R.J.M., and Bale, A.J. (1978). A filtration unit for use with continuous autoanalytical systems applied to highly turbid waters. *Estuar. & Coast. Mar. Sci., 6,* 105-109.

Stainton, M.P. (1974). Simple, efficient reduction column for use in the automated determination of nitrate in water. *Analyt. Chem., 46,* 1616.

Strickland, J.D.H., and Parsons, T.R. (1972). A manual of seawater analysis, 2nd. edition. *Bull. Fish. Res. Bd., Can., 125,* 203pp.

II. SPATIAL HETEROGENEITY AND PROCESSES

R. F. C. Mantoura and A. W. Morris

Natural Environment Research Council, Institute for Marine Environmental Research, Prospect Place, The Hoe, Plymouth, PL1 3DH, Devon, UK

ABSTRACT

The spatial distributions of salinity, temperature, nitrate, phosphate, silicate dissolved organic carbon and chlorophyll a within a 60km^2 rectangular grid in lower Swansea Bay are discussed in terms of water circulation, inputs and biological processes. Increased winter run-off into Swansea Bay markedly affects the orientation of isohalines and associated chemical isopleths, and is accompanied by a clockwise rotation of the saline intrusion from the west in summer to the south in winter. A 2-4km wide plume of chemically distinct water originating from the anticlockwise eddy in upper Swansea Bay, protrudes around Mumbles Head and into the northern sectors of the grid. This results in pronounced north to south gradients of chemical anomalies which are associated with biological depletion of nutrients and production of organic matter in summer, and freshwater discharge in winter.

KEYWORDS

Spatial heterogeneity; Circulation; Nutrient chemistry; Dissolved organic carbon; Pollution; Swansea Bay; Bristol Channel.

INTRODUCTION

Chemical processes in coastal and estuarine waters are considerably more complicated than in open ocean systems in that there are a greater number of controlling factors and mechanisms in operation. This can give rise to both sharp concentration gradients and fluctuating or non-steady state distribution of chemicals in these regions. Swansea Bay is no exception, since the waters are subject to a multiplicity of distinct inputs from rivers, domestic and industrial outfalls, all discharging into a tidally asymmetric system. The purpose of this Chapter, is to extend the general chemical description provided in Part I (Morris and Mantoura, this Chapter) to include the spatial variability of salinity, temperature, nutrients and dissolved organic carbon in order to resolve those processes that most strongly affect the chemistry in Swansea Bay. (For data on inputs to the Bay see Chapter 20).

The physiographic description of the survey area, tidal regime, experimental procedures, cruise details and general seasonal variation of mean concentrations have already been introduced in Part I. Shown in Fig. 28.7 are the principal geographic

454   R. F. C. Mantoura and A. W. Morris

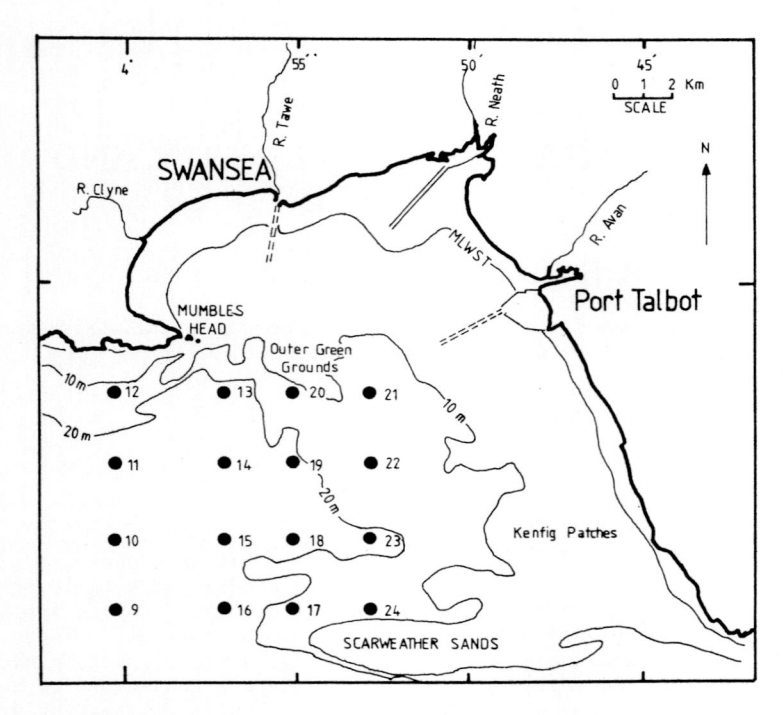

Figure 28.7. Location of study area within Swansea Bay showing grid stations
     Nos. 9-24, bathymetric controus (10m intervals below chart datum;
         Admiralty Chart 1179), and principal rivers draining into
                              Swansea Bay.

and bathymetric features which will be referred to later.

The spatial resolution of chemical determinands is set by, on the one hand, the overall response times of the various continuous monitoring systems (salinity (S), temperature (T)),turbidity and *in vivo* chlorophyll fluorescence, and on the other hand the sampling frequency of discrete chemical measurements (nutrients and dissolved organic carbon (DOC) auto analysers) in relation to the cruising speed of the research vessel (8-10km/h). Fine scale variability in the order of 30m for S, T, turbidity and fluorescence, and ∿300m for nutrients have been recorded and these have proved very useful in cross correlation studies (see Joint, Chapter 29). However, this resolution is incompatible with mixing and tidal excursion scales (0-10 ± 1km) which must be invoked to correct for the non-synoptic sampling and is thus of limited use in observing regional variability. In order to obtain compatability of scales, the continuous and discrete data bases were reduced to a discrete format based on a 4 x 4 grid of 16 stations (see Fig. 28.7).

     RESULTS

The distribution of S, T, nitrate (NO_3), phosphate (PO_4), silicate (Si) dissolved organic carbon (DOC) and chlorophyll a in surface waters of Swansea Bay is shown in Figs. 28.8-28.12 as a series of concentration isopleths contoured by linear interpolation between 16 grid stations, and where possible, cross checked against continuous records.   Five surveys were selected (B7/77/1, B2/77/2, B9/77, B1/78/1 and

B1/78/2; see Table 28.2, Morris and Mantoura, this Chapter, Part I) from a total of nine since these exhibit most clearly the seasonal changes in the chemistry of Swansea Bay. With the exception of the 20 January 1978 Survey (B1/78/1), all these surveys were carried out during flood tide conditions (see Table 28.2, Morris and Mantoura, this Chapter, Part I).

Salinity and Temperature

The annual average salinity of the Swansea Bay grid is 32.34 ± 0.63°/oo, which represents an estuarine mixture comprising of 91.7% sea water (using Celtic Sea of 35.28°/oo, 1 June 1977, as marine end-member) and 8.3% fresh water. However, this overall mean does not take into account the considerable heterogeneity in salinities resulting from varying inputs and circulation patterns which are encountered within the 60km^2 sampling grid.

The spatial distribution of S and T in Swansea Bay are illustrated in Figs. 28.8a-28.12a as overlapping sets of isohaline and isothermal contours, both of which show marked seasonal changes in value and orientation. In August, the salinity range is only ∼0.3°/oo but the isohaline distribution (Figs. 28.8a and 28.9a) is sufficiently well resolved to indicate a westerly intrusion of saline waters (>33.1°/oo) running parallel to the South Gower coastline, and a south easterly source of lower salinity waters (<32.8°/oo) originating from central Bristol Channel. The abrupt change in curvature of the 33.0°/oo isohaline coincident with the 18.0°C isotherm in Fig. 28.8a points to a northerly input of isohaline but warmer waters from Mumbles Head. With increasing influence fresh water run-off from rivers within Swansea Bay during autumn and winter months, the dominant fresh water input switches from a weak south easterly input, to the northeast in autumn (Fig. 38.10a) and eventually to a strong winter input from north-northeast (Fig. 28.11a and 28.12a). This is accompanied by an anticlockwise rotation in the direction of the saline intrusion from the west in the summer to the southwest in autumn (Fig. 28.10a) and veering to the south in winter surveys. The east-west running isohalines in the southern sectors of the winter grids converge with the main Bristol Channel system of isohalines which assume a northwest-southeast orientation in the winter (unpublished IMER data).

The distribution of temperature within Swansea Bay is complex and contrasts with normal offshore waters in that the isotherms do not relate in a simple or consistent way with the isohaline distribution (see also Part I, this Chapter). Both parallel (positively and negatively correlated) and orthogonal distribution patterns may coexist within the same grid (e.g. Figs. 28.8a, 28.9a and 28.11a). These are due to the combined effects of (1) seasonal thermal inversion in the T/S structure typical in temperate estuaries, and (2) the mixing of different water masses. For example, in the sectors of the grid in which isotherms and isohalines are parallel, temperature is found to increase with salinity in the winter and decrease with salinity in the summer. All surveys show a temperature anomaly in the northwest pointing to the input of a plume of Swansea Bay water from around Mumbles Head. This Mumble Head plume is particularly accentuated during ebb tide and low water surveys (e.g. Fig. 28.11a). Thus the use of T/S relationship in Swansea Bay is restricted to qualitative assignment of water types and cannot be used as a quantitative oceanographic tool.

Nutrients

The seasonal variation in mean concentrations of nutrient salts (NO_3, PO_4, SiO_2) in Swansea Bay follows the classical pattern of low concentrations in the summer and high concentrations in winter, and these have been discussed in Part I of this chapter. However, examination of nutrient distributions within the survey grids (Figs.

Figures 28.8. - 28.12. show the distribution of:

(a) salinity (°/oo, -) and temperature (°C, ---).
(b) nitrate (µg-at - NO_3 - N/l).
(c) phosphate (µg-at - PO_4 - P/l).
(d) silicate (µg-at - Si/l).
(e) dissolved organic carbon (mg DOC - C/l).
(f) chlorophyll a (µg/l)

in the Swansea Bay grid for five surveys. A list of tidal states corresponding to all the surveys is to be found in Table 28.2. in Part I of this Chapter.

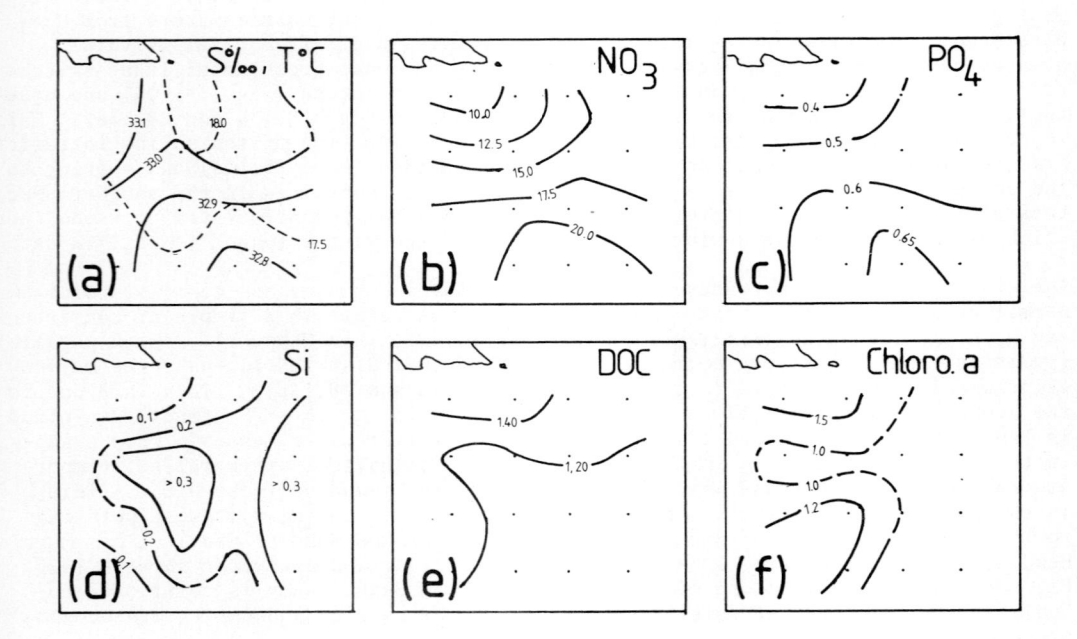

Figure 28.8. Survey date 7 August, 1977 (B7/77/1).

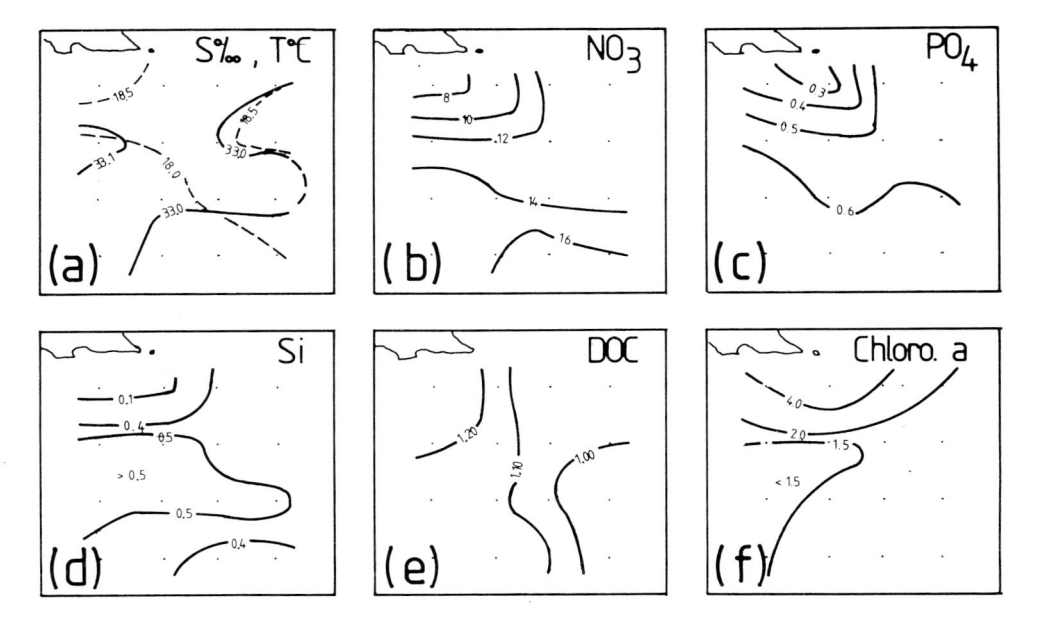

Figure 28.9. Survey date 12 August, 1977 (B7/77/2). For explanation see Figure 28.8.

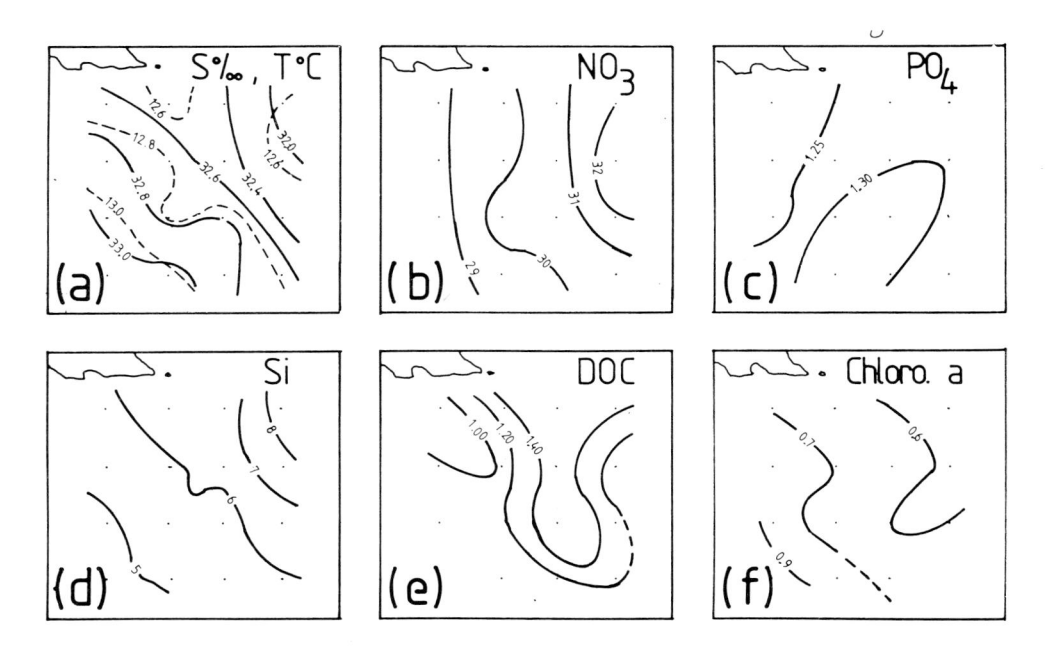

Figure 28.10. Survey date 4 November 1977 (B9/77). For explanation see Figure 28.8.

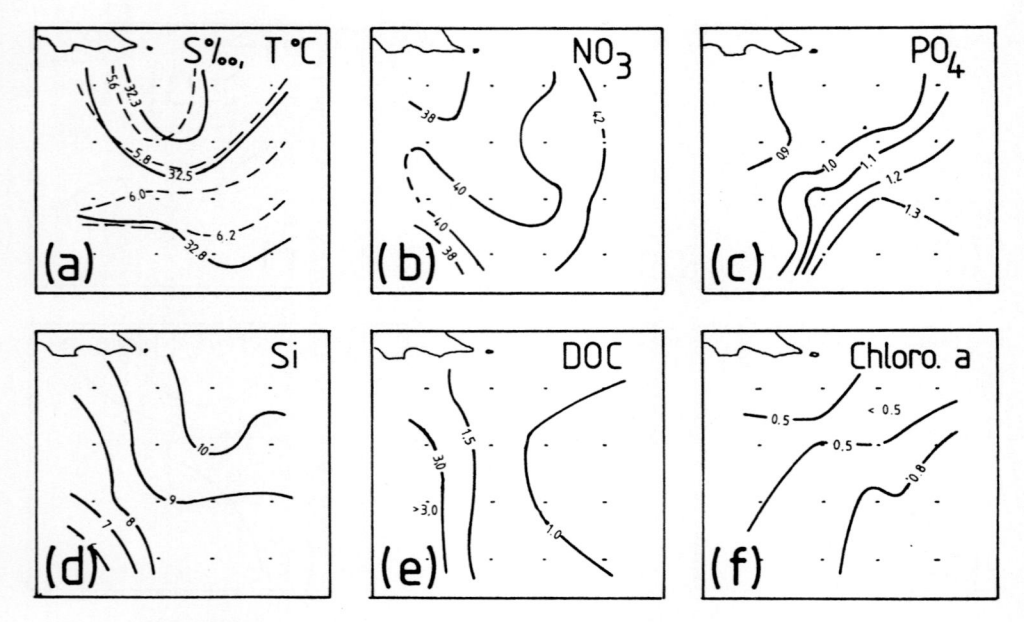

Figure 28.11. Survey date 20 January, 1978 (B1/78/1). For explanation see Figure 28.8.

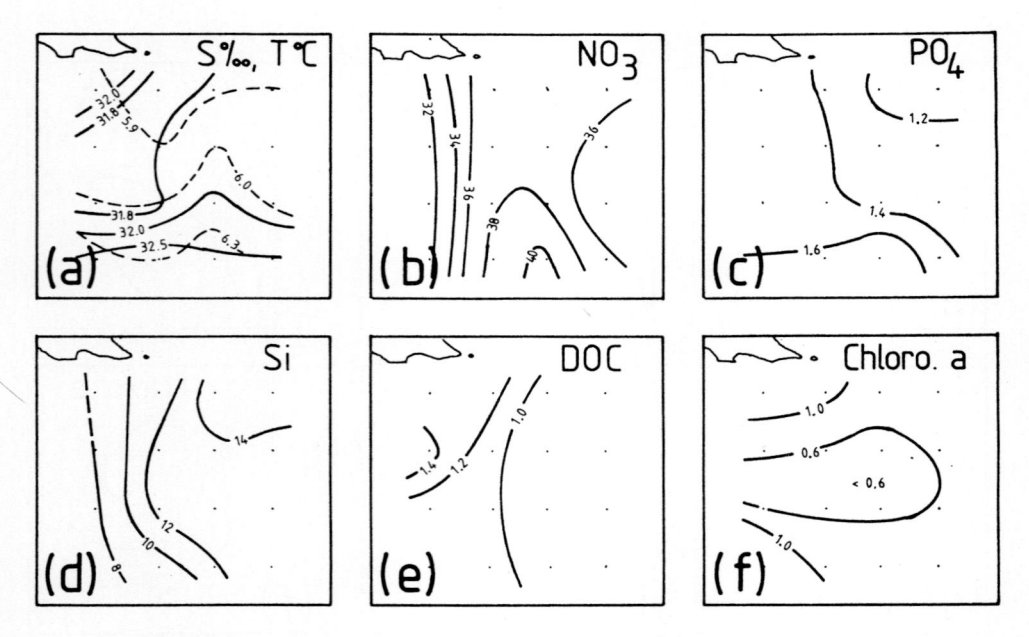

Figure 28.12. Survey date 24 January, 1978 (B1/78/2). For explanation see Figure 28.8.

28.8b, c, d. - 28.12b, c, d) shows unusual properties specific to Swansea Bay, namely, that the three nutrients do not necessarily covary but can display significantly different distributions and are on these occasions controlled by different processes. The concentration pattern of NO_3, PO_4 and Si in the two August surveys is dominated by a north westerly inflow of a highly productive (see chlorophyll a distributions Figs. 28.8f and 28.9f), warm and nutrient-depleted plume of water originating from Mumbles Head, balanced in the southeast by a supply of Bristol Channel waters relatively richer in nutrients. Thus, in the northern half of the August grids, nutrient isopleths covary showing overall depletion of NO_3, PO_4 and Si, along a southeast-northwest transect, of 58.2%, 42.4% and 100%, respectively, on 12 August and increasing to 59.5%, 56.9% and 100%, respectively, on 17 August. In addition, the relative depletion of Si coincident with the high chlorophyll a patch in the southwest, suggest that there are qualitative differences between this phytoplankton population and that associated with the Mumbles Head plume.

In contrast, the November orientations of the NO_3 and Si isopleths (Fig. 28.10b, d) are parallel to and negatively correlated with the isohaline distribution showing the gradually dominating effect of increasing run-off from rivers in Swansea Bay on the nutrient distribution. The slight negative skewness between the NO_3 and salinity isopleths in the northwest corner of the grid is associated with a localised input of NO_3 - poor waters from Mumbles Head. This effect is more pronounced during the low water survey of 20 January 1978 (B1/78/1; Fig. 28.11b), where the plume of low NO_3 concentration extends to the centre of the grid. The November PO_4 isopleths show little or no variation ($\sim$3%) with salinity, and assume an orthogonal configuration with respect to the NO_3 and Si isopleths.

Much larger PO_4 gradients ($\sim$30% variation) are encountered in both January surveys (Figs. 28.11c and 28.12c), with the higher concentrations (1.3 - 1.6µg-at. - PO_4 - P/l) associated with a southeasterly input of Bristol Channel waters, and low concentrations in the north and northeast from PO_4 poor waters originating from upper Swansea Bay. An opposite distribution is observed for Si with high concentrations coinciding with low salinity region in the northwest sectors of the grid, and orthogonality of Si isopleths with respect to isohalines in the southwest where mixing with waters from Central Bristol Channel assumes greater importance.

Dissolved Organic Carbon and Chlorophyll

Precise determinations of DOC are required in order to observe the small ($\pm$ 0.1mg DOC-C/l) but important changes associated with biological and chemical processes. During summer months, high DOC concentrations (>1.3mg DOC-C/l) are found in the biologically productive, nutrient depleted waters in the northwest regions of the grid, with the DOC isopleths showing strong correlation with concomitant distribution of chlorophyll a (see Figs. 28.8f and 28.9f). However, the mid grid tongues of high DOC (1.8mg DOC-C/l) evident in the November survey (Fig. 28.10f) and the particularly high concentrations (>3.5mg DOC-C/l) found in the westernmost stations of the 20 January survey (Fig. 28.11f) do not appear to be related to other chemical and biological features of the Bay.

DISCUSSION

Chemical data presented in this and a companion paper (Morris and Mantoura, this Chapter, Part I) clearly show that the hydrodynamics and chemistry of lower Swansea Bay are affected by but distinct from those of the Bristol Channel. In a general chemical survey of the Bristol Channel, Abdullah et al. (1973) showed that elevated values of water temperature and integrated UV absorbance were associated with specific Swansea Bay effects. More recently, Collins et al. (1979) reported detailed results of hydrodynamic and sedimentological investigation of Swansea Bay. They concluded that the protrusion of Mumbles Head into an essentially rectilinear tidal current system of the Bristol Channel results in tidal assymetries within Swansea Bay causing an anticlockwise eddy system in the western half of the Bay, and an area of divergence between the eddy and the main channel flow. In particular, Eulerian observations of tidal currents at Mumbles Head show a swift southerly ebb current lasting 9 hours of the tidal cycle and attaining maximum speeds of 1m/s, and alternating with short lived (3h) flood currents of maximum speed of 0.03m/s (Collins et al., 1979).

Our salinity and temperature distributions clearly show this Mumbles Head flow as a 2-4km tongue of water extending 4-5km in a south-southeasterly direction at low water conditions. This plume invariably shows up as the dominant hydrochemical feature in the north-western regions of all grids. Based on these and on the seasonal changes in the orientation of isohalines and isotherms a simple 3 component circulation model (Fig. 28.13a, b) can be proposed to explain the distribution of chemical constituents within the grids.

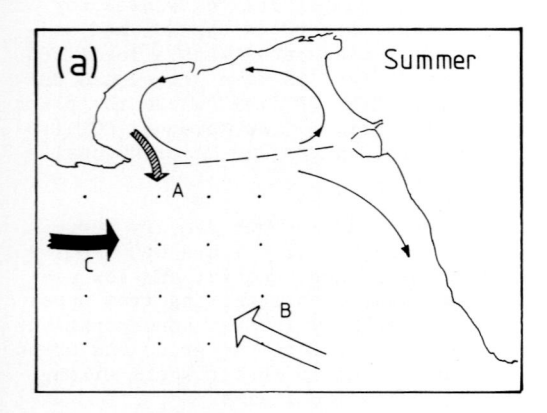

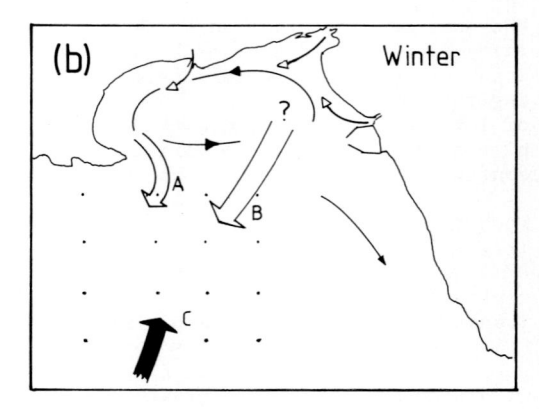

Figure 28.13. Simplified summer (a) and winter (b) circulation models for lower Swansea Bay constructed from the isohaline distribution in Figs. 28.8-28.12. The models consist of three advective components (A) Mumbles Head plume (B) Central Bristol Channel Input and (C) saline intrusion. Component (B) in winter circulation model corresponds to fresh water influence originating from within Swansea Bay. Residual currents: (⟶); river run-off: (⟶); current divergence zone: (-------).

In summer months the Mumbles Head outflow (current A in Fig. 28.13a) is isohaline with the saline flood stream from the west (current C in Fig. 28.13a) because the anticlockwise eddy system receives little or no freshwater contributions in the summer from rivers draining into Swansea Bay. Under these conditions, salinity cannot be used to resolve the Mumbles Head plume, but the associated chemical and thermal anomalies can clearly delineate the plume (see Figs. 28.8 and 28.9). The main freshwater influence is from a south-easterly input of intermediate salinity (32.8 °/oo) water from the Bristol Channel (current B, Fig. 28.13a). During winter, increased run-off in Swansea Bay not only reduces the salinities and temperature at Mumbles Head (see for example, Fig. 28.11a) but also produces a strong secondary advection of Swansea Bay water in the northeast (Fig. 28.10a; current B in Fig. 28.13b).

The mean volume (V) and approximate residence time (T) of waters in upper Swansea Bay enclosed in the south by an east-west line from Mumbles Head to Port Talbot is

Chemistry: Spatial Heterogeneity and Processes

$4.3 \times 10^8 m^3$ and ~ 3.5 days, respectively (Dr. R. Uncles; IMER, *pers. comm.*). Under average combined run-off conditions (Q) of $2.5 \times 10^6 m^3$/day for rivers Avan, Neath, Tawe and Clyne (Stoner, *pers. comm.*), it is possible to calculate the overall salinity depression caused by complete mixing of these waters using the relationship: $\Delta S = S_i \times Q \times T/V$ where S_i is the initial salinity - say $33.24°$/oo (annual average for grid). A salinity depression ΔS of $0.68°$/oo is obtained which is comparable to the salinity gradients for Mumbles Head plume during the low water (Fig. 28.11a) survey in January 1978.

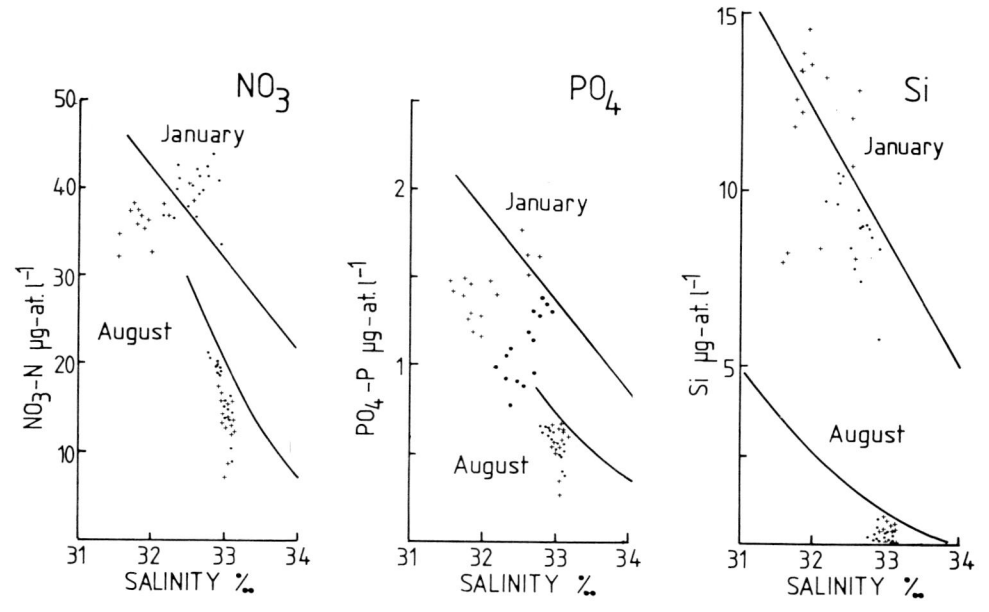

Figure 28.14. The relationship between salinity and the concentrations of nitrate, phosphate and silicate in the surface water of Swansea Bay (Grids 1(.) and 2(+)) and of the Bristol Channel (———). 12, 17 August 1977 (B7/77/1,2) and 20, 24 January 1978 (B1/78/1,2).

The nutrient distributions in Swansea Bay (Figs. 28.8-28.12) result partly from mixing with Bristol Channel waters and partly from *in situ* chemical and biological processes specific to Swansea Bay. These two components can be resolved through nutrient-salinity regressions of the Swansea Bay data in relation to the Bristol Channel. Shown in Fig. 28.14 are the NO_3, PO_4 and Si - salinity correlations for Swansea Bay as well as the corresponding curves for the Bristol Channel (see Morris and Mantoura, this Chapter, Part I). The concentrations of the three nutrients in the Bristol Channel consistently show an inverse relationship with salinity suggesting these are to a large extent influenced by run-off into the Channel (see also Abdullah *et al.*, 1973). Biological utilisation of the nutrients during productive summer months results in the non-conservative curvature in the salinity relationships and accounts for most of the concentration decreases observed in the August survey. At the same time, the nutrients in Swansea Bay are even further depleted, falling well below the Bristol Channel curves, and in the case of NO_3 and PO_4 still displaying a negative correlation with salinity. The vertical deviation of the Swansea Bay concentrations from the Bristol Channel relationship is referred to as the negative concentration anomaly (ΔNO_3 for NO_3, etc.) and provides a quantitative estimate of those processes leading to the supply or utilisation of nutrients in Swansea

Bay. Shown in Fig. 28.15 are the nutrient anomaly isopleths for 12 August 1977 and 20 January 1978 surveys. These anomaly isopleths clearly show the dominant effect of the Mumbles Head plume on the generation of negative NO_3, PO_4 and Si anomalies in August, with Si showing particularly good correlation with concurrent chlorophyll a distribution (Fig. 28.8f). The nutrient anomalies covary in the north-

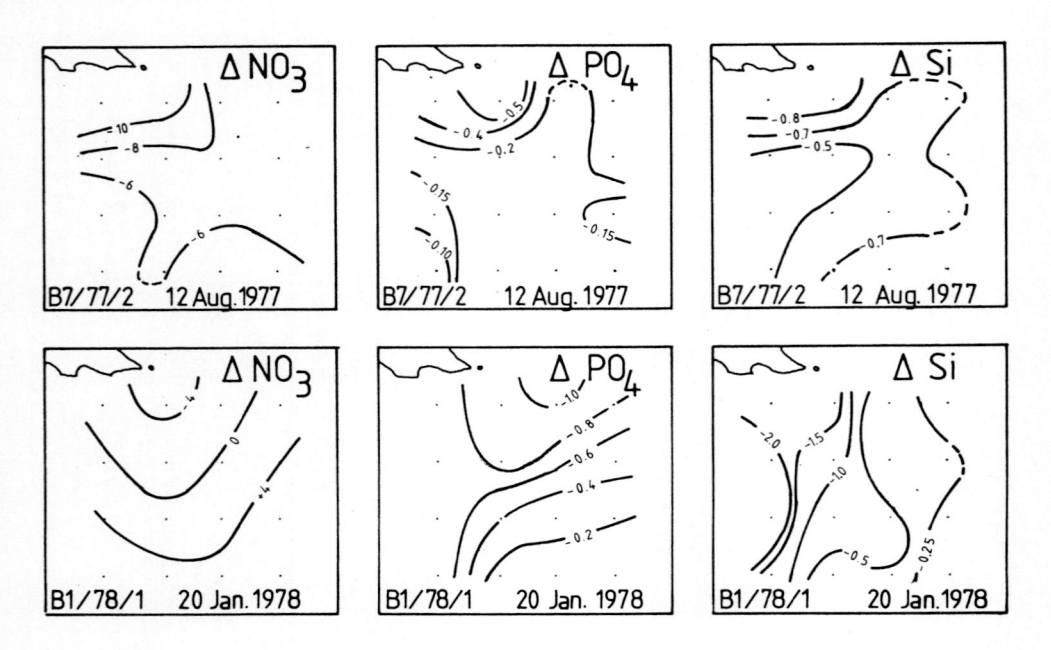

Figure 28.15. The distribution of nitrogen, phosphorous and silicon anomalies, (ΔNO_3, ΔPO_4, ΔSi; µg at/l) in the surface waters of Swansea Bay Grid; 12 August 1977 (B7/77/2) and 20 January 1978 (B1/78/1).

west region of the August grids with a mean anomaly ratio ($\Delta N : \Delta P : \Delta Si$) of 27.5: 1.0:>2.5, which is indicative of a silicon-selective biological removal mechanism. However this ratio can covary considerably throughout the grid. For example, $\Delta Si: \Delta P$ ratios change from 5.4 at Station 9 to <1.9 at Station 13 where silicon is depleted below the detection limit (0.10µg - at. Si/l). Thus depletion stoichiometry of silicon is not constant with respect to NO_3 and PO_4, is the main contributor to the variability in the anomaly ratios, and is possibly the growth limiting element. The phytoplanktonic production required to generate an average nitrogen anomaly of $\Delta N = -10$µg-at. N/l at Mumbles Head over the 3.5 day residence time of water in upper Swansea Bay is equivalent to $0.23 g/m^3/day$ (assuming an atomic C:N ratio of 6.63, Richards (1965), and complete mixing). This is approximately twelve times the average primary production reported by Joint (Chapter 29) for the 20m water column at the centre of the grid and suggests that the utilisation of nutrients is by benthic diatoms located in the shallow and intertidal regions of upper Swansea Bay (see also Chapter 30).

In winter, the Si-salinity distribution for Swansea Bay is similar to that of the Bristol Channel, but both NO_3 and PO_4 appear to be positively correlated with salinity, with PO_4 concentrations falling well below the Bristol Channel line. This is caused by the freshwater inputs into Swansea Bay being overall less concentrated in NO_3 and, particularly, in PO_4 relative to Bristol Channel inputs. This also provides an explanation for the constancy in PO_4 concentration over the large salinities encountered in the November survey (Fig. 28.10c), in terms of a transition state between a negative PO_4 - salinity correlation in summer and positive PO_4 - salinity relation in winter. It is noteworthy that despite the fact that 24.2% of the total PO_4 discharged into Swansea Bay is via the domestic sewage outfall at Mumbles Head (see Chapter 20), a negative ΔPO_4 of -1.0µg-at. PO_4-P/l is still maintained in the Mumbles Head plume.

The DOC concentration in Swansea Bay may not only reflect biological production gradients (as in the August surveys) but may also be used as a non specific tracer of organic pollution. It is likely that the elevated levels of DOC in the central regions of the November grid coincide with the dumping of dredged organic rich sediments, and the high DOC values in January correspond to a flood tide transport of sewage sludge originating from Avonmouth and Newport and dumped in the central Bristol Channel. The molecular composition and consequences of these anthropogenic patches of DOC are as yet unknown.

ACKNOWLEDGEMENTS

The authors wish to thank many colleagues at IMER for help with the collection and analysis of samples during work, the assistance given by A.J. Bale and R.J.M. Howland warrants particular credit. Thanks are also due to the Master, Officers and crew of the R.R.S. *John Murray*. This work forms part of the Estuarine Ecology Programme of the NERC and was partly supported by the Department of the Environment under Contract No. DGR 480/48.

REFERENCES

Abdullah, MI., Dunlop, H.M., and Gardner, D. (1973). Chemical and hydrographic observations in the Bristol Channel during April and June 1971. *J. mar. biol. Ass. UK.*, *53*, 299-319.

Collins, M., Ferentinos, G., and Banner, F.T. (1979). The hydrodynamics and sedimentology of a high (tidal and wave) energy embayment (Swansea Bay, Northern Bristol Channel). *Estuar. Coast. Mar. Sci.*, *8*, 49-74.

Richards, F.A. (1965). *In:* Riley, J.P., and Skirrow, G. (Eds.). *Chemical Oceanography*. Vol. 1, Academic Press, 197-225.

DISCUSSION VI

Britton: Could I ask either Dr. Morris or Dr. Mantoura whether their measurements were all surface measurements and, if so, whether they took account of wind drift of the water during each group of measurements?

Mantoura: All our measurements were sampled at a depth of 1.5 - 2m using submersible pumping system. It is possible that the consistently low surface concentrations of phosphate encountered in north-western sectors of the grid indicate that we missed the significant subsurface inputs of phosphate from the Mumbles Head outfall (See Humphrey et al., Chapter 27). However, we haven't carried out vertical profiling at Mumbles Head to confirm this. In the centre part of the grid, however, we carried out several vertical profiles and no significant gradients in salinity, temperature or any other determinand were observed. We did not investigate the effect of winds on the distributions shown.

Wakefield: Do you, when you're sampling, make sure that you obtain a sample from the Tawe or other main freshwater inputs into the Inner Bay area, because you seem to be implying that the silica and phosphate is quite often due to freshwater input.

Mantoura: What I've done is not something which is recommended by estuarine chemists. I've taken the limited salinity range that we've worked in, and extrapolated the data to the freshwater end member. For the winter phosphate data, this procedure shows that the phosphate concentrations (or rather input) is about 1/2 to 1/3 what it is in the Bristol Channel, which is approximately 10µg-atoms per litre and this agrees with the phosphate input data that was provided by Chubb et al (Chapter 20). We can't do the same thing for nitrate, because of complications with ammonia. We have done some ammonia measurements on more recent cruises, but we can't confirm the source of nitrate as being the nitrification of ammonia as was suggested earlier on.

Collins: Could I provide information about that north westerly area. Here there is both an anticlockwise eddy, which possibly brings round the water from the River Tawe, and a sewage effluent outfall (at Mumbles). Your surveys were carried out mostly during the flood tide, so sewage discharge shouldn't effect your stations; but certainly, on the ebb, there is the possibility of influence from the sewage outfall there.

Mantoura: Some of the surveys, in January and May, 1977 were low water surveys and we have four possible ways of detecting the effects of outfalls - the three nutrient concentrations and, more particularly, in the DOC concentration. The DOC concentration in the outfalls is 100-1,000 times the concentrations we are reporting in this grid. We do occasionally see high DOC, and this may well be associated with dilution of the outfall water.

Collins: May I clear up a comment about the physical complexity of flow in the vicinity of Mumbles Head.

At Mumbles Pier, the flood flow lasts about 3 hours and the ebb flow for 9 hours. We have deployed a series of current meter stations in the littoral zone (within the Bay) and have confirmed this flow asymmetry and the existence of an anticlockwise eddy. 3 hours of flood water enter the Bay which is then overtaken by the eddy. As a result of this circulation pattern, water comes around the Bay; this water can be distinguished from the effluent from the outfall at Mumbles Head. This flow poses a slight problem, in that we might assume that water coming down the River Tawe is picked up in that eddy and comes round the embayment.

Another confusing factor to water masses here is the outfall at Mumbles, which was originally designed to operate on the ebb. As we saw in Mr. Borthwick's results (Chapter 24), the effluent does tend to move a short distance offshore and then drift alongshore, so this whole area here is affected by effluent dispersing from the outfall at Mumbles. Now there was a time and there have been times, when this effluent was discharged at the wrong time within the eddy system in Swansea Bay, but Dr. Stoner has now convinced us that it is discharged on the ebb. The *effluent disperses down the Gower coastline at a fairly high rate.*

The above discussion demonstrates that there are two systems and I hope that this helps to clear up any problems, or maybe even adds to the confusion. There are two separate systems: one is the natural physical system whereby the eddy is developed, within which waters from the Tawe and sand, raised in suspension from the intertidal zone, is transported by easterly winds; the other is this dispersion of material from Mumbles, which is dispersed subsequently along the coastline.

<u>Mantoura</u>: *Could I comment on the contribution of the Tawe to this anticlockwise gyre. Our chemical evidence suggests that it does, because we see a depleted phosphate plume coming round Mumbles Head into our sampling grid. This is in agreement with the phosphate concentration in terms of the overall input of phosphate given by the W.W.A. (Chapter 20). How wide is this plume that comes around Mumbles Head and is the outfall discharging into the plume?*

<u>Collins</u>: *This could certainly extend the length of the Mumbles Pier and probably a bit further. Outside of Mumbles Head there is a plume of material a couple of hundred meters wide, when sand is picked up into suspension. It is very distinct and confined to the coastal zone. Aerial photographs show that secondary eddies are also associated with the main eddy.*

<u>Cronshaw</u>: *(Subsequent Written Contribution): I would like to make a point about the Mumbles outfall. I have never been convinced that this outfall in itself was a serious pollution threat except over a very localised area. The pollution attributed to this outfall along the Swansea coastline was based on some ignorance of the conditions in the trunk sewer. For instance, the input from the Clyne Valley was always suspect as were the several stormwater overflows discharging to the foreshore at various points between Mumbles and the City Centre. It might be of interest to know that, in 1967, it was certainly true that it was difficult in practice and, under the conditions existing in the trunk sewer at the time, to conform to the timing of discharges from the Mumbles storage tanks as laid down in an Act of 1918. As I now understand the present position, some relief of the trunk sewer has comparatively recently been provided by better surface water arrangement nearer to the City Centre and the Welsh Water Authority have, during this Symposium, stated that they are now able to conform to the statutory conditions. A further point of interest is that I also understand that the bacteriological work carried out by the W.W.A. in the vicinity of the Mumbles outfall has indicated localised pollution effects, which did not suggest that the input from the outfall itself was of such major significance as was originally thought.*

A further point was that various papers at the Symposium had indicated an anticlockwise water movement within the Bay itself and it might well be that the pollution arising from the Tawe and the Neath could be influencing the pollution loads noted along the Swansea coastline including the seaward flow round Mumbles Head.

<u>Jones</u>: *Dr. Mantoura has presented a very nice story about the chemical characteristics of water bodies and he also discusses currents. Is there any reason why these two approaches shouldn't be combined in approaching the chemical work done in the northern parts of the Bay?*

<u>Mantoura</u>: *I don't see why not. One thing that is characteristic of near-shore or estuarine waters, is temperature inversion, that is to say, in summer the freshwater temperature is higher than the seawater and in winter the freshwater is colder. This means that there are marked seasonal changes in salinity/temperature characteristics and therefore S/T studies are only useful in restricted localised short-term circulation studies.*

Certainly the chemical elements measured so far by W.W.A. and our surveys show that some of these constitutents are reasonably good markers for various inputs. Maybe it would be a logical progression to use these markers to try and establish the fate of the freshwater inputs. But for marine inputs, I should emphasise this, the gradients are much too small in chemical concentration in the offshore area of the Bay. South of Mumbles Head, where the summer salinity gradient is much lower, it is very difficult to assign chemical markers. Certainly, chemical markers can be used to solve the water movement problem elsewhere, for example in dye studies.

29. PHYTOPLANKTON PRODUCTION IN SWANSEA BAY

I. R. Joint

Natural Environment Research Council, Institute for Marine Environmental Research, Prospect Place, The Hoe, Plymouth PL1 3DH, U.K.

ABSTRACT

The standing stock of phytoplankton in Swansea Bay in August 1977 was measured by continuously recording the fluorescence due to chlorophyll in a pumped water sample as the ship steamed round a grid of twenty nautical miles. The salinity, temperature and turbidity of the water were also measured continuously and the concentration of nitrate, phosphate and silicate were analysed continuously with an autoanalyser system. The highest biomass of phytoplankton was measured in the shallow, inshore waters to the north of the bay; phytoplankton biomass was positively correlated with water temperature and negatively correlated with water turbidity and with the nitrate, phosphate and silicate concentrations. These plant nutrients were estimated to be removed by phytoplankton in the atomic ratio of 17 N:2 Si: 1 P. The rates of primary production measured on two successive days in the centre of the bay were .41 gCm^2/day and .34 ^2gCm /day.

KEYWORDS

Bristol Channel; Swansea Bay; Phytoplankton production; Temperature; Turbidity; Spatial variability.

INTRODUCTION

There has been considerable, recent interest in the spatial heterogeneity of phytoplankton and zooplankton in the sea and in the factors controlling patchiness over a wide range of spatial scales from centimetres to kilometres. Early studies of spatial variability were often hampered by the use of point sampling and did little more than give a qualitative description of patchiness; it is only comparatively recently that techniques of continuous sampling of water have enabled progress to be made in relating spatial variability in phytoplankton biomass to variations in physical parameters.

One of the first attempts to study spatial variability was by Armstrong and La Fond (1966) who sampled continuously from a research tower and showed that the fluctuations in nitrate and silicate concentration were correlated with changes in water temperature and turbidity. They did not attempt to measure phytoplankton biomass but they attributed most of the turbidity changes to phytoplankton biomass. Platt,

Dickie and Trites (1970) used a more sophisticated statistical treatment, power spectral analysis, to study phytoplankton patchiness but, because they used discrete sampling, they were severely restricted in the range of variability scales that they could study. Using continuous measurements of chlorophyll and temperature, Denman and Platt (1975) presented coherence spectra between chlorophyll $\underline{a}$ and temperature from a number of field situations. All these measurements were made at a single depth but Denman (1976) increased the sophistication of these studies by considering data obtained from multiple-depth horizontal tows; he found high coherence between temperature and chlorophyll when the chlorophyll variance was low and suggested that most of the variance was due to vertical mixing effects. When the chlorophyll variance was high, Denman suggested that the patches were due to high phytoplankton growth rates. Lekan and Wilson (1978) included nutrient analyses in their consideration of phytoplankton patchiness and found that the chlorophyll $\underline{a}$ structure at wavelengths greater than 20km was related to the distribution of ammonia but that at wavelengths from 5 to 20km, physical processes were important in producing the observed structure. All these studies involved measurements from a moving ship but Demers and co-workers (1979) sampled over a Spring tide - Neap tide cycle from a single anchor station in the St. Lawrence Estuary; they found that the chlorophyll distribution during Neap tides was controlled by physical processes but, during Spring tides, with decreased stability of the water column and increased vertical mixing, they found less primary production and less chlorophyll $\underline{a}$ per cell, indicating that the phytoplankton were in a poor physiological state.

From these studies it is clear that phytoplankton distribution is closely related to water temperature changes and to changes in other physical variables such as water turbidity. The present study in Swansea Bay was not designed to look at spatial heterogeneity *per se* because it was assumed that any patchiness would be short lived in such a tidally dynamic area. However, the data obtained in August 1977 show that spatial variability is an important aspect of phytoplankton ecology even in this area.

METHODS

The ship steamed at a constant speed through the water of 6 knots (*ca* 3m/s) round the grid of stations from 9 to 24 (Fig. 29.1) on the 7th and 12th August 1977. On both occasions, sampling began about one hour before low water when the ship was at station 11 on the first day and at station 13 on the second day. Water was sampled from 1 metre depth with a submersible pump at a flow rate of approximately 3 m/s, so sampling most of the horizontal structure of the water column. Samples were taken at only one depth because on previous occasions the water column had been found to be thoroughly mixed. All measurements made on the pumped water supply were recorded continuously. Salinity and temperature were measured with a Plessey 6600T recording thermosalinograph and salinity readings were calibrated against discrete samples which were measured with an inductive bench salinometer. Water turbidity was measured with a Partech Suspended Solids Monitor, calibrated against gravimetrically determined, standard turbidity water. Estimates of phytoplankton chlorophyll fluorescence were made with a Turner model 111 flow through fluorometer; discrete samples of seawater taken at each station were filtered through a glass filter (Whatman GF/C), frozen and subsequently analysed for chlorophyll $\underline{a}$ concentration by the method of Strickland and Parsons (1968). The regression of *in vivo* fluorescence against extracted chlorophyll $\underline{a}$ (Fig. 29.2) was used to convert all fluorescence measurements into chlorophyll $\underline{a}$ concentration. Plant nutrients (phosphate, silicate and nitrate) were analysed by autoanalyser as described by Morris (Chapter 28a). All measurements were recorded on chart recorders and digitized by hand at a fixed time interval of two minutes; this is approximately equal to a reading every 370 metres through the water column.

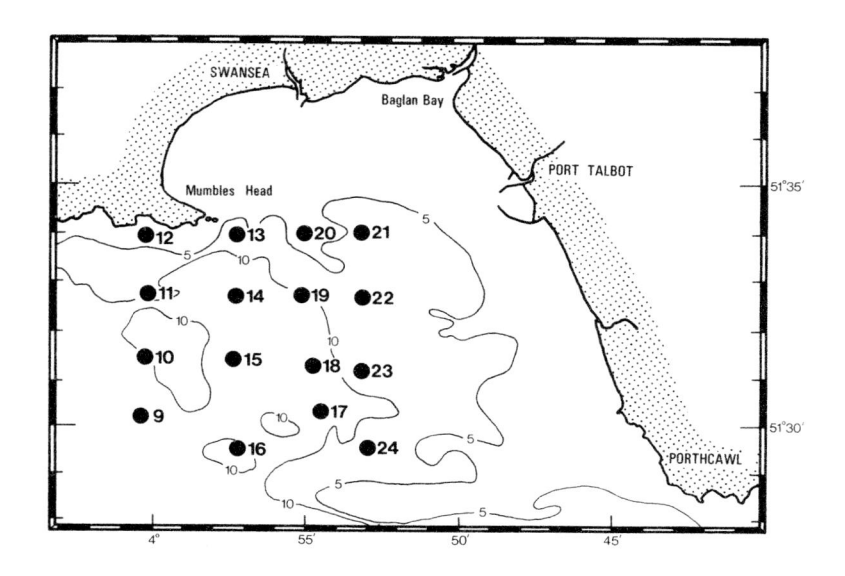

Figure 29.1. Chart of Swansea Bay showing the grid of sampling stations and depth contours in fathoms.

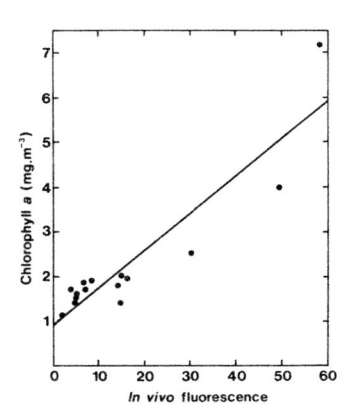

Figure 29.2. Calibration curve of *in vivo* fluorescence and extractable chlorophyll <u>a</u>. The regression is Y = .083X + .907 with a correlation coefficient of .85.

Primary production was measured using the ^{14}C technique of Head (1976) with six neutral density filters to simulate depth in the water column. Water samples were collected from the depths which approximated to the light regime of the neutral density filters and incubated for nine hours with 5μ Ci Na$_2$^{14}CO$_3$ under ambient light conditions, with pumped seawater to maintain the samples at ambient temperature. At the end of the incubation period, the samples were filtered through a .45μ Millipore^R filter under a vacuum of less than 200mm Hg and frozen for transport to the laboratory. The filters were dried to remove unfixed $^{14}CO_2$, dissolved in 2-methoxy-ethanol and toluene scintillant and counted in a liquid scintillation counter, the counting efficiency being determined by the external standard, channels ratio method.

RESULTS

Phytoplankton Standing Stock

Figure 29.3. shows the distribution of chlorophyll a in Swansea Bay on two occasions in August 1977; on the 7th August (Fig. 29.3a), there were two peaks of chlorophyll concentration between station 11 and 13 and again between 16 and 20 where the concentration was about twice that found over the rest of the grid. On the

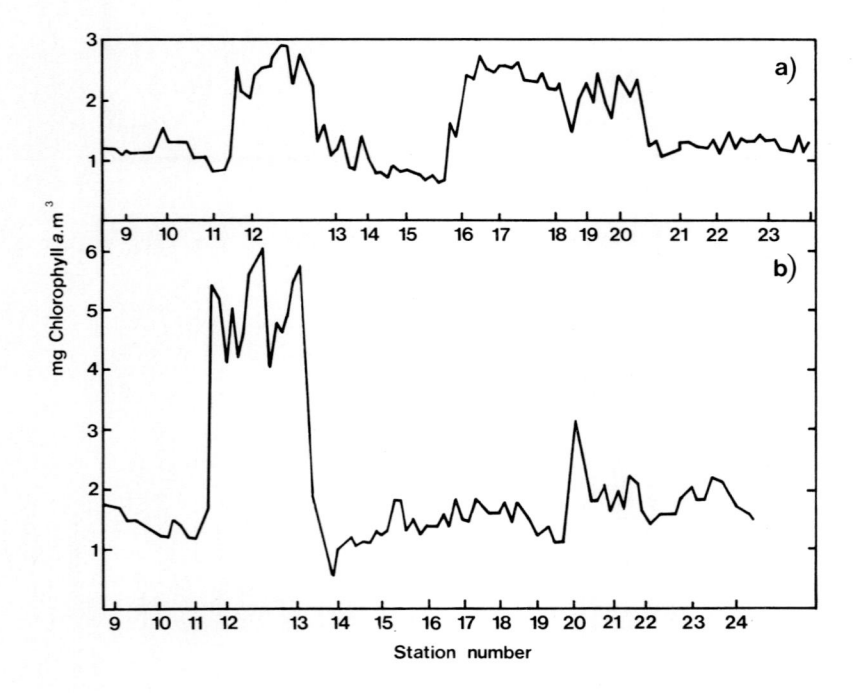

Figure 29.3. The chloropyll a distribution measured, estimated from *in vivo* fluorescence on a) 7th August 1977 and b) 12th August 1977.

12th August (Fig. 29.3b), there was only one peak in chlorophyll a abundance, again between station 11 and 13 where the chlorophyll a concentration was double that found at these stations five days earlier. There were no elevated chlorophyll a levels between station 16 and 19 although there was an increase around station 20.

Physical Variables

The time series data for salinity (Fig. 29.4a) show only small variations round the grid with the lowest values recorded between station 16 and 17 in the south. The temperature record (Fig. 29.4b) also shows a minimum in the same region, with warmer

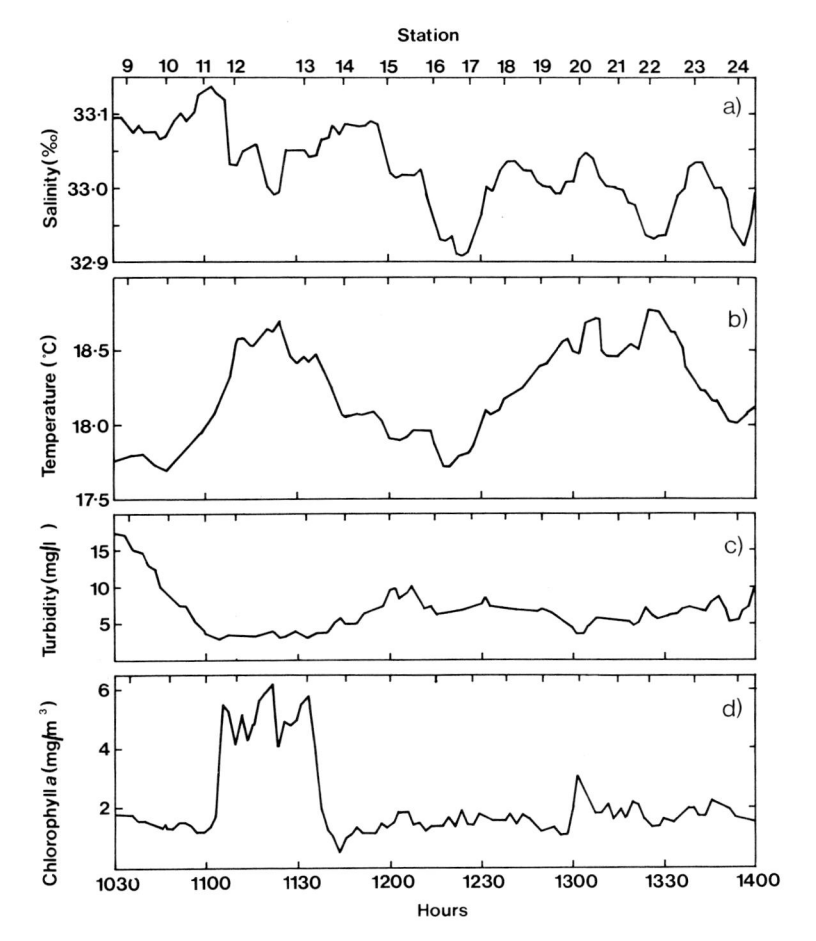

Figure 29.4. The distribution of a) salinity, b) temperature, c) turbidity and d) chlorophyll a measured on 12th August 1977.

water between stations 12 and 13 and between 20 and 22, i.e., within the shallow inshore region (<10.5m). There was also a minimum in water turbidity (Fig. 29.4c) in these shallow waters, especially between stations 11 and 14. The chlorophyll a data from Fig. 29.3b are also plotted (Fig. 29.4d), for comparison with the physical variables.

Chemical Variables

The same chlorophyll a data are plotted on Fig. 29.5a for comparison with the data obtained on nitrate, silicate and phosphate. The nitrate maximum (Fig. 29.5b) was measured at station 16 in the water of lowest salinity in the south of the grid. There was a minimum in nitrate concentration between stations 12 and 13 corresponding to the region with the high biomass of phytoplankton; there was also an obviously lower concentration of nitrate at station 20 where the chlorophyll a level was also high. Similarly, silicate (Fig. 29.5c) was dramatically reduced in concentration in the water with high phytoplankton biomass between station 11 and 14

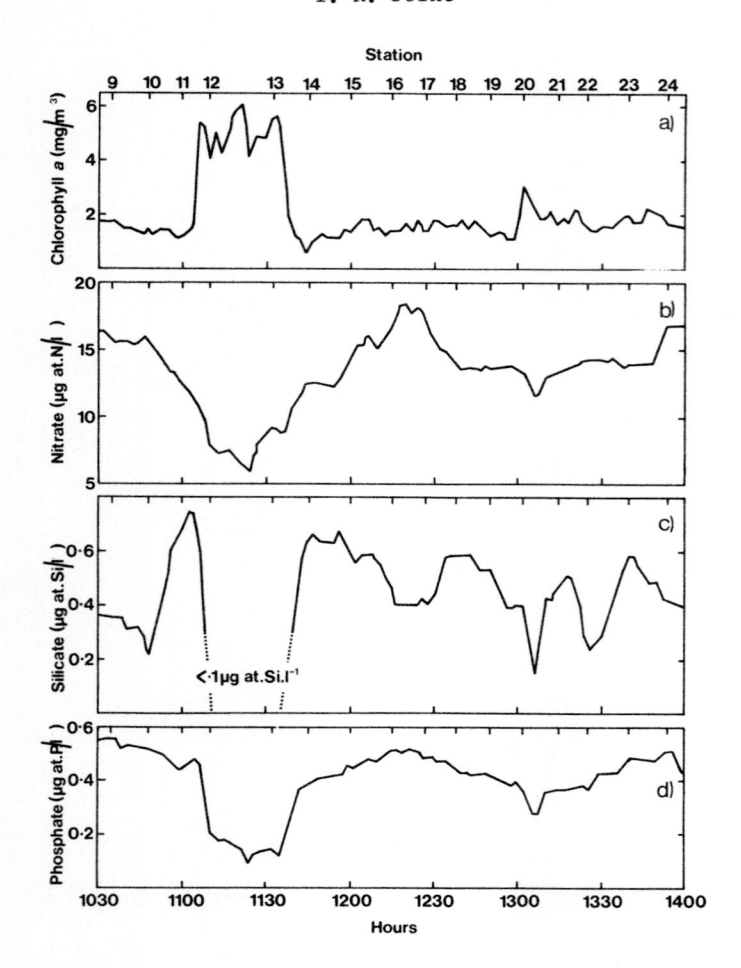

Figure 29.5. The distribution of a) chlorophyll a, b) nitrate, c) silicate, and d) phosphate measured on 12th August 1977.

and at station 20; indeed, the concentration of silicate between station 11 and 14 was less than the limit of detection of the autoanalyser method (<.05 g at Si/l). The low salinity water round station 16 which had elevated nitrate levels had less silicate than the rest of the grid not dominated by the phytoplankton growth. Phosphate (Fig. 29.5d) showed the same feature as nitrate with depletion in the regions of high phytoplankton biomass and an increased level in the low salinity waters round station 16.

Statistical Analysis

The 106 data points for each of the seven sets of data were compared in a multiple regression analysis (Table 29.1). Chlorophyll a was positively correlated with temperature and negatively correlated with turbidity, nitrate, silicate and phosphate; temperature was negatively correlated with turbidity, nitrate, silicate and phosphate and the plant nutrients were highly correlated with each other. In an

TABLE 29.1. Multiple regression of data from complete grid.

	Chlorophyll a	Salinity	Phosphate	Silicate	Nitrate	Turbidity
Temperature	.453	-.232	-.687	-.426	-.642	-.590
Turbidity	-.472	.086	.664	.238	.643	
Nitrate	-.760	-.342	.892	.540		
Silicate	-.711	.142	.699			
Phosphate	-.753	-.058				
Salinity	.048					

Values underlined, significant at $P < .001$.

TABLE 29.2. Multiple regression of data from west half of grid.

	Chlorophyll a	Salinity	Phosphate	Silicate	Nitrate	Turbidity
Temperature	.805	-.403	-.959	-.634	-.969	-.767
Turbidity	-.508	.121	.730	.233	.796	
Nitrate	-.807	.240	.938	.623		
Silicate	-.758	.406	.732			
Phosphate	-.786	.401				
Salinity	-.380					

Values underlined, significant at $P < .001$

TABLE 29.3. Multiple regression of data from east half of grid.

	Chlorophyll a	Salinity	Phosphate	Silicate	Nitrate	Turbidity
Temperature	.173	.351	-.727	-.357	-.807	-.418
Turbidity	-.467	-.010	.468	.445	.309	
Nitrate	-.330	-.778	.683	-.005		
Silicate	-.084	-.438	.391			
Phosphate	-.262	-.352				
Salinity	.331					

Values underlined, significant at $P < .001$.

attempt to remove from the data analysis the influence of the dominant phytoplankton patch, multiple regressions were done on the data from the first (west) half of the grid, which include the high chlorophyll a values, and from the second (east) half of the grid. The correlation coefficients for the west half of the grid, up to station 16 are shown in Table 29.2 and the correlation coefficients for all pairs of data are better than in Table 29.1, with the exception of nitrate and salinity which are no longer significantly correlated. Considering the data from the east half of the grid (Table 29.3), chlorophyll a is still correlated with turbidity but with no other variable, nitrate is negatively correlated with salinity and temperature but positively correlated with phosphate and temperature is negatively correlated with phosphate and nitrate.

Primary Production Measurements.

Measurements of primary production were made at a station in the centre of the grid and on the 10th and 11th August, 1977. The depth of the euphotic zone, assumed to be twice the Secchi disc reading, was between 5 and 6 metres and the temperature at the time of sampling on both days was 17.8°C. On the 10th August, the daily primary production was estimated to be .412 g C/m^2; the chlorophyll a concentration of the water sampled at the beginning of the experiment was .8 mg/m^3. On the following day, the chlorophyll a concentration was 1.0 mg/m^3 and the estimated primary production was .343 g Cm^2/day; the water was slightly more turbid on the second day when the depth of the euphotic zone decreased to 5m.

DISCUSSION

These data demonstrate the power of continuous analysis at sea; features of chemical and biological heterogeneity can be discerned which would be missed by discrete sampling on the stations of the grid. However, it is unlikely that all of the structure of the water column was sampled using these procedures: the flow of water from the pump was at approximately the same rate as the ships speed through the water, but friction in the pump tubing and variable responses of the instruments would result in smoothing of the data. This was a particular problem with the autoanalyser system and the reason that the data presented in this paper were read off at two minute intervals from a continuous recording. Therefore these data are a series of discrete measurements taken at close time intervals and some of the information obtained by the continuous measurement are lost.

The chlorophyll a distribution in Swansea Bay was very different on the two sampling occasions. There was always a high phytoplankton biomass between station 11 and 13 but the concentration doubled over a five day period; the elevated levels present between stations 16 and 20 on the first day had been halved over the five day period. However, there is no reason to believe that the same water mass was present in the bay on the two occasions and these data may not be directly comparable.

The high concentration of chlorophyll a between stations 11 and 13 on the 12th August, occurred in water of elevated temperature and reduced turbidity, i.e., high light penetration. Armstrong and La Fond (1966) ascribed most of the water turbidity off Southern California to phytoplankton cells but in Swansea Bay, the turbidity of the water is due to inorganic particles in suspension; therefore, water turbidity is a contributory factor to rather than the result of phytoplankton production. The peak of chlorophyll a at station 20 is probably part of the same patch of phytoplankton as at station 13 since the water temperature, salinity and turbidity are all approximately the same; the high phytoplankton biomass was confined to the shallow inshore waters of depth less than 5 fathoms.

There was no correlation between chlorophyll a and salinity or between salinity and temperature suggesting complex inputs to Swansea Bay and that *in situ* changes in temperature by insolation are important. There was a significant correlation between salinity and nitrate for the east half of the grid (Table 29.3) suggesting an intrusion of low salinity, high nitrate water into this part of the bay. None of the other nutrients were significantly correlated with salinity.

The most biologically significant correlation occurred between chlorophyll a and nutrients. The high biomass of phytoplankton in the west half of the grid is negatively correlated with all the nutrients (Table 29.2) but there was no correlation in the data from the east of the grid. The high phytoplankton biomass and the resulting reduction in nutrient concentration allowed an estimate to be made of the nutrient removal by phytoplankton. Only the data from station 20 were considered; although there was significant nutrient depletion, the silicate concentration was still detectable and an estimate of silicate removal could be made. The nutrient depletion was calculated by subtracting the nutrient concentration at station 20 from the mean value for the whole grid, excluding the data between station 11 and 13 where the high phytoplankton biomass occurred. Clearly the nutrient concentrations in Swansea Bay are not homogenous, but it is a reasonable approximation for this calculation. The estimated removal of nitrate at station 20 was 2.76µg at N/l, of silicate was .328µg at Si/l and of phosphate was .160µg at P/l. The elemental ratio for the uptake of nutrients by phytoplankton was 17 N:2 Si:1 P which compares with the well known ratio for phytoplankton nitrogen and phosphorus of 106 C:16 N:1 P (Richards 1965). The silicon: phosphorus ratio of 2 suggests that although diatoms were clearly present in the bloom and effectively removed all of the silicon from the water column, they were not the major component of the phytoplankton bloom. Lisitsyn and co-workers (1967) gave a mean silicon : phosphorus ratio of 25 for diatoms with a range of variation of 9 to 70. Clearly, the silicon: phosphorus ratio found in the Swansea Bay phytoplankton bloom was too low for all of the bloom to be diatoms and this must be a mixed bloom; no attempt was made to identify the phytoplankton present to confirm this.

Although there was good agreement with published values for the nitrogen:phosphorus ratio, the ratio of carbon to nitrogen and phosphorus does not appear to hold. The chlorophyll a peak at station 20 was 1.75 mg/m^3 and, assuming the published carbon: phosphorus ratio (Richards 1965) the ratio of carbon to chlorophyll a for the bloom must be 109. This value is too high. Eppley and co-workers (1971) found carbon: chlorophyll a ratios of 90 and 112 only with stationary growth phase phytoplankton cells but a ratio of 46 and 58 with log. phase cells. Antia and co-workers (1963) reported a carbon chlorophyll a ratio of 25 for vigorously growing phytoplankton with excess nitrate but this ratio increased to 60 for unhealthy phytoplankton cells. However, the carbon element of the C:N:P ratio is quite variable and Goldman, McCarthy and Peavey (1979) working with continuous cultures of phytoplankton suggested that the ratio of 106 C:16 N:1 P is only obtained at high growth rates. The uncertainty of the carbon:phosphorus ratio for phytoplankton makes it impossible to determine a meaningful carbon:chlorophyll ratio for this bloom in Swansea Bay but the variable amount of organic detritus in the water of Swansea Bay also precludes a meaningful chemical estimate of phytoplankton carbon.

If it is assumed that the chlorophyll a measured on the two occasions between station 11 and 13 (Fig. 29.3) was due to the same phytoplankton bloom, there was an increase in chlorophyll a of 3 mg/m^3. If the rate of primary production measured in the slightly colder water at the centre of the grid was applicable to this bloom, if a carbon:chlorophyll ratio of 50 is assumed and, if no grazing or dispersion occurred, then the observed increase in chlorophyll a would require about 7 days primary production; there were 4 days of daylight between the two sets of data. It is possible that there was no integrety in the phytoplankton bloom but that the source of the high chlorophyll a values was removal of benthic algae from the intertidal areas of Swansea Bay. However, the observed correlations between chlorophyll a concentration and temperature and turbidity might not then be expected.

It is perhaps surprising if discrete patches of phytoplankton could be maintained over several days in such a complex hydrographic region as Swansea Bay. Collins, Ferentinos and Banner (1979) described the hydrography of the region and found the main tidal stream ran parallel to the Gower coastline with an anticlockwise eddy system in the west half of the inner bay; they also described asymmetry in the duration of the flood and ebb currents with 8 to 9 hours effective ebb. Since low water occurred when the ship was at the same point in the grid on both sampling occasions, the high chlorophyll a values could have been derived from the inshore water of Swansea Bay. However, the hydrodynamic characteristics of Swansea Bay are not known in sufficient detail to distinguish between *in situ* production of a discrete bloom and transport of phytoplankton into the bay from another region.

Continuous sampling has been extremely valuable in describing the patchiness of phytoplankton in Swansea Bay and has given details of the relationships between phytoplankton biomass and water temperature and turbidity which would not have been apparent from discrete sampling. However, it is clear that more data are required from the adjacent sea areas before a definitive description of phytoplankton abundance and distribution can be made.

ACKNOWLEDGEMENTS

I am grateful to P.J. Radford for advice in statistics. This work forms part of the estuarine and nearshore research programme of the Institute for Marine Environmental Research, a component of the Natural Environment Research Council.

REFERENCES

Antia, N.J., McAllister, C.D., Parsons, T.R., Stephens, K., and Strickland, J.D.H. (1963). Further measurements of primary production using a large-volume plastic sphere. *Limnol. Oceanogr.*, *8*, 166-183.

Armstrong, F.A.J., and La Fond, E.C. (1966). Chemical nutrient concentrations and their relationship to internal waves and turbidity off Southern California. *Limnol. Oceanogr.*, *11*, 538-547.

Collins, M.B., Ferentinos, G., and Banner, F.T. (1979). The hydrodynamics and sedimentology of a high (tidal and wave) energy embayment (Swansea Bay, Northern Bristol Channel). *Estuar. Coastal Mar. Sci.*, *8*, 49-74.

Demers, S., La Fleur, P.E., Legendre, L. and Trump, C.L. (1979). Short term covariability of chlorophyll and temperature in the St. Lawrence Estuary. *J. Fish. Res. Bd. Can.*, *36*, 568-573.

Denman, K.L., and Platt, T. (1975). Coherences in the horizontal distribution of phytoplankton and temperature in the upper ocean. *Mem. Soc. r. Sci. Liege, 6th series*, *7*, 19-30.

Eppley, R.W., Carlucci, A.F., Holm-Hansen, O., Kieffer, D., McCarthy, J.J., Venrick, E., and Williams, P.M. (1971). Phytoplankton growth and composition in shipboard cultures supplied with nitrate, ammonia or urea as the nitrogen source. *Limnol. Oceanogr.*, *16*, 741-751.

Goldman, J.C., McCarthy, J.J., and Peavey, D.G. (1979). Growth rate influence on the chemical composition of phytoplankton in oceanic waters. *Nature*, *279*, 210-215.

Head, A. (1976). Primary production in an estuarine environment= a comparison of *in situ* and simulated *in situ* ^{14}C techniques. *Estuar. Coastal Mar. Sci.*, *4*, 575-578.

Lekam, J.F., and Wilson, R.E. (1978). Spatial variability of phytoplankton biomass in the surface waters of Long Island. *Estuar. Coastal Mar. Sci.*, *6*, 239-251.

Lisitsyn, A.P., Belyayev, Yu. I., Bogdanov, Yu. A. and Bogoyavlenskiy, A.N., (1967). Distribution relationships and forms of silicon suspended in waters of the world ocean. *Int. Geol. Rev., 9,* 253-274.

Platt, T., Dickie, L.M., and Trites, R.W. (1970). Spatial heterogeneity of phytoplankton in a near shore environment. *J. Fish. Res. Bd. Can., 27,* 1453-1473.

Richards, F.A. (1965). Anoxic basins and fjords. In: Riley, J.P., and Skirrow, G. (Eds.). *Chemical Oceanography, Vol. 1,* Academic Press, London, 611-645.

Strickland, J.D.H., and Parsons, T.R. (1968). A Practical Handbook of Seawater Analysis. *Bull. Fish. Res. Bd. Can., 167,* 311pp.

30. THE PHYTOPLANKTON OF INSHORE SWANSEA BAY

P. J. Paulraj* and J. Hayward

Department of Botany and Microbiology, University College, Swansea, S. Wales, U.K.
*Vidyalankara University, Kelaniya, Sri Lanka

ABSTRACT

A study of the inshore phytoplankton of Swansea Bay is reported. This includes estimates of net phytoplankton and chlorophyll concentrations, together with the results of the analyses of the sea water for nitrate, phosphate, silicate and salinity, for the period July, 1973 - June, 1974. The interrelationships of these parameters is discussed; emphasis is placed upon the comparatively high levels of mineral nutrients present in the sea water. The relationship of these to the variation in chlorophyll concentration is considered.

KEYWORDS

Swansea Bay; Phytoplankton; Mineral nutrients; Annual variation.

INTRODUCTION

Projecting into Swansea Bay for a distance of c. 60m is Mumbles Pier, which allows access, at its seaward end, to the inshore waters of the Bay. This water differs appreciably in character, appearing to contain much more suspended particulate matter, than is present in deeper water some 200-300m off the end of the Pier. An investigation was carried out in this nearshore water during 1973-74 with the object of following the annual cycle of phytoplankton growth and the variation in the concentrations of mineral nutrients present in the sea water.

MATERIALS AND METHODS

The phytoplankton was sampled by means of a net (180 meshes/inch) to give the net plankton. After collection, the plankton was preserved in Lugol's iodine, concentrated by sedimentation and then counted using the inverted microscope (Utermöhl, 1936); identification of the algae present was carried out, after gentle heating with concentrated nitric acid, using an oil immersion objective on a binocular microscope.

The top 3m of the water column was sampled by means of a plastic tube weighted at one end. The 4-litre sample so obtained was filtered through Whatman GF/C paper and the chlorophyll concentration of the particulate matter retained by the filter paper determined after acetone extraction by the method described by Strickland and Parsons (1968).

A surface sample of water was collected at the same time and this water was used in the determination of the concentrations of nitrate, phosphate and silicate by the methods described in Strickland and Parsons (1968). The salinity of this sample was determined by means of a temperature-salinity conductivity bridge. All sampling was carried out, as far as possible, at approximately 1 hour after full tide and the samples were returned to the laboratory within 30 mins of collection; analyses were begun immediately on return to the laboratory. Sampling was carried out at weekly intervals throughout the period 1973-74.

RESULTS

Figure 30.1 shows the results obtained by the methods used for the analysis of the concentrations of nitrate, phosphate and silicate, together with the results of the salinity determinations. The investigation commenced in July 1973 and was ended in June 1974.

Figure 30.2. shows the results obtained from counting the total number of net phytoplankton organisms sampled. Microscopic examination showed that diatoms dominated the flora throughout the 12-month period and that dinoflagellates were never present in any quantity. The peaks shown in the net plankton are due to the dominance of one or more species of diatoms, *viz:-*

August, 1973.   *Rhizosolenia hebetata.*
September, 1973.   *Cocconeis Spp: Leptocylindrus danicus.*
October, 1973.   *R. hebetata: Cocconeis Spp: Coscinodiscus Spp.*
March, 1974.   *Skeletonema costatum.*
April, 1974.   *R. hebetata.*
May, 1974.   *Biddulphia Spp.*

An examination of Fig. 30.3 also reveals a variation in the concentration of chlorophyll a throughout the period. There are sometimes marked fluctuations in the net plankton and chlorophyll a concentrations from week to week, these being particularly well defined in the autumn and late spring periods of phytoplankton growth. A comparison of net plankton numbers and chlorophyll concentrations shows little, if any, correlation between these two parameters.

DISCUSSION

A striking feature of the chemical analyses is the lack of any seasonal variation in the concentration of nitrate-nitrogen present in the water. This ranged from 15.7 to 19.2µg at NO_3-N/l and compares with 0.36-15µg at/l in the Menai Straits (Ewins and Spencer, 1967), 0.0-10.5µg at/l in the English Channel (Armstrong and Butler, 1960a,b), 0.36-25.2µg at/l in Cardigan Bay (Sykes and Boney, 1970). For the offshore area of Swansea Bay, Abdullah, Dunlop and Gardner (1973) obtained values for NO_3-N concentrations of 1-70µg at/l. The comparatively high level of nitrate-nitrogen maintained throughout the year would appear to be due to a constant level of input from the areas of agricultural land surrounding the Bay.

The range of variation in concentration of phosphate-phosphorus throughout the period of investigation shows an annual fluctuation; the highest concentrations (0.7-1.14µg at/l) occurred during the period November to February with the minimum concentration of approximately 0.25µg at/l occurring during June and July. The range

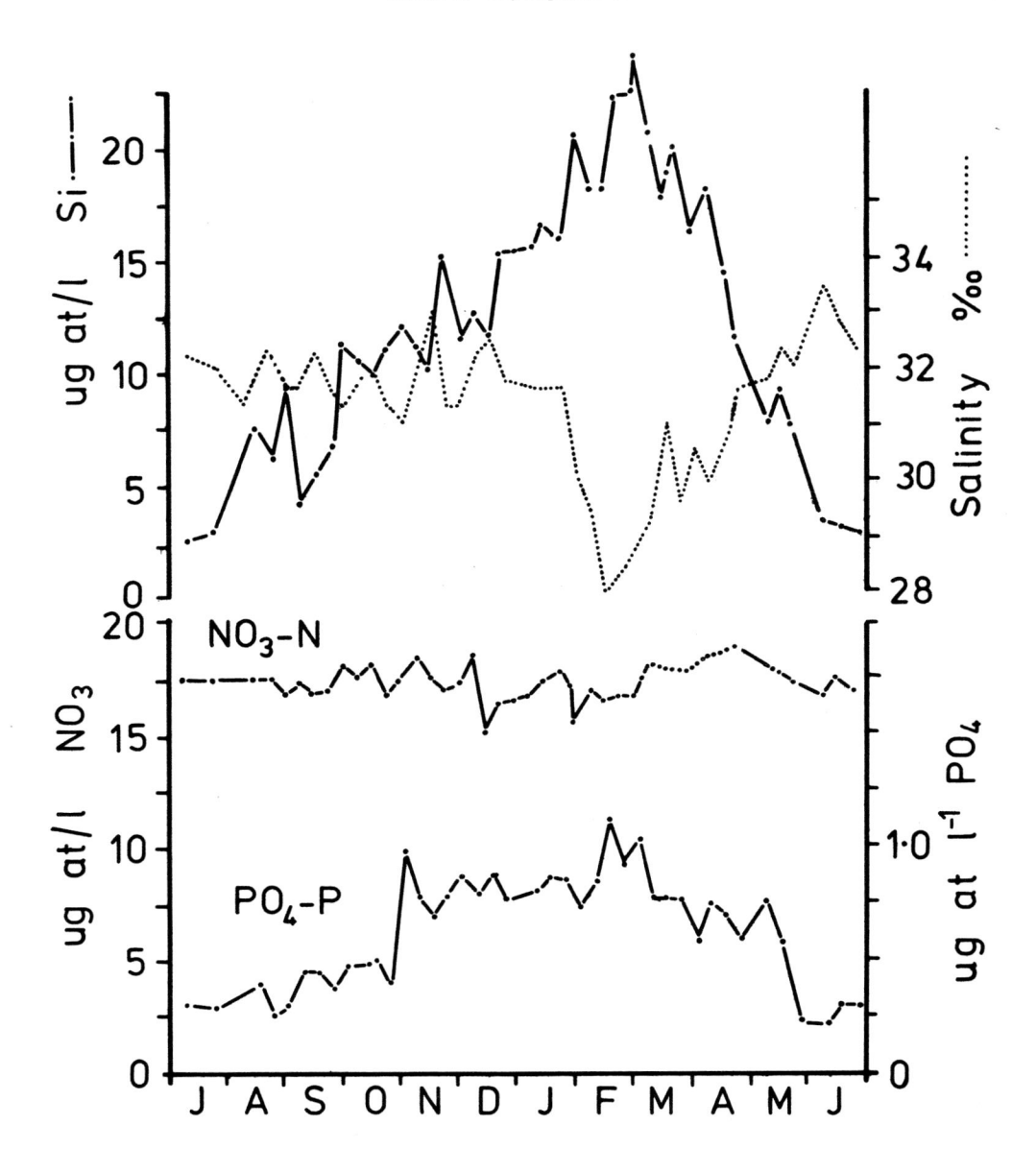

Figure 30.1. Annual variation in concentration of PO₄-P (μg at/l), NO₃-N (μg at/l) SiO₄-Si (μg at/l) and salinity (°/oo) for period July, 1973 to June, 1974.

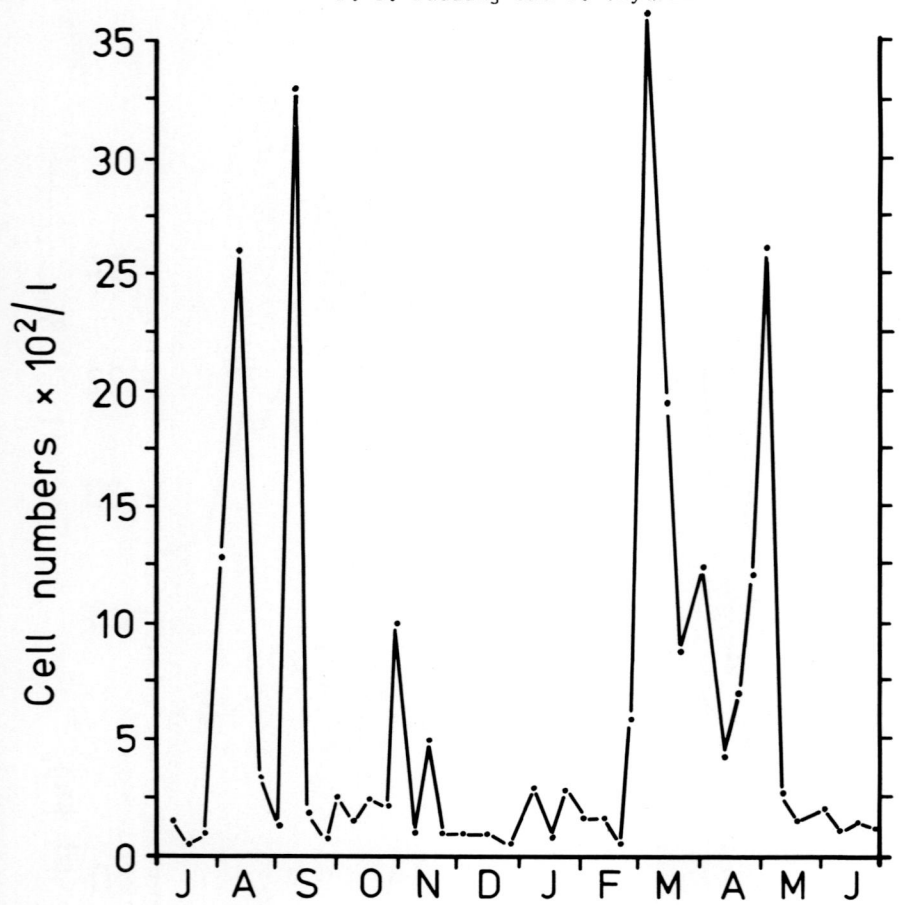

Figure 30.2. Annual variation in net phytoplankton (No. of cells/l).

of concentration of phosphate-phosphorus is of the same order as obtained by the authors mentioned in connection with nitrate.

Silicate-silicon shows a similar annual variation to that exhibited by phosphate-phosphorus, with the maximal concentration of 23µg at/l being attained in February 1974. This maximal concentration is much higher than any reported from similar areas (Armstrong and Butler, 1960a, b; Ewins and Spencer, 1967; Sykes and Boney, 1970) but is exceeded by the concentration of 35µg at/l reported by Abdullah, Dunlop and Gardner (1973) for the Bristol Channel. The minimal concentration of silicate-silicon is of the order of 2.5µg at/l which corresponds with the Menai Straits (2.0µg at/l) reported by Ewins and Spencer (1967) but this minimum is 40 times higher than that reported as the minimum for the English Channel (Armstrong and Butler, 1960a, b).

The variation in salinity exhibits a minimum in February, 1974 of 28.6°/oo. This low value may be explained by the high rainfall exhibited in the previous month and the occurrence of a current gyre in Swansea Bay which tends to circulate water within a comparatively restricted area of the bay and thus allow the retention of the

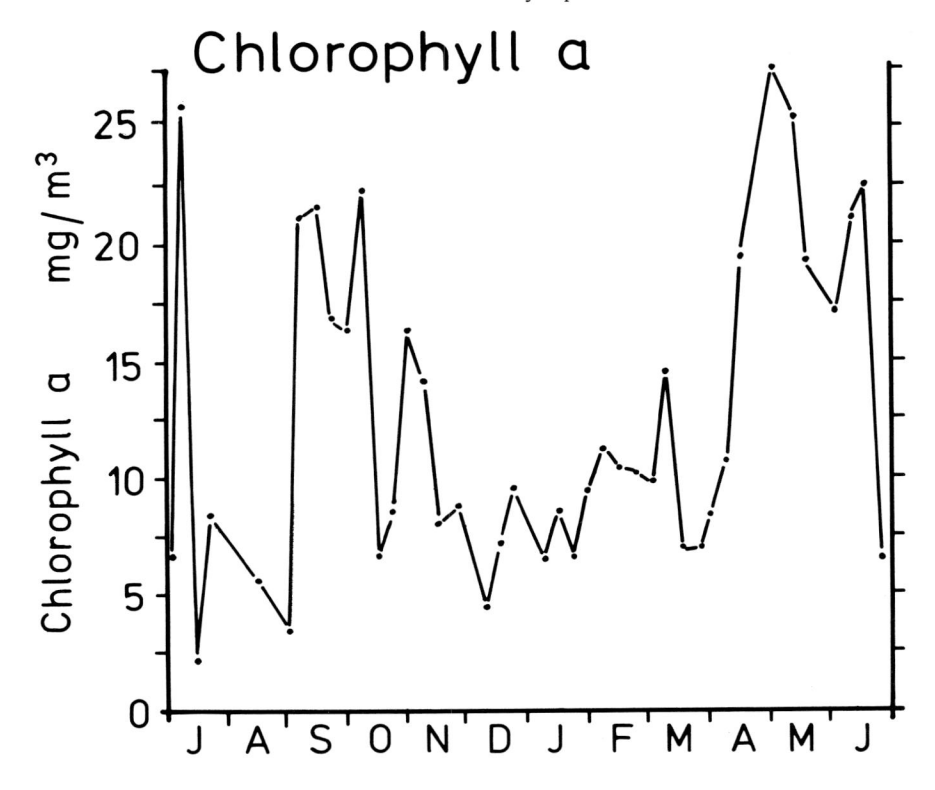

Figure 30.3. Annual variation in chlorophyll a (mg/m³)

increased input of fresh water from the rivers. This minimal salinity corresponds with the maximal concentration of silicate-silicon obtained during the period of investigation and with the maximal concentration of phosphate-phosphorus; this tends to confirm the suggestion of increased input and gyre circulation made above.

A comparison of the annual variation in chlorophyll a concentration and concentration of nitrate-nitrogen shows that there is no correlation between the phytoplankton and nitrate-nitrogen concentration. A puzzling feature of this almost constant nitrate-nitrogen level is this lack of correlation despite growth, sometimes considerable, of the phytoplankton. It would suggest that there is reservoir of nitrate-nitrogen present in the area, possibly on the sea bed, which is in a state of fluctuating equilibrium with that dissolved in the water and that nitrate-nitrogen is not a factor which is limiting phytoplankton activity. The fact that phosphate-phosphorus and silicate-silicon vary on an annual cycle would suggest that it is not input which controls the level of nitrate-nitrogen but possibly bacterial action upon the plentiful supply of organic matter available in the region.

The fluctuation in chlorophyll a concentration from a minimal figure of 1.7mg/m³ in July 1973 to the maximum of 26.6 mg/m³ in May 1974 shows a wide range, which is greater than that shown by Joint in his paper 'Phytoplankton of Swansea Bay (See Chapter 29). The weekly variation in chlorophyll a concentration may be partly explained by the variation in the degree of turbulence in the water due to weather conditions. A microscopic examination of the net phytoplankton during the autumn and spring blooms in particular, shows that the flora contains numbers of benthic diatoms. These organisms normally live on the bottom sediments but are swept up into the water column by the turbulence brought about by stormy weather. There does appear to be some correlation between the occurrence of benthic diatoms in the net phytoplankton and wind conditions prior to their collection. Periods of calm weather result in the occurrence of non-motile diatoms in the plankton.

The comparatively high level of production, as measured by chlorophyll $\underline{a}$ determinations, could result in the inshore area of Swansea Bay acting as a source of supply of phytoplankton organisms for the areas further offshore. The complex current system would tend to distribute these organisms over a wide area, beyond the immediate region of production. In the inshore region the concentration range of chlorophyll $\underline{a}$ in the surface 3m is from 5 - 25 mg/m^3. These figures compare with 0.3 mg/m^3 in the English Channel (Holligan and Harbour, 1977) and 1 - 5 mg/m^3 in the Indian Ocean (Shah, 1973) and serve to illustrate the high chlorophyll $\underline{a}$ concentrations of the inshore area. A comparison of net plankton numbers and chlorophyll $\underline{a}$ concentration reveals little correlation and this suggests that nannoplankton organisms may play a large part in this high level of production.

REFERENCES

Abdullah, M.H., Dunlop, H.M., and Gardner, D. (1973). Chemical and Hydrographic observations in the Bristol Channel during April and June, 1971. *J. mar. biol. Ass. UK.*, *53*, 299-319.

Armstrong, F.A.J., and Butler, E.I. (1960a). Chemical changes in the sea water off Plymouth during 1958. *J. mar. biol. Ass. UK.*, *39*, 299-302.

Armstrong, F.A.J., and Butler, E.J. (1960b). Chemical changes in the sea water off Plymouth during 1959. *J. mar. biol. Ass. UK.*, *39*, 525-528.

Ewins, P.A., and Spencer, C.P. (1967). The annual cycle of nutrients in the Menai Straits. *J. mar. biol. Ass. UK.*, *47*, 533-542.

Holligan, P.M., and Harbour, D.S. (1977). The vertical distribution and succession of phytoplankton in the western English Channel in 1975 and 1976. *J. mar. biol. Ass. UK.*, *57*, 1075-1093.

Shah, N.M. (1973). Seasonal variation of phytoplankton pigments and some of the associated oceanographic parameters in the Laccadive Sea off Cochin. *In:* Zeitzschel, B. (Ed.). *Ecological Studies, 3. The Biology of the Indian Ocean.* Chapman and Hall, London.

Strickland, J.D.H., and Parsons, T.R. (1968). A Practical Handbook of Sea Water Analysis. *Fish. Res. Bd. Canada, Ottawa Bull. 167.*

Sykes, J.B., and Boney, A.D. (1970). Seasonal variation in inorganic phytoplankton nutrients in the inshore waters of Cardigan Bay. *J. mar. biol. Ass. UK.*, *50*, 819-827.

Utermöhl, H. (1936). Uber das umigekehrte Mikroskop. *Arch. Hydrobiol.*, *22*, 643-645.

31. THE ZOOPLANKTON OF SWANSEA BAY

M. J. Isaac

Swansea Museum and Zoology Department, University College, Swansea, U.K.

ABSTRACT

Fortnightly plankton hauls taken from Mumbles Pier, Swansea, for about two years yielded a mixture of euryhaline and oceanic forms. Differences between the two years may be explained in part by the fact that 1971 was warmer than 1970. Some species occurred in most samples, some seasonally, and some irregularly. Copepods showed peak numbers after phytoplankton peaks, but were more diverse in winter than in summer. Offshore sampling showed an increase in numbers of oceanic species further down the Bristol Channel

KEYWORDS

Zooplankton; Larvae; Seasonal variation; Diversity; Swansea Bay; Bristol Channel

INTRODUCTION

There has been very little previous work on the plankton of Swansea Bay, with the exception of Pearce (1967), who compared the plankton of the Queen's Dock (Swansea), Mumbles and Pembrokeshire. He concluded that the plankton at Mumbles was characterised by the presence of euryhaline species, such as the mysid *Mesopodopsis slabberi* and the copepod *Eurytemora hirundoides*, whereas Pembrokeshire was characterised by oceanic forms, such as the euphausiid *Meganyctiphanes norvegica* and the copepod *Centropages typicus*. Rees (1939) worked on the plankton of the upper reaches of the Bristol Channel, mainly off Penarth, and concluded that the low salinity, along with excessive siltiness, was probably the reason for the paucity of the plankton in that area. He also found euryhaline species, such as *Eurytemora*, whilst Dias (1960) found the same species in the areas of reduced salinity in Milford Haven.

The reasons for this investigation were (a) to compile a list of planktonic organisms which can be caught in the surface waters off Mumbles Pier at different times of the year; (b) to see what correlation there might be between the animals present and the variations in sunlight and temperature; (c) to analyse the arthropods present in more detail, and compare them with those present in plankton hauls taken lower down the Bristol Channel in July (see Isaac, 1974).

MATERIALS AND METHODS

For about three hours after high tide, a current of approximately 154cm/s flows from the west of Swansea Bay, under the Mumbles Pier, and out, between the Mumbles Head Islands, into the Bristol Channel. Thus, a plankton net attached to the pier is held open by the current, and the force of the water is so great that, unless the net has a weight attached, it stays in the surface waters. The net used was of medium mesh size, 52 m.p.i., and was left in the water for half an hour during the period between 0900 and 1030, usually commencing at about an hour after a morning high water spring tide. In this way, samples were taken approximately once a fortnight, from December 1969 to January 1972. The position of attachment to the pier was at low water mark of spring tides, so the water would have been approximately 8m deep at the time the net was put in (from Admiralty Tide Tables). The sea water temperature at Mumbles was recorded each time a plankton haul was taken. Sunshine readings were obtained from the Swansea Corporation's meteorological station in Victoria Park (which finished in June 1971) and from the British Steel Corporation's meteorological station at Margam. During the summer tourist season, Mumbles Pier is illuminated and open after dark, so night plankton hauls could be taken at this time. Throughout the rest of the year, the pier is locked up by 1700 hr, and access is impossible.

Unless otherwise stated, the Fiches d'Identification du Zooplancton (Conseil Permanent International pour l'Exploration de la Mer) were used to identify specimens.

RESULTS AND DISCUSSION

As mentioned above, Pearce (1967) found that the plankton of Swansea Bay was characterised by the presence of euryhaline animals. Some of these, such as *Centropages hamatus* and *Mesopodopsis slabberi*, were found to be quite numerous during certain seasons in the course of this study; others, such as *Eurytemora hirundoides*, were found to be extremely rare. Also, certain more oceanic species, such as *Evadne, Podon* and *Muggiaea*, which Pearce never found at Mumbles, were found during this study. It would seem, therefore, that there may have been a change in the water characteristics in Swansea Bay between 1966 and 1970. Certain possible changes in the currents around Gower had been noticed over the previous few years, which had caused clay to be deposited on some of the South Gower beaches, such as Oxwich Bay. A likely explanation is the dumping of silt in the outer reaches of Swansea Bay which was carried out during the excavations for the tidal harbour at Port Talbot. This silt has since disappeared from where it was deposited, and might well have been in part removed to some of the local beaches by water currents (F.T. Banner, *pers. comm.*). Southward (1962) has suggested that most changes in the composition of plankton are due to changes of temperature and changes in the emphasis of water movements, and also states that the temperature of the Celtic Sea and other areas has risen over the past 70 years, which has resulted in southern species, such as *Muggiaea* and *Chthamalus*, to be far more abundant around the southern shores of Britain and Ireland. Thus it is possible that the difference in the plankton at Mumbles between 1966 and 1971-72 was due to such factors as water movement and temperature changes.

It is possible to divide the adult planktonic forms at Mumbles roughly into three groups:- (i) those present more or less all the time, usually with peaks of occurrence; (ii) those which are present at certain seasons only, and (iii) those which occur occasionally, more or less at random. Those species which are usually benthic, but which get lifted into the plankton by the turbulence after rough weather would constitute a fourth category.

Examples of the first group are *Pleurobrachia pileus, Acartia clausi* (Fig. 31.2), *Centropages hamatus, Temora longicornis* and *Sagitta setosa*. *Acartia clausi* was

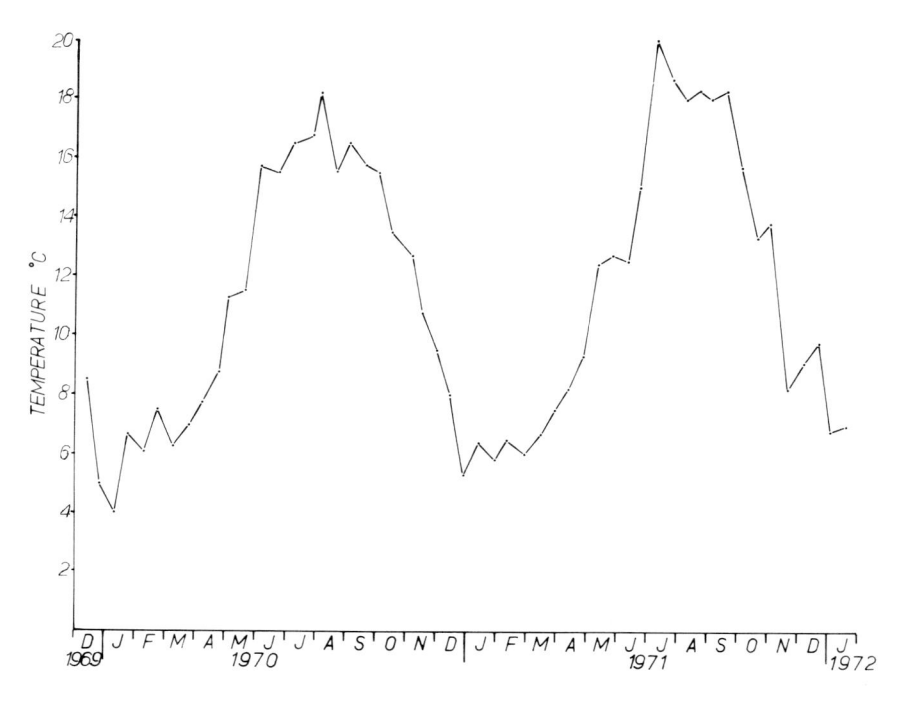

Figure 31.1. Sea water temperature at Mumbles from December 1969 to January 1972

the only species which was present in every haul taken off Mumbles Pier. The three copepod species, *A. clausi*, *C. hamatus* and *T. longicornis* usually peak at the same time, and often with other species of copepods. Fig. 31.3 is a graph of the total number of copepods, and a number of peaks can be seen each year. The plankton net used for this study was not fine enough to trap many of the smaller phytoplankton cells. However, Gabriel (1973), who was working on the phytoplankton of the area, found a similar patchiness of numbers, and the peaks of the copepod numbers were all found to follow a phytoplankton peak. Bainbridge (1953) has put forward a theory to explain the patchy occurrence in the open sea of high concentrations of either phytoplankton or zooplankton, which do not necessarily follow the classical theory of outbursts of phytoplankton in spring and autumn (*sensu* Newell and Newell, 1963). Bainbridge's experiments showed that most zooplankton species that grazed on phytoplankton were attracted to higher concentrations of phytoplankton cells. Thus if a diatom species grew and divided in an area where there was not much zooplankton, a high concentration of diatoms would result in that area. Grazing zooplankton would then be attracted to the area and would start to concentrate there. Once the zooplankton reached such a concentration that the grazing rate exceeded the rate of division of the phytoplankton cells, the diatoms would quickly be grazed down, leaving a high concentration of zooplankton. Harvey *et al.* (1935) found that some species of zooplankton appear to eat greatly in excess of their needs when diatoms are abundant, and this, along with Bainbridge's theory would explain the peaks of grazing copepods coming soon after phytoplankton peaks at Mumbles.

Although the plankton net used was not fine enough to trap the smaller phytoplankton cells, some larger species were caught. The one which occurred most frequently

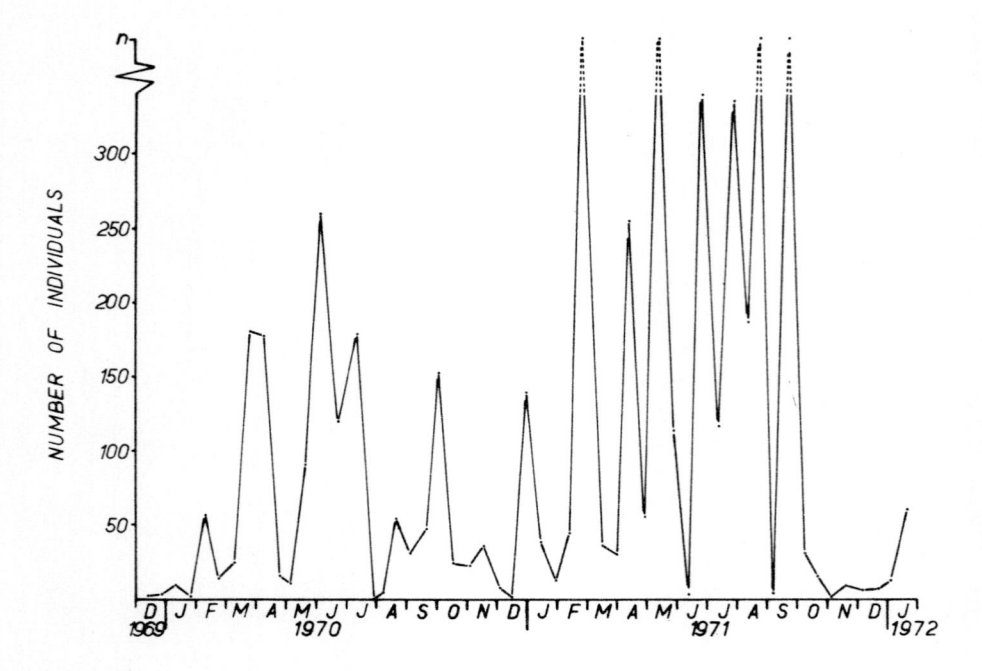

Figure 31.2. Temporal distribution of the calanoid copepod *Acartia clausi* at Mumbles.

was the diatom *Biddulphia sinensis* which was present all the year round, except for June (Fig. 31.4). This species, a native of the Indo-Pacific region, suddenly appeared in 1903 in the North Sea (Lebour, 1930) and has since spread into many parts of the seas around Britain. It is tolerant of a wide range of temperature and salinity (Newell and Newell, 1963), which may explain its abundance in Swansea Bay in winter, when the temperature is low, and the salinity is about 30°/oo. *Bacillaria paradoxa* was also present during most months of the year.

In the second group, *Pseudocalanus minutus* was the only species which was present during the winter, and not in the summer or autumn. Thus, it did not peak with other species of copepods, apart from an unusually early peak in February, 1971. Species which occurred only in summer included the Cladocera. *Podon intermedius* was present between May and August both years, quite abundantly in August 1971. *Evadne spinifera* and *Evadne nordmanni* were present only in July both years, but in quite large numbers. According to Newell and Newell (1963), *Evadne* is a warm water genus, which may explain why it was present only when the temperature was above 16°C.

The medusa of *Phialidium hemisphaericum* (Fig. 31.5) and the larvacean *Oikopleura dioica* were present in the summer and autumn only, and *Euterpina acutifrons* and *Mesopodopsis slabberi* (Fig. 31.6) were present in the autumn and early winter. *Oikopleura dioica* was present from August to November 1970, and May 1971 to January 1972. It was far more abundant in 1971 than 1970, presumably due to the warmer sea temperature (Fig. 31.1). It is a euryhaline species, commonly occurring in estuaries (Newell and Newell, 1963), and was the only larvacean found.

The mysid *Mesopodopsis slabberi* was present during the autumn and winter, sometimes in quite large numbers (Fig. 31.6). This is a brackish water species, having been

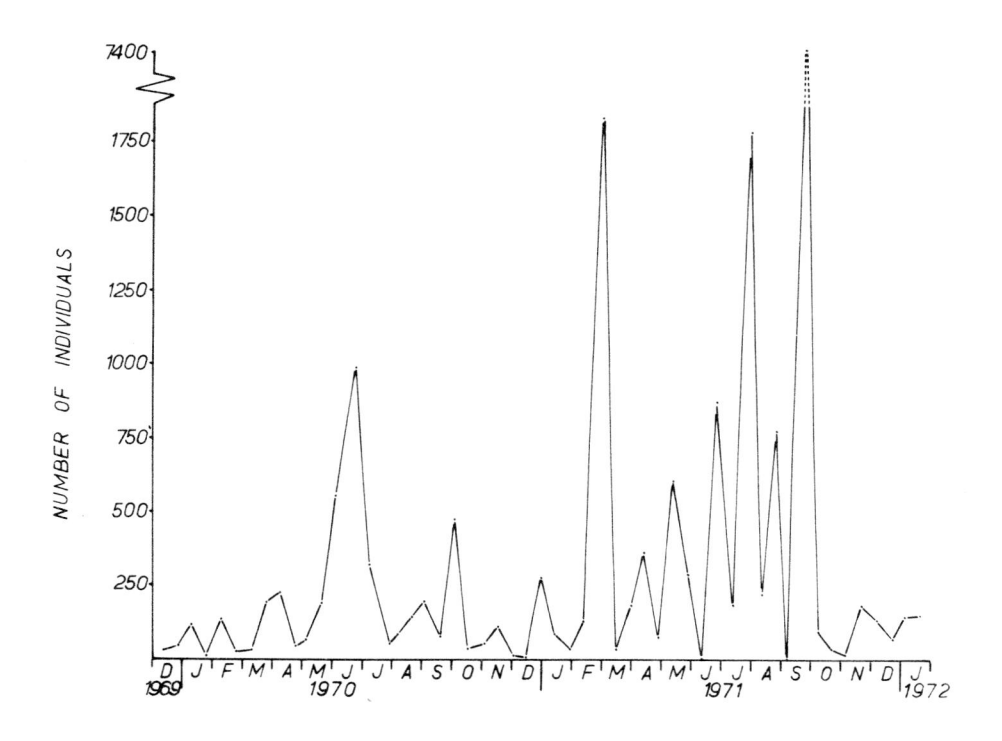

Figure 31.3. Total number of copepods caught in fortnightly plankton hauls at Mumbles.

found in water of as little as 1.3°/oo, along with freshwater plants and animals (Tattersall and Tattersall, 1951). This species used to be considered rare, because it is so difficult to see and catch, but is now known to swarm in astonishing abundance in many estuaries. It is believed by some observers to have a diurnal rhythm of migration, coming to the surface waters at night and going back into deeper waters by day, but other work has shown that this may not be so (*vide* Tattersall and Tattersall, 1951), except when the animals are in breeding condition. Since this species breeds only in spring and summer in this area, it is probable that the animals were always in deeper waters during the day. Once the autumn came, sexual activity ceased and some animals may then have remained in the upper waters during the day, and thus got caught in the plankton net.

Those species which are in the third group include the copepod *Paracalanus parvus*, and many others, most of which were sparce in appearance. All of them are mentioned in the Appendix, as are the tachoplanktonic species, raised during rough weather.

All the larval forms were present seasonally, though some, such as those of *Elminius modestus* (Fig. 31.7) and *Carcinus maenas* (Fig. 31.8) were present for very long seasons. The seasons of abundance of the larval forms will obviously reflect the breeding seasons or seasons of larval release of the adults.

The egg cases of the periwinkle *Littorina littorea* showed an interesting change as

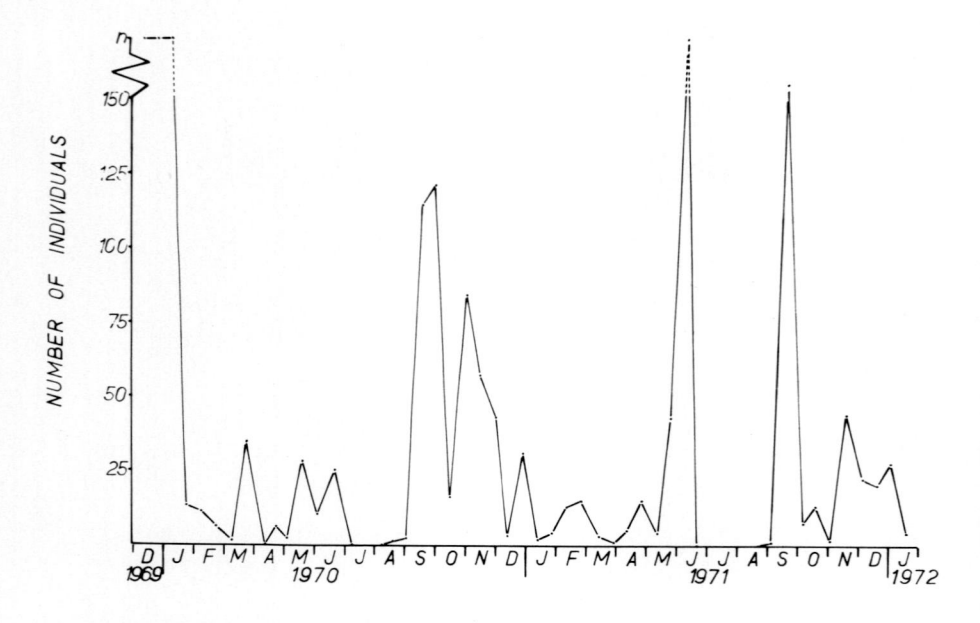

Figure 31.4. Temporal distribution of the diatom *Biddulphia sinensis* at Mumbles.

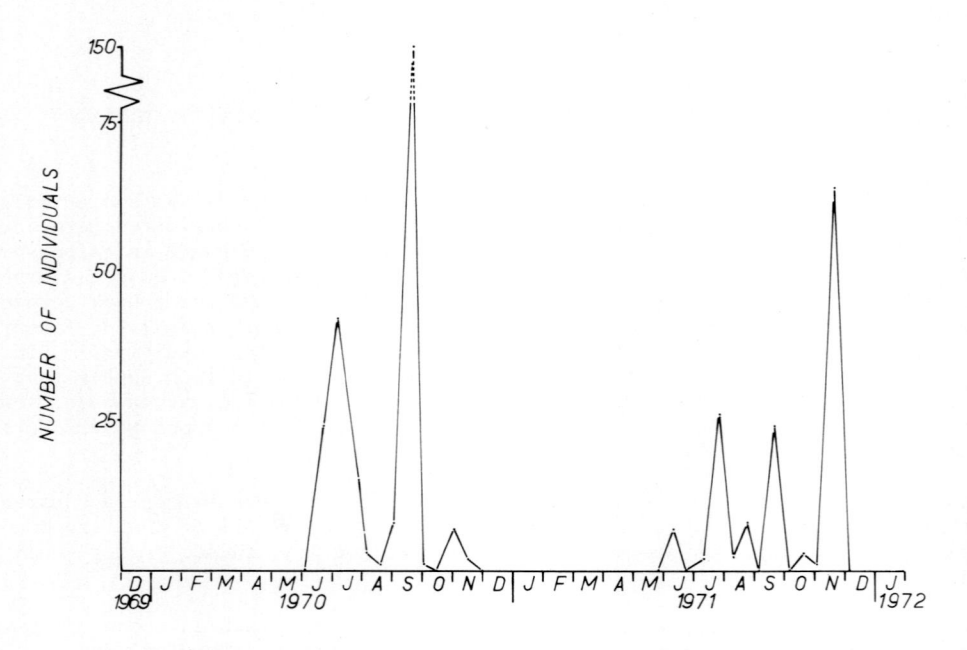

Figure 31.5. Temporal distribution of the hydromedusa of *Phialidium hemisphaericum* at Mumbles.

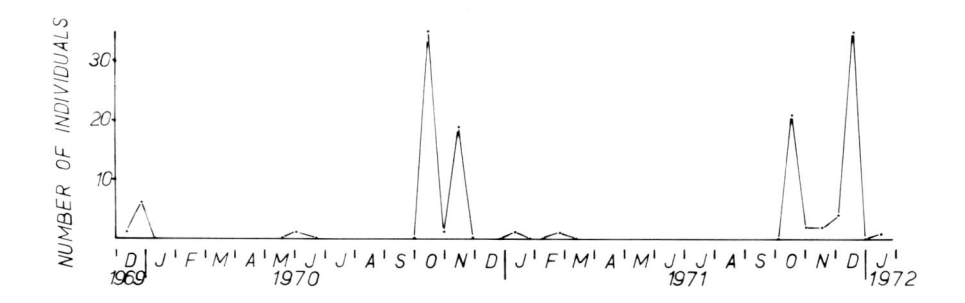

Figure 31.6. Temporal distribution of the mysid *Mesopodopsis slabberi* at Mumbles.

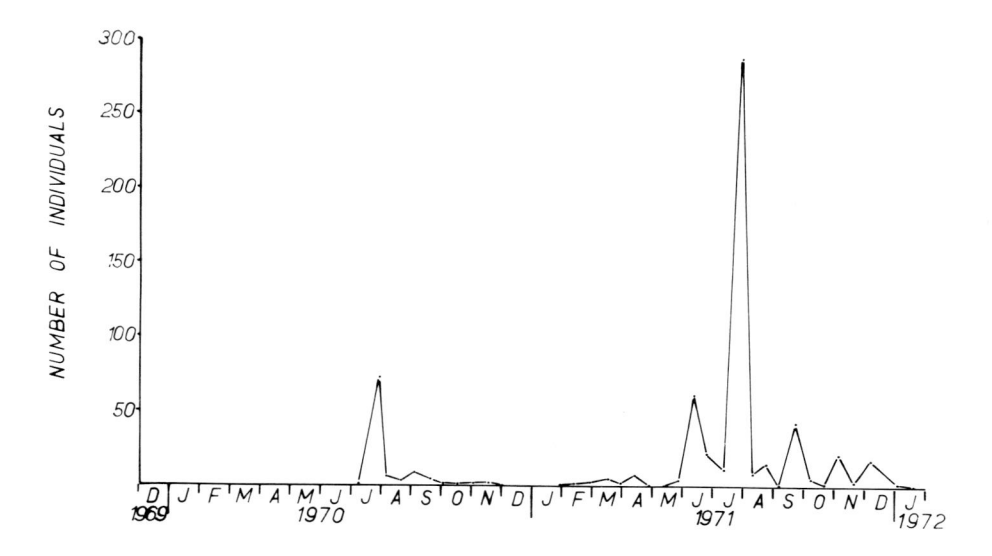

Figure 31.7. Temporal distribution of the nauplius and cyprid larvae of the cirripede *Elminius modestus* at Mumbles.

the season progressed (Fig. 31.9). The increase in the proportion with two eggs per case is probably due to the adults feeding better as the littoral algae grow in the spring. Triple and quadruple eggs do not appear at all until April, whereas there is a certain proportion of double egg cases throughout the year.

As has been stated previously, 1971 was a warmer year than 1970, both during winter and summer. During 1971, for three months (July, August and September) the sea temperature was at or above 18°C, whereas there was only one reading in this range in 1970, on August 5th (Fig. 31.1). The temperature difference was probably the main reason for the differences seen in the plankton between the two years.

Some species were more numerous in the warmer year (1971). Three of the abundant species of copepod, *Centropages hamatus*, *Acartia clausi* and *Pseudocalanus minutus*,

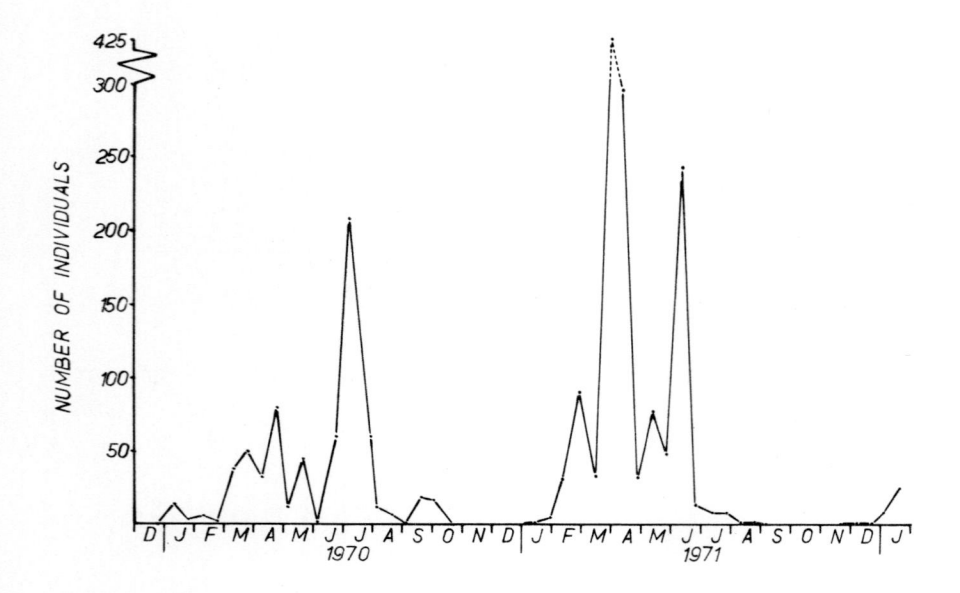

Figure 31.8. Temporal distribution of the zoea larva of the decapod crustacean *Carcinus maenas* at Mumbles.

came into this category. In the case of the first two species, this is not surprising, since they have a wide distribution, but *Pseudocalanus minutus* is a northerly species (Sars, 1903), and it is therefore perhaps unexpected that it would be more abundant during a warmer winter. However, the *Pseudocalanus* season in 1971 coincided with the very early "spring" outburst of phytoplankton in February, and the copepod peaked then, which helps to explain its greater numbers in that year. Two other species whose adults were much more abundant in 1971 were the cladoceran *Podon intermedius* and the larvacean tunicate *Oikopleura dioica*. The latter is a southerly species (Newell and Newell, 1963), and it would therefore be expected to do better at higher temperatures. However, it was present late in the year, after the highest temperatures had occurred and the sea was rapidly cooling, so it is possibly less directly dependent on the water temperature alone.

The characteristically oval eggs of the anchovy, *Engraulis encrasicholus*, were present in greater numbers and over a longer period (May to July) in the warmer 1971 than in 1970 (June only). This species, along with the crab *Pilumnus hirtellus* and one or two others, was one of the few to show an earlier breeding season or time of larval release in 1971 than in 1970. The fact that most eggs and larvae were not earlier in 1971 is rather surprising, as one would have expected the mild winter to have accelerated the breeding cycle of many species, and to have caused the eggs of animals such as crabs, in which the females lay the eggs and then carry them for a few months as they develop, to hatch earlier. However, from the study of the larval forms in the plankton, it is evident that in most species this did not occur. This could be due to breeding cycles being affected by day length as well as temperature.

The larval forms of a number of species were more abundant in the warmer year. The polychaete *Spiophanes bombyx* was one such species, and it also showed much earlier larval release and a longer season of larval occurrence in 1971 (February to June) than in 1970 (May to July). From these dates it would seem that this species

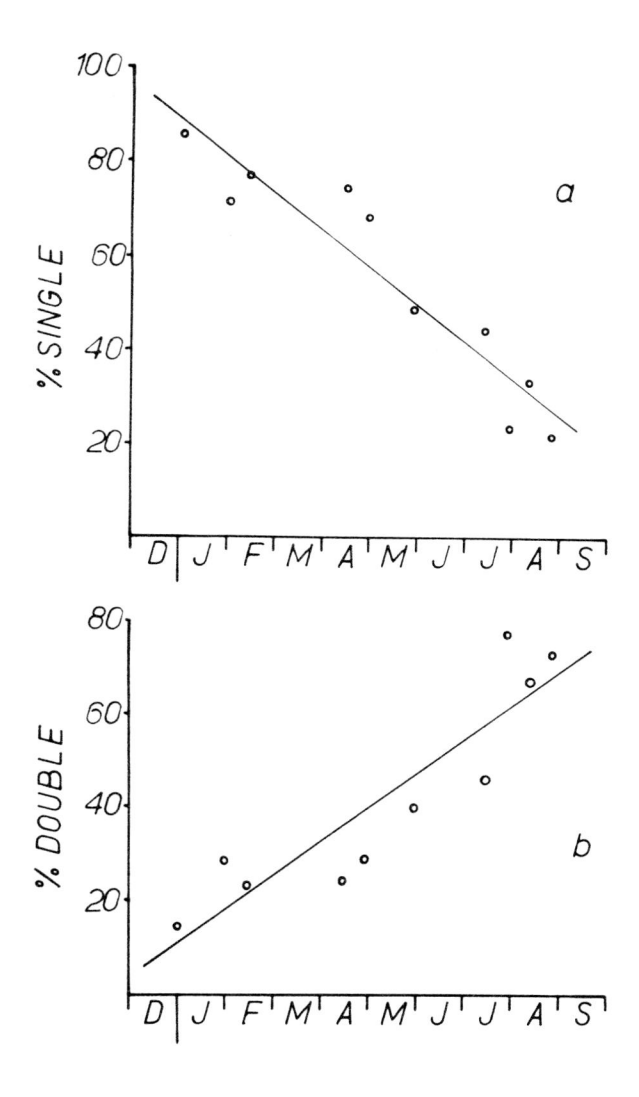

Figure 31.9a. Percentage of egg capsules of the gastropod
               Littorina littorea containing one egg.

Figure 31.9b. Percentage of egg capsules of the gastropod
               Littorina littorea containing two eggs.

Both sets of results are from December 1970 to September 1971 at Mumbles.

would formally breed in spring, and that the colder winter of 1969-70 not only reduced the number of larvae present, but delayed the breeding season in 1970. Polychaete larvae are small, so most of them would not be trapped by the medium mesh net. *S. bombyx* larvae must therefore have been very abundant in the plankton for so many to have been caught in 1971. The medium mesh size would also explain the low numbers caught of species such as *Polydora*, whose adults are very abundant in the locality.

A number of different arthropod larvae were more abundant in the warmer 1971, including the barnacle *Elminius modestus* (Fig. 31.7) and the crabs *Pagurus bernhardus, Carcinus maenas* (Fig. 31.8) and *Maia squinado*. The southern barnacle *Chthamalus stellatus* was totally absent from the 1970 plankton. *Elminius* released a small number of larvae earlier in 1971 than in 1970, but the main peak for both years was in July. *Carcinus,* with its very long season of larval release, did not show an earlier release in 1971, and *Maia* first released earlier in 1970 (June) than in 1971 (July) which seems unexpected not only in being a reversal of the trends shown by most species, but also since *Maia* larvae were more abundant in 1971, although released later in the year.

A number of species showed the opposite effect to that mentioned above, and were more abundant in the cooler year (1970). Three species of hydromedusans, *Sarsia eximia, Rathkea octopunctata* and *Obelia ? lucifera* showed this phenomenon. *S. eximia* is a more northern species (Russell, 1953), so one would expect it to be more abundant when the sea is cooler, but *R. octopunctata* has a very wide distribution both north and south of Britain, so the effect is more surprising with this species. The distribution of the *Obelia* species is not known, since the medusal and hydroid stages of each species have not, as yet, been identified (Russell, 1953). The ctenophore *Beroë cucumis* is another species which was more abundant in 1970 than in 1971.

The copepod *Microcalanus pygmaeus*, a polar species (Sars, 1903), was present in the colder 1970, but completely absent in 1971. The only other copepod to show a similar behaviour was *Paracalanus parvus*, which, though present in 1971, was more abundant in 1970. This is most surprising, since this species has a southern distribution (Sars, 1903).

Many larvae were less abundant in 1971 than in the colder 1970, including *Philocheras fasciatus, Pisidia longicornis, Cancer pagurus* and *Pilumnus hirtellus*. Some, such as *Porcellana platycheles* and *Pagurus pubescens,* were completely absent in 1971. This could be partly due to the warmer temperature of the sea affecting them directly, especially those species with a more northerly distribution, such as *Pagurus pubescens* (Newell and Newell, 1963). Another possible reason is that the first ("spring") outburst of phytoplankton in 1971 was in February, and the larvae missed this outburst by being released too late, since some of these species, such as *Pisidia* and *Porcellana,* are widely distributed (Smaldon, 1972), and would thus presumably not be directly affected by the warmer temperatures of 1971.

A large number of species seem to have been unaffected by the temperature differences of the two years. In some cases, such as the copepods *Temora longicornis* and *Euterpina acutifrons,* the distribution of the species is very wide (Sars, 1903, 1921), and therefore temperature might not have such a marked effect, although it does seem to have had an effect on other widely distributed species. Other species, such as the pea crab larva *Pinnotheres pisum* are very rare, and there are usually not more than two or three present in any one sample. Thus, unless the species did not breed at all in the colder summers, the number of larvae present was too small small for any noticeably significant difference. Other species, such as the siphonophore *Muggiaea atlantica* and the copepod *Calanus helgolandicus,* are southern (and western) in their distribution, so one would perhaps expect them to have been more abundant during the warmer year. *Muggiaea,* however, like *Oikopleura* (mentioned above) is present in the autumn, after the maximum sea temperatures have past, and the water is cooling, so perhaps the temperature is not so important to this species. Another possible explanation of why some species are not more abundant during the warmer year, or why they are less abundant, as in the case of *Rathkea,* is that other species which have done better due to the warmer weather compete successfully for the same food, and thereby check the numbers of the less abundant species.

As mentioned earlier, plankton hauls were taken at night only during August and September 1970. The main difference between these samples and the daylight samples was the much greater number of animals present at night, though most of the species present were also in the daylight hauls. The only species which were caught solely at night were the polychaete *Flabelligera affinis*, the pycnogonid *Nymphon gracile*, some caprellid amphipods and the pipe-fish *Syngnathus rostellatus*. Otherwise, the species present were the same as for the day-time hauls of the same period.

The diversity of the copepods present in the daylight hauls was studied using two formulae (Margalef, 1958). The index of diversity d of Gleason (1922) is given by

$$d = \frac{S - 1}{\log_e N}$$

where S is the number of species, and N the number of individuals. The expression of Brillouin (Quastler, ed., 1953, quoted by Margalef, 1958) gives the entropy of a system of N individuals consisting of N_1 individuals of a first species, N_2 of a second species....,N_s if an s-th species, where

$$E = \log \frac{N!}{N_1! N_2! \ldots N_s!}$$

with a maximum E max. = logN! (S = N) and a minimum E min. = 0 (S = 1). If dealing with a series of samples consisting of varying numbers of individuals, then one

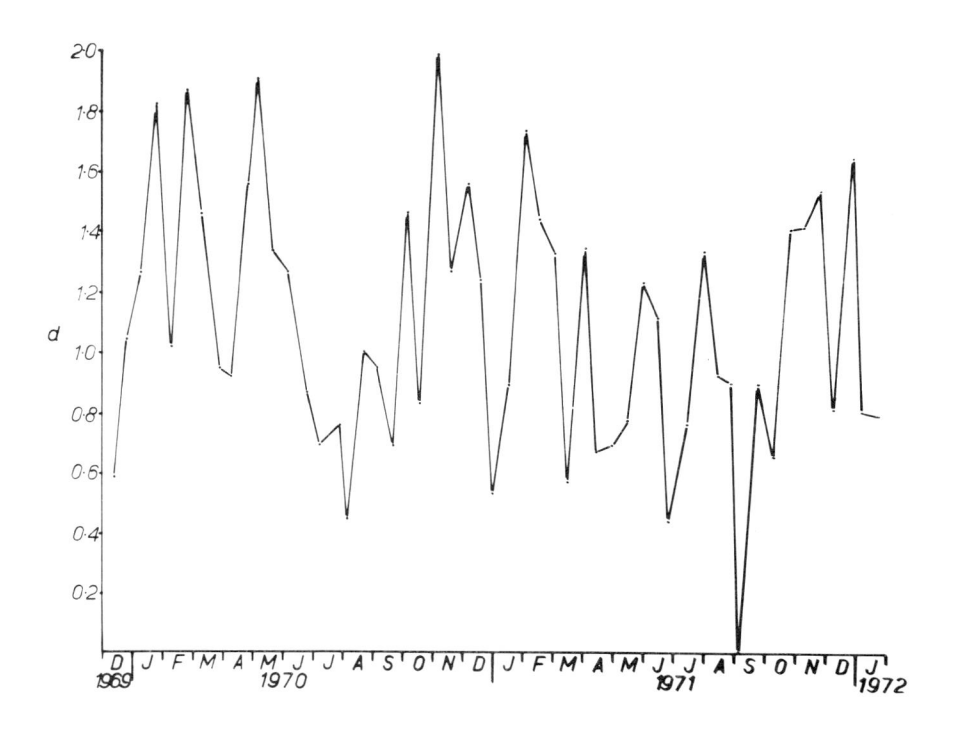

Figure 31.10. Index of diversity, d, for all the copepods caught in fortnightly plankton hauls taken at Mumbles.

uses

$$E_m = \frac{E}{E\ max.}$$

Both d (Fig. 31.10) and Em (Fig. 31.11) were obtained for the copepods in the samples from Mumbles. The correlation between the two was extremely good, with a probability of no correlation very much less than 0.001 (tables in Murdoch and Barnes, 1968). These statistical estimates were compared with the temperature and sunlight (Fig. 31.12) readings, and there was a negative correlation with both (0.02 probability with sunlight, 0.05 probability with temperature). Thus, the copepods of the plankton were more diverse when the water was cooler, and there was less sunlight. This was partly due to the fact that certain benthic harpacticoids were more often present in the winter plankton, due to the rough weather lifting them off the bottom. However, when calculated for the pelagic species only, both d and Em were still higher in winter than in the summer, notwithstanding the fact that there were certain pelagic species, such as the monstrillids and *Centropages typicus*, which were only present during summer and autumn. One could argue that the monstrillids ought to be left out of the calculations, since they are meroplanktonic, but this would make the diversity even lower during the summer. The species,

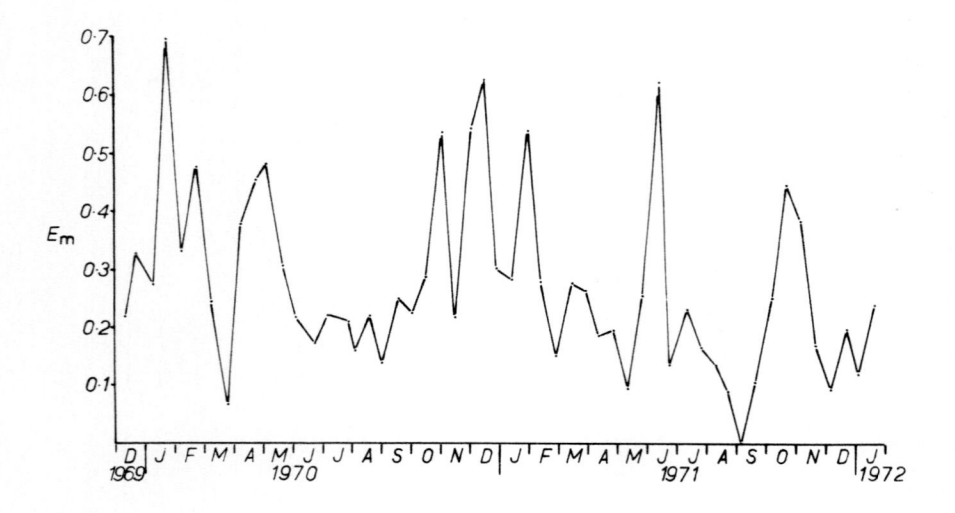

Figure 31.11. A measure of the entropy, Em, of the copepods caught in fortnightly plankton hauls taken at Mumbles.

such as *Labidocera wollastoni*, *Centropages typicus*, *Oithona* spp. and *Cyclopina* spp., which were present only during summer and autumn, were found in very small numbers, whilst the abundance of the few common species was so high in comparison that the diversity index is low. During the winter, the total number of copepods was low, and since there were often a few different species present, the diversity index was bound to be much higher. Strømgren (1971) and Bainbridge (1972) found similar seasonal effects in their plankton studies, which were carried out respectively in Skjomen, off the Ofotfjorden, and within the Gulf of Guinea.

During a field trip on the R.V. "*Ocean Crest*" in 1971, plankton hauls were taken at different locations in the Bristol Channel, and one was taken in the waters just south of St. Agnes, in the Scilly Islands. The arthropods in these samples were

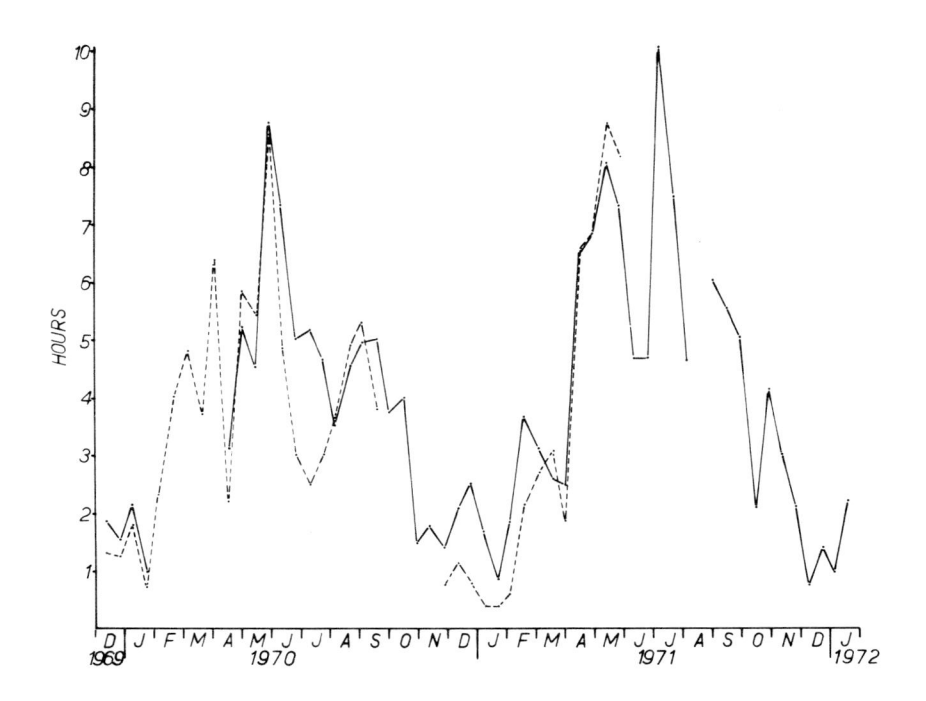

Figure 31.12. Average number of hours of sunshine per day for each fortnight from December 1969 to January 1972.
Continuous line: British Steel Corporation, Margam.
Broken line: Swansea Corporation, Victoria Park.

identified, and the species present compared with those at Mumbles. The plankton hauls taken off Lundy Island had a number of more oceanic species of calanoid copepod, such as *Candacia armata* and *Anomalocera patersoni,* and the cyclopoids *Corycaeus anglicus* and *Oithona helgolandica,* but euryhaline forms, such as *Centropages hamatus* and *Eurytemora hirundoides* were also present. As with all the hauls taken lower down the Bristol Channel, the variety of decapod (Crustacea) larvae was more diverse than that at Mumbles. The hauls taken near Gulland Rock, off Padstow, Cornwall, contained more oceanic species, such as *Parapontella brevicornis* and *Labidocera wollastoni,* which were absent from the Lundy hauls. There was also a great variety of monstrillid copepods, and a mysid, *Gastrosaccus sanctus* was present. One euryhaline species, *Centropages hamatus* was present but this, unlike *Eurytemora,* is often present in offshore water.

The plankton haul with the most oceanic forms was taken north of Land's End at 50° 11½'N, 5°45'W. This contained the calanoids *Candacia varicans, C. elongata,* and *Metridia lucens,* as well as the mysids *Anchialina agilis* and *Erythrops elegans,* whilst *Centropages hamatus* was absent. The haul taken south of St. Agnes, Scilly Islands, was much less varied and most oceanic forms were absent. The euryhaline *Mesopodopsis slabberi* was present as well as *Centropages hamatus.*

Thus, not surprisingly, it can be seen that the number of oceanic forms present in the plankton of the Bristol Channel increased as one moved down the Channel towards the Irish Sea. The only surprising result came from the haul taken south of St.

Agnes, since the species present indicate a lower salinity, whereas, according to Southward (1962) the salinity at the Scillies is greater than that further up the Bristol Channel, and the same as that north of Land's End, where the haul with most oceanic forms was taken. It is possible that the water currents carry the small amount of fresh water that comes off St. Agnes, or one of the other islands, to the point where the plankton haul was taken, with minimum mixing, since *Mesopodopsis slabberi* is a euryhaline form which is very rarely taken in oceanic water (Tattersall and Tattersall, 1951).

All the plankton hauls from further down the Bristol Channel had a much greater variety of decapod larvae than those taken off Mumbles. All the hauls were taken further offshore than the Mumbles hauls, and many of the larvae not present at Mumbles were of sub-littoral, as well as littoral, species. Divers working off Lundy, Gulland Rock and the Scillies have found a much greater variety and abundance of benthic fauna than they find around Swansea and Gower (A.L. Osborn and R.J.A. Atkinson, *pers. comm.*), so one would expect this much richer fauna to be reflected in a greater variety of larvae present in the plankton of these areas

REFERENCES

Admiralty Hydrographic Department (1969-71). *Admiralty Tide Tables. I. European Waters.* H.M.S.O. London.

Bainbridge, R. (1953). Studies on the interrelationships of zooplankton and phytoplankton. *J. mar. biol. Ass. UK.*, 32, 385-447.

Bainbridge, V. (1972). The zooplankton of the Gulf of Guinea. *Bull. mar. Ecol.*, 8, 61-97.

Conseil Permanent International par l'Exploration de la Mer (1939-). *Fiches d'Identication du Zooplancton.* Høst, Copenhagen.

Dias, N.S. (1960). *Studies on the plankton of Milford Haven.* Unpub. M.Sc. Thesis, University of Wales.

Gabriel, P.L. (1973). *The Plankton of Polluted Waters.* Unpub. Ph.D. Thesis, University of Wales.

Gleason, H.A. (1922). On the relation between species and area. *Ecology*, 3, 156-162.

Harvey, H.W., Cooper, L.H.N., Lebour, M.V., and Russel, F.S. (1935). Plankton production and its control. *J. mar. biol. Ass. UK.*, 20, 407-441.

Isaac, M.J. (1974). *Studies on Planktonic Arthropods.* Unpub. Ph.D. Thesis, University of Wales.

Lebour, M.V. (1930). *The planktonic diatoms of northern seas.* Roy. Society, London.

Margalef, R. (1958). Temporal succession and spatial heterogeneity in phytoplankton. *In:* Buzzati-Traverso, A.A. (Ed.). *Perspectives in Marine Biology.* University of California Press, 323-349.

Murdoch, J., and Barnes, J.A. (1968). *Statistical tables for science, engineering and management.* Macmillan, London.

Newell, G.E., and Newell, R.C. (1963). *Marine plankton - a practical guide.* Hutchinson, London.

Pearce, D.W. (1967). *Studies on the plankton of the Bristol Channel Region.* Unpub. M.Sc. Thesis, University of Wales.

Quastler, H. (Ed.)(1953). *Information theory in biology.* University of Illinois Press, Urbana.

Rees, C.B. (1939). The plankton of the upper reaches of the Bristol Channel. *J. mar. biol. Ass. UK.*, 23, 397-425.

Russell, F.S. (1953). *The medusae of the British Isles.* Cambridge University Press.

Sars, G.O. (1903). Copepoda Calanoida. *An Account of the Crustacea of Norway*, 7, 1-121.

Sars, G.O. (1921). Copepoda supplement. *An Account of the Crustacea of Norway*, 7,

1-121.
Smaldon, G. (1972). Population structure and breeding biology of *Pisidia longicornis* and *Porcellana platycheles*. *Mar. Biol.*, *17*, 171-179.
Southward, A.J. (1962). The distribution of some plankton animals in the English Channel and approaches. II. Surveys with the Gulf III high speed sampler, 1958-60. *J. mar. biol. Ass. UK.*, *42*, 275-375.
Strømgren, T. (1971). Zooplankton investigations in Skjomen. Preliminary report, Nov. 1969 - Jan. 1971. *Tromsø Mus. Skjomenunders. Mar. Unders.*, *18*, 1-25.
Tattersall, W.M., and Tattersall, O.S. (1951). *The British Mysidacea*. Roy. Society, London.

APPENDIX

A list of all the plants and animals caught in plankton hauls taken once a fortnight off Mumbles Pier, Swansea, December, 1969 to January, 1972.

Key

1. Present more or less all the time (with peak, if any).
2. Seasonal (with season(s)).
3. Occasional and/or sporadic.
4. Benthic and only present in rough weather.
5. Very rare (with season(s), if any).
6. Night haul in August/September only.

a. Spring; b. Summer; c. Autumn; d. Winter; * Graphed on Figure.

PLANTS

BACILLARIOPHYCEAE

Melosira sp. 3
Paralia sulcata (Ehrenberg). 2 c.
Coscinodiscus excentricus Ehrenberg. 1 b, d.
Coscinodiscus ?lineatus Ehrenberg. 1 c, d.
Coscinodiscus radiatus Ehrenberg. 3.
Coscinodiscus granii Gough. 3.
Thalassiosira decipiens (Grunow). 3.
Thalassiosira gravida Clève. 1 a, b.
Leptocylindricus ?danicus Clève. 5 b.
Rhizosolenia alata Brightwell. 2 b.
Rhizosolenia stolerfothi Peragallo. 5 b.
Rhizosolenia shrubsolei Clève. 2 b.
Rhizosolenia setigera Brightwell. 1.
Rhizosolenia styliformis Brightwell. 5 d.
Chaetoceros ?densus Clève. 2 b.

Chaetoceros decipiens Clève. 5 c.
Biddulphia aurita Lyngbye. 5 a.
Biddulphia regia Schultze. 5 d.
Biddulphia sinensis Greville. 1 b,c.
Biddulphia alternans (Bailey). 5 a, d.
Bellarochia malleus (Brightwell). 2b,c.
Lithodesmium undulatum Ehrenberg. 5 b.
Ditylium brightwelli (West). 5 c.
Eucampia zoodiacus Ehrenberg. 5 b.
Streptotheca thamensis Shrubsole. 5 b.
Asterionella japonica Clève & Muller 2a.
Navicula sp. 5 a.
Pleurosigma sp. 2 a, c, d.
Bacillaria paradoxa Gmelin & van Heurck 1 b, d.

XANTHOPHYCEAE

Halosphaera viridis Schmitz. 2 a.

DINOFLAGELLATA

Peridinium granii Ostenfeld. 5 d.
Procentrum micans Ehrenberg. 5 b.

Noctiluca scintillans (Mcartney). 2b.

ANIMALS

PROTOZOA

Tintinnopsis sp. 5 c.

HYDROMEDUSAE

Sarsia eximia Allman. 2 a, b.
Sarsia prolifera Forbes. 5 b.
Sarsia gemifera Forbes. 5 b.
Hybocodon prolifer L. Agassiz. 5 a.
Steenstrupia nutans M. Sars. 2 b.
?Cladonema radiatum Dujardin. 5 b.
Turritopsis nutricula McCrady. 5 c.
Podocoryne minima Trinci. 6.
Rathkea octopunctata M. Sars. 2 a, d.
Lizzia blondina Forbes. 5 d.

Amphinema dinema Péron & Lesueur. 5 b.
Leuckartiara octona Fleming. 5 a, c.
Leuckartiara brevicornis Murbach & Shearer 6.
Mitrocomella brownei Kramp. 5 b.
**Phialidium hemisphaericum* L. 2 b. c.
Obelia ?lucifera Browne. 2 b.
Lovenella clausa Hincks. 5 c.
Eucheilota maculata Hartlaub. 5 b.
Phialella quadrata Forbes. 2a, b, c.
Gossea corynetes Gosse. 5 c.

SIPHONOPHORA

Muggiaea atlantica Cunningham. 2 b, c.
Muggiaea kochi Will. 5 c.
?Rosacea sp. 5 a, c.
?Nanomia sp. 5 a.

?Clausophyes sp. 5 b.
?Hippopodius hippopus Forskål. 5 c.
?Eudoxides spiralis Bigelow. 5 c.

SCYPHOZOA

Aurelia aurita (L.) (Ephyra larva). 2 a, d.

CTENOPHORA

Beroë cucumis Fabricius. 3.
Bolinopsis infundibulum (O.F. Müller). 5 a.

Pleurobrachia pileus (O.F. Müller). 1 b,c.

TURBELLARIA

?Euplana sp. 5 d.

ROTIFERA

Unidentified. 5 b, c.

NEMATODA

Unidentified. 3.

POLYCHAETA

Autolytus brachycephalus (Marenzeller). (stolon). 3.
Autolytus alexandri Malmgren. (epitoque). 5 a.
Autolytus ?langerhansi Gidholm. (stolon). 5 c.
Proceraea cornuta (A. Agassiz). (stolon). 3.
Proceraea prismatica (Fabricius). (stolon). 3.
Procerastea sp. (stolon). 5 c.   *Flabelligera affinis* M. Sars. 6.
Harmothoë johnstoni (McIntosh). 5 a.

Larvae

Lanice conchilega (Pallas). 2 a, b, c.
Spio martinensis Mesnil. 5 c.
Spio sp. 5 b.
Pygospio elegans Claparède. 5 b.
Spiophanes bombyx Claparède. 2 a, b, d.

Polydora caulleryi Mesnil. 5 a.
Polydora flava Claparède. 5 b.
Polydora sp. 5 b.
Scolelepis girardi Quatrefages. 5 a.
Poecilochaetus serpens Allen. 5 a.

GASTROPODA

Hydrobia ulvae (Pennant). 3
Littorina littoralis (L.). 5 d.

Littorina neritoides (L.). 5 d.

Larvae

?*Velutina* sp. 2 b.

Eggs

Littorina littorea (L.). 1 a. *Littorina neritoides* (L.). 2 a.

LAMELLIBRANCHIA
Larvae

Mytilus edulis L. 2 a, d.
Tellina crassa Pennant (=*Arcopagia crassa*). 5 a, c.
Tellina fabula Gmelin. 5 c, d.
?*Spisula eliptica* (Brown). 5 b, d.

Cardium edule L. (=*Cerastoderma edule*). 5 d.
Cardium ?ovale Sowerby. 5 a, d.
Cardium ?crassum Gmelin. (= *Laevicardium crassum*). 5 b, c.

CEPHALOPODA

Sepioid larva. 5 b.

PYCNOGONIDA

Nymphon gracile Leach. 6.   *Anoplodactylus petiolatus* (Kröyer). 5 c.

INSECTA

Lipura maritima (Laboulbène). 5a, b, c.

ACARINA

Unidentified. 3.

CUMACEA

Diastylis rugosa G. O. Sars. 4.   *Iphinoë trispinosa* Goodsir. 4.
Diastylis tumida Lilljeborg. 4. *Vaunthompsonia cristata* Bate. 4.

CLADOCERA

Podon intermedius Lilljeborg. 2 b.   *Evadne spinifera* P.E. Muller. 2 b.
Podon polyphemoides Leuckart. 5 b.   *Evadne nordmanni* Lovén. 5 b.
Podon leuckarti G.O. Sars. 5 b.

CIRRIPEDIA
Larvae

Balanus balanoides (L.). 2? a.   *Verruca stroemia* (O.F. Müller). 2 a, b, d.
Balanus crenatus Bruguière. 2? b. *Chthamalus stellatus* (Poli). 2 a, b.
Elminius modestus Darwin. 1 b.

COPEPODA
Calanoida

Calanus finmarchicus (Gunnerus). 5.   *Isias clavipes* Boeck. 5 a, d.
Calanus helgolandicus Claus. 3.   *Temora longicornis* (O.F. Müller). 1 b.
Paracalanus parvus (Claus). 3.   *Eurytemora hirundoides* (Nordqvist). 5 a.
Pseudocalanus minutus Kröyer. (=*Pseudo-   Anomalocera patersoni* Templeton. 5 d.
  calanus elongatus*). 2 d.   *Labidocera wollastoni* (Lubbock). 5 b.
Microcalanus pygmaeus G.O. Sars. 5 a, d.*Acartia clausi* Giesbrecht. 1 a, b, c, d,
Centropages typicus Kröyer. 5 b.   *Acartia discaudata* (Giesbrecht). 5 b.
Centropages hamatus (Lilljeborg). 1b, d.

Harpacticoida

Tigriopus fulvus (Fischer). 5 a, c, d.
Alteutha interrupta (Goodsir). 3.
Idya ?furcata (Baird). 4.
Idya gracilis T. Scott. 4.
Idya longicornis T. Scott & A. Scott. 4.
Thalestris longimana Claus. 4.
Thalestris ?rufoviolacens Claus. 4.
Euterpina acutifrons (Dana). 2 c, d.
Clytemnestra rostrata (Brady). 5 d.

Cyclopoida

Oithona helgolandica Claus. 5 b.
Oithona nana Giesbrecht. 5 c.
Cyclopina longicornis Boeck. 5 b, d.
Corycaeus anglicus Lubbock. 5 c.

Monstrilloida

Monstrilla helgolandica Claus. 5 b, d.
Monstrilla grandis Giesbrecht. 2 b, c.
Thaumaleus rigidus (Thompson). 5 b.

ISOPODA

Eurydice pulchra Leach. 3.
Eurydice inermis Hansen. 5 d.
Idotea pelagica Leach.
Idotea neglecta G.O. Sars. 4.
Idotea baltica Pallas. 4.
Idotea linearis Pennant. 4.
Idotea viridis Slabber. (= *Idotea chelipes* Pallas). 4.
Epicaridean (microniscus stage). 5 c.

AMPHIPODA

Calliopius laeviusculus (Kröyer). 4.
Corophium volutator (Pallas). 4.
Lysianassidae. 4.
Gammaridae. 4.
Caprellidae. 6.

MYSIDACEA

*Mesopodopsis slabberi van Beneden. 2c,d.   *Gastrosaccus sanctus* van Beneden. 5 c.

EUPHAUSIACEA

Calyptopis larva. 5 c.

DECAPODA

Larvae

Alpheus macrocheles (Hailstone). 5 b.
Palaemon sp. 2 b.
Leander sp. 2 b.
Crangon crangon L. (=*Crangon vulgaris* Fabricius). 2 a, b, c.
Crangon allmani Kinahan. 2 b, c.
Philocheras trispinosus (Hailstone) 5a,b.
Philocheras fasciatus (Risso). 5 b.
Galathea strigosa (L.). 5 d.
Porcellana platycheles (Pennant). 5 b.
Pisidia longicornis (L.). 2 b, c.
Upogebia sp. 5 d.
Pagurus bernhardus L. 2 a, d.
Pagurus pubescens Kröyer. 5 a, d.
Ebalia sp. 5 d.
Corystes cassivelaunus (Pennant). 5 a.
Pirimela denticulata (Montagu). 2 b, c.
Thia polita Leach. 5 b.
Cancer pagurus L. 2 b, c.
Macropipus puber L. 2 a, d.
Macropipus holsatus (Fabricius). 2 b, c.
Macropipus pusillus (Leach). 5 b.
Macropipus depurator L. 5 b.
Bathynectes longipes (Risso). 5 b.
*Carcinus maenas (L.). 1 a, b.
Xantho incisus Leach. 5 b.
Pilumnus hirtellus (L.). 2 b.
Pinnotheres pisum (Pennant). 2 b.
Maia squinado (Herbst). 2 b, c.
Inachus sp. 5 b, c.
Macropodia longirostris (Fabricius). 5 c.
Macropodia rostrata (L.). 5 b.

CHAETOGNATHA

Sagitta elegans Verril. 5 d.
Sagitta ?serratodentata Krohn. 5 c.

Sagitta setosa J. Müller. 1 b, c.

PHORONIDEA
Larva

Phoronis mulleri de Selys Longchamps. 5 c.

BRYOZOA
Larvae

Membranipora membranacea (L.). 5 b, c.   *Electra pilosa* (L.). 5 a.

ECHINODERMATA
Larva

Ophiothrix fragilis (Abildgaard). 5 c.

ENTEROPNEUSTA
Larva

Balanoglossus clavigerus Delle Chiaje. 5 b.

TUNICATA

Oikopleura dioica Fol. 2 b, c.

PISCES

Syngnathus rostellatus Nilsson. 6.

Young

Anguilla anguilla (L.). 5 a.   *Trigla gurnardus* L. 5 b.
Ammodytes lancea Yarrell. 5 a.

Larvae

Scomber scombus L. 5 b.   *Pleuronectes platessa* L. 5 a.
Merluccius merluccius (L.). 5 a.

Eggs

Engraulus encrasicholus L. 2 a, b.   *Onos mustela* L. 2 a, d.
Solea solea (L.). 5 b.   *Serranus cabrilla* L. 5 a.

32. NEARSHORE SUBLITTORAL ECOSYSTEMS ALONG THE GOWER COAST

K. Hiscock, D. Cartlidge and S. Hiscock

Field Studies Council Oil Pollution Research Unit, Orielton Field Centre, Pembroke, Dyfed, U.K.

ABSTRACT

A survey of nearshore sublittoral habitats and plant and animal communities was carried out along the Gower coast during one week in June 1978. The study was part of a primary descriptive survey of south-west Britain commissioned by the Nature Conservancy Council. Twenty-one sites were studied from Worms Head to Mumbles Head at locations selected to ensure that as wide a range of habitats as possible were surveyed. Communities of plants and animals mainly from sublittoral rocks are described from the Gower coast. The distribution of the species present in relation to local environmental conditions is discussed. Changes in the flora and fauna from South Pembrokeshire to the Gower and from the Gower to areas east of Swansea Bay are described and discussed in relation to environmental conditions and pollution in the Bristol Channel.

KEYWORDS

Bristol Channel; Biogeography; Communities; Conservation; Ecosystems; Sublittoral organisms; Sublittoral zones; Underwater surveys.

INTRODUCTION

The Gower survey was part of a study of nearshore sublittoral ecosystems in southwest Britain being carried out for the Nature Conservancy Council. The aims of the three-year study are: to describe the distribution of conspicuous species; to assess the range of variability in sublittoral communities and the environmental factors causing variability; to classify sublittoral nearshore ecosystems; and to provide a basis for the assessment of the conservation interest of near-shore sublittoral areas in south-west Britain.

The Gower peninsula from Worms Head to Mumbles Head includes a predominantly rocky shore and shallow sublittoral area bordered to the west and east by large sandy bays. Along the Gower coast and to the west, industrial and urban development is slight whilst to the east, coastal areas are extensively developed to both towns or cities and by industry. Of added significance to the present study is the substantial part of the Gower coastline which is of nature conservation or scenic interest.

Although a wide range of biological investigations have been carried out along the Gower coast and the area is used for teaching and collecting, no descriptions of nearshore rocky sublittoral fauna and flora have been published. For nearshore sediments, Tyler (1976) and Tyler and Banner (1977) have described the communities present in Oxwich Bay. Work carried out in August 1978 to the west of Gower along the South Pembrokeshire coast (Cartlidge and Hiscock, 1979) and to the east off Porthcawl, Nash Point and St. Donats (authors' unpublished data) using the same methods provide a basis for the comparison of the Gower flora and fauna with areas to the west and east as well as an assessment of the importance of Carmarthen Bay and Swansea Bay as areas of change in rocky sublittoral communities.

ENVIRONMENTAL CONDITIONS

The environmental conditions most likely to determine the rocky sublittoral species and communities present along the Gower coast are: 1) extent and type of hard substrata present, 2) exposure of the seabed to wave action and tidal streams, 3) direction of residual water flow along the coast, 4) amount of suspended material in the water and its effects on light penetration, 5) temperature, 6) salinity, 7) pollution.

The depth to which rock extends is important in providing suitable surfaces for the development of rocky sublittoral communities and species which occur only in particular depth zones. Stability of the rock substratum is important in enabling the development of communities of long-lived species with a low level of recruitment whilst stones and cobbles moved during storms will most likely support a community of fast-growing species with a high level of recruitment. Rock type is important to boring organisms. No published information has been found indicating the extent of sublittoral rock along the Gower coast. Admiralty Chart 1165 provides a little information on the distribution of sediments along the coast and much of the seabed is indicated to be of fine sand with some shell material. Mud is indicated as present in west Oxwich Bay. For the purposes of the present study, most site surveys were therefore commenced adjacent to the rocky shore and continued in an offshore direction. All of the bedrock along the Gower coast is limestone.

The strength of both tidal streams and wave action is important in determining the communities present through the tolerance of species to disturbance by strong water movement, their ability to withstand siltation in areas of slight water movement and the importance of water movement for feeding. Almost all of the coastline studied faces south-south-west and is therefore open to prevailing winds and swell. However, local shelter is present in the lee of Port Eynon Point, Oxwich Point, Pwll-du Head and Mumbles Head. In the terminology described by Hiscock (1979a) areas of sublittoral seabed studied during the present survey ranged from 'Very Exposed' at Worms Head to 'Sheltered' on the west side of Oxwich Bay. Tidal streams are not strong along the coast studied with maximum flows present around the headlands. For instance, Tyler and Banner (1977) suggest maximum tidal stream velocities of 41cm/s (about 0.8 knot) within Oxwich Bay to 121cm/s (about 2.4 knots) on the seabed off Oxwich Point. However the most important feature of tidal flow adjacent to the coast is the predominantly westerly direction of currents which ensures that the supply of water along the Gower coast is mainly from Swansea Bay (Hamilton, 1973; Collins, Ferentinos and Banner, 1979. See also Chapter 10 and 14).

The volume of suspended sediment in the water increases from west to east along the South Wales coast. Along the Gower coast, suspended sediment levels are usually high. Such high levels result in poor light penetration and will affect the depth to which algae can grow. Suspension feeding animals might benefit from the much more abundant source of food in turbid waters but must also survive adverse effects such as clogging of feeding organs.

Temperature and salinity maxima and minima and the range through the year are important to the survival and reproduction of benthic species. The Conseil Permanent International pour l'Exploration de la Mer (1962) record surface temperatures in the region of the Gower as varying between 7°C and 16°C and salinity as varying between 32°/oo and 33°/oo through the year. These figures are similar to the ranges for open coast areas of Britain.

Residual water flow carries pollutants from Swansea Bay westwards along the Gower coast and a large sewage outfall which carries some industrial waste is situated at Mumbles Head. The likely effects of such pollutants on benthic communities are little known though it is notable that Stebbing (1979) found that the stolon growth of *Campanularia flexuosa* was significantly different in water collected near to the outfall at Mumbles Head compared to growth in water collected away from effluents and other sources of stress. It is therefore necessary to consider that the coastline studied might be affected by pollution and that the area of Mumbles Head might be subject to high level of pollution stress.

METHODS

A full description of survey methods together with copies of check lists, recording cards and abundance scales are given in the report of the Gower survey made to the Nature Conservancy Council (Hiscock, 1979b). The survey was carried out by eight persons from June 25th to 30th 1978. The authors of the present chapter were responsible for systematic species recording of plant and animal communities. The remaining staff were responsible for some species recording, for the description of habitats present and for the collection of material for laboratory identification. Sites were selected by the inspection of maps and charts to include as wide a range of habitats as possible particularly in relation to the strength of wave action and tidal streams but also with a fairly even distribution along the coast. Onshore positions were located according to shore topographical features whilst offshore positions were plotted using sighting compasses. All sites were surveyed using diving. Check lists of algae, animals and habitat categories together with abundance scales were used throughout the survey to ensure thorough recording and comparable data from person to person and site to site. At most sites, a general survey was carried out listing habitats present, species observed, their abundance, and the different communities present in different habitats. At selected sites, detailed studies of the abundance of algae and animals in different biological zones at different depths were carried out. Field records were made on laminated plastic writing boards whilst one of us (KH) used an underwater tape recorder. Species which could not be identified with certainty in the field were usually collected and subsequently identified. Photographs of different habitat types, communities and species were taken for illustration and to assist the description of sites with a Nikonos underwater camera, electronic flash and, where required, a supplementary lens or extension tube for close-up photography. All of the field data together with identifications of collected specimens were tabulated to provide species lists, details of distribution with depth and the sites at which each species was found.

RESULTS

Introduction

The 21 sites studied are shown in Fig. 32.1. The survey recorded 66 species of algae and 134 species of animals in a wide variety of habitats and to a maximum depth of 20m. A summary of the results is presented here whilst full records of the distribution of species with notes on their habitats are given in Hiscock (1979b).

Substrata and habitats present at sites studied: Rock throughout the area studied

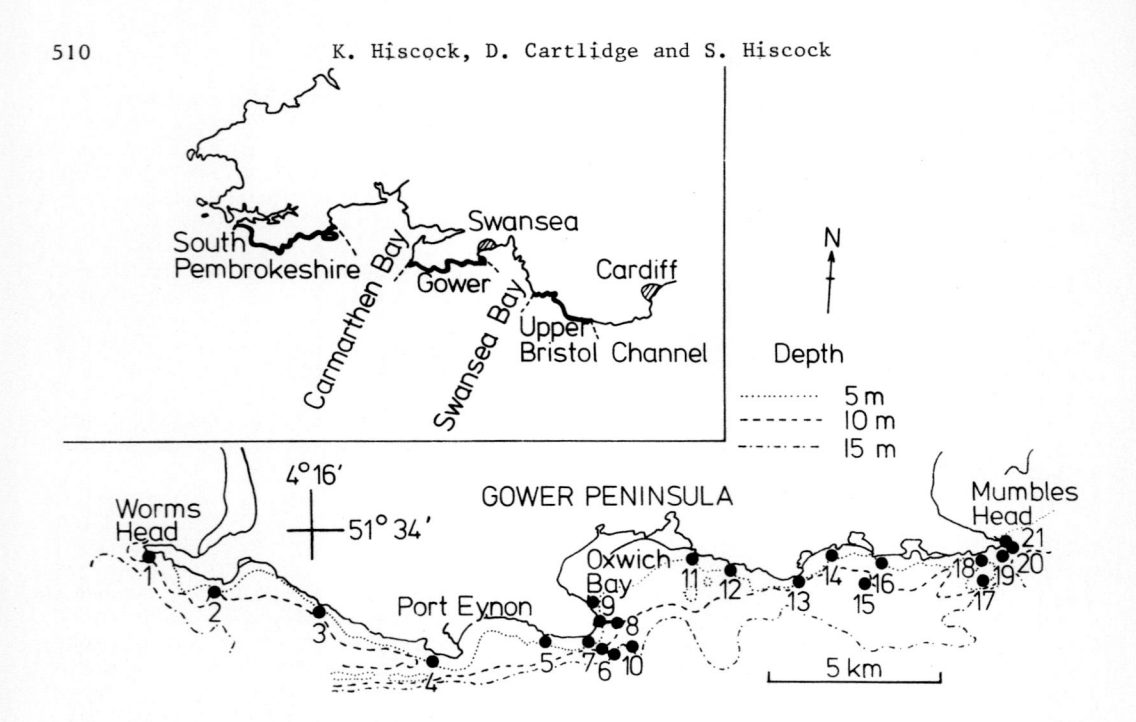

Figure 32.1. Location of survey areas mentioned in the text along the South Wales coast and position of survey sites along the Gower coast. Site names and full Ordnance Survey Grid References are given in Hiscock (1979b).

was of limestone. Along much of the coast investigated, rock surfaces adjacent to the shore extended only to 1 to 3m below Chart Datum where a clean sand or muddy sand plain was present. However, the gradual slope meant that rock surfaces were often extensive. Deeper areas of rock to 6m were studied at Worms Head (sites 1 and 2), west of Port Eynon Point (site 4), south and east of Oxwich Point (site 7), and Shire Combe (site 11). Offshore of Oxwich Point (site 6), broken bedrock with areas of cobbles was studied to 20m. Large areas of hard substrata were present offshore of Mumbles Head (site 20) and Caswell Bay (site 15). Areas of bedrock were predominantly of upward facing surfaces with gullies, vertical surfaces and some overhangs. At many sites, stones and cobbles were present in gullies or over extensive areas of seabed between bedrock reefs or between bedrock and the sand plain. Other habitats which held distinctive communities included kelp stipes and stable rocks adjacent to or partly covered in sand. Sand and muddy sand areas of seabed were usually studied where rock surfaces terminated but observations were also made offshore at Oxwich Point (site 10) and Mixon Shoal (site 17).

Communities Present in Different Habitats

Upward-facing bedrock surfaces: Horizontal and upward-facing surfaces were covered at most locations by a rich and varied epibiota. Extensive areas dominated by mussels and some areas recently bared of mussels but with a few colonising species present were also recorded.

The infralittoral (algal dominated) zone was very compressed and there was no clear infralittoral fringe though *Laminaria digitata* was usually present in small amounts at about +1m relative to Chart Datum. *Laminaria hyperborea* was present from about +1m to at or just below Chart Datum but nowhere formed a dense forest. Foliose algae formed a dense cover over rocks to a depth of about 0.5m wherever rock was not dominated or until recently dominated by mussels. Foliose algae which formed more than about 10% cover at several of the sites studied included *Cryptopleura ramosa*, *Polyneura gmelinii*, *Callibepharis ciliata*, *Plocamium cartilagineum*, *Phyllophora pseudoceranoides*, *Chondrus crispus*, *Dictyota dichotoma* and *Palmaria palmata*. The greatest variety of algae were observed in the west of Oxwich Bay along the most sheltered part of the coast studied. The maximum downward extent of foliose algae was to about 3.5m, but was difficult to assess because of the shallow downward extent of rocks at most sites and the presence of extensive mussel beds at many sites. Algae characteristic of the lower infralittoral were *Rhodymenia pseudopalmata* var. *ellisiae*, *Polyneura gmelinii* and *Hypoglossum woodwardii*.

Sessile and sedentary animals dominated rock in shallow water wherever algae were sparse or absent and rocks had not recently been bared by the loss of a mussel bed. Animal species which formed the main rock cover in the circalittoral (animal dominated) zone included *Halichondria panicea*, *Nemertesia antennina*, *N. ramosa*, *Aglaophenia* sp., *Halecium halecinum*, *Kirchenpaueria pinnata*, *Alcyonium digitatum*, *Tealia felina*, *Bugula plumosa*, *B. turbinata*, *Clavelina lepadiformis*, *Polyclinum aurantium*, *Sidnyum turbinatum* and *Distaplia rosea*. *Tubularia indivisa* was frequent at the tops of rock pinnacles in tide-exposed areas. *Flustra foliacea* dominated patches of seabed offshore of Oxwich Point in depths below 20m. A bed of *Ophiothrix fragilis* with associated large numbers of *Sagartia elegans* was present off Worms Head. *Polydora* sp. dominated extensive areas of shallow rock north of Mumbles Head. Dense populations of Jassidae and Caprellidae were recorded in tideswept areas at some sites, usually attached to hydroids. *Sabellaria spinulosa* was very common though often obscured by other species. In many areas, the tubes of *Sabellaria* formed a continuous crust several millimetres thick over the limestone rock.

Dense beds of the mussel *Mytilus edulis* were present at most of the locations studied. Large mussels were observed only in depths shallower than 3m below which the beds were of small individuals. Large populations of the predatory starfish *Asterias rubens* were present on the mussel beds and at some sites formed a distinctive front of very dense individuals with dead mussel shells on one side and a dense live bed on the other. Extensive areas of bared rock with byssus threads still attached were also present in some locations. Re-colonisation of areas previously smothered by mussels (byssus threads still attached to rocks) had started at a few locations. *Enteromorpha* sp., *Ulva* sp., *Taonia atomaria*, *Obelia dichotoma* and *Sertularia argentea* were noted as colonisers.

<u>Vertical and overhanging rock</u>: Vertical and overhanging surfaces were characterised by frequent dense patches of *Bugula plumosa* with some *B. turbinata* and by occasional or frequent colonies of the ascidians *Polyclinum aurantium*, *Sidnyum turbinatum*, *Botryllus schlosseri*, *Botrylloides leachi*, *Clavelina lepadiformis* and *Polycarpa pomaria*. The hydroids *Aglaophenia* sp. and *Kirchenpaueria pinnata* formed dense clumps in some areas whilst *Alcyonium digitatum* was present, generally in small amounts, at most sites. Several species of encrusting sponges occurred in small patches and *Dysidea fragilis* was frequent at some sites. The sabellid *Jasminiera elegans* was present in dense colonies on some overhangs.

<u>Kelp stipes</u>: Stipes of *Laminaria hyperborea* held a characteristic assemblage of a small variety of algae. *Membranoptera alata*, *Palmaria palmata* and *Cryptopleura ramosa* were most commonly observed whilst *Plocamium cartilaginium*, *Phycodrys rubens* and *Polysiphonia* sp. were also recorded.

<u>In limestone rock</u>: The rock observed at many sites was bored by several species. Polychaete worms were particularly abundant and included very high densities of *Polydora* sp. north of Mumbles Head (site 21) and *Jasminiera elegans* at several sites. Large holes made by boring bivalves were observed at many sites but only a few

siphons of live individuals, identified as *Hiatella arctica* in collected material, were found. Occasional colonies of boring *Cliona* sp. were present throughout the area and *Phoronis hippocrepia* was often abundant in rock adjacent to sand.

<u>Loose-lying rocks</u>: Cobbles and other mobile rock substrata were largely covered by *Balanus crenatus* and *Pomatoceros triqueter* usually with very few other species present. *Tealia felina* occurred frequently amongst the stones. To the north and east of Mumbles Head, the encrusting bryozoa *Conopeum reticulum* and *Cryptosula pallasiana* dominated some stones.

<u>Rocks adjacent to sand</u>: Rocks adjacent to or partly covered in sand were characterised by large colonies of *Phoronis hippocrepia,* frequent *Hydrallmania falcata* and *Sertularia cupressina*. At Graves End (site 13), several large groups of *Ciocalypta penicillus* were observed. A few algae were noted as present only or mainly on rocks adjacent to sand: *Rhodymenia delicatula, Radicilingua thysanorhizans* and *Taonia atomaria*

<u>Sediments</u>: A sparse visible fauna of a small variety of species was observed on muddy sand adjacent to rocks. Species included *Cereus pedunculatus,* another species of burrowing anemone probably *Peachia hastata, Corymorpha nutans, Lanice conchilega, Sabella penicillus, Pagurus* sp.*, Macropipus holsatus, Nassarius reticulatus* and small species of brittle star.

<u>Areas affected by the Mumbles Head sewage outfall</u>: The area south of Mumbles Head which receives water, sewage and some industrial waste from the large sewage outfall off Mumbles Head had communities present with a high biomass but largely dominated by mussels. The overhang communities, where mussels were sparse, were similar to those present elsewhere in Gower. *Carcinus maenas,* a species very rarely observed on the open coast, was present in large numbers. Only 19 species of algae were recorded and kelp stipes were mostly bare of epiphytes, suggesting that algal communities might be impoverished.

DISCUSSION

Comparison of the Gower with Areas to the West and East

The numbers of species in different groups of organisms present at locations along the coast of South Wales is summarised in Table 32.1.

Comparison of the results of the Gower survey with those of the South Pembrokeshire survey reveal a continuation from South Pembrokeshire of a gradual change in the communities present. The shallow downward extent of the kelp forest and of foliose algae and the absence of a well-defined infralittoral fringe along the Gower coast is clearly an extension of the gradual reduction in depth penetration of algae from west to east along the South Pembrokeshire coast. Here, the kelp forest extended to 7m in the west and 1.6m in the east whilst dense foliose algae extended to 10m in the west compared to 2.6m in the east.

Southern or oceanic species noted as occurring only on the offshore islands of Pembrokeshire and not on the mainland coast were also absent on the Gower. Several species which were most abundant or only present to the west of the survey area in South Pembrokeshire were not recorded along the Gower coast, for instance *Aglaozonia parvula, Zanardinia prototypus, Alaria esculenta, Clathrina coriacea, Caryophyllia smithi, Corynactis viridis, Pentapora foliacea, Marthasterias glacialis* and *Molgula manhattensis*. Others only rarely present included *Corallina* sp., 'Lithothamnia' *Polymastia mammilaris, P. boletiformis* and *Pachymatisma johnstonia*. Of the species noted as most abundant in the east of the South Pembrokeshire survey area some were not recorded or rarely recorded along the Gower coast, including *Rhodophyllis*

TABLE 32.1. Numbers of Species in the Main Groups of Conspicuous Rocky Sublittoral Organisms Present Along the Coast from Sheep Island (Entrance to Milford Haven) to Reynards Cave (Near Llantwit Major). Blocks of About Seven Sites are used to Provide Comparison with the Survey Area with the Lowest Number of Sites and to Ensure the Inclusion of Locations where a Wide Variety of Habitats are Represented and with Full Records of Algae and Animals at Several of the Sites.

Coastline included	SOUTH PEMBROKESHIRE							GOWER				UPPER BRISTOL CHANNEL
	Sheep Island to Crow Rock	Pen-y-Holt Bay to The Castle	St Gowans Shoals to Stackpole Head	N. Stackpole Head to Westmoor Cliff	Eastmoor Cliff to West Beacon Point	The Flats to St Catherines Island	CARMARTHEN BAY	Worms Head to S. Oxwich Point	E. Oxwich Point to Seven Slades	Off Caswell Bay to Mumbles Head	SWANSEA BAY	Fairy Rock, Porthcawl to Reynards Cave, Llantwit Major
Linear distance included west to east (km)	4.5	6.6	3.9	4.4	9.5	4.5*	22.5	12.9	6.9	5.2	19.3	12.1
Number of survey sites	7	8	7	7	7	7		7	7	7		6
Algae	57	60	49	50	49	40	no survey sites	45	52	19	no survey sites	17
Porifera	19	20	18	17	17	13		16	15	11		5
Hydrozoa	11	9	12	13	11	9		12	14	10		8
Anthozoa	7	8	10	6	7	7		9	6	6		5
Polychaeta	4	4	4	7	8	4		7	6	6		6
Decapoda	4	6	9	8	10	9		10	8	6		2
Bryozoa	14	14	13	16	18	10		10	12	12		10
Echinodermata	7	7	8	6	8	5		2	2	2		3
Ascidiacea	11	12	13	13	11	7		13	14	10		2
Total number of species	134	140	136	136	139	104		124	129	82		58

*South to north

divaricata, *Lomentaria orchadensis* and *Antedon bifida*.

Several species which were present in South Pembrokeshire in apparently similar amounts all along the coast were not recorded along the Gower: *Myriogramme bonne-*

maisonii, *Dictyopteris membranacea*, *Umbonula littoralis*, *Cellepora pumicosa*, *Pycnoclavella aurilucens* and *Stolonica socialis*.

Only three species of echinoderms were recorded compared to 18 in South Pembrokeshire indicating a considerable impoverishment of this group across Carmarthen Bay.

The number of species and the abundance of bryozoa were also considerably reduced off the Gower compared to South Pembrokeshire. It is particularly notable that the abundance of *Cellaria* spp., Crisiidae and Scrupocellariidae, groups often dominant on sublittoral rocks, was very low on the Gower compared to open coast areas of south-west Britain. The abundance of encrusting bryozoa was also low and *Cellepora pumicosa*, which was characteristic of many areas off South Pembrokeshire, was not recorded. However, the encrusting bryozoan *Conopeum reticulum*, which is characteristic of estuarine areas, was present in large amounts off Mumbles Head.

The shallow downward extent of algae and the absence of several species common in open coast areas of south-west Britain gave the impression of impoverishment in the Gower flora. However, it is clear from Table 32.1 that along most of the coast almost as many species of algae were recorded as along similar lengths of coastline off South Pembrokeshire. Off the coast from Caswell Bay to Mumbles Head, only 19 species of algae were recorded and this low number is accounted for partly by the impoverishment of the area south of Mumbles Head, the only location where algae were studied.

A few species were present in greater amounts on the Gower coast than off the South Pembrokeshire coast. The very extensive populations of *Mytilus edulis* and the large numbers of *Sabellaria spinulosa* forming a continuous crust over some rocks were particularly notable. Also, the domination of rocks north of Mumbles Head by *Polydora* sp. appears to be a feature of turbid water areas or areas affected by pollution stress. The high density of Caprellidae and Jassiidae observed at some sites along the Gower is unusual compared to other areas studied in south-west Britain.

Although extensive beds of *Mytilus edulis* are noted as a feature of the Gower coast, it seems that the presence of these beds is a recent occurrence. A great increase in the abundance of mussels has been noted since 1974 along the Gower coast with only localised occurrence in the previous 15 years (A. Osborn, *pers. comm.*).

Comparison of the Gower coast sublittoral flora and fauna with areas surveyed at Fairy Rock, Tusker Rock, Nash Point, St. Donats and off Llantwit Major to the east of Swansea Bay, reveals a very sharp change in the communities present from the west to the east side of Swansea Bay.

No *Laminaria* was observed to the east of Swansea Bay, there was no infralittoral zone, and the number of sublittoral algae present was reduced to a total of 17 species compared to a total of 66 recorded from the Gower. The number of animals recorded to the east of Swansea Bay was also much reduced compared to the Gower with only 41 noted. The reduction in the number of species and the abundance of bryozoa and echinoderms along the Gower coast compared to South Pembrokeshire was also noted east of Swansea Bay. In addition a large fall in the numbers of species of sponges, decapods and ascidians was observed. The most striking feature of communities present on sublittoral rocks to the east of Swansea Bay was the dominance of large areas of rock by *Sabellaria spinulosa, S. alveolata* and by *Dendrodoa grossularia*.

Thus, Carmarthen Bay is seen as a transition rather than a boundary area between open coast and enclosed coast flora and fauna whilst Swansea Bay appears to be a major boundary zone across which considerable impoverishment in rocky sublittoral communities occurs and key or dominant species change.

Environmental Factors Important in Determining the Communities Present

Local differences in the plant and animal communities present along the Gower coast are considered here to be mainly the result of the stability or mobility of rock substrata and the range of habitats provided by different topographical features including upward facing, vertical and overhanging surfaces as well as the effects of scour where sand is present adjacent to rock. Although the limestone rock is bored by several species, these do not form a conspicuous part of the rocky sublittoral biota. It also seems probable that the layer of *Sabellaria spinulosa* tubes or the remains of tubes found over many rock surfaces below overgrowth of other species, may prevent the settlement or smother species boring into the rock.

Since most of the Gower coast faces south-south-west and is subject to similar exposure to wave action and tidal streams, little difference in sublittoral communities as a result of this feature were observed. However, the distinctive communities present off Worms Head and Oxwich Point where tidal streams are strong, and the rich algal communities present in the shelter of West Oxwich Bay have most likely developed due to the different regimes of tide and wave exposure compared to most of the coast.

Residual water flow from east to west may have some effect in restricting the dispersion of larvae of benthic species eastwards when the nearest populations of some rock-living species, many of which will have short-lived larvae, might be over 20km to the west of the Gower across Carmarthen Bay. However, no particular species are suggested here as being absent from the Gower because of the effects of residual flow on larval distribution. Residual flow is seen as most important in the distribution of water masses of different quality and in particular in the supply of water along the Gower coast mainly from Swansea Bay.

Any gross effects of pollution appear to be limited to the area of Mumbles Head where the impoverishment of the flora and the presence of large numbers of *Carcinus maenas, Polydora* sp. and of the estuarine bryozoan *Conopeum reticulum* possibly indicate some stress.

Many of the characteristics of the Gower coast rocky sublittoral flora and fauna are doubtless brought about by the high turbidity of the water for most of the year. Such a high level of suspended sediment reduces light penetration and accounts for the shallow downward extent of the algae. Also, the suspended material provides a large food supply for suspension feeders such as mussels, Jassiidae and Caprellidae. Species which might be particularly liable to clogging include the hydrozoa and bryozoa and the latter group has been described as particularly impoverished along the Gower coast.

It is notable that similar changes to those described in rocky sublittoral communities from South Pembrokeshire to the Gower and from the Gower to areas east of Swansea Bay are similar to those which occur from open coast to enclosed marine areas (for instance, in the region of Abereiddy Quarry in Pembrokeshire, Hiscock and Hoare, 1975; in the region of Lough Ine, south-west Ireland, Hiscock, 1976; or from open Irish Sea to Liverpool Bay coasts of Anglesey, Hiscock, 1976) or along a severe pollution gradient such as that near to the bromine extraction plant on Anglesey (Hoare and Hiscock, 1974). It is therefore difficult to identify the effects of specific environmental factors such as turbidity or sewage pollution on rocky sublittoral communities on the Gower coast or to the east of Swansea Bay but many species are clearly subject to increasing environmental stress from west to east along the coast of South Wales with a sharp increase in the region of Swansea Bay.

ACKNOWLEDGEMENTS

This work was commissioned by the Nature Conservancy Council as part of its programme of research into nature conservation. The survey was carried out by the authors, Reh Rashid, Christine Webb, Julia Stubbs, Shaun Thorogood and Colin Shelley. Laboratory and air compressor facilities were provided by the Zoology Department of University College Swansea, and we are particularly grateful to Alan Osborn and Nigel Bowden for their help before and during the survey.

REFERENCES

Cartlidge, D. and Hiscock, K. (1979). *Field survey of sublittoral habitats, and species in South Pembrokeshire.* Nature Conservancy Council, Huntingdon/Field Studies Council Oil Pollution Research Unit, Orielton Field Centre, Pembroke. (Unpublished report).

Collins, M., Ferentinos, G. and Banner, F.T. (1979). The hydrodynamics and sedimentology of a high (tidal and wave) energy embayment (Swansea Bay, northern Bristol Channel). *Estuar. and Coast. Mar. Sci., 8,* 49-74.

Conseil Permanent International pour l'Exploration de la Mer: Service Hydrographique (1962). *Mean monthly temperature and salinity of the surface waters of the North Sea and adjacent waters from 1905 to 1954.* Charlottenlund Slot: CPIEM.

Hamilton, P. (1973). The circulation of the Bristol Channel. *Geophys. J.R. Astr. Soc., 32,* 409-422.

Hiscock, K. (1976). *The influence of water movement on the ecology of sublittoral rocky areas.* Unpub. Ph.D. Thesis, University of Wales.

Hiscock, K. (1979a). Systematic surveys and monitoring in nearshore sublittoral areas using diving. *In*: Nichols, D. (Ed.). *Monitoring the marine environment*, Institute of Biology, London, 55-74.

Hiscock, K. (1979b). *Field survey of sublittoral habitats and species along the Gower coast.* Nature Conservancy Council, Huntingdon/Field Studies Council Oil Pollution Research Unit, Orielton Field Centre, Pembroke. (Unpublished report).

Hiscock, K. and Hoare, R. (1975). The ecology of sublittoral communities at Abereiddy Quarry, Pembrokeshire. *J. mar. biol. Ass. U.K., 55,* 833-864.

Hoare, R. and Hiscock, K. (1974). An ecological survey of the rocky coast adjacent to a bromine extraction works. *Estuar. and Coast. Mar. Sci., 2,* 329-348.

Stebbing, A.R.D. (1979). An experimental approach to the determinants of biological water quality. *Phil. Trans. R. Soc. Lond., B, 286,* 465-481.

Tyler, P.A. (1976). Sublittoral community structure of Oxwich Bay, South Wales in relation to sedimentological, physical, oceanographic and biological parameters. *In*: Keegan, B.F., O'Ceidigh, P., and Boaden, P.J.S. (Eds.). *Biology of Benthic Organisms.* Pergamon Press, Oxford, 559-566.

Tyler, P.A. and Banner, F.T. (1977). The effect of coastal hydrodynamics on the echinoderm distribution in the sublittoral of Oxwich Bay, Bristol Channel. *Estuar. and Coast. Mar. Sci., 5,* 293-308.

33. ANNUAL MACROFAUNA PRODUCTION IN AN *ABRA* COMMUNITY

R. M. Warwick and C. L. George

Natural Environment Research Council, Institute for Marine Environmental Research, Prospect Place, The Hoe, Plymouth, U.K.

ABSTRACT

A single station representative of the *Abra* community in Swansea Bay was sampled at regular intervals between March 1975 and January 1976 with a Day grab and naturalist's dredge. Estimates of production of the major component species in the community have been made by cohort growth analysis. In order of productive importance, the species studied were: *Spisula elliptica, Nucula turgida, Abra alba, Diastylis rathkei, Nephtys hombergi, Ophiura texturata, Pectinaria koreni, Spiophanes bombyx* and *Ampharete acutifrons*. The faunal assemblage proved to be highly unstable numerically and the reasons for this, and the problems arising from it, are discussed. This instability is reflected in the life histories of the individual macrofauna species, but not in certain properties of community structure. The total annual production was 14.2g dry wt/m^2, and the mean annual biomass 11.1g/m^2, giving an annual P/$\bar{\text{B}}$ of 1.28.

KEYWORDS

Macrobenthos; Production; Population dynamics; Growth rates; Community structure; Bristol Channel; Swansea Bay.

INTRODUCTION

This paper reports the continuation of a study designed to determine the net secondary production of the major component species which comprise the macrobenthos communities of the Bristol Channel. The rationale behind this study was introduced by Warwick and Others (1978). Warwick and Davies (1977) have shown that the *Abra* community in the Bristol Channel takes three forms, the purest of which is found in sheltered inshore muddy bottoms, where *Nucula turgida* and *Nephtys hombergi* are prominent constituents of the community.

AREA OF INVESTIGATION AND METHODS

Station 62 (51°33.5'N, 3°52.0'W) of Warwick and Davies (1977) in Swansea Bay has a species composition typical of the pure *Abra* community and was selected for study. The water depth at this station is 18.2m at MHW Springs and 9.7m at MLW Springs. The bottom salinity ranges between 29.8 and 33.5°/oo depending on the degree of

TABLE 33.1. Numerical Abundance/m^2 of all Species (* = Species for which Production Estimates have been made).

Species	Mar.	May	Jly.	Sep.	Nov.	Jan.	MEAN
* Spisula elliptica	21	14	216	1950	2472	147	803.33
* Nucula turgida	358	127	1774	1817	400	70	757.67
* Nephtys hombergi	123	23	733	854	793	73	433.17
* Diastylis rathkei	62	81	242	193	152	-	146.0
* Abra alba	30	38	96	108	35	10	52.83
* Spiophanes bombyx	9	7	63	164	9	2	42.33
* Ampharete acutifrons	-	-	7	73	7	-	14.5
* Ophiura texturata	-	-	5	52	1	1	9.67
Polydora antennata	-	-	-	38	-	-	6.33
* Pectinaria koreni	-	1	7	19	8	2	6.16
Pharus legumen	1	-	1	1	12	1	2.67
Macoma balthica	-	-	13	-	-	-	2.17
Musculus sp.	7	-	-	2	-	-	1.50
Bulla sp.	-	-	-	-	9	-	1.50
Scalibregma inflatum	-	-	-	7	-	-	1.17
Lanice conchilega	-	-	1	3	-	1	0.833
Corystes cassivelaunus	-	-	1	2	-	-	0.50
Acronida brachiata	-	-	-	-	1	1	0.33
Pholoe minuta	-	-	-	2	-	-	0.33
Aphrodite aculeata	-	-	1	-	-	-	0.16
Gari fervensis	-	-	-	-	-	1	0.16
Natica catena	-	-	1	-	-	-	0.16
Orbinia cuvieri	-	-	-	1	-	-	0.16
Tharyx marioni	-	-	-	1	-	-	0.16
amphipods	1	-	10	46	3	-	10.00
other cumaceans	-	-	7	56	14	-	12.83
oligochaetes	29	2	2	196	11	6	41.0
polyclads	-	-	-	2	-	-	0.33

fresh water inflow into the Bay. Bottom water temperatures reach a minimum of 6.7°C in February/March and a maximum of 17.7°C in late August.

The sediment consists of a variable depth of sandy-mud, averaging about 6cm, overlying a bed of very fine cohesive clay. Nearly all the animals are confined to this upper sandy-mud layer.

The Day grab penetrated well into the sediment and, in view of the animal's confinement to the surface layers, sampled even the deepest burrowing species adequately. A series of fourteen 0.07 m² Day grab hauls, covering a total area of 1m² was taken on each occasion (March, May, July, September and November, 1975 and January 1976). Large non-quantitative samples of epifauna were also collected with a naturalist's dredge to obtain data on the growth rates of certain large but rare surface-living species. Samples were collected and processed as described by Warwick and others (1978) for the *Venus* community in Carmarthen Bay. However, the numbers of individuals proved to be very variable both between months and between samples taken in the same month, the latter possibly being a result of the variable thickness of sandy-mud overlying the clay. Changes in species numbers were difficult to interpret in terms of predation and recruitment (see Discussion), and we have therefore calculated approximate net production figures for each species by multiplying the weight increment of each year-class by the mean number of individuals in that year-class throughout the year. The production estimates are strictly for 10 months (March-January), but since production is minimal from January-March the figures will be very close to the annual production.

PRODUCTION ESTIMATES

Nine species were present in sufficient numbers for production estimates to be made (Table 33.1): these together made up 93% of the biomass of the whole assemblage averaged over the year.

Mollusca

Spisula elliptica: Shells were easily aged by ring counts and were also widely separated on the size frequency histograms (Fig. 33.1), except for the 1974/1973 year-class division from July onwards. The 1975 settlement first appeared in July, by which time many specimens were quite large (7mm), indicating that settlement probably begins in late May or early June. Settlement is evidently very patchy: nearly all the shells of the 7mm modal size-class were found in a single 0.07m² Day grab sample, with only one in the remaining thirteen grabs (Fig. 33.2). In subsequent months this group was divided more evenly between the samples, indicating post-settlement dispersal or mechanical disturbance and mixing by tidal currents. Small spat were also present in subsequent months suggesting a long settlement period. '0' group animals settling early in the year reach 10mm by the following winter, whilst late settlements only reach 2-3mm. Apparently there is differential survival of these settlements from year-to-year as the bulk of the overwintering population in March 1975 had a shell length of 3mm, but in January 1976 10mm.

Production was calculated by the method described by Crisp (1971, p.220), using monthly values for the mean individual weight of animals in each year-class, but assuming numbers remained constant at the mean value. Year-class weights have been determined from the size-frequency histograms using length/ash-free dry weight equations established for each month. The production calculation is given in Table 33.2. The annual production is 10.285g/m² and the mean biomass 6.227g/m².

Nucula turgida: Only a small proportion of shells could be aged by winter growth rings, and age cohorts could not be determined from the size frequency histograms

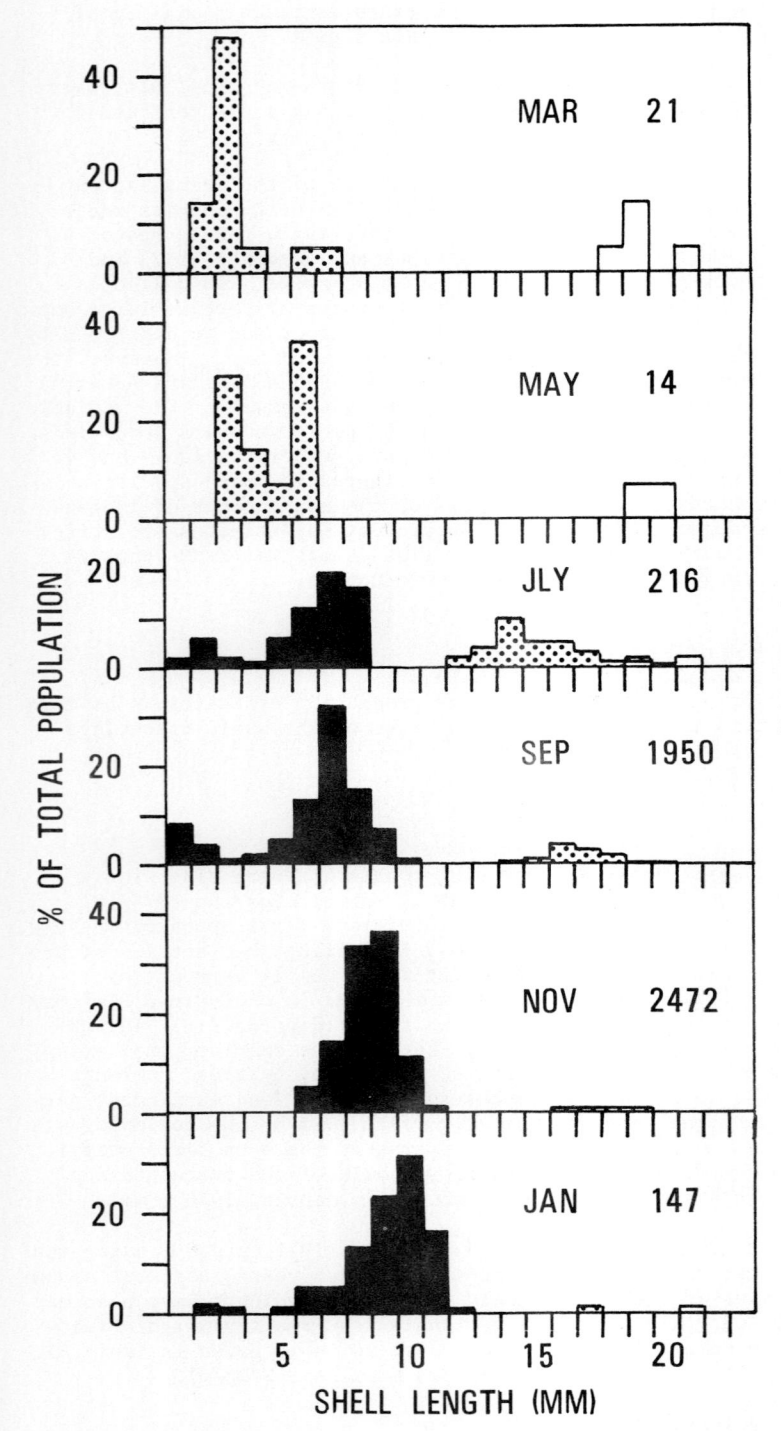

Figure 33.1. *Spisula elliptica*: size frequency histograms. 1975 year-class black, 1974 dotted, 1973 white. Numbers measured beside months.

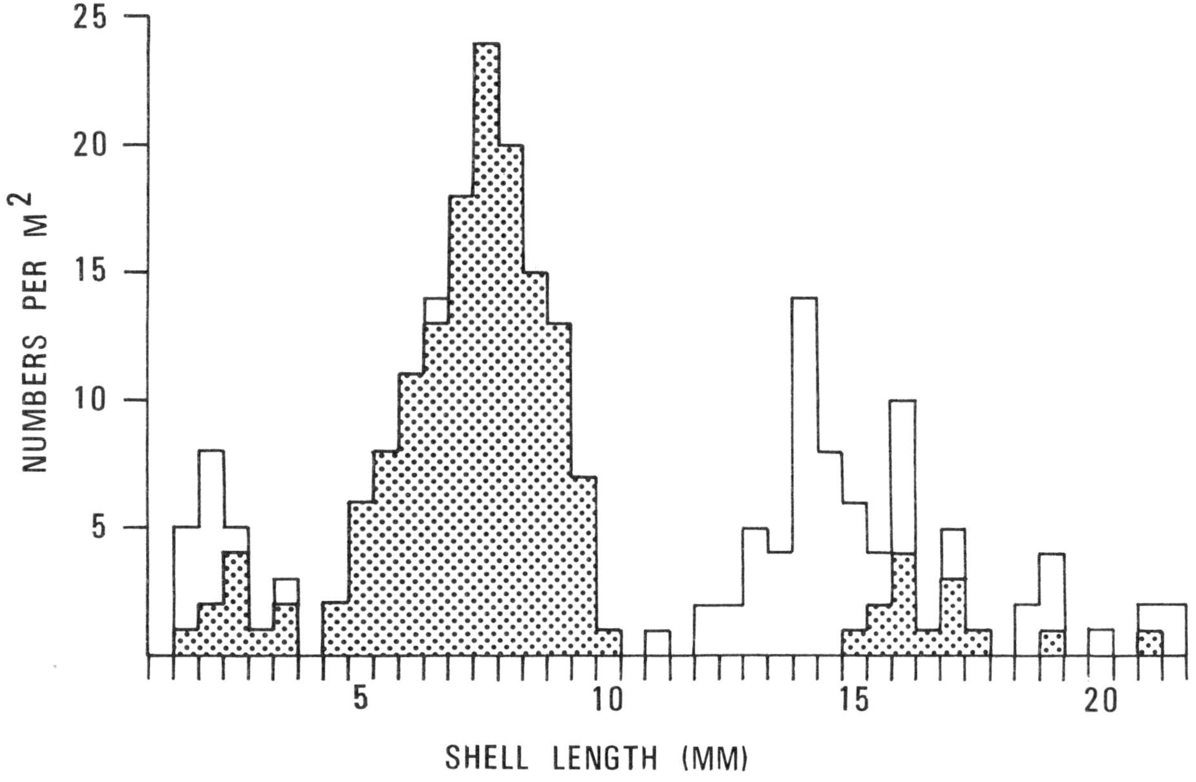

Figure 33.2. *Spisula elliptica*: size frequency histograms for a single grab sample in which a strong '0' group was represented, compared with the 13 other grabs where it was virtually absent (see text).

TABLE 33.2. Year-Class Production for *Spisula elliptica*

Year-class (year of settlement)	Mean No/m² in year class	Initial wt/ind (mg)	Final wt/ind (mg)	Annual Production (g/m²)
1975 (late)	73.5	0.037	0.074	0.005
1975 (early)	1047.8	2.777	7.326	7.675
1974	52.7	0.399	49.659	2.594
1973	3.0	71.389	99.461	0.084
			TOTAL	10.285

because of year-class overlap. We have therefore adopted the procedure used by Warwick and others (1978) for *Tellina fabula*. A Ford-Walford plot was constructed using shells on which clearly consecutive age-rings were discernible; it is described by the equation:

$$L_{t+1} = 3.653 + 0.588\ L_t \quad \text{(lengths in mm)}$$

From this, a growth curve was constructed (Fig. 33.3) using an initial length of 3.159mm, which is the mean length of the '0' ring measured on 123 specimens. Using this curve the size limits of each cohort were defined as in Fig. 33.2, and the size frequency histograms divided into cohorts (Fig. 33.4) assuming linear growth in shell length from May to September and no increase at any other time. Cohort weights were calculated from a length/ash-free dry weight regression determined from a sample of 40 animals comprising representatives of all months:

$$\log_{10} \text{wt.(mg)} = -1.4182 + 2.6278\ \log_{10} \text{length (mm)}$$

The annual production calculated as for *Spisula* (Table 33.3) was 1.351g/m² and the mean biomass 2.615g/m², giving a P/B̄ of 0.52. This compares with an average annual

TABLE 33.3. Year-Class Production for *Nucula turgida*

Year-class (year of settlement)	Mean No/m² in year class	Initial wt/ind (mg)	Final wt/ind (mg)	Annual Production (g/m²)
1975	248	0.149	0.952	0.236
1974	164	1.122	3.965	0.466
1973	125	3.749	6.404	0.329
1972	118	5.944	8.001	0.243
1971	48	8.175	9.621	0.069
1970	10	9.620	10.573	0.010
1969	7	10.329	11.239	0.006
1968	6	11.239	11.581	0.002
1967 and earlier	10	14.022	13.016	-0.010
			TOTAL	1.351

P/B̄ of 0.62 for populations in the German Bight (Rachor, 1976). The growth rate determined from the Ford Walford plot was fractionally slower than that of the German Bight populations (Fig. 33.3), which Rachor regarded as growing under suboptional conditions.

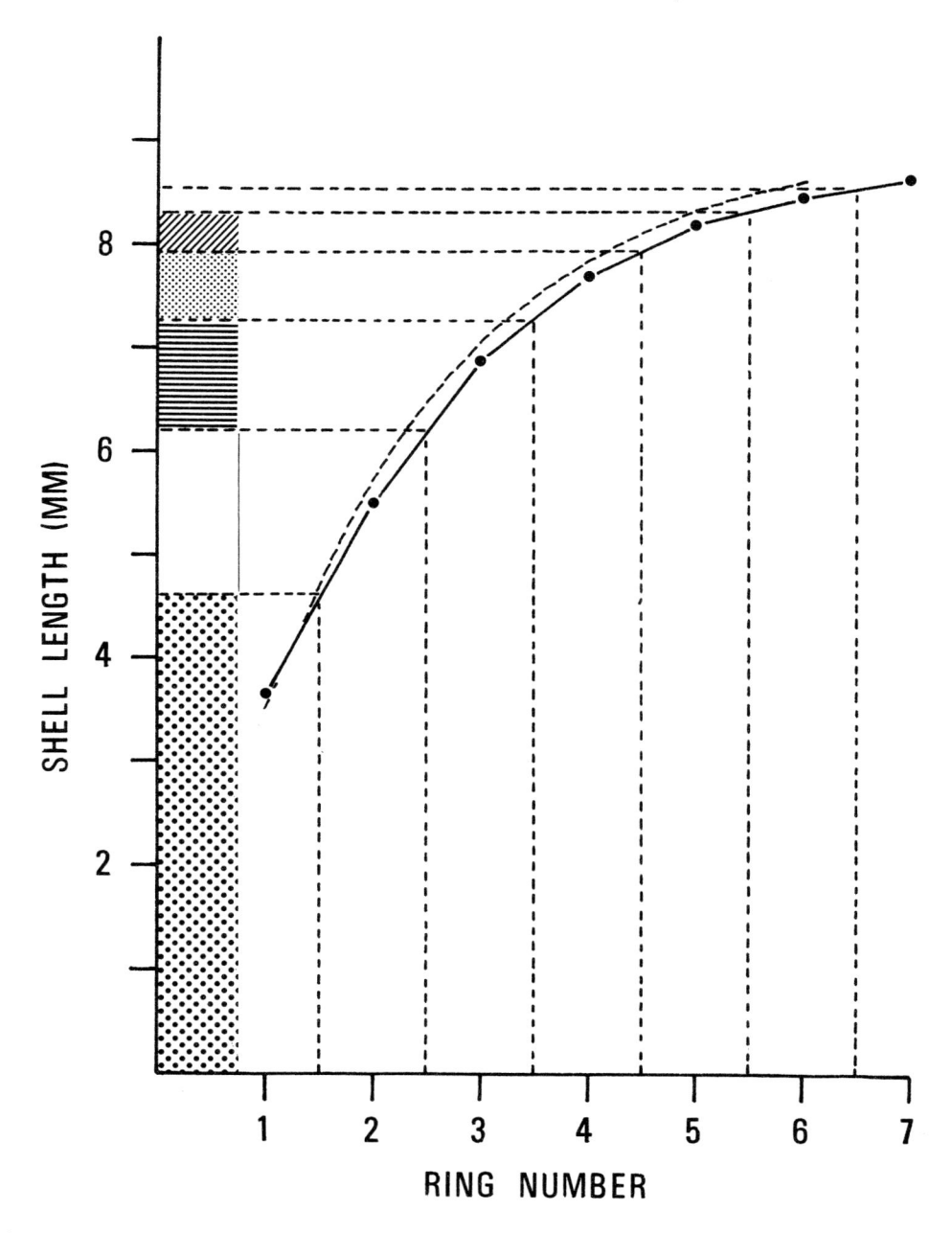

Figure 33.3. *Nucula turgida*: growth curve showing size limits of year-classes. Shading conventions as Fig. 33.4. Dotted line shows growth in the German Bight from Rachor (1976).

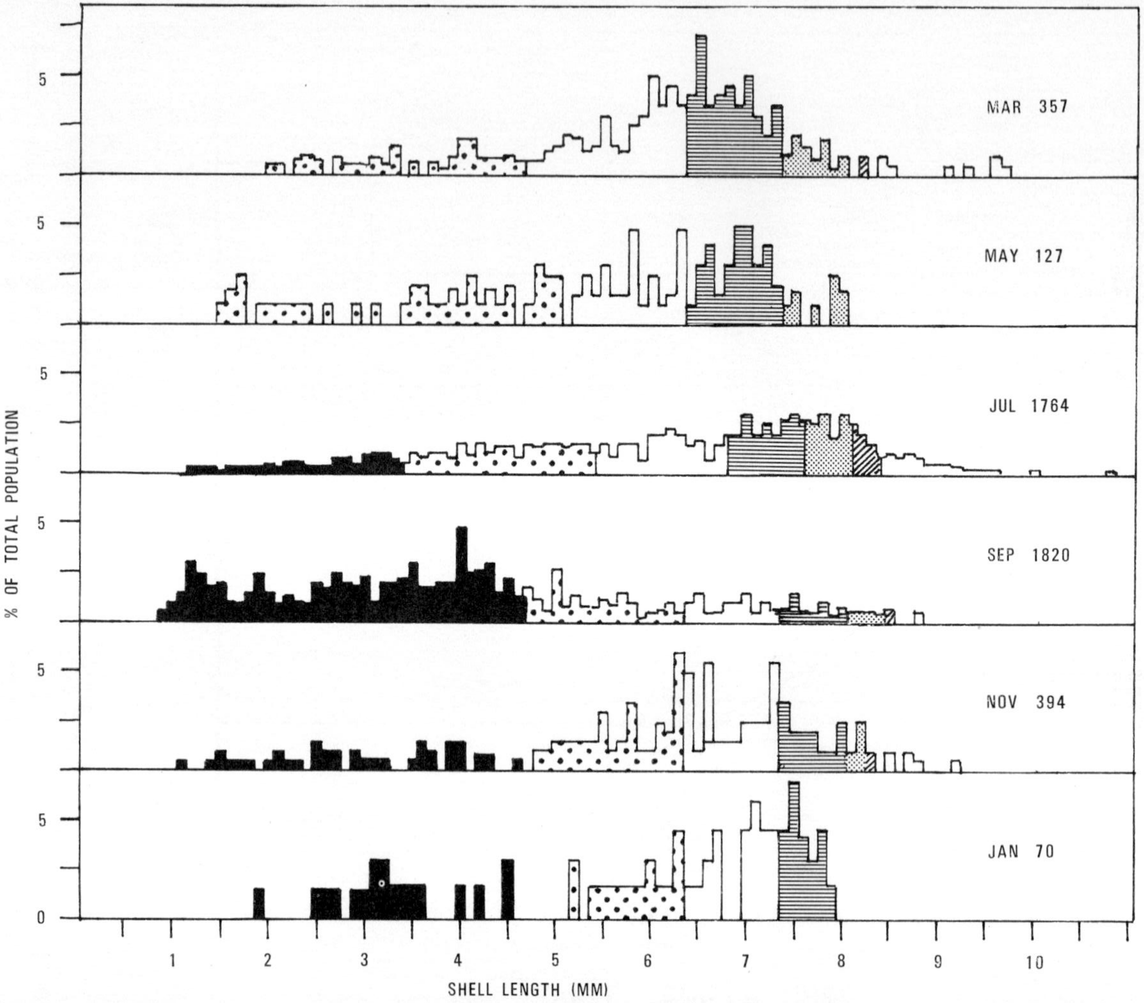

Figure 33.4. *Nucula turgida*: size-frequency histograms with limits of year-classes defined from Fig. 33.3. 1975 year-class black, 1974 dotted, 1973 white, 1972 transverse hatch, 1971 fine stipple, 1970 oblique hatch.

In samples dredged from the Cumbrae Deep, Allen (1953, 1954) recognised distinct size groups within the population which he regarded as year-classes. However, his nine histogram peaks occur at absolutely regular intervals and all correspond with exact whole millimeters, which led Ansell and Parulekar (1978) to infer an unconscious measuring bias. Despite measuring an even larger number of shells than Allen, both in July and September, we were unable to recognise such peaks, nor are they evident in the histograms of Rachor (1976). Furthermore, Allen's data are at variance with our Ford Walford plot which indicates a gradual decline from year-to-year in the rate of growth in shell length, a phenomenon supported by measured growth in laboratory maintained populations (Rachor, 1976).

Mortality in the Swansea Bay population is evidently rather low, which in combination with the slow growth rate of older animals produces a bias in the size frequency histograms towards larger shell size.

Such a bias is also present in Allen's samples, although he attributes the low numbers of small animals to mesh selection in the dredge, and in many of Rachor's (1976) samples. Low mortality rates are also found in other nuculanids (Ansell and Parulekar, 1978) and the implied life span of 5+ years is in accord with Rachor's (1976) data for the same species, and with *Nuculana minuta* (7 years; Ansell and Parulekar, 1978) and *Nucula pernula* (5 years; Tabunkov, 1974).

Abra alba: Shells could not be aged by ring counts, but in the summer months (July and September), when relatively large numbers were present, two distinct size classes were present. These were taken to represent the 1975 and 1974 settlements, and the size frequency histograms before and after these months were interpreted accordingly (Fig. 33.5). The 1975 settlement first appeared in the sieved samples in July, but very small shells were still present in November, indicating the probability of settlement over a long period of time. Production was calculated by the same method as for *Spisula* (Table 33.4). Growth of the 1974 year-class was rapid between May and July, resulting in a rather high production of $0.408 g/m^2/y$ in relation to the mean biomass of $0.302 g/m^2$, with a P/B of 1.35.

TABLE 33.4   Year-Class Production for *Abra alba*

Year-class (year of settlement)	Mean No/m² in year class	Initial wt/ind (mg)	Final wt/ind (mg)	Annual Production (g/m²)
1975	16.5	0.863	1.370	0.008
1974	41.83	0.377	9.951	0.400
			TOTAL	0.408

The initial year-class present in March 1975 comprised shells of very small size (modal length 3mm). These must have settled rather late in 1974, so that not much growth occurred before winter. Stephen (1932) found no new settlement by June in Loch Striven, Scotland, with a new year-class of 3-11mm shells appearing in August, but on the other hand Ford (1925) recorded newly settled 2-3mm spat in May in the Plymouth area (Bigbury Bay). An alternative explanation for the small size of the March 1975 year-class in Swansea Bay might therefore be that they settled early in 1975, or may be a mixture of early 1975 and 1974 settlements. Settlement of this species is notoriously erratic from year-to-year (Ford, 1925; Stephen, 1932; Thorson, 1946).

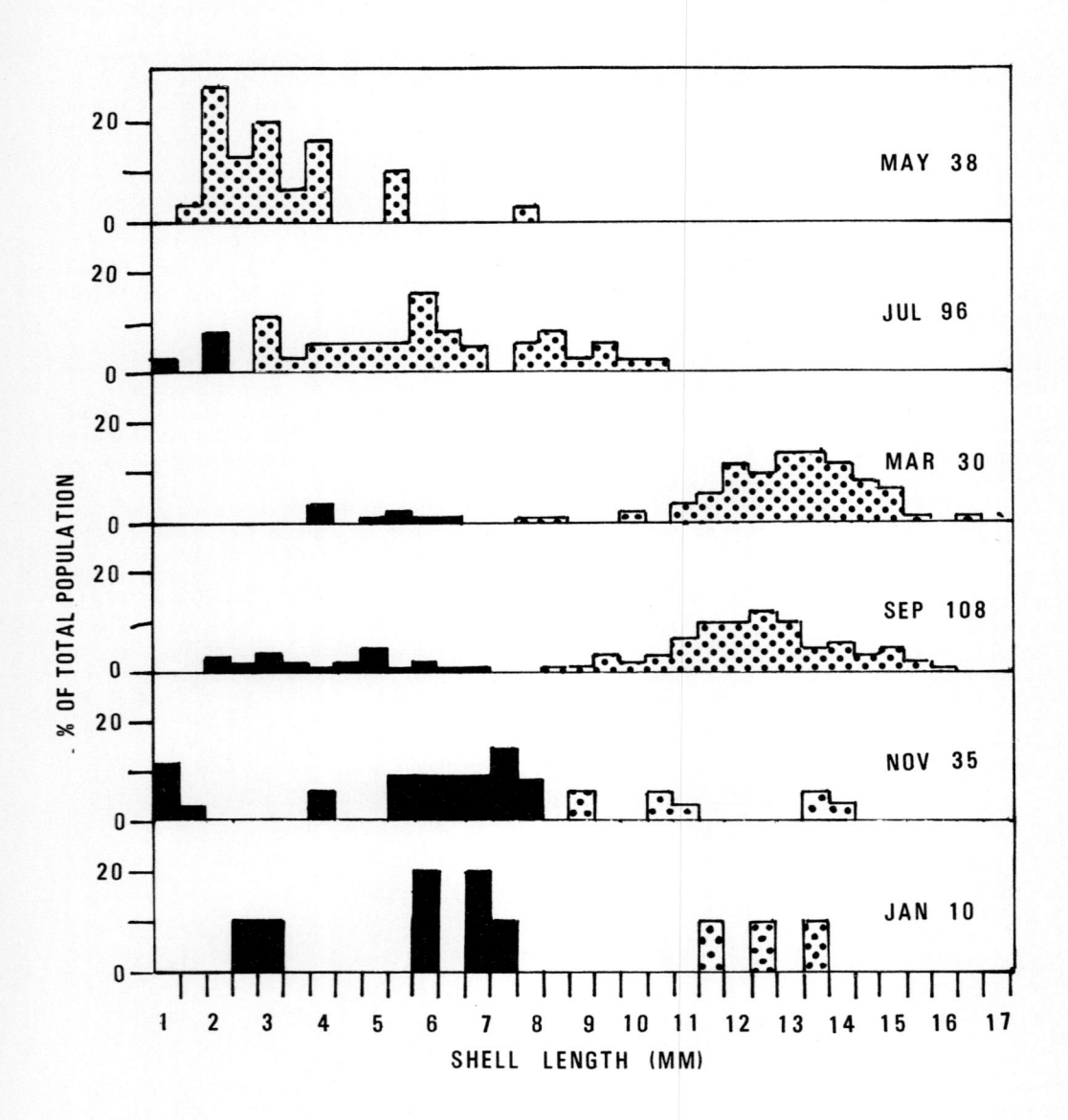

Figure 33.5. *Abra alba:* size frequency histograms. Shading conventions as Fig. 33.4.

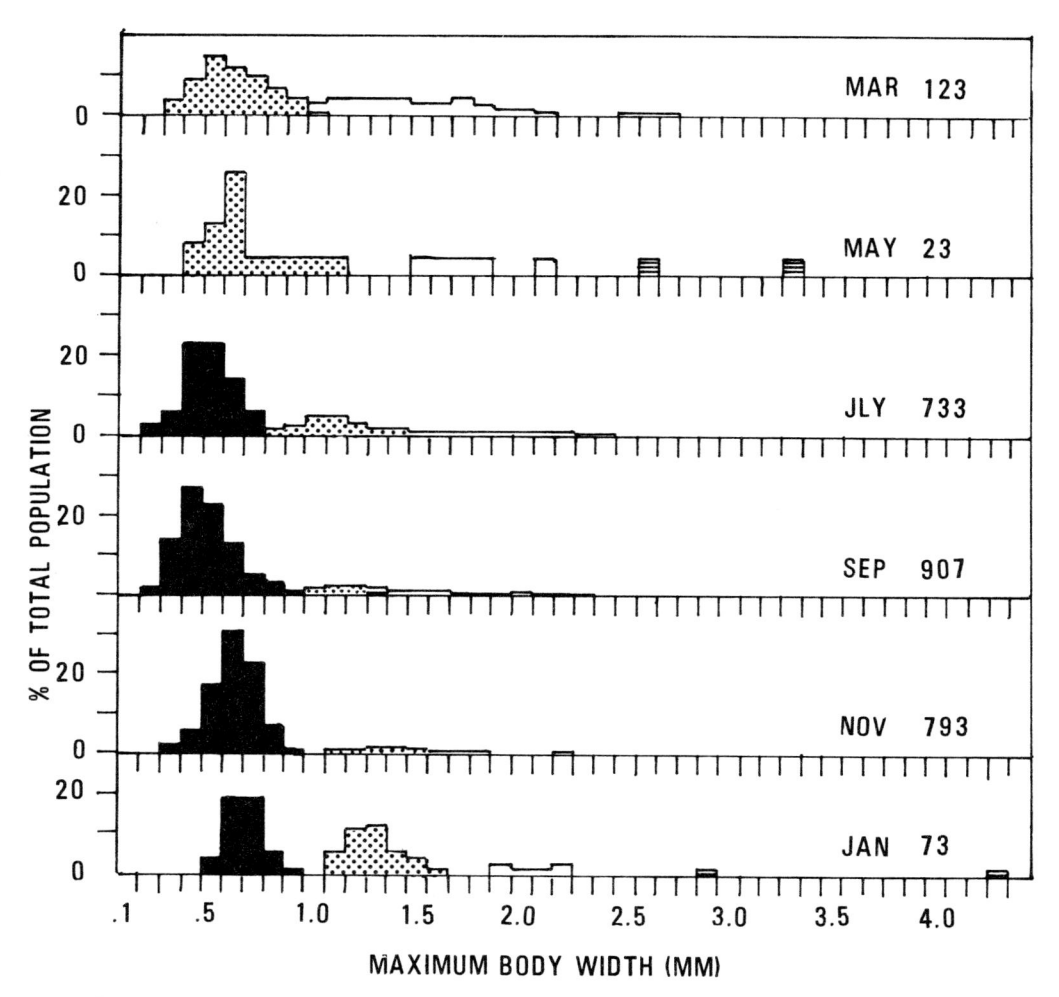

Figure 33.6. *Nephtys hombergi:* size frequency histograms. Shading conventions as Fig. 33.4.

Polychaeta

Nephtys hombergi: Size frequency histograms (Fig. 33.6) indicated that three main size-classes were present from July onwards, with occasional larger animals in very small numbers. This situation has also been found for intertidal populations (Warwick and Price, 1975; Olive, 1977): the first two classes correspond to single year groups, but the third class may comprise animals representing more than one year (Olive, 1977). A new settlement was recorded in July, much earlier than the intertidal population studied by Warwick and Price (1975), who postulated that animals initially settled in the sublittoral, not appearing in their intertidal samples until September.

Individual weights of animals in each size-class were determined from the histograms using size/weight regressions computed for each month by Warwick and Price

(1975): few large animals in the present study were suitably intact for original regressions to be calculated. The production calculation is given in Table 33.5. Annual production amounted to 0.368g/m², and the mean biomass 0.458g/m², giving a P/B̄ of 0.80. Price and Warwick (in press) found that the P/B̄ of an intertidal population varied over a five year period between 0.81 and 1.42, the lower values occurring in years of poor settlement resulting in an age distribution biased towards older animals. In the Swansea Bay population there was a strong settlement in 1975, and the low P/B̄ can be attributed to the generally slower growth rate of 1+ and older animals.

TABLE 33.5. Year-Class Production for *Nephtys hombergi*

Year-class (year of settlement)	Mean No/m² in year class	Initial wt/ind (mg)	Final wt/ind (mg)	Annual Production (g/m²)
1975	513.5	0.224	0.289	0.033
1974	71.7	0.312	2.234	0.138
1973	28.0	3.994	9.194	0.146
1972	1.3	19.430	58.346	0.051
			TOTAL	0.368

Spiophanes bombyx: In Carmarthen Bay this species is known to have several separate larval settlements each year (Warwick and others, 1978). This, together with the fact that adequate numbers of this species were only present in the July and September samples, makes interpretation of the size-frequency histograms for Swansea Bay (Fig. 33.7) particularly difficult in terms of the continuity of cohorts from month to month. Using the size/weight regression given in Warwick and others (1978), and interpreting cohorts as in Fig. 33.7, the annual production is 0.076g/m². The mean annual biomass is 0.058g/m² (Table 33.6) giving a P/B̄ of 1.31 compared with 4.86 in Carmarthen Bay. This comparison, however, is of little significance in view of the fact that the Swansea Bay size frequency data are open to alternative interpretations.

TABLE 33.6. Cohort Production for *Spiophanes bombyx* (January sample ignored).

Cohort	Mean No/m² in Cohort	Initial Wt/ind (mg)	Final Wt/ind (mg)	Annual Production (g/m²)
A(black)	29	0.394	0.356	-0.001
B(dotted)	34	0.921	1.890	0.033
C(white)	9	0.736	4.462	0.034
D(hatch)	2	2.219	6.977	0.010
			TOTAL	0.076

TABLE 33.7. Production Calculation for *Pectinaria koreni*.

Mean No/m²	Initial Wt/ind (mg)	Final Wt/ind (mg)	Annual Production (g/m²)
10.75	4.186	11.675	0.081

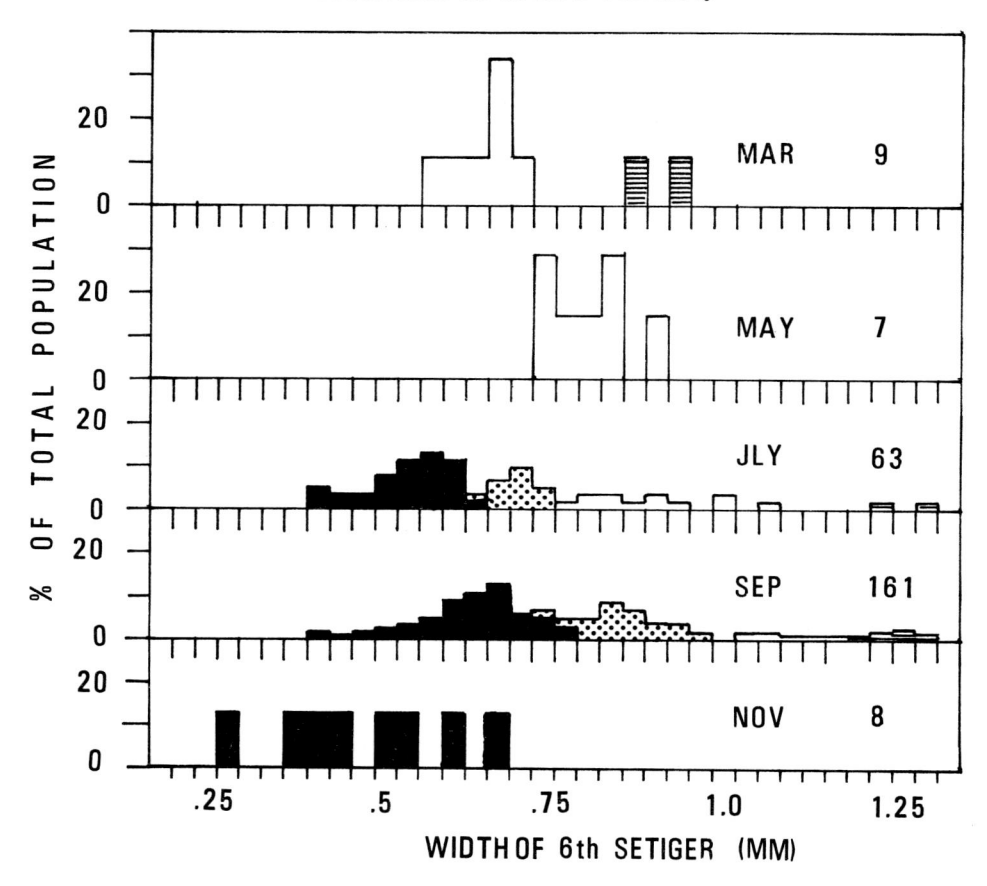

Figure 33.7. *Spiophanes bombyx:* size frequency histograms. Shading conventions represent individual settlements and not separate year-classes.

Pectinaria koreni: Low numbers of this species again precluded a definitive estimate of production. Length frequency histograms (showing actual numbers of each length-class) are given in Fig. 33.8. No specimens were found in March or May. Despite the rather large spread of size, there are no discernible peaks in the histograms, and we have treated the data as a single year-class of undetermined age. Annual production is estimated as $0.081g/m^2$ (Table 33.7) and the mean annual biomass is $0.039g/m^2$ giving a P/B̄ of 2.08.

Ampharete acutifrons: High numbers of this species were found only in September, when three rather distinct size-cohorts were present (Fig. 33.9). Low numbers were present in July and November, but none at any other time. Cohort weights were determined from a length/weight regression established from a wide size-spectrum of worms representative of all months in which the species was found. Interpreting the growth of these cohorts as in Fig. 33.9, the annual production is 0.030 g/m^2, the mean annual biomass $0.023g/m^2$ and the P/B̄ 1.30. Elsewhere, this species has been found to be an annual sublittorally in Long Island Sound (Richards and Riley, 1967) and intertidally in a Cornish estuary (Warwick and Price, 1975) with P/B̄ ratios of 4.58 and 5.5. respectively. The lower P/B̄ of the Swansea Bay populations is commensurate with its apparent three-year life-cycle in this locality.

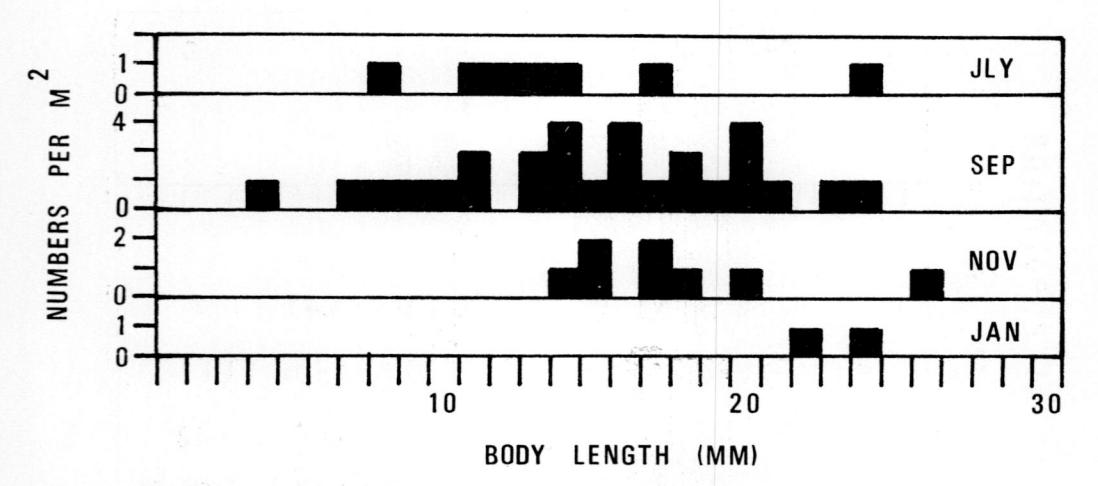

Figure 33.8. *Pectinaria koreni*: size frequency histograms. Single year-class of uncertain age.

Ampharete finmarchica (wrongly designated as *A. acutifrons*) also has a 3-year life-cycle off the Northumberland coast (Buchanan and Warwick, 1974).

TABLE 33.8. Year-Class Production for *Ampharete acutifrons*.

Year-class (year of settlement)	Mean No/m^2 in year class	Initial wt/ind (mg)	Final wt/ind (mg)	Annual Production (g/m^2)
1975?	22.5	0.542	1.040	0.011
1974?	18	1.301	2.371	0.019
1973?	6	5.206	-	-
			TOTAL	0.030

Crustacea

Diastylis rathkei: This species was consistently present in considerable numbers except in January: the latter samples were taken between 2000 and 2250 hrs, which coincides with the period of maximum intensity of vertical migration into the water column (Anger and Valentin, 1976), whilst samples for all other months were taken during daylight hours. In Table 33.9 we have divided these samples into the easily recognisable stages of maturity listed by Buchanan and Warwick (1974) for *Eudorella emarginata*, and a clear annual cycle emerges, with males living for about one year and females a little longer. An annual cycle is also recorded for this species in the Skagerak (Forsman, 1938) and Western Baltic (Kruger, 1940; Valentin and Anger, 1977).

Each stage was bulk-weighed. Annual production is estimated as 0.399g/m^2 (Table 33.10), and the mean biomass is 0.325g/m^2 (total biomass in this case has been divided by 5 to give the mean, since animals were assumed to be present in January) giving a P/$\bar{B}$ of 1.23.

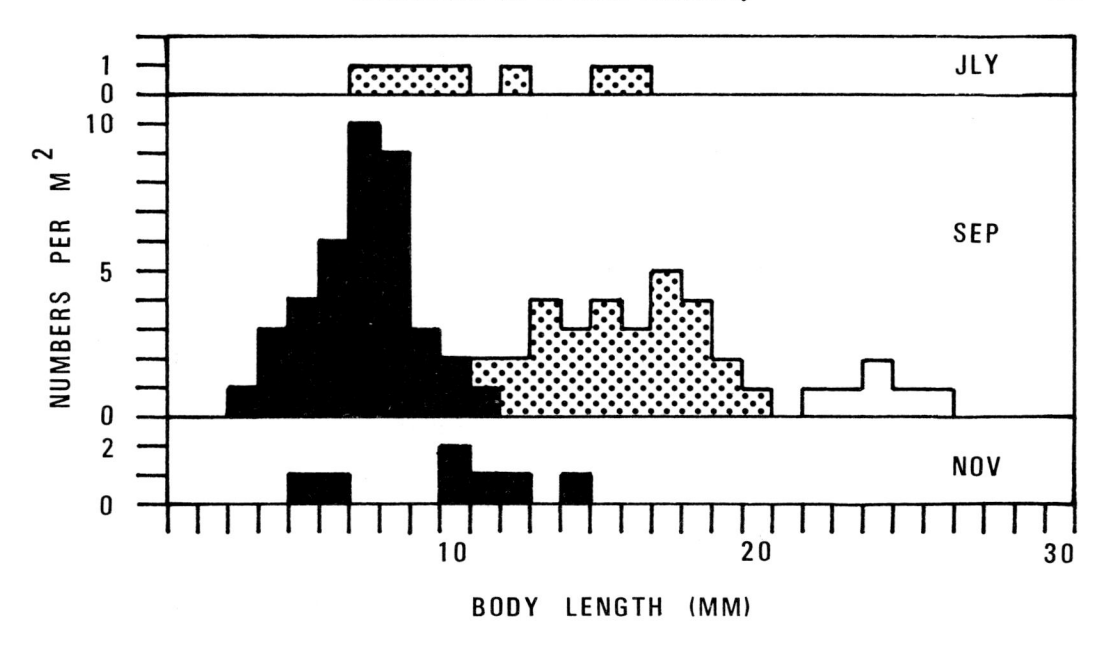

Figure 33.9. *Ampharete acutifrons:* size frequency histograms. Shading conventions as Fig. 33.4.

TABLE 33.9. Age Structure of the *Diastylis rathkei* Population.

	Mar	May	Jly	Sep	Nov
Small unsexable juveniles	55	80	-	-	-
Young ♂♂ with pleopod buds	-	-	109	76	23
♀♀ without marsupium	-	-	133	117	75
Adult ♂♂ with fully-developed pleopods	-	-	-	-	17
♀♀ with eggs in marsupium	-	-	-	-	37
♀♀ with post-larvae in marsupium	-	-	-	-	-
♀♀ with empty brood pouch					

Echinodermata

Ophiura texturata: This species was found in low numbers in the grab samples, and size frequency histograms have been constructed using the grab and dredge samples combined (Fig. 33.10). It was not possible to collect a dredge sample in November. '0' group animals with a disc daimeter of 1mm first appeared in September and had increased to a disc diameter of 3mm by the following winter. This growth increment is the same as that found for a population in Carmarthen Bay (Warwick and others, 1978), but here the '0' group first appeared in June. Like the Carmarthen Bay population, animals representing the 1974 settlement appeared to migrate to the area, since they were not found in March or May but were present by July with a modal disc diameter of about 7mm. 1973 animals were consistently present but were smaller and grew much less than the equivalent (1972) year-class in Carmarthen Bay. In March 1975, however, when both Carmarthen and Swansea Bays were sampled, the size frequency of the 1973 year-class was very similar at the two sites, indicating that perhaps the 1972 animals in Carmarthen Bay had enjoyed an exceptionally

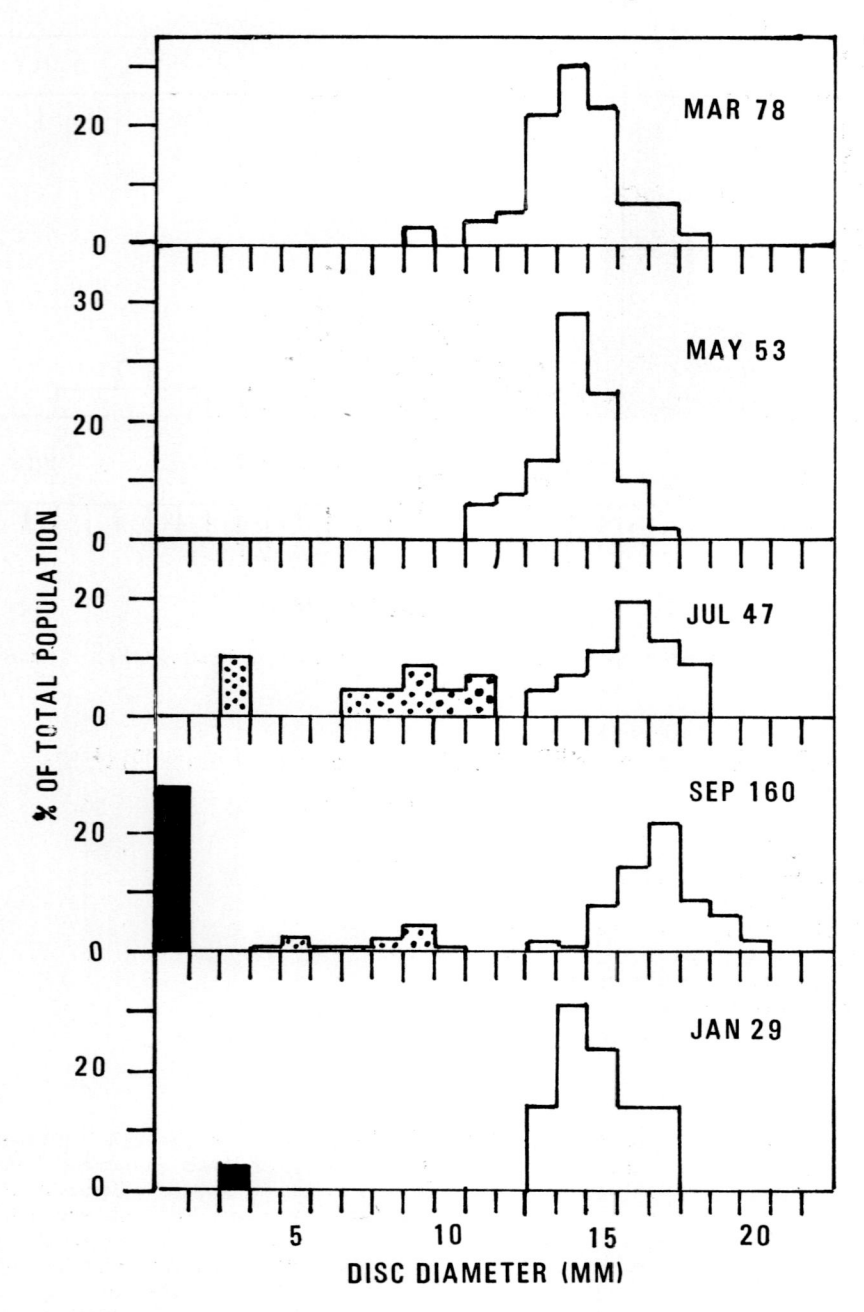

Figure 33.10. *Ophiura texturata:* size frequency histograms from dredge and grab samples combined. Shading conventions as Fig. 33.4.

TABLE 33.10. Production Calculation for *Diastylis rathkei*

	Mean No/m²	Initial Wt/ind (mg)	Final Wt/ind (mg)	Annual Production (g/m²)
♂	58.5	0.038	2.370	0.136
♀	87.5	0.038	3.041	0.263
			TOTAL	0.399

favourable period of growth. In Swansea Bay we have treated the 1973 group of animals as a single year-class, although evidence from Carmarthen Bay suggests that a few animals a year older than this could be present.

The biomass of each year-class has been determined from the histograms using the size-weight regression given in Warwick and others (1978). The annual production (Table 33.11) is 0.095g/m² and the mean biomass is 0.198g/m², giving a P/B̄ of 0.48. This compares with the P/B̄ of 0.68 for the Carmarthen Bay population in the previous year when, as already stated, growth of the 2+ year-class was greater.

TABLE 33.11. Year-Class Production for *Ophiura texturata*.

Year-class (year of settlement)	Mean No/m² in year class	Initial wt/ind (mg)	Final wt/ind (mg)	Annual Production (g/m²)
1975	22.5	0.216	2.541	0.052
1974	5.9	4.801	9.158	0.026
1973	1.8	82.311	91.963	0.017
			TOTAL	0.095

DISCUSSION

Assuming that the residue of rare species has the same average P/B̄ as that of the more abundant species studied, and accepting the possible inaccuracies inherent in the method of calculating production, the total community production amounts to 14.2g/m². The mean annual biomass is 11.1g/m² giving an overall P/B̄ of 1.28 (Table 33.12). Comparative values of P/B̄ for other communities are discussed by Warwick and others (1978): lower values have been recorded in a *Venus* and a *Brissopsis lyrifera/Amphiura chiajei* community, and higher values (on average) for *Macoma* communities. In Carmarthen Bay the community P/B̄ was lower (0.56) than in Swansea Bay. In both communities a single species dominates the total production. In the Carmarthen Bay *Venus* community the dominant was *Pharus legumen*, a species which lived for up to six years and had a correspondingly low P/B̄ of 0.56: in Swansea Bay the dominant was *Spisula elliptica*, which at this site had a maximum lifespan of 2.5 years and a correspondingly high P/B̄ of 1.65. The comparative lifespans, and hence P/B̄ values, of these two species are probably a reflection of the relative stability of the two habitats, the stable fine sand of Carmarthen Bay providing a more favourable environment for long-lived species.

The causes for the instability in the Swansea Bay *Abra* community are uncertain.

TABLE 33.12. Total Production Estimate.

Production Rank	Species	Production (g/m²/y)	% of Total P	Cumulative %	Mean Biomass (g/m²)	P/B̄
1	*Spisula elliptica*	10.285	72.5	72.5	6.227	1.65
2	*Nucula turgida*	1.351	9.5	82.0	2.615	0.52
3	*Abra alba*	0.408	2.9	84.9	0.302	1.35
4	*Diastylis rathkei*	0.399	2.8	87.7	0.325	1.23
5	*Nephtys hombergi*	0.368	2.6	90.3	0.458	0.80
6	*Ophiura texturata*	0.095	0.7	90.9	0.198	0.48
7	*Pectinaria koreni*	0.081	0.6	91.5	0.039	2.08
8	*Spiophanes bombyx*	0.076	0.5	92.0	0.058	1.31
9	*Ampharete acutifrons*	0.030	0.2	92.2	0.023	1.30
	Others	(1.100)	7.8	100.0	0.860	(1.28)
	Total	14.193	100.0		11.105	1.28

Such communities are inherently unstable (Arntz & Brunswig, 1975; Eagle, 1975): the burrowing and feeding activities of the animals themselves act in conjunction with storms and tidal currents in such a way that whole species assemblages may completely disappear and be replaced by others. In Swansea Bay the species composition of the faunal assemblage did not change significantly during the period of study but the numbers were highly variable: nearly all species were present in low numbers during winter and spring, large numbers being present in summer and autumn with a rapid decline to low numbers in winter again (Table 33.1). This could not be explained in terms of patchy distribution and inaccurate relocation of the station, because a random search within about a 0.5 mile radius of the station failed to reveal significantly higher populations during the low density periods. Neither can increased numbers have resulted from plantkonic settlements, since in most instances 1+ and older year-classes were also involved. One can only assume that strong currents resulted in an influx and subsequent re-establishment of benthic species from remote areas of the Bay. The only species which could survive this rigorous treatment are suitably robust sedentary infaunal species and mobile epibenthic forms. Inspection of the list of dominant species shows that most fulfil one or other of these criteria, a notable exception being *Abra alba* which has a thin fragile shell in contrast to the robust *Spisula* and *Nucula*. It is perhaps significant to note that the *Abra* population during the period of highest density (July and September) was dominated by large 1+ shells, with very few '0' group animals which are obviously more delicate.

If our assumptions about a shifting fauna are correct, any attempts to discuss the absolute level of production in relation to other communities or water depths are invalid. It might be expected that such physical instability would affect certain properties of the macrofaunal community, and we have investigated two of these: the partitioning of the total production amongst species and the distribution of numbers of individuals amongst species. These two properties are likely to be independent of the actual species involved and we have compared the Carmarthen Bay and Swansea Bay communities in these respects: the former area is relatively unpolluted with a stable sediment and the latter subject to both domestic and industrial pollutants (both from the shore and dumped at sea) with, we presume, an unstable sediment.

The partitioning of production amongst individual species within the community is remarkably similar in the two Bays (Fig. 33.11). In both cases a single species of filter feeding bivalve contributes two-thirds or more of the total production. Perhaps, then, the similarity between the sites in this respect is simply fortuitous,

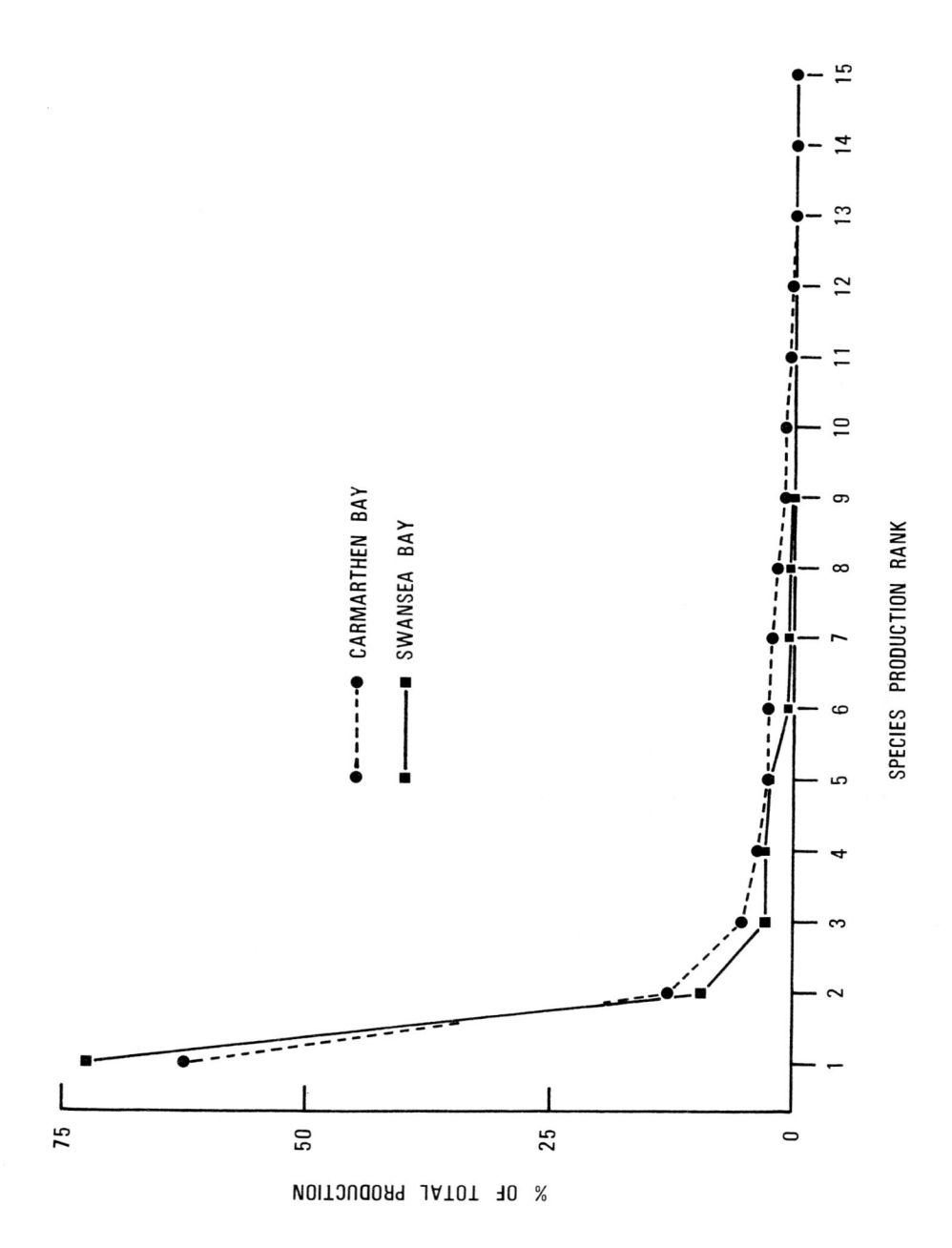

Figure 33.11. Partitioning of production amongst species in Swansea Bay and Carmarthen Bay.

since filter feeding species have varying levels of production in shallow water depending on the amount of food made available to them by local current regimes (Warwick, 1980). All that can be said is that in Swansea Bay there is no obvious shift in this partitioning which can be attributed either to pollution or disturbance.

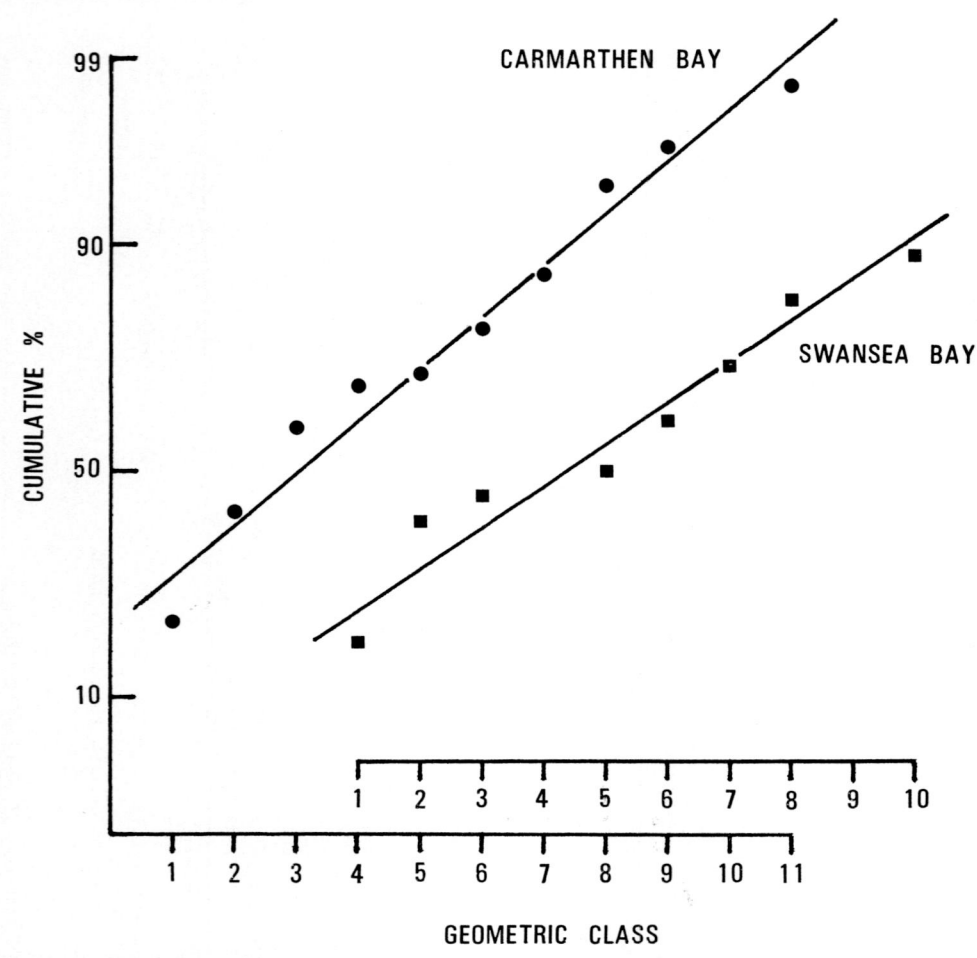

Figure 33.12. Log-normal plots of numerical species data from Swansea Bay (September 1975) and Carmarthen Bay (February 1974)(see Text).

Recently Gray and Mirza (1979) and Gray (1979) have indicated that there is a departure from the log-normal distribution of individuals amongst species (apparently typical of undisturbed equilibrium communities) under conditions of slight or prolonged disturbance. When the cumulative percentage of species is plotted against geometric classes of individuals per species on a probability scale a straight line is produced for equilibrium communities. With slight disturbance some species become more abundant while the rarer species are unaffected, producing a discontinuity in the plot with the line for more abundant geometric classes having a shallower slope. After a long period under stress the community achieves a new equilibrium but the log-normal plot has a shallower slope and extends over more geometric classes. Data for Carmarthen Bay and Swansea Bay plotted in this way (Fig. 33.12) show no marked departure from a straight line plot: for Swansea Bay the line has a slightly shallower slope but extends to one less geometric class than the Carmarthen Bay line. However, the difference is only marginal and certainly not as great as the differences Gray and Mirza suggest separate polluted from unpolluted communities.

Although we have not observed changes in either of these community properties which might be associated with the obvious physical disturbance at this site, such disturbance is certainly reflected in the life histories (particularly growth rate and longevity) of individual species. For example, the dominant species *Spisula elliptica*, which lives for about $2\frac{1}{2}$ years and reaches a maximum shell-length of 21mm at this site, may grow much larger and have a greater longevity elsewhere in the Bristol Channel, where it is a prominent member of the *Spisula* subcommunity of the *Venus* community (Warwick and Davies, 1977).

ACKNOWLEDGEMENTS

This work forms part of the estuarine and nearshore research programme of the Institute for Marine Environmental Research, a component of the Natural Environment Research Council.

REFERENCES

Allen, J.A. (1953). Observations on *Nucula turgida* Marshall and *N. moorei* Winckworth. *J. mar. biol. Ass. U.K., 31,* 515-528.
Allen, J.A. (1954). A comparative study of the British species of *Nucula* and *Nuculana*. *J. mar. biol. Ass. U.K., 33,* 457-472.
Ansell, A.D., and Parulekar, A.H. (1978). On the rate of growth of *Nuculana minuta* (Muller)(Bivalvia; Nuculanidae). *J. moll. Stud., 44,* 71-82.
Anger, K., and Valentin, C. (1976). *In situ* studies on the diurnal activity pattern of *Diastylis rathkei* (Cumacea, Crustacea) and its importance for the "hyperbenthos". *Helgolander wiss. Meeresunters, 28,* 138-144.
Arntz, W.E., and Brunswig, D. (1975). An approach to estimating the production of macrobenthos and demersal fish in a Western Baltic *Abra alba* community. *Merentutkimuslait. Julk./Havsforskningsinst. Skr., 239,* 195-205.
Buchanan, J.B., and Warwick, R.M. (1974). An estimate of benthic macrofaunal production in the offshore mud of the Northumberland coast. *J. mar. biol. Ass. U.K., 54,* 197-222.
Crisp, D.J. (1971). Energy flow measurements. *In:* Holme, N.A., and McIntyre, A.D. (Eds.). *Methods for the Study of Marine Benthos,* I.B.P. Handbook No. 16, Blackwell, Oxford.
Eagle, R.A. (1975). Natural fluctuations in a soft bottom benthic community. *J. mar. biol. Ass. U.K., 55,* 865-878.
Ford, E. (1925). On the growth of some lamellibranchs in relation to the food-supply of fishes. *J. mar. biol. Ass. U.K., 13,* 531-559.
Forsman, B. (1938). Untersuchungen uber die Cumacean des Skageraks. *Zool. Bidr. Upps., 18,* 1-356.
Gray, J.S., and Mirza, F.B. (1979). A possible method for the detection of pollution-induced disturbance on marine benthic communities. *Mar. Pollut. Bull., 10,* 142-145.
Gray, J.S. (1979). Pollution induced changes in populations. *Phil. Trans. R. Soc. Lond., B.286,* 545-561.
Kruger, K. (1940). Zur Lebensgeschichte der Cumacee *Diastylis rathkei* (Kroyer) in der westlichen Ostsee. *Kieler. Meeresforsch., 3,* 374-402.
Olive, P.J.W. (1977). The life-history and population structure of the polychaetes *Nephtys caeca* and *Nephtys hombergi* with special reference to the growth rings in the teeth. *J. mar. biol. Ass. U.K., 57,* 133-150.
Price, R., and Warwick, R.M. (In press). Temporal variations in the annual produc-

tion and biomass of two estuarine polychaetes, *Nephtys hombergi* and *Ampharete acutifrons*. *J. mar biol. Ass. U.K.*

Rachor, E. (1976). Structure, dynamics and productivity of a population of *Nucula nitidosa* (Bivalvia, Protobranchiara) in the German Bight. *Ber. dt. wiss. Kommn. Meeresforsch.*, 24, 296-331.

Richards, S.W., and Riley, G.A. (1967). The benthic epifauna of Long Island Sound. *Bull. Bingham Oceanogr. Coll.*, 19, 89-135.

Stephen, A.C. (1932). Notes on the biology of some lamellibranchs in the Clyde area. *J. mar. biol. Ass. U.K.*, 18, 51-68.

Tabunkov, V.D. (1964). Growth, productive properties and population development in *Nuculana pernula* (Taxodonta, Nuculanidae) off south-western Sakhalin Island. *Zool. Zh.*, 53, 1616-1622. (In Russian with English summary).

Thorson, G. (1946). Reproduction and larvae development of Danish marine bottom invertebrates. *Medd. Komm. Danm. Fisk. -og Havunders.*, ser. *Plankton*, 4, 1-523.

Valentin, C., and Anger, K. (1977). In situ studies on the life-cycle of *Diastylis rathkei* (Cumacea: Crustacea). *Mar. Biol.*, 39, 71-76.

Warwick, R.M. (1980). Population dynamics and production of benthos. *In:* Tenore, K.R., and Coull, B.C. (Eds.). *Marine Benthic Dynamics*. Univ. South Carolina Press, Columbia.

Warwick, R.M., and Davies, J.R. (1977). The distribution of sublittoral macrofauna communities in the Bristol Channel in relation to the substrate. *Estuar. and Coast. Mar. Sci.*, 5, 111-222.

Warwick, R.M., George, C.L., and Davies, J.R. (1978). Annual macrofauna production in a *Venus* community. *Estuar. and Coast. Mar. Sci.*, 7, 215-241.

Warwick, R.M. and Price, R. (1975). Macrofauna production in an estuarine mudflat. *J. mar. biol. Ass. U.K.*, 55, 1-18.

34. THE BENTHIC ECOLOGY OF LINEAR SANDBANKS: A MODIFIED *SPISULA* SUB-COMMUNITY

P. A. Tyler* and S. E. Shackley**

Department of Oceanography and Department of Zoology***
University College of Swansea, Singleton Park, Swansea SA2 8PP, U.K.

ABSTRACT

Examination of the linear sand banks of the northern Bristol Channel demonstrate an extremely high energy physical environment dominated by tidal current and wave action. The linear sandbanks are maintained by tidal current action moving medium sand towards the banks. Growth of the banks is limited by water depth and the down-bank removal of sand by wave action. The faunal diversity in this high energy environment is greatly reduced, being dominated by the peracarid crustaceans *Gastrosaccus spinifer* and *Pontocrates arenarius*, and the polychaete worm *Nephthys cirrosa*, suggesting that these linear sand banks represent a reduced *Spisula* community. The relationship of mobile sands of the linear banks and more exposed beaches is discussed.

KEYWORDS

Benthic Ecology; Linear Sandbanks; Wave Action; Tidal Currents; Exposure; *Gastrosaccus*

INTRODUCTION

Linear sandbanks are found on wide continental shelf areas which have both an adequate sediment supply, and the tidal current energy to move this sediment (Off, 1963). After the early studies of van Veen (1935; 1936) in the North Sea, the sedimentology of a number of banks of both the NW European and eastern North American shelf have been described in detail (Cloet, 1954; Houboult, 1968; Smith, 1969; Kenyon, 1970; Caston, 1971; Duane, et al., 1974; Turner, 1976; Britton, 1978).

Culver (1979) and Culver and Bull (Chapter 4) have postulated that northeastward wave bedload transport during the Flandrian transgression created accumulations of sand in the encroaching littoral and immediate sublittoral of the northern side of the Bristol Channel, enabling the development of linear sand banks only on this side of the Channel by sediment recirculation (tidal current and wave regimes) during the present sealevel stand.

The mechanism for the maintenance of these linear banks is tidal current energy with asymmetric flow round the banks moving sediment obliquely to the bank crest (Houboult,

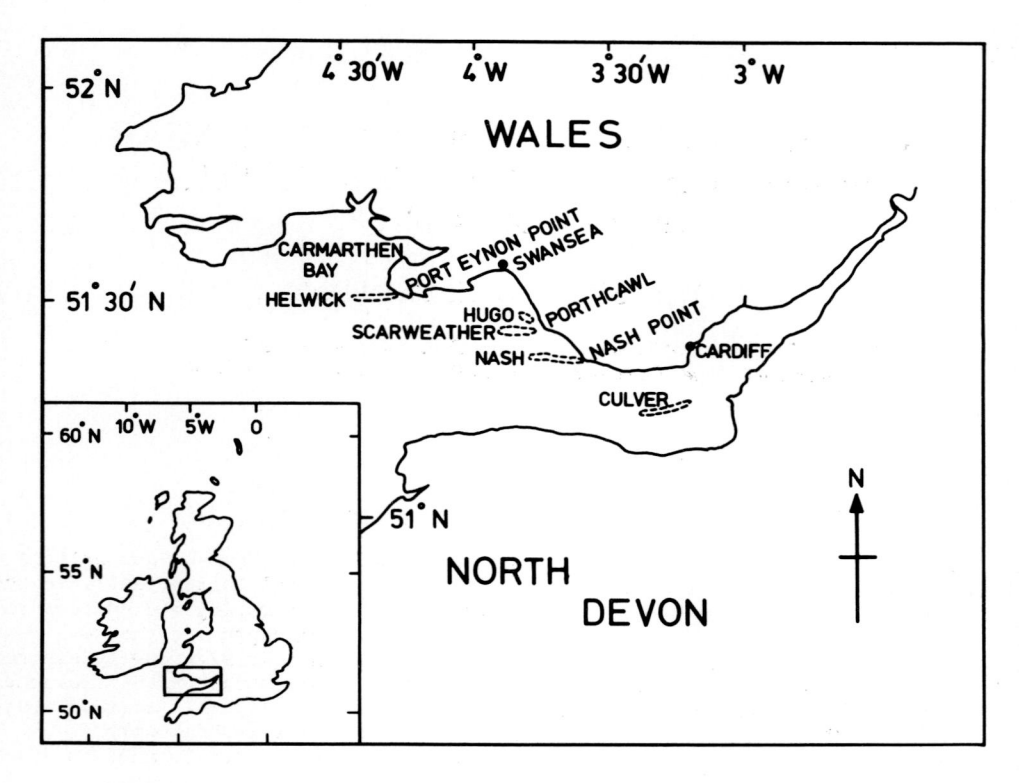

Figure 34.1. The Bristol Channel. Distribution of Helwick, Scarweather, Hugo and Culver linear sandbanks.

1968; Caston & Stride, 1970; Duane, et al., 1974).

Due to the high energy environment, the benthic ecology of linear sandbanks has received little attention, although the surrounding area of the Bristol Channel has been surveyed (Warwick & Davies, 1977).

The linear sandbanks examined include the Helwick, Scarweather, Nash and Culver Sands and the smaller Hugo Bank (Fig. 34.1). Of these banks, the sedimentology has been previously examined for only Helwick and Scarweather Sands. This Chapter presents an analysis of the physical environment of these banks as a habitat for a marine invertebrate fauna.

METHODS

Fieldwork for this study was carried out aboard R.R.S. "John Murray" Cruise 1/79. 113 stations were sampled on or around the linear banks of the Bristol Channel (Figs. 34.2, 34.3 and 34.4). Stations situated on the linear banks were as close to the crest axis as possible. Due to possible lateral movement of the banks since the Admiralty Charts were published, and the position fixing error, some stations do not appear at the bank crest. Decca Mk 21 was used for position fixing corrected against radar fixes.

At each station five $0.1m^2$ Day grab (Warwick & Davies, 1977) samples were taken.

Due to the variable sampling ability of this grab (Tyler & Shackley, 1978) sediment volume retrieved by each grab was measured. This grab was not fully effective on stoney or gravel bottoms but performed well on all other substrates.

For each station, a small sediment sample was removed for grain size analysis and determination of organic carbon content. The remaining sediment was sieved through a 1.00mm sieve screen and all fauna retained was preserved in 5% seawater formalin for identification in the laboratory.

For grain size analysis of the sediment the sample was dried at 110°C, dry sieved and mean grain diameter and sorting coefficient calculated. For the determination of organic carbon a small sediment sample was dried at 60°C and then analysed by the wet titration method of Gaudette et al. (1974).

OBSERVATIONS AND RESULTS

General Sedimentological Features of the Linear Sandbanks of the Bristol Channel.

The linear sandbanks of the Bristol Channel (Fig. 34.1) are steep-sided ribbon shaped sedimentary bodies arising in 20-30m of water in a region with a Spring Tidal Range of about 10m. With the exception of the Culver Bank all these linear sandbanks have their origin associated with headlands. Each sandbank is a discrete body overlying Pleistocene or older deposits separated by a definite reflector surface (Price, pers. comm.). In cross-section, the banks are asymmetric, commonly with a steep south-facing slope and a more gentle north face. The degree of asymmetry of the essentially rectilinear Helwick sand is slight, but is more marked in the Scarweather; the Nash is elongate sigmoidal in plan, with a changing asymmetry; the West Nash contrasting with the Middle and East Nash in being anomalously steeper on its north flank. Normal to, and surrounding the Helwick, Scarweather and Nash Sands are asymmetric sand waves with their steep slopes facing the prevailing current direction (Turner, 1976; Britton, 1978; Britton & Britton, Chapter 13). Excepting Helwick Bank, all these linear sandbanks have their most shallow parts exposed at extreme low water, the areal extent of exposure varying with each bank.

Helwick Sands: This linear sandbank is 14km long and up to 2.5km wide. Tidal current data for the area of the bank is very limited (Fig. 34.2a). Surface rectilinear reversing tidal currents have speeds of up to 120cm/s with flow subparallel to the bank (Admiralty, 1974). Ebb and flood bed flow appears to be towards the bank, and this flow crosses the bank diagonally during periods of high water (Britton, 1978, Admiralty, 1974, Britton & Britton, Chapter 13). The tidal flow to the north of the bank is determined more by coastal configuration than by the bank itself (Britton, 1978).

Helwick Bank is the most exposed bank of the banks in the Bristol Channel to the prevailing southwesterly swell (Fig. 34.2a). The SW swell has a predominant wave period between 5 and 11 seconds with a maximum recorded wave height of 10.4m (Darbyshire, 1963), almost the same as the tidal range! These long period waves will already have started to shoal on entry into the Bristol Channel. On reaching the Helwick Bank they will steepen rapidly and the wave orthogonal will refract northwards imparting the wave energy to the southern edge of the bank. Northern sector winds will produce only local seas, whilst waves from the S and SE will have a maximum wave period of 5 seconds.

Along the crest of the Helwick banks the sediment consists of well sorted medium sand (*sensu* Folk, 1961). The mean grain size decreases westwards along the crest of the bank (Fig. 34.2b). This well sorted medium sand is found to the north of the bank

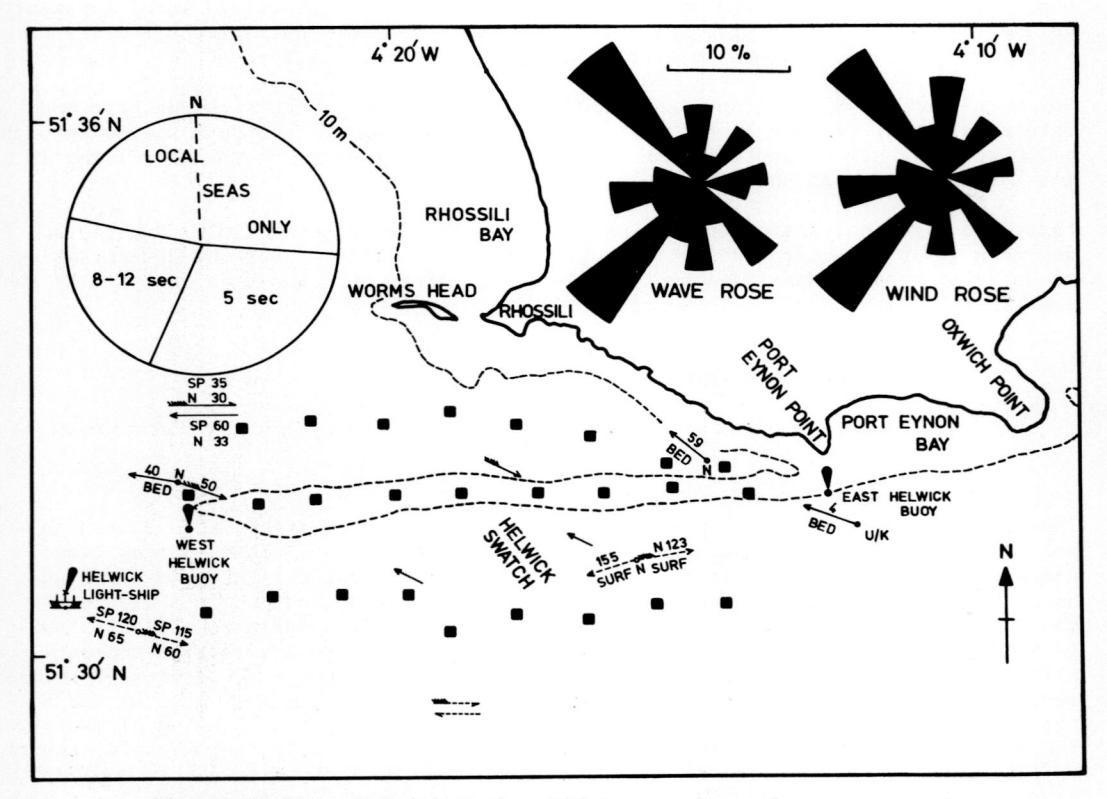

Figure 34.2a. Helwick Bank: Tidal currents and wave approach.

Legends for Figures 34.2a, 34.3a and 34.4a:

Solid lines:- near bed tidal currents; Hatched lines:- surface currents; SP = Spring Tidal Current Speed; N = Neap tidal current speed (cm/s). The circle represents direction of wave approach of long period (8-12s), short period (5s) and local seas at the western end of the bank. Wave-wind rose based on Ferentinos (1978).

Figures 34.2b, 34.3b and 34.4b. Hatched area represents medium sand with mean diameter (above line) and sorting coefficient (below line). G = Gravel, gS = gravelly sand, sG = sandy gravel, CS = Coarse sand, MS = Medium Sand and FS = Fine sand.

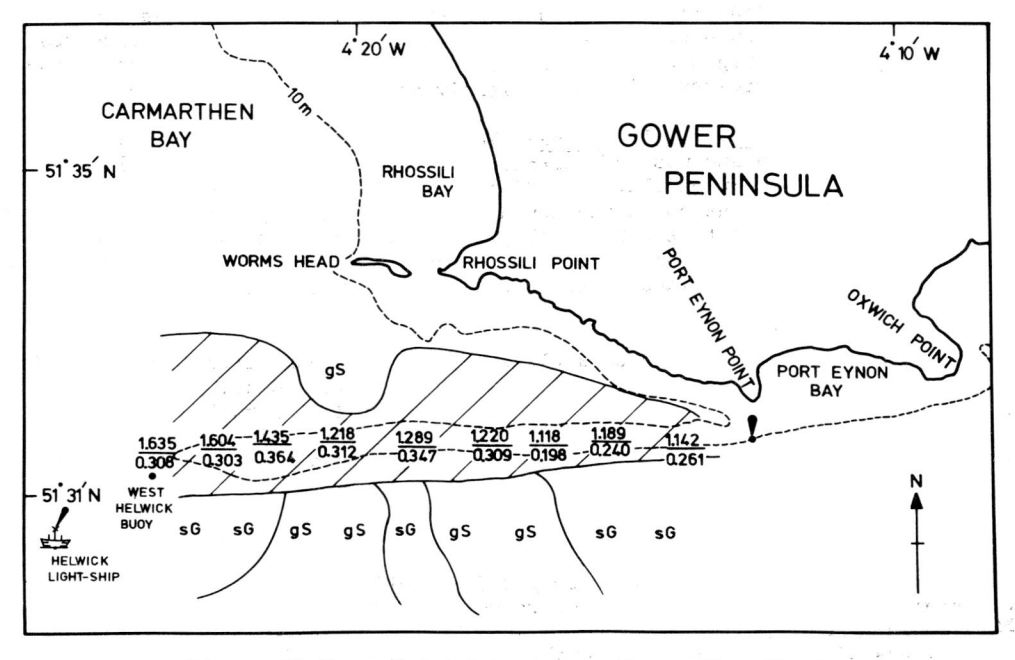

Figure 34.2b. Helwick Bank: sediment distribution.

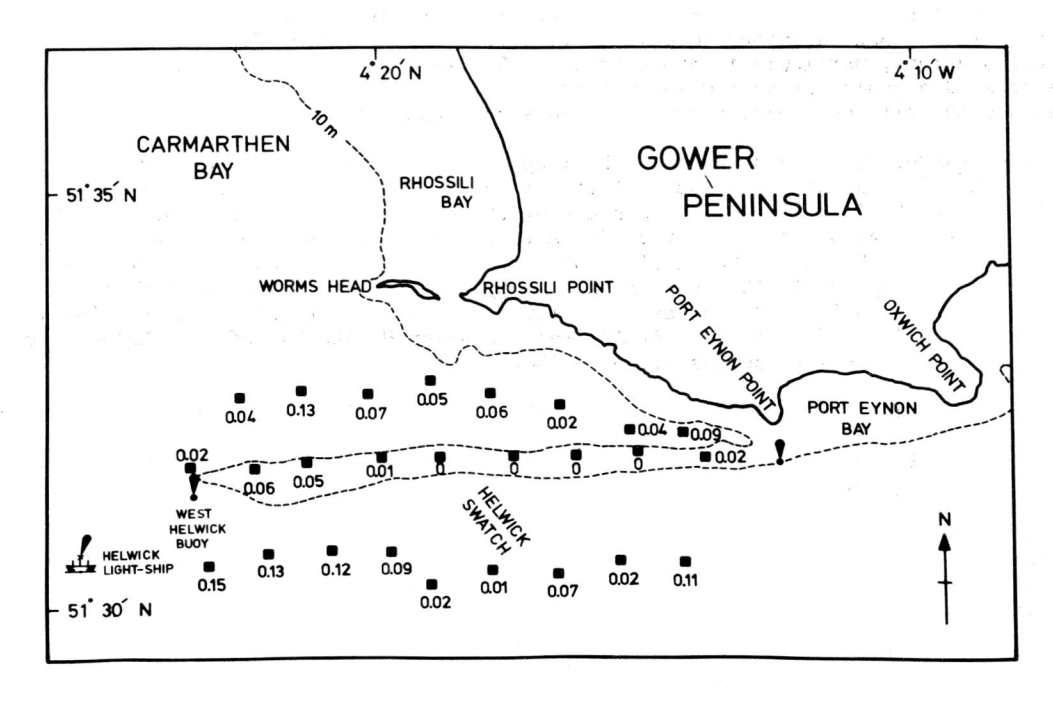

Figure 34.2c. Helwick Bank: % organic carbon.

whereas a mixture of gravelly sands and sandy gravels are found to the south. These sandy gravels to the south of the bank represent patches of sand, as sandwaves, moving round the bank. Organic carbon content at stations along the crest of the bank is negligible, and increases only very slightly at off-bank stations (Fig. 34.2c).

Nash, Scarweather and Hugo Bank Complex: These three banks form a complex of linear sandbanks to the south and west of Porthcawl. The tidal current circulation round these three banks is complex (Turner, 1976; Britton & Britton, Chapter 13). Tidal current data from stations north and south of these banks suggest a rectilinear reversing flow subparallel to the banks (Fig. 34.3a). At stations near the banks, near-bed flow appears to be obliquely across the bank. At the eastern end of the banks the influence of the land causes the tidal currents to run parallel to the coastline.

This current pattern gives rise to a clockwise rotating ebb current round the banks (Turner, 1976). Due to coastal configuration, clockwise rotation occurs on the flood tide. Both Scarweather and Nash sands are ebb dominated to the south and flood dominated to the north. Recent work (Ferentinos & Collins, 1979) suggests that tidal current flow round Nash Bank is stronger than that round Scarweather Bank. These three banks are less exposed to the dominant SW swell than is the Helwick Bank, but are more prone to the westerly swell. Seas from the south are short period and only local seas develop to the north of these banks (Fig. 34.3a).

The crestline of all three banks is composed of well sorted medium sands except at the western end of Scarweather Bank where well sorted fine sands are found (Fig. 34.3b). The Shord Channel consists of well sorted medium sands except for occasional patches of gravelly sand. South of Scarweather Sand and eastwards north of Nash Sand, the off-bank stations consist of poorly sorted gravels with occasional patches of sand. South of the Nash Bank clean gravel is found. As with Helwick Bank, the on-bank stations show low levels of organic carbon (Fig. 34.3c). Off-bank stations, particularly those south of Scarweather and north of Nash Bank, show increased organic carbon (>0.1%) whilst those in the vicinity of the Ogmore River sewage outfall show relatively high values of organic carbon.

Culver Sands: This sandbank is 8.5km long and 0.6km wide. No near-bed tidal current data is available for the vicinity of Culver Sands. Rectilinear reversing tidal currents flow E-W north and south of the bank with spring tide surface speeds of 230cm/s (Fig. 34.4a). At the Admiralty tidal current station A, 9km north of West Culver Light (Chart No. L(D1) 1152) spring tide ebb speeds of 220cm/s are found with a flood speed of 215cm/s. At Admiralty tidal station C, 5.5km SSW of West Culver Light, spring tide speeds reach 150cm/s. At both these stations, flow is in a West-East-West direction. At Admiralty station H, 9km ENE of East Culver buoy, the flow is SW-NE with speeds of up to 150cm/s.

Of all the linear sandbanks in the Bristol Channel, this bank is the most sheltered from wave action. The bank is exposed to only a narrow band of long period westerly swell, and is protected from the dominant southwesterly swell by the north Devon coastline. From all other wind directions, only local seas are formed (Fig. 34.4a).

5km of the most shallow part of this sandbank may be exposed at low water spring tides. This sandbank is also composed of well sorted medium sand showing a westward decrease in mean grain size. A single station at the extreme eastern end contains organically rich mud. Off-bank stations consist of a variety of substratum types. In the channel to the south of Culver Sand, there are clean gravels, whilst in the shoaling waters south of this line are a mixture of sands, sandy gravels and gravel (Fig. 34.4b). To the north of Culver Bank are a mixture of medium sands, gravelly sands and gravels. With the exception of the station by East Culver buoy, all stations show very low organic carbon content (Fig. 34.4c).

Benthic Ecology of Linear Sandbanks 545

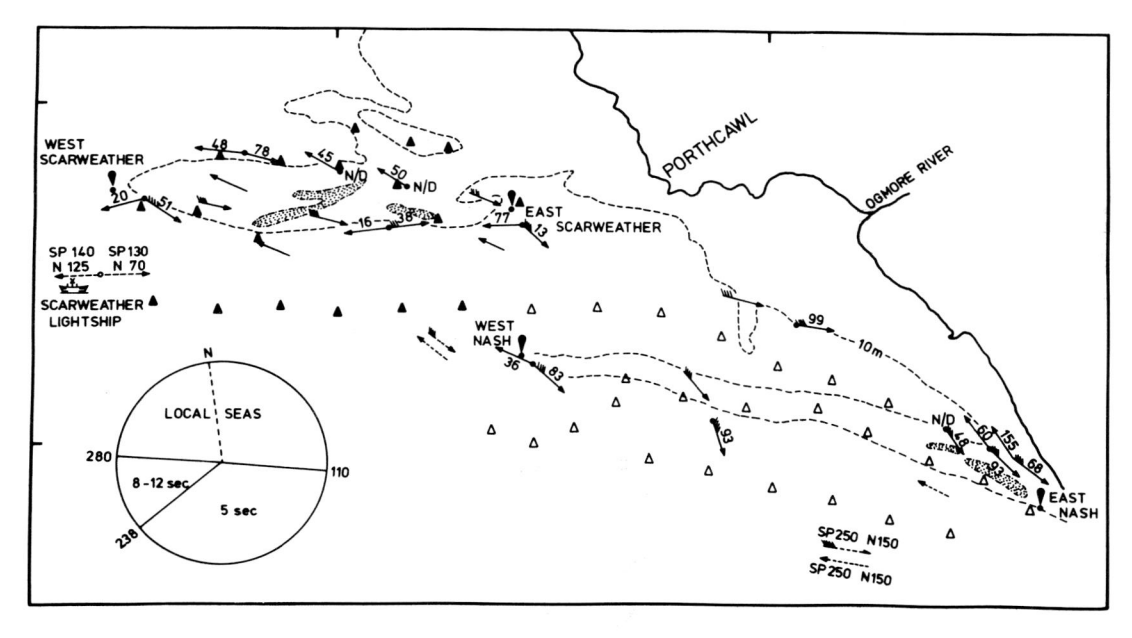

Figure 34.3a. Hugo, Scarweather and Nash Banks:
Tidal currents and wave approach.

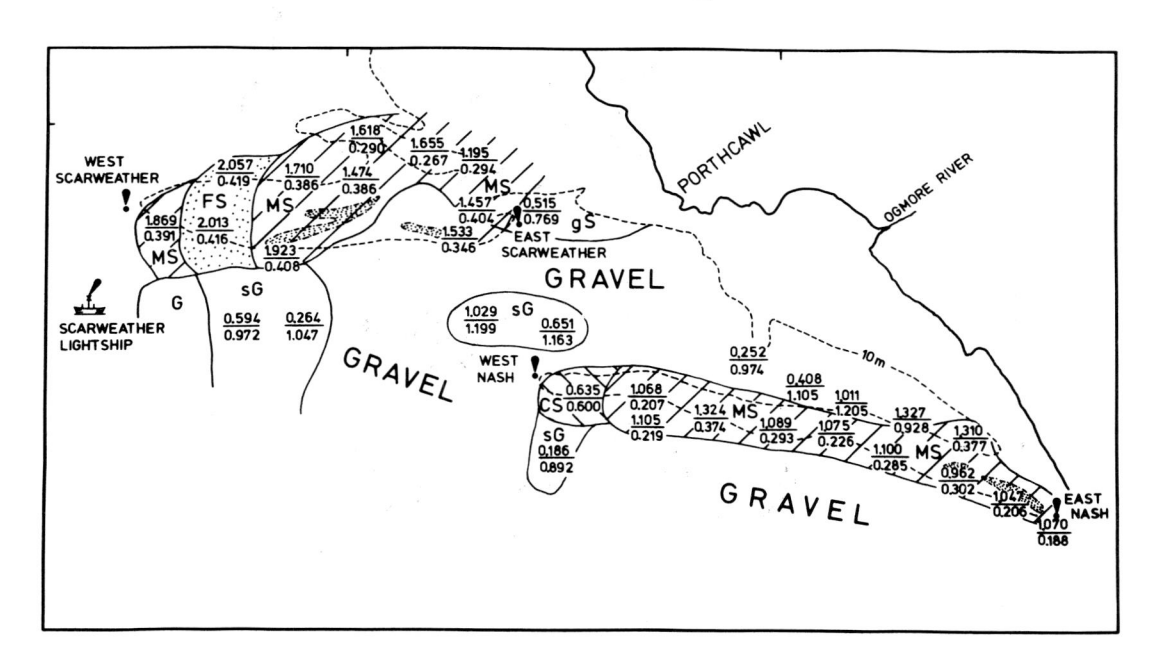

Figure 34.3b. Hugo, Scarweather and Nash Banks:
Tidal currents and wave approach.

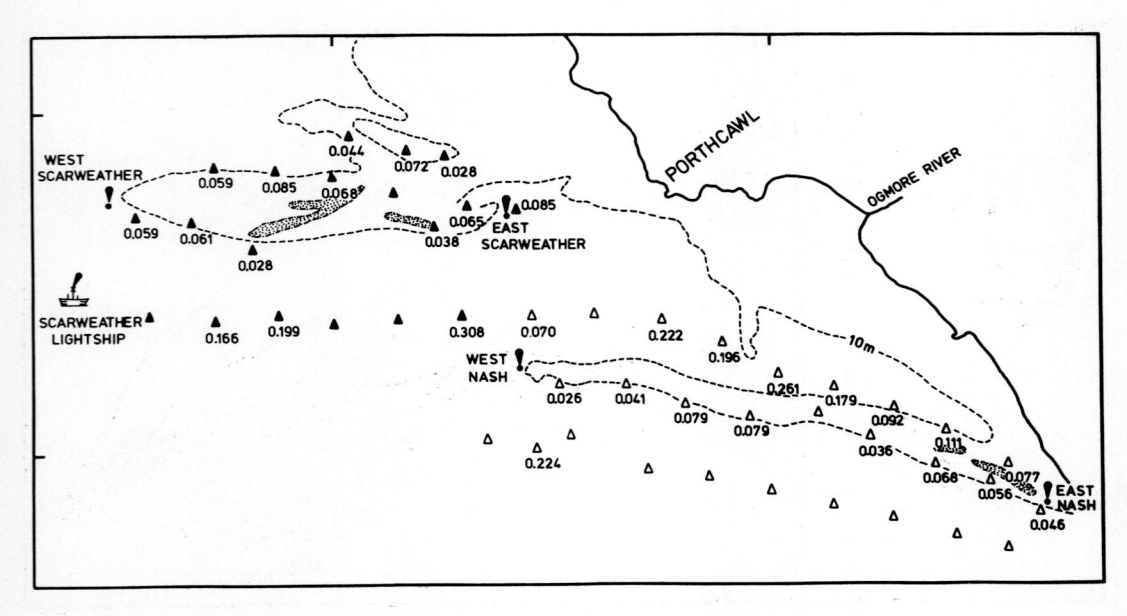

Figure 34.3c. Hugo, Scarweather and Nash Banks: % organic carbon.

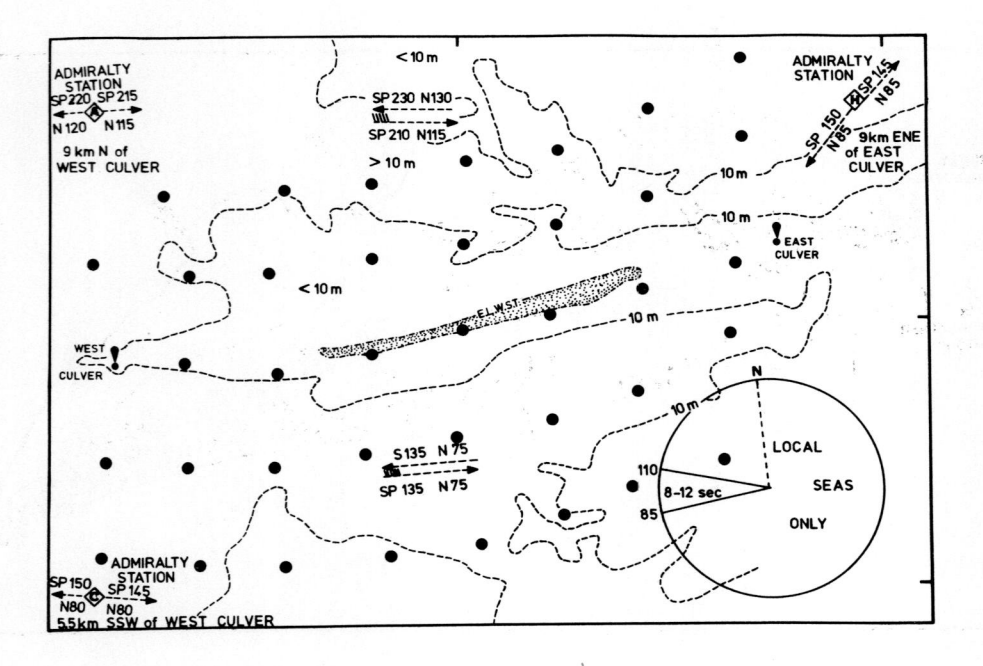

Figure 34.4a. Culver Bank: tidal currents and wave approach.

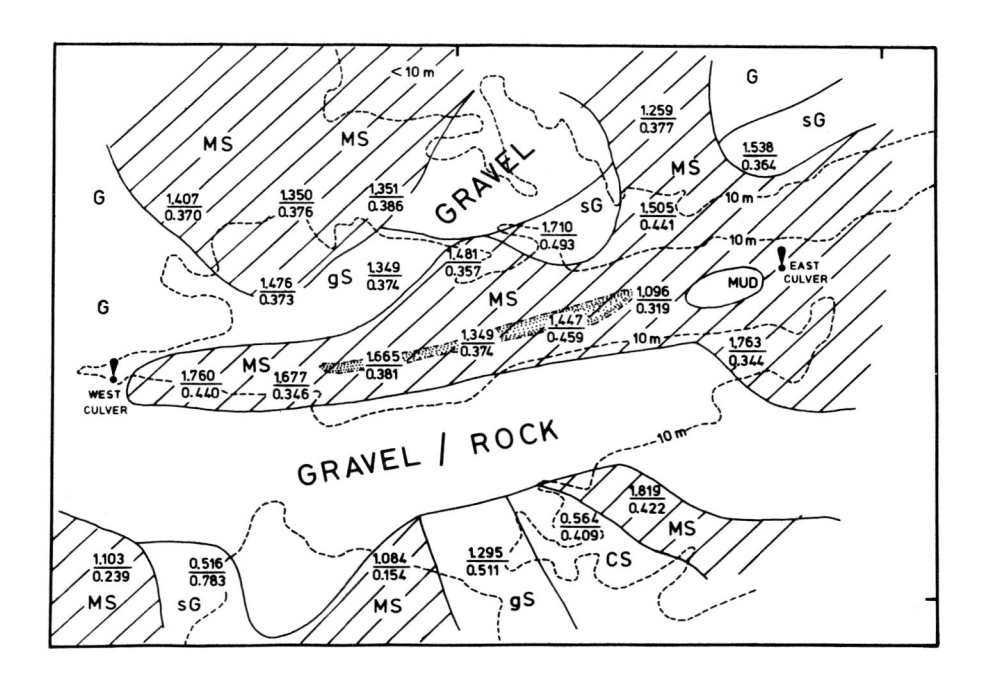

Figure 34.4b. Culver Bank: sediment distribution.

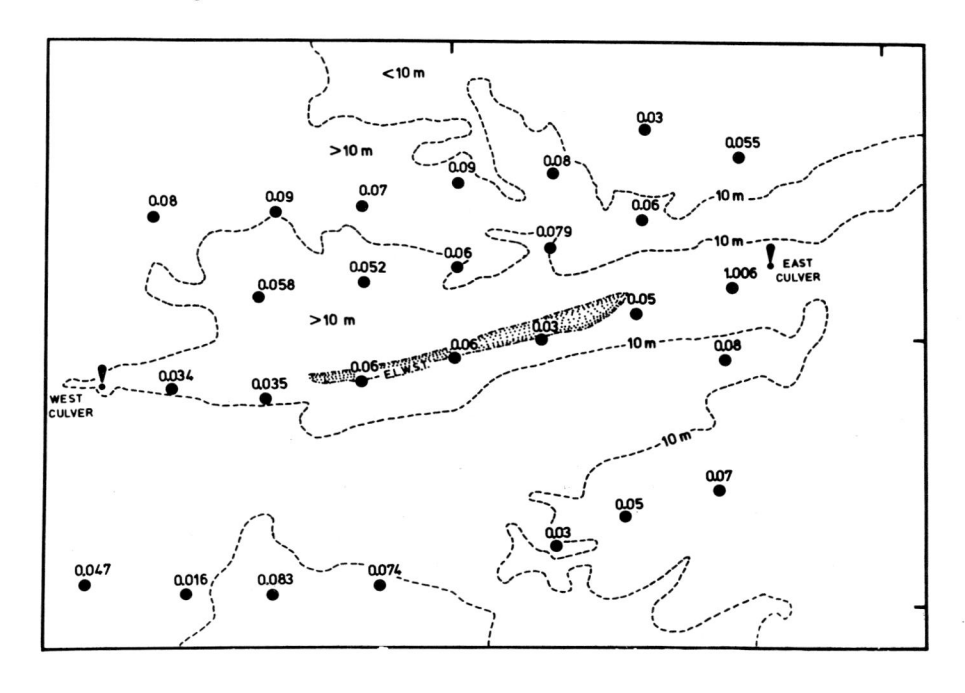

Figure 34.4c. Culver Bank: % of organic carbon.

The salinity of seawater round the Helwick Bank varies from 32-33.5°/oo. This decreases eastwards and the Culver Bank experiences 28-30°/oo (I.M.E.R., 1974). The annual temperature range in the Bristol Channel is 6-17°C. The water column is virtually homohaline and homothermal throughout the year.

DYNAMICAL SEDIMENTOLOGY AND FAUNAL DIVERSITY

Although the shapes in plan of the linear sandbanks in the Bristol Channel are maintained by tidal current action, wave action controls their height and contributes to their sediment supply. The balance between these two mechanisms dominates the environment of any fauna inhabiting the linear sandbanks.

The asymmetry of particularly the Helwick and Nash Banks would suggest variation in the ebb and flood paths around the banks (Off, 1963). Present evidence suggests these ebb/flood currents create an eddy where the tidal current is modified by the coastline, i.e., the widening of the Bristol Channel at Nash Point and Port Eynon Point cause tidal current deceleration and sediment deposition (Turner, 1976). Ferentinos & Collins (1979) have suggested that the shapes of the banks are maintained by topographically induced eddies on an ebbing tide, which reconcentrate sediment dispersed by wave action. Tidal current speeds are, in themselves alone, generally inadequate (especially in the deeper, more offshore Bristol Channel) to initiate or maintain the movement of medium sands. It is probable that the combined action of southwesterly swell and flood currents transports sediment to the areas of the banks (as they did during the earlier Flandrian) but that this sediment is maintained as offshore bank accumulations (i.e., is prevented from migrating onshore) by the tidal current circulation during its semidiurnal ebb and flood cycle around the banks.

Tidal currents move sediment round the banks, as seen in sandwaves with crests normal to the axis of the bank, and also obliquely towards the crest of the bank as the tidal currents off the bank are stronger than those at the bank. Houboult (1968) believes that this variation in tidal current sets up horizontal helical flow moving sediment onto a linear bank. The deflection of the tidal currents to the bank crest may cause a 'line of convergence' (Caston, 1971).

If tidal currents are responsible for the formation and maintenance of the linear bank, vertical growth will be limited by water depth. The relatively large 'intertidal' areas of Scarweather, Nash and Culver Sands are due to the high tidal range of the Bristol Channel. Britton (1978) and Britton & Britton (Chapter 13) have also suggested that by comparison with older charts of the area, the Helwick Bank has extended westwards during the last 200 years. This westward migration is supported by the decreasing mean grain size diameter inferring westward movement of sediment (Turner, 1976).

The medium sand forming the banks is believed to have been winnowed out from glacial till during the Flandrian marine transgression (Turner, 1976). The residual material forms the gravels and sandy gravels surrounding the banks. These tidal currents are rarely strong enough to move these gravel size fractions is evidenced by the occurrence of live *Sabellaria* tubes on one side of the gravel. The sandy gravels are usually poorly sorted, showing evidence of bimodality in their grain size analysis. These sandy gravels are evidence of a boundary where tongues of sand extend over the gravel as seen in the English Channel (Flemming & Stride, 1967).

The upward migration of sediment due to tidal current action is balanced by the downward migration of sand due to wave action, particularly during storms. Thus the degree of exposure and direction of dominant wave advance will modify both the sedimentology and benthic ecology. The restrictive effect of wave action is expressed in the relative exposure at low water of each bank. Helwick Bank, which has the maximum exposure (WNW to SSW) to long period waves, is never exposed at low water, suggesting that sediment transported to the crest by tidal current action is rapidly removed by wave action.

Moving eastward the Nash, Scarweather, Hugo Bank complex is exposed to a narrower sector of approach of long period destructive wave action than is Helwick Bank. Long period waves from west to southwest only will affect the bank. As a result of this decrease in destructive wave activity, both Scarweather and Nash Bank dry to about 2m. Further up channel, Culver Bank is exposed only to the less frequent long period westerly wave action. As a result, 5km of the crest of the bank is exposed as much as 4m at ELWST.

Wave action modifies the benthic ecology by destabilizing the substratum and winnowing out organic matter. Severe wave action has also been shown to be responsible for destruction of sublittoral communities (Orton, 1929; Rees, et al., 1977).

Preliminary investigations (pers. obs.) suggest that the faunal diversity is reduced on the bank crests, where the fauna consists wholly of the mysid *Gastrosaccus spinifer*, the amphipod *Pontocrates arenarius* and the polychaete *Nephthys cirrosa*.

Gastrosaccus spinifer shows considerably increased densities on the bank crests compared to off-bank stations. This species is indicative of the *Spisula* subcommunity in the sand wave area of the outer part of the Bristol Channel (Warwick & Davies, 1977). *Gastrosaccus* usually lives in swarms near the sea bed and exhibits vertical migration (Tattersall & Tattersall, 1951). However, Rasmussen (1973), on keeping *Gastrosaccus* in an aquarium, found it continually burrowing into the sediment if disturbed, an ideal strategy in the mobile sands of the linear sandbank. *Nephthys cirrosa* is modified for sand dwelling by the long setae attached to the parapodia and is considered to be indicative of clean sands (Clark, et al., 1962). The burrowing habits of *Pontocrates arenarius* still need further elucidation.

Recruitment and survival of juveniles within this high energy environment would only occur in those adapting their reproductive strategies by brooding or decreasing the larval life (McIntyre, 1970). Other species would not find either protection or food at the mobile substrate as in other sand areas of the Bristol Channel (Tyler & Banner, 1977; Tyler, 1977).

The physical environment of the linear sandbanks may be analogous to that of exposed beaches (Scott, 1960; McIntyre, 1970; Seed & Lowry, 1973; Eleftheriou & Nicholson, 1975; Withers, 1977), intertidal sandbanks (Withers & Thorp, 1978) and sandwave fields (Jones, et al., 1963). Sand beaches exposed to oceanic swell of low refraction are usually composed of sediment of grain size greater than 220μm, the fauna consisting of active swimmers with the severe wave action limiting species diversity (Eleftheriou & Nicholson, 1975; Withers, 1977). On the most exposed beaches of Scotland and the Western Isles (Scott, 1960; McIntyre, 1970), the faunal diversity is considerably reduced, with *Pontocrates arenarius* and *Nephthys cirrosa* being amongst the very few species present. The fauna of sand waves on Warts Bank, south of the Isle of Man, also appear to be severely reduced due to the unstable nature of the sediment (Jones, et al., 1963). McIntyre (1970) suggested that only *Eurydice* is indicative of impermanent sands but this species was found only rarely on the linear sandbanks of the Bristol Channel.

From this study, and those of extremely exposed beaches and intertidal sandbanks (Scott, 1960; McIntyre, 1970; Eleftheriou & Nicholson, 1975; Withers, 1977; Withers & Thorp, 1978), it is suggested that wave action modifies the fauna so that on the most wave-exposed sands (particularly in linear sandbanks) the faunal diversity is greatly reduced, resulting in a reduced *Spisula* community consisting mainly of peracarid crustaceans. Decrease in wave exposure permits the introduction of *Nephthys* spp. and wave action would have to be considerably reduced before a mollusc fauna could survive in this habitat to produce a true *Spisula* sub-community, ultimately leading to a *Venus* community under low energy conditions.

ACKNOWLEDGEMENTS

We wish to thank Professor F.T. Banner for facilities in the Department of Oceanography and for his critical reading of the manuscript; to the Master, Officers and Crew of R.R.S. "John Murray"whose navigation skills ensured the successful completion of the cruise; to N.E.R.C. for ship time and R.V.S. Barry, to Ms. J. Greengo for typing the manuscript and Mr. K. Naylor for final preparation of the figures.

The following are gratefully thanked for their assistance on board ship: R.J. Evans, G. Farmer, K. Naylor, A. Wilding and S. Williams.

REFERENCES

Admiralty (1974). *West Coast of England and Wales Pilot*. Pub. Hydrographer of the Navy, Taunton.

Britton, R.C. (1978). *Structure of Some Marine Sedimentary Bodies and their Dynamic Environments*. Unpub. Ph.D. Thesis, University of Wales, 255pp.

Caston, V.N.D. (1971). Linear sand banks in the southern North Sea. *Sedimentology, 18*, 63-78.

Caston, V.N.D., & Stride, A.H. (1970). Tidal sand movement between some linear sand banks in the North Sea off northeast Norfolk. *Marine Geology, 9*, M38-M42.

Clark, R.B., Alder, J.R., & McIntyre, A.D (1962). The distribution of *Nephthys* on the Scottish Coast. *Journal of Animal Ecology, 31*, 359-372.

Cloet, R.L. (1954). Hydrographic analysis of the Goodwin Sands and the Brake Bank. *Geographical Journal, 120*, 203-215.

Culver, S.J. (1979). Holocene patterns and modes of sediment transportation in the Bristol Channel and Severn Estuary. *Marine Geology, 29*, (In press).

Darbyshire, M. (1963). Wave measurements made by the N.I.O. In: Bretschneider, C.L. (Ed.). *Ocean Wave Spectra*, Prentice Hall, London, 285-291.

Duane, D.B., Field, M.E., Meisburger, E.P., Swift, D.J.P., & Williams, S.J. (1974). Linear Shoals on the Atlantic Inner Continental Shelf, Florida to Long Island. In: Swift, D.J.P., Duane, D.P., & Pilkey, O.H. (Eds.). *Shelf Sediment Transport: Process and Pattern*. Pub. Dowden, Hutchinson & Ross, Penn., 447-498.

Eleftheriou, A., & Nicholson, M.D. (1975). The effects of exposure on beach fauna. *Cahiers de Biologie Marine, 16*, 695-710.

Ferentinos, G. (1978). *Hydrodynamic and sedimentation processes in Swansea Bay and along the central northern Bristol Channel coastline*. Unpub. Ph.D. Thesis, University of Wales, 147pp.

Ferentinos, G. & Collins, M.B. (1979). Tidally induced secondary circulations and their associated sedimentation processes. *Journal of the Oceanographical Society of Japan, 35*, 65-74.

Flemming, N.C., & Stride, A.H. (1967). Basal sand and gravel patches with separate indications of tidal current and storm-wave paths, near Plymouth. *Journal of the Marine Biological Association of the U.K., 47*, 433-444.

Folk, R.L. (1961). *Petrology of Sedimentary Rocks*, University of Texas, 154pp.

Gaudette, H.E., Flight, W.R., Toner, L., & Folger, D.W. (1974). An inexpensive titration method for the determination of organic carbon in recent sediments. *Journal of Sedimentary Petrology, 44*, 249-253.

Houboult, J.J.H.C. (1968). Recent Sediments in the Southern Bight of the North Sea. *Geologie en Mijnbouw, 47*, 245-273.

I.M.E.R., (1974). *Report 1973-1974*. Institute for Marine Environmental Research, Plymouth, 71pp.

Jones, N.S., Kain, J.M. & Stride, A.H. (1963). The movement of sand waves on Warts Bank, Isle of Man. *Marine Geology, 3*, 329-336.

Kenyon, N.H. (1970). Sand ribbons in European Tidal Seas. *Marine Geology, 9,* 25-39.
McIntyre, A.D. (1970). The range of biomass in intertidal sand, with special reference to the bivalve *Tellina tenuis*. *Journal of the Marine Biological Association of the U.K., 50,* 561-575.
Off, T. (1963). Rhythmic linear sand bodies caused by tidal currents. *Bulletin of the American Association of Petroleum Geologists, 47,* 324-341.
Orton, J.H. (1929). Severe environmental mortality among *Abra (=Syndosmya) alba, Donax vittatus* and other organisms off the Lancashire coast. *Nature, 124,* 911.
Rasmussen, E. (1973). Systematics and ecology of the Isefjord Marine Fauna (Denmark). *Ophelia, 11,* 1-495.
Rees, E.I.S., Nicholaidou, A. & Laskaridou, P. (1977). The effects of storms on the dynamics of shallow water benthic associations. In: Keegan, B.F., O'Ceidigh, P., & Boaden, P.J.S. (Eds.). *Biology of Benthic Organisms.* Pergamon Press, Oxford, 465-474.
Scott, A. (1960). The fauna of the sandy beach, Village Bay, St. Kilda: A dynamical relationship. *Oikos, 11,* 153-160.
Seed, R., & Lowry, R.J. (1973). The intertidal fauna of seven sandy beaches of County Down. *Proceedings of the Royal Irish Academy, B. 73,* 217-230.
Smith, J.D. (1969). Geomorphology of a sand ridge. *Journal of Geology, 77,* 39-55.
Tattersall, W.M. & Tattersall, O.S. (1951). *The British Mysidae.* Ray Society Publication, *136,* 460pp.
Turner, S.R. (1976). *Some aspects of sedimentary bodies in parts of the Bristol Channel.* Unpub. Ph.D. Thesis, University of Wales, 235pp.
Tyler, P.A. (1977). Sub-littoral community structure of Oxwich Bay, South Wales in relation to sedimentological, physical oceanographic and biological parameters. In: Keegan, B.F., O'Ceidigh, P. & Boaden, P.J.S. (Eds.). *Biology of Benthic Organisms.* Pergamon Press, Oxford, 559-566.
Tyler, P.A. & Banner, F.T. (1977). The effect of coastal hydrodynamics on the Echinoderm distribution in the sublittoral of Oxwich Bay, Bristol Channel. *Estuarine and Coastal Marine Science, 5,* 293-308.
Tyler, P.A. & Shackley, S.E. (1978). Comparative efficiency of the Day and Smith-McIntyre Grabs. *Estuarine and Coastal Marine Science, 6,* 439-445.
Van Veen, J. (1935). Ondulations de sable dans la mer du Nord. *Hydrogr. Rev., 12,* 21-29.
Van Veen, J. (1936). *Onderzoekingen in de Hoofden* Algemeene Landsdrukkerij, The Hague, 252pp.
Warwick, R.M. & Davies, J.R. (1977). The distribution of sublittoral macrofauna communities in the Bristol Channel in relation to the substrate. *Estuarine and Coastal Marine Science, 5,* 267-288.
Withers, R.G. (1977). Soft-shore Macrobenthos along the south-west coast of Wales. *Estuarine and Coastal Marine Science, 5,* 467-484.
Withers, R.G. & Thorp, C. (1978). The macrobenthos inhabiting sand banks in Langstone Harbour, Hampshire. *Journal of Natural History, 12,* 445-455.

DISCUSSION VII

Jones: I get the distinct impression that this area must be "physically" dominated. The biologists have come to this conclusion, and, it seems to me, so have the physicists and chemists. However, there are a couple of points I can't understand. Dr. Hayward said that the phytoplankton round Mumbles Head occurs there because of the turbidity of the water in the area and that it was due to material stirred up from the intertidal zone and brought up into the water column; conversely, Dr. Joint was saying that the bloom he observed was south of there, because there was less turbidity. How does this fit into the pattern of circulation in Swansea Bay?

Joint: I can't say anything about the inner area; however, in the outer area, where the water is less turbid, we do find more primary production. I think the point I was trying to make about that high bloom of phytoplankton is that we do not really know if it is the result of *in situ* production, or transport from another area (i.e., the removal of benthic algae from intertidal and other areas). If there is a large removal of algae from intertidal areas, that in itself may increase the turbidity of the water.

Kent: Did Dr. Tyler find any seasonal variation in the fauna of the linear sandbanks, and, if so, what seasonal variation occurred?

Tyler, P: This was a one-off survey, with the R.R.S. John Murray for a 5-day period. We intend to carry out seasonal sampling, but this will be confined to one bank - most likely the Scarweather Bank.

Carr: I would like to make three points. Firstly, Dr. Tyler said he felt the impoverished benthos was related to the degree of exposure; this seems to be a reasonable conclusion. At the same time, it was the Culver Bank which had the most impoverished fauna of these banks. Perhaps he could comment on this apparent anomaly? The second point is that, in both this paper and that presented by Dr. Britton, sediment grain sizes tended to fine towards the western end of the Banks. If one accepts the argument that sediment fines in the direction of transport, this is evidence towards the progression of sediment down the Bristol Channel, towards the west. Thirdly, while I agree that linear sanbanks are progressively lower (with respect to mean tide level) as we go from east to west, it could also be argued that there might be some sort of relationship of the height of the banks to the available sediment supply as well as to wave energy. This would indicate a supply from up the Bristol Channel.

Tyler, P: There are two possible explanations for the reduction of fauna at Culver. Firstly, salinity in the region is low and water is very turbid. The area corresponds to one of the reduced communities of Warwick & Davies (1977) and I don't think there is much of a local fauna there. Secondly, we sampled right along the crest axis of Culver and I think it is so exposed (i.e., it is out of the water at LW) that there is considerable drainage through the sand along the crest, especially at LW Spring Tides; such conditions would make it relatively uninhabitable and a very reduced fauna would result.

I would like to add support to Richard Warwick's comments on the disappearance of animals. We have found it very frustrating ourselves. We have tried to follow the reproductive periodicity of a number of benthic invertebrates in the *Abra* community in Oxwich Bay and we find we get a 9-month sample and suddenly the species disappear. There appears to be no physical reason and we can only suggest migration or mortality of the community. Could Dr. Warwick suggest a reason for the migration of this community? Further, we have sampled the epibenthos of Oxwich Bay regularly since 1973 with an Aggaziz trawl. During 1973, and 1974, *Ophiura albida* was dominant, now *O. texturata* is very common. I wonder if Dr. Warwick would like to comment if he considers this an inward migration of adult *O. texturata* or as the result of larval competition?

Warwick: We found *O. albida* was generally found on coarser sediments in the Channel, often on mixtures of stones, pebbles, shells and sand in the central Channel, whereas *O*. *texturata* is found on finer sediments of sand or muddy-sand. Did Dr. Tyler observe any changes in the nature of the sediment in Oxwich Bay?

Tyler, P: Not noticeably. We are still getting *O*. *albida*, but in considerably reduced proportions.

Warwick: I would like to ask Dr. Isaac a question as there appears to be some mismatch between our data and his. We found very large numbers of cumaceans at the bottom during the daytime, but none at night, when they are supposed to swarm up into the plankton. Dr. Isaac did not find any of these in his night plankton hauls. I was wondering if these night hauls might be spurious because the lights were so bright on the pier that upward migration was inhibited?

Isaac: The lights on the pier are not that bright. I did, in fact, find cumaceans in both day and night hauls at Mumbles Pier.

35. FISH AND FISHERIES IN GREATER SWANSEA BAY

S. E. Shackley*, P. E. King* and J. Rhydderch**

*Department of Zoology, University College Swansea, U.K.
**South Wales Sea Fisheries Committee, Cambrian Place, Swansea, U.K.

ABSTRACT

The history of fishing in the Greater Swansea Bay area is traced over the last centuries. The causes, both artificial and natural, for the steady decline in the fishery and the collapse of the shellfish industry are discussed. The present distribution of potential commercial and sport fish is described and the possibilities of a future small fishery are presented

KEYWORDS

Oysters; Fish; Fisheries; Ichthyoplankton; Swansea Bay; Bristol Channel.

THE MUMBLES OYSTER FISHERY

Evidence suggests that the Mumbles Oyster fishery originated in ancient times. Excavations on Roman sites at Caerleon and Caerwent showed that oysters formed a part of the inmates' diet and presumably originated from the Bristol Channel. The fisheries existed in the reign of Elizabeth I and George Owen in his description of Pembrokeshire published in 1603 refers to the oyster beds at Milford Haven, Caldy and Stackpole. Most beds of importance were situated between Stackpole Head and Porthcawl in a moderate depth of water (Fig. 35.1), the most important beds being between Port Eynon and Mumbles Head, and in Swansea Bay (Matheson, 1933). When Thomas Dineley accompanied Henry Somerset, First Duke of Beaufort, in 1684, he recorded that Swansea Bay had "the best bed of oysters in Great Britain".

In the early days dredging was carried out from small, open rowing boats towing a single dredge fishing inside Swansea Bay or just outside Mumbles Point. A few larger boats may have joined the fleet from time to time from the newly formed (1776) Swansea Fishery. From 1840 smacks from Essex and Kent dredged the area when some Swansea oysters were used to restock the beds in the Thames estuary. In 1860 French luggers took large numbers to St. Malo and the Arcachon Basin to establish beds.

By the mid 19th century most oyster boats had masts and sails, some with a single dipping lug sail, but the majority with two masts each with gaff-headed sail (the

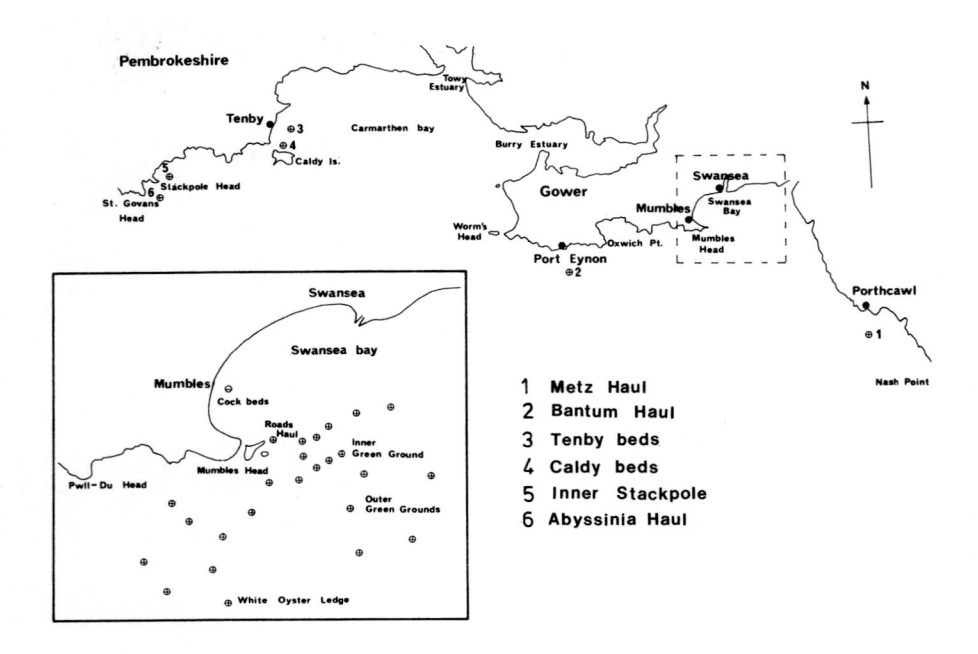

Figure 35.1. Oyster beds fished by Mumbles boats.

shallop rig). It is thought that the Swansea Bay pilot boats were later developed from this (Lloyd, 1954).

In the 1850's a group of Mumbles oyster fishermen travelled to Colchester to examine the local boats and acquired a boat named the "*Seven Sisters*", a decked sailing boat or skiff. Evidence suggests that similar decked skiffs were introduced at the time until by 1860 there were an estimated 66 at Oystermouth, 8 at Swansea and 22 at Port Eynon.

The skiffs weighed 8-10 tons, were 30-40ft long and had a single mast with a cutter rig. The advantages over the smaller open boats were that they could go further afield, were more manoeuverable and could tow two dredges (Lloyd, 1954). Skiffs were built at Appledore, St. Ives, Cardiff and Swansea but a few were built onshore at Oystermouth.

For 6 months of the year some dredged off Pembrokeshire returning to Tenby each night, and some even went north to work in the Solway Firth for several weeks, but the majority dredged in Swansea Bay from September to November, e.g. for the large roadster from the Roads haul, on the Metz haul, the Green Grounds and Jersey haul. All the patches had local names (Fig. 35.1). Few skiffs carried a compass relying on shore marks which made location of the hauls impossible in poor visibility. The skiffs sailed to windward over the patches, went about and sailed downwind towing the dredges. The dredges were unique to the area, made by John Libby of Oystermouth (King and Osborn, 1969).

When landed, oysters were placed in perches on the foreshore which were rented from the Duke of Beaufort.

The traditional boat lay-up was behind a horse-shoe shaped storm pebble beach formed alongshore in front of the Antelope and Prince of Wales Inns. It was open to the north so that the boats sailed in at high water. In 1892 the Swansea-Mumbles steam tramway was extended to Mumbles Head and a large portion of the beach, including the skiff lay-up was enclosed by the railway embankment. A wooden breakwater was built but proved inadequate and fell into disrepair.

The oyster fishery at Mumbles was at its peak in the 1870's. In 1871, 600 people were involved in the fishery (500 crewing the fleet, 40 bagging on the perches, and 10 hauliers to Swansea). After 1870 the numbers of boats declined as did the catch (Table 35.1) until in 1930 only a single skiff and two motor fishing vessels remained.

TABLE 35.1. Decline in the Oyster Fishery.

Decline in numbers of oyster boats

Year	Nos.
1869	154
1871	188*
1879	100
1883	47
1885	25
1900	20
1903	18
1906	19
1914	9
1920	10

Decline in numbers of oysters taken

Year	Nos.
1873	9,050,000
1874	6,600,000
1875	3,810,000
1895	1,600,000
1912-13	2,376,400
1920	1,256,000
1924	10,000
1925	None

*Including 12 Colchester and Jersey boats.

Opinions vary regarding the cause for the decline. Overfishing has been blamed, the removal of the skiff lay-up in 1892, and the "oyster disease" of 1920-21. However, some recovery since that date would have been expected if these had been the sole causes. In 1949 the South Wales Sea Fisheries Committee investigated the possibility of reviving the fishery. The offshore beds required restocking which was not practicable whilst the inshore beds were strongly polluted with sewage and chemical waste.

This year (1979) the 1931 Swansea Fishery order, regulating the oyster and mussel fishery in the area, has been revoked. The long history of the Mumbles oyster fishery must now be regarded as closed

THE HISTORY OF SWANSEA AS A FISHING PORT

In the 16th century a white fish industry was conducted by a line of fish weirs, nets and traps, 700 yards of net in total, extending along the foreshore between Mumbles and Swansea. This stake net fishery supplied Mumbles and Swansea, including the Swansea Valley, from the 16th to the 19th century. In the 19th century, the oyster fishermen fished in Swansea Bay during the closed season, supplementing the stake net fishery.

In 1887 Swansea's history as a fishing port started when steam tugs began to carry trawl nets and professional fishermen. This was a purely economical measure to ensure that time and fuel were fully utilised while waiting for trade. Some trawled in Swansea Bay but the main grounds were off Lundy and on other grounds in the Bristol Channel. This continued until 1895 when the tugs lost the right to fish within the 3 mile limit.

At the turn of the century Swansea's fishing industry changed from inshore to mid and deep water. In 1904 Castle Steam Trawlers, Ltd. transferred their shore base and fleet from Milford Haven to Swansea. The main reasons for this move were:-
(i) The geographical advantages of Swansea including its proximity to the South Wales coalfield.
(ii) The availability of a large tonnage of coal required for bunkering the steam trawlers.
(iii) The railway which could despatch daily landings directly to the highly populated mining valleys.
The Castle fleet boats, named after Welsh Castles, fished the exposed western grounds off Ireland for hake.

Post World War I, the Castle Fleet was taken over by Consolidated Steam Fishing and Ice Co. (Grimsby) Ltd., later to be known as Consolidated Fisheries, Ltd., whose fleet of 124 trawlers was the largest steam fleet in the world. Under the management of Major Ronald the fleet continued fishing through the Depression until World War II. Overfishing on the western grounds and economic pressures caused the eventual decline and closure of the fishery. In 1957 Consolidated Fisheries, Ltd., withdrew from all operations at Swansea.

Today, three wooden motor fishing vessels operate commercially out of Swansea Docks under the auspices of Swansea Fishermen Ltd. Several smaller motor fishing vessels are berthed in the Tawe. All Swansea's fishing boats now are inshore trawlers operating within the 3 mile limit in Swansea, Oxwich and Carmarthen Bays and also the larger boats fish downchannel off Lundy and Tenby. Landings for Swansea Bay are incorporated in landings records for these other areas, none fishing exclusively in Swansea Bay. Landings have declined in recent years but the reasons for this are unknown.

Drag-netting, stake-netting and trammel-netting are carried out by part-time fishermen alongshore between Mumbles and Swansea, at Porthcawl and Ogmore.

SPORT FISHING IN SWANSEA BAY.

Sport-fishing is a very popular recreational pursuit in the area, mostly carried on from the shore, piers and jetties or from small boats a short distance offshore. A survey of sea angling clubs in the area in 1972 (Nelson-Smith, 1972) revealed the information presented in Table 35.2.

Clubs were again circularised this year (1979) but response has been poor. The Swansea Sea Angling Club again mention bass and mackerel as being scarcer and dogfish being more abundant, with catches being smaller but in relatively good condition. A National Survey of Coastal Sport Fishing in Britain (Clark, 1971) showed that the Bristol Channel and its approaches appeared to have experienced a decline in a greater variety of fish than most other parts of the country. This survey

TABLE 35.2. Survey Sea Angling Clubs Using Swansea Bay Area. (Nelson-Smith, 1972).

	No of Members Active/Using Area	Average Use Hrs/Year	Average Spent £	Non-Club Anglers
Average for Club	50 38	360	25	9 : 1
Estimated Total	1900 1250	450,000	31,250	

Anglers using area - Absolute Total: 15-20,000

Questionnaire on Catches		Percentage of Respondents
Species fewer in area:	Cod	60
	Whiting	40
	Pouting	(listed)
	Bass	50
	Mackerel	(listed)
	Plaice	40
	Conger	(listed)
	Skate	5
	'Flatfish'	>50
Species more numerous:	Dogfish	50
Catches smaller:		70
Condition poorer:		30
Bait rarer:	(lugworm, peeler crab)	40

suggested causes of changes in abundance of fish to be due to (a) natural fluctuations; (b) overfishing; (c) pollution.

Fish populations are expected to show natural fluctuations in numbers depending on many factors. But the majority opinion of anglers (in 1971 and now) is that inshore trawling has intensified so much that fish are fewer and smaller. This opinion is probably caused by a clash of interests between the two groups. Anglers and commercial fishermen are in direct competition for some species, notably plaice, sole and skate. Fishing intensity preventing survival to large sizes and great age is not detrimental to the fishery provided fish survive to breeding size to maintain stocks. It is, however, damaging to the sport fisherman who is more interested in old, large fish for record size catches. The stringent control of net mesh size is thought to maintain reasonably healthy inshore fisheries, but it is difficult to control the meshes of the part-time drag net, etc. fishermen.

Some claims of pollution damage spring from local prejudice, but there is a *prima facie* case that pollution is causing deterioration in angling along the Bristol Channel.

ICHTHYOPLANKTON IN SWANSEA BAY

Fig. 35.2 is a chart of the area showing the sampling stations at which plankton hauls have been made using the 2m diameter Plymouth ring trawl. Hauls were made at monthly intervals over a two year period (Townley and King, 1979). Fig. 35.3 shows the average catch/haul/month of combined day and night hauls but minus the night haul sprat and goby data. This figure shows that the main spawning period at all stations is from April to July. The postlarvae caught late in the year are gobies,

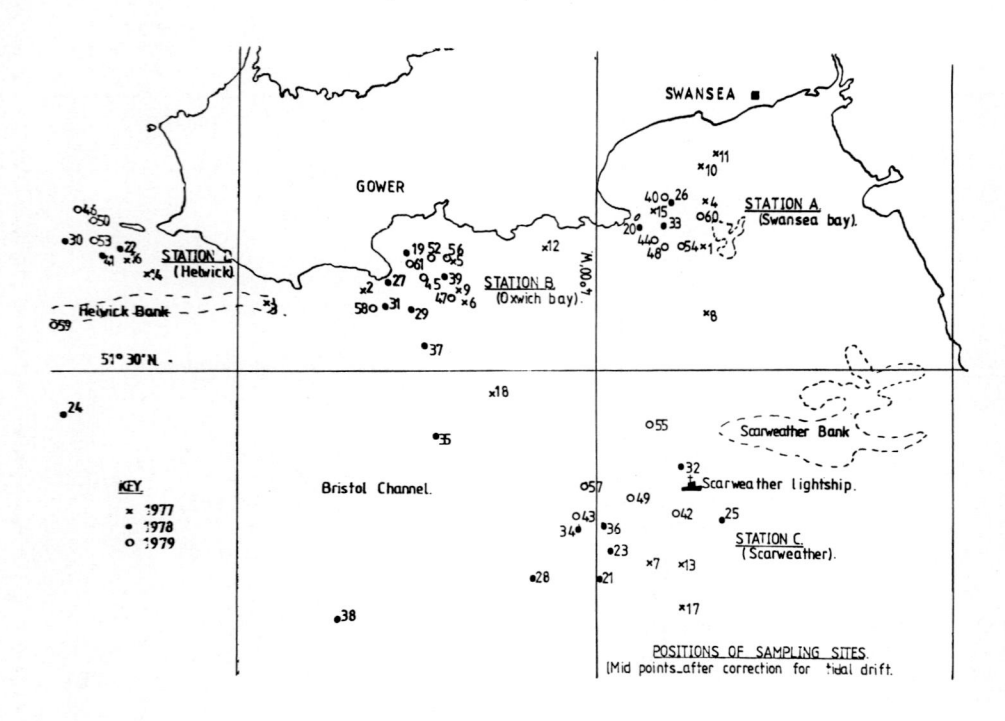

Figure 35.2. Stations in the Greater Swansea Bay used for the collection of Ichthyoplankton.

which show an extended spawning season not noted in other areas. The large numbers of eggs at Oxwich in May are of *Ciliata* spp (rockling). No such large congregations of eggs of other species were recorded.

Swansea and Oxwich samples are dominated by inshore species, e.g. *Agonus cataphractus, Liparis montagui, Taurulus bubalis* and *Blennius* spp whilst the Helwick and Scarweather samples contain more offshore species, e.g. eggs of gadoids.

The night haul data for June, July and August 1979 (Fig. 35.4) clearly shows the reason for the exclusion of sprat and goby data from the previous figure. Sprats and gobies occur in large numbers in the night hauls suggesting that the day hauls do not give a true representation of their populations.

Table 35.3 lists the Ichthyoplankton species found in the Greater Swansea Bay area. There is a general paucity of Ichthyoplankton when compared with a fifth station further west at Lundy, and with other regions, e.g. Plymouth (Russell, 1926-1973). Trends of species occurrence are similar to other areas except that the peak of occurrence of postlarvae occurs later in Swansea Bay (July) than in other regions (April/May).

COMMERCIAL IMPLICATIONS

Sprats (whitebait) occur almost all year round in large numbers so there is a possibility of a small whitebait fishery. The eggs of sole and bass indicate large

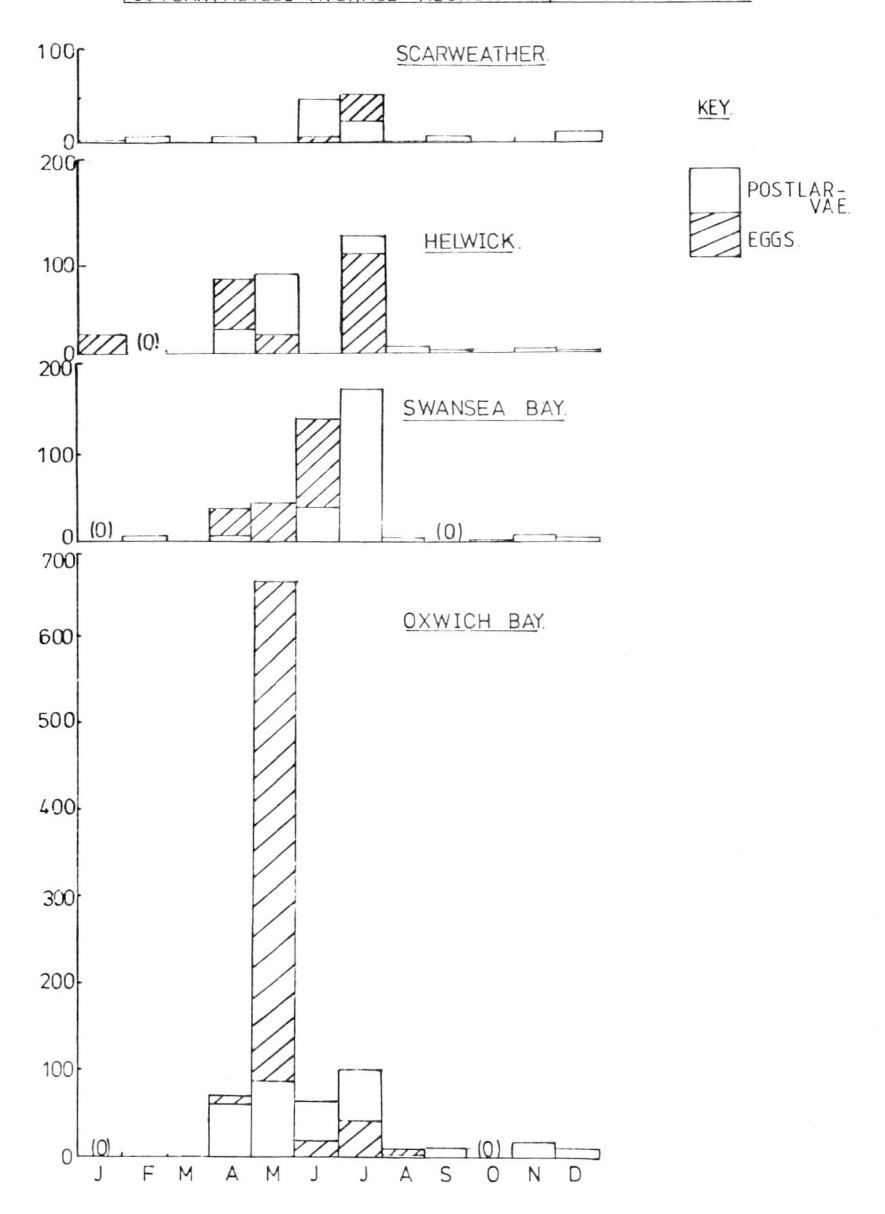

Figure 35.3. The average catch/haul/month for combined day and night hauls (omitting night haul sprat and goby data).

TABLE 35.3. Greater Swansea Bay Ichthyoplankton Species List.

1. Agonidae: *Agonus cataphractus* [PL].

2. Ammodytidae: *Ammodytes tobianus, A. marinus* [PL] *Hyperoplus lanceolatus, H. immaculatus* [PL] *Gymnammodytes semisquamatus* [PL].

3. Belonidae: *Belone belone* [PL].

4. Blenniidae: *Blennius pholis, B. ocellaris, B. gattorugine* [PL].

5. Bothidae: *Arnoglossus lanterna* [E/PL], *Zeugopterus punctatus* [E].

6. Callionymidae: *Callionymus lyra, C. reticulatus* [PL].

7. Clupeidae: *Sprattus sprattus* [PL], *Sardina pilchardus* [PL], *Engravlis encrasicolus* [E/PL].

8. Cottidae: *Taurulus bubalis* [PL].

9. Gadidae: *Merlangius merlangus* [PL], *Trisopterus luscus, T. minutus* [E/PL], *Ciliata* spp. [E/PL], *Gaidropsarus vulgaris* [PL], *Gadus morhua* [E/PL].

10. Gobiesocidae: *Apletodon microcephalus* [PL].

11. Gobiidae: *Pomatoschistus minutus, P. norvegicus, P. microps, Buenia jeffreysii, Aphia minuta, Gobius paganellus, Crystallogobius linearis* [PL].

12. Labridae: *Labrus mixtus, L. bergylta* [PL], *Crenilabrus melops* [PL], *Ctenolabrus rupestris* [PL].

13. Liparidae: *Liparis montagui* [PL].

14. Pleuronectidae: *Pleuronectes platessa* [E], *Limanda limanda* [E/PL], *Microstomus kitt* [E/PL].

15. Scombridae: *Scomber scombrus* [PL].

16. Serranidae: *Dicentrarchus labrax* [PL].

17. Soleidae: *Solea solea* [PL], *Pegusa lascaris* [E/PL], *Buglossidium luteum* [E/PL], *Microchirus variegatus* [E/PL].

18. Syngnathidae: *Syngnathus rostellatus* [PL].

19. Trachinidae: *Trachinus vipera* [E/PL], *T. draco* [PL].

20. Triglidae: *Trigla lucerna* [E/PL], *Eutrigla gurnardus* [E/PL].

N.B.: Eggs of *B. pholis, Gobius* spp. and *Cyclopterus lumpus* were found on the shore as were the postlarvae of *Atherina prebyster*.

[E/PL] = Eggs and postlarvae.

Fish and Fisheries 563

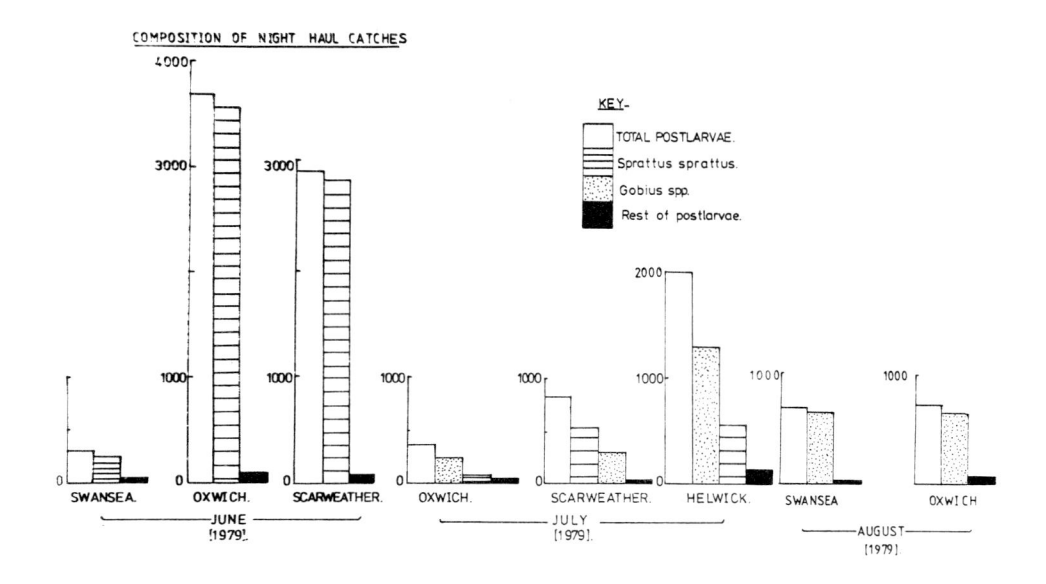

Figure 35.4. Night haul data for June, July and August, 1979.

numbers of spawning adults in the vicinity. But it is clear that there is no likelihood of the fishing industry in Swansea ever again returning to its former size and importance.

REFERENCES

Clark, R.B. (1971). Changing success of coastal sport fishing. *Mar. Poll. Bull.*, 2, 153-156.
King, P.E., and Osborn, A. (1969). Oyster Dredging. *Gower*, 20, 1-5.
Lloyd, R.J.H. (1954). The Mumbles Oyster Skiffs. *Mariners Mirror*, 40, 258-269.
Matheson, C. (1933). The Oyster Fishery at Mumbles, Glamorgan. *Trans. Cdff. Nats. Soc.*, LXVI, 81-86.
Nelson-Smith, A. (1972). Sport fishing in Swansea Bay. Unpub. Report to the Expert Working Group on Possible Pollution in Swansea Bay.
Russell, F.S. (1973). A summary of the observations on the occurrence of planktonic stages of fish off Plymouth, 1924-1972. *J. mar. biol. Ass. UK.*, 53, 347-355.
Russell, F.S. (1976). *The eggs and planktonic stages of British marine fishes.* Academic Press, 524pp.
Townley, M., and King, P.E. Seasonal abundances of Ichthyoplankton in the Bristol Channel. (In preparation).

36. DOCK AND HARBOUR PLANNING, MAINTENANCE AND DEVELOPMENT IN RELATION TO THE SWANSEA BAY PORTS

B. L. Flower

British Transport Docks Board, Swansea and Port Talbot, Adelaide Street, Swansea, U.K.

ABSTRACT

The various principal phases of developments and their relationship with the changing pattern of trade for Swansea and Port Talbot in particular, and the general pattern for other South Wales Ports, are described.

An account is given of the maintenance of the present facilities and how this is influenced by development of new materials and methods; also, the effect which the economic climate has had on port operations and the pattern for the future are noted.

The relationship of the development of the ports to the industrial and commercial development of the hinterland is described.

Planning for trade needs in the future and the developments which will be necessary to cope with them are discussed.

KEYWORDS

Docks; Harbours; Swansea Bay.

THE DEVELOPMENT OF SWANSEA DOCKS

Swansea's association with maritime trade goes back many centuries but it was the arrival of industry in the area which set in motion a great period of development and expansion for the port. The copper-smelting industry started in the Landore area in 1717 and, linked as it was with the development of coal mining, laid the foundation of Swansea's industrial growth. For many years, ore was imported exclusively from Cornwall and carried in small flat-bottomed coasting vessels which did the return voyage with cargoes of coal.

694 ships' entries in 1768 had increased to 2028 by 1793. Due to the poor communications in the Tawe Valley, as there was no turnpike road, goods for shipment were conveyed mainly by pack horse and vessels were constantly failing to get supplies on time. This led to the construction of the Swansea Canal extending from Abercrave to Swansea. Opened in 1798, its influence was quickly felt in accelerating the trade of the port. 159,633 tons of shipment coal was carried in 1816, increasing

PLATE 36.1. The Development of Swansea Docks.

to 386,058 tons by 1839. Copper and iron works along the river were rendered accessible and production rapidly increased.

1824 saw the construction of the Neath and Swansea Junction Canal, a private venture by the Tennant family from whom the canal was to take its name in later years. The project extended from the Vale of Neath to the mouth of the River Tawe. Both canals served Swansea Harbour well until the second half of the 19th century when traffic declined in the face of increased competition from the railways.

It became necessary in the course of time to go further afield for the copper ore and Chile became the main source of supply. The dimensions of ships using the port inevitably became larger and made imperative the construction of an enclosed dock.

In 1852, the Town Float - later known as the North Dock - was constructed by enclosing part of the River Tawe and making a new cut for the river. This development was closely followed in 1859 by the construction of the South Dock.

The local copper smelting industry reached its peak in 1866, when 17 of the 18 copper works in Britain were located in the Swansea area, but thereafter it began to decline.

By 1879, the Port of Swansea had become extremely congested, with 5745 ship entries in that year, and it is on record that at this time there was no harbour in the kingdom of equivalent water area where so much traffic was handled. Steps were therefore taken to provide additional dock accommodation and construction of the Prince of Wales Dock was completed in 1881.

The pattern of the port's trade was beginning to change by this time. Iron smelting in the district had progressed to steel making and the production of tinplate. This latter commodity, along with coal, was to become Swansea's main export and shipments of tinplate through the port grew from 12,000 tons in 1878 to 250,000 tons in 1885. The principal buyer at this period was the U.S.A.

The Prince of Wales Dock was extended in 1898 and then, in 1909, the King's Dock was opened, providing the port with accommodation for the largest cargo vessels of the day.

As shipping developed so did the industries associated with the port, reaching the peak of their prosperity in 1913 when 546,854 tons of tinplate and galvanised sheet were exported (three quarters of the total U.K. production) and shipments of coal and patent fuel exceeded 5 million tons.

Indeed, at this period patent fuel exports exceeded those of any port in the world. In addition, substantial tonnages of grain, chemicals, timber and nickel were passing through the port.

In 1920 the Queen's Dock was opened with its extensive tanker berthage and pipe lines connecting with the Anglo-Iranian Oil Company's refinery at Llandarcy.

This development was the only bright spot during the inter-war years and thanks to it Swansea was not to feel the full effect of the decline in trade which was experienced by the other South Wales Ports during this period. Swansea had never been so dependent on coal as the other South Wales Ports; for example, in 1913, the peak year for coal exports, only 60% of the trade handled at Swansea was coal, whereas the corresponding figure for Cardiff and Newport was about 80%.

In the 1950's, overall traffic handled at Swansea reached its peak and for each of three successive years exceeded 10 million tons, but, following the loss of Abadan and the construction of the B.P. pipe line from Milford Haven to Llandarcy, there

PLATE 36.2. View of Swansea Docks, c.1852, Showing the New Cut and the North Docks.

PLATE 36.3. View of the Entrance of Swansea Docks, c. 1870 showing Fabian Bay.

PLATE 36.4. View of Swansea Docks showing North, South and Prince of Wales Docks, and the industrial smoke from Swansea Valley, c. 1890.

has been a reduction in the tonnage of oil handled at the Port of Swansea.

The improvements which have been carried out in Swansea in recent years include the construction of the Ferryport in 1968 and the building of numerous roads to replace the narrow roads, many of which had cobble stones, as well as the construction of two modern breakwaters and a lay-by berth at the Locks.

Mechanical appliances have also been updated and Fork Lift Trucks have been introduced in the comparatively recent past and now form part of the modern cargo handling equipment: also, seven newer cranes have recently been transferred to Swansea.

THE DEVELOPMENT OF PORT TALBOT

Developments at Port Talbot commenced in 1837 when the Old Dock was built to enable coal to be shipped from the nearby collieries. Coal exports increased and the establishment of steel works at Port Talbot necessitated the enlargement of the dock and this took place in 1894 when the new lock was constructed. Before the war, the wagons bringing coal to Port Talbot were turned round three times within a day. This is probably a record for wagons, which has not been achieved elsewhere. Prior to the construction of the Harbour, iron ore was brought into Margam Wharf in 10,000 tonne vessels which were unloaded right alongside the blast furnaces.

However, with the need to reduce transport costs and the economies of scale which applies to large vessels, it was decided in the 1960's to construct a Tidal Harbour capable of accepting 60,000 tonne vessels. Work began in 1966 and was completed in 1970.

During the early stages of construction it was decided to increase the capacity to 100,000 tonne vessels and space has been left for a second Jetty to be constructed which will then take vessels up to 150,000 tonnes. The benefits of being able to provide such facilities in close proximity to the Steel Works undoubtedly brings benefits to the British Steel Corporation and it is likely that in due course these works will probably be further extended.

About 2 million tonnes of iron ore for the Llanwern Works is unloaded at the Jetty at Port Talbot and transferred by train to Newport, making the total handled approximately six million tonnes per annum.

It would be wrong not to include the two ports of Neath and Briton Ferry in this summary and over the years considerable quantities of trade have been handled by both ports. In former years this was, of course, largely coal, but, at the present time, the Neath River also handles a number of vessels which are broken up for scrap.

In the 1960's it was realised that there were too many ports in the U.K. vying with each other for the reduced amount of trade and therefore the Government set up an enquiry headed by Lord Rochdale particularly to study the situation regarding major ports. This published its findings in 1962 and, since then, the developments in ports have been monitored by the National Ports Council which now must give its permission before any port development costing more than £1 million can take place.

HARBOUR CONSTRUCTION AND MAINTENANCE

The development of new materials has influenced the method of construction of the various docks, particularly with regard to the type of construction of the quay walls.

The early quays of about 150 years ago were largely constructed of cribs, i.e., boxes made out of logs and filled with stone. In fact, this type of construction was used even up to the turn of this century, for River training walls at Port Talbot. Thereafter, most quay walls were constructed of masonry or brick, and these were used at the North and South Docks at Swansea.

Mass concrete (used in the Swansea Lock) and reinforced concrete (in some wharves in 1909) have now generally given way to steel piles. Breakwaters which were formerly always built of natural rock are now sometimes reinforced in exposed locations by concrete blocks of different shapes and locally we have employed tetrapods, slice blockwork and tripods to great effect.

The change has largely been as a result of better materials becoming available often as a means of reducing costs. Lock gates which used to be fabricated in wood, and then in wrought iron, are now generally made of steel or even reinforced concrete. The very high cost of replacing our Lock Gates at Swansea, which are 70 years old, has dictated that we now very carefully investigate the possibility of extending their life still further.

The recent storms must bring home to all that the forces of nature are very strong, and it is necessary to build maritime structures to resist these storms.

Mr. Jackson will mention (Chapter 37) that Port Talbot Harbour is exposed to the Atlantic gales with "fetch" of the order of 4,000 miles. Therefore the height of the waves is considerable and, even after they have been reduced after entering the Bristol Channel and Severn Estuary, the wave height is frequently of the order of 7 metres. This has caused some damage at the seaward end of the Breakwater at Port Talbot and one of the tasks of the Docks Engineer is to keep that Breakwater repaired. In 1974 we repaired it with natural rock armour, but this was not successful as we could not place it as far down the slope as we needed. Therefore, in 1976 we pumped ready-mix concrete into fibre glass moulds *in situ*, but although

PLATE 36.5. Port Talbot Main Breakwater at the time of the repairs in 1976.

these blocks weighed approximately 20 tons they tended to roll. However, in 1978/79, after model tests had been carried out at our Research Station at Southall, we decided that tripod blocks would be satisfactory. The bad storms, which occurred in mid-December 1978 and mid-August 1979, have shown that these tripods are very good.

THE PRESENT AND THE FUTURE

The high cost of construction of marine works is because such structures have foundations which are often in deep water. The present day replacement cost of Swansea Docks may well be of the order of £200 million.

The main fabric of the Port of Swansea has been fully depreciated, so interest costs are low, which helps to keep the port competitive. Although Port Talbot Harbour is of recent construction, it was built before the very high inflation of the last few years and therefore, again, this helps to keep the Port competitive.

A few years ago it looked as though there would be a continual need for expansion. Many ports, therefore, prepared a long term plan, and a well known example is the Maplin Plan for the Port of London. Swansea also had its grandiose scheme, but changing patterns of trade, including the reduction of oil handled, has dictated otherwise.

The world container revolution has reduced the number of cargo vessels and even the advent of the large passenger jet liner has altered the pattern of shipping; therefore, it is necessary for ports to modernise to take account of the changing circumstances. Even the possible construction of the Severn Barrage will have an effect on the South Wales Ports. This does not mean that these ports are finished. In fact, Swansea and Port Talbot are some of the most profitable ports in the U.K. but it is necessary to change with the times and provide the facilities for the efficient handling of cargo, and it is likely that the next few years will see the construction of new coal handling facilities, better Workshops, and probably new cargo sheds, to name but a few.

The involvement of Docks Engineers in the running of Ports involves a number of aspects such as:-
- (a) Identification of the need for developments.
- (b) Design of such developments.
- (c) Supervision of their construction.
- (d) Maintenance after they have been built.
- (e) Sometimes the Docks Engineer must also be involved with the closing down of assets after they have ended their useful life.

In this Chapter, I have tended to concentrate on the Port of Swansea, because it has had the greatest influence in the developments of the area, and had it not been for the port then the industrial development, and indeed the expansion of the City, could not have taken place to the same degree.

Therefore, it is seen that the prosperity of the area has been closely linked with the prosperity of the Port.

37. PORT TALBOT - ACCRETION AND DREDGING IN THE HARBOUR AND ENTRANCE CHANNEL

W. H. Jackson and D. R. Norman

British Transport Docks Board, Research Station, Hayes Road, Southall, Middlesex, U.K.

ABSTRACT

This Chapter describes a research project undertaken to find why the accretion and, hence, maintenance dredging in the channel and harbour at Port Talbot were greater than had been estimated and why the rate of accretion should vary between one year and another.

Different mechanisms of sediment movement are considered, including tidal currents, density currents and wave action. Preliminary results have been obtained from an underwater package placed alongside the entrance channel, from which velocity and sediment-load near to the bed are recorded under calm and storm conditions.

The purpose of the study is strictly practical, *viz.* to enable maintenance dredging to be planned and carried out in the most economic way.

KEYWORDS

Harbours; Dredging; Sedimentation; Swansea Bay.

INTRODUCTION

Swansea Bay is relatively clean when it is compared with some other parts of the Bristol Channel and Severn estuary, at least as far as fine sediment is concerned. Most of the suspended material is moving forwards and backwards further upstream in the Cardiff, Newport, Bristol and Sharpness areas, where concentrations of several thousand grams per cubic metre are common. Because of the general lack of a high sediment concentration, the problem of maintaining entrance channels and other areas to depths in excess of the natural depths is less than would be experienced at Newport, for example. Nevertheless, it costs the British Transport Docks Board £300,000 per year to maintain the required depths in the entrance channel and dock at Swansea and over twice that amount to maintain the required depths in the entrance channel and harbour at Port Talbot.

Because of the large continuing expenditure on dredging the Docks Board is interested in how the silt and sand moves in Swansea Bay. This chapter outlines Port Talbot's dredging problem and describes the research project which was carried out

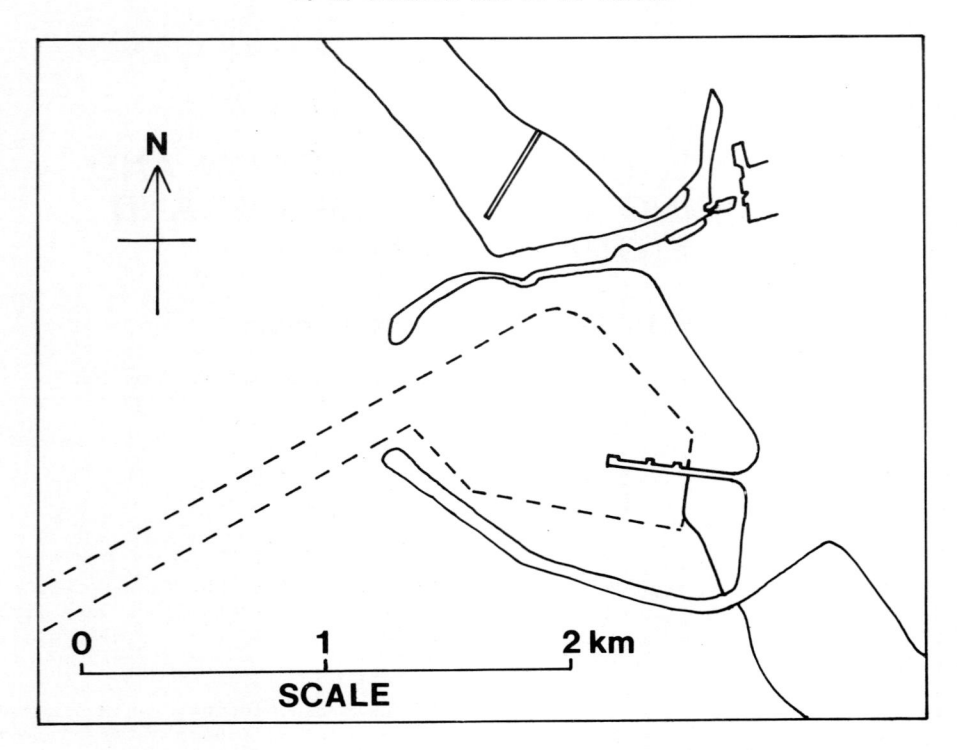

Figure 37.1. Plan of Port Talbot harbour and channel.

by the British Transport Docks Board Research Station which is situated at Southall on the West side of London. The B.T.D.B. is the only port authority which has its own research station.

PORT TALBOT

Prior to building the harbour at Port Talbot in 1969 (Fig. 37.1), an experimental channel was dredged and the rate of accretion in it was observed. Based on this and the limited amount of other data available at that time, it was estimated that the channel and harbour could be maintained using one trailer suction dredger, with a hopper capacity of 1530cu.m., working one week in the channel at Port Talbot, one week in the harbour and one week at Swansea. A grab dredger was also used as required to maintain the deep dredged pocket near to the berth, where carriers of 100,000 tonnes and larger part-laden ships have to float at all states of the tide. Figure 37.2 shows how, with this programme of dredging, the depths in the channel and harbour have varied since the harbour was built.

It will be seen that, when the harbour was completed in 1969, the level of the bed in the inner channel was approximately 0.6m and in the harbour 1 metre in excess of the required maintenance level. It can also be seen that, until the end of 1971, the allocated dredging effort was adequate to maintain the depth but that, during 1972 and subsequently, both the channel and the harbour lost depth and by early 1975 the bed level had risen to half a metre and more above the required depth and a large contract dredger had to be commissioned. After two months of intensive dredging with a large dredger, the bed was restored to the depth ruling at the end of

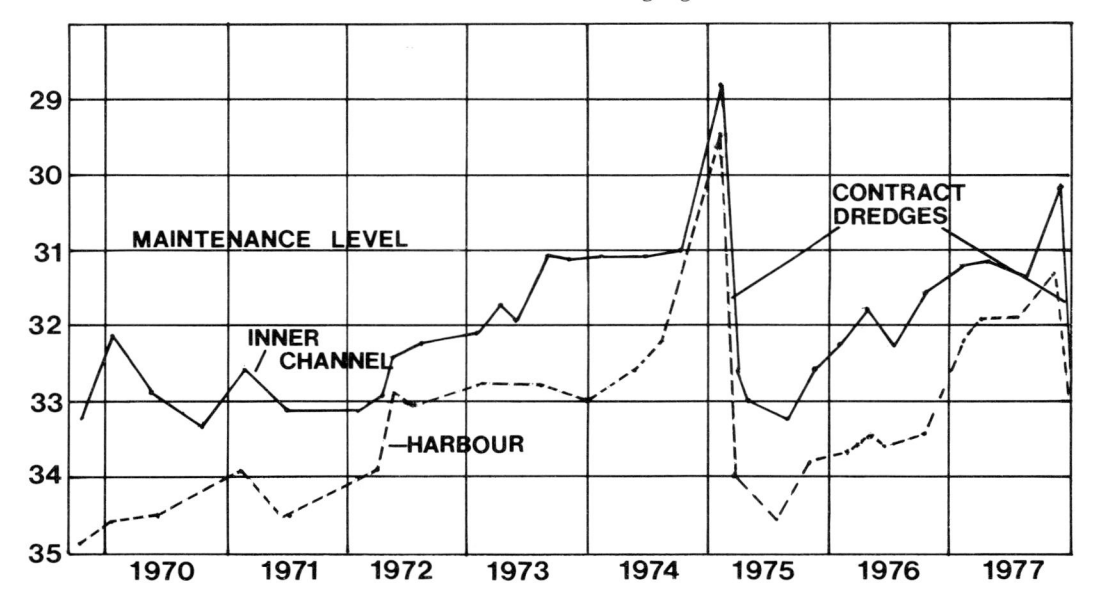

Figure 37.2. Port Talbot channel and harbour depths, averaged in feet below (old) datum; changes over the years 1970-1977.

the original capital dredge. Following this, the bed then built up again so that during the winter of 1977 a second contract dredge was needed. As each contract dredge costs in the order of £500,000, a large scale research project was initiated to study this accretion and to provide information from which the dredging effort could be optimised.

The Bed Material

At the extreme seaward end of the channel, the bed material is coarsely graded with particle sizes ranging from fine sand down to clay (Fig. 37.3). As the material is transported up the channel, it is separated by natural processes, resulting in fine sand (median size 0.06mm) settling just outside the harbour entrance and the finer silts and clays (median size 0.015mm) being carried and deposited inside the harbour.

Mechanisms of Silt Movement

Material can be eroded from the bed, moved and redeposited by a number of different mechanisms including tidal currents, density currents, and wave action. Each of these three mechanisms are considered separately.

Tidal Currents: Tidal currents in the vicinity of Port Talbot are relatively low. Typical values for the velocities on a spring tide are shown in Figure 37.4. With velocities only reaching 0.3m/s on the flood and 0.2m/s on the ebb on a spring tide, the amount of material which can be moved is relatively low (sediment concentrations are usually well below 100g/m^3). With both low velocities and low sediment concentrations, sediment flux and mass transport is correspondingly low. The values of mass transport for flood and ebb tides for several positions between the harbour and the outer deposit grounds are set out in Table 37.1.

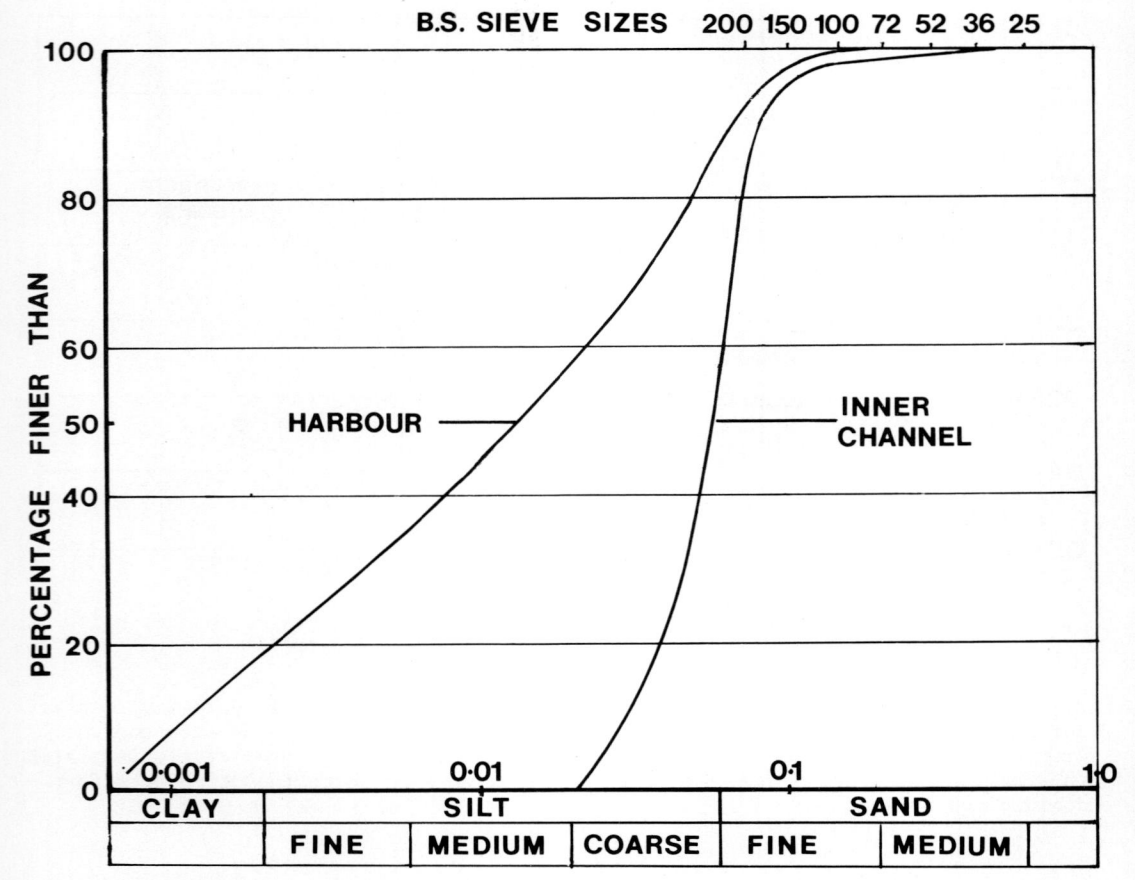

Figure 37.3. Port Talbot - Typical particle size distributions.

TABLE 37.1. Mass Transport (Tonnes per Metre Width).

Location	Ebb	Flood	Difference
Between Breakwaters	1.5	1.0	+0.5
200m W. of Lee Breakwater	2.4	4.2	-1.8
500m W. of Lee Breakwater	0.6	0.9	-0.3
In approach channel between inner and outer buoys	3.1	3.4	-0.3
At outer deposit ground	19.7	16.9	+2.8

Because of the low values of mass transport, tidal currents alone cannot account for the accretion known to be taking place in the channel and harbour.

Density Currents: Density currents can be caused by differences in salinity, temperature or suspended load. The salinity at Port Talbot varies very little either with depth or with state of tide. The average salinity is 31.0°/oo. With density currents and sediment concentrations both low the transport of material by this mechanism must also be low.

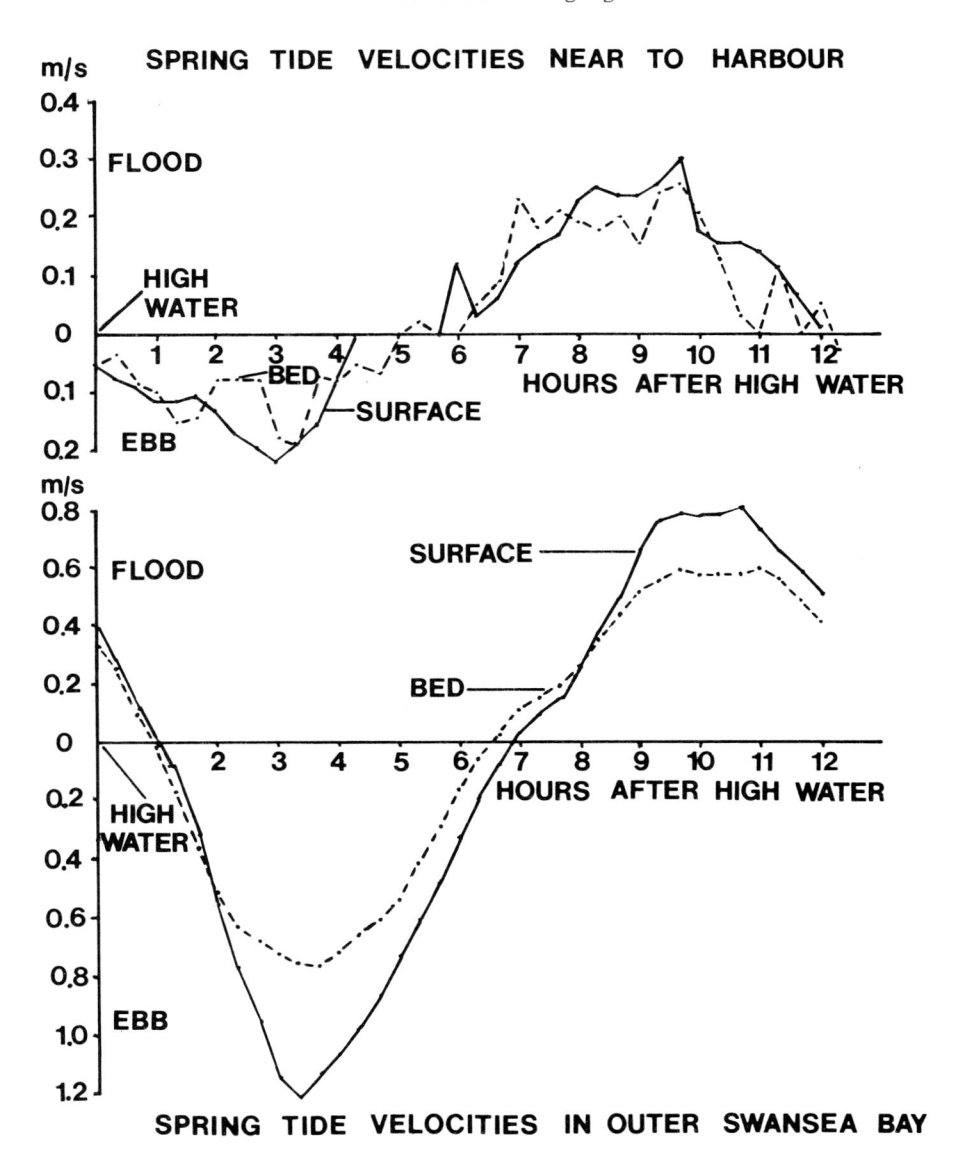

Figure 37.4. Spring tide velocities

<u>Wave Action</u>: Port Talbot is subject to large amplitude waves from the Atlantic. Occasional wave heights in excess of 7 metres have been recorded and wave heights of up to 5 or 6 metres are not uncommon in times of storm.

During 1973 an exercise was carried out jointly with the Atomic Energy Research Establishment to ascertain the movement of dredged spoil deposited within the bay. Figures 37.5 show the distribution of the radio-active tracer at the beginning of the test and at 2, 14 and 64 days afterwards.

The main direction of movement of the material is approximately 56° to the east of

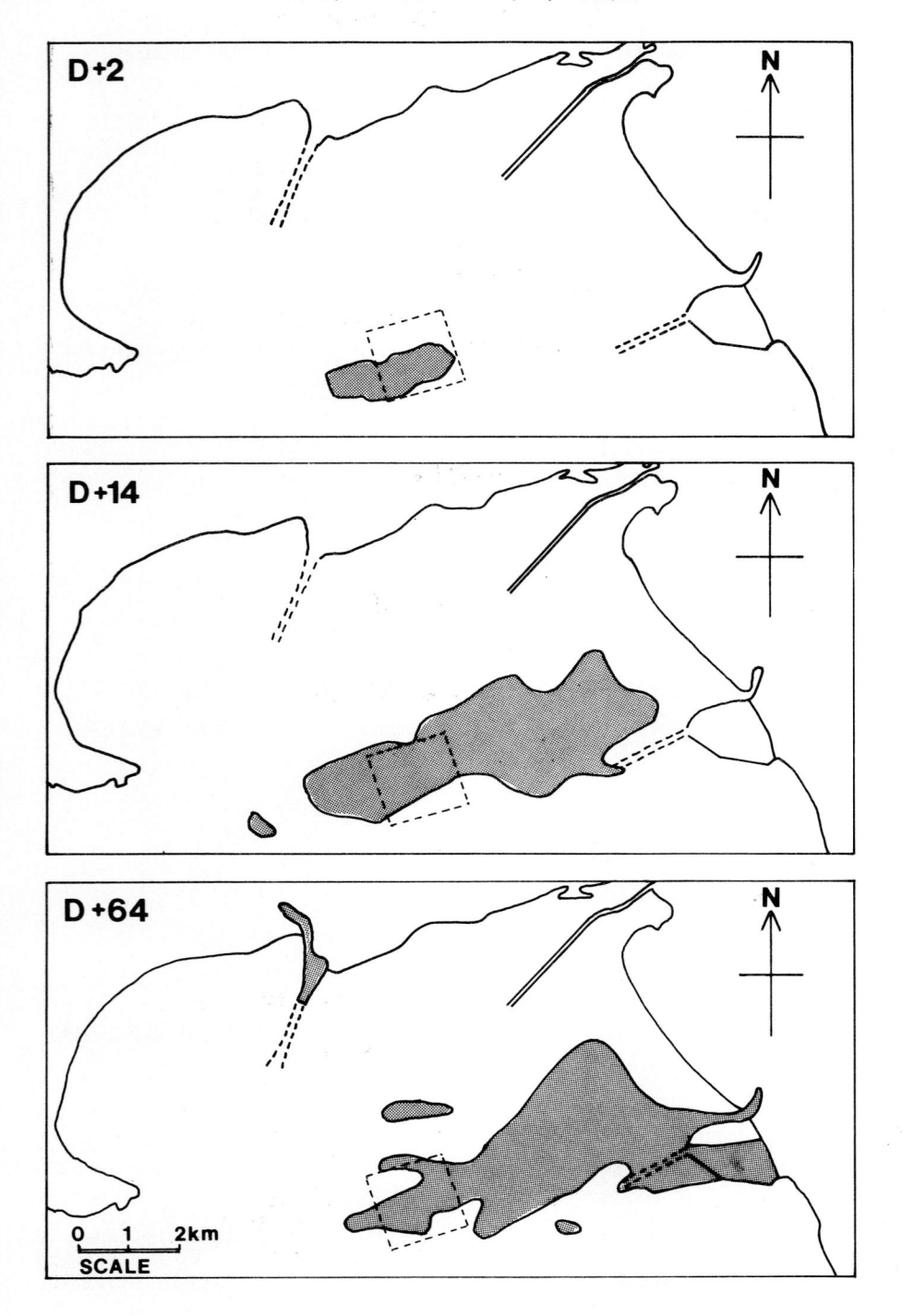

Figure 37.5. Radioactive tracer distribution from inner spoil ground.

Accretion and Dredging 579

north until it reaches the shore, after which it tends to spread in the north-westerly and south-easterly directions and much is deposited in the inner channel and harbour at Port Talbot. As a consequence of these tests, the spoil disposal site was moved out of the Bay, i.e., to the outer spoil ground.

The predominant waves are from the south or south-west, with the largest waves tending to come from the south west. As the direction of movement of the deposited material was not in the direction of the currents but in the direction of the predominant waves, it was deduced that the most probable cause of the sediment movement in this part of Swansea Bay was by wave action (compare Chapter 14).

Relationship Between Wind and Accretion

Although wave records have been taken in the approaches to the estuary and within the estuary for several years, there are gaps in the information which makes it difficult to obtain a clear relationship between accretion and waves. Continuous wind records have been taken over many years and Figure 37.6 shows the total cumulative wind from the south-west (in knot-hours) over the period 1970-77, plotted against the cumulative accretion as an apparent change in channel depth. This loss is despite routine maintenance dredging, which has been included.

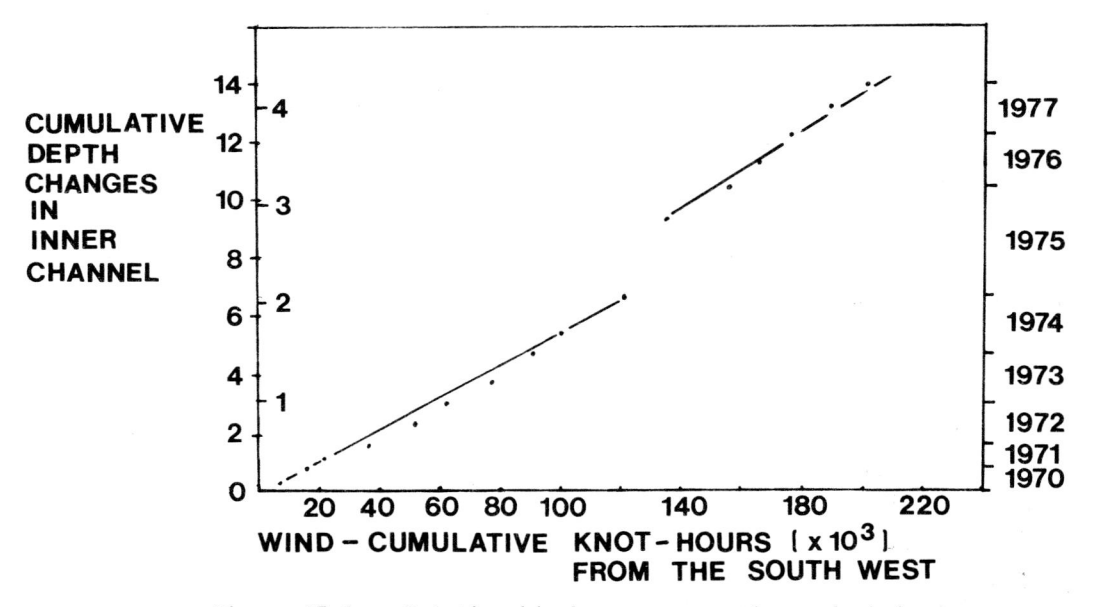

Figure 37.6. Relationship between accretion and wind

The correlation between the wind in knot-hours from the south-west and the rate of accretion is not immediately obvious and there is no simple quantitative relationship between the two. Nevertheless, the periods of maximum accretion usually either coincide with, or immediately follow, periods of high wind. The rates of accretion are greater in winter than in summer. This could be due to the greater viscosity of the water in winter, due to the lower temperature, as well as to the greater preponderance of storms.

Underwater Instrument Package

An alternative approach to the problem was to collect data on sediment transport during periods of calm and during periods of storm. As data during storms cannot be collected from a launch, some form of underwater recording equipment needed to be developed. Particularly important are velocities and sediment concentrations close to the bed.

The equipment, which was designed and built at the B.T.D.B. Research Station, consisted of a tripod-like structure which rested on the bed and to which was attached instruments to measure velocities (in two directions at right angles, at a single position about 200mm above the bed) and sediment concentrations (at two levels within the bottom metre). A pressure transducer was also fitted to measure the level of the water above the instruments. The output from these instruments was transmitted to a data-logger housed in a building at the end of the main breakwater. The package was deployed for two periods, the first of approximately two months and the second of approximately one month duration. The latter measurements were cut short when the cable was severed by a moving rock on the main breakwater during a severe storm.

The data obtained from this exercise has not yet been fully analysed, but a method has been developed which enables wave velocities to be separated from the tidal currents. Based on a preliminary study of the data the following conclusions have emerged.

1. Although the direction of the waves in the area tend to be at a slight angle to the channel, the resultant direction of flow in the channel near to the bed is in the direction of the channel into the harbour for much of the time.

2. Sediment concentrations of about $2,000 g/m^3$ have been recorded within 200mm of the bed during moderate storms. This is adequate to account for the known accretion.

3. During such storms, peak velocities recorded were about 0.8m/s, which is more than twice that recorded near to the harbour on spring tides in calm weather.

APPLICATION OF DATA

The purpose of the B.T.D.B. Research Station is not to do basic research as an end in itself, but to find economic solutions to strictly practical problems. The aim of the study outlined in this paper is to reduce dredging costs. As the research progressed it became apparent that the relatively low accretion which occurred during the first two years of the life of the harbour was the exception and not the rule. The rate of accretion is now known in sufficient detail to enable a dredging programme to be planned based on known quantities. There will be variation from year to year, but the likely occurrence of light and heavy dredging years is not known. Based on the information obtained, recommendations have been made as to the most economic way of dealing with the maintenance dredging problem.

FUTURE RESEARCH

It is proposed to continue monitoring the accretion and dredging in the harbour and channel, using data on soundings and dredged quantities supplied by B.T.D.B. South Wales.

Further measurements will also be taken using the underwater package at a different position. As the previous measurements were taken on the south side of the channel, these later measurements will record similar information on the north side of the channel. The indications so far are that most of the mobile material moves up the channel rather than in from the sides. It is expected that the additional measurements taken from the package and a more detailed computer analysis of this data will confirm or refute this statement. If it is concluded that the material moves chiefly from the outer to the inner channel, then it may be more economic to intercept the material before it reaches the inner channel, particularly if the material there, which is less closely graded, can result in better loads in the dredger hopper.

DISCUSSION VIII

<u>Heathershaw</u>: I would have thought that it was perfectly obvious that if you've got a navigation channel aligned with the direction of wave approach, you almost certainly get, during periods of storm activity, sediment being moved up the navigational channel.

<u>Banner</u>: Before Mr. Jackson spoke, I was pretty sure, and after he spoke, I was totally convinced that the sediment supply for the Bay is from the southwest. I cannot see any evidence whatever of anything more than a negligible supply from the east. First of all, where are the sources of a possibly supply of sediment? We know that towards the southwest and southeast of the Bay the seabed is bare; it is bedrock and it is scoured. To the west, and only to the west, there is a mobile sediment cover; this is being derived continuously from the reworking and erosion of the drift deposits, which cover much of the Channel and have covered it for the last 9,000 years. The pattern of sediment distribution within the Bay shows a belt of mobile sand. (The <u>Abra</u> community lives in such a mobile environment, and it is the only one which is). The mobile sand, seen in Culver's map (Chapter 4) is the only mobile sand moving in the Bay and it stretches from the southwest to the northeast, from the southwast approaches towards Port Talbot Harbour and that part of the embayment. That distribution, in itself, must be significant. We know that much of the rest of the Bay is covered by relict deposits which could be concrete as far as dynamical sedimentologists are concerned; these deposits haven't moved for 18-20,000 years.

If we look at the mineralogy of the sediments (Chapter 16), we see that the heavy mineral composition of the sediments of the inner part of the Bay links up with that of the west, not of the east. We can also examine the grain size and constitution of sediments of the Nash and Scarweather Banks. Firstly, we've heard from Dr. Britton (Chapter 13) there is no evidence whatsoever of any connection between the banks; even if there were, the material which is present in the Bay is not that which is present in the banks and, consequently, it could not travel through or across those banks. Secondly, we have <u>Arctica islandica</u> shells present in the Bay; they are quite heavy, have a threshold higher than that of fine or medium sand, and live in the deeper water to the south and west (not to the east). Finally, we have seen that tracer movement, reported by Mr. Jackson (Chapter 37) moves from southwest to east and northeast.

One can go on. All I can say is, if our quantitative records do not substantiate this evidence, then our quantitative records are deficient. Mr. Jackson's comment that storm waves are important was the simplest and truest statement we have heard. For example, in August (1979), we had waves breaking over the lighthouse at Mumbles. Could they not move sand? But there are <u>no</u> records. If we have 8-ton breakwater boulders moved (this Symposium),this surely is a sign that sediment can be moved by waves even if we don't have the quantitative wave records to analyse. I'm not really concerned with the mean of the significant waves, the highest 1/3rd which were measured while the wave recorder was there. I'm thinking of the storm waves which may occur once per year, or maybe once in two years; these can transport a mass of material. I must say that the material comes from the southwest, not from the east; it comes from the reworked drift deposits of the approaches to the Bay and is transported by current and wave action combined. Within the Bay, it is resorted and redistributed, probably ending up onshore (where the approach to the eastern part of the Bay is a wave normal approach) ultimately to be lost to the Bay, to the sand dunes to the east. Even in the west, we can have storm beaches; Dr. Shackley's paper (Chapter 35) showed that they existed once upon a time. It is ultimately distributed and spread.

<u>Vivian</u>: I would like to add to what Professor Banner has said. At a recent Symposium elsewhere, there was a paper about the movement of sediment in the New York Bight; here, all the movement of sediments was due to storms and, in 3 or 4 days, the transport would be as much as would happen in a normal year and under normal tidal conditions.

Carr: There is a big contrast between the tidal current dominated areas of northwest Europe and the northeastern American seaboard, where tidal currents are very weak; consequently, there is just a different order of magnitude. I accept a lot of the sedimentological data point towards transport from the southwest. Similarly, Mr. Jackson has pointed out (Chapter 37) the massive quantities of sediment moving up, on occasional years, towards Port Talbot Tidal Harbour. On the beaches immediately to the south of the Harbour, we have collected monthly profiles, one month after another, one year after another, over a period of three and a half years. Over the whole of this period, the beach in the mid-tidal zone has not altered by more than 8cm. This variation is minute. If you have sediment coming up in large quantities, and unless it is spread along the coastline as a north and south longshore drift, you would expect a remarkable quantity to reach the foreshore. So, I think there are lots of questions still left unanswered. Similarly, the linear sandbanks might not be part of the main structure of the Bay and transport may be peripheral to that in the Bay itself.

Banner: May I briefly comment? Firstly, three and a half years is not a very long time. We are dealing with a Bay which has been in existence for around 10,000 years and in which change can occur catastrophically overnight. Maybe next year we will see a very big change or maybe this may have happened in the year before you started taking records. This is no fault of the contract; however, sudden catastrophic change can alter the whole picture and can throw sediment out of what would be equilibrium in the preceding and ensuing, rather quieter, environments. Secondly, although the level of the beach may not have changed, it is evident to everybody that there must be a very considerable natural aeolian loss from the beach (See also Chapter 14). There undoubtedly has been a loss of sand over several thousands of years, certainly since the 12th century catastrophic storm beaches. There is no reason to suppose that this will not happen again. Loss is not alongshore and we can accept that the longshore drift is negligible (cf. Chapter 12); this again indicates that the linear banks, the Scarweather/Nash complex, are not particular sources of material for the Bay.

Carr: Of the order of 120m tons of material was in the sand dunes sytem at one time; this compares with, say, 1.5m tons during one storm event at Port Talbot. If you have 80 of those events at Port Talbot, blocking the main approach channel, you will have got the whole volume of the sand dunes system. Since the sand dunes took 5-6,000 years to develop, there cannot have been many major storm events; perhaps the Channel causes atypical results.

Banner: An awful lot of material was shown to be moved in the records presented by Mr. Jackson (Chapter 37). Similarly, people shovel sand off the road at Oystermouth even, which is the protected area of the embayment (see Plate 14.3). I think the catastrophic and rarer event is that which dominates the Bay, not the continual ebb and flow of the tide.

Langdon: I was the engineer responsible for the (Port Talbot) tidal harbour and I wish to emphasise what Professor Banner has said. During a single storm in 1974, one year's annual maintenance dredging was deposited in the approach channel: in the Harbour, 3 year's of annual maintenance dredging was deposited in 10 weeks.

I.K. Brunel once gave advice on the siting of Swansea docks. Brunel suggested that the docks be continued along the foreshore westwards, towards Mumbles. Now that was in direct conflict with his own interests for railway lines, since they came in on the east side of Swansea. I just wondered what the effect would have been had they (the docks) been built the other way around, towards Mumbles? During the last war, Mumbles Point was occupied by the army and a causeway was built between the Middle and Outer Islands. It was discovered, or alleged, that this particular causeway was causing the (approach) channel at Swansea to silt up. In the 1950's the War Department was forced to demolish the causeway; however, it appears to me that, if such a causeway were built, it would be possible to retain the sand in the Bay.

Collins: I have also heard that the dredging was increased because of the Mumbles causeway. If it was re-established, then deposition would occur in the eddy. As a more general comment, engineering constructions at a particular location along the coastline will cause sand to be deposited elsewhere.

Banner: May I ask Dr. Shackley a question about the oyster fisheries? One of the suspicious things about the foreshore in the western side of the Bay, is the number of dead oyster shells, which often look extremely fresh. No-one seems to record living oysters in the Bay. Are the shells really thirty or forty years old? Are there any living oysters in the Bay? If not, where do they come from?

Shackley: To my knowledge, only one oyster has been dredged alive, that was off the White Oyster Ledge. Those shells which I have seen come from that area.

Banner: So, the only source of the littoral oyster shells is from the southwest approaches to the Bay?

Shackley: Yes.

APPENDIX

THE POTENTIAL INFLUENCE OF INDUSTRIALISATION ON SEDIMENT DISTRIBUTIONS IN WESTERN SWANSEA BAY

A. D. Moran

Department of Oceanography, University College, Swansea SA2 8PP, U.K.

ABSTRACT

This Appendix describes the result of sediment sampling of the intertidal zone in western Swansea Bay (South Wales, U.K.). Samples of sand sized sediment from the intertidal zone were sieved and analysed; the latter was performed using computerised techniques, which produced a range of statistical analyses within samples (cumulative frequency/histogram plots of distributions samples and plots of percentage (by weight) of samples retained within a given sieve size) for the whole area (i.e., between samples).

The industrial and commercial activity undertaken in the vicinity of the study area are considered; these range, in time, from 1319 A.D. to the early part of the 20th Century. The pattern of modern (sand sized) sediment distribution is described. The grain size described above is considered in terms of historical (industrial) events. Finally, it is postulated that modern sediments of sand size and above may owe their location on the intertidal zone as much to artificial (related to human interference) effects as to other natural causes (sediment supply, wave and tidal action).

KEYWORDS

Sediment distribution; Industrial and commercial activity; Swansea Bay; Bristol Channel.

INTRODUCTION

Although former environmental conditions have influenced the modern sediments of the inter-tidal zone of western Swansea Bay (see Chapter 4), there is evidence to suggest that artificial (man-made) influences were, and are still, important. These artificial influences may, in combination with various transport mechanisms and the 'original' grain size distributions, result in anomalous grain size distributions in the modern sediments; such influences include:

(i) Flandrian, post-Flandrian and Recent oceanographic/meteorological events, such as storm surges, and geological/sedimentological events, such as differential transport of sediments by glacial meltwater;

(ii) Historical (artificial) change in the nature of the beach sediments due to industrial/commercial activity; and
(iii) Changes in the effect of wave action, tidal currents and sediment supply to the area due to (ii) and, to a lesser extent, (i) above.

PHYSICAL SETTING

In Swansea Bay, modern sediments cover Flandrian, post-Flandrian and Recent sediments to a depth of 0.5 to 1m (Ferentinos and Collins, 1978). In the intertidal zone, these modern non-cohesive sediments are of medium grain size (with a mean of 1.67ϕ to 1.83ϕ) and are moderately well to very well sorted (0.6 to 0.35)(Ash, 1976). The mean grain size of these surface sediments appears to decrease to the west, from the mouth of the River Tawe (inset to Fig. A1).

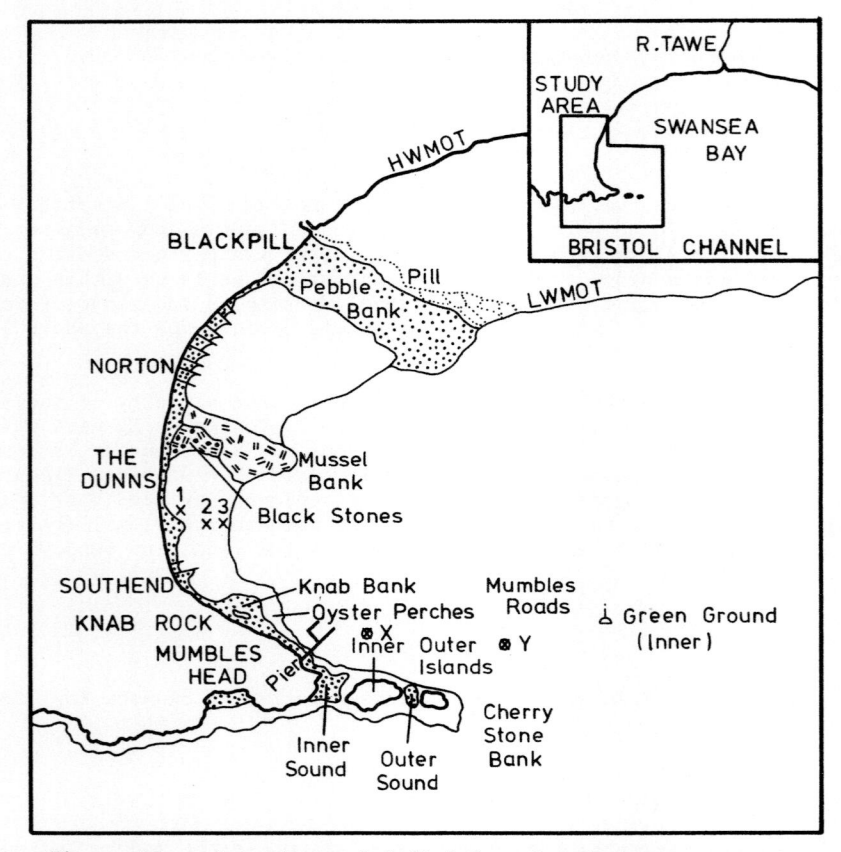

Figure A1. Location and definition sketch (not to scale).
Stations 1, 2 and 3 are sampling sites 10K, 10E and 6K (Figure A3).
Stations X and Y are current metering sites (see text).

In the zone immediately offshore from the Low Water Mark of Ordinary Tides (LWMOT, defined as the Low Water Mark calculated as the mean value of Low Water Neap and Low Water Spring Tides) the modern sea-bed surface is a muddy sand and the mean grain size of the sand fraction of these deposits varies from 1.9ϕ to 2.6ϕ; it is also moderately well sorted (Ferentinos and Collins, 1978). The boundary between this zone and the intertidal zone, at LWMOT, is marked by a break of slope. The gradient here changes from approximately 1:130 (intertidal zone) to 1:90 (below LWMOT).

The High Water Mark of Ordinary Tides (HWMOT) (calculated as the mean High Water Mark of High Water Neap and High Water Spring Tides) is almost everywhere coincident with a largely artificial embankment which separates the beach from former dune (at Blackpill) or cliff-systems (Southend). During Neap tides, water depth (at High Water) is approximately .5m; at High Water (Springs) the depth ranges from 2 to 4m.

Wave conditions in the area vary according to the direction of the local prevailing wind and the presence of westerly (oceanic) swell in the Northern Bristol Channel. Waves produced by wind conditions within the bay have H_b (breaker height) of up to 0.53m for southeasterly winds (Ash, 1976); angle of approach to the beach for these waves varies from approximately 80° (at Blackpill, see Fig. A1) to 20° for south-southeasterly waves here. At Knab Rock (Fig. A1), wave angles vary from 100° to 170° for the same winds. This example demonstrates that wave conditions due to local winds are varied both in direction and type; this may result in sediment transport along the beach either from Swansea to Mumbles, or in the reverse direction. Swell waves from the west and southwest are more frequent than those from the east and southeast; however, due to the sheltering effect of Mumbles Head and the Inner and Outer Islands, they rarely exceed .2m height at Knab Rock and 0.4m at Norton (see Fig. A1); angles of wave approach are also small (Carter, 1970).

Tidal currents in western Swansea Bay have been studied by Gibson, 1972; Borthwick and Collins, 1976; Ferentinos and Collins, 1978; Collins, Ferentinos and Banner, 1979 and Moran and Collins, 1979. Collins, Ferentinos and Banner (1979), postulated the presence of an anti-clockwise eddy system in the western half of Swansea Bay, with current speeds ranging from 7cm/s (flood) and 12 cm/s (ebb) at Station X to 20cm/s (flood) and 1.2m/s (ebb) at Station Y (Fig. A1). More recent observations (Moran and Collins, 1979) relate to current vectors in the area; these appear to confirm the presence of the postulated eddy. Further confirmation of the flow pattern is provided by a study of currents measured (using an N.B.A. DNC2 meter, in recording mode) over 60 tides at Mumbles Pier (Moran and Collins, *op.cit.*). These data confirm that the tidal currents show a time-tidal asymmetry and can be divided into: a short (2 hour) phase, immediately after LW when they flow northwest and parallel to the coastline; and a longer (approx. 10 hour) phase, in which the current direction is approximately southerly. Near-bed current speeds at Mumbles Pier were at a maximum of 65cm/s at about 3 hours before LW. During the time of the flood phase in the Northern Bristol Channel (i.e., about 3 hrs after LW), the maximum recorded current speed is .35m/s, but, more importantly, the current is southgoing.

DATA COLLECTION AND ANALYSIS

Sample Collection

70 surface sediment samples were collected from the intertidal zone in the Knab Rock/Norton region (Figs. A1 and A2). The samples were taken along lines which ran perpendicular to the coastline.

Each sample was washed, dried and sieved through sieves ranging in size from 2000 μm to 63μm (mesh sizes were at 1/4 phi intervals (see Table A1)). The fraction retained by each sieve was determined and coded for computer processing.

Data Processing

A computer program was developed (SANDJOB) which undertook two main functions:

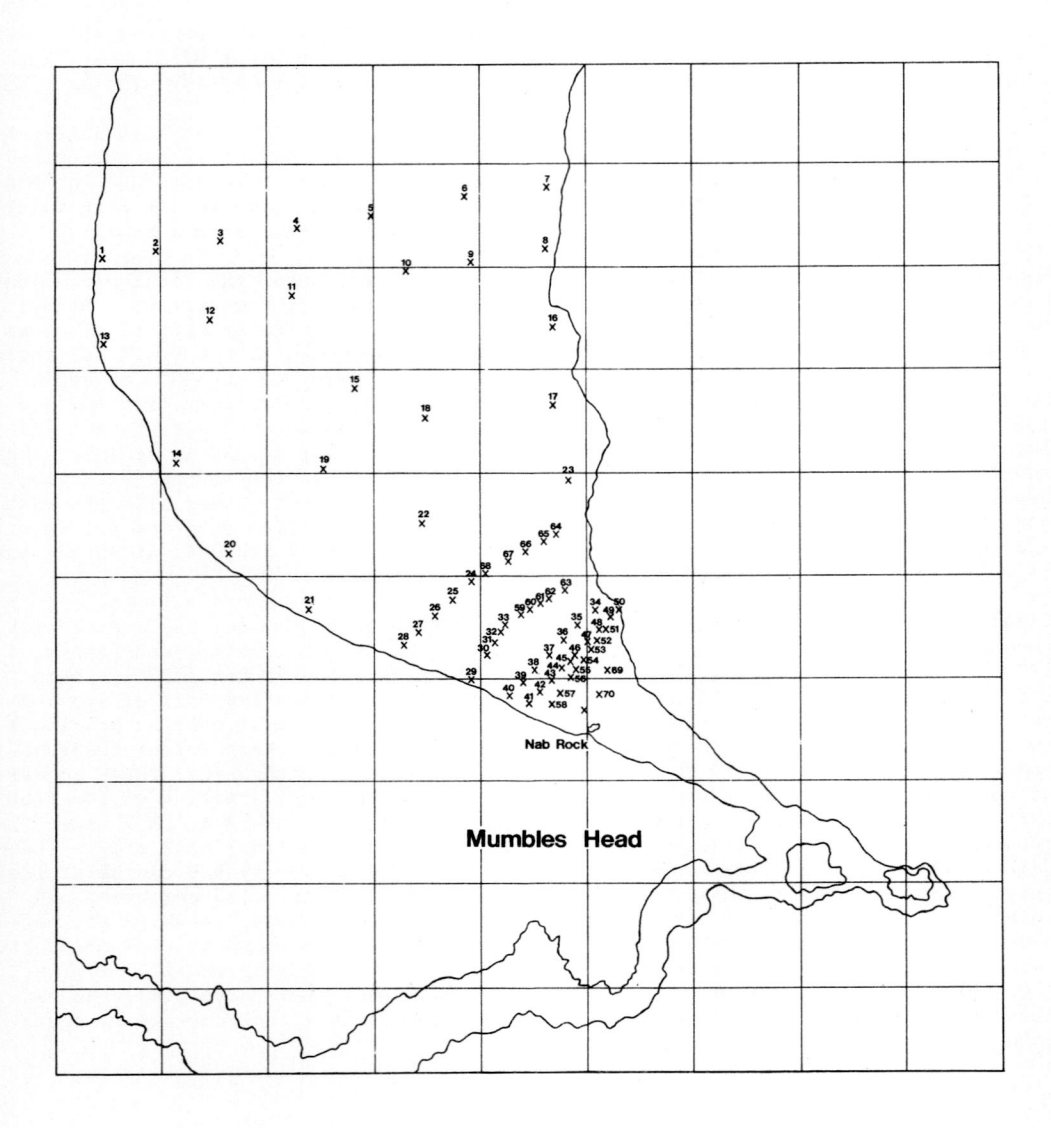

Figure A2. Location of beach sampling sites.

(a) the calling of DSAND79 (U.C. Swansea Computer Centre Library), which statistically analyses the weights of the fractions retained after sieving, and, using GINO-F subroutines (CADC, 1975) produces cumulative frequency/histogram curves (Fig. A3).
(b) the accumulation of percentage weights, from a given sieve size, into a storage array; this was conjoined to another array containing the grid reference points of the outline of the intertidal zone and to a final array containing the grid references of the sample sites. Titles, dates and labels were inserted into the main array by the program. The whole array was then plotted using SYMAP routines (UERCC, 1977).

TABLE A1.   Grain Size Scale for Sands.

Millimeters	Microns	Phi (ϕ)	Wentworth Size Class
2.00		-1.0	
1.68		-0.75	
1.41		-0.5	Very coarse sand
1.19		-0.25	
1.00		0.0	
0.84		0.25	
0.71		0.5	Coarse sand
0.59	500	1.0	
0.42	420	1.25	
0.35	350	1.5	Medium sand
0.30	300	1.75	
0.25	250	2.0	
0.210	210	2.25	
0.177	177	2.5	Fine sand
0.149	149	2.75	
0.125	125	3.0	
0.105	105	3.25	
0.088	88	3.5	Very fine sand
0.074	74	3.75	
0.0625	62.5	4.0	

A second, much simpler program, STATMAC, was written in order to compare the statistics output from the DSAND79 section of program SANDJOB; this used the same data as SANDJOB for the outline of the area and for the locations of the data points, but the values to be plotted were entered separately.

The total output from SANDJOB was 70 cumulative frequency/histogram plots, and 20 (areal) distribution plots of the percentage retained, for each sample on each sieve.   Program STATMAC produced 16 maps via SYMAP; one for each statistical test employed by DSAND79.

The major advantage of using the program was the display of sampling results, for examination of within and between sample variability.   Typical outputs from SANDJOB are shown in Figs. A3, A4 and A5 and from STATMAC in Fig. A6.

Fig. A3 shows the cumulative frequency/histogram plots produced for the samples taken at Stations 1 to 3 (Fig. A1).   Figs. A4 and A5 show the output from the SYMAP section of SANDJOB, and Fig. A6 is a representative output from STATMAC.   It should be noted that SYMAP divides the range of data values by a given number of classes; it then assigns a type of diagrammatic shading to each class.   Thus, the heaviest shading in Fig. A4 represents retained weights varying between 5.62% and 6.38% of sample (by weight): in contrast, the same level of shading in Fig. A5 represents a range of retained weight of 18.35% to 21.05% of the sample.   This computing characteristic could be confusing and *must* be borne in mind in subsequent interpretations: the degree of intensity of the shading in Figs. A4, A5 and A6 is, therefore, relative within each Figure only.

HISTORIC EVENTS AND THEIR POTENTIAL SEDIMENTOLOGICAL INFLUENCE

Normally sedimentological evidence (grain size distributions, etc.) would be interpreted merely in terms of sediment transport modes and sources: however, the intertidal zone of western Swansea Bay has been subjected to a number of events, which had potential significance in terms of its sedimentological characteristics.   The events described here date from AD 1319 and are more likely to affect directly modern sediment grain size distributions than those described in more detail elsewhere.

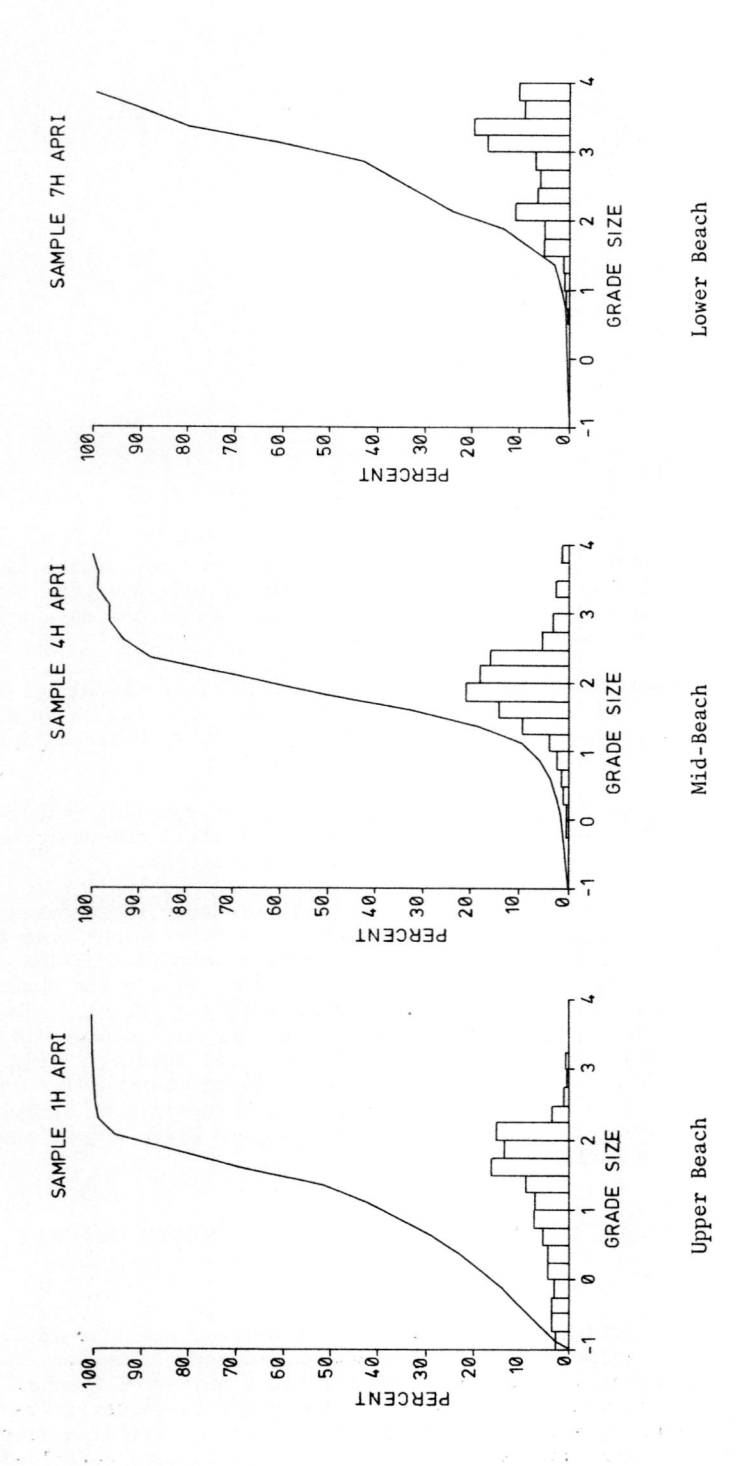

Figure A3. Cumulative frequency curves/histograms for sediments from sites 1, 2, 3 (see Figure A1).

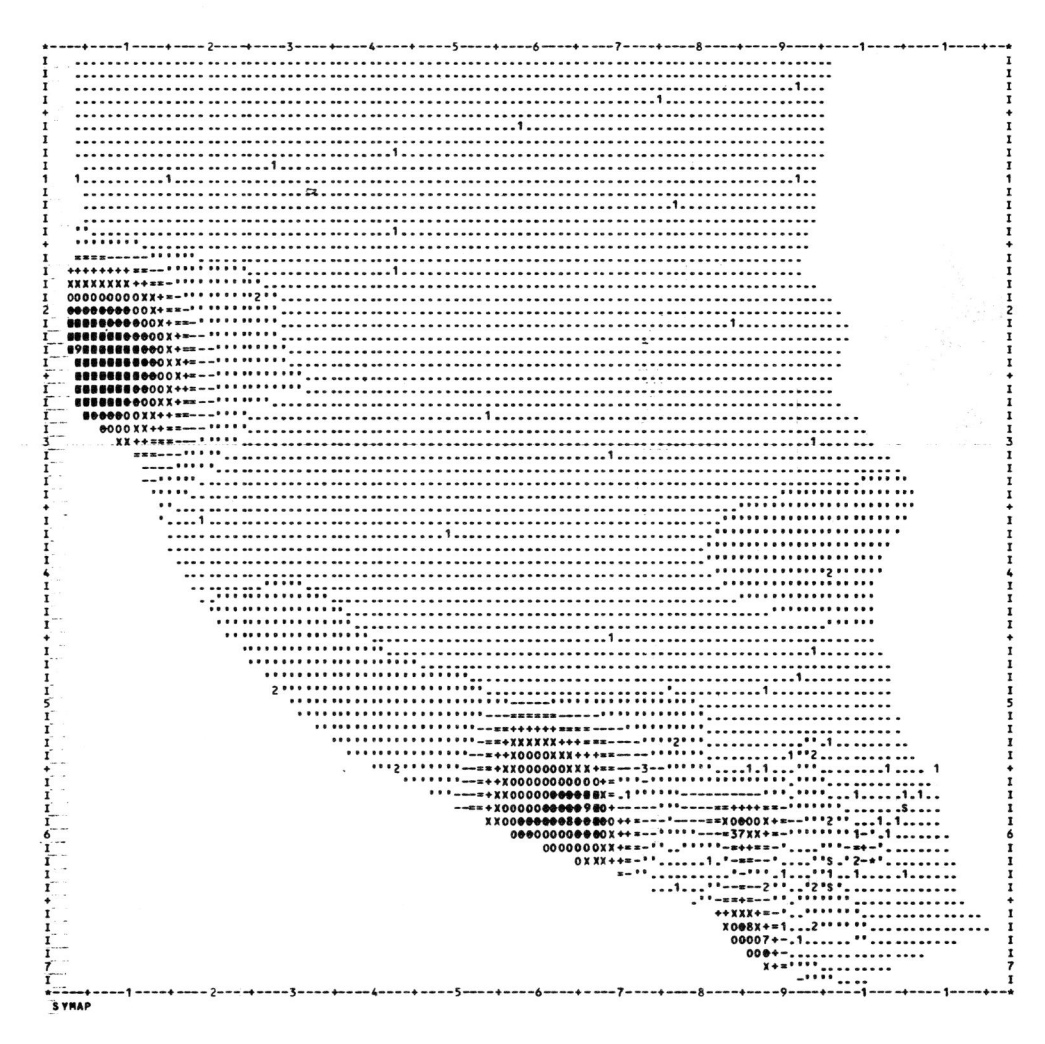

Figure A4. Plot of weight of sand fraction retained by .6mm mesh (Mumbles, April 1979). Values range from 0% to 6.3% of sample.

KEY (% of sample)

■ 0.0 - 0.7
θ 0.7 - 1.4
O 1.4 - 2.1
X 2.1 - 2.8
+ 2.8 - 3.5
= 3.5 - 4.2
- 4.2 - 4.9
' 4.9 - 5.6
. 5.6 - 6.3

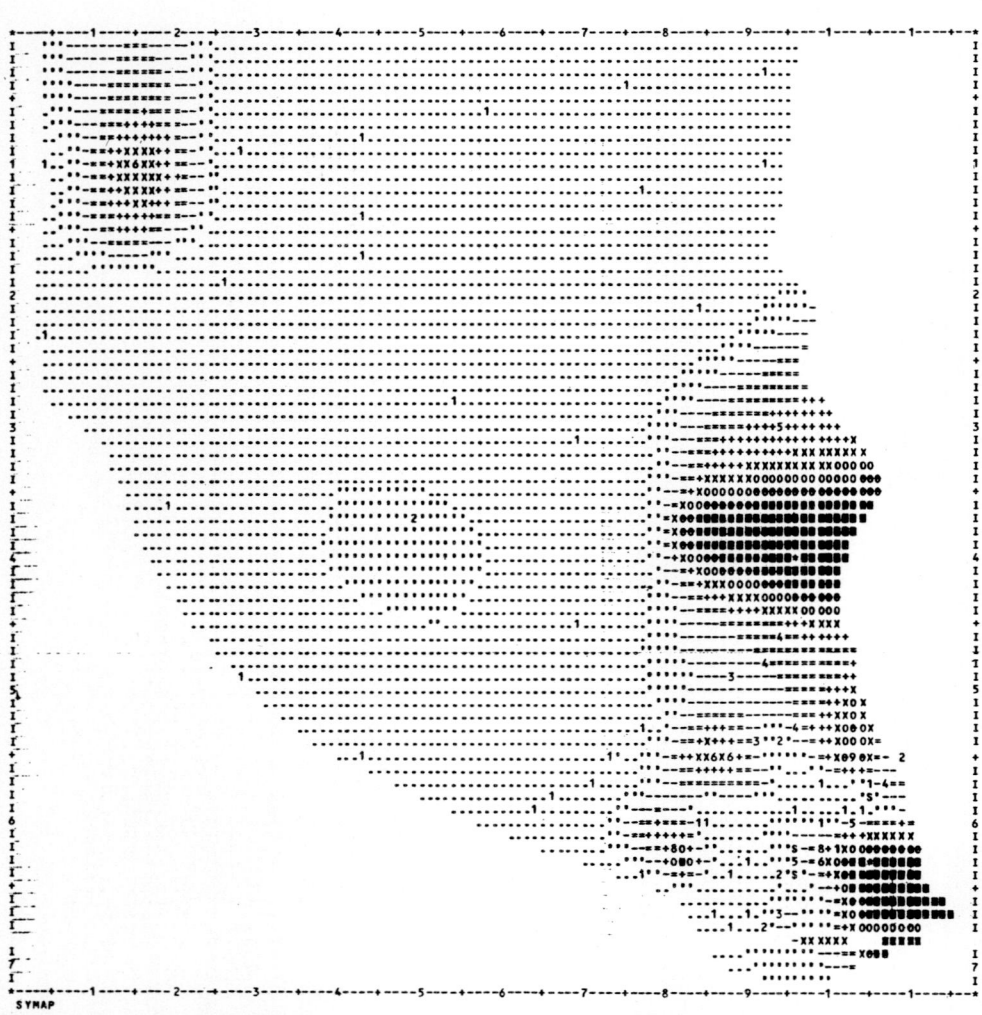

Figure A5. Plot of Weight of sand fraction retained by .09mm mesh (Mumbles, April 1979). Values range from 0% to 21% of sample.

KEY (% of sample)

■ 0.0 - 2.3
θ 2.3 - 4.5
0 4.6 - 7.0
X 7.0 - 9.3
+ 9.3 -11.6
=11.6 -14.0
-14.0 -16.3
'16.3 -18.7
.18.7 -21.0

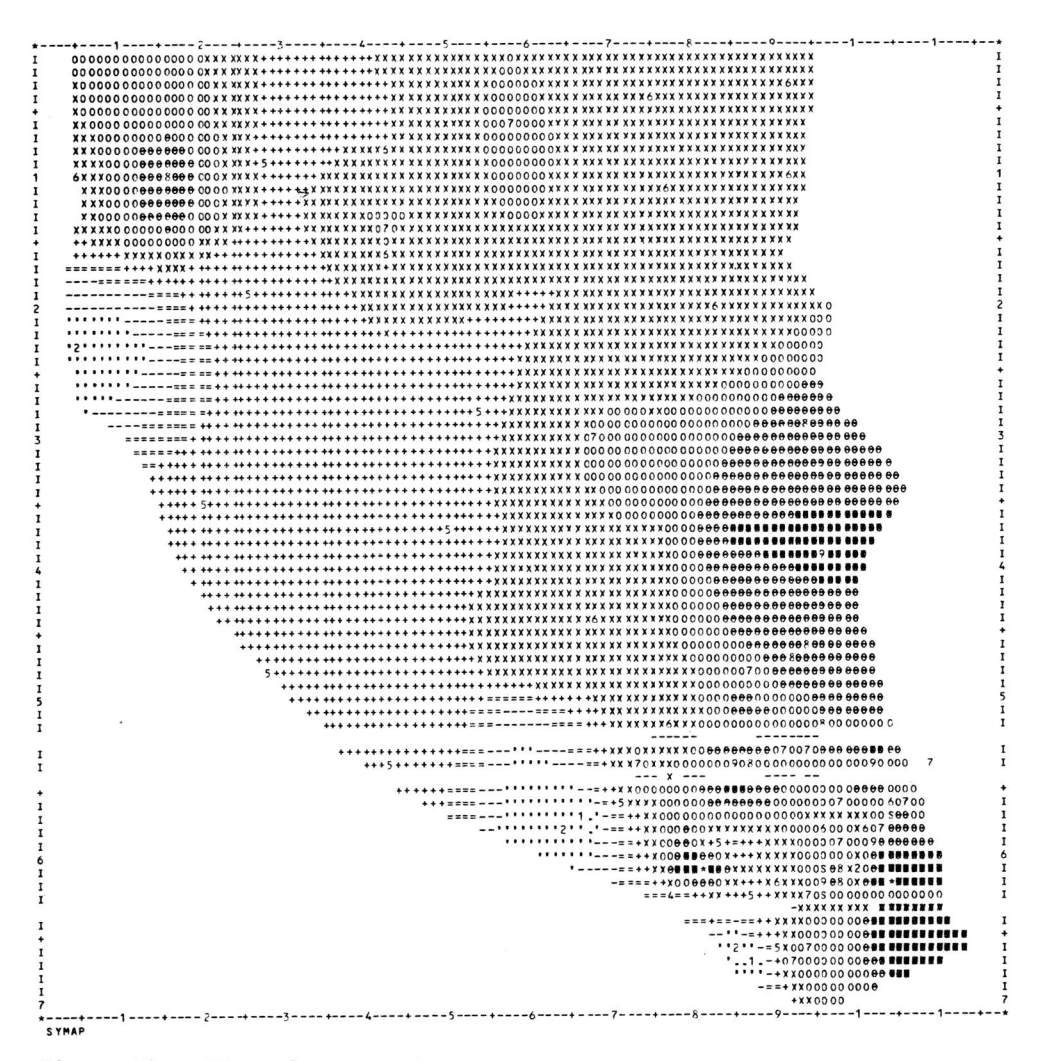

Figure A6. Plot of mean grain size distribution (sand fraction)(Mumbles, April 1979). Values range from .707φ to 3.067φ.

KEY (Mean grain size ranges (φ)).

■ .7 - .96
θ .96- 1.20
0 1.20- 1.40
X 1.40- 1.70
+ 1.70- 2.0
= 2.0 - 2.2
- 2.2 - 2.5
' 2.5 - 2.8
. 2.8 - 3.06

(Moran and Collins, 1979).

Firstly, an "inquisition" of 1319 mentions one John de Horton whose lands contained "mines of sea coal near le Clun" (Clyne)(Thomas, 1978, p.23); these may have been responsible for a build-up of the beach at Blackpill, due to outwashed spoil from the coal workings. Under such conditions, longshore drift of material from Swansea towards Mumbles (Fig. A1) may well have been halted, at least temporarily, by a "spoil" barrier.

In the late Medieval period, the influence of natural events seems to have been more important than those of "artificial" origin (see also Chapter 14). Hall (1899, p. 6) states that "violent iruptions of the sea" took place during the time of Henry VIII and of Queen Mary. Certainly, damage from one of these storms was bad enough to warrant mention in an Act of Parliament (1 Mary cap.xi, 1584)(G. Grant Francis, 1867, p.161).

Several authors (Thomas, 1978, p.20; Hall, 1899, p.6) refer to the "great flood" of 1607. This event, they maintain, was almost certainly the most important recent factor in determining the modern shape of Swansea Bay; it covered coastal areas that were probably already sinking.

Reference to the year 1624 gives some indication of the increasingly important role of industry in affecting the general sedimentology of the Bay. In this year, the common attorneys (the borough treasurers of the day) recorded that they had 'rec'd. of brokalew (Berkeley, Bro Clwyd?, *author*) men for throwing of blast (ballast, *author*) coming from the rode, vij s. vj d.'; again, in 1626, 'Rec'. of John Wine, of W'th in the p'ishof barnestable the 27th ffebruarij 1626, for throuinge Balest in the Roode, viij s.'. These men were being fined under an ordinance of the mid-sixteenth century, which forbad the dumping of ships' ballast within the harbour and bay of Swansea and within the 'Rode' (i.e., the Mumbles Road, the area of open sea off Mumbles, Fig. A1). This activity was a considerable nuisance to shipping within the Bay and was to leave noticeable effects in the form of deposits of pebble and cobble size on the beach at Mumbles (see below).

Cromwell's Gower Survey of 1650 records that, at this time, Richard Seys had a grant from Walter Thomas to dig coal in 'Clyn fforest'; this grant dated from 1642 (Jones, 1922, p.332). In addition to the reference to coal, this survey also provides details of the tolls paid on loading and discharging cargoes at the 'Key of Mumbles' (Jones, 1922, p.352), which may be the same one as that shown in Figure A7 (dated 1794) on the beach opposite Blackpill, since the (then) parish of Mumbles extended as far as the Pill. We may speculate that the remains of this Quay, together with any supplementary dumped ballast and the outwashed morainic material and pit spoil, may compose the pebble bank which can be seen today at Blackpill (see Figs. A1 and A6). This pebble bank extends to seaward, from Blackpill to the LWMOT, in a broad band of poorly-sorted material (Fig. A1).

A map of 1663, by Griffith Griffiths, records the name and property of the Maddocks family at "the Dunns" (see Fig. A1). The property protruded into the sea beyond the modern HWMOT (Jones, 1922, p.355). A later map (Fig. A8) records that this area was subsequently known as the 'Blackstones' and the modern sedimentological evidence (Sample 10K in Fig. 3A) reveals that the sediment here contains comparatively large proportions of the coarser grain sizes.

During the 17th Century, a small and irregular trade in general cargoes was probably being carried out from Mumbles. The mention of a fee for the loading and unloading of iron ore at the Mumbles quay, in Cromwell's (1650) Gower Survey, may be significant to an understanding of the area immediately to seaward of the Knab Rock (see below). By 1707, coasters were picking up and/or depositing ballast at Mumbles

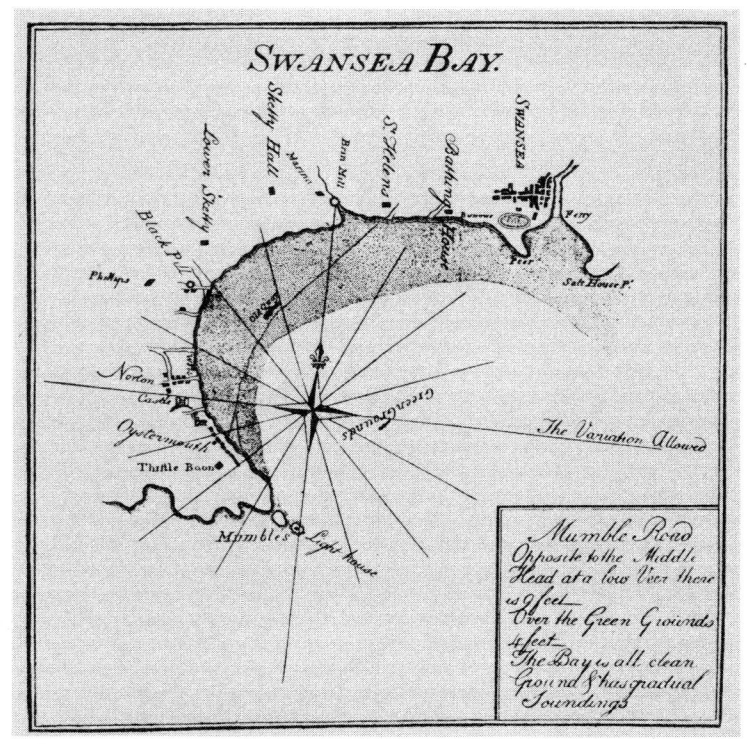

Figure A7. Map of Swansea Bay (1794), from Jones, 1922.

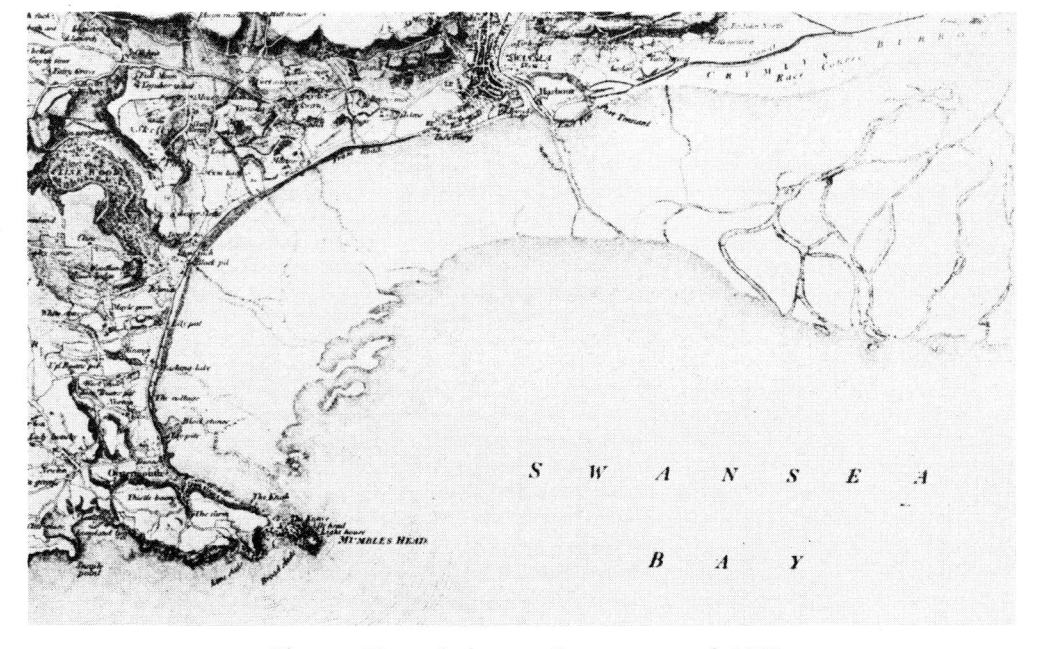

Figure A8. Ordnance Survey map of 1825.

(Jones, 1922, p.356); this probably happened over several centuries, as small coasting vessels were the main goods transport of the time (the coastal road connecting Mumbles, Blackpill and Swansea was not built until about 100 years after this). The surface of the intertidal zone in the Mumbles Head - Norton area is covered, in part, by areas of relatively unweathered pebbles and cobbles; these may date from these periods of dumping, or other subsequent industrial activity on the foreshore.

From the 1790's, there is an upsurge in the amount of information available on the effects of industry on western Swansea Bay. The Harbour Acts of 1791 and 1796 (31 Geo. 3, cap. lxxxiii, 1791 and 36 Geo. 3, cap. xciii, 1796)(G. Grant Francis, 1867, p.162) set up the Swansea Harbour Trust, with powers to regulate navigation within the harbour at Swansea and within the Bay. In 1793/4, the Trust employed a surveyor, named Huddart, to survey the harbour. One of Huddart's observations was that the waters of the Bay were then 'receding' and ships anchoring in the Mumbles Roads (Fig. A1) were being forced to anchor ever further offshore; this led to increasing expense, due to greater wear on the ships' cables in the more exposed moorings. Huddart also recommended the construction of the piers, whose successors now flank the constrained River Tawe (see Fig. A8). The original piers were probably completed around 1802; in this year, Mr. Jernegan (afterwards to design the Mumbles Lighthouse) tendered a design for a light for the western pierhead at Swansea (Jones, 1922, p.100)

Due to rapidly increasing industrialisation, there appears to have been increased erosion in the Swansea Valley at this time (1800-1810)(Jones, 1922, p.103). This may have resulted in increased water and sediment discharge, from the River Tawe, into the Bay; such sediment supply might also account for the recession of the sea over the western side of the embayment.

The map shown as Fig. A7 (dating from 1794) clearly indicates the presence of a bridlepath running almost directly from Mumbles to St. Helens. Such a path would be virtually impassable to either foot passengers or pack animals today, due to the softness of the surface sediments; this may be further evidence of a change in the nature of the sediments in the late 18th Century/early 19th Century. The modern nature of the sediments (e.g., Fig. A6) shows two areas of sediment with a large proportion of fine grain size (non-cohesive) particles on the lower beach, in the vicinity of the Knab Rock. In general, the mean grain size of such sediments are low throughout the southern part of the area; an exception is the upper beach region near HWMOT.

Although Fig. A7 may provide fairly reliable evidence for a particular quality of sediments on the beach (i.e., 'fairly hard' sand) around 1800, it may be less accurate in defining the lateral extent of the material. It is tempting to speculate that the lack of fine grained sediment in the upper intertidal zone, towards Knab Rock (see Fig. A6), provides evidence of an 'original' deposit prior to the sudden increase in sedimentation referred to above. However, such maps can be unreliable where large expanses of intertidal flat are concerned due to the relative unstability of some sediments; therefore no conclusion can be reached safely from the combined interpretation of Figs. A7 and A8.

The next event of significance which could have influenced the sedimentological history of the beach at Mumbles was the construction of the Mumbles Railway. This development was first "mooted" in 1803 and the Bill for presenting it to Parliament was approved, by the Town Corporation, in 1804 (Jones, 1922, p.121). The Bill was passed by Parliament and entered the record as a 'Tramway Act for Constructing a Tram or Railroad from Swansea to Oystermouth with Powers to make Branches Thereto' (44 Geo. 3. cap. lv, 1804(2))(G. Grant Francis, 1867, p.162). The purpose of the line was to open up communication with limestone quarries and iron ore mines at Southend and coal mines at Clyne. As it was first constructed, the line ran across the burrows and sand-hills which, themselves, had been slightly levelled for the purpose. The sea broke into these constructions at least twice, in 1815 and 1824; after the latter, Sir John Morris rebuilt the line on the seaward side of the land now occupied by the contemporary road (Jones, 1922, p.126). The gradual strengthening of the railway line and its advance to seawards may have been responsible for changes in the nature of tidal and wave-induced currents in the area around the High Water Mark. Wave action would have been affected by the steepening of existing beach surfaces. At present, the upper beach immediately adjacent to the embankment in the Dunns/Norton/Blackpill coastline is characterized by coarse sand (mean grain size of.78ϕ) (Fig. A6) and a relatively steep beach face (slope of 1:30). The changes brought about by modifications to the railway may have intensified longshore drift around High Water by increasing wave flow/action and causing an acceleration, by compression,of the tidal current system there. Groynes, constructed during the final stage of strengthening the railway embankment, have trapped east-going sediments of up to pebble size along the whole upper beach.

Although Fig. A8 is labelled 'Ordnance Survey Map of 1825', it is, in fact, only the 1825 edition of a map whose origins go back as far as 1804, when the earliest surveys for this series of Ordnance Survey Maps were made. The absence of a quay on the beach in this particular map probably dates the map from the later part of the survey; however, deterioration of the quay is likely to have taken place over an extended period of time. Several points of interest may be noted in Fig. A8:

(i) the comparatively large and naturally braided estuary of the River Neath, to the east. Later editions of the Ordnance Survey maps show that, after the River Neath was channeled, the beach in the vicinity decreased to about 2/3rds the lateral extent shown in Fig. A8. This was due perhaps to a change in the nature of sediment transport in the area; Amos (1974) has noted that multiple, braided channels in an intertidal zone may act as a barrier to the longshore transport of sediment, so the removal of such an obstruction may have accelerated sediment transport here.

(ii) the apparent presence, within the area of the Knab Rock, of a "knoll" immediately to the north of the Inner Island at Mumbles. This deposit *could* be related to material deposited during a phase of increased erosion in the Swansea Valley by the River Tawe at this time; the areas of fine sand in the lower intertidal zone in modern time (Figs. A3 and A6) may be the remnants of this "knoll".

(iii) the presence, between Norton and the Dunns (Fig. Al), of a pebbles bank (see text); this is called 'Blackstones'. Slightly to the south of this, in Fig. A8, is the word 'Claypits'. There is a bank of pebbles in this position today, but there is not much evidence now for 'clay' in the immediate vicinity. Modern sediments in this area have relatively high percentages of coarse-grained sand in them (Figs. A3, A5 and A6); this may reflect the history of the area. Finally,

(v) in Fig. A8, the influence of the short piers at the mouth of the River Tawe may be noted.

Towards the middle of the 19th Century, there was public concern over the amount of limestone which was being removed from the cliffs at Southend (see Fig. Al) and from the Inner and Outer sounds. Removal from the latter locations commenced in 1847 (Thomas, 1978, p.124); this could have had deleterious effects on the safety of the roadstead and this came to the notice of the Harbour Trust. At a public enquiry, held in 1850, a number of issues relating to this area were discussed. These were: the amount of limestone quarried annually; the shoaling of the inner (Mumbles) roadstead, caused by the dumping of ships ballast; the undermining of sections of the cliff edges, caused by blasting for limestone; and the effects of erosion here by the sea. In evidence, Mr. Phillips, who was the tenant of much of the land concerned, claimed that he had been responsible for the quarrying since 1814; since that time, some 2 acres of land had been added to the land area at Southend by the spreading of quarry spoil. He also stated that the sea had been originally to within

11 feet (3.6m) of his door, but that it was now some 60ft (18.1m) away. Mr. Phillips concluded his evidence by claiming that the had abandoned quarrying in the area of the Inner Sound in 1847. However, George Abernethy, another witness, claimed that he had seen blasting going on at the Inner Sound which was 'taking away the jagged points elevated about seven feet above the bottom of the Inner Sound'. He also thought that 'the silt carried through the Sounds is very prejudicial to the roadstead (Thomas, 1978, p.123). An expert witness, Mr. John Rosser, a Swansea Pilot for 37 years agreed with (Mr.) Abernethy and went even further in his comments; he claimed that it would be beneficial to the shipping community if the Sounds were blocked off. Captain Washington, one of two presiding commissioners, gave as his conclusion that shoaling of the (Mumbles) roadstead was due largely to the practice of discharging ballast there. The considerable amounts of pebble-sized material, distributed both as individual pebbles and as banks of loosely accumulated material on top of the beach sands throughout the western part of the intertidal zone, may have resulted from this practice. The presence of the material may also be due, in part, to the barrow method of loading limestone, via planked gangways laid out over the beach. Although both types of material (ballast and quarried limestone) are visually similar, it is probable that deposits in the upper beach zone are principally from spillage of quarried limestone and those in the lower area are largely dumped ballast.

In addition to the trade in limestone, the cliff immediately behind the Knab Rock was, at this time (c. 1847) being mined for iron ore (Thomas, 1978, p.207); however, this ran out after about 5 years and the miners turned their attention to limestone quarrying (Libby, undated, p.9).

Figure A9. The former embayment at Southend is in the centre part of the picture, with "the Dunns" at upper centre.

The Mumbles coastline was, in the 1850's, indented between (approximately) the site of "the Dunns" and Southend (Fig. A9). Photographs of this area show the land sur-

Figure A10. Within the former embayment at Southend, the beach surface appears to be of small, rounded pebbles (see text).

face, within the embayment, to have been covered with rounded, light-coloured pebbles; these are probably the "native" limestone or glacial drift material reworked by the sea (Fig. A10). The land in front of the houses in Fig. A9 and to seaward of them may be the land referred to as having been 'gained' in the Report of the Commissioners of 1850 (p.11). In Fig. A9, the faint outline of the Blackstones Bank can be seen (upper centre of picture).

Further along the coast, towards the Knab Rock, the foreshore seems to have been composed then, as it is now, of a mixture of deposits (Fig. A11); angular pieces, probably of limestone, of up to 50 x 50 x 50cm^3 in size and rounded limestone pebbles of approximately 20 x 15 x 10cm^3. The latter are similar in appearance to the pebbles which occur as storm beaches throughout the South Gower Coastline. The contrast between the two types is shown in Fig. A11, with the more angular material in the foreground. It is significant that this area was known locally as the 'Ballast Bank'. At the time of the photograph (c. 1875), the two deposits do not appear to have become mixed as they are today. Fig. A12 (from about the same time) shows a similar pattern of slightly irregular and mixed deposits, which appear to have been emplaced as a series of piles or heaps and to have become subsequently scattered. This is in agreement with the assumption that not only was ships' ballast dumped in the Mumbles roadstead and on the lower foreshore, but that the upper foreshore received spoil from the limestone/iron ore trades.

At the western end of the embayment, there was an eastward running pebble spit in the 1880's, approximately 70m in length. Fig. A13 shows the complete arrangement of the lay-up, including the spit. It is possible that the pebble bank was built by the action of waves, generated by southeasterly winds, and causing a net easterly drift of sediment in the upper foreshore. The close-up photograph of the lay-up (Fig. A14) confirms that the surface material here, at least of the spit, was angular limestone fragments. Although smaller in size than the material shown in Fig. A11, it is almost certainly of similar origin, i.e., quarry waste or spillage from

Figure A11. The 'Ballast Rock' towards the Knab Rock.

Figure A12. The 'Ballast Bank', showing two main types of deposit (see text).

Industrialisation and Sediment Distribution 603

Figure A13. The Dunns/Southend embayment with the spit shown left centre.

Figure A14. The southern portion of the Dunns/Southend embayment, showing the nature of the surface material of the spit.

the loading of beached ships. Examination of the modern grain-size distribution maps, Figs. A4 to A6, show that there are two areas of coarser sand-sized sediments in the upper beach area, approximately on the sites of the "flanks" of the embayment, with the more southerly representing the beach associated with the former spit.

The next major development in the (artificially-induced) sedimentological history of the coastline at Mumbles is the granting, in 1889, of permission to extend the railway from Oystermouth to Mumbles Head (Abram, 1973). This extension had been authorised originally in an Act of Parliament of 1865 (28, 29 Vict. cap. cccxlix, 1865)(G. Grant Francis, 1867, p.163)(the Act under which the pier was built followed in 1866 (28, 29 Vict. cap. cclxxxix, 1866)(G. Grant Francis, 1867, p.163)) and was granted to the then Oystermouth Railway Company. A series of long-lasting financial manoeuvres followed, with the ownership of the line changing hands several times. Construction work was put in hand, however, and some 61 chains of line from Oystermouth to Southend were built and opened between 1889 and 1893. The period between these years was probably occupied with raising capital for the building of the embankment across the mouth of the embayment (Fig. A15) and arranging an alternative to this 'natural' lay-up for the fishing craft. This alternative took the form of a short recurved jetty (see below). Comparison between Figs. A15 and A16 reveals that the former is of an earlier date - as indicated by the presence of infill behind the embankment in Fig. A16 which is not present in Fig. A15. Fig. A15 shows the shorter extension of the railway to Southend, whilst Fig. A16 shows the whole extension of the line to Mumbles Head.

Fig. A15 provides the first indication that there was a sizeable road leading to Mumbles Head at this time: according to Hall (1899, p.31), this was built in 1888. Evidence suggests that this road was built partly by blasting against the side of the cliff, towards Mumbles Head, and partly by being embanked on readily available rubble at Southend. Both Figs. A15 and A16 show the presence of the short jetty, recurved towards the east, which was constructed as compensation for the loss of the lay-up (as agreed between the railway company and local fisherman (Libby, undated, p.15)). The details of the jetty are difficult to discern precisely in the Figures; however, it appears that the jetty was about 70m long, with a recurvature of some 25m from the seaward end. The jetty was constructed of timber piles, as the modern remains show; these were inserted into the beach at 1-2m spacings and were, it appears from the Figures, further supported by struts on their landward sides (running diagonally from the heads of the piles to ground level). The plates show also that the piles were joined by closely spaced horizontal boards. It seems that this arrangement, together with what may have been a deliberately constructed shingle/ballast bank, adjacent to the jetty, was responsible for the bank of coarse-grained sediment shown north of the jetty in Fig. A16. The bank was not present in 1880 (cf. Fig. A13); therefore, it would appear to have accumulated in a comparatively short time (i.e., about 13 years). Unfortunately, more information on this development is not available; nevertheless, photographic evidence would appear to confirm the hypotheses of Collins and Ferentinos (1979) concerning differences between the direction of sediment type and movement here, between the upper and lower foreshore.

Fig. A17 shows the Bay as it was in 1896. This map may be slightly unreliable, since it does not depict the new jetty which was known to have been constructed earlier. However, the embankment is shown in Fig. A17, so the map was probably up to date at the time that this was built. It is interesting to compare this 1896 map with the 1804 (onwards) one of Fig. A8. The channeling of the River Neath and the building of extensions to the piers flanking the River Tawe seem to have led to considerable erosion of the beach (assuming, that is, that the maps have been based on the same datum). This erosion may have been due to the interruption of supplies of sediment towards the west; it could, however, be due to the gradual subsidence of the land surface or a rise in sea level. There is some evidence for this relative

Figure A15. The Dunns/Southend area, showing the embankment for the railway sealing off the former embayment.

Figure A16. The embankment and jetty, *circa* 1890.

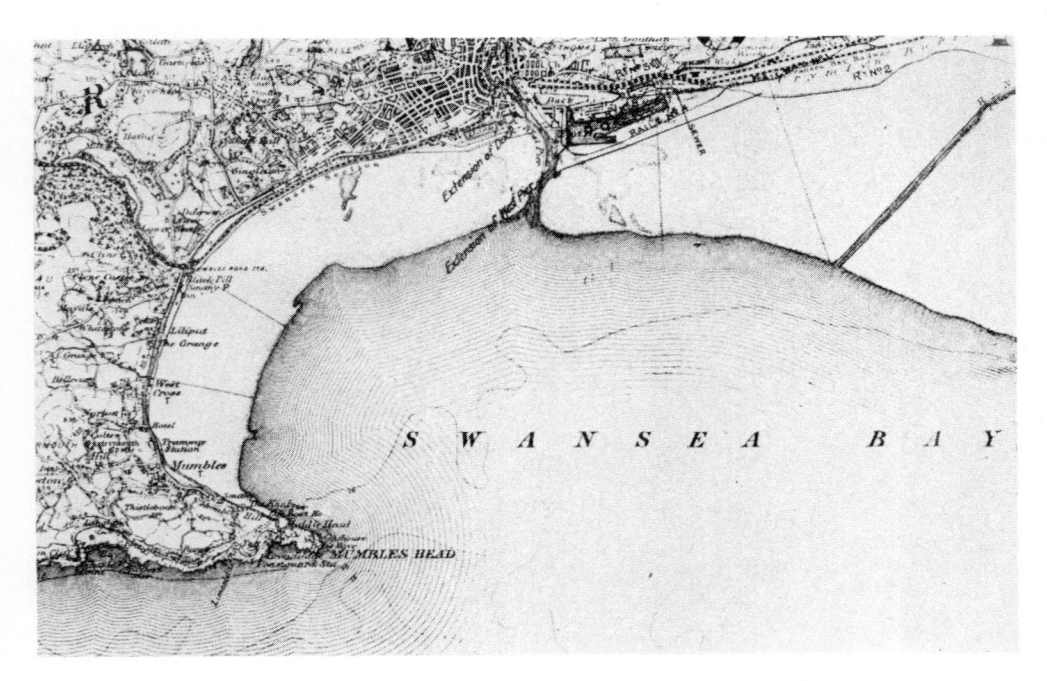

Figure A17. The Ordnance Survey map of 1896.

Figure A18. Mumbles in 1904, showing the jetty.

displacement from examination of the relative LWMOT's of the wave-cut platforms in the cliff sections of the coastline of southeast Gower (Figs. A8 and A17).

The general condition of the beach at the beginning of the 20th Century is shown in Fig. A18. The new extension to the railway, completed in 1901, and the new pier at Mumbles may be seen in the photograph. It is difficult to assess the exact importance, in terms of sediment transport, of the construction of the pier; however, photographs taken throughout the 20th Century often show little change, or even conflicting evidence as to its exact influence on the sediments of the area. The completion of the extension to the railway line to Mumbles (and its associated embankment) may have restricted and intensified the flow of water out of the Bay. In the same area, the flow may have been affected already by the amount and type of artificial deposits on the beach. The construction of the jetty, for laying-up oyster boats, with the subsequent accumulation of sediment behind it may be considered to be of more significance than the effect of the railway construction. A comparison of the position and of the amount of surface water on the beach in the area of "the Dunns" in Figs. A16 and A18 would appear to indicate a rise in the level of the beach in the latter Figure (although such evidence is not terribly reliable in terms of possible tidal stage variations).

Sometime between 1904 (Fig. A18) and 1917 (Fig. A19) wooden groynes were built at Southend; these were located between the site of the new jetty and the Knab. It is difficult now to assess the purpose of the construction of the groynes, unless they were intended to retain sediment moving towards the west, infilling the Knab embayment. In Fig. A19, the now-deteriorating jetty can also be seen. (The railway company originally built the jetty as an alternative to the previous lay-up, but had not been contracted to maintain it). Fig. A19 also shows that the sand in the nearer section in the photograph appears to have been transported into an extensive shallow embayment running parallel to the coastline from the seaward end of the jetty, towards Swansea.

Some time soon after 1900 the railway company again rebuilt the section of the line between Blackpill and Oystermouth. The rails were moved from their original location on an embankment, against the low moraine cliff in the area, and were relaid on a low embankment built on the beach (Thomas, 1978, p.121). This relocation had the effect of further straightening and moving to seawards the line of HWMOT in the area; this may have accelerated any longshore tidal current and wave-induced currents in the area. There may be modern sedimentological evidence for this increased energy in the coarse nature of sediments in the upper foreshore at this location. It is also possible that there may be a connection between the rebuilding of the line and the comparatively sudden increase in the amount of sediment in the area in front of "the Dunns" at this time.

Further degeneration of the jetty is shown in Fig. A20. In the Figure, the process has reached the stage where the jetty is no longer an effective barrier to the passage of sediment. The bank deposit which had built up on its leeward side seems to have decreased in extent, changing from sand and pebbles in composition to pebbles only (probably due to the fact that, in the absence of the jetty, the bank was exposed to wave action from the southeast, which would have removed the finer sediments). Fig. A20 suggests that the material removed from here may have been redeposited in the Knab embayment and, to a lesser extent, adjacent to the groynes at the eastern end of the embayment. The groynes also appear to have decayed in Fig. A20; indeed, they are scarcely visible.

Photographs (not presented here) taken since the construction of the pier, demonstrate that the pier does not appear to have had any effect on the nature of the sediments in the area. The pier is an open framework construction, which presents no significant barrier to the passage of tidal flows which are predominantly towards the south; thus, any depositional effects will only be felt in the deep water to the

Figure A19. Mumbles in 1917, showing the deterioration of the jetty, and the sediment adjacent to it. The groynes at Southend are also shown.

Figure A20. Mumbles in 1925, showing the gradual build-up of sediments in the region of the groynes at Southend.

south of the area.

Finally, a survey of a number of post Second World War photographs has revealed no significant changes in the nature of the beach during this period; consequently, with the possible exception of highly localised disturbance (such as that due to the extension of a speedboat slipway at Southend) sedimentological change has probably been minimal. The beach has remained similar, therefore, to its condition in 1939. A singular event whose significance cannot be accurately assessed is the construction, and eventual removal, of a causeway to the Outer Island during and after the Second World War. The causeway was located within a particularly critical area of the embayment, in that it may have affected the outflow of water and fine grained sediment from Swansea Bay. Local observations refer to the need for increased dredging rates during the existence of the causeway. Water may have been deflected by the causeway and recirculated into the Bay; this would have led to increased deposition of sediment within the central portion of the embayment.

CONCLUSIONS

The sedimentological history of the area may be summarised as follows:

(a) the deposition, during Flandrian and post-Flandrian times, of peats, muds, silts and clays;
(b) a gradual lowering of the relative level of the land surface in the area since glacial times, ending during the 16th and 17th Centuries; this may be due to local isostasy, but historical evidence indicates that this would have been effective in combination with wave and current action and short-term changes in sea level due to oceanographic/meteorological causes;
(c) from Medieval times until the beginning of the 20th Century, the area was exploited industrially: the major activities affecting the sediments of the beach were the quarrying of limestone, with its attendant spoil, and the practice of dumping ships' ballast on the beach;
(d) the construction of the Mumbles Railway line, involving straightening of the coastline and the seaward advance of HWMOT which has constricted the flow of the predominantly south-going tidal currents in the area resulting in increased longshore tidal current speeds at around HWMOT (subsequent removal of unconsolidated sands and the spreading of the artificial debris from (c) above may have occurred: the evidence of the cumulative frequency/histogram plots (Fig. A3) would tend to support this view.
(e) the building of a jetty in association with (d) above, and the construction of groynes in the area may have to some extent, stabilised some small areas of sediment at Southend. (Plots of mean grain size Figs. A4, A5 and A6, and grain fraction distributions tend to support this view).
(f) general leisure activity on the foreshore during the 20th Century has probably contributed to the spreading of the spoil; so too has the practice, now ceased, of using debris in the form of limestone pebbles and boulders to mark individual holdings of the oyster perches between the Knab Rock and Mumbles Pier.

The above conclusions are summarised in Tables A2 and A3.

TABLE A2. Summary of Historical Events Which Could Have Influenced the Distribution of Sediments in Western Swansea Bay.

Date	Event
Late Medieval Period	Mining sea-coal at Clyne

1624 *et. seq*	The dumping of ballast in Mumbles Road first evident.
1650	First evidence of the existence of a quay on the beach, at Blackpill.
1663	Griffith's map of "the Dunns".
1707	First record of cargo being loaded on the intertidal zone at Mumbles.
1790	Harbour Acts; increased erosion in Lower Swansea Valley and subsequent increased supply to the Bay; shoaling of the Mumbles Roads.
1802	Construction of piers either side of the River Tawe.
1803-1820	The commencement of the Mumbles Railway: construction of the line along the sandhills.
1824	Reconstruction of railway on foreshore, between Norton and Blackpill.
1825	First Ordnance Survey (OS) Map of the Bay, showing the extent of Neath and Tawe estuaries and a knoll in the region of the Knab Rock.
1850's	De La Beche (1851) publication on sediment transport within Swansea Bay; public enquiry over loss of limestone from cliffs at Mumbles during quarrying.
1865-1893	Closing off of embayment at Southend and the associated construction of a jetty; final extension of the railway to Mumbles Head.
1896	Ordnance Survey Map represents changes in the extent of the intertidal area throughout the Bay.

TABLE A3.   The Nature, Location and Possible Origin of Beach Sediments in the Mumbles Area of Swansea Bay.

Nature of Deposit	Location	Suggested Origin/Transport Mechanism
Muddy Sands/Peats/Silts	Lower intertidal zone Knab Rock.	Sediment transported from Lower Swansea Valley (c.1800)?
Coarse Grained Sands	Around HWMOT, throughout the area.	Winnowed by wave action, with longshore drift eastwards/ aeolian source.
Pebble/Cobble Bank (a)	From HWMOT and to seawards, at Blackpill.	The remains of spoil from the quay and from mining, together with morainic deposits.
Pebble/Cobble Banks (b)	At Knab Rock.	Spoil from the iron ore mine.
Pebble/Cobble Bank (c)	Blackstones Bank, "the Dunns".	Unknown, but may be related to Maddocks Farm.
Loose Pebbles/Cobbles	Scattered over the whole area from "the Dunns" to Mumbles Head.	(i) Upper beach may be limestone/iron ore spoil. (ii) Lower beach may be dumped ships' ballast.

Medium Grained Sands	Throughout the area, where the above are not present; predominant in the Norton/Blackpill area in the mid-intertidal zone.	Of glacial origin, or normally distributed modern material

Note: (a), (b) and (c) are not shown in the sediment distribution maps (Figs. A4 to A6), which represent non-cohesive material in the sand-size range.

ACKNOWLEDGEMENTS

The author wishes to thank Dr. M.B. Collins for his critical appraisal and correction of the manuscript. He also wishes to thank Mr. D.E. Price and Mr. A. Cutliffe (Department of Geography, University College, Swansea) for their help with the photographic work, and Mr. K. Naylor (Department of Oceanography, University College, Swansea) for his help in draughting the diagrams.

REFERENCES

Abram, R.C. (1973). The first passenger railway in the world. *In: Ostreme, 73*, Ostreme Festival Committee, Swansea, 32pp.

Ash, J.A. (1976). *Sediment movement in Swansea Bay*. Dissertation for degree of B.Sc., Department of Oceanography, University College, Swansea, (Unpublished) 76pp.

Borthwick, I., and Collins, M.B. (1976). *Tidal movements around Mumbles Head and the South Gower Coast*. Final Report to Swansea City Council, Department of Oceanography, University College, Swansea, 16pp.

C.A.D.C. (1975). *Gino-F*. Computer Aided Design Centre. Cambridge, 163pp.

Carter, T.G., (1970). *Ocean wave refraction and spectral analysis in the Mumbles area of Swansea Bay, using computational methods*. Dissertation for degree of B. Sc., Department of Oceanography, University College, Swansea, (Unpublished) 94pp.

Collins, M.B., Ferentinos, G., and Banner, F.T. (1977). The hydrodynamics and sedimentology of a high (tidal and wave) energy embayment (Swansea Bay, Northern Bristol Channel). *Estuar. Coast. Mar. Sci.*, 8, 49-74.

Ferentinos, G., and Collins, M.B. (1978). *Sediment transport through the area south of eastern Gower, as related to the sediment budget of Swansea Bay*. Final Report to I.O.S. (Taunton), Vol. 1. Department of Oceanography, University College, Swansea, (Unpublished), 120pp.

Francis, G. Grant (1867). *Charters granted to Swansea, the Chief Borough of the Seignory of Gower in the Marches of Wales in the County of Glamorgan*. Report to Swansea Town Council (Unpublished) 201pp.

Gibson, S.J. (1972). *A study of tidal currents off Mumbles Pier*. Dissertation for degree of B.Sc., Department of Oceanography, University College, Swansea (Unpublished), 108pp.

Hall, A.A. (1899). *A History of Oystermouth, with illustrations*. Alexandra Printing Co., Swansea, 44pp.

Jones, W.H. (1922). *The Port of Swansea*. Spurrell and Sons, Carmarthen, 253pp.

Libby, H. (Undated). *The mixture: Mumbles and Harry Libby*. Published in Mumbles? 106pp.

Moran, A.D., and Collins, M.B. (1979). *Sediment transport in the vicinity of Knab Rock, Western Swansea Bay*. Interim Report to Swansea City Council, Department of Oceanography, University College, Swansea, 41pp.

Thomas, N.L. (1964). *The Story of Swansea Districts and Villages*. The Guardian Press, Neath, 352pp.

Thomas, N.L. (1978). *The Mumbles past and present.* Gwasg Gomer, Llandysul, 118pp.
U.E.R.C.C. (1977). *SYMAP and SYMVU Manual.* University of Edinburgh Regional Computer Centre, Edinburgh, 104pp.

CONTRIBUTING AUTHORS

F.T. BANNER	Department of Oceanography, University College of Swansea, Singleton Park, Swansea, SA2 8PP, S. Wales, UK.
J.V. BARRIE	C-CORE, Memorial University of Newfoundland, St. Johns, Newfoundland, A1B 3XS, Canada.
J.L. BIRKS	Department of Medical Physics, Singleton Hospital, Swansea SA2 8PP, S. Wales, UK.
M.W.L. BLACKLEY	Institute of Oceanographic Sciences, Crossway, Taunton, Somerset, TA1 2DW, UK.
I. BORTHWICK	Department of Biology, Memorial University of Newfoundland, St. Johns, Newfoundland, A1B 3XS, Canada.
E.M. BRIDGES	Department of Geography, University College of Swansea, Singleton Park, Swansea, SA2 8PP, S. Wales, UK.
R.C. BRITTON	Department of Land Surveying, North East London Polytechnic, Forest Road, London, E17 4JB, UK.
S.R. BRITTON	B.P. Exploration Co. Ltd., Research Centre, Chertsey Rd. Sunbury-on-Thames, TW16 7KN, UK.
M. BROOKS	Department of Geology, University College, P.O. Box 78, Cardiff, CF1 1XL, S. Wales, UK.
R. BRYANT	Department of Chemical Engineering, University College of Swansea, Singleton Park, Swansea, SA2 8PP, S. Wales, UK.
P.A. BULL	School of Geography, University of Oxford, Mansfield Rd. Oxford, OX1 3TB, UK.
A.P. CARR	Institute of Oceanographic Sciences, Crossway, Taunton, Somerset, TA1 2DW, UK.
D. CARTLIDGE	Field Studies Council, Oil Pollution Research Unit, Orielton Field Centre, Pembroke, Dyfed, SA71 5EZ, UK.
C.J. CHUBB	Welsh Water Authority, Cambrian Way, Brecon, Powys, LD3 7HP, UK.
M.B. COLLINS	Department of Oceanography, University College of Swansea, Singleton Park, Swansea, SA2 8PP, S. Wales, UK.
H. CRONSHAW	Directorate of Engineering, The Welsh Office, Pearl House, Greyfriars Road, Cardiff, S. Wales, UK.
S.J. CULVER	Department of Paleobiology, National Museum of Natural History, Smithsonian Institution, Washington, D.C. 20560, U.S.A.
R.P. DALE	Welsh Water Authority, Cambrian Way, Brecon, Powys, LD3 7HP, UK.
C.M. DAVIES	Department of Maritime Studies, University of Wales, Institute of Science and Technology, King Edward VII Ave, Cardiff, CF1 3NU, S. Wales, UK.
G. FERENTINOS	Tay Estuary Research Group, Department of Geology, University of Dundee, Dundee, Scotland.
B.L. FLOWER	British Transport Docks Board, Adelaide Street, Swansea, S. Wales, UK.
C.L. GEORGE	Institute for Marine Environmental Research, Prospect Place, The Hoe, Plymouth, PL1 3DH, UK.
F.D.C. HAMMOND	Institute of Oceanographic Sciences, Crossway, Taunton, Somerset, TA1 2DW, UK.
J. HAYWARD	Department of Botany and Microbiology, University College of Swansea, Singleton Park, Swansea, SA2 8PP, S. Wales, UK.
A.D. HEATHERSHAW	Institute of Oceanographic Sciences, Crossway, Taunton, Somerset, TA1 2DW, UK.
K. HISCOCK S. HISCOCK	Field Studies Council, Oil Pollution Research Unit, Orielton Field Centre, Pembroke, Dyfed, SA71 5EZ, UK.

N.C. HUMPHREY	Welsh Water Authority, Cambrian Way, Brecon, Powys, LD3 7HP, UK.
M.J. ISAAC	Swansea Museum and Zoology Department, University College of Swansea, Singleton Park, Swansea, SA2 8PP, S. Wales, UK.
A.E. JAMES	Department of Oceanography, University College of Swansea, Singleton Park, Swansea, SA2 8PP, S. Wales, UK.
W.H. JACKSON	British Transport Docks Board, Research Station, Southall, Middlesex, UK.
I.R. JOINT	Institute for Marine Environmental Research, Prospect Place, The Hoe, Plymouth, PL1 3DH, UK.
P.E. KING	Department of Zoology, University College of Swansea, Singleton Park, Swansea, SA2 8PP, S. Wales, UK.
R.F.C. MANTOURA	Institute for Marine Environmental Research, Prospect Place, The Hoe, Plymouth, PL1 3DH, UK.
A.D. MORAN	Department of Oceanography, University College of Swansea, Singleton Park, Swansea, SA2 8PP, S. Wales, UK.
A.W. MORRIS	Institute for Marine Environmental Research, Prospect Place, The Hoe, Plymouth, PL1 3DH, UK.
D.R. NORMAN	British Transport Docks Board, Research Station, Southall, Middlesex, UK.
T.R. OWEN	Department of Geology, University College of Swansea, Singleton Park, Swansea, SA2 8PP, S. Wales, UK.
C.B. PATTIARATCHI	Department of Oceanography, University College of Swansea, Singleton Park, Swansea, SA2 8PP, S. Wales, UK.
C. PATTINSON	Welsh Water Authority, Cambrian Way, Brecon, Powys, LD3 7HP, UK.
J.P. PAULRAJ	Vidyalankara University, Kelaniya, Sri Lanka.
C.R. PRICE	COMAP Project Management Services Ltd., Trafford House, Chester Road, Stratford, Manchester, M32 ORS, UK.
J. RHYDDERCH	South Wales Sea Fisheries Committee, Queen's Buildings, Cambrian Place, Swansea, S. Wales, UK.
J.K. RIGLER	Department of Oceanography, University College of Swansea, Singleton Park, Swansea, SA2 8PP, S. Wales, UK.
S.E. SHACKLEY	Department of Zoology, University College of Swansea, Singleton Park, Swansea, SA2 8PP, S. Wales, UK.
J.H. STONER	Welsh Water Authority, Cambrian Way, Brecon, Powys, LD3 7HP, UK.
C. TAYLOR	Department of Civil Engineering, University College of Swansea, Singleton Park, Swansea, SA2 8PP, S. Wales, UK.
G.D. TONG	Department of Civil Engineering, University College of Swansea, Singleton Park, Swansea, SA2 8PP, S. Wales, UK.
J. TYLER	Welsh Water Authority, Virology Laboratory, Gowerton, Swansea, S. Wales, UK.
P. TYLER	Department of Oceanography, University College of Swansea, Singleton Park, Swansea, SA2 8PP, S. Wales, UK.
C.M.G. VIVIAN	Lancashire and Western Sea Fisheries Committee, University of Lancaster, Bailrigg, Lancaster, UK.
S.J. WAKEFIELD	Department of Oceanography, University College of Swansea, Singleton Park, Swansea, SA2 8PP, S. Wales, UK.
R.M. WARWICK	Institute for Marine Environmental Research, Prospect Place, The Hoe, Plymouth, PL1 3DH, UK.
A.J. WILDING	Marine Information Advisory Service, Institute of Oceanographic Sciences, Wormley, Nr. Godalming, Surrey, UK.
R.A. WILKINSON	Institute of Oceanographic Sciences, Crossway, Taunton, Somerset, TA1 2DW, UK.
D.J.A. WILLIAMS	Department of Chemical Engineering, University College of Swansea, Singleton Park, Swansea, SA2 8PP, S. Wales.

CONTRIBUTING AUTHORS

F.T. BANNER	Department of Oceanography, University College of Swansea, Singleton Park, Swansea, SA2 8PP, S. Wales, UK.
J.V. BARRIE	C-CORE, Memorial University of Newfoundland, St. Johns, Newfoundland, A1B 3XS, Canada.
J.L. BIRKS	Department of Medical Physics, Singleton Hospital, Swansea SA2 8PP, S. Wales, UK.
M.W.L. BLACKLEY	Institute of Oceanographic Sciences, Crossway, Taunton, Somerset, TA1 2DW, UK.
I. BORTHWICK	Department of Biology, Memorial University of Newfoundland, St. Johns, Newfoundland, A1B 3XS, Canada.
E.M. BRIDGES	Department of Geography, University College of Swansea, Singleton Park, Swansea, SA2 8PP, S. Wales, UK.
R.C. BRITTON	Department of Land Surveying, North East London Polytechnic, Forest Road, London, E17 4JB, UK.
S.R. BRITTON	B.P. Exploration Co. Ltd., Research Centre, Chertsey Rd. Sunbury-on-Thames, TW16 7KN, UK.
M. BROOKS	Department of Geology, University College, P.O. Box 78, Cardiff, CF1 1XL, S. Wales, UK.
R. BRYANT	Department of Chemical Engineering, University College of Swansea, Singleton Park, Swansea, SA2 8PP, S. Wales, UK.
P.A. BULL	School of Geography, University of Oxford, Mansfield Rd. Oxford, OX1 3TB, UK.
A.P. CARR	Institute of Oceanographic Sciences, Crossway, Taunton, Somerset, TA1 2DW, UK.
D. CARTLIDGE	Field Studies Council, Oil Pollution Research Unit, Orielton Field Centre, Pembroke, Dyfed, SA71 5EZ, UK.
C.J. CHUBB	Welsh Water Authority, Cambrian Way, Brecon, Powys, LD3 7HP, UK.
M.B. COLLINS	Department of Oceanography, University College of Swansea, Singleton Park, Swansea, SA2 8PP, S. Wales, UK.
H. CRONSHAW	Directorate of Engineering, The Welsh Office, Pearl House, Greyfriars Road, Cardiff, S. Wales, UK.
S.J. CULVER	Department of Paleobiology, National Museum of Natural History, Smithsonian Institution, Washington, D.C. 20560, U.S.A.
R.P. DALE	Welsh Water Authority, Cambrian Way, Brecon, Powys, LD3 7HP, UK.
C.M. DAVIES	Department of Maritime Studies, University of Wales, Institute of Science and Technology, King Edward VII Ave, Cardiff, CF1 3NU, S. Wales, UK.
G. FERENTINOS	Tay Estuary Research Group, Department of Geology, University of Dundee, Dundee, Scotland.
B.L. FLOWER	British Transport Docks Board, Adelaide Street, Swansea, S. Wales, UK.
C.L. GEORGE	Institute for Marine Environmental Research, Prospect Place, The Hoe, Plymouth, PL1 3DH, UK.
F.D.C. HAMMOND	Institute of Oceanographic Sciences, Crossway, Taunton, Somerset, TA1 2DW, UK.
J. HAYWARD	Department of Botany and Microbiology, University College of Swansea, Singleton Park, Swansea, SA2 8PP, S. Wales, UK.
A.D. HEATHERSHAW	Institute of Oceanographic Sciences, Crossway, Taunton, Somerset, TA1 2DW, UK.
K. HISCOCK S. HISCOCK	Field Studies Council, Oil Pollution Research Unit, Orielton Field Centre, Pembroke, Dyfed, SA71 5EZ, UK.

N.C. HUMPHREY	Welsh Water Authority, Cambrian Way, Brecon, Powys, LD3 7HP, UK.
M.J. ISAAC	Swansea Museum and Zoology Department, University College of Swansea, Singleton Park, Swansea, SA2 8PP, S. Wales, UK.
A.E. JAMES	Department of Oceanography, University College of Swansea, Singleton Park, Swansea, SA2 8PP, S. Wales, UK.
W.H. JACKSON	British Transport Docks Board, Research Station, Southall, Middlesex, UK.
I.R. JOINT	Institute for Marine Environmental Research, Prospect Place, The Hoe, Plymouth, PL1 3DH, UK.
P.E. KING	Department of Zoology, University College of Swansea, Singleton Park, Swansea, SA2 8PP, S. Wales, UK.
R.F.C. MANTOURA	Institute for Marine Environmental Research, Prospect Place, The Hoe, Plymouth, PL1 3DH, UK.
A.D. MORAN	Department of Oceanography, University College of Swansea, Singleton Park, Swansea, SA2 8PP, S. Wales, UK.
A.W. MORRIS	Institute for Marine Environmental Research, Prospect Place, The Hoe, Plymouth, PL1 3DH, UK.
D.R. NORMAN	British Transport Docks Board, Research Station, Southall, Middlesex, UK.
T.R. OWEN	Department of Geology, University College of Swansea, Singleton Park, Swansea, SA2 8PP, S. Wales, UK.
C.B. PATTIARATCHI	Department of Oceanography, University College of Swansea, Singleton Park, Swansea, SA2 8PP, S. Wales, UK.
C. PATTINSON	Welsh Water Authority, Cambrian Way, Brecon, Powys, LD3 7HP, UK.
J.P. PAULRAJ	Vidyalankara University, Kelaniya, Sri Lanka.
C.R. PRICE	COMAP Project Management Services Ltd., Trafford House, Chester Road, Stratford, Manchester, M32 0RS, UK.
J. RHYDDERCH	South Wales Sea Fisheries Committee, Queen's Buildings, Cambrian Place, Swansea, S. Wales, UK.
J.K. RIGLER	Department of Oceanography, University College of Swansea, Singleton Park, Swansea, SA2 8PP, S. Wales, UK.
S.E. SHACKLEY	Department of Zoology, University College of Swansea, Singleton Park, Swansea, SA2 8PP, S. Wales, UK.
J.H. STONER	Welsh Water Authority, Cambrian Way, Brecon, Powys, LD3 7HP, UK.
C. TAYLOR	Department of Civil Engineering, University College of Swansea, Singleton Park, Swansea, SA2 8PP, S. Wales, UK.
G.D. TONG	Department of Civil Engineering, University College of Swansea, Singleton Park, Swansea, SA2 8PP, S. Wales, UK.
J. TYLER	Welsh Water Authority, Virology Laboratory, Gowerton, Swansea, S. Wales, UK.
P. TYLER	Department of Oceanography, University College of Swansea, Singleton Park, Swansea, SA2 8PP, S. Wales, UK.
C.M.G. VIVIAN	Lancashire and Western Sea Fisheries Committee, University of Lancaster, Bailrigg, Lancaster, UK.
S.J. WAKEFIELD	Department of Oceanography, University College of Swansea, Singleton Park, Swansea, SA2 8PP, S. Wales, UK.
R.M. WARWICK	Institute for Marine Environmental Research, Prospect Place, The Hoe, Plymouth, PL1 3DH, UK.
A.J. WILDING	Marine Information Advisory Service, Institute of Oceanographic Sciences, Wormley, Nr. Godalming, Surrey, UK.
R.A. WILKINSON	Institute of Oceanographic Sciences, Crossway, Taunton, Somerset, TA1 2DW, UK.
D.J.A. WILLIAMS	Department of Chemical Engineering, University College of Swansea, Singleton Park, Swansea, SA2 8PP, S. Wales.

ADDITIONAL PARTICIPANTS

D.V. AGER.	*Department of Geology, University College of Swansea, Singleton Park, Swansea, SA2 8PP, S. Wales, UK.*
R. ALLEN.	*Department of Civil Engineering, University College of Swansea, Singleton Park, Swansea, SA2 8PP, S. Wales, UK.*
E.A. BOWERS.	*Open University in Wales, Pearl Assurance House, Greyfriars Road, Cardiff, S. Wales, UK.*
M.S. BROADBENT.	*Wimpey Laboratories, Springfield Road, Hayes, Middlesex, UK.*
R.P. CHAPLIN.	*B.P. Oil Llandarcy Refinery, Neath, S. Wales, UK.*
A.E. CHAPMAN.	*B.P. Chemicals, Belgrave House, Buckingham Palace Road, London, SW1W 0SU, UK.*
D.J. EVANS-ROBERTS.	*Hydraulics Research Station, Wallingford, Oxford, UK.*
P.H. GRANT.	*Department of Geography, Univerity of Aberdeen, Aberdeen, AB9 2UA, Scotland, UK.*
D. JOHN.	*B.P. Chemicals, Baglan Bay, Port Talbot, S. Wales, UK.*
N.V. JONES.	*Department of Zoology, University of Hull, Hull, HU6 7RX, UK.*
S. KENT.	*Welsh Water Authority.*
S. LANCASTER.	*Department of Oceanography, University College of Swansea, Singleton Park, Swansea, SA2 8PP, S. Wales, UK.*
K. LANGDON.	*Department of Civil Engineering, University of Liverpool, Brownlow Hill, Liverpool.*
R.E. LEWIS.	*I.C.I. Ltd., Brixham Laboratory, Freshwater Quarry, Brixham, Devon, UK.*
J. MASKELL.	*Hydraulics Research Station, Wallingford, Oxford, UK.*
E. MORGAN.	*Department of Biological Sciences, The Polytechnic, Wolverhampton, W. Midlands, UK.*
K. NAYLOR.	*Department of Oceanography, University College of Swansea, Singleton Park, Swansea, SA2 8PP, S. Wales, UK.*
L.A. NELSON.	*Thames Water Authority, 177, Rosebery Avenue, London, EC1 R4TP, UK.*
M.G. NORTON.	*Ministry of Agriculture, Fisheries and Food, Fisheries Laboratory, Burnham-on-Crouch, Essex, UK.*
R. PADGHAM.	*Natural Environmental Research Council, Polaris House, North Star Avenue, Swindon, Wilts, UK.*
C.P.G. PEREIRA.	*Department of Oceanography, University College of Swansea, Singleton Park, Swansea, SA2 8PP, S. Wales, UK.*
K. PROBERT.	*Nature Conservancy Council, Huntingdon, Cambridge, UK.*
I. REES.	*Nature Conservancy Council, 44, The Parade, Roath, Cardiff, S. Wales, UK.*
A.M. RIDDLE.	*I.C.I. Ltd., Brixham Laboratory, Freshwater Quarry, Brixham, Devon, UK.*
C. ROUSE.	*Department of Geography, University College of Swansea, Singleton Park, Swansea, SA2 8PP, S. Wales, UK.*
J. SAUNDERS.	*The Welsh Office, Pearl Assurance House, Greyfriars Road, Cardiff, S. Wales, UK.*
N.F. SIMONS.	*Edge Hill College of Higher Education, St. Helens Road, Ormskirk, Lancs, UK.*
A.J.E. SMITH.	*Binnie & Partners, Artillery House, Artillery Row, London, SW1, UK.*
S.C. SUGGITT,	*Department of Geography, Edge Hill College of Higher Education, St. Helens Road, Ormskirk, Lancs, UK.*
R.V. TAIT.	*Central London Polytechnic, London, UK.*
T.D. WATERS.	*Department of Zoology, University College of Swansea, Singleton Park, Swansea, SA2 8PP, S. Wales, UK.*
W.D.A. WATERS.	*The Welsh Office, Pearl Assurance House, Greyfriars Road, Cardiff, S. Wales, UK.*
D.G. WEBB.	*Hydraulics Research Station, Wallingford, Oxford, UK.*
D. WEBBER.	*Department of Botany and Microbiology, University College of*

Additional Participants

	Swansea, Singleton Park, Swansea, SA2 8PP, S. Wales, UK.
J. WELSBY.	Hydraulics Research Station, Wallingford, Oxford, UK.
H. WILLIAMS.	British Steel Corporation, Port Talbot, S. Wales, UK.
S.J. WILLIAMS.	Department of Oceanography, University College of Swansea, Singleton Park, Swansea, SA2 8PP, S. Wales, UK.
J.G. WILSON.	Department of Zoology, University of Dublin, Trinity College, Dublin, Ireland.
C. WOOLDRIDGE.	Department of Maritime Studies, University of Wales, Institute of Science and Technology, King Edward VII Avenue, Cardiff, S. Wales, UK.